Accounting Guide for Government Contracts

NINTH EDITION — 1988

by Paul M. Trueger
Certified Public Accountant

COMMERCE CLEARING HOUSE, INC.
PUBLISHERS of TOPICAL LAW REPORTS
4025 W. PETERSON AVE., CHICAGO, ILLINOIS 60646

Accounting Guide
for Government Contracts

Ninth Edition — 1988

FOREWORD

The many significant government actions in recent years have had a profound impact on government contractors and on government procurement, audit, and investigative officials. The major changes in contract administration and in the buyer-seller relationships have dictated the need for the Ninth Edition of this text to provide a current guide for both the private and public sector participants in the government procurement process, particularly in defense areas.

Defense expenditures, never popular except in periods of major, publicly supported warfare, continued to encounter more than usual resistance and hostility as the government experimented with formula solutions to reduce the huge federal deficit. Constituents for many social programs have been more numerous and influential than those advocating essential defense spending, and military funding requests continued to suffer from the adverse publicity of horror stories alleging fraud, waste, abuse, and excessive profits. The fact that many of these allegations proved to be unfounded or exaggerated did not lessen the unfavorable climate generated by the initial charges.

In this environment the government further increased fraud investigations and prosecutions; enacted legislation and promulgated regulations prescribing additional criminal and civil penalties; demanded that contractors voluntarily disclose any circumstances that might suggest potential wrongdoings and actively assist federal investigations of such circumstances; prohibited reimbursement of many normal business expenses; eliminated judicially recognized contractor defenses against government demands for price reduction because of alleged defective cost data; reduced profit margins on defense contracts; aggrandized the power and influence of contract auditors and inspectors and concomitantly undercut the authority of contracting officers and program managers; and increased contractor income taxes by further circumscribing the use of the completed contract method for income recognition under long-term contracts.

Fraud

In the Eighth Edition of this text, we noted the sharp increase in the government's efforts to detect fraud in procurement, especially in connection with DOD contracts where that Department's Office of Inspector General, DCAA, and a dedicated DOD-Department of Justice (DOJ) procurement fraud unit concentrated and competed in this effort and publicized "successful prosecutions." In the years since the publication of the previous edition, this activity continued to intensify as DCAA auditors were instructed by the DOD OIG and DOJ that almost any mischarging and almost every instance of defective pricing should be viewed as potential fraud.

The chapters on Fraud, Waste, and Abuse and Federal Inspectors General were revised and updated in the Ninth Edition. The Appendix on Indicators of Fraud in Defense Procurement, containing excerpts from the DOD OIG's pamphlet on this subject, was updated to cover the revised (1987)

iii

publication, and appendices were added to provide excerpts from the DOD OIG's publications of Handbook on Labor Fraud Indicators, Handbook on Fraud Indicators: Material, and Handbook on Scenarios of Potential Defective Pricing Fraud. The continuing DOD OIG admonitions to contract auditors to "think fraud" in their audits have resulted in superimposing and emphasizing fraud detection over conventional contract audit techniques. We have recommended that these publications be integrated, to the extent appropriate, into contractors' internal audit programs.

Contractor Self-Governance and Voluntary Disclosure

The President's Blue Ribbon Commission on Defense Management (Packard Commission) reported in 1986: "Our study of defense management compels us to conclude that nothing merits greater concern than the increasingly troubled relationship between the defense industry and government." The Commission offered a number of major suggestions to improve this relationship, so vital to the country's national defense.

As the Commission reported in its update a year later, DOD had failed to implement many of the recommendations. However, the Department quickly and vigorously pursued the recommendations directed at defense contractors, particularly exhorting them to improve their self-governance and to voluntarily disclose all potential wrongdoings. The strong emphasis on voluntary disclosure, particularly at the outset when proposed regulations and contract clauses would make the voluntary actions mandatory, when the DOD OIG, DCAA and the Department of Justice were overzealously viewing accounting and administrative errors as potential fraud, and when neither DOD nor Justice offered any encouragement for voluntary disclosure other than promises to expedite government investigations, created considerable concern among contractors and their legal and accounting advisors.

At this writing, signs of a rule of reason have appeared as DOD has reversed its initial proposals to mandate voluntary disclosures and, together with the Justice Department, has given some indications that consideration will be accorded to companies making voluntary disclosures and even to those who may not have done so but who had cooperated effectively in government investigations when potential wrongdoings were detected by federal auditors and investigators.

Effective self-governance, including the improvement of controls through vigorous programs participated in by both company and outside attorneys and accountants, continues to occupy close attention by contractor officials at every level.

Unallowable Costs

Following a series of investigations and related congressional hearings at which contractors were castigated for submitting, and contracting officers for accepting, allegedly unallowable costs, the legislators engaged in a major micro-management exercise in defense contracting in the DOD 1986 Authorization Act. Although implementation of the statute was mandated only for defense contracts, many of the actions were taken through FAR and thus affected all government departments and agencies and their contractors.

Ten categories of indirect costs were declared unallowable by fiat, and DOD was directed to "clarify" the allowability of sixteen additional categories. The direction to define more specifically the allowability of the latter sixteen categories was generally intended to limit, and resulted in limiting, the allowability of these costs.

Among other provisions of this legislation, P.L. 99-145, were shifting the burden of proof as to reasonableness of indirect costs from the government to the contractor; increasing and/or adding civil and criminal penalties against contractors found to have submitted unallowable costs; providing subpoena power for the DCAA Director; forbidding contracting officers from resolving any costs questioned by contract auditors until they secured "adequate" documentation and opinion of the auditor; requiring the contract auditor's presence at all negotiations and discussions with contractors concerning allowability of costs; and eliminating "bottom line" negotiations by requiring settlements to reflect specific disposition of indirect costs questioned by contract auditors.

Defective Cost or Pricing Data

In the middle 1980s representatives of the DOD OIG, GAO and DCAA continued their criticisms before congressional committees of the manner in which P.L. 87-653 was being implemented. Any ruling by the courts or boards of contract appeals in which a contractor successfully defended against a government allegation of defective pricing was censured by these critics, who alleged that contracting officers were negotiating lower or zero price reductions because of their apprehensions concerning adverse judicial decisions.

The continuing attacks, many with little if any merit, nevertheless persuaded Congress to enact the Truth in Negotiations Act Amendments as Section 952 of the DOD 1987 Authorization Act. This legislation eliminated most of the defenses recognized by courts and boards of contract appeals against government demands for contract price reductions as a result of allegedly defective cost or pricing data.

Profit

In June 1985, DOD issued a report on an 18-month comprehensive study of pricing, financing and profit policies and their interrelationships—Defense Financial and Investment Review (DFAIR). Although GAO disagreed with certain aspects of its findings, recommendations and methodology, DFAIR was influential in the formulation of a new DOD profit policy reflecting considerably greater weight to contractor investment and risk, lesser weight to estimated cost, and overall lower profit margins.

Continuing its criticisms of DFAIR, the current profit policy, etc., GAO proposed legislation to require OFPP to establish appropriate methodologies for the conduct of profit studies and thereafter conduct such studies on a periodic basis. A prominent feature of GAO's proposal was the provision that GAO be given complete access to the records of the contractors involved in these studies, to the working papers and reports of the certified public accountants who would attest to the data submitted by the contractors, and to the records of OFPP used in compiling, evaluating and reporting thereon. Several legislative proposals have been introduced to implement GAO's plan.

Contractor Surveillance and Oversight

The Packard Commission was not favorably impressed, to state it mildly, with the contribution of contract audit to effective defense procurement and sound relationships between government and industry. Noting DOD's increased attention and resources to detecting unlawful practices, the Commission stated: "But a plethora of departmental auditors and other overseers ... also have tended to establish a dysfunctional and adversarial relationship between DOD and its contractors." The report acknowledged the need for government oversight but pointed out that "no conceivable number of additional auditors, inspectors, investigators and prosecutors can police it fully, much less make it work effectively."

The Commission believed that real opportunities for improvement were available in effective contractor self-governance, including effective internal auditing. In this regard it recommended: "To encourage and preserve the validity of such internal auditing and reporting process, DOD should develop appropriate guidelines heavily circumscribing the use of investigative subpoenas to compel disclosure of contractor internal auditing materials."

The Commission was also concerned with the redundant contractor surveillance and recommended: "Oversight of defense contractors must be better coordinated among DOD agencies and Congress. Guidelines must be developed to remove undesirable duplication of official effort ... The new Under Secretary of Defense (Acquisition) should establish appropriate overall contract audit policy." The new Under Secretary, who resigned after a year's frustration over DOD's failure to provide him the authority he believed was contemplated by the Commission and Public Law 99-500 to enable him to formulate and direct a cohesive DOD acquisition policy, apparently encountered sufficient problems without addressing contract audit policy.

Regardless of the Commission's findings and recommendations, and more critical comments from both the private and public sectors, the Defense Contract Audit Agency (DCAA) flourished, expanded its authority at the expense of the contracting officer, took heavy-handed action to further extend its access to contractors' records and, unless constrained by Gramm-Rudman, may soon operate with twice the number of auditors it was authorized at its establishment.

As described in Chapter II of this text, the provisions of DOD Directive 7640.2 and P.L. 99-145 virtually stood the traditional contracting officer-contract auditor relationship on its head, the auditor in effect becoming a full (and potent) partner in all contract cost matters instead of an advisor. During the period since the publication of the Eighth Edition of this text, the Deputy Secretary of Defense directed that the responsibilities for determining billing and final indirect cost rates be transferred from the contracting officer to the contract auditor, and the responsibility for conducting contractor compensation reviews transferred from DLA and DCAA. These decisions were made over the strong protests of procurement officials in OSD and in the Army, Navy, Air Force and DLA.

When the DCAA Director obtained subpoena power through P.L. 99-145, the accompanying committee report emphasized that this provision was not intended to expand the scope of books, documents, papers or records to which the defense contract audit agency has access and that the subpoena power should be used sparingly and only in the performance of the functions and proposes ascribed to the contract audit agency.

In contrast to the Packard Commission's recommendation that DOD "heavily circumscribe the use of investigative subpoenas to compel disclosure of contractor internal auditing materials" and the congressional mandate that the subpoena authority be used "sparingly," DCAA moved out vigorously and demanded, through the use of or threat to use its new power, unrestrained access to all contractor internal audit materials, as well as long-term budgetary data, board of directors' minutes, and other records regardless of their remoteness or possible irrelevancy to the agency's basic mission of evaluating contractors' cost representations under proposed, ongoing, completed or terminated contracts.

In its July 1987 evaluation of actions taken on its original report, the Packard Commission stated: "Policy decisions have been made ... that severely undercut the role of contracting officers ... Auditors have been given responsibilities outside their competence and have been afforded a separate chain of command in a way that, in effect, makes them rivals of contracting officers ...."

Completed Contract Method for Income Determination

Initially authorized for federal income tax purposes in 1918, the completed contract method (CCM) was heralded as the practical and equitable answer to the problems involved in annual estimates of profits or losses on long-term contracts under the percentage of completion method (PCM).

Allegations that certain contractors were using CCM to defer reporting of profits under government and other long-term contracts resulted in legislative revisions in the Tax Equity and Fiscal Responsibility Act of 1982 (TEFRA) and the Tax Reform Act of 1986 (TRA). As implemented by the Internal Revenue Service, the use of CCM has been sharply curtailed and, even when used, the changed requirements for capitalizing expenses have substantially altered its impact.

Current efforts to produce revenues for federal deficit reduction under Gramm-Rudman include provisions to further limit or virtually eliminate CCM with few exceptions.

Cost Accounting Standards

Efforts to reestablish the CAS function began when the then Comptroller General and CASB Chairman became convinced that further funding would not be provided for the original Board. Over the years, numerous legislative proposals were introduced, each failing when government-industry agreement could not be reached as to the focus, nature, and composition of a new CAS function and the scope of its authority.

After obtaining an opinion from the Department of Justice that it had the authority "to adopt the CAS in whole or in part and ... once such adoption occurs, to reject or grant exemptions to the CAS," DOD attempted to establish a CAS Board of its own. This effort failed under the virtually unanimous opposition from both the private and public sectors. As an alternative, DOD moved to incorporate CAS into FAR where, under the agreed-upon assigned responsibilities between the DAR and CAA Councils, DOD would have the primary responsibility for Part 30, which contains CAS regulations. Despite the wide opposition to this proposal in June 1986, it was issued as a final rule, effective September 30, 1987.

On almost the same date, HR 3345 was introduced, establishing an independent CAS Board to be chaired by the OFPP Administrator and comprised of six additional members, one each from DOD and a civilian agency, two from industry and two from the public accounting profession. This measure encountered difficulties because, among other things, it contained other controversial provisions expanding OFPP's authority. Meanwhile CAS has been formally incorporated into FAR and revisions have been initiated.

CCH and the GUIDE

The publication of this Ninth Edition of the Accounting Guide for Government Contracts marks 35 years of our association with Commerce Clearing House, Inc., which began with the First Edition of what was then the Accounting Guide for Defense Contracts in April 1953. The CCH GOVERN-MENT CONTRACTS REPORTER and related publications offer the most comprehensive coverage of the entire field of federal government procurement, and we believe this GUIDE presents an appropriate supplement designed to provide special, concentrated assistance to contractor and government officials charged with the administrative and accounting responsibilities for these contracts.

As in the past, we welcome the constructive comments received on our efforts and attribute to them many of the improvements we hope have been reflected in each succeeding edition. We hope our readers will continue to write.

Paul M. Trueger, C.P.A.

April 1988

Table of Contents

Detailed Table of Contents

Chapter IV—Significant Clauses Included in Government Contracts

Chapter V—Government Contract Pricing

Chapter XX—Limitation of Cost Provisions of Government Cost-Reimbursement Type Contracts—Policies, Practices, and Case Law

Introduction and History

HISTORY OF GOVERNMENT CONTRACTING AND RELATED LAWS AND REGULATIONS

Legislation governing procurement of supplies and services by the federal government can be traced back to the 18th century, and the initial statutes appear to be directed to military procurement. Concern about possible fraud, waste, and other abuses, so much in the spotlight in recent years, existed 200 years ago as well. Then and now, the complex problems frequently proved beyond congressional expertise to solve; but, then and now, the lawmakers were not inhibited, enacting numerous statutes that they hoped would cure all of the real and imaginary ills.

Procurement by negotiation has always been considered suspect by many, and this view was reflected over the years in legislation mandating the use of formal advertising. This method, however, was found wanting during times of war, other periods of perceived urgency, and when the government needed to buy sophisticated and expensive equipment that very few companies were capable of producing. As World War II spread and United States military expenditures for our allies and our own preparedness increased, negotiation was increasingly endorsed in both legislation and government regulations. Today, as for many years, negotiated contracts are fewer in number but involve larger dollar amounts than those awarded by formal advertising.

Among the complexities that confuse understanding of procurement policy is the view still held by some that negotiated contracts abet favoritism, waste, and other abuses and do not permit competition. On the latter point, federal departments and agencies, particularly DOD, have made considerable efforts to demonstrate that, except where sole source procurement is necessary, negotiation can and does involve competition.

COMPETITION IN CONTRACTING ACT OF 1984 (CICA)

In July 1984, President Reagan signed into law P.L. 98-369, the Deficit Reduction Act of 1984, a weighty combination of related and unrelated taxing, spending and procurement measures. Our major interest in this brief summary focuses on Title VII of Division B of the law, referred to as the Competition in Contracting Act of 1984. Significant provisions relating to GAO's role in bid protests are discussed in Chapter XXVIII of this text, The General Accounting Office.

The CICA provisions of the Deficit Reduction Act were effective April 1, 1985, imposing upon the acquisition regulation writers a monumental task of revising the regulations to incorporate the new policies and procedures. In consonance with the designated caption of Title VII, the emphasis was on increasing competition in procurement, and the provisions focused on limiting circumstances under which sole source procurement could be used rather than on the previous distinctions between formal advertising and negotiation. The term "formal advertising" was replaced by the designation "sealed bidding." FAR Subsection C—Contracting Methods and Contract Types, at this writing, includes:

Part 13—Small Purchase and Other Simplified Purchase Procedures

Part 14—Sealed Bidding

Part 15—Contracting by Negotiation

Part 16—Types of Contracts

Part 17—Special Contracting Methods

THE FAR SYSTEM AND ITS PRECURSORS

After the hectic years of World War II, the combined talents of government and industry focused on the need for comprehensive legislation and regulations to control government procurement. A dual approach developed: military and civilian.

Military Procurement

The Armed Services Procurement Act, Public Law 80-413, was enacted in 1947 and was implemented by the Armed Services Procurement Regulation (ASPR). Uniformity could no more be achieved in those days than it can now: ASPR was supplemented by regulations issued by the individual military departments and defense agencies. In March 1978, for reasons some private sector observers considered arcane, DOD changed the name of ASPR to the Defense Acquisition Regulation (DAR).

Civilian Procurement

The basic legislation for civilian procurement was the Federal Property and Administrative Services Act, enacted in 1949, and the implementing regulations were the Federal Procurement Regulations (FPR), initially issued in March 1959. The FPR System, the responsibility of the General Services Administration (GSA), consists of the basic FPR and the individual agency procurement regulations that implement and supplement the FPR. Uniformity was much more difficult to come by for civilian agencies than for the military departments and defense agencies. Thus, the FPR System included supplements by most civilian agencies, with particularly comprehensive issuances by GSA and the Department of Energy (DOE).

Over the years, DOD generally led the way to new initiatives in the procurement area and related changes to ASPR/DAR. Many of these changes were subsequently adopted and incorporated into FPR. Thus, a company performing under both military and civilian contracts was required to refer to DAR, FPR, and the regulations of the civilian agency that awarded the contract.

The FAR System

We should distinguish the Federal Acquisition Regulation (FAR) and the Federal Acquisition Regulations System. The latter incorporates FAR but also includes the acquisition regulations published by the various agencies that implement or supplement FAR. The FAR System replaces the FPR System, DAR, and NASA PR.

A single regulation covering acquisition (or procurement) by all federal agencies has been a gleam in the eyes of many since the days of the early Hoover Commission studies and was vigorously revived by the Commission on Government Procurement in the early 1970s. Projects of this kind take many years to mature, and it was not until 1978 that the actual preparation of FAR was assigned, mainly to representatives of DOD and GSA. The task forces concluded early that the preparation of a completely new regulation was neither feasible nor desirable. Accordingly, the job was essentially to study DAR and the FPR System and to select what appeared to be the best coverage of each subject, sometimes choosing the coverage in either DAR or FPR, and sometimes taking parts of each. The final preparation was designed to reflect improved style and language, moving away from jargon where possible and seeking simplicity and clarity.

Some dreamers thought that FAR would be the bible for every federal agency and that virtually no deviations would be permitted. The dream was shattered early when DOD and a number of other agencies argued that differences in their missions and operations demanded supplements and deviations to meet their specific needs. These arguments led to the establishment of the FAR System. To set some limit to the implementing and supplementary regulations, those issued by the military departments and defense agencies are subject to the authority of the Secretary of Defense; those issued by NASA activities are subject to the authority of the Administrator of NASA; and those issued by other civilian agencies are subject either to the overall authority of the Administrator of General Services or to whatever independent authority the agency may have.

Revisions to the FAR are issued through coordinated action by two councils, the Defense Acquisition Regulatory Council (DAR Council) and the Civilian Agency Acquisition Council (CAA Council). The latter is chaired by a representative of GSA and includes representatives of about a dozen major civilian departments and agencies. The former is chaired by a representative of the Secretary of Defense and includes representatives of the military departments, DLA, and NASA. Each Council is responsible for designated parts of FAR and must secure agreement of both councils before forwarding any proposed change to the FAR Secretariat, operated by GSA, for printing and publishing.

Views of agencies and the private sector are sought for proposed "significant revisions of the FAR." This term means alterations of substantive meanings of any coverage having a substantial impact on the public and excludes editorial revisions that do not alter the contents. When views are invited, the opportunity to submit them is announced in the *Federal Register,* but these notices need not include the text of the proposed change or related explanations. The notices advise where this information can be obtained.

For those using the Code of Federal Regulations (CFR), FAR has been assigned Chapter 1 of Title 48 CFR. Individual agency regulations that implement or supplement FAR have been assigned Chapters 2 through 59 of

Title 48 CFR. These agency publications are required to parallel the FAR in format, arrangement, and numbering systems.

FAR was published in the *Federal Register* on September 19, 1983, to be effective April 1, 1984, and not long thereafter the Defense Department and other federal agencies published their FAR Supplements.

It is widely agreed that the FAR Project culminated in a useful product and enhanced uniformity in government acquisition regulations. However, some of the individual agency FAR Supplements are extensive, and government contractors must have reference to both the FAR and the FAR Supplement issued by the agency awarding the contract. The complexities and problems bidders and contractors continue to encounter are aggravated, as in the past, by informal or unwritten procedures, practices, and interpretations by government buying offices and by individuals responsible for the various aspects of contracting. In addition, many thousands of decisions and interpretations affecting government contracts are issued annually by federal courts, boards of contract appeals, the General Accounting Office, and other bodies.

Doing business with the government in an atmosphere of reasonable assurance that the final contract price will reflect recovery of pertinent costs and a fair profit requires an extensive library and experienced accountants, attorneys, and contract administrators to identify, interpret, and apply the relevant rules. Government contractors subscribe to publications and attend meetings and seminars in an effort to learn and keep abreast of the voluminous and constantly changing regulations. Although many of these efforts are generally beneficial, there remains a very real need for a comprehensive, up-to-date text on federal contracting—a single volume to bring together in an orderly fashion the essential accounting and administrative information required to do business with the government successfully. This has been the objective of our prior eight editions and is our goal for this, the Ninth Edition of the ACCOUNTING GUIDE FOR GOVERNMENT CONTRACTS.

ORGANIZATION OF THE GOVERNMENT ACQUISITION FUNCTION

The executive branch of the government includes 13 major departments and some 60 agencies that buy goods and services from the private sector. A detailed review of these organizations and how they buy would be an appropriate subject for another volume. Such information is available in Commerce Clearing House, Inc.'s GOVERNMENT CONTRACTS REPORTER and other commercial publications and in publications available from the U.S. Superintendent of Documents, Government Printing Office, such as *Selling to the Military, Selling to the U.S. Government, Doing Business with the Federal Government,* and *U.S. Government Procurement and Sales Directory.* For the purpose of this text, we have limited our comments to presenting a brief, overall picture of the organization of the government acquisition function.

Office of Management and Budget (OMB)

OMB is in many respects an extension of the White House and assists in formulating the federal budget and policies affecting the operations of the executive branch of the government. For our purposes, OMB is of interest in that (1) the OFPP Administrator (see below) reports to the OMB Director and (2) certain cost principles and other directives affecting government contracting are published by OMB's Finance and Accounting Division, including the following Circulars:

A-21 Cost Principles for Educational Institutions

A-87 Cost Principles for State and Local Governments

A-122 Cost Principles for Nonprofit Organizations

Office of Federal Procurement Policy (OFPP)

The number one recommendation of the Commission on Government Procurement was the establishment of a central government agency to formulate "a system of government-wide coordinated, and to the extent feasible, uniform procurement regulations." Pursuant to this recommendation, OFPP was established in 1974 as part of OMB to spearhead the implementation of this objective.

The precise authority of OFPP has been a controversial issue ever since its establishment. Strong proponents of maximum uniformity in procurement policy, located particularly in Congress and industry, have devoted the past decade to providing OFPP sufficient authority to achieve this goal. The major opposition has come from the Defense Department, which continues to contest any effort that would require it to yield any of its authority. DOD prefers an arrangement under which OFPP would enunciate broad policy but each agency would have wide latitude to promulgate implementations it deems appropriate to accomplish its mission.

Up to a point, DOD's position has merit. Certainly, the defense of this country is accomplished in a different environment than, for example, providing oversight for the nation's educational or environmental problems. Carried to an extreme, however, as it is by DOD from time to time, this attitude is not supportable. An example was DOD's insistence on a harsher cost principle governing allowability of so-called lobbying and related costs than that promulgated by OFPP and agreed to by the civilian agencies and NASA. Through its advocates in Congress, DOD has been successful in limiting OFPP's authority. The effort has been considerably helped by OMB, where the powerful DOD has much more clout than the tiny OFPP.

During 1983, Congress debated legislation extending the life of OFPP. Despite wide support for providing meaningful authority for OFPP, DOD and OMB succeeded in diluting such proposals. In a compromise measure enacted as Congress rushed to adjournment in November 1983, the life of OFPP was extended for four years. The statute permits the OFPP Administrator, with the approval of the OMB Director, to issue binding procurement regulations but only if DOD, GSA, and NASA are unable to agree upon, or have failed to issue, government-wide regulations in a timely manner. Where DOD or other agencies issue directives that are inconsistent with OFPP promulgations, rescissions may be made, but they are to be made by the OMB Director, not by the OFPP Administrator. Although no match for the huge bureaucracies, the OFPP has been successful in promoting and motivating a reasonable degree of uniformity in government-wide profit policies and in other areas. If the Cost Accounting Standards Board function is reinstated and placed in the executive branch, this authority and responsibility will likely be assigned to either OFPP or OMB.

Executive Departments and Agencies

The Department of Defense is the largest and best known buyer of goods and services and the leader in establishing procurement, contract administration, and contract audit policies and practices. Review of FAR and comparison of its provisions with those of DAR and FPR clearly establish the heavy influence of DOD views.

As the result of a project initiated in 1962, the Defense Contract Administration Services (DCAS) was established as part of the Defense Logistics Agency (DLA). Currently, DCAS administers all contracts awarded by DLA (the military counterpart of GSA) and virtually all contracts awarded by the Army, with the exception of that department's government-owned, contractor-operated (GOCO) plants. DCAS administers all of the Navy contracts except those awarded to shipyards and a few of its major weapons systems suppliers and those awarded by the Office of Naval Research (ONR). The Air Force has retained contract administration responsibility for some twenty large aerospace firms performing on Air Force contracts for major weapons systems. DCAS administers many contracts awarded by NASA as well as some contracts awarded by the smaller civilian agencies. The assumption by DCAS of contract administration responsibility beyond DOD will continue to increase as the policy for governmentwide coordination in this area progresses.

The contract audit counterpart to DCAS is DCAA. As commented upon in Chapter II, the Defense Contract Audit Agency performs all contract auditing for NASA and some or all of this work for a number of civilian agencies.

The General Services Administration was created in 1949 to consolidate dozens of agencies involved in carrying out the myriad "housekeeping" functions of the federal government, such as purchasing common supplies, providing communications, keeping records, and providing and maintaining facilities for government offices. GSA was responsible for maintaining the Federal Procurement Regulations System, which consisted of the FPR promulgated by GSA and the supplementing regulations published by the other civilian agencies. GSA was assigned a major role in working with DOD in formulating FAR, with the overall guidance of OFPP.

Some of the other federal agencies with significant buying activities include the Departments of Energy, Health and Human Services, and Transportation. Mention should also be made of the Environmental Protection Agency (EPA). Although direct procurement represents a relatively small portion of its appropriation, EPA's major impact is felt through its multibillion dollar program in grants-in-aid to states and local governments. The largest portion of these funds finds its way to the private sector through contracts awarded by the grantees.

KEY GOVERNMENT ACQUISITION PERSONNEL

Many thousands of government people participate in the acquisition process, from policymakers at very high levels in the federal departments and agencies to clerical support. It is not particularly important to know and understand the roles of all of the functionaries in government procurement. It is extremely important, however, for contractors to have a clear understanding of the authority and limitations of some of the people they deal with, whether in person or through correspondence.

The most important government official is generally the contracting officer, defined in FAR Subpart 2.1 as "a person with the authority to enter into, administer, and/or terminate contracts and make related determinations and findings." FAR states that this term also "includes certain authorized representatives of the contracting officer acting within the limits of their authority as delegated by the contracting officer."

The term "contracting officer" is properly applied to the individual known in DOD as the "procuring contracting officer" (PCO), the representative of the buying office who enters into the contract and signs it on behalf of the government. A contracting officer *may* perform all of the functions described in the FAR definition cited above. In DOD and other federal agencies, however, it is customary to assign the responsibilities of administering the contract after its award to an "administrative contracting officer." This individual is widely referred to as the ACO. DOD and certain other agencies assign the responsibilities incident to settling terminated contracts to a specialist in this area, referred to as the "termination contracting officer" (TCO).

When performed at the source, that is, at the contractor's plant, the inspection function is usually the responsibility of a member of the ACO's staff.

The audit of a contractor's records incident to evaluating pricing or indirect cost proposals, costs incurred, compliance with cost accounting standards, etc., and submitting recommendations thereon to the contracting officer is the responsibility of the contract auditor. As described in the following chapter, under DOD, NASA, and certain contracts awarded by some civilian agencies, this work is done by a member of the Defense Contract Audit Agency (DCAA), an independent DOD agency reporting to the Assistant Secretary of Defense (Comptroller). In the civilian agencies, the contract audit function is the responsibility of the agency's office of inspector general, through an assistant inspector general for contract audit.

As stated earlier, the contracting officer is generally the most important official representing the government. However, as developed in the next chapter, the DCAA auditor has become increasingly powerful in recent years and has eroded some of the contracting officer's authority. The contract auditor has taken over the authority for establishing billing rates and determining indirect cost rates, although the latter determination is appealable to the contracting officer. The DCAA Director has subpoena power which has been exercised to obtain almost every kind of contractor record, without the need for coordination with the contracting officer. While always an official for contractors to reckon with, the DCAA auditor has steadily increased his importance at the expense of the contracting officer.

CONTRACT COST PRINCIPLES

The earliest attempt at a consistent and concerted effort to establish cost accounting requirements in connection with government contracts can be traced back to military procurement during World War I. The aim of limiting profits earned on war contracts generally failed of fulfillment. The unsuccessful efforts during the first great war have been attributed largely to the method of procurement prevailing at that time. The cost-plus-percentage-of-cost (CPPC) contract served only to limit the percentage of profit that could be earned but did not restrict the amount of profit.

What is considered an even greater defect of this early "cost-plus" contract was its failure to provide any incentive for cost control. As a matter of fact, a minority of contractors took the opportunity to accumulate exorbitant profits by extravagant and wasteful expenditures. Even the great majority of sincere and honest companies experienced difficulties in effectively controlling and reducing costs when the profits to be earned increased in direct proportion to the costs incurred. The CPPC type of contract was ultimately made illegal by statute.

Legislation enacted during the period betweeen World War I and World War II did not reflect a real appreciation of the basic deficiencies encountered in prior years. The Vinson-Trammell Act of 1934 and the Merchant Marine Act of 1936 applied only to contracts for naval vessels and aircraft and merely required payment to the U.S. Treasury of profits earned in excess of a fixed percentage of the contract price. The efforts to modify and revise these statutes after the demise of the Renegotiation Act in 1979 are described in Chapter XXV of this text.

The major efforts to provide contract cost principles for government contracts were concentrated for many years in the military procurement area. The antecedents of the current cost principles include Treasury Decision 5000 (1940), the "Green Book" (1942), Joint Termination Regulations (1943), and ASPR/DAR (1949-1984). Cost principles for contracts awarded by civilian agencies were set forth in the FPR, with some exceptions. Agreement among the civilian agencies was not achieved with respect to independent research and development (IR&D) and bid and proposal (B&P) costs and cost of money. Additionally, DOE and DHEW (later DHHS) operated under many formal or informal cost principles that differed from those in FPR.

Substantial uniformity in applying contract cost principles was achieved with the promulgation of FAR.

Defense Contract Audit Agency (DCAA) and Other Federal Contract Audit Organizations

The history of the contract auditor in the Department of Defense has been marked by continuing growth in influence and importance. The success of DOD's Defense Contract Audit Agency has been instrumental in raising the status of contract audit organizations throughout the federal government. Led by DCAA, federal contract audit agencies have waged successful bureaucratic struggles to achieve increasing levels of potency. In these efforts, contract auditors are greatly indebted to the General Accounting Office (GAO), which has published numerous reports criticizing contracting officers for failing to accord appropriate recognition to audit advice. GAO has also taken the contract audit agencies to task on occasion, but its reports generally faulted the agencies for not doing enough and provided them excellent opportunities for complaining about lack of sufficient staff or failure of procurement officials to use their services.

As the leader in the contract auditor's ascendency, DCAA has been involved in controversies with both industry and other DOD components ever since its inception in 1965. Within DOD, there have been several serious efforts to make DCAA a real member of the "pricing team" by consolidating it into DCAS or integrating the auditors into whichever contract administration groups they were involved with, e.g., Air Force Plant Representative Offices (AFPROs), Navy Plant Representative Offices (NAVPROs), etc. On several occasions, DCAA's prized "independence" was in serious jeopardy as the logic of consolidating all factions of contract administration was favorably considered at high levels in the Pentagon. In each instance, however, with valuable assistance from the GAO and congressional supporters, DCAA not only withstood the efforts but appeared to emerge more powerful and independent than ever. While lagging behind their DOD colleagues, the contract auditors in most civilian agencies benefitted from DCAA's successes and also increased their influence.

ROLES OF CONTRACTING OFFICERS AND CONTRACT AUDITORS AND THEIR RELATIONSHIPS

This important and complex subject has defied precise clarification in the past and controversies and confusion have increased. There is a broad consensus in the public and private sectors that the contracting officer is the representative of the government "with the authority to enter into, administer, and/or terminate contracts and make related determinations and findings" (FAR Subpart 2.1). It is similarly understood and accepted that the DCAA auditor is responsible for "providing DOD officials responsible for procurement and contract administration with financial information and advice on proposed or existing contracts and contractors, as appropriate" (Department of Defense Directive 5105.36, sometimes referred to as DCAA's "charter"). Moving beyond these broad "roles and missions" statements, however, one encounters a number of issues that require further clarification, including the following:

What are the contracting officer's authority and responsibility with respect to the recommendations ("information and advice") contained in DCAA audit reports?

Who shall have access to which contractor's records and for what purpose?

We shall explore these issues by citing the authoritative but inconsistent provisions of FAR and DOD Directive 7640.2 and the nonauthoritative but important provisions of DCAA's Contract Audit Manual (CAM).

Federal Acquisition Regulation (FAR)

As we shall discuss later in connection with DOD Directive 7640.2, certain congressional committees, GAO, and DOD's Inspector General have been quite exercised over resolution of contract audit findings. Essentially, interest has been focused on whether contracting officers should accept and endorse each and every recommendation by contract auditors as to which costs submitted by contractors should be allowed. Presently, if a contract auditor recommends that a specific cost not be allowed but the contracting officer, after consultation with his other advisors and technical specialists, decides to allow the cost, the contract audit finding must be resolved; i.e., the contracting officer must forward the files to higher echelons along with reasons for not accepting the auditor's recommendations. With this preoccupation over specific cost elements, it is interesting to consider the government pricing philosophy as set forth in FAR 15.803(d):

The contracting officer's primary concern is the price the Government actually pays; the contractor's eventual cost and profit or fee should be a secondary concern . . . . Therefore, the contracting officer should not become preoccupied with any single element and should balance the contract type, cost, and profit or fee negotiated to achieve a total result and a price fair and reasonable to both the Government and the contractor.

It would appear difficult indeed to achieve the objectives of trade-offs and negotiation to reach a fair and reasonable price where the contracting officer must justify each decision to depart from the auditor's recommendation on every cost element.

As we shall see later in this chapter, DOD Directive 7640.2 seems to establish the contract auditor as almost coequal with the contracting officer in the cost aspects of contract pricing, while government acquisition philosophy differs significantly, recognizing the auditor as only one of the advisors whose recommendations should be taken into account. FAR 15.807(a) states this philosophy:

> In setting the prenegotiation objectives, the contracting officer shall analyze the offeror's proposal, taking into account the field pricing report, if any; any audit report and technical analysis whether or not part of a field pricing report; and other pertinent data such as independent Government cost estimates and price histories.

One can only wonder about the seeming indifference among government officials responsible for promulgating regulations and directives toward the publications issued by other such officials. DOD Directive 7640.2, issued on December 29, 1982, did not reflect substantive changes from the provisions of DOD Directive 5000.42, issued in August 31, 1981. And yet FAR, the regulation issued on September 19, 1983, to establish policy for government-wide acquisition, appears to ignore the DOD Directive in its coverage of contracting officer/contract auditor relationships.

On the issue of who must be given access to which contractor's records and for what purpose, the question surfaced early in DCAA's history with the agency's complaints that price analysts and other members of the contracting officer's or field pricing support's staffs were performing audits or engaging in equivalent activities, a function allegedly assigned exclusively to DCAA. Procurement and contract administration officials denied that their staffs were performing audits but would not concede that DCAA had the sole authority for examining contractors' records for pricing purposes. The controversies continued for many years and, although still not completely settled, are fairly well under control. The basic policy is set forth in FAR 15.805-5(d):

> Only the auditor shall have general access to the offeror's books and financial records. This limitation does not preclude the contracting officer, the ACO, or their representatives from requesting any data from or reviewing offeror records necessary to the discharge of their responsibilities. The duties of auditors and those of other specialists may require both to evaluate the same elements of estimated costs. They shall review the data jointly or concurrently when possible, the auditor rendering services within the audit area of responsibility and the other specialists rendering services within their own areas of responsibility.

On another aspect of access to contractors' records, both the ACO staffs and DCAA asserted authority to conduct reviews of contractors' estimating systems, purchasing systems, compensation structure, financial capability and other matters related to government contracts. Most of the rival claims have been settled, formally or informally. FAR 15.811 states that "cognizant audit activities ... shall establish and maintain regular programs for reviewing selected contractors' estimating systems or methods ...." Contractors' Purchasing System Reviews (FAR 42.302(a)(50) and Part 44) are assigned as contract administration office functions, as are reviews of contractors' compensation structure (FAR 42.302(a)(1)) and monitoring contractors' financial condition (FAR 42.302(a)(16)). Despite these assignments, DCAA auditors frequently review areas established as the responsibility of contract administration offices. For example, CAM 6-310 contains audit requirements for reviewing every facet of contractors' purchasing and subcontracting systems and operations.

Neither FAR nor its predecessor agency regulations recognized the contract auditor as having coequal authority with the contracting officer. However, in certain circumstances it is considered administratively desirable to assign to the auditor certain responsibilities slightly beyond purely advisory ones. In these instances, the conditions under which the auditor will assume such additional responsibilities and the manner in which they will be discharged are spelled out specifically, as illustrated in the policies and procedures prescribed in FAR Subpart 42.7 for billing rates and final indirect cost rates. Except for agencies whose procedures require contracting officer determination, this responsibility may be assigned to either the contracting officer or the contract auditor in accordance with the provisions of FAR 42.705-1 and 42.705-2, excerpted below:

42.705-1 Contracting officer determination procedure.

(a) *Applicability and responsibility.* Contracting officer determination shall be used for the following, with the indicated cognizant contracting officer responsible for establishing the final indirect cost rates:

(1) Business units of a multidivisional corporation under the cognizance of a corporate administrative contracting officer (see Subpart 42.6), with that officer responsible for the determination, assisted, as required, by the administrative contracting officers assigned to the individual business units. Negotiations may be conducted on a coordinated or centralized basis, depending upon the degree of centralization within the contractor's organization.

(2) Business units not under the cognizance of a corporate administrative contracting officer, but having a resident administrative contracting officer (see 42.602), with that officer responsible for the determination. For this purpose, a nonresident administrative contracting officer is considered as resident if at least 75 percent of the administrative contracting officer's time is devoted to a single contractor.

(3) Business units not included in subparagraph (1) or (2) above, but where the predominant interest (on the basis of unliquidated contract dollar amount) is in an agency whose procedures require contracting officer determination. In such cases, the responsible contracting officer will be as designated under that agency's procedures.

* * * *

42.705-2 Auditor determination procedure.

(a) *Applicability and responsibility.* (1) The cognizant Government auditor shall establish final indirect cost rates for business units not covered in 42.705-1(a).

(2) In addition, auditor determination may be used for business units that are covered in 42.705-1(a) when the contracting officer and auditor agree that the indirect costs can be settled with little difficulty and any of the following circumstances apply:

(i) The business unit has primarily fixed-price contracts, with only minor involvement in cost-reimbursement contracts.

(ii) The administrative cost of contracting officer determination would exceed the expected benefits.

(iii) The business unit does not have a history of disputes and there are few cost problems.

(iv) The contracting officer and auditor agree that special circumstances require auditor determination.

(b) *Procedures.* (1) The contractor shall submit to the cognizant contracting officer and auditor a final indirect cost rate proposal reflecting actual cost experience during the covered period, together with supporting cost or pricing data.

(2) The auditors shall—

(i) Audit the proposal and seek agreement on it with the contractor;

(ii) Obtain from the contractor a Certificate of Current Cost or Pricing Data, if required (see 15.804-4);

(iii) In coordination with the affected contracting officers, prepare an indirect cost rate agreement conforming to the requirements of the contracts;

(iv) Prepare an audit report including the information required by 15.805-5(e);

(v) If agreement with the contractor is not reached, forward the audit report to the contracting officer designated by the agency with the predominant interest (on the basis of unliquidated contract dollar amounts) or, where applicable, the contracting officer designated in 42.705-2(a)(2) above, who will then resolve the disagreement; and

(vi) Distribute resulting documents in accordance with 42.706.

Another illustration of FAR provisions that assign to the auditor responsibilities beyond those considered to be purely advisory relates to the disallowance of costs after incurrence. Depending on the procedures of the individual agency, vouchers submitted by contractors for payments under cost-reimbursement-type contracts may be directed to either the contracting officer or the contract auditor. FAR 42.803(b) prescribes the contract auditor's authority to handle such vouchers:

(b) *Auditor receipt of vouchers.* (1) When authorized by agency regulations, the contract auditor may be authorized to (i) receive reimbursement vouchers directly from contractors, (ii) approve for payment those vouchers found acceptable, and (iii) suspend payment of questionable costs. The auditor shall forward approved vouchers for payment to the cognizant contracting, finance, or disbursing officer, as appropriate under the agency's procedures.

(2) If the examination of a voucher raises a question regarding the allowability of a cost under the contract terms, the auditor, after informal discussion as appropriate, may, where authorized by agency regulations,

issue a notice of contract costs suspended and/or disapproved simultaneously to the contractor and the disbursing officer, with a copy to the cognizant contracting officer, for deduction from current payments with respect to costs claimed but not considered reimbursable.

(3) If the contractor disagrees with the deduction from current payments, the contractor may—

(i) Submit a written request to the cognizant contracting officer to consider whether the unreimbursed costs should be paid and to discuss the findings with the contractor;

(ii) File a claim under the Disputes clause, which the cognizant contracting officer will process in accordance with agency procedures; or

(iii) Do both of the above.

DOD Directive 7640.2

In the review of FAR, we learned that the contracting officer is the government's representative authorized to make determinations concerning contracts, with the focus on negotiating a fair and reasonable price rather than on individual elements of cost and profit or fee. We also learned that the contracting officer should obtain and consider the recommendations of various advisors, one of whom is the contract auditor, but that the final decision is the contracting officer's. Provisions of DOD Directive 7640.2, however, appear to describe a different world. Before commenting on this Directive, it would be useful to trace the events leading to its publication.

Prior to the establishment of DCAA, the audit organizations in the Military Departments were responsible for both contract audits and internal audits. Under this organizational structure, it was possible for an Army Audit Agency auditor to submit an advisory contract audit report to a contracting officer and then, donning his internal audit hat, to criticize the contracting officer if the price negotiated appeared to reflect the allowance of a cost element that the auditor had "questioned." When DCAA was established in 1965, it was assigned the function and staff related to contract audit while the function and staff related to internal audit remained with the department. The new arrangement resulted in what most people in both the private and public sectors believed was a complete separation of the two missions. However, the precise role of the DCAA auditor and his relationship with the contracting officer evolved into rather complex patterns.

The DCAA auditor was assigned to perform contract audits on request and to submit reports to contracting officers making recommendations concerning cost accounting aspects of contract negotiation, administration, and settlement. It was never intended or conceived that the contract auditor would be evaluating the contracting officer's decisions on these recommendations and even questioning or challenging the latter's decisions.

Not too long after DCAA was established, some of its officials became perturbed on learning that contract audit recommendations were not always followed. The fledgling agency was not prepared to challenge the authority of contracting officers head-on in the early years. Instead, it mounted a successful drive to require contracting officers to furnish copies of negotiation memoranda to the auditors in order to ascertain the details of the contracting officer's determinations. The stated purpose of obtaining these memoranda was to gain a better understanding of the contracting officer's actions. This enhanced understanding would be used to improve audits and related reports.

About this time, GAO issued a series of reports alleging that there were instances of substantial differences between audit recommendations and the ultimate negotiations; i.e., contracting officers were sometimes allowing costs that auditors believed should not be allowed. Although it was evident that GAO personnel then (and since) generally tended to side with their fellow auditors, it was difficult to ignore the major point that there was something wrong when two organizations within a department reached widely different conclusions about the allowability of the same costs.

DCAA then initiated the practice of instructing its auditors to make every effort to obtain copies of the negotiation memoranda and, when substantial costs questioned in audit reports were allowed by contracting officers, to carefully review such instances and discuss them with contracting officers. If, after such a review and discussion, a DCAA regional office concluded that the contracting officer's decision lacked merit, the matter was to be referred to the Agency's headquarters. At headquarters, referrals were carefully screened and a small number were submitted both to the DOD Comptroller and to what was then the Office of the Assistant Secretary of Defense for Installations & Logistics.

Though relatively few in number, these submissions rankled procurement and contract administration officials. The most disturbing feature of DCAA's new practice was the concept that the contract audit advisors had assumed the authority to question and second-guess the contracting officers. The unhappiness in the acquisition community led to complaints to then Deputy Secretary of Defense David Packard. In a significant memorandum of October 1970, Packard established that, while audit advice was essential to good contracting and had to be considered by contracting officers, the ultimate decisions on pricing required taking into account many factors in addition to those presented by the auditors. Secretary Packard concluded:

> We should avoid actions by auditors in their advisory capacity which appear to dispute or question specific decisions by the contracting officer. I want our contracting people to exercise judgment in their day-to-day work. The escalation of possible disputes relative to specific decisions should be avoided.

Just about 11 years later, the Defense Department issued Directive 5000.42, later revised and renumbered 7640.2, which appears to turn the Packard policy on its head. The contract auditor is now encouraged to dispute or question specific decisions by the contracting officer, and the two appear to be established as almost coequals in matters relating to the determination of costs. What led to the publication of these Directives and the drastic turn-around in DOD policy?

A series of GAO reports and related congressional hearings appeared to reflect what some observers believed to be a myopic view of procurement and other government activities: they apparently concluded that the majority of the deficiencies in government operations were attributable to the failure of managers, contracting officers, and other officials to comply with the recommendations of their auditors. The government's ills, some argued, could be substantially cured if the federal agencies would "develop, implement and use more effective means in resolving audit findings." Since the Defense Department is the largest federal agency and spends most of the federal funds, it drew most of the criticism.

Under considerable pressure, augmented by Secretary of Defense Weinberger's own increasing emphasis on detection and prevention of fraud, waste, and abuse, DOD revised its directives governing resolution of audit findings. At first, DOD officials attempted to explain to GAO and congressional committees that there were significant differences between internal and contract audit. The officials conceded that internal audit recommendations should be "resolved," that is, if a commander or other official did not decide to implement an internal audit recommendation, the official should explain the basis for the disagreement and some higher authority should be the final arbiter, deciding whether the audit recommendation should be followed.

But, in the area of contracting, a different condition obtained, as DOD officials unsuccessfully attempted to explain. Here the contracting officer had a warrant to sign contracts on behalf of the government and both the legal responsibility and the authority to make final decisions. The point was also made that the contracting officer has many advisors on staff in addition to the independent DCAA auditor, including attorneys, price analysts, and specialists in such areas as production, engineering, and quality assurance. If a formal "resolution" process were to be promulgated with respect to recommendations by contract auditors, might there subsequently be a requirement to develop similar procedures for recommendations by all of the other advisors to contracting officers?

The contentions and explanations were not persuasive to GAO or to certain congressional elements. The pressures from such sources continued, and their views were adopted by the highest levels in DOD and in the Office of Management and Budget (OMB), the latter presumably expressing the views of the Administration. The result was DOD Directive 5000.42, later 7640.2.

Few observers seriously question that this directive significantly dilutes the authority of the contracting officer and aggrandizes the role of the contract auditor. In the past, the contracting officer was admonished to obtain the advice of the contract auditor and the appropriate specialists on the contracting officer's own staff, and then to exercise his best judgment in negotiating a contractor's cost and price submissions. It is not unusual to find some differences among the recommendations received from the various advisors, and it was the contracting officer's responsibility to select those he considered most appropriate in the circumstances. Today, the contracting officer is still free to consider the suggestions of DOD staff, to arrive at his own conclusion, and to act on it; but it is not so with respect to the recommendations contained in the contract audit report.

One of the provisions of 7640.2 requires that,

From the time of audit report receipt to the time of final disposition of the audit report, there shall be continuous communication between the auditor and the contracting officer.

This provision is widely interpreted as meaning that, unless the audit recommendation is accepted, the contracting officer is in effect required to negotiate with the auditor in an effort to "resolve" their differences.

In a number of instances, contracting officers have apparently lacked the time or inclination for these negotiations and have found it more expedient to furnish the audit report or its conclusions to contractors as their own initial determinations, sometimes even suggesting that the contractors work out their differences with the contract auditors. Where the contractor is adamant in a disagreement, the contracting officer may seek to negotiate a price, the allowability of a cost, or the compliance with a cost accounting standard, with the aim of arriving at a conclusion acceptable to all parties. It sometimes develops into a three-party affair.

If these negotiating efforts fail, the contracting officer has two options: endorse the audit recommendation or accept the contractor's submission. If the contracting officer chooses the former rate and the contractor will not yield, and if the issue is along the lines of allowability of costs incurred, defective pricing, compliance with CAS, etc., the disagreement moves to a formal dispute and litigation before a board of contract appeals and/or the federal courts.

There are circumstances in which this route cannot be taken. If the issue involves preaward contract negotiations, particularly in the case of urgently needed supplies, the contracting officer must arrive at a negotiated price even if it does not reflect acceptance of all of the auditor's recommendations.

What if the contracting officer is more favorably impressed with the contractor's position than with the auditor's, the latter will not agree to modify the initial advice, and the contracting officer decides to accept the contractor's submission? In these instances, 7640.2 directs as follows:

> When the contracting officer's proposed disposition of contract audit report recommendations differs from the contract auditor's recommendations ... the contracting officer's proposed disposition shall be brought promptly to the attention of a designated independent senior acquisition official (DISAO) or board for review.

This official or board will receive the contracting officer's views plus any supporting data and the DCAA report, review this material, and request additional material from either the contracting officer or auditor, if required. Thereafter, "a clear, written recommendation" will be provided to the contracting officer with a copy to the contract auditor. This procedure is required with respect to the following:

(1) All audit reports covering estimating system surveys, accounting system surveys, internal control reviews, defective pricing reviews, cost accounting standards noncompliance reviews, and operations audits.

(2) Audit reports covering incurred costs, settlement of indirect cost rates, final pricings, terminations, equitable adjustment claims, hardship claims, and escalation claims if total costs questioned equal $50,000 or more and differences between the contracting officer and auditor total at least 5 percent of questioned costs.

(3) Prenegotiation objectives for forward pricing actions when questioned costs total at least $500,000 and unresolved differences between the auditor and contracting officer total at least 5 percent of the total questioned costs.

In addition to the other questionable aspects of these provisions, the thresholds established for initiating the cumbersome submissions to higher levels appear to be extremely low. In the audit reports described in paragraph (2) above, once total costs questioned equal $50,000, an unresolved difference of only $2,500 triggers the audit resolution process. In forward pricing actions, where total questioned costs equal $500,000, a difference of only $25,000 will bring the contract negotiation to a screeching halt while submissions are prepared, forwarded, and reviewed and an official or board transmits "a clear, written recommendation."

While industry as well as DOD acquisition people objected to these provisions as diluting the authority of the contracting officer, congressional elements voiced objections of a different kind. They criticized the provision under which the Designated Independent Senior Acquisition Offical (DISAO) or board made a recommendation to the contracting officer. In their view, the contracting officer should be stripped of authority in these circumstances and the higher authority should direct the contracting officer as to just how the difference with the auditor should be resolved.

On a realistic level, the difference between a recommendation and a direction from a higher level is not all that great. Theoretically, a recommendation, even one from a superior, permits the contracting officer to exercise judgment in making the final decision. Practically, neither contracting officers nor other officials are likely to view recommendations from higher levels lightly. The contracting officer must also bear in mind that, under 7640.2, each military department and defense agency must designate a senior management official (SMO) "to serve as a focal point for the audit followup function." In addition to the surveillance by the SMO, there will also be departmental internal auditors, DOD Inspectors General, GAO, and congressional committees looking over the contracting officer's shoulder through on-site reviews and analyses of status reports that must be provided to show all information regarding differences and how they were resolved.

DCAA Contract Audit Manual (CAM)

For a viewpoint on the contracting officer/contract auditor relationship from another government publication, we turn to DCAA's CAM. As mentioned earlier, this Manual lacks statutory or regulatory authority and is directed only to DCAA auditors. The thinking of the agency, however, should be of interest to contractors and contracting officers.

A CAM subsection on "Relationships with DOD Procurement and Contract Administration Organizations" advises DCAA auditors what actions to take in the event of disagreements with contracting officers concerning audit recommendations. It should be noted that this guidance is apart from the so-called audit resolution process in DOD Directive 7640.2:

1-403.3 Major Audit Issues

DCAA Forms 1 and audit report recommendations may lead to disagreements between the auditor and contracting officer. There must be continual communication between the parties to promote understanding and improve the potential for satisfactory resolution of the issue before final contracting officer action.

The following excerpt is from CAM Chapter 15, Section 6, which provides additional guidance to the agency's auditors with regard to implementing DOD Directive 7640.2:

15-604.2 Monitor All Final Disposition and Negotiation Memorandums

a. Each DCAA field audit office will monitor all final disposition and negotiation memorandums to determine when their contents:

(1) Fail to explain differences between the proposed disposition and the final disposition of audit recommendations.

(2) Indicate that disputed audit findings meeting the threshold criteria in 15-603.3 were not referred to DISAO review.

(3) State the audit position incorrectly; or indicate that the disposition, whether endorsed by a DISAO or not, was significantly adverse to the interests of the Government.

b. When the negotiation memorandum indicates one or more of the situations in a. above, the FAO will contact the DISAO to attempt to resolve the issue. Failing local resolution, the FAO will refer the situation to the regional director, through the cognizant RAM, for resolution at the regional level. If the regional director is unable to resolve the situation with appropriate counterparts in the acquisition community, a memorandum will be prepared from the regional director to Headquarters, Attention O, outlining the nature and current status of the problem, as well as actions taken to resolve it. Headquarters will contact the DOD Component Contract Audit Followup Official (CAFO) to attempt to resolve the situation.

c. Annually, by 31 December, the FAO, through the Regional Office, will provide the CAFO of each Military department a listing of all negotiation memorandums and/or final dispositions not received as of the previous fiscal year end, including all forward pricing assignments (Code 210) closed without receipt of PNM. This listing should identify the DFARs Appendix N activity code if furnished in the audit request.

DCAA CURRENT POLICIES, PROCEDURES AND PRACTICES

In the eighth edition of this text, we wrote that, with assistance from GAO and its congressional supporters, DCAA "appears to have established a solid base in the Department of Defense and in the federal government at large." We noted that its reception in the private sector was mixed, with many of its auditors having "earned respect and recognition for their professional competence, expertise, and fairness." We also addressed the other side of the coin, including the sharply adversarial relationships which other DCAA officials created with contractors, in their hostility to industry and their preoccupation with allegations of fraud, and in their overzealousness in efforts to compile impressive statistics on costs recommended for disallowance and on noncompliances with cost accounting standards.

With Congress increasingly involved in numerous facets of DOD procurement micromanagement, DCAA has come in for its share of attention at congressional hearings. The agency has also attracted considerable notice from defense contractors, the objects of increasing and redundant government oversight and surveillance. Add the continuing attention by the DOD Inspector General and GAO and the picture emerges of an agency very much in the public eye. Most comments from within the government were generally favorable to the audit agency, largely because of dissatisfaction with contractors and contracting officers. This dissatisfaction led to suggestions to increase DCAA's power and authority at the expense of contracting officers. However, there were also adverse views based on DOD IG and GAO allegations that the agency was not active enough in fraud detection and not tough enough on contractors in demanding access to records and disallowing costs.

In an effort to present a picture of DCAA in the late 1980s, we have compiled the varying views from both the public and private sectors, presenting them in the following categories:

Relationships with higher DOD authorities.

Relationships with contracting officers.

Relationships with contractors.

Access to records.

Critiques by DOD IG and GAO.

Congressional views and actions.

Who's in charge?

Office of Management and Budget (OMB) Circular A-50, Audit Follow-up.

DCAA Relationships with Higher DOD Authorities

As discussed in more detail under some of the following headings, congressional investigations, aided at times by GAO and DCAA auditors, have alleged widespread charging of improper costs by DOD contractors. These investigations revealed that some costs questioned by DCAA auditors were subsequently allowed in negotiations between contractors and contracting officers. This led certain congressmen to the conclusions that contracting officers should be stripped of some of their authority and that DCAA should be given a greater say in cost determination.

Such high level officials as the Secretary and Deputy Secretary of Defense have recognized the fact of life that it is the contracting officer who has the warrant and who is the major government representative in contractual dealings with industry. However, in order to appease their congressional critics, these officials have assigned increasing authority to DCAA, most recently for establishing interim billing rates and final rates for indirect costs.

As to the determination of final indirect cost rates, at one time considered the unquestionable authority of the contracting officer, FAR 42.705-2 adopted the previous DOD policy of assigning this responsibility to the contract auditor in limited instances where the contractors perform mainly on firm fixed-price contracts, have no history of disputes, and have no resident ACO. Benefitting from congressional criticism of contracting officers for allegedly allowing inappropriate indirect costs questioned by contract auditors, DCAA had little difficulty in persuading higher authority to assign to it indirect cost responsibility at all locations. On August 5, 1985, the Deputy Secretary of Defense sent the following memorandum to the Assistant Secretaries of Defense (Acquisition and Logistics) and (Comptroller):

SUBJECT: Audit Determination of Indirect Cost Rates

I have decided to assign responsibility for final indirect cost rate determination for all contractor locations to the Defense Contract Audit Agency (DCAA). This extends the same procedures currently used by DCAA to determine final overhead rates at smaller contractors to the larger contractor locations where final overhead rates are currently established through procurement negotiation. These procedures are to be applied only to contracts with commercial organizations, and, thus, will not affect overhead determination procedures for educational and similar institutions.

New guidelines should be developed in coordination with the military components and DLA that provide safeguards to ensure that a single DOD voice is maintained with contractors and that litigation is minimized. These guidelines should include provisions to permit DCAA to accomplish the role of rate determination effectively and to emphasize the need for close communication between auditors and administrative contracting officers.

Please proceed as quickly as possible to develop the new guidelines, initiate the necessary changes to the FAR and implementing DOD regulations, and establish a transition plan for those contractor locations where the rates are now determined through procurement negotiation.

It is to be noted that the aforegoing order was silent on the determination of interim billing rates. However, DFARS required that the agency responsible for establishing final indirect cost rates also be responsible for establishing interim billing rates.

As a result of the above, the DAR Council in April 1986 proposed a change to the DFARS implementing the Deputy Secretary's memorandum. Obviously, this action met certain resistance from the existing procurement related authorities. Ultimately, the Deputy Assistant Secretary of Defense for Procurement, on July 22, 1986, ordered the DAR Council to initiate the aforementioned proposed changes to the DFARS, as evidenced by the following "DOD Proposed Rule" dated March 2, 1987, with comments thereon due by May 1, 1987. This rule gives the auditor the authority to determine interim billing and final overhead rates for DOD contractor locations where DOD has the predominant interest.

Apparently this further deterioration of the contracting officer's authority and responsibility was not acceptable to the civilian agencies because the proposed implementation of the directive was published as proposed revisions to the DOD FAR Supplement (DFARS) rather than to the FAR. Inasmuch as these proposed revisions were promulgated by the DFARS Council, which is subordinate to the high level DOD authorities that initiated this proposed rule, it would appear to the author that this rule will be implemented in its final form accordingly, without further change, at an early date.

DOD Proposed Rule

242.704 Billing rates.

(a) The auditor is responsible for determining billing rates for those contractor entities listed at FAR 42.705-1(a)(1) through (6).

3. Section 242.705-1 is amended by adding paragraph (a), and by redesignating the existing paragraph (a)(1) as paragraph (1), as follows:

242.705-1 Contracting officer determination procedure.

(a) Responsibility for determination of final indirect cost rates is being transitioned to DCAA. Contracting officer determination procedures will continue to apply at individual contractor locations until transitioned to DCAA responsibility.

* * * * *

4. Section 242.705-2 is amended by adding paragraphs (a), (b)(1), (b)(2)(i), and (b)(2)(ii); by revising paragraph (b)(2)(iii); by adding paragraph (b)(2)(iv), and by revising paragraph (b)(2)(v) to read as follows:

242.705-2 Auditor determination procedure.

(a) Auditor determination procedures will be used for commercial contractor locations where DoD has the predominant interest (on the basis of unliquidated dollar amount). Transition years for contractor locations will be published at a later date. This procedure, as it applies to DoD contractor locations meeting the FAR criteria for contracting officer determination will be reevaluated at a subsequent date.

(b)(1) For multidivisional contractors, the proposal for each segment shall be submitted to the auditor responsible for conducting audits of that division and the divisional ACO. The cognizant auditor shall forward copies of the proposal to the corporate ACO and auditor. The contractor's proposal must contain an executed Certificate of Overhead Costs.

(b)(2)(i) Upon completion of the audit, the auditor will issue to the contractor a written notification setting forth audit exceptions to the contractor's proposal. The notification will state that the contractor has 90 days to provide its agreement or rebuttal comments. A copy of the notification will be furnished to the cognizant ACO. The auditor may grant the contractor one 30-day extension upon receipt of a written request from the contractor. Upon receipt of the contractor's response to the written notification of audit exceptions, the auditor will evaluate the response and issue the audit report required in FAR 42.705-2(b)(2)(iv) to the cognizant ACO within 60 days. If the contractor fails to respond to the notification by the required date (initial or extended), the auditor will issue the audit report. Regardless of the agreement or disagreement, the audit report will cover, as a mimimum:

(A) The contractor's indirect cost rate proposal;

(B) The audit findings;

(C) Reconciliation of all costs questioned, with identification of all individual elements of cost and amounts allowed to disallowed in the final settlement if agreement was reached, or recommended for disallowance if agreement was not reached;

(D) Disposition of period costing or allocability issues; and

(E) Identification of cost or pricing date submitted subsequent to the proposal and relied upon in reaching a settlement.

(ii) See paragraph (b)(2)(iii) of this section.

(iii) If the audit report details that agreement has been reached, the auditor will obtain from the contractor the Certificate of Current Cost or Pricing Date required in FAR 42.705-2(b)(2)(ii) and prepare an indirect cost rate agreement in accordance with FAR 42.705-2(b)(2)(iii). The agreement shall be signed by the contractor and the designated audit official.

(iv) See paragraph (b)(2)(i) of this section.

(v) If the audit report details that agreement with the contractor cannot be reached, the auditor will also issue DCAA Form 1 detailing the items of exception. Upon receipt of a DCAA Form 1, the contractor can submit a request, in writing, to the cognizant ACO to reconsider the auditor's determination and/or file a claim under the Disputes Clause. Such request or claim shall be submitted within 60 days. In considering the contractor's request, the ACO will not resolve any questioned cost without obtaining adequate documentation and the opinion of the auditor. To the maximum extent practicable, the auditor should be present at any negotiation or meeting between the ACO and contractor regarding the questioned costs. If agreement between the parties is reached, the ACO will obtain the Certificate of Current Cost or Pricing Data, prepare the indirect cost rate agreement, and prepare a negotiation memorandum containing the elements set forth in FAR 42.705-1(b)(5)(iii). Failure of the parties to reach agreement will be treated in accordance with FAR Subpart 33.2.

5. Section 242.706 is amended by revising paragraph (a), by removing paragraph (b)(1), and adding paragraph (b) to read as follows:

242.706 Distribution of Documents.

(a) When the auditor executes the overhead rate agreement (see 242.705-2(b)(2)(iii)), copies of the agreement will be furnished to the contractor, the cognizant CACO (if assigned), and the cognizant ACO. In addition, copies will be distributed to other Departments, and (upon specific request) any other interested Government agencies. Department may make further distribution to activities within their Departments and shall insert one copy in each contractor general file (see S2-101.2 and S2-102.4). When the ACO executes the overhead rate agreement (see 242.705-2(b)(2)(v)), distribution is the same except that a copy will also be provided to the cognizant auditor.

(b) The audit report issued to the cognizant ACO pursuant to 242.705-2(b)(2)(i) will also be furnished to the cognizant CACO (if assigned). If the ACO prepares a negotiation memorandum pursuant to 242.705-2(b)(2)(v), copies will furnished to the cognizant auditor and the cognizant CACO (if assigned). Upon specific request, a copy of the auditor's report and/or the contracting officer's negotiation memorandum will be furnished to other Departments or Government agencies.

Of course, the contracting officer has not been completely eliminated. Where agreement between the contractor and contracting officer cannot be reached, DFARS 2.705-2(b)(2)(v) requires the auditor to issue DCAA Form 1, along with his audit report, upon the receipt of which the contractor may request the ACO to reconsider the determination and/or file a claim under the contract disputes clause. If the ACO should consider allowing any costs questioned by the auditor, he picks up a heavy burden indeed, including obtaining documentation which would fully support any such decision, and to once more obtain the opinion of the potent contract auditor. If negotiations are to be attempted in an effort to reach some agreement and avoid the time-consuming and costly litigation process, the contracting officer is required to have the auditor attend any negotiation conference "to the maximum extent practicable," which adds up to something approaching a mandatory requirement. If the ACO should exercise his judgment and overrule the DCAA auditor, he must go through the "resolution" process of DOD Directive 7640.2.

Some aspects of the new procedure are not completely different from the past, e.g., obtaining the auditor's opinions, inviting him to negotiation conferences, laboring through the "resolution" process, and so on. Among the major proposed changes is the extent to which the DCAA auditor would negotiate with the contractor for a substantial period before the ACO formally enters the picture on a written request by the contractor. By that time, positions would probably have substantially solidified, making it all the more difficult for anyone to persuade the auditor to move away from a position he had taken and continued to hold over this period of time.

DCAA next persuaded the Assistant Secretary of Defense (Comptroller) that responsibility for indirect cost determination and establishment of billing rates should not be separated. Following discussions at the Pentagon, the DAR Council was directed to further revise DFARS, particularly 2.704, to transfer the additional authority to DCAA.

During most of the 1980s, the position of Assistant Secretary of Defense (Comptroller) has experienced a higher than usual turnover rate. The occupant of this post has been most important to DCAA, whose director reports to the ASD(C) and, as the incumbents came and went, the audit officials have enjoyed considerable success in obtaining their strong support for increased authority for the contract auditor. In these endeavors, DCAA has been assisted greatly by the aforementioned congressional criticisms of contractors and contracting officers. On January 31, 1985, for example, the Assistant

Secretary of Defense (Comptroller) wrote the DCAA Director that DOD's emphasis on acquisition improvement initiatives "requires that extraordinary attention be given to maximizing the role and effectiveness of the DCAA. The Secretary of Defense, Deputy Secretary of Defense, and I regard DCAA as essential to the process of ensuring that DOD procurement occurs in the most efficient, businesslike, and proper fashion possible. I intend to give special emphasis to make sure that the unique capabilities of DCAA in this regard are fully utilized and its full potential realized."

With these introductory comments, the ASD (C), with what many believe to be the close coordination of DCAA officials, requested the agency to take on certain tasks, one of which was to "[d]evelop and *strengthen* the role of DCAA as *primary* advisor to the contracting officer on accounting and financial matters." (Emphasis added.) Subtasks in this category included: "A. Identify existing conflicts of responsibility and changes needed to clarify roles and missions. B. Increase auditors' participation at negotiations."

As to subtask A, some DCAA officials have been displeased from time to time when cost and price analysts at PCO and ACO levels reviewed audit reports and submitted recommendations to contracting officers which differed from those of the auditors. Questions now arose as to whether DCAA would attempt to assert even greater power than it has under DOD Directive 7640.2, and whether efforts may be made to subordinate or eliminate the functions of the cost and price analysts. That there is cause for concern about DCAA's growing clout at the expense of acquisition officials and their staffs was indicated by one of the numerous "clarifications" to the Certification of Overhead Costs project.

In a letter to two industry associations, the DOD General Counsel advised contractors that if they were uncertain about the allowability of a cost, they "may request the opinion of the Department of Defense auditor reviewing the contractor's accounts prior to submitting the contractor's request for approval of overhead costs." This statement by DOD's top legal official raised questions as to whether he was unaware of the contracting officer's legal and contractual authority for cost determination or whether changes in this area were under consideration.

Another task assigned to DCAA by the ASD (C) was "[t]o develop a legislative proposal that gives subpoena authority to DCAA." Although this task, too, was under development within DOD, its culmination was short-circuited by the 1986 DOD Authorization Act with the following provision:

> The Director of the Defense Contract Audit Agency (or any successor agency) may require by subpoena the production of books, documents, papers, or records of a contractor, access to which is provided the Secretary of Defense by subsection (a) or by Section 2306(f) of this title.

Although subpoena authority for DCAA seemed to have wide support in the Congress and at high DOD levels, the nature and extent of the records that the agency could demand by subpoena were not clarified in the legislation. Importantly, the language of the conference report accompanying this legislation emphasizes that there was no intention to expand the scope of the records beyond whatever the government is presently entitled to, and that the subpoena power should be used sparingly:

This provision is not intended to expand the scope of books, documents, papers or records to which the defense contract audit agency presently has access, but rather to provide the director of the agency with an enforcement mechanism if a contractor does not make such books, documents, papers or records readily available. The conferees believe that *the subpoena power should be used sparingly,* and generally only when alternative investigatory methods have proven inadequate to obtain the materials that are sought. In addition, it should be used only in the performance of the functions and purposes ascribed to the contract audit agency. (Emphasis added.)

As discussed below in connection with DCAA's thrust for increasing access to records, most industry observers have concluded that DCAA has not accorded consideration to the conference report, sharply expanding the scope of records to which it has demanded access. As to the sparing use of the subpoena power, DCAA has been seen by some as circumventing this direction by enforcing a few subpoenas and then using the threats of issuing additional ones to achieve its purpose.

DCAA was also requested by the ASD (C) to "develop a plan to increase and strengthen DCAA's audits of the defective pricing program." Related subtasks establish that DCAA should follow the recommendations by GAO and DOD IG to increase the manpower devoted to these audits and view findings of alleged defective pricing as possible fraud. In this regard, one of the subtasks specifically directs DCAA to "[e]xplore changes in statutory language that would establish a connection between defective pricing and improper actions such as false statements or false claims, and whether penalties should be incorporated in the statute."

The fraud hysteria in the government is sparked by the all-too-numerous disclosures of fraudulent practices which some contractors have agreed did occur. DCAA officials continue to allege that the agency concentrates on its mission of contract auditing but these allegations have lost some credibility as the agency, as a result of outside pressure, and on its own, accords increasing attention to fraud detection.

As initially established, DCAA had two lawyers on its staff, transferred from the U.S. Army Audit Agency (neither the Navy or Air Force audit organization staffs included attorneys). It was widely recognized that the contract audit mission was to provide financial advice to contracting officers and that legal advisors were needed in contracting rather than audit agencies. Possible internal matters requiring legal advice, such as adverse personnel actions, could be handled by the legal staffs of the military departments and, subsequently, of the DOD comptroller. As in every other aspect of its operations, DCAA moved beyond its predecessor audit agencies, increasing its own legal staff. The requirement to formulate statutory changes involving access to records, changes in regulations, statutory language relating to possible false claims, etc., will establish the need for further expansion of the legal staff. There seems to be no end to this expansion, as witness the further implications of giving the agency subpoena authority.

One of the other tasks assigned by the ASD(C) was for DCAA to "assess audit coverage of labor and fringe benefits at major contractors." Compensation reviews, including "insurance and pension costs," have been cited in industry complaints about duplicative, costly audits, reviews, inspections, etc., by DCAA, contract administration staffs, DOD IG, etc. A subtask assigned by ASD(C) refers to coordination between DCAA and contract administration teams. However, as described by industry witnesses at hearings held by the Defense Acquisition Policy Subcommittee of the Senate Armed Services Committee on January 30 and March 12, 1985, coordination alone is not always the problem. In many instances each group believes the review comes under its aegis and will not accept the work of the others.

In addition to all of these additional tasks DCAA is being charged with there are the increasing special overhead and should-cost reviews directed by Secretary Weinberger and Deputy Secretary Taft. Inasmuch as DCAA is frequently delinquent in performing its normal work, industry and contracting agencies have expressed concern as to how the agency can take on the additional duties. Senate and House panels, too, have questioned DOD officials as to whether the DCAA has sufficient manpower to search out possible unallowable costs and pursue other allegations of fraud, waste and abuse.

DOD Comptroller Helm sought to allay these apprehensions when he testified at the above-mentioned March 12, 1985 hearing. He told the Senators that DCAA's current strength was 4,147, which included the 401 additional spaces authorized by Congress for 1984. The budget request was for 485 new spaces in 1985 and for 222 more spaces in 1986, which would bring the audit agency's strength to an awesome 4,854, closely rivaling in size the GAO, with its government-wide responsibilities. To view the 4,854,854, closely rivaling in size the GAO, with its government-wide responsibilities. To view the 4,854 number in perspective, it should be noted that DCAA's initial authorized strength was 3,600, and in its early years, this authorization was subjected to reductions. Additionally, actual strength, we are advised, was generally quite a bit below the authorization. The proposed authorization represented a 35% increase from the original 3,600, most of it since 1983.

There are serious questions as to whether DCAA can recruit and effectively train this great influx of auditors. The agency does most of its hiring from college campuses, and progression from trainee to journeyman auditor and higher levels is extremely rapid. Very real problems are encountered when the young college graduates, most without any previous exposure to manufacturing, research or other company operations, undertake to evaluate contractor operations to determine whether they are being conducted with maximum economy and efficiency, whether indicated defective pricing can be reported as fraud, whether compensation and other expenses are reasonable in the circumstances, whether contracting officers are correct in allowing indirect expenses which these young auditors have questioned, and to perform many other tasks which DCAA has assumed or which have been imposed upon it.

DCAA Relationships with Contracting Officers

This area was discussed earlier in this chapter and only a few words of summary are considered appropriate.

Almost 20 years have passed since the then Deputy Secretary of Defense issued a policy memorandum emphasizing that, while auditor advice was a valuable tool, the ultimate pricing decisions must be made by contracting officers, and that DCAA auditors should stop disputing or questioning specific decisions by contracting officers. The changes in this area have been nothing short of dramatic as congressional committees, GAO and DOD IG have joined in criticizing contracting officers' judgments, especially when they have been contrary to auditor recommendations. One major result was the previously discussed DOD Directive 7640.2, which imposes onerous burdens upon contracting officers to justify their decisions when not in strict conformance with DCAA recommendations. The climate created by this Directive has hardly improved the so-called team effort of contracting and auditing personnel.

A number of provisions of the DOD 1986 Authorization Act, together with implementing and related actions by DOD, served further to increase the friction between contracting officers and the DCAA auditors who seemed to be moving to usurp further authorities of those holding the warrants. These actions included requirements for further justifications of allowing costs questioned by contract auditors, all but prohibiting so-called "bottom-line" negotiations, requiring contracting officers to include in renegotiation memoranda full specifics as to the ultimate conclusions relating to each individual expense item.

Additionally, the presence of DCAA auditors at negotiation conferences was made virtually mandatory. To cite just one other directive, contracting officers were ordered to vacate any and all agreements they might have made with contractors regarding arrangements for access to records, and refrain from entering into any such agreements in the future. Access to records, it appeared, became the sole prerogative of the DCAA auditor, especially now that he is armed with the subpoena power, something not available to contracting officers to whom the auditors are supposed to be advisors.

DCAA Relationship with Contractors

There is little question but that DOD-industry relationships have deteriorated to just about the lowest point in their history, and there is a strong consensus that DCAA bears a strong responsibility for these unfortunate circumstances. Unassailable support for the seriousness of the unsatisfactory government-industry relationship is reflected in the respected and objective conclusions of the Packard Commission report, excerpts from which are cited below:

> Our study of defense management compels us to conclude that nothing merits greater concern than the increasingly troubled relationship between the defense industry and government.

*   *   *   *

> With notable results, DOD has devoted increased attention and resources to detecting and preventing unlawful practices affecting defense contracts. But *a plethora of departmental auditors and other overseers*—and the burgeoning directives pertaining to procurement— also have tended to establish a *dysfunctional and adversarial relationship between DOD and its contractors.* (Emphasis added.)

*   *   *   *

Though government oversight is critically important . . . *no conceivable number of additional auditors, inspectors, investigators, and prosecutors can police it fully, much less to make it work more effectively.* Nor have criminal sanctions proved to be a reliable tool for ensuing contractor compliance. (Emphasis added.)

Access to Records

One activity that has contributed significantly to the deterioration of government-industry relationships, primarily in the defense area, has been DCAA's insatiable drive for access to contractor records.

The basic contractual provision supporting the contract auditor's right to the contractor's records is quoted in Chapter IV of this text, together with a review of the relatively few instances of litigation which have resulted from the many controversies generated by DCAA's continuing expansion of its demands. Judgments as to which records auditors require in order to examine the allowability of contractors' cost representations run a very wide gamut. There were many differences among the military department audit agencies before DCAA was established in 1965. Since that time, aided in recent years by DOD IG and GAO, the audit agency has moved to extremes never imagined in the past. These overreachings and excesses included not only demands for virtually every piece of paper generated by a company doing business with DOD, but extended to "interviews" with contractor employees at every level.

Budgetary Data

Prior to the establishment of DCAA, demands for contractor budgetary data were sporadic and not vigorously pursued when forcefully denied. A concerted effort to obtain such data was initiated by DCAA beginning in 1970-1971 and, while achieving some success with some smaller, weaker contractors, met with strong opposition from larger companies. The continuing controversies were ultimately escalated to formal meetings at the Pentagon between high level DOD officials, the DCAA Director, and officials of the Aerospace Industries Association, representing defense industry.

The culmination of the many conferences, debates, etc., was a memorandum issued by the Assistant Secretary of Defense (I&L) to the Army, Navy, Air Force, DSA and DCAA, on January 17, 1973. This memorandum noted that the signatory and the Assistant Secretary of Defense (COMP) agreed that certain budgetary data must be made available and that when agreements cannot be reached, the controversy should be escalated from the DCAA auditor, to the ACO, to the PCO, to the appropriate level within the Service, and "in rare cases unresolved problems concerning access to records and data will be brought to the attention of OSD."

The major import of this memorandum is the attachment captioned: DOD Access to Contractor Budgetary, Forecast and Related Records and Data. The January 17, 1973 memorandum and the attachment thereto were distributed throughout the Department of Defense and, both formally and informally, throughout the entire defense community, but a summary of the salient points is useful to reiterate here.

It is DOD policy to require access to budgetary data because it can have a significant impact on incurred and estimated costs . . . access to such data will be limited to the term of the longest existing contract for the proposed program.

*   *   *   *

Forecasts and budgets meet the definitions of "data" under ASPR 7-104.41(b) and "records" under ASPR 7-104.41(c) the provisions of which, as they are pertinent to this matter, are acceptable and agreed to by contractors as they submit pricing proposals . . . and as they execute contracts . . .

. . . access to the overall budgetary system is required (1) to establish that the forecasts and projections prepared specifically for individual contract pricing or overhead proposals are based on or reconciled with management objectives and expectations contained in the company's overall budgetary system, and (2) to ascertain whether the contractor has established and is effectively implementing an adequate system for planning and controlling costs.

The memorandum also cites three broad circumstances which "illustrate the Government's needs for access to budgetary data":

1. Evaluation of Contract Pricing and Overall Rate Proposals.

2. Evaluating Current Operations and Costs and Cost-Schedule Control Systems (C/SCS).

3. Postaward Review. (P.L. 87-653)

The memorandum further illustrates the types of specific budgetary data which contractors are required to make available as well as those which they are not required to make available. Included in the first category are: forecast volume, projected acquisition or disposition of plant facilities, projections of direct and indirect manpower requirements, forecasts of estimated indirect fixed and variable costs, performance reports and variance analyses, and program budgets including estimates to complete.

As mentioned above, this directive also cites "certain restrictions which we believe can justifiably be placed on access to certain data under normal operating conditions":

Sales dollars are unnecessary if cost of sales and units of production or similar volume type data are available. Details concerning the identity of commercial customers can generally be obscured if summary data is available. Forecasts or predictions concerning outstanding claims or future negotiations, market strategies, forecasts of profits, analyses of competitive positions, and pro forma profit and loss statements including related cash flow projections are not required in the reviews of price proposals, costs incurred, or defective pricing. However, some of these data may be required in times of extreme financial problems which might adversely affect Government contracts, advance funding or guaranteed Government loans.

Early implementation of the "Access to Budgetary Data Memorandum" of January 17, 1973 was uneven, including amicable agreements at some locations, disputes and hair-splitting debates about terms in others, and out-and-out refusal to comply in still other instances. Over the next decade, with very few exceptions, contractor-government accord was reached and matters proceeded fairly smoothly until DCAA escalated its demands beyond any and all limitations of the January 1973 ground rules. Further comments on the current demands in this area are contained under the discussion of DCAA's subpoena authority.

Internal Audit Reports and Other Data

Emanating from its own increasing militancy and prodding by the DOD IG, DCAA's intensified drive for access to contractor records has emphasized demands for internal audit reports, working papers, and just about every paper generated by contractor internal audit departments.

Contractors have generally considered their internal audit reports to be proprietary data, not specifically and directly related to government contracts, and hence most companies have not furnished such reports to government contract auditors. The former policies of the old Army, Navy and Air Force audit agencies did not specifically demand that auditors aggressively pursue access to these reports and related working papers and, where requests to obtain such access were firmly denied by contractors, the military department contract auditors generally sought compromise or backed off.

DCAA formal policy generally followed those of its predecessors, and even the current Contract Audit Manual (CAM) addresses contractor internal audits in terms of whether the audits and resulting reports are suitable for use by DCAA auditors as a method for reducing their own checking. Guidance not formally published, however, urges DCAA auditors to obtain access to internal audit reports, working papers, etc., and to aggressively pursue these demands where access is denied. This current practice departs significantly from those of the past. The more rational and reasonable DCAA leadership of its first decade sought to persuade contractors that mutual benefits would be derived if DCAA were granted access to internal audit reports and working papers and could thereby reduce the extent of its own auditing. Where contractors were adamant in their denials, DCAA auditors used alternative techniques, but we have no record in prior years of instances when the costs of the internal audit departments were disallowed or subpoenaed or when further, formal action was taken to obtain such data by force.

In line with its increasingly aggressive attitude toward contractors, DCAA began to vigorously pursue its demands for information about the activities and reports of contractors' internal audit departments, and a series of impasses has been reached with a number of contractors who have held to their positions that the demands for internal audit reports are beyond the requirements of law and reason.

The Westinghouse Electric Corporation was one of the major contractors which had been locked in a dispute with DCAA over the agency's demand for internal audit reports. In keeping with its policy at that time, DCAA requested assistance from the DOD IG, which issued a subpoena for such reports on behalf of DCAA. *U.S. v. Westinghouse Electric Co.,* DC WPa No. 11710, 33 CCF par. 73,922, 8/14/85. Westinghouse refused to obey the subpoena, contending that the issue was beyond the IG's authority, since it constituted a dispute over access to records which should be resolved at the contracting officer level. Westinghouse also argued that these reports were not directly related to government contracts and hence not subject to subpeona by the government. After the contractor's refusal, the IG filed the aforementioned suit to enforce the subpoena, arguing among other things that such reports may reveal instances of "mischarging, employee defalcations or mismanagement."

In addition to obtaining the subpoena through the DOD IG, DCAA disallowed the costs of the Westinghouse internal audit department. There are indications that the government contracting authorities involved were not all that enthusiastic about supporting the disallowance; however, influenced by DOD Directive 7640.2 and the IG's position, the contracting officer issued a final decision upholding the disallowance in order to create a test case concerning the government's right to access to these records.

This action occurred prior to the time DCAA obtained its own subpoena authority. In this connection it is interesting to note that industry spokesmen had been objecting to DCAA's practice of threatening contractors with a DOD IG subpoena if internal audit reports and other controversial records were not furnished. These assertions were denied by top level DCAA officials who publicly stated at industry and professional seminars that DCAA would never request the DOD IG to issue a subpoena on its behalf. The Westinghouse case once again called DCAA's credibility into doubt.

The Westinghouse controversy may be said to have started in February 1984, when DCAA advised the contractor that it would initiate an operational audit of the Westinghouse internal audit function and, among other things, would want access to internal audit reports and related files. When Westinghouse declined to submit to such investigation and release of confidential data, DCAA advised that if the company failed to comply with the demands, the audit agency would suspend payment of the costs relating to the Westinghouse internal audit function in all Westinghouse cost reimbursement contracts, recommend reduction of progress payments to Westinghouse on its fixed-price contracts, and report the company's "lack of cooperation" to government contracting officers as a factor to be considered in negotiating future Westinghouse contracts. This hard line approach dovetailed with the agency's "get tough" policy and with recommendations of the DOD IG.

It is of interest that after over 20 years of assertedly protecting the government's interests through its audits, DCAA suddenly concluded that it could not accomplish its mission without full access to all information relating to contractors' internal audit departments and took the extreme action of requesting the DOD IG to issue a subpoena to force the contractor to comply with its demands.

The current strong hostility toward defense contractors emanating from Congress, GAO, the news media, and some DOD officials, has encouraged DCAA to assume an increasingly hard-line and adversarial posture in its demands for records and its intrusions in other areas. Additionally, as described elsewhere in this text, DCAA has been under pressure from the DOD IG to be more aggressive in its demands for access to records, and to initiate immediate, punitive action against any companies which deny them. The

Audit Agency obediently issued a directive to its field offices "to promptly question and/or suspend cost amounts that are determined to be unsupported for lack of access to contractor records."

DCAA's actions have understandably aroused considerable concern in the private sector and have contributed to the steady deterioration of DOD-industry relationships. Many DOD contracting officials are also quite unhappy over this course of events although, for obvious reasons, the latter views have been generally muted.

A number of interesting commentaries have addressed this problem including:

"Cost Disallowances, Offsets and Access to Records: A New Battlefield," *Federal Contracts Report* (BNA), 42 FCR 901.

Fenster and Lee, "The Expanding Audit and Investigative Powers of the Federal Government," 12 *Public Law Journal* (1982).

Adams and Gallagher, "Has DCAA Overstepped Its Authority Under the Audit Clause?", *Contract Management* (November 1982).

Starrett, "DCAA Access to Internal Audit Records," *Contract Management* (December 1984).

"The Scope of the Defense Contract Audit Agency's Access to Contractor Books and Records: A Continuing and Growing Controversy," *Machinery and Allied Products Institute* (February 1985).

Kipps, Carlson and Brown, "Confronting the DOD 'Access to Records' Offensive," *Federal Contracts Report* (BNA) 43 FCR 1025.

The adversary and hostile government-industry environment, generated by DCAA and strongly aided and abetted by the DOD IG and GAO, can be gleaned from portions of the titles of the above-mentioned commentaries, for example: "... A New *Battlefield*," "*Expanding Audit and Investigative* Powers ...," "Has *DCAA Overstepped Its Authority* ...," "... A Continuing and *Growing Controversy*," and "... DOD '*Access to Records' Offensive*." (Emphasis added.) As mentioned earlier, the antagonistic and punitive attitude toward defense contractors emanating from Congress and the news media, joined by high level DOD officials, further encourages DCAA's hard-line approach.

Whatever the rationale offered by DCAA, the strong role of the DOD IG was established in the affidavit of the Assistant IG for Policy and Oversight, which accompanied the government's Petition for Enforcement of Administrative Subpoena in the *Westinghouse* case. The OIG official referred to his oversight review of DCAA activities initiated in June 1983 and stated that "(o)ne of the matters selected for review concerned DCAA's access to contractor-originated documents necessary for its completion of comprehensive and reliable audits." Included within the scope of review was the question of *"whether DCAA auditors were obtaining internal audit reports and supporting workpapers."* (Emphasis added.)

The affidavit describes the selection of DCAA field offices for review: "Some of the locations were chosen because of suspected problems; the remaining locations were selected more or less at random. The DCAA Suboffice at

Westinghouse was selected because of a history of controversy and resistance concerning the Government's ability to fully audit the contractor's records."

The Assistant IG further states in his affidavit that a representative of his office visited that location and confirmed the existence of controversies, noting specifically that Westinghouse had denied access to its internal audit reports. "Subsequent to this visit," according to the affidavit, "DCAA formally requested copies of Westinghouse's internal audit reports . . . After exchanges of correspondence proved unsuccessful, DCAA . . . requested the issuance of an Inspector General's subpoena to compel Westinghouse to grant access to 'all demands generated by (Westinghouse's) internal audit department . . . '"

We agree with what would appear to be the unanimous view held in the private sector that DCAA has offered no cogent reasons for the sharp reversal of its 20 year old policy. This policy recognized that demanding these records, and instituting punitive actions against the contractors who resisted such demands, could not be supported by public policy, law, regulation, or contract provisions. Accordingly, the Audit Agency had traditionally requested access but had made no threats against companies who declined to comply with such requests, and certainly did not contemplate the extreme actions taken against Westinghouse.

In his "rebuttal," *Contract Management* (December 1984), the then DCAA Director Starrett devoted most of his attention to asserting that the Audit Agency's current demands are in conformance with generally accepted auditing standards (GAAS), issued by the American Institute of Certified Public Accountants (AICPA), and the Standards for Audit of Governmental Organizations, Programs, Activities and Functions, issued by GAO. These assertions seem to ring hollow considering that both these standards had been published long before DCAA's sudden initiation of battles with contractors over access to their internal audit records.

A wide consensus finds that DCAA's sudden discovery of commercial and GAO standards, as reflected in the above-referenced article by Starrett, is not persuasive, particularly inasmuch as neither of these standards has changed in any substantive respect over the years. And, the same may be said about the audit clause in DOD contracts from which DCAA seeks to draw comfort.

DCAA's letters to contractors demanding access to internal audit records sometimes include references to decisions by federal courts and boards of contract appeals. As a number of legal analyses have established, not a single case cited appears directly relevant, especially the one relating to a contractor that made all requested records available but would not permit the auditors to remove their working papers with this information from the company's offices. *Kleinschmidt Divn. of SCM Corp.* ASBCA No. 21022, 78-1 BCA par. 13,127, *SCM Corporation v. U.S.,* 227 Ct. Cl. 12, 24, (1981). Significantly, the board in this case specifically stated that DCAA adoption of GAAS was a voluntary rather than a mandatory action.

Considerably more to the point, it seems to us, although we do not recall reading references to it in this controversy, was the decision in *Grumman Aerospace Corp. v. U.S.,* 587 F.2d 498 (Ct. Cl. 1978), (25 CCF par. 82,892). The company had sustained a loss in 1971 and applied the related New York

State tax refund to reduce that year's G&A expenses. Grumman's position was supported by expert witnesses who demonstrated that it was in accordance with generally accepted accounting principles (GAAP). The government contended that the refund constituted a credit that should be applied to 1968, the year in which the tax was paid. The court and the board before it were persuaded that the then existing procurement regulations (ASPR 15-205.41(c)), and contract clause (Allowable Costs, Incentive Fee and Payments) required the credit to be carried back to 1968. In the significant language of the court:

> Without regard to how GAAP and sound accounting logic might treat the refund . . . the contract language controls here.

It would appear that this decision, as well as others, establishes a clear precedent that various accounting and auditing principles and standards may be taken into consideration by the courts, provided they do not conflict with applicable government regulations and contract clauses. On this basis, the ex-DCAA Director's theoretical exposition on GAAS in the *Contract Management* and elsewhere, while of academic and professional audit interest, would appear to lack relevance in the current controversy.

The DCAA rebuttal declines to discuss the comments by Adams and Gallagher relating to board of contract appeals rulings cited by some of the agency's field offices, stating they would "leave that to the lawyers." They do not leave to the lawyers, however, opinions on laws and contract clauses that, they argue, support the Agency's current drive for access to all of the records of contractors' internal audit departments. We shall leave this matter as well "to the lawyers" except to note again that the law and contract clauses cited have either been in existence for many years or the recent changes have been editorial in nature rather than substantive. Inevitably, the question must be raised as to why the same legal and contractual provisions that did not generate the vigorous efforts to obtain access to contractors' internal audit records in the past have suddenly been discovered as mandating the current intrusion.

To summarize, in the first 19 years of its existence, DCAA had not taken the punitive actions it initiated in the *Westinghouse* case and threatened in others. The practices of demanding internal audit records, and recommending cost disallowances and subpoenas when they are not made available, constitute a sharp break with precedent, and no new legal or contractual provision has been cited in support of this drastic reversal of the Agency's policy.

As an appropriate transition from the subject of access to contractor internal audit reports and related data to the following subject of DCAA's subpoena authority, it would appear appropriate to quote a passage from the Packard Commission report, referred to earlier and reviewed at some length in Appendix 4 to this text. The Commission's comments and suggestions relating to the improvement of industry accountability and self-governance included recommendations for more effective internal auditing. In discussing the need for structures and procedures to assure "frank reporting and prompt action on internal audit results," the Commission stated:

> To encourage and preserve the vitality of such internal auditing and reporting process, *DOD should develop appropriate guidelines heavily*

circumscribing the use of investigative subpoenas to compel disclosure of contractor internal auditing materials. (Emphasis added.)

DCAA Subpoena Power

The Commission was probably concerned with the action by the DOD IG in the *Westinghouse* case, referred to earlier, and perhaps even more by the provision of the 1986 DOD Authorization Act, P.L. 99-145, enacted on November 8, 1985, granting subpoena power to the DCAA Director. At this writing, unfortunately, this sage recommendation of the Commission has not been heeded.

Section 935 of the aforementioned statute amends section 2313 of Title 10 of the U.S. Code by adding a new subsection (d). This new provision was included as one of the "reference statutes" in DCAA publication DCAAR 5500.5, which was issued very promptly to assure quick implementation of the law. The pertinent provisions of these "reference statutes," as further amended by P.L. 99-661, are set forth below:

10 U.S.C. Sec. 2313(d).

(1) The Director of the Defense Contract Audit Agency (or any successor agency) may require by subpoena the production of books, documents, papers, or records of a contractor, access to which is provided to the Secretary of Defense by subsection (a) [of sec. 2313] or by section 2306a of this title.

(2) Any such subpoena, in the case of contumacy or refusal to obey, shall be enforceable by order of an appropriate United States district court.

(3) The authority provided by paragraph (1) may not be redelegated.

(4) The Director (or any successor official) shall submit an annual report to the Secretary of Defense on the exercise of such authority during the preceding year and the reasons why such authority was exercised in any instance. The Secretary shall forward a copy of each such report to the Committees on Armed Services of the Senate and House of Representatives.

10 U.S.C. Sec. 2313(a).

An agency named in section 2303 of this title is entitled, through an authorized representative, to inspect the plant and audit the books and records of—

(1) a contractor performing a cost or cost-plus-a-fixed-fee contract made by that agency under this chapter; and

(2) a subcontractor performing any subcontract under a cost or cost-plus-a-fixed-fee contract made by that agency under this chapter.

10 U.S.C. Sec. 2306a.

(f) RIGHT OF UNITED STATES TO EXAMINE CONTRACTOR RECORDS.—(1) For the purpose of evaluating the accuracy, completeness, and currency of cost or pricing data required to be submitted by this section with respect to a contract or subcontract, the head of the agency, acting through any authorized representative of the head of the agency who is an employee of the United States or a member of the armed forces, shall have the right to examine all records of the contractor or subcontractor related to—

(A) the proposal for the contract or subcontract;

(B) the discussions conducted on the proposal;

(C) pricing of the contract or subcontract; or

(D) performance of the contract or subcontract.

(2) The right of the head of an agency under paragraph (1) shall expire three years after final payment under the contract or subcontract.

(3) In this subsection, the term 'records' includes books, documents, and other data.

A section on policy in the regulation follows closely the statutory provisions and establishes that a subpoena may be issued to a company performing under cost-reimbursement prime or subcontracts issued by DOD or to a company required to submit cost or pricing data prior to the award of a DOD prime or subcontract.

Paragraph D addresses the responsibilities of the DCAA Director, the Assistant Director, Operations, the agency's General Counsel, and the regional managers, and paragraph E sets out the procedures to be followed.

Enclosure 1, Preparation of Request for DCAA Subpoena, describes the elements which must be included in such a request to DCAA headquarters; background, describing the history of the audit; access effort, discussing the efforts made to gain access; precise description of records to be sought; justification and relevancy, discussing the need for the records, applicable contract clauses, GAO and AICPA audit standards, demonstration of need, and consequences of failure to gain access; name and title of recipient; time and place of return; and a proposed subpoena duces tecum, illustrated in enclosure 2. Enclosure 3 illustrates the form of a certificate of return of service.

The regulation provides for the application of the procedures contained in the agency's Contract Audit Manual (CAM), Paragraph 1-504, before requesting a subpoena. This paragraph contains rather detailed guidance about actions to be taken when access to records is denied, including oral and then written requests at the point of denial and where necessary, evaluating the request to higher contractor and DCAA levels. Where the audit agency is unsuccessful, the field people are to seek the assistance of the plant representative/ACO, affected PCOs, and any other government personnel who might be able to help.

Where all of these efforts do not gain access, the regional director steps in, and, if he concludes it is necessary to do so, prepares a request for subpoena and forwards it to the headquarters Assistant Director Operations. The latter reviews the request and forwards it to the agency's General Counsel for a legal review. If the headquarters staff concludes a subpoena is appropriate, the General Counsel submits the subpoena to the Director for signature. The subpoena is then returned to the General Counsel, who transmits it to the regional manager for service.

The ink had hardly dried on DCAA's regulation, and full distribution had not yet been accomplished, before then-acting director Newton made his first strike, selecting Ford Aerospace and Communications Corp., and its parent Ford Motor Company, as the first targets. The records without which the audit agency allegedly could not conduct an appropriate audit (although it had done so for many years) were the internal audits and reviews conducted by both the parent and subsidiary for the previous five years.

The subpoena was broad and included just about every conceivable document relating to the contractor's internal audits, their scheduling follow-up action, and personnel records of the employees assigned to those functions.

Although Ford Aerospace was singled out as the first contractor to be subjected to DCAA's new subpoena power, agency officials who spoke on a non-attribution basis stated that more would follow unless industry opened virtually all of its records to the auditors. Internal audits and related working papers and other files have been selected as the first battleground.

DCAA next proceeded against Bath Iron Works Corp. and its parent company, Congoleum Corp. (Complete data is not available as to the number of contractors who may have yielded to DCAA demands based on threats of subpoenas.)

DCAA demanded all internal audit reports and related papers, all documents related to the annual and five-year plans, and all documents generated in meetings of the boards of directors. All of these data were to cover the five-year period 1981-1985, and to include both Bath Iron Works and its parent. These demands, as set forth in DCAA's subpoena, are quoted below:

a. Production is required of internal audits generated by Bath Iron Works and by the parent company, Congoleum Corporation, for the period 1 January 1981 through present. The documents should include, but not be limited to, schedules of audits, working papers generated during the audit, written reports summarizing the results of audit, follow-up action taken to implement the recommendations and personnel records documenting the time spent by the employees assigned to the internal audit department.

b. Production is required of any and all documents generated by the Bath Iron Works Corp. and by the parent company, Congoleum Corp. in developing the Annual and Five Year Plans during 1981 through 1985. The documents should include, but not be limited to the plans, executive summaries, business and economic forecasts and related data objectives/goals, financial forecasts reports summarizing the results of audit, follow-up action taken to implement manpower forecasts, capital appropriation summary, and capital expenditure summary.

c. Production is required of any and all documents generated by Bath Iron Works Corp. and by the parent company, Congoleum Corp. regarding the Board of Director's Meetings conducted during 1981 through 1985. The documents should include, but not be limited to, the minutes of the meetings, the notes or transcription of the meetings, and any summaries.

The impropriety of demands for contractor internal audit documents and practices, their resulting chilling effect on the candor and effectiveness of internal auditing, and the Packard Commission's strong objection to the use of subpoenas for these purposes have been discussed earlier. The additional impositions reflected in the seemingly punitive demands upon Bath Iron Works include the unusual (five-year) period, follow-up actions and personnel records.

As to budgetary data, we previously referred to the lengthy DOD-industry discussions which led to a January 1973 understanding which had been widely and substantially followed. While recognizing the need for contracting officers and contract auditors to have access to certain budgetary data, particularly in connection with evaluating pricing proposals, the policy memorandum, consistent with the rule of reason which prevailed in those days, set out certain exceptions and restrictions, mentioned earlier. Generally, the purpose which the government and industry representatives tried to achieve was to provide the data required by the government without unnecessarily encroaching upon industry's interests in protecting confidential, proprietary data. Restraints were also provided against prying contract auditors and other officials who might demand data not really needed to protect the government's interests. The Bath Iron Works subpoena clearly establishes that DCAA does not recognize these restraints.

Minutes of boards of directors' meetings are not a new area in the access to defense contractors' records controversy, but they are sufficiently remote that only the most aggressive contract auditors have made an issue of them. Today, armed with its new subpoena authority, DCAA has not hesitated to extend its demands to these records. Any possible information such minutes usually provide in terms of legitimate contract audit purposes is infinitesimal compared to DCAA's basic objective of establishing the principle of unlimited access to records authority.

DCAA's subpoena duces tecum to Bath Iron Works contained an appendix setting forth alleged authority and rationale for the demand for these records. Contractors subjected to DCAA audits over the years recognized that, except for some dressing up of the language, this appendix, quoted below, contained nothing new or persuasive. The difference lies in DCAA's new subpoena authority.

DCAA is responsible for advising contracting officers on the reasonableness, allocability and allowability of all costs proposed or claimed on Government contracts. Furthermore, DCAA is responsible for responding to requests of DOD officials on questions relating to the veracity of proposed, claimed and unclaimed costs. In order for DCAA to adequately audit the books and records of the contractor as required under 10 USC 2313(a), and to render an opinion on costs, the DCAA auditor must obtain sufficient competent and relevant evidential matter as prescribed by the government auditing standards published by the General Accounting Office.

Bath Iron Works has also submitted certified cost or pricing data in support of proposals that have resulted in its being awarded Government contracts. Under 10 USC 2306(f)(5):

> For the purpose of evaluating the accuracy, completeness and currency of cost or pricing data required to be submitted by this subsection (2306(f)), any authorized representative of the head of the agency who is an employee of the United States Government shall have the right, until the expiration of three years after final payment under the contract or subcontract, to examine all books, records, documents and other data of the contractor or subcontractor related to the proposal for the contract, the discussions conducted on the proposal, pricing, or performance of the contract or subcontract.

The documents in this subpoena are necessary for the evaluation of the accuracy and completeness of the certified cost or pricing data submitted by Bath Iron Works Corp. Without having access to the documents in this subpoena, we are unable to discharge our responsibility to determine that Bath Iron Works is in compliance or noncompliance with the requirements of the cost or pricing clauses of their Government contracts. The expiration of three years after final payment under the contracts has not occurred.

The records are required for audit for the following additional reasons:

A. The internal audit records required to be produced are relevant to the audit of Department of Defense contracts and/or to the evaluation of cost or pricing data submitted under such contracts as follows:

1. The costs of Bath Iron Works' and Congoleum's internal audit organizations are charged to Government contracts and contract proposals through indirect cost allocations.

2. The effective functioning of Bath Iron Works' and Congoleum's internal controls, as these are reflected in the internal audits, assures the proper allocations of costs to Government contracts.

3. Bath Iron Works' and Congoleum's internal audit organizations are responsible for reviewing controls that assure that only reasonable and allowable costs are charged to Government contracts.

4. Bath Iron Works' and Congoleum's internal audit organizations determine whether Bath Iron Works' and Congoleum's accounting records are reliable for proposal evaluations and audits of costs.

5. Bath Iron Works' and Congoleum's internal audits reflect any instances of mischarging of costs to Government contracts.

B. The records relating to the Annual and Five-Year Plan (budgets/forecasts) required to be produced are relevant to the audit of Department of Defense contracts and/or evaluations of cost or pricing data submitted under such contracts as follows:

1. The cost of Bath Iron Works' and Congoleum's budget data is charged to Government contracts and contractor proposals through indirect cost allocations.

2. A sound budgetary system operates effectively as a managerial function in producing maximum efficiency and economy of operations.

3. The budgetary system provides for a quantative expression of management plans and defines what is expected of each member of management at every level responsible for cost control in terms of business objectives and the costs expected to be incurred to accomplish assigned tasks.

4. The plans show the current need for each function and the reasonableness of the predicted cost level for those functions considered necessary.

5. The plans indicate whether management has effectively coordinated department (budget unit) managers' objectives with those of the company as a whole.

6. The system provides for early notice of contractor plans and changes to plans which may affect future work load and resources, such as increases and decreases in plant population, asset acquisitions and dispositions, and physical moves. Sound plans include all significant economic factors in the development of contractor budgets. The contractor plans permit an opportunity for timely discussions prior to actions which will be costly to reverse.

7. A valid system contains adequate monitoring techniques to curb unnecessary cost growth, such as sound and documented rationale for make-or-buy decisions, adequate benchmarks to determine direct and indirect manpower levels, guidelines for evaluating indirect cost projections, and requirements for performing adequate facility studies.

8. The plans permit the company to control planned cost levels by comparing actual direct and indirect costs to agreed plans in the budget and through the continuing appraisal of variances. The budget determines whether each management level is held responsible for explaining the reasons for variances, defining any necessary corrective actions, and generating required changes in the company's future plans.

C. The minutes of the Board of Directors' Meetings and associated data required to be produced are relevant to the audit of Department of Defense contracts and/or to the evaluation of cost or pricing data submitted under such contracts as follows:

1. The cost of the Board of Directors' Meetings of Congoleum Corp. are charged to Government contracts and contract proposals at Bath Iron Works through indirect cost allocations.

2. The Board of Directors establishes overall policy for Congoleum Corp. Its policy decisions impact all aspects of the company

including costs charged to Government contracts at Bath Iron Works.

3. The policy decisions of the Board of Directors which affect the level of costs relate to matters such as: (a) organizational structure; (b) plant layout; (c) budgeting; (d) make or buy; (e) plant cutback or expansion; (f) lease or purchase; and (g) personnel policies and compensation.

4. The minutes are reviewed to determine whether the Board of Directors is setting policies for utilization of its resources, personnel, property space, etc. in an economical and efficient manner.

5. The minutes are reviewed to ascertain that the policies which are set and influence the financial aspects of operation are:

(a) consistent with prudent business practices;

(b) adequate to provide proper control, accomplish the desired results, and meet the test of reasonableness; (c) in conformity with promulgated Cost Accounting Standards, Government regulations and contract requirements; and (d) effectively implemented by adequate procedures.

In other times and in the absence of DCAA's subpoena authority, it is safe to assume that the contractor would have continued to resist these demands. In today's circumstances, Bath Iron Works capitulated, requesting only some additional time to accumulate the records and seeking DCAA's consideration of some modification of its broad demands. As to copies of all internal audit reports and related papers for both Bath Iron Works and Congoleum for five years, the contractor noted the immense and costly effort required to produce them and proposed providing DCAA with an inventory listing of all such reports, from which the audit agency could select any it wished, which would be furnished. DCAA graciously agreed to this proposal.

As to the budgetary data, DCAA would only agree to immediate access to the current and outyear plans. The audit agency will develop a timetable for access to the prior years' plans.

The only concession DCAA would make regarding the minutes of the Board of Directors was an agreement that the resident auditor would examine them at the Congoleum corporate headquarters.

What are the indications for the future with respect to DCAA's demands for contractor records, enforced by subpoenas and threats of subpoenas? Considerable thought has been devoted to this subject and some believe relief may be found through the judicial process.

No relief is expected from higher DOD levels. This Department is not likely to chance antagonizing Congress by an action that could be misinterpreted as favorable to the defense industry, which currently meets a hostile reception among many legislators.

Section 2313(d) of 10 U.S.C., as added by P.L. 99-145, provides that the DCAA Director shall submit an annual report to the Secretary of Defense on the exercise of the subpoena authority and that copies of such report shall be forwarded by the Secretary to the Committee on Armed Services of the Senate and House of Representatives. Some observers are hopeful that the extremes to which DCAA is using (and threatening to use) its subpoena authority may be challenged and restrained by these committess. We see very little prospect of congressional action in this regard: for any congressman who might question the misuse of this authority, there would be many who would encourage the agency to be even more aggressive.

Before concluding this review of DCAA's drive for access to all records maintained by firms supplying goods and services for this country's defense, we should discuss the agency's assault on the attorney-client privilege and the attorney work product rule, set out in a memorandum of June 18, 1986, from the audit agency's general counsel to its major field offices. The memorandum is quoted in full:

SUBJECT: Denials of Records Based on the Attorney-Client Privilege and the Attorney Work Product Rule.

We have been informed that some contractors have refused audit access to certain corporate records and justified this refusal with assertions of privilege. These assertions may take one of two forms; the attorney-client privilege, and the attorney work product rule. In some cases, both may be claimed for one document or collection of documents. Each doctrine has a firm policy foundation for the protection of documents in litigation, or in anticipation of litigation. However, neither doctrine has been tested against DCAA's contractual or statutory rights to audit.

Attorney-Client Privilege

The attorney-client privilege is often used to shield documents and communications in adversary proceedings. The privilege protects communications by the client, and it is the client, not the attorney, who may either exercise or waive it. Although the communications are protected, the underlying facts are not.

It is well settled in law that: (1) where legal advice of any kind is sought (2) from a professional legal advisor in his capacity as such, (3) the communications relating to that purpose, (4) made in confidence (5) by the client, (6) are at his instance permanently protected (7) from disclosure by himself or by the legal advisor, (8) except when the protection be waived.

In determining the applicability of the privilege to contractor records, the following factors should be considered:

(1) The privilege was judicially created primarily for the purpose of limiting disclosure of information in a litigative setting. Under normal conditions it should not be used for denial of needed evidential matter for routine contract audits.

(2) It applies only to confidential communications to an attorney. Preexisting documentation, such as previously written internal audit reports and accompanying workpapers, probably would not be shielded, even in litigation.

(3) By contractually consenting to permit examination of all necessary audit information in exchange for monetary consideration, a waiver
of the privilege may have occurred.

Attorney Work Product Rule

In litigation, the work product rule is a limitation on discovery. A
high degree of protection is afforded to "the mental impressions, concu-
sions, opinions or legal theories of an attorney or other representative of a
party concerning the litigation." The most important element of the rule
is that the material be prepared in anticipation of litigation. The work
product rule does not apply to documents prepared in the normal course
of business. Thus, the purpose of which documents were gathered by the
attorney is quite relevant.

The rule differs from the attorney-client privilege in that it is the
attorney, not the client, who may invoke it. Inasmuch as the rule
primarily relates to the discovery process, it may be argued that it does
not operate to deny records in a normal contract audit. Furthermore,
many records do not meet the requirement that they were assembled in
anticipation of litigation. For example, where a corporate counsel has
overseen the performance of an otherwise normal internal audit function,
and there are no apparent prospects of litigation, access to DCAA should
not be denied under the work product rule.

Conclusions

Contract auditors should examine closely every claim of either the
attorney-client privilege or the work product rule, particularly if there
are indications that contractor records are being "laundered" through an
attorney. Both doctrines are primarily designed for the litigation setting.
Sound legal arguments are available to challenge their applicability to
routine contract audit. Because of a justifiable reverence for these rules
which is held by judges and attorneys (including government attorneys),
there must be a demonstrable audit need for any materials for which an
access claim is made. Auditors should consult with DCAA counsel in any
instance where they are confronted with a claim of privilege.

In keeping with our practice, we shall not comment on the purely legal
aspects of this memorandum. We do observe that at the outset the head of
what we understand is the growing legal staff of DCAA alerts the auditors
that neither the attorney-client privilege nor the attorney work product rule
doctrine "has been tested against DCAA's contractual or statutory rights to
audit." This would appear designed to place auditors-investigators on notice
that they should not be warded off by assertions of such doctrines.

Further, the audit agency's lawyer advises that the attorney-client privilege "was judicially created primarily for the purpose of limiting disclosure of
information in a litigative settting. Under normal conditions it should not be
used for denial of needed evidential matter for routine contract audits."

One of the problems with this statement is that today's fraud-minded
auditors have changed the rules of the game and created a new climate. How
would a contractor recognize "normal conditions" today, and how would he
know when a contract audit is "routine" and, if it appears to begin as such,

when might it suddenly and covertly turn into a fraud investigation? We do not believe that experienced contractor officials or their consultants should consider any DCAA forays into their offices and plants as *routine*. The audit agency has increasingly fostered a climate in which their representatives must be viewed as investigators or at least potential investigators.

We leave it to contractors' legal advisors to counsel them on the validity of the conjecture that contractors may have waived the attorney-client privilege "by contractually consenting to permit examination of all necessary audit information in exchange for monetary consideration . . . . " In addition to that legal question, there is the important consideration of the meaning of "all necessary audit information." Necessary in whose opinion? Under current DCAA policy and assertions, there appears to be very little paper generated by a contractor, that might not be viewed as necessary audit information.

In discussing the attorney work product rule, DCAA's lawyer again refers to "a normal contract audit" and we would again observe that it is difficult indeed these days to know when a contract audit is normal, and where it appears to have been initiated as one, at what point it may abruptly turn into a fraud investigation. A somewhat similar point may be raised with respect to "prospects of litigation." With DCAA, DOD IG, GAO and congressional staffs in sharp competition to detect fraud, when can a contractor be assured that "there are no apparent prospects of litigation"?

The attitude of the audit agency is emphasized in its general counsel's advice that auditors should examine closely any privilege claim and should be on the lookout for indications "that contractor records are being 'laundered' through the attorney." The advice is reiterated that both these privilege doctrines "are primarily designed for the litigation setting. Sound legal arguments are available to challenge their applicability to routine contract audit."

The legal memorandum concludes by telling the auditors that they "should consult with DCAA counsel in any instance where they are confronted with a claim of privilege."

We do not suggest that DCAA has abandoned the basic purpose for which it was created or that its auditors no longer conduct what might be termed "routine" audits. Indeed, most of the current audits fall into this cateogry. On the other hand, the auditors are increasingly impressed with fraud detection possibilities, some of them having been influenced to view accounting or administrative errors in labor charges, defective pricing, etc., as potential fraud.

We further do not suggest that all accounting and billing henceforth must be subjected to legal scrutiny. We do emphasize the importance of understanding the current, unfortunate climate which requires contractors to be unusually sensitive to the hostile and suspicious attitudes of some DCAA auditors, attitudes which sometimes blur the distinctions between these auditors and the investigators on the staffs of the DOD IG, GAO and congressional committees.

Industry's critique of this highly inappropriate legal memorandum was prompt and forceful, as reflected in a letter from NSIA to the DCAA director dated January 5, 1987.

NSIA advised that "DCAA's memorandum appears to misstate certain aspects of the privileges, and may be substantially misleading to DCAA auditors who attempt to apply the stated guidance." Noting that neither privilege protects "contractor documentation in the ordinary course of business, including internal audit reports prepared as part of a contractor's normal internal audit program," the Association stated that the memorandum "goes beyond" a justified complaint of the misuse of this privilege and "would intrude into the very heart of the area protected by the privilege. As such," NSIA's letter continues, "it represents a direct and potent threat to the legally protected interests of American corporations and their employees and has no support in the law."

The Association noted that DCAA's position will frustrate DOD's major ongoing effort to implement the Packard Commission's recommendation relating to Contractor Self-Governance, which involves contractor action to purge themselves of improper conduct through internal mechanisms:

> The attorney-client privilege is one of the most important and effective tools available to a contractor to encourage the type of employee frankness necessary to make a corporate self-governance program effective. The demise of the attorney-client privilege will greatly undermine the effectiveness of any corporate self-governance program, to the detriment of both the contractor and the Defense Department, ...

According to the NSIA, one of the misstatements in DCAA's memorandum was the assertion that the attorney-client privilege "was judicially created primarily for the purpose of limiting disclosure of information in a litigative setting." NSIA explained that this privilege "applies to *any* situation in which legal advice is sought from an attorney, and, contrary to the assertion, was created in large part to help clients resolve legal concerns while avoiding litigation." The Association's letter cited case law in support of its position, including rulings by the United States Supreme Court.

Among the other propositions in DCAA's memorandum with which the NSIA took issue was the assertion that "by contractually consenting to permit examination of all necessary audit information in exchange for monetary consideration, a waiver of this privilege may have occurred." As NSIA bluntly stated: "DCAA's guidance is plainly wrong." Again citing case law in support of its position, the Association explained: "Contractor assent to a Government contract containing the standard audit clause does not in and of itself waive the attorney-client privilege. A Government contract is a contract of adhesion . . . The [audit] clause does not speak to the matter of privilege directly and constitutes nothing more than a routine access to records provision."

"It is well-settled," NSIA advised DCAA, "that the Government's contractual or regulatory right to inspect records does not affect a client's right to assert the attorney-client privilege." The Association quoted the following from a federal court ruling denying a government's writ of mandamus to compel a railroad's counsel to disclose certain confidential correspondence between the railroad and its attorneys:

> The desirability of protecting confidential communications between attorney and client as a matter of public policy is too well known and has been too often recognized by textbooks and courts to need extended

comment now. If such communications were required to be made the subject of examination and publication, such enactment would be a practical prohibition upon professional advice and assistance.

While recognizing that the attorney work product rule is a limitation to discovery, DCAA's counsel concluded that "the most important element of the rule is that the material be prepared in anticipation of litigation." NSIA again objected to the erroneous impression in the audit agency's memorandum by explaining that "a business need not be engaged in actual litigation . . . before the work-product privilege can attach to the attorney-directed work." A federal court decision was cited which ruled that "litigation need not be imminent, so long as the primary motivating purpose behind the creation of the document was to aid in possible or prospective future litigation." Similarly, a recent GSBCA ruling concluded that "for the work product privilege to apply, it is necessary only to show that the information sought was prepared or obtained because of the prospect of litigation."

NSIA also cited Supreme Court and other federal court rulings emphasizing "special protection to work product revealing the attorney's mental processes." The DCAA memorandum correctly noted that "the purpose for which documents were gathered by the attorney is quite relevant." However, NSIA pointed out that courts have held "that investigation by a federal agency presents more than a 'remote prospect' of litigation and provides grounds for anticipating litigation sufficient to invoke the work product rule." In this regard, as we have reported elsewhere, under the DOD IG's exhortations to "think fraud," and through its own increasing proclivities, many DCAA audits are taking on the characteristics of fraud investigations.

The NSIA letter represents a carefully researched, documented and presented effort to place the subjects of attorney-client privilege and attorney work product rule in proper perspective and it would be well for DCAA to accord this communication careful consideration and revise its guidance. Unfortunately, as we have noted in the past, the major problem seems to be that while the Assistant Secretary of Defense (Comptroller), DOD IG, and more recently the new Under Secretary of Defense (Acquisition), all appear to have some authority for DCAA's operations, the audit agency seems to be under no real control by any DOD office and is only subjected to criticism by DOD IG for such things as not performing more defective pricing audits and not reporting more allegations of fraud.

Critiques of DCAA by DOD IG and GAO

DCAA has received much welcome support as well as sometimes less desirable prodding and criticisms from the DOD IG and GAO. Even the critical comments, however, tend to have favorable connotations to the extent that they require DCAA to extend its efforts further, to such matters as defective pricing audits, concentration on fraud, etc., and yield increased manpower authorizations.

In a hearing conducted in March 1984, then DOD IG Joseph Sherick testified that his organization had issued only one final report on the audit agency to date.

(However, the Deputy IG had criticized DCAA at a prior congressional hearing for failure to devote what he considered sufficient manpower for postaward audits for defective pricing.) The report referred to by Sherick covered evaluations of subcontractors' pricing proposals where DCAA performance was found to be adequate but "overall effectiveness of such audit services could be enhanced if reported deficiencies in cost and pricing data and contractor management systems were reported by DCAA to higher authorities for resolution. . . ." He also discussed two draft reports on DCAA that were in the process of being finalized: access to contractors' records and reporting of fraud.

On the matter of access to records, the IG "examined 28 [DCAA] field audit offices and found no significant problems at 15 of them. Access problems were found at 13 of the offices, particularly with respect to extended delays in resolving the access issues . . . We conclude that more aggressive action and improved controls were required to insure that DCAA obtained timely access to needed records." According to Sherick, the resolution of access to records disputes is "hindered by the lack of any incentive for contractors to provide required records" and is delayed by DCAA policies that take too much time in resolving the problems at local levels. He recommended that DCAA revise its policies "to provide contractors 30 days notice from the date of first denial that costs (i.e. payments) will be suspended if records are not provided."

The IG recommendation would surely be a very drastic measure and a simplistic approach to a complex problem. As many contractors, and contracting officers as well, are aware, the interests of some DCAA auditors in contractors' records and activities are virtually insatiable. These auditors seek access to records far beyond those needed to satisfy themselves that the contractors' cost representations are acceptable. As we observed earlier in this analysis, Senator Roth quoted DCAA officials as challenging the IG's requests for the audit agency's records on the ground that the IG investigators were "rummaging through files on fishing expeditions." It is the same kind of rummaging through contractors' files on fishing expeditions by DCAA auditors that companies resist. It is significant to recognize that the contract audit clause and judicial decisions have established certain restrictions on auditors' curiosities and ruled that auditors may not roam unrestricted through a contractor's plant and records.

There are, of course, considerable differences in contractors' attitudes toward auditors' demands for access to records, employees, and facilities, and it may well be that some companies deny or delay access to records that are required to establish the acceptability of cost representations. On the other hand, in the overwhelming majority of instances of which we are aware where controversies developed over access to records, DCAA auditors were definitely over-reaching and frequently demanding access to records to which they did not appear entitled from any contractual, legal, or logical viewpoint.

Mr. Sherick's review of the 28 contractors disclosed access to records problems in pricing proposals at three locations. He noted that these contractors continue to receive contracts despite the fact that the access to records problems "have existed for years." He voiced dissatisfaction with DCAA's practice of issuing qualified reports in such instances and recommended that

DCAA "refuse to perform an audit until needed records and supported data are provided . . . ." Apparently quite exercised on this issue, the DOD IG stated: "The use of qualified reports by DOD procurement officials dilutes the internal control role of DCAA in the procurement process" (a role which, to the author's knowledge, is not spelled out in any regulation). The DCAA's continued issuance of such highly qualified reports compromises its independence.

According to legal, contractual, and regulatory pronouncements, the contracting officer is authorized to enter into contracts on behalf of the United States Government. Under certain circumstances, the contracting officer obtains assistance from technical, financial, and accounting people in arriving at a fair and reasonable price. DCAA's "independence", as it is generally understood, consists of performing audits upon requests from the contracting officers. Such audits are performed by methods and to the extent deemed appropriate, and the auditors' reports are their independent opinions on the contractors' representations. DCAA's independence would indeed be compromised if the contents of the reports were subject to direction from outside the agency. Where the auditor "calls it as he sees it" and elects to include qualifications because the contractor did not furnish each and every document demanded during the audit, it would certainly appear illogical to suggest a compromise of the agency's independence.

Sherick was also critical of contracting officers because of some instances where contracts were negotiated without DCAA audit. We feel that contract audits represent an important but by no means exclusive tool for contracting officers in evaluating contractors' pricing proposals. The Armed Services Procurement Regulation Manual for Contract Pricing (ASPM No. 1), still effective today, describes the intricate and comprehensive process of price analysis and cost analysis and the roles of the many technical and financial specialists, including contract auditors. It is the contracting officer's responsibility to use these resources to the extent necessary to arrive at a fair and reasonable price. It seems to us that contracting officers should be subjected to criticism if they fail to arrive at appropriate contract prices rather than for using or not using specific specialists.

The DOD IG told the Senate committee that he recommended that DCAA desist from furnishing advisory reports on evaluation of pricing proposals where they encounter "denials and/or delays in access to records." He also testified that he had recommended to the Under Secretary of Defense that the Under Secretary instruct contracting officers "to withhold awards until contractors provide, during audit, sufficient cost or pricing data." He did not explain who would make the determination as to what constituted "sufficient cost or pricing data."

Sherick also discussed his draft report on DCAA's reporting of fraud. As we discussed earlier, DCAA has been placing increasing emphasis on fraud detection. The DOD IG noted with satisfaction that "DCAA had increased the awareness of its auditors to the type of contract fraud. This increased awareness has undoubtedly contributed to an increase in fraud referrals." He further testified that "during the last *six* months, DCAA referred 59 potential fraud cases to DOD investigators, compared with 46 cases for the preceding *12 months.*" (Emphasis added).

Despite this increased activity in fraud detection, the DOD IG was still not satisfied. For one thing, he concluded that there were extended delays in processing reports in 20 of 60 DCAA fraud reports examined. He thought there was some confusion at DCAA field offices and recommended new DCAA policies to require field auditors to promptly communicate with investigative agencies without awaiting the preparation of a formal "fraud report." In light of the many formal reports of suspected fraud that were determined to lack merit and basis for actions by investigative agencies, we wonder about the effect of such a new policy where DCAA auditors, admittedly not trained as investigators, would run to investigative agencies before appropriate reviews by DCAA officials.

Sherick was also not satisfied with controls over processing of fraud cases within DCAA. His staff concluded that there were difficulties in reconciling DCAA field and headquarters records and stated that "a formal system is now needed to insure the timely referral and tracking of fraud reports."

The DOD IG expressed concern over DCAA procedures in discussing potential fraud cases with local contract administration or procurement officials and recommended this practice be discontinued "especially when local DOD procurement officials may be involved."

Sherick closed with some complimentary words for the beleaguered agency. He noted with satisfaction that "on February 28, 1984, DCAA issued tougher instructions regarding suspending payments for denial of access."

Other reports and testimony by representatives of the DOD IG relating to DCAA are discussed in Chapter XXVI, Federal Inspectors General. Most criticisms of the audit agency tend to resemble paternal admonishings and encouragement to do more rather than the kind of sharp censures reserved for contractors and DOD contracting officers.

As discussed in Chapter XXVIII—The General Accounting Office—, the congressional watchdog has long played the role of a friendly critic to DCAA. Perhaps even kinder than the office of the DOD IG, the GAO's reports, with few exceptions, combine some mild criticisms with encouragement to DCAA for devoting increased efforts in such GAO-favored areas as defective pricing.

In February 1986, GAO did issue a report to a congressional committee which was critical of DCAA's planning system and management of its resources. We have summarized this report as a matter of interest in terms of a picture of the management of an agency which considers itself expert in evaluating the economy and efficiency of multibillion dollar companies. The GAO report is unfortunately somewhat flawed by the fact that its 1986 release date has little relevancy to the period in which the review was performed (May 1983—June 1984), and still less to the DCAA activities reviewed (July 1981—December 1982).

The report emphasized the importance of a sound planning system, consistently implemented, particularly in view of DCAA's highly decentralized organization and operations involving 4,000 (now approaching 5,000) personnel. In 1984, DCAA's personnel strength included 113 in its Washington headquarters, 416 in the six regional offices, and the others in its field audit offices. The Washington headquarters is responsible for policy, planning, and relations with higher DOD levels and others in the Nation's capital; the regional offices manage and review the field audit offices within their assigned geographical areas; and the field audit offices perform the actual audit work.

GAO concluded that DCAA's planning system was adequate "for identifying and prioritizing its work and for computing the resources needed . . . . However, inconsistencies in implementing the system among (its) field offices detract from the value of the planning system and reduce assurances that the agency is effectively using its resources." DCAA conducts a "peer review" consisting of reviews of each of its regions by personnel of the other regions, and GAO noted that some of the weaknesses it found had also been reported in the peer reviews but adequate corrective action had not been taken.

Inasmuch as reallocation of manpower among the audit offices to meet shifting workloads and priorities is very difficult because of a wide resistance to geographical moves by the auditors, the determination and definition of workloads and priorities for field audit offices, and computing their resource requirements, were identified by GAO as extremely important activities not effectively carried out.

DCAA's planning begins at field offices, where familiarity with a contractor (resident staff) or contractors (branch offices performing "mobile" audits) should permit identification of specific discretionary work and estimates of demand (requests from contracting officers) audits. GAO reported, however, that these offices have a limited perspective of DCAA's total responsibilities, and it falls to the regional offices and ultimately to the headquarters to make the necessary allocation judgments which should result in staffing offices in a manner permitting the accomplishment of the agency's most important work.

As is well known, it is much easier to criticize than to perform, and DCAA, which criticizes contractors for planning failures, was found to be itself deficient in this area.

DCAA field offices are supposed to survey contractors' operations, internal controls, etc., and to maintain permanent files, including results of prior work, necessary to identify the necessary audit work and time required. The audit agency has also formulated various techniques which are designed to more closely identify the government's exposure to fraud, waste and error, and to assess the risks involved in not auditing the various areas. This "vulnerability assessment" is mandated for all contractors with an annual incurred cost volume of $3 million or more. This process is further required to be prioritized by another technique designated as Workpackage Risk Analysis Procedure (WARP), designed to identify the workpackages or audit areas which have the greatest potential for unallowable costs. After the relative risks are established, the auditors are instructed to estimate savings (cost questioned) per audit hour and, where manpower is insufficient to audit the total contractor operations each year, priorities are supposed to be established on the basis of selecting those which are expected to yield the larger amounts of questioned costs.

GAO concluded that if the system were effectively implemented it would provide DCAA with reasonable assurance that the most important work was being identified and serve as a basis for managing its personnel resources. However, GAO found the implementation at the field level to be consistent.

The vulnerability assessments, considered so important, were not performed at all or not performed adequately in six of the twenty field offices visited. Some DCAA auditors told GAO that they found these assessments useless, too time-consuming, or otherwise not worthwhile.

GAO also found that some of the permanent files were outdated or otherwise inadequate, while some field audit offices had no general survey files. In this regard, the report also faulted DCAA headquarters for failing to provide appropriate guidance concerning such files.

It appeared that DCAA headquarters had introduced various resource management concepts but was not doing very much to assure that these concepts were being implemented. As a matter of fact, GAO found that in recent years the audit agency's personnel requests to DOD were based more on judgmental estimates by the headquarters than on data submitted by the field audit offices and approved by the respective regional offices. The lack of credibility in the data originating at the audit sites seems particularly significant in the light of the substantial personnel increases DCAA has been receiving.

One of the indicators used by DCAA to justify additional resources is an estimate for unaudited cost from prior years or a backlog of discretionary audit work. This backlog increased from $28 billion in 1980 to a projected $92 billion by the end of 1987. Although such data could be viewed as reflecting an unacceptable volume of unaudited costs and requirement for a substantial increase in manpower resources, GAO found it to be an "unverifiable indicator of audit risk or staff needs."

When DCAA was established, the initial organization included a review and evaluation group at the headquarters level which performed periodic reviews of the regional offices and selected field audit offices. Headed by a high-level official reporting directly to the DCAA Director, this group had a fair amount of clout. The work also included re-visits to the field to ascertain whether the approved recommendations had been implemented. This organizational group was eliminated in the late 1970s and, some years later, the function was undertaken by so-called peer review teams, groups of six to twelve field office chiefs selected from regions other than the one under review. GAO found that some of these peer reviews disclosed the same deficiencies as GAO found but that DCAA had no formal follow-up process to assure that any action was taken on the findings and recommendations.

GAO concluded that the "inconsistencies in implementing DCAA's planning system and the apparent lack of action on its peer review results cast doubts as to the sufficiency of top management oversight of field operations, and the credibility of the information generated by the system." It was recommended that the Secretary of Defense instruct the DCAA Director "to ensure that all field audit offices adhere to the planning system to provide information which is reliable for approving work plans and managing resources."

DOD essentially agreed with the GAO recommendations, stated that DCAA was taking necessary action, and that the office of the Assistant Secretary of Defense (Comptroller) would monitor DCAA's progress in these areas, had a management review of DCAA's planning system underway.

As mentioned earlier, most GAO reviews of DCAA conclude that DCAA should be expending more manpower in specified areas but do not couple such findings with suggestions as to where manpower could be reduced, thus assisting DCAA efforts to support its continuing requests for additional people. However, GAO has questioned DCAA's statistics relating to the astronomical amounts of asserted "savings" resulting from costs questioned by the auditors.

Congressional Views and Actions Relating to DCAA

DCAA reception by Congress has been pretty much a mixed bag. While being criticized in several areas during subcommittee hearings, the audit agency comes out well in the end, as indicated by its regular increase in authorized personnel strength and funding during periods when appropriations for other needs were cut.

DCAA was sharply criticized in a hearing conducted by the Senate Committee on Governmental Affairs on March 1, 1984. Chairman Roth opened the hearing by saying:

> Let me start by saying that I am concerned about the performance of the Defense Contract Audit Agency . . . .

> There are indications . . . that the current condition of DCAA management in many areas is poor and that it is leaving the taxpayers' defense dollar defenseless against excessive pricing and cost growth . . . .

Echoing allegations by the DOD IG and GAO that DCAA was subservient to contracting officers and not tough enough on contractors, the Senator concluded his opening remarks:

> We hope to examine today the nature of these problems and determine what can be done to solve them. If the hearings confirm our initial findings, I fully intend to do all I can to reform DCAA's management as soon as possible. If that means putting DCAA under the IG, then I am willing to give that step serious consideration.

Before the hearings concluded, Senator Sasser, a member of the Committee, introduced a bill to abolish DCAA and transfer its functions to the DOD IG. This proposal apparently never received serious consideration from the Senator's colleagues.

In addition to the critical testimony from then DOD IG Joseph Sherick, the Committee heard from two ex-DCAA auditors, one of whom had been allegedly discriminated against for whistle-blowing. Ernest Fitzgerald, Management Systems Deputy to the Air Force Assistant Secretary for Financial Management, was also scheduled to testify but decided not to appear when he was advised by DOD officials that his testimony was at odds with Air Force policy and, if he was to testify, it would have to be as a private citizen without Air Force sanction. However, his original testimony, later obtained by the

Committee, sharply criticized DCAA for inadequate auditing and reporting, and for being nonresponsive to Air Force requests for special studies.

Despite the occasionally hostile environment encountered by DCAA before congressional committees, the agency, as noted earlier, has fared quite well on the whole. In the lengthy hearings leading to the enactment of the 1986 DOD Authorization Act, more fully commented upon in subsequent chapters relating to contract cost principles, Congress provided the DCAA Director with subpoena power, directed that contract auditor participation at price negotiation conferences be virtually mandatory, prohibited contracting officers from negotiating on a "bottom line" basis, thus requiring meticulous explanations for allowing any costs questioned by DCAA, and included other provisions further strengthening the role of the contract auditor at the expense of the contracting officer.

Who's In Charge?

As discussed earlier, the DCAA Director reports to the Assistant Secretary of Defense (Comptroller), and in recent years that post has seen a succession of incumbents, none of whom appeared to exercise much if any supervision over the audit agency. The DOD 1983 Authorization Act added the DOD IG to the group of Inspectors General established by the Inspector General Act of 1978. In addition to the duties and responsibilities established by the 1978 legislation, the DOD IG was specifically given the authority to:

*　　*　　*　　*

(3) provide policy direction for audits and investigations relating to fraud, waste, and abuse and program effectiveness;

*　　*　　*　　*

(6) monitor and evaluate the adherence of department auditors to internal audit, contract audit, and internal review principles, policies and procedures;

Exercising the latter oversight authority, the DOD IG has performed numerous reviews of every facet of DCAA activities. Although, theoretically, DCAA asserts that it is not required to comply with all of the DOD IG recommendations, in practice, the audit agency has closely conformed to them.

The Packard Commission recommended an Under Secretary of Defense (Acquisition) whose authority was to include responsibility to:

Oversee DOD-wide establishment of contract audit policy, particularly policy for audits conducted in support of procurement and contract administration;

Except for criminal investigations and DOD internal audits, supervise establishment of policy for all DOD oversight of defense contractors, including oversight performed by procurement and contract management organizations;

*　　*　　*　　*

Delineate clearly respective responsibilities of jurisdiction of DOD oversight organizations;

Develop guidelines and mechanisms for DOD oversight organizations to share contractor data and otherwise to rely more extensively upon each other's work; and

Improve audit strategies for the conduct, scope, and frequency of contract auditing.

The several recommendations relating to the delineation of the responsibilities of the various organizations engaged in the oversight of defense contractors and the coordination of their efforts to relieve the redundancy of this surveillance were based on a number of studies by congressional committee staffs, the DOD IG, and independent organizations engaged by the Packard Commission, all of which found substantial duplication in the efforts of DCAA, contract administration groups, and others.

Shortly after the new USD(A) was appointed by the President and confirmed by the Senate, Secretary Weinberger announced that his responsibilities would include:

setting policy for the administrative oversight of defense contractors;

developing appropriate guidance concerning the auditing of defense contractors.

From the time the new position of USD(A) was created by the Military Retirement Reform Act of 1986, July 1, 1986, DCAA and its proponents lobbied against assigning any responsibilities to the Under Secretary which might jeopardize the audit agency's "independence." The DOD IG was also concerned in Washington's traditional "turf" competition. Through the combined efforts of GAO, DOD IG, DCAA, and critics of DOD acquisition officials, P.L. 99-500, the 1987 continuing appropriations resolution, muddied the waters by including the following provisions:

(d)(1) The Under Secretary shall prescribe policies to ensure that audit and oversight of contractor activities are coordinated and carried out in a manner to prevent duplication by different elements of the Department.

(2) In carrying out this subsection, the Under Secretary shall consult with the Inspector General of the Department of Defense.

(3) Nothing in this subsection shall affect the authority of the Inspector General of the Department of Defense to establish audit policy for the Department of Defense under the Inspector General Act of 1978 and otherwise to carry out the functions of the Inspector General under that Act.

The question of "who's in charge" in contractor audit and surveillance will, unfortunately, require time to fully resolve. It would appear that the USD(A) has clear and uncontested authority to reduce, if not eliminate, the redundancy in compensation, insurance, and operations reviews, now duplicated by DCAA and various contract administration groups. Aspects of contract audit policy, such as the current DCAA efforts to access virtually all of defense contractors' records, including internal audit reports, board of directors' meeting minutes, income tax returns, etc., will require more time to resolve. Industry groups have expressed cautious optimism that, ultimately, some restraints will be developed within DOD to curtail the current DCAA practices.

Office of Management and Budget (OMB) Circular A-50, Audit Follow-up

Government-wide policy for audit followup was promulgated in this OMB Circular in October 1982 and applies to a wide range of audit reports, including those issued by inspectors general, other agency audit organizations (both contract and internal), GAO, and nonfederal auditors.

Written comments are required on audit reports. Where agency officials agree with the recommendations, the response must include a statement of planned corrective action. Disagreements must be fully explained and referred for resolution to a higher level management official or to the audit followup official. Audit followup is applicable to preaward contract audits. "However," according to the Circular, "since such reports are resolved by negotiation of a contract price, they are not subject to the time limits or reporting requirements . . . . The requirements for records on the status of reports . . . may be met by records maintained in official contract files."

Audit recommendations require resolution within six months after the issuance of the audit report, and semiannual reports must be submitted on the status of any unresolved audit reports over six months old.

The Circular apparently joins in the views of GAO and certain congressional elements that the statutory and contractual role of the contracting officer does not require any special consideration in the audit followup process. In discussing responses to audit reports and resolution of disagreements with audit recommendations the expression "management and contracting officials" is used without any distinction between the two categories of officials.

DCAA ORGANIZATION AND STRUCTURE

The Defense Contract Audit Agency was formally established on July 1, 1965, with a total strength approximating 3,600, consisting of audit and administrative people identified as involved in contract audit activities in the Army, Navy, Air Force, and the Defense Supply Agency (DSA), now the Defense Logistics Agency (DLA). During the agency's almost quarter of a century of existence, its authorized strength has fluctuated. In recent years, however, with increased congressional interest in contractor oversight, cost disallowance and fraud detection, DCAA has enjoyed annual increases and its authorized manpower now approximates 5,000.

DCAA's charter Directive (DODD 5105.36) initially provided for the chain of command to run from the Agency's Director to the Secretary of Defense, with the ASD(C) assigned the responsibility for staff supervision of the Agency. In 1978, the Directive was revised to provide: "DCAA is established as a separate agency of the Department of Defense under the direction, authority and control of the Assistant Secretary of Defense (Comptroller)." As commented upon previously, it would appear that the ASD(C), DOD IG, and the new USD(A), all have some responsibility for contract audit activities in the Defense Department. The proliferation of this responsibility, it is feared, will inhibit effective, consistent direction of this important function.

DCAA's headquarters is located with DLA and DCAS at Cameron Station, Alexandria, Virginia, some five miles from the Pentagon. Operational responsibility is divided geographically among six regional offices (originally seven—New York abolished) of varying sizes: Boston, Philadelphia, Atlanta, Chicago, San Francisco, and Los Angeles. In addition to the New England States and portions of New York, the Boston Region includes Europe and the Middle East. The San Francisco Region covers an immense expanse of land (and water), including Northern California and extending north and east as far as Missouri and as far west as Hawaii and the Far East.

Each of the regions is headed by a director and deputy director, with approximately five regional audit supervisors (RAMs) and about fifteen technical and administrative people. The actual auditing is performed by field audit offices (FAOs). Companies with a continuing large volume of government contracts subject to audit have DCAA audit staffs permanently stationed at their plants and offices. Where the number of auditors exceeds five, the FAO is referred to as a resident office or residency, with the resident auditor reporting to the regional director through one of the RAMs. Where the permanent staff is five or less, DCAA uses the term "suboffice" and the auditor in charge reports to an FAO, usually a branch office. These offices, ranging in size from twenty or so to over fifty people, are located in areas of heavy incidence of government contractors. In most instances, branch offices perform their missions by conducting "mobile" audits, that is, through occasional visits to the contractors in contrast to maintaining resident staffs. The branch office chiefs also report to their respective regional directors through assigned RAMs.

A contractor's route to challenge or appeal an auditor's conclusions within DCAA channels, while not at all as simple as DCAA officials describe publicly, is still not too cumbersome. At a residency, the path is to the resident auditor (although intervening levels of supervisory auditors are encountered), then to the RAM, the Regional Director, and finally DCAA headquarters. Companies audited on a mobile basis follow a similar path with the branch chief substituted for the resident auditor. In either case, if the route extends to DCAA headquarters, it is best to telephone or write directly to the Director. Of course, the Director will review of all the facts in the case and the views of subordinates before meeting with the contractor, or may even refer the matter to a top assistant. However, the approach through the Director will assure that the matter is not lost in the bureaucratic shuffle. Furthermore, it is rare indeed for a DCAA Director to refuse to see a contractor's representative on a matter of consequence.

The author would strongly suggest that contractors advise all of the auditors at intervening levels of their intentions to carry the matter to higher authority and keep everyone involved abreast of developments. This procedure not only affords the local auditor and the auditor's immediate superiors the appropriate courtesy but reflects a logical process, inasmuch as all involved will sooner or later be advised of the contractor's actions and will be requested to submit their views.

OTHER FEDERAL CONTRACT AUDIT ORGANIZATIONS

The Department of Defense awards by far the largest number of contracts subject to audit and, with very few minor exceptions, all are audited by DCAA. This agency also performs all contract auditing for NASA and a substantial amount of such work for other civilian agencies. There are few if any federal departments or agencies, including such quasi-federal agencies as the U.S. Postal Service and the U.S. Railway Association, for whom DCAA has not performed some contract audit services. These services are performed under reimbursable, cross-servicing agreements in accordance with the following policy (DCAAM 1-303b., c.):

b. Cross-servicing agreements with non-DOD agencies provide for audit requests to be forwarded directly to the cognizant field office. Audit requests will be honored at locations where DCAA maintains a continuing audit interest under recurring DOD contracts.

c. Requests ... for audit services at locations where DCAA does not maintain a continuing audit interest will be referred to the regional office. The following criteria will be used to determine whether to accommodate or decline a request:

(1) Is the requested service compatible with normal DCAA responsibilities?

(2) Would acceptance/refusal to perform the work result in establishment of duplicative audit activity?

(3) Is another Government agency performing audit work at the contractor location that could perform the requested work?

Quite logically, where DCAA maintains a resident staff or even visits the location from time to time and has thus acquired a familiarity with the contractor's records and people, it would be wasteful and disruptive for another federal agency to assign auditors to review its contracts. As mentioned previously, DCAA maintains a large number of field audit offices throughout the United States and abroad. From time to time, civilian agencies will award contracts to companies at locations far removed from their audit offices but reasonably proximate to a DCAA field audit office. Here again, logically, the agency will request the nearby DCAA FAO to perform the required work.

The thought of a single contract audit agency to perform all of this work for all federal departments and agencies has not gone unnoticed. The proposal was seriously considered by the Commission on Government Procurement in the early 1970s and by others since then. Apart from bureaucratic rivalries, there are many serious reservations about the wisdom of this idea. The pros and cons include many familiar debates concerning the relative merits of centralization and decentralization and questions regarding the optimum size of an effective organization, audit or otherwise. At this writing, it would appear that efforts will continue to make maximum use of DCAA but most of the federal departments and agencies will continue to maintain varying degrees of their own contract audit capability.

DCAA AUDIT PUBLICATIONS, POLICIES AND PRACTICES

As we mentioned previously, the Defense Contract Audit Agency is an important organization to virtually all government contractors. It is the largest contract audit group and audits most contracts. Former DCAA officials are found in key positions in other departments and agencies. Additionally, DCAA has a well developed training program, which encompasses every facet of audit and related management from orientation courses for incoming junior auditors to MBA and other executive level courses for the agency's higher level people. A very limited number of spaces at DCAA's Contract Audit Institute are made available to other federal agencies.

DCAA's audit publication system is by far the most advanced and many agencies have adopted it in whole or in part for guidance to their auditors. The major and best known publication is the Defense Contract Audit Manual, officially referred to as DCAAM but more commonly known as CAM.

The original CAM, published July 1, 1965, was "not available for public distribution," a position that was sharply criticized by industry and the accounting profession. As a result of challenges under the Freedom of Information Act and other legislation, the agency subsequently released limited portions of the manual but continued to withhold the major sections. The proclivity to secrecy was apparently attributable to the agency's first director because shortly after his retirement, and the appointment of the second director, the entire CAM was made available to the public. It still may be purchased from the Superintendent of Documents, U.S. Government Printing Office, Washington, DC 20402. The author strongly recommends the purchase of this manual by companies whose records are subject to audit by government contract auditors.

CAM is a comprehensive compilation of policies, procedures, and techniques for auditing and reporting in connection with government contracts. On balance, it is a well-thought-out, professional auditing text, containing competent guidance in its chapters and appendices. The manual includes some of the most advanced techniques for auditing of and through automatic data processing systems, and for use of statistical sampling, improvement curve analysis and graphic and computational analysis. It also includes many controversial instructions, such as those relating to operations audits and access to a broad spectrum of contractors' books, records, and facilities. Some of the significant guidance contained in CAM is discussed in other portions of this text. A quick picture of CAM's contents (in the December 1987 edition) can be gleaned from the following listing of its chapters and appendices.

Chapter

1	Introduction to Contract Audit
2	Contract Auditing and Reporting Standards
3	Audit Planning
4	General Audit Requirements
5	Review of Policies, Procedures, and Internal Controls Relative to Accounting and Management Systems
6	Incurred Costs Audit Procedures
7	Selected Areas of Cost
8	Cost Accounting Standards

Appendix

For many companies doing business with the government that entails contract audits, the acquisition of CAM with a subscription to assure receipt of the periodic revisions is quite sufficient to anticipate, understand, and cope with the government auditors. Some contractors, however, especially large companies with a substantial volume of government contracts subject to audit, are interested in some of the other lesser known and informal DCAA releases. In the controversial field of the agency's operations audits, for example, DCAA has published pamphlets providing guidelines to its staff in such areas as facilities management, automatic data processing systems, contractors' reproduction operations, maintenance and calibration of test equipment, and production scheduling and control.

Other DCAA pamphlets cover such subjects as Delay and Disruption, Terminated Contracts, Auditors' Responsibility for Fraud Detection, and Postaward Reviews under P.L. 87-653. Although none of these pamphlets is restricted, to the author's knowledge, they are not as readily available as CAM. For one thing, one must know of the existence of a particular pamphlet to obtain it. Thereafter, the process involves communication with DCAA headquarters to ascertain its cost and sending a check in the requisite amount.

Chapter III

Types of Government Contracts

Viewed as a buyer of goods and services, the federal government is a vast, complex, heterogeneous bureaucracy, consisting of 13 major departments, approximately 60 agencies, hundreds of contracting officers and tens of thousands of individuals involved in the award and administration of contracts. The substantive differences in the missions and needs of the departments and agencies, the large numbers of federal employees engaged in contracting activities, and the virtually countless laws and implementing regulations related to these activities contribute to the difficulties encountered by the private sector in understanding how to sell to the government. In this light, it has been observed with some justification that there is no such thing as a typical government contract.

With the publication of the long awaited FAR, uniformity in the types of contracts used by federal agencies in various circumstances has been considerably enhanced, although differences still remain. This text is not designed to provide coverage of all facets of government contracting, but rather to furnish guidance on the accounting and certain administrative aspects of costing and pricing. This chapter summarizes the basic policies underlying government procurement and the major types of contracts used by federal agencies. Detailed regulatory provisions are contained in FAR Subchapter C:

Part 13—Small Purchase and Other Simplified Purchase Procedures

Part 14—Sealed Bidding

Part 15—Contracting by Negotiation

Part 16—Types of Contracts

Part 17—Special Contracting Methods

The view that the government can buy at the lowest price where it obtains maximum competition, and the suspicion created when purchases are made from a sole source or even under limited competition, have generated continuing pressure upon federal agencies to buy on the most competitive basis possible. Inasmuch as sealed bidding is generally considered to yield the most competitive form of procurement, federal laws and regulations require its use wherever possible. The need for negotiation is recognized in the Competition in Contracting Act of 1984 (CICA), but the emphasis on competition in lieu of the previous specific circumstances permitting the use of negotiation was intensified.

A wide variety of goods and services can be and are acquired through sealed bidding or negotiation on a competitive basis. By far the largest number of government contracts are awarded pursuant to significant competition. When it comes to dollar volume, however, conditions are different and we find considerable procurement, especially in the Department of Defense, made under limited competition or from sole sources. How many companies can deliver major weapons systems required for our national defense?

SEALED BIDDING

Policies and procedures for procurement by sealed bidding are contained in FAR Part 14. The first step in the process is the government's preparation of the invitation for bid (IFB), which should describe "the requirements of the Government clearly, accurately, and completely. Unnecessarily restrictive specifications or requirements that might unduly limit the number of bidders are prohibited." The IFBs are required to be appropriately publicized and to permit sufficient time for interested companies to prepare and submit bids. The bids are publicly opened and the contract is awarded "to that responsible bidder whose bid, conforming to the invitation for bids, will be most advantageous to the Government, considering only price and the price-related factors included in the invitation." The qualifying language is generally not too significant beyond the basic requirements that the low bidder be a responsible company and its bid conform to the terms of the IFB.

Contracts awarded under sealed bidding are generally firm fixed price contracts, but they may contain provisions for economic price adjustment. In the absence of such provisions, no cost or pricing data is required for government audit. Even where economic price adjustments are involved, the necessary computations are frequently resolved with the contracting officer and price analysts.

However, in the event of contract changes exceeding $100,000, cost or pricing data must be submitted in the same manner as if the original contract had been awarded after negotiation. In these instances, all of the accounting and government contract audit problems described throughout this text may be encountered. Also, where a sealed bid contract is terminated for the convenience of the government, the contractor will be required to submit the same kinds of data and be subject to the same types of audits experienced under negotiated contracts.

PROCUREMENT BY NEGOTIATION

As noted earlier, implementation of the CICA provisions required substantial changes to a number of FAR Parts, some minor, others of considerable consequence. FAR 15.101 now defines negotiation as meaning "contracting through the use of either competitive or other-than-competitive proposals and discussions. Any contract awarded without using sealed bidding procedures is a negotiated contract." FAR 15.102 further describes this contracting method as follows:

> Negotiation is a procedure that includes the receipt of proposals from offerors, permits bargaining, and usually affords an opportunity to revise their offers before award of a contract. Bargaining—in the sense of discussion, persuasion, alteration of initial assumptions and positions, and give-and-take—may apply to price, schedule, technical requirements, type of contract, or other terms of a proposed contract.

Negotiated contracts begin with the issuance of requests for proposals (RFPs). The contractor's response to an RFP can be accepted by the government to create a binding contract, usually following negotiations, but under specified circumstances (FAR 15.610) without discussion. In contrast, a request for quotation (RFQ) is not an offer and a response thereto cannot be accepted by the government to create a binding contract. An RFQ is intended for use when the government is not prepared to award a contract but is interested in obtaining information as to price, delivery, or other matters for planning purposes.

For negotiated contracts and modifications entered into after June 4, 1987, the Assistant Secretary of Defense for Production and Logistics, Robert Costello, authorized a class deviation to the DOD FAR Supplement that raises the thresholds for requiring field pricing reports. Under the class deviation, the threshold for requiring field pricing reports is increased from $100,000 to $500,000 for fixed-price contracts, from $250,000 to $500,000 for fixed-price incentive contracts, and from $500,000 to $1 million for cost-type contracts. Contracting officers may waive the higher thresholds with "adequate written justification." However, if the contracting officer is aware of deficiencies in the contractor's cost estimating system, the thresholds for requiring field pricing reports shall be $250,000 for fixed-price contracts and $500,000 for cost-type contracts. The higher thresholds are intended to speed up and simplify the acquisition process and to increase contracting officers' authority. The class deviation, at the time, was an interim measure to be formalized via changes to DFARS 15.805-5(a)(1).

GOVERNMENT PRINCIPLES FOR SELECTION OF NEGOTIATED CONTRACTS

The principles for selecting negotiated contracts are set forth in FAR 16.103, from which the following is excerpted:

(a) Selecting the contract type is generally a matter for negotiation and requires the exercise of sound judgment. Negotiating the contract type and negotiating prices are closely related and should be considered together. The objective is to negotiate a contract type and price (or estimated cost and fee) that will result in reasonable contractor risk and provide the contractor with the greatest incentive for efficient and economical performance.

(b) A firm-fixed-price contract, which best utilizes the basic profit motive of business enterprise, shall be used when the risk involved is minimal or can be predicted with an acceptable degree of certainty. However, when a reasonable basis for firm pricing does not exist, other contract types should be considered, and negotiations should be directed toward selecting a contract type (or combination of types) that will appropriately tie profit to contractor performance.

(c) In the course of an acquisition program, a series of contracts, or a single long-term contract, changing circumstances may make a different contract type appropriate in later periods than that used at the outset. In particular, contracting officers should avoid protracted use of a cost-reimbursement or time-and-materials contract after experience provides a basis for firmer pricing.

(d) Each contract file shall include documentation to show why the particular contract type was selected, except for (1) small purchases under Part 13, (2) repetitive purchases on a firm fixed-price basis, and (3) awards made on the set-aside portion of sealed bid solicitations partially set aside for either small business or labor surplus area concerns.

FAR 16.104 advises the contracting officer that the following are some of the factors that should be considered in selecting and negotiating the contract: price competition, price analysis, cost analysis, type and complexity of the requirement, urgency of the requirement, period of performance or length of production run, contractor's technical capability and financial responsibility, adequacy of the contractor's accounting system, concurrent contracts, and extent and nature of proposed subcontracting.

DESCRIPTION OF SPECIFIC TYPES OF NEGOTIATED CONTRACTS

Firm-Fixed-Price Contract

A firm-fixed-price contract provides for a price that is not subject to adjustment by reason of the contractor's cost experience. The favored status of this type of contract is indicated in the comment (FAR 16.202-1) that "(i)t provides maximum incentive for the contractor to control costs and perform effectively and imposes a minimum administrative burden upon the contracting parties."

Fixed-Price Contract with Economic Price Adjustment

The fixed-price contract with economic price adjustment provides for the upward and downward revision of the stated contract price, but only upon the occurrence of certain contingencies, which are specifically defined in the contract. This contract may be used in unstable market conditions, and the contingencies will generally relate to possible increases or decreases in the price of materials or in wage rates.

Fixed-Price Incentive Contract (Firm Target)

This is a fixed-price contract where, at the outset, there is negotiated a target cost, a target profit, a price ceiling (but not a profit ceiling or floor), and the formula for establishing final profit and price. Upon completion, the final cost is negotiated and the final price is then established in accordance with the formula. Within the price ceiling established, the formula provides for the government and the contractor to share the responsibility for the difference between the costs originally estimated and those finally negotiated. To the extent that the final cost is less than the target cost, the final profit will be greater than the target profit. To the extent that the final cost exceeds the target cost, the final profit will be less than the target profit or the result may even be a loss.

Fixed-Price Incentive Contract (Successive Targets)

This fixed-price contract provides for the negotiation of an initial target cost, an initial target profit, a price ceiling, a formula for fixing the firm target profit, and a production point at which the formula will be applied. This production point is generally fixed at a time prior to delivery or shop completion of the first item. When this point is reached, the firm target cost is negotiated and the firm target profit is automatically determined in accordance with the formula. At this point a firm fixed price may be negotiated; as an alternative, a formula for establishing final profit and price may be negotiated using the firm target profit and the firm target cost. As in the case of the firm target type of contract described above, the final cost is negotiated at the completion of the contract. The final contract price is then established in accordance with the formula for establishing final profit and price.

In order to arrange for payments under fixed-price incentive contracts, whether firm target or successive targets, a billing price is established. This billing price may be adjusted within ceiling limits, upon request of either party to the contract, when it becomes apparent that final negotiated costs will be substantially different from the target cost.

Use of the fixed-price incentive contract is conditional upon the availability of reliable cost and pricing information and upon the determination that the contractor's accounting system is adequate for the purpose.

Fixed-Price Contract with Prospective Price Redetermination at a Stated Time or Times During Performance

This type of contract provides for a firm fixed price for an initial period of contract deliveries or performance and for prospective price redetermination either upward or downward at a stated time or times during the performance of the contract. It is intended for use in quantity production contracts where it is possible to negotiate fair and reasonable firm fixed prices for an initial period but not for subsequent periods.

Fixed-Price Contract with Retroactive Price Redetermination After Completion

This type of contract provides for a ceiling price and a retroactive price redetermination after completion of the contract. Its use is limited to research and development contracts at an estimated cost of $100,000 or less.

Firm-Fixed-Price, Level-of-Effort Term Contract

This contract requires (a) the contractor to provide a specified level of effort, over a stated period of time, on work that can be stated only in general terms and (b) the government to pay the contractor a fixed dollar amount. It is considered suitable for investigation or study in a specific research and development area where the final product is a report. It is not to be used where the contract price exceeds $100,000 without the approval of the chief of the contracting office.

Cost Contract

This is a cost-reimbursement type contract without a provision for fee, usually employed for research and development with nonprofit organizations and for facilities contracts.

Cost-Sharing Contract

This is a cost-reimbursement type contract, for use in research and development procurement, under which the contractor is reimbursed only for an agreed portion of allowable costs. Generally, the basis for the contractor's agreement to absorb a portion of the cost is the expectation of compensating benefits.

Cost-Plus-Incentive-Fee (CPIF) Contract

This is a cost-reimbursement type contract with a fee that is adjusted by formula in accordance with the relationship between the total allowable cost and the target cost. Initially, there is negotiated a target cost, a target fee, a minimum and maximum fee, and the fee adjustment formula. The final fee is determined in accordance with the formula after the completion of the contract. The final fee will exceed the target fee when total allowable costs are less than the target cost and, conversely, the final fee will be less than the target fee when the total allowable costs exceed the target costs. The use of the CPIF contract is encouraged under certain circumstances where CPFF (cost-plus-fixed-fee contract, see below) contracts were previously used. For example, its use is encouraged where it is highly probable that the development is feasible and the Government generally has determined its desired performance objectives. Here the CPIF contract would be used in conjunction with performance incentives in the development of major systems and in other development programs.

Cost-Plus-Award-Fee (CPAF) Contract

The CPAF contract is a cost-reimbursement contract that provides for (1) a base amount fixed at the inception of the contract and (2) an award fee amount that the contractor may earn in whole or in part during performance. The fee is sufficient to provide motivation for excellence.

Cost-Plus-Fixed-Fee (CPFF) Contract

The CPFF contract provides for reimbursement of actual costs to the extent prescribed and a fixed fee that does not vary unless subsequent changes in scope are negotiated. It offers no incentive, hence its use is discouraged.

Time-And-Materials Contract

This type of contract provides for payment for direct labor hours expended at specified fixed hourly rates (which rates include direct and indirect labor, overhead, and profit) and for materials at cost.

Labor-Hour Contract

The labor-hour type of contract is a variant of the time-and-materials contract, except that materials are not supplied by the contractor.

Contract with Performance Incentives

Whereas the incentive type contracts previously discussed usually provide for increased profits or fees for the betterment of cost targets, contracts with performance incentives provide for increases in fees or profits to the extent that performance targets are increased. Conversely, of course, fees or profits will fall below the target amounts to the extent that the performance targets are not met. A performance incentive should relate to specific performance characteristics such as range of a missile, speed of an aircraft or ship, thrust of an engine, maneuverability of a vehicle, and fuel economy. This type of contract is considered particularly appropriate for major weapons and equipment.

Basic Ordering Agreement (BOA)

A BOA is a written instrument of understanding that contains (1) terms and clauses applicable to future contracts (orders) between the parties during its term, (2) a description, as specific as practicable, of supplies or services to be provided, and (3) methods for pricing, issuing, and delivering future orders under the basic ordering agreement. A BOA is not a contract.

Indefinite Delivery Contract

There are three versions of this type of contract: definite-quantity contracts, requirements contracts, and indefinite-quantity contracts.

A definite-quantity contract provides for delivery of a definite quantity of specific supplies or services for a fixed period, with deliveries to be scheduled at designated locations upon order.

A requirements contract provides for filling all actual purchase requirements of designated government activities for specific supplies or services during a specified contract period, with deliveries to be scheduled by placing orders with the contractor. A requirements contract is generally used for commercial or commercial-type products where the government anticipates recurring requirements but cannot predetermine the precise quantities that designated government activities will need during a definite period.

An indefinite-quantity contract provides for supplying indefinite quantities within stated limits of specific supplies or services during a fixed period, with deliveries to be scheduled by placing orders with the contractor. An indefinite-quantity contract is used when the government cannot predetermine, above a specified minimum, the precise quantities of supplies or services that will be required during a contract period. As in the case of a requirements contract, funds are obligated by each delivery rather than by the contract itself.

Letter Contract

A letter contract, the use of which has been frequently criticized by GAO, DOD IG and some congressmen, is a written preliminary contractual instrument that authorizes a contractor to begin immediately manufacturing supplies or performing services. It is used when the government requires a binding agreement so that the work can start immediately but negotiating a definitive contract is not possible. It requires approval of higher authority, definitization within 180 days (except upon special authorization in unusual instances), and may not commit the government to a definitive contract in excess of the funds available at the time the letter contract is executed.

Chapter IV

Significant Clauses Included in Government Contracts

Government contracts are considerably more voluminous and complex than most agreements reached in the private sector for procuring supplies or services. The question of whether government contracts really require so many complex clauses has been long debated. The fact is that, depending on the type of contract and individual circumstances, the number of clauses may approximate 100—a staggering adventure to encounter, particularly for small or medium-sized companies that do not have large staffs of experienced government contract administrators. And unfortunately, we see no relief in sight. On the contrary, our extensive experience in the government contracting field and our close review of government procurement regulations convince us that the number of contract clauses is much more likely to increase than to decrease.

ORIGINS OF GOVERNMENT CONTRACT CLAUSES

It is understandable that a contract should contain provisions for the goods or services to be supplied, prices to be paid, time and place of delivery, and similar essential features. Government contracts, however, contain numerous clauses extending far beyond these essentials. There are special clauses requiring that the company's books and records be made available to the procuring agencies' representatives and the General Accounting Office for audit; clauses permitting the government to terminate the contract, for default or for its convenience; provisions under which the government can compel changes of numerous kinds as long as they are "within the scope of the contract"; innumerable clauses, most of them mandatory in all or certain types of contracts, emanating from statutes involving socioeconomic objectives, e.g., utilization of small business and small disadvantaged business concerns, statutorily required provisions to favor American goods, and so on.

Other government contract clauses originate in specific regulations promulgated by the various federal agencies, and many have found their way into the vast maze of clauses because of the perceived need to formalize trade practices.

REFERENCE SOURCES

A major accomplishment by the FAR writers is Part 52, which (a) gives instructions for using provisions and clauses in solicitations and contracts, (b) sets forth all of the solicitation provisions and contract clauses prescribed by FAR, and (c) presents useful matrixes listing the FAR provisions and clauses applicable to each principal contract type and purpose (e.g., fixed-price supply, cost-reimbursement research and development).

Subpart 52.2 sets forth the texts of all FAR solicitation provisions and contract clauses, each in its own subsection. The subpart is arranged by subject matter, in the same order as, and keyed to, the parts of FAR. Each provision or clause collected in Subpart 52.2 is specifically prescribed elsewhere in FAR where the subject matter of the provision or clause receives its primary treatment.

For each provision or clause, Subpart 52.2 includes certain useful supplementary information in addition to the text of the provision or clause. A preface provides (1) a cross-reference to the location in the FAR subject text that prescribes its use and (2) directions for inserting it in solicitations or contracts.

Contracting officials in both the government and industry faced substantial problems in the transition from using the clauses with which they had been familiar and which they had learned to locate in DAR, FPR, or agency regulations. These officials found considerable assistance in the information following each provision or clause, setting forth its derivation. This helpful information is explained in FAR 52.106, Derivation of FAR Provisions and Clauses:

(a) Nearly all FAR provisions and clauses have been derived from Defense Acquisition Regulation (DAR) and/or Federal Procurement Regulations (FPR) provisions and clauses. In order to enable the user of this regulation to understand the derivation, a notation has been added at the bottom of each FAR provision or clause underneath the words "(End of provision)" or "(End of clause)." The notation shows the nature of the derivation by one of the following codes:

"NM" means *new material* not in the DAR or FPR.

"R" means the FAR coverage is *rewritten* from the DAR, FPR, or other material from which it is derived.

"AV" means the FAR coverage repeats a provision or clause in the DAR, FPR, or other source *almost verbatim.* In the text of the provision or clause, titles of organizations, officials, or documents are changed or personal pronouns deleted. The language is substantially the same, with no substantive differences from that of the DAR, FPR, or other provision or clause from which it is derived.

"V" means the FAR coverage repeats a DAR, FPR, or other provision or clause *verbatim.*

(b) In addition, when the derivation is from the DAR or FPR, the citation (and date when appropriate) of the DAR or FPR provision or clause from which the FAR material is derived has been included. The acronyms DAR and FPR have not been used when citing these former provisions or clauses, since their citations are distinctive: DAR citations generally begin "7-" and are dated, while the FPR citations all begin "1-" and are undated.

(c) When a provision or clause is revised or the FAR reissued, the derivation notations will be deleted.

FAR SUPPLEMENTS

As in most other subject areas covered in FAR, the various executive departments and agencies have included in their "FAR Supplements" additional or different clauses they concluded were needed. The Department of Defense, as in all other matters, has the heaviest coverage. But all of these DOD modifications were not considered adequate, and the Army, Navy and Air Force have added special clauses of their own. Outside of DOD, many other departments and agencies, such as NASA, Energy, Transportation, and GSA, have also included special clauses of their own in their FAR Supplements.

COVERAGE IN THIS TEXT

This text is not a legal treatise, and no effort has been made to provide comprehensive coverage of government contract clauses. Emphasis is placed on clauses of particular interest to accountants and financial managers. The commentary in this chapter identifies many of the clauses in this category. Where the subject of the clause is covered elsewhere in this text, appropriate reference is made to the related chapter. In other instances, the essence of the clause is described to the extent considered necessary. For ready reference purposes, the selected contract provisions are listed in alphabetical sequence rather than in the unstructured and differing sequences found in the original sources.

ADVANCE PAYMENTS (See Chapter VI)

ALLOWABLE COST AND PAYMENT

The Allowable Cost, Fee and Payment clause has been replaced by separate clauses for (1) Allowable Cost and Payment and (2) Fixed Fee (or Incentive Fee). Payment provisions, particularly regarding allowable costs for reimbursement, have expanded over the years, and the FAR clause (52.216-7) represents a substantial rewriting effort and consolidation of clauses formerly contained in DAR and FPR. For these reasons, a verbatim quotation of this clause is appropriate for this text:

(a) *Invoicing.* The Government shall make payments to the Contractor when requested as work progresses, but (except for small business concerns) not more often than once every 2 weeks, in amounts determined to be allowable by the Contracting Officer in accordance with Subpart 31.2 of the Federal Acquisition Regulation (FAR) in effect on the date of this contract and the terms of this contract. The Contractor may submit to an authorized representative of the Contracting Officer, in such form and reasonable detail as the representative may require, an invoice or voucher supported by a statement of the claimed allowable cost for performing this contract.

(b) *Reimbursing costs.* (1) For the purpose of reimbursing allowable costs (except as provided in subpararaph (2) below, with respect to pension, deferred profit sharing, and employee stock ownership plan contributions), the term "costs" includes only—

(i) Those recorded costs that, at the time of the request for reimbursement, the Contractor has paid by cash, check, or other form of actual payment for items or services purchased directly for the contract;

(ii) When the Contractor is not delinquent in paying costs of contract performance in the ordinary course of business, costs incurred, but not necessarily paid, for—

(A) Materials issued from the Contractor's inventory and placed in the production process for use on the contract;

(B) Direct labor;

(C) Direct travel;

(D) Other direct in-house costs; and

(E) Properly allocable and allowable indirect costs, as shown in the records maintained by the Contractor for purposes of obtaining reimbursement under government contracts; and

(iii) The amount of progress payments that have been paid to the Contractor's subcontractors under similar cost standards.

(2) Contractor contributions to any pension, profit-sharing, or employee stock ownership plan funds that are paid quarterly or more often may be included in indirect costs for payment purposes; *provided,* that the Contractor pays the contribution to the fund within 30 days after the close of the period covered. Payments made 30 days or more after the close of a period shall not be included until the Contractor actually makes the payment. Accrued costs for such contributions that are paid less often than quarterly shall be excluded from indirect costs for payment purposes until the Contractor actually makes the payment.

(3) Notwithstanding the audit and adjustment of invoices or vouchers under paragraph (g) below, allowable indirect costs under this contract shall be obtained by applying indirect cost rates established in accordance with paragraph (d) below.

(4) Any statements in specifications or other documents incorporated in this contract by reference designating performance of services or furnishing of materials at the Contractor's expense or at no cost to the Government shall be disregarded for purposes of cost-reimbursement under this clause.

(c) *Small business concerns.* A small business concern may be paid more often than every 2 weeks and may invoice and be paid for recorded costs for items or services purchased directly for the contract, even though the concern has not yet paid for those items or services.

(d) *Final indirect cost rates.* (1) Final annual indirect cost rates and the appropriate bases shall be established in accordance with Subpart 42.7 of the Federal Acquisition Regulation (FAR) in effect for the period covered by the indirect cost rate proposal.

(2) The Contractor shall, within 90 days after the expiration of each of its fiscal years, or by a later date approved by the Contracting Officer, submit to the cognizant Contracting Officer responsible for negotiating

its final indirect cost rates and, if required by agency procedures, to the cognizant audit activity proposed final indirect cost rates for that period and supporting cost data specifying the contract and/or subcontract to which the rates apply. The proposed rates shall be based on the Contractor's actual cost experience for that period. The appropriate Government representative and Contractor shall establish the final indirect cost rates as promptly as practical after receipt of the Contractor's proposal.

(3) The Contractor and the appropriate Government representative shall execute a written understanding setting forth the final indirect cost rates. The understanding shall specify (i) the agreed-upon final annual indirect cost rates, (ii) the bases to which the rates apply, (iii) the periods for which the rates apply, (iv) any specific indirect cost items treated as direct costs in the settlement, and (v) the affected contract and/or subcontract, identifying any with advance agreements or special terms and the applicable rates. The understanding shall not change any monetary ceiling, contract obligation, or specific cost allowance or disallowance provided for in this contract. The understanding is incorporated into this contract upon execution.

(4) Failure by the parties to agree on a final annual indirect cost rate shall be a dispute within the meaning of the Disputes clause.

(e) *Billing rates.* Until final annual indirect cost rates are established for any period, the Government shall reimburse the Contractor at billing rates established by the Contracting Officer or by an authorized representative (the cognizant auditor), subject to adjustment when the final rates are established. These billing rates—

(1) Shall be the anticipated final rates; and

(2) May be prospectively or retroactively revised by mutual agreement, at either party's request, to prevent substantial overpayment or underpayment.

(f) *Quick-closeout procedures.* When the Contractor and Contracting Officer agree, the quick-closeout procedures of Subpart 42.7 of the FAR may be used.

(g) *Audit.* At any time or times before final payment, the Contracting Officer may have the Contractor's invoices or vouchers and statements of cost audited. Any payment may be (1) reduced by amounts found by the Contracting Officer not to constitute allowable costs or (2) adjusted for prior overpayments or underpayments.

(h) *Final payment.* (1) The Contractor shall submit a completion invoice or voucher, designated as such, promptly upon completion of the work, but no later than one year (or longer, as the Contracting Officer may approve in writing) from the completion date. Upon approval of that invoice or voucher, and upon the Contractor's compliance with all terms of this contract, the Government shall promptly pay any balance of allowable costs and that part of the fee (if any) not previously paid.

(2) The Contractor shall pay to the Government any refunds, rebates, credits, or other amounts (including interest, if any) accruing to

or received by the Contractor or any assignee under this contract, to the extent that those amounts are properly allocable to costs for which the Contractor has been reimbursed by the Government. Reasonable expenses incurred by the Contractor for securing refunds, rebates, credits, or other amounts shall be allowable costs if approved by the Contracting Officer. Before final payment under this contract, the Contractor and each assignee whose assignment is in effect at the time of final payment shall execute and deliver—

(i) An assignment to the Government, in form and substance satisfactory to the Contracting Officer, of refunds, rebates, credits, or other amounts (including interest, if any) properly allocable to costs for which the Contractor has been reimbursed by the Government under this contract; and

(ii) A release discharging the Government, its officers, agents, and employees from all liabilities, obligations, and claims arising out of or under this contract, except—

(A) Specified claims stated in exact amounts, or in estimated amounts when the exact amounts are not known;

(B) Claims (including reasonable incidental expenses) based upon liabilities of the Contractor to third parties arising out of the performance of this contract; *provided,* that the claims are not known to the Contractor on the date of the execution of the release, and that the Contractor gives notice of the claims in writing to the Contracting Officer within 6 years following the release date or notice of final payment date, whichever is earlier; and

(C) Claims for reimbursement of costs, including reasonable incidental expenses, incurred by the Contractor under the patent clauses of this contract, excluding, however, any expenses arising from the Contractor's indemnification of the Government against patent liability.

Significant provisions are directed to limitations and restrictions placed on reimbursable costs. For example, for other than small business concerns, costs of items or services purchased directly for the contract are reimbursed only to the extent actual payment has been made. Another significant restriction relates to contractor contributions to pension, profit-sharing, or employee stock ownership plan (ESOP) funds. Where such payments are made quarterly, they will be reimbursed provided the contractor pays the contribution to the fund within 30 days after the close of the period. If payments are made less often than quarterly, accruals are not reimbursable and reimbursement is made only upon payment by the contractor.

AUDIT AND RECORDS

The two major clauses on this subject are Examination of Records by Comptroller General, FAR 52.215-1, discussed in Chapter XXVIII of this text, and Audit—Negotiation, FAR 52.215-2, quoted below:

(a) *Examination of costs.* If this is a cost-reimbursement, incentive, time-and-materials, labor-hour, or price-redeterminable contract, or any combination of these, the Contractor shall maintain—and the Contracting Officer or representatives of the Contracting Officer shall have the right to examine and audit—books, records, documents, and other evidence and accounting procedures and practices, sufficient to reflect properly all costs claimed to have been incurred or anticipated to be incurred in performing this contract. This right of examination shall include inspection at all reasonable times of the Contractor's plants, or parts of them, engaged in performing the contract.

(b) *Cost or pricing data.* If, pursuant to law, the Contractor has been required to submit cost or pricing data in connection with pricing this contract or any modification to this contract, the Contracting Officer or representatives of the Contracting Officer who are employees of the Government shall have the right to examine and audit all books, records, documents, and other data of the Contractor (including computations and projections) related to negotiating, pricing, or performing the contract or modification, in order to evaluate the accuracy, completeness, and currency of the cost or pricing data. The right of examination shall extend to all documents necessary to permit adequate evaluation of the cost or pricing data submitted, along with the computations and projections used.

(c) *Reports.* If the Contractor is required to furnish cost, funding, or performance reports, the Contracting Officer or representatives of the Contracting Officer who are employees of the Government shall have the right to examine and audit books, records, other documents, and supporting materials, for the purpose of evaluating (1) the effectiveness of the Contractor's policies and procedures to produce data compatible with the objectives of these reports and (2) the data reported.

(d) *Availability.* The Contractor shall make available at its office at all reasonable times the materials described in paragraphs (a) and (b) above, for examination, audit, or reproduction, until 3 years after final payment under this contract, or for any shorter period specified in Subpart 4.7, Contractor Records Retention, of the Federal Acquisition Regulation, or for any longer period required by statute or by other clauses of this contract. In addition—

(1) If this contract is completely or partially terminated, the records relating to the work terminated shall be made available for 3 years after any resulting final termination settlement; and

(2) Records relating to appeals under the Disputes clause or to litigation or the settlement of claims arising under or relating to this contract shall be made available until such appeals, litigation, or claims are disposed of.

(e) The contractor shall insert a clause containing all the terms of this clause, including this paragraph (e), in all subcontracts over $10,000 under this contract, altering the clause only as necessary to identify properly the contracting parties and the Contracting Officer under the Government prime contract.

As discussed in Chapter II and elsewhere in this text, contract audits by DCAA and other federal agencies have always generated controversies that have increased as the scope of these audits has increased to the point that audits are full reviews of contractor operations and include efforts to detect possible fraud, waste, and abuse.

Many observers are surprised that the legality of the extended audit scope has not yet been tested through litigation. Decisions by boards of contract appeals and the federal courts in this area have generally been limited to disputes over access to or availability of records that most contractors maintain. In *Grumman Aircraft Engineering Corporation,* ASBCA No. 10309, September 15, 1966, 66-2 BCA par. 5846, the contractor denied the DCAA auditor's request to examine the New York State franchise tax return, whereupon the allocation of the tax payment to the contract was disallowed. Grumman argued that it had provided sufficient evidence to support the tax payment and that there was no need to furnish a copy of the return.

Portions of this decision have been cited with approval by both government contract auditors and industry. The government, of course, was satisfied with the bottom line, i.e. the rule that the return was a "document" and, hence, should be made available for audit. Private sector observers have been impressed by other language in the decision suggesting limitations to the scope of contract audit. For example, the board noted that the tax return was a document in existence and that the government was not requesting the contractor to create new records. This point is significant in light of just such requests sometimes made by contract auditors.

It is important, too, to study the board's emphasis on the fact that this was a cost-reimbursement type contract. In these circumstances, in the opinion of the ASBCA, ". . . that contractor has also invited the Government into his office to determine what those costs are. Thereafter a Government auditor looks over his shoulder." Even in these circumstances, according to the board (and this portion of the ruling is considered particularly significant): "That auditor certainly has no right to roam without restriction through all of the contractor's business documents which have no connection with the Government contract."

Another dispute in this area involved the right of government auditors to copy pertinent information from a contractor's records and documents and to remove the audit working papers containing such information from the contractor's premises. The dispute was decided in favor of the government in ASBCA No. 21022, 78-1 BCA par. 13,127, and affirmed in *SCM Corporation v. U.S.,* Ct.Cls. No. 6-76, March 11, 1981, [28 CCF par. 81,113].

This was an unusual dispute and one in which the overwhelming majority of observers both in the public and private sectors believed the contractor could not prevail. SCM advised DCAA of certain rules the auditors would be required to follow in an audit relating to the repricing of a completed phase of a CPIF contract, including a prohibition against removal from the contractor's premises of information or copies of data described as proprietary, including vendors' names. DCAA refused to conduct an audit under such rules. Although this six-year litigation has many interesting ramifications, it is sufficient for the purpose here to note that the board and court were impressed by testimonies from expert witnesses, including an official of the American Institute of Certified Public Accountants (AICPA), that (1) matter to be accumulated in the working papers should be resolved by the exercise of independent judgment by the auditor, (2) vendors' names and other data in dispute were appropriate for inclusion in the working papers, and (3) such papers must be removed from the contractor's premises so that they may be available for supervisory review.

In two disputes decided by the General Services Board of Contract Appeals, the government prevailed where the contractors failed to maintain and furnish basic records. In *American Business Systems,* GSBCA Nos. 5140, 5141, April 21, 1980, 80-2 BCA par. 14,461, the contractor appealed the contracting officer's actions in terminating for default two contracts for repair and maintenance of government-owned typewriters. The contracts included detailed requirements regarding the labor cost records to be maintained by the contractor, and an examination of records clause provided the government the right to examine books involving transactions related to the contract. ABS either lacked or failed to submit payroll records, the auditor advised that he could not make a satisfactory audit in the circumstances, and the contracts were terminated for default. The GSBCA found that ABS's failure to maintain or refusal to disclose records it did maintain constituted nonperformance:

> Granted, the Government did not enter into the contract ... so that it could audit appellant's books and records. But in a time-and-materials contract, where payment is based on labor hours and material costs, the Government has a significant pecuniary interest in examining the contractor's records, and the contract therefore requires the contractor to allow Government auditors to examine them.

The default termination was upheld with respect to one of the contracts; in the other, the default termination was converted to a termination for the convenience of the government on the auditor's testimony that the work was almost entirely performed under flat rates and that he was not significantly hindered by the lack of records.

In *Loyal E. Campbell, d.b.a. House of Typewriters,* GSBCA No. 5954, June 30, 1982, 82-2 BCA par. 15,916, apparently involving a similar contract for servicing typewriters and containing similar contractual requirements for detailed labor cost records, the contractor failed to maintain such records, and the government auditor reported that it was impossible for him to find any support for any of the labor costs claimed. The contracting officer made his own computation of the contract cost based on hours required per typewriter, using information obtained from other companies in this line of work, extended by the hourly rate set forth in this time and materials contract. Using this computation, the contracting officer determined an amount that he alleged represented the contractor's overbillings and deducted such amount from payments due on another contract. The board concluded that the contractor's failure to maintain the labor records specifically required by the contract constituted a breach and that the House of Typewriters was not entitled to any compensation. However, finding a common law obligation under which "... the party in breach is entitled to restitution for any benefit he has conferred by way of part performance ...," the board concluded that the only compensation to which the contractor was entitled was the fair value of the repairs, and the government's computation did reflect a fair value.

We feel that none of these cases involved the really significant concerns and problems inherent in the access to records controversies. Absent salient facts that did not surface in these rulings, we would be inclined to agree with the conclusions of the boards and court. Still to be decided, however, is whether the right to examine and audit books, records, documents, and other evidence and accounting procedures and practices, sufficient to properly reflect all costs claimed to have been incurred or anticipated to be incurred in performing this contract, authorizes contract auditors to determine whether contractors are performing economically and efficiently in such areas as maintenance and calibration of test equipment, make or buy decisions, production layouts, determination of labor standards through independent time-and-motion studies, quality assurance, shipyard welding, computer-aided design and manufacturing functions, production scheduling and control, and other contractor operations that are under review by DCAA or for which audit programs are being formulated and tested.

DCAA's degree of success in moving into some of these operations varies considerably among contractors. Some companies offer little or no objection to the so-called "extended audit scope" while others strongly resist some or all of these extensions into areas not generally considered to be included in conventional or generally accepted auditing standards. In the latter instances, both sides generally give and take to arrive at a compromise or uneasy truce.

Controversies also continue over the contents of questionnaires used by DCAA in conjunction with their floor checks. Floor checks have been accepted by most contractors as a part of the government audit of direct and indirect labor charged to contracts, but a number of firms have objected to some of the items in the questionnaires and have refused to permit their employees to respond to them. No instance of cost disallowances for failure to respond to the questionnaires has come to our attention.

DCAA auditors' seemingly insatiable interest in access to contractors' records has led to demands for minutes of boards of directors' meetings, internal audit reports, income tax returns, and many other records, including some which appear to have only a remote connection, if any, to the appropriate review of contractors' cost representations. As discussed in Chapter II of this text, DCAA's demands had met with mixed success until the audit agency acquired its subpoena power. Since that time, either because of use of this power or of the DCAA's frequent threats to use it, most contractors have ultimately been forced to accede to these demands. The final answer as to which records DCAA is entitled to request or subpoena has yet to be litigated.

LIMITATION OF COST

Because of the significance, sensitivity, and controversy arising in connection with this subject, extended coverage is provided in Chapter XX of this text, Limitation of Cost Provisions of Government Cost-Reimbursement Type Contracts—Policies, Practices, and Case Law.

PROGRESS PAYMENTS (See Chapter VI)

PRICE REDUCTION FOR DEFECTIVE COST OR PRICING DATA (See Chapter XXII)

TERMINATIONS

Principles, procedures, and contract clauses applicable to the termination of government prime and subcontracts are discussed in Chapter XXI, Termination of Government Contracts.

Chapter V

Government Contract Pricing

SCOPE OF CHAPTER

Government procurement policies and procedures are frequently difficult to understand because (1) at any given time they reflect so many diverse and even contradictory goals and objectives and (2) the policies undergo continual changes. Who establishes procurement policy for the federal government? The proliferation of laws and regulations negates any simple answer. As described in Chapter I of this text, the publication of FAR has reduced somewhat the difficulties involved in coping with numerous and contradictory regulations by federal agencies and has enhanced uniformity. However, many compromises were necessary as FAR was developed, with the result that agencies were authorized to issue supplementary regulations limited only by restrictions against (1) repeating, paraphrasing, or otherwise restating FAR and (2) promulgating regulations inconsistent or in conflict with DAR. The latter restriction is further diluted by authorizing the agencies to seek deviations from FAR where the deviation is not precluded by law, executive order, or regulation.

The FAR System includes FAR and any agency supplements (which most of the agencies have issued, differing only in size). As might be expected, DOD's supplement is by far the largest, rivaling FAR in size. The civilian agencies, NASA, and the military departments have also issued supplements. Although the supplements are less voluminous than the acquisition regulations previously published by these agencies, and although FAR has become the center for many regulations for the entire federal government, April 1, 1984, did not provide the comfort and convenience some contractors had hoped for in terms of having only one regulatory source to consult.

TYPES OF CONTRACTS AND CONTRACT CLAUSES AS FACTORS IN PRICING

Chapter III of this text discusses types of contracts used by federal agencies, and Chapter IV comments on some of the significant clauses included in these contracts. Government procurement regulations instruct contracting officers to consider contract types and clauses as among the factors related to prenegotiation profit objectives. The significance placed on the contract type and some of the specific clauses by the government in negotiating a contract price suggests that contractors must accord equal consideration to these matters.

Sealed Bidding Contracts

In the instance of contracts awarded through sealed bidding, the contractor has the least opportunity to accord special consideration to the type of contract as an element in pricing. In these instances, sources of supply are generally numerous. In the light of the anticipated heavy competition, a bidder needs to consider estimated costs (discussed in subsequent sections of this chapter), plus the desired profit, and relate the total to the expected competing bids and the extent to which a particular award is desired. Even in these instances, however, close attention must be directed to specific contract provisions for economic price adjustments, particularly in periods of high inflation, as well as contract clauses relating to transportation, discount, government financing, and government furnished property.

Negotiated Contracts

There is a far greater variety of types of negotiated contracts (see Chapter III of this text), and, accordingly, the selection of the contract type becomes more significant. The general policy of the government is to view the firm-fixed-price contract as preferable inasmuch as it results in the contractor assuming all of the cost risk. According to procurement regulations, this type of contract is best calculated to stimulate outstanding performance. At the other extreme is the cost-plus-a-fixed-fee (CPFF) contract where the cost responsibility is said to be entirely with the government and the fixed nature of the fee is perceived to offer no incentive to the contractor for economy and efficiency. Between the two are various contracts with incentive and redetermination provisions.

Close observers of government contracting have noted the shift over the years in the type of contract preferred. At one time, cost-reimbursement type contracts outnumbered any other category. In the 1960s, led by the Department of Defense and certain members of the Congress, substantial efforts were made to "emulate the commercial market place" and "harness the profit motive to reduce government expenditures through ultimately lower prices." These voices, strongly supported by GAO, resulted in a significant shift from cost-reimbursement type contracts to fixed-price type contracts, with the firm-fixed-price contract held out as the ultimate objective. But pendulums in the government usually swing too far, and the strong move to firm-fixed-price contracts led to severe difficulties for both the government and industry when this type of contract was used to procure major weapons systems that had not been fully developed.

As administrations and major government procurement officials changed, the successors invariably identified the problems in government procurement and attributed them to the policies of their predecessors. Over the years, the federal government has frequently tended to overreact. We hope that we have entered a period when appropriate recognition will be given to the need for a variety of types of contracts, depending on the circumstances; we hope to see fewer efforts to impose a particular type of procurement simply because of personal predilection or a precept that newly assigned government officials responsible for procurement policies must ultimately work toward a complete reversal of the policies established by their predecessors.

As discussed elsewhere in this text, recent years have witnessed an unprecedented increase in congressional micromanagement of defense procurement. The Competition in Contracting Act of 1984 (CICA), for example, emphasized and extended the notion that negotiation meant lack of competition, and higher costs to the government. No amount of testimony by DOD officials was successful in persuading certain congressmen that substantial competition was achieved in major procurements where contracts were necessarily awarded through negotiation. Somehow, in the views of these congressmen, negotiated contracts were frequently characterized by various evils that could only be corrected by further increases in procurement by sealed bidding.

GOVERNMENT FINANCING AS A FACTOR IN PRICING

Chapter VI of this text contains a comprehensive discussion of government financing regulations, policies, and procedures, including commentaries on customary and unusual progress payments, guaranteed loans, and advance payments. FAR 32.107 indicates that the need for contract financing will not be treated as a handicap for a contract award and that a contractor will not be disqualified from receiving contract financing because of a failure to indicate a need for such financing prior to contract award. While progress payments and advance payments are available under most contracts awarded by the federal government, guaranteed loans are authorized by law and executive order only in contracts for national defense.

The government's continuing adamant position of refusing to recognize interest paid as an allowable cost, particularly in periods of high interest rates, has made it imperative that companies doing business with the government make every effort to assure that their contracts provide for optimum financing available from the government. The importance of financing, of course, increases when fixed-price contracts with long lead times are involved. As further discussed in Chapter VI of this text, government contract financing policies are more favorable for small business concerns.

Under cost-reimbursement type contracts, contractors may submit public vouchers and obtain reimbursement on a biweekly basis. In the case of both progress payments under fixed-price contracts and periodic reimbursements under cost-type contracts, continuous coordination with government contracting, audit, and disbursing offices is essential to assure that government payments are made promptly as established by the regulations.

UNALLOWABLE COSTS AS A FACTOR IN PRICING

Subsequent chapters (see particularly Chapter XVI—Concepts Underlying Government Principles for Determining Allowable and Unallowable Contract Costs and Chapter XVII—Application of Government Contract Cost Principles to Specific Costs and Expenses) contain extensive comments regarding this significant area. As discussed in those portions of this text, the status of some costs has changed from time to time and has been subjected to drastic revisions by some of the promulgations of the Cost Accounting Standards Board.

To the extent that certain costs, recognized under generally accepted accounting principles and Internal Revenue Service regulations, are not allowed under government contracts, contractors must seek to recover them in other ways. Accordingly, close consideration must be accorded to the so-called unallowable costs in negotiating contract prices.

In recent years, congressional and GAO investigations, with DCAA support, led to reports that costs questioned by the contract auditors were at times allowed by contracting officers. As a result, P.L. 99-145 mandated that ten specific costs shall be unallowable and directed the Secretary of Defense to clarify the allowability of sixteen additional expenses. As used in the law, the term "clarification" contained heavy overtones of congressional desires that such costs be regulated as unallowable in whole or in part.

GENERAL PRINCIPLES OF PRICE NEGOTIATION

The government attaches a very high degree of importance to the promulgation of price negotiation principles and supporting procedures and to the selection and training of its pricing team and personnel. Led by the Department of Defense, government agencies have increasingly emphasized that contracting officers be qualified and evidence appropriate experience, training, education, business acumen, and judgment.

While contracting officers are expected to be highly qualified in price negotiation, they are also directed to make maximum use of other government specialists in awarding and administering contracts. For example, FAR 15.805-5 instructs the contracting officer to use field pricing support as needed. "Field pricing support personnel include, but are not limited to, administrative contracting officers, contract auditors, price analysts, quality assurance personnel, engineers, and small business and legal specialists."

The contractor meets many of the government's pricing team members; others do most of their work behind the scenes. In any case, these extensive specialists' services are available to the government contracting officer and are used as circumstances dictate. It is thus obvious that contractors must also avail themselves of expert advice and counsel. Where all of the expertise required is not available within a contractor's own organization, assistance should be obtained from outside consultants experienced in this field.

To negotiate, according to Webster's dictionary, is "to confer, bargain, or discuss with a view to reaching an agreement." Sometimes the elementary but critical fact that all of the discussions should be pointed toward reaching an agreement is forgotten. Certainly, the government personnel become very firm in their positions at times and contractors must be equally firm when they are convinced of the propriety of their side. On the other hand, where a firm stand develops into an adamant stand, negotiation is ended. FAR 15.803(d) provides that "If . . . the contractor insists on a price or demands a profit or fee that the contracting officer considers unreasonable and the contracting officer has taken all authorized actions (including determining the feasibility of developing an alternative source) without success, the contracting officer shall then refer the contract action to higher authority."

Another point in this general context relates to the requirement for the contractor to furnish cost or pricing data under circumstances described in Chapter XXII of this text. In this regard, FAR 15.804-6(e) states that "[i]f the offeror still persists in refusing to provide the needed data or to take corrective action, the contracting officer shall withhold the award or price adjustment and refer the contract action to higher authority . . . ." FAR 15.805-5(d) requires the DCAA auditor to report any denial by the contractor of access to records or cost or pricing data which the auditor considers essential to the preparation of a satisfactory report.

All of the foregoing comments are certainly not intended to recommend that contractors accede to all government requests and suggestions. Throughout this text, we have identified and emphasized the statutory and regulatory ground rules governing the doing of business with the government and have advised contractors to protect their interests and privity. Our basic point here is that contractors should be represented by skilled, knowledgeable negotiators and that these negotiators should really negotiate, that is, continue discussions with a view to reaching an agreement.

PREPARATION FOR NEGOTIATION

When a contractor receives a request to submit a proposal for a negotiated contract, the contractor should be aware that the effective contracting officer has done quite a bit of preparatory work. Guidance to the contracting officer is provided in FAR Subparts 15.4 through 15.9 and merits review by prospective contractors.

If the contracting officer has adhered to instructions and prepared effectively, the contracting officer should be well ahead of the contractor when the request for a proposal is transmitted. Of course, there are many things that the contractor can do to reduce this gap, including the maintenance of proper liaison with the buying offices to permit advance knowledge of the government's needs and programs.

SELECTION OF OFFERORS FOR NEGOTIATION AND AWARD

With certain exceptions, FAR 15.610(b) requires that "the contracting officer shall conduct written or oral discussion with all responsible offerors who submit proposals within the competitive range."

PRICING OBJECTIVES AND METHODS

FAR emphasizes, as did DAR and FPR before it, the government policy of obtaining supplies or services from responsible sources at fair and reasonable prices calculated to result in the lowest ultimate cost to the government. This is indeed a worthwhile and even noble objective, although questions have been raised as to whether it is possible to simultaneously achieve the lowest cost to the government and a fair and reasonable price, a price that will enable the contractor to recover the cost of doing business and a profit commensurate with what could be obtained in selling to commercial customers, given comparable risk, investment, and efforts.

Newcomers to the government contracting field are frequently confused about the differences in policies and practices of contract pricing. One of the areas of confusion is the emphasis contained in government procurement regulations, and enunciated by many government contracting officers, that it is the total price that is significant rather than the individual cost elements and the prenegotiation profit objectives. However, other provisions in FAR stress the need for cost analysis, audit, and separate, careful establishment of the profit objective. The emphasis on individual cost elements rather than the total price is constantly abetted by DCAA, other executive agency contract auditors, and GAO. In many instances, after extensive audits of contract proposals and heavy discussions and controversies over the profit element, contractors find it impossible to believe that the government pays more than lip service to the emphasis on the total price rather than on its individual elements. The confusion between emphasis on the reasonableness of the bottom line and preoccupation with individual cost elements was aggravated by DOD Directive 7640.2 as discussed in Chapter II of this text.

The previously mentioned congressional micromanagement in P.L. 99-145 and elsewhere has extended the prohibition against bottom line negotiation to indirect expenses, requiring the contracting officer to include in his negotiation memorandum specific information as to which expenses or the portions thereof were allowed or not allowed in arriving at the indirect expense rates.

EVALUATION OF PROPOSALS UNDER NEGOTIATED CONTRACTS

Government procurement regulations require some form of review and evaluation of pricing proposals submitted under negotiated contracts. Unless the price negotiated is based on adequate price competition or established catalog or market prices of commercial items sold in substantial quantities to the general public, or prices set by law or regulation, or unless (in exceptional cases) waiver is obtained from the head of the agency or an authorized designee, contractors must submit cost or pricing data in connection with contracts or modifications expected to exceed $100,000. (The threshold was originally $100,000 but the law was changed to increase it to $500,000 here and in related areas because of the inflation during the quarter century since the legislation was introduced. However, at the urging of GAO, DOD IG and DCAA, Congress restored the lower threshold.) The terms "adequate price competition" and "established catalog or market prices of commercial items sold in substantial quantities to the general public" have been developed over many years and are now formally stated in FAR 15.804-3. Despite the efforts devoted to defining these terms, they still generate controversy.

If the exceptions described above do not obtain, contractors are required to submit cost or pricing data. This is another difficult term that has been honed over many years and has generated disputes between the General Accounting Office and the procuring agencies and a series of significant decisions by boards of contract appeals and federal courts. This important area is discussed in Chapter XXII of this text, Price Reduction for Defective Cost or Pricing Data (Public Law 87-653).

Price Analysis

FAR 15.805-2 suggests various price analysis techniques such as comparison of the price quotation submitted in connection with the proposal under consideration, comparison of prior quotations and contract prices with current quotations for the same or similar items, use of rough yardsticks (such as dollars per pound or other units), comparison with prices set forth in published price lists, and comparison of the proposed prices with estimates of cost independently developed by the government.

Cost Analysis

Cost analysis is required by government procurement regulations when the prospective contractor is required to submit cost or pricing data. Cost analysis, described in FAR 15.805-3, includes the verification of the specific cost elements included in the cost or pricing data and the projection of these data. Cost analysis, on occasion, resembles a mini-audit, including visits to the prospective contractor's offices by government cost analysts. More frequently, a decision by the contracting officer that cost analysis is required triggers an almost automatic request to the cognizant government contract audit agency to review the pricing proposal, including an audit of the contractor's records.

Audit

Chapter II of this text, Defense Contract Audit Agency (DCAA) and Other Federal Contract Audit Organizations, describes the policies and procedures of contract auditors in connection with pricing proposals where cost or pricing data are required to be submitted.

PROFIT

Profit, generally, is a proportionately small but obviously significant component of a negotiated contract price. It has been and continues to be a very complex and controversial subject and merits careful consideration.

Doing business with the government continues to be an adventure characterized by many complexities and frustrations, and the subject of profit is still among the most troublesome. Government contractors, especially those providing goods and services for the defense of this country, have traditionally served as whipping boys for critics so inclined politically or socially. And yet, under our form of government, the government looks to the private sector to furnish its requirements whether they be in support of our defense effort or part of the many and growing nondefense programs of the federal government.

The federal government has formally recognized that the best interests of the country are served when competent members of the private sector perform under contracts supplying goods and services, and competent companies are attracted when the government procurement policy recognizes their need to earn fair and reasonable profits on these contracts.

An endless number of profit studies over many years has failed to satisfy GAO and certain congressional elements that government contractors, particularly those performing under DOD contracts, are not reaping high profits. A comprehensive review of the many studies and other attention directed to this subject is contained in Chapter XXV of this text.

ARMED SERVICES PRICING MANUAL (ASPM)

The Federal Acquisition Regulation (FAR) and the DOD FAR Supplement (DFARS) contain voluminous material on all facets of acquisition/ procurement, supplemented also by the Air Force FAR Supplement (AFFARS), Army FAR Supplement (AFARS), Navy Acquisition Regulations Supplement (NARSUP), and the Defense Logistics Agency Acquisition Regulation (DLAR). Most of the various non-defense departments and agencies, of course, also publish their own FAR Supplements.

Despite all of the instructions and guidance to DOD acquisition officials in the above-named regulations (and we will not mention the various other less official publications by DOD components, some authorized and some not), it was determined that a need existed for a special manual dealing not only with policy, but with the nuts and bolts of contract pricing. This manual is well justified.

The Manual has a long history, originally published in October 1965 as the Armed Services Procurement Regulation Manual for Contract Pricing, ASPM No. 1. Follow-on editions, revising and expanding on the original, were published in February 1969 and September 1975. The current 1986 ASPM, together with Volume 2 thereof published in 1987, substantially revises the 1975 edition.

ASPM differs in a number of material respects from other DOD acquisition regulations. While referring to laws and other regulations, ASPM itself provides guidelines for DOD contracting people and is not binding on contractors. As explained in the opening paragraph, it "examines the conceptual and philosophical bases for [acquisition policies contained in FAR and DFARS]. It sets forth principles, tools, and techniques for estimating and evaluating costs, profits, and prices. It tells how to analyze direct and indirect costs, how to negotiate agreements on prices and pricing arrangements, and how to handle various specialized pricing tasks."

ASPM recognizes that it conforms to policies which existed at the time of its writing and that these policies will continue to change to reflect the dynamic procurement field. The Manual is not in loose leaf form and not designed to keep current with the myriad changes generated within both the legislative and executive branches. And, as a matter of fact, in a number of areas, such as profit, it is already out of date.

On balance, however, we found the 1986/1987 ASPM a worthwhile working tool for government people responsible for contract pricing. To a large extent, we believe this Manual can be very valuable for industry in pricing subcontractors.

This Manual may be purchased from the Superintendent of Documents, Attention Mail List Section, U.S. Government Printing Office, Washington, DC 20402. It is also available from Commerce Clearing House, Inc., 4025 West Peterson Avenue, Chicago, IL 60646.

We recommend this Manual for prime and subcontractors who acquire substantial portions of their goods and services from lower tier contractors. Highlights of the Manual are reviewed below.

Chapter 1—The Procurement Process and Contract Pricing

This opening chapter begins with comments on concepts of contract pricing and the various people and techniques available to assist the contracting officer in achieving the asserted objective of acquiring supplies and services "of the desired quality, in a timely manner, at fair and reasonable prices." The major contents discuss pricing arrangements, ranging from the relatively uncomplicated sealed bidding procedures leading to firm fixed-price contracts, to negotiated contracts, including fixed-price and cost type with various incentive and redetermination arrangements. The tables and illustrations of the manner in which these arrangements work out would be of interest particularly to firms not fully experienced with the manner in which the wide range of government contracts work out.

Chapter 2—Prices and Price Analysis

As the title suggests, this chapter concentrates on pricing techniques and the tools available to the contracting officer and those who assist him. The point is emphasized that a contracting officer may agree to a contract price, based on price analysis, and without cost analysis, but should not price a contract on the basis of cost analysis without price analysis. Price analysis is described as including:

a. Comparison of competitive quotations.

b. Comparison of prior quotations and contract prices with current quotations for the same or similar end items.

c. Use of yardsticks or parametric relationships to point up apparent gross differences. Examples are: dollars per pound or per horsepower, square foot cost of a building, daily cost of a hospital room, cost of washing a single window, or any other unit that can be compared with some familiar unit that has been bought before.

d. Comparison of prices on published price lists issued on a competitive basis with published market prices of commodities, together with discount or rebate schedules.

e. Comparison of proposed prices with independent estimates of cost developed within the purchasing office.

Chapter 3—Costs and Cost Analysis

This chapter is the first of several devoted to analysis of costs and profit objectives.

Will-cost and should-cost concepts are compared and the latter emphatically established as the more effective pricing consideration. The Manual recognizes the complexities of an effective should-cost study but suggests that forming an ad hoc team of experts in connection with a major program proposal is not the only available approach. "It also may be built into day-to-day analysis by implementing the work measurement standard and by challenging existing and proposed procedures, processes, manning, skills, and other aspects of the proposal."

Cost analysis is described as moving considerably beyond analyzing cost data submitted by the contractor to ascertain the allowability of the individual items. "It also involves analyzing design features, materials, manufacturing processes, organization and manning, and estimating assumptions . . . ." Factors involved in cost analysis are described as:

a. Need to incur costs.

b. Reasonableness of amounts estimated for necessary costs.

c. Extent of uncertainties of contract performance and realism of any allowances for contingencies.

d. Bases for allocation of overhead costs.

e. Appropriateness of allocations of specific overhead costs to the contract.

Where data are available, cost analysis would also include: actual costs incurred previously; last prior estimate, or series of prior estimates, for the same or similar item; current estimates from other offerors; and prior estimates of historical costs of other companies for the same or similar work.

An interesting observation advises the reader: "Contract cost analysis is performed by accountants, auditors, price analysts, negotiators, engineers, and production specialists; in short, by almost anyone who can be drafted by the contracting officer to help with this part of the job. Who does the job is not important, but it is important that it be done thoroughly and with imagination." Realistically, this broad observation somewhat overstates the matter and is the kind of comment which has disturbed DCAA auditors, who frequently assert they have the sole right to examine contractors' records, conceding only that qualified technical personnel may examine some of the records to determine the reasonableness of projections of labor hours and quantities of materials.

The Manual provides general guidance regarding uncertainties or contingencies, stressing that the pricing arrangements should consider the nature and extent of such uncertainties.

The subject of cost accounting is treated very briefly, the complexity of this subject is noted, and the reader is advised: "If you have any questions about accounting matters, consult the auditors."

Considerably more extensive coverage is devoted to cost estimating, with emphasis on the need to understand the estimating methods and procedures of the contractor with which the procurement office does business.

When DCAA was established in 1965, one of the intramural disputes between the audit agency and ACOs concerned who had the responsibility for estimating system surveys and contractor procurement system reviews. The compromise agreement, which still obtains today in one form or another, concluded that DCAA would be responsible for the first and ACO staffs for the second. As reported from time to time by GAO and DOD IG, this solution has apparently not produced the desired results.

On an estimating system survey, a DCAA auditor is the "captain" of the team that is supposed to have representation from appropriate contract administration people. Sometimes this assistance is provided and at other times it is not. In any event, in its early years DCAA accorded considerable emphasis to a program which involved periodic estimating system surveys of the larger contractors who performed and were expected to continue to perform under DOD contracts. As the DCAA workload grew and the program failed to generate satisfactory results or eye-catching cost savings or fraud detection, this program languished.

One factor that adversely affected the program was the difficulty in achieving realistic results. To begin with, DCAA auditors tended to be quick to criticize contractors' estimating systems and to recommend significant and sometimes expensive changes. Contractors were not always persuaded that DCAA auditors were correct as to the extent of the deficiencies or the propriety of the recommended changes. Since there were no costs questioned or other penalties associated with contractors' refusals to comply with auditors' suggestions, DCAA apparently concluded, formally or informally, that the time and effort were not worthwhile.

DOD IG reports in recent years have criticized DCAA for not devoting sufficient time to this subject area, and the audit agency has stepped up its efforts.

ASPM briefly describes round-table estimating and estimating by comparison, and devotes more extensive coverage to detailed estimating.

A discussion of cost or pricing data appears to be the kind of guidance industry would like to see, but never expects from DCAA. Although advising that additional information should be requested when necessary, ASPM cautions contracting officers and their staffs that preparation of detailed data in a particular form may be expensive and suggests that unnecessary data should not be insisted upon.

In a section on estimating techniques and tools for quantitative measurements, the Manual describes measures of central tendency, measures of variability, indices, probability, sampling, hypothesis testing, forecasting, the learning curve, cost estimating relationships, and computers and cost models. None of these subjects is covered to the extent needed by individuals without prior theoretical and practical background in them. The discussions are quite useful, however, in introducing the subjects so that the reader may perform the necessary study. Additionally, this and the other chapters contain useful "suggested readings." This is not to suggest that the coverage of techniques is inadequate. The brief comments on the learning curve could be helpful to a reader with some mathematical and statistical background.

An extended discussion of contract pricing proposals guides the reader through the contractor's submission and supporting data, the regulatory requirements, and the suggested approach to follow.

Chapter 4—Profit Analysis

Although made obsolete in part by revisions to DoD profit policy subsequent to its publication, ASPM contains useful guidance for contracting officers and, in turn, for contractor officials who negotiate with them.

Chapter 5—How to Analyze Direct Costs

This is the lengthiest and probably the most informative chapter in the Manual, covering materials, factory labor, engineering labor, tooling, and other costs.

The coverage of materials includes subcontracted items, standard commercial items, interorganizational transfers, raw material, and purchased parts. For each of these, the Manual offers examples of the manner in which the contractor might submit his estimates and suggests the kinds of questions the government representatives should be framing in performing the analysis. This guidance seems well thought out, practical, and informative, and we recommend its review by government contractors.

Direct factory labor is explained and differentiated from various catego-ries of indirect labor. Estimating direct labor based on historical costs is briefly explained and, appropriately, more extensive coverage is provided for standard costs. This section closes with a series of questions appropriate for the analyst to formulate in satisfying himself that a proper evaluation of the direct labor estimate has been made.

Direct engineering labor represents a technical and frequently difficult factor to estimate and to analyze. This complex subject is adequately treated, although greater emphasis could have been placed on obtaining the assistance of qualified government technical people. As elsewhere, ASPM provides a series of questions which the analyst should ask himself when he believes his analysis is completed. The questions relating to direct engineering labor are listed below to provide an illustration of the types of questions presented for the various cost elements.

a. Is the engineering labor estimate prepared in accordance with the contractor's estimating methods? Have the estimating methods been reviewed by Government personnel? Are the methods consistent with cost accumulation practices? If they are, is the portion that relates to engi-neering labor acceptable?

b. Is the estimate broken down by specific engineering tasks describ-ing the work to be performed? Is the level of engineer required to perform each task identified? Is the level commensurate with the task?

c. If the estimate covers tasks previously performed, is it supported by historical data? What do the data show? Has nonrecurring effort been identified? Is it treated properly?

d. If the estimate covers tasks not previously done, is it supported by historical data for similar tasks adjusted for differences in requirements?

e. Does the estimate for design engineering include redesign effort which, if it becomes necessary, would be priced separately?

f. If the estimate includes manufacturing engineering tasks for developing and implementing equipment and method improvements to increase productivity of direct factory workers, does the direct factory labor estimate reflect savings resulting from the engineering?

g. If the estimate includes manufacturing engineering tasks for development of advanced production technology, is that effort really necessary or would the current technology be just as efficient and less costly?

h. If the estimate includes reliability and maintainability tasks aimed at the manufacture of parts to meet these requirements, are the efforts duplicated under design engineering tasks?

i. If the estimate includes sustaining engineering, is all or any part of it duplicated under any of the tasks for other types of engineering effort?

j. If the estimate includes separate tasks for documentation, are the efforts duplicated in any design engineering tasks? Is the estimated documentation effort commensurate with the estimated design engineer-ing effort? Is it commensurate with the documentation requirement?

k. If any part of the estimate is based on learning curves, is such an approach feasible? Should the estimate be developed or tested by alternate means?

The balance of this chapter provides guidance for analyzing special tooling, preproduction costs, preservation packaging and packing, royalties, etc.

Chapter 6—How to Analyze Indirect Costs

A portion of the introductory guidance is based on a close analysis of the requirements of the Standard Form 1411, Contract Pricing Proposal Cover Sheet, as set forth in FAR 15.804-6(b) and FAR Table 15.2. The Manual quotes each significant word or phrase of these requirements and indicates the nature and extent of the information the contractor should be expected to furnish with his submission or by identification. Although the Manual instructs the contracting officer to analyze every facet of indirect costs, major emphasis is placed on trend analysis with guidance on reviewing indirect cost behavior and measuring the reasonableness of past, present and future overhead dollars.

A number of overhead examples are furnished for the various pools—material, engineering, and manufacturing overhead, and G&A expenses. In each instance the contractor has been required to furnish data for the prior year, the current year (actual to the date available, and forecast for the balance of the year), and the projection for the following year, supported by budgetary data. The same information is required for the respective allocation bases. Contracting officers are advised that longer-term projections should be obtained for long-term contracts.

DCAA auditors and some contracting officers insist on long-term budgetary data—five years and even longer where available. Some companies do develop such projections but are reluctant to furnish them to the government because some of the auditors and analysts do not appear to fully appreciate how the uncertainties of the forecasts increase with every future year. With all of the possible changes in defense policy on the optimum mix of weapons systems, national budgetary considerations and related political considerations, companies substantially involved in defense work face great difficulties in forecasting the future, difficulties which increase with each year, as the current contracts are completed.

ASPM provides a brief introduction of indirect cost behavior, with illustrations of the behavior of fixed, variable and semivariable expenses as impacted by activity volume.

The Manual also offers guidance relating to methods of allocating indirect costs and the analysis of individual expenses for allowability. The relatively brief attention to these facets suggests a recognition that a major effort in this direction will probably be made by the contract auditor.

Chapter 7—How to Analyze Labor Rates

Guidance on evaluating quantity (number of hours) was contained in Chapter 2 with respect to direct labor, and in Chapter 6 as to indirect labor. Labor rates are the subject of this chapter.

Geographical location, skill levels, time period of the contract, and conditions in the contractor's work force are identified as four general factors that have a significant impact on labor rates. Contracting officers are advised of various sources, such as the Bureau of Labor indexes, that can be used in verifying quoted labor rates, and are reminded that verification of rates can be expected from the contract auditor.

ASPM briefly introduces its readers into the complexities involved in projecting direct labor rates, particularly for long-term contracts, using graphic and computational analysis. Background in these areas is required in order to use these sophisticated techniques.

Chapter 8—How to Negotiate and Justify a Price

Six steps are identified in the process of reaching final contract negotiations after the receipt of proposals or offers:

1. Evaluate and rank offers in light of the evaluation criteria specified in the solicitation.

2. Identify proposals within a competitive range.

3. Identify and eliminate unacceptable proposals (those containing such deficiencies in price and/or technical merit as to preclude further meaningful negotiations).

4. Conduct written or oral discussions with offerors identified in Step 2 and, if necessary, permit revision of individual proposals to correct deficiencies.

5. Notify each offeror with which discussions have been conducted of a final, common cutoff date for submission of best and final offers.

6. Select the source or sources for final negotiation and award.

ASPM then guides the contracting officer through the procedure from the time the source is selected to the negotiation conference. After discussing the preparatory work toward developing a government position and achieving a good understanding of the contractor, the industry, product, money and competition involved, and time available, the Manual discusses the composition of the government's negotiation team. The significance the government places on the team (as needed, specialists in pricing, auditing, production, packaging, maintenance, quality control, administration, contract law, various fields of engineering and technical matters) suggests strongly, as we have mentioned elsewhere, the need for contractors to give similar consideration to this matter. From time to time, particularly but not exclusively in smaller companies, the negotiation team consists of one individual or is unrealistically limited.

The negotiator, who may or may not be the contracting officer, is usually the individual considered to be the most effective at negotiating. If this individual is not the contracting officer, understandings are reached as to how far the negotiator may go and the manner in which the contracting officer will signal his approval. Again, similar procedures may be considered by contractors.

The next step prior to the negotiation conference is identified as fact-finding, which consists of a review of all of the data prepared by the team after analyzing the pricing proposal, to assure that the contracting officer has a clear idea of factual data and assumptions and to permit further analysis where needed. The fact-finding phase may also include a preliminary or exploratory conference with the contractor. The decision on the price would not be made at this conference.

The final prenegotiation step is the final review, at which the negotiation team establishes the price objective and the contracting officer presents this information to his superior for approval. (In the case of a contractor, the final review, depending on the size and organization of the company and the amount and significance of the contract, may be performed by the vice president for contracts or other official higher or lower in the organization.)

The ASPM comments on the negotiation itself are sound but subject to some modification in light of legislative and regulatory changes since its publication. The emphasis, logically, is on negotiating a fair and reasonable price. While efforts should be made to reach understandings on the various components—e.g., actual and estimated costs, allowable and unallowable costs, costs and profit—the contracting officer is reminded that the total price is the real objective. As a matter of fact, separate agreements are faulted as hampering perspectives on the interrelationships of the components, causing substantial delays, discouraging reasonable trade-offs, and leading to "bad pricing," in that, according to the Manual, precise agreements on each cost element and profit may result in an unsound and inequitable total price.

The amount of specific documentation contracting officers and negotiators are required to prepare in support of the final decision on the allowability of each and every expense item has discouraged bottom line negotiation in the case of indirect costs. While no specific law or regulation governs price negotiations at this writing, the trend, reflecting lack of confidence by Congress in both contractors and contracting officers, seems to be in the same direction as indirect cost negotiations. In this connection, ASPM devotes considerable space to requirements for documentation of the negotiation results and preparation of the Procurement Negotiation Memorandum (PNM).

Chapter 9—Special Pricing Tasks

This chapter provides guidance to contracting officers for negotiation of items covered by the catalog or market price exemption, spare parts, warranties, procurement for foreign military sales, and data items on DD Form 1423, Contract Data Requirements List.

Section 9.1 explains the use of Standard Form 1412 and how to determine if prices are based on catalog or market prices of commercial items sold in substantial quantities to the general public, and furnishes explanations and illustrations that supplement the related provisions of FAR 15.804-3. The guidance is well summed up in a "logic chart," reproduced below:

LOGIC CHART FOR THE CATALOG OR MARKET PRICE EXEMPTION

EXEMPTION CRITERIA, QUESTIONS, AND ACTIONS	IF YES, GO TO	IF NO, GO TO
1. Is there an established catalog or market price?		
a. Is there a printed catalog, price list, published price, or other formal document showing prices and discounts?	2	b
b. Is there common knowledge of a marketplace procedure, such as auction, or regulated price?	2	c
c. If there is a formal price listing with optional discounts, do accompanying sales data validate the discount offered?	2	d
d. Can field contract administration personnel (or audit) validate from offeror's records that the price offered is a regular catalog or market price with appropriate discounts?	2	5
2. Is the item or service a commercial item?		
a. Is the item or service identical to that described in the catalog or obtained in the marketplace?	3	b
b. Is the item or service so similar it can be priced by reference to catalog or market?	3	c
c. Can the differences be identified and priced as add-ons or deducts from catalog or market prices by value analysis or from other known prices?	3	d
d. Can the differences be identified and the cost/price difference determined by cost analysis using data submitted by the offeror (and certified if over $100,000)?	3	5
3. Are there sales to the general public?		
a. Is there general knowledge of large public sales of products regularly stocked by dealers or regularly traded in the marketplace?	4	b
b. Does the offeror's data show sales over the appropriate past period as between Government and commercial customers?	4	c
c. Can field contract administration personnel validate from the offeror's records that sales have been made to commercial customers?	4	d
d. Can audit personnel make the validation?	4	5
4. Are there substantial sales to commercial customers who meet the test of the general public?		
a. Are reported sales to commercial customers at least 55% of total sales and those at catalog price at least 75% of this amount?	6	b
b. Are reported sales to commercial customers at least 35% of total sales and those at catalog price at least 55% of this amount and can you determine this is a reasonable commercial market?	6	c
c. Can field contract administration personnel verify from the offeror's records that commercial sales meet the regulation's criteria?	6	d
d. Can audit verify the data?	6	5
5. With no *yes* to these four questions, the proposal does not meet the test for exemption. Get cost or pricing data and, if over $100,000, certification after negotiation		
6. Exempt. Document file. Determine reasonableness of price		

Part 9.2 addresses the complex procurement of spare parts, made more complex for government buyers when competition cannot be obtained and sole source procurement is required. The Manual refers to fair and reasonable prices for spare parts as those approximating the cost to the seller and, at the

same time, the value to the buyer. As discussed later, legislation and regulations apparently promulgated after the Manual was written carried this difficult concept much further.

Obtaining cost or pricing data in Standard Form 1411 and performing cost analysis is recommended in purchasing high dollar value spares. However, when the quantity is large and unit prices relatively low, simple or stratified sampling is suggested.

Considerable emphasis is placed on learning and evaluating the contractor's system of pricing spare parts. A "spare parts pricing package" is suggested, consisting of (a) a written agreement between the contractor and government describing how spare parts will be priced, (b) a written description of how local government representatives will check spare parts lists, (c) a negotiation memorandum covering pricing factors, and (d) a certificate of current cost or pricing data executed by the contractor at the completion of the negotiations with clear identification of what it covers.

Pricing formulas are discussed as are the advantages of their use in terms of expediting the procurement process. The Manual describes the procedures required for evaluating these formulas.

The early 1980s witnessed increasing congressional investigations and criticisms directed to many facets of defense procurement, including a number of "horror stories" about alleged overpricing of spare parts. The communications media eagerly reported these allegations, causing severe public image damage to the entire defense community, industry and DOD alike. Legislation and implementing regulations followed.

Federal Acquisition Circular (FAC) 84-10, dated July 3, 1985, contained several revisions to implement some of the legislation—the Defense Procurement Reform Act of 1984 (Title XII of the Department of Defense Authorization Act of 1985, P.L. 98-525), and the Small Business and Federal Procurement Competition Enhancement Act of 1984 (P.L. 98-577).

FAC 84-10 added a new Section 15.812, Unit Prices. Paragraph 15.812-1(a) recognizes that, although direct and indirect costs are generally allocated to contracts in accordance with CAS, where applicable, or otherwise in accordance with Cost Principles contained in Part 31, ". . . for the purpose of pricing all items of supplies, distribution of those costs within contracts shall be on the basis that ensures that unit prices are in proportion to the item's base cost (manufacturing or acquisition costs). Any method of distributing costs to line items that distorts the unit prices shall not be used." FAC 84-28, effective April 16, 1987, expands on the implementation of the aforegoing 15.812-1(a) with respect to the application of pertinent CAS objectives, in that it does not apply to items based on established catalog or market prices of commercial items sold in substantial quantities to the general public.

Paragraph 15.812-1(b) requires that, "when contracting by negotiation, without full and open negotiation, contracting officers shall require that offerors identify in their proposals those items of supply which they will not manufacture, or to which they will not contribute significant value." This information is required even "when contracting by negotiation, with full and open competition if adequate price competition is not expected (see 15,804-3(b)."

This paragraph explains that such information "shall be used to determine whether the intrinsic value of an item has been distorted through application of overhead and whether such items shall be considered for breakout." Contract clause 52.215-26, Integrity of Unit Prices, was added to implement these provisions.

FAC 84-10 also added a new Section 15.813, Commercial Pricing Certificates, which provides that, with certain stated exceptions, the offeror is required ". . . to certify that the price offered is not more than its lowest commercial price or to submit a written statement specifying the amount of any difference and providing justification for that difference." The paragraph in which this requirement appears (15.813-1) sets forth the policy that "The Government should not purchase items of supply offered for sale to the public at a price that exceeds the lowest price at which such items are sold by the contractor unless the difference is clearly justified by the seller or unless exempt under 15.813-3."

A new clause 52.215-32 and paragraph 15-813-2 require that, in most instances, "commercial pricing certificates are required to be submitted with any offer/proposal covering any item or items that are offered for sale to the public . . ." when contracts are not awarded "on the basis of full and open competition." Under this clause, contracting officers or their representatives "shall have the right to examine and audit all books, records, documents and other data of the Contractor related to the pricing of the commercial items covered by [his] offer/proposal."

If the price is found to have been increased "because the certification in . . . the Certificate or the information provided as justification . . . was inaccurate, incomplete, or misleading, the price or cost shall be reduced accordingly and the contract shall be modified to reflect the reduction."

Contracts awarded prior to the promulgation of these provisions have also been subjected to intensive reviews and audits by the DOD IG and DCAA, and the Defense Department has demanded "voluntary" price reductions where the government has concluded that the items were "overpriced." In the light of the adverse publicity generated by reports of overpricing, several major contractors have voluntarily offered refunds or credits for parts where prices were established as excessive. This entire area, however, is complicated by a number of factors. Criteria are lacking for determining "excessive" prices and different views have been expressed regarding the time limitations in which DOD must assert overpricing to establish eligibility for credits or refunds. Obviously, contractors are not inclined to agree to indefinite periods. On the other hand, where parts are to be returned before credit is given, considerable difficulties are encountered in instances in which parts have been installed on equipment, especially when the equipment is located overseas.

After consideration of various comments from within DOD and from industry, Secretary of Defense Weinberger issued a memorandum dated November 1, 1985, providing guidance for seeking refunds or negotiated price adjustments. Introducing his memorandum by stating that "An integral part of our acquisition improvement program is to pursue refunds aggressively whenever overpricing has occurred," Weinberger directed:

> The Department of Defense will seek a refund/negotiated price adjustment whenever the Department believes a price paid for spare parts or items of support equipment is unreasonable, as determined by the Government. The Department will make every effort to identify quickly and return an item where a refund will be sought; however, where factors preclude an early identification we will seek a refund regardless of when the unreasonable pricing is identified. When military readiness prohibits the return of an item(s), DOD will continue to seek negotiated price adjustments consistent with the public trust. This guidance is applicable to all spare parts and support equipment items regardless of dollar value. DOD will continue to emphasize the initiatives already undertaken by Industry and the Department to ensure a fair value is received for every taxpayer dollar spent.

According to the Weinberger directive, which is tough enough to satisfy even the DOD IG, GAO and severe congressional defense critics, DOD will seek refunds "regardless of when the reasonable pricing is identified." Further, even if DOD will not return the item, it will nevertheless seek a negotiated price adjustment.

Although DOD has long followed a policy of seeking to breakout components and replenishment parts, it has recognized the many risks which such actions entail. The DOD FAR Supplement, for example (17.7202-4 Breakout Guidelines) includes 12 different criteria which must be considered in deciding whether a component should be broken out. Essentially, the inclination not to breakout is based on the understandable desire of DOD to assign the full responsibility for quality control, reliability, technical support, logistics support, compliance with delivery requirements, etc., to the prime contractor. In many instances, spare parts and support equipment could be purchased at (initially) lower prices from subcontractors and vendors. However, the government would then be required to assume the many responsibilities of the major contractor, the cost of which might well exceed the savings achieved from buying directly.

On November 18, 1986, the Defense Acquisition Regulatory (DAR) Council issued interim guidance regarding circumstances under which commercial pricing certification is required in contracts for spare and repair parts. Proposals for revisions to FAR on this subject had been drafted on three previous occasions by the DAR and Civilian Agency Acquisition (CAA) Councils, but the provisions had been disapproved by OMB.

Action with regard to defense contracts was mandated by the 1987 Continuing Resolutions under P.L. 99-591 and the 1987 DOD Authorization Act, P.L. 99-661. The Act provides that a firm that submits an offer "to enter into a contract for the supply of spare or repair parts under a contract awarded using procedures other than competitive procedures, and who also offers such parts for sale to the general public," shall be required to:

> (1) certify in such offer that, to the best of the knowledge and belief of the offeror, the price proposed in the offer does not exceed the lowest commercial price at which such offeror sold such parts during the most

recent regular monthly, quarterly, or other period for which sales data are reasonably available; or

(2) Submit with such offer a written statement—

(A) specifying the amount of the difference between the price proposed in the offer and the lowest commercial price at which such offeror sold such parts during a period described in paragraph (1); and

(B) providing a justification for that difference.

The Act authorizes exceptions to these requirements where a contracting officer makes a written determination that the use of the lowest commercial price is not appropriate because of national security considerations or because of significant differences between the terms under which the commercial sales have been made and the terms of the contract. Such differences may relate to quantity, quality, delivery requirements, or other terms and conditions.

The Act further provides that an offeror required to submit the certification or written statement quoted above shall make available for audit or examination "all records of sales (including contract terms and conditions) maintained by or for the contractor that are directly pertinent to sales by the contractor of spare or repair parts identical to those covered by the contract during the period covered by such certification or statement."

Further stress is placed upon the limitations on access to records for these purposes by the following provision relating to regulatory implementation of the Act:

Such regulations may not require the disclosure or submission of any data related to any element underlying the price of a commercial product not otherwise required by law.

The Act defines "spare or repair part" as "any individual piece, part, subassembly, or component which is furnished for the logistic support or repair of an end item and not as an end item itself."

The term "lowest commercial price" is defined as "the lowest price at which a sale was made to the general public of a particular part. Such term does not include the price at which a sale was made—

(A) to any agency of the United States;

(B) to any person for resale by such person after such person performs a service or function in connection with such part that increases the cost of the part, unless the agency procuring the part can demonstrate that the agency is procuring the part before such service or function has been performed by any such person;

(C) to a subsidiary, affiliate, or parent business organization of the contractor, or any other branch of the same business entity;

(D) to any person at a price that, for the purpose of making a donation, has been substantially discounted below the fair market value or regular price of such part; or

(E) to a customer located outside the United States.

A further exemption is provided for contracts entered into using simplified purchase procedures.

The DFARS interim guidance conforms to the provisions of P.L. 99-661 and further advises contracting officers to clearly identify in a contract or solicitation those items which are spare and repair parts. No specific solicitation provision or contract clause was included in the interim guidance in view of the ongoing effort to revise FAR in a manner acceptable to OMB. In the meantime, DOD contracting officers and contractors were required to negotiate clauses based on the statutory and regulatory provisions.

Despite the severity of the legislation in this area and the implementation in FAR and DFARS, the Navy, which had demonstrated it could be as hard on industry as GAO or Congress, began work on a policy for mandatory refunds. The proposed provisions were obviously inequitable and industry could not understand why a separate Navy regulation was needed in light of the FAR and DFARS promulgations. The proposed Navy action provided further evidence, if any were needed, of the failure of FAR to provide uniform acquisition policy (surely spare parts pricing was not a matter unique to the Navy).

About the middle of 1985, the Navy initiated communications with industry concerning methods of burdening spares under varying circumstances ranging from "pass through" items, which the prime acquires from another source and furnishes the government without adding any value, to items actually manufactured by the prime. CODSIA presented thoughtful comments, including suggestions for direct shipments from the vendor where the prime would add no value, and for possible separate prime contractor facilities for processing spares that required only such functions as inspection, etc., which special facilities would not be burdened with normal factory support costs. The industry association cautioned, however, that consideration must be accorded to the probability that any changes in burdening methods would result in violations of specific cost accounting standards or failure to follow practices set forth in the Disclosure Statement.

While industry awaited further discussions and coordination, the Navy published a regulation on June 3, 1986, under which its contracting officers would "request a refund whenever the contract price of any spare part or item of support equipment significantly exceeds the item's intrinsic value after considering the impact of specified delivery terms and quantity." Military departments may issue their own supplements governing situations peculiar to their operations upon approval of the DAR Council. Such deviation approval had been obtained by the Navy from the DARC, but the question raised by industry was what was unique to the Navy about spare parts pricing?

On August 4, 1986, CODSIA requested the Deputy Secavy about spare parts pricing?

On August 4, 1986, CODSIA requested the Deputy Secretary of Defense to withdraw the deviation approval and the Navy's rule. The disappointing reply on September 16 advised that the Navy publication had been reviewed prior to its issuance and was considered to be in line with Secretary Weinberger's refund policy statement. CODSIA was urged to work with the Navy and to "offer positive suggestions for improving the clause."

The Navy issued a further modified proposed rule on October 18, 1986, which continued to draw strong objections. It was pointed out, for example, that voluntary refunds by contractors obviated the need for a mandatory refund clause. This argument was rejected on the grounds that "voluntary refunds are inadequate to protect the Navy's interests." The pertinent advice for the Navy to remain within the Defense Department and await DOD action in this area was dismissed with the comment that such department-wide action did not appear to be forthcoming. The response begged the question concerning the validity of the go-it-alone policy, inasmuch as the Navy had not asserted that spare parts pricing was unique to its activities.

Other objections were similarly dismissed. The Navy refused to change "intrinsic" to "reasonable" value, maintaining its determination to ascertain whether the price exceeded "what a person would normally expect to pay for the item" regardless of the fact that the price was reasonable "in accordance with FAR cost principles."

Some concessions were made in the final rule issued on December 24, 1986. Refusing to adopt industry's proposal to reduce to one year the four-year period in which the Navy could request refunds, it compromised at two years. The clause was revised to permit return of an item for full refund only upon the contractor's agreement. Other changes included making the clause inapplicable to items with a unit price in excess of $100,000, or in excess of $25,000 if the contractor had submitted a certification as to the currency, accuracy and completeness of the pertinent cost or pricing data.

Many of the critics and initiators of punitive measures in this area refuse to recognize that while some of the prices for spare parts may be unreasonable in relation to their "intrinsic value," actual profits based on costs computed in accordance with existing government regulations were not excessive. Many other factors further complicated this area, a partial listing of which was identified by General Kammer, Jr., writing at that time in the *Army Logistician*. The Commander of the Defense Electronics Supply Center included as complicating factors:

> ordering significantly small quantities; higher military requirements for testing to ensure reliability; higher military requirements for packing to provide necessary protection in storage; manufacturers' start-up costs for items which companies had discontinued; added overhead costs by sole source suppliers where breakout has not been feasible; imposition of minimum charges for unusual low quantity orders; clerical errors in pricing; incorrect impressions of overpricing due to comparison with obsolete price data; requirements for more expensive versions because the less expensive are not interchangeable; and emergency buys.

"Horror stories" alleging overcharges by contractors for spare parts have largely disappeared from congressional hearings and the news media. Most observers understand the problems involved in this area and would concede that, for some of the reasons cited by General Kammer, Jr., and others, overpricing has occurred. The legislative and regulatory actions, however, largely fail to take the problems into consideration and certainly have not attempted to grapple with the questions arising from instances where the alleged overpricing was based on close adherence to cost accounting standards with modest profit add-ons.

Returning to ASPM, the balance of Chapter 9 addresses warranties, pricing procurements for FMS, and pricing data items on DD Form 1423.

Chapter 10—Postaward Pricing Actions

The final chapter of ASPM covers contract changes, interim pricing, final pricing, cost accounting standards, monitoring indirect costs and support for cost estimating.

Section 10.1 on contract changes presents a general picture of actual and constructive changes, requests for equitable adjustments, and pricing of changes. The very complex problems in delay and disruption claims, reviewed in depth in Chapter VII of this text, are addressed very briefly in ASPM.

As mentioned earlier, ASPM is a useful guide for government contracting officials and can also be used to advantage by contractors. It should be reviewed together with related regulations such as FAR Part 15 and DoD FAR Supplement Part 15. The civilian agencies' supplements to the FAR provisions on negotiation are very modest in comparison to DoD's.

ARMED SERVICES PRICING MANUAL (ASPM)—VOLUME 2

A companion piece to ASPM Volume 1 was published in June 1987. As indicated in its title, the 1987 publication focuses on price analysis, as distinguished from cost analysis, which constitutes the major coverage of the first volume.

Contract pricing includes both cost analysis and price analysis. In non-competitive procurements of major weapons systems and research and development, cost analysis, that is, the review and analysis of the separate cost elements and profit factor contained in the contractor's proposal, is necessarily the major consideration in arriving at a contract price. In contrast, most defense awards are for more commonplace goods and services and frequently are not expected to exceed $100,000. In these instances, price analysis, that is, examining and evaluating a proposed price without evaluating its separate cost elements and profits, is the predominant and frequently the only contract pricing technique required.

ASPM Volume 2 identifies the following factors that may be used in price analysis to determine whether the proposed price is fair and reasonable: competitive quotations, market prices, past prices, past quotations, estimating yardsticks such as dollars per pound, and independent estimates.

Chapter 11—Prices and Pricing

The chapters in Volume 2 follow those in the first volume and begin with Chapter 11—Prices and Pricing, offering conceptual considerations of fairness and reasonableness, the sellers' and the government's approaches, and the steps in contract pricing.

Chapter 12—Planning the Acquisition

The first step in contract pricing, "planning the acquisition," is the subject matter of Chapter 12. Considerable emphasis is placed on the efforts to obtain maximum competition by eliminating, where possible, any barriers to full and open competition. Table 12-2 identifies the following barriers to full, open and effective competition: unnecessarily restrictive specifications, unnecessarily restrictive solicitations that include requirements not fully justified and not in the government's interests, noncompliance with publicizing requirements, organizational bias, invalid selection criteria, and administratively created exigencies. The table shows the likely effects and remedies for each of the "barriers."

Chapter 13—Price Analysis but Not Cost Analysis

Table 13-5, Price Analysis/Cost Analysis Decision Chart, summarizes the guidance contained in this chapter:

IF ...	AND ...	THEN ...
The anticipated dollar value exceeds $100,000	● No exemption to cost or pricing data requirements applies	You must require submission of cost or pricing data and conduct both price analysis and cost analysis.
The anticipated dollar value exceeds $100,000	● An exemption applies	No cost or pricing data shall be required. You shall rely on price analysis.
The anticipated dollar value is between $25,000 and $100,000	● Price analysis alone cannot establish price reasonableness; or ● The purchase is for a new or complex item with significant potential for follow-on buys; or ● You determine for other reasons that available pricing data are not sufficient	You may request cost or pricing data and analyze costs in addition to prices but only to the extent necessary to establish price reasonableness
The anticipated dollar value is between $25,000 and $100,000	● Available competition and price analysis data are sufficient to establish price reasonableness	You shall not request cost or pricing data and shall rely on price analysis
The anticipated dollar value is less than $25,000		Certification of cost or pricing data shall not be required; price analysis usually will be relied upon.

Chapter 14—Price Analysis Techniques

This chapter describes the hierarchy of these techniques, as illustrated in Figure 14-1:

FIGURE 14-1. HIERARCHY OF PRICE ANALYSIS TECHNIQUES

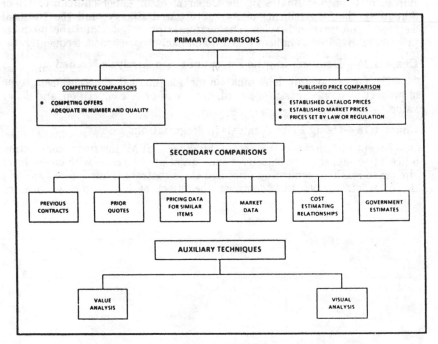

Chapter 15—Comparability

This chapter discusses factors that affect comparability among or between items to be acquired, adjustments required to establish comparability, and actions to be taken when comparability cannot be established. Time, quantity or size, geographic location, inflation, extent of competition, technology and special terms and conditions are described as factors affecting comparability. The optimum conditions, of course, are where comparability of prices can be obtained; otherwise, efforts should be made to apply adjustments that would approximate comparability.

Guidance is offered for making the following adjustments: estimated quantity, assumed change (trend analysis), product variance, ratio analysis, and additional techniques. Where comparability cannot be established, the data can either be disregarded or discounted. In the latter instance, it may be possible to consider comparability after noting and taking into account the gaps or differences.

Chapter 16—Getting Adequate Data for Price Analysis

Generally, there are four major sources of data for price anlaysis: offeror-supplied data, historical data, other government data, and market data. The major source of government data is the independent estimate, but the contracting officer is advised to also explore information available from such government sources as the Department of Commerce (Census Bureau and

Bureau of Economic Analysis), the Department of Labor (Bureau of Labor Statistics), the Departments of Agriculture and Energy, and the National Technical Information Service. The consumer price index and the producer price index are cited as indices which would likely be used most frequently.

Chapter 17—Determining the Extent of Price Analysis Needed

The factors for this determination include: method of procurement, type of product or service, basis for award, quality of price competition, and dollar value.

Chapter 18—Using Price Analysis in Negotiations

Except in instances of sealed bidding, ASPM instructs contracting officers to establish price objectives and "negotiate (bargain) with one or more offerors to reach agreement on price and other contract terms before awarding the contract." Table 18-1 describes the effect of key factors on a price objective:

FACTOR	EFFECT ON PRICE OBJECTIVE
Past and projected volume of sales; past and present dollar amount of purchases	Larger volume or amount usually means lower prices. Potential loss of income puts pressure on the offeror. Lower volume or amount might mean higher prices. In either case, consider total volume or added dollars, not just your order.
Current market conditions	A seller's market with high demand weakens your position. Similarly, an inflationary market indicates higher prices. Excess capacity can create a buyer's market and strengthen your position.
Extent of competition	Market forces tend to drive prices down when competition is strong. If competition slacks but demand stays strong, balance shifts to seller. Your expectations for lower prices are weaker.
Desire for Government business	An offeror eager for work can be expected to propose attractive prices. The relationship between idle capacity and fixed costs should indicate the offeror's need for business. Similarly, an offeror's interest may lag when it operates at capacity.
Inventory	An offeror with excess inventory is likely to propose attrative prices to reduce inventory carrying costs.
Differences between Government and other customers	Prices should tend to be lower because of assured and prompt payment, centralization, and volume of purchases.
Most favored customer determination	If terms and circumstances of a Government purchase are equivalent to a firm's pricing arrangement with its most favored customers, the prices also should be equivalent.
Special concessions, terms, and conditions	If the Government demands extra rights or concessions from the offeror, prices will tend to be higher. Government concessions should be reflected by lower prices.
Financing	Banks may give special concessions to firms holding Government contracts. These concessions may reduce the cost of doing business.
Type of product	A mass-produced commercial product should be priced lower than a product unique to the Government. Studies indicate that the Government pays more when buying to its own specifications.
Price adjustment provisions	An offeror should accept lower prices when contract provisions reduce risk.
Urgency of purchase	Purchases requiring additional effort because of short delivery normally command higher prices

Chapter 19—Situations and Discussions

This chapter discusses a number of procurement situations to illustrate pricing problems.

Appendix A contains a list of acronyms used in ASPM.

Appendix B provides a glossary of terms.

Appendix C consists of a table (9-2), providing a useful Logic Chart for the Catalog or Market Price Exemption.

Appendix D is the lengthiest coverage in ASPM Volume 2 and provides technical but instructive explanations and examples of some quantitative tools of analysis: graphic analysis, algebraic analysis, fitting a line, index numbers, cost estimating relationships (CERs), and experience or earning curves.

Appendix E contains a comprehensive listing of commodity, industrial, government and other sources of pricing information.

Most government prime and subcontractors will find the ASPM Volumes 1 and 2 useful additions to their purchasing reference libraries.

Chapter VI

Methods of Financing Government Contracts

The need for adequate financing of government contracts is recognized by both the private and public sectors, and controversies are generally limited to the nature and extent of the financing. FAR 32.104(a), for example, provides that "Prudent contract financing can be a useful working tool in Government acquisitions by expediting the performance of essential contracts .... Contract financing shall be administered so as to aid, not impede, the acquisition." And FAR 32.104(b) states: "If the contractor is a small business concern, the contracting officer shall give special attention to meeting the contractor's contract financing need."

The government's financing of its contracts is essential to broadening the industrial base. It enables awards to qualified companies who do not have the capability of performing without some financing, particularly in long lead contracts where considerable costs will be incurred before shipments begin and invoices are submitted. An alternative to government financing would be to permit as allowable costs interest paid on borrowed money and imputed interest in working capital. For a number of reasons, discussed in Chapter XVII of this text, the government has elected to treat these costs as unallowable, with certain exceptions relating to equitable price adjustments. One of the reasons for this decision is the government's ability to borrow money at lower interest rates than would be available to most contractors.

FAR 32.107 is captioned "Need for contract financing not a deterrent" and provides:

(a) If the contractor or offeror meets the standards prescribed for responsible prospective contractors at 9.104, the contracting officer shall not treat the contractor's need for contract financing as a handicap for a contract award; e.g., as a responsibility factor or evaluation criterion.

(b) The contractor should not be disqualified from contract financing solely because the contractor failed to indicate a need for contract financing before the contract was awarded.

BACKGROUND OF GOVERNMENT CONTRACT FINANCING

Obtaining appropriate provisions for financing is a significant consideration in contract negotiation and administration. Before reviewing the current regulations on this subject, it may be useful to provide a background summary tracing the continuing controversies in this area. The Defense Department's 1985 report on Defense Financial and Investment Review (DFAIR) provides considerable information, and the following material is an excerpt, with footnotes omitted, from that report.

The need for uniform policies on contract financing was proclaimed by the Deputy Secretary of Defense on October 14, 1950. Up to that time, the Military Departments had been free to grant progress payments as considered traditional for the goods and services being acquired. The Military Departments' application of contract financing proved to be uneven, sometimes resulting in overpayments to defense contractors. During this period, DoD was transitioning from wartime acquisition policies and procedures to the more businesslike approach that would be required in the post-World II era. The initial Joint Regulation on contract financing was published on March 17, 1952.

More specific guidance on progress payments soon became necessary, particularly as DoD began relying more on fixed-price contracts than cost-type contracts. In a memorandum to the Service Secretaries on February 12, 1954, the Secretary of Defense stated that use of progress payments was proper on contracts involving large pre-delivery expenditures in relation to contract price and working capital. The Secretary, however, also set the following limits:

It should be seldom necessary for progress payments based on costs to exceed 90 percent of direct labor and material costs, or 75 percent of total costs, of the work done under the undelivered portion of the contract. Lesser percentages and bases may often be adequate.

The Secretary's direction was subsequently issued on April 22, 1954, as DoD Directive 7840.1, "Defense Supply Contract Financing—Progress Payments Based on Costs." This directive also introduced the concept of customary and unusual progress payments. On December 17, 1956, the Joint Regulation on contract financing was amended to incorporate DoD Directive 7840.1 verbatim as Appendix 5, and it served as DoD's basic policy statement throughout the remainder of the 1950's. In 1959, the Joint Regulation was absorbed into the Armed Services Procurement Regulation as Appendix E. Simultaneously, the progress payment rate limitations for large businesses were lowered to 85% of direct labor and material costs and 70% of total costs. According to a Defense Industry Advisory Council (DIAC) Working Group paper, this action was taken because defense expenditures were higher than expected and posed a conflict with the national debt ceiling at that time. Small business concerns were allowed to continue receiving progress payments at the higher rates. This marked the point at which small business concerns began receiving progress payments at a higher rate than for large business. It coincided with legislative action under Public Law 85-100 in 1958 to "improve opportunities for small business concerns to obtain a fair proportion of Government purchases."

Several changes were made to the progress payment policies in 1968. First, effective March 1, 1968, the customary progress rates were increased from 70% to 80% for large businesses and from 75% to 85% for small business concerns. This action was taken as a result of a DIAC study completed in 1967. DIAC observed that interest had become the largest item of unallowable costs and, therefore, had degraded the realized profits earned by defense contractors. DIAC concluded that interest expense should remain unallowable, but the progress payment rate should be increased. In addition to the rate increase, a uniform standard for rates was established in lieu of the discretionary provisions for lower progress payments that were previously allowed. The Total Costs clause and the Direct Labor and Materials Cost clause were eliminated, and the Progress Payments clause was created.

Another important study, conducted in 1971 by DIAC, laid the foundation for other policy changes. It was determined that the policy toward certain expenditures needed further refinement in order to preclude the possibility of negative contractor investment in the work-in-process inventory (i.e., more financed by DoD than actually spent by the contractor). As a result, the following policy changes became effective on January 1, 1972:

1. Progress payments were limited to no more frequently than bi-weekly,

2. Items purchased directly for the contract were not eligible for progress payments until actually paid by the contractor (did not apply to small business concerns), and

3. The inclusion of profit expectations in progress payment liquidations from contract deliveries (i.e., use of alternate liquidation method) was to be more controlled.

It was recognized by DoD that these policy changes would result in increased financing costs to defense contractors. To offset this increase, contracting officers were instructed to add a factor to profit. This factor was mandatory and was to be computed as follows: the factor for new cash disbursement policy (item 2 above) was .8% of direct purchases and the factor for new bi-weekly frequency policy (item 1 above) was .07% of total costs. Combined, the added profit would have equated to roughly .4% of total costs.

With two exceptions, DoD's policies on progress payments, especially as they related to levels of contract financing, were basically unchanged throughout the remainder of the 1970's. In 1973, DoD required that contractors make cash contributions to pension fund accounts within 30 days after the close of the accounting period covered by the contribution. In 1976, Cost Accounting Standard (CAS) 406, "Cost Accounting Period," required contractors to use annualized indirect expense rates instead of cumulative year-to-date actual amounts.

In 1980, there was considerable opinion that the level of progress payments needed to be raised. The increase in the volume and cost of contract financing undertaken by defense contractors was believed to have had an adverse impact on the viability of the defense industrial base. Volume increases were caused by changes in the acquisition environment, such as more fixed-price contracts, longer lead-times, reduced government-furnished property, higher asset replacement costs, etc. The increased costs of financing were reflected in the Short Term Commercial

Loan Rate which rose from 6% in 1968 (when the rate was set at 80%) to 20% in 1979. In their report entitled, "The Ailing Defense Industrial Base: Unready for Crisis," the Defense Industrial Base Panel of the House Armed Services Committee concluded the following:

> The panel realizes that progress payments provide a degree of protection to the Government against the failure of a contractor to perform under the contract. However, in view of high inflation and interest rates, current progress payments may be placing an inordinate burden on defense industry . . . While progress payments at the 80% rate may provide a higher degree of protection to the Government, other aspects may well work against the Government's interests in improving productivity.

On January 14, 1981, the Deputy Secretary of Defense approved two actions: (1) raise the progress payment rate to 85% as an interim measure, and (2) develop a flexible progress payment policy which would give more attention to the variables affecting levels of actual contract financing. The action in the latter instance was prompted by a November 1980 study performed by the Deputy Under Secretary of Defense for Acquisition Policy. This study observed that, even though uniform standard progress payment rates are used, the actual levels of contract financing received on individual contracts may vary considerably. This is due to several variables affecting cash flow (i.e., period of contract performance, contractor payment lags, Government payment lags, etc.). The first action was taken on March 3, 1981. The second action was completed on August 28, 1981, when the following additional policy changes were made:

1. Raise customary progress payment rate from 85% to 90%,

2. Reduce progress payment frequency from bi-weekly to monthly, and

3. Allow optional flexible progress payments which would base the progress payment rate (up to 100%) on the contractor's average investment of 5% in the work-in-process inventory. This would be accomplished via the CASHII computer model.

ORDER OF PREFERENCE FOR CONTRACT FINANCING

FAR 32.106 addresses this subject as follows:

The contracting officer shall consider the following order of preference when a contractor requests contract financing, unless an exception would be in the Government's interest in a specific case:

(a) Private financing without Government guarantee. It is not intended, however, that the contractor be required to obtain private financing (1) at unreasonable terms, or (2) from other agencies.

(b) Progress payments based on costs at customary rates . . . .

(c) Loan guarantees.

(d) Progress payments based on costs with unusual terms . . . .

(e) Advance payments . . . .

LOAN GUARANTEES FOR DEFENSE PRODUCTION

FAR Subpart 32.3 prescribes policies and procedures for "Guaranteed loans" or "V loans," defined as "a loan, revolving credit fund, or other financial arrangement made pursuant to Regulation V of the Federal Reserve Board, under which the guaranteeing agency is obligated, on demand of the lender, to purchase a stated percentage of the loan and to share any losses in the amount of the guaranteed percentage" (32.301). These loans are made to expedite national defense production and the following agencies are authorized to guarantee loans through Federal Reserve Banks: the departments of Defense, Energy, Commerce, Interior, and Agriculture, and GSA and NASA.

Except under unusual circumstances, the guarantee is for less than 100% of the loan.

Procedures for Obtaining Guaranteed Loans

FAR Section 32.304 sets forth the procedures for obtaining guaranteed loans. Essentially, a contractor, subcontractor, or supplier who needs operating funds to perform work related to a national defense contract applies for a loan to a financial institution. If the institution will grant the loan only on the condition that the government guarantees some percentage of it, the institution applies to the Federal Reserve Bank for the bank's district. The aforementioned FAR section includes the details of the procedures and required documentation.

Subsection 32.304-2 describes the certificate of eligibility that must be prepared by the contracting officer for submission to the guaranteeing agency, including the determinations that the contracting officer must make for an affirmative recommendation. Subsection 32.304-3 describes the asset formula used to limit guarantees, usually to 90 per cent or less of the contractor's investment (e.g., payrolls and inventories) in defense production contracts.

Except where found unnecessary because of conditions spelled out in 32.304-5, contractors receiving guaranteed loans will be required to execute an assignment of claims.

ADVANCE PAYMENTS

Advance payments are generally considered by the government to be the least preferred method of contract financing. When approved, this method of financing is subject to numerous statutory and regulatory restrictions. Government agencies are admonished to avoid advance payments "if other types of financing are reasonably available to the contractor in adequate amounts." However, as provided in FAR 32.402(b): "Loans and credit at excessive interest rates or other exorbitant charges, or loans from other Government agencies, are not considered reasonably available financing."

Certain statutory requirements and standards must be met as prerequisites for agencies to authorize advance payments (FAR 32.402(c)):

(1) The statutory requirements are that—

(i) The contractor gives adequate security;

(ii) The advance payments will not exceed the unpaid contract price (see 32.410(b), subparagraph (a)(2)); and

(iii) The agency head or designee determines, based on written findings, that the advance payment—

(A) Is in the public interest (under 32.401(a) or (b)); or

(B) Facilitates the national defense (under 32.401(c)).

(2) The standards for advance payment determinations are that—

(i) The advance payments will not exceed the contractor's interim cash needs based on—

(A) Analysis of the cash flow required for contract performance;

(B) Consideration of the reimbursement or other payment cycle; and

(C) To the extent possible, employment of the contractor's own working capital;

(ii) The advance payments are necessary to supplement other funds or credit available to a contractor;

(iii) The recipient is otherwise qualified as a responsible contractor;

(iv) The Government will benefit from performance prospects or there are other practical advantages; and

(v) The case fits one or more of the categories described in 32.403.

The above referenced FAR 32.403 is quoted below:

32.403 Applicability.

Advance payments may be considered useful and appropriate for the following:

(a) Contracts for experimental, research, or development work with nonprofit educational or research institutions.

(b) Contracts solely for the management and operation of Government-owned plants.

(c) Contracts for acquisition at cost of facilities for Government ownership.

(d) Contracts of such a highly classified nature that the agency considers it undesirable for national security to permit assignment of claims under the contract.

(e) Contracts entered into with financially weak contractors whose technical ability is considered essential to the agency. In these cases, the agency shall closely monitor the contractor's performance and financial controls to reduce the Government's financial risk.

(f) Contracts for which a loan by a private financial institution is not practicable, whether or not a loan guarantee under this part is issued; for example, if—

(1) Financing institutions will not assume a reasonable portion of the risk under a guaranteed loan;

(2) Loans with reasonable interest rates or finance charges are not available to the contractor; or

(3) Contracts involve operations so remote from a financial institution that the institution could not be expected to suitably administer a guaranteed loan.

(g) Contracts with small business concerns, under which circumstances that make advance payments appropriate often occur (but see 32.104(b)).

(h) Contracts under which exceptional circumstances make advance payments the most advantageous contract financing method for both the Government and the contractor.

Letters of Credit

Letters of Credit are favored by the Treasury Department because they tend to generate a lower cash impact upon the government, and this procedure is favored by a number of civilian agencies. Using letters of credit, contractors may withdraw government funds only as actually needed to cover their own cash disbursements for contract purposes.

Interest on Advance Payments

With limited exceptions provided in FAR 32.407(a), the government will charge interest on the daily unliquidated balance of all advance payments at the higher of "(1) [t]he published prime rate of the banking institution . . . in which the special bank account . . . is established; or (2) [t]he rate established by the Secretary of the Treasury . . ." (32.407(a)).

Application for Advance Payments and Recommendation for Approval

FAR provisions for applications and approval recommendations are quoted below.

32.408 Application for advance payments.

(a) A contractor may apply for advance payments before or after the award of a contract.

(b) The contractor shall submit any advance payment request in writing to the contracting officer and provide the following information:

(1) A reference to the contract if the request concerns an existing contract, or a reference to the solicitation if the request concerns a proposed contract.

(2) A cash flow forecast showing estimated disbursements and receipts for the period of contract performance. If the application pertains to a type of contract described in 32.403(a) or (b), the contractor shall limit the forecast to the contract to be financed by advance payments.

(3) The proposed total amount of advance payments.

(4) The name and address of the bank at which the contractor expects to establish a special account as depository for the advance payments. If advance payments in the form of a letter of credit are

anticipated, the contractor shall identify the specific account at the bank to be used. This subparagraph (4) is not applicable if an alternate method is used under agency procedures.

(5) A description of the contractor's efforts to obtain unguaranteed private financing or a V-loan (see 32.301) under eligible contracts. This requirement is not applicable to the contract types described in 32.403(a) or (b).

(6) Other information appropriate to an understanding of (i) the contractor's financial condition and need, (ii) the contractor's ability to perform the contract without loss to the Government, and (iii) financial safeguards needed to protect the Government's interest. Ordinarily, if the contract is a type described in 32.403(a) or (b), the contractor may limit the response to this subparagraph (6) to information on the contractor's reliability, technical ability, and accounting system and controls.

* * * *

32.409-1 Recommendation for approval.

If recommending approval, the contracting officer shall transmit the following, under agency procedures, to the approving authority:

(a) Contract data, including—

(1) Identification and date of the award;

(2) Citation of the appropriation;

(3) Type and dollar amount of the contract;

(4) Items to be supplied, schedule of deliveries or performance, and status of any deliveries or performance;

(5) The contract fee or profit contemplated; and

(6) A copy of the contract, if available.

(b) The contractor's request and supporting information.

(c) A report on the contractor's past performance, responsibility, technical ability, and plant capacity.

(d) Comments on (1) the contractor's need for advance payments and (2) potential Government benefits from the contract performance.

(e) Proposed advance payment contract terms, including proposed security requirements.

(f) The findings, determination, and authorization (see 32.410).

(g) The recommendation for approval of the advance payment request.

(h) Justification of any proposal for waiver of interest charges (see 32.407).

PROGRESS PAYMENTS BASED ON COSTS (FAR SUBPART 32.5)

These payments are distinguished from (1) payments under cost-reimbursement contracts and (2) progress payments based on a percentage or stage of completion, used in contracts for construction or for shipbuilding or ship conversion, alteration, or repair.

CUSTOMARY PROGRESS PAYMENTS

Consideration for Progress Payments

Under circumstances described later in this chapter, customary progress payments are generally readily obtainable, and the contractor need not provide separate consideration therefor. However, this coverage should be included in the terms of the contract when it is awarded because if it is obtained subsequent to award "adequate new consideration is required" (FAR 32.501-4).

Use of Customary Progress Payments

The following criteria are provided in FAR 32.502-1 for the use of customary progress payments:

(a) Subject to paragraphs (b) and (c) below, the contracting officer may provide for customary progress payments if the contractor (1) will not be able to bill for the first delivery of products, or other performance milestones, for a substantial time after work must begin (normally 4 months or more for small business concerns; 6 months or more for others), and (2) will make expenditures for contract performance during the predelivery period that have a significant impact on the contractor's working capital. Progress payments may also be authorized, particularly for small suppliers, if the contractor demonstrates actual financial need or the unavailability of private financing (see 32.106(a)).

(b) To reduce undue administrative effort and expense, the contracting officer generally should not provide for progress payments on contracts of less than $1,000,000 unless—

(1) The contractor is a small business concern and the contract will involve approximately $100,000 or more; or

(2) The contractor will perform a group of small contracts at the same time and the total impact on working capital is equivalent to a single contract of $1,000,000 or more.

(c) The contracting officer shall not provide for progress payments if the contract items are quick turnover types for which progress payments are not a customary commercial practice. Examples of items customarily not subject to progress payments include (1) subsistence, (2) clothing, (3) medical and dental supplies, and (4) standard commercial items not requiring a substantial accumulation of predelivery expenditures by the contractor.

(d)(1) In considering whether to provide for progress payments in circumstances under which a series of orders are awarded (e.g., indefinite delivery contracts or basic ordering agreements contemplating requisitions, task orders, etc., or their equivalent), the contracting officer shall apply the standards in paragraphs (a) through (c) above, based on—

(i) An estimate of the total work to be done; and

(ii) The probable impact on working capital of the predelivery expenditures and production lead times of the majority of the individual orders.

(2) In authorizing progress payments under multiple-order contracts, the contracting officer should establish a single liquidation rate applicable to all orders.

Government Supervision and Administration of Progress Payments

The extent of government surveillance over progress payments varies considerably, based on such considerations as the contractor's experience, performance record, reliability, quality of management, financial strength, and adequacy of the contractor's accounting system and controls. For well-established contractors with high passing grades in the criteria mentioned above, progress payment requests are approved by the contracting officer "as a matter of course." If the evaluations are negative, of course, the government authorizes review of the matter by its specialists. In some instances, progress payments are not approved without audit by the cognizant contract audit agency. FAR provisions in these areas are set forth in 32.503-2, -3, -4, -5, and -6.

Liquidation of Progress Payments

As described in FAR 32.503-8 and 32.503-9, progress payments are recouped through the deduction of liquidations from payments that would otherwise be due to the contractor for completed contract items. The amount of liquidation is determined by applying the liquidation rate to the contract price of items delivered and accepted. The ordinary method uses a liquidation rate that is the same as the progress payment rate. An alternate method, designed to permit the contractor to retain the earned profit element of the contract prices for completed items, is described in FAR 32.503-9.

Progress Payment Contract Clause (FAR 52.232-16)

This clause is lengthy, detailed, and informative and should be reviewed carefully. Allowability of costs for progress payment purposes is limited in the case of supplies and services purchased directly for the contract to those where actual payment has been made (cash basis). This limitation does not apply to small businesses.

The accrual basis is acceptable for (1) materials issued from stores and placed in the production process for use on the contract; (2) direct labor, direct travel, and other direct in-house costs; and (3) properly allocable and allowable indirect costs. In the case of contributions under employee pension, profit-sharing, and stock ownership plans, for both small businesses and others, accrued costs shall be excluded until actually paid unless "(A) [t]he Contractor's practice is to contribute to the plans quarterly or more frequently; and

(B) the contribution does not remain unpaid 30 days after the end of the applicable quarter or shorter payment period . . . ."

Cost of money that would be allowable under FAR 31.205-10 is deemed an incurred cost for progress payment purposes.

Progress payments to subcontractors made under the provisions of paragraph (j) of the Progress Payment clause are includable in the contractor's progress payment requests.

Customary Flexible Progress Payments

This progress payment method, at this writing unique to the Defense Department, is set forth in the DOD FAR Supplement at 32.502-1(71):

(1) Paying progress payments assists in financing a contractor's performance and reduces the contractor's investment in its work in process inventory. The actual investment held by a contractor in work in process inventory is influenced by a number of factors in addition to progress payments, such as delivery schedules, cash management practices, and Government payment practices. Progress payment amounts that are determined by using uniform, standard progress payment rates are insensitive to these other factors influencing investment and, as a consequence, result in investments by contractors in work in process inventory that vary among contractors and across contracts; on the other hand, flexible progress payment rates (expressed as a percentage that will be applied to costs to determine the amount payable as a progress payment in the same manner as uniform, standard progress payment rates) are designed to tailor more closely the progress payment rate to the cash needs for financing performance of a particular contractor for a given contract.

(2) For flexible progress payments, cash needs are measured and projected in relation to investment underlying the work in process inventory over the life of the contract. Total investment is measured by a weighted average of total costs paid by the contractor to complete performance of the contract, and the contractor's investment is the weighted average of the amount not paid by the Government. The Department of Defense (DoD), as a matter of policy, has concluded that a contractor should retain at least a 25% investment in work in process inventory over the life of the contract. Accordingly, the DoD will make progress payments at a rate (expressed as a whole number) that is the highest rate which yields a corresponding investment by the contractor in work in process inventory of not less than 25%. The progress payment rate is to be determined by the DoD Cash Flow Computer Model. In no event will the progress payment rate be greater than 100%, or less than the uniform, standard progress payment rate that would have been applied to the contract absent flexible progress payments.

(3) Contracting officers shall use a flexible progress payment rate in lieu of the uniform standard rates if:

(i) The contractor requests the use of flexible progress payments rates,

(ii) The contractor agrees to the requirements of this section, and

(iii) The criteria in paragraph (a)(5) below are met.

(4) The flexible progress payment rate shall be determined through application of the DoD Cash Flow Computer Model, available to contracting officers on the COPPER IMPACT computer time sharing network under the computer file name "CASH IV." The model takes into account key cash flow factors, such as contract cost profile, delivery schedules, subcontractor progress payments, liquidation rates, and payment/reimbursement cycles. Operating instructions and cash flow data requirements are retrievable within the model in a conversational mode. Contractors may obtain copies of the DoD Cash Flow Computer Model User's Guide from the Defense Technical Information Center, Building 5, Cameron Station, Alexandria, VA 22314. Contracting officers shall not grant contractor access to Government leased COPPER IMPACT time sharing computer network.

(5) Contractors who submit certified cost or pricing data, as defined in FAR 15.804-2, for negotiated fixed-price contracts in excess of $1 million may request flexible progress payments. Formally advertised contracts are not eligible for flexible progress payments. Flexible progress payments are not available for contracts awarded and performed entirely outside of the United States, its possessions and territories.

(6) Contractors will furnish to the contracting officer cash flow data in the form and context specified by the DoD Cash Flow Computer Model. These data include: actual and projected incurred cost broken down by element of cost and by month for the duration of the contract, float times for each element of cost, progress payment receipts and delivery payments receipts and associated contract prices and profit percentage. Contracting officers will verify the cash flow data in accordance with normal procedures used to verify contractor cost and pricing data. Administrative contracting officers are encouraged to establish advance agreements at contractor locations for float and payment lag which are common to several contracts. Such agreements should be established when administratively practical.

(7) A redetermination of the flexible progress payment rate shall be made upon the request of the Government or contractor if measurement of the contractor's cumulative investment in work in process inventory using actual and projected cash flow data indicates an investment level above 27% or below 23%. The cash flow computer model is designed to generate a progress payment rate that yields a target investment of 25%, based on a weighted average. Accordingly, there should normally be no need to request actual and projected contract cash flow data unless delivery schedules are revised, Government progress payment lag times are substantially changed from those used in the establishment of the progress payment rate, or substantial new work (e.g., option) is added to the contract.

(8) As noted in FAR 32.504, the standards for progress payments to subcontractors ought to be the same as those applicable to prime contractors. Accordingly, subcontractors who request a flexible progress payment

rate, meet the criteria in paragraph (a)(5) above and agree to the requirements of this section are to receive a flexible progress payment rate. The subcontract flexible progress payment rate will be determined by the prime contractor without regard to the progress payment rate in the prime contract. The DoD Cash Flow Computer Model and associated procedures will be used by the prime contractor and a reasonable review of the cash flow data provided by the subcontractor will be made.

(9) When flexible progress payments are contemplated for use on a definitive contract superseding a letter contract or an unpriced BOA order, the applicable standard progress payment clause at 52.232-7007 shall be used until definitization.

UNUSUAL PROGRESS PAYMENTS

Customary progress payments are those made in accordance with procedures previously described, including the customary progress payment rate, the cost base, frequency of payment, and liquidation rate. Any other progress payments are considered unusual and may be used only in exceptional cases when authorized in accordance with FAR 32.501-2, quoted below:

32.501-2 Unusual progress payments

(a) The contracting officer may provide unusual progress payments only if—

(1) The contract necessitates predelivery expenditures that are large in relation to contract price and in relation to the contractor's working capital and credit;

(2) The contractor fully documents an actual need to supplement any private financing available, including guaranteed loans; and

(3) The contractor's request is approved by the head of the contracting activity or a designee . . . .

(b) The excess of the unusual progress payment rate approved over the customary progress payment rate should be the lowest amount possible under the circumstances.

(c) Progress payments will not be considered unusual merely because they are on letter contracts or the definitive contracts that supersede letter contracts.

DOD Progress Payment Policies Under Review and Criticism

A series of hearings conducted by the Senate Committee on Governmental Affairs focused on criticisms of a wide range of DOD procurement and financial policies and practices. As usual, representatives of the General Accounting Office joined in (or led) these attacks. Beginning early in 1983, however, the congressional critics of the Department have been joined by another source of fault-finding, the DOD Office of Inspector General, represented by the Deputy IG.

Testifying on May 19, 1983, the Deputy IG expressed concern that current progress payment rates were too high and decried the DOD implementation of CAS 408 (Accounting for Costs of Compensated Personal Absence), because the accrual basis results in government payments to contractors before they make payments to their employees.

The Deputy IG expressed concern about DOD's flexible progress payment procedures because it was widely used without audit to ascertain the accuracy of the flexible progress payment model. "Computer models," he announced, "are notorious for the ways they can be 'gamed' to produce a desired outcome." He did not indicate who might have "gamed" this computer model, but his statement was recognized by most observers as having serious implications.

The witness advised the committee that he would not be as concerned about the reimbursement of accrued vacation expenses "if current progress payment rates were lowered to where they were a few years ago, 80 percent for a large business and 85 percent for a small business." In view of the decrease in inflation and interest rates, according to the witness, "I believe that it is time for DOD to reconsider its current progress payment rates to ensure that contractors are not provided additional profits through the interest-free use of government funds."

Defending DOD policies and practices, the Deputy Under Secretary of Defense (Acquisition Management) agreed to an audit of the flexible progress payment computer model but did not agree that progress payment rates should be reduced at this time. She testified that the 80 and 85 per cent rates had been established when the prime interest rate was between 5 and 6 per cent and, if the prime rate should return to those levels, DOD would seriously consider reducing the progress payment rates.

Reduction of Progress Payment Rates Recommended by President's Private Sector Survey on Cost Control in the Federal Government

In a series of reports by its Task Forces, the Private Sector Survey issued recommendations which, it asserted, could result in savings amounting to many billions of dollars. One of the recommendations of the Task Group on Financial Asset Management was "that DOD scale back progress payment rates to February 1981 levels of 80 per cent for not-small businesses and 85 per cent for small businesses." According to the report, "The conditions justifying past increases are no longer present."

DFAIR Findings and Recommendations Concerning Progress Payments

The Defense Department's 1985 report on Defense Financial and Investment Review (DFAIR) noted the criticisms by the Grace Commission and the DOD IG, the latter supplementing his previously mentioned 1983 complaints at congressional hearings with an April 1985 report that again asserted that progress payment rates should be reduced.

The Grace Commission has drawn praise for strenuous efforts identifying federal government policies and practices which, in the Commission's opinion, were wasteful, and presenting recommendations that allegedly would save astronomical sums of money. These efforts have also been criticized to the extent that a number of the claimed savings appeared, upon close analysis, to be lacking in documented support. Both the Congressional Budget Office and GAO have questioned the Commission's estimated savings.

Alleged savings envisioned in the DOD IG report were similarly rejected by Department of Defense officials as based on faulty reasoning.

The DFAIR report reflected a serious and objective study of this area without trumpeting horror stories or claims of huge savings by the simple expedient of reducing progress payment rates. Another major difference was DFAIR's recognition of the interrelationships among financing, profits and pricing, a significant consideration which seemed to have been overlooked by the above-mentioned critics and their congressional counterparts.

An in-depth DFAIR study included contractor financing costs, considering government financing and commercial interest rates required to carry the unfinanced portions of the work in process inventories. The study attempted to establish criteria for a "typical" contract. The contractor's financing costs of the "typical" contract were found to have averaged 2%, fluctuating in the range between 1.5% and 2.5%. Consideration was also accorded to such factors as contractor cost profile, delivery schedules and contract length. The following recommendations were offered:

1. Interest on working capital should remain unallowable.

2. Alternative methods should continue to compensate contractors for working capital financing. Two percent of total contract costs was recommended as the requisite level.

3. Establish a mechanism for adjusting markup (DFAIR term used for profit) objectives in situations which vary substantially from baseline expectations, e.g., with respect to contract length, delivery schedules, and fluctuating interest rates.

4. Retain payment policy of five to ten days for progress payments.

5. Establish payment policy of 30 days for delivery (invoice) payments.

6. Progress payment frequency should remain on a monthly basis.

7. Revised progress payment rates upward to 90% for small businesses and 85% for other firms.

On May 1, 1985, DoD had lowered the rates to 90% for small businesses and 80% for other firms, with the proviso that these rates would be reconsidered based on the conclusions of DFAIR.

On May 27, 1986, the Deputy Secretary of Defense issued a series of recommendations relating to contract profits, financing and pricing after considering the DFAIR conclusions. Some recommendations were intended for immediate implementation through FAR or DFARS, and others were to be further studies:

1. A long-term study resulting in FAR changes would integrate contractor financing, government progress payments and changes in interest rates into the profit weighted guidelines.

2. The bank prime rate, approximating 12% during the DFAIR study, had dropped to about 8.5% and DOD concluded that progress payments should remain at 80% for firms other than small businesses. DFAIR had recommended that the differential between small and other businesses be narrowed to 5% and this led DOD to reduce the rates for small businesses to 85%.

3. DFAIR's review of flexible progress payment structures concluded that the minimum level for contractor investment should be increased from 5% to 15%. DOD directed that the level be raised to 20% and it has since been further raised to 25%.

In its continuing micromanagement of DOD acquisition policies and hostility to defense contractors, Congress enacted on October 18, 1986, P.L. 99-500, which directed the further reduction of progress payment rates to 80% for small business firms and 75% for others. As executive and legislative actions continued to reduce the progress payment rates, no consideration was apparently accorded to the fact that when the rates were increased in 1981 because of the high interest rates, industry was forced to pay for this largess through the elimination of the provision that progress payment billings could be submitted bi-weekly and the expansion of the frequency to monthly submissions. With the lowering of the rates, it seemed apparent to many that equity demanded restoring the bi-weekly practice; however, the perception of equity was not served.

On December 1, 1986, DOD issued a final rule, effective October 18, 1986, implementing the provisions of P.L. 99-500 that lowered the progress payment rates.

GAO Disputes DFAIR Findings and Recommendations

About 18 months after the issuance of the DFAIR report (about the same length of time required for the entire DFAIR study and report preparation), GAO issued a scathing criticism of virtually every DFAIR finding and recommendation. Much of GAO's December 23, 1986, blast is addressed to profit and is covered in Chapter XXV of this text. Some of the legislative watchdog's views on contract financing are summarized below.

Essentially, GAO took issue with DFAIR's methodology in developing a "typical" contract model that indicated that contractors historically incur a cost equal to approximately 2% of the total contract cost to finance their working capital requirements. GAO's own calculations led to the conclusion that DFAIR's approximation was greatly overstated.

The Department of Defense disagreed with virtually all of the GAO's conclusions. With respect to contract financing, DOD noted that GAO's computation of the contractors' cost was limited to interest paid on borrowed money, whereas DFAIR's correctly considered cost of working capital indifferent to the source, thus including the cost of equity financing. As DOD's reply states: "The GAO approach does not recognize such equity financing and is not based on an accounting concept shared by others who evaluate the cost of capital in either a defense or non-defense firm."

ASSIGNMENT OF CLAIMS (FAR SUBPART 32.8)

As defined in FAR, this term means "the transfer or making over by the contractor to a bank, trust company, or other financing institution, as security for a loan to the contractor, of its right to be paid by the Government for contract performance" (FAR 32.801). Assignment of claims is authorized by the Assignment of Claims Act of 1940, as amended, 31 U.S.C. 203, 41 U.S.C. 15, and implemented by the FAR provisions.

PROMPT PAYMENTS BY THE GOVERNMENT

The enactment of the Prompt Payment Act (P.L. 97-177) on May 21, 1982, culminated a long and successful effort for financial equity, an effort that was opposed by a number of federal agencies. The Act is applicable the first calendar quarter beginning more than 90 days after the date of its enactment. This established the effective date as October 1, 1982. It further provided that implementing regulations were to be promulgated not later than 90 days after its enactment.

Although some contractors have been successful in arranging for prompt payments, and GAO has even found government agencies that pay their bills prior to the due dates, a large number of companies have suffered late payments. The latter group includes contractors that have long agonized over relations with government agencies that have consistently paid late.

Numerous bills had been introduced in Congress to alleviate this problem. However, despite the obvious need to correct the inequities, and although it had been clear that some government paying offices simply would not or could not pay bills promptly, provisions requiring the government to pay interest on late payments were strongly opposed by some government agencies. A GAO study indicated that government contractors might be hurt by as much as $375 million annually because they were required to borrow money and pay interest on the loans attributable to late payments from the government. However, GAO opposed legislation requiring government agencies to pay interest on late payments because such a requirement "could result in an administrative burden." GAO saw the solution in effecting "managerial reforms" to prevent late payments. The OFPP Administrator also opposed such legislation, seeing provisions to be incorporated in FAR as resolving the problem.

The government witnesses in congressional hearings proved hardly a match for representatives of the private sector who furnished cogent arguments and case studies establishing the inequity of late payments by the government and the frustrations of contractors who tried to obtain relief. Attention was also drawn to the injustice and illogic of the government paying its bills late while disallowing interest on money contractors were forced to borrow because of government delinquency.

The Act provides that government agencies will pay interest penalties on late payments under contracts for property or services in accordance with regulations prescribed by the Director of OMB. These regulations were to specify a required payment date, which date shall be set forth in the contract or, if a date is not specified in the contract, it must be "thirty days after receipt of a proper invoice for the amount of the payment due." The OMB regulations were also to require that: "within fifteen days after the date on which any invoice is received, Federal agencies notify the business concern of any defect or impropriety in such invoice which would prevent the running of the time period specified . . . ."

Except for contracts for meat and agricultural products, interest runs "for the period beginning on the day after the required payment date and ending on the date on which the amount due is paid, except that no interest penalty shall be paid if payment for the complete delivered item . . . is made on or before . . . the fifteenth day after the required payment . . . ." The interest rate is that established by the Treasury under Section 12 of the Contract Disputes Act of 1978. This rate, originally established for Renegotiation Act purposes, is commonly referred to as the "Treasury Rate."

Any amount of an interest penalty which remains unpaid at the end of any thirty-day period shall be added to the principal amount of the debt, and thereafter interest penalties shall accrue on such added amount.

Some government disbursing offices take advantage of the discount provided for in the contract, although they pay on a date beyond the discount period. This unfair and frustrating practice has been extremely difficult to correct. The Prompt Payment Act addresses this practice and provides that agencies deducting discounts although paying beyond the discount period "shall pay an interest penalty on any amount which remains unpaid in violation . . ." of the contract.

Where an agency has failed to pay interest penalties for late payment as required by this Act, the contractor may appeal under the provisions of the Contract Disputes Act.

Congress did not walk away from this Act. It required that each agency submit a detailed annual report to OMB, including "the number, amounts, and frequency of interest penalty payments, and the reasons such payments were not avoided by prompt payment . . . ." The OMB Director, in turn, must submit annual summaries to several congressional committees including, for each agency, an analysis of the progress made.

In accordance with the provisions of the Act, the OMB issued implementing instructions. The OMB Circular was dated August 19, 1982.

OMB's implementation generally followed the provisions of P.L. 97-177 and drew relatively few major recommendations for revision. One of the questions concerned the applicability date, with commentors suggesting that the Act should be applicable to existing contracts. However, OMB held to the interpretation that the Act was applicable only to contracts awarded on or after October 1, 1982. In its supplementary information, however, OMB stated: "Nothing in this Circular prohibits business concerns from proposing amendments to contracts entered into before October 1, 1982."

Selected sections of OMB Circular A-125, issued June 9, 1987, are excerpted below:

3. *Policy.* Agencies will make payments as close as possible to, but not later than, the due date, or if appropriate, the discount date. Payment will be based on receipt of proper invoices and satisfactory performance

of contract terms. Agencies will take discounts only when payments are made within the discount period. When agencies take discounts after expiration of the discount period or fail to make timely payment, interest penalties will be paid. Agencies will pay interest penalties automatically, without the need for business concerns requesting them, and will absorb interest penalty payments within funds available for the administration or operation of the program for which the penalty was incurred.

*   *   *   *

8. *Payment of Interest Penalty.*

a. An interest penalty will be paid automatically when due without regard to whether the business concern has requested payment when all of the following conditions are met:

—There is a contract or purchase order with a business concern.

—Acceptance of property or services has occurred and there is no disagreement over quantity, quality, or other contract provisions.

—A proper invoice has been received (except where no invoice is required, e.g. some periodic lease payments) or the agency fails to give notice that the invoice is not proper within 15 days of receipt of an invoice (3 days for meat or meat food products, and 5 days for perishable agricultural commodities).

—Payment is made to the business concern more than 15 days after the due date (3 days for meat or meat food products, and 5 days for perishable agricultural commodities). This includes payment of amounts retained by the Government upon final settlement of the contract.

b. An interest penalty will also be paid when an agency takes a discount after the discount period has expired and fails to correct the underpayment within 15 days of the expiration of the discount period (3 days for meat and meat food products and 5 days for perishable agricultural commodities).

c. Interest penalties are not required when payment is delayed because of a disagreement between a Federal agency and a business concern over the amount of the payment or other issues concerning compliance with the terms of a contract; nor are they required when payments are made solely for financing purposes, payments are made in advance, or for a period when amounts are withheld temporarily in accordance with the contract. Claims concerning disputes, and any interest that may be payable with respect to the period while the dispute is being settled will be resolved in accordance with the provisions in the Contract Disputes Act of 1978 (41 U.S.C. 601 et. seq.).

The DOD implementing policy was originally set forth in a memorandum from the Deputy Under Secretary (Acquisition Management) dated January 4, 1983. This memorandum was published in full in DAC 76-42 and pertinent portions are cited below:

All existing and new contracts which contain financing provisions (advance payments, progress payments or cost reimbursement provisions) will continue to have all payments made in an expeditious manner (normally within 5 to 10 days after receipt of a proper request).

Payments on all existing and new contracts for items or services being purchased against commercial specifications or descriptions (except meat and meat products, and perishable agricultural commodities), and which do not contain financing provisions, will be made on the specific due date required by the contract, or in the absence of a specific due date on the 30th day (or, if applicable, on the early payment discount day), after receipt of a proper invoice. Payments for meat and meat products will be made on the 7th day after delivery, and for perishable agricultural commodities will be made on the 10th day. This requirement will be put into effect upon receipt.

Payments on all existing and new contracts for items or services being purchased against military specifications, and which do not contain financing provisions, will be made on the specific due date required by the contract, or in the absence thereof on the 30th day (or if applicable on the early payment discount day) after receipt of a proper invoice. This requirement will be put into effect on payment requests received on or after March 1, 1983. Contracting officers should notify paying officers as soon as possible of the contracts which are in this category.

Contracts currently in existence, which do not contain financing provisions, but which can meet the requirements of DAR E-503 may, at the request of the contractor be amended to include such financing provisions. Consideration should be addressed, however, separately identifiable financial consideration is not required.

With respect to all contracts which do not contain financing provisions, and which are entered into after January 31, 1983, contracting officers are authorized to negotiate a specific due date for payments. This date should be based on prevailing industry practice for the same or similar goods or services. In most cases, the due date should be 30 days and in no case should be less than 5 days after receipt of a proper invoice.

FAR SUPPLEMENT COVERAGE

Comments on regulatory provisions relating to contract financing have centered essentially on FAR. As indicated elsewhere in this text, that publication fell far short of the envisioned uniform federal acquisition guidance. DOD's FAR Supplement and the supplements of the Army, Navy, Air Force, DLA, and some civilian agencies include coverage which dwarfs the contents of FAR.

Companies doing business with the Defense Department must become familiar with DOD FAR Supplement Part 32 and related contract clauses, as well as these Parts in the Army, Navy, Air Force and DLA FAR Supplements. GSA, NASA, and the Departments of Energy and Transportation are among the civilian agencies which have published supplemental coverage on contract financing.

Chapter VII

Government Contract Changes and Equitable Price Adjustments

SCOPE OF CHAPTER

The government buys just about every kind of goods and services purchased by commercial organizations, plus a large dollar volume of sophisticated military hardware and other items not ordinarily involved in commercial transactions. Government requirements include many standard commercial and off-the-shelf items, which are frequently acquired with little or no change or adaptation, and also special items, requiring advances in the state of the art or substantial modifications. Once special military or other specifications are involved, the possibilities for changes during the contract performance are sharply increased. In recognition of these circumstances, government contracts for many years have included standard Changes clauses.

When the government orders changes to be made, contract costs are usually affected, a fact recognized in the Changes clause by providing for "an equitable adjustment . . . in the contract price or delivery schedule, or both . . . ." The full text of the Changes clause for a fixed-price contract for supplies (FAR 52.243-1) is cited below:

(a) The Contracting Officer may at any time, by written order, and without notice to the sureties, if any, make changes within the general scope of this contract in any one or more of the following:

(1) Drawings, designs, or specifications when the supplies to be furnished are to be specially manufactured for the Government in accordance with the drawings, designs, or specifications.

(2) Method of shipment or packing.

(3) Place of delivery.

(b) If any such change causes an increase or decrease in the cost of, or the time required for, performance of any part of the work under this contract, whether or not changed by the order, the Contracting Officer shall make an equitable adjustment in the contract price, the delivery schedule, or both, and shall modify the contract.

(c) The Contractor must submit any "proposal for adjustment" (hereafter referred to as proposal) under this clause within 30 days from the date of receipt of the written order. However, if the Contracting Officer decides that the facts justify it, the Contracting Officer may receive and act upon a proposal submitted before final payment of the contract.

(d) If the Contractor's proposal includes the cost of property made obsolete or excess by the change, the Contracting Officer shall have the right to prescribe the manner of the disposition of the property.

(e) Failure to agree to any adjustment shall be a dispute under the Disputes clause. However, nothing in this clause shall excuse the Contractor from proceeding with the contract as changed.

It is to be noted that item (c) above provides that any "proposal for adjustment" must be submitted under this clause within 30 days from the date of receipt of the written order. Prior to FAR, the longstanding clauses (DAR 7-103.2 and FPR 1-7.102.2) provided, in part, that "any claim by the contractor for adjustment under this clause must be asserted within 30 days from the date of receipt by the contractor of the notification of change."

FAR was published in the *Federal Register* on September 19, 1983, with an effective date of April 1, 1984. Before its effective date, during a series of government-industry FAR workshops conducted around the country, government representatives were asked whether, in connection with government-initiated changes, contractors were to be required to actually submit proposals reflecting the additional cost resulting from the changes within 30 days rather than simply asserting that a proposal would be submitted.

The responses from the government representatives uniformly indicated that the language change was not intended to bring about any substantive change in requirements. Uncomfortable with these informal assurances, as early as April 30, 1984, the National Security Industrial Association (NSIA), in separate letters to the Director of the Defense Acquisition Regulatory Council and the Chairman of the Civilian Agency Acquisition Council, requested confirmation of these understandings and more specifically a revision to the FAR clauses to establish clearly that the contractor's responsibility within the 30-day period was only to notify the contracting officer that there was a cost impact as a result of the change and not to actually submit his request (proposal) for an equitable adjustment within this period.

NSIA's letters explained that, except for the simplest of changes, there was no way in which contractors could compute their own additional costs, let alone compile the costs of subcontractors, some of whom might be several tiers down.

The need for a FAR revision to restore the previous DAR and FPR language was obvious, but the government regulators continued to drag their feet despite NSIA follow-up letters on July 23 and September 28, 1984, the latter finally drawing a DOD reply that the DAR Council had established a case for this subject and that the series of contract clauses was under active consideration.

On November 14, 1984, NSIA wrote to the Deputy Under Secretary of Defense (Acquisition Management), pointing up the mass confusion on the part of the government and the related problems visited upon contractors as a result of these misdirected FAR clauses. The DOD FAR Supplement had authorized the "assert" clause but only for stevedoring contracts. The NASA FAR Supplement authorized the "assert" clause but provided 60 days for the contractor's submission. The Air Force Supplement to the DOD FAR Supplement authorized contracting officers to use a claim adjustment assertion period of up to 60 days if considered desirable.

NSIA's November 14, 1984, letter also advised that the Association's member companies found themselves having to condition their proposals for equitable adjustments to meet the 30-day submission requirement, which in turn required subsequent proposal amendments in order to submit complete and accurate cost and pricing data.

After more than a year of confusion and repeated industry requests for resolution of this problem, the FAR Secretariat finally took formal notice of this matter in the *Federal Register* of May 17, 1985. However, the simple FAR revisions to restore the prior DAR and FPR language were not effected.

Almost another year went by before the FAR Secretariat announced in the *Federal Register* of May 2, 1986, a proposal to change the language in the Changes clauses—FAR 52.243-1 through 52.243-4. More than two years after industry clamored for the restoration of the DAR and FPR language, the regulators stated in the supplementary information accompanying the proposal that the clauses would be revised "to provide that the contractor must 'assert its right to an adjustment' rather than 'submit a proposal for adjustment,' within 30 days from the receipt of a written order. These proposed revisions," continued the background information, "essentially impose the same requirements on the contractor as those previously in effect in the Defense Acquisition Regulation and the Federal Procurement Regulations Changes clauses."

The text of the proposed changes essentially deletes the requirement for the contractor to "submit any 'proposal for adjustment' . . . under this clause within 30 days . . . ." and substitutes: "The Contractor must assert its right to an adjustment under this clause within 30 days . . ." To date, the foregoing has not been formally implemented in the FAR, but apparently it is being administered according to the prior DAR and FPR format.

Finally, after approximately four years the foregoing was revised to reinstate the pre-FAR requirements under FAR clauses 52.243-1, -2, -3 and -4 as delineated in the *Federal Register,* dated August 12, 1987, which is cited below:

> FAR clauses 52.243-1, 52.243-2, 52.243-3, and 52.243-4 are amended to reinstate the pre-FAR requirement that the contractor must "assert its right to an adjustment" rather than "submit its proposal for adjustment" within 30 days from the receipt of a written order. While this action corrects an unintended policy change which occurred during drafting of the FAR, contractors should not construe this action as a relaxation of the FAR 43.204 requirement for prompt definitization of unpriced change orders.

Although the impact of the great majority of changes is negotiated to the mutual satisfaction of both parties, controversies arising from the Changes clause have generally been at or near the top of the list of disputes leading to litigation. In recent statistics published by the Armed Services Board of Contract Appeals, about one-third of the cases disposed of involved changes.

There are a number of circumstances not specifically covered by the Changes clause where the government's actions or failure to act can result in increased costs for which contractors are entitled to equitable price adjustments. Some of these circumstances are covered by such contract clauses as Government Property and Government Delay of Work (Suspension of Work in construction contracts). The Government Property clauses provide that the government will deliver specified property at specified times. Where the government is unable to do so, or decides to make substitutions in type, condition, or dates, and the cost of performing the contract is increased, the contractor is entitled to an equitable adjustment in the delivery or performance dates, or the contract price, or both.

The Government Delay of Work clause (FAR 52.212-15) is quoted below:

(a) If the performance of all or any part of the work of this contract is delayed or interrupted (1) by an act of the Contracting Officer in the administration of this contract that is not expressly or impliedly authorized by this contract, or (2) by a failure of the Contracting Officer to act within the time specified in this contract, or within a reasonable time if not specified, an adjustment (excluding profit) shall be made for any increase in the cost of performance of this contract caused by the delay or interruption and the contract shall be modified in writing accordingly. Adjustment shall also be made in the delivery or performance dates and any other contractual provision affected by the delay or interruption. However, no adjustment shall be made under this clause for any delay or interruption to the extent that performance would have been delayed or interrupted by any other cause, including the fault or negligence of the Contractor, or for which an adjustment is provided or excluded under any other provision of this contract.

(b) A claim under this clause shall not be allowed (1) for any costs incurred more than 20 days before the Contractor shall have notified the Contracting Officer in writing of the act or failure to act involved, and (2) unless the claim, in an amount stated, is asserted in writing as soon as practicable after the termination of the delay or interruption, but not later than the date of final payment under the contract.

In addition to the coverage in this chapter of formal change orders issued by the contracting officer under the appropriate contract clauses, we shall discuss the complex and significant subject of constructive change orders—actions by contracting officers or other *authorized* government representatives which, without the issuance of written change orders, have the effect of requiring contractors to perform the contract differently in time or manner from that prescribed by the original contract terms. As the boards of contract appeals and courts have stated, where the government has in fact made a change but failed to issue a change order or contract modification, the contractor's claim for the cost of complying with the change will be treated as if the proper change order had been issued.

This is not a legal text and, although the author has had extensive experience in negotiations and litigation involving contract changes and equitable price adjustments, the major focus of this chapter is on the accounting and administrative actions necessary to assure that contractors obtain adequate recovery when, through formal or constructive change orders, they are required to perform at costs greater than they would have incurred under the original provisions of the contract.

Ideally, the parties would negotiate equitable price adjustments without expending substantial time, effort, and expense. When the contracting officer recognizes the contractor's *entitlement* to an adjustment, usually a process involving first the technical people and then, if necessary, the attorneys, the next question to be addressed is *quantum*—the amount of the adjustment. In many instances, quantum can be resolved through negotiations following review of the contractor's proposal by the contracting officer. Where the claim is large and complex, the contracting officer will request an audit by the cognizant contract audit agency. The resulting audit report, as all reports by contract auditors, is advisory, and the contracting officer is expected to arrive at a judgment after considering the audit report as well as the advice available from the technical, financial, legal and other officials of his organization.

Where the two sides are unable to reach agreement, the contracting officer hands down a unilateral, final determination from which the contractor can appeal under the provisions of the contract Disputes clause. In this regard, the Contract Disputes Act of 1978, Public Law 95-563, effective March 1, 1979, has resulted in several major changes in the appeals process. Chapter XXIII includes commentary concerning the Act, its implementation by the executive agencies of the government, and references to selected judicial and quasi-judicial decisions to indicate its application in litigation.

This chapter deals primarily with government contract changes where agreement on the equitable price adjustment could not be reached between the parties and settlement of the resulting disputes required decisions by boards of contract appeals or courts. Based on our extensive research and study of this area and our substantial practical experience with, and participation in, such litigation, we have presented suggestions for the preparation and documentation of claims for equitable price adjustments, together with analyses of selected decisions by boards of contract appeals and courts, to establish the pattern of judical thinking and rulings.

PREPARATION AND DOCUMENTATION OF CLAIMS FOR EQUITABLE PRICE ADJUSTMENTS

The basic purpose of government procurement is to obtain needed services and supplies at fair and reasonable prices. The negotiation of equitable price adjustments in consideration of changes to the original contractual agreement is inherent in this goal. Contractors who do not avail themselves of their rights in law and equity in these cirumstances are usually those failing in one or more of the following responsibilities.

Complete Knowledge of Contract Requirements—The first and rather obvious condition precedent to the recovery of additional costs resulting from changes to requirements is the intimate knowledge of the exact original contract obligations. In some instances, this knowledge is monopolized by a limited number of the contractor's staff instead of being available to the required personnel concerned with the manufacturing, engineering, purchasing, accounting, and legal aspects of contract performance.

Timely Notification to and Coordination with Contracting Officer—The "government" in the broad sense is a large, complicated, mysterious, heterogeneous mass. The contracting officer, however, is a single human being who represents the basis by which the huge government mass is reduced to an understandable and accessible working contract. The contracting officer should be notified immediately upon the discovery that the performance of the contract will need to proceed under changed conditions, and a basis must be established for close follow-up and coordination, which will continue until the matter is concluded.

Documentation—Perhaps the major and most frustrating cause of difficulties and controversies is the impatience and disregard for documentation on the part of "executives," "scientists," and others, who just cannot be bothered with compiling the files necessary to support required future action. Life would be infinitely easier for those who are called upon to effect final resolutions if everyone concerned did his part throughout. As soon as the need for changes involving additional costs is determined, historical files should be initiated and carefully maintained. Telephone calls and conferences should be supported by memoranda; all matters of importance should be confirmed by letters, and written replies thereto insisted upon; basic approvals should be sought as early as possible and from authoritative sources; files should be complete as to all the implications of the changes required—additional or more costly methods and materials, additional engineering requirements, exact periods of interruptions or slowdowns, impact of terminations of subcontractors and suppliers, precise data as to period and effect of idle machines and manpower. The matters to be included in the files should be prepared by the appropriate experts under the supervision of one individual designated to coordinate the entire case.

Cost Data in Support of Price Adjustment—All of the data cited in the above paragraph must be expeditiously translated into monetary effects in preparation for the ultimate submission of the adjustment and/or claim. Too often contractors submit some of the more obvious cost increases, but overlook the less apparent factors, which may actually constitute the more significant factors. The following check list, while not all-inclusive, will serve to suggest the types of costs that should be considered in developing the cost of changes to government contracts.

(1) Research, Development and Engineering—direct salaries and wages of the personnel involved, direct materials and supplies, and applicable overhead.

(2) Purchasing—suppliers' termination charges, cost of additional materials required.

(3) Material Control—cost of material made obsolete by changes, plus the expense of segregating, removing, storing, diverting, disposing, etc.

(4) Other production costs—direct labor costs incurred on obsolete materials, direct labor additionally required, plus all related manufacturing overhead, costs of all tools, equipment and facilities made obsolete or additionally required by the changes.

(5) Applicable General and Administrative Expense—including direct items where applicable, and pro rata share of total pools of such expenses.

(6) Special Costs—particularly in the event of changes resulting in decreases in quantities, stretch-outs, etc., substantial costs may be incurred, both of a direct nature, where direct productive employees are idle and cannot be diverted, and of an indirect category, in terms of unabsorbed burden. The latter category is often difficult to develop. Where a precise basis cannot be found, a satisfactory expedient may be used by comparing the engineering, manufacturing and administrative expense rates that obtained (or projected) in the periods of interruptions or stretch-outs with the rates experienced during periods of full production.

Final Review and Processing—If the coordination with the contracting officer has been effective, a meeting of minds attained and documented, files carefully compiled to support all factors that require consideration, and the effects monetized accurately, the contractor may expect to submit a proposal and satisfactorily and promptly negotiate an equitable price adjustment that will permit full recovery of all costs incurred in excess of those contemplated by the original contract terms. Breakdowns in any of these categories, or misunderstandings with procurement officials, however, will result in prolonged negotiations or even appeals to boards of contract appeals or the courts. A high premium must be placed on effective procedures, which will obviate disputes, including the all-important final review to determine that all the facts are carefully marshalled, supported, and presented and the equitable price adjustment formalized by a formal change order.

Constructive Change Orders—Special attention is required with respect to constructive change orders. First, it is essential that everyone in the contractor's organization who may become involved in a constructive change order clearly understand its meaning and implications. Suggestions for additional, different, or any other kind of changed performance may originate from government engineers, project managers, inspectors, and other officials. These suggestions may be conveyed in writing or orally, and they may be conveyed to the contractor's engineers, administrators, production people, or others. All of these possibilities establish clearly the need for a broad orientation program to assure that anyone receiving government requests regarding performance that departs from the contract terms immediately notify a predesignated individual with responsibility for full coordination with legal, contract administration, and other officials who may be involved.

Paperwork in our society, especially with the proliferation of better and cheaper reproduction equipment, sometimes threatens to swamp all of us and has been identified as a major cause of extra work and extra costs. However, in the area of contract changes, and especially with regard to constructive change orders, it is vital to compile and maintain files of correspondence, memoranda of telephone discussions, etc. These files are part of the documentation that, in our experience, has made or unmade successful claims.

The importance of records and other documentation is illustrated in *Litton Systems, Inc., Ameco Division*, ASBCA No. 15554, 73-2 BCA par. 10,155.

The decision contains lengthy, technical recitations of the board's analysis of the conflicting testimonies by government and contractor witnesses. The board found that the contractor was entitled to some additional compensation where the problems were attributable to inadequate drawing packages or government-furnished property. The contractor's major difficulty in obtaining anything close to the amount claimed was apparently due to lack of documentation or other support, which the following excerpts from the decision illustrate:

> However, appellant's claim rests, for the most part, on its contention that electrical redesign work far in excess of that contemplated in the contract as awarded had to be performed in order to satisfy the repackaging requirement. It is apparent that a great deal of electrical design work was performed. *But, the record presented provides us with no basis to measure the difference between the effort contemplated under the contract and the work actually performed.* Such a measure might have been provided if appellant had explained in some detail the engineering design approaches for the various subassemblies in appellant's stillborn production unit. This might have shown how appellant put into practice the aspirations of its proposal. But, this was not done. (Italics added.)

> Moreover, without an explanation of the technical effort envisaged at the time of contract award, we are unable to ascertain the extent of design work performed as a result of the government specifications as distinguished from faulty engineering judgements made by appellant during its performance thereafter. Through Mr. Fink's testimony appellant has sought to explain the nature of the effort which ultimately resulted in the end items. However, his testimony was for the most part hearsay, very general in character, and does not furnish an adequate explanation of the redesign specifies, the cost of which appellant claims. In certain instances we have accepted Mr. Fink's testimony as a partial basis for making the allowances indicated above. However, except for those allowances, we are constrained to conclude, for lack of proof, that appellant is not entitled to additional compensation.

The government did not cross-examine the contractor's main witness, nor did it present estimates of its own, leaving it to the board to cope with a claim lacking support in major degree. In a manner sometimes resorted to in these kinds of cases, the board somehow concluded that $30,000 was adequate settlement of the contractor's $290,000 claim:

> In view of the lack of corroboration for, or detailed explanation of, appellant's estimates, we are unable to make an allowance specifically based thereon. However, it is clear from our findings and conclusions on entitlement that appellant is entitled to partial recovery. In our opinion the age of this dispute, and the difficulties involved in obtaining precise cost information, would render further proceedings on quantum fruitless. We determine, on the basis of the record as a whole and after weighing the evidence, that appellant is entitled to total recovery in the amount of

$30,000 with respect to those individual claim items on which we have decided that appellant is entitled to additional compensation. (Italics added.)

We are not familiar with details of the actual events in this matter. It is possible that the claim could have been prepared and argued in a manner that would have persuaded the board that the contractor was entitled to a larger amount. In any case, what does seem evident is that maintaining records of some of the effort expended because of the government's changes would certainly have assisted the contractor in obtaining a better settlement.

PRICING OF CLAIMS FOR EQUITABLE PRICE ADJUSTMENTS

With very few exceptions, contract performance in a manner different from that required under the original terms will result in increased costs to the contractor. In a very well-known, frequently cited case, *Bruce Construction Corp. v. U.S.,* 163 Ct.Cls. 97, 324 F.2d 516 (1963), the Court of Claims said that the basic purpose of the equitable price adjustment is "to keep the contractor whole when the government modifies a contract." The other side of the coin, of course, as frequently stressed by government officials, is the need to ascertain the extent to which the contractor's costs were altered because of the change. This point has been made in numerous decisions; see, for example, *Turnbull, Inc. v. U.S.,* 180 Ct.Cls. 1010, 389 F.2d 1007 (1967) and *Hol-Gar Manufacturing v. U.S.,* 175 Ct.Cls. 518, 524, 360 F.2d 634, 638 (1966).

Throughout this text, we have referred to significant areas where the procurement regulations and the accounting profession have made little or no real contribution to developing principles for cost determination. In these instances, boards of contract appeals and courts have been forced to step into the breach and establish by case law the principles the responsible parties had abdicated. These include principles relating to limitation of cost provisions, Chapter XX, and implementation of P.L. 87-653, Chapter XXII. Determination of costs under claims for equitable price adjustments arising out of changes, delays, etc., covered in this chapter, is certainly another significant area.

Estimated v. Historical Costs

The standard changes, delay, and suspension contract clauses reflect the government's objective for the contractor to submit an estimate of the increased costs as early as possible and for the negotiations to be conducted based on such estimates. This procedure is frequently followed. In many instances, however, and particularly in those that culminate in controversies and disputes, the amount of the equitable adjustment is not resolved until after the additional costs have been incurred. The principle has been well established that historical costs (actual costs) best support a claim for equitable adjustment. In questions concerning reasonableness, for example, the Court of Claims in *Bruce Construction Corp. v. U.S., supra,* stated that historical costs are the best measure of reasonable costs. The principle established in this decision is far-reaching and includes the basic premise that the incurrence of costs will constitute a presumption of reasonableness even if the contractor can be proven to be less efficient than others. There is a limitation here, of course, but the burden of proving incurred costs to be unreasonable is upon the government, and it has been a heavy burden.

The views of the Armed Services Board of Contract Appeals regarding estimated v. actual costs in pricing equitable adjustments are illustrated in the appeal of *Missile Systems of Texas, Emtex Division*, ASBCA No. 8306, 1964 BCA par. 4434, MFR denied 10/22/64.

The principal matter under dispute was the number of direct labor hours that should be allowed for the performance of the change order. The contractor's proposal consisted essentially of an estimate prepared in advance of the actual work under the change order. The government considered this estimate to be highly excessive and sought to obtain actual costs or at least estimates prepared during the performance. The contractor maintained no records of costs of contract changes, the total costs of each contract being accumulated in a single job order. The contractor also refused to permit the government to time work performance or to otherwise arrive at current estimates.

The board was not persuaded that the contractor's proposal was reasonable and, on the basis of evidence presented by the government's engineering experts, became more favorably inclined toward the government's estimates. Of considerable interest here are the board's views in this very important area of change order pricing, including the consideration accorded to estimates and actual costs:

> This appeal presents at the outset the fundamental issue of whether the pricing of a change order should be based on an advance estimate of the cost of performance or whether it should reflect consideration of experienced costs of performance, when the pricing of the change has to be done after the completion of the work. Throughout performance of the contract, appellant's position with respect to the pricing of the proof testing change order was that, consistent with the policy favoring forward pricing, the price adjustment for the change order should be based on an advance estimate and that the actual costs experienced in performance of the change were irrelevant. In keeping with its concept of price adjustment, appellant declined to maintain records showing the actual costs incurred in performing the change order, restricted the government in its attempts to find out the costs being incurred during performance and declined to cooperate with the government in ascertaining the labor costs being incurred in performing the change order while the work was in progress, although appellant was well aware while the work was in progress that there was a wide divergence of opinion between it and the government as to the reasonable estimated costs of performing the change order. Also, in keeping with its theory that experienced costs are irrelevant to the pricing of change orders, appellant refused after completion of the work to make available to the government such job order labor cost records as it had, its position being that, since its advance estimate was reasonable, such advance estimate should be controlling in determining the amount of the price adjustment.

> *   *   *   *

> *While we do not take exception to the principle that forward pricing based on advance estimates is preferable to retroactive pricing based on*

historical costs when the parties are able to agree on a fair and reasonable price in advance of performance of the work, it does not follow by any means that retroactive pricing based on advance estimates is preferable to retroactive pricing that takes into consideration factual data concerning performance, including historical costs. In this case the parties were unable to agree on a fair and reasonable price before or during performance of the change order, and we are forced to resort to retroactive pricing. We do not discount the value of estimates in both forward pricing and retroactive pricing of change orders, and we do not wish to overemphasize the importance of historical costs. The ultimate objective is to arrive at a fair and reasonable price for the change order. In the accomplishment of such objective, *historical costs are relevant, and, to the extent that they are reasonably available, they should be considered along with other pertinent factors.* (Italics added.)

This position is expressed in other cases as well. See, for example, *Elliott Machine Works,* ASBCA No. 16135, 72-2 BCA par. 9501, where the board said that "the making of an equitable adjustment under a changes clause is a pricing operation that calls for the consideration of all factors involved in the price including actual cost of performance."

Total Cost and Jury Verdict Methods

The preference for actual costs emphasizes the need for contractors to expeditiously establish job order records to accumulate all the costs incident to a contract change. (We would reiterate here that our references to contract changes are usually made in broad terms and include delays and suspensions of work.) Companies experienced in government contracting and their outside accounting consultants are keenly aware of this requirement. And yet, because of the complexity inherent in changes, including lack of timely awareness of constructive change orders, contractors frequently fail to accumulate these costs or fail to accumulate all of the costs involved. Where entitlement has been established but the contractor is unable to substantiate the actual costs, companies frequently resort to the total cost method. Although this method has been accepted by boards of contract appeals and courts in some instances, it is more often denied. Where the board or court cannot determine actual costs but is strongly persuaded that the contractor should be granted some amount for an equitable adjustment, it sometimes resorts to the jury verdict method. Because of the significance of this area, we have reviewed and cited a number of cases involving both methods.

Lane-Verdugo, ASBCA Nos. 16327, 16328, 73-2 BCA par. 10,271

In these appeals, the parties agreed that the board would rule on entitlement only, with the subject of quantum subject to negotiation dependent on the board's decision. Although the board denied the appeals, and the issue of quantum was not before it, the board nevertheless elected to address the quantum issue and made clear the disfavor in which the total cost method is held:

> Although quantum is not at issue before the Board, we are constrained to note that this Board and the Court of Claims have consistently held that the total-cost approach adopted by the appellant in this

appeal usually is not an acceptable method for establishing entitlement or amounts of compensation to which a contractor may be entitled. *WRB Corporation et al. v. U.S.*, 183 Ct.Cls. 409, 426 (1968); *W.C. Shepard v. U.S.*, 125 Ct.Cls. 724, 736 (1953); *Turnbull, Inc. v. U.S.*, 180 Ct.Cls. 1010, 1025 (1967); *Air-A-Plane Corporation*, ASBCA No. 3842, 60-1 BCA par. 2547.

One of the fundamental reasons for these decisions by this Board and the Court is the fact that such an approach is frequently employed by contractors when they have failed to maintain data reasonably required to establish entitlement or damages for specific events. The fact that the Government may have erred does not relieve a contractor from the burden of establishing with a reasonable degree of specificity the claimed results of such acts by the Government.

National Mfg., A Teledyne Co., ASBCA No. 15816, 74-1 BCA par. 10,580

The total cost method of computing the amount of a claim for an equitable price adjustment involves, in its simplest form, deducting the originally estimated cost from the total actual cost incurred and assuming the difference to represent the cost attributable to the change. As mentioned above, this method is not viewed with favor.

Where little or no information is available, but the board is persuaded that the contractor should be compensated for additional costs, it may use the "jury verdict" method. Here the board somehow estimates what it believes to be a reasonable amount, usually less than the contractor claims and more than the government believes appropriate. The printed decisions seldom provide any tangible clue to just how the jury verdict amounts were arrived at.

The case here discussed involves an appeal by National Mfg., Inc., a subsidiary of Teledyne, Inc. The contractor's claim for additional costs resulting from defective specifications and drawings totaled $1.8 million. The board ruled for the contractor on entitlement and sustained the appeal in the amount of $1.2 million.

The decision on quantum seems to have relied heavily on a comprehensive DCAA audit report on the actual cost of contract performance. Thereupon, the board considered the contractor's claimed amounts and reached its conclusion on what seemed to be a combination of a jury verdict and total cost approach. National had physically moved several times during the performance of this contract, and the data supporting its original bid had been lost or misplaced. As a substitute, National "reconstructed what they thought would constitute the costs under the contract but for the various problems which appellant encountered due to the claimed defective drawings and specifications. A simple arithmetical subtraction of one from the other (actual cost of performance as verified by DCAA) resulted in appellant's claim."

Direct labor of $533,000 constituted a major portion of the claim, and the government argued that "appellant uses a total cost approach which prevents any recovery for its claim." The board conceded that National "did not have the actual costs and figures attributable to the claims. . . ." On the other hand, it observed that the contractor "cannot be completely barred from recovering on that basis alone." It added that "Appellant's books and records were kept on a cost basis and not per defective problem or claim." After considering the efforts of National to arrive at some estimates, the board stated:

> In our opinion appellant has presented sufficient evidence to allow us to make a jury verdict as to some amount which appellant would be entitled to recover. In reaching this amount we have borne in mind the failure of the Government to introduce any evidence other than the DCAA audit pertaining to this problem, its failure to get a technical evaluation as recommended by the DCAA auditor and the persuasive details of the appellant's evidence. On the other hand we have also borne in mind that appellant, although it knew of these possible claims from almost the inception of the contract, did not make an extra effort to keep the types of records which it knew or should have known would be required for recovery in such instances.

The board was thus critical of the government's failure to have technically evaluated the contractor's initial proposal. On the other hand, it was critical of the contractor for not having "eliminated from its overall direct labor claim an amount attributable to faulty worksmanship or to problems which it encountered with poor components from its suppliers for which it is not claiming reimbursement." It also disagreed with the hourly rate used by the contractor for additional labor costs, concluding on the basis of the DCAA audit report that they could not have been as high as claimed. After all of these considerations, and without supplying details, the board said: "Bearing all these things in mind in our opinion a reasonable allowance to appellant for direct labor would be $400,000." This illustrates a jury verdict.

Another major portion of the claim related to additional material costs of $289,000, and here the contractor did better, in terms of percentage of the claim approved by the board. Essentially, National accepted the DCAA auditor's extensive analysis of the original purchase orders and materials that were costed by extending the quantities by the unit prices. The amounts so determined were subtracted from actual cost to arrive at a portion of the claim. Added thereto were other materials, tools, and testing equipment, which the contractor stated were specifically necessitated by the defective drawings and specifications.

As in the case of direct labor, the government argued that the claim should be denied because it was based essentially on the total cost method. The board's reaction and reasoning for rejecting the government's argument, and ultimately reaching an amount of $240,000 via the jury verdict method, are best described in the following excerpt from the decision:

> The Government argues that appellant should not be entitled to the difference between what a component actually costs it and what the original purchase order price would have been but for the defective drawings and specifications. Rather, the Government argues that we should look to the amount which was contained in appellant's bid for these various items. Some of these could be identified by other evidence which is in the record ... We are not persuaded by the Government's argument. When a contractor receives an equitable adjustment as a result of a change in the contract, he is entitled to recover the difference

between its actual costs, reasonably incurred, and what it should have cost him but for the change. When appellant prepared its bid it was under great pressures due to lack of time. It did not even receive all of the bid documents until the date of the pre-award conference. This was also true of some other potential bidders and as a result the bid was extended for a two-week period. However, this still was a very limited time in which to compute the costs of devices as complicated as the MK 37 and MK 49. Appellant apparently used figures in preparation for its bid which it knew it could better at the time of placing orders. We have discussed this in our findings of fact earlier in this opinion, insofar as appellant's dealings with Nytronics are concerned where Norman Burnell had informed appellant that it would better the prices it quoted if in fact appellant was awarded the contract. We are convinced this must have been taken into consideration by appellant in its bid preparation. Therefore, we find that the amount to be considered as the original cost for each of the components is that amount for which appellant would have purchased it but for the defective drawings and specifications. We, therefore, find that appellant is entitled to recover the difference between the original purchase order price and what it actually cost it for each of the components.

Henry Products, ASBCA No. 16128, 74-1 BCA par. 10,502; 73-2 BCA par. 10,348

As indicated by the following pertinent excerpts from the decision, the board expressed reservations about the total cost method but apparently reached its conclusions closely in accordance therewith.

> Given the fact of contract changes directed by the Government which increased the cost of performance it is not essential to determine with precision the exact cost of each change involved. The ascertainment of an equitable price adjustment is not an exact science. All that is required is adequate evidence from which a fair and reasonable approximation of the dollar amount of adjustment can be made. See: *Specialty Assembling & Packing Co., Inc. v. U.S.,* 174 Ct.Cls. 153, 184 (1966).

> The reasonableness of a claimed cost must be viewed in the light of the appellant's costs. Where costs are incurred and claimed as a result of a contract change order, a presumption arises that such costs are reasonable. In attacking the reasonableness of the expenditure, the Government assumes the very heavy burden of showing that the claimed cost was of such a nature that it should not have been expended, or that the contractor's costs were more than were justified in the particular circumstances. See: *Itek Corporation, Applied Technology Division,* ASBCA Nos. 13528 and 13848, 71-1 BCA par. 8906; *Bruce Construction Corporation et al. v. U.S.,* 163 Ct.Cls. 97, 102 (1963).

> The comments set forth in the Government's Brief concerning the significance of the changed work can hardly be said to equal the Government's burden. This evaluation of the change orders is an affirmative defense requiring pleading and proof. It is not possible for this Board to appraise the technical quality, work impact and cost effect of a change order in a vacuum.

Here the board noted that there were limitations on what Henry could recover and established the dimensions of the total cost approach:

This does not mean, however, that the appellant is automatically entitled to either the entire period of delay claimed or the total money demanded. The total cost theory of recovery urged by the appellant hinges on proof that (1) the nature of the changes makes it impossible to determine actual costs with accuracy in any reasonable degree; (2) the bid price was realistic; (3) its actual costs were reasonable; and, (4) it was not responsible for the additional expenses. See: *WRE Corporation et al. v. U.S.*, 183 Ct.Cls. 409, 426 (1968). In this case we are persuaded that the appellant was responsible for some of the additional costs claimed.

* * * *

With respect to quantum, we think it would be highly improper to base the price adjustment for the established changes on the difference between the contract price and the total costs of performance since ordinarily total costs of performance are irrelevant to a price adjustment for changes. However, in the situation here presented where it is known that the changes directed by the Government affected the overall cost of performance but it is impossible to make an accurate assignment of costs to specific changes, and where determination of the amount of price adjustment for the changes must of necessity depend upon judgment, lacking accurate cost data, we believe that consideration of the overall costs provides a proper prospective for evaluating the costs to be allowed for the changes. See: *Tenney Engineering, Inc.*, ASBCA No. 7352, 1962 BCA par. 3471; *H. John Homan Co., Inc. v. U.S.*, 189 Ct.Cls. 500, 509 (1969).

United-Mack Construction Co., ASBCA No. 12223, 68-1 BCA par. 7052

This decision illustrates the board's lack of sympathy for a contractor who failed to maintain performance records, its unhappiness with the proposed use of the total cost method, and the ultimate ruling based on a jury verdict, without indication as to how the final amount was reached.

The board was not sympathetic to the contractor's pleas of unawareness of the enormity of the problem, in view of the time involved between the contractor's first knowledge of it and subsequent communications with the government. Nor did the board look with favor upon the contractor's request for a "jury verdict." In this regard, the board quoted at some length from *WRB Corporation et al. v. U.S.*, Ct.Cls. No. 67-62 (1968), which treated both the total cost method and the jury verdict. As to the former, the Court stated:

* * * This theory has never been favored by the court and has been tolerated only when no other mode was available and when the reliability of the supporting evidence was fully substantiated. See *Turnbull, Inc. v. U.S.*, 180 Ct.Cls. —, slip op. at 13-14 (July 1967); *J.D. Hedin Construction Co. v. U.S.*, 171 Ct.Cls. 70, 86-87, 347 F.2d 235, 246-47 (1965); *River Construction Corp. v. U.S., supra*, 159 Ct.Cls. at pages 270-71; *Oliver-Finnie Co. v. U.S.*, 150 Ct.Cls. 189, 200, 279 F.2d 498, 505-06 (1960); *F.H. McGraw & Co. v. U.S.*, 131 Ct.Cls. 501, 510-12, 130 F.Supp. 394 399-400 (1955). The acceptability of the method hinges on proof that (1) the nature of the particular losses make it impossible or highly impracticable to determine them with a reasonable degree of accuracy; (2) the plaintiff's bid or estimate was realistic; (3) its actual costs were reasonable; and (4) it was not responsible for the added expenses. See *J.D. Hedin Construction Co. v. U.S., supra,* 171 Ct.Cls. at pages 86-87, 347 F.2d at pages 246-47; *Oliver-Finnie Co. v. U.S., supra,* 150 Ct.Cls. at pages 197, 200, 279 F.2d at pages 505-06; *F.H. McGraw & Co. v. U.S., supra* 131 Ct.Cls. at page 511, 130 F.Supp. at page 400.

This case clearly fails some of these tests. A large measure of our present uncertainty is due to the Plaintiff's complete failure to maintain accurate cost records during performance. The only excuse for this lack of diligence was that plaintiff did not expect to become embroiled in litigation over the Fort Hood project. That is feeble justification for taking refuge in total-cost approach. * * *

The Board found considerable analogy in the *WRB Corporation* case:

This case bears marked resemblance to the situation the court is describing. In particular, we think that appellant has not met the first criterion cited by the court for invocation of the total cost approach. Some additional time and record keeping effort would have been involved, but we cannot believe that an experienced contractor, considering that it was faced with unexpected extra work because of excess water in houses, could not easily have established, on a contemporaneous basis, a simple method of recording the extra labor hours, materials, and equipment being expended because its forces were redoing or correcting work already finished. We would also expect that a contractor would promptly and forcefully call to the Government's attention that it considered it was performing extra work and that it was keeping such a record of the same.

The court treats the Commissioner's recommendation of "jury verdict" on some of plaintiff's claims in the following language:

* * * Because of the inadequate records kept by the plaintiff and the paucity of data—both affirmative and rebuttal—on damages, the trial commissioner was hard pressed to determine the extent of the builder's injuries on claims . . . Convinced that the plaintiff did incur some losses, the commissioner recommended entry of "jury verdicts" on each of those counts. The plaintiff now claims more money, while the defendant contends that the commissioner's assessment are munificent.

In the past we have allowed so-called 'jury verdicts' if there was clear proof that the contractor was injured and there was no more reliable method for computing damages—but only where "the evidence adduced (was) sufficient to enable a court or jury to make a fair and reasonable approximation." *Specialty Assembling & Co. v. U.S.,* 174 Ct.Cls. 153, 184, 355 F.2d 544, 572 (1966); see *River Construction Corp. v. U.S.,* 159 Ct.Cls. 254, 271 (1962); *Western Contracting Corp. v. U.S.,* 144 Ct.Cls. 318, 320, 333-36 (1958); *Brand Investment Co. v. U.S.,* 102 Ct.Cls. 40, 45, 58 F.Supp. 749, 751 (1944), *cert. denied,* 324 U.S. 850 (1945). Though we agree with the commissioner that the plaintiff was undoubtedly injured, the evidence as to the extent of its losses on the 'jury verdict' claims is very loose, and we are not happy to endorse the employment here of a 'jury verdict'. However, the parties' conduct during the litigation, taken together with the age of the case and the great doubt that further proceedings would produce any better foundation for an award, leave us with no alternative but to accept that approach.

The contractor had claimed $410,000 and the government had evaluated the amount due as not to exceed $100. Although looking with disfavor at the proposal for a jury verdict, the board finally reached a conclusion that $30,000 represented "a fair and reasonable approximation of the appellant's increased costs . . . ." The decision offers no clue as to how the latter amount was reached.

Hedin Construction Co. v. U.S., 347 F.2d 235 (Ct.Cls. 1965)

As we pointed out in introducing our commentary on the total cost method, while it is not automatically rejected by boards and courts, the number of appeals in which it has been accepted seems to be outweighed by those in which it has been turned down in whole or in part. In both favorable and unfavorable decisions, boards and courts frequently cite the successful *Hedin Construction* appeal. Accordingly, we have presented below an excerpt from this decision and commend it for careful study by contractors who find no alternative way of seeking to recover additional costs attributable to the government but the total cost method:

Defendant challenges the manner in which these costs were computed by arguing that the commissioner's report erroneously accepts the "total Cost" theory expressly rejected by us in *River Construction Corp. v. U.S.*, 159 Ct.Cls. 254 (1962) and in *F.H. McGraw & Co. v. U.S.*, 131 Ct.Cls. 501, 130 F.Supp. 394 (1955). We are aware that we have on a number of occasions expressed our dislike for this method of computing breaches of contract damages, and we do not intend to condone its use as an universal rule. However, we have used this method under proper safeguards where there is no alternative, since we recognized that the lack of certainty as to the amount of damages should not preclude recovery. *Oliver-Finnie Co. v. U.S.*, 150 Ct.Cls. 189, 279 F.2d 498 (1960); *MacDonald Construction Co. v. U.S.*, 122 Ct.Cls. 210 (1952); *The Great Lakes Dredge & Dock Co. v. U.S.*, 119 Ct.Cls. 504, 96 F.Supp. 923 (1951), *cert. denied* 342 U.S. 953 (1952). In all these cases the fact of government responsibility for damages where no other method was available, *River Construction Corp. v. U.S., supra* at 271. We think this is such a case. The exact amount of additional work which plaintiff had to perform as a result of the foundation problem is difficult, if not impossible to determine because of the nature of the corrective work which was being performed. The adverse weather conditions during the extended period in which the excavations remained open caused a myriad of problems. Additional trenching, form construction, and pumping of surface water became necessary. Reexcavation by hand was sometimes required. The extreme muddy conditions caused difficulties and slowed down performance. There is no precise formula by which these additional costs can be computed and segregated from those costs which plaintiff would have incurred if there had been no government-caused difficulties. However, the reasonableness and accuracy of plaintiff's estimate, which was prepared by an experienced engineer whose qualifications have been unchallenged, have been established. Defense counsel stated that the estimate was not challenged. The closeness of the bids gives support to the reasonableness of the estimate. The bidders were three extremely experienced contractors of large construction projects. Plaintiff on prior occasions had successfully constructed a number of large projects for the Veterans Administration. Plaintiff has established the fact that it performed additional work. Moreover, the responsibility of defendent for these damages is clear. The only possible method by which these damages can be computed is by resort to the "total cost" method. Under such circumstances, as stated earlier, we think that the Government should not be absolved of liability for damages which it has caused, because the precise amount of added costs cannot be determined.

Parsons of California, **ASBCA No. 20867, 82-1 BCA par. 15,659**

While we do not wish to abate our emphasis on the adverse reception that usually faces a claim based on the total cost method, it is important to identify circumstances where this method, especially when modified to meet some of the criteria established in *WRB Corporation,* supra, has been accepted.

Parsons was unable to establish actual costs of all of the modifications to this contract, and its claim was based in large part on estimates. The government also presented estimates of the changed work, which totaled considerably less than the contractor's.

The government argued that the claim should be denied because the actual costs of each ECP were not determined, and the board said:

Of course, the preferred method of providing the equitable adjustment is proof of actual costs. However, the failure to produce such data if it were available or could easily have reasonably been made available may cause us to look with disfavor upon appellant's estimates.

The board concluded, however, that it was unable to find that Parsons "could have easily and readily determined its actual costs of performing the work for the ECPs included in the contract modification."

These modifications included 394 ECPs with 744 engineering orders, 46 revised drawings and 16 new drawings. Appellant's accounting system only kept track of costs by product and department. *It would not have been feasible to expect each of appellant's employees to keep track of how much time was spent on each of these many EOs and ECPs.* (Emphasis added).

Having concluded that the determination of actual costs was not feasible, the board addressed the question of ". . . which, if any, of the parties' estimates represent the reasonable cost of performing the work . . . ."

The government estimates were not highly regarded because the board found that the government estimators ". . . lacked experience in estimating manufacturing and manufacturing related activities (and) . . . estimates failed to include a detailed breakdown of the manufacturing sequence or steps to perform the manufacturing aspects of the changes." In contrast, the board found that Parsons estimators did possess the estimating experience that the government people were lacking. The government unsuccessfully attacked the Parsons estimate on several counts.

The board addressed the "definitization of the delay and loss of efficiency caused by the drawing defects," and we quote the following from the decision:

> Appellant's claim is presented on a modified total cost basis. The total cost method must be rejected in this case unless the claimed costs can be attributed solely to the drawing defects. *James A. Boyajian v. United States* [14 CCF par. 83,467], 191 Ct.Cl. 2(2)33, 423 F.2d 1231, (1970). Appellant contends its method of computing its equitable adjustment meets this exacting standard by subtracting from its total labor costs the sum of the labor costs included in its bid, its other claims, and other ECP's for which the Government is not responsible and excluding from its calculations changes in material and subcontract costs. A total cost method has been approved when all possible reasons for the additional costs other than defective specifications had been eliminated. *Teledyne McCormick-Selph v. United States* [25 CCF par 82,891], 218 Ct.Cl. 513, 588 F.2d 808 (1978). The exacting standards which must be met before the total cost method can be applied have been summarized in *WRB Corporation et al. v. United States* [12 CCF par 81,781], 183 Ct.Cl. 409 (1968), as follows:

> "The acceptability of the method hinges on proof that (1) the nature of the particular losses make [sic] it impossible or highly impracticable to determine them with a reasonable degree of accuracy; (2) the [appellant's] bid or estimate was realistic; (3) its actual costs were reasonable; and (4) it was not responsible for the added expenses." 183 Ct.Cl. at 426.

> *   *   *   *

> The Government has failed to point to any other method of pricing the cost of the delay and lost efficiency caused by the drawing defects. We have previously determined that it was impracticable to segregate the historical or actual costs of the direct effort involved in the compensable 367 ECP's and for the same reasons find it even less practicable to determine the actual costs of the delay and lost efficiency due to these ECP's. The contracting officer admitted it was impracticable and we also find it impracticable because of the large number of overlapping ECP's
> . . . .

DEFECTIVE GOVERNMENT-FURNISHED DRAWINGS, DESIGNS, SPECIFICATIONS, MATERIALS, ETC.

One of the most frequently encountered categories of circumstances leading to changes in government contracts comprises defective drawings, designs, or specifications. The changes may be initiated by the government for the reasons mentioned earlier, or they may be proposed by the contractor where production discloses that the originally furnished government specifications are not suitable. These types of changes are usually the readiest to support a contract price adjustment. As a matter of fact, boards of contract appeals will go to great lengths to assure that a contractor receives equity, as illustrated by the following cases.

ASBCA No. 6966 is of interest in this area for a number of reasons, including the citations of various precedents by the board. The basic point involves a contract for 100 sets of equipment, with the bid based on a model to be furnished by the government. This model did not meet the stated specifications, and, accordingly, the contractor appealed for an entitlement to an equitable adjustment for extra work. The government did not deny that the model failed to meet the specifications but stated that, under proper interpretation of the contract, the contractor was required to meet the specifications, without additional compensation, regardless of the fact that the government-furnished model did not meet such requirements.

The board decided that the government-furnished model did not meet the requirements of the contract. The board also concluded that the terms of the contract made it impossible for the contractor to have performed the contract without following the model. Here are some of the points considered by the board, together with the conclusions reached and the precedents cited. To indicate the exact climate established by the board and to maintain continuity, a portion of the decision is quoted in full:

> When the Government contracts for supplies to be manufactured in accordance with Government specifications, ordinarily there is an implied warranty on the part of the Government that, if the specifications are followed, a satisfactory product will result. The rule as to construction, contracts is stated by the Supreme Court in *U.S. v. Spearin,* 248, U.S. 132, as follows:

> ... But if the contractor is bound to build according to plans and specifications prepared by the owner, the contractor will not be responsible for the consequences of defects in the plans and specifications. *MacKnight Flintic Stone Co. v. The Mayor,* 160 N.Y. 72; *Filbert v. Philadelphia,* 181 Pa. St. 530; *Bently v. State,* 73 Wisconsin, 416. See *Sundstrom v. New York,* 213 N.Y. 68. This responsibility of the owner is not overcome by the usual clauses requiring builders to visit the site, to check the plans, and to inform themselves of the requirements of the work, as is shown by *Christie v. U.S.,* 237 U.S. 234; *Hollerback v. U.S.,* 233 U.S. 165, and *U.S. v. Utah Etc., Stage Co.,* 199 U.S. 414, 424, where it was held that the contractor should be relieved, if he was misled by erroneous statements in the specifications.

The rule for construction contracts as stated by the Supreme Court applies in principle to contracts for supplies to be manufactured in accordance with Government specifications. The rule is stated in *R.M. Hollingshead Corporation v. U.S.,* 124 Ct.Cls. 681 as follows:

> The plaintiff urges that, because of a mutual mistake as to a material fact, the parties made a contract which was impossible of performance. It says that, since the Government prepared the contract which specified that the liquid should be shipped in metal containers, it implicitly represented that if the specifications were complied with, satisfactory performance would result. We think that, in the instant situation, that is a correct statement. . . . But we think that when the Government, through one of its important

agencies, orders the production of a specified thing by specified means, it would be a rare instance when the supplier could reasonably be expected to investigate for himself whether compliance with the specifications would, in fact, produce the desired result. See *Spearin v. U.S.* 51 Ct.Cls. 155, 161, affirmed 248 U.S. 132; *Steel Products Engineering Co. v. U.S.,* 71 Ct.Cls. 457, 472; *Whitlock Coil Pipe Co. v. U.S.,* 72 Ct.Cls. 473. The same view is expressed by the Comptroller General in Comp. Gen. Dec. B-75619, August 10, 1948.

When the Government specifies in detail the design and construction to be followed by the contractor in the manufacture of equipment and also specifies performance requirements for such equipment, and the contractor manufactures the equipment in a workmanlike manner in accordance with the Government design, but the equipment does not meet the performance requirements of the specifications, the contractor will not be denied compensation for the reason that it finally develops that the work done in accordance with the Government plans does not produce the intended results. *Dayton-Wright Company v. U.S.,* 64 Ct.Cls. 544.

Under the circumstances of this case, the government-furnished procurement model was a part of the contract specifications, and there was an implied warranty by the government that the model met the performance requirements of the specifications except as noted in the Invitation for Bids and, hence, that a product made in conformity with the model would meet the performance requirements of the specifications with exceptions noted. There was also a representation by the government official charged with responsibility for briefing bidders that the model met the requirements of the specifications with exceptions noted. "Mistake" is defined as a state of mind that is not in accord with the facts (Restatement of Contracts, Sec. 500), and when the contract was entered into there was mutual mistake in the belief by both parties that the model met the performance requirements of the specifications except as noted in the Invitation for Bids. In the absence of any provision for administrative relief, the contractor might, under the circumstances recited above, obtain relief in an action at law on the basis of breach of implied warranty or misrepresentation or mutual mistake.

However, there is a basis for administrative relief under the contract. In numerous appeals, this Board has held that a contractor is entitled to a price adjustment under the Changes clause for the increased costs of performance caused by erroneous or deficient Government specifications. See *Regent Manufacturing Co., Inc.,* ASBCA No. 5397 et al., 23 February 1961, 61-1 BCA par. 2956, (specification requirements that were impracticable of attainment); *Spencer Explosives, Inc.,* ASBCA No. 4800, 26 August 1960, 60-2 BCA par. 2795 (faulty specifications and defective Government-furnished property); *J.W. Hurst & Son Awnings, Inc.,* ASBCA No. 4167, 20 February 1959, 59-1 BCA par. 2095 (erroneous drawings and incomplete specifications); *Guntert & Zimmerman Construction Division, Inc.,* ASBCA No. 1544, 11 June 1954 (faulty design and mistakes in specifications); *F.G. West & Company,* ASBCA No. 2233, 12 August 1955 (requirement of a special hardener made Government painting specifications incapable of producing a satisfactory job).

In *Western Engine & Equipment Co.,* ASBCA No. 3918, 20 November 1957, 57-2 BCA par. 1523, the Board held that defective Government specifications explicitly made subject to the Government-furnished Property clause constituted Government-furnished property "of a type not suitable for use" so as to entitle the contractor to a price adjustment under the Government-furnished Property clause. Whether or not the Government model is regarded as a part of the Government specifications, it is closely analogous to Government-furnished patterns to be used by a contractor in making a product. In *P.M. Manufacturing Company,* ASBCA No. 1909, 21 December 1954, the Board held that defective Government-furnished patterns were not suitable for use for the production of caps under the contract so as to entitle the contractor to an equitable adjustment in price under the Government-furnished Property clause of the contract.

A decision by the Armed Services Board of Contract Appeals (*Fletcher Aviation Corp.,* ASBCA Nos. 7669 and 8542, 1964 BCA par. 4192; 65-1 BCA par. 4651) involved increased costs incurred by a contractor as a result of defective drawings and specifications furnished by the government. Our analysis of this case reveals that the circumstances and issues involved should be of broad interest to firms doing business with the government.

The Fletcher Aviation Corp. was awarded a Navy contract for aircraft fuel tanks under which it was required to construct and test a preproduction sample tank, and, after approval by the government, it was to commence production on a large number of such tanks.

A series of seven tests on six tanks, produced in accordance with the government-furnished specifications and drawings, failed to produce satisfactory results, and the contractor recommended design changes at an increase in price, for which it was prepared to accept full responsibility. The change order was issued, and the first tank fabricated under the contractor's proposed changes was accepted after it had passed all of the required tests.

One of the issues involved in this case was the contractor's claim for extra costs incurred as a result of constructing and testing the preproduction sample tanks under the government's faulty specifications. The government alleged that the contractor did not really prove that the original design was faulty. Additionally, it alleged that the same tanks, built by another manufacturer to the same specifications, had successfully passed all of the required tests. The board found, however, that the government's position was not a good one. First of all, it produced no evidence that the six tanks that failed to pass the tests had not been produced in accordance with the contract specifications. Secondly, the board noted that the government was not able to show to its satisfaction that the successful tanks of the previous manufacturer were constructed from drawings and specifications that were identical to those furnished to Fletcher. In this connection, the contractor introduced as evidence a Navy report that stated, among other things, that the predecessor contractor had made many structural changes to the original design as a result of which the Navy concluded that "the tank configuration which the Fletcher Aviation Corporation contracted to build has never been subjected to qualification tests." This was good enough for the board, which found that the government's contention, that a tank with the same specifications had been successfully built and tested by another contractor, was not supported.

Another interesting point here involved the discussions that had been going on where the contractor had contended that the specifications were faulty whereas the government alleged that another contractor had fabricated successful tanks to the same specifications. At one point, Fletcher offered, at its own expense, to test the tank built by the other contractor. The government agreed and the tests apparently showed that this tank failed in the same way as Fletcher's. Further, Fletcher introduced evidence that the government had made an independent test of a tank produced by the predecessor contractor and that it, too, had failed.

The board concluded that Fletcher was right, whereupon it addressed itself to the government's subsequent contention that, even with this finding, Fletcher's contention constituted a "breach of contract theory" and thus was outside the board's jurisdiction. This motion was denied. The board noted that it had held many times that "a contractor may recover under the Changes article the costs of attempting to perform under deficient drawings and specifications." The board cited, as precedent, its ruling in *Pastushin Industries, Inc.,* in ASBCA No. 7663, 1963 BCA par. 3757, handed down in May 1963.

Another case involving defective government-furnished specifications is discussed here particularly because the board has cited numerous judicial and quasi-judicial references which should be of interest to defense contractors.

The Air Force issued a contract under formal advertising for fuel tanks to be constructed in accordance with specifications under which fuel tanks had never before been manufactured. The successful bidder was not aware that the government had not tested a tank to these specifications and attempted without success to construct a tank to meet the testing requirements. Ultimately, he claimed additional costs (1) in connection with attempting to perform an allegedly impossible contract and (2) for designing a new tank in substitution for that originally specified. The contracting officer ruled against the contractor, who filed an appeal.

The board found that the design specified in the contract would not produce a tank that could meet the test requirements. It observed that, while some of the failures probably resulted from faulty fabrication, it would be incredible to think that a manufacturer with the contractor's experience would have failed to make at least one tank in accordance with the design. The board also observed that it found no proof that anyone else had manufactured a tank in accordance with this design.

In reaching its decision in favor of the contractor, the board discussed the entire area of deficient designs, plans, and specifications and cited a number of leading decisions by the various courts and by the board in connection therewith. This section of the board's decision is of substantial interest to all government contractors and is quoted verbatim.

Where the government issues deficient plans and specifications, the contractor is entitled to recover costs in attempting to perform under them. *L&O Research & Development Corporation,* ASBCA No. 5013, 59-1 BCA par.

2107. In so holding, this Board said in *J.W. Hurst & Son Awnings, Inc.*, ASBCA No. 4167, 59-1 BCA par. 2095, on pages 8964 and 8965:

When the Government contracts for supplies to be manufactured in accordance with Government specifications ordinarily there is an implied warranty on the part of the Government that, if the specifications are followed, a satisfactory product will result. *U.S. v. Spearin*, 248 U.S. 132; *Hollingshead v. U.S.*, 124 Ct.Cls. 681. While we do not believe that the errors in the specifications and drawings were so serious as to give the contractor a right to rescind the contract as soon as the errors were discovered; nevertheless, when the errors were brought to the attention of the Government, and the Government refused to recognize the existence of the errors and initially disapproved appellant's requests for changes to correct the errors, appellant was no longer under any legal obligation to proceed with performance. *U.S. v. Spearin, supra.* A dispute had arisen, and the "Disputes" clause of the contract required the contractor to proceed diligently with the performance of the contract in accordance with the contracting officer's decision pending a final decision on the matter in dispute. We have held that where a contracting officer requires a contractor to perform work not called for under the terms of its contract, his order to perform such work constitutes a change in the work called for under the contract entitling the contractor to an equitable adjustment in contract price in accordance with the provisions of the "Changes" article. Appeals of *Polan Industries*, ASBCA No. 3996 *et seq.* (1958); *Inca Metal Products Corporation*, ASBCA No. 4239, 58-1 BCA par. 1719; *Fields Corner Brass Foundry, Inc.*, ASBCA No. 2226, 56-2 BCA par. 1101; *Luton Manufacturing Company*, ASBCA No. 3100, 58-1 BCA par. 1692; *Julio Laabes*, ASBCA No. 1366 (1954); *M.M. Sundt Construction Company*, ASBCA No. 1414 (1953); *S.S. Ganick Corporation*, ASBCA No. 1428 (1953). Faulty design and mistakes in specifications causing extra work have been held to provide a basis for price adjustment under the "Changes" clause, *Guntert and Zimmerman Construction Division, Inc.*, ASBCA No. 1544 (1954); *White Star Heating & Supply, Inc.*, ASBCA No. 2015 (1954), even though the change constituted a relaxation of the specifications to achieve an attainable result *General Electric Company*, ASBCA No. 2458, 56-2 BCA par. 1093; *Robbins Mills, Inc.*, ASBCA No. 2255 (1956); *Measurements Corporation*, ASBCA No. 2444 (1955). We are of the opinion that this appeal is governed by the principles there enunciated. That a Board of Contract Appeals has jurisdiction to decide a claim for extra compensation for mistakes in Government plans is indicated by the court's decision in *Wells & Wells v. U.S.*, 164 F.Supp. 26 (1958), where the board's decision under the contract "Disputes" clause was held to be final and conclusive on the contractor. Where, as here, the change is necessitated by defective specifications and drawings, the equitable adjustment to which a contractor is entitled must, if it is to be equitable, i.e., fair and just, include the costs which it incurred in attempting to perform in accordance with the defective specifications and drawings. *General Electric Company, supra; Robbins Mills, Inc. supra.* Under the circumstances, the equitable adjustment may not be limited to costs incurred subsequent to the issuance of the change orders.

It is not necessary that performance be impossible. The contractor may recover if the specifications are defective in the sense that they make consistent results impossible, resulting in extra work. *Spencer Explosives, Inc.,* ASBCA No. 4800, 60-2 BCA par. 2795.

Here the design specified by the government would not produce a tank meeting other requirements of the contract. The contracting officer refused either to recognize the deficiencies or to allow the appellant to make changes. Appellant was compelled to continue in its attempts to perform under the deficient design. This was extra work for which the appellant was entitled to an equitable adjustment in the contract price.

The government was under the duty to correct the design deficiencies. Instead, the appellant was compelled to engineer the new design. When the government accepted this design, it became obligated to pay the appellant its costs in making it.

CHANGES IN METHODS OF SHIPPING OR PACKING, PLACE OF DELIVERY

Shipping or packing changes frequently result when experience early in the contract discloses the failure of the originally planned methods to effect delivery at the time and in the condition intended. Also, packing changes are required when items intended for use at military installations within the continental limits of this country are diverted to our armed forces stationed overseas, or vice versa. Changes by the government as to places of delivery become important when the contractual terms are FOB destination.

In *Design Center, Inc.* (1956), ASBCA 3039, 56-2 BCA par. 1029, the board ruled that the contractor was entitled to reasonable compensation for the additional costs that were occasioned by changes in the shipping instructions. The original instructions required the shipment of 122 items to 9 destinations in 11 exterior containers. As a result of subsequent changes, the contractor was required to ship 122 items to 75 destinations in 75 exterior containers. The contractor claimed additional costs resulting from the increase in destinations and the number of containers required in excess of those originally contemplated. The board ruled that the contractor was entitled to an equitable adjustment in the contract price.

DELAY AND SUSPENSION OF WORK—COMPUTATION OF UNABSORBED OVERHEAD

Controversies relating to delays, disruptions, and suspensions of contract performance continue to present difficulties and constitute a major cause of disputes and litigation. As in the case of changes, these controversies involve two major elements: entitlement and quantum. Where the government's action (or inaction) prevents the contractor from completing the contract within the period contemplated in the contract, the costs of performance are almost invariably increased beyond what was contemplated, either in the contractor's preparation of the bid for a formally advertised contract or in the negotiations of the parties for a negotiated contract. To recover the increased costs, the contractor must establish (1) that the delays were indeed attributable to the government (entitlement) and (2) the amount of the additional costs caused by the delays (quantum).

Additional costs arising from delays frequently include direct material and direct labor, especially in periods of high inflation, other direct costs and, perhaps one of the most complex areas, overhead. Although we have often been involved in establishing entitlement, and some of the ensuing comments and case law will relate to this issue, entitlement is essentially a matter for attorneys and technicians to establish. The major role of the accountant involves quantum, and the remainder of this chapter will emphasize computation of unabsorbed overhead.

Procurement regulations governing today cover almost every conceivable issue that has emerged over the years in connection with contracts awarded by government agencies to the private sector. Strangely, however, these regulations have studiously avoided the complex but significant subject of unabsorbed overhead. As a matter of fact, one cannot find this term in the current procurement regulations. Equally strange is the fact that the accounting profession has taken no formal notice of this issue despite the large and increasing portion of our national economy represented by government contracts for goods and services. The Cost Accounting Standards Board, which many believe promulgated standards in some inappropriate and nonessential areas, indicated on several occasions its intentions to research this area, but ultimately did nothing. Because the procurement and accounting authorities in the public and private sectors abdicated their responsibilities, in terms of issuing formal regulations or standards, the ground rules for computing unabsorbed overhead had to be established by boards of contract appeals and the courts through case law.

Definition of Unabsorbed Overhead

An approach to understanding the concept of unabsorbed overhead is through a hypothetical situation of a company which prices and accounts for the cost of its contracts by considering direct material, direct labor, other direct costs, manufacturing overhead allocated in the ratio of direct labor cost, general and administrative expenses allocated in the ratio of total manufacturing costs, and profit. It may be said that manufacturing overhead is absorbed by the individual contracts by prorating it among them as a percentage of direct labor. General and administrative expenses are absorbed by the individual contracts by prorating the total of such expenses as a percentage of manufacturing costs.

Under normal conditions, let us assume manufacturing overhead ($1.5 million) would have amounted to 150% of direct labor ($1 million), and general and administrative expenses ($500,000) would have equated to 10% of total manufacturing costs ($5 million). As the operations progress during the year, for each direct labor dollar expended on a contract the contractor would have allocated $1.50 of manufacturing overhead. If total direct labor on a contract totaled $20,000, the contractor would have allocated $30,000, and it and every other contract on which work was performed during the year would have absorbed manufacturing overhead at the rate of 150% of direct labor cost. Similarly, if the total manufacturing cost of that contract amounted to $100,000, the contractor would have allocated general and administrative expenses to it on the basis of 10% of its manufacturing cost. The contract thus would have absorbed $10,000 of general and administrative expenses.

Pursuing the hypothetical case further, assume a contract other than the one we have been discussing was planned for completion during the year in which the above percentages obtained. However, due to delays attributable to the government, the contractor was forced to stop work on several occasions. Because less direct labor was expended on the contract, the contractor was unable to allocate as much manufacturing overhead to it as planned, and because the total costs of the contract were lower, the contractor could not allocate as much general and administrative expenses thereto as it would have but for the delay. Now, if the manufacturing overhead and general and administrative expenses could not be reduced, the same amounts of indirect expenses would be allocated over smaller allocation bases, with the result that the contracts that were worked on during the year would be forced to bear (absorb) more indirect expenses than they should have.

As the Armed Services Board of Contract Appeals succinctly described it in *Essex Electro Engineers, Inc.,* ASBCA No. 21066, 79-2 BCA par. 14,035, a decision we shall be commenting upon later:

> A claim for unabsorbed overhead is really for a decrease in allo-cability to the other in-house work performed during the scheduled period of original contract performance, which other work bore too great a portion of the plant's indirect costs because of the delay associated with the incurrence of direct labor and materials.

While the concept of unabsorbed overhead can be stated succinctly and simply by a board of contract appeals, the methods of computing appropriate amounts under various differing circumstances are complex and have been a source of controversy and litigation for many years. In the great majority of cases where the contractor, through the expertise of its accounting and legal staff or the engagement of outside consultants, has employed a computation method that the boards and courts had found in the past to be appropriate in those circumstances, the contractor has prevailed. However, in many instances, the victories were very difficult to achieve because the government, particularly DCAA and other contract audit agencies, dislikes and takes adverse positions against claims for unabsorbed overhead in general and against certain methods in particular, despite the parade of board and court decisions that have with considerable consistency upheld the principle and, where appropriate, the method. Because of the extent of the controversies and complexities, we have summarized a number of significant decisions. A careful study of the circumstances involved and the decisions rendered should be helpful to companies whose contracts have been delayed or disrupted because of the government. We would emphasize, however, that this complex area does not permit a "do it yourself" recipe type of commentary, and we would recommend the engagement of accountants and attorneys who have estab-lished their expertise in the field.

Carteret Work Uniforms, ASBCA No. 1647, 6 CCF par. 61,561 (1954)

One of the truly pioneer efforts culminating in a successful appeal to a board of contract appeals for unabsorbed overhead, *Carteret* has a special significance for the author because of personal involvement in the case. The method approved by the board may be used where the delayed contract represents the only work in progress at the time and in other circumstances as appropriate:

1. Actual overhead rate during delay period less normal overhead rate equals excess rate during the delay period.

2. Excess rate during delay period multiplied by total base costs equals unabsorbed overhead during the delay period.

Allegheny Sportswear Division, ASBCA No. 4163, 58-1 BCA par. 1684

Another major formula for computing unabsorbed overhead surfaced in the 1950s in the appeal of *Allegheny:*

1. Overhead rate for actual period of contract performance less overhead rate anticipated for contract performance equals excess overhead rate.

2. Excess rate multiplied by actual direct labor or other direct contract costs equals unabsorbed overhead.

The Allegheny formula found much favor with the Defense Contract Audit Agency, as reflected in its "Audit Guidance—Delay and Disruption Claims," Pamphlet DCAAP 7641.45. Basically, DCAA preferred this method over the Eichleay formula (discussed hereafter) because it invariably arrives at a lower cost recovery to the contractor than the amount computed by Eichleay. For many years, despite numerous rejections by boards of contract appeals and federal courts, DCAA objected to equitable adjustment claims computed according to Eichleay and substituted its own calculations, reflecting Allegheny or some other method that would reduce the claim. Unfortunately, contracting officers accepted the audit agency's advice in the past, their decisions were overturned in the judicial arena, and needless time and expense were incurred by all concerned.

Eichleay Corp., ASBCA No. 5183, 60-2 BCA par. 2688; 61-1 BCA par. 2894

Undoubtedly the best known and most widely used method of computing unabsorbed overhead, especially but by no means exclusively in connection with construction contracts, is the Eichleay formula:

1. $\dfrac{\text{Contract Billings}}{\text{Total billings for contract period}} \times$ Total overhead for contract period
= overhead allocable to the contract.

2. $\dfrac{\text{Allocable Overhead}}{\text{Days of Performance}}$ = Daily contract overhead.

3. Daily contract overhead × Number of days delay = Amount claimed.

This formula determines the amount of overhead for the contract period, establishes the portion applicable to the contract, computes the daily amount, and multiplies this daily amount by the number of days of delay to secure the amount claimed. The use of hypothetical figures may serve to further illustrate this procedure. Assume the following facts:

Direct billings = $500,000.
Total billings for contract period = $10,000,000.
Total overhead for contract period = $1,000,000.
Days of performance = 500.
Number of days of delay = 200.

The application of the contractor's formula to the above figures would result in the following:

1. $\dfrac{\$500,000}{\$10,000,000} \times \$1,000,000 = \$50,000.$

2. $\dfrac{\$50,000}{500 \text{ days}} = \$100.$

3. $\$100 \times 200 \text{ days} = \$20,000.$

The contractor's insistence on computing delayed costs by applying the Eichleay formula in this appeal, as contrasted with the government proposed computation, enabled the company to achieve an equitable adjustment of the contract price. The contractor was a construction firm; however, as discussed later in this chapter, the principles have far wider applications.

With regard to the overhead portion of the claim, the prime and subcontractors asserted over $153,000 of excess costs. The contracting officer disallowed all but $36,000. The final ruling of the ASBCA substantially accepted the contractor's proposal (such reductions as were made by the board related to specific elements considered not appropriate or not allocable, did not affect the basic issues of excess overhead computation, and are not discussed here).

As to the salient facts in the case, the contracts involved construction of a NIKE missile site. There were numerous changes to each of the contracts, including government motivated suspension of work. Contractual clauses relating to suspension of work provided for equitable adjustment in price where work was suspended for an unreasonable length of time, if the suspension caused additional expense and was not due to the fault of the contractor. Agreement was achieved between the contractor and the contracting officer as to the facts that work was suspended by the government through no fault of the contractor and that additional costs were incurred, and as to the number of days of unreasonable delay caused by the suspensions. Agreement was also reached as to the additional direct costs involved. The dispute arose with regard to the manner in which the excess overhead costs occasioned by the delay should be computed.

Aside from the fact that the board accepted the contractor's formula in preference to the government's proposal, the case involved much significance in terms of many important statements and opinions of the board, including citation of many leading court decisions. Quotations or excerpts of some of these follow:

The problem out of which this dispute arises is how to allocate home office expenses incurred during a period of suspension of work. These expenses continue during temporary or partial suspensions, and it was in this case not practical for the contractor to undertake the performance of other work which might absorb them. There is no exact method to determine the amount of such expenses to be allocated to any particular contract or part of a contract. It has been held a number of times that it is not necessary to prove a specific amount, but only to determine a fair allocation for the purpose of compensating a contractor for delay by the Government. *Fred R. Comb Co. v. U.S.,* 103 Ct.Cls. 174, 184 (1945); *B. W. Construction Co. v. U.S.,* 104 Ct.Cls. 608, 643-644 (1945), *cert. den.* 327 U.S. 785; *Irwin & Leighton v. U.S.,* 101 Ct.Cls. 455, 481 (1944); *Brand Investment Co. v. U.S.,* 102 Ct.Cls. 40, 58 F.Supp. 749 (1944), cert. den. 324 U. S. 850.

Appellant has based its claim on an allocation of the total recorded main office expense to the contract in the ratio of contract billings to total billings for the period of performance. The resulting determination of a contract allocation is divided into a daily rate, which is multiplied by the number of days of delay to arrive at the amount of the claim. This method of computation relies primarily on the duration of the suspension as the criterion for allocating the contract expenses of the main office. The same formula has been used by the Court of Claims in *Fred R. Combs Co. v. U.S.,* 103 Ct. Cls. 174, 181, 183-184 (1945); *Houston Ready-Cut House Co. v. U.S.,* (Ct.Cls. 1951) 96 F.Supp. 639, 119 Ct.Cls. 120, 172-173, 192-193 (1951). In other cases, the daily rate and total for the delay period have been determined after allocation of contract overhead according to monthly gross, *B. W. Construction Co. v. U.S.,* 104 Ct.Cls. 608, 643-644 (1945), *cert. den.* 327 U. S. 785, or cost of work, *Irwin & Leighton v. United States,* 106 Ct. Cls. 398, 431, 457, 65 F.Supp. 794, 800 (1946); *Anthony P. Miller, Inc. v. U.S.,* 111 Ct. Cls. 252, 321-322, 329-330, 337, 77 F.Supp. 209 (1948); *S. C. Sachs v. U.S.,* 104 Ct. Cls. 372, 379-383, 386, 394, 63 F.Supp 59 (1945); *James Stewart & Co., Inc. v. U.S.,* 105 Ct. Cls. 284, 321, 330, 63 F.Supp. 653 (1946); *Henry Ericsson Co. v. U.S.,* 104 Ct.Cls. 397, 414-415, 423, 427-428, 62 F.Supp. 312 (1945).

The government raised various objections to the principles and techniques involved in the contractor's method of computation. For one thing, the government claimed that the contractor had not proved that the overhead rate had increased during the suspension period. The board noted, however, that the point involved was not an increase in overhead rates, but rather that the overhead continued during the period of suspension. It noted that "it had, however, been sufficiently demonstrated by the mere fact of prolongation of the time of performance, and the continuation of main office expenses, that more of such expenses were incurred during the period of performance than would have been except for the suspension."

The government raised as another objection the point that the contractor had been inconsistent in using various methods of computation before the final determination that led to this appeal. The board did not recognize the objection as relevant. The government objected to the use of total contract billings in the computation since the suspension applied to only about one-half of the work. The board found, however, that it was appropriate to use the entire contract as a measure of the entire overhead allocable to the contract. Near the close of its decision, the board stated:

The Government supports its computations on the basis that it is the normal accounting practice in construction contracts to apply the company overhead factor to direct costs. It suggests that the excess overhead in the period of suspension, when there were little or no direct costs, should be the difference between actual overhead computed on that basis and overhead that would have been incurred had there been no suspension, and the direct costs had been incurred when they should have been. The formula suggested on this basis, however, does no more than redistribute the indirect costs actually incurred, without taking into account those additional indirect costs which are incurred during and because of the suspension periods. The Government's theory stresses the conventional percentage relationships between overhead and direct costs, and between the Government contract work and the commercial work. On the other hand, the very nature of this claim is such that these relationships must of necessity be distorted because of the relatively small direct costs incurred during and as a result of the period of delay.

In the following pages, we have reviewed a number of judicial rulings in the 1970s and 1980s, most of which have accepted Eichleay, despite opposition led by DCAA, so long as this method was used in appropriate circumstances and applied in the manner originally approved. Since the rulings by the Court of Appeals for the Federal Circuit in *Capital Electric Company v. U.S.* and *Savoy Construction Company, Inc. v. U.S.* in 1984, the remaining doubts about Eichleay have evaporated.

In *Robert McMullen & Son, Inc.*, ASBCA No. 19023, 76-1 BCA par. 11,728, it appears that the board itself selected the Eichleay method. A review of that decision reveals that the formula was completely consistent with the one in the original *Eichleay* decision and differed in many respects from the formula set forth in DCAA's audit guidance. The same observations are applicable to the board's decision in the appeal of *Charles W. Schroyer, Inc.*, ASBCA No. 21859, 78-2 BCA par. 13,513.

The appeal of *Essex Electro Engineers, Inc.*, ASBCA No. 21066, 79-2 BCA par. 14,035, aff'd on rec. 79-2 BCA par. 14,151, is of special interest in illustrating the acceptance of the Eichleay formula in manufacturing situations. One of the major issues in the dispute was the contractor's use of Eichleay. The DCAA auditor understood the methodology used by Essex and, according to the decision, admitted it was a recognized method of determining unabsorbed burden. However, the auditor preferred, and his preference was supported by the contracting officer, to use the Allegheny formula.

In view of the lengthy stretchout of the contract, Essex also claimed burden fluctuation expense to compensate the company for having performed in a higher cost period than originally bargained for in entering into the contract. In the words of the board,

This is distinguishable from the unabsorbed burden claim which is simply requiring other in-house work to be reduced with respect to the overhead allocation forced upon such work by the delay in the performance of this contract. The auditor considered the two burden claims to be duplications of each other. The auditor agreed that if the claim is to be allowed that the appellant's computation is the correct method to use. We find the claim allowable.

We found portions of the decision particularly clear and persuasive and cite them below with a suggestion that they warrant careful reading. Attention is especially invited to the board's dismissal of the auditor's preference for the exclusive use of the Allegheny method over the Eichleay method for computing unabsorbed overhead for manufacturing operations as immaterial to the allowance of this element of the claim. In this regard, the board noted that it used Eichleay in prior cases involving manufacturing operations.

We also invite attention to the board's conclusion that the government failed to support a contention of duplication between the unabsorbed burden and burden fluctuation. Salient aspects of the decision are quoted below:

> This claim is predicated upon the Changes clause of the contract which clearly envisions the difference between the original contract cost and the cost incurred as a result of Government changes as the proper measurement of the equitable adjustment due. The weight of authority holds that it is the reasonable cost of both the unchanged and the changed work which must be employed to the extent it can be gleaned from available records and pertinent financial data. *Itek Corp. Applied Technology Division,* ASBCA Nos. 13528, 13848, 71-1 BCA par. 8906.

> In general, an administrative determination of the amount due as an equitable adjustment constitutes a question of fact. The contractor appellant has the burden of proof. However, it need only meet this proof burden by a preponderance of the evidence. *Teledyne McCormick-Selph v. The U.S.* [25 CCF par. 82,891], 588 F.2d 808 Ct.Cl. (1979).

> Proof of quantum need not be exact. Damages need not be proven with absolute certainty or mathematical certitude. It is sufficient if a reasonable basis for computation is furnished provided liability, causation and injury are established as we have found under the entitlement case presented by the appellant. *Wunderlich Contracting Co. v. The U.S.* [11 CCF par. 80,069], 173 Ct.Cl. 180, 199-200 (1965).

*   *   *   *

> The appellant's method of computing burden may have been objectionable to the auditor but this also is immaterial since the appellant's methodology was its norm and previously approved by the Government.

> The auditor also may prefer the exclusive use of the Allegheny method of computing unabsorbed overhead for manufacturing facilities rather than the Eichleay method but this preference also is immaterial to the allowance of this element of the claim. The auditor contends that the Allegheny method more properly applies to manufacturing facilities and the Eichleay method only to construction claims. This Board, however, has recognized the applicability of the Eichleay method to manufacturing facilities in the *Appeal of Therm-Air Mfg. Co., Inc.,* ASBCA 16453, 73-1 BCA par. 9983 and the *Appeal of Allied Materials and Equipment Co.,* ASBCA No. 17318, 75-1 BCA par. 11,150. See also *Public Contract Newsletter,* Vol. 9, No. 2, January 1974, Recovery of Unabsorbed Overhead.

> We are not persuaded that a claim for unabsorbed burden expense is duplicated by a claim for burden fluctuation. No proof was presented as

to this Government contention. Only the auditor's unsupported statement that this is so appears in the record. A claim for unabsorbed burden expense is really for a decrease in allocability to the other in-house work performed during the scheduled period of the original contract perform- ance, which other work bore too great a portion of the plant's indirect costs because of the delay associated with the incurrence of direct labor and materials. *Allied Materials and Equipment Co., Inc.*, ASBCA No. 17318, 75-1 BCA par. 11,150.

Burden fluctuation is a claim based upon the necessity to perform the original contract work in a later time period in which increased costs were incurred, a reasonable result of the Government caused delay.

The Government's defense of this claim is based upon an unreasona- ble refusal to accept responsibility for the delayed performance; unfounded assumptions that claimed expenses are unallowable; a prefer- ence for a different methodology of computing burden without establish- ing that the one used was improper and an unsupported claim that burden fluctuation duplicates unabsorbed burden.

The Government's evident dislike of the appellant's claim is not a sufficient basis for disallowance. We are persuaded that the appellant has computed its claim in a reasonable manner and on a reasonable basis. This presumption of reasonableness has not been rebutted. The Govern- ment's failure to rebut the claim as modified requires us to conclude that it is the correct equitable adjustment due this appellant.

The virtually unbroken series of decisions supporting the use of the Eichleay method continued in two appeals decided in September 1980. In *Schindler Haughton Elevator Corporation*, GSBCA No. 5390, 80-2 BCA par. 14,671, the government had admitted responsibility for a 325-day delay in Schindler's access to the work site to manufacture and install elevators in a government building. Schindler calculated its unabsorbed home office over- head costs attributable to the delay on the basis of the Eichleay method. As the board pointed out, the government initially opposed the use of Eichleay "on the ground that any decision to use the formula was an unwarranted restriction on the scope of its defense. At the hearing, however, the Govern- ment abandoned its opposition to the use of the Eichleay method and presented no alternative formula. *In fact, the Government used the 'Eichleay Formula' to arrive at what it contended was the proper quantum of adjust- ment of the appellant's claim.*"

Unabsorbed overhead was again an issue in the appeal of *Salt City Contractors, Ltd.*, VACAB No. 1362, 80-2 BCA par. 14,713. One of the major issues in dispute was a delay of 266 calendar days caused by the government's late delivery of government-furnished equipment.

Salt City Contractors computed the delay costs by the use of the Eichleay formula, and we found the following excerpt from the decision significant:

> The Government does not object to this method, which has been held by this and other Boards to be an established and acceptable method of approximating home office expenses allocable to a particular job and the duration of a particular period of performance.

A controversy then ensued over the nature of overhead that should be used in the formula, with the government holding that only fixed overhead expenses should be considered while Salt City Contractors argued that both fixed and variable expenses should be used.

The home office overhead for the contract period as calculated by the contractor included over two dozen individual expense accounts approximating $300,000. The government disputed all but four items amounting to about $100,000: depreciation, utilities, officers' salaries, and rent.

The board expressed the view that "the equitable results sought by utilization of the Eichleay formula may be distorted by including in the computation home office expenses which vary *substantially* with the degree of performance of work." (Emphasis added.) However, the board did not find that any of the expenses included by Salt City "are variable to such an extent that they should be excluded."

The board cited with approval the ASBCA ruling in the appeal of *Eichleay Corporation:*

> There is no exact method to determine the amount of such (home office) expenses to be allocated to any particular contract or part of a contract. It has been held a number of times that it is not necessary to prove a specific amount but only to determine a fair allocation for the purpose of compensating a contractor for delay by the Government.

The board's following commentary with particular regard to fixed and variable expenses is especially pertinent and is cited below (footnotes excluded):

> The *Eichleay* formula for computing overhead expenses of the contractor during periods of delay was based on a formula used by the Court of Claims. A review of those cases, cited by the Armed Services Board of Contract Appeals in its decision in the appeal of *Eichleay Corp.,* disclosed that although the Court at times rejected certain items claimed as allocable home office expense, *no absolute distinction was made between costs which were fixed and costs which were* variable, as defined by the Government in the appeal we have before us.

> The *Eichleay* formula, in determining an average daily rate of home office expense, uses the total home office expense incurred during the period of performance. This necessarily includes some costs which may vary during such period. Even those costs which the Government defines as "fixed" costs may vary. For example, the rent for office space may increase or decrease, and the utility bills certainly vary, but these are, without question, allocable overhead cost items. It is generally accepted that the Eichleay formula is used primarily for construction contracts, where there is an assumption that almost all overhead is fixed rather than variable, but *this is not to say that overhead costs which do not remain constant are to be excluded solely on this basis.* The Goverment contends that any costs for which the contractor has an option as to how much, if anything, it will incur, are to be excluded. Such a position is in direct contradiction to the cost principles contained in Part 1-15 of the Federal Procurement Regulations (FPR), which are applicable to this contract in

accordance with Clause 20 of the General Provisions. For example, the Government would reject such costs as dues and subscriptions, or advertising which, with certain qualifications, are allowable under the FPR cost principles. (Emphasis added.)

In its final decision, the board allowed all of the expenses other than those that it found specifically unallowable under the provisions of FPR 1-15.205, such as interest and donations.

Kemmons-Wilson, Inc., and South & Patton, Inc., ASBCA No. 16167, 72-2 BCA par. 9689

The contractor prevailed on the major issue, which involved the use of the Eichleay formula. A portion of the claim, however, relating to certain jobsite expenses was denied. The board ruled that the cost of the home office was "almost 100% a fixed expense, and will not vary solely because one job out of many is running longer than expected." Jobsite expenses were found to include both fixed and variable expenses, and the latter were not considered appropriate for reimbursement.

Propserv, Inc., ASBCA No. 20768, 78-1 BCA par. 13,066

The contractor's claim for an equitable adjustment was based on the Eichleay formula, which the government rejected. The pertinent portion of the decision in favor of Propserv is quoted below:

> Turning first to the method of allocation of the unabsorbed G&A expense, we note that the respondent's position is similar to the position taken by the Government in the appeal of *Kurz & Root Company, Inc.,* ASBCA No. 14665, 72-2 BCA par. 9552, wherein we stated:
>
>> The Navy agrees that unabsorbed overhead amounted to $11,604, but it argues that K&R should not recover unabsorbed general and administrative expense 'since general and administrative expenses, under generally accepted accounting principles, are relatively stable costs applicable to total company operations irrespective of the nature of individual production jobs.' We do not follow this argument. If the claim is for 'unabsorbed' expense, it is really for a decrease in allocability to other work, which bore too great a proportion of all indirect costs because of the disruption and delay. In this aspect, general and administrative expense stands on the same footing as other overhead expense.
>
> Hence, the fact that no specific increase in G&A expenses has been shown herein is immaterial. We find the "Eichleay" method employed by the appellant to allocate these expenses as a function of time to be particularly appropriate in cases of suspension of work where the direct costs incurred are minimal or non-existent. This formula, as used in the appellant's complaint and set out above, has been cited with approval and used in numerous construction cases. (Cf. *Robert McMullan & Son, Inc.,* ASBCA No. 19023, 76-1 BCA par. 11,728; *Eichleay Corp.,* ASBCA No. 5183, 60-2 BCA par. 2688) We find this method to be appropriate for implementation herein.

Charles W. Schroyer, ASBCA No. 21859, 78-2 BCA par. 13,513

The following excerpts of the decision are pertinent:

Since the parties eliminated the question of entitlement as an issue before the Board, the sole question is the amount, if any, to which appellant is entitled for such delay. The major dispute concerns overhead as the result of Government-caused delay in contract completion for 67 days, 31 January - 7 April 1976. Appellant has used the so-called "Eichleay" formula to compute the amount. The Government challenges both the use of the "Eichleay" formula, and, if we use such approach, the figures used by appellant in its calculations for the total contract billings for the period and for the overhead figure to which the formula is applied. Further, the Government argues appellant was able to utilize the labor on other contracts and that if we allow any amount it should be based on application of labor by appellant rather than on billings.

First, we will address the use of the formula itself. Most of the arguments offered by respondent have been made on numerous occasions before the Board and previously answered. See *Proserv. Inc.,* ASBCA No. 20768, 78-1 BCA par. 13,066; *Robert McMullan & Son, Inc.,* ASBCA No. 19023, 76-1 BCA par. 11,728; *Eichleay Corp.,* ASBCA No. 5183, 60-2 BCA ¶ 2688 and cases cited. The Government argues that appellant was able to utilize its direct labor elsewhere and, therefore, no overhead was unabsorbed. That begs the question since direct labor is only one of the costs involved in contract performance. The "Eichleay" formula has been developed to be used where direct costs are low or proof of actual allocation difficult or impossible. It is an effort to arrive at an approximate allocation. We conclude it is an appropriate approach to use here.

Dawson Construction Co., Inc., GSBCA No. 4956, 79-2 BCA par. 13,989

This appeal provides another example of the government vainly contesting the Eichleay method while offering alternative formulas designed to reduce the contractor's claim. The board's rejection of the government's argument was to the point:

. . . However, the Eichleay Formula is more precise than the method proposed by the Government which fails to take into consideration the period of delay over the term of the contract. Accordingly, we conclude that in the absence of a contractually-prescribed method for allocating overhead, the Eichleay formula is not only acceptable but preferable to the method proposed by the Government.

Excavation-Construction, Inc., ENG BCA No. 3858, 82-1 BCA par. 15,770, MFR denied, 83-1 BCA par. 16,203

The appeal involves delay in the construction of certain Washington Metrorail facilities. With respect to the claim for home office overhead, the government (Washington Metropolitan Area Transit Authority) objected to the use of the Eichleay formula on the grounds that the prime contractor ". . . has not proved that home office overhead was affected by the delay, either by increasing it or by causing it to be less than fully absorbed." The board put down this argument by ruling that it was satisfied that ". . . the record here clearly establishes that the share of home office overhead reasonably allocable to the instant contract was not, and could not feasibly have been, absorbed by substituted work during this relatively short period of delay."

The Authority then tried another form of argument against Eichleay, saying it might not be "unreasonable" but "home office overhead should preferably be based on a percentage of direct costs attributable to the delay, in accordance with 'the recognized method of allocation.' " But, the board was equally unimpressed with this argument and found the use of Eichleay more appropriate "in dealing with a suspension or delay where, in the extreme case, direct job costs may nearly have ceased while overhead costs continued unabated." Citing case law, the board further said: "Home office expense accumulates at a more or less constant rate over a given span of time regardless of how much direct job input cost a suspended contractor may be able to prove."

The government's motion for reconsideration centered entirely on its request that "the board declare that home office overhead costs should not be allowed for failure to prove that any such costs were affected by the delay." Most of the Authority's arguments and the cases it cited were repetitive of those originally presented. However, although it would not normally present the detailed discussion in a motion for reconsideration, it elected to do so here in view of the Authority's great interest in this point and the fact that the issue was covered in an abbreviated form in the original decision.

The board reiterated that the government caused delay was well supported as was the fact that both the prime and subcontractor remained mobilized. Further supported was the fact that the uncertainty as to when the notice to proceed would be issued was attributable solely to the government. In the circumstances, said the board, "it is abundantly clear . . . that E-C and Dyghton could not feasibly have obtained substitute work during the delay period to absorb the home office overhead reasonably allocable to this period." The board further ruled:

> It is not necessary that they show futile attempts to obtain other work which somehow could have been substituted for this major project during this relatively short and uncertain period of delay . . . .

Some of the cases cited in rebuttal by the Authority were not considered germane. In *W.G. Cornell Co., etc. v. Ceramic Coating Co.*, 626 F.2d 990 (D.C. Dir. 1980), the trial court found that overhead costs are not automatically recovered in delay situations and that the plaintiff had failed to show that the delay had affected its operations. The court of claims "observed that there was *scant evidence* in the record of how the delay had affected the plaintiff's operations and that there was no basis to conclude that the trial court's findings were clearly erroneous." (Emphasis added). Here and elsewhere, the Corps of Engineers Board and other authorities would go so far as to require a showing that a delay did affect a company in the sense that overhead costs continued and additional work to absorb such overhead could not be readily obtained. Once this point is reasonably established, the Eichleay formula is generally accepted.

Referring further to *W.G. Cornell,* the board noted: "The Court of Appeals expressly recognized that home office overhead could be awarded under appropriate circumstances," citing *Brand Investment Co. v. United States* (2 CCF par. 826), 102 Ct.Cl. 40, 58 F.Supp. 749 (1944). In that decision, the court said,

> We are allowing the plaintiff a proportionate part of main office overhead. While such an element of damage can never be proved with mathematical precision, it is standard accounting practice to attribute main office expense to various company operations on some fair basis.

The government also cited *Berley Industries, Inc. v. City of New York,* 385 N.E.2d 281, 45 N.Y.2d 683 (1978), a decision "discovered" by some government agencies and cited in an effort to defeat Eichleay. *Berley* has not been favorably received by most boards and courts. Some of the reasons are indicated in the following comments by the Corps of Engineers Board:

> Only a small portion of the work remained to be done at the beginning of a 335-day delay period for which recovery of overhead was sought, and there was no evidence of how the delay had affected the plaintiff's operations. Nevertheless, the trial court had allowed the issue to go to the jury based simply on testimony about the *Eichleay* formula. The principal opinion of the New York Court of Appeals does appear to be critical of the *Eichleay* formula itself. However, it is clear that the formula had been misused in the trial court and that the facts rather than the formula justified reversal. Indeed, three judges of the Court of Appeals concurred on that basis, even observing that the *Eichleay* formula might appropriately be used upon retrial if a suitable foundation were laid.

As indicated earlier, the government seemed to have pulled out all stops in its efforts to deny the prime and subcontractors recovery of home office overhead. It cited, for example, *Kansas City Bridge Co. v. Kansas City Str. Steel Co.,* 317 S.W.2d 370, 377 (1958), where the court denied recovery of home office overhead during the delay period apparently because the plaintiff failed to present sufficient proof that "... but for the delay, the plaintiff would have obtained other work sufficient in amount to have absorbed the portion of the overhead allocated." However, the board noted that this decision had been considered "exacting" by some courts and "rejected as an aberration by others." e.g., *Southern New England Contracting Company v. State,* 165 Conn. 644, 345 A.2d 550 (1974).

Capital Electric Company, GSBCA Nos. 5316, et al., 83-2 BCA par. 16,548

The Eichleay formula has survived for over two decades, but the survival has been made difficult and complex at times by several factors. As mentioned previously, government contractors, boards of contract appeals, and federal courts have been subjected to a barrage of rhetoric by government auditors and others seeking to discredit this method and substitute a variety of alternative calculations, all characterized by a common objective—the reduction of the contractor's claim. Second, some contractors have unfortunately viewed Eichleay as a kind of magic wand, which, when waved, will provide automatic recoveries of funds in contract delays regardless of the circumstances and regardless of the manner in which the claims are presented and supported. Where the Eichleay formula is used in inappropriate circumstances, contractors will not prevail and, most unfortunately, such cases are subsequently cited by government opponents in efforts to defeat valid claims based on this formula.

Another factor which formerly raised obstacles to the survival of Eichleay is the occasional decision which collegial judicial and quasi-judicial bodies view as aberrations. All of these factors, in various degrees, appear to have been present in *Capital Electric Company,* a decision by the General Services Board of Contract Appeals, later reversed by the Federal Circuit in Capital Electric Co. v. U.S., CA FC No. 83-965 [31 CCF par. 72, 119] and remanded back to the GSBCA for favorable treatment April 18, 1984, 84-2 BCA par. 17351.

The contractor was awarded a contract to furnish and install electrical, mechanical, and plumbing work within a federal building that was under construction. When the work was completed, the parties stipulated that Capital was unreasonably delayed for 303 days. The issues before the board related to quantum, both as to Capital's claim and the claims of its first and second tier subcontractors. While a number of controversies were involved, we have confined our analysis to Capital's claim for "extended home office overhead."

Capital calculated its extended home office overhead by using a "modified" Eichleay formula based on the May 1975 DCAA pamphlet (DCAAP 7641.45). As an alternative, the contractor used the formula accepted in *Eichleay Corp.,* ASBCA No. 5183, 60-2 BCA par. 2688, aff'd. 61-1 BCA par. 2894.

The government auditors of course rejected the Eichleay concept, even in its modified form, and argued that ". . . if appellant's home office overhead had been affected by the conceded delay, any damage that might have occurred in 1977 had been eliminated in 1978 when the contract work shifted into that accounting period had significantly reduced what he took to be the normal rates of allocation of home office overhead." The auditor similarly ran roughshod over the subcontractors' claims for extended home office overhead, leading the contractor to characterize the auditor's report and testimony as a "kamikaze mission to discredit a valid, supportable claim."

The GSBCA seemed to have approached this case as if it had been assigned a mission to revise and rewrite the legal, technical, economic, and accounting principles of delay claims. It identified underabsorbed overhead as applicable to "manufacturing cost accounting" and "extended overhead" as "a concept unique to construction contracting." The direction of the decision was evident early on in the assertion that extended overhead "has as its premise (a false premise, as it turns out) that extending the performance period will increase overhead costs." In labeling this premise as a false one, the board castigates the many federal judges and administrative judges who have explicitly accepted this premise for over 40 years. Included among these judicial authorities was the General Services Board of Contract Appeals itself which, on the very same project but involving the structural concrete phase, embraced this concept and the Eichleay formula in *Dawson Construction Co.,* GSBCA No. 4956, 79-2 BCA par. 13,989.

Nor was *Dawson* the only instance of GSBCA's acceptance of the premise and the Eichleay formula. There have been many others, two of which were referred to in this decision: *Marlin Associates, Inc.*, GSBCA No. 5663, 82-1 BCA par. 15,739, and *Schindler Haughton Elevator Corp.*, GSBCA No. 5390, 80-2 BCA par. 14,671. It is to be noted that the three decisions referred to above are hardly ancient. However, these precedents and the many reflected in the decisions of the ASBCA, other administrative boards, and federal courts bothered this panel not at all. "We expressly overrule our previous determination to the contrary in *Dawson . . .*" stated the ruling.

Formulating a decision that would achieve a breach with the 40-year precedent of judicial and quasi-judicial rulings was not easy. The GSBCA was forced to acknowledge its finding in *Dawson* "that the concept of recovery of extended home office overhead during periods of delay had its origin in *Fred R. Comb Co. v. United States*, 103 Ct.Cl. 174, 183 (1945), and that the *"Eichleay formula was simply an appropriate method for calculating extended home office overhead."* (Emphasis added). The board further acknowledged that "*Comb* was not a departure from existing law on recovery of breach damages due to performance delay. It was preceded by *Brand Investment Co. v. United States* [2 CCF 826], 102 Ct.Cl. 40, 44, 58 F.Supp. 749, 751 (1944), and *Coath & Goss, Inc. v. The United States* [2 CCF 844], 101 Ct.Cl. 702, 710 (1944). There are other and older cases but further citation would not be useful."

Having thus established the clear precedent for granting recovery of extended home office overhead in instances of performance suspension, the board found that Capital reflected a performance extension; however, said the board, "we do not think that such a distinction is meaningful, for the truth of the matter is that even in cases of performance suspension, home office overhead is seldom affected." So, suddenly, the board turned the precedent of 40 years of case law on its head.

The board then assumed the role of accounting experts and stated:

The daily rate concept of recovery of extended overhead that *Eichleay* represents comports with neither the pervasive principles nor the broad operating principles that encompass generally accepted accounting principles.

The board's brief attempt at an accounting treatise failed to provide any authoritative reference or support for its sweeping conclusion. This failure is hardly surprising inasmuch as the accounting profession, including the American Institute of Certified Public Accountants (AICPA) and the Financial Accounting Standards Board (FASB), has not promulgated accounting principles for computing the costs incurred by a contractor where contract performance is delayed.

Searching further for support for its revisionist conclusion, the board stated: "The matters that we adjudicate, claims under federal contracts, are governed by federal law . . . . Our rule of decision has as one of its sources the common law . . . . Our analysis thus far convinces us that the common law of construction contracts permits the recovery of underabsorbed home office overhead and precludes the recovery of extended home office overhead." Details as to the precise nature to the "common law of construction contracts" and the circumstances under which it supersedes the "federal law" of federal construction contracts were not provided.

Capital Electric Company v. The United States, CA FC No. 83-965, 31 CCF par. 72,119

After the incredible decision in *Capital Electric Co.* by the General Services Board of Contract Appeals, some observers became apprehensive that this ruling might influence other tribunals. These apprehensions were allayed before long. Some four months later, the Veterans Administration Board of Contract Appeals sustained an appeal for delay damages in *Ascani Construction & Realty Company,* VABCA Nos. 1572, 1584, 83-2 BCA par. 16,635. Significantly, the dispute involved a construction contract, and the Eichleay formula, which formed the basis for computing the amount allowed the contractor, was used originally by the government contracting officer.

Five months later, another appeal involving government-caused delays on a construction contract was decided with quantum based on the Eichleay formula. *Miles Construction,* VABCA No. 1674, November 30, 1983, 84-1 BCA par. 16,967. As in *Ascani,* the use of the Eichleay formula was initiated by the government. There were no signs that the curious trumpet call sounded by the GSBCA panel had persuaded anyone to follow.

But, the real blow to the presumptuous GSBCA ruling came on February 7, 1984, when its decision was overturned by the U.S. Court of Appeals for the Federal Circuit in *Capital Electric Company v. The United States,* CA FC No. 83-965, 31 CCF par. 72,119.

The court pointed out that both the government and the GSBCA had recognized that the Eichleay formula "has been the prevailing method adopted by the appeals boards" and the GSBCA itself had approved this method "in *Dawson Construction Co., Inc.* GSBCA No. 4956, 79-2 BCA par. 13,989 at 68,635 (1979), for the structural concrete phase of the same Fort Lauderdale project at issue here . . . ." It also noted the more recent Corps of Engineers Board of Contract Appeals decision in *Excavation-Construction, Inc.,* ENG BCA No. 3858, 82-1 BCA par. 15,770, at 78,068 (1982), also permitted the use of Eichleay for computing extended home office overhead.

The GSBCA had attempted to find support for its views in *Savoy Construction Company, Inc.,* ASBCA No. 21218 *et al.,* 80-1 BCA par. 14,392, recon. denied, 80-2 BCA par. 14,724, affirmed by the Claims Court, 2 Cl.Ct. 338 (1983). However, in an unpublished ruling on February 7, 1984, concurrently with its decision in *Capital Electric,* the Court of Appeals for the Federal Circuit reversed the Claims Court and remanded the case for further proceedings in the light of its ruling in *Capital Electric.*

The court took cognizance of the GSBCA observations in *Capital Electric* and the government's arguments "that an automatic application of the Eichleay formula allows a contractor to escape the burden of proof faced by all claimants, namely: establishing the facts of injury." But the court was not persuaded and we quote the following from the Discussion portion of its opinion:

> Although these points have some degree of validity, we are not persuaded that they correctly reflect the concept of the Eichleay formula, at least as far as Capital is concerned. In this case, *compensable* delay was stipulated before the board. Moreover, Capital introduced unrebut-

ted evidence that it could not have taken on any large construction jobs during the various delay periods due to the uncertainty of the delays and (except after the original contract period, when a major portion of the project had been completed and accepted) due to the limitation on its bonding capacity.[4] Thus, Capital has not actually used an *ipso facto* approach. Indeed, as stated in *Eichleay,* 61-1 BCA par. 2894 at 15,117: "The mere showing of these facts[5] is sufficient to transfer to the Government the burden of going forward with proof that Appellant suffered no loss or should have suffered no loss." Amicus American Subcontractors Association stated: "When the evidence adequately proves the existence of damages owing to a delay in work on the project, the extent of those damages need not be quantified to a mathematical certainty," citing *Story Parchment Co. v. Paterson Parchment Paper Co., 282* U.S. 555 (1931). [footnote not reproduced—CCH.]

Although the board recognized that calculation of contract damages is difficult and admitted that the method it used is an approximation, it faults the Eichleay formula for not being precise. Amicus Associated General Contractors of America points to a basic flaw in the method of calculation applied by the board ... in a case where no work is being performed during a suspension, for example, and application of a percentage overhead charge (e.g. 9.2) to the direct costs of work performed (zero) would produce zero for overhead that nonetheless continues on.[6] Capital lists examples of such overhead: weekly payrolls, Davis-Bacon reports, checks, W-2's, 941's and other required tax forms, cost records, review submittals from subcontractors, weekly and monthly progress reports to the Government, and "the myriad similar tasks which are as critical as the on-site work but which can more easily be performed at a central location." Amicus American Subcontractors Association adds: salaries, dues and subscriptions, auto and travel, telephone, and photocopying. [footnote not reproduced—CCH.]

Capital argues that the *Comb* decision remains binding precedent with regard to Government contracts, citing *Luria Brothers & Co. v. United States,* 369 F.2d 701, 709-10 (Ct.Cl. 1966) and *J.D. Hedin Construction Co. v. United States* [10 CCF par. 73,076], 347 F.2d 235, 259 (Ct.Cl. 1965). It asserts that the board had "no authority to disregard the binding precedents established by the Court of Claims." However, in fairness it should be said that if the board believed these precedents were wrongly decided, it was not improper for the board to act accordingly. At the same time, it must be recognized that, as held by the Court of Appeals for the Federal Circuit, sitting *en banc, South Corporation v. United States,* 690 F.2d 1368 (1982), these Court of Claims precedents are binding precedent and can only be overruled by the Federal Circuit sitting *en banc.*[7] [footnote not reproduced—CCH.]

As far as this panel is concerned, we do not believe these precedents should be overruled. They are of such long standing and have been followed in so many decisions of the various boards of contract appeals that such action should more properly be taken by the Congress. Nor are we persuaded that this would be an appropriate case for breaking precedent. [Emphasis added].

In concluding its decision, the court noted that Capital had proposed that its damages be calculated according to a modified Eichleay formula or, alternatively, according to the original Eichleay formula. The court decided that Capital's damages should be computed according to the basic Eichleay formula but approved an "Eichleay-type" formula for two of the subcontractors where the differences were negligible.

One of the three judges concurred but submitted a separate opinion, the major thrust of which seemed to be that Eichleay was well-established and that there was no reason to invite the full court to reconsider the decision *en banc.* Judge Friedman's concurring opinion is instructive. Because it does add some points to the basic opinion and because this decision is so important to the government contracting community, we quote it in full below:

> Although I agree with the court that the appellant is entitled to recover, the analysis through which I reach that conclusion differs somewhat from that of the court.

> For almost 40 years the Court of Claims consistently has held that the delay damages a government contractor may recover include extended home office overhead incurred during the period of delay. The leading case is *Fred R. Comb Co. v. United States,* 103 Ct.Cl. 174 (1945), which the court subsequently followed and approved a number of times. E.g., *Luria Brothers & Co. v. United States,* 369 F.2d 701, 709-10 (Ct.Cl. 1966); *J.D. Hedin Construction Co. v. United States* [10 CCF par. 73,076], 347 F.2d 235, 359 (Ct.Cl. 1965). Similarly, the various boards of contract appeals repeatedly allowed the recovery of this element of delay damages.

> The government now asks us to jettison this settled line of authority on the ground that all of those cases were wrongly decided. It argues that since the delay in performance ordinarily does not increase the total amount of office overhead the contractor incurs in connection with the particular contract, but merely spreads it over a longer period, allowing the contractor to recover for such overhead for the period of delay would result in compensating the contractor for losses it did not actually incur. According to the government, the only situations in which a contractor may recover for such extended office overhead is where the delay in performance: (1) requires the contractor to hire additional personnel or incur other additional expenses; or (2) prevents the contractor from taking on other work it would have been able to assume had there not been the delay.

> Although superficially plausible, the government's argument does not withstand more penetrating analysis based upon the theory on which extended office overhead is allowed as an element of delay damages. By definition this type of overhead cannot be directly attributed to the performance of a particular contract, yet it is an essential part of the contractor's total cost of doing business. Some basis, therefore, must be found for allocating this total overhead among the various contracts in connection with which it is incurred.

> A contractor's estimate of its costs necessarily includes its overhead costs, which it calculates on the basis of the time required to perform the

contract. Where performance of a contract has been delayed, the overhead expenses of performing that contract continue for the additional time. A portion of the total overhead for that additional period accordingly is allocable as a cost of performing that contract.

As the Court of Claims explained in *Comb,*

> It would not be expected that a contractor would enlarge his main office staff and facilities at a time when one of his jobs was merely marking time. But unless his office was understaffed before the suspension, it too would, *pro tanto,* mark time during the suspension, unless the useful work which it would have been doing in regard to this job, if the job had not been suspended, had been replaced by extra work made necessary by the suspension. So the fact that no extra help was hired seems both natural and immaterial. If some employees had been laid off, that would have been material, since it would have enabled the contractor to pay the full staff which he would need during the extra time that the work was in process, because of the delay, with the money he had saved by laying off employees during the period of suspension.

> But it is, ordinarily, not practicable to lay off main office employees during a short and indefinite period of delay such as occurred here. So the contractor, instead of saving the salary of that proportion of his main office staff which is attributable to this contract is obliged, in effect, to waste it, and to spend a similar amount at the end of the contract for the extra time made necessary by the delay. This waste is caused by the breach of contract, and it ought to be paid for by the party guilty of the breach.

103 Ct.Cl. at 183-84.

In other words, a portion of the overhead incurred during the entire period of performance must be charged against the revenue received during that period as a cost of performing the contract. The Court of Claims decisions, as well as the Eichleay formula used to calculate the amount of such extended office overhead, are based upon and reflect the economic realities of the construction business. I think those decisions are correct, and I see no reason for the panel (which is bound by those decisions) to invite the full court to reconsider them en banc.

The court did not dismiss the arguments that the automatic application of Eichleay could allow a contractor to escape the burden of proof of establishing the fact of injury. It found, however, that these circumstances did not prevail in Capital's case, and that the company had demonstrated that it was unable to take on large construction jobs during the various periods of government-caused delays. On this basis, and quoting *Eichleay Corp.,* the court found that "[t]he mere showing of these facts is sufficient to transfer to the Government the burden of going forward with proof that Appellant suffered no loss or should have suffered no loss." This point, of course, is extremely significant because Eichleay opponents generally concentrate on placing the burden of proof of injury entirely on the contractor to prove with precision damages that cannot be calculated with precision. Because reasonable people recognize that damages are almost always suffered by contractors in delay situations, and because precise calculations have defied accountants, lawyers, and judges, the Eichleay formula is accepted as a reasonable approach to estimating such damages.

Aftermath of *Capital Electric* and *Savoy Construction* Rulings

The decisions of the Court of Appeals for the Federal Circuit in the above cases did not result in a sudden end to judicial rulings involving unabsorbed and extended overhead. For one thing, a number of controversies had proceeded too far at that time and for another, some government officials continued to seek ways of undermining equitable price adjustment claims computed by the Eichleay formula.

In *R.W. Contracting, Inc.*, ASBCA No. 24627, 84-2 BCA par. 17,302, although finding the particular circumstances inappropriate for the Eichleay formula, the board made this significant statement:

> The *Eichleay* formula furnishes a necessary surrogate for the normal accounting practice of applying an overhead rate to the appropriate direct cost base in situations where the contractor is delayed and direct costs that normally would have been incurred in the performance of the contract decreased or were eliminated during the period of delay. It is a practical and necessary expedient to compensate the contractor in situations where the direct cost base is eroded thus making use of the normal indirect cost allocation percentage rate inappropriate. Derivation of a daily overhead rate is merely a necessary substitute designed for such situations where achieving a more precise measurement is impracticable and/or use of the percentage rate on direct costs would be inequitable. The *Eichleay* formula is a time-honored means of approximating a "fair allocation" of unabsorbed indirect costs in situations where direct costs have been reduced during periods of compensable suspensions of work and its validity and efficacy recently have been reaffirmed by the Court of Appeals for the Federal Circuit. *Capital Electric Company v. United States* [31 CCF ¶ 72,119], Fed. Cir. No. 83-965, dec'd February 7, 1984.

In *Landgraf Construction Co.*, EBCA No. 286-4-83, 84-2 BCA par. 17,307, the government contested the claim for extended overhead on the ground that "Appellant has not demonstrated that its work was unfairly burdened by the increased overhead as required by application of *Eichleay*." The government also argued that Eichleay should be rejected based on the rulings in *Capital Electric* by GSBCA and *Savoy Construction Co., Inc. v. U.S.* by the U.S. Claims Court. However, the U.S. Court of Appeals for the Federal Circuit had reversed both decisions by the time the Department of Energy board handed down its decision. The EBCA stated:

> Evidence was introduced to show the disruptive effect of the delays to Klein's [subcontractor submitting claim through the prime] work and operations .... Additionally, Klein suffered inability to take on other work during the delay periods due to the uncertainty of the delays and to the effects which the delays and the retained payments had on its bonding capacity, as well as its bidding posture for additional work.

In *George E. Jensen Contractor, Inc.*, ASBCA No. 29772, 85-1 BCA par. 17,833, the government computed the adjustment for extended home office overhead by applying the contractor's audited overhead rate to the direct costs it had incurred during the delay period, whereas Jensen used the *Eichleay* formula.

The board stated that "[a]s appellant correctly points out, the Court of Appeals for the Federal Circuit specifically rejected the Government's method and approved the appellant's approach in *Capital Electric Co. v. United States* [31 CCF par. 72,119], 729 F.2d 743 (Fed. Cir. 1984)." It then noted the various arguments offered by the government and the bases for rejecting them.

The government would "distinguish *Capital Electric* by arguing that work under this contract was suspended under the Changes rather than the Suspension of Work clause and that equitable adjustments under the Changes clause for overhead are computed by a percentage markup to direct cost . . . ." This argument was rejected on the basis that "the delays incurred here . . . were pure delays where the Government caused a suspension of the work without changing either the sequence of performance or end product to be constructed under the contract."

Another argument offered by the government was that Jensen knew of the delays in advance and "should have planned for them." This contention was equally unsuccessful, the board finding that Jensen did not know exactly when the delays would occur, and the uncertainty, short periods of delay, etc., prevented the contractor from making any such plans.

The government's third argument was one which has been offered from time to time by contract auditors and discredited by the boards and federal courts. The board's succinct description of the argument and the basis for its rejection are quoted below:

> Finally, the Government argues that the home office or extended overhead costs are fixed costs which would have been incurred even if there had been no delay. Its argument continues that to allow relief by utilizing the *Eichleay* formula would permit recovery of overhead costs much greater than the direct costs incurred during the periods of delay.

> This argument misses the point. Home office expenses are indirect costs usually allocated to all of a contractor's contracts based upon each contract's incurred direct costs. When a Government caused delay causes a contractor's direct costs to decline greatly, that contract does not receive its fair share of the fixed home office expenses. The *Eichleay* formula is one method approved by boards and courts over a long period of time which corrects this distortion in the allocation of these indirect expenses.

The George Hyman Construction Co., ENG BCA No. 4541, 85-1 BCA par. 17,847, was one of a series of disputes between the Washington Metropolitan Area Transit Authority (WMATA) and a number of prime and subcontractors involved in the construction and extension of a rapid transit system in Washington, D.C. and neighboring Virginia and Maryland suburbs. WMATA continued to resist the application of the *Eichleay* formula even after most federal departments and agencies had accepted it.

The board observed that WMATA disputed the use of *Eichleay* for a number of reasons:

It contends that Hyman did not incur any additional overhead expense because its auditor was unable to determine that there was any "unabsorbed overhead." . . . A less absolute position is that Hyman should recover home office overhead only as a percentage mark-up of some direct costs. It suggests using other methods or hybrid methods because they would presumably produce lower figures.

This comment has a very familiar ring in view of the many experiences with government contract auditors who have offered various alternatives to *Eichleay*, apparently because those alternatives would provide lower recoveries for contractors. Although we have cited a number of other sound judicial opinions in support of *Eichleay*, we believe the following excerpt from this decision is worth reciting:

In a pure suspension situation where no work at all was being performed, WMATA's principle would result in the allocation to the suspended job of no charges whatsoever for the home office even though it would continue to function to perform its corporate responsibilities and accrue costs. The manifest unfairness of keeping a contractor engaged on, or liable to perform, a job but postponing or extending his performance well beyond what he had a right to expect and upon which he bid, demands a means of compensating him for his costs of operating his home office during such extended period. *Eichleay* represents such a method. It may not be the only possible method of doing so, but it is a tested and long judicially-approved method. *Capital Electric v. The United States, 729 F.2d 743 (1984).* The majority of the panel of the Court of Appeals for the Federal Circuit in the cited case places substantial emphasis on precedent in reaching its conclusion to overturn the General Service Board of Contract Appeals decision disavowing the *Eichleay* approach to extended home office overhead. While precedent is certainly for consideration, more fundamentally, we believe, *Eichleay* should be affirmed because it is a rational, workable, and fair way to approach a somewhat difficult conceptual problem. *Excavation Construction, Inc.* ENG BCA No. 3858, 82-1 BCA par. 15,770, 83-1 BCA par. 16,293; affirmed *sub nom. Excavation Construction, Inc. v. WMATA,* Civ. Action No. 83-1125 (D.C. DofC, June 21, 1984). This is what Judge Friedman is saying in his concurrence in *Capital Electric.* Some of the confusion engendered by recent debate over the use of *Eichleay* may be lessened if the principle is viewed properly as a method of allocation of an overhead (indirect cost) pool to a particular contract and among all contracts performed by a contractor. So viewing the *Eichleay* concept and formula largely answers questions about "increased" overhead because of a suspension—there are more overhead charges and higher allocation because of longer engagement on a contract; "unabsorbed" overhead—all overhead must be absorbed by the totality of work the contractor is performing and parceled out to the constituents of that totality; availability of or engagement in other work—other contracts performed by the contractor will increase the denominator of the allocation fraction and reduce the portion of overhead to be charged to a particular job.

Comments on another delay dispute are considered instructive in view of certain additional conclusions by the board in *Shirley Contracting Corp.,* ASBCA No. 29848, 85-1 BCA par. 17,858; aff'd 85-2 BCA par. 18,019.

Shirley's claim was audited by a DCAA auditor who rejected the contractor's use of the *Eichleay* formula and recommended an allowance of home office overhead based on applying a G&A rate to the jobsite costs during the period of delays. Unfortunately, the contracting officer accepted the DCAA advice. The board, however, rejected this approach, quoting the following from the court decision in *Capital Electric:*

> A basic flaw in the method of calculation applied by the board . . . in a case where no work is being performed during a suspension . . . the application of a percentage overhead . . . to the direct costs of work performed (zero) would produce zero overhead that nonetheless continues on.

In its motion for reconsideration, the government conceded the applicability of *Eichleay* but took issue with the number of days of delay previously stipulated by both parties.

One of the government challenges to the length of delay related to the board's finding in its initial decision that Shirley was "hampered by its overall bonding limitation to bid large projects." The government now pointed out that Shirley had in fact taken on three contracts in the $3-4 million range during the delay period.

In rejecting the government's motion, the board stated that Shirley's ability to bid on two of the contracts "was made possible by other projects it had completed . . . . The Government had nothing to do with those other projects. We see no reason why the Government should now benefit from the completion of those projects." It further stated that had Shirley been allowed to complete the delayed contract as scheduled, it would have been able to bid, and perhaps obtain, an additional large project. As to the third contract obtained, the board noted the award was not until the month of the government contract completion and the bonding arrangement authorized it only because the work would not start for months thereafter.

With further references to the two earlier contracts obtained by Shirley, the board stated they were "irrelevant to the determination of whether appellant was damaged by the Government-caused delays . . . . What is significant is the fact that without completing the [contract in dispute], appellant was unable to replace *that* project with another." [Emphasis in board's decision.]

It would appear that this ruling affirmed the view some of us have argued in the past and presented a new dimension in the opinion of others. The government particularly had asserted that so long as a contractor obtains new business, he can not demonstrate damages for which an equitable adjustment is called. In Shirley, the board properly refined the issues to establish that an equitable adjustment for delays, computed by the use of the *Eichleay* formula, is appropriate where the contractor cannot replace *the project delayed by the government* with another.

Although the *Eichleay* formula is now well-established, we thought it would be useful to review two later rulings in this area to indicate the various kinds of arguments which the government has presented in an effort to defeat or dilute contractors' claims.

R.G. Beer Corporation, ENG BCA No. 4885, 86-3 BCA par. 19,012, involved a contract for the construction of pumping stations for local flood protection. Delays occurred because of late delivery of government-furnished pumps and motors and late completion of the levee or floodwall by a third party. The contractor's claim was computed on the basis of a modified *Eichleay* formula, and the board made the following comments regarding the use of *Eichleay* in general:

> The issues in this appeal concern computation of the additional price adjustment due Appellant for unabsorbed or extended overhead. Appellant argues that the amount of the recovery should be calculated pursuant to a modified *"Eichleay"* formula. *See Eichleay Corp.,* ASBCA No. 5183, 60-2 BCA ¶ 2688, *aff'd on recon* 61-1 BCA ¶ 2894. The so-called *Eichleay* formula actually originated in much earlier decisions of the Court of Claims. *See e.g. Fred R. Combs v. U.S.,* 103 Ct.Cl. 174 (1954) and cases cited by the ASBCA in *Eichleay, supra,* 60-2 BCA at 13,574. Since the hearing of this appeal, use of that formula has been reaffirmed as the generally-accepted method of computing the recovery of home office overhead due contractors for delays compensable under construction contract "Suspension of Work" clauses. *Capital Electric Co. v. United States* [31 CCF ¶ 72,119], 729 F.2d 743 (Fed Cir 1984); *George Hyman Construction Co.,* ENG BCA No. 4541, 85-1 BCA ¶ 17,847. Where such suspensions occur, "relationships [between overhead and direct costs] must of necessity be distorted because of the relatively small direct costs incurred during and as a result of the period of delay" *Eichleay, supra,* 60-2 BCA at 13,576. As stated in *R.W. Contracting, Inc.,* ASBCA No. 24627, 84-2 BCA ¶ 17,302 at 86,219:

>> The *Eichleay* formula furnishes a necessary surrogate for the normal accounting practice of applying an overhead rate to the appropriate direct cost base in situations where the contractor is delayed and direct costs that normally would have been incurred in the performance of the contract decreased or were eliminated during the period of delay. It is a practical and necessary expedient to compensate the contractor in situations where the direct cost base is eroded thus making use of the normal indirect cost allocation percentage rate inappropriate. Derivation of a daily overhead rate is merely a necessary substitute designed for such situations where achieving a more precise measurement is impracticable and/or use of the percentage rate on direct costs would be inequitable. The *Eichleay* formula is a time-honored means of approximating a "fair allocation" of unabsorbed indirect costs in situations where direct costs have been reduced during periods of compensable suspensions of work . . . .

One of the government's arguments was that the use of *Eichleay* in this instance was inequitable because the delays occurred in the late stages of the contract. The board found this contention without merit:

> However, as emphasized by Appellant, the Government has cited no precedent where the stage of completion of the job has militated against use of *Eichleay*. In fact, that the delaying events transpired during later stages of contract performance has not precluded application of the formula. *See, e.g., Shirley Contracting Corp.*, ASBCA No. 29848, 85-1 BCA ¶ 17,858 at 89,399, *aff'd on recon.* 85-2 BCA ¶ 18,019. In this case, we also note that approximately 11-18% of the contract work remained to be completed at the time of the suspension, based on contract billings. Moreover, substantial GFP remained to be installed. It took Appellant 4½ months to complete the work once it returned to the site in September 1981. The total period of performance, excluding the shutdown period was 18½ months. Therefore, approximately 24% of the total performance period was required to finish the project. Under these circumstances, we do not agree that use of *Eichleay* is inequitable to the Government.

Another argument advanced by the government was that Beer could or should have performed other work during the suspension period to mitigate its damages and absorb its overhead. Because such contentions are frequently made in these instances and because the board addressed (and rejected) this argument in such depth and clarity, we believe that citing this portion of the decision would prove useful and instructive to contractors facing similar circumstances:

> Where it is practicable for the contractor to shift its work force productively and efficiently to other contracts, part or all of the otherwise unabsorbed indirect costs will be allocable to direct costs expended in the performance of the other work, Accordingly, good faith, successful reassignment of qualified workers during periods of suspended work effectively mitigates the contractor's damages and generally reduces the unabsorbed indirect cost recovery. *See Gulf & Western Industries, Inc.*, ASBCA No. 18406, 79-2 BCA ¶ 13,960 at 68,524 (appellant was able to divert employees and fully use them on other work during delay); see also *Brand Investment Co. v. U.S.* [2 CCF 826], 162 Ct.Cl. 40, 58 F.Supp. 749 (1944). Thus, if it is practicable for the contractor prudently to use the suspension period for other work, the Government is entitled to receive the benefits of such damage mitigation efforts. Extra work under the disputed contract, ordered pursuant to the Changes clause and performed during the suspension period, also should be considered in determining the degree of underabsorption. See discussion, *infra.* We agree in principle that the contractor has an obligation to mitigate damages by absorbing indirect costs through performance of other work where it is possible to do so effectively, productively and practicably.

> However, the Government's contention that the contractor could or should have taken on other work has often been made but, as in this case, is rarely supported by the facts. *See, e.g., Robert McMullan & Son, Inc.*, ASBCA No. 19023, 76-1 BCA ¶ 11,782 at 55,966. This is in large part understandable because such contentions frequently are grounded upon a

series of guesses, that Government contract tribunals traditionally have been unwilling to make, concerning what work the contractor reasonably could or should have taken on during delay periods. In addition, particularly in the Government contract context where anticipated and/or ordinary profit are not recoverable under the "Suspension of Work" clause, the failure to take on other work during delay periods would be economically senseless if it is reasonably possible for the contractor to obtain substitute work. It stands to reason that contractors are not idly waiting around, with their work force dispersing, for an *Eichleay* "windfall" rather than attempting to earn a profit on other jobs.

Numerous, largely subjective factors are involved in determining whether the contractor could or should have taken on other work. These include: (1) the amount of notice and certainty as to the length of the delay period; (2) bidding, mobilization, geographic and submittal constraints attendant upon starting other work; (3) the size, resources, capabilities and expertise of the contractor; (4) the size and degree of completion of the job[5] [footnote not reproduced—CCH.] and the amount of work planned for the delay period. Unlike many single-location manufacturing operations, often sizable investments in time and money are required to transfer men and expensive equipment from one site to another. Mitigation of damages is, at best, difficult despite the contractor's best efforts. In particular, constructive suspensions of work normally are unplanned, of uncertain duration, and often sporadic. Moreover, the nature of the Government action may only partially delay or slow down the work permitting neither full efficiency on the contract work itself nor the shifting of the work force to other contracts. The contractor need not be absolutely "precluded" from taking on other work in order to fulfill its duty to mitigate damages. It need only act reasonably with due consideration given to all the facts and circumstances of each case.

In the face of the factors and uncertainties noted above, the Federal Circuit recognized that the burden shifts to the Government to come forward with proof that no injury was suffered where the contractor has adduced evidence that it was impracticable to take on additional projects. *Capital Electric Co. v. U.S., supra,* citing *Eichleay Corp., supra,* 61-1 BCA at 15,119. Here, we have found that it was impossible or impracticable for the contractor to obtain replacement work due to a combination of the uncertain length of the delay, long lead times inherent in acquiring substantial new projects and impairment of Appellant's bonding capacity. This conclusion has not been substantively rebutted by factual evidence from the Government. Accordingly, in the absence of such evidence to the contrary, we conclude that damages have been mitigated to the maximum degree possible.

We are also constrained to note that the *Eichleay* formula has a built-in corrective mechanism to reflect the extent of other projects performed during the delay period. To the degree other work is performed and billed, the billings ratio denominator is increased, automatically shifting overhead costs from the delayed contract to such other work proportionate to the amount billed. *George Hyman Construction Co., supra* at 89,354.

We consider the above rationale and analysis extremely lucid and persuasive, and for that reason quoted the board at some length. Note that the board agrees that a contractor indeed has an obligation to mitigate damages during delays by performance of other work "where it is possible to do so *effectively, productively and practicably*" [Emphasis added]. Note, too, the board's observation that the government's contention along these lines ". . . has often been made but, as in this case, is rarely supported by the facts." In effect, the board seems to be saying that such contentions amount to government knee-jerk reactions to delay claims based on the Eichleay method.

Although a contractor's failure to attempt to mitigate damages by obtaining other work can, if proven, be very harmful to his case, the above cited portion of the decision reveals the board's view that contractors generally make such efforts, especially since recoveries under the contract suspension provisions do not include any profit. It doesn't make good business sense to deliberately remain idle in order to recover unabsorbed indirect costs where new business could be obtained from which recovery of both costs *and profits* would be possible. The board also takes the position that a contractor need not prove with strong evidence that he was *"precluded"* from taking on other work. Rather, where he can adduce evidence that such action was *"impracticable,"* the burden shifts to the government to demonstrate otherwise.

The government in *R.G. Beer* filled its case with just about every tired argument advanced by *Eichleay* opponents. DCAA and others, for example, have argued that no unabsorbed indirect costs are incurred where the contract is substantially completed in the same period in which the delay occurred. Conversely, some have sought to persuade judicial tribunals that when two or more accounting periods are involved there still should be no recovery of unabsorbed or extended overhead because, somehow, the underrecovery in one period will be offset by an overrecovery in the next period. The lack of logic inherent in these contentions was clearly exposed by the board as it rejected them:

> The Government further asserts that recovery should be denied since the work was substantially completed during the same accounting period. Arguments that unabsorbed indirect costs should not be awarded where the contractor completes performance in less than one fiscal year (or accounting period) generally have been rejected implicitly. *See, e.g., Proserv, Inc.,* ASBCA No. 20768, 78-1 BCA ¶ 13,066. These arguments are premised upon the thesis that when the direct costs are incurred eventually during the same accounting period they will then absorb, if belatedly, their fair share of indirect costs.

> The principal problem with the argument is that it ignores the fact that it is generally impossible or impracticable for a construction contractor to use its work force assigned to the contract on other contracts during the actual period of delay (assuming damage mitigation efforts have failed) *as well as* during the extended performance period. Each day the contractor is delayed it loses the opportunity to do the work when planned and to complete on time or improve upon the scheduled completion date. It is forced to forego the opportunity of beginning new work and completing old jobs expeditiously. In addition, the opportunity of

taking on other work during the period when the delayed work is performed may be lost as a result of uncertainties concerning timing and manpower and diminution of bonding capacities inherent in most suspension situations. Although the Government is entitled to benefit from the contractor's mitigation of damages efforts (through effectively shifting its resources to other work) during the period of delay, it should not be permitted to delay the contractor beyond anticipated completion dates without liability, even in the case of single period delays.

As discussed in greater detail below, the *Eichleay* award properly considers only a residue of fixed overhead expenses that are not directly allocable. Such fixed costs, unlike variable expenses, are not and cannot be deferred and "recovered" when the work is performed. Accounting time periods for accumulation and reporting of costs serve a number of useful and necessary purposes, most importantly for financial reporting under generally accepted accounting principles. However, these accounting conventions are not intended to be employed to obscure the potential non-recovery of fixed expenses related to the delay period.

In the case of multiple period delays, there is concern that "under-recovery" in one period will be "offset" by an "over-recovery" in a later period. First, it should be noted that such an offsetting effect only will occur if projected indirect cost pricing rates are established without regard for the increased direct base costs that would have been incurred during the delay period and fixed costs assignable to the extended period do not increase. Moreover, it again ignores the lost opportunity associated with not working during the period of delay and/or not performing other contracts during the extended period. Unabsorbed indirect fixed costs are not "recovered" unless compensation therefor is forthcoming from the Government or the contractor itself compensates for their loss by adjusting his bids on future contracts, thereby risking loss of its competitive position. Simply because there may be a larger base over which to "spread" indirect costs in the later period does not mean that fixed, indirect costs related to the prior delay periods are "recovered." Allocation is *not* synonymous with recovery in a fixed price contracting environment. Likewise, the fact that indirect costs accruing *during* the delay period would, of necessity, have been allocable to other on-going contracts should not be interpreted as meaning that they were "recovered" in the contract price of those other contracts. Instead, they are a true "cost" of the delayed contract.

When the government finally acknowledged that the Eichleay formula should be used, it contended that a modified version was required because the delay occurred in the late stages of contract performance. Instead of the basic formula shown earlier in this chapter, the government proposed substituting the unbilled portion of the original contract price for total contract billings; adding the unbilled portion of the contract to total billings; and substituting the original contract period for the total days of contract performance. This distorted "modification" would obviously and seriously reduce the amount of the claim. This government attack was likewise rejected by the board:

... A principal problem with the Government approach is that the numerator it advocates is inconsistent with the total billings (irrespective of the degree of completion of other contracts) it proposes for use in the denominator. In essence, the Government is relating apples and oranges. More importantly, the question is not what or how overhead is to be related to the remaining work. The issue before us is how best to determine the amount of overhead that was unabsorbed as a result of the delay. The Government ratio does not represent a meaningful, much less a more accurate, approach to measurement of Appellant's delay damages. The result of the proposal is to approximate what portion of total overhead is allocable to the *remaining* work based on a modified billings ratio, *irrespective* of whether the remaining work was delayed.

The government was not alone in proposing some modifications to the basic *Eichleay* formula. The contractor's claim reflected the original contract price in the numerator of the first fraction instead of in the contract billings. The denominator was increased by the unbilled portion of the contract at issue. Among other modifications, the contractor proposed the use of the original contract period instead of the entire actual contract period. The contractor's efforts were no more successful than the government's, and the board stated strongly that an appropriate recovery requires the use of the original, well-accepted *Eichleay* formula. The decision included references to many prior rulings in support of the conclusion to reject both the government's and contractor's modifications and to apply the "unmodified *Eichleay* computation."

There may be instances where some modification of this formula is appropriate. However, this decision reiterates the point made many times previously that boards of contract appeals and federal courts have reviewed the *Eichleay* formula over many years and, while recognizing that it is less than perfect, have concluded that it is a "time-honored means of approximating a 'fair allocation' of unabsorbed indirect costs in situations where direct costs have been reduced during periods of compensable suspensions of work ...." It would thus appear that, in most instances, contractors could more effectively present and support a claim if it rests on the solid rock of the original *Eichleay* formula.

Where a close analysis reveals that the unmodified *Eichleay* formula yields an inequitable recovery and some revision is therefore considered appropriate, we would suggest considerable and careful thought before offering an alternative. Further, any alternative should be supported by strong, logical arguments. We would not counsel proposed revisions that a board or court will recognize as merely an attempt to increase the amount of recovery.

The final facet of this case which we will address in this analysis is the nature of the indirect expenses that should be considered in the *Eichleay* formula. Obviously, expenses established as unallowable or directly allocable to other work should be excluded. The further point originally made by the contract auditors in this controversy, and which has surfaced in other cases as well, relates to whether the total residual, allowable costs should be considered, or only those termed "fixed" in accounting parlance.

It has been argued that variable expenses are allocated to contracts when incurred and thereby recovered at that time. According to this reasoning, only fixed expenses should be considered for the purpose of the *Eichleay* formula. This point has presented many problems, including the difficulties experienced by accounting experts in distinguishing among fixed and variable expenses, with the problem further complicated by differing views on semi-variable, semi-fixed, and other categories of expenses, depending on the precision attempted. These problems take on much importance and complexity in the manufacturing environment. In construction contracts, however, where unabsorbed or extended overhead relates mainly to off-site home office expenses, the case has been made effectively that all of these expenses are fixed and thus appropriate for allocation. This was the conclusion adopted in this dispute:

> We agree in principle with the initial contention of the Government auditors in this case, that only fixed overhead expenses should be used in computing the *Eichleay* award. Fixed expenses are those that do not vary with construction or production volume during a given time period. Variable expenses, on the other hand, fluctuate directly with increases or decreases in such volume, and will be recovered when the delayed work is performed. In most construction contracts, job cost accounting systems, variable costs generally are allocable and allocated directly to contracts when incurred. Only by restricting the formula amount to fixed home office costs are the significant, theoretical objections to use of *Eichleay* overcome. However, the Government has apparently abandoned its initial audit position and we have been unable to find that any portion of Appellant's home office expenses were variable. The fixed versus variable character of home office overhead items is not self evident. Proof of the amount of variable expenses is required. We observe that home office expenses of most construction contractors are fixed, due in part to the prevalence of direct allocation of job site expenses. *See, e.g., Salt City Contractors, Ltd.,* VACAB No. 1362, 80-2 BCA ¶ 14,713 at 72,559. In the construction contract environment there is a presumption, rebuttable by the Government, that home office costs are fixed and no reduction to eliminate variable costs is necessary. *See id; see also Kemmons-Witson, Inc. (Florida) and South & Patton, Inc., A Joint Venture,* ASBCA No. 16167, 72-2 BCA ¶ 9689 at 45,254 (distinguishing job site overhead costs which often are of a fixed and variable nature; caveat: such jobsite costs, even if variable are directly allocable to the job during the suspension period and thus recoverable to the extent allowable, including reasonable). In the supply/manufacturing contract context, the distinction between fixed and variable indirect costs generally is of considerably greater importance. *See, e.g., A.C.E.S., Inc.,* ASBCA No. 21417, 79-1 BCA ¶ 13,809.

The final, significant ruling we have selected in the discussion of the *Eichleay* method is *G.S. and L. Mechanical and Construction, Inc.,* DOT CAB No. 1640, 86-3 BCA 19,026. Work under the contract was suspended for a lengthy period pursuant to the Suspension of Work clause, and the contractor filed a claim using a modified version of the Eichleay formula. Consistent with most previous BCA and court decisions, the board rejected any major modifications to the basic formula. Its sharpest criticisms, however, were directed at the government for accepting DCAA's reckless disregard of judicial precedent approving *Eichleay.*

DCAA audit reports referred to in this appeal reiterated the audit agency's consistently rejected theory that where the work is delayed but may be completed within the same fiscal period, there can be no such thing as unabsorbed overhead because "once the delayed G&A base is incurred, any G&A shifted during the delay period will shift back to the contract as if there were no delay because the contract will be completed in the same accounting period as originally scheduled."

The government placed the DCAA auditor on the stand, and the board commented on his testimony as follows:

> . . . It is clear from his testimony that the conclusions reached therein were driven by the DCAA policy that whenever there is a suspension of work, if the contractor had other contracts, no part of home office overhead during the suspension period should be borne by the suspending agency, so long as work is recommended and completed during the accounting period in which the suspension order was issued . . . . The auditor testified that DCAA considered cases such as *Eichleay Corp.,* ASBCA No. 5183, 60-1 BCA ¶ 2688, aff'd on recon., 61-1 BCA ¶ 2894, and *Capital Electric Company v. United States* [31 CCF ¶ 72,119], 729 F.2d 743 (Fed. Cir. 1984), to only apply to situations where the suspended contractor has no other work to bear the home office overhead and, because of the possibility of a lifting of the suspension, cannot take on other work . . . . He also acknowledged that he had never approved the application of the *Eichleay* formula on any contracts and that DCAA audit guidance calls for an attack on *Eichleay* because it is based solely on time and discounts all other factors.

DCAA further argued that there was other ongoing work during the suspension period and that such work should absorb all of the home office overhead including, apparently, that amount which would have been absorbed by the contract at issue but for the government's suspension of work. The auditor also opined that the number of days required to complete the contract was unchanged, only the time period was altered, and therefore "home office overhead incurrence will not be altered." The DCAA argument was demolished by the board:

> This argument is precisely the argument which was considered and rejected by the Court of Appeals for the Federal Circuit in deciding *Capital Electric Company v. United States* [31 CCF ¶ 72,119], 729 F.2d 743 (Fed. Cir. 1984). We quote from the concurring opinion of Circuit Judge Friedman, 729 F.2d at 747-748;
>
> > For almost 40 years the Court of Claims consistently has held that the delay damages a government contractor may recover include extended home office overhead incurred during the period of delay . . .
>
> The government now asks us to jettison this settled line of authority on the ground that all of those cases were wrongly decided. It argues that since the delay in performance ordinarily does not

increase the total amount of office overhead the contractor incurs in connection with the particular contract, but merely spreads it over a longer period, allowing the contractor to recover for such overhead for the period of delay would result in compensating the contractor for losses it did not actually incur. According to the government, the only situations in which a contractor may recover for such extended office overhead is where the delay in performance: (1) requires the contractor to hire additional personnel or incur other additional expenses; or (2) prevents the contractor from taking on other work it would have been able to assume had there not been the delay.

Although superficially plausible, the government's argument does not withstand more penetrating analysis based upon the theory on which extended office overhead is allowed as an element of delay damages. By definition this type of overhead cannot be directly attributed to the performance of a particular contract, yet it is an essential part of the contractor's total cost of doing business. Some basis, therefore, must be found for allocating this total overhead among the various contracts in connection with which it is incurred.

Judge Friedman goes on to quote from Judge Madden's decision in *Fred R. Comb Company,* 103 Ct.Cl. 174 (1945). Judge Madden's decision is premised upon the realization that a contractor is not free to utilize its facilities and staff on other work during the period when it is marking time under a suspension while the Government attempts to make a decision as to the future progress of the work. As a consequence, according to Judge Madden, some of these facilities and staff are "wasted." 103 Ct.Cl. at 183-184.

In *Capital Electric,* after quoting from *Comb,* Circuit Judge Friedman concludes, "In other words, a portion of the overhead incurred during the entire period of performance must be charged against the revenue received during that period as a cost of performing the contract. The Court of Claims decisions, as well as the *Eichleay* formula, are based upon and reflect these economic realities of the construction business." 729 F.2d at 748.

DCAA in the case before us is presenting the argument that a period of suspension does not increase the aggregate amount of overhead costs, but the total overhead costs for the contract remain the same. As we noted immediately prior to quoting from Circuit Judge Friedman, the arguments by the Government to which he refers are precisely the arguments respondent and the DCAA present here. While DCAA audit guidance may direct an attack upon the application of the *Eichleay* formula in a situation such as we have here, and indeed upon the entire concept of paying any home office overhead during a period of suspension (except when "unabsorbed"), the fact remains that the Court of Appeals has spoken, and it is their precedents which we must follow.

The strength of the board's convictions in this appeal and its aversion to DCAA's continuing presentation of opinions which had been sharply and consistently rejected in the judicial arena are reflected in the following portion of the decision:

Even if we were not bound by the precedents of the Court of Appeals, we would reach the same result, for the arguments advanced by respondent and the DCAA fly in the face of logic.

From the date that a contract is awarded (if not before) until the date performance under that contract is completed (if not later), a contractor's home office staff will be performing some functions with regard to that contract, *even if contract work is in a total state of suspension.* For example: there may be negotiations regarding compensation due under the Suspension of Work clause for additional direct costs; or the contractor may be discussing some technical problem which has caused the suspension (as here); or there may be acquired materials which must be protected, a direct cost which will involve home office effort, etc. In sum, the home office staff will be working on this particular contract over a longer time period than would have been contemplated at the time the contract was priced and bid.

If we accept DCAA's contention that, during a period of suspension while there is other work ongoing, there is no home office overhead for the Government to bear, since all such overhead is "absorbed" by the other contracts, we are ignoring this reality of continuing (albeit probably at a reduced rate) expenses caused by the prolonged existence of the suspended contract. We would be ignoring the fact that a contractor would be ill-advised to reduce home office expenses during a period of suspension, especially an undefined period of suspension such as we have here, by reducing staff.[2] It might be called upon at any time to resume work and would risk being unable to find qualified or experienced people. See *Fred R. Comb Company v. United States,* above, at 183-184. What DCAA is seeking is to have someone else bear the expenses which result from the Government's delay. We reject this approach: There is no such thing as a free lunch.[3] [footnotes not reproduced—CCH.]

We therefore acquiesce in another Board's statement: "It has, however, been sufficiently demonstrated by the mere fact of prolongation of the time of performance, and the continuation of main office expenses., that more of such expenses were incurred during the period of performance than would have been except for the suspension, *Fred R. Combs [sic] v. United States, supra,* at 183-184; *Henry Ericsson v. United States* [3 CCF ¶ 1157]," 104 Ct.Cl. 397, 414-415, 423, 427-428, 62 F.Supp. 312 (1945). *Eichleay Corp.,* ASBCA No. 5183, 60-2 BCA ¶ 2688, at 13,574-13,575, affirmed on reconsideration, 61-1 BCA ¶ 2894.

There is another separate reason for rejecting appellant's arguments, in addition to our holding that a prolongation of a performance period in itself increases overhead costs. The appellant has brought itself within the ambit of another principle, that the impairment of its bonding capacity caused by the suspension has precluded it from using its home office's capacity to support other construction projects. Therefore, to use Judge Madden's term from *Fred Comb,* there is wasted capacity. This is the position which the Government acknowledged in the above quotation from *Capital Electric* (q.v.), namely that a contractor may recover when a delay precludes him from taking on other substantial work which could pick up overhead costs.

We reach this conclusion because appellant has proved that, but for the impairment of its bonding capacity wrought by the continued existence of this contract, an existence which would have been earlier expired but for the excessively long suspension of work, it would have entered upon performance of the Navy contract already awarded to it subject to the furnishing of performance and payment bonds. We shall not allow an owner (respondent) to suspend a contractor's right to proceed for such a long period, precluding it from obtaining more than a modicum of other work over which to spread its overhead costs, and then claim that such owner is not liable for a proportionate share of the overhead costs during the period of suspension. Such an argument falls upon very unsympathetic ears.

* * * *

... When a contractor has exhausted its bonding capacity, it is effectively precluded from accepting further public or private contracts for all but very small, unbonded construction work until it has completed substantial portions of the work under bonded contracts. As a result of the suspension of work by the FAA, and the prolonged duration of that suspension, GS&L found itself in this position: unable to accept additional contracts and IN FACT precluded from proceeding on the Navy contract which had been awarded to it.

Before concluding this lengthy and thoughtful decision, the board probed deeply into the essence of the *Eichleay* formula, the arguments advanced in opposition to it, the formula's imperfections but basic fairness, and the government's failures to provide a suitable alternative. It noted DCAA's preference for computing a percentage of G&A expenses to total costs and applying such percentage to the costs incurred under a contract, and the suitability of this method in certain contractual circumstances but not in situations such as occur during suspension of work:

... However, when parties are negotiating after-the-fact to agree on compensation for a Government-directed suspension of work (as opposed to a change, in which work continues although altered), this approach is not appropriate, for the direct costs incurred by a contractor during a suspension period are negligible. The Court of Appeals recognized the inappropriateness of this method of computing overhead for a suspension period, in *Capital Electric v. United States,* above, because applying any overhead rate to a $0.00 direct cost base yields $0.00 reimbursement for overhead. To illustrate, when the circumstances of a suspension preclude a contractor from accepting other work, the dollar amount of the direct cost base is reduced while home overhead costs remain unaltered. As a result, the overhead rate (overhead expressed as a percentage of direct costs) increases, but the increased rate will not avail a contractor whose direct cost incurrences on his contract are in the neighborhood of $0.00 due to the suspension.

In its analysis of what it perceived to be imperfections in the *Eichleay* method, the board noted the inherent presumption that home office overhead is "straight-lined" over the period of contract performance whereas, in its view, less home office is expended on an inactive contract under suspension than on one proceeding at "full steam." The board thought there might be a second inaccurate presumption in believing that unabsorbed overhead recovery computed by *Eichleay* would yield the same amount of G&A expense included in the original contract price.

The board felt strongly that the selection of the period for applying *Eichleay* was very important. The selection of fiscal years, in its view, might be suitable for accounting conventions in other circumstances. For applying *Eichleay*, however, distortions should be avoided by using the entire contract period.

The board also observed that *Eichleay* will not yield precise results because after the extended or unabsorbed overhead is recovered under the suspended contract, other work will be left with more or less than its appropriate share, and the contractor would not, nor does the board recommend that he should, attempt to open and revise the prices of his other fixed-price contracts, a practice the board refers to as a "devastation of the firm fixed-price contracting philosophy." On the other hand, using the same premises, the board pointed to what it saw as the fallacy in the government's argument "that reimbursement only lies if there is unabsorbed overhead, and since appellant had other ongoing work, all home office overhead is considered to have been absorbed by the other contracts, leaving nothing unabsorbed to be picked up by this contract." To the contrary, the board said:

> . . . We accept the premise that an extended performance period in itself results in a contractor incurring increased home office overhead costs. Having done so, then to hold that such additional overhead cost is to be "absorbed" by other contracts, contracts which for the most part have been prospectively priced based on an estimate of future allocable overhead costs, is in reality to hold that such additional costs are to be borne by the contractor out of his profit under those other contracts and this contract. This is because there is no way to pass on increased overhead costs, or decreased overhead costs, to the owner under an existing fixed-price construction contract.

After probing deeply into the problems of cost recovery during periods of contract work suspensions, the board concluded that while there were some imperfections in the Eichleay method, it had not found any better alternative. As to DCAA's recommendation to simply apply the percentage of total G&A expenses to total costs, the board said: ". . . we shall not apply the thoroughly discredited approach of applying a G&A rate to direct costs incurred during the suspension period. This approach has been rejected by the courts, and we reject it again."

OTHER FACTORS WARRANTING PRICE ADJUSTMENTS UNDER THE "CHANGES" CLAUSE

There are numerous other conditions arising in the course of government contracts which result in additional costs and for which the contractor should seek price adjustment. Some of these circumstances are illustrated below, extracted from cases in which the contractors successfully obtained compensation.

In *Specialty Assembling and Packing Co., Inc.,* 1956, ASBCA 3562, 3715, 56-2 BCA par. 1049, the cost of developing detailed drawings required to manufacture certain equipment, which the government had failed to furnish according to the contract terms, was allowed as additional compensation. The contract provided for the manufacture of certain electronic equipment and stated that detailed drawings "will be furnished to the contractor upon his application." The contractor requested the drawings, but the government did not furnish them. Accordingly, the contractor had to develop the necessary information, including dimensions, manufacturing processes, detailed listing of bills of materials, etc. The contractor claimed that the price should be increased by the amount of engineering costs which had been incurred in the preparation of the drawings. The contractor's appeal was sustained.

There are also instances where contractors manufactured supplies under processes or specifications stated in the contract, and the supplies failed to pass inspection. The additional costs are recoverable under the Changes clause.

Delays in delivery schedules may be occasioned by a wide variety of factors. Some are identified as "excusable" and some as "inexcusable." Where a contractor fails to meet the delivery schedules, and the government is not at fault, the contractor may or may not be excused. By the terms of the standard government clauses, contractors will be excused when delays are beyond their control or without their fault or negligence (e.g., acts of God). In these cases, the contractor will be permitted to perform without being charged for default or excess costs. Otherwise, in reverse, the contract may be terminated for default, and/or excess costs may be levied. Frequently, delays are attributable directly to acts of omission or commission on the part of the government. In the latter circumstances, excess costs resulting from these delays are properly borne by the government, and the contractor is entitled to full reimbursement.

As to excusable delays, it is generally held by boards of contract appeals and courts that a contractor is presumed to have the capability to perform competently in terms of money, technical knowledge, personnel, and equipment. Generally, where delays are occasioned by contractor deficiencies in these areas, they are held to be inexcusable and the contractor is subject to financial penalties or termination for default. In each of these instances, however, a showing of extenuating circumstances may establish the delay to be excusable. For example, while the contractor is charged with having the proper labor force available, strikes are specifically mentioned as excusable delays. Financial difficulties are much more difficult to establish as a basis for an excusable delay. With very few exceptions, courts and administrative boards have not excused delays caused by lack of finances unless the contractor could show that financing had been promised by the government and that the government had failed to keep its commitment. Finally, delays attributable to subcontractors will generally be held excusable only where it can be shown that the fault was beyond the control of both the prime and subcontractor.

As mentioned previously, delays attributable to faults by the government are excusable, and related excess costs incurred by the contractor should be recovered from the government. This point is obvious when viewed in terms of considerations of law and equity. And yet, this entire field is one of substantial difficulty for contractors and has resulted in probably more disputes and appeals than any other in the field of government contracting. The two major problems encountered are (1) establishing that the government was at fault and (2) determining and supporting the amount of financial injury to the contractor.

An interesting and rather complicated situation, a case in which the author of this text was involved, is described below to illustrate the complexities that may arise in contract delay controversies. (*Northbridge Electronics Inc. v. U.S.*, Ct.Cls. No. 42-64, April 13, 1966)

The company entered into a contract with the Army for the manufacture of 230 units of electronic equipment. The contract contained a provision for "bounce conditioning." This required that each unit, after the final assembly, be bounced prior to inspection in order to shake out loose bits of wire and solder and to show up any possible loose connections.

The bounce equipment was very inexpensive, but the contractor did not have one. In submitting a list of proposed tests to the government, the contractor did not include a reference to the bounce conditioning.

In the initial production phase, the Army sent a specialist to the contractor's plant. This field engineer stayed there until 50 units had been produced, even though an Air Force resident inspector was at the site. During his stay, the Army specialist learned that the bounce test was not being performed and thereupon increased the supervision and inspection in order to accomplish visually the objectives sought by the government through the bounce test. The 50 units were accepted by the government after inspection by the resident inspector, who was also aware of the fact that they had not been bounce conditioned. Thereafter, the contractor produced 85 additional units without bounce conditioning, all of which were likewise accepted by the resident government inspector with full knowledge that bounce conditioning had not been performed. In this connection, it was ultimately established that the government never contended that these 135 units were defective. It was also established that the contractor had not realized any overall saving on account of the omission of bounce conditioning.

After the 135 sets had been produced and accepted, another Army electronics specialist visited the contractor's plant, noted the absence of bounce conditioning equipment, learned there was no written waiver for this test, and, unaware of the substitution of the increased visual inspection for bounce conditioning, reported to the contracting officer that the contractor was not complying with the contract. The contracting officer directed the inspector not to accept any more units unless they were bounce conditioned.

The contractor protested on the grounds that the Army's previous approval of its production procedures constituted an agreement to omit bounce conditioning. The contractor also ascertained that the requirement to initiate the bounce test, including obtaining the necessary equipment, would require 60 to 90 days during which the production line would have to be shut down and many employees laid off. The contractor's request for a waiver of bounce conditioning for the remaining 95 units was concurred in by the resident government inspector but denied by the contracting officer.

The contractor ultimately secured the necessary equipment and completed the contract. It then filed a claim under the contract's Changes clause for an equitable adjustment for delay costs—approximately three months during which the production line was shut down. The contractor's claim was denied by the contracting officer, and an appeal was made to the ASBCA.

The ASBCA ruled for the government, holding that the bounce conditioning was a contractual requirement, that there was no evidence to establish a binding agreement to eliminate this requirement, and that the government was within its contractual rights in ordering compliance therewith for the 95 units. It was reasoned that, if the contractor were, in effect, contractually required to perform the bounce test, he could not claim an equitable adjustment for costs associated with the contractual requirement. The board failed to find evidence of an agreement between the contractor and the government for eliminating the bounce-conditioning requirement. It held that discussions on this matter involved only government representatives (Army field engineer and Air Force resident inspector) and were not participated in by the contractor and that the most that could be said of the Army field engineer's act was that it was one "of forbearance, than of an agreement."

The contractor appealed the board's decision to the Court of Claims. The appeal asserted "that the Board's conclusion that the evidence did not establish the existence of a valid and binding agreement is a legal conclusion not entitled to finality and that, to the extent that it constitutes a question of fact, it is arbitrary and capricious and not supported by substantial evidence."

The Court of Claims reversed the decision of the ASBCA in a most unequivocal manner and ruled for the contractor. The court found that the record clearly established a valid agreement between the contractor and the government to omit bounce conditioning and accomplish the same function by increased visual and mechanical inspection. It pointed to "undisputed testimony before the board," given by the Army's field engineer and the contractor's vicepresident, establishing the Army's engineer's awareness of the lack of bounce conditioning equipment and his agreement with the government resident inspector to the substitution of more rigid visual and mechanical inspection procedures. The contractor's representative and the Army engineer agreed in their respective testimonies that the contractor had initiated, on request, intensified inspection procedures that, in the opinion of the government representative, accomplished the objectives of the bounce test. The Army engineer also testified that he had the authority to waive the bounce test and to agree to the alternative procedure.

The court was particularly impressed by the fact that the Army engineer was assigned to the contractor's plant during the production of the first 50 items to exercise surveillance over the pilot run in order "to set up standards and procedures to govern performance through the contract." The court found that the Army engineer and the resident inspector, not in any casual manner, but deliberately and with full knowledge and consent of both parties, modified the procedures.

EQUITABLE ADJUSTMENT FOR INCREASED COSTS ARISING FROM PARTIAL TERMINATION

In one of its lengthier and more complex decisions, the ASBCA rejected several different proposals offered by the contractor for computing an equitable adjustment in the contract price for the unterminated items as a result of a partial termination. However, although the computation method ultimately developed by the board yielded a much smaller amount than would have been realized by the use of the contractor's methods, it is important that the board reiterated the basic concept of the contractor's entitlement to an adjustment in these circumstances. "In our view," said the board, "an equitable adjustment should give appellant a price for the units produced equivalent to what would reasonably have been agreed upon had the parties known that the total number of engines to be manufactured under the contract was the unterminated quantity (266) rather than the original quantity (322)." (For reference purposes, the case involves the appeal of *Fairchild Stratos Corporation*, ASBCA No. 9169, 67-1 BCA par. 6225 and 68-1 BCA par. 7053, originally decided by the board on March 20, 1967, and reaffirmed on May 29, 1968.)

This was a Navy contract for aircraft engines. The initial quantity of 74 was increased by 248 to 322 and in October 1958 was decreased by 56 by a partial termination, which makes up the issue in this case. An event which made this case particularly complex, and overshadowed this partial termination, was an action by the Air Force about two and a half months later terminating all of the Air Force engine contracts. The Air Force terminations ultimately led to the closing of the Fairchild plant that was involved.

All of the contractor's attention was focused on the termination settlement with the Air Force, and the claim to the Navy for equitable adjustment was not filed until more than two years after the partial termination.

Some chronological data are essential to keep in mind here. The Navy partial termination occurred in October 1958; the Air Force terminated all its contracts in January 1959; the Navy contract (with the revised quantities) was completed in April 1959; and the plant was closed in October 1959. From the time the Air Force cancelled, the contractor's operations were expectedly and completely disrupted and overhead rates skyrocketed despite mass layoffs and other economy measures.

Although Fairchild tried various approaches in computing an equitable adjustment, the various methods appeared to have in common the objective of having the Navy assume a share of the costs incurred during the period when production dwindled to zero and the contractor vainly attempted to secure new business. The details of the negotiation of the major terminations by the Air Force were not given in the decision; however, it appears that the Air Force did assume a considerable portion of the continuing costs. It appeared also that the contractor concentrated on the more significant Air Force matter and assumed that the smaller Navy claim could be settled by the use of similar approaches and methods.

The hoped-for settlement of the Navy claim did not materialize. The Navy would have no part of the significant and unusual costs leading to the closing of the plant, which it had attributed to the major Air Force terminations. The board agreed with the Navy.

The contractor did not argue that the Navy was bound by the allocations made in the Air Force settlement; on the other hand, Fairchild strongly suggested that it would be inappropriate for two government departments to assume different positions.

The board emphasized that there was nothing in the Navy fixed-price contract binding it to pay any costs other than those attributable to the partial termination. The ASBCA saw no obligation on the part of the government to make the contractor whole. "The interplay of the Air Force and Navy contracts is not such that necessarily if an item is not paid for under one, it must be paid for under the other." The board also emphasized "that if appellant does not recover all of these costs (going out of business) in some way from the Government it does not mean it has not received an equitable adjustment since the Government has never committed itself to bear the costs of going out of business."

One of Fairchild's proposals was termed the "Dunbar Kapple Method" (*Dunbar Kapple, Inc.,* ASBCA No. 3631, 57-2 BCA par. 1448, 23 Sept. 1957). Essential to this method is the assumption that a learning curve was used in the original contract pricing and that an equitable adjustment for partial termination must include an adjustment for abbreviation of the learning curve or unamortized starting load and adjustment for change in overhead rates. Although the board conceded that an increase in efficiency should follow increase in production, it rejected the contractor's method because it found no evidence that learning curves had been employed by Fairchild in connection with pricing the contract at issue. As a matter of fact, the board alleged that in procurement plans for the same or similar engines, the contractor had been estimating virtually identical anticipated labor hours per unit.

Fairchild proposed the use of the 1959 actual overhead rates and again cited *Dunbar Kapple.* The Navy was of the opinion that the situations were dissimilar in that "Dunbar Kapple did not have a catastrophic shock to its overhead rates similar to that which Fairchild received upon the complete termination of its Air Force contracts." The Navy argued and the board agreed that this unusual situation warranted the use of data other than the actual experience for 1959. The Navy recommended, and the Board again agreed, that the contractor's budget estimates, made after and with consideration of the Navy's partial termination, but before and without consideration of the Air Force terminations, would constitute a reasonable basis.

In rejecting the use of actual experience in 1959 in favor of the estimate, the board used language that should be carefully considered and stored for the future by defense contractors: "Reasonable actual figures generally are preferred to estimates, but not when they distort the significant facts."

Although the board rejected Fairchild's claim for recovery of what it computed to be the Navy share of 1959 unabsorbed overhead, it acknowledged "that there may be instances where allowance of unearned or unabsorbed dollar overhead would be appropriate." In arriving at an appropriate method here, the board said:

> It is pertinent then to inquire what overhead rates would have been quoted on the total contract quantity as terminated for comparison with the overhead rates quoted on the original contract quantity. To the

extent that those rates change because of partial termination, appellant is entitled to an adjustment by the application of the increase to remaining labor expended.

The board did not compute the specific amount of the equitable adjustment because the parties asked for a ruling only on whether the appellant was entitled to an equitable adjustment, and, if so, how the equitable adjustment should be computed. The essence of the board's conclusion and decision was:

Appellant's failure of proof as to the learning curve results in no adjustment for starting load costs. We find that appellant is entitled to an equitable adjustment in its contract price for the increase in its overhead rates during the period January-June 1959 by reason of the partial termination of its contract. This represents the approximate period during which the contract would have been completed but for termination ... the rate adjustment should be computed on the difference between the rates used for contract pricing ... and the average rates forecast for the first half of 1959 in appellant's budget ... the increased percentages ... should be applied to the full manufacturing and engineering labor figures used for Pricing Amendment No. 1 to the contract and multiplied by the 55 engines delivered in 1959. If the G&A rate increased in the forecast for the first one-half of 1959 ... an appropriate adjustment should be made therefore. To the figure thus computed there should be added profit of 10% but not interest.

LEARNING CURVE TECHNIQUES

The decision in the appeal of *Celesco Industries, Inc.,* ASBCA No. 21928, 81-2 BCA par. 15,260, involved a number of important principles applicable to preparing and supporting claims for equitable price adjustments. Inasmuch as most of them are discussed elsewhere in this chapter under specific topic captions, comments on *Celesco* are limited to the acceptability of learning curve techniques, and we cite the board's view on this subject:

We agree with the parties that the unamortized labor costs on the unterminated or completed quantity of the simulators is best represented by the difference between the average labor hours per unit expended on the smaller quantity of completed units and the average labor hours per unit which would have been experienced if the contract had been completed. *Henry Spen & Company, Inc.,* ASBCA No. 20766, 77-2 BCA par. 12,784 at 62,180.

Both parties computed this difference on the basis of a learning improvement curve that has been defined as follows:

"The theory of the learning curve is that for a particular design of aircraft, trailer or other manufactured product the direct labor hours per unit progressively decline in accordance with a mathematical formula, and the rate of decline is expressed as a percentage of labor reduction between doubled quantities." *Dunbar Kapple, Inc.,* ASBCA No. 3631 57-2 BCA par. 1448 at 4875.

Appellant considers without foundation in the law respondent's argument that the claim for loss of learning should be denied because appellant failed to demonstrate that it had used learning curve principles in calculating the expected cost of fabrication when preparing its bid. We agree with appellant that by closer examination the case cited by respondent, *Fairchild Stratos Corporation*, ASBCA No. 9169, 67-1 BCA par. 6225, does not stand for such a broad proposition. In that case the contract for aircraft engines had been partially terminated for the convenience of the Government in the middle of the production and the board refused to grant an equitable adjustment based on a learning curve on two grounds: the contractor's failure to prove that there would be some increase in efficiency with production of greater numbers of engines and that it had utilized such assumption in pricing this contract (at 28,798). The board also noted that the learning curves the contractor proposed were not based on experience with the engine involved. On the contrary, on three consecutive prior procurements of the same engines, the contractor had quoted virtually identical amounts of labor hours. This in effect eliminated or disregarded any possibility of improvement in labor efficiency and thus "belied . . . [the] estimates and assumptions for application of a learning curve at all." (*Ibid.* at 28,793)

This is not the case here. There seems to be no disagreement that in the production of this type of simulator there is involved a learning factor which is demonstrated by the actual labor effort expended in the performance of the contract. In such a situation it would be proper to use the learning curve in computing the equitable adjustment due the contractor on account of having been able to complete only about one- half of the initial contract quantity. "Where a fixed unit price is to be paid for all contract quantities, and where the costs of production are shown to decline as production continues, then recovery of unamortized labor learning experience is proper. *Continental Electronics Manufacturing,* ASBCA No. 14749, 71-2 BCA par. 9108." *Bermite Divn. of Tasker Industries,* ASBCA No. 18280, on motion for reconsid. 77-2 BCA par. 12,731 at 61,879, aff'ng 77-1 BCA par. 12,349.

We may add that the use of learning curve technique in determining equitable adjustments has been accepted by this board, in addition to the cases already cited, on a number of previous occasions. See *Lockley Manufacturing Co., Inc.,* ASBCA No. 21231, 78-1 BCA ¶ 12,987; *Ortronix, Inc.,* ASBCA No. 12745, 72-2 BCA ¶ 9564; *Lake State Manufacturing Corp.,* ASBCA No. 17286, 73-2 BCA ¶ 10,190; *Hicks Corporation,* ASBCA No. 10760, 66-1 BCA ¶ 5469.

We offer the following observations regarding improvement (learning) curves. Most of the major contractors have experts in this area and, in significant disputes, engage outside experts with appropriate credentials. In contrast, many medium-sized and most of the smaller companies neither employ such experts nor engage outside consultants. A number of considerations are involved in these decisions and certainly the amount of the claim at issue would be a very important one. If the amount involved is significant, we believe the contractor *should* engage an expert in this field because the government agency is very likely to include such an expert among its witnesses. Lacking a counterpart would place the contractor at a distinct disadvantage.

INTEREST AS A COST IN CLAIMS FOR EQUITABLE ADJUSTMENTS

Significant changes involving allowability and timing of interest as a cost in claims for equitable price adjustments were made by the Contract Disputes Act of 1978, as discussed in Chapter XXIII of this text. The discussion of interest below applies to appeals which were not taken under this Act.

S.S. Silberblatt, Inc. v. The United States, Ct.Cl. No. 209-76, 29 CCF par. 81,610

A comprehensive commentary on interest on borrowings and allowance for the use of equity capital during delay periods is found in the appeals of S.S. Silberblatt, Inc. The case took a complex path to the Postal Service Board of Contract Appeals, PSBCA No. 297, 80-1 BCA par. 14,263, then to the U.S. Court of Claims for the decision cited in the above caption, then back to the Postal Service Board of Contract Appeals, PSBCA No. 297, 82-2 BCA par. 16,096. Because of the thorough review of leading board and court rulings, we include an extended analysis of this series of appeals and exclude digests of a number of disputes that appeared in prior editions of this text.

In the initial appeal, Silberblatt argued that the interest paid during the period of delay was an increase in the cost of performing the contract. It further argued that the claim was based solely on delay and, therefore, did not fall within the series of board and court decisions concerning interest on borrowed funds for changed work.

The government argued that under this 1965 contract Silberblatt was prohibited from recovering interest by both statute and case law. The government cited 28 U.S.C. 2516(a): "Interest on a claim against the United States shall be allowed in a judgment of the Court of Claims only under a contract or act of Congress expressly providing for payment thereof." As to case law, the government relied mainly on *Dravo Corporation v. The United States,* 25 CCF par. 82,542, 594 F.2d 842 (Ct.Cl. 1979), and decisions cited therein, and contended that Silberblatt had not shown that the interest paid was increased by or should be attributed to the suspension of work.

Studying the question of the payment of interest on contractor claims, the PSBCA started, as do most judicial and quasi-judicial bodies, with *Bell v. United States,* 13 CCF par. 82,406, 186 Ct.Cl. 189 (1968), which involved a delay under a 1953 contract that did not include a suspension of work provision. Bell had financed the contract work with a substantial bank loan and sought to recover interest on that loan during the period of delay. The court ruled that the board should have applied the "constructive change doctrine" and instructed the contracting officer to issue a change order. Inasmuch as the Silberblatt contract provided for a price adjustment for "any increase in the cost of performance" during a delay, and in view of the court's observation in *Bell* that extra interest on borrowed money "undoubtedly" is an increased cost of performance during a period of delay, it appeared to the board to this point that Silberblatt should prevail.

However, the board then reviewed subsequent court of claims decisions: *Framlau Corp. v. United States,* 24 CCF par. 81,906, 215 Ct.Cl. 185 (1977); *Singer Co. v. United States,* 24 CCF par. 81,914, 215 Ct.Cl. 281 (1977); *Coley*

Properties Corp. v. United States, 25 CCF par. 83,084, 593 F.2d 380 (Ct.Cl. 1979); and *Dravo Corp. v. United States supra* (the last two decided February 21, 1979). It then cited a lengthy portion of the *Coley* decision from which we quote the following portion:

> . . . it is clear that this Court still holds to the view that direct tracing to a specific loan or a necessity for increased borrowing is still required to be proven in order for a contractor to recover interest costs under an equitable adjustment theory.

> * * * *

> Fact finders should not have to speculate as to whether any borrowing was necessitated by changed work . . . .

> * * * *

> This Court requires that a clear necessity for borrowings occasioned by the change be proven.

The PSBCA concluded that the court had thus clarified its ruling in *Bell,* and that its present position ". . . is that a contractor is entitled to receive payment for interest on borrowings only when the contractor clearly demonstrates that its borrowings were incurred or increased as the direct result of a requirement for additional funds to finance a contract change or a government-caused delay. The board concluded that Silberblatt had not met these requirements and denied the claim.

Silberblatt also argued that it had committed approximately $5 million of its own funds to the contract, that such funds were impounded during the period of delay, and that it was entitled to be compensated for the loss of use of those funds during that period.

The government cited *Dravo, supra,* where the court found an argument of this kind had a "certain appeal" without granting the claim:

> Although plaintiff has ably argued its position in this regard, the Court must apply the law as it finds it, and it finds 28 U.S.C. § 2516(a) (1970) precluding recovery under these factual circumstances. This Court is not free to substitute its view of what the law ought to be; that function is reserved for the Congress.

In denying Silberblatt's claim, the board said: "We perceive no authority for this board to do that which the court finds it is unable to do."

Silberblatt appealed to the U.S. Court of Claims, which upheld the board with respect to its ruling denying recovery for Silberblatt's use of its own funds. The court found the board's decision "correct as a matter of law" and noted that "the use of equity capital is generally regarded as an element of profit." The court further ruled:

> The suspension of work clause contained in the contract before us expressly excludes any allowance for profit. In view of this contractual provision and 28 U.S.C. § 2516(a), we hold that plaintiff is not entitled to recover any compensation for the use of its risk capital during the period of delay.

The dispute was considerably less clear-cut to the court with respect to Silberblatt's claim for interest on borrowed money. During the delay period, Silberblatt had two outstanding loans, one for $17 million and one for $1 million in another bank. During the delay period, the latter loan was increased to $2 million. As the board viewed it, except for the facts that the loans continued to run and that Silberblatt continued to pay interest on them, Silberblatt presented no evidence showing a change in its borrowing as a result of the delays.

The following views of the court are very significant and we invite our readers' close attention to them:

> The board then concluded that, as a result of these later decisions [*Dravo*, *Singer* and *Framlau*], it is the present position of the court "that a contractor is entitled to receive payment for interest on borrowings only when the contractor clearly demonstrates that its borrowings were incurred or increased as the direct result of a requirement for additional funds to finance a contract change or government-caused delay." We hold that the Board has misconstrued our decisions in the cited cases; that our decision in *Bell* has not been modified or limited, and that under the suspension of work clause, the contractor is entitled to recover extra interest paid or incurred on existing loans as a direct result of the Government's delay.

But then the court was unable to make a specific ruling and remanded the question to the board to make additional findings of fact and conclusions of law as may be required.

> ... if it is found that [Silberblatt] was required to pay or that it incurred additional interest on either or both of the outstanding loans as a direct result of the 3½ month delay, [Silberblatt] would be entitled to recover the amount of interest so paid. On the other hand, if it is found that in view of [Silberblatt's] loan arrangements and other circumstances [Silberblatt] would have paid or incurred the claimed interest on either or both of the loans even if the delay had not occurred, [Silberblatt] would not be entitled to recover.

On remand from the U.S. Court of Claims, Silberblatt did not fare very well. The contractor had incurred interest of $282,625 on the $17 million loan and $29,358 on the $1 million dollar loan that had been increased to $2 million. The board allowed the smaller interest cost and denied the larger. Although Silberblatt's recovery was much lower than it had expected, the court's ruling and the board's decision on remand establishes a basis for more equitable recoveries for government contractors.

The contract was for the construction of a Postal facility upon the completion of which the contractor was to lease the facility to the Postal Service. The government acknowledged its responsibility for the 3½ months' suspension of work that resulted in a delay in the execution of the lease by that amount of time. As to the larger loan, the contractor argued it should be viewed as two separate borrowings for two separate periods—the construction period and the operations period. As the construction period was delayed or protracted, Silberblatt paid extra interest on the building loan, which it said it was entitled to recover. The contractor's expert witness, however, conceded that if the loan had been paid off at the maturity date, the total interest on the building and permanent loans would not have increased. The board found no distinction between the construction and operations financing and noted that the maturity date for the note was unaffected by the delay. It concluded Silberblatt had presented no evidence to show an increase in its overall interest obligation on the larger loan.

On the smaller loan, however, it was clear that the loan had been increased because of the delay, and the basis for the board's denial of the interest claim in the initial decision was difficult to explain. The difficulty is increased by the board's finding in the initial decision that the funds from this loan were used exclusively for the Postal Service facility. Despite this finding and despite the unrebutted testimony of Silberblatt's witnesses that the loan would have been paid but for the delay, the government apparently continued to argue against allowing this interest, contending that the contractor had produced no records to show the conditions of the loan or when it was finally paid and that other factors may have prevented the loan being paid.

The board agreed that Silberblatt "has not presented the kind of documentary evidence that would establish a precise sequence of events." On the other hand, it found that the government had stipulated to "certain critical matters" and presented virtually no rebuttal. The preponderance of evidence, in the opinion of the board, established that Silberblatt had incurred additional interest during the delay period, which additional interest was the direct result of the delay. Nor did the board find anything in the loan arrangements to indicate the contractor would have incurred the interest costs regardless of the delay.

The board's allowance of the interest on the smaller loan on remand is obviously correct. Its denial of the interest on the larger loan is certainly debatable. The major point in this series of appeals by Silberblatt is the establishment of the fine distinction between the board's initial understanding of the nature of the evidence required by a contractor to support a claim for interest on a government-caused delay under a suspension of work clause provision and the criteria established by the U.S. Court of Claims. The board's initial and more rigid requirement was for a contractor to "clearly demonstrate that its borrowings were incurred or increased as a direct result of a requirement for additional funds to finance a contract change or a government-caused delay." In contrast, the court established that if a contractor "was required to pay or . . . incurred additional interest . . . as a direct result of the . . . delay, [the contractor] would be entitled to recover the amount of interest paid."

New York Shipbuilding Co., a Division of Merritt-Chapman & Scott Corporation, ASBCA No. 16164, 76-2 BCA par. 11,979, MFR denied, 83-1 BCA par. 16,534

In our judgment, no study of recovery of interest on equity capital in equitable adjustment claims would be complete without careful consideration of a separate opinion filed by Administrative Judge John Lane, Jr., in the ruling on the motion for reconsideration of *New York Shipbuilding Co.*

In its initial ruling in 1976, the board concluded that the contractor was entitled to recover imputed interest, regardless of whether the contractor had borrowed money and paid out interest or whether it used its own capital and lost interest because that money was unavailable for other purposes. The board handed down other similar rulings in that period but departed from this course after what appeared to be adverse rulings by the Court of Claims, e.g. *Dravo Corp. v. The United States,* 25 CCF par. 82,542, 219 Ct. Cl. 416, 594 F.2d 842 (1979).

Some seven years after the board's decision, the government concluded that it had found a basis for filing a motion for reconsideration. The legal implications of the motion are not germane to the major issue nor appropriate for coverage in this text. Accordingly, we shall not comment on the merit of the government's arguments nor the board's decision, which denied the motion as untimely by a unanimous vote of the five-judge panel.

The point of interest here, however, is that Administrative Judge Lane, Jr., who wrote the opinion, also filed a lengthy separate opinion representing his own view that the board's initial decision to grant interest on equity capital was and remains correct. Unfortunately, the other four judges did not join in the opinion on the ground that "it deals with matters irrelevant to the disposition of this motion." Two of the four went even further and noted their disagreement "with the substance of Judge Lane's separate opinion in view of the Court of Claims' clear position on this issue."

With due respect to the four judges who did not join in Judge Lane's opinion, we share the views of many attorneys and others well versed in government contracting matters that this separate comprehensive opinion is an excellent scholarly analysis of a complex problem. We further believe that a well presented appeal, giving full consideration to the problems the court found in *Framlau* and *Dravo,* could ultimately prevail before the U.S. Court of Appeals for the Federal Circuit, or, if unsuccessful because the court elected to follow precedent of the Court of Claims, could prevail before the U.S. Supreme Court. Space does not permit the kind of analysis of Judge Lane's opinion that would do it justice. We strongly recommend that all seriously concerned with government contracting issues study it with great care.

Citing numerous decisions by boards of contract appeals and federal courts, evolution of laws and regulations, and views of recognized commentators, Judge Lane traces the history of reimbursing interest in claims. He concludes that the court's decision in *Dravo* does not overrule the board's decision in *New York Shipbuilding.* After his careful review of the court's ruling in that case, as well as in *Singer, Framlau,* and the more recent *Silberblatt,* he concludes that, if the necessary evidentiary support were provided, the court's position would have to be regarded as "still open." He also reviewed recent BCA decisions, some denying interest on equity capital citing *Dravo,* but was not persuaded that under other circumstances and with other evidence the contractors would not have recovered. We would note in this regard that the claims of *Creative Electric, Inc.,* ASBCA No. 21498, 83-1 BCA par. 16,363, February 24, 1983, was denied by a 3-2 divided court. The dissenter, (Judge Lane not involved) cited cases where the board had allowed a profit factor "in recognition of 'financing effort,'" citing for example *R.L. Spencer Construction Co., Inc.*, ASBCA No. 18450, 75-2 BCA par. 11,604.

While not exactly on point, the board's decision in *Blue Cross Association & Blue Shield Association (In the Matter of Pennsylvania Blue Shield)*, ASBCA No. 21113, July 20, 1982, 82-2 BCA par. 15,966, is of interest. The same panel that sat in *New York Shipbuilding* ruled that imputed cost of equity capital, referred to as Return on Investment (ROI), was properly reimbursable as an administrative expense. Different contract provisions and the absence of specific application of FPR or DAR separate this decision from the others under discussion, but the principle appears to be similar. Here the contractor prevailed in a 4-1 decision, also written by Judge Lane, with three of the judges who parted company with him in *New York Shipbuilding* joining him in *Blue Cross.*

As mentioned earlier, space does not permit the kind of review of Judge Lane's erudite opinion that would do it justice and we commend its study. We do quote below the very end of his opinion, beginning with his views on recent board cases and ending with his final conclusion. The reader would do well to remember that judicial history is not without instances where minority opinions of one period became majority opinions of another and where minority opinions of administrative boards and lower courts became the majority opinion of higher courts.

Examination of the facts of those cases, however, will reveal that in virtually all of them the claim was either a bare assertion of entitlement to extra profit without evidentiary support of the kind discussed earlier, or a claim based on commercial interest rates rather than conservative moneymarket rates reflecting the pure timecost of money, or a claim for an extra allowance over and above a profit factor that was already adequate to compensate for the capital invested in the changed work or at least had not been shown inadequate, or a claim in the nature of damages for a pure delay in paying money due (such as liquidated damages or progress payments).

In particular, the facts in *Schwam* indicate that the Board felt an allowance of extra profit for the use of capital would have been a double recovery, because "appellant has elected to compute its profit on the weighted guidelines which includes an allowance for its investment." 79-2 BCA 68,332. In *Praxis,* the facts indicate that the contractor had already agreed to the equitable adjustment pricing of changed work and was asserting a separate damages claim for late progress payments and loss of interest on money used to finance the changed work.

Moreover, in at least two of the cases (*Herley* and *Parsons*), the contractor was found entitled to interest from the date of appeal under the Payment of Interest on Contractor's Claims clause, so that the time period and the dollars involved in an application of the rule of his case might well have been de minimis. In one case (*Washington Patrol*), no entitlement to an equitable adjustment for changes was found, where a delay in payment was caused by late formalization of a contract extension, so there was no investment of capital in changed work; and if there had been, the Payment of Interest on Contractor's Claims clause would have applied and might well have covered all or most of the capital investment.

Understandably, too, absent the kind of evidentiary showing that would require careful reexamination of *New York Shipbuilding* in light of *Framlau, Singer,* and *Dravo,* there has been a tendency to cite recent Court of Claims comments on the issue, even if they were not authoritative holdings.

It is precisely because of the resulting confusion that I have provided here a thorough review of the *New York Shipbuilding* holding and rationale and of the Court of Claims' comments.

*   *   *   *

Our original decision in this case, properly understood with respect to the theoretical and historical basis of recovery, the appropriate measure of recovery, and the evidentiary prerequisites, is still good law and has not been overruled. It is squarely within the rule of *United States v. New York,* 160 U.S. 598 (1896). *Chelsea Factors, Inc. v. United States* [7 CCF ¶ 71,232], 149 Ct.Cl. 202, 181 F.Supp. 685 (1960), and *Bell v. United States,* 186 Ct.Cl. 189, 404 F.2d 975 (1968), allowing the payment of compensation for capital IN an equitable adjustment claim as part of the Government's payment for end items, and outside the scope of the statutory and common-law prohibition against recovery of interest ON a claim against the Government as damages for delay in payment of money due and owing. It is fully supported by long-standing and generally understood DOD policy and practice governing both initial contract pricing and repricing actions. The commonlaw bar against recovery of interest from the Government for delay in payment is premised on the "general rule, in the practice of the Government," *United States ex rel. Angarica v. Bayard,* 127 U.S. 251 (1888). The "general rule, in the practice of the Government" with respect to contract pricing and repricing over more than forty years *permits* recovery of compensation for both borrowed and equity capital as outside the commonlaw bar and the implementing statute, 28 U.S.C. § 2516(a).

Gevyn Construction Company, ENG BCA No. 3031, 83-1 BCA par. 16,428; *Gevyn Construction Company v. United States,* U.S. Claims Court, No. 158-74 [33 CCF Par. 74,851]

We have included a brief analysis of this case, reflecting a court ruling near the close of 1986, to indicate that there have been no significant changes in the judicial outlook with respect to (1) the refusal to recognize imputed interest on equity capital for profit-making organizations, and (2) insistence on proof and tracing of borrowed funds to the increased costs resulting from changes or delays before interest on borrowed money is allowed.

Gevyn was the prime contractor on a contract to rehabilitate a VA hospital and Potomac Metal Products, Inc., a major subcontractor. Gevyn filed a claim on its own behalf and on behalf of Potomac for increased costs resulting from government changes and delays. The claims were denied by the contracting officer and his decision was upheld by the ENG BCA. The ENG BCA was reversed by the Court of Claims, which directed the contracting officer to negotiate an equitable adjustment on those claims for which the government was ruled liable. In the negotiations, Gevyn reserved the right to pursue claims for itself and Potomac for the cost of financing the extra work. These claims—the prime's for imputed interest on its equity capital and the subcontractor's for interest on borrowed money—were subsequently submitted and denied by the contracting officer.

On appeal to the ENG BCA, Gevyn's claim was denied on the grounds that Gevyn had been well compensated throughout the contract by progress payments and had earned a reasonable profit before taking into consideration the additional amount received as a result of the equitable adjustment. The board also noted that Gevyn's financial position had been further enhanced by its slow payments to Potomac.

Gevyn had relied on *New York Shipbuilding Co.*, ASBCA No. 16164, 76-2 BCA par. 11,979, and *Fischbach & Moore*, ASBCA No. 18146, 77-1 BCA par. 12,300, where imputed interest on equity capital had been allowed. However, the board noted that these decisions had been overcome by subsequent court rulings in *Dravo Corporation v. U.S.* [25 CCF par. 82,542], 219 Ct. Cls. 416, 594 F. 2d 842 (1979) and *Framlau Corporation v. U.S.* [24 CCF par. 81,906] 215 Ct. Cls. 185, 568 F. 2d 687.

Potomac's claim for interest on borrowed money was also denied. The board ruled that borrowings could not be traced to the additional costs for which the equitable adjustment had been provided. Further, it ruled that Potomac's need for borrowing was attributable to Gevyn's delays in making payments to Potomac despite Gevyn's receipt of timely progress payments and its performance of the contract at a fair profit.

The United States Claims Court upheld the board's decisions with respect to both the prime and subcontractor. As to Gevyn, the court noted that the contractor's legal basis was correctly rejected by the board based on the *Framlau* decision. Whatever be the merits of Gevyn's appeal, we have always had doubts about the propriety of the *Framlau* ruling which, at least up to this time, has destroyed contractors' chances of recovering imputed interest on equity capital in equitable adjustment claims. Our doubts increased sharply after the promulgation of CAS 414, which specifically recognized cost of money. The portion of the *Framlau* ruling cited by the court here and in other cases to support denial of imputed interest is that "the cost to the contractor of borrowing capital is clearly determinable, while the [imputed interest value] to him of the use of equity capital is not so readily ascertainable."

It is difficult to accept such a wide-ranging, precedent-setting ruling on what, from accounting and economic viewpoints, seems to be such a weak point. We can concede that the imputed interest value of equity capital "is not so readily ascertainable" but do not see this as a strong enough basis for rejecting the entire concept, noting, again, the promulgation of CAS 414 and CAS 417. It may well happen some day that a contractor will appeal a denial of imputed interest on equity capital to higher courts where, perhaps, this issue will be treated more logically and fairly.

The court also upheld the board's denial of Potomac's claim for interest on borrowed money, agreeing that the borrowings were attributable to Gevyn's delays in making payments to Potomac rather than to actions by the government.

Chapter VIII

Cost Accounting Standards and Related Regulations

The promulgations of the Cost Accounting Standards Board (CASB), the implementing regulations in FAR, the impact on government and industry, and the legal controversies are susceptible to various methods of presentation. Based on our extensive experience with companies performing on CAS-covered contracts and our review of the many educational and training efforts in this area, we developed a pragmatic approach that we believe integrates the cost accounting standards into the other government cost and financial principles and regulations in an optimum manner. This approach is designed to facilitate the reader's understanding of this subject within the total context of government contracting.

This chapter includes (1) the background leading up to the creation of the CASB, (2) a history of its ten-year life and events leading to its termination, (3) the significant regulations (as contrasted to standards) it promulgated, (4) the implementation of these standards and regulations by the executive agencies, and (5) by the legislative and executive branches of the government, since the demise of the CASB, culminating in the incorporation of CAS into FAR, effective September 30, 1987.

As discussed more fully in describing the FAR revision incorporating CAS (FAC 84-30), efforts were made to facilitate references in the transition from the CASB publications to FAR. FAR Subparts 30.2, CAS Program Requirements, and 30.3, CAS Rules and Regulations, include the rules and regulations, in somewhat different order, which were contained in CAS Subchapters C and E, Part 331, Contract Coverage, Part 332, Modified Contract Coverage, and Part 351, Disclosure Statement. The Disclosure Statement form itself is omitted, companies being advised to secure copies from their contracting officers.

The text of the standards, contained in CASB Subchapter G, were relocated to FAR Subpart 30.4. The conventional FAR paragraph numbering procedure was modified to facilitate referencing. For example, CAS 401 is cited as FAR 30.401, and so on. As to the commentaries in this text on the standards published by the defunct CASB, our discussions with observers in both the public and private sectors indicated that the reader would find it easier if we continued to refer to the standards as CAS 401, etc., instead of FAR 30.401, and we have done so. Our comments on the related rules and regulations, however, cite the old CASB and/or FAR references as it appears appropriate.

Chapter IX—Management Practices and Accounting Systems for Government Contracts includes the Disclosure Statement, Part 351 of the Board's regulations, and standards 401, 402, 405, 406, and 407.

Chapter X—Accounting Methods and Controls for Material includes standard 411.

Chapter XI—Accounting Methods and Controls for Labor includes standard 408.

Chapter XIII—Accounting Methods and Controls for Manufacturing Overhead includes standard 418.

Chapter XIV—Accounting Methods and Controls for Engineering and Research and Development Expenses includes standard 420.

Chapter XV—Accounting Methods and Controls for Selling, General and Administrative Expenses includes standards 403 and 410.

Chapter XVII—Application of Government Contract Cost Principles to Specific Costs and Expenses includes standards 404, 409, 412, 413, 414, 415, 416, and 417.

BACKGROUND OF EVENTS LEADING TO CREATION OF THE CAS BOARD

Public Law 90-370 -- Feasibility Study

The Defense Production Act of 1950, as periodically amended, includes Title VII, which prohibits discrimination by government contractors against contracts to which priorities are assigned by charging higher prices or imposing different terms and conditions. During the congressional hearings on the extension of the Act in 1968, Admiral Rickover testified that this provision was unenforceable because in the absence of uniform cost accounting standards the government had no way of ascertaining what the costs were, whether profits were excessive, or whether there was discrimination in the form of higher pices. Rickover's vigorous espousal of congressional action to correct these alleged problems by requiring contractors to use uniform cost accounting standards was countered by almost unanimous opposition from both the private and public sectors. The American Institute of Certified Public Accountants (AICPA), industry associations and individual government contractors, the Department of Defense and even the General Accounting Office (GAO) either strongly opposed such legislation or asserted the concept was vague and argued that it was neither feasible nor desirable to impose a standard accounting system for the myriad defense contractors. (The extension to nondefense contractors had not been discussed at that time.)

The strong and pervasive opposition to imposing this new regulation upon industry almost sealed the doom of the Rickover proposal. However, in an eleventh hour maneuver, the congressional CAS proponents succeeded in enacting a compromise measure—a study to determine the feasibility of applying uniform cost accounting standards to negotiated prime and subcontracts in excess of $100,000. P.L. 90-370 required the Comptroller General, in cooperation with the Secretary of Defense and the Director of the Bureau of the Budget (now the Office of Management and Budget—OMB), to conduct this study, including consulting with the accounting profession and the defense industry, and to report back to the Congress within 18 months.

The feasibility study was a mammoth undertaking, with the Comptroller General soliciting advice from just about every interested organization and individual in both the public and private sectors. A very considerable portion of the work, including the preparation of the final report to Congress, was performed by members of GAO and DCAA, although significant inputs, including preparing and analyzing questionnaires and submitting views, were received from academia and from industry associations.

The final report, consisting of some 550 pages, concluded that it was both feasible and desirable "to establish and apply cost-accounting standards to provide a greater degree of uniformity and consistency in cost accounting as a basis for negotiating and administering procurement contracts." The Comptroller General recommended that the standards be made applicable to all negotiated prime and subcontracts government-wide and that "new machinery should be established for the development of cost-accounting standards." The report reviewed the following and concluded they were "not adequate for contract costing because they have been designed for different purposes: generally accepted accounting principles, regulations of the Internal Revenue Service, Regulations of the Securities and Exchange Commission, and rules adopted by the Renegotiation Board." ASPR Section XV was also considered inadequate for a number of reasons, including its dependence on generally accepted accounting principles and IRS rules and because it included provisions stating that "in ascertaining what constitutes costs, any 'generally accepted method' of determining or estimating costs that is 'equitable under the circumstances' may be used."

The recommendation that "new machinery" was needed for promulgating CAS reflected strong GAO and DCAA views that government procurement authorities would not formulate the very strict accounting rules that those auditors prefer. However, the report also included some caveats and limitations regarding CAS, which many observers feel the CAS Board and its proponents subsequently failed to consider, e.g.: "It is not feasible to establish and apply cost-accounting standards in such detail as would be necessary to ensure a uniform application of precisely prescribed methods of computing costs for each of the different kinds of costs, under all the wide variety of circumstances involved in Government contracting."

Enactment of Public Law 91-379

The report on the feasibility study was submitted in January 1970, and congressional hearings on legislation to implement its recommendations began that March. The hearings in both houses attracted many witnesses with strong feelings on the issue. GAO, of course, to be consistent with the conclusions of the feasibility study, changed its position and the Comptroller General spoke in favor of CAS. The AICPA also withdrew its objections and endorsed the concept, albeit without much enthusiasm. Industry associations and the Financial Executives Institute provided the major voices of opposition.

After the hearings, congressional debates continued for months, but P.L. 91-379 ultimately passed both houses in August 1970 by very wide margins. In signing the bill, President Nixon expressed the view that the Board should be in the Executive Branch and requested Congress to amend the statute accordingly. The provisions of the statute we believe to be of the greatest significance to the government contracting community are set forth below:

(a) There is established, as an agent of the Congress, a Cost-Accounting Standards Board which shall be independent of the executive departments and shall consist of the Comptroller General of the United States who shall serve as Chairman of the Board and four members to be appointed by the Comptroller General. Of the members appointed to the Board, two, of whom one shall be particularly knowledgeable about the cost accounting problems of small business, shall be from the accounting profession, one shall be representative of industry, and one shall be from a department or agency of the Federal Government who shall be appointed with the consent of the head of the department or agency concerned.

* * * *

(g) The Board shall from time to time promulgate cost-accounting standards designed to achieve uniformity and consistency in the cost-accounting principles followed by defense contractors and subcontractors under Federal contracts. Such promulgated standards shall be used by all relevant Federal agencies and by defense contractors and subcontractors in estimating, accumulating, and reporting costs in connection with the pricing, administration and settlement of all negotiated prime contract and subcontract national defense procurements with the United States in excess of $100,000, other than contracts or subcontracts where the price negotiated is based on (1) established catalog or market prices of commercial items sold in substantial quantities to the general public, or (2) prices set by law or regulation. In promulgating such standards the Board shall take into account the probable costs of implementation compared to the probable benefits.

* * * *

(h)(1) The Board is authorized to make, promulgate, amend, and rescind rules and regulations for the implementation of cost-accounting standards promulgated under subsection (g). Such regulations shall require defense contractors and subcontractors as a condition of contracting to disclose in writing their cost-accounting principles, including methods of distinguishing direct costs from indirect costs and the basis used for allocating indirect costs, and to agree to a contract price adjustment, with interest, for any increased costs paid to the defense contractor by the United States because of the defense contractor's failure to comply with duly promulgated cost-accounting standards or to follow consistently his disclosed cost-accounting practices in pricing contract proposals and in accumulating and reporting contract performance cost data. Such interest shall not exceed 7 per centum per annum measured from the time such payments were made to the contractor or subcontractor to the time such price adjustment is effected. If the parties fail to agree as to whether the defense contractor or subcontractor has complied with cost-accounting standards, the rules and regulations relating thereto, and cost adjustments demanded by the United States, such disagreement will constitute a dispute under the contract dispute clause.

(2) The Board is authorized, as soon as practicable after the date of enactment of this section, to prescribe rules and regulations exempting from the requirements of this section such classes or categories of defense contractors or subcontractors under contracts negotiated in connection with national defense procurements as it determines, on the basis of the size of the contracts involved or otherwise, are appropriate and consistent with the purposes sought to be achieved by this section.

(3) Cost-accounting standards promulgated under subsection (g) and rules and regulations prescribed under this subsection shall take effect not earlier than the expiration of the first period of sixty calendar days of continuous session of the Congress following the date on which a copy of the proposed standards, rules, or regulations is transmitted to the Congress; if, between the date of transmittal and the expiration of such sixty-day period, there is not passed by the two Houses a concurrent resolution stating in substance that the Congress does not favor the proposed standards, rules, or regulations. For the purposes of this subparagraph, in the computation of the sixtyday period there shall be excluded the days in which either House is not in session because of adjournment of more than three days to a day certain or an adjournment of the Congress *sine die.* The provisions of this paragraph do not apply to modifications of cost accounting standards, rules, or regulations which have become effective in conformity with those provisions.

(i)(A) Prior to the promulgation under this section of rules, regulations, cost-accounting standards, and modifications thereof, notice of the action proposed to be taken, including a description of the terms and substance thereof, shall be published in the *Federal Register.* All parties affected thereby shall be afforded a period of not less than thirty days after such publication in which to submit their views and comments with respect to the action proposed to be taken. After full consideration of the views and comments so submitted the Board may promulgate rules, regulations, cost-accounting standards, and modifications thereof which shall have the full force and effect of law and shall become effective not later than the start of the second fiscal quarter beginning after the expiration of not less than thirty days after publication in the *Federal Register.*

*   *   *   *

(j) For the purpose of determining whether a defense contractor or subcontractor has complied with duly promulgated cost-accounting standards and has followed consistently his disclosed cost-accounting practices, any authorized representative of the head of the agency concerned, of the Board, or of the Comptroller General of the United States shall have the right to examine and make copies of any documents, papers, or records of such contractor or subcontractor relating to compliance with such cost-accounting standards and principles.

In an amendment enacted in 1975, the last sentence in paragraph (g) was changed to read as follows: "In promulgating such standards and major rules and regulations for the implementation of such standards, the Board shall take into account, and shall report to the Congress in the transmittal required by section 719(h)(3) of this Act, the probable costs of implementation, including inflationary effects, if any, compared to the probable benefits, including advantages and improvements in the pricing, administration, and settlement of contracts."

THE COST ACCOUNTING STANDARDS BOARD, 1971-1980, A BRIEF HISTORY

Although P.L. 91-379 was enacted on August 15, 1970, Congress adjourned without appropriating funds for its operations and the Comptroller General concluded he could not move to implement the statute until the funds were appropriated. Congress passed the necessary bill toward the end of the year and it was signed into law early in January, 1971. Later that month, the Comptroller General named the other four members, and the first CASB meeting, largely ceremonial in nature, was held on February 9, 1971. The following month the Board's first executive secretary was named and he assumed his duties on April 1. Thereafter, recruitment of the other staff members began, as did planning and research for the promulgation of standards and regulations to meet the requirements established by law.

Initial CASB Promulgations

On December 30, 1971, the Board published in the *Federal Register* and requested comments on its regulations relating to Contract Coverage (Part 331), Disclosure Statement (Part 351), and CAS 401 and 402. After considering the comments and making some revisions, the regulations and standards were forwarded to Congress on February 24, 1972, for approval.

Cost Accounting Standards

A complete list of the standards issued by the CASB, and their effective and applicability dates, are set forth below.

401. Consistency in Estimating, Accumulating and Reporting Costs—effective and applicable July 1, 1972.

402. Consistency in Allocating Costs Incurred for the Same Purpose—effective and applicable July 1, 1972.

403. Allocation of Home Office Expenses to Segments—effective July 1, 1973, required to be followed as of the beginning of the next fiscal year after September 30, 1973.

404. Capitalization of Tangible Assets—effective July 1, 1973, applicable to accrued expenditures for acquisition of tangible capital assets during the contractor's next fiscal year beginning on or after October 1, 1973.

405. Accounting for Unallowable Costs—effective and applicable to all solicitations issued on or after April 1, 1974.

406. Cost Accounting Period—effective July 1, 1974, required to be followed by each contractor as of the start of his next fiscal year beginning after receipt of a contract to which this standard is applicable.

407. Use of Standard Costs for Direct Material and Direct Labor—effective October 1, 1974, required to be followed by each contractor as of the start of his next fiscal year beginning after the receipt of a contract to which this standard is applicable.

408. Accounting for Costs of Compensated Personal Absence—effective July 1, 1975, required to be followed by each contractor as of the start of his next fiscal year beginning after the receipt of a contract to which this standard is applicable.

409. Depreciation of Tangible Capital Assets—effective July 1, 1975, required to be followed by each contractor for all tangible assets acquired on or after the start of his next fiscal year beginning after the receipt of a contract to which this standard is applicable.

410. Allocation of Business Unit General and Administrative Expense to Final Cost Objectives—effective October 1, 1976, required to be followed by each contractor after the start of his next fiscal year beginning after January 1, 1977.

411. Accounting for Acquisition Costs of Material—effective January 1, 1976, required to be applied to materials purchased or produced after the start of the contractor's next fiscal year beginning after receipt of a contract to which this standard is applicable.

412. Composition and Measurement of Pension Cost—effective January 1, 1976, required to be followed by each contractor on or after the start of his next cost accounting period beginning after the receipt of a contract to which this standard is applicable.

413. Adjustment and Allocation of Pension Cost—effective March 10, 1978, required to be followed by each contractor on or after the start of his next cost accounting period beginning after the receipt of a contract to which this standard is applicable.

414. Cost of Money as an Element of the Cost of Facilities Capital—effective October 1, 1976, but not applicable to contracts awarded, or on which final agreement on price was reached, prior to the effective date.

415. Accounting for the Cost of Deferred Compensation—effective July 10, 1977, required to be followed by each contractor for awards of deferred compensation made on or after the start of his next cost accounting period beginning after the receipt of a contract to which this standard is applicable.

416. Accounting for Insurance Costs—effective July 10, 1979, required to be followed by each contractor on or after the start of his next cost accounting period beginning after the receipt of a contract to which this standard is applicable.

417. Cost of Money as an Element of the Cost of Capital Assets Under Construction—effective December 15, 1980, required to be followed by each contractor on or after the start of his next cost accounting period beginning after the receipt of a contract to which this standard is applicable.

418. Allocation of Direct and Indirect Costs—effective September 20, 1980, required to be followed by each contractor on or after the start of his

second fiscal year beginning after the receipt of a contract to which this standard is applicable.

419. (withdrawn and not replaced)

420. Accounting for Independent Research and Development Costs and Bid and Proposal Costs—effective March 15, 1980, required to be followed by each contractor as of the start of his *second* fiscal year beginning after the receipt of a contract to which this standard is applicable.

In terms of output, the CASB promulgated 19 standards in the ten years of its operations: 1971—0; 1972—3; 1973—3; 1974—2; 1975—3; 1976—3; 1977—1; 1978—1; 1979—1; 1980—2.

CASB RULES AND REGULATIONS

P.L. 91-379 authorizes the Board to promulgate standards, rules, and regulations. Most of the promulgations in the rules category are not of major import to government contractors. They cover the Board's organization and operations, responsibilities and conduct of the CASB members and staff, release of information, and bylaws. One rule of interest to the private sector is Part 303—Release of Information. Although the CASB is a legislative arm and hence not required to comply with the Freedom of Information Act, it has adopted the essence of the provisions of that statute.

The major regulations are Part 331—Contract Coverage, Part 332— Modified Contract Coverage, and Part 351—Disclosure Statement. Some of the regulations have been extremely controversial since their initial issuance in draft in February 1972. They have been amended several times, the latest revision having been promulgated at the Board's last meeting on September 18, 1980, with an effective date of April 1, 1981.

Part 331 - Contract Coverage as Amended, Effective April 1, 1981

Paragraph 331.20 contains a number of key definitions, including "national defense" and "negotiated subcontract," terms that are not always understood. The major portion of this paragraph defines a "cost accounting practice" and a "change to a cost accounting practice," and provides a series of illustrations of changes and the related accounting treatment, categorized as to whether they constitute changes to cost accounting practices. The illustrations merit careful study to develop a thorough knowledge of these terms as defined in the CASB regulations, because a change to a cost accounting practice requires a contractor to compute the impact on CAS-covered contracts and to negotiate an equitable adjustment to the contract price as provided in paragraph (a)(4)(C) of the CAS contract clause.

Paragraph 331.30 addresses applicability, exemption, and waiver. The major change reflected in the April 1, 1981, revision was the addition of the following exemption:

> Any firm fixed price contract or subcontract awarded without submission of any cost data: *Provided,* that the failure to submit such data is not attributable to a waiver of the requirement for certified cost or pricing data. (Italics in original.)

This provision reflects a partial concession to vigorous urging by a broad spectrum of the government contracting community, beginning as far back as February 1972, to exempt all procurements awarded based on adequate price competition. After turning a deaf ear to these recommendations for many years, the Board proposed on February 8, 1980, to exempt "any firm fixed price contract or subcontract awarded without submission of any cost data." Industry objected that this provision failed to meet the objective of exempting firm fixed price contracts where costs play no part in determining the price. The Council of Defense and Space Industry Associations (CODSIA) pointed out that the submission of some cost data by a contractor does not necessarily mean that the buyer has relied on that cost data in making the award and recommended the adoption of the P.L. 87-653 (Truth in Negotiations) ground rules, which require the contractor to submit a certificate of cost or pricing data and an indication that the government relied on that data. The CASB was not only adamant in rejecting this recommendation, but moved a step back by heeding an apprehension expressed by a government agency that the proposed language might prove to be an incentive for a potential contractor to seek to avoid submission of cost data. To allay these apprehensions, the Board added the proviso cited in the above excerpt.

The other exemptions remained pretty much unchanged, but government contractors should be fully aware of those relating to small business concerns, firms that are elegible to use Part 332—Modified Contract Coverage, and others.

Provisions relating to waivers remained unchanged, requiring so much effort, documentation, and attention by very high level DOD officials that the granting of the waiver by the CASB was indeed a rare occurrence in its ten years of operations. As we shall discuss later in this chapter, efforts to transfer the Board's functions to OMB failed after the CASB was forced to cease operations for lack of appropriations. The CASB chairman refused to delegate the waiver authority to DOD and it appeared that no organization had the authority to approve a waiver. The manner in which DOD subsequently asserted the waiver authority is described later in this chapter.

Paragraph 331.50 contains the CAS contract clause and 331.70 provides related interpretations, provisions that were born and continue to live in controversy. The major issue involved the provision in 331.70(b) that, for firm fixed price contracts, increased cost to the government because of the contractor's failure to follow its cost accounting practices or comply with applicable cost accounting standards would ". . . be measured by the difference between the cost estimate used in negotiation and the cost estimate that would have been used had the contractor proposed on the basis of the practices actually used during the contract performance."

For many years industry had vainly tried to persuade the Board that this provision should be changed because, as many people saw the issue, once a firm fixed price contract was properly priced and awarded, subsequent cost shifts to other firm fixed price contracts or to commercial work, as a result of changes to cost accounting practices or failure to follow applicable standards, cannot and do not result in increased costs paid by the government. As far back as August 1978, CODSIA wrote the Board:

> Increased costs can arise only where the change in practice or failure to comply results in additional *payments* by the government caused by the change or failure. A mere difference between what costs are to be and those considered at the time of pricing, in and of itself, does not warrant a contract price change absent additional *payments* caused by the change or failure. (Emphasis added.)

Years of study and submission of cogent papers failed to persuade the CASB, and these regulations remained substantially unchanged, except for the final version that offered the minor concession with respect to firm fixed-price contracts: "The determination of the contract price that would have been agreed to will be left to the contracting parties and will depend on the circumstances of each case."

Part 332 - Modified Contract Coverage as Amended, Effective April 1, 1981

Although not revised in the April 1981 version, Part 332 represents another illustration of many years' efforts by industry and belated action by the CASB.

Subparagraph (h)(2) of P.L. 91-379 authorizes the Board ". . . as soon as practicable . . . to prescribe rules and regulations exempting from the requirements of this section such classes or categories of defense contractors or subcontractors . . . as it determines on the basis of the size of the contracts involved or otherwise, are appropriate and consistent. . . ."

From the very early days of the CASB, both industry and DOD urged exemptions for contractors whose national defense awards represented minor portions of their total business. It appeared illogical to most observers for a company with a small percentage of defense procurements to be required to change its costs accounting practices to comply with CAS. Nevertheless, the Board delayed action for years while it demanded various data and conducted numerous studies. It was not until March 10, 1978, that modified contract coverage was provided for a "business unit which in its immediately preceding cost accounting period received less than $10 million in award of covered contracts: Providing, That the sum of such awards equals less than 10 percent of the business unit's total sales during that period." As an additional restriction, the regulation provides that, if a business unit receives a single contract award of $10 million or more, that contract must contain the regular CAS clause, as must any other covered contract awarded in the same cost accounting period.

Under the contract clause that may be used by contractors qualified under Part 332, compliance is required only with respect to CAS 401 and 402, and the company's cost accounting practices must be followed consistently. The submission of a Disclosure Statement is not required unless the contractor is a business unit of a company *required* to submit a Disclosure Statement.

Part 332 is a relatively short regulation and reasonably clear and so requires little discussion here. One provision, however, is important and should be given attention. Paragraph 332.70(a) discusses the mechanics of determining whether the sum of contract awards equals less than 10% of the business unit's total sales and provides that ". . . an order received by the one segment from another segment shall be treated in the same way that a subcontract award to the receiving segment would be treated. In measuring sales for a year, transfer by one segment to another shall be deemed to be a sale by the transferor."

Subchapter E - Disclosure Statement, Part 351 - Basic Requirements

The initial threshold requirement for filing disclosure statements was $30 million in national defense procurements in fiscal year 1971. From that time (1972), the CASB continually lowered the threshold. Current regulations require:

> . . . any defense contractor which, together with its segments, received net awards of negotiated national defense prime contracts and subcontracts subject to Cost Accounting Standards totaling more than $10 million in its most recent cost accounting period, must submit a completed Disclosure Statement . . . Any business unit which receives a negotiated national defense contract or subcontract which is subject to Cost Accounting Standards and is for $10 million or more must submit a completed Disclosure Statement . . . Each corporate or other home office which allocates costs to one or more disclosing segments performing covered contracts shall file a Part VIII of the Disclosure Statement.

From time to time, additional contractors become subject to this regulation when the total of their CAS-covered contracts and subcontracts in the preceding fiscal year exceed $10 million or they receive a single CAS-covered contract for $10 million or more. In these instances, the companies should secure the necessary form (CASB-DS-1) from the contracting officer and complete it. For those exposed to this requirement, it can be a difficult chore, particularly if they lack adequate accounting manuals containing their policies and procedures. DCAA and other contract audit agencies are required to determine the adequacy of the disclosure statements, that is, whether they reflect the contractor's accounting practices accurately, completely, and currently. If the government auditors find the statements inadequate, contractors may be involved in considerable additional efforts.

Contractors must be advised by their cognizant contracting officers whether their disclosure statements are adequate. However, although they may receive any number of notices that their practices are noncompliant with cost accounting standards and/or FAR, they seldom if ever are advised that they are in compliance. A major problem resulting from this government policy is that contractors may have followed certain cost accounting practices for many years without complaints from the government and then suddenly receive notice that such practices are in noncompliance with various standards. In the case of practices followed under FAR cost principles, a long series of BCA and court decisions will generally deter the government from attempting to impose retroactive adjustments. While this issue has not been specifically litigated at this writing, a legal consensus suggests that the statutory status of cost accounting standards may permit retroactive adjustments by the government back to the date of the initial noncompliance. In the author's view, such action would be patently unfair.

IMPLEMENTATION OF CASB PROMULGATIONS BY EXECUTIVE AGENCIES

Implementation of CASB regulations and standards by the executive departments and agencies of the federal government may be divided into several categories, ranging from the formal and official to the informal. Those that will be discussed here, regardless of the categories in which they fall, are important for companies bidding for or performing under CAS-covered contracts.

INCORPORATION OF CAS INTO FAR

As noted earlier, while legislation to reestablish a CAS Board was still under consideration in both houses of Congress, a final rule effective September 30, 1987, incorporated CAS into FAR. At this writing, it cannot be predicted with certainty whether this Administration-supported action will end the arguments of many years over the placement of the CAS function or whether legislation urged by GAO and DOD critics in Congress will establish an independent board. And, if such legislation should pass both houses, the question would arise as to whether it would encounter a presidential veto and, if so, whether sufficient support for such a measure could be generated to overcome a veto.

Rules and Regulations

Parts 331, 332, and 351 of the CASB promulgations contained the rules and regulations relating to requirements, administration, and other guidance, including the Disclosure Statement. Additionally, FAR Part 30 contained guidance related to Disclosure Requirements, CAS Contract Requirements, and CAS Administration. Virtually all of the material, exclusive of the actual standards, have now been consolidated into FAR Subparts 30.2 and 30.3. The contents of each Subpart are listed below:

30.201	Contract requirements
30.201-1	CAS applicability
30.201-2	Types of CAS coverage
30.201-3	Solicitation provisions
30.201-4	Contract clauses
30.201-5	Waiver
30.202	Disclosure requirements
30.202-1	General requirements
30.202-2	Impracticality of submission
30.202-3	Amendments and revisions
30.202-4	Privileged and confidential information
30.202-5	Filing Disclosure Statements
30.202-6	Responsibilities
30.202-7	Determinations
30.202-8	Subcontractor Disclosure Statements
30.301	Definitions
30.302	Definitions, explanations, and illustrations of the terms, "cost accounting practice" and "change to a cost accounting practice"
30.302-1	Cost accounting practice
30.302-2	Change to a cost accounting practice
30.302-3	Illustrations of changes which meet the definition of "change to a cost accounting practice"
30.302-4	Illustrations of changes which do not meet the definition of "change to a cost accounting practice"
30.303	Effect of filing Disclosure Statement

On balance, the changes resulting from consolidating the former CASB and FAR provisions and the several changes in the sequence appear to have resulted in an easier to follow and study regulation. Some of the significant sections of these subparts are quoted here.

SUBPART 30.2—CAS PROGRAM REQUIREMENTS

30.201 Contract requirements.

30.201-1 CAS applicability.

(a) This subsection describes the rules for determining whether a proposed contract or subcontract is exempt from CAS. (See Subpart 30.4.) Negotiated contracts not exempt in accordance with 30.201-1(b) shall be subject to CAS. A CAS-covered contract may be subject to either full or modified coverage. The rules for determining whether full or modified coverage applies are in 30.201-2.

(b) The following categories of contracts and subcontracts are exempt from all CAS requirements:

(1) Sealed bid contracts.   *

(2) Negotiated contracts and subcontracts not in excess of $100,000.

(3) Contracts and subcontracts with small businesses.

(4) Contracts and subcontracts with foreign governments or their agents or instrumentalities or, insofar as the requirements of CAS other than 30.401 and 30.402 are concerned, any contract or subcontract awarded to a foreign concern.

(5) Contracts and subcontracts in which the price is set by law or regulation.

(6) Contracts and subcontracts when the price is based on established catalog or market prices of commercial items sold in substantial quantities to the general public (see 15.804-3(c)). A prospective contractor requesting exemption from CAS on this basis must provide supporting justification in accordance with 15.804-3(e). When the contracting officer determines that the justification is adequate, this exemption from CAS shall be used even though the award is made on the basis of adequate price competition.

(7) Contracts and subcontracts of $500,000 or less if the business unit is not currently performing any national defense CAS-covered contracts.

(8) Nondefense contracts awarded based on adequate price competition (see 15.804-3(b)).

(9) Nondefense contracts and subcontracts awarded to business units that are not currently performing any CAS-covered national defense contracts.

(10) Contracts and subcontracts with educational institutions other than those to be performed by Federally Funded Research and Development Centers (FFRDC's) operated by such institutions.

(11) Contracts awarded to labor surplus area concerns pursuant to a labor surplus area set-aside (see Part 20).

(12) Contracts and subcontracts awarded to a United Kingdom contractor for performance substantially in the United Kingdom, provided that the contractor has filed with the United Kingdom Ministry of Defense, for retention by the Ministry, a completed Disclosure Statement (Form No. CASB-DS-1) which shall adequately describe its cost accounting practices. Whenever that contractor is already required to follow U.K. Government Accounting Conventions, the disclosed practices shall be in accord with the requirements of those conventions. (See 30.201-4(d).)

(13) Subcontracts under the NATO PHM Ship program to be performed outside the United States by a foreign concern.

(14) Contracts and subcontracts to be executed and performed entirely outside the United States, its territories, and possessions.

(15) Firm-fixed-price contracts and subcontracts awarded without submission of any cost data; (*provided,* that the failure to submit such data is not attributable to a waiver of the requirement for certified cost or pricing data).

30.201-2 Types of CAS coverage.

(a) *Full coverage.* Full coverage requires that the business unit comply with all of the CAS in effect on the date of the contract award and with any CAS that become applicable because of later award of a national defense CAS-covered contract. However, the award of a new nondefense CAS-covered contract shall not trigger application of new CAS having effective dates later than the award date of the last national defense CAS-covered contract. Full coverage applies to contractor business units that—

(1) Receive a single national defense CAS-covered contract award of $10 million or more;

(2) Received $10 million or more in national defense CAS-covered contract awards during its preceding cost accounting period; or

(3) Received less than $10 million in national defense CAS-covered contract awards during its preceding cost accounting period but such awards were 10 percent or more of total sales.

(b) *Modified coverage.* (1) Modified CAS coverage requires only that the contractor comply with Standard 401, Consistency in Estimating, Accumulating, and Reporting Costs, and Standard 402, Consistency in Allocating Costs Incurred for the Same Purpose. Modified, rather than full, CAS coverage may be applied to a covered contract of less than $10 million awarded to a business unit that received less than $10 million in national defense CAS-covered contracts in the immediately preceding cost accounting period if the sum of such awards was less than 10 percent of the business unit's total sales during that period. For the purpose of determining whether the sum of covered contract awards equals 10 percent of the business unit's total sales, an order received by the one segment from another segment shall be treated in the same way that a subcontract award to the receiving segment would be treated. In measuring sales for a year, a transfer by one segment to another shall be deemed to be a sale by the transferor.

(2) If any one contract is awarded with modified CAS coverage, all CAS-covered contracts awarded to that business unit during that cost accounting period must also have modified coverage with the following exception: if the business unit receives a single national defense contract award of $10 million or more, that contract must be subject to full CAS coverage. Thereafter, any covered contract awarded in the same cost accounting period must also be subject to full CAS coverage.

(3) A contract awarded with modified CAS coverage shall remain subject to such coverage throughout its life regardless of changes in the business unit's CAS status during subsequent cost accounting periods.

(c) *Nondefense contracts.* Nondefense contracts subject to CAS shall have the same type of CAS coverage as the most recently awarded national defense contract currently being performed by the same business unit.

(d) *Subcontracts.* Subcontract awards subject to CAS require the same type of CAS coverage as would prime contracts awarded to the same business unit.

(e) *Foreign concerns.* Contracts with foreign concerns subject to CAS shall only be subject to modified coverage.

* * * *

30.201-5 Waiver.

(a) In some instances, contractors or subcontractors may refuse to accept all or part of the requirements of the CAS clauses (52.230-3, Cost Accounting Standards and 52.230-5, Disclosure and Consistency of Cost Accounting Practices). If the contracting officer determines that it is impractical to obtain the materials, supplies, or services from any other source, the contracting officer shall prepare a request for waiver describing the proposed contract or subcontract and containing—

(1) An unequivocal statement that the proposed contractor or subcontractor refuses to accept a contract containing all or a specified part of a CAS clause and the specific reason for that refusal;

(2) A statement as to whether the proposed contractor or subcontractor has accepted any prime contract or subcontract containing a CAS clause;

(3) The amount of the proposed award and the sum of all awards by the agency requesting the waiver to the proposed contractor or subcontractor in each of the preceding 3 years;

(4) A statement that no other source is available to satisfy the agency's needs on a timely basis;

(5) A statement of alternative methods considered for fulfilling the need and the agency's reasons for rejecting them;

(6) A statement of steps being taken by the agency to establish other sources of supply for future contracts for the products or services for which a waiver is being requested; and

(7) Any other information that may be useful in evaluating the requests.

(b) (1) For national defense contracts of the DOD, waivers shall be controlled and approved by the Deputy Assistant Secretary of Defense (Procurement) and shall be processed for review by the Defense Acquisition Regulatory (DAR) Council in accordance with agency procedures.

(2) For national defense contracts of National Aeronautics and Space Administration (NASA), waivers shall be controlled and approved by the Assistant Administrator for Procurement after consultation with the Deputy Assistant Secretary of Defense (Procurement). Requests for waiver shall be processed in accordance with agency regulations.

(c) For nondefense contracts, and defense contracts of agencies other than DOD or NASA, the agency head or designee may waive CAS requirements. Agencies shall ensure consistent treatment of—

(1) Waivers within the agency; and

(2) Contractors performing under both defense and nondefense contracts.

(d) For purchases of substantially the same product from the same contractor for which a waiver was previously granted, approval authority is redelegated in the Department of Defense to the Secretaries of the Military Departments and the Director, Defense Logistics Agency.

30.202 Disclosure requirements.

30.202-1 General requirements.

(a) A Disclosure Statement is a written description of a contractor's cost accounting practices and procedures. The submission of a new or revised Disclosure Statement is not required for any nondefense contract or from any small business concern. However, if a Disclosure Statement has been submitted in connection with a CAS-covered defense contract, the contractor must also comply with such disclosed practices under nondefense CAS-covered contracts (see subparagraph (a)(1) of the clause at 52.230-3, Cost Accounting Standards).

(b) Completed Disclosure Statements are required in the following circumstances:

(1) Any business unit that is selected to receive a CAS-covered negotiated national defense contract or subcontract of $10 million or more shall submit a Disclosure Statement before award.

(2) Any company which, together with its segments, received net awards of negotiated national defense prime contracts and subcontracts subject to CAS totaling more than $10 million in its most recent cost accounting period must submit a Disclosure Statement before award of its first CAS-covered contract in the immediately following cost accounting period. However, if the first CAS-covered contract is received within 90 days of the start of the cost accounting period, the contractor is not required to file until the end of 90 days.

(c) When a Disclosure Statement is required, a separate Disclosure Statement must be submitted for each segment whose costs included in the total price of any CAS-covered contract or subcontract exceed $100,000 unless the contract or subcontract is of the type or value exempted by 30.201-1. If the cost accounting practices are identical for more than one segment, then only one Disclosure Statement, clearly identifying each such segment, need be submitted. A Disclosure Statement will also be required for each corporate or group office whose costs of any amount are allocated to one or more segments performing CAS-covered contracts.

(d) Each corporate or other home office that allocates costs to one or more disclosing segments performing CAS-covered contracts must submit a Part VIII of the Disclosure Statement.

(e) Foreign contractors and subcontractors who are required to submit a Disclosure Statement may, in lieu of filing a Form No. CASB-DS-1, make disclosure by using a disclosure form prescribed by an agency of its Government, provided that the official designated to approve waivers in 30.201-5 determines that the information disclosed by that means will satisfy requirements of Subpart 30.2. The use of alternative forms has been approved for the contractors of the following countries:

(1) Canada.

(2) Federal Republic of Germany.

30.202-2 Impracticality of submission.

The agency head may determine that it is impractical to secure the Disclosure Statement, although submission is required, and authorize contract award without obtaining the Statement. This authority may not be delegated.

30.202-3 Amendments and revisions.

(a) Contractors and subcontractors are responsible for maintaining accurate Disclosure Statements and complying with disclosed practices. Amendments and revisions to Disclosure Statements may be submitted at any time and may be proposed by either the contractor or the Government. Resubmission of complete, updated, Disclosure Statements is discouraged except when extensive changes require it to assist the review process.

(b) Should the obligation to maintain the Disclosure Statement cease because the contractor no longer meets the financial thresholds, the contractor shall still be required to follow the disclosed practices for those contracts awarded during a period in which the contractor was obligated to submit a Disclosure Statement.

30.202-4 Privileged and confidential information.

If the offeror or contractor notifies the contracting officer that the Disclosure Statement contains trade secrets and commercial or financial information, which is privileged and confidential, the Disclosure Statement shall be protected and shall not be released outside the Government.

30.202-5 Filing Disclosure Statements.

(a) Disclosure must be on Form Number CASB-DS-1. Forms may be obtained from the cognizant administrative contracting officer (ACO).

(b) Offerors are required to file Disclosure Statements as follows:

(1) Original and one copy with the cognizant ACO; and

(2) One copy with the cognizant contract auditor.

(c) Amendments and revisions shall be submitted to the currently cognizant ACO and auditor.

30.202-6 Responsibilities.

(a) The contracting officer is responsible for determining when a proposed contract may require CAS coverage and for including the appropriate notice in the solicitation. The contracting officer must then ensure that the offeror has made the required solicitation certifications and that required Disclosure Statements are submitted.

(b) The contracting officer shall not award a CAS-covered contract until the ACO has made a written determination that a required Disclosure Statement is adequate unless, in order to protect the Government's interest, the contracting officer waives the requirement for an adequacy determination before award. In this event, a determination of adequacy shall be required as soon as possible after the award.

(c) The cognizant auditor is responsible for conducting reviews of Disclosure Statements for adequacy and compliance.

(d) The cognizant ACO is responsible for determinations of adequacy and compliance of the Disclosure Statement.

30.202-7 Determinations.

(a) *Adequacy determination.* The contract auditor shall conduct an initial review of a Disclosure Statement to ascertain whether it is current, accurate, and complete and shall report the results to the cognizant ACO, who shall determine whether or not it adequately describes the offeror's cost accounting practices. If the ACO identifies any areas of inadequacy, the ACO shall request a revised Disclosure Statement. If the Disclosure Statement is adequate, the ACO shall notify the offeror in writing, with copies to the auditor and contracting officer. The notice of adequacy shall state that a disclosed practice shall not, by virtue of such disclosure, be considered an approved practice for pricing proposals or accumulating and reporting contract performance cost data. Generally, the ACO shall furnish the contractor notification of adequacy or inadequacy within 30 days after the Disclosure Statement has been received by the ACO.

(b) *Compliance determination.* After the notification of adequacy, the auditor shall conduct a detailed compliance review to determine whether or not the disclosed practices comply with Part 31 and the CAS and shall advise the ACO of the results. The ACO shall take action regarding noncompliance with CAS under FAR 30.602-2. The ACO may require a revised Disclosure Statement and adjustment of the prime contract price or cost allowance. Noncompliance with Part 31 shall be processed separately, in accordance with normal administrative practices.

30.202-8 Subcontractor Disclosure Statements.

(a) The contractor or higher tier subcontractor is responsible for administering the CAS requirements contained in subcontracts.

(b) If the subcontractor has previously furnished a Disclosure Statement to an ACO, the subcontractor may satisfy the submission requirement by identifying to the contractor or higher tier subcontractor the ACO to whom it was submitted.

(c)(1) If the subcontractor considers the Disclosure Statement (or other similar information) privileged or confidential, the subcontractor may submit it directly to the ACO and auditor cognizant of the subcontractor, notifying the contractor or higher tier subcontractor. A preaward determination of adequacy is not required in such cases. Instead, the ACO cognizant of the subcontractor shall (i) notify the auditor that the adequacy review will be performed during the postaward compliance review and, upon completion, (ii) notify the subcontractor, the contractor or higher tier subcontractor, and the cognizant ACO's of the findings.

(2) Even though a Disclosure Statement is not required, a subcontractor may (i) claim that CAS-related reviews by contractors or higher tier subcontractors would reveal proprietary data or jeopardize the subcontractor's competitive position and (ii) request that the Government perform the required reviews.

(d) When the Government requires determinations of adequacy or inadequacy, the ACO cognizant of the subcontractor shall make such recommendation to the ACO cognizant of the prime contractor or next higher tier subcontractor. ACO's cognizant of higher tier subcontractors or prime contractors shall not reverse the determination of the ACO cognizant of the subcontractor.

(e) Postaward submission of the subcontractor's Disclosure Statement must be approved by the ACO having cognizance of the prime contractor. Before authorizing postaward submission, the ACO shall coordinate with the ACO cognizant of the subcontractor to ensure that this action will not have an adverse impact on other contracts and subcontracts subject to the CAS requirements, and with the contracting officer to obtain the information needed to make the required written determination.

(f) Any determination that it is impractical to secure a subcontractor's Disclosure Statement must be made in accordance with 30.202-2.

SUBPART 30.3—CAS RULES AND REGULATIONS

*   *   *   *

30.302 Definitions, explanations, and illustrations of the terms, "cost accounting practice" and "change to a cost accounting practice."

30.302-1 Cost accounting practice.

"Cost accounting practice," as used in this part, means any disclosed or established accounting method or technique which is used for allocation of cost to cost objectives, assignment of cost to cost accounting periods, or measurement of cost.

(a) "Allocation of cost to cost objectives," as used in this part, includes both direct and indirect allocation of cost. Examples of cost accounting practices involving allocation of cost to cost objectives are the accounting methods or techniques used to accumulate cost, to determine whether a cost is to be directly or indirectly allocated to determine the composition of cost pools, and to determine the selection and composition of the appropriate allocation base.

(b) "Assignment of cost to cost accounting periods," as used in this part, refers to a method or technique used in determining the amount of cost to be assigned to individual cost accounting periods. Examples of cost accounting practices which involve the assignment of cost to cost accounting periods are requirements for the use of specified accrual basis accounting or cash basis accounting for a cost element.

(c) "Measurement of cost," as used in this part, encompasses accounting methods and techniques used in defining the components of cost, determining the basis for cost measurement, and establishing criteria for use of alternative cost measurement techniques. The determination of the amount paid or a change in the amount paid for a unit of goods and services is not a cost accounting practice. Examples of cost accounting practices which involve measurement of costs are—

(1) The use of either historical cost, market value, or present value;

(2) The use of standard cost or actual cost; or

(3) The designation of those items of cost which must be included or excluded from tangible capital assets or pension cost.

30.302-2 Change to a cost accounting practice.

"Change to a cost accounting practice," as used in this part, means any alteration in a cost accounting practice, as defined in 30.302-1, whether or not such practices are covered by a Disclosure Statement, except for the following:

(a) The initial adoption of a cost accounting practice for the first time a cost is incurred, or a function is created, is not a change in cost accounting practice. The partial or total elimination of a cost or the cost of a function is not a change in cost accounting practice. As used here, function is an activity or group of activities that is identifiable in scope and has a purpose or end to be accomplished.

(b) The revision of a cost accounting practice for a cost which previously had been immaterial is not a change in cost accounting practice.

*   *   *   *

30.303 Effect of filing Disclosure Statement.

(a) A disclosure of a cost accounting practice by a contractor does not determine the allowability of particular items of cost. Irrespective of the practices disclosed by a contractor, the question of whether or not, or the extent to which, a specific element of cost is allowed under a contract remains for consideration in each specific instance. Contractors are cautioned that the determination of the allowability of cost items will remain a responsibility of the contracting officers pursuant to the provisions of the applicable procurement regulations.

(b) The individual Disclosure Statement may be used in audits of contracts or in negotiation of prices leading to contracts. The authority of the audit agencies and the contracting officers is in no way abrogated by the material presented by the contractor in his Disclosure Statement. Contractors are cautioned that their disclosures must be complete and accurate; the practices disclosed may have a significant impact on ways in which contractors will be required to comply with Cost Accounting Standards.

30.304 Concurrent full and modified coverage.

Contracts subject to full coverage may be performed during a period in which a previously awarded contract subject to modified coverage is being performed. Compliance with full coverage may compel the use of cost accounting practices that are not required under modified coverage. Under these circumstances the cost accounting practices applicable to contracts subject to modified coverage need not be changed. Any resulting differences in practices between contracts subject to full coverage and those subject to modified coverage shall not constitute a violation of CAS 30.401 and CAS 30.402. This principle also applies to contracts subject to modified coverage being performed during a period in which a previously awarded contract subject to full coverage is being performed.

30.305 Materiality.

In determining whether amounts of cost are material or immaterial, the following criteria shall be considered where appropriate; no one criterion is necessarily determinative:

(a) *The absolute dollar amount involved.* The larger the dollar amount, the more likely that it will be material.

(b) *The amount of contract cost compared with the amount under consideration.* The larger the proportion of the amount under consideration to contract cost, the more likely it is to be material.

(c) *The relationship between a cost item and a cost objective.* Direct cost items, especially if the amounts are themselves part of a base for allocation of indirect costs, will normally have more impact than the same amount of indirect costs.

(d) *The impact on Government funding.* Changes in accounting treatment will have more impact if they influence the distribution of costs between Government and non-Government cost objectives than if all cost objectives have Government financial support.

(e) *The cumulative impact of individually immaterial items.* It is appropriate to consider whether such impacts (1) tend to offset one another, or (2) tend to be in the same direction and hence to accumulate into a material amount.

(f) *The cost of administrative processing of the price adjustment modification shall be considered.* If the cost to process exceeds the amount to be recovered, it is less likely the amount will be material.

30.306 Interpretations.

In determining amounts of increased costs in the clauses at 52.230-3, Cost Accounting Standards, and 52.230-5, Disclosure and Consistency of Cost Accounting Practices, the following considerations apply:

(a) Increased costs shall be deemed to have resulted whenever the cost paid by the Government results from a change in a contractor's cost accounting practices or from failure to comply with applicable Cost Accounting Standards, and such cost is higher than it would have been had the practices not been changed or applicable Cost Accounting Standards complied with.

(b) If the contractor under any fixed-price contract, including a firm fixed-price contract, fails during contract performance to follow its cost accounting practices or to comply with applicable Cost Accounting Standards, increased costs are measured by the difference between the contract price agreed to and the contract price that would have been agreed to had the contractor proposed in accordance with the cost accounting practices used during contract performance. The determination of the contract price that would have been agreed to will be left to the contracting parties and will depend on the circumstances of each case.

(c) The Government policy underlying this interpretation is that the United States not pay increased costs, including a profit enlarged beyond that in the contemplation of the parties to the contract when the contract costs, price, or profit is negotiated, by reason of a contractor's failure to use applicable Cost Accounting Standards, or to follow consistently its cost accounting practices. In making price adjustments under the Cost Accounting Standard clause at 52.230-3 in fixed price or cost reimbursement incentive contracts, or contracts providing for prospective or retroactive price redetermination, the Federal agency shall apply this requirement appropriately in the circumstances.

(d) The contractor and the contracting officer may enter into an agreement as contemplated by subdivision (a)(4)(ii) of the Cost Accounting Standards clause at 52.230-3, covering a change in practice proposed by the Government or the contractor for all of the contractor's contracts for which the contracting officer is responsible, provided that the agreement does not permit any increase in the cost paid by the Government. Such agreement may be made final and binding, notwithstanding the fact that experience may subsequently establish that the actual impact of the change differed from that agreed to.

(e) An adjustment to the contract price or of cost allowances pursuant to the Cost Accounting Standards clause at 52.230-3 may not be required when a change in cost accounting practices or a failure to follow Standards or cost accounting practices is estimated to result in increased costs being paid under a particular contract by the United States. This circumstance may arise when a contractor is performing two or more covered contracts, and the change or failure affects all such contracts. The change or failure may increase the cost paid under one or more of the contracts, while decreasing the cost paid under one or more of the contracts. In such case, the Government will not require price adjustment for any increased costs paid by the United States, so long as the cost decreases under one or more contracts are at least equal to the increased cost under the other affected contracts, provided that the contractor and the affected contracting officers agree on the method by which the price adjustments are to be made for all affected contracts. In this situation, the contracting agencies would, of course, require an adjustment of the contract price or cost allowances, as appropriate, to the extent that the increases under certain contracts were not offset by the decreases under the remaining contracts.

30.307 Cost Accounting Standards Preambles.

Following Part 30, an Appendix containing the nonregulatory preambles to the Cost Accounting Standards and preambles to related Rules and Regulations is provided in the looseleaf edition only. The preambles are not regulatory, but are intended to explain why the Standards and related Rules and Regulations were written, and to provide rationale for positions taken relative to issues raised in the public comments. The preambles are printed in chronological order to provide an administrative history. As revisions are made to Part 30, preambles will be published under the FAR system. Part I, Preambles to the Cost Accounting Standards, and Part II, Preambles to the Related Rules and Regulations published by the Cost Accounting Standards Board, were originally published in Title 4 of the Code of Federal Regulations. Part III is reserved for preambles to be published under the FAR System.

Cost Accounting Standards

The initial proposal to incorporate CAS into FAR did not include the CASB preambles or prefatory comments to the standards. This omission was met with objections because the preambles contain useful and informative material, particularly with respect to comments submitted on the preliminary drafts and the consideration accorded thereto by the CASB. The final version of the FAR revision adopted the recommendations to include the preambles, as explained in FAR 30.307, cited above.

The texts of the standards in FAR Subpart 30.4 are taken verbatim from the CASB publications, with certain exceptions. As to the minor deviations, paragraphs .10, .30, .70, and .80 are omitted as no longer necessary. These paragraphs covered the CASB's authority, definitions (now covered in the rules and regulations), exemptions, and effective dates.

A major exception was the inclusion of Interpretation No. 1 to CAS 403, Allocation of Home Office Expenses to Segments. As described in Chapter XV of this text, the allocation of state and local income and franchise taxes generated some of the heaviest and most expensive litigation for which the CASB was responsible. In the major decisions described in the aforementioned chapter, the ASBCA rebuked the CASB for attempting to intervene in the judicial process by ramming through an interpretation favoring the government while the litigation was in process. It also stated ". . . we do not consider the purported Cost Accounting Standards Board 'interpretation' as binding or determinative as to the proper interpretation of the standard."

If it is ultimately determined that the executive branch properly included CAS in FAR and has the authority to modify promulgated standards, it would appear that the rejected interpretation to CAS 403 could be proposed. In any event, the background information to FAC 84-30, incorporating CAS into FAR, was misleading in stating that "No changes to the substance of the Cost Accounting Standards or existing rules have been made."

Department of Defense CAS Steering Committee and Working Group

While the CASB was promulgating cost accounting standards and regulations, increasing controversies arose regarding their interpretation. One school of thought was that all required interpretations and amplifications should be issued by the Board. Another saw the standards as very similar to statutes, which are normally interpreted by the executive agencies.

In the Spring of 1975, DOD decided to take the initiative and form an organization that would issue interpretations of cost accounting standards and regulations. This group began to work and was formalized in Department of Defense Instruction 5126.45, issued June 23, 1976. The Instruction established a CAS Steering Committee and CAS Working Group. The Committee consisted of high level officials responsible for establishing policy guidelines for administration of CAS, promulgating guidances appropriate for timely and efficient administration of CAS, conducting liaison with CASB on major issues, and responding to congressional inquiries on this subject. In accordance with the usual bureaucratic procedures, the actual work was assigned to a lower level CAS Working Group "operating under the general guidance and direction of the CAS Steering Committee for the purpose of carrying out the detail work. . . ." The Working Group was chaired by a representative of the then Office of the Assistant Secretary of Defense (I&L) and the other members consisted of the representatives of the military departments, DLA, DCAA, and the Assistant Secretary of Defense (COMP).

With the approval of the Steering Committee, the CAS Working Group has issued 24 Working Group Papers, generally designated as W.G. followed by the number and date:

W.G. No.	Date	Subject
76-1	2-24-76	Interim Guidance for Implementing CAS 412.
76-2	2-24-76	Application of CAS to Contract Modifications and to Work Orders Placed Under Basic Agreements.
76-3	3-11-76	Application of CAS to Subcontracts.
76-4	10-1-76	Determining Increased Costs to the Government for CAS-Covered FFP Contracts.
76-5	10-1-76	Treatment of Implementation Cost Related to Changes in Cost Accounting Periods.
76-6	10-1-76	Application of CAS Clause to Changes in Contractor's Established Practices when a Disclosure Statement has been Submitted.
76-7	10-1-76	Significance of "Effective" and "Applicability" Dates Included in Cost Accounting Standards.
76-8	12-17-76	Use of the Offset Principle in Contract Price Adjustments Resulting from Accounting Changes.
76-9	12-17-76	Measurement of Cost Impact on Firm Fixed-Price Contracts.
77-10	2-2-77	Retroactive Implementation of CAS when Timely Compliance is not Feasible.
77-11	2-2-77	Implementation of CAS 410.
77-12	3-29-77	Deliberate Noncompliance and Inadvertent Noncompliance.
77-13	3-29-77	Applicability of CAS 405.
77-14	3-29-77	Early Implementation of New Cost Accounting Standards.
77-15	3-29-77	Influence of CAS Regulations on Contract Terminations.
77-16	6-14-77	Applicability of Cost Accounting Standards to Letter Contracts.
77-17	6-14-77	Identification of Cost Accounting Standards Contract Universe at Contractor's Plant.
77-18	6-14-77	Implementation of CAS 414—Cost of Money as an

		Element of the Cost of Facilities Capital; and DPC 76-3.
77-19	8-18-77	Administration of Leased Facilities Under Cost Accounting Standard 414, Cost of Money as an Element of the Cost of Facilities Capital.
77-20	6-14-77	Policy for Withdrawing Determination of Adequacy of Disclosure Statement.
78-21	1-16-78	Implementation of CAS 410, Allocation of Business Unit General and Administrative Expenses to Final Cost Objectives.
78-22	3-27-78	CAS 409 and the Development of Asset Service Lives.
79-23	1-21-79	Administration of Equitable Adjustment for Accounting Changes not Required by New Cost Accounting Standards.
79-24	1-26-79	Allocation of Business Unit G&A Expenses to Facilities Contracts.
81-25	2-10-81	Change in Cost Accounting Practice for States Income and Franchise Taxes as a Result of Change in Method of Reporting Income From Long-Term Contracts.

As discussed in Chapter XV of this text, CAS 410 has been one of the most controversial and unpopular standards issued by the Board. W.G. 78-21 substantially worsened the problem by interpreting CAS 410 in a manner that most observers were persuaded had no justification or basis. After years of intensive effort, industry finally persuaded the Defense Department that W.G. 78-21, which asserted that the total cost input base was the preferred method for allocating G&A expenses, did not correctly reflect the plain meaning of CAS 410. On April 10, 1981, an amendment to 78-21 revised the arbitrary provisions of the original Working Group Paper. Although the amendment was viewed as an improvement, there was a wide consensus in the private sector that the Defense Department was still misinterpreting CAS 410. The correctness of this belief was affirmed in ASBCA No. 23833, August 31, 1983, 83-2 BCA par. 16,813. In sustaining the appeal of *Ford Aerospace and Communications Corp., Aeronutronic Division,* the board destroyed the misconceptions of both the original and amended 78-21. This significant decision is discussed in Chapter XV of this text.

It is essential for companies performing under CAS-covered contracts to clearly understand the status of the Working Group Papers. It is the overwhelming consensus, indeed probably the unanimous view, of the attorneys involved in government contracting that the guidance furnished in these papers has no force or effect. The Papers were not prescribed by statute and were neither formally incorporated in DAR nor included or referred to in government contracts. On the other hand, the Guidance Papers are directive upon the Department of Defense contracting officers and contract auditors. Inasmuch as these officials are required to adhere to the provisions of the Papers, it is incumbent upon government contractors to be familiar with them.

Defense Contract Audit Manual—Chapter 8

As most of our readers are aware, the Defense Contract Audit Manual (CAM) is directive only to DCAA auditors. Nevertheless, as we pointed out in Chapter II and elsewhere, DCAA auditors, while serving in an advisory capacity, are extremely influential. For this reason, we recommend that companies performing on contracts with the federal government obtain copies of CAM and become familiar with the manner in which the DCAA people perform their audits and report the results of these audits to contracting officers.

Chapter 8 of CAM is titled Audit Guidance—Cost Accounting Standards, Rules and Regulations. Chapter 8 contains considerable useful information as to how the Agency reviews Disclosure Statements and determines proposals. Additionally, the major portion of Chapter 8 consists of analyses and explanations of the individual standards, together with illustrations over and above those contained in the formal standards.

Despite the contracting officer's fundamental authority, most experienced government contractors have found that the major issues involving cost accounting standards are raised by DCAA auditors and that contracting officers frequently follow DCAA recommendations. Accordingly, careful study of CAM Chapter 8 is extremely important in order to understand the guidance under which the contract auditors perform the CAS reviews.

THE SUN SETS ON THE CASB AND EFFORTS PROCEED TO REESTABLISH CAS FUNCTION

For a number of reasons, including the CAS Board's unpopularity in both the public and private sectors, and the Board's own periodic statements that boasted of substantial accomplishment of its intended purpose and, in contrast, allegations that additional work was required to evaluate the implementation of its promulgations, the CASB's support in Congress eroded, culminating in the congressional refusal to continue to fund this activity in the fiscal year beginning October 1, 1980.

Knowledge of this impending action generated considerable effort on the part of the then Comptroller General and CASB Chairman Staats to transfer the CAS function to GAO. Virtually unanimous opposition from federal departments and agencies and industry resulted in the abandonment of this scheme in favor of an alternative proposal to place the authority in OFPP, a proposal which OFPP and OMB were persuaded to accept. Enabling legislation, however, never moved out of committee because of sharp disagreements regarding the nature of OFPP's authority. Staats would provide that office with all of the authority possessed by the CASB, while the opposing consensus would limit OFPP to revising existing standards where necessary and would not permit the issuance of new standards.

The subject of the reestablishment of the CAS function never died, surfacing from time to time in congressional hearings. When or if concrete action in this area would have developed is difficult to surmise, but a series of actions by the Department of Defense in 1983 brought this matter unusual attention.

The Comptroller General had adamantly refused suggestions for assigning CAS authority to DOD and, in an effort to strengthen the arguments favoring OFPP, declined to transfer waiver authority to federal departments and agencies involved. Accordingly, at the demise of the Board, there appeared to be no way to grant waivers regardless of the needs that could be established in the interests of the national defense.

In the Fall of 1983, in an exchange of correspondence between DOD and the Department of Justice, DOD was advised that it "continues to have the authority to adopt the CAS in whole or in part and the Department of Defense has the authority, once such adoption occurs, to reject or grant exemptions to the CAS." Moving quickly to assert this newly discovered, broad authority, DOD proposed to establish, in effect, a CASB of its own.

DOD's "concept paper" proposing its own CASB, issued in January 1984, resulted in congressional hearings and heavy opposition from members of Congress, GAO, and industry. In an effort to block DOD's proposed action and move to a resolution of the problem of reestablishing the CAS function, Congressman LaFalce introduced a bill in April 1984 which, with a minor difference, would create a new CASB in the image of the original one. Hearings on the LaFalce measure drew wide opposition, even including GAO whose representative testified that his organization alone had the objectivity, independence, and expertise to perform this function and, therefore, the CAS authority should be assigned to GAO. Other witnesses, of course, opposed the measure and in particular objected to the presence of the Comptroller General or any other GAO member on a CASB.

In April 1985, Senator Roth introduced a five-part measure that included penalties for contractors submitting defective pricing proposals or claiming unallowable costs, reestablished the Renegotiation and CAS Boards, required DOD to conduct periodic profit studies, and placed 18-month limitations for contractors to submit claims against the government on DOD contracts. With each of the five titles stirring controversies of its own, this legislation predictably failed to move out of the committee.

In June 1986, the proposal to incorporate CAS into FAR was printed in the *Federal Register* and was met with the expected vigorous and near unanimous opposition from both the public and private sectors. In a rare display of agreement, both industry associations and GAO asserted that the staffs of the FAR Councils lacked the objectivity, accounting expertise and integrity to do the job.

Congressman LaFalce made another effort to reestablish an independent CASB, this time with the major improvement of substituting the OFPP Administrator as board chairman instead of the GAO chief. We thought that industry should have supported many features of this proposal. However, it appeared that the industry associations and some of the major contractors again failed to adopt a unified position, facilitating the ultimate CAS incorporation into FAR.

During the Fall of 1986, GAO was active in a series of vigorous attacks upon DOD's profit study (DFAIR), as discussed in Chapter XXV of this text, which culminated in the legislative watchdog's proposal for a law that would require OFPP to both conduct periodic profit studies and assume responsibility for CAS. A bill to implement GAO's proposal was introduced by Senator Proxmire in March 1987.

GAO's proposal and the related legislation were viewed by many observers as a devious effort to assign the CAS responsibility to OFPP on paper but to actually place the power in GAO. This was to be accomplished by establishing an Advisory Council, chaired by the Comptroller General and comprised of four additional members appointed by him, who were to advise the OFPP Administrator, which advice would be in the form of "formal comments for inclusion in the annual report submitted to the Congress." It hardly required an intensive analysis to discern the real intent of this legislation, especially upon noting the provisions which assigned no additional staff to OFPP for this purpose, in effect placing all of the authority in the GAO-directed "Advisory Council."

In the Fall of 1987, several members of Congress were considering bills that would establish a CASB independent of the FAR system. However, congressional priorities in other areas and DOD opposition strongly contested these efforts. In conjunction with legislation reauthorizing the OFPP, Brooks' House Government Operations Committee reported out a bill (H.R. 3345) that would assign that office authority not only for CAS but for determining allowability of costs. The Board responsible for both allocability and allowability of costs would be chaired by the OFPP Administrator and include six additional members, one each from DOD and a civilian agency, two from industry, and two CPAs.

Among problems encountered by H.R. 3345 were its additional provisions assigning OFPP increased authority to prescribe government procurement regulations, authorize debarment of contractors, propose a methodology for assessing contractor profits, and other matters. The sweeping authority proposed for OFPP generated unusually strong action by DOD, with the Secretary and Deputy Secretary of Defense seeking the support of the Armed Services Committees in both the House and Senate to defeat a measure that assertedly encroached on DOD's prerogatives.

Amidst the controversies generated by this and other proposed legislation, FAC 84-30 incorporated CAS into FAR and, unless rooted out of this Regulation by specific legislation, a DOD-controlled FAR committee would be responsible for initiating procurement regulations relating to cost allocability and cost allowability.

Without addressing the specific merits of all of the provisions of H.R. 3345, we believe that industry would be well advised to support the kind of board envisioned by this bill, providing the balance and expertise of private sector representation, and ending the confusion that has surfaced between cost accounting principles and cost accounting standards.

Chapter IX

Management Practices and Accounting Systems for Government Contracts

GOVERNMENT'S ROLE IN AFFAIRS OF DEFENSE CONTRACTORS

The government's intensive and extensive participation in the affairs of its contractors has virtually no counterpart in the commercial marketplace. To begin with, it establishes various social and economic ground rules that influence the selection of companies that may be considered as potential contractors and subcontractors in specific circumstances. Thus, there are set-asides for small business concerns, small "disadvantaged" firms, labor surplus area concerns, etc. The contracts must include a clause whereby the contractor warrants that the contract was not secured through payment of a contingent fee (with certain exceptions), and for breach of this warranty, the contract may be annulled. In addition, government contracts contain an incredible volume of clauses and provisions covering almost every aspect of performance.

Where prices are negotiated, contracts frequently provide that price reductions can be effected by the government where the cost or pricing data submitted by the contractor is deemed "defective"; however, similar provisions are not available for price increases. Contractors' books and records are subject to inspection by contracting officers, technical specialists, cost and price analysts, and auditors. In addition, contractors' plants and records may also be inspected by officials of agencies' Offices of Inspectors General, the General Accounting Office, Department of Justice, and staffs of congressional committees.

Approval may be required from the government before a contractor makes a decision as to whether a component should be manufactured or purchased and, if purchased, sometimes how and from whom. For example, FAR sets forth government policies and procedures as to component breakout. As discussed further in Chapter X of this book, under certain circumstances the government may decide to break out a component, that is, purchase the component and furnish it to the contractor. FAR Subpart 15.7 establishes conditions under which the contractor decides whether to make or buy, and, assuming approval by the contracting officer is obtained or not needed, the contractor may still be faced with other participation by the government. The contractor's purchasing and subcontracting system may be reviewed, and certain individual subcontracts may require prior approval. Contractors may be required to seek a large number of bids even where they know that only a limited number of firms can produce the item needed. They may also have to offer many explanations for failing to award a subcontract to the lowest bidder though they may know that the lowest bidder could not have performed. A contractor may also be required to expend considerable effort to place subcontracts with small businesses and labor surplus area concerns.

On October 24, 1978, the President signed into law Public Law 95-507 amending the Small Business Act and the Small Business Investment Act of 1958. Section 211 of P.L. 95-507 relates to subcontracting under federal contracts. The provisions of this law were implemented by OFPP Policy Letter 80-2, dated April 29, 1980, with an effective date of June 1, 1980. The law and implementing regulations resulted in a furor among administrators, attorneys, and accountants involved in government contracts. The problem was not the statement of government policies and objectives for greater utilization of small business concerns and small business concerns owned and controlled by "socially and economically disadvantaged individuals," but the many and very real problems in implementing the law, both for government agencies and for prime contractors. The problems include the definition of adequate subcontracting percentage goals, which must be established for each contract award, the difficulties in identifying small business and small disadvantaged business concerns for commercial products, and so on. OFPP Policy Letter 80-2 has been implemented in FAR Subpart 19.7, and most people in the government contracting community have been making good faith efforts to implement this legislation, which is characterized by worthy objectives but almost impossible implementation problems.

By contractual terms, the contract may be terminated by the government either for default or at the government's convenience. Even where the contract is terminated for the government's convenience, the contractor's claim may be subjected to unilateral determination by the contracting officer if the two parties are unable to negotiate a settlement.

Under certain circumstances, the government may acquire or reserve the right to acquire the principal or exclusive rights throughout the world in and to any inventions made in the course of or under a contract.

Standard contract clauses make it mandatory for the contractor to carry certain types of insurance.

Part 22 of FAR contains DOD policies, procedures, and contract clauses relating to labor. Among the matters in which the government is involved in all its contracts, or in specific circumstances, are overtime, use of convict labor, compliance with the Contract Work Hours Standards Act, compliance with Walsh-Healey Public Contracts Act, compliance with Fair Labor Standards Act of 1938, and antidiscrimination (equal opportunity) policies.

Theoretically, contractors may expend sums of whatever nature and amount they deem appropriate for salaries, maintenance, rentals, and other overhead expenses. As a practical matter, they are substantially influenced and restricted in their expenditures by the government contract cost principles and procedures. As detailed in FAR Part 31 and Parts 31 of the DOD and other agencies' FAR Supplements, many items of expense, even though appropriate under generally accepted accounting principles and practices and allowable for income tax purposes, may nevertheless be declared unacceptable in connection with cost determination of defense contracts. Thus, the portion of such a cost applicable to government contracts cannot be recovered against them and must come out of profits or equity.

In the preceding paragraphs we have presented a dark but realistic picture of some of the ways in which the government participates in the affairs of its contractors.

Chapter VIII of this text contains a historical summary of the Cost Accounting Standards Board and discusses its regulation, relating mainly to the administration of the Board's promulgations. In this chapter, we shall comment in further detail on the Disclosure Statement and move into the serious business of the standards themselves. This chapter will cover CAS 401, 402, 405, 406, and 407.

In some respects, the impact of the standards on companies performing CAS-covered contracts may exceed the government's role in its contractors' cost accounting matters, based on the requirements of FAR Part 31.

REQUIREMENTS AS TO COST ACCOUNTING SYSTEMS

The simplest definition of a cost accounting system is the extension of the systematic recording of financial transactions reflected in the general accounting system, and controlled by or reconciled thereto, for the purpose of disclosing the material, labor, and burden costs of manufacturing and selling a product. Although numerous types of cost systems are in use, adapted in most instances to the specific needs of particular industrial operations, any and all can generally be classified within or as combinations of six basic categories, shown below. It will be noted that the vertical listing relates to the manner in which costs are charged, i. e., historically as incurred or on a predetermined basis. The horizontal designation refers to the method of accumulating costs of production, whether by total costs of groups of items produced or by stages of production.

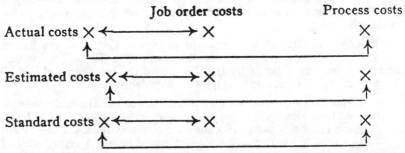

The foregoing diagram is intended to illustrate that costs may be charged as actual, estimated, or standard and in any of these cases may be accumulated on the basis of either jobs or processes. It is also desirable to specifically avoid the less logical classification of cost systems often encountered that contemplates a segregation among standard cost, job order cost, and process cost. It is obvious that cost systems may (and frequently do) reflect costs charged at standard and accumulated on the basis of jobs, processes, or a combination of the two.

VARIATIONS IN COST SYSTEMS

In addition to or as variations from the basic job order and process cost systems, the particular types of cost systems individually employed are as unlimited as is man's ingenuity. Class costs, parts costs, departmental costs, and assembly costs are only a few of the better known cost systems utilized. Moreover, many firms successfully employ more than one type in order to effectively determine product costs. The most common illustration of this is found in companies that, otherwise committed to the use of standard costs, consistently resort to actual costs for research activities and for initial operations on new production articles.

COST ACCOUNTING SYSTEMS FOR GOVERNMENT CONTRACTS

Prior to the issuance of the revised contract cost principles in November 1959, there existed very little in the way of authoritative government regulations regarding cost accounting systems. As mentioned later in this chapter, the Department of Defense Contract Audit Manual discusses systems of internal control and accounting. However, the contract audit manual is considered binding only on DCAA auditors.

GOVERNMENT CONTRACT COST PRINCIPLES AND GOVERNMENT COST ACCOUNTING STANDARDS (CAS)

Government contract cost principles and procedures, as set forth in FAR Part 31, consist of subparts dealing with the following topics: contracts with commercial organizations; contracts with educational institutions; contracts with state, local, and federally recognized Indian tribal governments; and contracts with nonprofit organizations. Detailed cost principles and procedures are provided only with respect to contracts with commercial organizations. More general provisions and references to OMB circulars are included for the other contracts.

In Chapter VIII, we discussed the origins of CAS, and the following provision of FAR 31.201-1, captioned "Composition of Total Cost," indicates the kind of reasonable flexibility that persuaded the proponents of CAS that the government contract cost principles were inadequate.

The total cost of a contract is the sum of the allowable direct and indirect costs allocable to the contract, incurred or to be incurred, less any allocable credits, plus any allocable cost of money pursuant to 31.205-10. In ascertaining what constitutes a cost, *any generally accepted method of determining or estimating costs that is equitable and is consistently applied may be used,* including standard costs properly adjusted for applicable variances. See 31.201-2(b) and (c) for Cost Accounting Standards (CAS) requirements. [emphasis added]

It was similar phraseology in previous regulations that enabled the CAS champions to persuade enough members of Congress to enact a law establishing a board designed to "enhance uniformity and consistency." It is important to bear in mind that the provisions of FAR are still governing for contracts that are not covered by cost accounting standards. Another important and considerably more complex point is that the standards promulgated by the CASB are intended to govern allocability only, while determinations of allowability remain the province of the executive departments and agencies. We shall discuss the problems of distinguishing between rules for allocability and those for allowability in subsequent chapters of this text.

Determination of Allowability

FAR 31.201-2(a) provides that the following factors shall be considered in determining whether a cost is allowable:

(1) Reasonableness.

(2) Allocability.

(3) Standards promulgated by the CAS Board, if applicable; otherwise, generally accepted accounting principles and practices appropriate to the particular circumstances.

(4) Terms of the contract.

(5) Any limitations set forth in this subpart.

The section further provides:

(b) Certain cost principles in this subpart incorporate the measurement, assignment, and allocability rules of selected CAS and limit the allowability of cost to the amounts determined using the criteria in those selected standards. Only those CAS or portions of standards specifically made applicable by the cost principles in this subpart are mandatory unless the contract is CAS-covered (see Part 30). Business units that are not otherwise subject to these standards under a CAS clause are subject to the selected standards only for the purpose of determining allowability of costs on Government contracts. Including the selected standards in the cost principles does not subject the business unit to any other CAS rules and regulations. The applicability of the CAS rules and regulations is determined by the CAS clause, if any, in the contract and the requirements of the standards themselves.

(c) When contractor accounting practices are inconsistent with this Subpart 31.2, costs resulting from such inconsistent practices shall not be allowed in excess of the amount that would have resulted from using practices consistent with this subpart.

The provisions of DAR 15-201.4 and FPR 1-15.201-4 with respect to the determination of allocability have been incorporated verbatim into FAR 31.201-4, quoted following.

A cost is allocable if it is assignable or chargeable to one or more cost objectives on the basis of relative benefits received or other equitable relationship. Subject to the foregoing, a cost is allocable to a Government contract if it—

(a) Is incurred specifically for the contract;

(b) Benefits both the contract and other work, and can be distributed to them in reasonable proportion to the benefits received; or

(c) Is necessary to the overall operation of the business, although a direct relationship to any particular cost objective cannot be shown.

These provisions are extremely important because they govern in the absence of a standard that may specifically establish a rule to the contrary. This definition of allocability is also extremely significant because some of its provisions (subsection (c) particularly) are unpopular with government contract auditors, and it is essential that government contractors understand the requirements and insist on adherence to them. The particular portion of FAR 31.201-4 that must be remembered provides that a cost is allocable to a government contract if it "is necessary to the overall operation of the business, although a direct relationship to any particular cost objective cannot be shown." Despite several decisions by boards of contract appeals and courts upholding contractors' assertions that certain expenses should be allocable to all of their activities under the above-cited provision, some government officials continue to take a hard line and incorrectly insist on a showing of benefit to the government work specifically before allowing an expense for inclusion in a pool for allocation to all of the work.

The major efforts in this direction have been through specific identification of necessary and ordinary business expenses as unallowable in FAR 31.205, Selected Costs. Additions to business expenses thus made unallowable have generally been initiated by DOD's DAR Council, frequently upon DCAA recommendations. A sledge hammer attack on allowability of business expenses was reflected in P.L. 99-145, which mandated that 10 categories of costs shall be unallowable and directed that the Secretary of Defense "clarify" the allowability of 16 additional cost categories. A review of the legislative history of this statute does not disclose any consideration accorded by Congress to allowing costs necessary to the overall operation of the business.

"Golden Parachutes"

As noted earlier, inadvertent or deliberate overlooking of FAR 31.201-4(c) has become increasingly widespread. Another illustration involves the allowability of "golden parachutes," guaranteed compensation to certain corporate officials in the event of a takeover. Although such costs have generally not been claimed by contractors, and disallowed when claimed, two congressmen wrote to Secretary of Defense Weinberger that the acquisition regulations do not specifically cite such compensation as unallowable. The angry letter was picked up by the usual media industry critics and resulted in expediting the ongoing work by the DAR Council, which led to a FAR revision specifying to the satisfaction of industry's harshest critics that such compensation is unallowable under government contracts.

In this analysis, we have not addressed the issue of whether such compensation should or should not be allowable but focus on some of the reasoning presented for establishing the expense as unallowable.

In a memorandum to the Military Departments and defense agencies dated March 17, 1987, Deputy Assistant Secretary of Defense for Procurement Spector stated in part:

Although the DOD regulation governing the allowability of contract costs does not specifically mention "golden parachutes," it does require that all costs charged to Government contracts be "reasonable." A "reasonable cost" does not exceed that which would be incurred by a prudent person in the conduct of competitive business. Additionally, costs charged to Government contracts must bear a causal or beneficial relationship to the work performed on such contracts. The DOD position holds that the costs of "golden parachutes" are not reasonable nor do they benefit government work. Accordingly, they are unallowable and should be questioned on Government contracts.

The description of a reasonable cost in the above excerpt is a partial citation of FAR 31.201-3, Determining Reasonableness. While incomplete and not a self-evident support for establishing this cost as unreasonable, the excerpt is from the FAR provision. In contrast, the statement that "costs charged to Government contracts must bear a causal or beneficial relationship to the work performed on such contracts," directly distorts the FAR allocability provision cited at the beginning of this analysis by deliberately omitting any reference to a cost "necessary to the overall operation of the business although a direct relationship to any particular cost objective cannot be shown" (FAR 31.201-4(c)).

As noted earlier, the issue addressed here is not the allowability of golden parachutes but the increasing undermining of the basic concept of allocability contained in government acquisition regulations for almost 30 years. In this connection, a press release prepared by the Office of the Assistant Secretary of Defense for Acquisition and Logistics on March 18, 1987, contains the same language, holding that the costs of golden parachutes are unallowable because they "are not reasonable nor do they benefit government work."

The subject of golden parachutes does not present the best opportunity for industry to re-acquaint senior DOD acquisition officials with acquisition regulations. However, at a more appropriate time, this action should be taken.

The prior editions of this text discussed the provisions contained in government procurement regulations regarding acceptable cost accounting systems and noted their relative reasonableness and flexibility—relative to current circumstances brought about by the promulgation of cost accounting standards and regulations by the CASB, regulations that are considerably more strict and severe and more potent because they have "the full force and effect of law."

In Chapter VIII, we discussed the implementation of CASB regulations and standards by federal agencies, including the publication of such new regulations as FAR Part 30, pertinent contract clauses included in FAR Part 52, Guidance Papers issued by the Department of Defense CAS Steering Committee and Working Group, and Chapter 8 to the DCAA Manual. Additionally, numerous changes have been made throughout DAR Section XV and FPR Part 1-15, now incorporated in FAR Part 31.

DISCLOSURE STATEMENT

The initial standards and regulations promulgated by the CASB, Disclosure Statement, CAS 401 and CAS 402, became effective July 1, 1972.

The requirement for a regulation relating to a disclosure of cost accounting practices stems directly from P.L. 91-379, which directed the CASB to require "defense contractors and subcontractors as a condition of contracting to disclose in writing their cost accounting principles, including methods of distinguishing direct costs from indirect costs and the basis used for allocating indirect costs. . . ."

Nature of Disclosure Statement

The following items comprise a Disclosure Statement, available from the contracting officer and authorized for reproduction.

1. General instructions describe requirements for filing, method in which questions should be answered, submission of amendments, and codes and classification descriptions selected from the Standard Industrial Classification Manual (SIC).

2. Cover sheet and certification. The cover sheet requires a contractor's official to certify that to the best of his knowledge and belief the Statement is complete and current as of the date indicated.

3. Part I requires replies providing general information, such as type of entity, principal products, total annual and government sales, categorization of cost accounting system, and fiscal year.

4. In Part II, Direct Costs, the contractor is required to define what direct material, direct labor, and other direct costs are or will be charged directly to government contracts. Further questions in Part II are directed toward obtaining information as to methods of charging these direct costs.

5. In Part III, Direct Vs Indirect Costs, the contractor is required, by both responding to specific questions and including a narrative continuation sheet, to describe criteria for determining whether costs are charged directly or indirectly to government contracts or similar cost objectives. Part III lists various direct costs and related expenses and requires the contractor to explain by a code provided in the Disclosure Statement whether these expenses are treated as direct material, direct labor, direct material and labor, other direct costs, sometimes direct/ sometimes indirect, indirect only, and other. In Part III and throughout the Disclosure Statement, contractors are encouraged to include continuation sheets where applying the "treatment code" to individual expenses may not be fully descriptive.

6. Part IV, Indirect Costs, is designed to obtain information about the nature of the contractor's various manufacturing, engineering, general and administrative, selling and service center costs, etc., and the number and nature of the pools of expenses and allocation bases.

7. A separate section of the Disclosure Statement, Part V, Depreciation and Capitalization Practices, is devoted to identifying the nature of the contractor's fixed assets by category and describing capitalization and depreciation practices.

8. Part VI, Other Costs and Credits, is a relatively short section of the Disclosure Statement, designed to obtain information regarding the

contractor's accounting practices for vacation, holiday and sick pay, supplemental unemployment benefit plans, severance pay, methods used to account for incidental receipts, and proceeds from employee welfare activity.

9. Deferred Compensation and Insurance Costs have long been areas of controversy. Part VII is designed to obtain information as to whether these costs are recorded at the corporate or subordinate organizational levels, the nature of pension plans and their extent of funding, actuarial methods, etc., a description of deferred incentive compensation plans and related cost accounting practices, and information on the nature of insurance and accounting treatment of the various plans, including self-insurance programs.

10. The final section of the Disclosure Statement is Part VIII, Corporate or Group Expenses, which requires the submission of information concerning home office, group office and other intermediate management offices. In addition to requiring certain information about sales, the basic questions in Part VIII are directed toward obtaining information as to the nature of expenses contained in the pools of those organizational elements and the allocation bases used for each.

Requirements for Filing Disclosure Statement

The Disclosure Statement has been a cornerstone of the CASB regulations and standards. There was some consideration at the outset of imposing the requirement for filing Disclosure Statements simultaneously on all prime and subcontractors as a condition of contracting. However, after discussions with officials of DCAA and others within the Department of Defense, the CASB realized that a review of all of the Disclosure Statements required to be filed constituted an impossible task for both auditors and contracting officers. Accordingly, it was decided to phase in the requirement for submitting Disclosure Statements. Initially, this requirement was limited to contractors who in the government's fiscal year 1971 had been awarded negotiated prime defense contracts of $30 million net or more. For several years thereafter, the dollar thresholds were modified by the Board to broaden the coverage. The requirements contained in the last regulation promulgated by the CASB before it went out of business (4 CFR 351.40) are quoted below:

(a) *Who must file.* (1) Any defense contractor which, together with its segments, received net awards of negotiated national defense prime contracts and subcontracts subject to Cost Accounting Standards totaling more than $10 million in its most recent cost accounting period, must submit a completed Disclosure Statement as specified in paragraph (b)(1) of this section.

(2) Any business unit which receives a negotiated national defense contract or subcontract which is subject to Cost Accounting Standards and is for $10 million or more must submit a completed Disclosure Statement as specified in paragraph (b)(2) of this section.

(3) Except as provided in 4 CFR 331.30(b) or except where the price is based on (i) established catalog or market prices of commercial items sold in substantial quantities to the general public or (ii) prices set by

regulation, a separate Disclosure Statement must be submitted covering the practices of each segment of a defense contractor whose costs included in the total price of any covered contract exceeds $100,000. If the cost accounting practices are identical for more than one segment of a contractor, only one statement need be submitted for those segments, but each such segment must be identified.

(4) Each corporate or other home office which allocates costs to one or more disclosing segments performing covered contracts shall file a Part VIII of the Disclosure Statement.

(b) *Time of Filing.* Any defense contractor required by paragraph (a)(1) of this section to file a Disclosure Statement must do so prior to award of the first covered contract received by the contractor or by a segment of such contractor in the cost accounting period immediately following the period in which the contractor receives awards totaling $10 million. If the first covered contract is received within 90 days of the start of the cost accounting period, the contractor is not required to file until the end of the 90 days.

(2) Any business unit required by paragraph (a)(2) of this section to submit a Disclosure Statement must do so as part of its proposal for such contract unless the business unit has already submitted a Disclosure Statement disclosing the practices used in the pricing of its proposal.

(3) A corporate or home office required by paragraph (a)(4) of this section to file a Disclosure Statement shall do so at the same time its disclosing segment files its Disclosure Statement.

(c) *Confidentiality of disclosure statement.* (1) If the business unit submitting a Disclosure Statement notifies the contracting agency and the CASB that the Disclosure Statement contains trade secrets and commercial or financial information which it regards as privileged and confidential, the Disclosure Statement will be protected and will not be released outside of the Government. (Persons submitting Disclosure Statements containing such information should place an appropriate legend on the face of the document at the time of submission.)

(2) If a subcontractor considers that the information in its Disclosure Statement is privileged and confidential and declines to provide it to the contractor or higher tier subcontractor, the contractor may authorize direct submission of that subcontractor's Disclosure Statement to the same Government offices to which the contractor was required to submit its Disclosure Statement.

(d) *Waiver.* In the event the agency head determines that it is impractical to secure a required Disclosure Statement, he may authorize award of a contract or subcontract without submission of a Disclosure Statement. He shall within 30 days thereafter submit a report to the Cost Accounting Standards Board setting forth all material facts.

In the above quotation, paragraph 351.40(a)(3) refers to an exception in paragraph 331.30(b). Parts 331 and 332 of the Board's regulations are discussed in Chapter VIII of this text.

Amendments of Disclosure Statements

As explained in paragraph 351.120, there are two circumstances under which Disclosure Statements must be amended: (1) when the cost accounting practices are changed to comply with new cost accounting standards and (2) when cost accounting practices are changed under other circumstances.

Paragraph 351.120(b) directs that amendments to Disclosure Statements shall be submitted to the same offices, including the CASB, with which the original Disclosure Statement was filed. When the CASB went out of business on September 30, 1980, its requirement that contractors submit to it copies of amendments or Disclosure Statements, where submitted for the first time, was rescinded. At this writing, legislation has not been enacted to transfer the CASB functions to another agency. Some assume such legislation will ultimately be passed. The successor to the CASB may or may not wish to continue receiving new Disclosure Statements or amendments to Statements previously filed.

The major reason for the CASB's requirement that copies of Disclosure Statements and related amendments be furnished to its staff was the belief that the information therein contained would be useful as part of the research required in connection with formulating new standards. All of the information contained in the Disclosure Statements was computerized by the CASB staff, and several of the Board's annual Progress Reports to Congress contained, as appendices, Aggregated Disclosure Statement Responses. These appendices represented a compilation, showing numbers and percentages, of the cost accounting practices followed by more than 1,000 units that had been required to submit the Statements.

Administrative procedures established by the executive agencies regarding prime and subcontractors' Disclosure Statements, reviews of such Statements, and other disclosure provisions are contained in FAR Part 30. Although not authoritative in the sense of having a statutory or regulatory basis, DCAA's Contract Audit Manual contains in Chapter 8 Section 2 guidance to its auditors with respect to Disclosure Statements. The auditor's initial review of an originally filed Disclosure Statement is essentially designed to determine the Statement's adequacy, i.e. whether it is accurate, current, and complete. These reviews may be made on an intensive basis at the site or through desk reviews. It is important to note that the auditor must and will express an opinion as to the adequacy of the Disclosure Statement, but will not express an opinion as to whether the cost accounting practices are in compliance with cost accounting standards and FAR Part 31 or other applicable regulations. However, when a contractor amends its Disclosure Statement, the auditor's examination must be sufficient to support an opinion as to both the adequacy of the change and whether the amended cost accounting practices are in compliance with CAS and applicable procurement regulations. As in regard to all of the government contract auditors' efforts, their reports to the contracting officers are advisory. The final determination regarding adequacy and compliance is the responsibility of the contracting officer. As a practical matter, in the author's experience, in the overwhelming preponderance of such reviews, the contracting officer tends to (at least initially) accept the contract auditor's conclusions and recommendations. This practice is particularly prevalent within civilian agencies, but many Department of Defense contracting officers also at times appear to delegate this area of judgment to the contract auditor although FAR does not authorize such delegation.

The significance of the real-life conditions should encourage contractors with CAS-covered contracts to make every effort to present their views clearly and persuasively to the contract auditor.

It is frequently the case that a contract auditor's report containing an opinion that an amendment to a Disclosure Statement is in noncompliance with cost accounting standards and/or FAR is almost routinely translated into a letter from the contracting officer to the contractor announcing an initial determination of noncompliance. At this point, the contractor should muster the best rationale and arguments to support a finding of compliance and include them in the response to the contracting officer. In this connection, it is extremely important that the contractor have full knowledge of the government contract auditor's basis for asserting noncompliance, which means obtaining a draft of the auditor's proposed report to the contracting officer. The contractor should, before responding to the contracting officer's initial determination of noncompliance, request a copy of the contract auditor's advisory report. In the author's experience, this request has never been denied.

If the alleged noncompliance cannot be satisfactorily negotiated or agreed upon, the contracting officer may issue a final determination of noncompliance. A final determination must state that it is final, and the contracting officer must advise the contractor of the right to proceed under the Disputes clause of the contract.

CAS 401 - CONSISTENCY IN ESTIMATING, ACCUMULATING AND REPORTING COSTS

The first standard appeared in final form on February 29, 1972, with an effective date of July 1, 1972. Its major provisions are cited below:

401.40 Fundamental requirement.

(a) A contractor's practices used in estimating costs in pricing a proposal shall be consistent with his cost accounting practices used in accumulating and reporting costs.

(b) A contractor's cost accounting practices used in accumulating and reporting actual costs for a contract shall be consistent with his practices used in pricing the related proposal.

(c) The grouping of homogeneous costs in estimates prepared for proposal purposes shall not per se be deemed an inconsistent application of cost accounting practices under paragraphs (a) and (b) of this section when such costs are accumulated and reported in greater detail on an actual cost basis during contract performance.

401.50 Techniques for application.

(a) The standard allows grouping of homogeneous costs in order to cover those cases where it is not practicable to estimate contract costs by individual cost element or function. However, costs estimated for proposal purposes shall be presented in such manner and in such detail that any significant cost can be compared with the actual cost accumulated and reported therefor. In any event the cost accounting practices used in estimating costs in pricing a proposal and in accumulating and reporting costs on the resulting contract shall be consistent with respect to: (1) The classification of elements or functions of costs as direct or indirect; (2) the indirect cost pools to which each element or function of cost is charged or proposed to be charged; and (3) the methods of allocating indirect costs to the contract.

(b) Adherence to the requirement of 401.40(a) of this standard shall be determined as of the date of the award of the contract, unless the contractor has submitted cost or pricing data pursuant to Public Law 87-653, in which case adherence to the requirement of 401.40(a) shall be determined as of the date of final agreement on price, as shown on the signed certificate of current cost or pricing data. Notwithstanding 401.40(b), changes in established cost accounting practices during contract performance may be made when authorized by the standards, rules, and regulations issued by the Cost Accounting Standards Board.

Illustrations designed to facilitate understanding of this standard are contained in CAS 401.60. Additional illustrations, although lacking authoritative status, are set forth in DCAA's Contract Audit Manual, paragraph 8-401.3.

Neither ASPR nor FPR required consistency between estimating costs for a contract proposal and accumulating and reporting costs under that contract after its award, and the Comptroller General's feasibility study report (see Chapter VIII of this text) cited this absence as a "problem area" in government auditing and pricing. The arguments against this consistency principle were relatively mild, especially compared with those evoked by some of the later standards. However, many recognized the potential problems resulting from the rigid rule, which would prohibit change regardless of whether circumstances dictated the need therefor.

Problems Emanating from CAS 401

Very shortly after the effective date, unmistakable signs surfaced that an unduly strict construction of this standard could result in widespread government allegations of noncompliance. One of the major problems involved engineering and other direct labor costs where contractors, at the request of the procuring activities, traditionally displayed more detail in their estimates than in their books of account. Another related to the general practice of estimating material costs by pricing a bill of materials and adding scrap, spoilage, and other factors thereto, while actual costs were recorded in total, without segregation of scrap and spoilage.

Credit is due the DCAA for identifying these problems very early and seeking authoritative interpretations. At that time, the CASB and its staff were heavily engaged in formulating new standards and resisted the diversion of its manpower to issue clarifications or interpretations. Efforts to obtain guidance within the Department of Defense were also fruitless. The DOD CAS Steering Committee had not been established, and the complicated DOD bureaucracy was unable or unwilling to initiate a solution. Finally, DCAA picked up the ball and after obtaining Pentagon coordination, issued the following guidance to its auditors:

> In our memorandum for Regional Managers dated 19 January 1973, Subject: Cost Accounting Standards (CAS), the DD Form 633, Contract Pricing Proposal, and the notes thereto were established as the base line for determining the amount of detailed information which must be displayed by the contractor in the accumulation of costs. As a result of numerous questions and recent field trips to review the implementation of CAS 401, it was determined that additional guidance is required concerning the acceptable level of detail which must be used in accumulating costs based on the level of detail which must be presented for cost estimating and reporting purposes.

> It is recognized that the DD Form 633 is not necessarily compatible with every accounting system and instruction 4 to the form states "The formats for the Cost Elements and the Proposed Contract Estimate are not intended as rigid requirements. These may be presented in different format with the prior approval of the contracting officer if required for more effective and efficient presentation."

> It is also recognized that contracting officers may on occasion request contractors to furnish a display of information which is in greater detail than required by the DD Form 633, and footnotes thereto, (subsequent references to DD Form 633 are intended to encompass footnotes thereto) or which is arranged in a way that is not consistent with the manner in which the contractor intends to accumulate the actual costs. As a general rule, a contractor is in compliance with CAS 401 if (1) his estimate is made in accordance with his normal accounting practices and (2) he accumulates his costs in the same manner.

> If in the performance of a review of a price proposal the auditor identifies estimates of significant items of costs which will not be comparable with the actual cost accumulated therefor discussions should be held with the contractor. As a part of these discussions the auditor should point out the areas of potential noncompliance and advise the contractor of the recommendations he proposes to make to the administrative contracting officer. Should the contractor contend that the display of detail in the price proposal was presented for negotiation purposes but that there was no intention to accumulate costs in such manner he should be informed that the contracting officer will be advised to request a summary of the estimate in accordance with the manner in which the costs will be accumulated. These summaries should be reviewed to determine if the details contained therein meet the requirements of the Request for Proposal and the audit report should contain the auditor's opinion on whether or not the summaries contain an acceptable level of detail for accumulating purposes. The following examples are furnished for guidance in reaching that decision:

>> a. A contractor in his proposal furnishes the cost of engineering labor by class, i.e., Engineer I, Engineer II, etc.. However, it is the practice of the contractor to accumulate engineering labor by type, i.e., Electrical Engineer, Design Engineer, etc.. If the contractor

submits a summary of the proposal by type of engineer which reconciles with the proposed cost by class of engineer and this summary meets the requirements of the DD Form 633 and further explains that this is the manner in which cost will be accumulated, then consistency with CAS 401 will have been achieved. A note of caution is necessary here, however, since it could be the intent of the procuring officer to buy a specific number of hours by class of engineers in which case the contracting officer should require the contractor to estimate and accumulate by the same classes of engineers. However, the general principle enunciated above is still valid: any special breakdown required by the contracting officer is a matter for discussion between the contracting parties and is not dealt with by CAS 401.

b. A second contractor estimates cost by line item, i.e., data, first article test and hardware, and then submits a single DD Form 633 for all three items. The contractor does not intend to accumulate the cost for the three items separately, but rather, in accordance with his established accounting practice, accumulate significant and disparate labor, material, and overhead costs for the contract as a whole rather than for each line item. The contractor must develop an estimate of these costs in accordance with the requirements of the DD Form 633 and footnotes thereto. The practice of estimating and accumulating the combined cost of the three items by categories of costs should not be considered a violation of CAS 401. However, the contracting officer should be advised of the contractor's intentions so that he may request the contractor for any additional detail of accumulation he may wish (i.e., line item costs) beyond the essential requirements of CAS 401.

If, however, the contractor is required to submit separate DD 633s for individual contract line items and the cost of each such line item represents a major item of cost, distinct in nature from other line items for which costs are accumulated, the contractor probably should be required to accumulate cost by such line items. In effect, where the contracting officer requires this, the cost of each line item should be estimated and accumulated as if each was a separate contract. Examples of contracts whose costs should be estimated and accumulated on such a basis are contracts which provide for (1) design, prototype development and production or (2) distinct and disparate end items of production.

c. A third contractor's estimate includes breakdowns of separate and disparate items of cost. Although he accumulates costs in his system in such a manner, his internal reporting system presents cost data in broad summary form only. Contractors are not required to report on a scheduled basis the cost breakdown set forth in the estimate. They need only provide for the accumulation of data in a manner so that it can be extracted from the accounting records on a demand basis within a reasonable period of time. It should be remembered that the use of supplemental or workpaper records are acceptable for CAS purposes.

It should also be remembered that the above examples are for illustration purposes and that each situation must be reviewed on its own merits. Thus, a contractor who has a process cost accounting system would be expected to estimate and accumulate cost by contract or contract items in accordance with that system. There is no requirement for such a contractor to establish and maintain a job order cost accumulation system.

The above DCAA paper had also been informally coordinated with the CASB staff. Shortly after its issuance, the executive secretary of the CASB distributed the DCAA letter to the ever-growing CASB mailing list; the covering letter stated, "The Cost Accounting Standards Board staff agrees that this guidance should facilitate administration of the Standard."

Interpretation No. 1. to CAS 401—Estimating and Accumulating Scrap, Spoilage, and Related Costs

The interpretation was apparently considered necessary because of the continuing controversies between government and industry people regarding provisions for scrap, spoilage, and other "materials not incorporated in end items."

ASPR 15-205.22 at the time stated that "In computing material costs consideration will be given to reasonable overruns, spoilage, or defective work . . . ." Such factors are included in contract price proposals and reflected in cost accounting records. However, few contractors indeed maintain records of sufficient detail and precision to isolate and identify these factors. Customarily, contractors will develop estimates based on pricing bills of materials and apply a factor or factors for scrap, spoilage, waste, etc. In many instances the cost records show the total cost of materials placed into production but do not separately identify the "materials not incorporated in end items."

Where the factors submitted by contractors are supported by some kind of records, even informal factory data, to indicate the reasonableness of the estimates, not too much difficulty is encountered in negotiations. Government auditors sometimes tend to be overly demanding and exacting, preferring the niceties of costly, sophisticated cost accounting systems. Contracting officers and their staffs usually adopt a more pragmatic approach. This sometimes results in scrap factors being questioned by auditors for lack of what they believe constitutes proper support, but all or major amounts are reinstated in negotiations.

The origins of Interpretation No. 1 are uncertain but appear to extend back to the early days of the Board or even beyond then when this area was identified by DCAA as a cost accounting problem requiring a standard. The CASB staff initially planned a separate standard for scrap but apparently concluded it was not warranted. Inasmuch as the crux of the problem was seen as a question of consistency in estimating and accumulating costs, the Board decided to approach it through an interpretation of CAS 401. The subject is introduced in the *Federal Register* in the following manner:

Section 401.40 requires that a contractor's "practices used in estimating costs in pricing a proposal shall be consistent with his cost accounting practices in accumulating and reporting costs". Many contractors estimate the costs of certain direct materials, such as materials expected to be scrapped, as a percentage of basic material requirements or some other base. A significant number of questions have been raised as to whether it is an acceptable practice to estimate the cost of such materials on the basis of percentage factors where a contractor's accounting system does not accumulate separately the corresponding actual costs.

The interpretation being proposed today provides criteria for determining whether contractors' practices used in estimating costs of direct materials are consistent with practices used in accumulating the costs of such materials.

The text of Interpretation No. 1 to CAS 401 is provided below in full for the convenience of our readers. We invite attention to the significant provisions, which we have identified by italics. To capsulize the salient points, where a contractor estimates a significant part of direct material costs by means of percentage factors and those factors are not supported by accounting or statistical data, and where the actual direct material costs are accumulating in an "undifferentiated account," the company will be in noncompliance with CAS 401. The second point involves the nature and amount of detail required to achieve compliance in these circumstances and this problem, in the opinion of the Board, "has been and continues to be a matter to be decided by Government procurement authority . . . ."

Part 401, Cost Accounting Standard, Consistency in Estimating, Accumulating and Reporting Costs, requires in Section 401.40 that a contractor's "practices used in estimating costs in pricing a proposal shall be consistent with his cost accounting practices used in accumulating and reporting costs".

In estimating the cost of direct material requirements for a contract, it is a common practice to first estimate the cost of the actual quantities to be incorporated in end items. Provisions are then made for additional direct material costs to cover expected material losses such as those which occur, for example, when items are scrapped, fail to meet specifications, are lost, consumed in the manufacturing process, or destroyed in testing and qualification processes. The cost of some or all of such additional direct material requirements is often estimated by the application of one or more percentage factors to the total cost of basic direct material requirements or to some other base.

Questions have arisen as to whether the accumulation of direct material costs in an undifferentiated account where a contractor estimates a significant part of such costs by means of percentage factors is in compliance with Part 401. The most serious questions pertain to such percentage factors which are not supported by the contractor with accounting, statistical, or other relevant data from past experience, nor by a program to accumulate actual costs for comparison with such percentage estimates. *In the opinion of the Board the accumulation of direct costs in an undifferentiated account in this circumstance is a cost accounting practice which is not consistent with the practice of estimating a significant part of costs by means of percentage factors.* This situation is virtually identical with that described in Illustration 401.60(b)(5), which deals with labor.

Part 401 does not, however, prescribe the amount of detail required in accumulating and reporting costs. The Board recognizes that the amount of detail required may vary considerably depending on the percentage factors used, the data presented in justification or lack thereof, and the significance of each situation. Accordingly, the Board is of the view that it is neither appropriate nor practical for the Board to prescribe a single set of accounting practices which would be consistent in all situations with the practices of estimating direct material costs by percentage factors. *The Board considers, therefore, that the amount of accounting and statistical detail to be required and maintained in accounting for this portion of direct material costs has been and continues to be a matter to be decided by Government procurement authorities on the basis of the individual facts and circumstances.*

Board of Contract Appeals Decisions Relating to CAS 401

Despite some initial thinking that the implementation of CAS 401 would generate relatively few problems, and even after the adoption of the DCAA guidance and Interpretation No. 1. to the standard discussed above, additional problems surfaced early and are continuing, with a number having reached the litigation stage.

AiResearch Manufacturing Company, ASBCA No. 20998, 76-2 BCA par. 12,150; 77-1 BCA par. 12,546

The first decision handed down by a board of contract appeals involving cost accounting standards concerned a contracting officer's final determination that AiResearch was in noncompliance with CAS 401 and CAS 406. However, neither the original decision nor the ruling on the motion for reconsideration addressed in any detail the nature of the noncompliances. The major issue was the contractor's assertion that the contracting officer had no authority to issue a final decision because the government admittedly was unable to determine the amount of increased costs, if any, which may have resulted from the noncompliances. The contractor also contended it could refuse to comply with any or all of the standards and pay such increased costs as might be determined.

The government argued that its inability to determine the cost impact of the alleged noncompliances was due to the condition of the contractor's records, which precluded the necessary auditing.

The ASBCA ruled initially, and reiterated on the motion for reconsideration, that no provision of the law or CASB regulations precluded a contracting officer from making a final determination without first establishing quantum. The ASBCA also emphatically disagreed with the contractor's assertion that it could refuse to comply with the standard as long as it paid the increased costs that resulted from such noncompliance. The board concluded: "Under the Cost Accounting Standards clause, the contractor undertakes an affirmative obligation, *inter alia,* to comply with all Cost Accounting Standards in effect."

Dayton T. Brown, Inc., ASBCA No. 22810, 78-2 BCA par. 13,484; 80-2 BCA par. 14,543

The Brown organization consisted of a corporate office and three divisions: Manufacturing, Laboratory and Technical. The first named had virtually no government contracts while the other two were heavily defense-oriented. Prior to 1975, apparently at the government's advice (although this is not entirely clear), Brown collected its bid and proposal (B&P) costs, incurred and originally recorded in each of its three divisions, in its corporate headquarters G&A pool and then reallocated these costs back to the divisions on a total cost input basis. The decision notes that this method had the effect of allocating a disproportionately large amount of B&P to the commercial Manufacturing Division in that it incurred little B&P work but had the largest cost input base. (Apparently the DOD auditors were quite content with this arrangement, which was described in the decision as having the effect of Brown's commercially oriented Manufacturing Division "subsidizing the B&P costs incurred by the other Government contract-oriented divisions".)

Brown was a small company and, because it was receiving payments from DOD for IR&D and B&P in amounts less than $2 million a year, was not required to negotiate advance agreements but rather was to use the formula set forth in DAR 15-205.3(d)(2)(B).

Brown had been following the practice described earlier since 1971. The government had offered no objections since the commercial work had been disproportionately burdened. Further, since total B&P costs varied only slightly in 1972, 1973, and 1974, DCAA did not consider applying the DAR formula described above.

The problem originated in 1975 when Brown's commercial business began to fall off and the company increased its B&P efforts in the Manufacturing Division, resulting in an increase in total company B&P costs and thereby requiring the application of the DAR formula.

In computing B&P costs for 1975 for application of the formula, Brown changed its procedure by applying the formula after the B&P costs had been allocated to the division. DCAA recomputed allowable B&P costs by applying the formula at the corporate level and arrived at a substantial amount of B&P costs questioned. The major portion of the amount disallowed by DCAA represented a lesser allocation of these costs to the defense-oriented Laboratory and Technical Divisions.

DCAA's formula was appealed by Brown to the ACO, the appeal noting that ASPR 15-205.3(d)(2)(B) permitted the application of the formula "either on a company-wide basis (Headquarters) or by profit centers (Divisions) . . . ." The ACO sustained Brown's appeal, but DCAA was persistent and refused to approve a reimbursement voucher for payment, advising the ACO that Brown's B&P cost limitation on a divisional basis violated CAS 401.

CAS 401 requires that "A contractor's practices used in estimating costs in pricing a proposal shall be consistent with his cost accounting practices used in accumulating and reporting costs." DCAA's reference to CAS 401 was apparently persuasive, and the ACO issued a second final determination, this time upholding DCAA's calculations and the related disallowance.

In arriving at its decision for Brown, the ASBCA agreed that CAS 401 prohibited "cost increasing changes in established cost accounting practices." However, it proceeded to address the question of whether Brown's application of the B&P limitation formula at its divisional level did indeed constitute a change in cost accounting practice within the purview of the CAS clause. Quoting the definition of "cost accounting practice," the ASBCA concluded that the term applied to "any accounting method or technique which is used for measurement of cost, assignment of cost to cost accounting periods, or allocation of cost to cost objectives." 4 CFR 331.20(h). The ASBCA further quoted from the above-referenced CASB regulation, referring to the citations of "measurement of cost encompassing accounting methods and techniques . . . assignment of cost to cost accounting periods . . . (and) allocation of cost to cost objectives . . . ."

The ASBCA seemed further to point up that, even if it were to find that Brown's application of the B&P formula was a cost accounting practice, "the application, *per se,* is neither a change nor in any way otherwise prohibited by the CAS clause and CAS 401." On this point, it referred to the CAS regulations, which establish that "the initial adoption of a cost accounting practice for the first time a cost is incurred, or a function is created, is not a change in cost accounting practice." Since both the government and Brown stipulated that the B&P limitation formula was applied for the first time in 1975, the ASBCA concluded that such initial application of the formula could not be construed as a change under the above-cited CAS regulation.

Moving on to another government argument, we find the contention that Brown was in violation of CAS 401 because its practice in 1975 of accumulating costs at the corporate G&A level was inconsistent with its practice of reporting B&P at the divisional level. The board concluded the government did not really understand CAS 401:

> The Government misreads CAS 401; that provision requires a consistency between appellant's cost accounting practices of accumulating and reporting costs, on the one hand, and estimating costs on the other not between accumulating costs and reporting costs. CAS 401 is considered inapposite for this reason alone. Moreover, since appellant did not use the formula for estimating in 1975, it would be an impossibility for there to be an inconsistency between its application of the formula in reporting its costs in 1975 and in estimating costs for that year. CAS 401 would therefore not be applicable for that additional reason.

The original dispute was decided by the board upon the documentary record, after both parties had stipulated the facts, agreed on the issues, and waived hearings and pleadings. When the case was heard under the government's motion for reconsideration, the board reversed itself and ruled against the contractor. The decision on the MFR stated in part:

> They (the parties) had certified and argued the following issue to the Board: whether application of the . . . B&P cost limitation formula set forth in ASPR 15-205.3(d)(2)(B) at appellant's divisional level in 1975 was violative of the . . . CAS clause, CAS 401, or otherwise inconsistent with the requirements of ASPR. We held that *such application of the*

formula, per se, did not constitute a violation of either CAS or ASPR. (Emphasis added.)

The primary issue now raised by the Government's Motion has not been previously addressed by the Board. Government counsel acknowledged that the "issues were not properly defined by the parties causing confusion and necessity of the instant additional proceedings" . . . and asks the Board to consider now whether appellant's *reporting of its incurred B&P costs at the division level constitutes an inconsistency prohibited by CAS 401 in view of appellant's accounting practice to estimate these costs by using indirectly allocated costs at the corporate level.* Additionally, the respondent (government) argues that *appellant's use of B&P costs at divisional level in computing the allowability of the B&P costs constitutes a change in accounting practices since appellant's established practice was to estimate and accumulate and report B&P costs at the corporate level using indirectly allocated costs.* (Emphasis added.)

The government now presented "Additional Findings of Fact." One of these facts was that Brown's method, previously described, was used in pricing its contracts in 1975 and in accumulating and finding costs of these contracts in the same manner. "However, in computing the allowable costs by the application of the cost limitation formula in ASPR 15-205.3, appellant used the B&P costs as they were actually incurred in the divisions, ignoring their allocation through the corporate G&A expense pool. . . ."

The ASBCA now appeared to be saying that its initial decision was incorrect because of the manner in which "the parties framed the issue." The board further stated: "Since the parties stipulated the results of their respective positions, we only concerned ourselves with the propriety, under the ASPR provisions, of appellant's computing its allowable 1975 B&P costs by applying the formula to its divisional level. We are now asked to determine whether appellant's use of the actually incurred B&P costs at the divisional level is inconsistent with its estimating practices regarding these costs, a practice prohibited by CAS 401."

A major point of contention here was Brown's argument that it had not violated CAS 401, with the following reasoning: "its use of incurred divisional B&P costs in the B&P cost limitation formula is consistent with the accounting practices it used in estimating costs and, thus, is proper under CAS 401. . . . Its accounting practice for estimating a G&A rate, including B&P expenses for 1975, was to use cost input as a base and to use B&P costs incurred for 1974 for estimating the 1975 rate."

The government argued that, in determining the final allowable B&P costs according to the ASPR cost limitation formula, Brown did not use B&P costs allocated to its divisions through the corporate G&A expense pool, "but instead used a hybrid of the allocated and divisionally incurred costs, and, in doing so, created an inconsistency with its established practice of estimating these costs." The government contended that the CAS 401 violation occurred when Brown failed to use its accounting practice of estimating, accumulating and reporting B&P costs at the corporate level in computing its 1975 allowable B&P costs utilizing the B&P cost limitation formula.

The board substantially reversed its initial decision by concluding that Brown had violated CAS 401. According to the board, "The violation occurred when appellant used raw incurred divisional B&P costs to compute the historical ratio required by the B&P limitation formula and to measure the disallowed B&P costs. This selection of accounting data clearly involves accumulating and reporting within the meaning of CAS 401."

After citing the definitions of accumulating costs and reporting costs set forth in CAS 401.30, the board found, "The inconsistency prohibited by CAS 401 arises from appellant's reporting its allowable B&P costs based on incurred divisional costs, which was inconsistent with its established accounting practice of estimating B&P costs on the basis of their allocation from the corporate G&A expense pool."

As the board saw it in its second decision, Brown's selection of divisional B&P costs for use in the B&P cost limitation formula constituted "accumulating 'relevant cost data' with the intention of ultimately reporting its allowable B&P cost for 1975." The board further found in its decision that, to the extent Brown "previously reported as B&P costs at the corporate level using allocated costs, we can perceive how the change in its accounting practice of reporting costs has occurred . . . when appellant selected the incurred divisional B&P costs for use in the formula, it was accumulating 'relevant cost data' with the intention of ultimately reporting its allowable B&P costs; this was an act of reporting." The board concluded as follows: "Appellant might now argue that it may select allocated B&P costs at the divisional level in the B&P cost limitation formula, which we would reject for the same reasoning. Regardless of whether appellant selects incurred or allocated costs for use in the formula, if it reports either at the divisional level it is changing its established cost accounting practice within the meaning of the CAS clause."

Texas Instruments, Inc., ASBCA No. 18621, 79-1 BCA par. 13,800; 79-2 BCA par. 14,184.

As summarized by the board, the government's position was that TI's "cost accounting practices in not accumulating and reporting costs by individual contracts, are inconsistent with its cost estimating practices which, in the Government's opinion, are based on a single contract. This would constitute noncompliance with CAS 401." As the board summarized TI's position, "It does not estimate costs for pricing purpose by a single contract and therefore no inconsistency exists between its practices and estimating costs on one hand and in accumulating the reporting costs on the other hand."

Important to an understanding of the controversy is TI's cost accounting system which, for fixed-price supply contracts, does not accumulate costs by individual contracts. Essentially, the contractor's computerized cost accounting system is based on accumulating costs by projects and these costs related to identical or similar products, based on commonalities of subassemblies, parts, etc., regardless of the origin for the order of the products. The system is described as a *product line accounting-cost accounting system,* and the project is the final cost objective for accumulating costs.

We understand that over the years DCAA has tried to persuade TI to accumulate and report costs by individual contracts and has suggested this could be done by use of supplemental memoranda and journal entries, although at a very significant additional cost that TI refused to incur.

The essence of the controversy was whether CAS 401 requires contractors to accumulate and report costs by individual contract. But the government moved from this position to one it considered more favorable—the consistency requirement of CAS 401: "Mainly, that the accumulation and reporting of costs must be on a single contract basis if the contractor estimated and proposed costs on a single contract basis as is the appellant's practice by using the DD Form 633." Zeroing in further on the identification of the DD Form 633 and estimating requirements, the government argued:

> Since Appellant's estimating practice is to estimate by contract using a DD Form 633, i.e., by estimating based on the requirements of the proposed contract such as the quantities or unique tasks or specification requirements set forth in the contract proposal, Appellant's practice used in the accumulating and reporting of costs for the resulting contract must be to allocate the costs to the contract as a final cost objective in order to meet the consistency and comparability requirements of CAS 401. It is the Government's position that this allocation is a requirement of CAS 401.40(b) regardless of what kind of cost accounting system a contractor uses or discloses on its Disclosure Statement.

TI, on the other hand, argued that its estimating practices were consistent with its cost accounting practices in accumulating and reporting costs since they both produced average costs of a unit or a part as necessary. The contractor further argued that the submission of a pricing proposal on a DD Form 633 for a single contract is not determinative as to the nature of its estimating practices. TI further indicated that the government "has improperly and erroneously equated the form of the proposal with estimating practices and thus has, in effect, asserted that 'accumulated cost must be consistent with the form of the proposal.' "

The board identified the basic issue as being what constitutes TI's practice in estimating costs for proposal purposes in connection with fixed-firm price contracts for supplies. The government pointed to the pricing proposal as represented by DD Form 633; TI insisted that its estimating practices are represented by the methods and techniques it uses in establishing the estimates that appear on the proposal form.

The board said that, if it agreed with the government that TI estimates for pricing proposals are on a single contract basis, then TI's practices in accumulating and reporting costs would not be consistent with its practices in estimating and consequently would be in noncompliance with CAS 401. However, the board did not agree with the government's contention. It found that, except for the base material, estimates for practically all other costs on the DD Form 633 were based on historical cost data derived from the various projects. The historical cost data used in the estimating processes represented the average costs of many units manufactured under many contracts; accordingly, they did not represent the costs incurred under a single contract. The board emphasized that the cost TI was estimating was the average cost within a project or product line.

The board concluded that CAS 401 does not require accumulation, reporting, and estimating of costs by individual contracts. Nor did the board find anything in the legislative or administrative history of this standard to support the government's position or to make TI's practices unacceptable. Quite the contrary, the board found that the legislation did not require accounting by individual contracts. The CASB, through its regulations, could have imposed that specific requirement but did not do so. As a matter of fact, the draft of CAS 401 had stated, "The purpose of this Cost Accounting Standard is to insure that each contractor's cost accounting practices used in estimating costs are consistent with those used by him in accumulating and reporting costs *on individual contracts*." (Emphasis added.)

The board pointed to other instances as well, where changes made from the draft to the finally promulgated CAS 401, by omitting such terms as "under each contract," would certainly suggest that the board did not intend the stringent requirements that the government was insisting on in this appeal. Nor was the board persuaded by the DCAA representative or the government trial attorney that it was the CASB's intention to require estimating and accumulating by individual contracts. To the contrary, the board said, "In a matter that is assigned by the Congress to the CAS Board for regulation, we would be very reluctant to supply by construction for CAS 401 the requirement for accumulating, reporting, and estimating costs by individual contracts when the CAS Board has shown an intention to omit it."

In summary, the board concluded that TI's estimating practices were not based on an individual contract, that the submission of a DD Form 633 reflecting a proposed price for a contract in no way changed TI's practices, and that CAS 401 did not require estimating, accumulating, and reporting by individual contract.

An important matter to which we invite attention is the limitation in the decision on descriptions of TI's cost accounting system. We have been concerned in the past about the extensive descriptions of contractors' cost accounting practices that appear in decisions of boards of contract appeals and courts. Industry expended such strong efforts and succeeded in retaining confidentiality of Disclosure Statements, which some contractors are required to file that it has seemed incongruous to us to see this confidential information in the judicial and quasi-judicial decisions. On this point, we were extremely interested in reading the following paragraph from the board's decision in the *TI* appeal and recommend this procedure for all contractors facing similar circumstances: "During extended prehearing and discovery activities the parties entered into an extensive stipulation regarding the description of the appellant's cost accounting system. . . . On appellant's motion, this document and two trial exhibits . . ., all found to contain confidential company financial and management information, were placed under a Board's protective order."

Consistent with its action in *Dayton T. Brown,* and its actions in other litigations where the ASBCA ruled in favor of the contractor on CAS-related issues, the government filed a motion for reconsideration. The board found the government's arguments lacking in substance and affirmed its decision.

CAS 402—CONSISTENCY IN ALLOCATING COSTS INCURRED FOR THE SAME PURPOSE

The second standard also appeared in final form on February 29, 1972, with an effective date of July 1, 1972. Its major provisions are cited below:

§ 402.40 Fundamental requirement.

All costs incurred for the same purpose, in like circumstances, are either direct costs only or indirect costs only with respect to final cost objectives. No final cost objective shall have allocated to it as an indirect cost any cost, if other costs incurred for the same purpose, in like circumstances, have been included as a direct cost of that or any other final cost objective. Further, no final cost objective shall have allocated to it as a direct cost any cost, if other costs incurred for the same purpose, in like circumstances, have been included in any indirect cost pool to be allocated to that or any other final cost objective.

§ 402.50 Techniques for application.

(a) The Fundamental Requirement is stated in terms of cost incurred and is equally applicable to estimates of costs to be incurred as used in contract proposals.

(b) The Disclosure Statement to be submitted by the contractor will require that he set forth his cost accounting practices with regard to the distinction between direct and indirect costs. In addition, for those types of cost which are sometimes accounted for as direct and sometimes accounted for as indirect, the contractor will set forth in his Disclosure Statement the specific criteria and circumstances for making such distinctions. In essence, the Disclosure Statement submitted by the contractor, by distinguishing between direct and indirect costs, and by describing the criteria and circumstances for allocating those items which are sometimes direct and sometimes indirect, will be determinative as to whether or not costs are incurred for the same purpose. Disclosure Statement as used herein refers to the statement required to be submitted by contractors as a condition of contracting as set forth in Part 351 of this chapter.

(c) In the event that a contractor has not submitted a Disclosure Statement the determination of whether specific costs are directly allocable to contracts shall be based upon the contractor's cost accounting practices used at the time of contract proposal.

(d) Whenever costs which serve the same purpose cannot equitably be indirectly allocated to one or more final cost objectives in accordance with the contractor's disclosed accounting practices, the contractor may either: (1) Use a method for reassigning all such costs which would provide an equitable distribution to all final cost objectives, or (2) directly assign all such costs to final cost objectives with which they are specifically identified. In the event the contractor decides to make a change for either purpose the Disclosure Statement shall be amended to reflect the revised accounting practices involved.

(e) Any direct cost of minor dollar amount may be treated as an indirect cost for reasons of practicality where the accounting treatment for such cost is consistently applied to all final cost objectives, provided that such treatment produces results which are substantially the same as the results which would have been obtained if such cost had been treated as a direct cost.

Continuing the precedent established in CAS 401, the CASB included, as paragraph 402.60, several illustrations. Additional examples, although lacking authoritative status, are set forth in DCAA's Contract Audit Manual, paragraph 8-402.1.

Although CAS 402 is considered a basic implementation of Public Law 91-379, the principle it established was not entirely new. Previous to promulgation of CAS 402, DAR 15-202(a) provided:

Costs identified specifically with the contract are direct costs of the contract and are to be charged directly thereto. Costs identified specifically with other work of the contractor are direct costs of that work and are not to be charged to the contract directly or indirectly. When items ordinarily chargeable as indirect costs are charged to Government work as direct costs, the cost of like items applicable to other work of the contractor must be eliminated from indirect costs allocated to Government work.

Interpretation No. 1. to CAS 402—Bid and Proposal Costs

Among the problems that surfaced in connection with the initial and final publications of CAS 402 was the application of this standard to bid and proposal (B&P) costs. There existed no authoritative accounting principles or regulations as to whether B&P costs should be charged direct or indirect, and a wide variety of methods were in use. Some contractors treated all B&P costs as indirect expenses while others charged some B&P costs as direct to the contract and the balance as indirect.

As published in its final form in the *Federal Register* of June 18, 1976, Interpretation No. 1. to CAS 402 states, essentially, that bid and proposal costs may be charged directly where they are incurred "pursuant to a specific requirement of an existing contract." However, the interpretation does not prohibit charging proposal costs as indirect if this practice is followed consistently by the contractor and if it provides "an equitable distribution to all final cost objectives."

The text of Interpretation No. 1. to CAS 402 is quoted below:

Part 402, Cost Accounting Standard, Consistency in Allocating Costs Incurred for the Same Purpose, provides, in Section 402.40, that ". . . no final cost objective shall have allocated to it as a direct cost any cost, if other costs incurred for the same purpose, in like circumstances, have been included in any indirect cost pool to be allocated to that or any other final cost objective."

This interpretation deals with the way Part 402 applies to the treatment of costs incurred in preparing, submitting, and supporting proposals. In essence, it is addressed to whether or not, under the Standard, all such costs are incurred for the same purpose, in like circumstances.

Under Part 402, costs incurred in preparing, submitting, and supporting proposals pursuant to a specific requirement of an existing contract are considered to have been incurred in different circumstances from the circumstances under which costs are incurred in preparing proposals which do not result from such specific requirement. The circumstances are different because the costs of preparing proposals specifically required by the provisions of an existing contract relate only to that contract while other proposal costs relate to all work of the contractor.

This interpretation does not preclude the allocation, as indirect costs, of costs incurred in preparing all proposals. The cost accounting practices used by the contractor, however, must be followed consistently and the method used to reallocate such costs, of course, must provide an equitable distribution to all final cost objectives.

The question of whether proposal costs are direct or indirect or may be either has been argued over as many years as we can remember. ASPR was silent on this point, leaving arguments to be resolved on a case-by-case basis between a contractor and government representatives, and the promulgation of CAS in 1972 highlighted and focused additional attention on this controversy.

CAS 402 and Disclosure Statement Prove Factors in Bid Protest

Several factors were involved in a bid protest by CACI, Inc.-Federal, sustained in Comptroller General's decision No. B-216516, November 19, 1984. This review and analysis is limited to the protester's contention that the government's evaluation of CACI's proposal was in violation of CAS 402.

The RFP solicited proposals for the performance of certain integration, assembly and warehousing services related to modular hospital units, and also encompassed options for shelter outfitting and preassembled module construction. The "offerors were advised that their proposals were 'acceptable' and 'substantially equal' technically and that the predominant factor in determining the awardee would be the lowest cost, as evaluated on the basis of the government's determination of a realistic cost." The best and final offers showed CACI with by far the lowest costs; however, the Navy's evaluation lowered the cost proposal of the highest bidder by some $900,000, and increased CACI's cost proposal by about $6.6 million or 69%. As a result of the evaluation, the Navy awarded the contract to the company with the highest cost proposal but lowest evaluated bid. CACI protested the award and simultaneously sought a temporary restraining order and preliminary injunction against further performance. The United States District Court for the District of Columbia (Civil Action No. 84-2971), September 26, 1984, issued a temporary restraining order requiring immediate cessation of work by the awardee, and it requested expedited treatment from GAO to CACI's protest.

The controversy discussed here concerns the treatment of the accounting function. In what it asserted constituted compliance with the accounting practice reflected in its Disclosure Statement, CACI treated the accounting function as indirect costs. The Navy contended that because the accounting function for this contract required the assignment of dedicated personnel, such costs should be considered direct and further that this treatment would be consistent with CACI's Disclosure Statement. In a portion of the decision, the Comptroller General wrote:

> . . . From our review, it appears that CACI consistently indicated to the Navy that this function would not be a direct charge to the contract under its accounting system, but rather would be included as a part of CACI's indirect pool costs charged under the contract. The Navy states that CACI's approach reflects a misunderstanding of the RFP's extensive cost reporting requirements and that only a dedicated accounting function can fulfill contract requirements. CACI states that the RFP did not require a dedicated accounting function and to require this now would necessitate an RFP amendment.

GAO reviewed CACI's Disclosure Statement and concluded that "the accounting function is not clearly indicated to be either a direct or indirect charge under that statement." This seems to be a curious point inasmuch as one would have thought that DCAA would have identified such a deficiency and requested the contracting officer to direct CACI to revise its Statement at the time it was first submitted.

Citing pertinent DAR provisions, the Navy argued that because dedicated accounting personnel are necessary, its cost must be charged as a direct cost to the contract because they can be identifiable with a particular final cost objective.

"However," wrote GAO, "the Navy fails to recognize that part 402 of the CAS supplements this general rule for CAS-covered contractors, such as CACI." Citing the provisions of this standard, GAO pointed out that if CACI charged the accounting function as indirect under other contracts, it must be consistent under this contract. The decision did recognize that: "If this contract required something different from CACI's ordinary accounting functions, it is possible that CACI could elect to charge this as a direct charge." However, GAO emphasized that "even in this event, it would be CACI's initial election of how it wanted to manage its accounting system, so long as CACI complied with CAS. The government cannot legally dictate how an offeror should establish his accounting system." GAO accordingly found that "the Navy improperly added the accounting function as a direct charge without proper verification of the appropriate treatment of this cost under CACI's accounting system and the CAS. Therefore, we sustain this aspect of the protest and recommend that revised proposals be submitted."

GAO's decision found no specific requirement in the RFP for a dedicated accounting staff and stated that if the Navy had a legitimate requirement for dedicated personnel not specifically designated in the RFP, "offerors should be advised and given an opportunity to submit proposals on that requirement in accordance with proper accounting practice and the Navy should evaluate the proposed approaches in accordance with CAS."

As stated earlier in this review, this Cost-Plus-Award-Fee RFP protest included controversies in addition to this CAS feature. CACI's protest was sustained in several respects and GAO concluded that "there should be further negotiations with the offerors in the competitive range and revised cost proposals should be solicited." It concluded that unless the firm having the lowest evaluated bid was judged "the successful offeror on this recompetition, its contract should then be terminated."

The other point on which the protest was sustained related to an alleged violation of the regulations concerning the maximum amount of the award fees. GAO's recommendations that contracts be terminated are rare and it is not known whether such conclusion would have been reached in the absence of the CAS issue.

CAS 405—ACCOUNTING FOR UNALLOWABLE COSTS

This is the third of the standards we considered appropriate for inclusion in this chapter on Management Practices and Accounting Systems for Government Contracts. It took effect January 1, 1974, and the final version fell far short of satisfying the vigorous and virtually unanimous criticisms of the private sector. The major provisions of CAS 405 are cited below:

§ 405.40 Fundamental requirement.

(a) Costs expressly unallowable or mutually agreed to be unallowable, including costs mutually agreed to be unallowable directly associated costs, shall be identified and excluded from any billing, claim, or proposal applicable to a Government contract.

(b) Costs which specifically become designated as unallowable as a result of a written decision furnished by a contracting officer pursuant to contract disputes procedures shall be identified if included in or used in the computation of any billing, claim, or proposal applicable to a Government contract. This identification requirement applies also to any costs incurred for the same purpose under like circumstances as the costs specifically identified as unallowable under either this paragraph or paragraph (a) above.

(c) Costs which, in a contracting officer's written decision furnished pursuant to contract disputes procedures, are designated as unallowable directly associated costs of unallowable costs covered by either (a) or (b) above shall be accorded the identification required by paragraph (b) above.

(d) The costs of any work project not contractually authorized, whether or not related to performance of a proposed or existing contract, shall be accounted for, to the extent appropriate, in a manner which permits ready separation from the costs of authorized work projects.

(e) All unallowable costs covered by paragraphs (a) through (d) above shall be subject to the same cost accounting principles governing cost allocability as allowable costs. In circumstances where these unallowable costs normally would be part of a regular indirect-cost allocation base or bases, they shall remain in such base or bases. Where a directly associated cost is part of a category of costs normally included in an indirect-cost pool that will be allocated over a base containing the unallowable cost with which it is associated, such a directly associated cost shall be retained in the indirect-cost pool and be allocated through the regular allocation process.

(f) Where the total of the allocable and otherwise allowable costs exceeds a limitation-of-cost or ceiling-price provision in a contract, full direct and indirect cost allocation shall be made to the contract cost objective, in accordance with established cost accounting practices and Standards which regularly govern a given entity's allocations to Government contract cost objectives. In any determination of unallowable cost overrun, the amount thereof shall be identified in terms of the excess of allowable costs over the ceiling amount, rather than through specific identification of particular cost items or cost elements.

§ 405.50 Techniques for application.

(a) The detail and depth of records required as backup support for proposals, billings, or claims shall be that which is adequate to establish and maintain visibility of identified unallowable costs (including directly associated costs), their accounting status in terms of their allocability to contract cost objectives, and the cost accounting treatment which has been accorded such costs. Adherence to this cost accounting principle does not require that allocation of unallowable costs to final cost objectives be made in the detailed cost accounting records. It does require that unallowable costs be given appropriate consideration in any cost accounting determinations governing the content of allocation bases used for distributing indirect costs to cost objectives. Unallowable costs involved in the determination of rates used for standard costs, or for indirect-cost bidding or billing, need be identified only at the time rates are proposed, established, revised, or adjusted.

(b) The visibility requirement of paragraph (a) above may be satisfied by any form of cost identification which is adequate for purposes of contract cost determination and verification. The Standard does not require such cost identification for purposes which are not relevant to the determination of Government contract cost. Thus, to provide visibility for incurred costs, acceptable alternative practices would include (1) the segregation of unallowable costs in separate accounts maintained for this purpose in the regular books of account, (2) the development and maintenance of separate accounting records or workpapers, or (3) the use of any less formal cost accounting techniques which establishes and maintains adequate cost identification to permit audit verification of the accounting recognition given unallowable costs. Contractors may satisfy the visibility requirements for estimated costs either (1) by designation and description (in backup data, workpapers, etc.) of the amounts and types of any unallowable costs which have specifically been identified and recognized in making the estimates, or (2) by description of any other estimating technique employed to provide appropriate recognition of any unallowable costs pertinent to the estimates.

(c) Specific identification of unallowable costs is not required in circumstances where, based upon considerations of materiality, the Government and the contractor reach agreement on an alternate method that satisfies the purpose of the Standard.

The more general criticisms directed to this standard included the view that this entire matter was an administrative issue and not a proper subject for a cost accounting standard. It was also argued that this standard would only add to current controversies and inhibit negotiation. The Board found these arguments unpersuasive. It emphasized (1) that existing regulations did not provide any guidance in this area, (2) that cost accounting (allocability) considerations were involved and were within the province of the Board, and (3) that the standard did not govern the allowability of costs, which was a function of the procuring authority.

Objections were raised regarding the additional cost and effort that would be required in identifying unallowable costs. The Board recognized the merit in these contentions and virtually all of CAS 405.50 is directed toward minimizing the recording and reporting requirements. Paragraph 405.50(b), for example, offers contractors the opportunity to select alternative practices under which unallowable costs could be recorded in separate accounts in the regular books of account, or in separate accounting records or work papers, or by the use of any other informal cost accounting technique so long as these costs are adequately identified and are susceptible of audit verification. In the case of rate determination for bidding or billing purposes, CAS 405.50(a) provides that the unallowable costs "need be identified only at the time rates are proposed, established, revised, or adjusted."

With further reference to the apprehensions that this standard will impose a substantial amount of additional work, CAS 405.50(c) addresses considerations of materiality and permits the government and the contractor, under certain circumstances, to agree that specific identification is not required where some alternative methods would satisfy the objective of this standard.

From the time that the first exposure draft on this standard was published, there were substantial controversies revolving around the term and concept "directly associated cost." Understandably unhappy with the adverse effects on profits of unallowable costs, industry has steadfastly, although not too successfully, resisted the enlarging impact attributable to various accounting devices employed by the government. These devices, by increasing unallowable costs through adding thereto so-called associated, corollary, or other expenses, resulted in further inroads on profits. Based on these considerations, industry opposed the introduction of this concept in the standard. In contrast, DOD's opposition was based on the principle that the standard did not go far enough. It objected to the Board's definition of directly associated costs: "Any cost which is generated solely as a result of the incurrence of another cost and which would not have been incurred had the other cost not been incurred." The Defense Department was of the view that this definition was too restrictive.

The final version of the standard, including the prefatory comments, indicates that the Board considered both sources of opposition and elected to make no concession to either. It did recognize that this concept might result in double counting in certain circumstances. Accordingly, CAS 405.50(e) provides that in those circumstances a cost shall not be classified as a directly associated cost but shall be retained in the indirect cost pool and allocated through the regular allocation process.

In an effort to accommodate some of the other objections, CAS 405.40(a) provides for the exclusion of only expressly unallowab.e or mutually agreed-to unallowable costs. Where the cost is designated as unallowable through the unilateral determination of the contracting officer, it must be identified, but it need not be excluded from billings, claims, or proposals (405.40(b)(c)).

Industry objected strongly but unsuccessfully to the provision that unallowable costs included in an allocation base for indirect expenses must remain in that base and thus be increased through the allocation of indirect expenses thereto. This provision, which in effect prohibits fragmentation of an indirect allocation base, paralleled DAR 15-203(c) and now FAR 31.203(c).

Finally, DOD auditors and contracting officers understandably encountered difficulties in interpreting the language of CAS 405, and the lack of uniformity and consistency in its implementation suggested the need for a Defense Department interpretation. The interpretation was also (if not primarily) generated by disagreements between DCAA and contracting officers over the manner in which the standard was being applied by the audit agency in its audits of defense contractors' Washington offices, initiated in the middle 1970s as a result of pressure from Senator William Proxmire.

As a general policy, where DCAA concludes that contractor personnel are engaged in "unallowable" activities, they are inclined to disallow or question a wide range of costs that they consider to be directly associated. These may include not only salaries and fringe benefits of the people involved but the entire gamut of space and support costs that can possibly be related to those individuals.

CAS 405.60(e) illustrates the CASB's thinking on treating directly associated costs as unallowable. In this illustration, a contractor's official takes a business entertainment trip. According to the Standard, the entertainment costs are expressly unallowable. This official's salary is usually included in G&A expenses, and the Standard states: "However, unless this type of activity constituted a significant part of the official's regular duties and responsibilities on which his salary was based, no part of the official's salary would be required to be identified as a directly associated cost of the unallowable entertainment expense."

Predictably, questions and controversies arose over the appropriate interpretation of "a significant part of the official's regular duties and responsibilities." We understand that DCAA issued unofficial guidance to its offices which established 5% as "a significant part." This position was sharply opposed by industry and by most DOD contracting officers as well. After lengthy studies, DOD concluded: "There shall be a conclusive presumption that a portion of an official's or employee's salary is a directly associated cost and significant and thus unallowable if such official or employee devotes *30%* or more of his time to the unallowable cost activity or objective." (Emphasis added.)

The interpretation was not favorably received by the private sector nor by the CASB staff. Ultimately, the essence of CAS 405, without use of arbitrary percentages, was incorporated into DAR (February 1982) and FPR (March 1983). After some editing, these provisions, quoted below, were included in FAR 31.201-6:

(a) Costs that are expressly unallowable or mutually agreed to be unallowable, including mutually agreed to be unallowable directly associated costs, shall be identified and excluded from any billing, claim, or proposal applicable to a Government contract. A directly associated cost is any cost which is generated solely as a result of incurring another cost, and which would not have been incurred had the other cost not been incurred. When an unallowable cost is incurred, its directly associated costs are also unallowable.

(b) Costs which specifically become designated as unallowable or as unallowable directly associated costs of unallowable costs as a result of a written decision furnished by a contracting officer shall be identified if included in or used in computing any billing, claim, or proposal applicable to a Government contract. This identification requirement applies also to any costs incurred for the same purpose under like circumstances as the costs specifically identified as unallowable under either this paragraph or paragraph (a) above.

(c) The detail and depth of records required as backup support for proposals, billings, or claims shall be that which is adequate to establish and maintain visibility of identified unallowable costs, including directly associated costs. Unallowable costs involved in determining rates used for standard costs, or for indirect cost proposals or billing, need be identified only at the time rates are proposed, established, revised, or adjusted. These requirements may be satisfied by any form of cost identification which is adequate for purposes of contract cost determination and verification.

(d) If a directly associated cost is included in a cost pool which is allocated over a base that includes the unallowable cost with which it is associated, the directly associated cost shall remain in the cost pool. Since the unallowable costs will attract their allocable share of costs from the cost pool, no further action is required to assure disallowance of the directly associated costs. In all other cases, the directly associated costs, if material in amount, must be purged from the cost pool as unallowable.

(e)(1) In determining the materiality of a directly associated cost, consideration should be given to the significance of (i) the actual dollar amount, (ii) the cumulative effect of all directly associated costs in a cost pool, or (iii) the ultimate effect on the cost of Government contracts.

(2) Salary expenses of employees who participate in activities that generate unallowable costs shall be treated as directly associated costs to the extent of the time spent on the proscribed activity, provided the costs are material in accordance with subparagraph (e)(1) above [except when such salary expenses are, themselves, unallowable]. The time spent in proscribed activities should be compared to total time spent on company activities to determine if the costs are material. Time spent by employees outside the normal working hours should not be considered except when it is evident that an employee engages so frequently in company activities during periods outside normal working hours as to indicate that such activities are part of the employee's regular duties.

(3) When a selected item of cost under 31.205 provides that directly associated costs be unallowable, it is intended that such directly associated costs be unallowable only if determined to be material in amount in accordance with the criteria provided in subparagraphs (e)(1) and (e)(2) above, except in those situations where allowance of any of the directly associated costs involved would be considered to be contrary to public policy.

CAS 406—COST ACCOUNTING PERIOD

CAS 406 is another of the standards that appears appropriate for discussion under the general subject of management practices and accounting systems. Its major provisions are cited below:

§ 406.40 Fundamental requirement.

(a) A contractor shall use his fiscal year as his cost accounting period, except that:

(1) Costs of an indirect function which exists for only a part of a cost accounting period may be allocated to cost objectives of that same part of the period as provided in paragraph 406.50(a).

(2) An annual period other than the fiscal year may, as provided in paragraph 406.50(d), be used as the cost accounting period if its use is an established practice of the contractor.

(3) A transitional cost accounting period other than a year shall be used whenever a change of fiscal year occurs.

(4) Where a contractor's cost accounting period is different from the reporting period required by Renegotiation Board regulations, the latter may be used for such reporting.

(b) A contractor shall follow consistent practices in his selection of the cost accounting period or periods in which any types of expense any types of adjustment to expenses (including prior-period adjustments) are accumulated and allocated.

(c) The same cost accounting period shall be used for accumulating costs in an indirect cost pool as for establishing its allocation base, except that the contracting parties may agree to use a different period for establishing an allocation base as provided in paragraph 406.50(e).

§ 406.50 Techniques for application.

(a) The cost of an indirect function which exists for only a part of a cost accounting period may be allocated on the basis of data for that part of the cost accounting period if the cost is (1) material in amount, (2) accumulated in a separate indirect cost pool, and (3) allocated on the basis of an appropriate direct measure of the activity or output of the function during that part of the period.

(b) The practices required by paragraph 406.40(b) of this Standard shall include appropriate practices for deferrals, accruals, and other adjustments to be used in identifying the cost accounting periods among which any types of expense and any types of adjustment to expense are distributed. If an expense, such as taxes, insurance or employee leave, is identified with a fixed, recurring, annual period which is different from the contractor's cost accounting period, the Standard permits continued use of that different period. Such expenses shall be distributed to cost accounting periods in accordance with the contractor's established practices for accruals, deferrals and other adjustments.

(c) Indirect cost allocation rates, based on estimates, which are used for the purpose of expediting the closing of contracts which are terminated or completed prior to the end of a cost accounting period need not be those finally determined or negotiated for that cost accounting period. They shall, however, be developed to represent a full cost accounting period, except as provided in paragraph (a) of this section.

(d) A contract may, upon mutual agreement with the Government, use as his cost accounting period a fixed annual period other than his fiscal year, if the use of such a period is an established practice of the contractor and is consistently used for managing and controlling the business, and appropriate accruals, deferrals or other adjustments are made with respect to such annual periods.

(e) The contracting parties may agree to use an annual period which does not coincide precisely with the cost accounting period for developing the data used in establishing an allocation base, provided (1) the practice is necessary to obtain significant administrative convenience, (2) the practice is consistently followed by the contractor, (3) the annual period used is representative of the activity of the cost accounting period for which the indirect costs to be allocated are accumulated, and (4) the practice can reasonably be estimated to provide a distribution to cost objectives of the cost accounting period not materially different from that which otherwise would be obtained.

(f) When a transitional cost accounting period is required under the provisions of paragraph 406.40(a) (3), the contractor may select any one of the following: (1) the period, less than a year in length, extending from the end of his previous cost accounting period to the beginning of his next regular cost accounting period; (2) a period in excess of a year, but not longer than fifteen months, obtained by combining the period described in (1) above with the previous cost accounting period; or (3) a period in excess of a year, but not longer than fifteen months, obtained by combining the period described in (1) above with the next regular cost accounting period. A change in the contractor's cost accounting period is a change in accounting practices for which an adjustment in the contract price may be required in accordance with paragraph (a) (4) (B) of the contract clause set out at 4 C.F.R. 331.50.

CAS 406 is one of the standards that encountered opposition from both the private sector and the Department of Defense. DOD expressed the very definite preference for its own regulation on this subject which, while accepting the premise that a contractor's fiscal year should normally be the base period, also recognized the equity and propriety of shorter periods in certain instances. Prior to the promulgation of CAS 406, ASPR 15-203(e) provided:

> A base period for allocation of indirect costs is the period during which such costs are incurred and accumulated for distribution to work performed in that period. Normally, the base period will be the contractor's fiscal year; however, use of a shorter period may be appropriate in case of (i) contracts whose performance involves only a minor portion of the fiscal year, or (ii) where it is general practice in the industry to use a shorter period. In any event, the base period or periods should be so selected as to avoid inequities in the allocation of costs. When the contract is performed over an extended period of time, as many such base periods will be used as will be required to represent the period of contract performance.

It seemed that just about everyone except the CASB and its staff and DCAA was more favorably impressed by the logic and flexibility of the procurement regulations than by the rigid requirements that increasingly characterized the cost accounting standards. On the other hand, it must be said that the question of the appropriate cost accounting period for determining overhead rates surfaced in a number of decisions by boards of contract appeals and the guidance in the boards' decisions was not always consistent. In *Itek,* NASA BCA No. 27, 65-1 BCA par. 4592, the government prevailed in requiring a period covering the last eight months of the fiscal year instead of the entire fiscal year because the first four months covered the beginning of Itek's business life and was devoted to organizational and other activities rather than contract performance.

In *America Scientific Corp.,* IBCA No. 576-666, 67-2 BCA par. 6670, the Department of Interior Board accepted the government's contention that the contractor maintained an inadequate accounting system and upheld the use of a full year for determining a rate for work done in about one month. Finally, a detailed inquiry and conclusion regarding ASPR 15-203(e) is found in *Nash-Hammond, Inc.,* ASBCA No. 15563, 71-2 BCA par. 9166. Here the contractor calculated its indirect expense rate on the basis of its full fiscal year, while the government ruled that the rate should be determined on the basis of the first six months. The government's argument seemed to be based mainly on the fact that direct costs decreased sharply during the second half of the fiscal year, resulting in a sharply increased indirect expense rate. The board found nothing in ASPR 15-203(e) that would support the government's position.

Illustrations to help the government and industry implement this standard are contained in CAS paragraph 406.60, and the significant but unauthoritative illustrations added by DCAA are contained in its CAM, paragraph 8-406.2.

FAR essentially incorporates the provisions of DAR and FPR as revised after the effective date of CAS 406. The requirements of that standard must be applied to contracts subject to full CAS coverage, while the more flexible provisions obtain for modified or non-CAS-covered contracts. FAR 31.203(e) is quoted below:

> (e) A base period for allocating indirect costs is the cost accounting period during which such costs are incurred and accumulated for distribu-

tion to work performed in that period. The criteria and guidance in CAS 406 for selecting the cost accounting periods to be used in allocating indirect costs are incorporated herein for application to contracts subject to full CAS coverage. For contracts subject to modified CAS coverage and for non-CAS-covered contracts, the base period for allocating indirect costs will normally be the contractor's fiscal year. But a shorter period may be appropriate (1) for contracts in which performance involves only a minor portion of the fiscal year or (2) when it is general practice in the industry to use a shorter period. When a contract is performed over an extended period, as many base periods shall be used as are required to represent the period of contract performance.

CAS 407 - USE OF STANDARD COSTS FOR DIRECT MATERIAL AND DIRECT LABOR

CAS 407 was effective October 1, 1974, and its major provisions are cited below:

§ 407.40 Fundamental requirement.

Standard costs may be used for estimating, accumulating, and reporting costs of direct material and direct labor only when all of the following criteria are met:

(a) Standard costs are entered into the books of account:

(b) Standard costs and related variances are appropriately accounted for at the level of the production unit; and

(c) Practices with respect to the setting and revising of standards, use of standard costs, and disposition of variances are stated in writing and are consistently followed.

§ 407.50 Techniques for application.

(a)(1) A contractor's written statement of practices with respect to standards shall include the bases and criteria (such as engineering studies, experience, or other supporting data) used in setting and revising standards; the period during which standards are to remain effective; the level (such as ideal or realistic) at which material-quantity standards and labor-time standards are set; and conditions (such as those expected to prevail at the beginning of a period) which material-price standards and labor-rate standards are designed to reflect.

(2) Where only either the material price or material quantity is set at standard, with the other component stated at actual, the result of the multiplication shall be treated as material cost at standard. Similarly, where only either the labor rate or labor time is set at standard, with the other component stated at actual, the result of the multiplication shall be treated as labor cost at standard.

(3) A labor-rate standard may be set to cover a category of direct labor only if the functions performed within that category are not materially disparate and the employees involved are interchangeable with respect to the functions performed.

(4) A labor-rate standard may be set to cover a group of direct labor workers who perform disparate functions only under either one of the following conditions:

(i) Where that group of workers all work in a single production unit yielding homogeneous outputs (in this case, the same labor-rate standard shall be applied to each worker in that group), or

(ii) Where that group of workers, in the performance of their respective functions, forms an integral team (in this case, a labor-rate standard shall be set for each integral team).

(b) (1) Material-price standards may be used and their related variances may be recognized either at the time purchases of material are entered into the books of account or at the time material cost is allocated to production units.

(2) Where material-price standards are used and related variances are recognized at the time purchases of material are entered into the books of account, they shall be accumulated separately by homogeneous groupings of material. Examples of homogeneous groupings of material are:

(i) Where prices of all items in that grouping of material are expected to fluctuate in the same direction and at substantially the same rate, or

(ii) Where items in that grouping of material are held for use in a single production unit yielding homogeneous outputs.

(3) Where material-price variances are recognized at the time purchases of material are entered into the books of account, variances of each homogeneous grouping of material shall be allocated (except as provided in par. (b) (4) of this section), at least annually, to items in purchased-items inventory and to production units receiving items from that homogeneous grouping of material, in accordance with either one of the following practices, which shall be consistently followed:

(i) Items in purchased-items inventory of a homogeneous grouping of material are adjusted from standard cost to actual cost: the balance of the material-price variance, after reflecting these adjustments, shall be allocated to production units on the basis of the total of standard cost of material received from that homogeneous grouping of material by each of the production units; or

(ii) Items, at standard cost, in purchased-items inventory of a homogeneous grouping of material, are treated, collectively, as a production unit; the material-price variance shall be allocated to production units on the basis of standard cost of material received from that homogeneous grouping of material by each of the production units.

(4) Where material-price variances are recognized at the time purchases of material are entered into the books of account, variances of each homogeneous grouping of material which are insignificant may be included in appropriate indirect cost pools for allocation to applicable cost objectives.

(5) Where a material-price variance is allocated to a production unit in accordance with paragraph (b) (3) of this section, it may be combined with material-quantity variance into one material-cost quantity variance for that production unit. A separate material-cost variance shall be accumulated for each production unit,

(6) Where material-price variances are recognized at the time material-cost is allocated to production units, these variances and material-quantity variances may be combined into one material-cost variance account.

(c) Labor-cost variances shall be recognized at the time labor cost is introduced into production units. Labor-rate variances and labor-time variances may be combined into one labor-cost variance account. A separate labor-cost variance shall be accumulated for each production unit.

(d) A contractor's established practice with respect to the disposition of variances accumulated by production unit shall be in accordance with one of the following paragraphs:

(1) Variances are allocated to cost objectives (including ending in-process inventory) at least annually. Where a variance related to material is allocated, the allocation shall be on the basis of the material-cost at standard, or, where outputs are homogeneous, on the basis of units of output. Similarly, where a variance related to labor is allocated, the allocation shall be on the basis of the labor cost at standard or labor hours at standard, or, where outputs are homogeneous, on the basis of units of output; or

(2) Variances which are immaterial may be included in appropriate indirect cost pools for allocation to applicable cost and objectives.

(e) Where variances applicable to covered contracts are allocated by memorandum worksheet adjustments rather than in the books of account, the bases used for adjustment shall be in accordance with those stated in paragraphs (b) (3) and (d) of this section.

The CASB provided illustrations in paragraph 407.60, and DCAA's additional informal examples are contained in CAM 8-407.

CAS 407 was not favorably received by most of the commentators in the private sector. However, despite some of the problems inherent in the rigidity of most of the Board's promulgations, it would be difficult to argue, as some industry and professional associations did, that ground rules for the use of standard costs were inappropriate or unnecessary. Prior to the publication of this standard, ASPR 15-201.1 and FPR 1-15.201-1 had only the following comment about standard costs: "In ascertaining what constitutes costs, any generally accepted method of determining or estimating costs that is equitable under the circumstances may be used, including standard costs properly adjusted for applicable variances."

Inasmuch as the government procurement regulations did not address how standard costs should be developed, or if or how such costs should be recorded in the books of account, it would be inconceivable that the CASB would not try to address this subject.

The reaction to the standard did not equal the volume of comments generated by some of the other standards because standard costs are used for government contracts by only about 25% of the contractors. Some of the comments that were received, however, reflected quite vigorous objections because, as mentioned above, government regulations hitherto were not particularly meaningful.

Most of the unfavorable comments argued that a standard cost system was a management tool, tailor-made for specific company operations, and that the requirements and constraints imposed by the CASB would defeat or impair the purposes for which such systems were established. Some companies stated they would not change their systems and would be required to establish "another set of books."

Chapter X

Accounting Methods and Controls for Material

DEFINITIONS

The terms "direct materials" and "indirect materials" have well-defined and established meanings in cost accounting theory and practice. Direct materials may be defined as material that enters directly on or into the product being made. That material which is used indirectly, but which is still necessary to complete the product and to operate the plant that completes the product, is known as indirect material.

Materials classified as direct should possess all three of the following characteristics:

(1) The materials should enter into or become a part of the product or process or the appurtenances or accessories thereof.

(2) The quantities of such materials, used on specific processes or products, should be determinable and measurable.

(3) The identification and measurement of such materials, as to specific processes or products, should be expedient and not disproportionately expensive.

Predicated on these requirements in respect of direct materials, indirect materials may be described as all materials necessary to manufacturing (exclusive of supplies) that do not possess all of the characteristics attributable to direct materials.

In connection with the above, consideration should be accorded to differences in various industries with respect to the nature of materials considered direct and indirect. As an illustration, packing and crating materials may be classified as direct materials by hosiery and electrical manufacturers, contrary to the procedures in most other industries, where such items are generally classified as indirect materials or manufacturing supplies.

FAR PROVISIONS

Provisions regarding material costs, as set forth in government contract cost principles, were expanded over the years. The current FAR provisions, set forth below, are unchanged from those previously contained in DAR 15-205.22 and FPR 1-15.205-22.

31.205-26 Material costs.

(a) Material costs include the costs of such items as raw materials, parts, sub-assemblies, components, and manufacturing supplies, whether purchased or manufactured, and may include such collateral items as inbound transportation and intransit insurance. In computing material costs, consideration shall be given to reasonable overruns, spoilage, or defective work (unless otherwise provided in any contract provision relating to inspection and correction of defective work). These costs are allowable, subject to the provisions of (b) through (e) below.

(b) Costs of material shall be adjusted for income and other credits, including trade discounts, refunds, rebates, allowances, cash discounts, and credits for scrap, salvage, and material returned to vendors. Such income and other credits shall either be credited directly to the cost of the material or be allocated as a credit to indirect costs. When the contractor can demonstrate that failure to take cash discounts was reasonable, lost discounts need not be credited.

(c) Reasonable adjustments arising from differences between periodic physical inventories and book inventories may be included in arriving at costs; *provided,* such adjustments relate to the period of contract performance.

(d) When materials are purchased specifically for and are identifiable solely with performance under a contract, the actual cost should be charged to the contract. If material is issued from stores, any generally recognized method of pricing is acceptable if that method is consistently applied and the results are equitable. When estimates of future material costs are required, current market price or anticipated acquisition cost may be used, but the basis of pricing must be disclosed.

(e) Allowance for all materials, supplies, and services sold or transferred between the contractor and divisions, subsidiaries, or affiliates of the contractor under a common control shall be on the basis of cost incurred in accordance with this subpart. However, allowance may be at a price when it is the established practice of the transferring organization to price interorganization transfers at other than cost for commercial work of the contractor or any division, subsidiary, or affiliate of the contractor under a common control, and when the price—

(1) Is or is based on an "established catalog or market price of commercial items sold in substantial quantities to the general public" in accordance with 15.804; or

(2) Is the result of "adequate price competition" in accordance with 15.804 and is the price at which an award was made to the affiliated organization after obtaining quotations on an equal basis from such organization and one or more outside sources which produce the item or its equivalent in significant quantity.

(3) Provided, that in either subparagraph (1) or (2) above—

(i) The price is not in excess of the transferor's current sales price to the most favored customer (including any division, subsidiary or affiliate of the contractor under a common control) for a like quantity under comparable conditions; and

(ii) The contracting officer has not determined the price to be unreasonable.

(f) The price determined in accordance with paragraph (e)(1) above should be adjusted to reflect the quantities being acquired and may be adjusted to reflect actual cost of any modifications necessary because of contract requirements.

It will be noted from the following that, except for interorganization transfers, the FAR approach to the definition of direct materials is consistent with CAS 411 and generally accepted cost accounting principles. An additional exception is found in certain instances where the items to be considered and reimbursed as direct materials are specifically enumerated in the contract. In such instances, of course, contractual provisions will determine cost classifications and will override any cost principle or procedure coming in conflict therewith. The exception, however, must be viewed in its proper perspective.

In this connection, it should be noted that, as a rule, defense contracts do not spell out precisely the particular items to be considered as direct materials, confining themselves usually to a general statement along the lines set forth in the previously cited paragraph of FAR, or a reference to generally accepted accounting principles. Moreover, when specific materials are enumerated, this procedure is effectuated as a result of an agreement between representatives of the government and the contractor and will often reflect the recognized practice of the particular industry.

With the foregoing exceptions, it can generally be stated that the determination of materials to be classified as direct will fall upon the contractor and that this determination will be accepted by the DCAA representatives after they have been satisfied by tests made that the following conditions obtain:

(1) The contractor's procedures are not contrary to generally accepted cost accounting principles.

(2) Such procedures are employed consistently with respect to other fiscal periods and other work.

COST ACCOUNTING STANDARDS PERTAINING TO MATERIAL COSTS

Several standards promulgated by the now-defunct Cost Accounting Standards Board addressed the subject of material costs.

Interpretation No. 1 to CAS 401 - Estimating and Accumulating Scrap, Spoilage, and Related Costs. Chapter IX of this text contains the background and provisions of this promulgation.

CAS 407 - Use of Standard Costs for Direct Material and Direct Labor. The major provisions of this standard are also contained in Chapter IX of this text.

CAS 410 - Allocation of Business Unit General and Administrative Expenses to Final Cost Objectives. As indicated by its title, this standard addresses G&A expenses. It is accordingly discussed in Chapter XV of this text—Accounting Methods and Controls for Selling, General and Administrative Expenses. The following provisions of CAS 410 relate to the manner in which G&A expenses are to be applied to material or inventory costs:

410.50 (i). For purposes of allocating the G&A expense pool, items produced or worked on for stock or product inventory shall be accounted for as final cost objectives in accordance with the following paragraphs:

(1) Where items are produced or worked on for stock or product inventory in a given cost accounting period, the cost input to such items in that period shall be included only once in the computation of the G&A expense allocation base and in the computation of the G&A expense allocation rate for that period and shall not be included in the computation of the base or rate for any other cost accounting period.

(2) A portion of the G&A expense pool shall be allocated to items produced or worked on for stock or product inventory in the cost accounting period or periods in which such items are produced at the rates determined for such periods except as provided in (3) below.

(3) Where the contractor does not include the G&A expense in inventory as part of the cost of stock or product inventory items, the G&A rate of the cost accounting period in which such items are issued to final cost objectives may be used to determine the G&A expenses applicable to issues of stock or product inventory items.

410.60(d)(2) - Illustration. During a cost accounting period, Business Unit D buys $2,000,000 of raw materials. At the end of that cost accounting period, $500,000 of raw materials inventory have not been charged out to contracts or other cost objectives. The $500,000 of raw materials are not part of the total cost input base for the cost accounting period, because they have not been charged to the production of goods and services during that period. If all of the $2,000,000 worth of raw material had been charged to cost objectives during the cost accounting period, the cost input base for the allocation of the G&A expense pool would include the entire $2,000,000.

410.60(e)(1) - Illustration. Business Unit E produces Item Z for stock or product inventory. The business unit does not include G&A expense as part of the inventory cost of these items for costing or financial reporting purposes. A production run of these items occurred during Cost Accounting Period 1. A number of the units produced were not issued during Period 1 and are issued in Period 2. However, those units produced in Period 1 shall be included in the cost input of that period for calculating the G&A expense allocation base and shall not be included in the cost input of Period 2.

(2) Business Unit E should apply the G&A expense rate of Period 1 to those units of Item Z issued during Period 1 and may apply the rate of Period 2 to the units issued in Period 2.

(3) If the practice of Business Unit E is to include G&A expense as part of the cost of stock or product inventory, the inventory cost of all units of Item Z produced in Period 1 and remaining in inventory at the end of Period 1, should include G&A expense using the G&A rate of Period 1.

410.60(f)(1) - Illustration. Business Unit F produced Item X for stock or product inventory. The business unit does not include G&A expense as part of the inventory cost of these items. A production run of these items was started, finished, and placed into inventory in a single cost accounting period. These items are issued during the next cost accounting period.

(2) The cost of items produced for stock or product inventory should be included in the G&A base in the same year they are produced. The cost of such items is not to be included in the G&A base on the basis of when they are issued to final cost objectives. Therefore, the time of issuance of these items from inventory to a final cost objective is irrelevant in computing the G&A base.

CAS 411 - Accounting for Acquisition Costs of Material. The major promulgation by the CASB on the subject of material costs was CAS 411. It is one of the shorter standards and can hardly be considered an important contribution to the subject. The meagerness of the coverage provoked little if any criticism because accounting literature and government procurement regulations seemed to supply ample information and guidelines. To the contrary, the major reactions to this standard were questions as to why a promulgation was necessary in an area that generated so few government-industry differences. Strong objections were also raised to certain provisions in the staff draft which, fortunately, were modified or eliminated in the final version.

The significant provisions are contained in paragraphs 411.40, Fundamental Requirement, and 411.50, Techniques for Application. We have cited them below, followed with our analysis and commentary.

§ 411.40 Fundamental requirement.

(a) The contractor shall have, and consistently apply, written statements of accounting policies and practices for accumulating the costs of material and for allocating costs of material to cost objectives.

(b) The cost of units of a category of material may be allocated directly to a cost objective provided the cost objective was specifically identified at the time of purchase or production of the units.

(c) The cost of material which (i) is used solely in performing indirect functions, or (ii) is not a significant element of production cost, whether or not incorporated in an end product, may be allocated to an indirect cost pool. When significant, the cost of such indirect material not consumed in a cost accounting period shall be established as an asset at the end of the period.

(d) Except as provided in paragraphs (b) and (c) of this Section, the cost of a category of material shall be accounted for in material inventory records.

(e) In allocating to cost objectives the costs of a category of material issued from company-owned material inventory, the costing method used shall be selected in accordance with the provisions of par. 411.50, and shall be used in a manner which results in systematic and rational costing of issues of material to cost objectives. The same costing method shall, within the same business unit, be used for similar categories of materials.

§ 411.50 Techniques for application.

(a) Material cost shall be the acquisition cost of a category of material, whether or not a material inventory record is used. The purchase price of material shall be adjusted by extra charges incurred or discounts and credits earned. Such adjustments shall be charged or credited to the same cost objective as the purchase price of the material, except that where it is not practical to do so, the contractor's policy may provide for the consistent inclusion of such charges or credits in an appropriate indirect cost pool.

(b) One of the following inventory costing methods shall be used when issuing material from a company-owned inventory:

(1) The first-in, first-out (FIFO) method,

(2) The moving average cost method,

(3) The weighted average cost method,

(4) The standard cost method, or

(5) The last-in, first-out (LIFO) method.

(c) The method of computation used for any inventory costing method selected pursuant to the provisions of this Standard shall be consistently followed.

(d) Where the excess of the ending inventory over the beginning inventory of material of the type described in par. 411.40(c) is estimated to be significant in relation to the total cost included in the indirect cost pool, the cost of such unconsumed material shall be established as an asset at the end of the period by reducing the indirect cost pool by a corresponding amount.

The very first "fundamental requirement" is for written statements of accounting policies and practices, and this encountered sharp objections. Some commentators just could not see this requirement as one contemplated for coverage by cost accounting standards. Others argued that such policies were already set forth in their Disclosure Statements of accounting manuals. In discussing the various objections in its prefatory comments, the Board addressed only one in a specific manner, i.e. by ruling that the Disclosure Statement argument was not valid because many companies subject to the standards are not required to file Disclosure Statements. Otherwise, the Board concluded that it "feels that written policies and practices are beneficial as evidenced by the many companies which have them." The same argument could obviously be used to require written policies for every area subjected to cost accounting standards. We share the view of those who doubt that this requirement was contemplated by P.L. 91-379.

The most controversial provision of CAS 411 related to the permissible costing methods to be used when issuing material from a company-owned inventory. As finally promulgated, paragraph 411.50(b) permits the use of the following methods:

(1) First in, first out (FIFO);

(2) Moving average cost;

(3) Weighted average cost;

(4) Standard cost; and

(5) Last in, first out (LIFO).

The fundamental requirement relating to costing methods, paragraph 411.40(e), states that the selected method "shall be used in a manner which results in systematic and rational costing of issues of material to cost objectives. The same costing methods shall, within the same business unit, be used for similar categories of materials."

In the first draft of this standard, LIFO was not included among the acceptable costing methods, and commentators were asked to identify any other methods they believed to be acceptable. As we predicted, the Board received many comments urging the inclusion of LIFO as one of the acceptable methods. A great number of reasons was given, including the acceptability of this method under "generally accepted accounting principles" and for IRS purposes, as well as the view that it represented a more realistic basis during inflationary periods.

Although the standard now permits LIFO, the Board's prefatory comments did not reflect a graceful acceptance of this method. First, the Board dismissed the arguments that LIFO was acceptable for tax and financial reporting purposes, stating that neither was concerned with cost allocations to particular contracts. Nor was the Board impressed with the need for LIFO to account for the impact of inflation. It noted that most of the companies recommending LIFO did not use this method for contract costing purposes; instead, they charged most of the material to contracts at the time the material was acquired or produced. And in any case, the Board expressed the view that the impact of inflation should be the subject of a separate standard, a project under intensive research by the CASB staff at that time (but ultimately abandoned).

Finally, the Board expressed concern with the techniques involved in using the LIFO method. The reason offered for excluding this method in the draft standard was that "Contractors which currently follow LIFO for Government contracts use it in a manner which does not permit systematic and rational identification of the cost and material issues to specific cost objectives." The prefatory comments pointed to the requirement in paragraph 411.40(e) for "systematic and rational costing" and explained that "The costing of such issues to cost objectives must be reasonably current; it would not appear rational to hold in abeyance for months, pending a LIFO determination, the cost of materials issued to a Government contract."

MAKE-OR-BUY

FAR Subpart 15.7 sets forth government policies and procedures by which prospective contractors' proposed make-or-buy programs will be evaluated or approved. Paragraph 15.703 requires contractors to submit make-or-buy programs for all negotiated acquisitions whose estimated value is $2 million or more, with certain exceptions. Where the contracting officer believes it necessary, prospective contractors may be required to submit make-or-buy programs for negotiated acquisitions whose estimated value is under $2 million.

Firms engaged in contracts involving government surveillance and approval of their make-or-buy policies and procedures would do well to review FAR Subpart 15.7. Also, government contractors should be informed that their make-or-buy programs are frequently subject to review even though the formal requirements are not present and even though the standard clause is not included in their contracts. Representatives of the cognizant administrative contracting officer often review this area in considerable detail. Additionally, it is not unusual to find DCAA auditors becoming involved in this aspect of the evaluation process. In this latter regard, the DCAA Contract Audit Manual specifically instructs the auditors (par. 6-309) to include make-or-buy considerations in the audit program.

SUBCONTRACTING POLICIES AND PROCEDURES

Policies and procedures for consent to subcontracts and for review, evaluation, and approval of contractors' purchasing systems are contained in FAR Part 44.

Contractor Purchasing System Review (CPSR)

FAR 44.302 provides that a CPSR shall be conducted for each contractor whose negotiated sales to the government are expected to exceed $10 million during the next 12 months (excluding contracts for which the negotiated price is based on established catalog or market prices of commercial items sold in substantial quantities to the general public or is set by law or regulation).

The extent of the CPSR and the nature of the surveillance required in the period between complete CPSRs are set forth in FAR 44.303 and 44.304. Although these reviews are to "be conducted by the cognizant contract administrative agency" DCAA auditors, particularly at plants of larger contractors, are also active in this area. Paragraph 6-310 of the DCAA Contract Audit Manual sets forth criteria for an adequate system of internal control and provides audit guidance in evaluating contractors' purchasing and contracting policies and practices.

Requirement for Consent to Subcontracts

FAR Subpart 44.2 sets forth policy and procedures for consent by the government to subcontracts awarded by prime contractors. Generally, consent to subcontracts is required when the subcontract work is complex, the dollar value is substantial, or the government's interest is considered to be not adequately protected by competition and the type of prime contract or subcontract.

FAR 44.203(a) provides:

> The contracting officer's consent to a subcontract or approval of the contractor's purchasing system does not constitute a determination of the acceptability of the subcontract terms or price, or of the allowability of costs, unless the consent or approval specifies otherwise.

This policy is incorporated in the subcontract clause (FAR 52.244-1).

Disputes and Arbitration Provisions in Subcontracts

Many attempts have been made over the years to accord subcontractors the right to obtain a direct decision of the contracting officer or the right of direct appeal to the ASBCA. The government has consistently held that it is entitled to the management services of the prime contractor in adjusting disputes between the prime and subcontractors. Accordingly, FAR 44.203(b) prohibits contracting officers from consenting to subcontracts that would oblige the contracting officer to deal directly with the subcontractor or make the results of arbitration, judicial determination or voluntary settlement by the prime contractor and subcontractor binding on the government. A further elaboration of the policy in this area is contained in FAR 44.203(c):

> (c) Contracting officers should not refuse consent to a subcontract merely because it contains a clause giving the subcontractor the right of indirect appeal to an agency board of contract appeals if the subcontractor is affected by a dispute between the Government and the prime contractor. Indirect appeal means assertion by the subcontractor of the prime contractor's right to appeal or the prosecution of an appeal by the prime contractor on the subcontractor's behalf. The clause may also provide that the prime contractor and subcontractor shall be equally bound by the contracting officer's or board's decision. The clause may not attempt to obligate the contracting officer or the appeals board to decide questions that do not arise between the Government and the prime contractor or that are not cognizable under the clause at 52.233-1, Disputes.

OTHER ASPECTS OF ACCOUNTING METHODS AND CONTROLS FOR MATERIALS

This book is not intended to serve as a cost accounting text; accordingly, no attempt has been made to include detailed comments as to accounting methods and controls for material. In discussing the various aspects of material costs in the following pages, primary emphasis has been placed on those methods and controls that are favored by government auditors.

Receiving and Inspection

Recommended procedures as to receipt and inspection of materials are set forth below.

(1) The receiving function is independent of the purchasing, invoice processing, and shipping functions.

(2) Incoming material is centrally controlled.

(3) Receiving reports, signed by an authorized representative, are prepared for all material received, and a copy is furnished the accounting department.

(4) The receiving department is advised, by copy of the purchase order, of the type of material purchased.

(5) Quantities of materials received are verified by actual count, weight, or measurement by the receiving department.

(6) Quality inspection is evidenced by inspection reports, notations on receiving reports, or other acceptable records.

(7) Procedures are in effect which control defective and damaged material, overshipments, returned material, material received but not ordered, and claims against carriers and vendors, with related responsibilities for the initiation of procedures for the issuance of debit memorandums.

(8) Where the contractor accepts and reworks defective vendor-furnished material instead of rejecting and returning it, government contracts are not charged with the cost of rework, unless this is clearly justified in the circumstances.

(9) Material returns are routed to the shipping department and are controlled by authorized shipping documents or material releases.

(10) Procedures are in effect for distributing material from the receiving area to stores or to production areas.

Storing and Issuing

After receipt and inspection, the materials physically flow from the Receiving Department to stores or production areas. A summary of procedures and related controls considered appropriate by the government is set forth below.

(1) Separate accountability is maintained for contractor-owned and government-owned materials for each class of material.

(2) Material received is delivered directly to the warehouse, storeroom, or production area, via an inspection area if appropriate. When material received is delivered directly to a production area, procedures insure that proper documentary and accounting control is maintained.

(3) Stores' records are maintained by employees and are functionally independent of storekeepers.

(4) There are adequate controls to prevent theft or diversion of materials. Unauthorized persons are denied access to storerooms. There are special safeguards for high dollar value material and material susceptible to personal use or sale.

(5) Materials are so stored as to facilitate locating, withdrawing, handling and counting.

(6) Procedures provide for the timely reporting of slow-moving, obsolete, and overstocked material.

(7) Procedures provide for the release of materials only upon the receipt of a properly approved requisition.

(8) Requisitions applicable to government-owned materials are distinguishable from requisitions for contractor-owned materials.

(9) Procedures provide that appropriate credits are issued when unused material is returned to stock or where material is diverted to other work.

(10) Procedures are in effect to control the collection, segregation, and disposition of scrap and the issuance of appropriate credits.

(11) Procedures are in effect which control and account for returnable items such as reels, containers, skids, boxes, and barrels.

(12) Procedures provide for issuing materials subject to spoilage or shrinkage on a first-in/first-out basis.

Handling of Purchase Invoices

The vendor's invoice is often received before the material arrives. The original invoice remains with the accounting department for payment, awaiting the arrival of the material. A copy of the invoice is sent to the purchasing department, which indicates that the material is en route. When the material is received and the accounting department obtains the original receiving report, it has a complete history of the transaction: the purchase requisition, showing the authorization of the purchase order; the purchase order, showing the quantity ordered, the price to be paid, and the items; and the receiving report, showing the quantities received and inspected. A copy of the receiving report is forwarded to the purchasing department so that its personnel can enter it in their records and maintain a completed and uncompleted status on each purchase order.

The original invoice is now checked against the purchase order and the receiving report and then stamped. The stamp provides for an initial indication of an authoritative person's determination as to (a) correctness of quantities, prices, and terms, (b) accuracy of extensions, (c) account to be charged, (d) receiving report and purchase order numbers, and (e) approval by the department head.

Appropriate internal control procedures would include the following:

(1) Receipt of partial shipments annotated on purchase orders or on separate sheets attached to purchase orders.

(2) Controls providing that cash discounts, trade discounts, quantity discounts, rebates, and freight allowances are taken.

(3) Transportation bills are compared with applicable invoices, purchase orders, and receiving reports.

(4) Subcontractor, interplant, or interdivisional invoices are subjected to the same internal procedures as invoices from outside vendors.

(5) Controls are in effect that prevent duplicate payments of invoices or transportation bills.

(6) Debit memorandums are prepared and applied for all reductions or adjustments in quantities or price resulting from shortages, overpricing, returned purchases, rework at the expense of vendors, or substitutions. Debit memorandums are serially numbered, accounted for, cross-referenced to related invoices, and introduced into the accounting system prior to payment of invoices.

(7) Invoices for services not supported by receiving reports that are approved by authorized personnel.

(8) Invoices and related documents are reviewed to ensure that all required actions have been taken and are evidenced by the initials or signatures of those responsible.

(9) Personnel who sign disbursement checks are responsible for reviewing the vouchers relating to the payment.

(10) Invoices and supporting documents are marked, mutilated, perforated, or controlled in such a manner that they cannot be submitted for payment a second time.

Inventory Taking

There should be written instructions for taking physical inventories, including the following:

1. Inventories should ordinarily be taken at least annually.

2. Inventories should be taken under the direction of an independent person.

3. Inventory cut-off procedures should be clearly defined and followed.

4. Physical inventory counts should be checked by independent personnel.

5. In-transit and consigned materials should be verified.

6. Differences between physical counts and perpetual inventory balance should be investigated, and the latter adjusted to agree with the physical count.

7. The approval of a responsible executive should be required on all adjustments resulting from physical inventories.

As to pricing, inventories should be consistently priced through a method that is in accord with generally accepted accounting principles, and transportation costs should be charged uniformly.

The accuracy of the physical inventory recapitulation should be verified as to quantities by using inventory sheets; unit conversions; prices; extensions; sheet totals and summary totals; material withdrawal or movement during the taking of the physical inventory.

ACCOUNTING METHODS

Under conventional procedures, accounting for materials closely follows their physical flow. Thus, materials are charged to raw material accounts when they are received, to work-in-process accounts when they are transferred to the production process, to finished goods accounts when they are completed and transferred to separate storage areas, and to cost of goods sold when they are shipped. There are, of course, several acceptable variations to these procedures. For example, materials purchased specifically for a government contract may be charged directly to such contract upon receipt. Also, the accounting step involving the transfer from work-in-process to finished goods inventories is frequently omitted when shipment is made immediately or very shortly after production is completed.

Few problems arise where materials are purchased directly for a government contract and charged thereto at actual cost. (See also comments later in this chapter regarding treatment of freight, purchase discounts, and material handling charges.) Some complications are encountered when materials used on government contracts are transferred from contractors' stores. From the physical viewpoint, the government auditor and/or technical specialist may review the quantities to establish that excessive amounts are not involved. From the financial side, the matter of pricing the stores' issues is of consequence.

Government auditors will accept the contractor's pricing procedure if it is in accordance with generally accepted accounting principles, consistently applied, and accurately calculated. If it results in reasonable charges to the contract, any of the following methods is appropriate: actual costs, average costs, first-in/first-out (FIFO), or last-in/first-out (LIFO). If the contract is subject to cost accounting standards, pricing of stores' issues must conform to CAS 411, described earlier in this chapter.

COST CONSIDERATIONS AT INTERIM TARGET POINTS

Unquestionably, the most complex problems arise in arriving at costs during the performance of the contract. Such determinations are required under incentive contracts. They are also required where follow-on contracts are being negotiated before the predecessor contract(s) is completed. The task here is twofold: (1) calculating the cost of the shipments made to date and (2) estimating the costs of future shipments.

The following reflect some of the commonly employed procedures for determining, prior to the time that the contract is completed (as required by an incentive contract), the cost of the materials contained in completed units:

(1) Estimates.

(2) Standards, plus applicable variances.

(3) Physical inventory.

(4) Establishment of job lots.

(5) Pricing a bill of materials.

The first mentioned is the least desirable for obvious reasons. It has been mentioned previously that a standard cost system represents an acceptable costing method under defense contracts. However, it must be understood that some qualifications surround this basic premise, and, in this connection, certain difficulties must be overcome by the contractor. At the outset, the fact must be faced that some of the so-called standard cost systems being employed today are really little more than glorified estimated costing procedures.

Standards should be scientifically established, subjected to continuous review, and revised from time to time in the light of actual experience. Moreover, variances should be accurately accumulated and should be segregated so as to avoid the application of over-all variance factors to particular products or processes with respect to which such over-all percentages may not be applicable. The standard cost system will normally be accepted by the government if it meets these requirements. If the contract is subject to cost accounting standards, a standard cost system must comply with the provisions of CAS 407 as described in Chapter IX of this text.

The above comments are not intended to discourage the use of standard costs in connection with interim pricing. A well-operated standard cost system may be the best answer to this problem, if appropriate in the circumstances. However, there are times when government production may not represent such circumstances. As an illustration, the first government contract for material substantially different from (1) the commercial line and (2) any product the company has previously manufactured may not be an appropriate spot for standards. On the other hand, standard costs may well be employed for subsequent contracts of this nature, or even later stages of the first contract, after sufficient experience has been gained.

Determining costs of a pricing period by the expedient of physical inventory-taking reflects certain advantages and disadvantages. This method has the merit of producing accurate costs, where the inventory is carefully counted and appropriately priced. On the other hand, the loss of time and the incurrence of expense required by physical inventory-taking serve to limit the advantages of this procedure. In addition, this method will not yield the information required in respect of cost data for forward pricing.

Redetermination of price before completion contemplates knowledge of cost experience to the target point and sufficient data to enable an intelligent forecast as to the uncompleted portion. The inventory method will serve for the first requirement but not for the second.

Probably the most desirable method for arriving at all the facts necessary to negotiate retroactive and prospective pricing at target point is the establishment of two or more job lots within the first pricing period. Under this method, assuming a total of 1,000 units contracted for and 400 units as the number fixed for the first price redetermination, two or more separate job orders could be established. The total costs of all the lots would represent, of course, the aggregate costs of the first pricing period. The first job lot could cover the first 100 units and would include all (or most) of the starting load costs. The second job lot could cover the cost of the next 200 units. The unit cost data derived therefrom should represent information more nearly indicative of future costs. A third lot of 100 would either confirm that the second lot was representative of the balance or indicate the trend.

This data, together with such other information as may be available at the target point (possible price changes, etc.), would constitute an appropriate basis for projecting costs for the subsequent pricing period. This procedure is most effective when employed in conjunction with such statistical techniques as efficiency and learning curves. The main difficulty encountered in the use of this method is the danger of incorrect accounting distributions between job lots, where certain operations are performed simultaneously for quantities in excess of those requested on the first lot. Appropriate control and care, however, will reduce this possibility.

Contractors maintaining costs on a job order basis, where separate lots have not been established and where inventory has not been taken, often find that the only means available to them to determine costs of deliveries during the first pricing period consists of pricing a bill of materials. This method involves many difficulties. In the first place, where many engineering changes have been encountered, substantial confusion will arise. Complete and accurate records are a prerequisite in respect to quantities under each change.

When changes have occurred in whether certain component parts are furnished by suppliers or fabricated by the contractor, the situation becomes more muddled. Yet other significant difficulties arise in pricing a bill of materials, in that the resulting data yield only base costs without provision for waste and spoilage and, unless satisfactory and complete records have been maintained in this regard, accurate costs will not be obtainable. In the absence of such records, estimates will need to be applied to the "bare" costs to reflect total costs. If these estimates for waste, scrap, and spoilage cannot be substantiated by auditable records, the contractor may be hard pressed to recover total costs. If the contract is subject to cost accounting standards, the contractor must comply with the provisions of Interpretation No. 1 to CAS 401, as described in Chapter IX of this text.

SPECIAL MATERIAL ACCOUNTING PROBLEMS

Inbound Freight

Direct charges to jobs for freight-in constitute the most accurate accounting for this cost element. In actual practice, however, the time and expense involved in matching material and freight invoices, and effecting apportionments where required, sometimes do not prove worthwhile. Government contract requirements are in conformance with generally accepted practice.

The inclusion of cost of inbound freight as part of manufacturing overhead may be acceptable if its aggregate effect on contract costs is not substantial. Where the cost is significant, the procedure may be questioned inasmuch as manufacturing overhead is generally apportioned in the ratio of direct labor cost or time, whereas the incidence of freight costs is more closely related to material costs. A separate material-handling charge, including certain purchasing and receiving costs in addition to freightin, and related to contracts or products in the ratio of direct material, would be acceptable. There are, of course, numerous other methods employed to apportion freight costs. It can usually be assumed that a procedure conforming to generally accepted accounting principles will be satisfactory to the DOD auditors.

Chapter XIII of this text, Accounting Methods and Controls for Manufacturing Overhead, contains an analysis of CAS 418—Allocation of Direct and Indirect Costs. This subject was covered in the draft stage in five, then three, proposed standards before the pressure of both the private and public sectors persuaded the CASB to promulgate a single standard with less rigid require-ments than those contained in the earlier proposals. One of the initially proposed five standards was titled Allocation of Material-Related Overhead Costs and would have *mandated* one or more overhead pools for expenses related to materials. Although CAS 418 as finally promulgated does not contain such rigid requirements, one of the illustrations (CAS 418.60(f)) states that a material-issued base would be appropriate for allocation of "an indirect cost pool containing a significant amount of material-related costs."

Scrap, Waste, Spoilage, Defective Work

These four terms, although often used interchangeably, actually represent four specific types of material. The term "scrap" is correctly applied to materials remaining after such operations as cutting, trimming, punching, etc. The most obvious illustration of scrap would be reflected in a sheet of metal that is used to punch out a number of pieces of a certain design and size. A considerable portion of the original sheet may remain, and the material may have significant sales value, although it cannot be utilized further in produc-tion of the particular product for which it was originally purchased.

The term "scrap" may also be applied to the materials remaining after changes in design or material content requirements result in such materials having no further use in the particular production. These materials, however, generally have a definite sales value. The term "waste" has often been applied to materials resulting from the same conditions as referred to above. The distinction is often made that, whereas scrap reflects a definite realizable sales value, waste may have only nominal value or perhaps none at all.

Whereas scrap and waste generally arise as a result of certain operations mentioned above, such as punching, cutting, etc., spoilage and defective work are related to the portion of the material actually selected for production and subsequently found unsuitable. Returning to the previous illustration of a sheet of metal from which a number of pieces of a certain design were punched out, it was stated that the remaining material could be termed scrap. Now if some of the actual pieces proved to be unsatisfactory for use in the end items, the latter material content could be termed spoilage or defective work. The latter two terms may be distinguished to the extent that defective work implies the possibility of reworking, while spoilage indicates generally that such material can be disposed of only through sales or use for purposes other than that originally intended.

The government's interests in the above types of material, by whatever term, are twofold: (1) adequate physical controls and safeguards and (2) appropriate accounting methods to insure that the government derives appli-cable credits. Acceptable procedures would include current and controlled records of scrap generated or otherwise accumulated, with fixed responsibility for its accumulation, handling, storage, and disposition.

Some government auditors prefer a complete segregation of all materials purchased for use on their contracts. This would include the extension of this segregation to all remaining quantities, including scrap and waste, and the accounting segregation of income derived from its sale. In instances where defense and commercial production are intermingled, particularly in respect to fixed-price contracts, objections cannot be raised to commingling scrap, both physically and for accounting purposes. Where the contractor can sustain the contention that segregation is not feasible, the government's requirements will be satisfied if the over-all procedures are satisfactory and if the methods employed to credit defense contracts with their pro rata share of any resulting income are fair and reasonable.

Here again, the necessity for appropriate accounting records is stressed. Unusual percentages of waste and spoilage may be questioned, and the recovery of such costs may be difficult in the absence of specific accounting support. Many small companies do not maintain adequate records of waste and spoilage. In other instances, certain fragmentary records are kept, but without control by, or reconciliation to, the books of account.

At the time of repricing, the contractor may contend that the bare material costs are subject to substantial increases to reflect unfortunate spoilage experience. Such increases are quite prevalent, particularly in procurement of new defense materials. However, where the actual experience in this regard is not reflected in auditable records, there is danger of incomplete recovery of costs.

Where waste and spoilage are significant items of cost, daily reports should be required. The information to be included in such reports will depend on the needs of the particular company. However, as a minimum, the reports should indicate date, department number, operation, identification as to contract or product, nature, reason, responsibility, disposition, and cost. The related costs may be integrated in the cost of completed units by dividing total costs (including costs of scrap) by the good units. A preferable method provides for dividing total costs by total units, including those ultimately scrapped. The total cost of the scrapped units is thus established and can be segregated for ultimate transfer to jobs or overhead, as desired.

Attempts by contract auditors to persuade the CASB to establish rigid accounting requirements for scrap, waste, spoilage, and defective work failed after heavy protests from both the private and public sectors. Chapter IX of this text describes these efforts, the draft proposals, and the final moderate promulgation in Interpretation No. 1 to CAS 401. Requirements for contracts not covered by cost accounting standards should certainly not be more exacting than those set out in that interpretation.

Purchase Discounts, Rebates

FAR 31.205-26(b) provides as follows:

Costs of material shall be adjusted for income and other credits, including available trade discounts, refunds, rebates, allowances, and cash discounts, and credits for scrap, salvage, and material returned to vendors. Such income and other credits shall either be credited directly to the cost of the material or be allocated as a credit to indirect costs. When the contractor can demonstrate that failure to take cash discounts was reasonable, lost discounts need not be credited.

The treatment accorded to these items has varied through the years. During World War II it was considered that the contractor was entitled to the first 1% earned on purchase discounts and that the balance should be used as a reduction of material costs. The trend thereafter was to consider all discounts, rebates, etc., as a reduction of material costs. For a time the pendulum swung too far and the DOD auditors deducted all available discounts (whether or not actually taken). This procedure was often grossly inequitable where the contractor was financially unable to take advantage of time discounts. Under current practices, all discounts actually earned will be deducted. As to discounts available but not taken, the attitude of the government will depend on the circumstances. Where the discounts were not taken as a result of financial inability, or other reasonable cause, the contractor will not be penalized.

Some government auditors prefer direct reduction of material costs to the extent of all discounts, rebates, etc., so that the charges to contracts will be the net of all such items. This procedure is recommended for rebates and trade discounts, especially where considerable differences exist among materials used for government contracts and commercial work. For normal cash discounts, however, this same need is not apparent, and fair apportionment of the resulting credits will be acceptable. In this connection, a percentage application, representing the relationship between purchases and discounts, would be satisfactory.

Reducing factory overhead by income from purchase discounts is also generally acceptable, although this method is defective by reason of the fact that manufacturing overhead is generally allocated to contracts in the ratio of direct labor time or costs, whereas purchase discounts are not considered to generate in relation to direct labor.

As described earlier in this chapter, CAS 411.50(a) indicates a preference for adjusting the purchase price of material by extra charges incurred or discounts and credits earned. However, this paragraph avoids rigid requirements with the statement, "except that where it is not practical to do so, the contractor's policy may provide for the consistent inclusion of such charges or credits in an appropriate indirect cost pool."

PRODUCTION SPECIAL TOOLING AND PRODUCTION SPECIAL TEST EQUIPMENT

The fiscal year 1987 Defense Appropriations Act, P.L. 99-500, directed that, with certain exceptions, contractors may not be reimbursed under a contract for more than 50% of the full acquisition cost of production special tooling (PST) and production special test equipment (PSTE). The statutory provisions are excerpted below:

> .... no contractor may be reimbursed directly under a contract awarded 90 days after the effective date of this Act, where the purchase of additional quantities of like items is contemplated in subsequent years, for more than 50 percent of the full acquisition cost of production special tooling and production special test equipment as a direct cost unless (a) such special equipment is to be used solely for final production acceptance test or (b) additional reimbursement that is in the best interest of the Government is approved in advance by the Service Secretary for programs reported on Selected Acquisition Reports or approved by an Assistant Service Secretary for all other programs: *Provided further,* That the contract may provide that if such a contract is terminated for any

reason that does not reflect a failure of the contractor to perform, the contractor shall be entitled to be paid by the United States for the cost of any special tooling and special test equipment which has not been fully amortized and the United States may elect to take title to such special tooling and special test equipment.

The House-Senate conferees "explanation" of this requirement is quoted below:

> The conferees have modified the Senate's provision to limit the amount of expected contractor exposure for special tooling and special test equipment to 50 percent of the contractor proposed requirements. Furthermore, authority is provided for the Service Secretary to finance more than 50 percent of the special tooling and test equipment if budgeted and approved in advance. It is expected that this authority will be used when it is in the best interest of the government when contractors cannot handle the additional financial exposure. But, it is clearly expected that contractors will carry as much of the financing as possible up to 50 percent. It is not the desire of the conferees that defense contractors "bet their companies" on any particular contract. It is the desire of the conferees to continue and accelerate the use of private investment in the defense industry.

> The conference agreement continues to require government funding of special tooling and special test equipment used for final government acceptance of items as proposed by the Senate.

> The policy statement has been clarified to permit direct reimbursement for tooling costs when there will be only a single year production contract available for amortization purposes.

> The conferees have added a final provision entitling a contractor to be paid by the United States for the unamortized balance of any tooling remaining in the event of contract termination for any reason other than failure of the contractor to perform. In which case the law would permit the government to take title to the special tooling and test equipment.

Regulatory implementation of the statutory requirements is provided in DFARS 15.873, which closely follows the language of the Act. The point is clearly made that the purpose is "to shift part of the burden of financing PST and PSTE to the contractor . . . ." However, the point is also made that there is no intention "to place the contractor at undue financial risk" and it is "not intended that any portion of [such costs] be made unallowable . . . ." Rather, these costs are to be amortized over future years production of the same items and are not to be assigned to other programs by charging such costs to indirect cost pools.

Solicitation and contract clauses provide for dollar ceilings, amortization schedules, and reimbursement in event of termination.

SPARE PARTS AND SUPPORT EQUIPMENT

The current thinking on the pricing of spare parts and support equipment, together with the required certificates and refund provisions thereunder, is covered in detail in Chapter V, Government Contract Pricing, under the discussion of the Armed Services Procurement Manual (ASPM), Chapter 9—Special Pricing Tasks.

GOVERNMENT AUDIT OF MATERIAL COSTS

In developing and improving methods and controls over material costs, contractors have found it useful to study the publications prepared by the government for its auditors and investigators. There are obvious benefits in understanding the objectives and procedures of those who review your records.

Defense Contract Audit Manual

We have referred from time to time to DCAA's Contract Audit Manual (CAM). On balance, based on many years of experience in auditing contractors' books and records, we believe it provides useful guidance for the agency's auditors.

Audit instructions relating to material costs are contained in several sections of CAM. Chapter 6, Section 3, addresses Audit of Incurred Purchased Services and Material Costs. The table of contents of this section indicates the nature of the guidance provided:

6-301   Introduction

6-302   Audit Objectives

6-303   Scope of Audit

6-304   Evaluation of Policies, Procedures, and Internal Controls

    6-304.1   Policies

    6-304.2   Procedures

    6-304.3   Internal Controls

6-305   Accounting for Material Cost

    6-305.1   Audit Objectives

    6-305.2   Internal Controls

    6-305.3   Audit Guidelines

6-306   Physical Inventories and Adjustments

    6-306.1   Audit Objectives

    6-306.2   Internal Controls

    6-306.3   Audit Guidelines

6-307   Scrap, Spoilage, and Obsolescence

    6-307.1   Audit Objectives

    6-307.2   Audit Guidelines—Scrap and Spoilage

    6-307.3   Audit Guidelines—Obsolete Materials

6-308   Determination of Requirements

    6-308.1   Audit Objectives

    6-308.2   Internal Controls

Chapter 9 of CAM is directed to the Review of Cost Estimates and Price Proposals, and Section 4 of this chapter addresses the Evaluation of Direct Material Cost Estimates. The following is the table of contents of this section:

As discussed in Chapter XXII of this text, Contract Price Reduction for Defective Cost or Pricing Data (Public Law 87-653), DCAA has been pressured by GAO and DOD IG to devote increasing attention and manpower to postaward reviews in search of defective cost or pricing data. Guidance for these reviews is contained in Chapter 14, Section 100 of CAM and in manuals and various memoranda issued by DCAA headquarters to its field offices. The CAM section alerts auditors to possibilities that contractors (1) had received, but had not disclosed, the existence of lower quotes from vendors, and (2) had not solicited quotes from known vendors when submitting proposals but had done so thereafter and awarded the purchase orders or subcontracts to such firms. A separate paragraph is also devoted to "Handling Subcontract Price Adjustments."

Department of Defense Inspector General

As referred to earlier and developed in other chapters of this text, the DOD IG has been instrumental in prodding DCAA to increase its attention to the so-called defective pricing audits. In addition to its conviction that defective pricing is "rampant," that office also believes, and has persuaded DCAA, that in many instances defective cost or pricing data can be developed into fraud cases. And detection of fraud and assistance in prosecuting the perpetrators, of course, is the major mission of the DOD IG.

Appendix 1 of this text contains excerpts from a DOD IG report on "Indicators of Fraud in Department of Defense Procurement." Several sections of this report relate to possibilities of fraud with respect to material costs. This area was developed at length in a subsequent DOD IG publication, "Handbook on Fraud Indicators: Material," reproduced in Appendix 3 to this text. The handbook is intended to alert all federal contract auditors to possible instances of fraud in connection with material costs.

Chapter XI

Accounting Methods and Controls for Labor

DEFINITIONS

The terms "direct labor" and "indirect labor" have well-defined and established meanings in cost accounting theory and practice. However, some differences are necessary to accommodate the requirements of certain industries and to take into account materiality in record keeping. "Direct labor" may be defined as labor identified with a particular final cost objective or work necessary to produce a product or provide a service. A logical modification to this definition is that the identification and measurement of such labor with regard to specific products or services should be expedient and not disproportionately expensive. "Indirect labor" would then be defined as labor that cannot be expediently identified with a final cost objective.

COVERAGE OF LABOR IN THIS TEXT

The government's interest in its contractors' labor policies and practices is extensive, having been expanded in various areas over the years. Additionally, numerous new regulations have been published by the executive departments and the CASB affecting determination of direct and indirect labor costs under government contracts.

This chapter contains reviews and analyses of government labor policies as contained principally in FAR Part 22, Application of Labor Laws to Government Acquisitions. It also covers government contract administrative surveillance and contract audit of labor costs, including monitoring and DCAA operations audits.

FAR Part 31 sets forth principles that spell out in considerable detail criteria for allowability of labor and other costs. These principles are studied in Chapters XVII and XVIII of this text together with the following promulgations of the CAS Board, which relate to labor costs:

CAS 408 Accounting for Costs of Compensated Personal Absence

CAS 412 Composition and Measurement of Pension Costs

CAS 413 Adjustment and Allocation of Pension Cost

CAS 415 Accounting for the Cost of Deferred Compensation

GOVERNMENT CONTRACT ADMINISTRATION POLICIES AND PROCEDURES

Some of the labor policies and procedures addressed in FAR Part 22 are listed below:

Labor disputes

Overtime work

Contract Work Hours and Safety Standards Act

Walsh-Healey Public Contracts Act

Fair Labor Standards Act of 1938

Equal employment opportunity

Nondiscrimination because of age

Employment of the handicapped

Affirmative action for disabled and Vietnam era veterans

Industry-Labor Relations and Labor Disputes

The government seeks to establish and maintain optimum industry-labor relations in order that it may obtain its required goods and services without delay. The basic policies concerning government action in labor disputes and during strikes are contained in FAR 22.101-1 and FAR 22.101-2, quoted below:

22.101-1 General.

(a) Agencies shall maintain sound relations with industry and labor to ensure (1) prompt receipt of information involving labor relations that may adversely affect the Government acquisition process and (2) that the Government obtains needed supplies and services without delay. All matters regarding labor relations shall be handled in accordance with agency procedures.

(b) Agencies should remain impartial concerning any dispute between labor and contractor management and not undertake the conciliation, mediation, or arbitration of a labor dispute. To the extent practicable, agencies should ensure that the parties to the dispute use all available methods for resolving the dispute, including the services of the National Labor Relations Board, Federal Mediation and Conciliation Service, the National Mediation Board and other appropriate Federal, State, local, or private agencies.

(c) Agencies should, when practicable, exchange information concerning labor matters with other affected agencies to ensure a uniform Government approach concerning a particular plant or labor-management dispute.

(d) Agencies should take other actions concerning labor relations problems, to the extent consistent with their acquisition responsibilities. For example, agencies should—

(1) Notify the agency responsible for conciliation, mediation, arbitration, or other related action of the existence of any labor dispute affecting or threatening to affect agency acquisition programs;

(2) Furnish to the parties to a dispute factual information pertinent to the dispute's potential or actual adverse impact on these programs, to the extent consistent with security regulations; and

(3) Seek a voluntary agreement between management and labor, notwithstanding the continuance of the dispute, to permit uninterrupted acquisition of supplies and services. This shall only be done, however, if the attempt to obtain voluntary agreement does not involve the agency in the merits of the dispute and only after consultation with the agency responsible for conciliation, mediation, arbitration, or other related action.

(e) The head of the contracting activity may designate programs or requirements for which it is necessary that contractors be required to notify the Government of actual or potential labor disputes that are delaying or threaten to delay the timely contract performance (see 22.103-5(a)).

22.101-2 Contract pricing and administration.

(a) Contractor labor policies and compensation practices, whether or not included in labor-management agreements, are not acceptable bases for allowing costs in contracts if they result in unreasonable costs to the Government. For a discussion of allowable costs for compensation resulting from labor-management agreements, see 31.205-6(c).

(b) Labor disputes may cause work stoppages that delay the performance of Government contracts. Contracting officers shall impress upon contractors that each contractor shall be held accountable for reasonably avoidable delays. Standard contract clauses dealing with default, excusable delays, etc., do not relieve contractors or subcontractors from the responsibility for delays that are within the contractors' or their subcontractors' control. A delay caused by a strike that the contractor or subcontractor could not reasonably prevent, can be excused only to the extent that a reasonably diligent contractor or subcontractor could resume the delayed performance by acting to end the strike by such actions as—

(1) Filing a charge with the National Labor Relations Board to permit the board to seek injunctive relief in court.

(2) Using other available Government procedures.

(3) Using private boards or organizations to settle disputes.

(c) Strikes normally result in changing patterns of cost incurrence. Certain costs may increase because of strikes; e.g., guard services and attorney's fees. Other costs incurred during a strike may not fluctuate (e.g., "fixed costs" such as rent and depreciation) but because of reduced production, their proportion of the unit cost of items produced increases. All costs incurred during strikes shall be carefully examined to ensure recognition of only those costs necessary for the performance of the contract in accordance with the Government's essential interest.

(d) If during a labor dispute, the inspectors' safety is not endangered, the normal functions of inspection at the plant of a Government contractor shall be continued without regard to the existence of a labor dispute, strike, or picket line.

Overtime, Extra-Pay Shifts and Multi-Shift Work

The government's definitions of normal workweek and workday in the United States, its possessions, and Puerto Rico generally mean a workweek of 40 hours. Policies and procedures relating to this area are contained in FAR 22.103. FAR 22.103-2 provides:

> Contractors shall perform all contracts, so far as practicable, without using overtime, particularly as a regular employment practice, except when lower overall costs to the Government will result or when it is necessary to meet urgent program needs. Any approved overtime, extra-pay shifts, and multishifts should be scheduled to achieve these objectives.

The entire subject of overtime and shift work, particularly with respect to the accounting treatment and reimbursability of the premium pay portion, is complex and significant in cost reimbursement type contracts. Companies doing business with the government should carefully study the relatively short provisions of the entire FAR 22.103. We also recommend close attention to the provisions of the Payment for Overtime Premium clause.

Questions relating to overtime and shift work fall into two major categories. The first, requirement for government approval, is covered in the procurement regulations and contract clause referred to above. The second concerns cost treatment, and here we are confronted with a surprising lack of specific government policies and procedures. Guidance is not available in the FAR cost principles, or in any of the promulgations by the CASB. There are, of course, many generally accepted accounting principles in this area. However, for the government's approach, we must turn to the DCAA's Contract Audit Manual, paragraph 6-410.

While reiterating the point we make throughout this text that the CAM is directive only to DCAA auditors and that the auditors' recommendations are advisory only to contracting officers, we must also repeat the fact that the contract auditors are indeed potent advisors, especially with respect to incurred costs. All too often this advice becomes the government's official position, because some contracting officers lack the business and accounting training to perform their own evaluations and others are not inclined to expend the time and effort to document their files as required when auditors' recommendations are overruled. The provisions of CAM 6-409 are therefore quoted below:

6-409 Review of Overtime, Extra-Pay Shifts, and Multi-Shift Work

The auditor should review the contractor's policies, procedures, and internal controls on overtime, extra-pay shifts, and multi-shift work, and the accounting and distribution of the premium costs. The auditor should be familiar with the provisions of FAR 22.103, which includes definitions and conditions under which overtime costs may be approved under Government contracts. When overtime work is required, the contractor's policies and procedures should comply with FAR 22.103 and insure that the operations will be limited to the actual need for the accomplishment of specific work. The auditor should ascertain that the amount of work performed at premium rates is equitably divided between Government and commercial operations.

6-409.1 Audit Objectives

The objectives of audit are to determine whether (1) management is properly authorizing, scheduling, and controlling overtime, extra-shift, and multi-shift work, (2) the contractor is obtaining the contracting officer's written approval when required by contract provisions, (3) the premium costs are reasonable and properly allocable to the Government contracts, (4) adequate control is exercised over productivity in the extra-pay periods, and (5) compensatory overtime work by salaried personnel is properly authorized, and application against subsequent working hours is properly monitored.

6-409.2 Audit Procedures

Audit procedures should include the following:

a. A determination as to whether the contractor's practices are consistent with the Government's interests. Effective procedures should include (1) acceptable standards to determine the need for overtime and premium shift work, (2) the establishment of categories of employees eligible to receive premium pay, (3) the proper levels of management authorization, approval, and continuing control over these operations, (4) the establishment of adequate procedures for authorizing compensatory overtime and effective monitoring of compensatory overtime credits against subsequent working time not actually worked, and (5) the continual review of overtime and shift data by management to control overtime and shift premium costs.

b. A review of contracts, when overtime and shift work is applicable, and an examination of the bid proposal and negotiating memoranda to ascertain the extent to which the contract price provided for overtime premium and shift premium expenses. If overtime and shift premiums were not considered in the contract price, the auditor should ascertain and evaluate the reasons for the overtime and shift premiums.

c. A determination that premium labor costs charged to the contract have been approved by the contracting officer, when required, and have been incurred in accordance with the contractor's normal policy.

d. A periodic review of the continuing need for the exception types of overtime operations cited in FAR/DFARS 22.103-4.

e. A review of the accounting treatment accorded overtime premium pay and the method of cost distribution. Overtime premium pay, although generally treated as indirect expense, may be acceptable as a direct charge when it is the contractor's regularly established policy and when appropriate tests clearly demonstrate that this policy results in equitable cost allocations.

f. A review of the accounting and distribution treatment accorded shift premium pay.

g. A review of the contractor's procedures for compensatory overtime work to determine that this type of work is properly authorized and performed according to an acceptable company policy and that proper monitoring is exercised by management in applying an employee's compensatory overtime to subsequent scheduled working time in which the employee does not work.

OTHER DCAA POLICIES AND PROCEDURES FOR AUDITING LABOR

The Defense Contract Audit Agency provides considerable guidance to its staff in the audit of virtually every aspect of incurred and estimated labor, including conventional techniques for auditing labor costs incurred, evaluations of contractors' estimates in initial pricing proposals and redetermination and incentive contracts that are repriced at a stage during performance, operations audits designed "to determine whether the costs are commensurate with the benefits derived, and to determine the reasonableness and efficiency of the labor utilization," and the increasing efforts to probe the possibility of fraud or other irregularities.

CAM Chapter 6, Section 4, provides audit guidance for labor costs incurred and includes reviews and evaluations of the following areas:

Audit Objective

Scope of Audit

Review of Labor Cost Charging and Allocation

Review of Compliance with Internal Controls

Review of Uncompensated Overtime

Review of Other Labor Costing Systems

Personnel Policies and Procedures

Recruitment Costs and Practices

Quantitative and Qualitative Utilization of Labor

Timekeeping Procedures and Observation of Work Areas (Floor Checks)

Payroll Preparation and Payment

Overtime, Extra-Pay Shifts and Multi-Shift Work

Verification of Labor Costs

We would recommend that the entire section be carefully studied by companies doing business with the government. The audit guidance relating to overtime, extra shifts, and multi-shift work was quoted earlier in its entirety. Comments and excerpts on some of the other significant audit areas are addressed below.

Evaluation of Quantitative and Qualitative Utilization of Labor

This high- and rather grandiloquent-sounding aspect of auditing labor consists, in large part, of DCAA's controversial operations audit. Some critics in both industry and within the Defense Department challenge the capabilities of auditors to perform the assigned evaluations. Although CAM 6-412.2 recognizes that these evaluations "*may* require the assistance of qualified Government technical personnel" (emphasis added), auditors are encouraged to go as far as they can, and, where the outside assistance is not available, they frequently go it alone. Some of the specific procedures which many consider to lie outside the auditors' expertise include:

6-412.2b. Ascertain whether the work performed by the contractor is required by the terms of the contract, properly authorized and directed to the appropriate operational unit.

6-412.2e. ... review and evaluate ... personnel files of employees assigned to Government contract work to determine whether qualifications of workers performing the contract are commensurate with the rates charged and all other requirements of the contract.

6-412.2g. Review the contractor's basis for assigning and phasing-out technical personnel for both Government production and commercial operations .... The auditor should also determine whether the contractor is assigning technical personnel in accordance with their skills ....

6-412.2j. Determine whether engineering on Government work is subcontracted rather than performed by the contractor and whether such practice results in unreasonable costs to the Government. Among the factors to be considered is whether, under the prevailing conditions, there is any necessity for subcontracting other than to meet temporary or emergency requirements.

6-412.2k. Review manual labor procedures for possible mechanization (capital investment opportunities 5-602) which will result in increased efficiencies and economies of the contractor's operation and less cost to the Government.

Audit of Incurred Labor Costs

This audit area is addressed in the CAM 6-400 section, and the title suggests a conventional and appropriate responsibility for contract auditors. However, as noted earlier, recent years have witnessed increasing efforts by government contract auditors to probe for fraud and other irregularities. At this writing, contract auditors in all federal departments and agencies except for the Defense and Justice Departments have been placed within organizations headed by inspectors general. Customarily, there is a presidentially appointed inspector general with an assistant for investigations and an assistant for audits. Investigators and auditors may work on separate assignments or join forces. This type of organization has resulted in increased emphasis on fraud, both real and imaginary.

As described in Chapter XXVI, DOD strongly resisted congressional efforts to establish an Office of Inspector General for the Defense Department, but proponents of this idea finally prevailed in the 1983 DOD authorization bill. The Defense Contract Audit Agency, which has always prized its independence, had joined in opposing the appointment of a single inspector general for DOD. However, it had become obvious to industry that DCAA, in the effort to demonstrate that it should continue as an independent agency, had sharply increased its efforts of detection in the much-discussed area of "fraud, waste and abuse." The increased efforts have included expanded audit guidance and special training of its staff. Illustrations of this type of guidance, under the caption Audit of Incurred Labor Costs, are summarized below.

The distribution of labor costs to projects, work orders, accounts, or contracts is a very fertile area of possible fraud or other unlawful activity. A number of fraud cases involve deliberately falsified labor distribution and payroll records. These include among others:

(1) padding payrolls with fictitious employees charged to contracts;

(2) charging cost-type contracts with labor applicable to firm-fixed price work;

(3) altering account numbers on time cards or labor distribution documents;

(4) ordering employees to mischarge their time;

(5) claiming overtime which was not worked;

(6) improperly recording the time of direct engineers to contracts, IR&D, B&P, or overhead, depending on monetary limitations of the contract or advance agreement.

DCAA Investigative Questionnaires and Employee Interviews During Floor Checks

Toward the latter part of 1980, Headquarters DCAA distributed to its field offices floor check audit guidelines with strong investigative overtones. As a result of vigorous opposition by many contractors, DCAA floor check audit guides were revised. The revisions were asserted to have the objectives of modifying some of the questions that were framed in a manner to place the employees in self-incriminating positions and to cause them to inadvertently make statements that could incorrectly be adverse to the company's interests. In response to industry criticisms, DCAA Headquarters issued the following revised guidance to its field auditors in the form of a memorandum and an accompanying "Floor Check Audit Guidelines for Direct/Indirect Employees."

Some months ago we sent you a copy of the floor check audit guides used by one of our regions. These guides have provoked some opposition from contractors, because they believed the manner in which some of the questions were framed caused the responders to place themselves in a self-incriminating position.

We have therefore modified the audit guides and are providing you a revised copy for FAO use. However, each application may well require some further local modification to fit the contractor's system and the results of audit analysis that may precede the floor check.

What is essential however, to any floor check, is the need for the auditor to confirm, verify, attest or otherwise assure that information already recorded in the contractor's system is accurate. Regardless of the type of audit tests performed it would appear that interviews of the employees are an essential and critical prerequisite to any conclusion on the adequacy, reasonableness, and reliability of labor records. Further, once it is established that labor costs require analysis because of materiality and relative risk considerations, the reasonable accuracy of the labor records must be resolved in the incurred cost audit to support audit approval of the costs. Accordingly, refusal to permit performance of floor checks by any contractor in these situations will be tantamount to an unsatisfactory condition (CAM 4-803) which requires reporting to this Headquarters. We would encourage auditors to follow these audit guides with the objective of evaluating contractors' labor recording and distribution systems for their adequacy to generate reliable costs charged to Government contracts. The labor floor checks are not investigatory procedures, nor are they preludes to possible criminal actions. We need to project to companies in the defense industry that we are not investigators, but that our program requires the performance of generally accepted audit procedures aimed at assuring the credibility of contractors' labor recording systems.

Please provide us any feedback on the implementation of the attached guides which you believe is of significance to the Agency's approach.

DEFENSE CONTRACT AUDIT AGENCY
FLOOR CHECK AUDIT GUIDELINES FOR DIRECT/INDIRECT EMPLOYEES

GENERAL INFORMATION

Contractor_____ Date_____

Location_____ Time_____

DCAA Auditor_____

Contractor Representative and Title_____

Technical Representative_____

Employee_____ Employee No._____

Job Title_____

Department_____ Supervisor_____

1. Establish identification of employee by badge or other means_____

2. Was the employee present? Yes____No____. If not present where was employee?_____

3. Absent employees must be interviewed either by telephone or in person at a later date. Interviewed by telephone? Yes____No____ Interviewed on_____

4. Record the entries which appear on the employee's time sheet or attach a copy of the time sheet._____

5. Request the employee to indicate the work/time change for a previous period. This should be compared to existing records and any differences should be explained. Comments_____

6. Time Card:	Yes	No
In the possession of the employee?	____	____
In ink?	____	____
Completed to the current date?	____	____
Completed for the remainder of the week?	____	____
Signed in advance?	____	____
Alterations?	____	____

Comments_____

7. Briefly describe what the employee is working on. (Job number, project name, indirect function)._____

8. What job number did the employee charge today?_____

9. When does the employee receive his/her time sheet?_____ From whom?_____

10. Does the employee prepare his/her own time sheet? Yes____No____

11. When does the employee complete the time sheet?_____

12. What instructions have been provided the employee for completing his/her time sheet? (Verbal, written manual, etc.)_____

13. Who approves the employee's time sheet?_____

14. When does the employee turn in the time sheet?_____ Does he/she retain a copy? Yes____No____. If yes, note several entries from prior time sheets and verify them to the regular time sheet.

15. How does the employee correct errors on the time sheet? (Erasure, crossout, whitened, etc.)_____

16. When the employee makes a correction, does he/she initial the change and indicate the reason why the change was made? Yes____No____

17. After the employee has submitted the time sheet, is it ever returned for correction? Yes____No____. If yes, why?_____

18. Does the employee ever turn in a blank, signed time sheet? Yes____No____

19. Does anyone else ever make a correction on the employee's time sheet? Yes____No____. If yes, who makes the change and under what circumstances?_____

20. Are there any circumstances in which the employee changes a job classification (technician, engineer, etc.) other than what he/she is classified as? Yes____No____. If yes, under what circumstances (e.g., maintenance projects, other)_____

21. Does the employee charge most of his/her time direct to contracts? Yes____No____. If yes, under what circumstances do they charge overhead or G&A costs?_____

22. Does the employee ever work overtime for which he/she does not get paid? Yes ____ No. ____. If yes, does he/she record the overtime on the time sheet? Yes ____ No ____.

23. In lieu of overtime pay, does the employee ever receive compensatory time? Yes ____ No ____. If yes, when they take compensatory time, what job or account number do they charge? _____

24. What assignments will the employee be working on for the remainder of the week?_____

A review of the above cited memorandum and guidelines indicates clearly the reasons for the contractors' continued dissatisfaction. A review of this situation should logically begin with the pertinent provisions of the Audit by Department of Defense ASPR/DAR 7-104.41* contract clause, which governs or should govern all of the government auditor's actions at a contractor location for negotiated type contracts including cost reimbursement, incentive, time and material, labor hour, price redeterminable, or any combination thereof.

*The Audit-Negotiation clause in FAR 52.215-2 is similar in all substantive respects.

... the Contracting Officer or his representatives shall have the right to examine books, records, documents, and other evidence and accounting procedures and practices, sufficient to reflect properly all direct and indirect costs of whatever nature claimed to have been incurred and anticipated to be incurred in the performance of this contract. Such right of examination shall include inspection at all reasonable times of the Contractor's plants, or such parts thereof, as may be engaged in the performance of this contract.

Where the contractor submitted cost or pricing data, unless otherwise exempt, the Audit clause gives the government the further right ". . . to examine all books, records, documents and other data of the Contractor related to the negotiation, pricing or performance of such contract . . . . The right of examination shall extend to all documents necessary to permit adequate evaluation of the cost or pricing data submitted, along with the computations and projections used therein."

The Audit clause is completely silent on floor checks and obtaining information from employees through questionnaires or interviews. However, floor checks have been employed by government contract auditors for several decades and, unless embellished by inappropriate questionnaires or interviews, are generally not challenged by government contractors. It is also important, of course, that the auditor not be permitted (in floor checks or other auditing procedures) to be unescorted by responsible officials, i.e. "not to roam unrestricted." Years of experience, however, have resulted in government contract auditors and contractors effecting mutually satisfactory arrangements that permit the floor checks to be performed on a surprise basis and yet have the auditor escorted.

The performance of effective floor checks without some discussions with the employees involved is hardly practicable. However, when the discussions become "interviews," contractors frequently encounter something much more than differences in semantics. Experience has indicated that some of the interviews take on investigative aspects, and this despite the above cited letter that asserts the floor checks are not "investigatory procedures" and exhorts the DCAA field personnel that: "We need to project to companies in the defense industry that we are not investigators . . . ."

A particularly chilling comment in the DCAA April 1, 1981, letter is the statement that ". . . refusal to permit performance of floor checks by any contractor in these situations will be tantamount to an unsatisfactory condition (CAM 4-803) which requires reporting to this Headquarters." The current version of the cited provision of the Defense Contract Audit Manual (CAM 12-702 later became 4-803) is quoted below:

4-803 Unsatisfactory Conditions (Serious Weaknesses, Mismanagement, Negligence, etc.)

a. Unsatisfactory conditions, such as repeated and significant deficiencies in accounting or estimating practices, excessive mismanagement or negligence, may result in significant monetary loss or cost to the Government.

b. Examples of unsatisfactory conditions could include, but are not limited to, the following:

(1) An estimating system and related practices so deficient that price proposals are consistently unreliable, resulting in widespread defective pricing.

(2) Significant and chronic violations of Cost Accounting Standards.

(3) Internal control weaknesses of a magnitude that could cause significant monetary loss to the Government.

(4) Excessive or premature contractor reimbursement because of inappropriate application or review of economic price adjustment provisions.

(5) A contractor's refusal to certify its overhead proposal as required by DFARS 42.770.

(6) A surplus or salvage dealer pursuing a Government contract to supply parts by using surplus parts acquired through normal Government disposition channels. This would appear to be an unsatisfactory condition within the Government's operation of its disposal process. While DCAA does not have primary responsibility for auditing Government operations, report this condition to Headquarters, Attention: OAD, to allow the compilation of data for transmission to the appropriate audit or investigative agency.

c. When serious weaknesses causing major audit problems are encountered during audit performance, the auditor should communicate these to contractor officials authorized to make a decision. The notification should be made at the earliest possible time. The auditor should not wait until the final exit conference or the issuance of the audit report. In addition, the communication should be written whenever possible. Document any oral discussions by appropriate memorandums or notations in the work papers.

d. When an FAO encounters unsatisfactory conditions in contractor or Government operations, notify the ACO. The regional office should become involved promptly and actively. If the condition is not or cannot be corrected after all FAO and regional office efforts have been exhausted, prepare a report in accordance with 10-1200 and submit it through the regional director to Headquarters, Attention O and DL. Before the report is submitted, the regional director will assure that it contains all pertinent facts and a comprehensive explanation of all actions taken to resolve the matter. Wherever determinable, it should include the monetary amount involved.

Inasmuch as the contract audit clause does not provide for floor checks, certainly not the kind used by DCAA embellished by interviews and questionnaires, contractors have been frustrated as to how a refusal to permit DCAA to use doubtful audit or investigative procedures could be identified in the category of "excessive mismanagement or gross negligence."

A review of DCAA's "Floor Check Audit Guidelines for Direct/Indirect Employees" reveals several questions that appear most inappropriate and fall in the category of self-incriminatory and investigatory aspects. This subject has been discussed by industry representatives with DCAA officials but the latter have proved rigid and unyielding.

Although some companies have raised little or no protest to the latest DCAA expansion in operations and investigative activities, a number of contractors have flatly refused to permit DCAA to use these procedures. A report within DCAA on "Unsatisfactory Conditions" in and of itself will have little impact other than to further exacerbate the unsatisfactory adversary relations between industry and the Audit Agency.

DCAA GUIDANCE ON "FRAUD OR OTHER UNLAWFUL ACTIVITY"

In the closing comments on DCAA's Audit of Incurred Labor Costs, the excerpt from CAM cited 4-700. This reference is to Chapter 4, Section 7— Responsibilities for Prevention, Detection, and Reporting of Fraud, Other Unlawful Activity, or Improper Practices. Because of the increasing emphasis by contract auditors in these areas and the many serious problems being created, ranging from expenditures of vast sums of monies by contractors in defense of ill-founded allegations to suspensions or debarments of individuals or entire firms, we have cited the complete texts of 4-702 Suspected Fraud and Unlawful Activity—General, 4-703 Suspected Contractor Provision of Gratuities to Government Personnel, 4-704 Suspected Violations of Anti-Kickback Statute, and 4-705 Suspected Improper Noncompetitive Procurement Practices. Although the quoted guidance includes areas other than labor costs, we elected to include it here in its totality to provide a full perspective of DCAA's guidance. The significance of the instructions is magnified by the practice of contract audit organizations in other federal departments and agencies in emulating DCAA's policies and procedures.

4-702 Suspected Fraud and Unlawful Activity—General

4-702.1 *General.* a. In the course of auditing a contractor's or subcontractor's records, auditors may encounter, or may receive from other sources, information which could constitute evidence or cause suspicion of fraud, criminal activity, violations of the Anti-Kickback law, improper noncompetitive procurement practices, or irregularities of a similar nature. This information may pertain to acts of:

(1) Military personnel or civilian employees of the Government in their relations with the Government.

(2) Military personnel or civilian employees of the Government in their relations with individuals or firms.

(3) Individuals or firms in their business relations with the Government.

(4) Individuals or firms in their business relations with other individuals or firms doing business with the Government.

b. *Definition*. For purposes of this chapter, the term "fraud" or "other unlawful activity" means any willful or conscious wrongdoing that adversely affects the Government's interests. It includes, but is not limited to, acts of cheating or dishonesty which contribute to a loss or injury to the Government. Some examples of the types of activities included in this definition: (1) falsification of documents, such as time cards or purchase orders; (2) charging personal expenses to Government contracts; (3) submission of false claims, such as invoices for services not performed or materials not delivered; (4) intentional mischarging or misallocation of costs; (5) deceit by suppression of the truth; (6) regulatory or statutory violations, such as bribery, corrupt payments which violate the Foreign Corrupt Practices Act, theft, graft, conflict of interest, gratuities, and kickbacks; (7) any unlawful or fraudulent acts resulting from accounting classification practices that are designed to conceal the true nature of the expenses, such as unallowable costs for advertising, entertainment, etc., being classified as office supplies to avoid detection or the concealment of accounting data comprising a proposed estimating factor, like a material decrement factor used to reduce proposed material costs; and (8) any attempt or conspiracy to engage in, or use, the above devices.

4-702.2 *Audit Responsibilities*. It would be prohibitive to apply the level of audit effort required to assure that all fraud or other unlawful activity will be discovered through extremely detailed transaction auditing. Although generally accepted governmental auditing procedures are not specifically designed for the detection of such activity and are not the ideal types of review for complete assurance of detection, numerous aspects of the DCAA auditor's responsibilities, as set forth in Chapters 6 and 9 particularly, require constant alertness to the possibility of fraudulent activities. This alertness, combined with the operation of the contractor's internal controls and the auditor's normally programmed tests of procedures and transactions, should afford a practical and reasonable degree of assurance for disclosure of fraud or other unlawful activity.

4-702.3 *Audit Procedures*. An auditor may suspect fraud or other unlawful activity in the course of a normal audit performed in accordance with generally accepted government auditing standards. The auditor may also become aware of such activities when allegations of wrongdoing are received from sources outside the Agency. These sources may be company employees, disgruntled participants, or other persons who make their allegations by letter, telephone, personal visit, or through a third party.

a. When the auditor observes or is alerted to any circumstances indicating fraud or other unlawful activities, he or she has a duty to initiate an investigative referral. It is emphasized that it is not necessary to establish evidence of intent to defraud the Government before referring suspicions for investigating. Proving intent is the responsibility of the investigative organization.

b. The auditor must recognize that suspicions of fraud or other unlawful activity may be so serious as to preclude the issuance of an unqualified audit report or lead to a recommendation that partial or progress payments be halted pending resolution. If additional time is required to develop factual information for an audit impact determination, the final audit report can usually be delayed in DCAA initiated assignments, such as operations auditing, estimating system surveys, or defective pricing reviews. However, when an audit report is scheduled within a specified time frame, such as a price proposal review, the suspected condition may have a serious impact on the auditor's ability to meet the due date, or may require a report qualification. When this is the case, the auditor should:

(1) Consult the Regional Office.

(2) Contact the Plant Representative/ACO or the representative of a non-DoD agency, as appropriate, to explain the condition and arrange for an extended report due date if required.

(3) If a due date cannot be extended, qualify the audit report and/or provide comments on the circumstances that impact on the procurement situation by separate letter.

(4) Question any costs improperly claimed as a result of the suspected wrongdoing.

c. All information related to the suspicion of fraud or other unlawful activity must be carefully protected and its dissemination strictly controlled, not only to protect reputations of innocent persons, but to ensure that such information is not prematurely and inadvertently disclosed to persons who may themselves be a party to the matter, thereby possibly compromising the Government's efforts to gather needed evidence. All related DCAA reports and correspondence will be marked "FOR OFFICIAL USE ONLY" (unless an actual security classification is otherwise required in connection with specific security classification guidance), and should be controlled and protected as follows:

(1) During normal duty hours, the documents should be in an out-of-sight location if the work area is accessible to non-government personnel. Non-government personnel includes all contractor personnel.

(2) After duty hours, the documents should be in locked receptacles such as file cabinets, desks, or bookcases.

When such information is being disseminated outside DCAA, reports and correspondence should be handcarried between appropriate officials whenever practicable, or otherwise transmitted in a manner which will preclude inadvertent release to unauthorized persons.

d. It is established DCAA policy that information relating to a matter which has been referred for investigation will be considered protected information and will not be released or disclosed to a contractor, or to a contractor's employee, representative, or attorney. This policy is based on the need to avoid the disclosure of information which might impede or compromise an investigation. A case-by-case exception to this policy may be made by a regional director or head of a principal staff element.

Representatives of a contractor seeking protected information might take unusual measures to contact the auditor away from the workplace. Such measures could include making an unannounced visit or making a telephone call to the auditor's home. Whether the contact occurs at the workplace or elsewhere, the auditor should decline to discuss any aspect of a matter referred for investigation. Any contractor contacts, whether related to an investigation or normal audit activity, should occur at the auditor or contractor's place of business during duty hours.

4-702.4 *Procedures for Referring Suspicions.*

a. The auditor is expected to exercise due professional care and be mentally alert, inquisitive, and responsible in the performance of his/her audits. This requires that the auditor be attentive for indications of fraud or other unlawful activity. Upon encountering or receiving information which raises suspicion of fraud, or other unlawful activity, the auditor will:

(1) Promptly refer suspicions by completing the DCAA Suspected Irregularity Referral Form (DCAAF 2000.0), by directly contacting an outside investigative agency, or by using the DoD Hotline (toll-free telephone number 800/424-9098). Use of DCAAF 2000.0 is preferred because it specifies the type of information needed by the investigators, and it assures appropriate consideration of audit impact.

(2) If the DCAAF 2000.0 is used, send the original to Headquarters, Attention: DL and submit two copies to the FAO manager. (If assigned to a regional office or Headquarters, submit the two copies to the applicable regional director or the Assistant Director, Operations.) See Figure 4-7-1 for a copy of DCAAF 2000.0.

(3) Continue with assigned duties, and pursue development of factual information as appropriate/required by 4-702.3. Coordinate any continuing review with the supervisor or the FAO manager.

b. The FAO manager will:

(1) Encourage auditors to discuss suspicions which relate to contract audit matters with their supervisor or FAO manager and to reflect the results of these discussions in whichever method the auditor decides to refer the suspicions. These discussions are not mandatory and should not in any way impede any referrals the auditor may choose to make.

(2) Should the auditor not refer the suspicions, consider whether the activity should be referred and do so if an affirmative conclusion is reached.

(3) Upon receipt of a DCAAF 2000.0, mark one copy "early alert" and promptly forward it by registered mail with return receipt requested to the local unit of the cognizant investigative organization. The cognizant investigative organization will be determined as follows:

Contract Administered by	Investigative Organization
DLA (DCAS)	DoD/OAIG Investigations
Navy	Naval Investigative Service
Air Force	AF Office of Special Investigations
Army	Criminal Investigative Command
Non-DoD	Applicable Inspector General

(4) Except where the contracting representatives may be involved or otherwise instructed, prepare a transmittal to the "early alert" copy of the DCAAF 2000.0 that states unless advised to the contrary within five days of receipt, a copy of the early alert will be furnished the ACO. The FAO manager may add appropriate comments to the transmittal. However, the DCAAF 2000.0 must be transmitted whether or not the manager considers it valid. All copies of the DCAAF 2000.0 and the transmittal memorandums will be marked "FOR OFFICIAL USE ONLY," unless a higher security classification is otherwise required by security classification guidance (see 4-702.3c).

(5) Unless the suspicions relate to a non-DoD contract, provide a copy of the DCAAF 2000.0 to the Defense Procurement Fraud Unit (DPFU) at the following address:

> Department of Justice
> Defense Procurement Fraud Unit
> 1400 New York Avenue N.W.
> Washington, D.C. 20005

(6) Treat as possible audit leads any allegation received from outside sources (telephone calls, anonymous letters, contractor employees, etc.). Complete a DCAAF 2000.0 if there exists a reasonable basis to suspect fraud or other irregularity. If the allegation does not provide a reasonable basis to suspect fraud or other irregularity, relay the allegations under Hotline procedures. Any DCAAF 2000.0 issued will normally be on a "stand alone" basis (i.e., without audit reports being used as enclosures).

(7) Notify regional representatives of suspicions as required by regional instructions. Coordinate/continue any necessary audit reviews to ascertain the extent of error without attempting to establish wrongdoing (an investigative responsibility). Furnish a copy of any resulting audit report to the appropriate investigative organization and the Defense Procurement Fraud Unit (DPFU). All future correspondence and/or updates will reference the DCAA case number assigned by DL.

(8) Fully support the investigators as provided in DCAA's 4 May 1983 Memorandum of Understanding with the DoD Investigative Organizations. Provide reasonable access to applicable DCAA work paper files, including contractor-generated material contained in them. Copies of work papers provided the investigators will be

listed for future reference. Physical custody of the work papers must be maintained by DCAA. Throughout the investigative process, continue to pursue administrative recoupment unless directed by the regional director or Headquarters, DCAA, to defer administrative recoupment actions. Before finalizing an administrative recoupment, the ACO should be advised to coordinate the action with the investigator/prosecutor responsible for the case.

(9) Notify his/her regional director of any multisegment contractors suspected of systemic fraudulent conditions that might be applicable to other contractor segments.

c. The regional director will decide, for multisegment contractors, if a suspected fraudulent condition indicates systemic problems that could be applicable to other contractor segments. In such situations, the regional directors cognizant of these other segments will be apprised of pertinent facts so that appropriate review measures can be taken.

4-702.5 *Audit Techniques.* The matters listed in the following subparagraphs should be noted as examples of audit techniques which should assist in the maintenance of an acceptable level of probability that fraudulent activities and other unlawful practices will be revealed.

a. Evaluations of the contractor's system of internal control should include the determination that there are sufficient checks and balances, especially those associated with control totals and divisions of duties. If the opportunity for fraud is decreased by internal control, the temptation therefor is also decreased. As an example, floor checks coupled with divisions of duties and control totals provide a major deterrent to padding of payrolls with fictitious employees.

b. Transactions testing should include the determination that the records being examined have not been falsified. A number of fraud cases involve deliberately falsified labor distribution and payroll records; these include, among others, charging cost-type contracts with costs applicable to firm-fixed price work; charging employee labor costs to other direct and indirect activities when contractor projects, budgets, contracting ceilings or advance agreement (e.g., IR&D/B&P) limitations are about to be exceeded; and charging material costs with inflated prices recorded from invoices from fictitious or "dummy" companies. A common method of making improper charges to flexible price contracts is to change the account number to which a labor distribution document or vendor invoice is to be charged. The auditor should be alert to accounting misclassification that may be intended to conceal the true purpose of the expenditure. In one case, unallowable election donations were passed through the accounts as consultant fees.

c. Physical observations (5-106) should be programmed as an integral part of the audit. They should be unannounced, and the auditor should be alert for evidence of fraud, waste, or mismanagement. This technique is especially useful in receiving, production, material control, and engineering areas; it is further emphasized in 6-405, 6-310, 6-312, and 6-607.1. Details and conclusions of the observations, in whatever area utilized, should be noted carefully in the work papers and promptly compared with the related accounting records.

d. The contractor should have a reasonable degree of physical control of plant areas to prevent unauthorized access to data and unauthorized removal of property. A high degree of potential pilferage exists whenever significant quantities of high dollar value consumer-type items are included in stock room inventories used by manufacturing, engineering, or other activities. These inventories include components and assemblies of consumer or highly saleable commercial items, such as automobile and truck parts, as well as specialized and saleable material such as copper, brass, or other high value alloys, all easily portable. Consequently, the matter of physical safeguards should receive attention in the development of the audit program.

e. Isolated cases of irregularities have been noted where continuous overtime or premium pay was paid to certain individuals or groups because they were willing to kick back a part of their pay to influential outsiders or company personnel. Where overtime, holiday, or other premium pay is significant, the contractor's control procedures should be such as to prevent, insofar as practicable, the continuing payment of such amounts to a select group or to certain individuals unless clearly justified. The auditors should ascertain that the approval process for premium work includes determination that (1) the premium work is needed in the quantity requested or charged, (2) the skills involved are appropriate, and (3) there is no undue concentration of this work in certain individuals or groups. In determining whether undue concentration exists, extreme care should be exercised inasmuch as it is the contractor's prerogative and responsibility to select the kinds and quantities of required labor, as well as the individuals to be used. If the above conditions are noted and appear to be of a pattern or repetitive nature which would suggest suspicion of wrongdoing, they should be considered for possible reporting under this paragraph or 4-803.

f. With the development of more advanced data processing systems, the possible perpetration of fraud is facilitated by two factors: (1) manually prepared records may be replaced by computer output and, (2) audit trails may be eliminated or difficult to follow. (See Section 3, Appendix C for additional guidance for the survey of EDP systems.)

(1) The decrease in manually prepared documentation at present is more prevalent in the labor area. Employees may insert the data which formerly appeared on job tickets into remote computer entry stations in the shop which relay this information directly to the computer for processing. The support for costs under this type of system normally consists of machine printouts which detail the data which formerly appeared on source documents. If it were desired to alter the distribution of costs under these circumstances, it could be done by programming the computer to prepare printouts supporting incorrect cost distribution. The effect would be the same as the manual alteration of records. However, the computer could do the job much more efficiently and without involving a large number of persons. In most cases, this type of manipulation

could be detected through floorchecking procedures including, as a minimum, tests of the correctness of the last recorded payroll distribution as described in 6-405.

(2) A more serious problem arises when the audit trail is nonexistent or difficult to follow. The use of auditing techniques described in C-300 will not necessarily provide full protection against fraud under these circumstances. It is possible to have the computer increase cumulative costs charged to one or more cost-type Government contracts with a balancing decrease in amounts charged to commercial products or fixed-price Government contracts, without having the transaction appear on detailed printouts. As an alternative, a contrived printout of a cost distribution could be substituted for a valid one. Another possibility would be to simply remove computer listing pages containing transactions that management or an employee does not want the auditor to review. If a listing includes a large number of transactions, it would be extremely laborious to manually ascertain whether the totals and/or accounting distribution at the end of the listing agree with the preceding detail. Use of a computer program for sample selection, as described in B-306, offers additional assurance against fraudulent practices of the type discussed in this paragraph, since the output includes the total dollar value of transactions charged to the account(s) under review, as well as a sample of the transactions which comprise the total.

(3) When a statistical sample of a universe is contemplated, the auditor should take the steps indicated in B-306.1 to assure that the integrity of the universe is maintained. Additionally, when the contractor's computer facilities are used to select audit samples, the auditor should be aware of the possibility of unknown alterations of such selections and take the appropriate steps indicated in B-306.2 to preclude sample manipulations.

4-703 Suspected Contractor Provision of Gratuities to Government Personnel.

Section VIII, "Gratuities," of DoDD 5500.7, "Standards of Conduct," prohibits DoD personnel from accepting any gift, gratuity, favor, entertainment, loan, or any other thing of monetary value either directly or indirectly from any person, firm, or corporation which: (1) is engaged in business or financial transactions with any agency of DoD, (2) conducts operations or activities that are regulated by any DoD agency, or (3) has interests that may be substantially affected by DoD employees' performance or nonperformance of official duties.

a. Noncompliance with section VIII of DoD Directive 5500.7 may become the subject of an investigation and can result in disciplinary action. DCAA has no responsibility to monitor DoD compliance with section VIII; consequently, audit programs do not contain specific steps to detect noncompliance. However, any apparent noncompliance, regardless of the dollar value or length of time since the suspected event occurred, coming to the auditor's attention is reportable. Suspected offers or acceptance of gratuities will be reported even though no recipient can be identified or no investigative lead is apparent to the auditor. Although the directive is not applicable to non-DoD personnel, the reporting requirements are the same where instances of non-DoD personnel have accepted gifts, gratuities, loans, favors, or entertainment.

b. To be responsive to the specific needs of cognizant Government officials, reports must be sufficiently informative to provide basic investigative leads. The use of accounting and auditing terminology which may not be familiar to report recipients should be avoided.

(1) The report (DCAAF 2000.0 may be used) must contain as much information as is available including identity of the offeror and recipient (names, position titles, and agency/department or contractor), type of gratuity, range in dollar value of the gratuity or benefit detected, estimated total dollar value, what records were reviewed, whether access to any records was denied, and why the auditor suspects that a gratuity has been offered and or received. Also, the auditor should indicate whether the contractor is aware of the condition, and if so, comments should be included on the nature of corrective action taken or contemplated, including the adequacy of any repayments to the government.

(2) Numerous copies of essentially duplicative documents from the contractor's records, such as expense vouchers, need not be forwarded with the report. Instead, one or two representative samples of such records may be forwarded along with a listing of pertinent information (names, dates, amounts, etc.) extracted from the records. All copies should be legible. If it is not possible to obtain a legible copy, state this fact in the report and briefly describe the document.

(3) The report will be sent to Headquarters, Attention: DL, with copies to the regional director. The report will be referred by Headquarters DL to the appropriate investigative agency.

4-704 Suspected Violations of the Anti-Kickback Act (41 U.S.C. 51 to 58)

4-704.1 *General.* a. The Anti-Kickback Act (4-7S1) prohibits the providing, attempting to provide, or offering to provide any kickback; the soliciting, accepting, or attempting to accept any kickback; or the including, directly or indirectly, of the kickback amount in the contract price charged by a subcontractor to a prime contractor or a higher tier subcontractor or in the contract price charged by a prime contractor to the government.

b. Kickback is defined as any money, fee, commission, credit, gift, gratuity, thing of value, or compensation of any kind which is provided, directly or indirectly, to any prime contractor, prime contractor employee, subcontractor, or subcontractor employee for the purpose of improperly obtaining or rewarding favorable treatment in connection with a prime contract or in connection with a subcontract relating to a prime contract.

4-704.2 *Examples of Questionable Practices.* Questionable practices under the Anti-Kickback Act may take such form as: payments of commissions to prime contractor personnel; entertainment provided for prime contract personnel; loans to prime or higher-tier contractor personnel which may not be repaid and may be subsequently recorded as an expense on the subcontractor's records; expensive gifts of varying treatment for particular subcontractors.

4-704.3 *Audit Responsibilities.* Ascertain that contractors have informed their personnel concerned with awarding or administering subcontracts or purchase orders and their subcontractors and suppliers regarding the provisions of the amended Anti-Kickback Act and questionable practices thereunder. If such action has not been taken by a contractor, the auditor should initiate recommendations to the contracting officer relative to the matter and cooperate to the extent necessary to assure that the contractor's procurement personnel are aware of the provisions of the Act.

4-704.4 *Reporting Requirements.* When there is reason to believe that a violation of the Act has occurred or when a violation by a prime contractor or subcontractor is suspected and further audit action is justified, the auditor shall immediately prepare a report thereon. The reports, properly classified, will state all known details of the transaction, and will be forwarded and coordinated in the same manner as those on suspected fraud. (See 4-702.4.)

4-705 Suspected Improper Noncompetitive Procurement Practices

a. Improper noncompetitive procurement practices are those designed to eliminate competition or restrain trade. They include but are not limited to collusive bidding, follow-the-leader pricing, rotated low bids, sharing the business, or identical bids. They do not include bona fide sole source procurement actions.

b. If information received from any source leads the auditor to suspect improper noncompetitive procurement practices by a contractor or subcontractor, the auditor shall determine by appropriate audit techniques whether sufficient evidence exists to reasonably indicate an improper practice. In such cases, the auditor shall promptly submit a report using the procedures in 4-702 to the responsible contracting officer.

DCAA GUIDELINES FOR A COMPREHENSIVE AUDIT OF LABOR COSTS

Despite the extensive coverage accorded to audit of labor costs in CAM and other publications, DCAA issued a separate Pamphlet (DCAAP 7641.88, September 1984) with the above-captioned title. Introductory comments to this Pamphlet state that "discovery of unlawful or fraudulent activities is not the primary audit objective" in this area, but hurriedly add that "the auditor should be alert to any condition which suggests that such a situation may exist." Encouragement to pursue fraud investigations is reflected here in the comment that "Comprehensive labor audits have resulted in a significant number of reports of suspected irregularities (CAM 4-702)."

Auditors are directed to ask such questions as:

"Where can the Government be overcharged?"

"How and where can the contractor benefit by misclassifying/ mischarging labor costs?"

(It becomes quite obvious that the various admonitions by the DOD IG to the auditors to "think fraud" have been well absorbed by DCAA.)

The Pamphlet recommends the desirability of a "current/comprehensive audit of labor," particularly at the larger contractors. However, recognizing that a complete audit of all labor ramifications cannot be performed at one time, it suggests the use of "risk/vulnerability assessment" techniques to establish priorities and areas of emphasis. DCAA "risk analysis" is an audit technique "performed to identify those problem areas most likely to result in a *significant* adverse cost impact to the Government." (Emphasis in original.) "Vulnerability assessments," according to the Pamphlet, "are performed to determine the extent of Government exposure to suspected irregular conduct."

The auditor is furnished numerous suggestions regarding where to probe for mischarging and irregularities, such as overrun contracts, charging work on fixed-price contracts to cost-reimbursable contracts, improper shifting of costs among IR&D, B&P and contract work, etc. He is encouraged to prepare "audit lead sheets" to direct future audits and auditors to suspected areas that cannot be examined very closely at the moment.

DCAA views auditing labor of great importance for a number of reasons. For example, whereas charges for materials and other costs usually originate in billings or related charges from external sources, labor charges originate within the contractor's organization through the preparation of time sheets, time clocks, etc. The audit agency views this factor as increasing the possibility of fraudulent or other irregularities in charges to government contracts. Labor also takes on importance in that it is a prime component in the ultimate price. For example, assuming an overhead rate of 200%, a G&A rate of 20% and a profit of 10%, a mischarged direct labor amount of $100 would overstate the price by $396.

The Pamphlet devotes considerable attention to floor checks and other employee "interviews." As noted earlier in this chapter, the extent and manner in which DCAA auditors have been known to interrogate contractor employees are extremely complex, controversial and sensitive matters, and it is essential that responsible contractor officials restrain the tendencies for these auditors/investigators "to roam unrestricted" throughout the plant and subject the employees to improper interrogations.

DOD INSPECTOR GENERAL LABOR FRAUD INVESTIGATIONS AND GUIDANCE

As discussed throughout this text, the DOD IG has been in the forefront of all federal inspectors general in fraud detection and in furnishing guidance to auditors in this area. A very substantial portion of both the alleged and proven cases of fraud involving accounting matters has been related to labor charges, and the DOD IG has placed considerable emphasis on this area.

Appendix 1 of this text contains excerpts from the DOD IG's "Indicators of Fraud in Department of Defense Procurement" and a lengthy Section E of this report addresses labor mischarges. This 1984 publication was followed by the issuance of the DOD IG's "Handbook on Labor Fraud Indicators" in August 1985, extensive excerpts of which are contained in Appendix 2 of this text. The stated purpose of the handbook is to "stimulate the contract auditor's imagination regarding the detection of fraud." The handbook further asserts: "Fraud does exist. It is the auditor's responsibility to identify and make examples of those contractors who consider themselves above the law."

These and other statements, together with the "scenarios" furnished, which might suggest that most contractors devote their attention to devising schemes to defraud the government, do not even pretend to present a well-rounded and balanced guidance to the audit of labor. The handbook has, however, to a large extent, achieved its objective of making contract auditors "think fraud."

It is important for contractors to be aware of this guidance in order to understand the thinking and actions of contract auditors today. This guidance could also be useful as a basis for reviewing contractors' accounting methods and controls for labor and their internal audit programs in this area.

Accounting Methods and Controls for Other Direct Charges to Government Contracts

It has been previously stated that the cost accounting viewpoint, which holds that accurate product costs are dependent upon the extent to which individual cost items are identified and charged directly thereto, is tempered by considerations of expense, convenience, and practicability. Accordingly, substantial factory and other costs that could conceivably be measured and charged directly to contracts are accumulated instead in overhead accounts. Accountants then rely on appropriate allocation bases to distribute such expenses to contracts in a manner that will reasonably measure the applicable portion, without seriously distorting product costs.

However, when certain costs are incurred in substantial amounts for the sole benefit of specific jobs, inclusion of such items in overhead and their proration to all final cost objectives, using a base such as direct labor, total cost, etc., may result in substantial inaccuracies. Therefore, cost accounting conventions recognize a class of costs variously termed but designated for the purposes of this discussion as Other Direct Charges. These are costs, other than direct materials and direct labor, which are or should be charged directly to jobs.

REQUIREMENTS AND LIMITATIONS UNDER GOVERNMENT CONTRACTS

Both government and industry recognize that a cost, unless it is immaterial in amount, that can be specifically identified with a final cost objective should be charged thereto, and both recognize the impropriety of charging a cost directly to a final cost objective if other costs incurred for the same purpose, in like circumstances, have been included in an indirect cost pool and allocated to that or any other final cost objective. Differences arise primarily because contractors are concerned with obtaining full recovery of costs incurred, particularly on variably priced contracts, and emphasize charging costs directly to such contracts whenever the costs are significant in amount. Government auditors, on the other hand, appear to concentrate their attention on assuring that (1) the cost accounting practices do not result in "double counting," the kind of practice described above as improper and (2) costs which may be identified specifically with nongovernment work are excluded from overhead pools.

Despite the differences in emphasis, the basic principle was always recognized, as indicated by the contract cost principles in ASPR 15-202(a) and (b) prior to the revisions in the DAR and FPR and the current FAR 31.202:

> A direct cost is any cost which can be identified specifically with a particular cost objective. Direct costs are not limited to items which are incorporated in the end product as material or labor. Costs identified specifically with the contract are direct costs of the contract and are to be charged directly thereto. Costs identified specifically with other work of the contractor are direct costs of that work and are not to be charged to the contract directly or indirectly. When items ordinarily chargeable as indirect costs are charged to Government work as direct costs, the cost of like items applicable to other work of the contractor must be eliminated from indirect costs allocated to Government work.

> This definition shall be applied to all items of cost of significant amount unless the contractor demonstrates that the application of any different current practice achieves substantially the same results. Direct costs of minor amount may be distributed as indirect costs . . .

COST ACCOUNTING STANDARDS

Although the government's contract cost principles appeared to clearly recognize and address the possible problems in charging certain costs as direct and indirect, the Comptroller General's "Report on the Feasibility of Applying Uniform Cost-Accounting Standards to Negotiated Defense Contracts" stated that there were numerous abuses, mostly involving "situations wherein the contractors charged directly to the Government work costs which were normally handled as indirect costs and did not adjust their indirect charges to eliminate similar costs from indirect costs also charged to the contract." The subject was even referred to in Public Law 91-379, creating the CASB: "Such regulations shall require defense contractors and subcontractors as a condition of contracting to disclose in writing their cost-accounting principles, including methods of distinguishing direct costs from indirect costs . . . ."

Was the problem attributable to an inadequacy of existing regulations or to the failure of DOD contracting and auditing officials to effectively implement those regulations? The Comptroller General's Task Force and Congress obviously were persuaded that the fault was in the regulations. In this instance, as in so many other areas, there are those who believe that enactment of additional legislation and promulgation of additional regulations will solve all problems. Accordingly, as discussed in Chapter IX of this text, among the CASB's first promulgations was CAS 402—Consistency in Allocating Costs Incurred for the Same Purpose, which had the following stated purpose:

> The purpose of this standard is to require that each type of cost is allocated only once and on only one basis to any contract or other cost objective. The criteria for determining the allocation of costs to a product, contract, or other cost objective should be the same for all similar objectives. Adherence to these cost accounting concepts is necessary to guard against the overcharging of some cost objectives and to prevent double counting. Double counting occurs most commonly when cost items

are allocated directly to a cost objective without eliminating like cost items from indirect cost pools which are allocated to that cost objective.

In terms of rules and regulations, what was the significant change brought by CAS 402 over the cost principles previously published by the federal departments and agencies? The reader may analyze the provisions of DAR 15-202(a), duplicated in FPR 1-15.202(a) (the provisions of FAR 31.202(a) are almost identical), and judge whether the cost accounting standard made any real difference in cost accounting principles:

> A direct cost is any cost which can be identified specifically with a particular final cost objective. . . . No final cost objective shall have allocated to it as a direct cost any cost, if other costs incurred for the same purpose, in like circumstances, have been included in any indirect cost pool to be allocated to that or any other final cost objective. Costs identified specifically with the contract are direct costs of the contract and are to be charged thereto. Costs identified specifically with other final cost objectives of the contractor are direct costs of those cost objectives and are not to be charged to the contract directly or indirectly.

We see then an exercise in language directed at assuring that the long-standing principles embodied in cost accounting conventions and government contract cost principles are stated in stricter and more rigid terms. But even the CASB recognized the difficulties of absolutism. For example, CAS 402.60(b)(1) recognizes the propriety of a contractor including as indirect costs and allocating to all of its work the costs of a fire-fighting force of 10 employees for the general protection of the plant, while at the same time allocating directly to a contract the cost of three fixed-post firemen on 24-hour duty to protect highly inflammable materials used on that contract.

SPECIFIC CONTRACT PROVISIONS

Contracts subject to either full or modified CAS coverage (see Chapter VIII of this text) will contain a clause requiring compliance with CAS 402. Contracts not subject to cost accounting standards, where cost is a factor in pricing, will generally incorporate FAR Part 31 and thus be subject to FAR 31.202. As described above, the ground rules for treating similar costs in like circumstances are virtually identical.

In certain cost-reimbursement type contracts, however, specific clauses spell out those items that are to be charged direct and those contemplated for recovery through indirect cost allocations. These specific provisions will prevail, and contractors need only assure that their cost accounting practices do not result in charging the same costs in similar circumstances both directly to specific final cost objectives and to indirect expense pools for allocation to all of the work. As a commonly encountered situation, certain contracts, particularly those requiring study and research involving considerable travel, provide that the travel costs of employees working directly on these contracts will be reimbursed directly. The illustration in CAS 402.60(a)(1) recognizes such circumstances under conditions where the contractor previously charged all of its travel expenses as indirect costs. This contractor must now revise its cost accounting practices to exclude from indirect expense pools all travel costs of employees whose time is accounted for as direct labor on this *and any other final cost objective.* However, the contractor may, and should, include in its appropriate indirect cost pools the traveling expenses of administrative and other employees whose time is not accounted for as direct labor on any final cost objective.

Many other specific costs may be identified in contracts for direct charging and direct reimbursement. For example, as discussed in Chapter IX of this text, the CASB was required to address the proper treatment of Bid and Proposal (B&P) costs because of (1) the variety of ways such costs were accounted for in industry, (2) the significance of this cost, and (3) the failure of CAS 402 to indicate what the appropriate cost accounting practice should be. The final conclusion was set forth in Interpretation No. 1 to CAS 402, which recognized that "costs incurred . . . (for) proposals pursuant to a specific requirement of an existing contract are considered to have been incurred in different circumstances from the circumstances under which costs are incurred in preparing proposals which do not result from such requirements." The former costs, therefore, may be charged directly and the latter indirectly without violating CAS 402.

Chapter 8 of DCAA's Contract Audit Manual, "Cost Accounting Standards," includes additional illustrations for the standards promulgated by the CASB. While not clothed with authoritative or official status, the audit guidance is worthy of study. In the case of CAS 402, DCAA's illustrations emphasize that, where a certain contract requires a greater degree of planning, engineering, or other effort than the other final cost objectives, this fact in and of itself does not justify direct charging of such effort while similar costs in like circumstances for other work, even though expended in lesser degree, are charged to an indirect expense pool for allocation to all work. The recommended solution is either to charge such costs direct to all final cost objectives or to charge the costs to overhead and develop an equitable distribution base.

TYPES OF DIRECT CHARGES

Almost any cost may be charged directly to final cost objectives at the contractor's election provided the practice does not conflict with its Disclosure Statement or the cost accounting standards, where applicable, or the contract cost principles contained in FAR. A complete listing is not feasible, but the following pages discuss many of the costs and expenses charged directly.

Special Tooling and Special Test Equipment Costs

FAR 31.205-40 provides:

(a) The terms "special tooling" and "special test equipment" are defined in 45.101.

(b) The cost of special tooling and special test equipment used in performing one or more Government contracts is allowable and shall be allocated to the specific Government contract or contracts for which acquired, except that the cost of (1) items acquired by the contractor before the effective date of the contract (or replacements of such items), whether or not altered or adapted for use in performing the contract, and

(2) items which the contract schedule specifically excludes, shall be allowable only as depreciation or amortization.

(c) When items are disqualified as special tooling or special test equipment because with relatively minor expense they can be made suitable for general purpose use and have a value as such commensurate with their value as special tooling or special test equipment, the cost of adapting the items for use under the contract and the cost of returning them to their prior configuration are allowable.

The charging of special tooling costs directly to final cost objectives and concurrently allocating thereto the costs of general purpose tooling is specifically approved in an illustration in CAS 402.60(b)(1):

Contractor normally allocates special tooling costs directly to contracts. The costs of general purpose tooling are normally included in the indirect cost pool which is allocated to contracts. Both of these accounting practices were previously disclosed to the government. Since both types of costs were not incurred for the same purpose in accordance with the criteria set forth in the contractor's Disclosure Statement, the allocation of general purpose tooling costs from the indirect cost pool to the contract, in addition to the directly allocated special tooling costs is not considered a violation of the standard.

It must be remembered that one of the difficulties in recovering costs as direct charges is the need to substantiate to the audit representatives that the related costs were incurred solely and specifically for a government contract or contracts. To obviate controversies on this score, contractors should follow through in every respect of their accounting procedures. In the instance of purchased tools, all the underlying documents, including purchase orders, vendor's invoices, etc., should clearly reflect the contract number or other identification to which the costs are charged.

When special tools are fabricated in the contractor's own shop, separate work orders should be established and identified to the related contract. All time cards, raw material purchases, etc., should show the contract number. Further, all of the tooling costs under a given contract should be accumulated in a separate ledger account, again clearly designated with the appropriate contract number. Any relaxation in the above procedures may invite difficulties and possibly preclude the total recovery. Another important step is the obtaining of an understanding with the contracting officer as to the tooling required. Such understanding should be reduced to writing. The preferable form, of course, is the contract itself. However, if for some reason this is not feasible, alternative procedures, including exchange of letters and minutes of meetings, may be employed. In this connection, it must be noted that government auditors are more interested in an expression of opinion from the contracting officer than from the contractor. Accordingly, presenting a letter written by the contractor to the contracting officer, without an acknowledgment, will do little good.

At one time the government spent a lot of time and effort in determining the appropriate basis for amortizing a special tooling program. The contractor, understandably enough, was primarily interested in recovering the monies expended in the shortest possible time. The government audit representatives, on the other hand, with some accounting precedent and principles on their side, sought to defer a portion of the charges to effect a pro rata write-off over all the contracts benefiting by the tools involved. The difficulties encountered were caused first by conflict in interests, as between a speedy recovery of expenditures and the deferment of such costs, and second by the complications involved in determining the proper period of amortization. There were questions about the actual length of the period of useful life for certain tools, the possibilities of obsolescence due to specification changes and the constant addition of new contracts, and upward and downward revisions to quantities called for under existing contracts. The trend in recent years, however, has pointed to the acceptance of industry's view that the government should pay the contractor immediately for expenditures of this nature.

As an illustration, in the instance of a contract subject to price revision at 40% completion, contractors were frequently paid in full for tooling costs incurred to that time, without any question of amortization. The government took no chances in this procedure inasmuch as such tools become its property and cannot be charged again. This approach seemed to satisfy all parties involved.

Funding Requirements for Certain Special Tooling and Test Equipment

Chapter X of this text contains a review of the statutory and implementing regulatory provisions under which, with certain exceptions, contractors may not be reimbursed under a contract for more than 50% of the acquisition cost of production special tooling and production special test equipment.

Starting Load Costs

This category of costs generally includes both preproduction costs and certain additional charges continuing over the early stages of production. Preproduction costs include the time spent by all personnel in planning, training, set-up, and related charges incident to the commencement of manufacturing. The other charges are those related to the early inefficiency and other factors resulting in higher unit cost experience encountered in the initial stages.

The question of amortization of starting load costs does not now present the problems of the past, and the trend has been towards the same procedure discussed under special tooling in the preceding paragraphs. The government has come to the realization that preproduction costs must be paid and is now, generally, willing to reimburse the contractor for such costs coincident with the first repricing action so long as the government representatives are assured that no danger exists for possible duplication of such charges in subsequent periods.

Starting load costs should be accumulated in a special account for each contract wherever feasible. This procedure is usually possible in respect of all such costs with the exception of the higher unit labor costs experienced in the initial stages. The isolation of such costs can be established by establishing two or more job lots within the first 20% to 40% period, or through a study of monthly cost trends.

Rearrangement

The cost of plant rearrangement is often combined with other starting load costs. This procedure is not objectionable except that, where the related costs are substantial in amount, it is advisable to accumulate the charges in a separate account. Here again, it is very important that all supporting data, including time tickets, purchase orders, vendors' invoices, stores requisitions, work orders, etc., be properly identified with the appropriate contract number and that the contracting officer's recognition for the need of the rearrangement program be reduced to writing.

As mentioned in the paragraphs dealing with special tooling and starting load costs, rearrangement costs can usually be recovered at the time of the first price revision. In the light of this thinking by the government, contractors should not miss the opportunity for prompt recoupment of such charges so that they may be enabled to place those funds back into the business.

Special Packing

Most government contracts, even those relating to an item not dissimilar to the contractor's commercial product, will contain packing provisions over and above commercial requirements. This is especially true where the contract calls for packing for overseas shipment. A careful study of the packing costs required under government and commercial work will often reveal that the former run considerably higher. When this is the case, recovery of all packing and shipping costs through overhead allocation will seldom result in accurate charges between the types of business but will serve to inequitably burden commercial orders.

Accordingly, a careful study should be made of all surrounding circumstances to determine the best procedure to follow. This study is highly essential. Many contractors have rushed procedures of this nature only to discover that the savings accomplished were insufficient to compensate for the time, effort, and expense generated.

Where it is established that the additional costs of packing and shipping under government contracts warrant effecting direct charges, several methods may be employed. One effective plan provides for the establishment of standard packing and shipping costs for each product (or category of products) shipped. Government contracts and commercial orders will then be charged on the basis of such standards and the over- or underabsorbed packing and shipping costs may be apportioned to all jobs in the ratio of the standards or any other reasonable basis.

Government auditors will probably accept the method and the results generated by it if they can be shown that the standards were scientifically established and if the variances are not so great as to cast a doubt as to the credibility of the standards. Another method entails identifying the special shipping and packing costs that are incurred only under a specific government contract or contracts and charging such costs directly to their related final cost objectives. The remaining packing and shipping, where appropriate, should be included as indirect expenses and allocated to all of the final cost objectives. This method should meet the requirement of CAS 402 that costs incurred for the same purpose in like circumstances should not be charged to final cost objectives and also included in indirect cost pools. A third method, if feasible under the circumstances, would be to requisition packing supplies as required under each contract and charge the contracts directly with the cost of packing supplies actually used.

Travel Expenses

FAR 31.205-46 provides that travel expenses, based on their nature and purpose, may be allowable as either indirect or direct costs. "Travel costs incurred in the normal course of overall administration of the business are allowable and shall be treated as indirect costs. ... Travel costs directly attributable to specific contract performance are allowable and may be charged to the contract under (FAR) 31.202." The cited reference, paragraph 31.202 of FAR, is quoted earlier in this chapter.

Before the contract cost principles were spelled out in their present comprehensive terms, difficulties were sometimes encountered with DOD auditors in connection with travel expenses. Certain audit offices seemed to be of the opinion that, unless direct charges for travel expenses were specifically provided for in the contract, such costs should all be treated as indirect. As an alternative, they would hold that, if certain travel costs were allowed as direct charges to the contract, all other travel costs included in overhead pools should be disallowed. Current FAR provisions, as cited above, make it quite clear that travel expenses may be appropriately charged to contracts, both as direct charges and through overhead allocations.

Consultants' Fees

The consideration of this cost as a direct charge is required mainly in the instances of small or medium-sized firms, performing under some form of research or developmental contracts, where the services of outside consultants are required to supplement the technical and scientific knowledge of the contractors' personnel. Where services of outside consultants are employed regularly for all work, establishing procedures for direct charges may not be advisable. However, where outside consultants are called in especially for government work, full recovery of their fees cannot be accomplished through overhead allocation and the costs should be recovered as direct charges. Inasmuch as the charging of consultants' fees directly does not ordinarily entail substantial effort or expense, the procedure is strongly recommended.

Other Expenses That May Be Charged Directly

Almost every item of overhead expense may conceivably be charged directly to government contracts. In addition to special tooling, starting load costs, rearrangement, special packing, traveling expenses and consultants' fees, mentioned in the preceding paragraphs, the following items have been found as direct charges: overtime and shift premium pay, expeditors' salaries, certain clerical salaries, shop supplies, freight-in, freight-out, telephone and telegraph expenses, plant protection, defective work royalties, bidding expenses, and possibly others.

As a specific rule, the costing approach to government contracts should be reviewed before the beginning of operations and periodically during the life of the contract to assure that full recovery is being effected for all elements of costs incurred. Where this full recovery is not provided through normal overhead apportionment procedures, consideration should be accorded to effecting direct charges for the items involved. In determining whether to recover charges directly or through overhead, studies should be made to ascertain whether the additional expense involved in the direct charge approach justifies the utilization of this method.

Another consideration involved in making the determination is the matter of consistency. It has been pointed out previously that the government contractor cannot be stopped from effecting direct charges for certain cost elements because it was not the contractor's prior consistent policy in regard to its commercial work. However, contractors subject to full or modified CAS coverage (see Chapter VIII of this text) must conform with their disclosed or established cost accounting practices and comply with the provisions of the CAS clause relating to changes in cost accounting practices.

DCAA Contract Audit Manual Audit Guidance Relating to Other Direct Costs and Credits

CAM Chapter 6, Section 5, contains guidance to DCAA auditors for auditing other direct costs. CAM emphasizes that other direct costs should be reviewed in conjunction with the audit of indirect costs to "provide assurance that when items ordinarily chargeable as indirect costs are charged to Government work as direct costs, the costs of like items applicable to other work of the contractor are treated in the same manner" (6-504). CAM 6-505 directs auditors to review "negotiation memorandum and contract provisions" to ascertain the intent of the parties as to whether certain costs were to be charged direct or indirect.

Chapter XIII

Accounting Methods and Controls for Manufacturing Overhead

GENERAL COMMENTS ON INDIRECT COSTS UNDER GOVERNMENT CONTRACTS

The allowability of indirect costs under government contracts has always posed the most difficult problems and generated the most controversies. The contract cost principles promulgated by the executive agencies have devoted by far the greatest amount of coverage to indirect costs, and, of the changes to these principles, those affecting indirect costs have been predominant. Indirect costs have also been the major source of litigation and legislation relating to contract cost principles. The enactment of Public Law 91-379 brought us cost accounting standards, designed to enhance uniformity and consistency in cost accounting practices. However, as illustrated throughout this text, the cost accounting standards have generated their own controversies, disputes, and litigation.

A discussion of indirect costs under government contracts may be approached in several ways. The one selected in this text, and covered in the next several chapters, first categorizes indirect costs into three broad groupings: Manufacturing Overhead; Engineering and Research and Development Expenses; and Selling, General and Administrative Expenses. Methods and controls for each of these categories, including broad regulations governing their allocability to government contracts, are addressed in this Chapter XIII and the following Chapters XIV and XV. Subsequent chapters cover in considerable detail the concepts underlying government principles for determining allowable and unallowable costs and the application of these principles to specific indirect costs.

ACQUISITION (PROCUREMENT) REGULATIONS

FAR contains extensive comments on the general subject of indirect costs:

31.203 Indirect costs.

(a) An indirect cost is any cost not directly identified with a single, final cost objective, but identified with two or more final cost objectives or an intermediate cost objective. It is not subject to treatment as a direct cost. After direct costs have been determined and charged directly to the contract or other work, indirect costs are those remaining to be allocated to the several cost objectives. An indirect cost shall not be allocated to a final cost objective if other costs incurred for the same purpose in like circumstances have been included as a direct cost of that or any other final cost objective.

(b) Indirect costs shall be accumulated by logical cost groupings with due consideration of the reasons for incurring such costs. Each grouping should be determined so as to permit distribution of the grouping on the basis of the benefits accruing to the several cost objectives. Commonly, manufacturing overhead, selling expenses, and general and administrative (G&A) expenses are separately grouped. Similarly, the particular case may require subdivision of these groupings, e.g., building occupancy costs might be separable from those of personnel administration within the manufacturing overhead group. This necessitates selecting a distribution base common to all cost objectives to which the grouping is to be allocated. The base should be selected so as to permit allocation of the grouping on the basis of the benefits accruing to the several cost objectives. When substantially the same results can be achieved through less precise methods, the number and composition of cost groupings should be governed by practical considerations and should not unduly complicate the allocation.

(c) Once an appropriate base for distributing indirect costs has been accepted, it shall not be fragmented by removing individual elements. All items properly includable in an indirect cost base should bear a pro rata share of indirect costs irrespective of their acceptance as Government contract costs. For example, when a cost input base is used for the distribution of G&A costs, all items that would properly be part of the cost input base, whether allowable or unallowable, shall be included in the base and bear their pro rata share of G&A costs.

(d) The contractor's method of allocating indirect costs shall be in accordance with standards promulgated by the CAS Board, if applicable to the contract; otherwise, the method shall be in accordance with generally accepted accounting principles which are consistently applied. The method may require examination when—

(1) Substantial differences occur between the cost patterns of work under the contract and the contractor's other work;

(2) Significant changes occur in the nature of the business, the extent of subcontracting, fixed-asset improvement programs, inventories, the volume of sales and production, manufacturing processes, the contractor's products, or other relevant circumstances; or

(3) Indirect cost groupings developed for a contractor's primary location are applied to offsite locations. Separate cost groupings for costs allocable to offsite locations may be necessary to permit equitable distribution of costs on the basis of the benefits accruing to the several cost objectives.

(e) A base period for allocating indirect costs is the cost accounting period during which such costs are incurred and accumulated for distribution to work performed in that period. The criteria and guidance in CAS 406 for selecting the cost accounting periods to be used in allocating indirect costs are incorporated herein for application to contracts subject to full CAS coverage. For contracts subject to modified CAS coverage and for non-CAS-covered contracts, the base period for allocating indirect costs will normally be the contractor's fiscal year. But a shorter period may be appropriate (1) for contracts in which performance involves only a minor portion of the fiscal year or (2) when it is general practice in the industry to use a shorter period. When a contract is performed over an extended period, as many base periods shall be used as are required to represent the period of contract performance.

(f) Special care should be exercised in applying the principles of paragraphs (b), (c), and (d) above when Government-owned contractor-operated (GOCO) plants are involved. The distribution of corporate, division, or branch office G&A expenses to such plants operating with little or no dependence on corporate administrative activities may require more precise cost groupings, detailed accounts screening, and carefully developed distribution bases.

FAR 31.203 reflects a considerable editorial revision of DAR 15-203 and FPR 1-15.203 but no substantive changes. Except for the necessary reminders that allocation of indirect costs to CAS-covered contracts must be in accordance with cost accounting standards, FAR retains the previous provisions, which were largely characterized by adherence to generally accepted accounting principles and practices and, with few exceptions (e.g., 31.203(c)), a general absence of rigid requirements or preferences. An indication of the practical and flexible approach is found in 31.203(b), which advises: "When substantially the same results can be achieved through less precise methods, the number and composition of cost groupings should be governed by practical considerations and should not unduly complicate the allocation."

ALLOCATION OF MANUFACTURING OVERHEAD TO FINAL COST OBJECTIVES

We provided a quotation in full of FAR 31.203 above. The predecessor DAR 15-203 and FPR 1-15.203 were similar in most major respects. The latter regulations provided that "indirect costs shall be accumulated by logical cost groupings" and cited manufacturing overhead as one of the groupings "commonly" used. These groupings should be distributed to appropriate cost objectives by selecting a distribution base that would "permit allocation of the grouping on the basis of the benefits accruing to the several cost objectives." DAR and FPR then cautioned, "The principle for selection is not to be applied so rigidly as to complicate unduly the allocation where substantially the same results are achieved through less precise methods."

There were substantial differences of opinion as to whether the guidelines set forth in the procurement regulations were adequate to achieve the ultimate objective of fairly and reasonably establishing the amounts of indirect costs allocable to government contracts. The vast majority in the private sector was joined by many procurement officials in the belief that the diversity of circumstances among industries and individual firms precluded the promulgation of more specific ground rules and that adherence to generally accepted accounting principles would provide sufficient guidance to arrive at reasonable agreements in this area. Other government officials, especially contract auditors, sharply disagreed and argued for more detailed and rigid regulations. The Comptroller General's "Report on the Feasibility of Applying Uniform Cost-Accounting Standards to Negotiated Defense Contracts" stated that allocation of indirect costs was one of the principal costing problems reported by GAO and DCAA field offices. The report further stated:

> Indirect costs, in the aggregate, represent the largest single class of expense incurred under Government contracts. The allocation of indirect costs is one of the most controversial areas in cost accounting for Government contracts and is subject to alternative approaches. *It is not a problem that can be solved by simple or rigid rules.* Indirect cost assignments of necessity cannot be as accurately determined as direct ones, but they still must be based on some demonstrable relationships between the reasons why costs were incurred and the cost objectives to which they are assigned. (Emphasis added.)

The italicized sentence reflects a thought that is found in several places in the report but was ignored by the CASB members and staff. The report did not state that the subject of indirect costs had been ignored by the writers of the procurement regulations. Indeed, as cited earlier, DAR 15-203 stated that "Indirect costs shall be accumulated by logical cost groupings with due consideration of the reasons for incurring the costs. Each grouping should be determined so as to permit distribution of the grouping on the basis of the benefits accruing to the several cost objectives."

A point that was identified in the Comptroller General's report but not specified in the procurement regulations was the necessity that each cost grouping "should contain only costs which are homogeneous—i.e., similar in the sense that they are amenable to adding together without distorting the significance of the results when spread among cost objectives on a single or common allocation base." The distance between the views of those who wrote about "logical" and those who recommended "homogeneous" cost groupings or pools was probably not a long one in concept. However, the possibilities for rigid rules and requirements for proliferation of indirect cost pools, reflected in the early versions of what was to become CAS 418, Allocation of Direct and Indirect Costs, could be seen in the following illustration contained in the Comptroller General's report: "For example, personnel-related costs, materials-related costs, and machine-related costs may not, in given situations, be logically grouped together and spread among objectives on a single common base." Considering that most manufacturing overhead pools contain all three of these categories, the example became a matter of concern to close readers of the report.

Convinced of the need to formulate standards for allocating indirect costs, the CASB moved very early and, as described in Chapter XV of this text, promulgated CAS 403, Allocation of Home Office Expenses to Segments, in December 1972. The Board early on also began its research on what was to become CAS 410, Allocation of Business Unit General and Administrative Expense. However, for a number of reasons commented upon in Chapter XV of this text, CAS 410 was not published until April 1976, almost three and one-half years later. Another lengthy period ensued before the CASB published

CAS 420, Accounting for Independent Research and Development Costs and Bid and Proposal Costs, in September 1979 (Chapter XIV of this text).

COST ACCOUNTING STANDARD 418 - ALLOCATION OF DIRECT AND INDIRECT COSTS

Background

The CASB and its staff devoted a considerable portion of its closing years to the development of CAS 418. The coverage is described as "indirect costs, including service center and overhead costs. . . ." It is obviously intended to encompass the wide area of indirect costs commonly referred to as manufacturing overhead and would also appear to provide criteria for engineering overhead. This standard completed coverage of indirect costs except for selling and marketing expenses. As described in Chapter XV of this text, a CASB Staff Issues Paper was disseminated for comment on selling and marketing expenses, but no standard relating to these expenses was ever promulgated. Had the CASB not been terminated, it is likely that a standard covering selling and marketing expenses would have been published.

CASB's First Proposal—Five Standards

The Board's first effort, published for comment in March 1978, included five proposed standards:

CAS 417—Distinguishing Between Direct and Indirect Costs

CAS 418—Allocation of Service Center Costs

CAS 419—Allocation of Material-Related Overhead Costs

CAS 420—Allocation of Manufacturing, Engineering and Comparable Overhead Costs

CAS 421—Allocation of Indirect Costs

This publication drew wide criticism from both government and industry. It did not appear to be well thought-out, and most commentators complained that the five proposed standards were replete with duplication and were unnecessarily detailed and restrictive. There was much concern that the standards would probably be implemented by DCAA to require contractors to establish numerous indirect expense pools at exorbitant cost. Commentators expressed the view that the proliferation of expense pools would not achieve more accurate contract costing and would have the serious disadvantage of destroying comparability with periods prior to the effective dates of these standards.

CASB's Second Proposal—Three Standards

About a year after the date on which comments on these standards were required, the Board reissued the Indirect Cost Allocation Standards. The July 23, 1979, version reflected consideration of many of the criticisms received, and, in some instances, revisions had been made to mitigate the detrimental effects of the initial publication.

The complete illogic of promulgating five separate standards with significant overlapping and redundancy was recognized by the Board. Although it did not move as far as we had suggested (two standards) or as CODSIA recommended (a single standard), the board did propose to cover its requirements in three standards. The transition from five to three is shown in the below tabulation:

March 16, 1978	July 23, 1979
417 - Distinguishing Between Direct and Indirect Costs.	417 - Distinguishing Between Direct and Indirect Costs.
418 - Allocation of Service Center Costs.)	418 - Allocation of Indirect Cost Pools.
421 - Allocation of Indirect Costs.)	(No. 421 deleted)
419 - Allocation of Material-Related Overhead Costs.)	419 - Allocation of Overhead Costs of Productive Functions and Activities
420 - Allocation of Manufacturing, Engineering and Comparable Overhead Costs.)	(No. 420 deleted)

Despite the improvements made by the Board, considerable concern remained that these standards would result in a proliferation of overhead pools and would have adverse effects on analyses involving comparison of prior periods. It would be difficult to find any evidence that these deleterious impacts would be in any way compensated for by comparable benefits to government or industry. As so many individual contractors and their consultants pointed out to the Board in commenting on the March 1978 proposals, maintaining fairly broad indirect cost pools tended to promote a relative stability, which facilitated forecasting. The requirement to fragment such existing indirect cost pools into many smaller ones that would be much more heavily impacted by changes in the nature of a company's business was bound to undermine forecasting capabilities. The advantages, if any, were highly theoretical. Increasing the number of indirect cost pools, in our judgment, would not appear to be beneficial for the requirement, either on the side of government or industry, to work effectively in preparing and evaluating proposals for government flexibly priced contracts.

CASB's Final Effort—One Standard

Almost a year from the date the Board proposed to cover the allocation of direct and indirect costs in three standards, it at last addressed the subject as a single standard in the final rule appearing in the *Federal Register* of May 15, 1980. The industry associations and their member firms were still unhappy with many provisions in the single standard, and some of their concerns were understandable, particularly in the light of the doubts regarding the manner in which the provisions of CAS 418 would be implemented. On the other hand, we understand that some members of the CASB staff and some officials of DCAA believed that the CASB had moved too far in the direction of flexibility. If the old view that a "good negotiated agreement" is one that leaves both sides somewhat dissatisfied is correct, CAS 418 may turn out to be the best product the Board could make considering the diametrically opposing views of both sides.

Salient Provisions of CAS 418

The Fundamental Requirements and Techniques for Application sections in CAS 418 are excerpted verbatim for the convenience of our readers.

§ 418.40 Fundamental requirements.

(a) A business unit shall have a written statement of accounting policies and practices for classifying costs as direct or indirect which shall be consistently applied.

(b) Indirect costs shall be accumulated in indirect cost pools which are homogeneous.

(c) Pooled costs shall be allocated to cost objectives in reasonable proportion to the beneficial or causal relationship of the pooled costs to cost objectives as follows: (1) If a material amount of the costs included in a cost pool are costs of management or supervision of activities involving direct labor or direct material costs, resource consumption cannot be specifically identified with cost objectives. In that circumstance, a base shall be used which is representative of the activity being managed or supervised. (2) If the cost pool does not contain a material amount of the costs of management or supervision of activities involving direct labor or direct material costs, resource consumption can be specifically identified with cost objectives. The pooled cost shall be allocated based on the specific identifiability of resource consumption with cost objectives by means of one of the following allocation bases: (i) a resource consumption measure, (ii) an output measure, or (iii) a surrogate that is representative of resources consumed. The base shall be selected in accordance with the criteria set out in § 418.50(e).

(d) To the extent that any cost allocations are required by the provisions of other Cost Accounting Standards, such allocations are not subject to the provisions of this Standard.

(e) This Standard does not cover accounting for the costs of special facilities where such costs are accounted for in separate indirect cost pools.

§ 418.50 Techniques for application.

(a) *Determination of direct cost and indirect cost.* (1) The business unit's written policy classifying costs as direct or indirect shall be in conformity with the requirements of this Standard.

(2) In accounting for direct costs a business unit shall use actual costs, except that:

(i) Standard costs for material and labor may be used as provided in 4 CFR Part 407, or

(ii) An average cost or pre-established rate for labor may be used provided that (A) the functions performed are not materially disparate and employees involved are interchangeable with respect to the functions performed, or (B) the functions performed are materially disparate but the employees involved either all work in a single production unit yielding homogeneous outputs, or perform their respective functions as an integral team.

Whenever average cost or pre-established rates for labor are used, the variances, if material, shall be disposed of at least annually by allocation to cost objectives in proportion to the costs previously allocated to these cost objectives.

(3) Labor or material costs identified specifically with one of the particular cost objectives listed in paragraph (d)(3) of this section shall be accounted for as direct labor or direct material costs.

(b) *Homogeneous indirect cost pools.* (1) An indirect cost pool is homogeneous if each significant activity whose costs are included therein has the same or a similar beneficial or causal relationship to cost objectives as the other activities whose costs are included in the cost pool. It is also homogeneous if the allocation of the costs of the activities included in the cost pool result in an allocation to cost objectives which is not materially different from the allocation that would result if the costs of the activities were allocated separately.

(2) An indirect cost pool is not homogeneous if the costs of all significant activities in the cost pool do not have the same or a similar beneficial or causal relationship to cost objectives and, if the costs were allocated separately, the resulting allocation would be materially different. The determination of materiality shall be made using the criteria provided in 4 CFR 331.71.

(3) A homogeneous indirect cost pool shall include all indirect costs identified with the activity to which the pool relates.

(c) *Change in Allocation Base.* No change in an existing indirect cost pool allocation base is required if the allocation resulting from the existing base does not differ materially from the allocation that results from the use of the base determined to be most appropriate in accordance with the criteria set forth in paragraphs (d) and (e) of this section. The determination of materiality shall be made using the criteria provided in 4 CFR 331.71.

(d) *Allocation measures for an indirect cost pool which includes a material amount of the costs of management or supervision of activities involving direct labor or direct material costs.* (1) The costs of the management or supervision of activities involving direct labor or direct material costs do not have a direct and definitive relationship to the benefiting cost objectives and cannot be allocated on measures of a specific beneficial or causal relationship. In that circumstance, the base selected to measure the allocation of the pooled costs to cost objectives shall be a base representative of the activity being managed or supervised.

(2) The base used to represent the activity being managed or supervised shall be determined by the application of the criteria below. All significant elements of the selected base shall be included.

(i) A direct labor hour base or direct labor cost base shall be used, whichever in the aggregate is more likely to vary in proportion to the costs included in the cost pool being allocated, except that

(ii) A machine-hour base is appropriate if the costs in the cost pool are comprised predominantly of facility-related costs, such as depreciation, maintenance, and utilities, or

(iii) A units-of-production base is appropriate if there is common production of comparable units, or

(iv) A material cost base is appropriate if the activity being managed or supervised is a material-related activity.

(3) Indirect cost pools which include material amounts of the costs of management or supervision of activities involving direct labor or direct material costs shall be allocated to:

(i) Final cost objectives;

(ii) Goods produced for stock or product inventory;

(iii) Independent research and development and bid and proposal projects;

(iv) Cost centers used to accumulate costs identified with a process cost system (i.e., process cost centers);

(v) Goods or services produced or acquired for other segments of the contractor and for other cost objectives of a business unit; and

(vi) Self-construction, fabrication, betterment, improvement, or installation of tangible capital assets.

(e) *Allocation measures for indirect cost pools that do not include material amounts of the costs of management or supervision of activities involving direct labor or direct material costs.* Homogeneous indirect cost pools of this type have a direct and definitive relationship between the activities in the pool and benefiting cost objectives. The pooled costs shall be allocated using an appropriate measure of resource consumption. This determination shall be made in accordance with the following criteria taking into consideration the individual circumstances:

(1) The best representation of the beneficial or causal relationship between an indirect cost pool and the benefiting cost objectives is a measure of resource consumption of the activities of the indirect cost pool.

(2)(i) If consumption measures are unavailable or impractical to ascertain, the next best representation of the beneficial or causal relationship for allocation is a measure of the output of the activities of the indirect cost pool. Thus, the output is substituted for a direct measure of the consumption of resources.

(ii) The use of the basic unit of output will not reflect the proportional consumption of resources in circumstances in which the level of resource consumption varies among the units of output produced. Where a material difference will result, either the output measure shall be modified or more than one output measure shall be used to reflect the resources consumed to perform the activitiy.

(3) If neither resources consumed nor output of the activities can be measured practically, a surrogate that varies in proportion to the services received shall be used to measure the resources consumed. Generally, such surrogates measure the activity of the cost objectives receiving the service.

(4) Allocation of indirect cost pools which benefit one another may be accomplished by use of (i) the cross-allocation (reciprocal) method, (ii) the sequential method, or (iii) another method the results of which approximate those achieved by either of the methods in paragraph (e)(4)(i) or paragraph (e)(4)(ii).

(5) Where the activities represented by an indirect cost pool provide services to two or more cost objectives simultaneously, the cost of such services shall be prorated between or among the cost objectives in reasonable proportion to the beneficial or causal relationship between the services and the cost objectives.

(f) *Special allocation.* Where a particular cost objective in relation to other cost objectives receives significantly more or less benefit from an indirect cost pool than would be reflected by the allocation of such costs using a base determined pursuant to paragraphs (d) and (e) of this section, the Government and contractor may agree to a special allocation from that indirect cost pool to the particular cost objective commensurate with the benefits received. The amount of a special allocation to any such cost objective made pursuant to such an agreement shall be excluded from the indirect cost pool and the particular cost objective's allocation base data shall be excluded from the base used to allocate the pool.

(g) *Use of pre-established rates for indirect costs.* (1) Pre-established rates, based on either forecasted actual or standard cost, may be used in allocating an indirect cost pool.

(2) Pre-established rates shall reflect the costs and activities anticipated for the cost accounting period except as provided in paragraph (g)(3) of this section. Such pre-established rates shall be reviewed at least annually, and revised as necessary to reflect the anticipated conditions.

(3) The contracting parties may agree on pre-established rates which are not based on costs and activities anticipated for a cost accounting period. The contractor shall have and consistently apply written policies for the establishment of these rates.

(4) Under paragraph (g)(2) and (g)(3) of this section where variances of a cost accounting period are material, these variances shall be disposed of by allocating them to cost objectives in proportion to the costs previously allocated to these cost objectives by use of the pre-established rates.

(5) If pre-established rates are revised during a cost accounting period and if the variances accumulated to the time of the revision are significant, the costs allocated to that time shall be adjusted to the

amounts which would have been allocated using the revised preestablished rates.

Supplementary Information and Prefatory Comments

A review of the prefatory comments accompanying CAS 418 makes it abundantly clear that the many written comments and oral presentations to the Board, expressing deep concern about unnecessary proliferation of expense pools and changes in cost accounting practices and the substantial costs that such changes would generate without producing any practical impact on government contract costs, were ultimately clearly understood. Comment (2) states:

... the Board recognizes that this Standard may have a pervasive impact on contractor accounting systems. Because of this, the Board here and in the Standard is emphasizing the necessity to evaluate any perceived need for change in cost accounting practices in terms of materiality. The need to evaluate the materiality of a change in cost accounting practice applies to all provisions of the Standard. It is not limited to those particular provisions of the Standard in which materiality is mentioned for emphasis.

These strong comments certainly indicate the Board's sharing of industry's concern about numerous changes and proliferation of overhead pools, and the statement cited above surely must be considered as guidance to future CAS staff implementation, DCAA auditors and contracting officers to think long and carefully before concluding that CAS 418 requires a change in cost accounting practice.

Efforts were made to persuade the Board to define materiality in terms of the net effect on the cost of the totality of government contracts in relation to the cost of implementing any accounting change pursuant to the standard. The Board refused to go this far, and, in our own personal judgment, it could not accede to these recommendations without finding itself in conflict with the terms of appropriation statutes. While it did not accede to this recommendation, the Board reiterated in several different ways the basic thought that it "intends that the creation of additional indirect cost pools or change of allocation base will be required only if the changes result in materially different allocations of cost."

Requirement for Written Policies to Distinguish Between Direct and Indirect Costs

CAS 418.40(a) and 418.50(a) require business units to have written statements of accounting policies and practices, and to consistently apply them for classifying costs as direct or indirect. These provisions were inserted in place of the restrictive and rigid criteria initially contained in CAS 417, criteria that drew heavy criticism from many commentators. If DCAA and the government contracting officers adopt a reasonable position on these provisions, it would appear to us that a Disclosure Statement adjudged as adequate should fulfill the requirements of these paragraphs with no further action required.

Average and Pre-Established Direct Labor Rates

A number of objections had been raised to the provision in the previously proposed CAS 417 which required as a prerequisite for the use of average or pre-established direct labor rates that the resources be "interchangeable." The Board was persuaded that the interchangeability requirement was too strict, particularly in view of the likelihood that the term might be interpreted to mean "identical" when implemented by the government. What industry could see here was the creation of many more labor rates. In conformance with its less rigid posture, the Board withdrew this requirement, and CAS 418.50(a)(2)(B) permits two groupings in addition to interchangeability. Average or pre-established direct labor rates may now be set for a group of employees who produce homogeneous output or form an integral team.

Blanket Costs

The proposed CAS 417 would have permitted labor or material costs accumulated in intermediate cost objectives and reallocated to final cost objectives as direct costs only if they were allocated by a measure of resource consumption or a measure of output. Most commentators believed this requirement too restrictive and were concerned that, as implemented, all blanket costs would be classified as indirect costs. Here again, the CASB saw the light and removed the requirement that blanket costs, in order to be classified as direct costs, must be allocated on the basis of direct measures of consumption or output.

Materiality

As mentioned earlier in discussing the Board's previous efforts on standards for direct and indirect cost allocation, industry's greatest concern was that the apparent rigidity and severity of the requirements of the proposed standards along with a heavy-handed implementation would require extensive and costly changes in cost accounting practices and proliferation of indirect cost pools. To alleviate this well-based apprehension, the Board had proposed a 5% materiality test. However, most commentators expressed serious reservations about the practicality of such a test or, for that matter, the use of any percentage. The question of materiality is an old and familiar one in the accounting field and has never been satisfactorily resolved because of the inherent subjectivity of arriving at such a determination.

The Board's final conclusion was to apply 4 CFR 331.71, which establishes materiality criteria. References to 331.71 are found in several sections of the prefatory comments as well as in the standard itself (418.50(a)(3), (b)(2), and (c)). The basic thinking that changes to cost accounting practices should not be required unless material differences in cost allocations would result permeates the standard and prefatory comments, and we hope that this point is well understood by the government officials charged with implementing the standard.

Homogeneous Indirect Cost Pools

The requirement of the previous proposed standard that an indirect cost pool must be homogeneous was viewed widely as an unnecessarily severe requirement and one susceptible to misunderstanding. Industry was persuaded that overzealous implementation of this requirement would result in an unnecessary proliferation of indirect cost pools.

The final rule provides in 418.50(b) that "an indirect cost pool is homogeneous if each significant activity whose costs are included therein has the same or a similar beneficial or causal relationship to the cost objective as the other activities whose costs are included in the cost pool." Materiality is stressed again, and an indirect cost pool is also considered homogeneous "if the allocation of the costs of the activities included in the cost pool result in an allocation to cost objectives which is not materially different from the allocation that would result if the cost of the activities were allocated separately."

Hierarchy of Allocation Bases

In our analysis of the previous effort by the Board, we noted that the hierarchy of allocation measures was based on a criterion that required the government to be satisfied that "the allocation base used is the best available representation of resource consumption." This term bothered many commentators, some of whom expressed the view that greater flexibility should be permitted among the alternative allocation bases that the Board listed in its July 23, 1979, version.

The entire subject of hierarchy of allocation bases is particularly sensitive in the case of CAS 410, which does not provide for any hierarchy but for which a hierarchy, total cost input, was nevertheless jammed into the implementation by DOD, by DCAA, and by W.G. 78-21. (See Chapter XV of this text.)

In the case of CAS 418, the Board's prefatory comments noted its view that the establishment of a hierarchy is essential to assure the basic concept of cost allocations. However, although it did not in many of the other standards, the Board for the first time seemed to be really paying attention to the views of the regulated defense industry and noted here the validity of the concerns expressed by many commentators. To reduce the rigidity and the undoubted future controversies to come, the Board substituted a new 418.50(e) in which the phrase "an appropriate measure of resource consumption" was substituted for "the best available representation of resource consumption." Paragraph 418.50(e) also provides expanded guidance with recognition of availability and quality of the data on which potential measures are based. 418.50(e) will require careful study.

The problems of the selection of an allocation base in the heirarchy of allocation bases raised many questions and criticisms with respect to the Board's July 23, 1979, three-standard proposal. Considerable clarification was required. In an attempt to clarify its objectives and minimize future implementation problems, the Board carefully rewrote certain sections of the standard, particularly 418.50(d) and (e).

Where an indirect cost pool includes a material amount of costs of management for supervision of activities involving direct labor or direct material costs, the base used should be one that is representative of the activity being managed or supervised (see 418.50(d)(3)). Where indirect cost pools do not include material amounts of the costs of management or supervision of activities involving direct labor or direct material costs, such a base would not be appropriate and 418.50(e) would provide for the use of an appropriate measure of resource consumption.

Casual Sales

We previously commented upon the criticism of the March 1978 five-version standard, which required that all costs of such service centers as special facilities would need to be allocated on a pro rata basis to all final cost objectives even where some of these objectives consisted of casual sales when these facilities were established primarily for certain contracts or classes of contracts. We noted, too, that this area has been a controversial issue for many years and has not been directly addressed in the government procurement regulations. Previous disputes required resolution by Boards of Contract Appeals and federal courts. The July 23, 1979, version was not responsive to industry recommendations that the Board consider this subject more carefully, and many commentators again recommended that casual sales of services in these instances be costed at other than full cost.

It is evident from paragraph (12) of the prefatory comments that the Board found itself unable to resolve this problem. It finally concluded that "for sales to be characterized as casual, they must be an immaterial part of the total activities of a cost pool." Thereupon, the Board reiterated its position that it will not deal with immaterial matters and concluded that, if the sales identified are casual or immaterial, "the contracting parties can determine the acceptability of the costing methods to be used." On the other hand, "where sales represent a material part of the total activities of a cost pool, they cannot be deemed to be casual." In these latter instances, the sales would be required to be costed at full cost.

Productive Activities

The terms "productive functions" and "productive activities" generated considerable confusion and concern, particularly because of the apprehension that, as set out in the previous versions of this standard, there appeared substantial possibilities for unnecessary proliferation of overhead pools and unwarranted government requirements for changes in cost accounting practices. In the final rule, these terms were at last eliminated. The emphasis is now on the concept of the homogeneity of indirect cost pools as set forth in 418.50(b).

Special Facilities

Accounting for the cost of special facilities has posed continual controversy between the government and industry. Absent specific guidance in the government procurement regulations, decisions on these controversies required settlement by Boards of Contract Appeals and courts.

The CASB and its staff certainly devoted sufficient time in the study of accounting for the cost of such special facilities as space chambers, wind tunnels, reactors, etc. And yet a sufficient consensus was not reached, and the Board failed to bite the bullet on this accounting problem. Prefatory comment (14) closes with the statement: "The board recognizes a need for particular attention to the accounting for the limited number of special facilities involved and has established a project in this area to review the cost allocation issues." However, the CASB did not survive long enough to issue a formal rule on this subject.

Prefatory Comment (15)

Prefatory comment (15), while not providing much in the way of specific guidance, is significant and should be carefully studied to prepare for the possible approaches that may be taken by different contract auditors in implementing it.

Prefatory comment (15) consists of two paragraphs. The first appears to establish the Board's conclusion that the many concerns expressed about the provisions of prior versions of this standard resulting in unnecessary proliferation of overhead pools were considered valid. Accordingly, the Board eliminated various references that seemed to require too much specificity, such as the definition of "productive activity" and the specific references to the treatment of special facilities, purchased labor, and overtime premiums and shift differentials in allocation bases. The second paragraph continues in the same vein and announces that the Board "decided to remove the references to those terms and provisions." However, the pull and tug between the more reasonable Board members on the one hand, and the hardliners and most of the staff on the other, can be seen in the closing sentences of prefatory paragraph (15). Although prefatory comments certainly do not carry the same force and effect as the specific provisions of the standard, they are used as guidelines, and industry was concerned with the form of implementation the DCAA would take based on its reading of the last two sentences of prefatory paragraph (15):

> The elimination of these terms and provisions does not reflect a change in position concerning the appropriate accounting for the cost involved. Rather, in consolidating the proposed 417, 418 and 419 into a single CAS 418 being promulgated today, the Board is providing a more general Standard incorporating the basic concept of cost allocation previously established in the *Board's Restatement of Objectives, Policies and Concepts.*

Discussions with DOD officials indicated that they believed the Board retreated considerably from its initial rigid requirements, which threatened to impose a large proliferation in overhead pools and change in cost accounting practices.

DCAA Guidance to Its Staff on CAS 418

Although DOD procurement officials found no need for publishing any implementation or other guidance relating to this standard, DCAA concluded that its auditors required direction in handling this standard, and policy guidance was issued in the form of a headquarters memorandum on August 25, 1980.

The guidance recognizes the similarity of CAS 418 and DAR. However, whereas many DOD contracting officials believe there is no tangible difference at all, DCAA accepts the similarity only as regards the "conceptual basis" and suggests that "the standard goes beyond the requirements of DAR and provides more definitive guidance for allocation base selection."

An important issue relates to the requirement of CAS 418 for a written statement of policy for classifying costs as direct or indirect. In our opinion, an adequate Disclosure Statement should serve this purpose, and we were gratified to note that the DCAA guidance concurred in this view. Of course, nothing comes all that easy from the contract auditors, and the guidance states that "... the Disclosure Statement *may* be sufficient to meet this requirement. It should be reviewed before requesting additional details from the contractor." One point is certain, if the DCAA auditor requests the written policy statement, the contractor should ascertain whether the auditor has reviewed the Disclosure Statement and ask for specific reasons why the statement previously judged adequate is not sufficient for this purpose.

We were pleased to note comments of the following kind in the DCAA interim guidance:

The creation of additional indirect cost pools should be required only if the changes result in materially different allocations of cost to cost objectives.

Even with regard to the fundamental requirement for homogeneous cost pools, the Board has said that a pool may be considered homogeneous if the separate allocation of costs of the dissimilar activities would not result in materially different allocations of cost to cost objectives.

Where there are no audit problems with the existing structure, it is anticipated that CAS 418 will not require further review of indirect cost pools. However, the allocation base for those pools should be reviewed for compliance with the requirements of the standard.

The audit agency's interim guidance, however, as might be expected, does contain certain instructions and suggestions that have caused some controversies. CAS 418, for example, is cited as providing "authoritative support and criteria" where there are current "problems." This provision is acceptable so long as DCAA auditors do not seek to twist the provisions of this standard to support a position they previously pursued without convincing the contractor or contracting officer. This DCAA interim guidance includes a "compliance review control schedule," the full text of which is provided at the end of the Guidance Memorandum for the information of our readers. It has been found useful in anticipating the scope of the DCAA review.

The DCAA Guidance Memorandum and Review Control Schedule follow:

CAS 418 which was promulgated by the Cost Accounting Standards Board on 15 May 1980 provides for a 20 September 1980 effective date. The standard must be followed by each contractor on or after the start of the second fiscal year beginning after receipt of a contract to which the standard is applicable.

An outline of the standard, as promulgated, is presented on the Compliance Review Control Schedule Format—Enclosure 1, to enable advance planning regarding its implementation.

CAS 418 requires that costs be consistently classified as direct or indirect, establishes criteria for accumulating indirect costs in indirect cost pools, and sets forth guidance for allocating indirect cost pools.

The standard's fundamental requirements provide that (a) a business unit have a written statement of accounting policies and practices for classifying costs as direct or indirect which shall be consistently applied; (b) indirect costs be accumulated in indirect cost pools which are homogeneous; and (c) pooled costs shall be allocated to cost objectives in reasonable proportion to the beneficial or causal relationships of the pooled costs to cost objectives. While the CAS and the DAR are similar with regard to the conceptual basis, the standard goes beyond the requirements of the DAR and provides more definitive guidance for allocation base selection.

The requirement for a written statement of policies for classifying costs as direct or indirect is a critical aspect for assuring consistent implementation of this standard. Information disclosed by the contractor in Item 3.1.0 of the Disclosure Statement may be sufficient to meet this requirement. It should be reviewed before requesting additional detail from the contractor.

In promulgating CAS 418, the Board emphasized evaluating any perceived need for change in cost accounting practices in terms of materiality. The materiality consideration should encompass all of the criteria in Part 331.71 of the CAS Board's rules and regulations. The creation of additional indirect cost pools should be required only if the changes will result in materially different allocations of cost. Even with regard to the fundamental requirement for homogeneous cost pools, the Board has said that a pool may be considered homogeneous if the separate allocation of costs of the dissimilar activities would not result in a materially different allocation of cost to cost objectives. Where there are no audit problems with the existing structure, it is anticipated that CAS 418 will not require further review of indirect cost pools. However, the allocation base for those pools should be reviewed for compliance with the requirements of the standard. Where current problems regarding the allocation of direct and/or indirect costs do exist, however, CAS 418 provides authoritative support and criteria that may be helpful in formulating an acceptable methodology. In addition, where the contractor is establishing new indirect cost pools, careful attention should be directed toward the pool structure and allocation base to assure conformity with the standard.

The first step in applying the standard's criteria for allocating pooled costs is to determine whether the pool includes a material amount of management or supervision costs relating to activities involving direct labor or material costs.

If the cost pool *does* contain a material amount of the costs of management or supervision of activities involving direct labor or direct material, the standard specifies criteria for selecting a base representative of the activity being supervised. Allocation bases include a direct labor hour or dollar base, a machine-hour base, a units-of-production base, or a material cost base, depending on which best relates to pooled costs of the managing activity. An example would be engineering direct labor cost as a base for allocating the engineering overhead cost pool or direct material input cost as a base for allocating the material-handling overhead pool.

If the cost pool *does not* contain material amounts of the costs of management or supervision of activities involving direct labor or direct material, the standard specifies criteria for selecting a base representing an appropriate measure of resource consumption. The standard establishes a hierarchy of acceptable representations of beneficial or causal relationship, the best representation being a direct measure of the resource consumption of the activities of the indirect cost pool. If such direct measures of resource consumption are unavailable or impractical to ascertain, the next best representation is a measure of the output of the activities of the indirect cost pool. If neither resources consumed nor output of the activities can be measured practically, the standard permits a surrogate that varies in proportion to the services received to be used as a measure of resources consumed. For example, an ideal measure of resource consumption attributable to a central reproduction cost center would be equipment usage (hours). However, the production equipment may not have time meters for purposes of measurement; therefore, the use of such a base for allocation of the cost center would be impractical. As an alternative, the next best representation of beneficial or causal relationship should be selected. A base consisting of the number of reproduced pages might be selected as an appropriate allocation measure of the output of the activities of the central reproduction cost center. However, if for some reason it is not practical to measure the number of pages reproduced for each requesting activity, a surrogate that varies in proportion to the services rendered may be used to measure the resources consumed. Such a surrogate could be based upon the number of personnel in each department where past experience has demonstrated that the number of requisitions vary in reasonable proportion to departmental population, thereby constituting a reasonable measure of the activity of the cost objectives receiving the service.

It should be noted that CAS 418 applies the same criteria for average and preestablished direct labor rates that are used in CAS 407. In addition, provisions are included governing variances and other aspects of preestablished indirect cost rates.

COMPLIANCE REVIEW CONTROL SCHEDULE

Requirements

I. Written statement of policies and practices for classifying costs as direct or indirect.

    A. Actual costs shall be used in accounting for direct costs; except:

        1. Standard costs may be used per CAS 407

        2. Average or preestablished labor rates may be used if:

            a. Functions performed are not disparate and employees are interchangeable with respect to function; or

            b. Functions performed are disparate but employees either work in a single production unit yielding homogeneous outputs, or perform their functions as an integral team.

c. The variances, if material, are disposed of at least annually by allocation to cost objectives in proportion to the costs previously allocated.

B. Labor and material costs shall be accounted for as direct labor or direct material costs if specifically identifiable to any of the following cost objectives:

1. Final cost objectives

2. Goods produced for stock or product inventory.

3. Independent research and development and bid and proposals projects.

4. Cost centers for accumulating costs identified with a process cost system.

5. Goods or services produced or acquired for other segments and other cost objectives of a business unit.

6. Self-construction, improvement or installation of tangible capital assets.

II. Indirect costs shall be accumulated in homogenous indirect cost pools.

A. Each significant activity whose costs are included in the pool must have the same or similar beneficial or causal relationships to cost objectives; or

B. The allocation of costs of activities included in the cost pool result in an allocation to cost objectives that is not materially different from that which would result if costs of the activities were allocated separately.

C. A homogenous cost pool shall include all direct costs identified with the activity to which the pool relates.

III. Pooled costs shall be allocated to cost objectives in reasonable proportion to the beneficial or causal relationship of the pooled costs to cost objectives:

A. If a material amount of the costs included in an indirect cost pool are costs of management or supervision of activities involving direct labor or direct material costs, a base shall be used which is representative of the activity being managed or supervised, determined as follows:

1. Direct Labor Hour or Cost Base - Whichever is likely to vary in proportion to the costs included in the pool;

2. Machine-Hour Base - Appropriate if the pool costs are predominately facility-related costs, such as depreciation, maintenance and utilities.

3. Units of Production Base - Appropriate if there is common production.

4. Material Cost Base - Appropriate if the activity being managed or supervised is a material related activity.

B. If the indirect cost pool does *not* contain a material amount of the costs of management or supervision of activities involving direct labor or direct material costs, the pooled costs shall be allocated on the basis of specific identifiability of resource consumption with cost objectives by means of one of the following bases:

1. Resource Consumption Measure - Best representation of beneficial or causal relationship.

2. Output Measure - Next best representation if consumption measures are unavailable or impractical to ascertain as a measure of the output of the activities of the cost pool; however, where the level of resource consumption varies among the units of output produced, and a material difference will result, the output measure shall be modified or more than one output measure shall be used.

3. Surrogate - If neither resource consumption nor output of the activities can be measured practically, a base that varies in proportion to the services received shall be used.

C. Allocation of indirect cost pools that benefit one another may be accomplished by the cross-allocation (reciprocal) method, the sequential method, or another method that produces comparable results.

D. Special Allocation - Government and contractor may agree to a special allocation from an indirect cost pool to a particular cost objective commensurate with benefits received.

E. Preestablished rates may be used in allocating an indirect cost pool; however:

1. Must be reviewed at least annually, and revised as necessary.

2. Material variances must be disposed of by allocation to cost objectives in proportion to the costs previously allocated.

3. If based on other than costs and activities anticipated for the cost accounting period, contracting party agreement in conformity with written and consistently followed policy must be evident.

COST PRINCIPLES FOR MANUFACTURING EXPENSES

This chapter essentially addresses controls and allocations of manufacturing overhead. Chapter XVII of this text, Application of Government Contract Cost Principles to Specific Costs and Expenses, describes the treatment accorded specific manufacturing expenses, including those related to the following:

Automatic data processing equipment leasing

Depreciation, including CAS 409

Employee morale, health, welfare, etc.

Gains and losses on disposition of depreciable property or other capital assets

Idle facilities and idle capacity

Insurance and indemnification, including CAS 416

Labor relations

Maintenance and repair

Indirect material

Plant protection

Plant reconversion

Rental

Special tooling and special test equipment

Transportation

In addition to the above, Chapter XVIII of this text, Compensation for Personal Services, includes considerable commentary relating to compensation of employees engaged in contractors' manufacturing operations, and discusses CAS 412 and 413 on pension costs and CAS 415 on deferred compensation.

Chapter XIV

Accounting Methods and Controls for Engineering Overhead

(Including Manufacturing and Production Engineering, Independent Research and Development, and Bid and Proposal Costs)

"Engineering as an industrial cost" is too broad a term for successful discussion. For the purposes of the ensuing comments, a distinction is made between engineering operations performed concurrently and side-by-side with production, termed manufacturing and production engineering, and that engineering which is further removed and which at times becomes a separate function, called research, development, and experimental engineering. Because of their close relationship to research and development costs, bid and proposal costs are also addressed in this chapter.

MANUFACTURING AND PRODUCTION ENGINEERING

Manufacturing and production engineering may be divided into two general phases. One relates to the problems involved in planning the most efficient plant layout, over-all methods of production, and related efforts of benefit to all products manufactured. The other phase is less general and is identified closely with specific products or processes. In either case, production engineering is generally performed by technical personnel working in the factory under the control of or in very close liaison with the production people.

The question treated here is the determination of a fair method of absorbing production engineering costs so as to recover them in the selling price of the products sold, with particular emphasis on procedures considered appropriate for government contracts.

Some firms provide for a segregation of manufacturing and production engineering salaries in their payroll distributions and, perhaps, a segregation of engineering department supplies. These accounts are contained among all other manufacturing overhead expenses. A more fully developed accounting system provides for the establishment of an engineering department and the accumulation of all salaries, wages, supplies, etc., as well as assessments for rent, light, heat, and power. The latter method is, of course, to be preferred unless the engineering costs are negligible in amount.

Assuming a logical and precise distribution of expenses is made so that the engineering department contains the total engineering direct labor and indirect expenses properly allocable to the production engineering function,

353

the next question relates to the method of recovering total engineering costs amortized over the products manufactured and sold. The most accurate, although not always the most practical, method contemplates allocations measured by actual services rendered. This may be accomplished by establishing a work order for each project assigned to or requested of the engineering department. This work order would indicate the department or product that will be the recipient of the work. All the direct time of the engineers employed on such projects should be charged thereto, as well as any materials or supplies, if substantial in amount. To the actual cost of labor and materials, if any, there can be added a pro rata share of the engineering department overhead, allocated to the various projects in the ratio of direct engineering hours. This method should accomplish the allocation, in an appropriate manner, of at least the greatest share of engineering costs to the products securing the benefits of the related services.

There will generally be certain functions of the production engineering department that represent projects which are not directly identifiable with any specific product or project. These costs also must be recovered. The allocation of such costs presents another problem which, however, will not be too significant if the substantial portion of the engineering costs has been allocated by the method outlined above.

The unallocated residue expenses may be apportioned to all operations reasonably expected to benefit from the services on any basis that can be sustained as a fair distribution in the circumstances. Methods employed include (1) total engineering costs allocated directly, (2) direct factory labor, and (3) direct factory costs. It is of course understood that the method employed must be based on a careful study of the existing conditions.

This category of engineering costs seldom introduces major problems with regard to cost determinations under government contracts except where government officials fail to distinguish correctly between manufacturing and production engineering and independent research and development costs. The provisions of the current cost principles are cited below (FAR 31.205-25).

31.205-25 Manufacturing and production engineering costs.

(a) The costs of manufacturing and production engineering effort as described in (1) through (4) below are all allowable:

(1) Developing and deploying new or improved materials, systems, processes, methods, equipment, tools and techniques that are or are expected to be used in producing products or services;

(2) Developing and deploying pilot production lines;

(3) Improving current production functions, such as plant layout, production scheduling and control, methods and job analysis, equipment capabilities and capacities, inspection techniques, and tooling analysis (including tooling design and application improvements); and

(4) Material and manufacturing producibility analysis for production suitability and to optimize manufacturing processes, methods, and techniques.

(b) This cost principle does not cover:

(1) Basic and applied research effort (as defined in 31.205-18(a)) related to new technology, materials, systems, processes, methods, equipment, tools and techniques. Such technical effort is governed by 31.205-18, Independent research and development costs; and

(2) Development effort for manufacturing or production materials, systems, processes, methods, equipment, tools and techniques that are intended for sale is also governed by 31.205-18.

(c) Where manufacturing or production development costs are capitalized or required to be capitalized under the contractor's capitalization policies, allowable cost will be determined in accordance with the requirements of 31.205-11, Depreciation.

MANUFACTURING AND PRODUCTION ENGINEERING COSTS v. INDEPENDENT RESEARCH AND DEVELOPMENT COSTS

Most contractors engaged in manufacturing of sophisticated products in the electronics, aerospace, and other industries expend considerable effort in acquiring and improving their manufacturing technology. These costs, frequently originating in commercial operations and ultimately benefiting government contracts, are variously classified as manufacturing engineering, production engineering, manufacturing technology, etc. Sometimes such expenses are readily identifiable and clearly segregated in the books of account; other times they are more difficult to specifically identify.

A problem common to this general cost category is the inclination of some government contracting, technical, and audit people to fail to understand their nature and to misclassify them as independent research and development (IR&D) costs.

Despite the need recognized in government and industry alike for continued incentives for increased expenditures in IR&D, unrealistic legislation and government regulations have prevented the government from bearing its fair share of IR&D costs when incurred by government contractors. As a result of the artificial ceilings, detrimental to government and business as well, the level of IR&D continues to fall.

The problems with IR&D have been aggravated by the tendencies mentioned above for government field people to misclassify manufacturing, production and engineering as IR&D. The gravity of this error was underscored in a policy guidance issued by the Defense Department to the Army, Navy, Air Force, DLA, and DCAA. In a memorandum dated September 25, 1979, the Deputy Undersecretary (Acquisition Policy) identified the problem and advised DOD personnel that manufacturing technology does not generally fit into the IR&D category. He admonished the military departments, DLA, and DCAA that, when contractors include manufacturing technology products under such categories as manufacturing and production engineering overhead, this classification should be accepted by the government "and we consider this to be appropriate, except when the projects clearly fall within the definition of IR&D." Because of the significance of the stated Department of Defense policy, we have included the text of the aforementioned September 25, 1979, memorandum.

SUBJECT: Classification of Manufacturing and Production Engineering

It has come to our attention that some confusion exists regarding the inclusion, in IR&D, of effort falling under the general heading of manufacturing technology. Some contractors allege that field personnel are pressing for classification, as IR&D, many items that properly belong in other cost classifications such as manufacturing and production engineering. To the extent that such misclassification takes place, IR&D costs will be overstated, and since the allowance of IR&D costs if limited by ceilings, the net effect is that contractors must either take greater cost disallowances or reduce the effort they put into production engineering. In terms of constant dollars, IR&D has already fallen below the level of several years ago, and any policies that tend to cause further reductions are very undesirable. With respect to manufacturing and production engineering, we have been striving for some time to encourage contractors to increase their effort in this area. Forcing these costs unnecessarily into IR&D will tend to reduce rather than increase this desirable cost reducing work.

Some years ago when we were developing the present cost principle on IR&D, we asked DCAA to sample and report on various types of technical effort that were being performed outside IR&D. As a result of that review, which continued over several years, we developed a definition for IR&D that encompassed all types of effort that fit into the IR&D category. Manufacturing technology did not generally fit into the IR&D arena, because it does not normally relate to product lines intended to be sold to a company's customers. At this time we see no reason to revise the policies that were adopted in the late 1960's and were understood by those involved with IR&D in the DOD, NASA, the GAO, and the U.S. Congress.

We understand that some companies may follow a practice of putting certain manufacturing technology projects into their IR&D program. It is not our intent to preclude this. Generally, however, it is the practice of contractors to include such costs in other overhead accounts, and we consider this to be appropriate, except when the projects clearly fall within the definition of IR&D.

DCAA AUDIT GUIDANCE ON MANUFACTURING AND PRODUCTION ENGINEERING

The Contract Audit Manual (CAM) addresses the subject essentially in connection with audits of incurred indirect costs, where the guidance centers on allocation of overhead, and in connection with reviews of estimates and proposals, where the discussion primarily treats such costs as direct charges.

Audit of Incurred Indirect Costs

The allocation of indirect engineering costs is included within the general discussion of allocation methods found in Section 6-606 of the current edition of the CAM. In the 1983 edition of the CAM, however, the allocation of engineering overhead was segregated. Because the philosophy has not changed and the prior treatment allows us to focus exclusively on the allocation of engineering overhead, we have quoted from the 1983 edition. CAM 6-603.3, Allocation of Engineering Overhead, provided:

a. The engineering cost pool is closely related to engineering labor. The usual basis for allocating this overhead category is either engineering direct labor costs or engineering direct labor hours.

b. When direct engineering labor cost is the basis for prorating the related engineering costs, adequate tests should be made of the salary or wage levels of employees engaged on Government contracts as compared to the over-all engineering salary and wage structure. If the average wage of employees engaged on Government contracts is substantially at variance with wages for the over-all operations, the direct labor cost method ordinarily will not be acceptable. In such instances, the auditor should consider using a direct engineering labor hour base.

c. The auditor should review and analyze direct and indirect engineering salary and wage accounts to ascertain whether there is consistent treatment between Government and commercial production. When salaries or wages of engineering personnel devoted to the contractor's own engineering projects have been charged to overhead accounts or have otherwise been excluded from engineering direct labor bases by the contractor, such costs should be reclassified to the direct engineering labor base.

d. When the contractor's accounting system does not provide for the segregation of engineering expenses from the total manufacturing pool, and when engineering costs represent significant costs to the Government, the auditor should make appropriate tests to determine the equity of the combined allocation, and if not equitable, separate rates should be determined.

e. When engineering costs are accumulated separately and allocated to cost objectives on a basis other than as described in a. above, sufficient tests should be made to establish the propriety of such basis. Use the applicable contract cost principles (such as DAR 15-201.4 and 15-203) and, if applicable, Cost Accounting Standard 418 as criteria. Special considerations in audit of overhead allocations to facilities contracts are discussed in 6-607.4.

Reviews of Estimates and Proposals

CAM 9-605.1, in the 1987 edition, provides the following audit guidance on engineering as direct costs:

Engineering costs included in other direct costs generally fall into two categories—design and production. The type of engineering effort included in each of these categories depends on the individual contractor's practices. The use of the two terms should be considered in relation to the definitions and applications of individual contractors. Because engineering effort required for a specific procurement of a complex product or for research and development involves technical determinations, assistance from Government technical personnel should be solicited in evaluating proposed engineering man-hour estimates. An understanding of the various fields of engineering specialists is important when fashioning requests for technical specialist assistance. The major engineering fields, industrial, mechanical, electrical, chemical, civil and several sub-specialties are discussed in Appendix D-300.4.

(a) Design Engineering

Data accumulated in the contractor's accounting system or adjunct statistical records which may be helpful to the auditor in evaluating estimates for design engineering include (1) the total number of basic design hours expended on previous contracts of similar complexity, (2) the number of various types of drawings required, and the average number of hours expended per type of drawing for prior contracts of varying degrees of complexity, (3) the percentage factors for support engineering (the direct engineering effort other than that expended by detailed designers working in the design department) and (4) percentage factors for engineering effort incidental to changes made during production which represent refinements of the product to attain improved performance. The auditor should be alert to the fact that the cost of design changes and revisions which are effected during the production of the contract may be commingled with production engineering.

(b) Production Engineering

Production engineering generally represents engineering effort expended during the life of a contract, and commences with the completion of the initial design. Initial design is usually segregated from other engineering effort in the contractor's accounting or statistical records. However, as indicated in the previous paragraph, design changes for which costs are not segregated may occur during the life of the contract. In evaluating the reasonableness of the estimate for production engineering, the auditor should review the contractor's methods and supporting data. The study should include a review of the number of similar type engineering hours expended on previously completed projects of like complexity.

(c) Analytical Techniques

The plotting of engineering hours of contracts of similar complexity, by month, will generally indicate the extent of design and production engineering effort in relation to significant points of contract performance. Graphic analysis may also indicate definite patterns of engineering contract costs in relation to deliveries. When the estimate involves a follow-on procurement, or the run-out portion of an existing contract, the use of graphic analysis of prior experience is of particular importance in evaluating the engineering costs included in a proposal. The analysis should provide:

(1) An appraisal of the reasonableness of the monthly production engineering hours estimated by the contractor,

(2) A determination as to whether there is a marked reduction in engineering hours after the initial delivery, and

(3) An appraisal, at an interim point, of the reasonableness of the contractor's estimated production engineering hours for the run-

out portion of contracts subject to price redetermination or for setting successive targets under incentive type contracts.

RESEARCH AND DEVELOPMENT

The larger companies and many medium-sized concerns maintain engineering staffs and facilities for performance of services that may not be intimately related to the current manufacturing operations. These functions may include independent research and development projects, the search for new products, and development of ways and means to improve current products. In addition, some engineering departments may also perform on specific orders from customers along engineering lines. Operations coming under the last-named function are closely aligned with the normal functions of engineering and research companies.

A commonly employed method of allocating the costs of engineering departments provides for the treatment of the aggregate of such costs as a below-the-line item, with apportionment to all products in the ratio of cost of sales, cost of production, or some similar basis. This method contemplates engineering expense as a secondary burden, comparable to selling and administrative expenses, and was generally acceptable to government agencies until the promulgation of CAS 420, Accounting for Independent Research and Development Costs and Bid and Proposal Costs.

The following is intended as an illustration of accounting procedures for an engineering department (performing functions other than production engineering).

(1) Every program or assignment to perform research, development, or other engineering work should be initiated by designated executive personnel. The authorization should be in writing, contain sufficient information to appropriately identify the work to be performed, and be controlled by a budgeted amount.

(2) The authorization should be given a project number for accounting purposes, which would serve as a basis for establishing an account in the project ledger.

(3) All engineers and draftsmen, other than clerical and top supervisory personnel, should be required to maintain daily (or weekly) time records setting forth the number of hours charged to each project worked upon, together with a brief description of the nature of work performed.

(4) Weekly payroll distribution should be prepared for the engineering department, and the total direct engineering salaries and wages should be charged to the appropriate projects. Indirect engineering salaries and wages, sick leave, vacation, etc., should be charged to separate accounts provided therefor in the engineering department's general ledger.

(5) Materials, equipment, and supplies, where acquired for specific projects and where significant in amount, may be charged directly to the applicable projects. General supplies may be charged to the respective engineering expense accounts.

(6) The costs accumulated in the various project accounts should be controlled by a projects-in-process account.

(7) In addition to the indirect salaries, wages, and supplies mentioned above, the indirect engineering expenses should also include all other direct overhead of the engineering department as well as appropriately assessed charges for light, heat, rent, insurance, etc. The aggregate of all such expenses should be allocated to projects on an equitable basis, appropriate in the circumstances. In this connection, it should be noted that direct engineering labor cost may not be the most accurate base for engineering overhead apportionment inasmuch as considerable ranges in salary rates are usually experienced. This factor could create considerable distortions in overhead allocation. As an illustration, let us assume that a specific project required the services of top engineers resulting in the average rate for the project of $30.00 per hour. If 100 hours were required to complete the work, the labor cost would amount to $3,000.00. On the other hand, let us assume that a concurrent project required the efforts of rank and file engineering personnel whose salary rates averaged $10.00 per hour. If 100 hours were required for this project too, the total labor cost would aggregate $1,000.00. If indirect expenses were allocated in the ratio of labor cost, the first project would absorb three times the overhead charged to the second. As a matter of fact, it is possible that the first project, far from generating three times as much overhead as the second, may actually generate less overhead as a result of a lesser requirement for supervision, etc. Accordingly, unless a scientific (and probably expensive) method is employed whereby various groups of expenses are allocated on different bases, direct labor hours could be a preferable basis to direct labor cost. The government has a real interest in this matter in view of the fact that projects undertaken for defense sometimes entail the services of higher-salaried engineers, and hence the use of the direct labor cost method could result in a much higher charge to government contracts than the direct labor hour base.

(8) Following the aforementioned procedures will result in the total costs of the engineering department being absorbed into the aggregate of projects performed within the fiscal period. This absorption is considered a prerequisite to all future considerations of recovering the cost against operations, current or future.

(9) The next step is to extract those projects that are of special benefit to particular operations. As an example, there is the category of "paid" projects, a term sometimes applied to specific engineering work performed pursuant to a definite order from a customer and for which billing will be effected. The costs of paid projects should be closed out to cost of sales. An alternative method, by which the income from paid projects is simply employed as a credit to total engineering costs, is not generally considered acceptable since this method serves to over- or understate the costs of the remaining projects to the extent of the profit or loss on the paid projects.

(10) After all paid projects have been closed out to cost of sales, the remaining costs may represent unallocable engineering costs to be borne pro rata by all operations. Two alternative methods are possible in this connection: One method provides for deferring the costs incurred and the subsequent amortization over a predetermined number of years; the other contemplates

charging the total costs to the current fiscal year. Before considering deferral of these costs to future fiscal years, consideration should be accorded to the provisions of FAR 31.205-18(d).

(11) In determining government contract costs, a pro rata share of the engineering expense should be apportioned thereto.

FAR 31.205-18

Before the comprehensive revision in 1959, Department of Defense cost principles cited as allowable "research and development specifically applicable to the supplies or services covered by the contract." "General research, unless specifically provided for elsewhere in the contract," was cited as unallowable. In addition, subjects requiring special consideration included "research programs of a general nature." These provisions, in the past, often resulted in an inconsistent approach to this area and were productive of much controversy and extensive negotiations.

The current provisions of the cost principles are considered more liberal, and the coverage devoted to the entire subject of research and development costs is much more comprehensive. Among the many useful editorial revisions in FAR has been the combining of the IR&D and B&P cost principles, which eliminated a substantial amount of redundancy. The new combined cost principle is quoted below:

31.205-18 Independent research and development and bid and proposal costs.

(a) *Definitions.*

"Applied research," as used in this subsection, means that effort which (1) normally follows basic research, but may not be severable from the related basic research, (2) attempts to determine and exploit the potential of scientific discoveries or improvements in technology, materials, processes, methods, devices, or techniques, and (3) attempts to advance the state of the art. Applied research does not include efforts whose principal aim is design, development, or test of specific items or services to be considered for sale; these efforts are within the definition of the term "development," defined below.

"Basic research," as used in this subsection, means that research which is directed toward increase of knowledge in science. The primary aim of basic research is a fuller knowledge or understanding of the subject under study, rather than any practical application thereof.

"Bid and proposal (B&P) costs," as used in this subdivision, means the costs incurred in preparing, submitting, and supporting bids and proposals (whether or not solicited) on potential Government or non-Government contracts. The term does not include the costs of effort sponsored by a grant or cooperative agreement or required in contract performance.

"Company," as used in this subsection, means all divisions, subsidiaries, and affiliates of the contractor under common control.

"Development," as used in this subsection, means the systematic use, under whatever name, of scientific and technical knowledge in the design, development, test, or evaluation of a potential new product or service (or of an improvement in an existing product or service) for the purpose of meeting specific performance requirements or objectives. Development includes the functions of design engineering, prototyping, and engineering testing. Development excludes: (1) subcontracted technical effort which is for the sole purpose of developing an additional source for an existing product, or (2) development effort for manufacturing or production materials, systems, processes, methods, equipment, tools, and techniques not intended for sale.

"Independent research and development (IR&D)" means a contractor's IR&D cost that is not sponsored by, or required in performance of, a contract or grant and that consists of projects falling within the four following areas: (1) basic research, (2) applied research, (3) development, and (4) systems and other concept formulation studies. IR&D effort shall not include technical effort expended in developing and preparing technical data specifically to support submitting a bid or proposal.

"Systems and other concept formulation studies," as used in this subsection, means analyses and study efforts either related to specific IR&D efforts or directed toward identifying desirable new systems, equipments or components, or modifications and improvements to existing systems, equipments, or components.

(b) *Composition and allocation of costs.* The requirements of CAS 420, Accounting for Independent Research and Development Costs and Bid and Proposal Costs, are incorporated in their entirety and shall apply as follows—

(1) *Fully-CAS-covered contracts.* Contracts that are fully-CAS-covered shall be subject to all requirements of CAS 420.

(2) *Modified-CAS-covered and non-CAS-covered contracts.* Contracts that are not CAS-covered or that contain terms or conditions requiring modified CAS coverage shall be subject to all requirements of CAS 420 *except* 4 CFR 420.50(e)(2) and 4 CFR 420.50(f)(2), which are not then applicable. However, non-CAS covered or modified CAS-covered contracts awarded at a time the contractor has CAS-covered contracts requiring compliance with CAS 420, shall be subject to all the requirements of CAS 420. When the requirements of 4 CFR 420.50(e)(2) and 4 CFR 420.50(f)(2) are not applicable, the following apply:

(i) IR&D and B&P costs shall be allocated to final cost objectives on the same basis of allocation used for the G&A expense grouping of the profit center (see 31.001) in which the costs are incurred. However, when IR&D and B&P costs clearly benefit other profit centers or benefit the entire company, those costs shall be allocated through the G&A of the other profit centers or through the corporate G&A, as appropriate.

(ii) If allocations of IR&D or B&P through the G&A base do not provide equitable cost allocation, the contracting officer may approve use of a different base.

(c) *Allowability.* Except as provided in paragraph (d) below, costs for IR&D and B&P are allowable only in accordance with the following:

(1) *Companies required to negotiate advance agreements.*

(i) Any company that received payments for IR&D and B&P costs in a fiscal year, either as a prime contractor or subcontractor, exceeding $4,400,000 from Government agencies, is required to negotiate with the Government an advance agreement which establishes a ceiling for allowability of IR&D and B&P costs for the following fiscal year. This agreement is binding on all Government agencies, unless prohibited by statute. The requirements of Section 203 of Pub. L. 91-441 necessitate that the Department of Defense (DOD) be the lead negotiating agency when the contractor has received more than $4,400,000 in payments for IR&D and B&P from DOD. Computation of IR&D and B&P costs to determine whether the threshold criterion was reached shall include only recoverable IR&D and B&P costs allocated during the company's previous fiscal year to prime contracts and subcontracts for which the submission and certification of cost or pricing data were required. (Also see paragraph (b) above and 15.804.) The computation shall include full burdening pursuant to CAS 420.

(ii) When a company meets the criterion in (i) above, required advance agreements may be negotiated at the corporate level and/or with those profit centers that contract directly with the Government and that in the preceding year allocated recoverable IR&D and B&P costs exceeding $550,000, including burdening, to contracts and subcontracts for which the submission and certification of cost or pricing data were required (also see paragraph (b) above and 15.804). When ceilings are negotiated for separate profit centers of the company, the allowability of IR&D and B&P costs for any center that in its previous fiscal year did not reach the $550,000 threshold may be determined in accordance with subparagraph (c)(2) below.

(iii) Ceilings are the maximum dollar amounts of total IR&D and B&P costs that will be allowable for allocation over the appropriate base for that part of the company's operation covered by an advance agreement.

(iv) No IR&D and B&P cost shall be allowable if a company fails to initiate negotiation of a required advance agreement before the end of the fiscal year for which the agreement is required.

(v) When negotiations are held with a company meeting the $4,400,000 criterion or with separate profit centers (when negotiations are held at that level under (ii) above), and if no advance agreement is reached, payment for IR&D and B&P costs shall be reduced below that which the company or profit center would have otherwise received. The amount of such reduced payment shall not exceed 75 percent of the amount which, in the opinion of the contracting officer, the company or profit center would be entitled to receive under an advance agreement. Written notification of the contracting officer's determination of a reduced amount shall be provided the contractor. In the event that an advance agreement is not reached before the end of the contractor's fiscal year for which the agreement is to apply, negotiations shall immediately be terminated, and the contracting officer shall furnish a determination of the reduced amount.

(vi) Contractors may appeal decisions of the contracting officer to reduce payment. The appeal shall be filed with the contracting officer within 30 days of receipt of the contracting officer's determination. (Also see Subpart 42.10.)

(2) *Companies not required to negotiate advance agreements.* Ceilings for allowable IR&D and B&P costs for companies not required to negotiate advance agreements in accordance with subparagraph (c)(1) above shall be established by a formula, either on a company-wide basis or by profit centers, computed as follows:

(i) Determine the ratio of IR&D/B&P costs to total sales (or other base acceptable to the contracting officer) for each of the preceding three years and average the two highest of these ratios; this average is the IR&D/B&P historical ratio;

(ii) Compute the average annual IR&D/B&P costs (hereafter called average), using the two highest of the preceding three years;

(iii) IR&D/B&P costs for the center for the current year which are not in excess of the product of the center's actual total sales (or other accepted base) for the current year and the IR&D/B&P historical ratio computed under (i) above (hereafter called product) shall be considered allowable only to the extent the product does not exceed 120 percent of the average. If the product is less than 80 percent of the average, costs up to 80 percent of the average shall be allowable.

(iv) However, at the discretion of the contracting officer, an advance agreement may be negotiated when the contractor can demonstrate that the formula would produce a clearly inequitable cost recovery.

(d) *Deferred IR&D and B&P costs.* (1) IR&D costs that were incurred in previous accounting periods are unallowable, except when a contractor has developed a specific product at its own risk in anticipation of recovering the development costs in the sale price of the product provided that—

(i) The total amount of IR&D costs applicable to the product can be identified;

(ii) The proration of such costs to sales of the product is reasonable;

(iii) The contractor had no Government business during the time that the costs were incurred or did not allocate IR&D costs to the Government contracts except to prorate the cost of developing a specific product to the sales of that product; and

(iv) No costs of current IR&D programs are allocated to Government work except to prorate the costs of developing a specific product to the sales of that product.

(2) When deferred costs are recognized, the contract (except firm-fixed-price and fixed-price with economic price adjustment) will include a

specific provision setting forth the amount of deferred IR&D costs that are allocable to the contract. The negotiation memorandum will state the circumstances pertaining to the case and the reason for accepting the deferred costs.

EVOLUTION OF CONTRACT COST PRINCIPLES FOR IR&D AND B&P

Prior to the effective date of FAR, the provisions of FPR 1-15.205-35, Research and Development, and FPR 1-15.205-3 were identical to the provisions of the 1959 ASPR for these costs, the civilian agencies, except for the Departments of Energy and the then HEW, having conformed their regulations to those of DOD. However, as the Defense Department substantially revised its cost principles for IR&D and B&P, in large part because of legislative pressures, the civilian agencies were unable to resolve their differences and FPR remained unchanged.

The 1949 ASPR cited as allowable "research and development specifically applicable to the supplies or services covered by the contract." "General research, unless specifically provided for elsewhere in the contract," was cited as unallowable. In addition, subjects requiring special consideration included "research programs of a general nature."

As in the instance of other items included under "selected costs," research and development have been treated at substantial length in the contract cost principles. Research and development, however, was a very difficult area, and it was doubtful that the commentary in the 1959 ASPR Section XV would achieve clarity or assure consistent treatment.

Requisite to the discussion of these costs are several definitions used in the 1959 cost principles. "Basic research," for example, was defined as that "directed toward increase or knowledge in science." The definition of "applied research" was closely aligned to that of basic research and, as a matter of fact, the 1959 cost principles indicated that the former follows the latter and may not be severable therefrom. "Applied research" was also defined as "attempts to determine and expand the potentialities of new scientific discoveries or improvements . . . and . . . to advance the state of art." As contrasted with research, "development" was defined as "the systematic use of scientific knowledge which was directed toward the production of, or improvements in, useful products to meet specific performance requirements, but exclusive of manufacturing and production engineering." One other definition required to analyze the treatment accorded to this cost area is "a contractor's independent research and development." It is described as "that research and development which is not sponsored by a contract, grant, or other arrangement."

With these definitions in mind, the Defense Department's views on research and development expenses in the 1960s may be analyzed as follows:

(1) As an initial prerequisite to considering a contractor's costs of independent research as allowable, these costs must be allocated to all work of the contractor. This compared with the specific citation of general research as unallowable, unless specifically provided for in the contract, in the 1949 cost principles.

(2) Allowability of a contractor's independent development costs was limited to the extent that such costs were "related to the product lines for which the Government has contracts ... reasonable in amount and are allocated as indirect costs to all work of the contractor on such product lines."

(3) "Independent research and development costs shall include an amount for the absorption of their appropriate share of indirect and administrative costs. ..." This point was injected into the cost principles in an attempt to settle the many controversies that have existed over this area and that of accounting methodology. However, this provision was almost completely negated by the immediately following language: "unless the contractor, in accordance with its accounting practices consistently applied, treats such costs otherwise."

(4) A rather strange provision stated that "research and development costs (including amounts capitalized) ... which were incurred in accounting periods prior to the award of a particular contract, are unallowable except where allowable as precontract costs." A strict application of this provision would indicate that, where a contractor follows a policy of capitalizing and then amortizing research and development costs, the annual amortization could be allowable under continuing contracts but unallowable for new contracts. If this provision were to be closely followed, separate overhead rates could be required each year for continuing and new contracts. (It is difficult to believe that this was intended.)

(5) Extensive comments were made with regard to attempts to control the amount of independent research and development to be borne by the government. First, the usual requirements for "reasonableness" were emphasized, and close scrutiny was particularly recommended for development costs incurred by firms whose work consisted predominantly of government contracts. Government procurement officials were encouraged to enter into advance agreements that would result in the government's bearing less than a pro rata share of the total cost of a contractor's independent research and development program. Three possible types of agreements were suggested. Under the first proposal, the government would accept the allocable costs of only certain specific projects; under the second, it would accept an allocable portion of an agreed-upon maximum dollar limitation of research and development costs; and under the third, it would accept an allocable share of only a percentage of the contractor's plant program.

As a result of the complexities of this area, the 1959 principles emphasized that advance agreements between the government and the contractor are particularly important.

The Defense Department's 1959 effort reflected more of a beginning than an end to the discussions and controversies over the optimum consideration to be accorded to IR&D and B&P costs. The Seventh Edition of this text contains a detailed analysis of the events during the period 1959 to 1972, from which we have condensed the following summary. Although some of the details are not essential to the current scene, scholars of the subject closely interested in how current thinking developed may wish to refer to the Seventh Edition.

The period from 1959 to 1972 witnessed considerable interest in this area, including several decisions by boards of contract appeals, reports by the General Accounting Office, and numerous studies including those performed by GAO, congressional committee staffs, and the Department of Defense. Although not the most important issue, the method of accounting was continually debated. One of the aspects of this issue was whether IR&D and B&P costs should be established as limited to direct costs or whether they should be "burdened," i.e., should overhead and G&A expenses be allocated to such costs. The compromise solution was that appropriate engineering overhead should be allocated but G&A expenses should not. This complex controversy is discussed later in this chapter in our analysis of CAS 420, Accounting for Independent Research and Development and Bid and Proposal Costs.

The debates also focused on the treatment of deferred IR&D expenses, whether research costs should be treated differently from development costs, whether bid and proposal expenses should be considered as limited to the administrative efforts of preparing proposals or should include the technical effort as well, treatment of R&D costs sponsored in part by others, identification of the differences between IR&D and B&P costs, and many other issues. As to the differences between IR&D and B&P costs and the difficulty of distinguishing among the various costs in these areas, the middle 1960s brought the proposal for combining all of these costs into a category to be called "CITE"—contractor independent technical effort. CITE seemed to be heading for incorporation into DOD regulations but became a victim of an adverse decision at high Pentagon levels.

GAO's contributions, including mammoth multiyear studies, brought criticisms of whatever the departments and agencies were doing, comments regarding lack of uniformity, hints that contractors were profiting by government IR&D in their commercial business, and the like, but no recommendations.

During the period from 1959 to 1972, congressional critics of defense spending began their efforts, continuing today, to place limits on the amount of money that DOD could pay for IR&D and B&P. Legislation was enacted requiring demonstration that such costs had a potential relationship to a military function or operation, and advance agreements were required with contractors who received more than a specified amount in payments for IR&D and B&P. Legislation originating in the early 1970s also introduced the requirement for the Secretary of Defense to submit annual reports to Congress identifying the companies receiving payments in excess of specified amounts and providing other information. The April 1972 revision to DAR reflected a substantial overhaul of the existing cost principles, including the incorporation of the congressionally mandated provisions.

In the following years, congressional resistance to expenditures for defense needs increased. The arbitrary legislative limitations on reimbursement of contractors' IR&D and B&P costs continued, but this area did not draw other major attention in either the executive or legislative branches despite the general assaults on cost allowability led by GAO, DOD IG and DCAA during the mid 1980s.

Informed observers note with increasing alarm the growing percentage of foreign-made components in our major weapon systems. The lower cost of labor in many countries, combined with their more modern facilities, cry out for government action to assist in the creation of a viable industrial base. One kind of action would be providing incentives for research and development by American industry, both in defense and nondefense fields. However, no such encouragement seems to be forthcoming in the current political environment, and recent income tax changes, if anything, appear to reflect disincentives to capital investments, which may reverse the favorable trend of recent years.

The extensive provisions of FAR 31.205-18, covering both IR&D and B&P costs, were quoted in full earlier in this chapter. Working with these provisions is considerably easier for defense contractors than for companies performing under contracts for civilian agencies because FAR, in substance, incorporates the prior DAR provisions. The major changes consisted of combining IR&D and B&P into one cost principle, as well as considerable editorial revisions. Contractors familiar only with FPR faced a completely different problem. Advance agreements had been recommended in FPR, whereas under FAR such agreements are mandatory for companies receiving payments exceeding $4.4 million a year for IR&D and B&P from government agencies. Also new for former FPR users was the provision for the use of a formula for determining ceilings for those contractors that were not required to negotiate advance agreements. To mention one other change, FPR provided that deferred IR&D costs were unallowable whereas FAR sets out certain circumstances under which such costs may be recognized.

BOARD OF CONTRACT APPEALS DECISIONS RELATING TO IR&D AND B&P

Selected board decisions are summarized to provide a flavor of the manner in which the accounting treatment of these costs has been viewed when controversies culminated in litigation. Although we believe these summaries will add to the understanding of this complex subject, the reader is cautioned to consider each decision in the perspective of the date on which it was issued and the regulations which governed on those dates.

Accounting Treatment for Excess of Costs Over Prices of R&D Contracts

Prior editions of this text contained analyses of several decisions by the ASBCA and the U.S. Court of Claims where the government disallowed what it categorized as losses incurred under R&D contracts when contractors deferred such amounts and amortized them in future years with portions allocated to government contracts. The boards and courts were not always persuaded that excesses of cost over prices for R&D contracts could not be properly amortized over future production contracts. As it has done on so many occasions when displeased with judicial rulings, DOD revised its regulations to state that such costs are unallowable unless allowable as precontract costs. This provision was carried over into FAR 31.205-48.

Allowability of IR&D Costs on Cosponsored Projects

As a matter of further interest with respect to IR&D, we might consider a decision by the Armed Services Board of Contract Appeals, ASBCA No. 10254, 66-1 BCA par. 5860.

The General Dynamics Corporation had been expending considerable effort and expense in connection with a research and development program. For a number of years, that company had entered into arrangements with a number of associations under which these associations agreed to share in the costs of some of the R&D projects in return for receiving data developed in connection therewith.

The total IR&D cost expended by the contractor was reduced by the amount contributed by and support received from the associations, and the net amount was submitted as part of the overhead cost claimed under Department of Defense contracts. It was the practice of the contractor and the DOD contracting officer to negotiate a cost-sharing type of arrangement under which a stipulated dollar ceiling was allowed for allocation to DOD contracts.

During 1960, General Dynamics submitted to DOD a brochure outlining its planned IR&D program for 1960. Based on a review of this brochure and other discussions, an agreement was negotiated under which the government agreed to share in 78% of an agreed-upon dollar ceiling cost. The evidence indicates that the R&D projects participated in by the several associations, as mentioned above, had been included in the brochure which formed the basis for this advance agreement.

The government disallowed the costs of the cosponsored projects because the cost principles identified IR&D as projects that were not sponsored and also because such costs might be considered unallowable as losses on the cosponsored projects.

The contractor's appeal was based on an interpretation of ASPR 15-205.35(c): "A contractor's independent research and development is that research and development which is not sponsored by a contract, grant, or other arrangement." The government's argument was broader. It held that the projects to which costs were contributed were "sponsored" as contemplated by the aforementioned provision. Additionally, the government argued that the costs of these projects should not be recoverable in any event because there was no benefit to the government flowing from these projects.

Taking up the latter point first, the board stated that it found nothing in ASPR 15-205.35 "requiring that the Government receive a direct benefit from an IR&D program carried on by a contractor in order for it to bear a portion of the program's cost. . . ." The board emphasized that it found no such limitations or requirements. It further pointed to the fact that the ASPR provisions recognized the necessity and desirability of basic research, together with the government's encouragement thereof through indirect contributions.

The board found nothing in the record to show that the government had specifically raised any objections regarding the nature or purpose of the projects involved; rather, the government's concern about reimbursement stemmed from a belief that reimbursement was prohibited under ASPR 15-205.35(c) rather than because of the propriety of the specific projects.

The board then undertook an effort to determine the precise meaning of ASPR 15-205.35(c). It found nothing which, in its opinion, shed any meaningful light on the intent of those writing this regulation. The board noted that the terms "contract" and "grant" had been interpreted by the contractor as relating solely to those let by the federal government. The board was not persuaded that this interpretation was necessarily logical.

The board was impressed with what it termed one of the contractor's "common-sense" arguments. In this argument, the contractor contended that the government would have raised no question about the costs of the projects involved if no financial assistance had been received from outside sources. The contractor then pointed out that it appeared "anomalous indeed that after it successfully seeks outside assistance in financing its research programs, the effect of which is to reduce the total amount to be applied against Government contracts, the Government refuses to recognize this reduced amount as properly includable in a pool to be allocated to Government contracts. The effect of this is to penalize the appellant for reducing the costs allocable to Government contracts."

The board concluded that ASPR 15-205.35(c) did not compel an interpretation of this kind and that it did not bar the contractor's recovery "of its 1962 IR&D costs above contributions by private sources on the projects involved in this dispute up to the limiting percentage agreed to in advance by the parties." The board found its conclusion strengthened by the action of the parties in previous years wherein such costs were accepted, particularly in the years prior to 1960, when the ASPR provisions then existing "may fairly be characterized as less liberal" than 15-205.35(c). The board was also impressed by the fact that the government had accepted such costs in the advance agreement for 1960. The board could not draw a clear conclusion with respect to 1961 but commented: "All that we can say is that in view of the practice as to the percentage of total IR&D costs to be recognized for the year before and the year after, it seems as likely as not, notwithstanding an apparent statement to the contrary, that costs for the projects here in dispute were included in the total IR&D costs accepted."

In reviewing the advance agreement for 1963, the board concluded that there was no evidence that the question was "faced, settled, or disposed of. . . ." On the other hand, the board found it significant that the Air Force allowed about 81% of the total 1962 IR&D costs and that this total included the questionable projects.

It is obvious that the board experienced considerable difficulties in reaching a conclusion in this case, and it ultimately handed down a split decision. The majority sustained the contractor's appeal; however, it felt "impelled to caution that we are deciding as to one year only, in the light of the actions of these parties, and within the ambit of the presentation made to us." It suggested that it had doubts as to some of the aspects of the contractor's research program, but apparently took no action adverse to the contractor "in view of the 'all-or-nothing' presentation of this appeal." The majority decision closed with the statement: "While we recognize that this decision may have set a pattern for the years 1963-1965, unless factual differences can be developed, the contracting officer clearly has available to him for future years the device of a detailed and specific advance understanding as to the costs herein questioned, which can set these questions to rest."

The minority dissent recognized the need for clarifying ASPR 15-205.35(c). However, until this might be accomplished, the minority opinion held that, while research costs could be considered independent even though an outside contribution is received, a different situation obtains when most of the costs are paid by other organizations. In the latter circumstances, the minority view held that the contractor's contributed portion should not be allowable.

Distinctions Among IR&D, B&P, and Selling Costs

A case decided by the Armed Services Board of Contract Appeals in September 1968 (Nos. 12814 and 12890, 68-2 BCA par. 7297), involving the Convair Division of General Dynamics Corporation, reflects several illustrations of the board's thinking and should be of interest to defense contractors as well as to DOD officials

The contractor incurred significant costs in the fabrication, testing, and flight of an aircraft and contended "that the costs concerned were reasonable, properly chargeable as either selling costs or bid and proposal costs pursuant to generally accepted accounting principles; correctly considered as an expense of its business; and therefore allowable in accordance with ASPR Section XV." In the opinion of the government, "[t]he costs were incurred in the performance of non-Government-sponsored research and development work." The government and the contractor had entered into an agreement for the years involved as to maximum dollar limitations for reimbursability of IR&D expenses. Based on that agreement, the costs involved would have been in excess of the negotiated ceiling and hence not reimbursable.

The history of the manufacture and testing of the aircraft is quite long and complex. The government offered testimony to establish the project as one of independent research and development and the contractor sought to persuade the board that generally accepted accounting principles would establish these costs as bid and proposal or selling expenses.

The contractor emphasized that the aircraft had been built to demonstrate its capabilities to the government and aid in the ultimate sale to one or more of the military departments. However, the board concluded that "Convair embarked upon the systematic knowledge it acquired in its admittedly research program, both to improve and later produce a useful product, i. e., a production aircraft." The board alleged that the record evidenced that the contractor itself referred to the aircraft as an experimental type, and it concluded that all the costs involved did constitute development work within the provisions of the contract and the cost principles. The board continued as follows: "Being company sponsored development work, it was independent (research and) development." Thereupon, with the contractor's concession that these costs would be in excess of applicable reimbursement ceilings set in IR&D agreements, the board found the government's disallowance of these costs to be appropriate, and the appeal was denied.

Having concluded that these costs represented IR&D, the board stated that it did not find it necessary to consider the reimbursability of these costs in the categories of bid and proposal or selling expenses. Having made this determination, the board proceeded, nevertheless, to discuss several other matters, including the positions it might have taken had these costs been classified as bid and proposal or selling expenses. Some of the board's commentaries seem to be at least as interesting as its major decision, and we have included certain summaries and excerpts.

Speaking to the contractor's argument relating to the manner in which the costs in question were charged, the board stated, "Ordinarily, it is of small moment whether a cost or an expense is recorded in one account or another. The pure academics of accounting principles do not, and should not, alter basic determinations regarding reimbursability."

The above quote is rather difficult to follow except possibly when viewed in the light of ensuing comments which seem to add up to a critical and summary dismissal of accounting principles and practices. Of course, this dismissal was not done in a vacuum entirely. As will be seen in the excerpt that follows, the board sought to emphasize that reimbursability is to be determined by law, regulations, or contract terms and not by "generally accepted accounting principles."

The board cited ASPR 15-201.2, which listed as factors to be considered in determining the allowability of individual items of cost "(i) reasonableness, (ii) allocability, (iii) applicability of those generally accepted accounting principles and practices appropriate to the particular circumstances, and (iv) any limitations or exclusions set forth in this contract as to types or amounts of cost items." We include now an excerpt from the decision which, while lengthy, we consider to be of considerable interest.

In this case allocability ((ii) above) is not an issue; reasonableness ((i) above) as to the nature of the costs concerned may be; limitations, etc. ((iv) above) is certainly an issue. Despite the concentrated preoccupation of the parties with the subject of generally accepted accounting principles and practices ((iii) above), we conclude that they cannot affect our decision herein.

One of the basic considerations in this appeal is to determine first, whether any one of the factors appearing in ASPR 15-201.2 is of overriding significance. We conclude that the limitations and exclusions ((iv) above) do not possess this overriding significance. If reimbursement is limited or excluded by a law (whether it is or is not referenced in the contract or incorporated cost principles), or applicable or incorporated regulations, such as ASPR, Section II, or by the contract otherwise, it is our opinion that that is the end of the inquiry. "Reasonableness" becomes unimportant, because such a limitation, in effect, proclaims the cost under discussion to be *ipso facto* unreasonable either as to type or amount, or both. "Allocability" can never become a factor until a cost is first established to be allowable and reasonable as to the type and amount; otherwise, there is nothing to allocate.

Generally accepted accounting principles and practices cannot conclusively control the interpretation of a limiting or exclusionary law, regulation or contract. In context, they may assist in such interpretation. These are questions for determination by either administrative bodies, such as this Board, or the courts. Nor can accounting principles and practices be relevant to the issue of whether it is reasonable for the contractor to engage at all in an activity in the expectation of reimbursement, or whether the extent of such engagement is reasonable. Such decisions are business or management-type decisions and not accounting problems. As we view this case, with one small possible exception it can be decided within the confines of issues as described above which are immune from the effect of accounting principles and practices. We believe that we need not reach this exception. Therefore, we reiterate that the extensive evidence and discussion of generally accepted accounting principles are not relevant to our decision.

We mentioned earlier that the board stated that its categorization of the costs as IR&D made it unnecessary to discuss the reimbursability of these costs as selling or bid and proposal expenses and that it then proceeded to do just that. Because all of these cost categories are of very significant current interest to the defense community (and have been, as a matter of fact, for more than 25 years), the board's views are quoted as follows: "As bid and proposal costs, we believe there is an unsurmountable question of reasonableness. ASPR 15-205.3 defines bidding costs as "the costs of preparing bids or proposals . . ., including the development of engineering data and cost data necessary to support the contractor's bids or proposals. Building and hardware cannot be said to have any function in the preparation of bid or proposal papers, not even as an enclosure to the package."

In the board's opinion there was no evidence that the building of the aircraft was necessary to support any proposal, and it expressed the view that "[t]his may be desirable from Convair's point of view, but that is not the same as necessary."

The board then considered the cost of building the aircraft as a selling or demonstration cost and offered the following view:

As "selling costs," we doubt strongly that the cost of building a demonstrator is reimbursable. Even if we dissociated an analysis of the applicability of ASPR 15-205.37 (Selling Costs) from the fact that building Charger was principally a development effort (as we have found above), we should have to arrive at the same conclusion.

Construction and Updating of Mock-Up, Competitive Systems and Other Analyses, and Wind Tunnel and Other Tests Held to Constitute B&P Costs

Close to $1 million in overhead costs disallowed by the government were involved in the appeal (*General Dynamics Corp., Convair Div.,* ASBCA Nos. 15394, 15858, 72-2 BCA par. 9533). The costs included the construction and updating of a mock-up built and displayed in support of the contractor's competitive proposal for an engineering development contract for a weapons system, competitive systems analysis, demonstration of its avionics capability on the plant system's avionics simulator, and demonstrations of aerodynamic characteristics in wind tunnel tests. The government did not question that the costs were incurred or that they were reasonable in amount. It contended, however, that (1) the costs were inappropriately classified as B&P expenses, (2) the contractor's efforts were not required by either the definition or sustaining contracts, (3) the costs were expended to enhance the contractor's competitive position, and (4) the work was performed gratuitously. The government argued that, inasmuch as it neither requested nor required this work, the related costs should either be considered as losses incurred under the respective contracts or classified as independent research or development costs. In the latter case, they would be considered unallowable because they exceeded the negotiated allowable amounts for the accounting periods in question.

The board found that the construction and updating of the mock-ups were essential to the refinement of the contractor's proposal and to the preservation of its competitive position. This latter point, however, did not suggest to the board that the costs were misclassified as B&P expenses. The board's decision emphasized testimony and other evidence, including views of DOD officials directly concerned, that all of the costs, especially the construction of the mock-ups, were essential to both the contractor and the government in evaluating the requirements of the weapons system. The board agreed with the contractor that the costs were not incurred because of the specific requirements of the contracts, but rather in an effort to obtain follow-up development and production contracts for this major weapons system. In the circumstances, the board viewed these expenses as properly classified as B&P.

In previous appeals, the board had taken what appeared to the government to be different positions with regard to the classification of B&P expenses, and the board considered it appropriate to comment and distinguish this appeal from the others:

> In this connection, appellant has persuasively shown that the cost of demonstrating the feasibility of its design effort as part of an overall proposal effort requested by the Government and identifiable at all times as the VS(X) program for the development of an ASW carrier-based aircraft was necessary to its continuance as a viable competitive factor for the VS(X) weapon system. This, we think, distinguishes this case from prior decisions in which we held that the fact that the ultimate goal of an independent design and proposal effort is the submittal of an unsolicited proposal is insufficient when standing alone to justify allowing such effort as a B & P expense.

> We believe the facts bring this case within the ambit of those decisions which hold that the cost of work undertaken in an attempt to verify and insure favorable consideration of a proposal effort requested and partially funded by the Government may, when reasonable and necessary, be allowable as a B&P expense. Compare *General Dynamics Corporation (Pomona Division)*, ASBCA No. 13869, 70-1 BCA par. 8143, at 37,834-835, with *North American Rockwell Corp.*, ASBCA No. 13067,

69-2 BCA par. 7812, at 36,301-302 and *General Dynamics Corpration*, ASBCA No. 9842, 65-2 BCA par. 5067 at 23,852-854.

Addressing another government contention, the board stated:

To the extent that the Government argues that if the costs in question are allowable they must be considered development costs, we note that if bidding and proposal costs are chargeable only to the contract toward which they are directed, reimbursement for unsuccessful bids and proposals would always be denied. We have interpreted ASPR 15-205.3 as requiring that bidding costs 'incurred prior to award of a contract not only may, but MUST be charged as current indirect expenses, unless some other established practice has been shown and approved.' *North American Rockwell, supra*, 69-2 BCA par. 7812, at 36,300. We find appellant was correct in charging its costs for construction and updating of the third mockup and verifying its design concept to its B & P accounts for 1968 and 1969.

The board then addressed the government's contention that the costs in question should properly be classified as IR&D. Here it stated that "[a]ssuming, without deciding," that the costs involved were similar to independent development efforts, the government had failed to prove that the contractor was required to classify such costs as IR&D. At this point the board developed further the aspects of this case which, in its judgment, distinguished it from some of the other appeals dealing with similar subjects:

In *General Dynamics Corporation (Pomona Division), supra.*, 70-1 BCA par. 8143 at 37,834 we held that the "cost of work which may represent both independent research and proposal preparation may within limits (see *General Dynamics Corporation, Convair Division*, ASBCA No. 12814, et al., 68-2 BCA par. 7297, the *"Charger"* case) be allowable as either one or the other as the contractor wishes to account for it." Accord, *North American Rockwell, supra*. This is not to say that Convair's subjective intent conclusively governs classification of the costs. Nor is it purely a question of applying "generally accepted accounting principles" since whether or not a cost is reasonable in nature requires the application of sound business judgment to all the extrinsic circumstances. In the area of overlap between independent development effort and bid and proposal effort there is obviously room for differences in judgment. In the final analysis the judgment adopted must be based upon a consideration of the record as a whole.

We believe that the key factor here, however, and the one that distinguishes this case from the *"Charger"* case, which involved the complete and secret research and development of a "flying prototype" to support an unsolicited proposal, is the fact that all of the effort involved was directed toward satisfaction of the Government's several requests for proposals to design and develop the VS(X) weapon system. In view of the long, joint and cooperative effort between appellant and the Government on the VS(X) program we find it was permissible for appellant to charge these costs to the identified cost objective of obtaining the development and production contracts. We also find "Charger" distinguishable on the ground that the undisputed evidence here shows that the design and development effort with respect to both "hardware" and "software" was clearly necessary to support appellant's proposal efforts for the development and production contracts for the VS(X) weapon system.

B&P Costs in Excess of Formula Held Allowable When Contracting Officer Was Found to Have Abused His Discretion by Refusing to Enter into Advance Agreement.

Many medium and small defense contractors can take considerable comfort from the board's ruling in the appeal of *Dynatrend, Inc.*, ASBCA No. 23463, 80-2 BCA par. 14,617. And we hope this decision will be carefully studied by DOD contracting officers, some of whom have consistently taken a hard line on the issue involved here, a line rejected and criticized by the Armed Services Board of Contract Appeals.

The author has had many personal experiences which parallel the controversy in *Dynatrend, Inc.* While we have succeeded in assisting some of our clients in this area, the discussions with ACOs have frequently been difficult, and we would expect to encounter more reasonable attitudes on the part of the government people in the future because of this decision.

Dynatrend had been receiving less than $2 million per year from the Department of Defense for IR&D and B&P; accordingly, the annual amounts allowed were computed in accordance with the formula set forth in DAR 15-205.3(d)(2)(B). In addition to the mechanics of the formula, similar to the current FAR provision, the regulation stated:

(B) Companies Not Required to Negotiated Advance Agreements (CWAS). Allowable B&P costs for companies not required to negotiate advance agreements in accordance with (A) above shall be established by a formula, either on a company-wide basis or by profit centers, computed as follows:

(i) Determine the ratio of B&P costs to total sales (or other base acceptable to the contracting officer) for each of the preceding three years and average the two highest of these ratios; this average is the B&P historical ratio;

(ii) Compute the average annual B&P costs (hereafter called average), using the two highest of the preceding three years;

(iii) B&P costs for the center for the current year which are not in excess of the product of the center's actual total sales (or other accepted base) for the current year and the B&P historical ratio computed under (i) above (hereafter called product) shall be considered allowable only to the extent the product does not exceed 120% of the average. If the product is less than 80% of the average, costs up to 80% of the average shall be allowable.

(iv) Costs which are in excess of the ceiling computed in (iii) above are not allowable except where the ceiling computed for IR&D cost under 15-205.35 is reduced in an amount identical to the amount of any increase over the B&P ceiling computed in (iii) above.

The above is extremely significant. The formula for determining the applicable amount of B&P was developed after some considerable thought and numerous discussions, and many people thought it was reasonable. However, and very importantly, there was a clear recognition that in certain instances the strict application of this formula could be inequitable to certain contractors, such as new and rapidly growing companies. The latter description fitted Dynatrend.

According to the text of the decision, the contractor wrote the contracting officer on September 29, 1977, requesting negotiation of an advance agreement with respect to B&P costs. In support of the request, the contractor pointed out that its sales volume had increased by 65% of its last three-year average. In the circumstances, the DAR formula would result in a clearly inequitable cost recovery. Dynatrend recommended a ceiling of $4\frac{1}{2}\%$ of sales for the past (1977) fiscal year and the current (1978) fiscal year.

The ACO requested DCAA to review the contractor's proposal. The audit agency, which is not generally known to be sympathetic to government contractors, reported that the 65% increase in sales volume had indeed occurred. However, the report also stated, gratuitously and apparently without clarification, that this increase "does not necessarily demonstrate that the formula produces a clearly inequitable cost recovery as required by the ASPR clause for an advance understanding."

A review of the ASBCA decision would suggest that DCAA did not include any constructive opinion as to the kind of data or information it believed was necessary to demonstrate "that the formula would produce a clearly inequitable cost recovery."

According to the decision the report also stated, "we have taken no exception to the cost data submitted by the contractor in support of its advance agreement request," but concluded that the 4.5% proposed ceiling was too high because the B&P costs were 4% of sales during FY 1977 and were projected to be 3.3% of sales during FY 1978.

The DCAA report was reviewed by the ACO's price analyst, who noted that Dynatrend exceeded the amount of B&P costs allowable under the formula and recommended a ceiling of 3.3% of government sales "as a negotiation objective for allowing B&P costs under an advance agreement, in lieu of the formula."

Although the price analyst was favorably inclined toward an advance agreement and the DCAA report indicated that the contractor's data were correct, the ACO refused to enter into an advance agreement and concluded: "On the basis of these reviews, it was determined that it has not been demonstrated or supported that application of the formula would produce a clearly inequitable cost recovery for the fiscal years 1977 and 1978." The ACO accordingly disallowed the B&P costs in excess of the amount computed by the formula and the contractor appealed.

Following Dynatrend's appeal, the ACO forwarded the file to DLA Headquarters requesting guidance for reaching a determination in similar circumstances in the future. The advice from DLA Headquarters was in the form of a position paper, and we excerpt below considerable portions of that paper as quoted or paraphrased by the ASBCA. The excerpts are somewhat lengthy, but we believe their inclusion is appropriate in view of the significance of the topside policy stated and our readers' need to avail themselves of this information in the event they confront contracting officers and/or contract auditors who arbitrarily and capriciously deny the propriety of entering into an advance agreement on B&P costs in appropriate circumstances:

On 12 March 1979, the Chief, Financial Services Division of DLA sent the ACO a "Position Paper" on the subject of reimbursement for B&P costs (Stip 40). The paper noted the concern expressed by the General Accounting Office (GAO Report No. B-167034, dated 17 Sept 73) over the application of the formula to young, fast growing companies, and the assurance provided to GAO by DoD in response to the GAO report that the proviso authorizing advance negotiated agreements would be invoked whenever the formula approach would lead to inequitable results. The position paper went on to compare appellant's position with the IR&D and B&P cost problems of two other companies where costs exceeded formula ceilings because of rapid growth. In these instances, actual costs were allowed because, "the intent of the cost principle— allowance of reasonable cost—was not being realized by insistence on the formula approach or the technicality of an advance agreement."

The position paper noted that the DCAA audit report did not question the reasonableness of appellant's B&P costs and that the report dismissed the appellant's 65% sales increase without substantive comment. The paper also stated that the DCASMA report of 17 July 1978 incorrectly advised the ACO that appellant did not qualify for an advance agreement under the terms of the regulation. The paper concluded with the following enunciation of policy:

"IR&D/B&P costs are necessary costs of doing business, and as such should be evaluated on the basis of reasonableness and allocability. Such costs directly support and encourage technical and price competition within the industrial sector. It is DoD policy to reimburse contractors for reasonable IR&D/B&P costs. Therefore, the DAR permits negotiation of voluntary advanced agreements whenever small or medium sized contractors would be penalized because: (i) their business posture dictated the expenditure of IR&D/B&P exceeding those amounts calculated through application of the DAR formula, or (ii) the contractor had incurred little or no IR&D/B&P expenses in prior years and therefore had no basis for the formula application."

Attached to the position paper was a list of 10 nonmandatory advance agreements negotiated by DCAS ACO's in similar circumstances. The attachment showed dollar amounts of sales and B&P/IR&D costs, with allowable costs ranging between 2.32% to 10.97% of sales.

The ASBCA decision was clear-cut and decisive, finding that Dynatrend's B&P costs for 1977 and 1978 were reasonable and that the cost recovery allowed by the ACO, based on the formula, was clearly inequitable. The board found further that the ACO had no justification for refusing to negotiate an advance agreement. It cited cases in support of the doctrine that "a contracting officer's exercise of discretionary authority may be overturned if it is shown to have been arbitrary, capricious, or an abuse of discretion." It concluded that all three of these characteristics fitted the ACO's final determination in this case.

CAS 420 - ACCOUNTING FOR INDEPENDENT RESEARCH AND DEVELOPMENT AND BID AND PROPOSAL COSTS

When visits to defense contractors by CASB staff members in the middle 1970s signaled the Board's increased attention to a cost accounting standard on IR&D and B&P, the major reaction in both the public and private sectors was to ask why. The historical summary presented in this chapter depicts vividly the extensive and intensive attention accorded this area by DOD and other federal agencies, GAO, Congress, and judiciary bodies. This summary surely suggests, too, that IR&D and B&P, perhaps more than any other costs, involve many considerations beyond accounting conventions. In the author's opinion, final judgments in this area should have given greater weight to United States national defense and economic interests than to rival schools of accounting theory.

This kind of thinking was apparently lacking among those responsible for the Comptroller General's "Report on the Feasibility of Applying Uniform Cost-Accounting Standards to Negotiated Defense Contracts." This report noted that IR&D and B&P costing problems were among those mentioned most frequently by GAO and DCAA field offices. It also observed that advance agreements were common with regard to IR&D, which established ceilings on the amounts the government would compensate the contractor and that "difficulties arise when ceilings are exceeded (overrun)." In the view of the report's authors, "IR&D overrun should not be charged, directly or indirectly, to the Government. In practice, some contractors change the classification of the IR&D expenditure and/or the account, which, in effect, defeats the intent of such agreement." Other "problems" presented in the report included "IR&D work tasks are often similar or identical to ... B&P costs ... (which) are usually not subject to a ceiling; consequently, IR&D projects are sometimes identified as B&P projects. IR&D overruns are sometimes included in indirect costs for allocation to both commercial and Government work."

The report also expressed concern about the failure of some contractors to charge "applicable factory overhead and/or G&A expenses" to IR&D and B&P. The authors favored charging IR&D and B&P projects with their "proportionate share of indirect costs, including G&A expenses. . . ."

The myopic observations totally failed to recognize the national interests involved. The GAO authors also ignored the fact that GAO itself had struggled with this area for many years and, as described earlier in this chapter, had utterly failed to provide any useful recommendations.

There is a broad consensus that CAS 420 did very little to resolve the problems identified as the reasons for formulating this standard.

CASB Staff Draft, April 1977

The Board's first public exposure on this subject required that "[t]he costs of IR&D and B&P shall be accounted for as if the effort were a final cost objective and shall include all allocable direct and indirect costs including home office expenses and general and administrative expenses." The staff draft provided that IR&D and B&P costs of a business unit would be allocated to final cost objectives using the cost input base for allocating G&A expenses, except that the base would exclude the base elements applicable to IR&D and B&P projects. Under another significant provision, "IR&D and B&P costs incurred in a cost accounting period shall be allocated to final cost objectives of that cost accounting period only."

The proposals to allocate home office and business unit G&A expenses to IR&D and B&P costs, and the unconditional prohibition against recognizing deferrals, reflected impositions that were more rigid and harmful to United States industry than those imposed by DOD or Congress.

Both industry and the Department of Defense strongly opposed the proposal to allocate home office and general and administrative expenses to IR&D and B&P costs "as if they were final cost objectives." It seemed obvious to just about everyone beyond the Board and its staff that IR&D and B&P costs are not final cost objectives and that no valid accounting or business basis existed for the proposed accounting treatment.

There was equally broad opposition to the proposal that IR&D and B&P costs should be allocated using the same bases as home office and business unit G&A expenses, respectively. Commentators clearly recognized that this arbitrary allocation method failed to take into consideration beneficial or causal relations that might exist at any location and would be bound to lead to an allocation of these expenses to segments and final cost objectives without any regard for such relations.

Both government and business objected to the provision in the staff draft for including administrative effort in B&P costs, both preferring the existing DAR provision that required that only technical effort must be included as B&P while the administrative costs may be classified in accordance with the contractor's normal accounting practice.

Objections were also raised to the prohibition against deferring IR&D costs. It appeared that this prohibition was based on a similar provision of Financial Accounting Standards Board (FASB) 2. The CASB had not hitherto established any firm policy to adhere to the promulgations of FASB, and the proposal in the case of IR&D seemed particularly inappropriate. DOD recommended that deferrals of IR&D and B&P costs be permitted where the government and the contractor agreed that the projects have a potential military relationship and have not been previously included.

Proposed Standard, July 1978

Some fifteen months after the issuance of the staff draft, the Board had digested the pervasive critical comments and issued a proposed rule on IR&D and B&P in the *Federal Register* (July 28, 1978). The proposed standard appropriately considered the unanimous objections to the requirement to allocate home office and G&A expenses to IR&D and B&P costs and eliminated this provision. The Board also made other modifications in response to the widespread criticisms from the public and private sectors; however, the revised CASB effort was still considered to represent an unsound and illogical accounting rule. CODSIA thought the best thing the Board could do would be to scrap it entirely, noting that it dealt almost exclusively with cost allocations and that this subject was adequately provided for in CAS 403 and 410, promulgated to date, and the proposed Indirect Cost Allocation Standards scheduled as 417-421, ultimately published as CAS 418 (Chapter XIII of this text). Commentators noted that the Board's proposal remained deficient in failing to provide appropriate consideration to the following recommendations, most of which emanated uniformly, although independently, from government and industry:

1. B&P administrative costs under circumstances provided in the DAR need not be considered B&P costs.

2. The recommendation to establish separate projects for each IR&D or B&P effort, regardless of the amount involved should be eliminated as unnecessary, uneconomical, and an intrusion of CAS into areas not associated with the charter of the Board.

3. Recommendations again were made to the Board that it scrub the requirement for allocating home office IR&D and B&P costs by means of a base representing the total activity of all segments. As they had a year earlier, commentators pointed out to the Board that, in accordance with its own fundamental policies, allocation should be based on beneficial or causal relations. An arbitrary and artificial requirement to allocate these home office costs to all segments would yield such completely illogical results as illustrated in the comments by the Department of Defense. The example is one of a company in the electronics field which has a subsidiary engaged in renting automobiles. By the terms of the proposed standard, the electronics IR&D effort would be allocated to the auto rental company despite the absence of any causal or beneficial relationship.

4. Numerous recommendations were made again to revise the requirement that segment IR&D and B&P costs must be allocated to the final cost objectives of that segment by means of a base representing its total activity. DOD thought the Board should recognize that such costs may be incurred in a particular segment for the benefit of other segments in which case provision for the appropriate allocation should be made. Industry complained about the Board's blind adherence to the mandatory use of a single broad base. CODSIA pointed out to the Board that, time and time again, it seems to lose sight of the objective for allocating costs on beneficial or causal relations and retreat to the artificial single broad base.

5. Recommendations were reiterated to revise the requirements that a business unit must use the same base to allocate IR&D and B&P costs as it does for its G&A expenses. The Board's single-minded absorption with a prescribed single base regardless of the existence of causal or beneficial relations was noted and objected to by many commentators.

We have noted only a few of the voluminous and serious criticisms made by both government and industry to the CASB's second effort in formulating a standard on IR&D and B&P costs. The author joined those who urged the Board to issue this standard as a proposed rule again because the latest issuance contained far too many serious deficiencies.

Proposed Standard, May 1979

Apparently sufficiently impressed by the vigorous opposition from both the private and public sectors, the Board complied with the recommendations for issuing this standard in draft form again. However, the reception to this (third) effort was negative. Many commentators remained convinced that the best course for the CASB to follow would be to scrap this effort entirely. CODSIA saw nothing in the Board's proposal which would improve DOD-industry relationships in this area. On the other hand, the Association and other commentators recognized that the proposed standard would introduce "more problems . . . in an area where few now exist." However, lacking a realistic basis for believing the CASB would scrub this project, commentators again offered suggestions.

Final Version of CAS 420, September 1979

The Fundamental Requirements and Techniques for Application sections of CAS 420, as finally promulgated, are quoted below:

§ 420.40 Fundamental requirement.

(a) The basic unit for the identification and accumulation of IR&D and B&P costs shall be the individual IR&D or B&P project.

(b) IR&D and B&P project costs shall consist of all allocable costs, except business unit general and administrative expenses.

(c) IR&D and B&P cost pools consist of all IR&D and B&P project costs and other allocable costs, except business unit general and administrative expenses.

(d) The IR&D and B&P cost pools of a home office shall be allocated to segments on the basis of the beneficial or causal relationship betweeen the IR&D and B&P costs and the segments reporting to that home office.

(e) The IR&D and B&P cost pools of a business unit shall be allocated to the final cost objectives of that business unit on the basis of the beneficial or causal relationship between the IR&D and B&P costs and the final cost objectives.

(f)(1) B&P costs incurred in a cost accounting period shall not be assigned to any other cost accounting period.

(2) IR&D costs incurred in a cost accounting period shall not be assigned to any other cost accounting period, except as may be permitted pursuant to provisions of existing laws, regulations and other controlling factors.

§ 420.50 Techniques for application.

(a) IR&D and B&P project costs shall include: (1) costs, which if incurred in like circumstances for a final cost objective, would be treated as direct costs of that final cost objective, and (2) the overhead costs of productive activities and other indirect costs related to the project based on the contractor's cost accounting practice or applicable Cost Accounting Standards for allocation of indirect costs.

(b) IR&D and B&P cost pools for a segment consist of the project costs plus allocable home office IR&D and B&P costs.

(c) When the costs of individual IR&D or B&P efforts are not material in amount, these costs may be accumulated in one or more project(s) within each of these two types of effort.

(d) The costs of any work performed by one segment for another segment shall not be treated as IR&D costs or B&P costs of the performing segment unless the work is a part of an IR&D or B&P project of the performing segment. If such work is part of a performing segment's IR&D or B&P project, the project will be transferred to the home office to be allocated in accordance with paragraph (e) below.

(e) The costs of IR&D and B&P projects accumulated at a home office shall be allocated to its segments as follows:

(1) Projects which can be identified with a specific segment(s) shall have their costs allocated to such segment(s).

(2) The costs of all other IR&D and B&P projects shall be allocated among all segments by means of the same base used by the company to allocate its residual expenses in accordance with 4 CFR Part 403; provided, however, where a particular segment receives significantly more or less benefit from the IR&D or B&P costs than would be reflected by the allocation of such costs to the segment by that base, the Government and the contractor may agree to a special allocation of the IR&D or B&P costs to such segment commensurate with the benefits received. The amount of a special allocation to any segment made pursuant to such an agreement shall be excluded from the IR&D and B&P cost pools to be allocated to other segments and the base data of any such segment shall be excluded from the base used to allocate these pools.

(f) The costs of IR&D and B&P projects accumulated at a business unit shall be allocated to cost objectives as follows:

(1) Where costs of any IR&D or B&P project benefit more than one segment of the organization the amounts to be allocated to each segment shall be determined in accordance with paragraph (e) above.

(2) IR&D and B&P cost pools which are not allocated under subparagraph (1) above shall be allocated to all final cost objectives of the business unit by means of the same base used by the business unit to allocate its general and administrative expenses in accordance with 4 CFR Part 410.50; provided, however, where a particular final cost objective receives significantly more or less benefit from IR&D or B&P costs than would be reflected by the allocation of such costs the Government and the contractor may agree to a special allocation of the IR&D or B&P costs to such final cost objective commensurate with the benefits received. The amount of special allocation to any such final cost objective made pursuant to such an agreement shall be excluded from the IR&D and B&P cost pools to be allocated to other final cost objectives and the particular final cost objective's base data shall be excluded from the base used to allocate these pools.

(g) Notwithstanding the provisions of paragraphs (d), (e) or (f), the costs of IR&D and B&P projects allocable to a home office pursuant to paragraph 420.50(d) may be allocated directly to the receiving segments, provided that such allocation not be substantially different from the allocation that would be made if they were first passed through home office accounts.

The final version of this standard reflected some additional improvements, but also retained a number of objectionable features. A major improvement was the elimination of the totally impractical requirement to allocate IR&D and B&P by product lines. Another help was the revision to permit allocation of these costs to final cost objectives on the same basis as used for G&A expenses, as compared with the requirement in the draft standard for the exclusive use of the total cost input base. The Board was also finally persuaded to eliminate the rigid and specific criteria it had established for deferral of IR&D costs and to permit the accounting treatment to be governed by the procurement regulations.

Although the revision to use the same base for allocating IR&D and B&P expenses as for G&A is certainly preferrable to the prior rigid and senseless requirement to use the total cost input base, this area will continue to be a problem. Most commentators argued effectively that IR&D benefits the in-house activity rather than the work of subcontractors and vendors. Accordingly, the use of the total cost input base would result in an illogical allocation, i.e., disproportionately more IR&D would be allocated to final cost objectives where material and subcontract costs were high. The CASB revision is insufficient in light of the heavy government bias in favor of the total cost input base for allocating G&A expenses (despite DOD's belated revision to W.G. 78-21, as described in Chapter XV of this text). In the author's opinion, the allocation of IR&D and B&P costs to final cost objectives should be based on beneficial or causal relations without an artifical tie-in to the manner in which G&A expenses are allocated.

Accounting Methods and Controls for Selling, General and Administrative Expenses

Probably the greatest sources of controversy and disagreement between industry and government representatives as to "allowable" and "unallowable" costs are found in the area of selling, general and administrative expenses. The controversies exist as to the nature of expenses that are to be allowed, the amount to be allowed, and the manner in which allowable expenses are to be allocated to government contracts.

Selling expenses in particular often contain expenditures that government representatives attempt to isolate and identify exclusively with the contractor's commercial business. The government's contention here holds that such expenses are not necessary or incident to the performance of its contracts and that, therefore, no portion of such costs should be borne by such contracts (an outdated T.D. 5000 concept, superseded by ASPR/DAR 15-201.4 and FAR 31.201-4).

General and administrative expenses generate problems because of the controversies that arise as to the "reasonableness" of such items as executive compensation, professional and consultant service costs, etc.

Appropriate methods for allocating selling, general and administrative expenses have been studied by government procurement and audit officials, courts and boards of contract appeals, the General Accounting Office, and the Cost Accounting Standards Board. However, the many regulations promulgated and judicial decisions rendered have failed to solve the complex problems and, if anything, may have served only to increase the controversies. This sad fact is clearly reflected in the wrangling and disputes generated by CAS 403 and 410, discussed later in this chapter.

GOVERNMENT LIMITATIONS ON EXPENSE RECOVERY

As discussed in Chapter XVI and elsewhere in this text, from the time of the earliest modern promulgations of contract cost principles the federal government has asserted that, where costs are a factor in pricing, it will not "allow" certain costs regardless of whether or not they represent necessary and ordinary expenses of doing business, and regardless of their treatment by the Internal Revenue Service and other government agencies. Over some 40 years of changing regulations, we can identify several trends. One major trend has been to expand the explanations of allowable and unallowable costs, ranging from the terse one-line statements contained in the 1940 and 1950 regulations to the voluminous commentaries of today.

Another trend of obvious and significant concern to companies doing business with the government has been the continuing expansion in the number of expenses mandated unallowable, which means that the government refuses to bear its fair share of such expenses and that they must come out of contractors' profits or equity. The very early cost principles reflected the notion that costs were unallowable unless they could be established as necessary for or incident to the performance of government contracts. This harsh and illogical concept, when carried to extremes, sometimes resulted in the disallowance of, or at least challenge to, many expenses obviously necessary to the conduct of the business where a hard-line government representative alleged that, somehow, they were not essential to contract performance.

This irrational concept was abandoned many years ago when ASPR/DAR, followed by FPR and now FAR, provided that a cost shall be considered allocable to government contracts if "it is necessary to the overall operation of the business, although a direct relationship to any particular cost objective cannot be shown." This victory for fairness and adherence to generally accepted accounting, economic, and business principles, however, was never fully achieved to begin with and the concept has been continually undermined by the increasing number of costs specifically identified as unallowable despite their clear relationship to the "overall operation of the business."

At this writing, the contract cost principles in FAR Part 31 address 51 "selected costs," most of which are established as unallowable in whole or in part even though a strong case can be made that virtually all of them are necessary for the overall operation of the business. The number of unallowable costs has increased over the years, but the rate of increase jumped sharply in the 1980s. In the early part of this decade, the additions were generally initiated by the Department of Defense, which, even with the publication of FAR, continued to exercise a dominant role with the respect to such regulations as contract cost principles. To support the requests for the necessary higher costs of defending this country and to counter congressional criticisms, DOD apparently concluded it needed to demonstrate cost effectiveness and control through various means, including limiting cost recovery by defense contractors.

As we moved into the mid-1980s, unfavorable publicity about a few major contractors who were accused of charging patently unallowable costs to defense contracts generated concerted attacks by congressional committees, GAO, DCAA and DOD IG, which culminated in the enactment of Public Law 99-145. This Act, among other things, established 10 categories of expenses as unallowable and 16 additional categories with respect to which the Secretary of Defense was directed to issue regulations clarifying their allowability in whole or in part.

A review of these provisions, as well as disallowance of costs initiated by the Defense Department, demonstrates the continual undermining of the basic concept that expenses shall be considered allowable if necessary to the overall operation of the business. Material, labor and other direct costs of contract performance are difficult to challenge. The further the costs are from the direct category, the more likelihood there is that they may be declared unallowable in whole or in part. Selling, general and administrative expenses, although as a group obviously necessary to the overall operation of a business, are usually the most remote from the actual manufacture, construction, or other requirement of contract performance. And this is the main reason why such expenses are so often the major targets of attack by the government.

Almost without exception, the 10 expense categories that P.L. 99-145 makes unallowable and the 16 concerning which, in effect, the Secretary of Defense was directed to establish as unallowable in whole or in part are selling, general and administrative expenses. With very few exceptions, these expense categories represent legitimate business costs and the federal government's arbitrary refusal to accept a fair allocation thereof to its contracts has little or no basis in equity or logic, nor in accounting or economics.

SELLING EXPENSES

Selling expenses, marketing expenses, distribution expenses, sales expenses, or expenses by whatever other term designated refer to expenditures made for the purpose of converting the company's product into ultimate cash. The current contract cost principles contain extensive provisions regarding these expenses, as illustrated by the several citations from FAR in this chapter.

31.205-1 Public Relations and Advertising Costs.

(a) "Public relations" means all functions and activities dedicated to—

(1) Maintaining, protecting, and enhancing the image of a concern or its products; or

(2) Maintaining or promoting reciprocal understanding and favorable relations with the public at large, or any segment of the public. The term public relations includes activities associated with areas such as advertising, customer relations, etc.

(b) "Advertising" means the use of media to promote the sale of products or services and to accomplish the activities referred to in paragraph (d) of this subsection, regardless of the medium employed, when the advertiser has control over the form and content of what will appear, the media in which it will appear, and when it will appear. Advertising media include but are not limited to conventions, exhibits, free goods, samples, magazines, newspapers, trade papers, direct mail, dealer cards, window displays, outdoor advertising, radio, and television.

(c) Public relations and advertising costs include the costs of media time and space, purchased services performed by outside organizations, as well as the applicable portion of salaries, travel, and fringe benefits of employees engaged in the functions and activities identified in paragraphs (a) and (b) of this subsection.

(d) The only advertising costs that are allowable are those specifically required by contract, or that arise from requirements of the Government contracts and that are exclusively for —

(1) Recruiting personnel required for performing contractual obligations, when considered in conjunction with all other recruitment costs (but see 31.205-34);

(2) Acquiring scarce items for contract performance; or

(3) Disposing of scrap or surplus materials acquired for contract performance.

Costs of this nature, if incurred for more than one Government contract or both Government work and other work of the contractor, are allowable to the extent that the principles in 31.201-3, 31.201-4, and 31.203 are observed.

(e) Allowable public relations costs include the following:

(1) Costs specifically required by contract.

(2) Costs of—

(i) Responding to inquiries on company policies and activities;

(ii) Communicating with the public, press, stockholders, creditors, and customers; and

(iii) Conducting general liaison with news media and Government public relations officers, to the extent that such activities are limited to communication and liaison necessary to keep the public informed on matters of public concern such as notice of contract awards, plant closings or openings, employee layoffs or rehires, financial information, etc.

(3) Costs of participation in community service activities (e.g., blood bank drives, charity drives, savings bond drives, disaster assistance, etc.)

(4) Costs of plant tours and open houses (but see subparagraph (f)(5) of this subsection).

(5) Costs of keel laying, ship launching, commissioning, and roll-out ceremonies, to the extent specifically provided for by contract.

(f) Unallowable public relations and advertising costs include the following:

(1) All advertising costs other than those specified in paragraph (d) of this subsection.

(2) Costs of air shows and other special events, such as conventions and trade shows, including—

(i) Costs of displays, demonstrations, and exhibits;

(ii) Costs of meeting rooms, hospitality suites, and other special facilities used in conjunction with shows and other special events; and

(iii) Salaries and wages of employees engaged in setting up and displaying exhibits, making demonstrations, and providing briefings.

(3) Costs of sponsoring meetings, symposia, seminars, and other special events when the principal purpose of the event is other than dissemination of technical information or stimulation of production.

(4) Costs of ceremonies such as corporate celebrations and new product announcements.

(5) Costs of promotional material, motion pictures, videotapes, brochures, handouts, magazines, and other media that are designed to call favorable attention to the contractor and its activities (but see 31.205-13(a), Employee morale, health, welfare, food service, and dormitory costs and credits; 31.205-21, Labor relations costs; 31.205-43(c), Trade, business, technical, and professional activity costs; and 31.205-44, Training and educational costs).

(6) Costs of souvenirs, models, imprinted clothing, buttons, and other mementos provided to customers or the public.

(7) Costs of memberships in civic and community organizations.

(8) All public relations costs, other than those specified in paragraph (e) of this subsection, whose primary purpose is to promote the sale of products or services by stimulating interest in a product or product line (except for those costs made allowable under 31.205-38(c), or by disseminating messages calling favorable attention to the contractor for purposes of enhancing the company image to sell the company's products or services. Nothing in this subparagraph (f)(8) modifies the express unallowability of costs listed in subparagraph (f)(2) through (f)(7). The purpose of this subparagraph is to provide criteria for determining whether costs not specifically identified should be unallowable.

(g) Costs made specifically unallowable under this subsection 31.205-1 are not made allowable under subsections of Subpart 31.2 such as 31.205-13, Employee morale, health, welfare, food service, and dormitory costs and credits; 31.205-22, Legislative lobbying costs; 31.205-34, Recruitment costs; 31.205-38, Selling costs; 31.205-43, Trade, business, technical, and professional activity costs; or 31.205-44, Training and educational costs. Conversely, costs that are specifically unallowable under these and other subsections of Subpart 31.2 are not made allowable under this subsection.

This relatively new (effective April 1986) cost principle establishes as unallowable many categories of public relations expenses that had been previously allowed by the Armed Services Board of Contract Appeals (ASBCA). It is the result of years of pressure by GAO, DCAA, and congressional critics of defense contractors. Craftily constructed, this cost principle combines the prior FAR 31.205-1, which was limited to advertising expenses, with the added coverage on public relations expenses in an effort to create a delusion of a close relationship between the two and thus buttress the argument for disallowing additional ordinary and necessary costs of doing business.

A comprehensive insight into this cost principle can best be achieved by tracing the origins of the initial prohibition of advertising expense and then augmentation of unallowable costs by including public relations expenses.

However, immediately subsequent to the delayed implementation of the aforegoing under the FY 1986 Appropriations Act (P.L. 99-145), the FY 1987 Continuing Appropriations Act (P.L. 99-500) was also being implemented, and it had included therein an innocuous statement to the effect that—"The foreign selling provision was never intended, or is now intended to apply to costs incurred in promoting American aerospace exports as domestic and international exhibits." Obviously, this statement is in direct conflict with the aforementioned input under P.L. 99-145, and it will be interesting to observe how this is reflected in the FAR regulation as it applies to contracts let under P.L. 99-500 and other appropriations from now on.

Thereafter, the conference reports associated with the FY 1987 and FY 1988 Appropriations Acts contained language with similar intent that such reasonable and applicable costs should be allowable. However, as of the date of this writing and pursuant to the request of the pertinent Appropriations Committees, the cognizant FAR people have not issued further implementing details regarding this item. Apparently, the direction would allow all direct and supporting costs necessary to participate in the subject exhibits to promote products for export. It will specifically exclude costs of a controversial nature in the areas of advertising, entertainment, and operating chalets as being unnecessary and unreasonable. Inasmuch as the foregoing only applied to contracts entered into under their respective Appropriations Acts as funded, it is understood that an attempt will be made to have this same blurb included in subsequent Appropriations Bills.

The major portion of advertising costs, previously allowable under defense contracts, was declared nonreimbursable in the Department of Defense Appropriation Act for 1962. Section 636 of this Act states as follows:

No part of the funds appropriated herein shall be available for paying the costs of advertising by any defense contractor, except advertising for which payment is made from profits, and such advertising shall not be considered a part of any defense contract cost. The prohibition contained in this section shall not apply with respect to advertising conducted by any such contractor, in compliance with regulations which shall be promulgated by the Secretary of Defense, solely for (1) the recruitment by that contractor of personnel required for the performance by the contractor of obligations arising under a defense contract, (2) the procurement of scarce items required by the contractor for the performance of a defense contract, or (3) the disposal of scrap or surplus materials acquired by the contractor in the performance of a defense contract.

The allowability of advertising costs under defense contracts is one of the oldest and most controversial problems in defense contract pricing. Probably the best rationale on the government's side of this subject was contained in the old "Green Book," which attempted a philosophical resolution of this matter and established a compromise, the fundamentals of which lived on for almost twenty years without substantial change. It was reasoned that advertising was not really necessary to do business with the government and, therefore, as a general rule, advertising should be considered as an inadmissible item of cost. On the other hand, it was recognized that "certain kinds of advertising of an industrial or institutional character, placed in trade or technical journals, not primarily with the object of selling particular products but essentially for the purpose of offering financial support to such trade or technical journals, because they are of value for the dissemination of trade and technical information for the industry are not really an advertising expense to effect sales so much as an operating expense incurred as a matter of policy for the benefit of the business and the industry."

The next official, defense-wide publication of consequence in this area was Section XV of ASPR, issued in March 1949. With respect to supply and research contracts with commercial organizations, the following types of advertising were included as examples of items of allowable costs.

"Advertising in trade and technical journals, providing such advertising does not offer specific products for sale but is placed for the purpose of offering financial support to journals which are valuable for the dissemination of technical information within the contractor's industry."

"Recruiting (including 'help wanted' advertisements) and training of personnel."

The 1959 DOD cost principles, generally characterized by fuller and more comprehensive commentaries, expanded the coverage on advertising costs but made no substantive change in concept.

Problems and controversies in determining allowability of advertising costs continued to grow. One of the causative factors for this growth was the increase in the number of publications that contain matters relating, in various measures, to defense. Also, proficiency in the artistic aspects of advertising copy became highly developed. As a result, larger and fancier advertisements were placed in an increasing number of magazines. As another point, unofficial (but official-sounding) publications more and more competed for advertisements by defense contractors. Congressional and other critics began to feel irritated at the sight of the multitude of lavish art works which, when contained in trade and technical journals, were usually allowed under defense contracts. The irritation probably reached its peak in the early 1960s when Congress was discussing the relative merits of two major weapons systems. The companies that fathered each of the systems, allegedly with the support of the military services involved, purportedly expended substantial sums of money on what some members of Congress considered an attempt to exercise undue influence.

What the final outcome of the congressional displeasure would have been without DOD participation is difficult to establish. However, while the House debated this issue, the Secretary of Defense and some of his top aides officially advised Congress that, in their opinion, no advertising expense should be allowed except (1) recruitment of personnel, (2) procurement of scarce items, and (3) disposal of scrap or surplus acquired for contract performance. The final language of the defense bill substantially incorporated these views.

Even before the enactment of the restrictive provisions contained in this law, the opinion was held by many that the provisions of ASPR XV were incorrect in principle. A substantial school of thought held that the only justifiable basis for questioning advertising expenses would be if the amount involved were unreasonable. Otherwise, even where the primary objective was to promote sales of commercial products, advertising could be considered a normal expense of doing business. In this connection, we would refer the reader to our comments on selling expenses. We establish the point that such expenses as product advertising, by increasing the company's sales volume, increase the total cost input or whatever basis is used to compute percentages for allocating the administrative and selling expenses. In this manner, the government actually derives a definite benefit from commercial product advertising through a lower expense rate.

However, as we mentioned earlier, the concept of some types of restriction on advertising expenses has been generally accepted for many years. This point was made clear in the various statements made before the Senate during the 1962 Appropriations Act hearings in the sense that no objections were raised to the general principle of restrictions on advertising costs. As a matter of fact, most of the witnesses appeared to concede that restrictions such as exclusion of product advertising were appropriate. There were, however, many objections raised to the prohibition against advertising costs other than help wanted, procurement of scarce items, and disposal of scrap or surplus materials.

Probably the major and most frequently mentioned objection involved the substantial usefulness of trade and technical journals in enhancing the state of the art and the various scientific and industrial fields in which interests are shared by the government. The point was repeatedly made that these magazines, useful for all engaged in a particular line of endeavor, from the student to the highest ranking government or industrial technician, could not live without the income derived from advertisements. And, where trade and technical journals would cease publication, what medium could substitute in the job of disseminating the valuable trade and technical information? In a somewhat different line, the argument was advanced that those firms that are engaged solely or substantially in defense work should be given an opportunity to maintain at least their names before the public. Modern technology being what it is, it is not unusual for the Defense Department to abandon a specific category of offensive or defensive weapons, leading to the termination of contracts held by prime and subcontractors involved in this program. Where it becomes necessary for a company to switch quickly into commercial business, or even if it must convert its capabilities into a somewhat different area within the defense activities, a failure to keep its name before potential customers (government and nongovernment) could be extremely costly.

ASPR was revised to reflect the provisions of the 1962 Appropriations Act and remained unchanged until August 1977 when subparagraph (c) was added to provide: "Advertising costs other than those specified above are not allowable."

PUBLIC RELATIONS COSTS

The origins of the addition of public relations expenses to the ever-growing list of unallowable costs may be traceable, at least in substantial part, to the decisions in *The Boeing Company,* ASBCA No. 14370, 73-2 BCA par. 10,325, and *Aerojet-General Corporation,* ASBCA No. 13372, 73-2 BCA pars. 10,307 and 10,164. In both disputes DCAA auditors questioned many corporate expenses of substantial dollar amounts, alleging they represented advertising or related expenses, unallowable then by ASPR. In both instances contracting officers were persuaded to sustain the audit recommendations. The board carefully studied dictionary definitions of the terms involved and reinstated substantial portions of the disallowances. Some of the costs allowed by the board were declared to constitute public relations expenses that were not designated as unallowable by the ASPR cost principle on advertising or by the governing statute upon which this provision was based.

As mentioned elsewhere, DOD frequently moves rapidly to revise its regulations to identify, as unallowable, costs that the ASBCA rules allowable. In the case of public relations expense, however, DCAA efforts to persuade the ASPR/DAR Committees to revise the DOD regulations to make such costs unallowable had thus far been unsuccessful.

Unable to find a statutory or regulatory base for disallowing public relations costs, DCAA devoted considerable attention to this subject in its Contract Audit Manual (CAM), Chapter 7, Section 12, in the current (December 1987) edition. The essence of the instructions to the field auditors is that public relations expenses should be carefully scrutinized, with special attention accorded to whether portions may be susceptible to classification as contributions, entertainment, or other expenses that are established as unallowable by acquisition regulations. Considerable emphasis is also directed to the reasonableness criteria, and the auditors are admonished that even though public relations costs were not currently unallowable per se, they may be so considered if they, for example, "represent a significant deviation from established business practices, increasing contract costs." In these circumstances, the audit agency concludes that the costs "are likely to be unreasonable."

Public relations costs charged to DOD contracts were the subject of an "oversight hearing" by the House Legislation and National Security Subcommittee of the Committee on Government Operations on July 25, 1984. In his opening remarks, Chairman Jack Brooks stated:

> Today we will examine another issue involving DOD's management of public funds—the practice of DOD paying defense contractor's public relations expenses—that is, expenses incurred to enhance the contractors' public image. We will hear testimony on recent studies which indicate that a loophole exists in contract cost principles which results in reimbursement to many contractors for such items as exhibits, ceremonies, promotional material and gifts.

> Each year the auditors of the Defense Contract Audit Agency question over a half billion dollars claimed by contractors as public relations expenses. However, many of these questioned costs are subsequently allowed by contracting officers and ultimately paid by DOD with taxpayers' dollars.

> During the course of this hearing, we hope to learn more about the extent of this wasteful practice and what should be done to prevent it.

An opening statement was also made by Senator David Pryor, who took the occasion "to praise Common Cause Magazine . . . . for the very fine article entitled "Lookin' Good" on this subject. The Senator was indignant about the allowability of public relations expenses and accused DOD:

> Time and again Pentagon officials have blocked conscientious auditors who were trying to protect public funds. Time and again, the military-industrial complex has worn down the watchdogs and the public has suffered.

Further indicating his feelings and distrust of responsible officials in the executive branch, the Senator called for legislation "to prohibit taxpayer reimbursement of public relations. I would like to think that regulations would suffice, but I am concerned about assuring a permanent change and avoiding undue pressure on regulations writers by the contractor community." The Senator did not appear to be aware how little effect any such alleged pressure has had, as the regulations writers have promulgated one harsh provision after another in recent years, e.g., disallowance of contractors' costs of defending themselves against fraud charges, disallowance of lobbying and goodwill, and elimination of CWAS.

The lead-off witness, of course, was a representative of GAO. He complained that although some of the FAR provisions regarding allowability of costs (31.205) are specific, "many are vague." He noted that public relations costs were not specifically addressed, but alleged that while such costs "are routinely questioned by DCAA as being unallowable advertising," they were being allowed under the provisions of selling costs. He supported this allegation by an incomplete citation of FAR 31.205-38. The full provision and actual practice would appear to sharply contradict this allegation.

Alleging that the considerable ambiguity in FAR results in different interpretations among contractors, DCAA, and contracting officers, the GAO official reported on a review of certain final overhead costs settlements. Instances were offered relating to costs of air shows, exhibits, technical public relations films, advertising, which included both employee recruitment and description of the company's products, etc. In these instances, DCAA auditors, of course, questioned the total of such expenses. Contracting officers, however, allowed all or portions of these charges. GAO's conclusion was that "clarification of FAR is needed," and the direction of the clarification desired by the watchdog agency was obvious from the testimony.

A DCAA official then testified that this subject "has long been of concern to DOD and particularly DCAA." He further stated:

> In a nutshell, our concern is that public relations costs of Government contractors comprise a very large amount of costs easily misclassified and lacking overall control. Some contractors tend to classify product advertising, donations, entertainment and other unallowable expense as public relations costs or some other categorization of costs. In addition, because contractors are not required to accumulate public relations costs in the accounts under a consistent definition, other expenses which are commonly considered public relations costs are dispersed throughout the accounts. This makes summarization for reasonableness assessments difficult or impossible.

These and other comments by the DCAA representative were the kinds of statements the congressmen wished to hear and they were well received. He assured the Subcommittee that "effort toward assuring adequate control of public relations costs charged to government contracts is taking place within the Department of Defense" and advised of the recommendation made on May 29, 1984, by the DOD comptroller (DCAA inspired). The recommendation was for a "broad study to precisely identify public relations activities, determine whether any of those activities benefit DOD contracts, consider the need to establish thresholds for determining reasonableness, and develop a DOD policy on the allowability of public relations costs."

The DCAA official's prepared testimony included an appendix containing a proposed definition of "public relations" and a copy of Chapter 7, Section 12 of CAM (December 1983). In advance of the hearing, the audit agency had furnished Chairman Brooks with certain information developed by a study of 28 contractor segments, including "public relations definitions, accounting treatment of public relations costs, and public relations costs questioned in the most recent contractor fiscal year." The letter summarized the results of the agency's survey as follows:

1. Where contractors have defined public relations, the definitions are broad and inconsistent among contractors.

2. Public relations costs are not consistently identified in the accounting records. This requires auditors to spend additional time to ferret out these costs and identify the corollary expenses.

The letter further advised that the DAR Council will establish a case to review this DCAA data, "along with other considerations, to determine whether or not a special group should be established to perform a study of public relations costs." To display the agency's continuous zeal in this area, its July 12, 1984, letter to Brooks stated: "DCAA is also continuing to consider alternative approaches for controlling public relations costs. Proposals for revising the cost principles may result from this consideration."

Although all of the witnesses agreed that there was a need to revise the regulations to provide better definitions of these costs and establish reasonableness criteria, all obviously designed to reduce the allowability of public relations costs, which the Armed Services Board of Contract Appeals had ruled on several occasions were allowable under existing statutes and regulations, none of them was prepared to offer specific recommendations regarding the treatment of public relations costs. This led the congressional committee to reiterate its lack of confidence in the executive branch to formulate regulations in this area restrictive enough to suit them. It became obvious that this latest attack on contractor cost recovery was in high gear and the alternative to regulatory action would be punitive legislation.

On February 21, 1985, the FAR Councils issued a proposed revision of 31.205-1 with provisions similar in many respects to the final version now incorporated in FAR.

As described earlier, the DOD 1986 Authorization Act, P.L. 99-145, directed that 10 expense categories be made unallowable and the extent, if any, to which 16 other expenses would be allowable should be clarified. These listings include public relations expenses both directly and indirectly.

Industry was understandably concerned over the sweeping and punitive provisions in the FAR February 1985 proposal, and CODSIA offered many serious objections with respect thereto. Recognizing the futility of trying to persuade the regulators to take no action with respect to this expense, the industry association sought to ameliorate some of its harsher aspects. Even P.L. 99-145 did not mandate the disallowance of all public relations expenses, but included this cost category among those which required clarification.

Industry's cogent suggestions for revisions of the proposed cost principle were accorded very little consideration by the DOD-dominated writers of the FAR Part on contract cost principles who were apparently much more concerned over continued congressional investigations and hearings. Staffed by GAO and DCAA auditors, the "Cofer" investigation led to one more report criticizing contracting officers for allowing costs questioned by DCAA. Public relations was one of the expenses prominently addressed. Accordingly, the final FAR provision, quoted earlier in this chapter, effective April 7, 1986, reflected few changes of substance from the February 1985 version.

Selling Costs

The FAR provision in effect immediately prior to July 30, 1987, is quoted below:

31.205-38 Selling costs.

(a) "Selling" is a generic term encompassing all efforts to market the contractor's products or services, some of which are covered specifically in other subsections of 31.205. Selling activity includes the following broad categories:

(1) Advertising.

(2) Corporate image enhancement including broadly-targeted sales efforts, other than advertising.

(3) Bid and proposal costs.

(4) Market planning.

(5) Direct selling.

(b) Advertising costs are defined at 31.205-1(b) and are subject to the allowability provisions of 31.205-1(d) and (f). Corporate image enhancement activities are included within the definitions of public relations at 31.205-1(a) and entertainment at 31.205-14 and are subject to the allowability provisions at 31.205-1(e) and (f) and 31.205-14, respectively. Bid and proposal costs are defined at 31.205-18 and have their allowability controlled by that subsection. Market planning involves market research and analysis and generalized management planning concerned with development of the contractor's business. The allowability of long-range market planning costs is controlled by the provisions of 31.205-12. Other market planning costs are allowable to the extent that they are reasonable. Costs of activities which are correctly classified and disallowed under cost principles referenced in this paragraph (b) are not to be reconsidered for reimbursement under any other provision of this subsection.

(c) Direct selling efforts are those acts or actions to induce particular customers to purchase particular products or services of the contractor. Direct selling is characterized by person-to-person contact and includes such activities as familiarizing a potential customer with the contractor's products or services, conditions of sale, service capabilities, etc. It also includes negotiation, liaison between customer and contractor personnel, technical and consulting activities, individual demonstrations, and any other activities having as their purpose the application or adaptation of the contractor's products or services for a particular customer's use. The cost of direct selling efforts is allowable if reasonable in amount.

(d) The costs of any selling efforts other than those addressed in paragraph (b) or (c) of this subsection are unallowable.

(e) Costs of the type identified in paragraphs (b), (c), and (d) of this subsection are often commingled on the contractor's books in the selling expense account because these activities are performed by the sales departments. However, identification and segregation of unallowable costs is required under the provisions of 31.201-6 and CAS 405, and such costs are not allowable merely because they are incurred in connection with allowable selling activities.

(f) Notwithstanding any other provision of this subsection, selling costs incurred in connection with potential and actual Foreign Military Sales as defined by the Arms Export Control Act, or foreign sales of military products or services are unallowable on U.S. Government contracts for U.S. Government requirements.

(g) Notwithstanding any other provision of this subsection, sellers' or agents' compensation, fees, commissions, percentages, retainer or brokerage fees, whether or not contingent upon the award of contracts, are allowable only when paid to bona fide employees or established commercial or selling agencies maintained by the contractor for the purpose of securing business (see 3.408-2).

The 1949 ASPR cost principles did not contain any specific reference to allowable selling expenses. On the other hand, "commissions and bonuses (under whatever name) in connection with obtaining or negotiating for a government contract" and "selling and distribution activities not related to the contract products" were specifically cited as examples of items of unallowable costs. The later ASPR/DAR cost principles, although failing to eliminate the controversies, did appear to constitute a somewhat more liberal attitude toward this cost category. For example, they stated that "selling costs are allowable to the extent that they are reasonable and are allocable to government business," and, in this regard, an advance understanding was recommended. As basic criteria in ascertaining whether the selling costs were allocable to government business, the cost principles suggested a determination "in the light of reasonable benefit to the government arising from such activities as technical, consulting, demonstration, and other services which are for the purposes such as application or adaptation of the contractor's products to government use." A reasonable application of this provision should result in uncontested allowance of all selling efforts relating to government contracts, subject only to possible discussion as to reasonableness of amounts.

A substantial change between the old and later DAR cost principles appears to have been made in relation to commissions. Whereas commissions "in connection with obtaining or negotiating for a government contract" were previously specifically cited as unallowable, the later principles stated: "salesmen's or agent's compensation, fees, commissions, percentages, retainer or brokerage fees, whether or not contingent upon the award of contracts, whether foreign or domestic (but see 6-1305), are allowable only when paid to bona fide employees (see 1-505.3) or bona fide established commercial or selling agencies (see 1-505.4) maintained by the contractor for the purpose of securing business."

The regulations and widespread attitudes in the government have consistently reflected an inherent, adverse bias against allowing selling expenses. And, even though the regulations in recent years, including the FAR provision prior to the April 1986 revision, recognize the allowability of certain selling expenses, they have always qualified the allowability by reminding government auditing and contracting officials that the allowance depended on a showing of benefit to the government and reasonableness of the amounts involved. Generally, there is no objection to the criteria of benefit and reasonableness. However, these criteria are adequately stated in FAR 31.201 for applicability to all costs, and the additional emphasis in the selling cost principle understandably provides government representatives, particularly auditors, with a basis for exercising additional attention and discrimination with respect to this cost. In this connection, the provisions of the DCAA's CAM are cited later in this chapter.

Congressional investigations and hearings in the mid-1980s, with the extensive participation of GAO and DCAA representatives, asserted that contracting officer reinstatements of costs questioned by DCAA ran high with respect to certain expenses. Selling costs were not identified as one of these areas per se; however, there were allegations that advertising and other unallowable costs of this nature were allowed by contracting officers when classified by contractors as selling costs. This led to the provision that selling cost be included in the 16 categories that required clarification.

The proposed implementation of P.L. 99-145 relating to selling costs was initially published on December 24, 1985, and reflected a substantial expansion of the prior FAR provision. Apart from what many observers believed to be unnecessary verbiage that might confuse as much as clarify, the major features of the proposal were the reiterations that other expenses should not be intermingled with selling expenses.

Recent FAR Provision Brings Slight Relief to Foreign Selling Costs (FSC) Policy

FAC 84-26, effective July 30, 1987, revised FAR 31.205-38(f), which had been interpreted as disallowing any and all costs and expenses related to Foreign Military Sales. The new language and explanatory comments are quoted below:

(f) Notwithstanding any other provision of this subsection, costs of direct selling efforts, as defined in paragraph (c) of this subsection, incurred in connection with potential and actual Foreign Military Sales, as defined by the Arms Export Control Act, or foreign sales of military products or services are unallowable on U.S. Government contracts for U.S. Government requirements.

Item XII—Selling and Marketing

FAC 84-15 dated April 7, 1986, substantially revised FAR 31.205-38, Selling Costs. This revision responsed to Section 911 of Pub. L. 99-145, which directed that the cost principle be clarified. As revised, FAR 31.205-38 establishes a comprehensive Government policy on the allowability of selling costs. In so doing, the new cost principle specifically incorporates elements of cost that are treated in separate cost principles, such as advertising, public relations, and bid and proposal costs. While incorporating separate cost principles into FAR 31.205-38 makes it more coherent and definitive, this express recognition has expanded the scope of "selling costs" beyond that covered previously by FAR 31.205-38.

After reviewing public comments on the original proposal, as well as internal input, the DARC and the CAAC have concluded that paragraph (f) of FAR 31.206-38 may, because of the expanded concept of "selling costs," have unintended side effects. More specifically, paragraph (f) disallows foreign selling costs on U.S. Government contracts for U.S. Government requirements. While the Councils intended this statement simply to preserve prior policy concerning foreign selling costs, as directed by Section 8071 of Pub. L. 99-190, FAR 31.205-38's generally expanded scope has the effect of making costs, principally bid and proposal costs associated with foreign sales, unallowable on U.S. Government contracts for U.S. Government requirements. To correct this unintended effect (i.e., expansion of the disallowance to categories of cost beyond those addressed by Congress when the funding limitation was enacted), the Councils have modified paragraph (f) to limit the restriction associated with foreign sales to "direct selling efforts," as defined in FAR 31.205-38(c). This category of costs most closely approximates those foreign selling costs which were made unallowable by paragraph (b) of FAR 31.205-38 as in effect on April 1, 1984, and whose compensation is prohibited by Pub. L. 99-190.

CAS Board Effort on Selling Costs

After conducting preliminary field research, the CASB issued a Staff Issues Paper on the subject of Allocating of Selling and Marketing Expenses. However, because the Board was then preoccupied with promulgating CAS 418 and 420, trying to revise CAS 403 and 410, and unsuccessfully seeking to prolong its existence, no further action was taken with respect to a possible standard governing selling expenses.

Selling Costs as Viewed by DCAA

Government contract auditors have traditionally taken a hard line against allowing any expenses included in the category of selling costs. The bias was carried over into DCAA and, despite this organization's professional training for its audit staff, instances are still encountered where any expenses so termed are questioned (recommended for disallowance) on the basis of a nomenclature review rather than an objective audit. The general attitude of contract auditors is important to consider because the likelihood of recovery of expenses within this group which were incurred in connection with, or would reasonably benefit, government contracts will often be improved to the extent of the contractor's ability to effect the necessary refinements and classifications in its accounts to substantiate those expenses properly chargeable to government business.

DCAA's close, hard-line approach to these expenses is reflected in its Contract Audit Manual, quoted below:

7-1302 General Audit Considerations

Selling expenses are subject to the same basic audit procedures and tests for allocability and reasonableness as manufacturing and administrative expenses. However, there are certain factors for special consideration. Where a significant amount of selling expense is involved there should be adequate tests of the individual items and accounts classified under this expense category to enable the auditor to fully understand (1) the type and size of the contractor's sales organization, (2) the basis of employee compensation, (3) the nature of the selling and distribution activities involved, (4) their relationship to the contractor's different operations, products or product lines, and (5) their applicability to Government and commercial business. A nomenclature review of account titles is not sufficient for this purpose.

7-1304.1 General Allocability Considerations

a. FAR 31.201-4 and 31.203 contain criteria regarding the allocability of costs to cost objectives. These sections also apply to the determination of the allocability of selling costs. Proper allocability is accomplished by (1) the direct charge or (2) apportionment to particular cost objectives such as products, product lines, classes of customers, or individual contracts, by means of a basis that will apportion the expenses in accordance with the benefits derived by the particular cost objectives, or the purposes for which the expenses were incurred. Also see 6-606 and 6-606.4 regarding allocability.

b. FAR 31.202(a) and 31.203(a) require, for costs incurred for the same purpose in like circumstances, consistency in the allocation of these costs as direct or indirect costs. Where a specific type or category of selling expense is allocated as a direct charge to Government contracts or other cost objectives, care must be exercised to assure that all items or transactions in the same type or category applicable to other cost objectives are likewise allocated as a direct charge.

c. FAR 31.203(b) addresses selection of appropriate bases for allocation of indirect costs. The selection of an appropriate base for the apportionment of selling expenses as an indirect charge involves certain considerations different from those applicable to manufacturing expenses. Manufacturing expenses are usually apportioned without regard to the specific end item being manufactured or the customer to whom the item may ultimately be sold. These latter factors, however, are important considerations in apportioning selling expenses which may indicate that an over all allocation of selling expenses on the basis of cost of sales or cost of goods manufactured may not be equitable. The auditor should perform a careful analysis of the time, effort and expense incurred for selling activities in relation to the company's products, product lines, classes of customers or other objectives to determine the most suitable base for apportioning selling expenses.

d. When a contractor, with contracts subject to the Cost Accounting Standards, includes selling costs in its G&A pool, those costs are subject to the provisions of CAS 410.40(d) and 410.50(b)(1). These sections require that marketing costs whose beneficial or causal relationship to business unit cost objectives can be best measured by a base other than a cost input base representing the total activity of a period be removed from the G&A expense pool and allocated on a representative base. If a total cost input or value added base is used to distribute G&A expenses, selling costs would then become part of the G&A allocation base. See also 8-410.

e. When a contractor, with contracts subject to the Cost Accounting Standards, allocates selling costs to final cost objectives using one or more burden pools other than the G&A pool, the requirements of CAS 418 apply. CAS 418 requires that costs be accumulated in homogeneous pools and allocated using bases best representing a beneficial or causal relationship of the pooled costs to cost objectives. For example, when commercial selling effort is disproportionate to that expended for government selling effort, separate pools should be established and allocation bases representative of each pool's activity should be selected to distribute the costs to the benefiting cost objectives. See also 8-418.

7-1305 Reasonableness of Selling Costs

Reasonableness involves consideration of (1) the nature and amount of these costs in the light of the expenses which a prudent individual would incur in the conduct of competitive business, (2) the proportionate amounts expended as between Government and commercial business, (3) the trend and comparability of the company's current period costs in relation with prior periods, (4) the general level of such costs within the industry, and (5) the nature and extent of the sales effort in relation to the costs thereof and to the contract value. The foregoing considerations may result in a determination that a particular item or category of selling expense is not reasonable either in total due to its nature or in part due to the excessiveness of the amount involved (see FAR 31.201-3). In determining reasonableness, the following factors should receive special consideration:

a. Some companies engaged in defense production expend substantial amounts to establish and maintain large staffs of salesmen and engineers whose primary function is obtaining new or additional Government business on a prime or subcontract basis for existing company products and to seek out other products required by the Government which the company can manufacture with its existing facilities. The submission of unsolicited bids and proposals and the preparation of brochures setting forth the company's capabilities and past accomplishments with respect to defense work usually represent an important aspect of this function. In periods of low volume, companies may divert normal production engineering personnel to augment their sales staff on a temporary basis or hire additional sales personnel to increase volume.

b. If appropriate safeguards are not maintained with respect to selling expenses, companies engaged wholly or substantially in Government production under flexible price type contracts may conceivably be encouraged to increase their selling activites without restraint since they would expect to be compensated therefor as a necessary cost of doing business. Other companies in the same industry with little or no existing flexible price Government business (cost-type or price-redeterminable contracts), would thus be placed in an unfavorable competitive position for new Government business as compared with those companies who in effect have been subsidized by the Government for their selling activities.

c. Each audit should also include an appraisal of the extent to which the sales promotion, consultation, technical, liaison and other related activities engaged in by the contractor's personnel produced a recognizable benefit to the Government in consonance with the amounts included in the contractor's claims or cost representations. "Benefit to the Government" should be considered, in a broad sense, as the acceptability of selling expense is not necessarily contingent upon a showing of proof that the performance of a specific item would not have been possible without the incurrence of such expenses. If it can be established that useful and desirable information was exchanged or that technical matters concerning existing contracts were discussed during visits by the contractors' personnel to Government procurement offices, the resulting costs may be considered to result in "benefit to the Government." This situation is contrasted with visits made for purely promotional purposes where a contractor's sales representative seeks Government contracts or related information and his or her visits do not result in any commensurate benefit to the Government.

d. While DFARS 25.7305 is applicable to acquisitions made for the purpose of Foreign Military Sales (FMS), DFARS 25.7305(d)(2)(iii) contains criteria for determining the reasonableness of sales agents' fees or commissions that can be applied in evaluating the reasonableness of sales agents' fees and commissions on non-FMS contracts as well. This section states "The basic test of reasonableness ... is an assessment of the services provided, or to be provided, compared to the amount of the fee. In addition to the fee breakdown of services, a comparative analysis may be made of the proposed fee/commission with recent payment for comparable services under commercial sales (non-FMS) of the same or similar items, and sales commissions and fees allowed on previous FMS of comparable scope and dollar amounts. In analyzing the fee, consideration should be given to whether the sale is the initial or follow-on sale because the effort for follow-on sales of additional quantities, spares, and support equipment would not normally be as great as the effort for the initial sale."

e. It will usually be necessary to request technical assistance from the contracting officer in evaluating the reasonableness of the agent's commissions or fees. The request will state all facts available to the auditor which could bear on the technical review. If the requested technical assistance is not provided before the report is issued, the acceptability of these costs should be qualified in the report (see CAM 10-303).

Direct Selling Expenses

Some accounting literature recognizes salesmen's salaries, commissions, and traveling expenses as direct selling expenses. To these expenses, purists would add a pro rata portion of related indirect selling expenses, including payroll taxes, clerical salaries, rent, light, etc. The aggregate of direct selling expenses would then be charged as a cost of specific products benefiting therefrom. In this regard, the contract cost principles provide that: "Selling costs are allowable to the extent they are ... allocable to Government business." This point emphasizes the need for careful segregation of those direct selling expenses that are incurred in connection with defense contracts so that recovery can be effected.

An important point in regard to the selling expenses identifiable with government costs is the method of their allocation. Many contractors have been guilty of the rather obvious error of spreading government selling expenses over all the products sold. It goes without saying that such expenses should be allocated only to government contracts. This procedure cannot be effected unless the contractor's records disclose not only the aggregate of such expenses, but also the related basis for allocation. In other words, assuming that such expenses are to be apportioned in the ratio of cost of sales, it is obvious that the total cost of government sales must be known in order to effect the allocations.

Credit and Collection Expenses

All expenses of this nature, including losses on bad debts, are frequently considered unrecoverable under government contracts by DCAA and other contract auditors. The rationale is that the government does not default on its just debts. By the same token, they argue, it would not appear necessary to incur collection expense of the type experienced with slow payers. Regardless of the obvious fallacy of the latter point, care must be exercised to ascertain that credit and collection expense categories do not contain such costs as normal billing expenses, etc. This separation is important for the reason that a credit and collection account or group of accounts may be "disallowed" by government auditors in their entirety. Accordingly, any expenses included in that group that may be applicable to government contracts should be segregated and disclosed.

In many instances the credit department may investigate the credibility of certain suppliers servicing both government and commercial contracts. If this is so, it can be used as a basis for sustaining at least a portion of the total expenses on government business.

Selling Costs in Connection with Foreign Military Sales

The many problems that contractors continue to experience in appropriately recovering selling costs under government contracts have taken on increased complexity in the case of foreign military sales (FMS). For readers who may not be completely familiar with the terminology, we might note that sales of U.S. arms to foreign governments may be accomplished generally by one of two methods. The foreign government may purchase either directly from the United States producer or from the United States government. Sales by the United States government to foreign countries, which may be either from existing stock or by new procurement, are referred to as FMS. The others are considered in the category of commercial sales.

Beginning probably some time before our entrance into World War II, sales of U.S. arms to foreign governments by both methods increased substantially. This activity has been plagued by considerable confusion, and American efforts have been deterred by various efforts, on both the legislative and executive sides, to move into this area and exercise controls. An example of legislative initiatives is found in the Arms Export Control Act, P. L. 90-627 as amended by P.L. 94-329. An example of executive involvement was President Carter's policy statement in 1977 reflecting his interest in restraining the support of American arms by any type of sale or by grant. As in the case of many other initiatives of this kind, the restraints on American sales of arms did not reduce either the desire or capacity of many countries to obtain them. All we accomplished was to enable the Soviet Union and other nations in the communist block, and a number of our allies as well, to substantially increase their arms sales.

In the area of contract pricing, in apparent connection with the policy to deter or at least not encourage foreign military sales, the Defense Department's weighted guidelines for computing profit were revised by removing a factor previously included that provided an additional 1% to 4% for FMS. The additional profit factor had originally been included in the recognition that additional costs and risks were initially incurred by contractors in sales to foreign countries. When DOD removed the 1% to 4% additional profit factor for FMS, there was an understanding within the industry that DAR Section XV would be revised to provide at least partial compensation. And it was in this context that DOD was understood to have undertaken the revision of DAR 15-205.37. Previous to that time, it had contained no reference to selling expenses related to foreign sales. Although those costs should have been included among all others as allowable subject only to tests for reasonableness and allocability, questions had been raised by some DOD officials concerning the allowability of foreign-related selling costs. It was understood that DOD was to revise DAR 15-205.37 to make it clear that such expenses were allowable.

On March 12, 1979, DOD published a revision (DAC 76-18) to 15-205.37. The portion applicable to FMS stated: ". . . Selling costs incurred in connection with potential and actual foreign military sales as defined by the Arms Export Control Act, or foreign sales of military products shall not be allocable to U.S. Government contracts for U.S. Government requirements."

Understandably, DOD contractors felt aggrieved. Under the language cited above, and so interpreted by government auditors and some contracting officers, selling costs related to sales to foreign governments would be disallowed even though they were properly allocated in accordance with other DAR provisions and cost accounting standards. As CODSIA pointed out in its letter of October 17, 1979, to DOD, this new prohibition or disallowance had not been included in the DOD proposal that had been distributed to industry for comments. Industry saw the adverse effect on recovery of selling costs as threatening a reduction of related selling efforts with a resultant loss in international sales. By this time, there was a wide consensus that the administration's unilateral constraints on foreign military sales were contrary to the best interests of the United States.

In its lengthy letter to the Department of Defense, CODSIA also explained that FMS provide benefits to all work of the contractors in the form of lower costs to DOD, which are attributable to production volume and learning curve effects as well as to the increased base for allocation of indirect costs. DOD was also advised that any proposal to allocate particular selling costs solely to FMS would be inappropriate and inequitable because selling costs are not usually incurred in the same year in which the products are produced or delivered.

CODSIA also suggested that the revision contained in DAC 76-18 could be interpreted as requiring one or more additional overhead cost pools and separate allocation bases by contractors involved in FMS or other foreign sales. There appeared to be a conflict with CASB concepts regarding allocation of overhead pools on the basis of causal or beneficial relationships. There also seemed to be a very real possibility that compliance with the new DAR 15-205.37 might result in an automatic noncompliance with one or more cost accounting standards.

The well-thought-out communication from CODSIA concluded by strongly urging that DOD promptly revoke the revision established by DAC 76-18.

DOD moves very slowly on a revision that may be in industry's interests. This pace is in sharp contrast to the Pentagon's speed when revising cost principles to make unallowable a cost that a board of contract appeals or court ruled allowable. (See for example our comments on goodwill in Chapter XVII.) In this case over a year after communications with CODSIA, the DAR Council offered for comment a revision to DAR 15-205.37 that deleted the prohibition against allowing selling costs in connection with FMS.

The principle on selling costs initially incorporated into FAR, however, substantially adopted the existing DAR provisions, ignoring all of the proposed changes, including the deletion of the prohibition against selling costs on FMS.

In view of a shift in national policy, which now monitored and regulated rather than deterred American sales of military material to selected countries, the retention of this prohibition seemed to many to lack any foundation other than the usual efforts of the usual DOD elements to restrict contractors' cost recovery. Industry continued its efforts and, after years of frustrating efforts, action was finally initiated at high DOD levels to remove this provision.

Formal notice of this decision was contained in a memorandum from the Principle Deputy Under Secretary of Defense (Research and Engineering) James P. Wade, Jr., Acting, to the Director, Defense Acquisition Regulatory System, dated April 4, 1984, quoted below:

SUBJECT: Allocability of Foreign Selling Costs to DoD Contracts

The DAR was changed on March 12, 1979, to prohibit allocation of any foreign selling costs to DoD contracts. Prior to the 1979 change DoD accepted and negotiated, as part of overhead, a fair share of selling costs for U.S. Government, foreign, and commercial sales activity on the basis of reasonable benefit to U.S. Government contracts.

The DAR change was made in 1979 because the existing coverage was considered to be inconsistent with President Carter's Presidential Decision No. 13 which was designed to discourage defense sales to foreign countries.

The Reagan Administration repealed PD No. 13, and has taken the position that arms sales are an "indispensable" component of foreign policy. Therefore, it is apparent that the restrictive disincentive objective that caused the original change to DAR 15-205.37 no longer exists, and the old policy should be restored based on the Current Administration's policy towards cooperative arms sales.

I, therefore, direct the DAR Council to initiate a revision to FAR 31.205-38 and the DoD FAR Supplement 25.7304 to (a) immediately return to the cost recovery policies that existed prior to the 1979 DAR change; and (b) open a FAR case to completely resolve any question on the reasonableness, allocability, and allowability of selling costs.

Although it appeared at that time that fairness and good cost accounting would be reinstated in this cost principle, opposition to the DOD proposal surfaced within both the Defense Department and Congress. The Navy, which in recent years has consistently adopted a more hostile attitude toward industry, objected on the grounds that " no measurable benefit" would accrue from these additional costs. When congressional objections were added, the Wade proposal was abandoned, and the current (April 1986) FAR provision retains the FMS selling cost prohibition.

Special and Inequitable Treatment of Foreign Selling Costs (FSC)

The history of foreign selling costs is lengthy and dismal, with proponents of disallowing such costs on domestic DOD contracts devoting little attention to equity, cost accounting principles, or cost accounting standards. The desirability of foreign military sales (FMS) was clearly recognized as in the interests of national policy and the risks inherent in such sales were recognized by special profit consideration. Major contractor recovery problems were most adversely affected by the Arms Export Control Act (AECA) of 1976, Public Law 94-329. The impact of this unfortunate legislation on costs and profits is probably best described in General Electric Company, ASBCA No. 24913, 83-1 BCA par. 16,130, although the dispute was essentially concerned with recovery of IR&D and B&P expenses under FMS contracts.

Special profit considerations for FMS were ultimately eliminated on the ground that such action was demanded by AECA. Additionally, the DOD cost principles group somehow concluded that this Act also required establishing FSC as unallowable under domestic contracts. Industry strongly protested and the Office of the DOD General Counsel agreed that the AECA indeed did not require such action but required only that "foreign customer must pay full value." Continued industry efforts led to DAR consideration to revising the prohibition against allowing FSC, but no revision was ever made and this prohibition ultimately was incorporated into FAR 31.205-38(f).

In one of the latest of the many controversies involving this area, a contractor included foreign selling costs (FSC), identified in this controversy as "costs incurred in foreign sales of military products, i.e., foreign military products selling costs," in his G&A expense pool at his Electronics and Space (E&S) Division and allocated them to all contracts using total cost input as the base. The government disallowed approximately 3 million dollars, representing the portion of such costs charged to domestic DOD contracts for the period October 1, 1979, through March 8, 1984, on the ground that they were unallowable under the then provisions of DAR 15-205.37. The government further charged that the contractor's practice violated CAS 405, Accounting for Unallowable Costs.

The contractor moved for summary judgment, supporting his appeal on the legal grounds: "(1) that foreign selling costs were not 'expressly unallowable costs' subject to the requirements of CAS 405 and (2) that the allocation requirement expressed in DAR 15-205.37(b) conflicts impermissibly with CAS 410 . . . and is without legal effect." The contractor's motion was denied and the parties directed to prepare for hearing on the merits. *Emerson Electric Co.,* ASBCA No. 30090, November 19, 1986, 87-1 BCA par. 19,478.

Although the hearing on the merits may provide information regarding acceptable alternative methods of treating FSC, it cannot solve the basic problem in the inequity of the acquisition regulations, particularly the even more definitive prohibitions in the current FAR.

The DAR provisions during the period involved in the dispute stated in part:

> (b) Selling costs are allowable to the extent they are reasonable and are allocable to Government business. . . . Selling costs incurred in connection with potential and actual Foreign Military Sales as defined by the Arms Export Control Act, or foreign sales of military products shall not be allocable to U.S. Government contracts for U.S. Government requirements.

In March 1982, DCAA issued an audit report to the ACO asserting Emerson was in noncompliance with CAS 405 and DAR 15-205.37, but did not issue a Form 1. The ACO issued an initial finding of noncompliance with CAS 405 thereafter. In the ensuing correspondence between Emerson and the ACO, Emerson disagreed and the ACO requested the contractor to submit a cost impact proposal. Correspondence, discussions, and further DCAA audits continued for about a year, and the parties finally agreed to revised procedures under which Emerson developed separate selling expense rates for foreign and domestic sales, and these costs were removed from the G&A pool and included in the total cost input base against which G&A expenses would be allocated.

The parties were unable to reach agreement on the original issues of noncompliance with CAS 405 and DAR 15-205.37. Upon further review of DCAA's reports and correction of errors contained therein, the ACO corrected the government's computation of the cost impact of the alleged noncompliance from $3 to $2.2 million.

Although Emerson's motion focused on only the CAS 405 violation and the parties had addressed only this issue and disregarded the disallowance issue, the board concluded that the scope of this appeal should properly extend to the allowability of FSC. The board further noted that the latter issue did not depend on establishing a CAS violation. Therefore, even if Emerson's motion were granted, it would not dispose of the entire appeal.

Emerson's arguments that FSC were not "expressly costs" under the then DAR provisions were based largely on the language that such costs were not "allocable" and did not state they were not "allowable."

The board rejected this argument, ruling that the language of the entire cost principle made it obvious that the intent was to establish FSC as unallowable. The first sentence of the paragraph in question stated that selling costs "are allowable to the extent they are allocable" to government contracts, and the third sentence, that foreign military products selling costs "shall not be allocable" to domestic government contracts. The board concluded that these two statements made up the first two legs of a syllogism, and the third leg would necessarily be: "Therefore, foreign military products selling costs are not allowable under domestic Government contracts."

While not directly "unallowable," the board concluded it was direct enough to come within the intended meaning of CAS 405, in its use of the term "expressly unallowable."

Emerson's second legal point contended that CAS 410 permitted the inclusion of selling costs in the G&A expense pool and required the allocation of G&A expenses on a cost input base, with the total cost intput base, the one used by Emerson preferred. DAR 15-205.37(b), argued the contractor, contradicts CAS 410 by requiring that foreign selling costs be separated and allocated over a fragmented cost input base that does not reflect the total activity of the business unit. Accordingly, Emerson contended:

> As the provisions of CAS take precedence over the DAR Cost Principles, the conflict must be resolved in favor of the CAS provision and DAR 15-205.37(b) is without legal effect.

In setting out this argument, the contractor relied on *The Boeing Co.*, ASBCA No. 28342, 85-3 BCA par. 18,435, aff'd *U.S. v. The Boeing Co.*, [33 CCF par. 74,612], CA FC No. 86-927, 10/1/86. (The board decision and the court's ruling are reviewed in Chapter XVIII.)

The board ruled that Emerson's reliance on *Boeing* was misplaced. As reviewed in the aforementioned chapter, Boeing successfully argued that DAR 15-205.6(f), while referring to allocability, actually imposed an allocation requirement for pension costs and this requirement was in conflict with CAS

412 and 413. While DOD could limit allowability based on various considerations, it could not do so with respect to allocability where the acquisition provision conflicted with CAS.

The board distinguished this case from *Boeing* in finding that the disallowance of FSC was based on "policy considerations, 'independent of cost accounting considerations,' including the understanding that foreign selling costs appeared 'disproportionate to the amounts related to U.S. Government contracts' and that such costs were 'not beneficial to the Government'."

The board observed that the reasons for prohibiting the allocation of FSC to domestic DOD contracts "are not clearly articulated in the record." However, after conjecturing on the reasons, the board concluded that they were based on the benefit concept, which was within the purview of acquisition regulations, and not on measurement, assignment, and allocation considerations, which are in the realm of CAS.

As to the arguments that CAS prefers a cost input base representing the total activity of a business unit while DAR required the allocation of FSC over a fragmented cost base, the board ruled that Emerson overstated the requirements of both the DAR and CAS provisions. CAS 410, the board found, "permits, but does *not* mandate, (a) including selling costs in the G&A pool and (b) allocation of that pool on a *single* total cost input base." As to the DAR provision, the board ruled that it is "silent regarding the measurement and assignment of foreign selling costs to allocation bases."

Even if a conflict could be discerned between the DAR and CAS provisions, the board opined that Emerson could devise an accounting practice compliant with both. In contrast, according to the board, in the *Boeing* case referred to, DAR required a cash basis of accounting whereas CAS provided for the accrual basis, and the conflict there was irreconcilable.

The board reiterated that the DAR and CAS provisions in this case were not in conflict and suggested that Emerson could remove FSC from the pool for allocation to government contracts and still use a single cost input base.

IR&D and B&P expenses in excess of negotiated ceilings are not allowable under DOD contracts but are allowable under DOD-FMS and direct foreign sales, and these expenses were added back to the G&A pool by Emerson in computing a G&A rate for such sales. The board suggested that Emerson could follow a similar procedure for the FSC.

ALLOWABILITY OF GENERAL AND ADMINISTRATIVE EXPENSES

General and administrative expenses include all the necessary costs of doing business, other than those appropriately classified as manufacturing, engineering, or selling expenses. They include the salaries and expenses of officers and executives (unless directly chargeable to one of the other groups), salaries and expenses of all clerical help not directly employed elsewhere, general legal, auditing, and other professional expenses, and all organizational and corporate expenses, including franchise and similar taxes. As a whole, the group of general and administrative expenses is considered allowable under government contracts, subject to (1) such considerations as reasonableness, etc., and (2) the exclusion of those expenses specifically cited as unallowable in the contract cost principles. The general and administrative expenses considered unallowable are discussed at length in Chapters XVI and XVII of this text.

Allocation of General and Administrative Expenses

The allocation of general and administrative expenses is surely one of the oldest and most controversial accounting problems confronting the government and those firms who do business with it. A significant share of the blame for the inability to resolve this problem must be borne by the accounting profession. We accountants must shoulder a large part of this responsibility because this problem is primarily an accounting one.

Traditionally, general and administrative expenses have not been allocated to products or contracts. There are several reasons. First, conventional, conservative accounting thought has opposed adding these expenses to the cost of inventory. The prevailing view has been to consider them as period costs, to be charged to profit and loss each year. Second, G&A expenses are frequently far removed from the manufacture of a product, and therefore it is just simply too complicated to devise a "good" way of computing the pro rata portion of these expenses to the individual product. Considering that problems are even encountered with determining direct material and labor costs, and that the difficulties are multiplied in ascertaining allocable factory or indirect manufacturing costs, it is easy to imagine the complexities involved in arriving at a basis for allocating G&A expenses.

In the years immediately preceding World War II, and particularly after this country's entrance into that conflict, government procurement rose to an unprecedented volume. It also changed substantially in form, including a tremendous increase in the use of CPFF and other flexibly priced contracts. Where the contract price was based entirely or significantly on cost, ground rules had to be devised to permit contractors and government contracting officers to find some common ground for establishing contract costs. In this search, accounting literature was of little assistance.

One of the earliest government efforts to establish ground rules in this area was reflected in the Green Book, an unofficial Army-Navy publication prepared to provide guidance in interpreting and applying Treasury Decision 5000. In paragraph 66, relating to administrative expenses, this 1942 publication advised that: "Such of the items as can be directly related to a specific contract or Government contracts in general, should be correspondingly apportioned. On the other hand, those items which clearly do not relate in any respect to doing business with the Government ... should be excluded from apportionment to Government contracts." Chapter 67 contained the following guidance:

> The remaining items ... then should be apportioned between Government business and other business on the most equitable basis. This basis frequently is to charge to government business a proportion of the total expenses equal to the ratio between manufacturing costs plus other contract performance costs and the total of such costs for the business as a whole. Sometimes the apportionment is made on the basis of percentage

to sales values. Under either or any other method the conditions and proportions of the bases between different kinds of business activities should be carefully considered in order that the resulting apportionment shall be equitable.

Although this Green Book guidance merits commendation for a first effort to provide guidelines, it can hardly be said that it provided much more than a hope or a goal of equity. And equity, of course, is a most subjective concept under which both parties to a dispute could well argue indefinitely.

It is useless and unseemly to criticize the past from a hindsight vantage point. It is even less productive when one finds that little if any improvement has been achieved in the decades which followed. For example, the 1949 ASPR Section XV contained the following provisions regarding all allowable indirect costs.

In establishing a method of equitably apportioning the indirect costs, consideration should be given to such factors as charges of subcontractors, fixed asset improvement programs, and any unusual circumstances involved in the contractor's operation; and such factors should be carefully reviewed from time to time, particularly when there is a change in the nature or volume of production, to determine whether the method of apportionment continues to be equitable. Whenever items ordinarily chargeable as indirect costs are charged to a government contract as direct costs, the cost of similar items applicable to other work of the contractor must be eliminated from indirect costs apportioned to the contract.

Seven years after the Green Book, DOD continued to think and write about equity. We see nothing in the 1949 ASPR which would improve the understanding of the government and its contractors or make their negotiations easier.

Chapter XIII of this text sets forth the current FAR Part 31 provisions relating to allocation of indirect costs to government contracts. As set forth in FAR 31.201-4 and 31.203, the current guidelines contain considerably more commentary and theory. The objective of equity is retained and is augmented by emphasis on the benefits concept.

DCAA Guidance for Allocating G&A Expenses

The most extensive and intensive DOD commentary on allocation of G&A expenses is found in the DCAA Contract Audit Manual, and we quote from paragraph 6-606 of CAM:

6-606.4 *Allocation Bases for General and Administrative Expense Other Than Corporate/Home Office Expense*

a. G&A expenses are any management, financial, and other expenses which are incurred by or allocated to a business unit and which are for the general management and administration of the business unit as a whole. When CAS 410 applies, the auditor should refer to the requirements of the standard and implementing audit guidance in 8-410. When CAS 410 does not apply, the auditor may refer to CAS 410 in conjunction with the guidance in this section. Audits of corporate/home office expense allocations, and G&A expense allocation under facilities contracts are discussed in 6-606.5 and 606.6.

(1) The pool grouping should be assessed using the principles set forth in FAR 31.201-4, Allocability, and 31.203, Indirect Costs. The expenses in the G&A pool should represent only the cost of those activities that are necessary to the overall operation of the business, although a direct relationship to any particular cost objective cannot be shown. The cost of those activities incurred specifically for a contract or that can be distributed to both Government and other work in reasonable proportion to the benefits received should be removed from the G&A pool and distributed to the final cost objectives on a more appropriate basis. Expenses which are not G&A expenses but are insignificant in amount may be included in the G&A expense pool.

(2) The distribution base should be evaluated to assure that it is common to all cost objectives to which the G&A pool is to be allocated. As stated in CAS 410.5(b)(1), the G&A allocation base should be a cost input base representing the total activity of the business unit. Cost input bases are discussed in 6-606.4b(1) and include total cost input, value added and single element. CAS also permits special allocations under certain conditions (CAS 410.50(j)) and permits variants of the foregoing cost input bases if they are representative of the total year's business activity and produce an equitable distribution of the G&A expenses to all final cost objectives (CAS 410 supplement). The auditor must recommend another distribution base when it is determined that the selected base does not adequately represent the total year's business activity or results in an inequitable distribution of the G&A expenses to final cost objectives.

All contractors are covered by FAR 31.203, which states "Indirect costs shall be accumulated by logical groupings ... (which) should be determined so as to permit distribution of the grouping on the basis of the benefits accruing to the various cost objectives." If a contractor which is not CAS-covered has a single pool, the auditor must evaluate its allocation base against this requirement.

b. The subparagraphs below provide comments on distribution bases which may be proposed for allocating G&A expense to contracts/jobs where Cost Accounting Standards do not apply. In the event any of these bases of allocation are used and accepted on the basis that no inequity results, such acceptance should be qualified in the audit report and the contractor notified that a more appropriate distribution base will be used in the future if it is determined that the selected base is creating an inequity.

(1) Cost Input. Cost input is the cost, except G&A, which for contract cost purposes is allocable to the production of goods and services during the cost accounting period. The most often used bases are: total cost input (TCI), all costs excluding G&A; value-added cost input, all costs excluding material, subcontracts, and G&A; and single-element cost input. Cost input bases are generally acceptable for Government contracts because they express the causal and beneficial relationship between

G&A expenses and all of the final cost objectives of a cost accounting period (matching principle).

(2) Cost of Goods Sold. The cost of goods sold base in often identical to TCI, and when identical it is acceptable. Its advantage is that the amount is generally available from the accounting records and does not require separate computation. Cost of goods sold bases may be unsatisfactory when the G&A expense allowable under Government contracts is more closely related to production for the period than to products distributed and sold. Distortions are most likely to result when some of the contractor's products require a long manufacturing cycle, or when commercial items are produced for stock or leasing rather than to fill sales commitments. G&A expenses which are not clearly a part of production may not be applied to inventory because to do so would violate generally accepted accounting principles. Distortion may also result if a contractor classifies all costs incurred under cost-type contracts as sales when the costs are incurred, but does not record sales under fixed-price contracts and other work until shipment of the completed product.

(3) Cost of Sales. Cost of sales includes selling costs whereas cost of goods sold does not. The cost of sales base is inequitable because the contractor is precluded from recovering allowable selling costs and must allocate G&A to all selling costs. All other considerations affecting cost of goods sold apply to cost of sales.

(4) Cost of Goods Manufactured. Cost of goods manufactured differs from cost of goods sold in that it includes ending inventories and excludes beginning inventories. Cost of goods manufactured is generally not an acceptable allocation base for G&A expense under Government contracts because it does not adequately represent the cost of production for the accounting period. Cost of goods manufactured includes prior period costs applicable to goods in process at the beginning of the accounting period and excludes current period costs applicable to goods remaining in process at the end of the accounting period. Distortions are most likely to result when (1) the contractor's products require varying manufacturing cycles, some longer than others, or (2) inventories of raw materials and work in process vary significantly between the beginning and end of the accounting periods.

(5) Total Sales. Total sales as a basis for allocating G&A expense is generally not acceptable for Government contracts because: (1) the concurrence of sales with production usually varies between the items produced for the Government and those produced commercially, (2) the margin of profit may vary appreciably among contracts and between Government and other work, and (3) the final selling price of incentive type contracts or other contracts which contain price revision terms is not known until the work has been completed and the price negotiated.

6-606.5 Allocation Bases for Corporate/Home Office Expense

a. When CAS 403 applies, reference should be made to the requirements of the standard and implementing audit guidance in 8-403. When CAS 403 does not apply, it may be used as general information in conjunction with the guidance in this section.

b. Home office expense is the cost of administering the overall operations of a multi-plant or multi-segment company. Home offices typically establish policy for and provide guidance to the segments in their operations. They usually perform management, supervisory, or administrative functions, but may also perform service functions in support of the operations of the various segments. The costs may include (1) those incurred for the benefit of a specific segment, such as specialized consulting services or leases for specific facilities; (2) those incurred for the benefit of several but not all segments, or for several segments in differing proportions, such as a central computer center or similar service operations or fringe benefit costs such as pensions and insurance; (3) those incurred for the common benefit of all segments, such as board of director expenses or top executive salaries. Costs of the third type, often referred to as "residual" corporate/home office expense, are typically allocated to all segments over a common allocation base except as discussed in d. below. Costs of the first two types, where significant, require separate allocation for equitable costing of Government contracts at the various segments.

* * * *

c. To evaluate the bases used by the contractor to distribute home office expenses, the auditor should carefully review the organizational structure and operations of the corporate office and each corporate segment, including details of the type of service and support rendered by the corporate office to each segment. This may require close cooperation among the contract auditors cognizant of the company sites. (See 15-200 for information on the contract audit coordinator (CAC) program which has been established to facilitate this coordination within DCAA.) In addition, the corporate/home office auditor is responsible for the necessary reviews of segments not involved in Government contract work. The objective is to see that the contractor's allocations proportionately distribute home office costs to all segments of the business on the basis of the relative benefits received. Use the applicable contract cost principles (such as FAR 31.201-4, 31.202, and 31.203) as criteria to evaluate the contractor's method.

d. Residual expenses generally have no discernible direct benefit to a particular segment but are necessary to the overall business operations. They may be categorized as costs relating to the prudent management of all resources at the disposal of the corporation. Residual expenses may include the salaries, fringe benefits, occupancy costs, taxes, and other administrative expenses of the board of directors, executive committees, corporate officers, and administrative/executive management officials. The basis of allocation of residual expenses should reflect the total activities of all segments of the business. However, certain segments may require special allocations of residual expense if their operations are relatively self-contained or self-sufficient and/or require minimal administrative support from the corporate/home office. Conversely, a segment may require special allocation in amounts greater than the average rate if it is highly dependent upon the home office staff for general administrative support. (See 6-606.6 regarding allocations to GOCO activities.)

e. The form of the business (foreign or domestic), the extent of ownership (wholly- or partially-owned), or the accounting treatment for financial accounting purposes (consolidated or unconsolidated) are not basic criteria for determining whether a particular segment should be included in or excluded from the residual allocation base. Also, the fact that an individual contract or group of contracts does not permit recovery of corporate office expenses is not a reason to exclude the operating segment performing the contract(s) from the base of allocation. Once an appropriate base for distributing indirect costs has been accepted, it should not be fragmented by removing individual elements (FAR 31.203(c)). Also see CAS 410.50(j) for a discussion of special allocations. To the extent that the home office provides necessary support for the segment, a proportionate share of the residual expenses should be allocated to that segment.

6-606.6 *Allocation Bases for Residual Corporate/Home Office Expense to GOCO Activities*

a. Special attention should be given to the appropriate allocation of residual corporate/home office expense to Government-owned contractor-operated (GOCO) plants. Contractor's GOCO activities are usually conducted on a basis substantially independent of supervision by higher corporate echelons. In addition, less administrative support is usually received from the central office since many corporate administrative services are paralleled by the GOCO administrative activity. In such circumstances, it would not be equitable to distribute a share of all the higher level supervisory or administrative expenses to these plants on a proportionate basis by any of the methods commonly used to allocate residual corporate/home office expense to segments.

b. Each auditor at a GOCO plant will provide the corporate/home office auditor information on the nature and extent of administrative functions performed at the GOCO plant. The auditor at the home office will review with the contractor whether portions of the home office expenses duplicate these functions, so that a suitable corporate allocation structure is developed for GOCO activities.

c. If it is appropriate to allocate less residual expenses to a GOCO, the contractor may accomplish this by developing two expense rates as follows: (1) a basic rate reflecting those corporate expenses which apply to all work of the contractor including GOCO plant operations, and (2) a rate in addition to the basic rate reflecting those corporate expenses which apply to all work of the contractor except GOCO plant operations. Figure 6-6-1 is a sample of the development of such rates.

d. Where CAS 403 applies, any special allocations of residual corporate/home office expenses to GOCO activities are established by agreement between the contractor and the Government in accordance with CAS 403.40(c)(3) and 403.50(d). Only a contracting officer may execute such an agreement, but the contract auditor will normally evaluate the proposed method before an initial agreement. The auditor will evaluate the continuing appropriateness of the contractor's method during each audit cycle, and advise the contracting officer if any formal agreement warrants revision.

*   *   *   *   *

6-607.4 G&A Allocation Per W.G. 79-24

DoD CAS Steering Committee Paper No. 79-24 (W.G. 79-24) states DoD policy on special allocation of segment G&A expense to facilities acquisition costs under facilities contracts. It states that facilities acquisitions usually receive less benefit from G&A expense than do other contracts, and requires a special allocation when this is the case. The paper applies CAS 410.50(j) to such situation. A DoD procurement office would likely follow the same approach in the event of a non-CAS covered facilities acquisition program, as an implementation of the general policy expressed in FAR 31.106-2. NASA and other non-DoD procurement offices may apply similar principles. Under W.G. 79-24, the contractor's normal G&A allocation will apply to facilities maintenance effort; the special allocation is only for the costs of contractor-acquired Government-funded facilities. Where needed, the contractor should (1) develop an appropriate allocation method for facilities contracts and any similar non-Government work and (2) propose and cost all such effort as consistently as possible.

Figure 6-6-1 (Ref. 6-606.6)
SAMPLE OF CORPORATE EXPENSE RATES—GOCO ACTIVITIES

		Rate Calculations	
	Totals	Basic	Additional
Residual Corporate Expenses:			
Basic (applicable to all segment activities)	$ 20,000	$ 20,000	——
Balance (applicable to non-GOCO segment activities)	40,000	——	$ 40,000
Total	$ 60,000	$ 20,000	$ 40,000
Base of Allocation:			
GOCO segment activities	$ 200,000	$ 200,000	——
All other segment activities	800,000	800,000	$ 800,000
Total	$1,000,000	$1,000,000	$ 800,000
Rates	——	2%	5%

Note: In this illustration, the corporate expense rate applicable to GOCO activities is 2%; the rate applicable to other activities of the contractor is 7%.

As indicated elsewhere in this text, the provisions of DCAA's Manual are generally informative even though they are directive only to the agency's auditors.

Judicial Decisions Relating to Allocation of G&A Expenses

The past forty years have witnessed many sharp differences between contractors and government contract auditors regarding allocation of G&A expenses. Where agreement could not be reached on differing accounting theories, the matter was usually resolved by negotiation between the contractor and the contracting officer. As discussed in Chapter XIII of this text, except for CAS-covered contracts, DAR and FPR have provided that allocation of indirect costs should be in accordance with generally accepted accounting principles appropriate to the circumstances involved and on a basis of the benefits accruing to the cost objectives. The benefit concept seemed logical and valid; however, the absence of specific guidelines enabled each party to assert that this concept supported its method. And even less help was available from the requirement to comply with generally accepted accounting principles because such principles classified G&A expenses as period costs, to be written off annually, and did not enunciate allocation bases appropriate in various circumstances.

Where the issue could not be resolved, the contracting officer made a unilateral final determination under the contract Disputes clause. When contractors appealed from these decisions, the agency boards of contract appeals and the U.S. Court of Claims encountered the same difficulties. Traditionally, judicial bodies looked to the language of the contract and applicable laws and regulations as bases for their decisions. When disputes involved such matters as conflicting methods of allocating G&A expenses, the judicial bodies found no help in the contracts, laws, or regulations. In some instances, these decisions were described as being based on generally accepted accounting principles although the specific principles, or the authority therefor, were seldom cited. In other cases, the boards and courts stated that (a) there were generally accepted accounting principles to support both methods in contention or that (b) no generally accepted accounting principles existed for allocating G&A expenses. A salient ruling relating to allocation of G&A expenses prior to CAS 410 is described below.

Litton Systems, ASBCA No. 10395, 66-1 BCA par. 5599; Ct.Cls. 228-66, 10/15/71.—Controversies involving cost of sales versus cost of input as the appropriate basis for allocating G&A expenses continued over many years until the CASB outlawed any cost output base for this purpose on CAS-covered contracts in Standard 410. Ironically, while DOD, led by its contract auditors, carried some of these controversies to the litigation stages, it concurrently accepted the cost of sales base in numerous other instances. (This situation was similar to the DCAA-led effort to prohibit many contractors from using any input base but total cost under CAS 410 while accepting the value-added or other cost input base at other locations.) An early leading case in which the government opposed the use of the cost of sales base, Litton Systems included decisions by the ASBCA and the Court of Claims.

Over a period of a number of years, beginning with 1955, the company computed its G&A rate as a percentage of its cost of sales. Manufacturing costs of CPFF contracts were charged to cost of sales at the time the contractor submitted reimbursement vouchers to the government. As to fixed-price contracts, however, most of which were completed within a year, manufacturing costs were not charged to cost of sales until the contract items were completed and delivered.

For the years 1955-1964, inclusive, with the exception of 1957, the company's year-end inventory showed an increase as compared with the inventory at the beginning of the year, with the first really substantial variance coming about in 1959. With respect to overhead determinations for that year, government auditors first raised the question of the propriety of the company's cost of sales base for G&A application. It was then apparent that because of (1) the above-mentioned difference in charging production costs to cost of sales as between CPFF and fixed price contracts, and (2) the substantial increase in ending over beginning inventories, G&A allocations to CPFF contracts on a cost of sales basis would be much higher than amounts allocated on an input basis. (The term "input," as used in the ASBCA decision and here, refers to total production costs, i. e., material, labor, manufacturing expenses, etc., exclusive of G&A expenses.) A series of discussions on this subject followed, culminating in the issuance of a DD Form 396, appeal and denial thereof by the Comptroller of the Navy, and finally the appeal to the ASBCA.

The contractor's major arguments were that the cost of sales basis is in accordance with generally accepted accounting practices and, as such, is in accordance with the intent of Section XV of ASPR, incorporated in the contract. In the company's circumstances, either a cost of sales base or a cost input base would serve the purpose, but neither method can be considered better than the other. As an accepted basis consistently used, the cost of sales method should not be changed because of a change in the nature or extent of the company's business. Consistency was stressed as one of the most important elements in the achievement of equity for both parties, and it was argued that it would be inequitable to require the contractor to shift from one method to another merely because the resulting allocation would be less.

The contractor also argued that any G&A allocation base that is representative of the year's activity is as good as another base and that, since the contractor was in existence to sell, cost of sales is representative of a year's activity.

The government took issue on this latter point and argued that a cost of sales base could not be considered representative of a year's activity when the ending inventory was substantially in excess of the opening inventory. In this connection, it was noted that ASPR 15-203(d)(ii) specifically cited significant changes in inventories as a factor requiring reexamination of a contractor's allocation methods. The government also cited the third edition of this text:

(4) Administrative and selling expenses are traditionally charged off annually to profit and loss. In terms of accounting principles, then, selection of a basis such as total input, cost of goods manufactured, etc., over cost of sales, would be questionable accounting-wise. However, for the purpose of contract cost computations, some form of "incurred cost" basis has the advantage of spreading administrative and selling expenses over all factory costs, and the resulting percentage will be free from possible distortions emanating from significant differences between opening and closing inventories. Such methods would appear to be particularly appropriate for use in allocating administrative and selling expenses to terminated contracts.

(5) The cost of sales basis is traditional, acceptable in accounting theory and practice, and the base is usually readily available for identification and for audit. It is therefore recommended for general use. It may not be appropriate when (a) closing inventories are substantially in excess

of opening inventories, and (b) the pattern and relationships of the manufacturing costs under a specific contract are substantially at variance from the overall pattern and relationships in the total cost of sales.

In its decision, the board narrowed the issue to whether the contractor's cost of sales basis met the requirements of Section XV of ASPR or whether the government had the contract right to require the contractor to shift to a cost input base (no alternatives to these two bases had been proposed by either party). Recognizing the cost of sales base as one generally accepted, commonly used, and previously approved by the government, the board further narrowed the question to (1) whether the government can prove that the cost of sales base produced an inequitable distribution of G&A expense to CPFF contracts, and (2) whether the shift to a cost input base would be prejudicial to the contractor's fixed-price contracts.

With respect to the first point, the board found that the old ASPR and more specifically, the new ASPR did not accept an allocation base or an accounting method just because it followed generally accepted accounting principles. Rather, the allocation method must be appropriate in the particular circumstances and must accomplish the objective of equitably apportioning G&A. The board emphasized the provisions of ASPR 15-203(d)(ii), mentioned above, which specifically required reexamination of a contractor's method under various circumstances including significant changes in inventories. The board also cited its 1958 decision (ASBCA No. 3438) where it ruled, under similar circumstances, that a cost input G&A allocation base should be used because the cost of sales base produced an inequitable apportionment.

The board found that the contractor's cost of sales base resulted in an inequitable apportionment of G&A because of the rising inventories and because of the contractor's use of different methods in its costing of fixed-price and CPFF contracts. At this point, it should be noted that the board was not critical of the contractor's procedure in charging production costs of CPFF contracts to cost of sales at the time of reimbursement. In this connection, it noted that the contractor's method was in accordance with Chapter 11 of AICPA Accounting Research Bulletin No. 43. On the other hand, it reasoned that, from both a legal and practical standpoint, there is no difference in substance between fixed-price work in process and CPFF work in process for the same items.

Earlier in its deliberations, the board had recognized that criteria for a proper allocation base would include benefit, cause and effect, and the test of representativeness. Applying any one of the three criteria, the board found no distinction between fixed-price work in process and CPFF work in process. On the other hand, it was of the opinion that a base which ignores a large inventory buildup, constituting the substantial part of the year's production, is not representative of the year's activity.

The ASBCA decision in favor of the government was upheld by the Court of Claims.

Judicial Decisions: Adjustments to Base for Allocating General and Administrative Expenses

One of the points of contention between contractors and government officials in this area related to adjustments that may be required to the base for allocating these expenses. Some contractors have contended that all manufacturing costs disallowed by the government should be removed from the cost of sales (or similar) base for allocating general and administrative expenses. Most government auditors have taken a position that such adjustments are not appropriate. On the one side, it is contended that failure to remove the disallowed manufacturing costs from the base, thus allocating G&A expenses thereto, results in disallowing otherwise allowable G&A expenses. The counterargument holds that all costs generated (pro rata) general and administrative expenses and that the allowability or unallowability of manufacturing costs under government contracts does not affect the basic principle.

Sunstrand Turbo, A Division of Sundstrand, ASBCA No. 9112, 65-1 BCA par. 4653.—The government had disallowed from the manufacturing overhead pool approximately $150,000 of "excess depreciation and amortization" as applicable to the increase in the valuation of fixed assets effected by the contractor upon acquiring such assets from a predecessor company.

While disallowing the excess depreciation as a charge against the contracts involved, the contracting officer retained this amount in the cost of sales base used to compute the percentage of G&A expense applicable to the contracts. The effect of this procedure was to reduce the amount of G&A expense applicable to the contracts since the ratio of G&A expenses to the larger cost of sales base resulted in a decreased percentage. The rationale for the government's position was that excess depreciation was properly includable in the base because it was a cost to the contracter although disallowed as a cost to the government.

The board showed little sympathy with the government position and expressed the following views:

> It is not necessary to decide or even to question the government's contention that its position accords with sound accounting practice. Under the circumstances of this matter, it appears to be unjust to treat a cost to the contractor as a cost to the government when it is not. The sole result, if not the purpose, is to reduce the reimbursable amount of G&A expense, yet it appears that the dollar amount of G&A expense actually incurred by the appellant has been affected not a whit ... The excess depreciation should, in this instance, be removed from the base for computing G&A.

American Electronic Laboratories, Inc., ASBCA No. 9879, 65-2 BCA par. 5020.—In accordance with procedures generally followed by Defense Department auditors, the amount of overtime premium pay established as unallowable under government CPFF contracts was not deducted from the total cost of sales base used to establish the percentage for applying G&A expenses. The reasoning behind this procedure is that, while such expenses do not constitute appropriate and reasonable costs under the government contracts involved, they nevertheless generate G&A expenses and therefore should be retained in the cost of sales base.

The board elected to sidestep the basic issue involved and stated: "The question presented is whether a disallowed manufacturing cost should be charged with a pro-rata share of the contractor's G&A pool for the purpose of reducing the amount of G&A expense that would otherwise be allocated to the government cost-reimbursement contract. We do not believe that a 'yes' or 'no' answer can be given to the question stated in such broad terms. We shall consider only the type of disallowed manufacturing costs here involved, namely, overtime premium."

Addressing itself to the point at issue, the board stated:

We must not lose sight of the fact that the basic objective is to cause the thing that generated the G&A cost to bear such cost or, in the words of ASPR 15-203, to cause the cost objective that benefits from the G&A to bear such cost. We do not believe that as a general rule man-hour of overtime work involves any more managerial effort or generates any more G&A expense than a manhour of straight time work, and to allocate G&A to overtime premium would have the effect of causing the thing that does not generate G&A or benefit from G&A to bear G&A expense . . . . we are not aware of any general accounting principle which requires that a cost item which has been eliminated from the cost of sales of the contract must, nevertheless, be retained in the total cost of sales base used for allocating G&A.

In both cases, the board elected to hand down its decision surrounded by limiting or qualifying expressions. In the *Sundstrand* case, it stated that it was not necessary to address the government's contention that its position accords with sound accounting practice and substantially rested its decision on the following statement: "Under the circumstances of this matter, it appears to be unjust to treat a cost to the contractor as a cost to the government when it is not."

In the *American Electronic Laboratories* case, the board again shied away from coming to grips with the basic issue as to whether a disallowed manufacturing cost should be retained in the base for allocating G&A expenses. Here the board stated: "We do not believe that a 'yes' or 'no' necessarily can be given to the question stated in such broad terms."

Martin-Marietta Corporation, ASBCA No. 14159, 71-1 BCA par 8783.—A significant aspect of this dispute involved the government's disallowance of G&A expenses computed as the portion allocable to unallowable base costs (the contractor used total cost input as the allocation base, and the propriety of this method was not in contention). In the periods involved, the contractor and the government agreed that certain costs included in the base were not allowable under government contracts. The text of the decision is neither complete nor clear as to the costs involved, but these are some of the items identified:

1. Engineering overhead for which the contractor ultimately elected not to bill the government, treating it instead as a participating contribution to a major weapons system program.

2. A pro rata portion of a communication system allocated by the contractor's Baltimore headquarters to Denver. It was subsequently

agreed that the allocation was in error, and the charge was transferred out of Denver costs to those of another location.

3. Erroneous charge for depreciation on fully depreciated assets, the elimination of which was agreed to by the contractor.

4. Credit to the government by the contractor for excess depreciation disallowed by the Internal Revenue Service.

In computing G&A expense rates for allocating such expenses to government contracts, the contractor, in effect, first deducted the above-mentioned and other unallowable base costs from the total input costs and then calculated the applicable percentages. Under this procedure, no G&A expenses were allocated to these unallowable base costs. The government's contention that the rate should be determined by the relationship between G&A expenses and the total input base was rebutted:

Appellant concedes that in accounting theory when a base cost generates overhead cost the disallowance of the base cost should result in the disallowance also of the overhead cost caused by the disallowed base cost. As an example of a proper disallowance of overhead generated by a disallowed base cost, appellant's controller and treasurer stated that, if the wages of an employee were found to be unallowable, it would be proper to disallow, not only the wages, but also payroll taxes and insurance and fringe benefits on the disallowed wages. He differentiated between fixed overhead costs and variable overhead costs and between base costs that caused additional overhead costs and base costs that do not cause any additional overhead costs and the elimination of which would not reduce the amount of overhead costs incurred. He testified that since some base costs have overhead costs associated with them and some do not, it should not be arbitrarily and automatically assumed that each item of base costs has a proportionate amount of overhead costs associated with it.

The government steadfastly maintained the position that a correlative relationship must and does exist between the base and the overhead pool (here, G&A), that the base, in effect, causes the incurrence of or generates the overhead pool, and that the G&A expenses must, therefore, be distributed to the total input base cost. On this reasoning, a pro rata share of the G&A expense would be allocated to the unallowable base costs.

The board ruled for the contractor. It found the government in error because of its requirement that the contractor retroactively change its accounting method. At considerable length, the board declared that the government was wrong in its contention that each element in the base generated a pro rata share of G&A expense and saw an allocation base as selected simply "because it provides an equitable method of allocating the G&A pool proportionately ...." Excerpts from the decision reflecting the board's formulation of cost accounting principles are set forth below:

... Appellant's accounting system causes its entire pool of allowable G&A expense to be distributed and allocated to its business operations, about 99½% of which consist of Government contracts. The G&A disallowance made by the contracting officer involves a change in appellant's method of allocation which will cause a portion of its pool of allowable G&A expense not to be allocated to any of its business operations.

The proposed G&A disallowance is premised on the erroneous theory that each and every cost element in the G&A allocation base generates its pro rata share of G&A expense. It was the resident auditor's theory that the contractor's selection of total input costs as the allocation base "creates the premise * * * that the dollars in the base in turn derived or caused to be incurred the expenses which are to be apportioned over the base." Under his theory, it would seem that prior to 1962 when the contractor used total direct labor cost as its G&A allocation base, only direct labor generated G&A expense, but when the contractor shifted to total input costs as its G&A allocation base, suddenly direct materials and manufacturing and engineering overhead which are included in total input costs began to generate for the first time their pro rata share of G&A expense.

* * * *

The accounting objective is to allocate indirect cost elements to direct cost objectives in proportion to the benefits assumed to have been derived, and this can be done when there is a flow down or traceable cause and effect relationship between the constituent elements of the indirect cost pool and the elements of the allocation base. However, this type of relationship is inapplicable to the pool of general and administrative expense which by its nature is the expense of the general operation of the business that cannot be related to any cost objective through the showing of a cause and effect relationship. A proper G&A allocation base must be representative of the year's business activity so as to cause the pool of G&A expense to be equitably apportioned over the year's business activities. Litton Systems, Inc., supra, at p. 26,167. The G&A allocation base is not selected because it generates the G&A expense but because it provides an equitable method of allocating the G&A pool proportionately to the contracts, jobs, departments, products, services, and types of customers that make up the firm's business activities. Whether and the extent to which the cost elements in the G&A allocation base generate G&A costs has no direct bearing on whether the G&A allocation base will serve its purpose of equitably apportioning the G&A expense to the contractor's business activities for the year.

The contracting officer's theory of burdening disallowed base costs with G&A expense confuses the G&A base with the cost objective. For the purpose of allocating G&A expense, the cost objective is the year's business activity, and the G&A allocation base is merely the vehicle by which the pool of allowable G&A expense is distributed to the year's business activity.

Since in this case the business activity of appellant's Denver Division consisted almost entirely of Government contracts, the proper type of G&A allocation base was one which would equitably apportion all of the pool of allowable G&A expense to such Government contracts, except the amount allocated on a proportionate basis to the small amount of commercial sales. Regardless of whether the G&A allocation base included all input costs incurred or only allowable input costs, it should accomplish the objective of causing the entire pool of allowable G&A expense to be allocated to the contractor's business activities.

There is no evidence that any of the unallowed input costs generated any G&A expense, and there is no valid basis for assuming without evidence that an unallowable item of input cost recorded in appellant's books of account generated any G&A expense.

Department of Defense Revision of ASPR 15-203(c)

In accordance with a practice considered inappropriate and incorrect by the private sector, the Department of Defense from time to time revises its cost principles to preclude the repetition of ASBCA decisions with which it does not agree. Some years following the ASBCA's refusal to permit the disallowance of otherwise allowable G&A expenses by allocating and attaching them to unallowable costs in the allocation base, DOD added the following to what was then ASPR 15-203(c):

Once an appropriate base for the distribution of indirect costs has been accepted, such base shall not be fragmented by the removal of individual elements. Consequently, all items properly includable in an indirect cost base should bear a pro rata share of indirect costs irrespective of their acceptance as Government contract costs. For example, when a cost of sales base is deemed appropriate for the distribution of G&A, all items chargeable to cost of sales, whether allowable or unallowable, shall be included in the base and bear their pro rata share of G&A costs.

Industry has vigorously opposed this provision primarily because it results in the disallowance of allowable G&A expenses. However, the many efforts were unsuccessful in persuading DOD to change its position or to prevent the incorporation of this concept into FAR 31.203(c).

CASB PROMULGATIONS RELATING TO G&A EXPENSES

In accordance with the recommendations in the Feasibility Study Report, the Board moved early to address the problems of allocating indirect costs. Beginning with G&A expenses, the CASB recognized that this group of expenses required separate treatment predicated on whether they were incurred at a corporate home or divisional office or at what the Board termed a "business unit" or "segment." Despite undoubted good intentions, however, history was to show that the cost accounting standards promulgated may have caused as many controversies as they resolved.

CAS 403—Allocation of Home Office Expenses to Segments

On December 14, 1972, the CASB published CAS 403 with an effective date of July 1, 1973, and a requirement that contractors who received net awards of applicable negotiated defense contracts in federal fiscal year 1971 totaling more than $30 million to start following its provisions at the beginning of their next fiscal year after September 30, 1973. Salient provisions of this standard are quoted below.

403.30(a) (2) *Home office.* An office responsible for directing or managing two or more, but not necessarily all, segments of an organization. It typically establishes policy for, and provides guidance to the segments in their operations. It usually performs management, supervisory, or administrative functions, and may also perform service functions in support of the operations of the various segments. An organization which has intermediate levels, such as groups, may have several els, such as groups, may have several home offices which report to a common home office. An intermediate organization may be both a segment and a home office.

*   *   *   *

403.30(a) (4) *Segment.* One of two or more divisions, product departments, plants, or other subdivisions of an organization reporting directly to a home office, usually identified with responsibility for profit and/or producing a product or service. The term includes Government-owned contractor-operated (GOCO) facilities, and joint ventures and subsidiaries (domestic and foreign) in which the organization has a majority ownership. The term also includes those joint ventures and subsidiaries (domestic and foreign) in which the organization has less than a majority of ownership, but over which it exercises control.

*   *   *   *

§ 403.40 Fundamental requirement.

(a)(1) Home office expenses shall be allocated on the basis of the beneficial or causal relationship between supporting and receiving activities. Such expenses shall be allocated directly to segments to the maximum extent practical. Expenses not directly allocated, if significant in amount and in relation to total home office expenses, shall be grouped in logical and homogeneous expense pools and allocated pursuant to paragraph (b) of this section. Such allocations shall minimize to the extent practical the amount of expenses which may be categorized as residual (those of managing the organization as a whole). These residual expenses shall be allocated pursuant to paragraph (c) of this section.

(2) No segment shall have allocated to it as an indirect cost, either through a homogeneous expense pool, or the residual expense pool, any cost, if other costs incurred for the same purpose have been allocated directly to that or any other segment.

(b) The following subparagraphs provide criteria for allocation of groups of home office expenses.

(1) *Centralized service functions.* Expenses of centralized service functions performed by a home office for its segments shall be allocated to segments on the basis of the service furnished to or received by each segment. Centralized service functions performed by a home office for its segments are considered to consist of specific functions which, but for the existence of a home office, would be performed or acquired by some or all of the segments individually. Examples include centrally performed personnel administration and centralized data processing.

(2) *Staff management of certain specific activities of segments.* The expenses incurred by a home office for staff management or policy guidance functions which are significant in amount and in relation to total home office expenses shall be allocated to segments receiving more

than a minimal benefit over a base, or bases, representative of the total specific activity being managed. Staff management or policy guidance to segments is commonly provided in the overall direction or support of the performance of discrete segment activities such as manufacturing, accounting, and engineering (but see subparagraph (6) of this paragraph).

(3) *Line management of particular segments or groups of segments.* The expense of line management shall be allocated only to the particular segment or group of segments which are being managed or supervised. If more than one segment is managed or supervised, the expense shall be allocated using a base or bases representative of the total activity of such segments. Line management is considered to consist of management or supervision of a segment or group of segments as a whole.

(4) *Central payments or accruals.* Central payments or accruals which are made by a home office on behalf of its segments shall be allocated directly to segments to the extent that all such payments or accruals of a given type or class can be identified specifically with individual segments. Central payments or accruals are those which but for the existence of a number of segments would be accrued or paid by the individual segments. Common examples include centrally paid or accrued pension costs, group insurance costs, State and local income taxes and franchise taxes, and payrolls paid by a home office on behalf of its segments. Any such types of payments or accruals which cannot be identified specifically with individual segments shall be allocated to benefited segments using an allocation base representative of the factors on which the total payment is based.

(5) *Independent research and development costs and bid and proposal costs.* Independent research and development costs and bid and proposal costs of a home office shall be allocated in accordance with 4 CFR Part 420.

(6) *Staff management not identifiable with any certain specific activities of segments.* The expenses incurred by a home office for staff management, supervisory, or policy functions, which are not identifiable to specific activities of segments shall be allocated in accordance with paragraph (c) of this section as residual expenses.

(c) *Residual expenses.* (1) All home office expenses which are not allocable in accordance with paragraph (a) of this section and subparagraphs (1) through (5) of paragraph (b) of this section shall be deemed residual expenses. Typical residual expenses are those for the chief executive, the chief financial officer, and any staff which are not identifiable with specific activities of segments. Residual expenses shall be allocated to all segments under a home office by means of a base representative of the total activity of such segments, except where subparagraph (2) or (3) of this paragraph applies.

(2) Residual expenses shall be allocated pursuant to subparagraph (1) of § 403.50(c) if the total amount of such expenses for the contractor's previous fiscal year (excluding any unallowable costs and before eliminating any amounts to be allocated in accordance with subparagraph (3) of

this paragraph) exceeds the amount obtained by applying the following percentage(s) to the aggregate operating revenue of all segments for such previous year:

3.35 percent of the first $100 million;

0.95 percent of the next $200 million;

0.30 percent of the next $2.7 billion;

0.20 percent of all amounts over $3 billion.

The determination required by this subparagraph for the 1st year the contractor is subject to this Standard shall be based on the pro forma application of this Standard to the home office expenses and aggregate operating revenue for the contractor's previous fiscal year.

(3) Where a particular segment receives significantly more or less benefit from residual expenses than would be reflected by the allocation of such expenses pursuant to subparagraph (1) or (2) of this paragraph (see § 403.50(d)), the Government and the contractor may agree to a special allocation of residual expenses to such segment commensurate with the benefits received. The amount of a special allocation to any segment made pursuant to such an agreement shall be excluded from the pool of residual expenses to be allocated pursuant to subparagraph (1) or (2) of this paragraph, and such segment's data shall be excluded from the base used to allocate this pool.

§ 403.50 Techniques for application.

(a)(1) Separate expense groupings will ordinarily be required to implement § 403.40. The number of groupings will depend primarily on the variety and significance of service and management functions performed by a particular home office. Ordinarily, each service or management function will have to be separately identified for allocation by means of an appropriate allocation technique. However, it is not necessary to identify and allocate different functions separately, if allocation in accordance with the relevant requirements of § 403.40(b) can be made using a common allocation base. For example, if the personnel department of a home office provides personnel services for some or all of the segments (a centralized service function) and also establishes personnel policies for the same segments (a staff management function), the expenses of both functions could be allocated over the same base, such as the number of personnel, and the separate functions do not have to be identified.

(2) Where the expense of a given function is to be allocated by means of a particular allocation base, all segments shall be included in the base unless: (i) Any excluded segment did not receive significant benefits from, or contribute significantly to the cause of the expense to be allocated and, (ii) any included segment did receive significant benefits from or contribute significantly to the cause of the expense in question.

(b) (1) Section 403.60 illustrates various expense pools which may be used together with appropriate allocation bases. The allocation of centralized service functions shall be governed by a hierarchy of preferable allocation techniques which represent beneficial or casual relationships. The preferred representation of such relationships is a measure of the activity of the organization performing the function. Supporting functions are usually labororiented, machineoriented, or spaceoriented. Measures of the activities of such functions ordinarily can be expressed in terms of labor hours, machine hours, or square footage. Accordingly, costs of these functions shall be allocated by use of a rate, such as a rate per labor hour, rate per machine hour or cost per square foot, unless such measures are unavailable or impractical to ascertain. In these latter cases the basis for allocation shall be a measurement of the output of the supporting function. Output is measured in terms of units of end product produced by the supporting function, as for example, number of printed pages for a print shop, number of purchase orders processed by a purchasing department, number of hires by an employment office.

(2) Where neither activity nor output of the supporting function can be practically measured, a surrogate for the beneficial, or causal relationship must be selected. Surrogates used to represent the relationship are generally measures of the activity of the segments receiving the service; for example, for personnel services reasonable surrogates would be number of personnel, labor hours, or labor dollars of the segments receiving the service. Any surrogate used should be a reasonable measure of the services received and, logically, should vary in proportion to the services received.

(c) (1) Where residual expenses are required to be allocated pursuant to § 403.40(c)(2), the three factor formula described below must be used. This formula is considered to result in appropriate allocations of the residual expenses of home offices. It takes into account three broad areas of management concern: The employees of the organization, the business volume, and the capital invested in the organization. The percentage of the residual expenses to be allocated to any segment pursuant to the three factor formula is the arithmetical average of the following three percentages for the same period:

(i) The percentage of the segment's payroll dollars to the total payroll dollars of all segments.

(ii) The percentage of the segment's operating revenue to the total operating revenue of all segments. For this purpose, the operating revenue of any segment shall include amounts charged to other segments and shall be reduced by amounts charged by other segments for purchases.

(iii) The percentage of the average net book value of the sum of the segment's tangible capital assets plus inventories to the total average net book value of such assets of all segments. Property held primarily for leasing to others shall be excluded from the computation. The average net book value shall be the average of the net book value at the beginning of the organization's fiscal year and the net book value at the end of the year.

(d) The following subparagraphs provide guidance for implementing the requirements of § 403.40(c)(3).

(1) An indication that a segment received significantly less benefit in relation to other segments can arise if a segment, unlike all or most other segments, performs on its own many of the functions included in the residual expense. Another indication may be that, in relation to its size, comparatively little or no costs are allocable to a segment pursuant to § 403.40(b)(1) through (5). Evidence of comparatively little communication or interpersonal relations between a home office and a segment, in relation to its size, may also indicate that the segment receives significantly less benefit from residual expenses. Conversely, if the opposite conditions prevail at any segment, a greater allocation than would result from the application of § 403.40(c)(1) or (2) may be indicated. This may be the case, for example, if a segment relies heavily on the home office for certain residual functions normally performed by other segments on their own.

(2) Segments which may require special allocations of residual expenses pursuant to § 403.40(c)(3) include, but are not limited to foreign subsidiaries, GOCO's, domestic subsidiaries with less than a majority ownership, and joint ventures.

(3) The portion of residual expenses to be allocated to a segment pursuant to § 403.40(c)(3) shall be the cost of estimated or recorded efforts devoted to the segments.

(e) Home office functions may be performed by an organization which for some purposes may not be a part of the legal entity with which the Government has contracted. This situation may arise, for example, in instances where the Government contracts directly with a corporation which is wholly or partly owned by another corporation. In this case, the latter corporation serves as a "home office," and the corporation with which the contract is made is a "segment" as those terms are defined and used in this Standard. For purposes of contracts subject to this Standard, the contracting corporation may only accept allocations from the other corporation to the extent that such allocations meet the requirements set forth in this Standard for allocation of home office expenses to segments.

§ 403.60 Illustrations.

(a) The following table lists some typical pools, together with illustrative allocation bases which could be used in appropriate circumstances.

Home office expense or function	*Illustrative allocation bases*
Centralized service functions:	
1. Personnel administration	1. Number of personnel, labor hours, payroll, number of hires.
2. Data processing services	2. Machine time, number of reports.
3. Centralized purchasing and subcontracting.	3. Number of purchase orders, value of purchase, number of items.
4. Centralized warehousing	4. Square footage, value of material, volume.
5. Company aircraft service	5. Actual or standard rate per hour, mile, passenger mile, or similar unit.
6. Central telephone service	6. Usage costs, number of instruments.

(b) The selection of a base for allocating centralized service functions shall be governed by the criteria established in § 403.50(b).

Home office expense or function	Illustrative allocation bases
Staff management of specific activities:	
1. Personnel management.	1. Number of personnel, labor hours, payroll, number of hires.
2. Manufacturing policies (quality control, industrial engineering, production, scheduling, tooling, inspection and testing, etc.).	2. Manufacturing cost input, manufacturing direct labor.
3. Engineering policies.	3. Total engineering costs, engineering direct labor, number of drawings.
4. Material/purchasing policies.	4. Number of purchase orders, value of purchases.
5. Marketing policies.	5. Sales, segment marketing costs.
Central payments or accruals:	
1. Pension expenses...................	1. Payroll or other factor on which total payment is based.
2. Group insurance expenses	2. Payroll or other factor on which total payment is based.
3. State and local income taxes and franchise taxes.	3. Any base or method which results in an allocation that equals or approximates a segment's proportionate share of the tax imposed by the jurisdiction in which the segment does business, as measured by the same factors used to determine taxable income for that jurisdiction.

(c) The listed allocation bases in this section are illustrative. Other bases for allocation of home office expenses to segments may be used if they are substantially in accordance with the beneficial or causal relationships outlined in § 403.40.

CAS 403 was initially proposed in the *Federal Register* of June 30, 1972, and the Board received over a hundred comments from industry and professional associations, government agencies, individual contractors, individual public accounting and legal firms, etc. Almost unanimously, differing only in degree and intensity, the commentators opposed specific portions or the entire proposed standard.

Objections were raised to the requirement for allocating home office expenses "directly to segments to the maximum extent practical." There was opposition from those who view home office expenses as costs incurred to protect and promote a company as a whole. This school of thought has little appreciation for efforts to identify any portion of the home office expenses with a specific segment. Despite the many problems envisioned in connection with the time and expense that would be required for the detailed record-keeping necessary to permit direct allocations, however, some companies already were adhering to this concept. This group was concerned with the possibility (or probability) that the contract auditors and others required to implement this standard would go beyond the stated provision that direct allocations should be made only "to the maximum extent practical."

Concern was also expressed regarding the requirement to establish "logical and homogeneous pools," because of the apprehension that this requirement would be implemented overzealously and that contractors would be required to set up numerous such pools, which would generate needless waste of time and money, pointless fragmentation of the cost of home office direction and administration, and yield no benefits to anyone.

The major industry spokesman, the Council of Defense and Space Industry Associations (CODSIA), expressed concern "that this standard in prescribing inflexible practices will set such a precedent for other standards that will follow." Quoting from the 1970 testimony by GAO chief and later also CASB Chairman, Elmer Staats, CODSIA argued that neither the GAO Feasibility Study nor P.L. 91-379 contemplated that the Board would prescribe single, specific methods of allocation. In addition to expressions of its overall displeasure with this proposed standard, CODSIA's lengthy comments included detailed disagreements on specific provisions, such as the three-part formula for allocating residual expenses. This author joined in opposing the requirement for the three-part formula, noting that the Board had provided no rationale or support for its use.

Prophetically, many commentators expressed concern about the listing of typical pools with illustrative allocation bases in CAS 403.60. The critics had had many experiences with government auditors who viewed illustrations in regulations as firm policy from which they could not deviate. The concern about the illustrative allocation bases, particularly the one for state and local income and franchise taxes, was shared by one of the Board members who expressed apprehension about the effects of a rigid application of this provision.

Many of the apprehensions about the various provisions of CAS 403 ultimately materialized. Although many problems and controversies developed, particularly as the Board broadened the application of this standard from relatively few companies to all with CAS-covered contracts, one specific provision resulted in probably more litigation to date than any other single cost principle or standard promulgated by a government agency. This result is ironic indeed in view of the Board's continued assertions that its promulgations were reducing industry-government disagreements regarding cost accounting practices.

The provision for allocating state and local taxes has resulted to date in litigation involving four major aerospace companies.

The Boeing Company, ASBCA No. 20998, 76-2 BCA par. 12,150; MFR Denied 79-1 BCA par. 13,708; 680 F.2d 132, 29 CCF par. 82,630 (Ct.Cl. June 2, 1982); petition for Writ of Certiori, Sup. Ct. No. 82-1024, denied 4/18/83. At issue was the accounting treatment of taxes paid by Boeing to the State of Washington and certain localities within that State; these taxes included real property, personal property, sales, use, business and occupation, and fuel and vehicle taxes. The contractor's consistent practice may be summarized as that of accumulating all such tax payments in an account in the corporate office records and then allocating percentages to Washington segments of the company according to a head count of employees located in the State of Washington. Boeing's rationale is bottomed mainly on the benefit theory of indirect expense allocation, although in a somewhat unusual application. The company explained that it reviewed the uses to which the various governments put the monies they received from tax collections and found that they were expended in support of elementary and secondary schools; human resources, including medical assistance, workmen's compensation, etc; transportation; sanitation; police and fire protection, parks and recreation; etc. In Boeing's opinion, the benefits of these services accrued to the residents of the respective localities, including the contractor's employees. Viewing the allocation from the causal theory, Boeing concluded that the cause of the taxes was the need for the services. Accordingly, viewed from either the beneficial or causal perspective, head count was considered the most logical basis for allocation.

As a quick summary of the government's position, it should first be noted that DCAA had disagreed with the head count allocation base over the years. When a contracting officer supported DCAA, the government lost in quasi-judicial and judicial forums because the head count basis was considered to be accommodated under the broad umbrella of generally accepted accounting principles. When CAS 403 became effective, DCAA believed its prior views were vindicated by the standard's provisions, and the audit agency moved quickly to conclude that the head count method would not be in compliance with CAS 403. The Air Force contracting officer agreed and handed down a unilateral determination, and this appeal followed.

The essence of the dispute is well captured by the ASBCA:

The parties are in agreement that the resolution of the dispute herein is dependent upon a proper interpretation of CAS 403.40(b)(4) with which the appellant's allocation of home office expenses to segments must comply. It reads:

"(4) *Central payments or accruals.* Central payments or accruals which are made by a home office on behalf of its segments shall be allocated directly to segments to the extent that all such payments or accruals of a given type or class can be identified specifically with individual segments. Central payments or accruals are those which but for the existence of a number of segments would be accrued or paid by the individual segments. Common examples include centrally paid or accrued pension costs, group insurance costs, State and local income taxes and franchise taxes, and payrolls paid by a home office on behalf of its segments. Any such types of payments or accruals which cannot be identified specifically with individual segments shall be allocated to benefitted segments using an allocation base representative of the factors on which the total payment is based."

The Government focuses on the first sentence and concludes most of the taxes here in issue must be "allocated directly to segments" because they "can be identified specifically with individual segments."

The appellant considers the operative requirement is the last sentence and concludes these central payments or accruals "cannot be identified specifically with individual segments" so must be "allocated to benefitted segments using an allocation base representative of the factors on which the total payment is based." Head count, as a surrogate, is a base representative of such factors, it argues.

The board unequivocally denied the appeal and ruled for the government:

We conclude that CAS 403.40(b)(4) requires each tax to be "allocated directly to segments" on its assessment base if the tax "can be identified specifically with individual segments" on such a base.

Each of the taxes in issue herein has a certain base upon which it is computed. Each tax can be specifically identified with a particular segment by that base and in fact is so identified by each segment prior to the home office pooling of all such taxes.

Referring to its prior decisions and that of the Court of Claims, the board noted that, prior to the promulgation of CAS 403, "the matter of such allocation was considered within the framework of the ASPR cost principles which did not specifically address the allocation of home office expenses to segments." The conditions then existing permitted a number of alternative methods for this purpose. Conditions changed drastically with the advent of Public Law 71-379, and the board found that "cost accounting standard 403 provides the first authoritative accounting statement concerned specifically with the allocations of home office expenses to segments."

Moving to the critical issue, the board observed:

At the very heart of this dispute is appellant's concept of benefit and cause. It asserts that the cause to be concerned with is the cause of the imposition of a tax. This it concludes is the community's need for services. So far as such need reflects the reason why the taxing authorities levy a tax, we agree it is certainly a cause. It also contends that the benefit to be concerned with is the benefit that the corporation and its segments, receive directly from the community services, and indirectly through benefits to its employees. So far as this is an assertion that there is a benefit to those within Washington from the services provided by the State and other communities there is certainly a benefit.

However, the board saw its major task as the need to resolve "how the CAS Board used the concepts of 'benefit' and 'cause,' with particular reference to taxes." The board found some assistance in the provisions of the standard:

CAS 403.60 provides some illustration of various home office expenses typically pooled and allocation bases which could be used in appropriate circumstances. Although the precise types of taxes in issue here are not alluded to, state and local income taxes and franchise taxes are mentioned as central payments or accruals. The illustrative allocation base is:

"Any base or method which results in an allocation that equals or approximates a segment's proportionate share of the tax imposed by the jurisdiction in which the segment does business, as measured by the same factors used to determine taxable income for that jurisdiction."

We believe that the CAS Board has hereby adopted an assessment base method of allocating these taxes, and, furthermore, by so doing has demonstrated that such a base comports with its concept of the beneficial or causal relationship alluded to in Sec. 403.40 as Fundamental Requirements. This conclusion is supported by the fact that in Section 403.60(c) where the CAS Board purports to permit other bases for allocation of home office expenses to segments, it restricts them to only such as are "substantially in accordance with the beneficial or causal relationships outlined in Sec. 403.40."

In the MFR, Boeing argued that the board should reconsider its decision for the following reasons:

"1. By interpreting CAS 403 as mandatorily requiring the allocation of any central payment or accrual to a single segment by merely because it can be 'identified specifically' to that segment by mechanical traceability without regard to any facts or circumstances, the decision is clearly erroneous as a matter of law.

"2. By holding that CAS 403.40 'does not accept the broad benefit test' and that costs such as Boeing's taxes which are paid by a home office must be allocated to segments by 'either specific identification or, if this cannot be done, on the basis of causality,' and thus giving no effect to the words 'benefit,' 'beneficial' and 'benefited' appearing in the Standard, the decision is clearly erroneous as a matter of law.

"3. The decision as it relates specifically to the allocation of Boeing's Washington state and local taxes to the business conducted by Boeing in the State of Washington is not equitable, is not supported by any findings of fact, nor is there any substantial evidence in the record to support the decision. On the contrary, there is ample evidence in the record to support a finding of fact that Boeing's method of allocating its taxes is equitable and the ASBCA has found as a fact (p. 44) that Boeing's method allocates its tax costs in accordance with both a beneficial and a causal relationship."

The Motion for Reconsideration was carefully considered but denied by the board, which concluded that "the CAS Board's treatment of tax cost allocation reflects its conclusion that an allocation of tax costs on the assessment base or any method not producing significantly different results does affect an allocation according to its concept of beneficial or causal relationship between the cost and the segment."

In June 1979, Boeing carried its appeal to the U.S. Court of Claims, which denied the company's appeal in June 1982. In this appeal, Boeing not only argued that the ASBCA decision was wrong as a matter of law, but also included a wide range of other arguments, such as that CAS 403 was improperly promulgated and that the CASB was unconstitutionally constituted and all its promulgations therefore void.

Boeing argued again that CAS 403 did "not mandate use of the assessment base method but is flexible in permitting any approach which measures benefits to the receiving segments from the tax expenditures."

The court then addressed the contractor's argument that the CASB was unconstitutionally constituted and therefore its acts, including the promulgation of CAS 403, were void.

The basis for the constitutionality issue lies in the manner in which the CASB members were appointed. The Comptroller General was established as chairman by P.L. 91-379, and he appointed the other four members. The Comptroller General was appointed by the President and confirmed by the Senate but only in his capacity as Comptroller and not as CASB Chairman. The "Appointments Clause" of the U.S. Constitution, Article II, Section 2, provides that officers of the United States shall be nominated by the President and appointed by the President by and with the advice of the Senate. In its decision, the court seems to be saying it need not rule on the constitutional issue because (1) DOD voluntarily adopted this (and the other) standards and (2) equity and practicality demand the past acts of the CASB should be accepted because of the problems and costs that retroactive invalidation would cause.

In December 1982, Boeing appealed to the Supreme Court, filing a petition for Writ of Certiorari, Sup. Ct. Dkt. No. 82-1024. Boeing asserted that "the Court of Claims' refusal to rule that the CASB was appointed in violation of the appointments clause (of the constitution) is in conflict with controlling decisions of this court." The Court of Claims' reason for refusing to rule on the constitutional issue was that "Equity and practicality demand that result. The number of contracts which would need to be altered, the amount of moneys involved, and the agreement by the contractors to CAS 403 standard would justify nonretrospective application of any current ruling of unconstitutionality of the method of appointment of the CASB members." Boeing noted, however, that, while many contractors did agree to accept CAS 403, Boeing did not, reserving its rights in its contracts to challenge the validity of this standard.

Boeing also cited case law in support of its arguments that the Court of Claims could have made its decision prospective only, with relief only to Boeing.

In another argument, one that was to assume unexpected, future significance, Boeing challenged the court's ruling that DOD itself had adopted CAS 403 although it had the independent authority to adopt or not to adopt this standard. Boeing asserted that DOD did not have such an option because the Act provided that that the CASB's standards *"shall* be used by all relevant Federal agencies . . . ." As discussed in Chapter VIII of this text, the court's view on this point was to lead the Department of Justice to issue a ruling based upon which DOD attempted to establish its own CAS Board.

The long road of this case seemed to have ended on April 18, 1983, when the Supreme Court declined to issue the writ Boeing had requested.

McDonnell Douglas, ASBCA No. 19842, 80-1 BCA par. 14,223; MFR Affirmed 80-2 BCA par. 14,508 and *Lockheed & Lockheed Missiles & Space,* ASBCA No. 22451, 80-1 BCA par. 14,222; MFR Affirmed 80-2 BCA Par. 14,509.—Seldom, if ever, in its history of litigating disputes involving costs under government contracts has the Department of Defense suffered such hard blows as it experienced in two decisions handed down by the ASBCA on December 26, 1979.

The specific sections of CAS 403 involved in these disputes are 403.40(b)(4), Central Payments or Accruals; 403.60(b)(3), containing an illustrative allocation base for state and local income and franchise taxes; and

403.60(c), which permits the use of bases other than those illustrated. These sections were quoted earlier in this chapter.

The McDonnell Douglas Decision.—As summarized by the administrative judge, "This appeal concerns the question of whether the manner in which the *McDonnell Douglas Corporation* (MDC) allocates California Franchise Tax (CFT) and Missouri Income Tax (MIT) is in compliance with . . . CAS 403 . . . ."

As described in the decision, the CFT "requires that every corporation (except those expressly exempted) 'doing business' within California, for the privilege of exercising its franchise in California, shall pay to California a tax based upon its net income." The decision further notes that "doing business" is defined as "conducting activities for gain or profit." The following additional excerpts from the decision further describe the CFT:

> In the case of corporations having net income from sources both within and without California, the California Revenue and Taxation Code provides that the tax proposed . . . should be measured by the net income derived from or attributable to sources within California. . . . The statutes set forth specific rules for allocating such income to California. . . .

> The (CFT) is based on the unitary concept. Under this concept of taxing the income of interstate business, due consideration must be given to the relative contributions of the business activities of the taxpayer in each of the several states to the production of the net income of the total unitary enterprise. . . .

> California apportions the unitary income of (MDC) to California by applying a three factor formula which gives equal weight to the geographical distribution of property, payroll, and sales . . .

> Then this percentage is multiplied by unitary income to determine the income attributable to the (MDC) business activity within California. This apportioned income is then multiplied by the tax rate to compute the actual tax obligation. . . .

In describing the Missouri income tax, the board noted that the three-factor apportionment formula is permitted only as an alternative to its one-factor sales formula. In describing the MIT, the board said:

> Missouri, like California, apportions unitary income to Missouri for the purpose of taxation. . . . Missouri looks to the activity in Missouri relative to the activity of the corporation everywhere. The primary formula uses a single factor: sales in Missouri plus one-half the sales partly within and partly without Missouri is the numerator and the taxpayer's corporate-wide sales is the denominator . . . (MDC) utilizes the primary formula, the single sales factor, to compute Missouri income tax.

In accordance with its consistent accounting practices, MDC allocated the CFT and the MIT to its segments in the ratio of gross payroll dollars. Under this method, all state income and franchise taxes are pooled at the MDC home office and then allocated without regard to the taxing jurisdictions to its segments in the ratio of gross payroll.

DCAA has never been happy with the gross payroll method and, as a matter of fact, had persuaded the contracting officer to disapprove the use of this method even before the effective date of CAS 403. MDC appealed this ruling, and its gross payroll method was found by ASBCA to be acceptable under DAR. In the appeal under discussion, the government advised MDC that its method was in noncompliance with CAS 403. MDC disagreed, whereupon a DCAA Form 1 was issued, which became the contracting officer's final decision from which this appeal was taken. The essence of the government's position as cited in the DCAA Form 1 is quoted below:

> MDC's basis for allocation of state and local income and franchise taxes as described above, is not representative of the factors on which the payment is based because (1) no effect is given to the factors for sales or assets involved in a significant way in the determination of the amount to be paid, and (2) no effect is given to the distribution by taxing jurisdiction of payroll, sales or asset factors of a segment in the determination of its share of the payment or accrual. Accordingly, MDC's method of allocation of these taxes fails to meet the requirements of CAS 403.40(b)(4). It also fails to meet the test for equivalence contained in CAS 403.60 which reads, "Any base or method which results in an allocation that equals or approximates a segment's proportionate share of the tax imposed by the jurisdiction in which the segment does business, as measured by the same factors used to determine taxable income for that jurisdiction."

Essentially, the government had advocated that the taxes involved be computed based on the so-called DCAA method. In the case of the CFT, the segment's tax expense would be the product of the total tax expense multiplied by the three-factor formula, a percentage representing an average of the ratios of property, payroll, and sales, respectively, within California to the total of such factors.

In computing each segment's tax expense for the MIT, the DCAA method as adopted by the government consisted of multiplying the total Missouri income tax expense by the sales formula previously described.

The board's ultimate conclusion was that neither the MDC gross payroll method nor the government's DCAA method was in compliance with CAS 403. The board therefore decided: "We, therefore, remand this dispute to the parties to negotiate an acceptable method giving consideration to the conclusions set forth in this opinion. In the event this proves unsuccessful appropriate steps would again have to be taken to bring a new appeal before the Board."

As key issues in arriving at its decision, the board identified these questions: "(1) what did CASB mean by 'factors' and (2) was a single benchmark established by the illustrative base against which other methods allowed by CAS 403.60(c) are to be measured?"

The board then addressed the first of the key issues mentioned above, i.e., what the CASB meant by "factors." The government argued that the term "factors" could relate only to the property, payroll, and sales equation. The government saw segment income and the tax rate as elements. The board's rejection of this government argument seemed to us one of the two most significant aspects of the decision, and we have quoted portions of the related discussions at some length:

> CAS 403 does not use the term "elements" nor does it define factors. While the prefactory comments might lead one to believe that at least for state and local income and franchise taxes the CAS Board intended to limit factors in that manner it could have said so clearly and specifically ... Nothing in the record convinces us that this was specifically what the CAS Board intended. Review of the record, both written and oral, fails to convince us that in changing the illustrative base example in CAS 403.60, the CAS Board intended to eliminate income as a factor in the allocation base. We view the change as broadening the base and giving consideration to all parts of the formula. We recognize respondent's argument to the contrary but interpret the evidence it relies upon in a different manner.

> *   *   *   *

> We, therefore, conclude that the term "factors" includes all portions of the equation used to calculate the tax being allocated. Thus, rate is also a factor. In most instances this is a constant but where it varies it must also be considered. In the case of state and local income taxes or franchise taxes using income in their computation, income must be included as one of the factors of the allocation base. To conclude otherwise could cause a distorted allocation of a cost one major factor or component of which is income. Therefore, such allocation would fail to meet the causal requirement of the standard. We recognize respondent's position concerning "cause" is that benefit and cause are essentially synonymous, namely the taxes are caused by doing business within the taxing jurisdictions (having property, payroll or sales in California, having sales in Missouri) and the segments doing business in the taxing jurisdiction benefit from the payment of the tax. This gets perilously close to the broad benefit test rejected in Boeing. We view the cause as contribution to any factor, including income, by a segment to the base.

> We, therefore, conclude that in referencing "factors" in both CAS 403.40(b)(4) and CAS 403.60, the terms means all figures used in an assessment base.

The second significant issue identified and considered by the board was whether CAS 403.40(b)(4) or CAS 403.60 did "establish a single benchmark for the allocation of state and local income or franchise taxes." The board's rationale for concluding that these provisions did not establish a single benchmark are significant and are quoted below:

> CAS 403.40(b)(4) provides that allocation of the second tier payments or accruals be made "using an allocation base representative of the factors upon which the total payment is based." CAS 403.60 sets forth an illustrative allocation base and also provides, as indicated previously, for any use of other bases if they are "substantially in accordance with the beneficial or causal relationships outlined in CAS 403.40." We do not

view the standard, considered as a whole, as establishing any specific "bench mark" against which all methods of allocation are to be measured. Rather, based upon our analysis of the standard, the legislative and administrative history and the evidence and testimony presented at the hearing we conclude that various assessment bases may comply with the standard. We further conclude that a contractor using the illustrative allocation base need not establish compliance but a contractor who uses some other base must prove it meets the beneficial or causal requirements of CAS 403.40 and is representative of the factors upon which the tax payment is based. The standard itself recognizes that many of these costs are difficult to allocate.

Having concluded that various allocation bases can achieve compliance with CAS 403, the board next considered which ones would be in compliance and which would not.

The MDC gross payroll method was adjudged not to comply with the illustrative allocation base of CAS 403.60. As the board pointed out, "It consists of a portion of one of the factors of the (CFT) and is not in the formula for (MIT)."

The board rejected the DCAA method because it "fails to meet the requirements of the illustrative allocation base in that it fails, in toto, to consider income—unitary or segment . . . ."

As mentioned earlier, the board rejected both MDC's and the government's methods and remanded the dispute to the parties to negotiate an acceptable method "giving consideration to the conclusions set forth in this opinion." For a further insight into a method that the ASBCA would find acceptable, we must review the board's concurrent decision in the Lockheed appeal.

The Lockheed Decision.—The ASBCA summarized this dispute as follows:

This is a test case under CAS 403 to resolve a dispute over Lockheed's allocation of California Franchise Tax to segments. The controversy centers on whether segment net income may be used as a factor in allocating the tax expense to segments. Lockheed's primary contention is that the tax expense cannot be specifically identified with individual segments and must be allocated to segments using a base representative of the factors on which the total payment is based. Lockheed's position is that an allocation base must include net income as a factor in order to be representative of the factors on which the total payment is based. . . . The government contends that an allocation base which includes segment net income as a factor is not representative of the factors on which the total payment is based.

Essential to an understanding of this decision is a clear description of the manner in which the California franchise tax expense was allocated to Lockheed's segments. This description is provided in the decision in the following succinct manner.

Lockheed allocated the Lockheed Affiliated Group's income year 1974 California Franchise Tax expense to Lockheed's profitable segments with

California sales, payroll, or property on essentially a two step basis. In the first step, each segment was treated as if it were a separate and distinct unitary business, and its "net income derived from or attributable to California sources" was computed by multiplying the segment's net income by an apportionment percentage which consisted of the average of the ratios of the segment's California to the segment's total payroll, property, and sales. In the second step, individual segment "net income derived from or attributable to California sources" was totaled for all profitable segments and the Lockheed Affiliated Group's California Franchise expense was allocated to individual profitable segments in the same proportion that each segment's "net income derived from or attributable to California sources" had to the total. Segments operating at a loss were not allocated any part of the Lockheed Affiliated Group's tax liability, nor did such segments receive any credit.

The *Lockheed* appeal came before the board much later than the *MDC* appeal, and the government used substantially the same arguments and proposals.

The board noted the concurrent opinion it issued in the appeal of *MDC,* ASBCA No. 19842, 80-1 BCA par. 14,223, and drew heavily upon that decision because it also involved the CFT and the application of CAS 403. The board also noted that many of the same issues were argued in both appeals and discussed in detail in the *MDC* opinion, and hence the pertinent summaries would suffice for the *Lockheed* decision.

In summarizing its decision in *MDC,* the board had said:

We concluded that the California Franchise Tax cannot be "identified specifically with individual segments" pursuant to the first sentence of CAS 403.40(b)(4) so that the last sentence of CAS 403(b)(4) applied and California Franchise Tax was to be allocated using an allocation base "representative of the factors on which the total payment is based." We further concluded that the word "factors" in that last sentence and also in the illustrative allocation base set forth in CAS 403.60 is not limited to the so-called statutory factors of property, payroll and sales but includes all of the factors upon which the tax was based, namely, income, statutory factors and rate. (Since here the rate is constant it is not a variable in the allocation). We, therefore, also concluded neither Government method A or Government method B was in compliance with CAS 403 because neither considered the contribution of segmental income to unitary income.

The board found the same conclusions applicable to the *Lockheed* dispute, and it saw the next question for resolution as being whether any of Lockheed's methods for allocating the CFT were in compliance with CAS 403. In *MDC,* the board concluded "that the test for compliance with the last sentence of 403.40(b)(4) was whether it complied with the illustrative allocation base in CAS 403.60 . . .," which we have cited earlier in this analysis.

The board also stated: "If so we concluded that is all that is required. We further concluded that such compliance is not limited to one allocation base but that various bases could conform."

Inasmuch as the government had identified the critical issue to be whether the CASB intended to include segment income as a factor, and inasmuch as the board then resolved this question affirmatively in *MDC,* it said "[p]erhaps our decision should end here with a determination (Lockheed's) method is in compliance and sustain the appeal." However, the board elected to go further and explain why Lockheed's specific method conformed to the illustrative allocation base set forth in CAS 403.60:

The allocation is limited to each segment in the "jurisdiction in which the segment does business." It further complies since the first-step is "measured by the same factors used to determine taxable income for that jurisdiction." The only question is whether by considering only those segments which had net income and disregarding segments which had net losses the allocation is not one which "equals or approximates a segment's proportionate share of the tax." In the case of California Franchise Tax we conclude allowance of credits (recognition of losses) is not appropriate. California has no provision for a refund of its franchise tax in a loss year by carryback or carry forward to a profitable year. To the contrary, it provides for a minimum tax of $200 per corporation under such circumstances. The corporation has already benefited since the loss by any particular segment reduces the unitary income and therefore decreases the corporate franchise tax. To allow a credit under such circumstances to a loss segment would result in a franchise tax allowance to the profitable segments in excess of the amount actually paid and a negative allocation (credit) to the loss segments even though their business activity factors contributed to the tax. We have also considered respondent's argument that segment book income is not always available and is somewhat suspect. Here the segment income information is available and whether inaccurate or unreliable is capable of proof by audit and analysis beyond any proof in this case. Raising a "spectre" of same is insufficient. We, therefore, conclude that this method of allocation, which allocates only to profitable segments, is in compliance with CAS 403.

Having found Lockheed's basic method in compliance with CAS 403, the board sustained the company's appeal.

The ASBCA decisions greatly upset the CASB and its staff, and DCAA, whose director painted a black picture suggesting that hundreds of contractors, who had been required to comply with the government's interpretation of CAS 403 with regard to the allocation of state income taxes, would now be in noncompliance.

Moving with urgency seldom found in the federal bureaucracy, the Board directed its staff to prepare an interpretation of CAS 403 that would state that its intent had been misunderstood by the ASBCA, that the allocation of such taxes must be determined by applying the statutory factor to the total income of the organization, and that the income of the individual segments must be ignored.

The directions to the staff were given at the Board's first meeting (February 8-9, 1980) following the publication of the ASBCA decisions in *MDC* and *Lockheed.* With the next Board meeting scheduled for late in March, the CASB took the unusual position of directing its staff to prepare the interpretation and obtain approval by correspondence and telephone. The interpretation seeking to overthrow the ASBCA decisions was completed and sent to the CASB members within a week. Approval was obtained, and the interpretation was published in the *Federal Register* on March 3, 1980, as a final rule, effective the same date.

Essentially (and incredibly) the CASB sought to intervene in the litigation in process (the government had filed Motions for Reconsideration in both the *McDonnell Douglas* and *Lockheed* disputes) and alleged that its "intent in CAS 403 has been misunderstood by the ASBCA." Rewriting this standard in a manner designed to insure the acceptability of only the DCAA method, the CASB stated in part:

> Most States tax a fraction of total organization income, rather than the book income of segments that do business within the State. The fraction is calculated pursuant to a formula prescribed by State statute. In these situations the book income or loss of individual segments is not a factor used to determine taxable income for that jurisdiction. Accordingly, in States that tax a fraction of total organization income, rather than the book income of segments within the State, such book income is irrelevant for tax allocation purposes. Therefore, segment book income is to be used as a factor in allocating income tax expense from a home office to segments only where this amount is expressly used by the taxing jurisdiction in computing the income tax.

On March 7, 1980, the ASBCA held hearings on the government's MFRs on *MDC* and *Lockheed*. The MFRs had been prepared prior to the CASB's promulgation of its interpretation, which it sought to make applicable retroactively to December 1972, the date CAS 403 was published in the *Federal Register*. In view of this new development, the parties involved were given further time to prepare briefs relating to the implications of the interpretation.

In decisions handed down on June 5 (*Lockheed*) and June 9, 1980 (*McDonnell Douglas*), the ASBCA affirmed its initial decisions and slapped down the CASB's effort to improperly intrude into judicial matters. The two decisions were prepared and issued concurrently. The one on *McDonnell Douglas* contained most of the ASBCA's reasoning and our analysis will accordingly devote greater attention to this decision.

At the oral hearings on the MFR, MDC, Lockheed and the government were requested to submit supplemental arguments relating to the CASB's Interpretation No. 1 of CAS 403. All of the parties did so.

In addressing the interpretation, the ASBCA first cited the CASB's 1973 "Statement of Objectives, Policies and Concepts" and its 1977 "Restatement of Objectives, Policies and Concepts." The ASBCA particularly noted that both the statement and the restatement contained a very clear provision: "The Board notes the existence of contractual and administrative provisions for the resolution or settlement of disputes arising under a contract, and the Board will not intervene in or seek to supercede such provisions."

The ASBCA also noted that the statement and restatement referred to the Board's authority to issue interpretations, at its discretion, and that "such interpretations will be published in the *Federal Register . . . .*"

However, a study of Public Law 91-379 (50 U.S.C. App. (1970)) persuaded the ASBCA that the CASB "is not granted statutory authority to issue interpretations. It is given authority to issue 'rules, regulations, cost-accounting standards, and modifications thereof' using certain, specifically prescribed procedures." The ASBCA then cited Section 719(i), which requires that all standards, rules and regulations, and modifications thereof must be published in the *Federal Register* and all parties affected shall be afforded a period of not less than thirty days to comment thereon. And only after the Board considers such comments may it promulgate standards and modifications "which shall have the full force and effect of law and shall become effective not later than the start of the second fiscal quarter beginning after the expiration of not less than thirty days after publication in the *Federal Register.*"

The ASBCA also quoted paragraph (h)(3) of the Act, which states that cost accounting standards shall take effect not earlier than the expiration of the first period of sixty calendar days of continuous session of the Congress following the date on which a copy of the standard is transmitted to the Congress.

The ASBCA also took cognizance of an exception to this requirement, which appeared in the Congressional Conference Committee Report accompanying the enactment of P.L. 91-379: "However, minor and technical modifications in already promulgated standards, rules or regulations which do not in effect constitute the issuance of new standards, rules or regulations would not have to be submitted to Congress prior to promulgation."

The ASBCA noted that the CASB had issued two prior interpretations and in each of these instances followed the requirements of law for publication and submission to Congress. In contrast, these procedures were not followed in the case of Interpretation No. 1 to CAS 403. The government's argument that the latter interpretation was of a minor or technical nature, and therefore did not require congressional review, was rejected by the ASBCA, which found that the interpretation set out a new definition for the significant term "factors" in CAS 403.40. As such, it certainly could not be considered minor or trivial.

The ASBCA also pointed to the contradictions in the government's arguments, where it on the one hand alleged that the interpretation was of a minor nature and on the other hand defended the unusual haste on the grounds that quick action was necessary because of concern among the contractors who had revised their cost accounting systems to conform with government Method B (the reference here is to the three-factor formula employed by DCAA).

The ASBCA acknowledged the CASB's authority to modify its promulgations as long as it followed the procedure prescribed by the statute. It concluded that the CASB's Interpretation No. 1 changed the ground rules for permissible formulas. This change was considered significant and in the words of the ASBCA: "However, we do not consider Interpretation No. 1 as a permissible 'short-cut' to such procedure. Therefore we do not consider the purported Cost Accounting Standards Board 'interpretation' as binding or determinative as to the proper interpretation of the standard."

The *MDC* decision on the government's MFR contains another significant comment, which addresses the alleged problems portrayed by the government regarding the consequences of this decision to the many companies that had, either voluntarily or through dictation by the government, adopted the three-factor formula for allocating state and local income taxes.

> We, therefore, consider concern about contractors who adopted Government Method B prior to our decision unnecessary. In our opinion, nothing precludes a contractor from continuing to use a method with Government approval either in compliance with CAS 403.40(b)(4) or under the consistency objective of the Cost Accounting Standards Board or by negotiation and settlement of a dispute. But Government may not dictate a surrogate allocation base to a contractor under CAS 403.60(c) where a more appropriate and equitable result would be reached by applying a base in keeping with the specific language of CAS 403.40(b)(4) and the illustration in CAS 403.60. Such is the case with *McDonnell Douglas*.

While we must leave the final legal evaluation of the above citation to the legal fraternity, our layman's view is that any contractor who has been using the three-factor formula in a state providing for such formula may, at its election, reach an agreement with the government to continue using this method. On the other hand, a contractor in these circumstances who wishes to change its practice and use the Lockheed method, or a variant thereof that includes the factors of segment income and the tax rate in addition to the statutory factors, may do so.

The ASBCA concluded its decision on the MFR by stating that no argument presented by the government persuaded it to reach a conclusion different from the original. This statement appeared to place the *MDC* appeal back on the same status as the December 26, 1979, original decision in which the ASBCA concluded that MDC's gross payroll method and both government Methods A and B were not in strict compliance with CAS 403 for failure to consider segment income as a factor.

The ASBCA decision on the government's MFR in the *Lockheed* case was considerably shorter in that the ASBCA referred to the *MDC* decision and noted that it would not repeat all of the discussions in the *Lockheed* case. The ASBCA did identify a major difference between the two in that MDC's method was determined to be not in compliance with CAS 403 whereas Lockheed's two-step method was adjudged to be in compliance with CAS 403.40(b)(4).

The *Lockheed* CAS 403 controversy, however, was far from concluded. DCAA was outraged that the accounting theory it had painstakingly developed in support of its application of CAS 403 was rejected by the ASBCA, and especially so after the "interpretation" of this standard, which it had assisted the CASB staff in contriving, was declared not binding because the CASB, in its unseemly haste to promulgate this interpretation to intervene in the ASBCA's deliberations, failed to process it in accordance with statutory requirements.

Equally disturbed or even more so were some of the Air Force officials, particularly one trial attorney who had compiled a record of unsuccessful verdicts before the ASBCA, and who was to sharply criticize the ASBCA at congressional hearings in connection with disputes involving P.L. 87-653 (see Chapter XXII of this text).

The contracts involved in the *Lockheed* dispute had been awarded prior to the effective date of the Contract Disputes Act of 1978 (CDA), which, for the first time, permitted the government to appeal ASBCA decisions to federal court. After the passage of this Act, the disappointed government officials entered into extensive efforts to prepare an appeal to the U.S. Court of Appeals for the Federal Circuit. This was accomplished by selecting some contracts awarded to Lockheed after March 1, 1979, the effective date of CDA, and rearguing before the ASBCA the allocation of the California Franchise Tax to segments according to the Air Force/DCAA notions. The board's ruling in favor of Lockheed was fully expected but the purpose of all of the time, cost and effort was to develop a basis for appeal to the federal court.

The expected ASBCA ruling sustaining Lockheed's appeal was handed down in *Lockheed Corporation and Lockheed Missiles & Space Company, Inc.,* ASBCA No. 27921, 86-1 BCA par. 18,614. Although this decision covers much of the ground previously addressed by the board, its review is recommended for those involved or interested in allocation of state and local income taxes and franchise taxes based on income pursuant to CAS 403. In the knowledge that the board's decision would be appealed to the federal courts, the government and the contractor presented extensive stipulations identifying all of the major facts and issues in the case. In turn, although the board noted that it could have sustained the appeal with a brief decision through reference to its prior ruling, it set out its views in a very comprehensive manner to facilitate the review by the court.

On April 15, 1987, the U.S. Court of Appeals for the Federal Circuit rejected the government's appeal and affirmed the board's ruling in favor of Lockheed. *U.S. v. Lockheed Corp. and Lockheed Missiles and Space Co.,* CA FC No. 86-1177 [34 CCF par. 75,258]. Unfortunately, the court's decision did not rule on the CASB's hasty "interpretation" of CAS 403, widely considered, and formally described by the ASBCA, as illegal. On this point the court stated:

> Although the government urges that we look beyond CAS 403.30(b)(4) to determine whether the Lockheed Method is in compliance with CAS 403.60 and Interpretation No. 1 to CAS 403, the question is moot in the light of the stipulation. The court in *Boeing I,* after noting that the standard of CAS 403 "does not necessarily mandate any particular allocation" . . . held that the examples in CAS 403.60 are illustrative only and were not intended to be exclusive . . . . In addition, Interpretation No. 1 to CAS 403 does not by its terms mandate for all purposes of CAS 403 that income taxes "are to be allocated only to those segments that do business in the taxing jurisdiction" . . . Rather it merely interprets an illustrative allocation base in CAS 403.60.

Since Interpretation No. 1 applies only to CAS 403.60, we need not, and do not, address the validity of Interpretation 1, nor its applicability in any other context.

The stipulation referred to in the above excerpt was by both parties: "if CAS 403 permits net income to be included as a factor in the allocation base, the Lockheed Method complies with CAS 403 and shall be used . . . ." The court found that CAS 403 indeed did permit segment net income to be included as a factor in the allocation base.

We understand the proclivity of boards of contract appeals and courts to confine their rulings to the extent necessary to decide a dispute and their reluctance to rule on matters not essential for this purpose. On the other hand, this practice frequently serves only to produce additional litigation and to defer the required decisions to another time. See for example Chapter XXII of this text where the judiciary is reluctant to face head on the availability of intentional understatements for offsets where the government asserts defective pricing under P.L. 87-653. In a 1973 ruling, *Lockheed Aircraft Corp., Lockheed-Georgia (Midwestern Instruments, Subcontractor) v. U.S.* [19 CCF par. 82,586], Ct.Cl. No. 250-67, with the subject of intentional understatements clearly at issue, the court elected not to address this issue, ruling for *Lockheed/Midwestern* on the ground that the ASBCA had "arbitrarily and capriciously cast upon plaintiff the burden of proof that the understatement . . . was unintentional."

The issue of intentional understatements, of course, did not "go away." It reappeared in the dispute involving *Rogerson Aircraft Controls,* ASBCA No. 27954, 85-1 BCA par. 17,725, also reviewed in Chapter XXII of this text. On a 3-2 vote, the ASBCA permitted the use of intentional understatements for offsets in this particular case but stated that it was not handing down a hard and fast rule and other disputes would require decisions based on the particular facts of each case. In its appeal to the U.S. Court of Appeals for the Federal Circuit, No. 85-2058, 33 CCF par. 14,262, the government requested the court to rule specifically on this subject but the court declined to do so, finding instead for Rogerson on the basis that the government was aware of the understatements at the time of negotiations. The court concluded:

Accordingly, we affirm the ASBCA, leaving still undecided by this court the issue whether a deliberate, deceptive (or misleading) understatement (*i.e.,* an intentional understatement which is unknown to the Government) can be offset in a "defective pricing" case.

The issue of intentional understatements may have been decided by the DOD 1987 Authorization Act, which provides that "A contractor shall not be allowed to offset an amount otherwise authorized to be offset under subparagraph (A) if—(i) the certification . . . with respect to the cost or pricing data involved was known to be false when signed . . . ."

The controversy over the invalid CAS 403 interpretation, however, because of the court's refusal to address it, may still remain and generate disputes if DOD succeeds in incorporating CAS into FAR.

In the *Lockheed* CAS 403 controversy, the court identified two major issues:

(1) Whether the Board correctly held that the California Franchise Tax for a multistate enterprise cannot be allocated directly to the individual segments of that enterprise pursuant to CAS 403.

(2) Whether the Board correctly held that the causal relationship required by CAS 403 mandates consideration of segment net income as one of the factors in the allocation base.

With the advantages of the comprehensive joint stipulations of the parties and equally comprehensive ruling by the ASBCA in anticipation of the appeal, the court was able to write its decision, affirming the ASBCA ruling, without the need for what would otherwise have been a very lengthy ruling.

As to the first issue, the court agreed with the ASBCA ruling that Lockheed's California Franchise Tax cannot be directly allocated to segments because a segment's contribution to the cause of the tax cannot be specifically identified. Citing the CASB's 1977 Restatement of Objectives, Policies and Concepts, which requires that the beneficial or causal relationship between the incurrence of cost and cost objectives be clear and exclusive in order to identify costs with final cost objectives directly, the court found that the "causal relationship between Lockheed's California Franchise Tax expense and Lockheed's individual segments is not exclusive or in any way directly traceable."

The court was equally (if not more) emphatically in agreement with the ASBCA decision upholding Lockheed's contention that net income must be considered a factor in the allocation base. The government was forced to agree that "net income subject to California tax could not be computed without including net income." However, it contended, through its expert witness, that net income was not a "factor" since it was not an apportionment factor.

The court agreed with the board "that the term 'factors' is used in the broad and generic sense, not being used as a term of art meaning the 'apportionment factors,' and that the major component (net income) for the tax variation could not be disregarded in finding compliance with the requirements of CAS 403." The court further states:

Thus, for Lockheed, the assessment base, or measure of the tax, is a portion of its net income determined by multiplying Lockheed's total net income by an apportionment percentage. Lockheed's net income and its apportionment percentage thus jointly measure or cause the tax expense and together determine the assessment base for the tax. Total net income—the sum of the incomes (losses) of the various segments—is a significant cause of the California Franchise Tax expense. An increase in Lockheed's net income causes a proportional increase in its tax expense, and a decrease in net income causes a proportional decrease in its tax expense. The causal relationship between Lockheed's net income and the tax expense is an arithmetical fact.

The clear and unequivocal rulings by the ASBCA and the Court of Appeals for the Federal Circuit should persuade the Air Force attorneys and DCAA auditors to stop wasting taxpayers' monies by continuing their efforts to impose their ill-advised views.

Grumman Corporation and Grumman Aerospace Corporation ASBCA No. 23219. 82-1 BCA par. 15,661; MFR Aff'd 82-2 BCA par. 15,993. This decision, as in the cases of *McDonnell Douglas* and *Lockheed,* climaxed a lengthy history where the disagreements between the government and the contractor were traceable to the promulgation of CAS 403. Although we find nothing objectionable in the method used by Grumman, we shall not devote any time in describing it because, during the hearings, the company stated that it would accept the method approved by the board in *Lockheed* if it were modified to take into consideration credit allocations to loss segments. From what we can gather of the case, Grumman was not giving up very much by accepting the *Lockheed* method, as modified, because it was moving to an accepted method (with the treatment of credits unknown) and this method would provide Grumman with essentially the amount it was looking for, and certainly much more than it could expect under the "DCAA Method."

A considerable portion of the decision was devoted to the nature of the New York State franchise tax, its purposes, and its complicated computation procedures. Throughout these descriptions, the ASBCA took the occasion time and time again to establish the significance of income, unitary and segment. It was particularly significant in this case because the New York business income of Grumman Corp. and its affiliates amounted to more than 90 per cent of the corporation's total business income.

We are not certain the adoption of the *Lockheed* method by Grumman required considerable arguments by the contractor over and above the citation of the *Lockheed* decision. Perhaps it did because one of the Grumman expert accounting witnesses obviously made a strong impression on the board as indicated in the ultimate ruling. He "presented statistical correlation and regression analyses confirming objectively the strength of the relationship between the income or loss of the segments and the amount of tax." The witness cited the feasibility study leading to the establishment of the CASB concluding that "cost measurement must be based upon objective evidence, logically and consistently analyzed and interpreted; no cost assignment should be made without a valid (statistically verifiable) justification." The witness also cited other authorities and, indeed, the DCAA Manual, which advocated the use of regression and correlation analyses in the selection of allocation bases. The testimony revealed a very strong (positive) correlation between income or loss and taxes due or refunded each year. On the other hand, there was little or no correlation between the so-called statutory factors and taxes due or refunded.

The board reiterated its decisions in *McDonnell Douglas* and *Lockheed* that these kinds of taxes are not "caused by doing business in the tax jurisdiction." The board found that the taxes have "multiple causes" and, referring to the regression and correlation analyses, found that "changes in the Grumman tax cost were significantly correlated with changes in income, whereas there was virtually no correlation between the apportionment factors and changes in the tax."

The board then turned to the issue vital to Grumman (the *Lockheed* decision having been rendered by then)—consideration of losses.

As mentioned earlier, Grumman moved to an acceptance of the Lockheed method, modified to allocate credits to the loss segments. The notion of credits to loss segments was intolerable to the government, which persisted in viewing the franchise tax as a tax for doing business. When the ASBCA established the causal effect of the N.Y. franchise tax as mainly segment income or loss, the underpinnings of the government argument crumbled. The ASBCA further saw segment net operating losses as "valuable legal and accounting assets." They reduce the total N.Y. franchise tax paid or increase the carryback and resulting refund. And, herein lay the major differences between the N.Y. and California taxes. In the latter case, the loss corporation would be subject to the minimum tax in the event it filed separately and could not carry back or carry forward the loss. Therefore, reasoned the board, a loss segment in California realized the full value of its loss when it joined in the combined return despite the fact that it did not receive an allocation tax cost or credit. On the other hand, the full value of a net operating loss in New York cannot be recognized by loss segments without the allocation to them of credits that compensate them for use of their legal accounting asset. The board further stated that, without allocation of credits, the loss segments would, in effect, be penalized by joining in the combined return and deprived of any opportunity to carry back or carry forward the loss without filing separately.

The board conceded that this method might result in an allocation to a profitable segment that would exceed the total tax paid. However, the amount allocated would not exceed what the profitable segment would pay were it to file separately. In essence, according to the ruling, the tax credit paid to loss segments would have been paid to the state in the form of an additional tax cost had the segments filed separately.

The government filed a motion for reconsideration and, on July 8, 1982, the board reaffirmed its ruling.

One of the government's main arguments was that the board's decision permitted unallowable credits in contravention to DAR 15-205.41—Taxes, since such credits do not represent franchise taxes paid to a state. The government also argued that the credits could not be an imputed cost since DAR requires the tax to be paid or accrued. *Physics International Company,* ASBCA No. 17700, 77-2 BCA par. 12, 612 was cited in support of this contention.

The board found that the differences between this case and *Physics* were so great as to make that decision inapplicable. Physics had acquired a subsidiary company, Cintra, which was anticipated to and did incur losses in the early years of its operations. Physics, Cintra, and another subsidiary recorded a loss approximating $900,000 on the combined California franchise tax return filed by the three corporations for that tax year. Physics made a credit allocation to Cintra for the amount of taxes Physics would have paid but for the loss incurred by Cintra. The corresponding debit was recorded in the G&A expenses of Physics and a portion thereof allocated to government contracts. This charge was disallowed by the government, the disallowance appealed by the contractor, and the board ruled for the government. Here, however, the board found many differences, chiefly that Physics never paid any tax (aside from nominal taxes for each of the three corporations), and its own expert witness testified that the tax recorded on Physics' books was an imputed cost as distinguished from one paid or accrued. Thus, the charge was ruled unallowable under DAR 15-205.41. There were also a number of other differences, including the fact that the New York tax law provided for carrybacks and carryforwards whereas the California tax law did not.

CAS 410—Allocation of Business Unit General and Administrative Expenses to Final Cost Objectives

The standard provides the following definition of G&A expense (410.30(a)(6)):

Any management, financial, and other expense which is incurred by or allocated to a business unit and which is for the general management and administration of the business unit as a whole. G&A expense does not include those management expenses whose beneficial or causal relationship to cost objectives can be more directly measured by a base other than a cost input base representing the total activity of a business unit during a cost accounting period.

The "Fundamental requirements" and "Techniques for application" paragraphs of this standard are quoted below:

§ 410.40 Fundamental requirement.

(a) Business unit G&A expenses shall be grouped in a separate indirect cost pool which shall be allocated only to final cost objectives.

(b) (1) The G&A expense pool of a business unit for a cost accounting period shall be allocated to final cost objectives of that cost accounting period by means of a cost input base representing the total activity of the business unit except as provided in paragraph (b)(2) of this section. The cost input base selected shall be the one which best represents the total activity of a typical cost accounting period.

(2) The allocation of the G&A expense pool to any particular final cost objectives which receive benefits significantly different from the benefits accruing to other final cost objectives shall be determined by special allocation, (410.50(j)).

(c) Home office expenses received by a segment shall be allocated to segment cost objectives as required by 410.50(g).

(d) Any costs which do not satisfy the definition of G&A expense but which have been classified by a business unit as G&A expenses, can remain in the G&A expense pool unless they can be allocated to business unit cost objectives on a beneficial or causal relationship which is best measured by a base other than a cost input base.

§ 410.50 Techniques for application.

(a) G&A expenses of a segment incurred by another segment shall be removed from the incurring segment's G&A expense pool. They shall be allocated to the segment for which the expenses were incurred on the basis of the beneficial or causal relationship between the expenses incurred and all benefiting or causing segments. If the expenses are incurred for two or more segments, they shall be allocated using an allocation base common to all such segments.

(b) The G&A expense pool may be combined with other expenses for allocation to final cost objectives provided that:

(1) The allocation base used for the combined pool is appropriate both for the allocation of the G&A expense pool under this Standard and for the allocation of the other expenses; and

(2) Provision is made to identify the components and total of the G&A expense pool separately from the other expenses in the combined pool.

(c) Expenses which are not G&A expenses and are insignificant in amount may be included in the G&A expense pool for allocation to final cost objectives.

(d) The cost input base used to allocate the G&A expense pool shall include all significant elements of that cost input which represent the total activity of the business unit. The cost input base selected to represent the total activity of a business unit during a cost accounting period may be: (1) total cost input, (2) value-added cost input, or (3) single element cost input. The determination of which cost input base best represents the total activity of a business unit must be judged on the basis of the circumstances of each business unit.

(1) A total cost input base is generally acceptable as an appropriate measure of the total activity of a business unit.

(2) Value-added cost input shall be used as an allocation base where inclusion of material and subcontract costs would significantly distort the allocation of the G&A expense pool in relation to the benefits received, and where costs other than direct labor are significant measures of total activity. A value-added cost input base is total cost input less material and subcontract costs.

(3) A single element cost input base, e.g., direct labor hours or direct labor dollars, which represents the total activity of a business unit may be used to allocate the G&A expense pool where it produces equitable results. A single element base may not produce equitable results where other measures of activity are also significant in relation to total activity. A single element base is inappropriate where it is an insignificant part of the total cost of some of the final cost objectives.

(e) Where, prior to the effective date of this Standard, a business unit's disclosed or establishecd cost accounting practice was to use a cost of sales or sales base, that business unit may use the transition method set out in Appendix A hereof.

(f) Cost input shall include those expenses which by operation of this Standard are excluded from the G&A expense pool and are not part of a combined pool of G&A expenses and other expenses allocated using the same allocation base.

(g) (1) Allocations of the home office expenses of (i) line management of particular segments or groups of segments, (ii) residual expenses, and (iii) directly allocated expenses related to the management and administration of the receiving segment as a whole shall be included in the receiving segment's G&A expense pool.

(2) Any separate allocation of the expenses of home office (i) central-ized service functions, (ii) staff management of specific activities of segments, and (iii) central payments or accruals, which is received by a segment shall be allocated to the segment cost objectives in proportion to the beneficial or causal relationship between the cost objectives and the expense if such allocation is significant in amount. Where a beneficial or causal relationship for the expense is not identifiable with segment cost objectives, the expense may be included in the G&A expense pool.

(h) Where a segment performs home office functions and also per-forms as an operating segment having a responsibility for final cost objectives, the expense of the home office functions shall be segregated. These expenses shall be allocated to all benefiting or causing segments, including the segment performing the home office functions, pursuant to disclosed or established accounting practices for the allocation of home office expenses to segments.

(i) For purposes of allocating the G&A expense pool, items produced or worked on for stock or product inventory shall be accounted for as final cost objectives in accordance with the following paragraphs:

(1) Where items are produced or worked on for stock or product inventory in a given cost accounting period, the cost input to such items in that period shall be included only once in the computation of the G&A expense allocation base and in the computation of the G&A expense allocation rate for that period and shall not be included in the computa-tion of the base or rate for any other cost accounting period.

(2) A portion of the G&A expense pool shall be allocated to items produced or worked on for stock or product inventory in the cost account-ing period or periods in which such items are produced at the rates determined for such periods except as provided in (3) below.

(3) Where the contractor does not include G&A expense in inventory as part of the cost of stock or product inventory items, the G&A rate of the cost accounting period in which such items are issued to final cost objectives may be used to determine the G&A expenses applicable to issues of stock or product inventory items.

(j) Where a particular final cost objective in relation to other final cost objectives receives significantly more or less benefit from G&A expense than would be reflected by the allocation of such expenses using a base determined pursuant to paragraph (d) of this section, the business unit shall account for this particular final cost objective by a special allocation from the G&A expense pool to the particular final cost objec-tive commensurate with the benefits received. The amount of a special allocation to any such final cost objective shall be excluded from the G&A expense pool required by section 410.40(a), and the particular final cost objective's cost input data shall be excluded from the base used to allocate this pool.

Accounting for Selling Costs.—CAS 410.30(a)(6) and 410.40(d) pro-vide certain limitations on the kind of indirect expenses that may be included as G&A. Additionally, the treatment of most other indirect costs is now governed by CAS 418 and 420. But what about selling costs? As mentioned earlier in this chapter, the Board had issued a Staff Issues Paper on selling and marketing expenses, but took no further formal action by the date Congress decided not to fund its activities any longer.

Although the "Fundamental requirements" and "Techniques for application" sections of CAS 410 do not refer to selling costs, reference thereto is made in the "Illustrations" section, 410.60 (c)(2) and (5) and (d)(1). The essence of these illustrations is that a company that included selling costs as part of its G&A pool may continue to do so and these costs must then be allocated over an appropriate cost input base. Companies that previously treated selling costs separately and allocated them on a base such as cost of sales, and companies that wished to adopt this procedure, may do so, but the selling costs will then become part of the total cost input base if such base has been selected for allocating G&A expenses.

In actual practice, the treatment of selling costs has created many controversies because DCAA and other DOD elements moved into the vacuum created by the Board and published their own implementations and interpretations in this area. DOD's Guidance Paper W.G. 78-21, discussed in detail later in this chapter, asks the provocative question: "May selling costs be included in the G&A expense pool if an inequitable distribution results?" A question so phrased necessarily leads to a negative response: in this case, that the selling costs "should be the subject of a separate distribution in reasonable proportion to the benefits received." DCAA, which played a major role in formulating the controversial W.G. 78-21, provides similar guidance in its Contract Audit Manual, paragraph 8-410. The net result seems to be that the CASB has simply multiplied the existing problems in this area, adding the selection of an allocation base to the previous controversies, discussed earlier in this chapter.

Base for Allocating G&A Expenses.—The major problem relating to G&A expenses has always centered on the selection of the allocation base, and this problem was certainly not resolved by the CASB. In some respects, the promulgation of CAS 410 served to exacerbate the controversies between industry and the government.

The initial storm of protest from the private sector related to the requirement that G&A expenses be allocated on a cost input base. The prohibition against cost of sales or other output base should not have come as a surprise in view of the steady movement in that direction by the government, including the judicial decisions cited earlier in this chapter. Nevertheless, many commentators criticized the proposal of only one base as unduly rigid. It is interesting, in connection with the potential for many future controversies over allocation methods, that the CASB's prefatory comments denied this charge. The Board said, "[t]he Standard is not limited to the use of one allocation base. . . . Under the Standard only a cost input base may be used. Three cost input bases have been provided and criteria have been established for selection of the appropriate base."

The prohibition against the cost of sales base, however, did not fully satisfy DCAA and certain other elements in DOD who seemed to be disturbed that the standard established criteria for using three alternative cost input bases rather than rigidly mandating one base for all. Under guidance from their headquarters, DCAA auditors challenged most contractors who elected (or continued) to use the value-added or single element cost input base. Although some contractors gave in to the pressure for the total cost input base, others found it illogical in their circumstances and resisted. Seeking support for its preference, DCAA, through its membership on the DOD CAS Steering Committee's Working Group, succeeded in persuading the Department to publish W.G. 78-21, quoted below in part, which was quickly recognized in the private sector as a biased interpretation, or a revision of CAS 410, rather than as guidance for the implementation of this standard as written.

W.G. 78-21—Implementation of CAS 410, Allocation of Business Unit G&A Expenses

Discussion

Since a variety of issues and related guidance are involved, the guidance will be presented in a question and answer format.

* * * *

3. *Question* - The standard says, "The cost input base selected to represent the total activity of a business unit during a cost accounting period may be: (1) total cost input, (2) value-added cost input, or (3) single element cost input." Is the total cost input base preferred?

Answer - Yes. The standard says, "A total cost input base is generally acceptable as an appropriate measure of the total activity of a business unit." The prefatory comments say, ". . . the term 'total activity' refers to the production of goods and services during the cost accounting period." Thus, unless circumstances exist where a significant difference is apparent between the activity involved in the production of goods and services during the cost accounting period and the costs of such activity, a total cost input base should be used. When circumstances exist where total cost input does not appear to be an appropriate measure of total activity of the business unit, other bases available in the standard should be considered. However, the conditions involved should be carefully considered before departing from a total cost input base. The value-added base shall be used where inclusion of material and subcontract costs would significantly distort the allocation and where costs other than direct labor are significant measures of total activity. What constitutes a significant distortion in this context will be addressed as a separate question below. The criteria for use of a single element cost input base are very specific. The standard says, "A single element base may not produce equitable results where other measures of activity are also significant in relation to total activity. A single element base is inappropriate when it is an insignificant part of the total cost of some of the final cost objectives." Considering the criteria for the use of the value-added and single element bases, the thrust of the standard is toward implementing a total cost input base in most situation. Purification of the G&A expense pool is the most viable approach to minimizing any potential inequities which may surface in implementing the total cost input base.

* * * *

5. *Question* - What type of circumstance would meet the value-added base criteria that inclusion of material and subcontract costs would significantly distort the allocation of the G&A expense pool in relation to the benefits received?

 Answer - Responding to this question requires consideration of the context in which the criteria is presented in the standard and of related comments published by the CAS Board.

In describing the G&A base in 410.50(d), the CAS Board said, "The cost input base used to allocate the G&A expense pool shall include all significant elements of that cost input which represent the total activity of the business unit." In the prefatory comments the CAS Board said, "... the term 'total activity' refers to the production of goods and services during a cost accounting period." What is being pursued for the base is a flow of costs which bears a reasonable relationship with the production of goods and services. The criteria for a value-added base appears to be referring to a significant distortion in that relationship.

The production of goods and services requires material, labor, overhead, and other direct and indirect elements in varying amounts. The fact that a variance in amounts occurs usually reflects a variance in activity involved rather than a distortion in the relationship of costs and activity. However, when the activity involved in cost objectives is similar but the costs vary significantly, this usually indicates that a distortion exists for which use of a value-added base should be considered.

W.G. 78-21 furnished two examples "in which significant distortions would likely lead to a decision to use a value-added base": government-furnished components and precious metals.

Another provision of W.G. 78-21 related to this subject was number 7:

7. *Question* - When may a single-element cost input base be used to allocate the G&A expense pool?

 Answer - A single-element cost input base may be used when a contractor can demonstrate that it best represents the total activity of a business unit and produces equitable results. Thus, a single-element base such as direct labor dollars may be used when the direct labor dollars are significant and the other measures of activity are less significant in relation to total activity. The contractor should periodically analyze the single element base to assure that it continues to best represent total activity and produces equitable results. When other measures of activity become significant, a single-element base may not produce equitable results. A single-element base is inappropriate when it is an insignificant part of the total cost of some of the final cost objectives.

* * * *

Although vigorous objections were raised regarding many of the provisions of W.G. 78-21, by far the strongest and most extensive protests were directed to questions and answers 3, 5, and 7. Inasmuch as CAS 410.50 (d) cites the total cost input base as generally acceptable, makes the use of the value-added cost input base mandatory ("shall be used") under certain circumstances, and establishes the single element cost input base as discretionary ("may be used where it produces equitable results"), industry questioned the DOD Working Group's authority and basis for asserting in question and answer 3 that the standard establishes the total cost input base as the preferred one.

The objections to question and answer 5 were based on the torturous reasoning used to discredit the value-added cost input base, the use of which was declared to be mandated by CAS 410 where inclusion of materials and subcontracts would create a distortion. Industry also correctly recognized that the two illustrations provided where value-added could be used, government-furnished materials and precious metals, would be viewed by DCAA auditors as the only justifications for this base.

Question and answer 7 were criticized because of the obvious bias against the single element cost input base, as evidenced in the emphasis that the total burden of proof be placed on the contractor electing to use this method and that such contractors be required to make periodic analyses to "assure that it continues to best represent total activity and produces equitable results." Why should such a requirement be placed on those electing to use the single element base but not on those selecting the total cost input base?

The Guidance Papers were issued by the DOD CAS Steering Committee, but were not incorporated into DAR and, while directive upon DOD personnel, carry no statutory, regulatory, or contractual weight. Accordingly, a number of contractors continued to conform to the provisions of CAS 410 and to select the value-added or single element cost input base when one of those bases is appropriate in the circumstances of a business unit. Such contractors have been subjected to continual pressures and harassment on the part of DCAA in that agency's efforts to impose a total cost input base on all companies.

In a number of instances, contractors were successful in persuading contracting officers to overrule DCAA and allow the use of a value-added or single element cost base. In most events, however, contracting officers endorsed the audit agency's single-minded views. Most contractors yielded at this point, but some carried their controversies into the formal disputes procedure where, as described later in this chapter, they met with considerable success.

CASB's Futile Effort to Revise CAS 410.—Earlier in this chapter we described how the CASB, ignoring its own stated policy and P.L. 91-379, attempted to rush through an interpretation to CAS 403 while the *Boeing, McDonnell Douglas, Lockheed,* and *Grumman* litigations were in process. The CASB's effort to recast CAS 403 to support the government's position and reject the methods used by the contractors failed when the ASBCA said "we do not consider the purported Cost Accounting Standards Board 'Interpretation' as binding or determinative as to the proper interpretation of the standard." Despite this rebuke to the CASB and its loss of face, and the obvious indications that it was slated to go out of existence on September 30, 1980, some of the CASB members and staff appeared unable to make a graceful departure.

The *Federal Register* of July 24, 1980, contained a proposed rule described as clarifying the Board's intent with respect to the base for allocating G&A expenses under CAS 410. As mentioned earlier, some of the problems generated by CAS 410 were the result of unclear language and the use of undefined terms, e.g., "distort." The proposed change was also generally considered ineptly written. However, the point that did come through quite distinctly was that the Board was seeking to revise rather than to clarify the standard. The proposal would remove all references to the value-added and single element cost input bases and require that "[a] total cost input base or any other cost input base which obtains allocations similar to those resulting from use of a total cost input base shall be used. . . ." The proposal did contain provisions that the total cost input base should be modified under certain vaguely described circumstances; however, the proposal would definitely strengthen the position of the total cost input base proponents while increasing the difficulties encountered by anyone using one of the alternatives specifically set forth in the original standard.

Fortunately, the CASB's existence ended before this ill-advised proposal could be acted upon.

DOD Revises W.G. 78-21.—Ever since DOD issued its ill-advised W.G. 78-21, many elements in the private sector continued their efforts to persuade the Defense Department to revise this guidance paper to remove such obvious misinterpretations of CAS 410 as those describing the total cost input base as the preferred method. After more than three years of correspondence and discussions, Defense Department officials were finally persuaded that some revisions were required, and, on April 10, 1981, DOD issued Amendment 1 to W.G. 78-21. Although the amendment fell far short of satisfying industry's complaints, the changes did move in the direction of deterring the imposition of personal preferences of DCAA auditors for the total cost input base. The text of the amendment follows.

Background

W.G. 78-21 provided guidance in response to specific questions which had been surfaced during the implementation of CAS 410. However, questions remain concerning the most appropriate cost input allocation base to be used in the distribution of G&A expenses to final cost objectives. Basically, the underlying issues concerned the answers to Question #3 and Question #5 in W.G. 78-21. Specifically, is total cost input the preferred allocation base (Question #3) and under what conditions would the inclusion of material and subcontract costs in the allocation base distort the assignment of G&A expense to final cost objectives, therefore, requiring selection of the value-added cost input base (Question #5)?

Discussion

Question #3

The question of whether the total cost input allocation base is the preferred base under CAS 410 has been emphasized beyond its relevance to the proper implementation of this standard. Therefore, the guidance contained in W.G. 78-21 is restated as follows:

Answer

There is no specific statement of preference in the standard. The standard says, "A total cost input base is generally acceptable as an appropriate measure of the total activity of a business unit." The prefatory comments say, "... the term, 'total activity' refers to the production of goods and services during the cost accounting period." Thus, unless circumstances exist where a significant difference is apparent between the activity involved in the production of goods and services during the cost accounting period and the costs of such activity, a total cost input base would satisfy the requirements of the standard. When circumstances exist where total cost input does not appear to be an appropriate measure of total activity of the business unit, other bases available in the standard should be considered. The value-added base shall be used where inclusion of material and subcontract costs would significantly distort the allocation *and* where costs other than direct labor are significant measures of total activity. What constitutes a significant distortion in this context is addressed in Question #5. The criteria for use of a single element cost input base are very specific. The standard says, "A single element cost input base, e.g., direct labor hours or direct labor dollars, which represents the total activity of a business unit may be used to allocate the G&A expense pool where it produces equitable results. A single element base may not produce equitable results where other measures of activity are also significant in relation to total activity. A single element base is inappropriate where it is an insignificant part of the total cost of some of the final cost objectives."

A perfect reflection of total activity may not be reasonably expected from any of the three cost input bases available in the standard. The selection of a cost input allocation base which best represents total activity must be predicated on an analysis of the relevant circumstances at each business unit. The relevant circumstances considered should be those experienced in a typical cost accounting period rather than unique circumstances existing at one time or within a single accounting period. Purification of the G&A expense pool is a viable approach to minimizing any potential inequities which may surface in implementing the standard.

Question #5

The criteria for establishing the existence of a significant distortion appears to have been confined in practice to the two examples contained in the W.G. 78-21 guidance: Government-furnished components and precious metals. These two examples had not been intended to be all-inclusive as instances where the value-added base must be selected. To illustrate this point the answer to Question #5 in W.G. 78-21 is amended to include another example where a significant distortion may exist, as follows:

Answer

c. Disproportionate Material and Subcontract Content. The existence of a wide range of material and subcontract content among contracts may signal the precondition for potential significant distortion.

For example, suppose that a contractor's material and subcontract content for most of a business unit's total activity normally ranges from 20 percent to 70 percent of total contract costs. This situation, in and of itself, does not prove that a significant distortion exists. Such a distortion may exist if the material and subcontract content of most contracts falls at the range's extremes. However, no significant distortion would likely exist if the material and subcontract content of most contracts fell within a relatively narrow band within the range (e.g., 30 percent to 50 percent). It should be noted that the percentages used in this example are for illustrative purposes only and are not intended to be uniform guidelines.

Whenever there is an indication that a significant distortion exists, further consideration of the circumstances is necessary to arrive at a conclusion. Disproportionate cost ratios may merely represent variations in activity. For example, analysis of the activity on the contracts with extremely high material cost content may disclose that the costs represent subcontracts which are designated procurements and drop-shipped to the customers. Such circumstances would support a determination that the costs do not fairly represent the activity performing the contract. On the other hand, the analysis may disclose that the costs represent subcontracts for work that is subject to make-or-buy decisions and in fact is being performed in-house on other contracts. Such circumstances would support a determination that the material costs are representative of the activity of performing the contract. Consideration of the particular circumstances is essential before making a determination.

DCAA Resistance to Amendment 1 to W.G. 78-21.—As mentioned earlier, DCAA early established a preference for the total cost input allocation base and challenged virtually every contractor that used one of the alternative bases provided for in CAS 410. Through its membership on the DOD CAS Steering Committee's Working Group, DCAA was influential in formulating Guidance Paper W.G. 78-21, which stated, among other things, that CAS 410 should be interpreted as intending that the total cost input base be considered the preferred one.

DCAA suffered a serious setback when the aforementioned Amendment 1 to W.G. 78-21 revised the Department of Defense guidance relating to the implementation of this standard and stated: "There is no specific statement of preference [as to the allocation base] in the standard." Some officials in DCAA were also quite disturbed about the statement in Amendment 1 to W.G. 78-21 that "[t]he existence of a wide range of material and subcontract content among contracts may signal the precondition for potential significant distortion." Prior to this amendment, most DCAA auditors would accord favorable consideration to the value-added cost input base only when significant amounts of government-furnished materials or precious metals, the illustrations contained in W.G. 78-21, were present.

In what appeared to be a disregard of the DOD CAS Steering Committee, DCAA distributed the amendment to its field offices with the following guidance:

Enclosed is Amendment 1 to Interim Guidance Paper W.G. 78-21 concerning the selection of an allocation base for general and administrative expenses in accordance with the provisions of CAS 410. Among other provisions, Amendment 1 eliminates the statement in W.G. 78-21 that CAS 410 contains a special preference for a particular allocation base. It also adds a third criteria [sic] "Disproportionate Material and Subcontract Content" to the systems that may justify use of a value-added allocation base. The amendment is effective immediately and remains in effect until it is either withdrawn or is suspended by permanent guidance in the Defense Acquisition Regulation.

Amendment 1 does not change the basic position that total cost input is the generally acceptable allocation base which should normally be used. A value-added or single element base still is appropriate only when the specific circumstances outlined in CAS 410 are present. Auditors should continue to pursue CAS 410 noncompliance issues and ASBCA cases where the contractor has not justified use of a particular allocation base.

Based on available information, DCAA issued this guidance without approval from or coordination with the Pentagon officials responsible for promulgating procurement policy, including the CAS Guidance Papers. The DCAA headquarters memorandum is curious in a number of respects. Questions were raised in field audit offices as to whether the order to "pursue CAS 410 noncompliance issues" intended that DCAA auditors should continue opposing any base but the total cost input regardless of the determinations of ACOs. Many field auditors also wondered how they should "pursue . . . ASBCA cases" inasmuch as appeals to the ASBCA (or the Claims Court under the Contract Disputes Act of 1978) can be generated only under the contract disputes clause after a final determination by the *contracting officer.*

Disputes and Litigation Relating to CAS 410.—At this writing, a number of disputes appear to have totally discredited the views of DCAA and the DOD Working Group.

General Dynamics, Convair Division, ASBCA No. 22461, 78-2 BCA par. 13,270.—The dispute involved the base for allocating G&A expenses, and, although the period involved preceded the effective date of CAS 410, the ruling contained certain observations that suggested a relationship to the standard.

The contractor had been allocating its G&A expenses on the basis of direct labor costs since January 1, 1969, a base that was not uncommon either then or now in the business in which the contractor is engaged.

DCAA initially found that the direct labor cost base was in accordance with generally accepted accounting principles, resulted in an equitable distribution, and simplified the task of calculating the base for distribution. In later years, the auditor reversed his position and found that the direct labor cost base resulted in an "inequitable allocation of general and administrative expense to Government contracts . . . ." DCAA continued to object to the contractor's method but was unsuccessful in persuading the ACOs until August 1976. It is difficult to determine whether the publication of CAS 410 in the *Federal Register* of July 2, 1976, affected the contracting officer's decision to support the auditor.

Although both sides agreed that CAS 410 did not apply to the contract at issue and that the disallowance was based on ASPR provisions, the language of the DCAA Form 1 revealed language clearly borrowed from CAS 410.

The contractor presented evidence that persuaded the board "that an allocation of its 1977 G&A between its government and commercial work on the basis of direct labor cost resulted in an allocation closer to the G&A actually incurred for those two categories of work than did a distribution based upon total cost."

The board ruled that ASPR 15-203 required indirect costs such as G&A to be allocated in accordance with generally accepted accounting principles and that the direct labor cost base for allocating G&A was in accordance with generally accepted accounting principles and was also a method consistently followed by the contractor since January 1, 1969. The board said a contractor cannot be required to change its accounting system merely because a change would benefit the government. A contractor's consistent method could be changed only if it were established that particular circumstances made it inequitable. It ruled that no such contention was proved by the government and, to the contrary, that the direct labor cost base resulted in a more equitable allocation than the total cost basis.

Significant to future disputes under CAS 410 was the government's opposition to the contractor's method on the grounds that "direct labor represented only about twenty-eight to thirty-two percent of the contractor's total cost of operations." The ASBCA decision stated, "We find nothing intrinsically wrong in an allocation base of the magnitude of twenty-eight to thirty-two percent of total cost." The further significance of this observation was the following footnote at the conclusion of the decision:

> Although the standard promulgated by the Cost Accounting Standards Board for allocation of G&A does not apply to the instant contract, we note that Section 410.50(d)(3) provides that a single element base such as direct labor cost is inappropriate where it is an insignificant part of the total cost of some of the final cost objectives. Twentyeight to thirtytwo percent could hardly be considered to be insignificant.

TRW, Inc., ASBCA Docket No. 23470.—TRW, Inc., a large defense contractor involved in a major dispute, advised the government that it intended to use a value-added base for allocating G&A expenses for pricing contracts beginning with the effective date of CAS 410. The ACO initially agreed with the contractor's proposal; however, after receiving a report from DCAA, he reversed himself and found the value-added allocation base in noncompliance with CAS 410.

An interesting point in this dispute, and one that has been involved in other controversies of this kind, related to the G&A allocation method previously used by TRW. For many years prior to the effective date of this standard, the contractor and the government had agreed to a reduced G&A rate for subcontracts and material purchases where the initial orders exceeded $300,000 and a regular rate for all other contract costs. As an illustration, the rates included in the proposals for one year reflected a G&A rate of 3.2% for those subcontracts and material purchases while the G&A rate for the other contract costs was 15.2%. This arrangement enabled the contractor to argue that the government had always recognized that the inclusion of all subcontract and material costs in the allocation base would create a distortion. Inasmuch as CAS 410 did not permit the continuation of such arrangements, TRW concluded that the value-added cost input base served best to effect an appropriate allocation of G&A expenses and closely paralleled the method that had been agreed upon by the contractor and the government for many years.

More than two and a half years after the case was docketed in accordance with formal dispute procedures, the government and the contractor entered into a settlement agreement in which the value-added cost input base was established as consistent with the provisions of CAS 410, and the case was removed from the docket.

Ford Aerospace & Communications Corporation, Aeronutronic Division, ASBCA No. 23833, August 31, 1983, 83-2 BCA par. 16,813.—The decision handed down in this dispute should finally put an end to the efforts of DCAA and certain other DOD groups to revise the plain meaning of CAS 410.

Aeronutronic had been using what it termed a "modified value-added allocation base" since 1973. The term "modified" related to Aeronutronic's inclusion of "other direct costs" with labor and overhead. When CAS 410 became effective, Aeronutronic proposed to continue using its same base because the language in the standard's preamble indicated that exceptions to the composition of a particular base would be acceptable if they were insignificant, and other costs at Aeronutronic at that time were less than 5 percent of a complete value-added base.

The almost three years that followed included an initial determination by the DCAA resident auditor that the value-added base was appropriate in the circumstances at Aeronutronic and in compliance with CAS 410 and his turnabout to an opinion of noncompliance after reversal by higher levels. This point, incidentally, reflected a widespread pattern wherein DCAA auditors who accepted any method other than total cost input were generally overruled by the Agency's headquarters. DCAA's hardened position in this area was attributable to a small group in its headquarters who concluded that rigid uniformity was required and devised the theory that the total cost input base was "preferred." DCAA's influence on this subject within DOD is indicated by the comment in the *Aeronutronic* decision (Findings of Fact, par. 48), that the guidance from the Audit Agency's headquarters in February 1977 resembled what appeared in W.G. 78-21, one year later.

The ACO, too, was favorably impressed with the contractor's proposal, but he likewise bowed to DCAA and his own headquarters "guidance" and found Aeronutronic in noncompliance.

It appeared that the contractor was involved in competition for major awards and apparently received the word that the noncompliance issue might be considered an unfavorable factor. Aeronutronic thereupon undertook the unusual course of requesting a review by a team consisting of DCAA headquarters and CASB staff representatives. As should have been expected, this team advised the contractor that its value-added allocation method was not in compliance with CAS 410.

Concerned about its competitive position and standing with DOD procurement authorities, Aeronutronic computed its revised proposal using the total cost input base. Subsequently, after considerable legal and administrative controversies, the contractor requested an equitable adjustment in all contracts impacted by the change. By final decision in March 1979, the ACO denied the contractor's request, and the issues in the ensuing dispute included both the propriety of the value-added base and the contractor's entitlement to the equitable adjustment arising out of being directed to use the total cost input base. We shall discuss first, and devote most of our attention to, the allocation base appropriate in Aeronutronic's circumstances in relation to the provisions of CAS 410.

As we have noted in the past, the facts of life are that management efforts and interest, reflected in G&A expenses, are much more heavily concentrated on in-house efforts than on the efforts of vendors and subcontractors, as reflected in the prices of materials and subcontracts. If a company's (or division's) total activity consists of labor-intensive development contracts or consists solely of production contracts where material and subcontract costs represent approximately the same percentage of total contract costs, the method for allocating the G&A expenses may not be all that important. However, for companies that work on both labor-intensive development contracts with a relatively low percentage of material and subcontract costs and production contracts with a heavy incidence of the latter costs, the total cost input base will not appropriately measure the benefit of G&A expenses to contracts. This is particularly the case where purchasing, receiving, and related expenses are included in a separate pool or in manufacturing overhead. In these circumstances, allocating G&A expenses on the basis of value added actually reflects the appropriate apportioning of these expenses to the contractor's total activities.

The major point of departure with DCAA and those it persuaded to its line of argument is the fallacy of including the *cost* of materials and subcontracts in the allocation base. This cost represents work done by others and creates an obvious distortion when included in the allocation base. Through the years, DCAA has consistently confused activity and cost and concluded they were one and the same. There is no basis for this concept, just as there is no basis for the assertion that the total cost input base is "preferred."

It has been our judgment from the outset that both the plain words of the standard and sound cost accounting practice establish the correctness of the value-added base in circumstances described above, and the burden of proof in the event this method is challenged should be on the government. Unfortunately, overly impressed with the need for rigid uniformity and regardless of the provisions of the standard that provided for three alternative allocation bases, DCAA, some DOD financial people, and certain staff members of the defunct CASB waged what had been up to this time a successful campaign to revise and distort the provisions of the standard to the point of convincing many in the government and even some in the private sector that the total cost input base was virtually mandated by the standard. They imposed upon contractors seeking to use one of the alternative methods provided in the standard a burden that most found impossible to bear. The burden was to "prove" that management activities, reflected in G&A expenses, were focused to a much greater extent on in-house work than on the prices paid to vendors and subcontractors. Aeronutronic accepted the challenge and successfully presented its proof to the ASBCA.

One of the major problems in establishing the focus of G&A activities on in-house work is that the kind of people whose salaries and related expenses, allocable occupancy, etc., are included in G&A do not maintain time cards or other detailed data. Accordingly, when estimates are presented, they are usually brushed off by DCAA auditors as subjective, unsubstantiated, and the like. This is what happened at Aeronutronic and in *General Dynamics Corp., Convair Division,* ASBCA No. 22461, 78-2 BCA par. 13,270. In the latter case, General Dynamics successfully demonstrated that the preponderance of the time of its people in G&A expenses was focused on in-house work, and the board ruled in the contractor's favor on the use of direct labor as the base for allocating G&A expenses. Although the period involved preceded the effective date of CAS 410, the decision suggested that the ruling might well be the same under CAS 410.

Aeronutronic listed the categories of expenses comprising its G&A, which consisted of the divisional general manager's office, controller's office, industrial relations, marketing, home office and sub-home office assessments, state and local taxes, and interim pool allocations. For each category, the company estimated the percentage related to material/subcontract activity. These percentages ranged from 2% to one at 33% with a weighted average of 12%. The care exercised in the estimates was indicated by Aeronutronic's elimination of the accounts payable function from the accounting activity.

The basis for deriving these percentages was substantiated by the head of each office involved, some using daily appointment calendars and others accumulating judgmental, point-in-time estimates prepared by managers who worked at this division over a number of years.

As expected, the government challenged these estimates as subjective and not susceptible of substantiation or audit verification. However, as the board noted, the government "has not introduced evidence rebutting or impugning the validity of the assumptions . . . ." The board reviewed each estimate and the manner in which it was arrived at. It found all of them accurate and reasonable and reiterated the government's failure to rebut them.

A DCAA headquarters official testified that the allocation base should be the one that best represents the contractor's total activity and that total activity refers to every activity involved in producing the company's goods and services. In accordance with the established DCAA position, he alleged that the CASB intended that total cost input serve as a surrogate for total activity.

The board agreed, and indeed Aeronutronic did not dispute, that total activity includes materials and subcontracts as well as labor and overhead. The board found the government's arguments fallacious, however, in concluding "that each dollar expended for materials and subcontracts necessarily bears the same beneficial relationship to incurrence of G&A expenses as each dollar of labor and overhead." Stressing the difference between the activity and the *cost* of the activity, the board provided the government with an education in this area, which many of us have tried so hard and so unsuccessfully to do over the years. Attention was particularly invited to the point apparently ignored by DCAA and other DOD elements that if the CASB intended that only the total cost input base should be used, it would have stated so in the standard. In contrast, the standard specifically provides for bases that include less than total cost. The board's comments follow:

> ... To the contrary, the total of the *cost* of each element comprising total activity may or may not "best represent total activity" depending on the individual circumstances of each business unit. The crucial question is not what activity elements comprise "total activity", but what "best represents total activity." CAS 410.50(d)(2) specifically recognizes that including the *cost* to the contractor of what others have produced may result in a distortion of the "benefits received" by contracts from G&A expenses incurred. Defining "total activity" to include subcontracts and materials does not eliminate the necessity for analyzing the beneficial relationships between G&A costs and cost objectives. Although the term "total activity" encompasses all elements necessary for "production", it does not and cannot refer to the total of the costs of those elements without rendering the other allocation bases superfluous. If "total activity" was the equivalent of the total of the costs of all elements of activity, only total cost input could "best represent total activity." Cost Accounting Standard 410 makes clear that a contractor's "total activity" may be measured or "represented" by less than the contractor's "total cost input." The Standard expressly authorizes cost input bases which include cost elements significantly less than total cost input, i.e., the value-added and single element cost input bases. In short, "total activity" and "total cost input" are not synonymous or interchangeable under CAS 410 (see finding 102(e)). In particular, were "total activity" to be "represented" only by adding up all costs of activities connected with producing goods or services, the CAS Board's approval of a direct labor base under the circumstances specified in CAS 410.50(d)(3) would present an irreconcilable incongruity. Each of the authorized bases properly may be the best surrogate for "total activity", depending on the individual circumstances of each business unit. If a base other than total cost input properly is selected, this does not mean that the material and subcontract elements of "total activity" necessarily are not represented. It simply means that exclusion of the *price paid* for materials and subcontracts results in a better, more accurate, more equitable allocation of G&A costs in the individual circumstances of that particular business. (Emphasis in original).

Failing to rebut Aeronutronic's estimates, which demonstrated that G&A expenses provided a closer relationship to in-house activities than to the contractor's cost or price paid for materials and subcontracts, the government shifted to another line of argument. It belittled the contractor's measurement of the value of its G&A efforts to contracts, contending that G&A expenses "are the 'most indirect of costs' and their relationship to cost objectives is not susceptible of analysis."

The board agreed that there were practical difficulties in tracing some G&A expenses to specific cost objectives. However, it strongly rejected the contention that the CASB intended to depart in CAS 410 from the principle of allocation on the basis of benefits received. It quoted provisions of this standard that specifically set out the objective to achieve allocation of G&A expenses to cost objectives "based on their causal or beneficial relationship." The remoteness of G&A expenses from final cost objectives does not negate the possibility and necessity of "applying CAS 410 to determine which method will allocate G&A expenses most realistically to contracts consonant with the benefits received."

The government's arguments, directly or indirectly, included the baseless position of DCAA that the total cost input base was preferred. This position was thrust into W.G. 78-21 and remained there until the amendment to that guidance paper retracted it. Addressing this contention, the board stated specifically, "[t]he provisions of CAS 410 . . . preclude any finding that a total cost input base is preferred." It continued:

> . . . The Standard expressly authorizes three cost input allocation bases, and, subject to limited restrictions stated in CAS 410.50(d)(1-3), provides that the determination of which allocation base is to be used should be judged according to individual company circumstances and on the basis of causal or beneficial relationships. Under the plain wording of the Standard as promulgated there is no "preference" for a total cost input base where inclusion of material and subcontract costs produces significant distortion requiring use of the valueadded base. Moreover, where the contractor can show that a single element base produces "equitable results" and otherwise satisfies CAS 410.50(d)(3), the contractor "may" use the base. In such circumstances, there is no "preference" for the total cost input base that eliminates or seriously erodes this permission. If the "causal or beneficial" relationship almost always could be obtained through the use of the total cost input base the Cost Accounting Standards Board could have so provided. It clearly did not do so.

Further clutching at straws, the government tried to make much of the words in the standard that "a total cost input base is *generally acceptable* as an appropriate measure of the total activity of the business unit." (Emphasis added.) This argument was struck down as decisively as the others when the board traced the origin of this term to early research by the CASB staff, which came to this conclusion on finding that, for a majority of the contractors surveyed, the proportion of material, labor, and manufacturing overhead across all government work and between government and commercial work was similar. In a penetrating analysis, the board said:

> . . . In other words a majority of contractors had homogeneous operations, without significantly disproportionate amounts of material and subcontract content in any particular class of its contracts. The term "generally acceptable" must be interpreted in the context of this preliminary research. Since the majority of contractors were found to have homogeneous operations, use of the total cost input base would not distort the "benefits received" by cost objectives and would be "generally acceptable" to that majority of business units surveyed. However, the Cost Accounting Standards Board's conclusion that the total cost input base is "generally acceptable" for the majority of contractors is far different

than the government's contention that the total cost input base, therefore, is "preferred" for all contractors.

CAS 410.50(d)(1) does not establish reliable criteria that can be applied in evaluating particular contractor circumstances. The evidence adduced in this appeal establishes that there are no other statistics or reliable objective standards on the basis of which a contractor conclusively may determine whether the total cost input base is "acceptable" without careful, subjective analysis of its own individual circumstances. Moreover, even if a contractor had apparently homogeneous operations and uniformly distributed material and subcontract activity, CAS 410.50(d)(1) states only that the total cost input base is "acceptable". The term "generally acceptable" reasonably cannot be construed to mean "required" in any given case or as establishing an express or implied preference for the total cost input base. It also reasonably does not connote that that method is "always" or "nearly always" acceptable. The term must be evaluated against the standard's requirement that the selection of allocation base be judged based on the circumstances of each business unit, as stated in CAS 410.50(d). In the overall context of CAS 410.50(d), "generally" logically cannot be interpreted to mean that the total cost input base is necessarily appropriate in any particular case. At most, therefore, CAS 410.50(d)(1) indicates that use of the total cost input base will be acceptable, provided its use does not produce significant distortion. It does not require a contractor first to disprove the appropriateness of such use before alternative bases may be considered. Nor does it otherwise establish a "preference" for the total cost input base.

The government also argued that the ASBCA should give "substantial deference" to the statement of preference in the original W.G. 78-21 and the alleged CASB endorsement thereof by a statement in the minutes of its March 9, 1979 meeting: "the (CAS) Board concluded that guidance contained in W.G. 78-21 reflected the Board's intent with respect to the provisions of CAS 410 concerning the selection of the allocation base."

This argument suffered the same fate as the other government contentions, and we cite a portion of the decision in which it was struck down:

Numerous infirmities associated with the guidance and minutes dictate against according them "substantial deference." With respect to W.G. 78-21, the DOD CAS Steering Committee amended the guidance paper in April 1981 to eliminate its prior conclusion that total cost input base is preferred. As amended, it now recognizes that "no specific statement of preference" exists in CAS 410. It acknowledges that its prior conclusion to the contrary was incorrect. In any event, the Government concedes that the guidance is not binding on contractors. Similarly, with respect to the "minutes" neither the Cost Accounting Standards Board then or the Government in this appeal contends that they constitute a formal "interpretation" of Cost Accounting Standard 410 promulgated in accordance with that Board's required procedures. Therefore, statements contained therein cannot be considered binding or determinative as to the proper interpretation of the standard. *McDonnell Douglas Corp.,* ASBCA

No. 19842, on motion for reconsideration, 80-2 BCA par. 14,508. Further-more, the minutes (if not the original guidance) were issued after actual or threatened litigation. This fact further detracts from the amount of deference due them.

*   *   *   *

... We conclude that if the Cost Accounting Standards Board meant by its 9 March 1979 minutes that the standard contained a preference for the total cost input base, this informal indorsement of W.G. 78-21 was contrary to the plain meaning of Cost Accounting Standard 410 itself, contrary to the only reasonable conclusion that can be drawn from the objective evidence attendant upon its development, and contrary to the CAS Steering Committee's own current position with respect to the matter. For the above reasons, among others, we cannot accord the original guidance and the Cost Accounting Standards Board minutes "substantial deference."

As noted earlier, the government had initially attacked Aeronutronic's analysis of its G&A expenses, which established that the preponderance of effort, and thus benefit received, related to the in-house work rather than the cost of materials and subcontracts.

The attack was based on allegations that the analysis was subjective and unverifiable. When that argument was lost, after the board found the esti-mates to be reasonable and the government lacking in effective rebuttal or alternative demonstration, the government switched gears and argued that any extensive, internal analysis was irrelevant because there was no "direct and precise" relationship between G&A expenses and benefiting cost objec-tives.

The government seemed to be making a point that CAS 410 did not intend that any judgment be exercised in selecting an allocation base, and the ASBCA went to substantial lengths to set out the fallacies of this argument. In the decision, reference was made, for example, to CAS 410.50(d), which stated in part: "The determination of which cost input base best represents . . . total activity . . . must be *judged* on the basis of the circumstances of each unit." (Emphasis in ASBCA decision.) Several sections of the preamble to the standard were cited to demonstrate that the CASB intended that judgment should and must be exercised. For example, in defending against assertions that the standard was unduly rigid because it permitted the use of only one allocation base, the CASB emphasized that it provided three cost input bases and that "the individual circumstances of a given business unit must be analyzed and the cost input that best represents the total activity of that business unit would be the base selected." The language so obviously estab-lishes the intent to provide alternatives and to require analyses of individual circumstances to determine which of the three was most appropriate in the circumstances as to totally destroy the government's argument, and indeed, to question its credibility.

Having dealt with issues relating to the selection of a base for allocating G&A expenses under CAS 410 generally, the board turned to the application of the criteria to Aeronutronic and concluded that "use of the value-added base is *required* because inclusion of material and subcontract costs *significantly*

distorts the benefits received by appellant's contracts from its G&A expenses."
(First emphasis in original; second emphasis added.) The two primary reasons
for this conclusion are summarized below:

> ... (1) The material and subcontract content of appellant's contracts is
> disproportionate and its general management expenses pertain more
> substantially to its "in-house" activity than its material and subcontract
> activity; and (2) Aeronutronic's general management expenses provide
> substantially more benefit to its labor intensive development contracts
> than its material intensive production contracts.

As to the first point, the board noted that, as a percentage of total cost
input, an average of approximately 53% of Aeronutronic's contracts consisted
of material and subcontract costs versus only 33% for its development and
engineering contracts. This was considered sufficient evidence of significant
distortion, the board finding no merit in the artificial position of the amendment to W.G. 78-21, which required clustering of contracts outside the 20-70%
range. The board agreed with the contractor's contention that, in addition to
its nonauthoritative status, the amendment's artificially restrictive provisions
were not a substitute for "more careful subjective analyses of the interrelation-
ship between G&A expenses and final cost objectives . . . ."

On the second point, the decision stated:

> We have found, based on uncontroverted testimony and evidence
> that the "benefit" of Aeronutronic's G&A management and related
> expense pertains most heavily to Aeronutronic's "in-house" or labor and
> overhead activities and only in small part to material and subcontract-
> related activities. That is, appellant's G&A expenses are incurred primar-
> ily for the benefit of labor and overhead effort and general management
> activity is devoted primarily to managing that effort. Based on appel-
> lant's estimates, we have found that only an approximate 12% of Aeronu-
> tronic's G&A expenses related to material and subcontract activities
> (Finding 94). Use of appellant's proposed value-added base implies that
> 10% of general management expenses relate to material and subcontract
> activity (Finding 96). Use of the current, government-advocated, total
> cost input base implies that 49% of general management expenses are
> related to or benefit such activity (Finding 96). Due to this disparity, the
> total cost input base significantly distorts the "benefits received by
> appellant's contracts from G&A expenses."

The board emphasized the "in-house" focus of Aeronutronic's G&A management effort and expense by noting the contractor's G&A pool excluded
virtually all purchasing-related functions, all of which were included in the
contractor's value-added base. This accounting procedure, according to the
board, ". . . tends to increase the homogeneity of appellant's G&A expenses
with respect to the relationship of G&A cost to material and subcontract
activity, reducing the 'benefits received' by such activity from G&A expenses
. . . . At the same time, inclusion of the cost of most purchasing and subcontract related functions, (other than the *price* of materials and subcontracts) in
appellant's value-added base recognizes and 'represents' Aeronutronic's material and subcontract activity . . . . Material and subcontract activity thus does
receive its fair share of G&A expenses." (Emphasis in original.)

Our analysis of this ruling is considerably more comprehensive and extensive than we generally accord to judicial and quasi-judicial decisions. The major reason for this unusual effort is our belief that the government's distortion of the plain meaning of CAS 410 has done great damage, both in terms of financial losses to many contractors who have been forced into using an incorrect allocation method and in the loss of credibility of those who thrust this incorrect method upon government contractors.

The most important question emanating from this ruling is what course should government contractors follow in the future with respect to allocating G&A expenses to CAS-covered contracts. The author is not an attorney and we are always careful to avoid offering recommendations that may be construed as legal advice. We would suggest, however, that contractors and their legal advisors accord consideration to the board's ruling in the motion for reconsideration in the *McDonnell Douglas* dispute involving CAS 403, discussed earlier in this chapter. Responding to the government's expressed concern as to the consequences for the many contractors who had adopted the so-called "DCAA method" for allocating state and local income and franchise taxes, a method the board found noncompliant with this standard, the board opined that "nothing precludes a contractor from continuing to use a method with Government approval ... under the consistency objective of the Cost Accounting Standards Board or any negotiation and settlement of a dispute. But Government may not dictate a surrogate allocation base to a contractor ... where a more appropriate and equitable result would be reached by applying a base in keeping [with] the specific language" of a standard.

DCAA's Adamant Position on Allocation of G&A Expenses

As previously discussed, the audit agency has been successful to a large extent in acting independently, not only of acquisition officials, but at times of the entire Defense Department. Among other areas in which it has largely ignored all officials, including even the ASBCA and FAR, has been the selection of the base for allocating G&A expenses. From the time CAS 410 was promulgated, DCAA developed a mindset that concluded that despite the plain language of the standard, which established that a contractor could use the cost input base appropriate in the circumstances, the only base that satisfied the agency was total cost input (TCI). Despite defeats at the hands of some of the contractors that contested the arbitrary audit position, including the ignominious defeat suffered in the *Ford Aerospace* litigation described earlier, DCAA continued to perpetrate its biases on other firms, including smaller contractors that were not required to comply with CAS.

In 1983, the National Security Industrial Association created a Smaller Company Subcommittee to address problems encountered by contractors in this category. One of the problems identified was DCAA's adamant and unreasonable insistence on the use of the TCI base where the circumstances clearly permitted the value-added or direct labor base. Faced with congressional criticisms of contracting officers who had the temerity to exercise their warrants and overrule DCAA "recommendations," many contracting officers refused to become involved in these arguments, and many smaller companies lacked the funds or expertise to initiate litigation.

To assist these companies, NSIA officials arranged meetings with DCAA headquarters representatives in May and August 1985, in an attempt to persuade the audit agency to issue guidance to its field officers to comply with the FAR and CAS provisions and accept an allocation base appropriate in particular circumstances, rather than to continue illogically to insist on TCI exclusively. These meetings were followed up with NSIA furnishing position papers for DCAA's consideration. Unfortunately, DCAA is much enamored of its own views and once it assumes a position, is loath to abandon or even modify it. The problems are exacerbated by the apparent lack of higher-level DOD control over the agency's operations.

With the audit agency continuing to stonewall, NSIA wrote to the DCAA Director in January 1987, noting that no guidance had been issued to the agency's field offices concerning the selection of an allocation base for G&A expenses appropriate to the circumstances. Finally, about two months after this letter, and some two years after the beginning of the discussions, a response was received over the signature of the agency's director.

After conceding that the Contract Audit Manual (CAM) can be interpreted as preferring TCI and advising that the Manual was being revised "to state the criteria that should be used in determining an appropriate G&A base," the response continued with argumentative verbiage that suggested to many that while DCAA was forced to accept the decision in *Ford Aerospace,* it was not happy about it, and contractors proposing a value-added or single element base would continue to face a hard road.

Citing DOD CAS Working Group Paper 78-21 (essentially the handiwork of DCAA), which has never been incorporated into FAR, DFARS or any other regulation binding upon contractors, and offering its own interpretation of *Ford Aerospace,* the response made it very clear that contractors who have previously been coerced by DCAA into using the TCI base would experience substantial difficulties in changing to a more appropriate base.

"It is our position," asserts the DCAA letter, once again assuming authority for acquisition regulations never assigned to it, "that a contractor should not be able to freely pick and choose any base it wants without limit." Of course, no such assertion had been made by NSIA. The letter continued with DCAA's concession that it would consider a proposed change from its previously mandated TCI, but only where contractors ". . . . perform either a detailed analysis which indicates that the G&A expense benefits some elements of cost more than others, or . . . demonstrate that a material amount of subcontract costs are costs of a few contracts which do not require close management, e.g., systems integration contracts where subcontracts can easily be provided Government Furnished Equipment, or under prime teaming arrangements."

DCAA has thus once against usurped the contracting officer's authority in interpreting CAS and FAR. Certainly, the director's letter does not contain a single reference to the government official with the warrant, the individual who at one time was supposed to have some say in these matters.

While quickly acknowledging that the burden imposed on Ford Aerospace by the ASBCA to support the value-added method was not a heavy one, the DCAA letter stresses the need for "a detailed analysis" or the demonstration of the above-cited circumstances, which are not to be found in any authoritative regulations or judicial rulings.

It seems now that after almost a decade of blind insistence on the TCI, the audit agency has been forced to acknowledge that other methods may be more appropriate in certain circumstances. However, some of the same hardliners who so vigorously insisted on TCI to the exclusion of any other base for allocating G&A expenses will continue to expend their best efforts to make it extremely difficult for contractors to use any other method. The *Ford Aerospace* decision should be studied very carefully, together with CAS 331.50(a)(4) and (5), before accepting DCAA's "positions" on the appropriate base. The basic problem continues to be the audit agency's unrestrained usurpation of the authority to interpret CAS and acquisition regulations and establish its own to fill any vacuums.

Concepts Underlying Principles for Determining Allowable and Unallowable Contract Costs

This book deals in considerable detail with cost and price aspects of government contracts. An integral and most significant factor in this area relates to the concept of the so-called unallowable costs. This aspect constitutes the source of many areas of disagreement between the representatives of government and of industry, and the impact on contract prices has been known to range as high as two to four percent. It is deemed of the utmost importance, therefore, that government contractors attain a full understanding of this concept.

The officials responsible for the successful operation of a business and in position to control its expenditures take justifiable pride in their ability to limit expenditures to only the minimum extent necessary to produce and market a saleable product. Hence it is often extremely difficult for them to understand how certain costs necessary for doing business can be considered unallowable.

ILLUSTRATION OF DIFFERENCES BETWEEN COMMERCIAL AND GOVERNMENT COST CONCEPTS

Generally speaking, where a selling price can be established to recover the company's costs plus a reasonable profit, rather than meet the competition of the market place, a vendor may compute the selling price of an article as the sum of (1) all direct costs (material, labor, etc.); (2) allocations of all indirect costs and taxes; and (3) profit. Very often it is neither practicable nor reasonable to effect considerable refinements of the indirect costs involved, and many companies are content to recover a pro rata share of all such costs in the selling price of each product, on an over-all basis. As an illustration, let us assume that the vendor seeks a profit of 10% and is guided by the following recent, condensed profit and loss statement for the company:

Net sales		$10,000,000
Cost of sales:		
Beginning inventory	$1,000,000	
Materials purchased	5,000,000	
Direct labor expended	1,250,000	
Manufacturing overhead	2,500,000	
Total	$9,750,000	
Less ending inventory	2,750,000	
Cost of sales		7,000,000

Gross profit		$ 3,000,000
Expenses:		
Administrative expenses.......	$700,000	
Selling expenses..............	600,000	
Research and		
development expenses.......	500,000	
Interest	300,000	
Total Expenses		2,100,000
Net profit before income taxes		$ 900,000
Provision for federal income taxes		500,000
Net profit for the year......................		$ 400,000

Based on the above experience, the company could effect the following calculation of the unit selling price:

Assuming that the unit material cost is known to be		$ 415
And assuming that the unit labor cost is known to be		75
Manufacturing overhead may be computed as 200% of direct labor, based on the over-all relationship reflected in the profit and loss statement (overhead—$2,500,000, and labor—$1,250,000)		150
Resulting in a factory cost of		$ 640
All other expenses on the profit and loss statement aggregate $2,100,000, or 21% of net sales. To recover such expenses the vendor would add		210
Taxes amount to 5% of net sales, and in recovery of this item, the vendor would add		50
Resulting in a total cost of		$ 900
Add a profit factor of 10% of the selling price		100
Resulting in a selling price, reflecting recovery of all expenses and 10% profit, of		$1,000

The above cost determination would not be acceptable to the government, whose calculation would reflect the exclusion of such costs, or portions thereof, which it deemed inapplicable to the contract, unreasonable in amount, or otherwise unallowable in accordance with existing regulations. The government might effect the following adjustments:

(1) Assuming that manufacturing overhead included depreciation, maintenance and other costs applicable to an idle plant in the amount of $125,000, such charges may be eliminated in accordance with FAR 31.205-17 and manufacturing overhead adjusted to $2,375,000 or 190% of direct labor.

(2) The following items could be deleted from the other expenses:

(a) Officers' compensation included in administration expenses, to the extent considered unreasonable in amount	$ 160,000
(b) Advertising contributions, bad debts and other charges included in the selling expense category and deemed inapplicable to the government or otherwise unallowable	440,000
(c) Independent research and development expenses in excess of the ceiling negotiated in accordance with FAR 31.205-18.......................................	100,000
(d) Interest, specifically cited as unallowable in FAR 31.205-20.......................................	300,000
Total adjustments	$1,000,000

The expenses of $2,100,000 are thus reduced to $1,100,000, and the ratio of this amount to total cost input would be 12.6% (total cost input equals $8,750,000—$5,000,000 plus $1,250,000 plus $2,500,000—divided into $1,100,000).

(3) Federal income and excess profits taxes may be treated as unallowable in accordance with FAR 31.205-41.

Giving effect to the foregoing adjustments, and assuming (1) no adjustments to direct material and labor and (2) acceptability of the 10% profit factor, the sales price as computed by the government would amount to $783.42 determined as follows:

Direct material (no change)	$415.00
Direct labor (no change)	75.00
Manufacturing overhead (recomputed as	
190% of direct labor)	142.50
Factory cost	$632.50
Expenses (recomputed as 12.6%	
of factory cost)	79.70
Federal Income taxes (deleted entirely)	
Total cost	712.20
Profit (10% of adjusted costs)	71.22
Revised selling price	$783.42

In the hypothetical case shown above, the vendor quoted a selling price of $1,000 per unit in good faith and based on the actual cost experience of the company. The government's counter offer is $783.42, a reduction of $216.58. The original bid contained no hidden profits, reserves for contingencies or the like, and the logical question arises as to what happened to $216.58. Assuming that the contract calls for 1,000 units, there is an indicated underrecovery of expenses aggregating $187,800 ($900 − $712.20 × 1,000 units) and no provision for profit.

Government contractors have often contended that the government procedures are inequitable. On the other hand, government generally believes that no inequity results from its procedures, and it would be the government's view in this instance that the contract for 1,000 units should yield the contractor a profit of $71,220. How can these divergent views be reconciled? How can actual costs be termed unallowable? In addition, what steps should a contractor take to recover these costs that are not applicable to government work, but presumably applicable to other work of a nongovernment contract nature?

Let us examine the basic principles of the unallowable costs concept for clues to these questions.

BASIC PRINCIPLES OF UNALLOWABLE COSTS

A careful study of government cost concepts will shed some light on the apparent irreconcilable factors commented upon above. Moreover, the understanding gleaned from the explanation of these principles will serve as a necessary vehicle to transport the reader through the succeeding chapters, which treat these matters in detail.

The bases upon which costs may be declared unallowable are summarized in FAR 31.201-2:

31.201-2 Determining allowability.

(a) The factors to be considered in determining whether a cost is allowable include the following:

(1) Reasonableness.

(2) Allocability.

(3) Standards promulgated by the CAS Board, if applicable; otherwise, generally accepted accounting principles and practices appropriate to the particular circumstances.

(4) Terms of the contract.

(5) Any limitations set forth in this subpart.

(b) Certain cost principles in this subpart incorporate the measurement, assignment, and allocability rules of selected CAS and limit the allowability of costs to the amounts determined using the criteria in those selected standards. Only those CAS or portions of standards specifically made applicable by the cost principles in this subpart are mandatory unless the contract is CAS-covered (see Part 30). Business units that are not otherwise subject to these standards under a CAS clause are subject to the selected standards only for the purpose of determining allowability of costs on Government contracts. Including the selected standards in the cost principles does not subject the business unit to any other CAS rules and regulations. The applicability of the CAS rules and regulations is determined by the CAS clause, if any, in the contract and the requirements of the standards themselves.

(c) When contractor accounting practices are inconsistent with this Subpart 31.2, costs resulting from such inconsistent practices shall not be allowed in excess of the amount that would have resulted from using practices consistent with this subpart.

The above general principles governing allowability are applicable specifically to contracts with commercial organizations. The Office of Management and Budget (OMB) Circular No. A-21, Cost Principles for Educational Institutions; OMB Circular No. A-87, Cost Principles for State and Local Governments; and OMB Circular No. A-122, Cost Principles for Nonprofit Institutions govern for those respective organizations.

DAR and FPR contained separate cost principles for the aforementioned organizations and also for construction and architect-engineer contracts and facilities contracts. The latter two categories are now subject to the cost principles for commercial organizations except as described in FAR 31.105 and 31.106, cited below:

31.105 Construction and architect-engineer contracts.

(a) This category includes all contracts and contract modifications negotiated on the basis of cost with organizations other than educational institutions (see 31.104), State and local governments (see 31.107), and nonprofit organizations except those exempted under OMB Circular A-122 (see 31.108) for construction management or construction, alteration or repair of buildings, bridges, roads, or other kinds of real property. It also includes architect-engineer contracts related to construction projects. It does not include contracts for vessels, aircraft, or other kinds of personal property.

(b) Except as otherwise provided in (d) below, the cost principles and procedures in Subpart 31.2 shall be used in the pricing of contracts and contract modifications in this category if cost analysis is performed as required by 15.805-3.

(c) In addition, the contracting officer shall incorporate the cost principles and procedures in Subpart 31.2 (as modified by (d) below) by reference in contracts in this category as the basis for—

(1) Determining reimbursable costs under cost-reimbursement contracts, including cost-reimbursement subcontracts thereunder;

(2) Negotiating indirect cost rates;

(3) Proposing, negotiating, or determining costs under terminated contracts;

(4) Price revision of fixed-price incentive contracts; and

(5) Pricing changes and other contract modifications.

(d) Except as otherwise provided in this paragraph (d), the allowability of costs for construction and architect-engineer contracts shall be determined in accordance with Subpart 31.2.

(1) Because of widely varying factors such as the nature, size, duration, and location of the construction project, advance agreements as set forth in 31.109, for such items as home office overhead, partners' compensation, employment of consultants, and equipment usage costs, are particularly important in construction and architect-engineer contracts. When appropriate they serve to express the parties' understanding and avoid possible subsequent disputes or disallowances.

(2) "Construction equipment," as used in this section, means equipment (including marine equipment) in sound workable condition, either owned or controlled by the contractor or the subcontractor at any tier, or obtained from a commercial rental source, and furnished for use under Government contracts.

(i) Allowable ownership and operating costs shall be determined as follows:

(A) Actual cost data shall be used when such data can be determined for both ownership and operating costs for each piece of equipment, or groups of similar serial or series equipment, from the contractor's accounting records. When such costs cannot be so determined, the contracting agency may specify the use of a particular schedule of predetermined rates or any part thereof to determine ownership and operating costs of construction equipment (see subdivisions (d)(2)(i)(B) and (C) of this section). However, costs otherwise unallowable under this part shall not become allowable through the use of any schedule (see 31.109(c)). For example, schedules need to be adjusted for Government contract costing purposes if they are based on replacement cost, include unallowable interest costs, or use improper cost of money rates or computations. Contracting officers should review the computations and factors included within the specified schedule and ensure that unallowable or unacceptably computed factors are not allowed in cost submissions.

(B) Predetermined schedules of construction equipment use rates (e.g., the Construction Equipment Ownership and Operating Expense Schedule published by the U.S. Army Corps of Engineers, industry sponsored construction equipment cost guides, or commercially published schedules of construction equipment use cost) provide average ownership and operating rates for construction equipment. The allowance for ownership costs should include the cost of depreciation and may include facilities capital cost of money. The allowance for operating costs may include costs for such items as fuel, filters, oil, and grease; servicing, repairs, and maintenance; and tire wear and repair. Costs of labor, mobilization, demobilization, overhead, and profit are generally not reflected in schedules, and separate consideration may be necessary.

(C) When a schedule of predetermined use rates for construction equipment is used to determine direct costs, all costs of equipment that are included in the cost allowances provided by the schedule shall be identified and eliminated from the contractor's other direct and indirect costs charged to the contract. If the contractor's accounting system provides for site or home office overhead allocations, all costs which are included in the equipment allowances may need to be included in any cost input base before computing the contractor's overhead rate. In periods of suspension of work pursuant to a contract clause, the allowance for equipment ownership shall not exceed an amount for standby cost as determined by the schedule or contract provision.

(ii) Reasonable costs of renting construction equipment are allowable (but see paragraph (C) below).

(A) Costs, such as maintenance and minor or running repairs incident to operating such rented equipment, that are not included in the rental rate are allowable.

(B) Costs incident to major repair and overhaul of rental equipment are unallowable.

(C) The allowability of charges for construction equipment rented from any division, subsidiary, or organization under common control, will be determined in accordance with 31.205-36(b)(3).

(3) Costs incurred at the job site incident to performing the work, such as the cost of superintendence, timekeeping and clerical work, engineering, utility costs, supplies, material handling, restoration and

cleanup, etc., are allowable as direct or indirect costs, provided the accounting practice used is in accordance with the contractor's established and consistently followed cost accounting practices for all work.

(4) Rental and any other costs, less any applicable credits incurred in acquiring the temporary use of land, structures, and facilities are allowable. Costs, less any applicable credits, incurred in constructing or fabricating structures and facilities of a temporary nature are allowable.

31.106 Facilities contracts.

31.106-1 Applicable cost principles.

The cost principles and procedures applicable to the evaluation and determination of costs under facilities contracts (as defined in 45.301), and subcontracts thereunder, will be governed by the type of entity to which a facilities contract is awarded. Except as otherwise provided in 31.106-2 below, Subpart 31.2 applies to facilities contracts awarded to commercial organizations; Subpart 31.3 applies to facilities contracts awarded to educational institutions; and 31.105 applies to facilities contracts awarded to construction contractors. Whichever cost principles are appropriate will be used in the pricing of facilities contracts and contract modifications if cost analysis is performed as required by 15.805-3. In addition, the contracting officer shall incorporate the cost principles and procedures appropriate in the circumstances (e.g., Subpart 31.2; Subpart 31.3; or 31.105) by reference in facilities contracts as the basis for—

(a) Determining reimbursable costs under facilities contracts, including cost-reimbursement subcontracts thereunder;

(b) Negotiating indirect cost rates; and

(c) Determining costs of terminated contracts when the contractor elects to "voucher out" costs (see Subpart 49.3), and for settlement by determination (see 49.109-7).

31.106-2 Exceptions to general rules on allowability and allocability.

(a) A contractor's established accounting system and procedures are normally directed to the equitable allocation of costs to the types of products which the contractor produces or services rendered in the course of normal operating activities. The acquisition of, or work on, facilities for the Government normally does not involve the manufacturing processes, plant departmental operations, cost patterns of work, administrative and managerial control, or clerical effort usual to production of the contractor's normal products or services.

(b) Advance agreements (see 31.109) should be made between the contractor and the contracting officer as to indirect cost items to be applied to the facilities acquisition. A contractor's normal accounting practice for allocating indirect costs to the acquisition of contractor facilities may range from charging all these costs to this acquisition to not charging any. When necessary to produce an equitable result, the contractor's usual method of allocating indirect cost shall be varied, and appropriate adjustment shall be made to the pools of indirect cost and the bases of their distribution.

(c) The purchase of completed facilities (or services in connection with the facilities) from outside sources does not involve the contractor's direct labor or indirect plant maintenance personnel. Accordingly, indirect manufacturing and plant overhead costs, which are primarily incurred or generated by reason of direct labor or maintenance labor operations, are not allocable to the acquisition of such facilities.

(d) Contracts providing for the installation of new facilities or the rehabilitation of existing facilities may involve the use of the contractor's plant maintenance labor, as distinguished from direct labor engaged in the production of the company's normal products. In such instances, only those types of indirect manufacturing and plant operating costs that are related to or incurred by reason of the expenditures of the classes of labor used for the performance of the facilities work may be allocated to the facilities contract. Thus, a facilities contract which involves the use of plant maintenance labor only would not be subject to an allocation of such cost items as direct productive labor supervision, depreciation, and maintenance expense applicable to productive machinery and equipment, or raw material and finished goods storage costs.

(e) Where a facilities contract calls for the construction, production, or rehabilitation of equipment or other items that are involved in the regular course of the contractor's business by the use of the contractor's direct labor and manufacturing processes, the indirect costs normally allocated to all that work may be allocated to the facilities contract.

COSTS UNREASONABLE IN NATURE OR AMOUNT

The FAR provisions were revised effective June 30, 1987, the major change being the shifting of the burden of proof of reasonableness from the government to the contractor, as discussed later in this chapter.

31.201-3 Determining reasonableness.

(a) A cost is reasonable if, in its nature and amount, it does not exceed that which would be incurred by a prudent person in the conduct of competitive business. Reasonableness of specific costs must be examined with particular care in connection with firms or their separate divisions that may not be subject to effective competitive restraints. No presumption of reasonableness shall be attached to the incurrence of costs by a contractor. If an initial review of the facts results in a challenge of a specific cost by the contracting officer or the contracting officer's representative, the burden of proof shall be upon the contractor to establish that such cost is reasonable.

(b) What is reasonable depends upon a variety of considerations and circumstances, including—

(1) Whether it is the type of cost generally recognized as ordinary and necessary for the conduct of the contractor's business or the contract performance;

(2) Generally accepted sound business practices, arm's length bargaining, and Federal and State laws and regulations;

(3) The contractor's responsibilities to the Government, other customers, the owners of the business, employees, and the public at large; and

(4) Any significant deviations from the contractor's established practices.

Reasonableness is one of the most complex factors affecting allowability of costs under government contracts and merits close analysis. At this point, we shall be considering costs already incurred inasmuch as the reasonableness of estimated costs found in contract pricing proposals, overhead projections, and the like involve different considerations.

Reasonableness Established by Regulation

Certain costs commonly incurred by firms have been specifically established as unallowable by government regulations, and the only basis appears to be that the government has decided they are unreasonable in nature or amount. Analyses of cost principles governing "selected costs" are contained in subsequent chapters. The brief commentaries below are designed to provide an indication of the extent to which the government has limited recovery of certain expenses based frequently on arbitrary concepts of reasonableness.

FAR 31.205-2, Automatic Data Processing Equipment Leasing Costs, limits recognition of such costs in several respects including requirements that the contractor demonstrate leasing will result in lesser costs to the government over the anticipated useful life than the costs of ownership, failing which allowability is limited to ownership costs.

By far the lengthiest and most complex cost principle is the one governing compensation for personal services, FAR 31.205-6. It is replete with restrictions as to allowability, many of them directly or indirectly involving the government's concepts of reasonableness. Compensation may be challenged as to reasonableness in whole or as to its various components, such as base pay, bonus, or other elements.

Reasonableness is established as a restriction on the amount to be recognized as costs of employee morale, health, welfare, food service, and dormitory costs and credits, FAR 31.205-13. In addition to a general, undefined monetary restriction, this principle specifically cites as unallowable losses from operating food and dormitory services in most instances unless the contractor can demonstrate an objective of operating on a break-even basis.

FAR 31.205-17, Idle Facilities and Idle Capacity Costs, provides reasonableness tests as the bases for recognition of these costs. Allowable costs are limited based on arbitrary periods of time.

Among the most arbitrary limitations based on artificial reasonableness concepts are those found in FAR 31.205-18, Independent Research and Development and Bid and Proposal Costs. Some of the limitations are attributable to congressional and other external pressures on the Department of Defense but have been extended by FAR to contracts with civilian agencies as well. Companies receiving payments for such costs exceeding $4.4 million in a fiscal year must negotiate advance agreements establishing ceilings for allowability, in other words, mandatory cost sharing. Contractors receiving payments of less than $4.4 million in a fiscal year are not required to negotiate advance agreements but allowability is limited by an arbitrary formula.

The government's heavy hand in imposing limitations and restrictions on recognition of costs predicated on reasonableness determinations is also found in FAR 31.205-33, Professional and Consultant Service Costs. After specifying such costs as unallowable for various other reasons, the regulation provides that recognition shall be limited to costs "when reasonable in relation to the services rendered." Problems are sometimes encountered when government representatives use government pay scales as criteria for evaluating professional and consultant fees.

In view of the widely recognized national needs for education and training, one might expect the government to provide strong encouragement for such programs by companies that have the wisdom to conduct them. While some training and educational costs are allowable, FAR 31.205-44 sets forth numerous limitations and restrictions premised on arbitrary concepts of reasonableness of time per year which employees may devote to enhancing their capabilities.

FAR 31.205-46, Travel Costs, reflects the continuing government efforts to preclude contractor recovery of legitimate business expenses incurred in employee travel. Disallowances allegedly based on reasonableness considerations have grown from restrictions on first-class accommodations and the use of contractor-owned, -leased, and -chartered aircraft, to the current provisions, which virtually nationalize the defense industry by substantially limiting recovery of travel costs to those allowed for federal employees.

A significant ruling in this area was in the appeal of *Stanley Aviation Corporation,* ASBCA No. 12292, 68-2 BCA par. 7081, discussed in part in Chapter XVII in connection with the cost principle on Idle Facilities and Idle Capacity Costs. A major issue, and one on which the government's case was crushed, was an attempt to disallow portions of total indirect expense pools on the grounds that the actual experienced expense rates were far in excess of those used in bidding, were unreasonably high, and were not "competitive."

After the award of the contract at issue, the government terminated another very large contract under performance by Stanley. As a result of this unexpected occurrence, and despite the contractor's efforts to replace the business, the indirect expense rates rose astronomically. The government was unable to, or in any case did not, present arguments that the specific expenses making up the pools were individually unreasonable in nature or amount. Instead, it defended the position of its contract auditor and contracting officer that total expenses, represented by the excess of the experienced rates over those considered reasonable by the government, were unallowable.

The ASBCA meticulously reviewed the existing provisions of the contract cost principles applicable to the contract in dispute and concluded that they did not (nor do the current ones) contain any support for the government's contentions. The notion that overhead rates were unreasonable to the extent they were noncompetitive was quickly rejected. The regulations simply did not establish competitiveness as a criterion in evaluating reasonableness.

The board likewise found that the cost principles emphasized the reasonablenss of specific costs in nature or amount and not of aggregate expense pools. It further found that the government could only defend a close scrutiny of overhead rates in the circumstances of significant increases. However, having done so, it would need to find actions by the contractor that it could show resulted in the incurrence of specific unreasonable costs. This it failed to do. As a matter of fact, indirect expenses were sharply reduced; however, because the direct costs dropped considerably more, the indirect expense rates increased. Having failed to demonstrate by specific reference to the cost principles regulations that any specific expenses were unreasonable, the government did not carry its burden and Stanley prevailed.

Burden of Proof as to Reasonableness of Incurred Costs

As indicated in the judicial decisions cited in this chapter, boards of contract appeals and federal courts have generally ruled that incurred costs, unless specifically cited as unreasonable by regulation or obviously unreasonable, were reasonable unless the government proved otherwise.

Section 933 of the 1986 DOD Authorization Act, P.L. 99-145, discussed in more detail later in this chapter, included the following provision:

> In a proceeding before the Armed Services Board of Contract Appeals, the United States Claims Court, or any other Federal court in which the reasonableness of indirect costs for which a contractor seeks reimbursement from the Department of Defense is in issue, the burden of proof shall be upon the contractor to establish that such costs are reasonable.

Many observers saw this provision, endorsed by GAO and DCAA, as virtually turning American law and concepts of justice on their heads, and viewed it as comparable to a position that one is guilty until proven innocent. The arguments in favor of this provision were considered devoid of logic or merit; rather, this provision was another of the punitive measures in this Act directed at firms doing business with the Department of Defense. GAO and DCAA proponents of this measure had complained that the judicial position on reasonableness was deterring the auditors' efforts to disallow costs.

To implement this statutory provision, the following sentence was proposed as an addition to FAR 31.201-3(a):

> No presumption of reasonableness shall be attached to the incurrence of costs by a contractor, and upon challenge of a specific cost by the contracting officer, the burden of proof shall be upon the contractor to establish that such a cost is reasonable.

Although industry representatives understood that DOD was required to implement the statutory provision, considerable opposition was raised with respect to the proposed FAR change. The regulators, led by DOD representatives, were found to have overreached in the implementation. As an obvious point, the statute specifically identifies "indirect costs" whereas the proposed implementation expanded the penalty to all costs. The Council of Defense and Space Industry Associations (CODSIA) directed attention to the legislative background of the provision, involving congressional concern over GAO and DCAA reports that contractors were charging unallowable indirect costs to

DOD contracts. The Senate version of the shift in burden was limited to general and administrative expenses and the House version, ultimately adopted, extended it to all indirect costs. No statutory basis existed for the further extension proposed in FAR. As inequitable and punitive as the statutory provision was considered, CODSIA recommended that the exact language of the law be incorporated into FAR rather than the proposed FAR language, which would override many years of judicial rulings.

As in most other instances, industry's comments were totally disregarded and the revised provision covering reasonableness, incorporated into FAR by FAC 84-26, effective July 30, 1987, includes the shifting of the burden to the contractor on all costs.

Other Government Efforts to Disallow Costs on the Basis of Reasonableness

Monitoring contractors' costs (DOD FAR Supplement Subpart 42.70) and DCAA operations audits have contributed to numerous controversies regarding reasonableness of costs incurred by government contractors. Both efforts have as their primary goals the evaluation of contractors' operations to determine if they are being conducted economically and efficiently. These efforts have drawn considerable criticism from government contractors, who have expressed alarm about the potential implications of government people assuming management's prerogatives and deciding whether the work was being performed in the most economical and efficient manner. The widely held view in the private sector has been that a determination as to whether the contractor is employing the most economical and efficient procedures generally requires a subjective judgment, a judgment which should properly be made by the managers of the business rather than by a government "Cost Monitoring Coordinator" or DCAA operations auditor who typically never held responsibility for managing a comparable operation. Despite the many protests, formal cost monitoring is being conducted at some of the larger contractor locations, and DCAA operations audits are sometimes performed on contractors with relatively small amounts of government business.

Judicial Views on Disallowance of Costs on the Basis of Reasonableness

A review of many years of decisions by boards of contract appeals and the Court of Claims reveals relatively few instances of litigation concerning costs asserted to be unreasonable in amount by the government. The reason is found in the fact that boards and courts, with a few blatant exceptions, are loathe to declare unreasonable those costs that have been actually incurred by contractors unless specifically identified by regulations. An illustration of the difficulties encountered by the government when contractors move these controversies to the litigation stage is found in *Lulejian and Associates,* ASBCA No. 20094, 76-1 BCA par. 11,880, where the board sustained salaries, bonuses, and contributions to pension funds for the contractor's executives, which were disallowed as unreasonable by the government.

The dispute and decision in *Data-Design Laboratories,* ASBCA No. 24534, June 16, 1983, 83-2 BCA 16,665, are of considerable interest to government contractors in several respects. For one thing, the board reiterated the principle that, when costs are incurred, the government bears an extremely heavy burden when it seeks to disallow them on the grounds of unreasonableness. Other points of consequence include the board's reluctance to permit the government to override a contractor's policies and substitute its own management for that of the contractor's officials.

Prior to July 1, 1976, the contractor's policy was predicated on obtaining maximum productivity from its employees by requiring that travel should be accomplished to the extent possible outside normal working hours. As partial compensation for the employees traveling on their own time and for not charging labor hours in travel status to its cost-type contracts, Data-Design permitted its employees first-class travel while on official business. During the hearing, the contracting officer conceded that, if labor costs associated with time spent traveling in connection with the performance of duties required by the contract were charged thereto, they would be allowable. He also testified that DAR allowed payment of overtime work provided no premium pay was involved, in which case prior approval was required.

After a DCAA audit, the contracting officer disallowed the differential between first-class and coach fare for the contractor's fiscal years 1973, 1974, and 1975. Data-Design thereupon revised its policy, discontinuing first-class air travel by other than corporate officers. The new policy further required that travel be conducted to the maximum extent possible during the normal work week, and, if travel beyond those hours could not be avoided, employees would be reimbursed for such hours as overtime but not including premium pay.

DCAA auditors were advised of the new policy and took exception thereto, alleging that it represented a deliberate attempt to circumvent the contracting officer's prior disallowance of the differential between first-class and less-than-first-class air travel costs. The contracting officer agreed with the auditor's opinion. Although the contracting officer cited various references in support of the disallowance, his final decision and testimony established that he relied solely on the reasonableness of DAR 15-201.3. These provisions were incorporated without major change into FAR 31.201-3, quoted earlier in this chapter.

During the hearings, the government introduced testimony by the DCAS compensation review boards, which recommended disallowance of overtime for travel, alleging that such practice was "atypical" based on the practices of other companies in that area. The latter allegation was disputed by the contractor on a number of counts, including a contemporaneous study by the American Management Association that indicated that many companies had policies similar to those of Data-Design.

The board saw the major thrust of the government's argument as based on the assertion that the contractor had instituted its overtime for travel policy because the government had disallowed reimbursement for first-class travel of its exempt employees. DataDesign did not deny this. However, while the government ascribed a "malevolent intent" to this change, the board viewed it as an attempt to obtain the maximum possible productivity for its employees.

The board addressed the government's specific arguments and we have quoted portions of the decision because we believe them to be of major importance for all contractors to remember when confronted by arbitrary positions of overzealous auditors and contracting officers, in many areas beyond the specific dispute here involved. Reviewing the provisions of DAR 15-201.3, the board said:

> ... We consider the specific criteria set forth to be used in determining whether a cost meets the reasonable requirements of the section as a whole. They are neither all inclusive nor conclusive of the question to be resolved. While the Government argues that appellant has failed to meet the four criteria set forth in this provision, we find its supporting evidence weak and, in some instances, far too speculative to constitute proof of the propositions it is attempting to establish. *The Government cannot merely superimpose its opinion in contradiction to that of the contractor. It must show why the contractor's actions were not those which a prudent business person would have taken. A presumption of reasonableness attaches to costs which were actually incurred by a contractor and is measured by the situation which existed at the time of performance.* Grumman Aerospace Corp., NASA BCA Nos. 673-8, 1273-17, 1273-18, 76-1 BCA par. 11,671; *The Boeing Co.* ASBCA No. 10524, 67-1 BCA par. 6350. (Emphasis added).

The board then turned to the arguments as to whether Data-Design's practice was in accordance with the practices of other contractors and again was not favorably impressed with the government's position:

> Each party has introduced evidence concerning industry policy for payment of overtime. We consider the Government's evidence inconclusive to establish that appellant's policy was contrary to industry practice. The survey of companies within the Los Angeles area, and other evidence of such nature is insufficient for reaching the conclusion sought by the Government. It is subject to many other interpretations. *Further, had such proof been sufficient to do so, we are not prepared to conclude that this in and of itself would make appellant's policy unreasonable.*

> *We, again, are compelled to look at the entire compensation package for such determination.* It may well be that other companies paid a higher base rate, bonuses, or other fringe benefits which would more than compensate an employee for travel outside of work hours. We find the record here insufficient to conclude that appellant's payment of overtime to exempt employees for travel under the circumstances here present was unreasonable under DAR 15-201.3(a)(1). (Emphasis added).

The board was likewise unimpressed with the other government arguments and, near the close of the decision, made a statement that we wish all government auditors and contracting officers would carefully study:

> The Government does not have a right to superimpose its definition or judgment for that of a contractor who has acted in a reasonable manner when incurring costs which are reasonable and allocable and permitted within the provisions of Chapter XV of the Defense Acquisition Regulations.

The above conclusion should be read in conjunction with the previous statements in the decision that when a cost is incurred, the government bears a heavy burden in asserting that it is unreasonable.

Contractor's Weighted Average Share in Cost Risk (CWAS)

The Seventh Edition of this text contained a comprehensive account of the background, principles, and practices of CWAS, concluding with the observation that the concept had been incorporated in preliminary drafts of FAR, which provided encouragement for the thinking that CWAS would evolve into a government-wide principle. Unfortunately, through an adverse chain of events, the Defense Department eliminated CWAS from DAR and used its influence to have this principle removed from an advanced draft of FAR.

The twenty-year story with a sad ending has its beginnings in 1964 congressional hearings where DOD was criticized for failing to provide adequate guidance for its contracting officers on evaluating the reasonableness of certain overhead expenses. Studies and discussions led to the thought that contractors with a preponderance of work in which they bore major shares of cost risk, e.g., firm fixed price contracts and commercial equivalent, did not require an army of auditors and administrators to conduct surveillance to determine whether their indirect costs were reasonable. Because for those contractors a substantial share of each dollar of indirect expenses incurred directly reduced their profits, the companies had an obvious incentive to maintain such costs at a reasonable level.

When a company's CWAS formula-developed rating reached a certain level, expenses would not be reviewed for reasonableness; however, the expenses would be examined in the normal manner to determine allocability, allowability, compliance with generally accepted accounting principles, and later compliance with CAS. CWAS-qualified contractors were also supposed to be relieved of some of the burden associated with purchasing system and other reviews. The CWAS concept was incorporated into ASPR/DAR; however, because agreement could not be reached among civilian agencies, this concept was not made a part of FPR.

CWAS never fulfilled the hopes of its advocates. It was under intermittent attack by GAO and congressional critics of DOD. Within the Defense Department, the concept was endorsed at higher levels but was received with little enthusiasm at lower levels where it was disliked by DCAA and never viewed warmly by DCAS and Navy and Air Force contract administration components who were supposed to eliminate or reduce certain aspects of surveillance over CWAS qualified contractors. Stranger than this opposition was the relative lack of strong support from industry where the attitude might be best described as a mixed bag. We know of no contractor who opposed the concept. On the other hand, many companies grew discouraged as they saw the ASPR/DAR provisions on CWAS yield virtually no difference in the extent of government surveillance, and they gave up their interest and sometimes even the efforts to seek CWAS qualification status. Some contractors also became preoccupied with the details of the formula that established CWAS qualification, particularly as DOD raised the threshold and made it increasingly difficult for companies to qualify.

In June 1982, the National Security Industrial Association (NSIA) wrote to the Deputy Secretary of Defense that "the CWAS concept, properly applied, can greatly lighten the administrative burden on both the government and the private sector. The government loses nothing by allowing the market place and the incentive for profit to establish the reasonableness of a cost." NSIA further pointed out that "a CWAS-qualified contractor can be expected to effectively control the reasonableness of costs incurred. Further, we believe it is unlikely that audit surveillance is an effective use of scarce resources." The NSIA letter included a number of cogent recommendations that, if adopted, would make CWAS an effective procurement tool and help in the Administration's objective to "get the government off the people's backs."

The Pentagon reply was carefully couched and advised that a review of this matter had been directed. The Deputy Secretary of Defense concluded his reply: "In my opinion if the concept is valid, we should apply it to as broad a base as possible. On the other hand, if it is not, we should eliminate the program."

The review was assigned to a CWAS Ad Hoc Group, which included auditors, cost and price analysts, and others who had not been among those with confidence in CWAS but rather believed in the need for a heavy government surveillance of defense contractors. It accordingly came as little surprise when this group issued a report on March 31, 1983, recommending the elimination of the CWAS concept and advising the FAR Project Office to eliminate the FAR equivalent (Waiver of Government Surveillance Requirements) from the draft, which had reached the executive coordination stage.

Industry considered the report recommendations to be based on data that CODSIA termed "inadequate, inconclusive, and in some areas inaccurate." The bias in favor of heavy government audit and other surveillance was evident, and CODSIA, complaining that industry was not given an opportunity to review the findings and rebut the inaccuracies, proposed that the study be assigned to a high-level, objective Blue Ribbon panel "consisting of industry and government leaders for a further in-depth analysis." These efforts proved to be in vain when the Deputy Secretary of Defense denied the Association's request and advised that "it was the unanimous decision of senior executives throughout DOD that the disadvantages of CWAS clearly outweighed its advantages."

The demise of CWAS was formally announced in Defense Acquisition Circular (DAC) 76-45, dated June 30, 1983, which advised that the Deputy Secretary of Defense had approved a DOD study that recommended the elimination of CWAS and that DAR was being revised accordingly.

COSTS NOT ALLOCABLE OR IMPROPERLY ALLOCATED TO GOVERNMENT CONTRACTS

This category also includes costs asserted to be in noncompliance with cost accounting standards, where applicable, or, otherwise, generally accepted accounting principles.

The definition of allocability, as stated in FAR 31.201-4, is well thought out and, if intelligently and objectively applied, could obviate many of the government-industry controversies:

31.201-4 Determining allocability.

A cost is allocable if it is assignable or chargeable to one or more cost objectives on the basis of relative benefits received or other equitable relationship. Subject to the foregoing, a cost is allocable to a Government contract if it—

(a) Is incurred specifically for the contract;

(b) Benefits both the contract and other work, and can be distributed to them in reasonable proportion to the benefits received; or

(c) Is necessary to the overall operation of the business, although a direct relationship to any particular cost objective cannot be shown.

The above definition, in the author's judgment, is well considered and articulated. In the absence of the various artificial limitations and reservations in FAR 31.205, e.g., advertising and selling costs, it would be possible for contractors to recover an appropriate pro rata share of their indirect costs under government contracts. Even with the limitations included in the cited sections, there would be fewer controversies by far if it were not for the proclivities of government contract auditors and some other government officials to ignore the intent of paragraph (c).

The selected costs, some of which we shall be discussing in Chapter XVII of this text, include expenses classified as unallowable because, although not so explained, they are considered not allocable to government contracts. An illustration is Bad Debts (31.205-3), which is not allocable on the basis that the government does not default on its just indebtedness.

Allocability of Indirect Costs—Procurement Regulations

In addition to the definition cited above, FAR 31-203 provides policies and procedures governing allocation of indirect costs. As we discussed in Chapter XIII of this text, these ground rules emphasize the selection of a distribution base that will permit allocation on the basis of benefits accruing to the cost objectives. Also, for contracts not subject to cost accounting standards, "the contractor's method of allocating indirect expenses . . . shall be in accordance with generally accepted accounting principles which are consistently applied."

Allocability of Indirect Costs—Generally Accepted Accounting Principles (GAAP)

The procurement regulations, in many respects, placed too much reliance on GAAP as criteria for allocability of indirect costs. Writing in the April 1969 issue of the *Journal of Accountancy,* Marshall S. Armstrong, CPA, practitioner and former member of the AICPA Accounting Principles Board and Chairman of the Financial Accounting Standards Board, described GAAP as "those principles which have substantial authoritative support." He went on to note that while "Opinions of the Accounting Principles Board constitute 'substantial authoritative support,' 'substantial authoritative support' can exist for accounting principles that differ from the Opinions of the Accounting Principles Board." Mr. Armstrong then cited about a dozen additional "sources of authority which, in and of themselves or in combination with other such sources, would constitute 'substantial authoritative support.' " These included "substantial practice within an industry," "accounting textbooks and references books of individuals whose views are generally respected," "publications of recognized industry associations," and "published articles and speeches of distinguished individuals." Within this framework, contractors experienced few difficulties in describing a wide variety of allocation methods as being in consonance with GAAP.

Another major problem in trying to apply GAAP to allocation of indirect costs to contracts has been the history of the accounting profession's emphasis on principles governing the financial condition of a business entity at a point in time and the results of its overall operations for a period ending on such date. These principles have necessarily included rules for measuring the value of assets and the portions of certain assets that should be charged to expense in the different accounting periods, as in the case of depreciation and amortization. The determination of costs of contracts, products, processes, etc., which constitutes the essence of cost accounting, has not been accorded much consideration by the present Financial Accounting Standards Board (FASB) or the prior AICPA Accounting Principles Board (APB). Cost accounting has evolved as a tool of management, and cost accounting principles, including methods of allocating indirect costs to contracts, have been the province of industrial cost accountants, their associations, and recognized authors of cost accounting text books.

Had the public accounting profession moved more vigorously into this area and established "generally accepted cost accounting principles," the government procurement regulations might have adopted them and the need for a Cost Accounting Standards Board might not have obtained sufficient credence to support the enactment of P.L. 91-379.

Despite what many observers, including practicing public accountants, believe to be the inadequate consideration given to cost accounting in formal accounting pronouncements, acccounting concepts are at the heart of the allocability concept. Most federal officials responsible for promulgating contract cost principles and the members and staff of the CAS Board have been accountants. From the earliest attempts to define the term "allocable" in federal acquisition regulations to the present time, the writers referred to an allocable cost as one that is assignable, chargeable, etc., to what is currently termed "cost objectives," on the basis of benefits received. To broaden this term somewhat, the words "or other equitable relationship" were added. The CAS Board favored the terms "beneficial or causal relationships."

Although controversies have been encountered with respect to all three of the subparagraphs of FAR 31.201-4, subparagraphs (b) and (c) have produced by far the greatest number. The controversies relating to an allocation or distribution base for indirect expenses accepted as allocable to all or a great number of cost objectives have been characterized by two distinct facets. One is a straightforward, objective, accounting consideration. Accepting the premise that there is no mathematically precise measurement, when a group of expenses is pooled and distributed in proportion provided by a selected base, which base, practically conceived and established, would best achieve the objective of allocating the indirect expenses on a beneficial, causal or other equitable basis?

As discussed at length in other chapters of this text, this question was extensively and intensively addressed by the CAS Board. Despite the gigantic effort, which included wide distribution of drafts of its standards, and the participation of so many knowledgeable representatives of both the private and public sectors, the Board's efforts met with mixed success as controversies and litigation in this area have continued.

A more troublesome facet of allocation base selection is the subjective element. Reiterating the absence of a mathematically precise method of selecting a base, we find an unfortunate but readily understandable conflict of interests. Assuming reasonable arguments can be advanced for two (or more) methods of allocation, and in the absence of a definitive statute or regulation accepting one and rejecting all others, it is not uncommon to find a contractor selecting a method that will yield a higher allocation to government contracts whereas the government, essentially DCAA auditors, recommending a basis that would result in a higher allocation to the commercial work.

In arguments generated by these circumstances, both sides can be quite persuasive and pose major problems for boards of contract appeals and the federal courts. While judicial rulings are sometimes difficult to predict, one can reasonably be assured that absent drastic changes in contractors' operations or organization, the party that defends the consistent use of an existing method will prevail over the party that seeks to change it.

As noted above FAR 31.201-4(c) provides that a cost is allocable if it is "necessary to the overall operation of the business, although a direct relationship to any particular cost objective cannot be shown." This sensibly worded provision is a far cry from the very early requirements for a cost to be "necessary for or incident to" a contract before its allocability can be established. Controversies in this area, too, involve both accounting considerations and subjective interests, and have posed major problems when they move into the judicial arena.

There is a further problem, of increasing proportions, relating to this allocability criterion, found in the continuing government promulgations arbitrarily ruling certain costs to be unallowable despite the often obvious evidence that such costs are "necessary to the overall operation of the business." It is difficult to believe that the legislative and executive branch officials responsible for the growing list of indirect expenses established as unallowable are really persuaded that many expenses in the categories of advertising, public relations, selling and marketing, and employee welfare, to mention but a few recently added to the "black list," are not necessary for the overall operation of the business. Actually, many observers believe that the government has simply ignored this allocability criterion cavalierly in arbitrarily designating certain costs as unallowable. It is significant, in this connection, that many of the newly specified unallowable costs were routinely found allowable in the past by boards of contract appeals and courts.

Allocability of Indirect Costs—Judicial Decisions

Generally accepted accounting principles have been frequently addressed by boards of contract appeals and federal courts. A review of the many such decisions provides a confusing picture of the judicial attitude toward GAAP.

In some cases, including one we shall be discussing in some detail below, the Armed Services Board of Contract Appeals ruled in favor of the contractor on the grounds that its allocation method was in accordance with GAAP. And yet, one could find no authoritative body that promulgated generally accepted accounting principles in the area covered (special facilities such as space chambers, wind tunnels, etc.).

Where one party to a dispute based its case on generally accepted accounting principles, and the other on specific provisions of government regulations or contract clauses, the latter always prevailed.

An illustration of judicial rejection of GAAP when found to be in conflict with procurement regulations or contract terms is reflected in the Grumman Corporation's unsuccessful appeals relating to the period in which a refund of the New York state franchise tax was to be credited.

In 1971, the Grumman Corporation (Grumman), essentially the defense-oriented Grumman Aerospace Corporation (GAC), incurred a substantial loss under a Navy contract for the F-14 aircraft. Under the carryback provisions of the New York State tax, Grumman received a refund of some $1,600,000 of which approximately $1,500,000 was allocable to GAC, the amounts being applied to the year 1968. As indicated in the decisions we shall be reviewing, there appear to have been no controversies regarding the refund, its computation, or the amount allocable to GAC. The dispute that gave rise to the litigation involved the year to which the refund should be applied. The contractor applied the refund to 1971; the government asserted that it should have been applied to 1968.

In the appeal to the Armed Services Board of Contract Appeals, ASBCA No. 18590, 75-2 BCA par. 11,492, the contractor argued that its method was in accordance with generally accepted accounting principles (GAAP). One of the specific GAAP references introduced was Accounting Principles Board (APB) Opinion No. 11, Accounting for Income Taxes, December 1967. The particular citation from APB 11 is quoted below:

> The tax effects of any realizable loss carrybacks should be recognized in the determination of net income (loss) of the loss periods. The tax loss gives rise to a refund (or claim for refund) of past taxes, which is both measurable and currently realizable; therefore the tax effect of the loss is properly recognizable in the determination of net income (loss) for the loss period.

The government argued that APB 11 was directed to published financial statements and did not govern determination of costs of government contracts.

Addressing Grumman's arguments, including the contractor's insistence that the carryback provision of the tax distinguished the recovery from a refund, the board stated:

> This "carryback" feature, however, does not change the nature of the refund as a reduction of appellant's 1968 franchise tax liability and a restitution of a portion of the tax paid in 1968 for which appellant had been reimbursed by the Government . . . thus this refund is "properly allocable" to the 1968 tax payment which represents the "costs for which the contractor has been reimbursed by the Government," within the

meaning of paragraph (f) of the "Allowable Costs, Incentive Fee, and Payment" clause.

The board's reasoning is further reflected in the following excerpt:

The Government's rights in the refund of the 1968 franchise tax are tied to and dependent upon the amount of costs which it has reimbursed to appellant. Hence, reduction in appellant's 1968 franchise tax liability should be applied to proportionately reduce the Government's cost reimbursement. "ASPR cost principles are concerned with assuring that if the Government pays a cost and later that cost is reduced, by whatever means, the Government receives the benefit of that reduction . . . ."

The board concluded that its decision was in full accord with the applicable provisions of ASPR Sections 15-201.1 and 15-205.41(c), as well as the contract clause.

The contractor appealed, but the Court of Claims upheld the ASBCA decision. *Grumman Aerospace Corp. v. U.S.,* Ct.Cl. No. 71-76 (25 CCF par. 82,892). The court agreed with the board's reasoning in looking particularly to the contractual terms, especially the Allowable Costs, Incentive Fee, and Payment clause, which contended the following: "(f) The Contractor agrees that any refunds, rebates, credits, or other amounts . . . accruing to or received by the Contractor . . . under this contract shall be paid by the Contractor to the Government to the extent that they are properly allocable to costs for which the Contractor has been reimbursed by the Government under this contract."

As the court read this contract clause and the provisions of ASPR 15-205.41(c), it concluded that both "are concerned with assuring that if the Government pays the cost and later that cost is reduced, by whatever means, the Government receives the benefit of that reduction."

The court further expressed the view that "[a]lthough the credit was obviously attributable to the carryback of a net operating loss from 1971 to 1968, the credit was, both literally and plainly, a 'refund' of, and a reduction in the amount of, Grumman's New York State Franchise Tax liability for 1968."

As succinctly summarized in its concluding comments, the court's decision emphasized: "Without regard to how GAAP and sound accounting logic might treat the refund for income tax accounting purposes, the contract language controls here."

In some decisions involving conflicting views of the parties regarding GAAP, boards and federal courts have made comments to the effect that both sides experienced little difficulty in obtaining expert accounting witnesses to testify that their allocation practices were in accordance with GAAP. For example, in *Wolf Research & Development Corporation,* ASBCA No. 10913, 69-2 BCA par. 8017; 68-2 BCA par. 7222, the board quoted the U.S. Court of Claims in a decision involving U.S. Steel to the effect that: "One must be cautious in using 'generally accepted accounting principles' as an aid in determining the allocability of costs to Government contracts." Pursuing this point further, the board said: "Not only must one be cautious in applying generally accepted accounting principles but one apparently must be diligent indeed even to find such principles."

Although similar views have been expressed by boards of contract appeals in other decisions, these bodies have been far from consistent and, from time to time, seem to accept and find satisfaction in the same principles that they summarily reject on other occasions. A case in point is the decision in the appeal of the *McDonnell Douglas Corporation,* ASBCA No. 12639, 69-2 BCA par. 8063. As we read this decision, the board appears to assert, without any citation of authority or other reference, that a certain cost accounting practice is in accordance with GAAP. Thereupon, this assertion, among others, is used to justify this practice.

Undisputed in the case is the fact that the contractor incurred costs of some $920,000 in operating wind tunnels and space chambers that, together with the costs of other special facilities, were allocated to jobs and projects "on the basis of direct labor dollars incurred in the appellant's engineering activities." There was also agreement that the issue was allocability. The contractor's method allocated wind tunnel and space chamber costs to some contracts in the performance of which these facilities were not used.

As to contracts on which such facilities *were* used, the contractor's method failed to allocate those costs in proportion to the hours used. The government complained that this method was inequitable and violated ASPR Section XV requirements that allocation be made in proportion to benefits received.

The contractor stated that its method was permitted by ASPR and, furthermore, had been used with the knowledge and consent of both parties for prior years. Since ASPR had not changed, nor had any change occurred in the contractor's business, the contractor argued that no basis existed for changing the method.

Interesting here is a comment in the ASBCA decision that a partner in one of the leading certified public accounting firms "states that the method is in accordance with generally accepted accounting principles." The partner did not address himself to the question of whether such method was appropriate to the particular circumstances.

The ASBCA was obviously impressed by the fact that a number of other leading aerospace firms had employed the same method as McDonnell Douglas during this period and that DOD had not questioned this method for the other firms. It also noted that the government had been attempting (unsuccessfully) to persuade other contractors to change to the usage method. Based on these facts: "The Board concludes that during the six-month period concerned appellant's method of allocating space chamber and wind tunnel costs was one 'generally accepted method of determining or estimating' such costs and that appellant applied 'generally accepted accounting principles and practices.' "

By way of summary, we quote sections of the decision:

> For a considerable number of years before this dispute arose both parties to the contracts understood that appellant's method of allocation was a method permitted by the contract terms and used it in allocating the costs concerned.

The Board concludes that the interpretation was one reasonable meaning of the contract terms. The contract does not specify that separate costs centers must be established for some or all of appellant's special facilities and the costs in such centers allocated on a usage basis only to the contracts on which such special facilities are used.

It is clear that during the period concerned appellant was using a generally accepted method of allocating the costs concerned.

The record does not show that appellant's method was not equitable under the circumstances or was not appropriate to the particular circumstances. The fact that the other contractors were permitted to use it during the same period is evidence that it is a method permitted by the contract terms concerned.

The Board's decision was based in part on the fact that the Government, as a class of customer, clearly benefitted directly from appellant's special facilities, including the wind tunnels and space chambers and in part on the fact that appellant's method did not discriminate against the government as a class of customer.

The accounting and auditing elements of DOD noted the board's statement that: "If the Government wants the indirect costs of a special facility allocated by appellant on usage basis, contracts negotiated with appellant should so specify." On the basis of this comment, a recommendation was made that ASPR Section XV be revised to satisfy the board's conclusion.

As indicated previously, concern was also felt that ASBCA No. 12639 would provide contractors with an option to choose any of the cost objectives cited in ASPR in allocating their indirect costs. There was apprehension that this could increase the cost to the government and run contrary to efforts towards accurate contract costing.

After a review of the board's decision and the other circumstances involved, the ASPR Committee submitted certain proposed revisions for industry comment in August 1970. A new cost principle was proposed to specifically cover special facilities. In addition, certain changes to ASPR 15-201.4 were proposed to more specifically enunciate DOD policies relating to allocability.

As a result of intense industry opposition and lack of a strong consensus within DOD, neither ASPR nor its successor, DAR, was revised to provide guidance for allocating costs of such special facilities as space chambers, wind tunnels, etc., nor have the authors of FAR elected to address this subject.

DCAA's Contract Audit Manual contains extensive guidance regarding the cost of operating special facilities such as wind tunnels and space chambers. Inasmuch as the CAM provisions are directive upon the DCAA auditors, we have cited them below for the information of our readers, with the cautionary note that the provisions of this manual have no statutory, regulatory, or contractual force.

7-301 Introduction. a. This paragraph provides guidance on the treatment to be accorded the operating costs of certain facilities, where costs, if not properly accounted for, could fail significantly to measure the benefits accruing to the several cost objectives.

b. The guidance includes (1) definition of facilities to which applicable, (2) criteria for determining whether the contractor is using an acceptable basis for charging or distributing costs to work benefited, and (3) criteria for determining billing or costing rates. Allocation of computer operating costs is covered in 7-100.

c. In the course of implementing the following guidelines, including the development of any recommendation to change an established and heretofore acceptable accounting procedure with respect to a particular facility, the principles below are not to be applied so rigidly as to complicate unduly the allocation where substantially the same results are achieved through less precise methods.

7-302 Criteria for "Special Facilities." Facilities to which this guidance is applicable cannot be specifically designated by name or type but rather must be determined by ascertaining whether they meet certain basic criteria. The first criterion to be met is that the costs involved in the operation of each facility must be significant in amount with respect to the contractor's overall operations. The second criterion is that the facility benefits only a limited portion of the contractor's total workload. Wind tunnels and space chambers are representative of facilities which, if they meet the criteria above, would be subject to the guidance provided in this section.

7-303 Basis for Allocating Costs to Benefiting Work. There are basically three methods for allocating costs related to facilities which meet the criteria in 7-302, although variations may be encountered. If a variation appears to reasonably measure the benefits accruing to the several cost objectives, its use should be satisfactory. The three basic methods are described below.

7-303.1 *Method 1—Full Costing on Usage Basis*

Under the first method, all readily identifiable direct costs are charged to projects, contracts, or other work involved. Additionally, all general operating costs of the facility, such as rentals, depreciation (including obsolescence), amortization, repairs, maintenance, supplies, general support salaries and wages, etc., are allocated to the using projects, contracts, or other work involved, on a usage or other quantitative basis. Generally, this method yields the most equitable results and should be used if cost and usage data for the facility can be economically accumulated with reasonable accuracy. Where it is determined that methods 2 or 3 below would yield inequitable cost allocations, cost data which will permit the determination of costs by this method should be maintained by the contractor.

7-303.2 *Method 2—Only Directly Identifiable Costs Allocated on Usage Basis*

Under the second method, readily identifiable direct costs are charged to the projects, contracts, or other work involved, as in method 1 above. However, all general operating costs of the facility, such as rentals, depreciation (including obsolescence), amortization, repairs, maintenance, supplies, general support salaries and wages, etc., are included in the distribution through one of the contractor's appropriate categories of indirect expense. Although this method is less precise than method 1, its use is satisfactory if it reasonably measures the benefits accruing to the several cost objectives.

7-303.3 *Method 3—General Indirect Cost Allocation*

Under the third method, all costs associated with the facility, including direct labor and material, are grouped and distributed through one of the contractor's appropriate categories of indirect expense. This method should be used only when the contractor demonstrates that (1) neither method 1 or 2 above is practical, and (2) its use is unlikely to result in any significant failure to measure the benefits accruing to the several cost objectives.

7-304 Determination of Costing Rates

7-304.1 *Basic Procedures for Costing Rates*

a. General operating costs of those facilities which meet the criteria in 7-302 and for which Method 1 above is considered appropriate should generally be charged to users by means of actual or predetermined billing or costing rates as provided below. This will require maintenance of a time log for each facility to record the hours of time spent by each user. The period covered by the billing or costing rates will not normally exceed twelve months. See 8-406 for CAS covered contractors and FAR 31.203(e) for non-CAS covered contractors.

b. Where only one rate for the facility is to be applied, it should consist of the actual or estimated applicable costs divided by the actual or estimated number of hours or other units composing the basis.

7-304.2 *Treatment of Real and Estimated Cost Differentials*

a. Where real cost differentials (such as certain services furnished during prime shifts only or by different facilities) exist and can be readily demonstrated, separate rates for such cost differentials may be used.

b. In the case of educational institutions, where rental or lease costs are based upon prime-shift usage, second and third shift usage may, with appropriate approval, be charged at reduced rates.

c. Under certain situations reasonably estimated differential costs may be used where cost differentials logically exist but cannot be determined precisely by contractor. For example, such differentials would permit priority or interrupt or short-turn-around time runs at premium rates and/or nonpriority or nonprime time or large-volume runs at reduced rates.

d. Whether a single rate or several rates are used, the rates should be so designed as to recover or closely approximate total recovery of costs from all users of the facility. Where differing rates are used, they should be applied to all users on a nondiscriminatory basis. The costing of accommodations sales at reduced rates is not considered appropriate.

7-304.3 *Treatment of Under- Over-Absorbed Rates*

Any immaterial underabsorption or overabsorption of costs resulting from application of predetermined rates may be charged or credited to an appropriate category of indirect expense. If the underabsorption or over-absorption is material, it should be treated in accordance with the CAS covered contractor's disclosed practices (See 8-418).

7-305 Treatment of Manufacturer Discounts to Educational Institutions

Where the manufacturer leases or sells the equipment below commercial prices to an educational institution as an allowance to education, the allowance should be treated as a reduction of the cost of leasing or purchasing.

7-306 Treatment of Grants for Special Facilities

Where the contractor (normally a university) has received a grant from the Government to be used in connection with a particular facility, application of the funds provided should be in accordance with the terms of the grant.

Controversies relating to allocation of costs of such special facilities to government contracts were identified by DCAA as problems warranting attention by the Cost Accounting Standards Board. The CASB made several efforts to provide ground rules in this area as its original proposal for five indirect cost allocation standards was reduced to three, then finally issued as a single standard, CAS 418. As we described in Chapter XIII of this text, the provisions of CAS 418 reflected a substantial dilution of the extensive and rigid requirements stated in the earlier multistandard drafts. As formally issued, CAS 418 contains no direct reference to allocation of costs of special facilities. However, paragraph (14) of the prefatory comments to this standard states:

> The Standard being promulgated today does not provide guidance for accounting for the costs of special facilities (e.g. space chambers, wind tunnels, reactors) accumulated in separate cost pools. These assets usually do not have application to all of the work of a business unit, and this circumstance creates difficult questions concerning the appropriate cost allocation techniques to be applied. The Board recognizes a need for particular attention to the accounting for the limited number of special facilities involved and has established a project in this area to review the cost allocation issues.

The CASB ceased operations before any substantive action was taken on this project.

Allocability of Indirect Costs—Cost Accounting Standards (CAS)

P.L. 91-379, as discussed in Chapter VIII and elsewhere in this text, established the Cost Accounting Standards Board with authority to promulgate cost accounting standards, and compliance with these standards was required with respect to specified national defense procurements. Over the years, the CASB provided additional exemptions, as contemplated by the law, both for specific contracts and for categories of contracts. Although the law did not apply to nonnational defense procurements as detailed in Chapter VIII of this text, FAR states that "the obligation to comply with CAS is extended to certain non-defense contracts as a matter of policy."

Cost accounting standards address allocability as contrasted with allowability; however, FAR 31.201-2 attaches allowability to the standards by providing that, for CAS-covered contracts, standards constitute a factor in determining the allowability.

COSTS SPECIFICALLY ESTABLISHED AS UNALLOWABLE IN FAR 31.205

As discussed earlier in this and previous chapters of this text, many of the "Selected Costs," established as unallowable in whole or in part in FAR 31.205, are based on considerations of reasonableness or allocability. Other costs are established as unallowable for other reasons or apparently without reason. For example, as discussed more fully in Chapter XVII of this text, contributions and donations are made specifically unallowable, without any rationale, by FAR 31.205-8.

COSTS SPECIFICALLY CITED AS UNRECOVERABLE BY CONTRACT CLAUSE

In addition to the above-mentioned categories of unallowable costs under government contracts, contractors may be subjected to additional restrictions on cost recovery by specific contract clauses. It is important to understand that these kinds of restrictions generally reflect local ground rules of procuring activities and are subject to negotiation. It is, accordingly, very important for contractors to carefully review the clauses in the proposed contracts to ascertain whether any such additional provisions for cost disallowances or limitations have been added and to assure that they do not cause the contractor to inadvertently effect agreement to such exclusions by signing contracts without full consideration of all such clauses.

ADVANCE AGREEMENTS (UNDERSTANDINGS) ON PARTICULAR COST ITEMS

Significant provisions of the procurement regulations, contained in FAR 31.109, recognize the difficulties of applying cost principles to the many different economic and accounting situations encountered in government contracts and encourage advance agreements or understandings between the government and the contractors, particularly with regard to special or unusual costs. Although there are specific limitations to advance agreements, such as the prohibition against a contracting officer agreeing in advance to allow a cost specifically established as unallowable, many needless controversies could be avoided through advance agreements.

The text of FAR 31.109, Advance Agreements, is quoted below:

31.109 Advance agreements.

(a) The extent of allowability of the costs covered in this part applies broadly to many accounting systems in varying contract situations. Thus, the reasonableness and allocability of certain costs may be difficult to determine, particularly for firms or their divisions that may not be under effective competitive restraints. To avoid possible subsequent disallow-ance or dispute based on unreasonableness or nonallocability, contracting officers and contractors should seek advance agreement on the treatment of special or unusual costs. However, an advance agreement is not an absolute requirement and the absence of an advance agreement on any cost will not, in itself, affect the reasonableness or allocability of that cost.

(b) Advance agreements may be negotiated either before or during a contract but should be negotiated before incurrence of the costs involved. The agreements must be in writing, executed by both contracting parties, and incorporated into applicable current and future contracts. An advance agreement shall contain a statement of its applicability and duration.

(c) The contracting officer is not authorized by this 31.109 to agree to a treatment of costs inconsistent with this part. For example, an advance agreement may not provide that, notwithstanding 31.205-20, interest is allowable.

(d) Advance agreements may be negotiated with a particular con-tractor for a single contract, a group of contracts, or all the contracts of a contracting office, an agency, or several agencies.

(e) The cognizant administrative contracting officer (ACO), or other contracting officer established in Part 42, shall negotiate advance agree-ments except that an advance agreement affecting only one contract, or class of contracts from a single contracting office, shall be negotiated by a contracting officer in the contracting office, or an ACO when delegated by the contracting officer. When the negotiation authority is delegated, the ACO shall coordinate the proposed agreement with the contracting officer before executing the advance agreement.

(f) Before negotiating an advance agreement, the Government nego-tiator shall—

(1) Determine if other contracting offices inside the agency or in other agencies have a significant unliquidated dollar balance in contracts with the same contractor;

(2) Inform any such office or agency of the matters under considera-tion for negotiation; and

(3) As appropriate, invite the office or agency and the cognizant audit agency to participate in prenegotiation discussions and/or in the subsequent negotiations.

(g) Upon completion of the negotiation, the sponsor shall prepare and distribute to other interested agencies and offices, including the audit agency, copies of the executed agreement and a memorandum providing the information specified in 15.808, Price negotiation memorandum, as applicable.

(h) Examples of costs for which advance agreements may be particu-larly important are—

(1) Compensation for personal services, including but not limited to allowances for off-site pay, incentive pay, location allowances, hardship pay, and cost of living differential;

(2) Use charges for fully depreciated assets;

(3) Deferred maintenance costs;

(4) Precontract costs;

(5) Independent research and development and bid and proposal costs;

(6) Royalties and other costs for use of patents;

(7) Selling and distribution costs;

(8) Travel and relocation costs, as related to special or mass personnel movements, as related to travel via contractor-owned, -leased, or-chartered aircraft, or as related to maximum per diem rates;

(9) Costs of idle facilities and idle capacity;

(10) Costs of automatic data processing equipment;

(11) Severance pay to employees on support service contracts;

(12) Plant reconversion;

(13) Professional services (e.g., legal, accounting, and engineering);

(14) General and administrative costs (e.g., corporate, division, or branch allocations) attributable to the general management, supervision, and conduct of the contractor's business as a whole. These costs are particularly significant in construction, job-site, architect-engineer, facilities, and Government-owned contractor operated (GOCO) plant contracts (see 31.203(f));

(15) Costs of construction plant and equipment (see 31.105(d));

(16) Costs of public relations and advertising; and

(17) Training and education costs (see 31.205-44(h)).

APPLICABILITY OF CONTRACT COST PRINCIPLES AND COST ACCOUNTING STANDARDS TO FIXED-PRICE CONTRACTS

Current Contract Cost Principles

The current contract cost principles are virtually identical for both cost-type and fixed-price contracts "whenever," in the words of FAR 31.103(a), "cost analysis is performed as required by 15.805-3."

The applicability of the FAR cost principles to all contracts and modifications negotiated with commercial organizations on the basis of cost is spelled out in FAR 31.103:

31.103 Contracts with commercial organizations.

This category includes all contracts and contract modifications for supplies, services, or experimental, developmental, or research work negotiated with organizations other than educational institutions (see 31.104), construction and architect-engineer contracts (see 31.105), State and local governments (see 31.107) and nonprofit organizations (see 31.108) on the basis of cost.

(a) The cost principles and procedures in Subpart 31.2 and agency supplements shall be used in pricing negotiated supply, service, experimental, developmental, and research contracts and contract modifications with commercial organizations whenever cost analysis is performed as required by 15.805-3.

(b) In addition, the contracting officer shall incorporate the cost principles and procedures in Subpart 31.2 and agency supplements by reference in contracts with commercial organizations as the basis for—

(1) Determining reimbursable costs under (i) cost-reimbursement contracts and cost-reimbursement subcontracts under these contracts performed by commercial organizations and (ii) the cost-reimbursement portion of time-and-materials contracts except when material is priced on a basis other than at cost (see 16.601(b)(3));

(2) Negotiating indirect cost rates (see Subpart 42.7);

(3) Proposing, negotiating, or determining costs under terminated contracts (see 49.103 and 49.113);

(4) Price revision of fixed-price incentive contracts (see 16.204 and 16.403);

(5) Price redetermination of price redetermination contracts (see 16.205 and 16.206); and

(6) Pricing changes and other contract modifications.

We stated earlier that the current contract cost principles are virtually identical for cost-type and fixed-price contracts. A difference, the significance of which is still debated on occasions, is found in FAR 31.102, which provides:

31.102 Fixed-price contracts.

The applicable subparts of Part 31 shall be used in the pricing of fixed-price contracts, subcontracts, and modifications to contracts and subcontracts whenever (a) cost analysis is performed, or (b) a fixed-price contract clause requires the determination or negotiation of costs. However, application of cost principles to fixed-price contracts and subcontracts shall not be construed as a requirement to negotiate agreements on individual elements of cost in arriving at agreement on the total price. The final price accepted by the parties reflects agreement only on the total price. Further, notwithstanding the mandatory use of cost principles, the objective will continue to be to negotiate prices that are fair and reasonable, cost and other factors considered.

Contract cost principles were originally applicable only to cost reimbursement-type contracts although contract auditors and some contracting officers used such principles as a "guide" in determining costs under variably priced fixed-price contracts. The Defense Department's revised 1959 contract cost principles represented the first official recognition of the applicability of such principles to fixed-price contracts. Although these principles were publicly heralded as providing a common set of principles for both types of contracts, various provisions emphasized that a less rigid application was intended for fixed-price contracts where the total price was the important matter. The 1959 principles contained a separate Part 6 to describe their application to fixed-price contracts.

APPLICABILITY OF CONTRACT COST PRINCIPLES TO SUBCONTRACTS

The contract cost principles were understood to be applicable to subcontracts where the price was based on cost unless the chain down to lower tier subcontracts was broken by an award where cost was not a factor in determining the price. The applicability of contract cost principles to subcontracts was explicitly stated for the first time in FAR 31.102, quoted above.

DOD 1986 AUTHORIZATION ACT, PUBLIC LAW 99-145

As mentioned elsewhere in this text, virtually every change to contract cost principles after the comprehensive 1959 revision further limited the ability of contractors to recover necessary and ordinary costs of doing business by establishing additional expenses as unallowable in whole or in part. The severest and most concentrated government attack in this area was reflected in the above-captioned statute, enacted November 8, 1985. Among its other provisions, the Act established that numerous expenses shall be considered "not allowable," and with respect to an even greater number, the Secretary of Defense was directed to "clarify" their allowability. Implementation in both instances was required within 150 days of enactment and, although the legislation was limited to the Department of Defense, virtually all of the revisions were effected through FAR and thus made applicable to covered contracts issued by all federal departments and agencies.

Costs Specified as Not Allowable

Section 911(e) of this Act provides that the following costs are not allowable under a covered contract (a contract for an amount more than $100,000 entered into by DOD other than a fixed-price contract without cost incentives):

(A) Costs of entertainment, including amusement, diversion, and social activities and any costs directly associated with such costs (such as tickets to shows or sports events, meals, lodging, rentals, transportation, and gratuities).

(B) Costs incurred to influence (directly or indirectly) legislative action on any matter pending before Congress or a State legislature.

(C) Costs incurred in defense of any civil or criminal fraud proceeding or similar proceeding (including filing of any false certification) brought by the United States where the contractor is found liable or has pleaded nolo contendere to a charge of fraud or similar proceeding (including filing of a false certification).

(D) Payments of fines and penalties resulting from violations of, or failure to comply with, Federal, State, local, or foreign laws and regulations, except when incurred as a result of compliance with specific terms and conditions of the contract or specific written instructions from the contracting officer authorizing in advance such payments in accordance with applicable regulations of the Secretary of Defense.

(E) Costs of membership in any social, dining, or country club or organization.

(F) Costs of alcoholic beverages.

(G) Contributions or donations, regardless of recipient.

(H) Costs of advertising designed to promote the contractor or its products.

(I) Costs of promotional items and memorabilia, including models, gifts, and souvenirs.

(J) Costs for travel by commercial aircraft which exceed the amount of the standard commercial fare.

Costs Requiring Clarification as to Allowability

The law required the Secretary of Defense to prescribe amendments to the acquisition regulations that "shall define in detail and in specific terms those costs which are unallowable, in whole or in part, under covered contracts. These regulations shall, at a minimum, clarify the cost principles applicable to contractor costs of the following:

(A) Air shows.

(B) Membership in civic, community, and professional organizations.

(C) Recruitment.

(D) Employee morale and welfare.

(E) Actions to influence (directly or indirectly) executive branch action on regulatory and contract matters (other than costs incurred in regard to contract proposals pursuant to solicited or unsolicited bids).

(F) Community relations.

(G) Dining facilities.

(H) Professional and consulting services, including legal services.

(I) Compensation.

(J) Selling and marketing.

(K) Travel.

(L) Public relations.

(M) Hotel and meal expenses.

(N) Expense of corporate aircraft.

(O) Company-furnished automobiles.

(P) Advertising.

Other Provisions of DOD 1986 Authorization Act

Some comments on the environment in which a law containing these and other provisions commented upon below are needed to understand the outpouring of punitive measures against defense contractors.

Actual and alleged instances of fraud, waste, and abuse had been providing the communications media and congressional committees with a continuing source for criticism of the Defense Department and firms that performed under contracts it awarded. The major trumpeters of the "horror stories" were the General Accounting Office, the Office of the DOD Inspector General, and DCAA. Further comments on the contributions of these agencies to the growing congressional criticisms are contained in Chapters II, XXVI, XXVII, and XXVIII of this text.

DOD had taken numerous actions on its own, and at all, including the highest, departmental levels, through increasing suspensions, debarments, referrals to the Department of Justice for prosecution of alleged fraud, public cost disallowances and denouncements of contractors who reportedly charged unallowable costs to government contracts, continuing additions to the list of costs established as unallowable, etc. These and other actions did not satisfy certain congressional critics, and various subcommittees competed for hearings at which GAO and DOD IG representatives criticized defense contractors on numerous accounts, including the submission of unallowable costs. These witnesses also criticized contracting officers for accepting certain costs that GAO and DOD IG viewed as unallowable, especially when the costs were accepted after being questioned by DCAA auditors.

DOD witnesses at these hearings, focusing on defending the Department, and in the vain effort to deter the continuing congressional investigations and repetitive hearings, boasted of the measures DOD had taken, such as conducting special reviews and investigations of certain contractors, requiring certification of cost submissions, and taking the other actions mentioned above. Despite the assurances that DOD had moved to take matters under control, House subcommittee chairmen Nichols and Bennett directed an independent investigation conducted by their staff members and representatives of DCAA and GAO.

The results of the investigation were included in a report that received considerable publicity as Congressmen Nichols and Bennett issued press releases and appeared on television shows. Instances of unallowable cost submissions were reported, together with DCAA recommendations and final contracting officer negotiations. The hearings that followed featured GAO officials who criticized contractors and contracting officers, and bore down hard on what had become a major matter of emphasis for GAO—inadequacies and ambiguities of FAR contract cost principles. The "watchdog" representatives insisted that the regulations should be overhauled to clearly establish the unallowability of many indirect costs that were being allowed by contracting officers in overhead negotiations.

GAO officials also expressed sharp opposition to "bottom line" overhead negotiations, a term used to describe agreements reached between contractors and contracting officers on indirect expense rates without specifically and formally recording the decisions on the disposition of each and every expense in dispute between the contractor and DCAA. They recommended that contracting officers be compelled to record the specific action taken on each item and, further, to justify the allowance of any expense questioned by DCAA auditors.

The congressional hearings culminated in the introduction of HR 2397, the "Allowable Cost Reform Act," which contained most of GAO's recommendations and additional measures to penalize contractors accused of submitting unallowable costs and to restrict contracting officers from allowing costs questioned by contract auditors. This proposed legislation, together with others relating to this subject, was ultimately folded into the DOD 1986 Authorization Act. We have commented above on the provisions of the latter statute relating to costs established as unallowable and costs with respect to which allowability must be clarified. Earlier in this chapter, we noted the provision regarding the change to the focus of the burden of proof where the reasonableness of a cost is in dispute. Some of the other provisions of P.L. 99-145 are summarized below.

Increasing and/or adding civil and criminal penalties against contractors found to have submitted unallowable costs.

Requiring certification by a contractor official that to his best knowledge and belief all indirect costs included in the submission to the government are allowable.

Increasing criminal fines and civil penalties for false claims in DOD procurement.

Giving subpoena power to the DCAA Director.

Requiring the Secretary of Defense to report within 60 days his views concerning eliminating G&A expenses from the base for calculating profit.

Requiring GAO to evaluate DOD's implementation of the statutory provisions to determine if consistent with the congressional objective of eliminating unallowable costs charged to defense contracts. (P.L. 99-190)

Requiring the contracting officer not to resolve any questioned costs until he obtains adequate documentation and the opinion of the contract auditor.

Requiring the auditor's presence at all negotiations and discussions with contractors concerning allowability of costs "to the maximum extent practicable."

Eliminating "bottom line" negotiations by requiring settlements to reflect specific disposition of costs questioned by contract auditors.

Penalties for Submitting Unallowable Indirect Costs

As noted earlier, one of the provisions of P.L. 99-145 required the Defense Department to issue regulations imposing penalties on contractors for submitting unallowable costs. The text of this statutory provision is quoted below:

Sec. 2324. Allowable Costs Under Defense Contracts

(a)(1) The Secretary of Defense shall require that a covered contract provide that if the contractor submits to the Department of Defense a proposal for settlement of indirect costs incurred by the contractor for any period after such costs have been accrued and if that proposal includes the submission of a cost which is unallowable because the cost violates a cost principle in the Federal Acquisition Regulation or the Department of Defense Supplement to the Federal Acquisition Regulation, the costs shall be disallowed.

(2) If the Secretary determines by clear and convincing evidence that a cost submitted by a contractor in its proposal for settlement is unallowable under paragraph (1), the Secretary shall assess a penalty against the contractor in an amount equal to—

(A) the amount of the disallowed costs; plus

(B) interest (to be computed based on regulations issued by the Secretary) to compensate the United States for the use of any funds which a contractor has been paid in excess of the amount to which the contractor was entitled.

(b) If the Secretary determines that a proposal for settlement of indirect costs submitted by a contractor includes a cost determined to be unallowable in the case of such contractor before the submission of such proposal, the Secretary shall assess a penalty against the contractor, in addition to the penalty assessed under subsection (a), in an amount equal to two times the amount of such cost.

(c) An action of the Secretary under subsection (a) or (b)—

(1) shall be considered a final decision for the purposes of section 6 of the Contract Disputes Act of 1978 (41 U.S.C. 605); and

(2) is appealable in the manner provided in section 7 of such Act (41 U.S.C. 606).

(d) If any penalty is assessed under subsection (a) or (b) with respect to a proposal for settlement of indirect costs, the Secretary may assess an additional penalty of not more than $10,000 per proposal.

Some of the provisions of this law were adopted by civilian agencies and those were implemented in FAR. Others, such as this penalty provision, have not been accepted by the other agencies. Accordingly, the implementation is through DFARS and its applicability is limited to DOD-covered contracts (contracts over $100,000 other than fixed-price without cost incentives).

Following the statutory language, DFARS 31.7001(a)(3) describes the penalties as follows: (Effective February 26, 1987).

(i) If the cost is unallowable based on clear and convincing evidence, the penalty is equal to the (A) amount of the disallowed cost plus (B) interest on the paid portion, if any, of the disallowance.

(ii) If the cost was determined to be unallowable before proposal submission, the penalty is equal to (A) the amount in (a)(3)(i) above plus (B) two times the amount of the disallowed cost.

(iii) If any penalty is assessed under (a)(3)(i) or (a)(3)(ii) above, an additional penalty of not more than $10,000 per proposal may be assessed.

DFARS 31.7001(a)(2) states that "(a)n unallowable cost is defined at FAR 31.001" but the regulation provides no explanation or interpretation of the words "based on clear and convincing evidence." DCAA auditors and some overzealous contracting officers may find clear and convincing evidence for declaring unallowable, costs that could be considered allowable. The only comfort for contractors is the established relationship to FAR, which should obviate including in this category costs that are not specifically so identified in that regulation. For example, DCAA auditors were "questioning" such costs as public relations, goodwill, etc., when FAR was silent on their treatment.

The cognizant ACO is responsible for determining whether the above penalties should be assessed and for initiating action leading to the assessment. "Departments/Agencies" are responsible for establishing procedures to review the ACO recommendations to assess penalties and to designate officials authorized to make the assessments.

In most instances, assessments will be initiated by contract auditors who are charged with making such recommendations to the ACO, and will include "documentation sufficient for a decision."

Subparagraph (a)(3)(ii), cited above, provides for the heavier penalty where the cost was determined to be unallowable before submission. The regulation lists certain documentation, described as not all inclusive, that may evidence prior determination of unallowability:

(A) A DCAA Form 1 (see FAR 42.705-2) which was not appealed by the contractor or withdrawn by DCAA.

(B) A contracting officer final decision which was not appealed under the Disputes clause.

(C) Prior ASBCA or Court decision which upheld a cost disallowance involving the contractor.

(D) Any determination of unallowability under the procedures provided in FAR 31.201-6, Accounting for unallowable costs.

An illustration is offered of the circumstances in which an additional penalty of $10,000 per proposal may be assessed in accordance with (a)(3)(iii)—"repeated submission of unallowable costs in a specific proposal."

Further implementation is provided by the requirement for insertion of Penalties for Unallowable Costs clauses for cost-type and fixed-price incentive contracts, DFARS 52.231-7001 and -7002, respectively.

With the assistance of Congress, GAO, its own IG, and DCAA, the Department of Defense has acquired a wide array of weapons for use against its contractors through civil and/or criminal avenues. In many instances the civil and/or criminal penalties are not exclusive but can be added one upon the other for maximum punishment of companies that agree to provide goods or services for the country's national defense.

GAO Report on DOD Implementation of 1986 Authorization and Appropriation Acts

In accordance with the statutory requirement, GAO issued its "initial report" on October 10, 1986, titled "UNALLOWABLE COSTS—Improved Cost Principles Should Reduce Inconsistent Treatment of These Costs." As the title indicates, GAO stated it "found that DOD has taken significant strides to comply with the Congress' intent by prescribing new and amended cost principles within the directed time period." Details of these "strides" are reflected in the chapters of this text that cite and comment on the individual contract cost principles as currently set forth in the acquisition regulations.

Acknowledging the point both DOD and observers in the private sector had been emphasizing over the years that "allowability criteria for all cost elements cannot be written in such a way as to remove all ambiguity," GAO expressed the view that DOD had appropriately addressed "most of the costs" that the DOD 1986 Authorization Act mandated be either established as unallowable or their allowability clarified. However, GAO stated it was not completely satisfied and reported it had recommended that DOD further toughen up the cost principles relating to entertainment and executive lobbying:

> The entertainment principle states that costs of amusement, diversion, and social activities are unallowable, but refers the reader to the principles covering advertising and public relations, 31.205-1, and employee morale, 31.205-13. The reference to other principles has been interpreted by some contractors, contracting officers, and contract auditors to mean that entertainment costs incurred as a result of employee morale or public relations activities are allowable. Others have concluded that all entertainment costs are unallowable. For example, costs for tickets to sports events have been claimed by contractors as improving employee morale or performance. These costs could be classified as either entertainment, public relations, or employee morale. Because the objective of changing the principle is to remove ambiguities and ensure consistent treatment of the costs, we believe entertainment costs should be unallowable under all circumstances. Therefore, we recommend that the reference to other cost principles be removed from the entertainment principle and that a statement be inserted that costs made specifically unallowable under this subsection, 31.205-14, are not allowable under other subsections of FAR subpart 31.2.

> The exective lobbying principle specifies that costs incurred in attempting to improperly influence an executive branch employee are unallowable. The principle refers to FAR 3.401 which defines improper influence, in essence, as an inducement to act regarding a contract on any basis other than the merits of the matter. The legislative lobbying principle, by contrast, lists specific costs that are unallowable without regard to whether the costs were incurred in connection with the merits of the matter. It also lists costs which are allowable and the circumstances under which they are allowable. To achieve consistency in the treatment of lobbying costs, we recommend that the executive lobbying principle be structured in a manner similar to the legislative lobbying principle.

GAO even reported that some of the implementing regulatory changes were "notable," which the private sector understood meant that the revisions were sufficiently severe to please even the demanding legislative watchdog:

For example, the advertising principle was expanded to include public relations costs. This principle contains definitions for the two terms, the specific advertising and public relations costs which are allowable, a declaration that all other advertising costs are unallowable, and a listing of numerous public relations costs that are unallowable. In addition, DOD added a new and important concept. This principle includes a declaration that costs which are unallowable under this principle cannot be allowable under other cost principles and vice versa.

In another example, the selling costs principle was rewritten to include a definition which lists the broad categories of activities performed by contractors to sell their products, such as advertising, public relations, entertainment, and market planning. The allowability of costs for these activities is controlled by the provisions of other cost principles. The fact that costs that are unallowable under these other cost principles may have been incurred in connection with allowable selling activities does not make them allowable.

Another notable change involves the compensation cost principle under which the contracting officer may challenge the reasonableness of any individual compensation element or the sum of the elements paid or accrued to particular employees or classes of employees. Once the compensation element is challenged, the contractor has the burden to demonstrate the reasonableness of that element.

GAO also took the occasion to express its satisfaction with an earlier action taken by DOD (but not adopted by other agencies and hence not incorporated into FAR) relating to resolution of costs submitted by contractors and questioned by contract auditors. The report noted that "on August 5, 1985, DOD assigned responsibility for determining final overhead rates for all contractors, except educational or similar institutions, to the Defense Contract Audit Agency."

Chapter XVII

Application of Government Contract Cost Principles to Specific Costs and Expenses

FAR 31.205 addresses the allowability of certain "selected costs," following the pattern of the previous DAR 15-205 and FPR 1-15.205. Although the coverage is extremely comprehensive, FAR provides the necessary qualification in 31.204(c) that it "does not cover every element of cost. Failure to include any item of cost does not imply that it is either allowable or unallowable. The determination of allowability shall be based upon the principles and standards in this subpart and the treatment of similar or related items."

FAR 31.205 is applicable to contracts with commercial organizations. As referenced in Chapter XVI of this text, cost principles for contracts with educational institutions, contracts with state and local governments, and contracts with nonprofit organizations are governed by the provisions of the related OMB Circulars. The selected costs also apply to construction and architect-engineer contracts and facilities contracts, subject to the exceptions described in the previous chapter of this text.

In previous editions of this text, in addition to our analyses and comments, we quoted some of the selected costs in whole or in part. The full text of all of the selected costs was contained in an appendix. A number of readers suggested that including the full text of all of the selected costs and our analyses within the chapters would assist study and reference and eliminate duplication. We have adopted these suggestions.

At this writing, FAR 31.205 contains commentaries regarding the allowability or unallowability of 51 "selected costs," most of which are reviewed in this chapter. Certain exceptions appeared appropriate. For example, FAR 31.205-18, Independent research and development and bid and proposal costs, seemed more logically positioned in Chapter XIV of this text, Accounting Methods and Controls for Engineering Overhead. Public relations and advertising costs, FAR 31.205-1, and Selling costs, FAR 31.205-38, were considered better fitted in the discussions of Accounting Methods and Controls for Selling, General and Administrative Expenses, Chapter XV. The cost principle for Compensation for Personal Services, FAR 31.205-6, is particularly lengthy and complex and we have addressed this subject separately in the following (XVIII) chapter.

Our commentary is not motivated to develop arguments for or against the contract cost principles. Rather, the objective is to provide a fair and comprehensive presentation of these principles, including historical background where it would appear to facilitate understanding, clarify the rationale for the conclusions reached in the regulations, and identify points of controversy. The author does not pretend to assume the role of a totally impartial observer—a close-to-impossible achievement for human beings; we therefore offer no apologies for any side-taking that may be reflected in this commentary. A real effort, however, has been made throughout to present the views of both government and industry on disputed matters.

PUBLIC RELATIONS AND ADVERTISING COSTS

This substantially revised and retitled cost principle is quoted and reviewed in Chapter XV of this text.

AUTOMATIC DATA PROCESSING EQUIPMENT LEASING COSTS

FAR 31.205-2 provides:

(a) This subsection applies to all contractor-leased automatic data processing equipment (ADPE), as defined in 31.001 (except as components of an end item to be delivered to the Government), acquired under operating leases, as defined in Statement of Financial Accounting Standard No. 13 (FAS-13), Accounting for Leases, issued by the Financial Accounting Standards Board. Compliance with 31.205-11(m) requires that ADPE acquired by means of capital leases, as defined in FAS-13, shall be treated as purchased assets; i.e., be capitalized and the capitalized value of such assets be distributed over their useful lives as depreciation charges or over the leased life as amortization charges as appropriate. Allowability of costs related to contractor-owned ADPE is governed by other requirements of this subpart.

(b)(1) If the contractor leases ADPE but cannot demonstrate, on the basis of facts existent at the time of the decision to lease or continue leasing and documented in accordance with paragraph (d) below, that leasing will result in less cost to the Government over the anticipated useful life (see paragraph (c) below), then rental costs are allowable only up to the amount that would be allowed had the contractor purchased the ADPE.

(2) The costs of leasing ADPE are allowable only to the extent that the contractor can annually demonstrate in accordance with paragraph (d) below (whether or not the term of lease is renewed or otherwise extended) that these costs meet the following criteria:

(i) The costs are reasonable and necessary for the conduct of the contractor's business in light of factors such as the contractor's requirements for ADPE, costs of comparable facilities, the various types of leases available, and the terms of the rental agreement.

(ii) The costs do not give rise to a material equity in the facilities (such as an option to renew or purchase at a bargain rental or price other than that normally given to industry at large) but represent charges only for the current use of the equipment, including incidental service costs such as maintenance, insurance, and applicable taxes.

(iii) The contracting officer's approval was obtained for the leasing arrangement (see subparagraph (d)(3) below) when the total cost of leasing—

(A) The ADPE is to be allocated to one or more Government contracts which require negotiating or determining costs, or

(B) ADPE in a single plant, division, or cost center exceeds $500,000 a year and 50 percent or more of the total leasing cost is to be allocated to one or more Government contracts which require negotiating or determining costs.

(3) Rental costs under a sale and leaseback arrangement are allowable only up to the amount that would have been allowed had the contractor retained title to the ADPE.

(4) Allowable rental costs of ADPE leased from any division, subsidiary, or organization under a common control are limited to the cost of ownership (excluding interest or other costs unallowable under this Subpart 31.2 and including the cost of money (see 31.205-10)). When there is an established practice of leasing the same or similar equipment to unaffiliated lessees, rental costs shall be allowed in accordance with subparagraphs (b)(1) and (2) above, except that the purchase price and costs of ownership shall be determined under 31.205-26(e).

(c)(1) An estimate of the anticipated useful life of the ADPE may represent the application life (utility in a given function), technological life (utility before becoming obsolete in whole or in part), or physical life (utility before wearing out) depending upon the facts and circumstances and the particular facilities involved. Each case must be evaluated individually. In estimating anticipated useful life, the contractor may use the application life if it can be demonstrated that the ADPE has utility only in a given function and the duration of the function can be determined. Technological life may be used if the contractor can demonstrate that existing ADPE must be replaced because of—

(i) Specific program objectives or contract requirements that cannot be accomplished with the existing ADPE;

(ii) Cost reductions that will produce identifiable savings in production or overhead costs;

(iii) Increase in workload volume that cannot be accomplished efficiently by modifying or augmenting existing ADPE; or

(iv) Consistent pattern of capacity operation ($2\frac{1}{2}$-3 shifts) on existing ADPE.

(2) Technological advances will not justify replacing existing ADPE before the end of its physical life if it will be able to satisfy future requirements or demands.

(3) In estimating the least cost to the Government for useful life, the cumulative costs that would be allowed if the contractor owned the ADPE should be compared with cumulative costs that would be allowed

under any of the various types of leasing arrangements available. For the purpose of this comparison, the costs of ADPE exclude interest or other unallowable costs pursuant to this Subpart 31.2; they include but are not limited to the costs of operation, maintenance, insurance, depreciation, facilities capital cost of money, rental, and the cost of machine services, as applicable.

(d)(1) Except as provided in subparagraph (3) below, the contractor's justification, under paragraph (b) above, of the leasing decisions shall consist of the following supporting data, prepared before acquisition:

(i) Analysis of use of existing ADPE.

(ii) Application of the criteria in paragraph (b) above.

(iii) Specific objectives or requirements, generally in the form of a data system study and specification.

(iv) Solicitation of proposals, based on the data system specification, from qualified sources.

(v) Proposals received in response to the solicitation and reasons for selecting the equipment chosen and for the decision to lease.

(2) Except as provided in subparagraph (3) below, the contractor's annual justification, under subparagraph (b)(2) above, of the decision to retain or change existing ADPE capability and the need to continue leasing shall consist of current data as specified in subdivisions (d)(1)(i) through (iii) above.

(3) If the contractor's prospective ADPE lease cost meets the threshold in 31.205-2(b)(2)(iii) above, the contractor shall furnish data supporting the initial decision to lease (see subparagraph (b)(1) above). If the total cost of leasing ADPE in a single plant, division, or cost center exceeds $500,000 per year and 50 percent or more of the total leasing cost is allocated to Government contracts which require negotiating or determining costs, the contractor shall furnish data supporting the annual justification for retaining or changing existing ADPE capability and the need to continue leasing shall also be furnished (see subparagraph (b)(2) above).

The changes from the prior DAR and FPR provisions are essentially editorial, and FAR continues to reflect the government's close interest in leasing costs and restrictions on the amounts considered allowable. Persuaded that purchasing is more economical than leasing, and unmindful of the problems of obtaining capital when interest is unallowable and of risks incident to obsolescence, the government provides various tests contractors must meet and demonstrations they are required to make before leasing costs will be allowed.

BAD DEBTS

FAR 31.205-3 states:

Bad debts, including actual or estimated losses arising from uncollectible accounts receivable due from customers and other claims, and any directly associated costs such as collection costs, and legal costs are unallowable.

The rationale for the unequivocal disallowance of bad debts is that the government pays its just indebtedness; accordingly, bad debts and directly associated costs presumably pertain to nongovernment business and hence are not allocable to government contracts.

BID AND PROPOSAL COSTS

A major editorial improvement by the FAR authors was the consolidation of B&P costs (see Chapter XIV of this text) with IR&D costs, which eliminated considerable redundancy.

BONDING COSTS

FAR 31.205-4 indicates:

(a) Bonding costs arise when the Government requires assurance against financial loss to itself or others by reason of the act or default of the contractor. They arise also in instances where the contractor requires similar assurance. Included are such bonds as bid, performance, payment, advance payment, infringement, and fidelity bonds.

(b) Costs of bonding required pursuant to the terms of the contract are allowable.

(c) Costs of bonding required by the contractor in the general conduct of its business are allowable to the extent that such bonding is in accordance with sound business practice and the rates and premiums are reasonable under the circumstances.

CIVIL DEFENSE COSTS

FAR 31.205.5 provides:

(a) Civil defense costs are those incurred in planning for, and protecting life and property against, the possible effects of enemy attack. Costs of civil defense measures (including costs in excess of normal plant protection costs, first-aid training and supplies, fire fighting training and equipment, posting of additional exit notices and directions, and other approved civil defense measures) undertaken on the contractor's premises pursuant to suggestions or requirements of civil defense authorities are allowable when allocated to all work of the contractor.

(b) Costs of capital assets acquired for civil defense purposes are allowable through depreciation (see 31.205-11).

(c) Contributions to local civil defense funds and projects are unallowable.

These provisions appear reasonable except for what would appear to be a restriction that suggestions or requirements of civil defense authorities constitute a prerequisite for the allowability of such expenditures. Another point of contention, raised by some contractors, is the requirement for allocating these expenses to all of the operations. This point is in contention because this category of costs is frequently incurred only in connection with those portions of the facilities devoted to defense efforts and not to the facilities used for the firm's regular commercial business. Although the basis for these contentions appears reasonable, the above-cited provisions can hardly be subject to misinterpretation. The provision that cites contributions to local civil defense funds and projects as unallowable is consistent with the government's overall position on contributions and donations. Comments on this subject are contained in the succeeding pages.

COMPENSATION FOR PERSONAL SERVICES

As explained earlier, this cost principle is covered separately in the following chapter.

CONTINGENCIES

FAR 31.205-7 provides:

(a) "Contingency," as used in this subpart, means a possible future event or condition arising from presently known or unknown causes, the outcome of which is indeterminable at the present time.

(b) Costs for contingencies are generally unallowable for historical costing purposes because such costing deals with costs incurred and recorded on the contractor's books. However, in some cases, as for example, terminations, a contingency factor may be recognized when it is applicable to a past period to give recognition to minor unsettled factors in the interest of expediting settlement.

(c) In connection with estimates of future costs, contingencies fall into two categories:

(1) Those that may arise from presently known and existing conditions, the effects of which are foreseeable within reasonable limits of accuracy; e.g., anticipated costs of rejects and defective work. Contingencies of this category are to be included in the estimates of future costs so as to provide the best estimate of performance cost.

(2) Those that may arise from presently known or unknown conditions, the effect of which cannot be measured so precisely as to provide equitable results to the contractor and to the Government; e.g., results of pending litigation. Contingencies of this category are to be excluded from cost estimates under the several items of cost, but should be disclosed separately (including the basis upon which the contingency is computed) to facilitate the negotiation of appropriate contractual coverage. (See, for example, 31.205-6(g), 31.205-19, and 31.205-24.)

A close reading of this cost principle suggests that provisions for contingencies are suspect under any circumstances and are likely to be disallowed. This point is clearly stated with respect to historical costs and such matters as pending litigation. Where stated to be allowable, as in the instances of "minor unsettled factors" in terminations and rejects and defective work in forward pricing, the intent clearly relates to what most of us would understand as estimates rather than contingencies.

CONTRIBUTIONS AND DONATIONS

Although these expenses remain unallowable, as they have been for many years, a few additional words were added to comply with the direction in P.L. 99-145 to clarify the allowability of designated costs. The cost principle now states:

> Contributions or donations including cash, property and service, regardless of recipient, are unallowable, except as provided in 31.205-1(e)(3).

The referenced exception states: Costs of participation in community service activities (e.g., blood bank drives, charity drives, savings bond drives, disaster assistance, etc.).

During World War II, the "Green Book" set out the principle that certain types of contributions, those "to local charitable or community and similar organizations, to the extent constituting ordinary and necessary business expense," would be allowable. Ground rules for the Army and Air Force, as reflected in TM 14-1000, similarly stated (Paragraph 222) that "such contributions will constitute reimbursable costs when made to charitable, religious, scientific, or educational organizations which are 'recognized' as such by the Treasury Department." The restrictive trend towards the elimination of all contributions and donations, as reflected in the ASPR/DAR and FPR and now FAR, has quite understandably proved to be unpopular.

In a narrow sense, contributions are not necessary or incident to the performance of government contracts. On the other hand, the types of contributions described above are made pursuant to the doctrines of a democratic society that contemplates that the individual citizens rather than the government will sustain charities. The related donations are in the interests of public welfare and no business should shirk its duty. Assuming then that a company is engaged in performing government contracts to a substantial extent, the condition would arise where such contributions would be made entirely out of profits or equity. This concept, of course, is contrary to the principles of income tax regulations, which provide for contributions as appropriate deductions from income in tax determinations.

Government regulators view this subject in a different light. Broadly speaking, a business can dispose of its profits through distribution to the owners, reinvestment in current funds or capital assets, or by any other method it deems appropriate.

Stretching a point, it may be considered that a business (similar to an individual wage earner) can elect the manner in which monies remaining will be disposed. One source of disposition is giving to charities. Following this conjectural line, if the government reimburses the contractor for contributions made, then the government and not the contractor is making the contribution. Accordingly, the government may say to the contractor, "Contributions are socially desirable. If you wish to make donations, do so, but if they are to be your donations, they must come from your profits." Some business people point out that certain contributions are required to maintain public good will and so they do not represent entirely voluntary contributions. This contention, however, is answered by the government to the effect that such contributions represent, in effect, advertising and thus are still unallowable.

The entire matter is complex, and much remains as yet unsaid. So long as contributions continue to be viewed as unallowable items of costs, there is little that a contractor can do except, inasmuch as the donations account will be disallowed in its entirety, effect a very careful screening of this account to ascertain that it contains nothing but donations. This screening is important in view of the fact that some companies often intermingle payments for memberships with payments for contributions.

FAR provides that costs of memberships in trade, business, technical and professional organizations and subscriptions to related periodicals are allowable.

In 1966, DOD was persuaded that a blanket disallowance of all contributions and donations was inequitable and inappropriate, and a revision to ASPR proposed that contributions made in accordance with IRS regulations, further restricted by a percentage of cost and average expenditures for prior years, would be allowable. While industry debated the merits of the proposed restrictions, extravagant criticisms from the press and some congressional sources led to the withdrawal of the proposal.

COST OF MONEY

The text of FAR 31.205-10 is set forth below:

(a) *Facilities capital cost of money.*

(1) *General* (i) Facilities capital cost of money (cost of capital committed to facilities) is an imputed cost determined by applying a cost-of-money rate to facilities capital employed in contract performance. A cost-of-money rate is uniformly imputed to all contractors (see subdivision (ii) below). Capital employed is determined without regard to whether its source is equity or borrowed capital. The resulting cost of money is not a form of interest on borrowings (see 31.205-20).

(ii) CAS 414, Cost of Money as an Element of the Cost of Facilities Capital, establishes criteria for measuring and allocating, as an element of contract cost, the cost of capital committed to facilities. Cost-of-money factors are developed on Form CASB-CMF, broken down by overhead pool at the business unit, using (A) business-unit facilities capital data, (B) overhead allocation base data, and (C) the cost-of-money rate, which is based on interest rates specified by the Secretary of the Treasury under 50 U.S.C. App. 1215(b)(2).

(2) *Allowability.* Whether or not the contract is otherwise subject to CAS, facilities capital cost of money is allowable if—

(i) The contractor's capital investment is measured, allocated to contracts, and costed in accordance with CAS 414;

(ii) The contractor maintains adequate records to demonstrate compliance with this standard; and

(iii) The estimated facilities capital cost of money is specifically identified or proposed in cost proposals relating to the contract under which this cost is to be claimed.

(3) *Accounting.* The facilities capital cost of money need not be entered on the contractor's books of account. However, the contractor shall (i) make a memorandum entry of the cost and (ii) maintain, in a manner that permits audit and verification, all relevant schedules, cost data, and other data necessary to support the entry fully.

(4) *Payment.* Facilities capital cost of money that is (i) allowable under subparagraph (2) above and (ii) calculated, allocated, and documented in accordance with this cost principle shall be an "incurred cost" for reimbursement purposes under applicable cost-reimbursement contracts and for progress payment purposes under fixed-price contracts.

(5) *Goodwill.* The cost of money resulting from goodwill (however represented) in the facilities capital employed base is unallowable.

(b) *Cost of money as an element of the cost of capital assets under construction.*

(1) *General* (i) Cost of money as an element of the cost of capital assets under construction is an imputed cost determined by applying a cost-of-money rate to the investment in tangible and intangible capital assets while they are being constructed, fabricated, or developed for a contractor's own use. Capital employed is determined without regard to whether its source is equity or borrowed capital. The resulting cost of money is not a form of interest on borrowing (see 31.205-20).

(ii) CAS 417, Cost of Money as an Element of the Cost of Captial Assets Under Construction, establishes criteria for measuring and allocating, as an element of contract cost, the cost of capital committed to capital assets under construction, fabrication, or development.

(2) *Allowability* (i) Whether or not the contract is otherwise subject to CAS, and except as specified in subdivision (ii) below, the cost of money for capital assets under construction, fabrication, or development is allowable if—

(A) The cost of money is calculated, allocated to contracts, and costed in accordance with CAS 417;

(B) The contractor maintains adequate records to demonstrate compliance with this standard; and

(C) The cost of money for tangible capital assets is included in the capitalized cost that provides the basis for allowable depreciation costs, or, in the case of intangible capital assets, the cost of money is included in the cost of those assets for which amortization costs are allowable.

(ii) Actual interest cost in lieu of the calculated imputed cost of money for capital assets under construction, fabrication, or development is unallowable.

(3) *Accounting.* The cost of money for capital assets under construction need not be entered on the contractor's books of account. However,

the contractor shall (i) make a memorandum entry of the cost and (ii) maintain, in a manner that permits audit and verification, all relevant schedules, cost data, and other data necessary to support the entry fully.

(4) *Payment.* The cost of money for capital assets under construction that is allowable under subparagraph (2) above of this cost principle shall be an "incurred cost" for reimbursement purposes under applicable cost-reimbursement contracts and for progress payment purposes under fixed-price contracts.

CAS 414—Cost of Money as an Element of the Cost of Facilities Capital

A discussion of FAR 31.205-10 requires concurrent consideration of its precurser, CAS 414—Cost of Money as an Element of the Cost of Facilities Capital. Cited below are the Fundamental Requirements and Techniques for the Application sections of this standard:

§ 414.40 Fundamental requirement.

(a) A contractor's facilities capital shall be measured and allocated in accordance with the criteria set forth in this Standard. The allocated amount shall be used as a base to which a cost of money rate is applied.

(b) The cost of money rate shall be based on interest rates determined by the Secretary of the Treasury, pursuant to Pub. L. 92-41 (85 Stat. 97).

(c) The cost of capital committed to facilities shall be separately computed for each contract using facilities capital cost of money factors computed for each cost accounting period.

§ 414.50 Techniques for application.

(a) The investment base used in computing the cost of money for facilities capital shall be computed from accounting data used for contract cost purposes. The form and instructions stipulated in this Standard shall be used to make the computation.

(b) The cost of money rate for any cost accounting period shall be the arithmetic mean of the interest rates specified by the Secretary of the Treasury pursuant to Pub. L. 92-41 (85 Stat. 97). Where the cost of money must be determined on a prospective basis the cost of money rate shall be based on the most recent available rate published by the Secretary of the Treasury.

(c)(1) A facilities capital cost of money factor shall be determined for each indirect cost pool to which a significant amount of facilities capital has been allocated and which is used to allocate indirect costs to final cost objectives.

(2) The facilities capital cost of money factor for an indirect cost pool shall be determined in accordance with Form CASB-CMF, and its instructions which are set forth in Appendix A. One form will serve for all the indirect cost pools of a business unit.

(3) For each CAS-covered contract, the applicable cost of capital committed to facilities for a given cost accounting period is the sum of the products obtained by multiplying the amount of allocation base units

(such as direct labor hours, or dollars of total cost input) identified with the contract for the cost accounting period by the facilities capital cost of money factor for the corresponding indirect cost pool. In the case of process cost accounting systems the contracting parties may agree to substitute an appropriate statistical measure for the allocation base units identified with the contract.

Computations of Cost of Money and Contract Facilities Capital Employed

CAS 414 is very brief on commentary but extremely and appropriately comprehensive on methodology. An Appendix A contains instructions for completing Form CASB-CMF, used in computing the cost of money factors, and Exhibit B is an example, providing a detailed, step-by-step development of these data.

After the facilities capital cost of money factors are computed, they are applied to the respective contract overhead allocation bases to arrive at the related facilities capital cost of money for each overhead pool. These amounts are added and the total is divided by the applicable facilities capital cost of money rate to arrive at the contract facilities capital employed. These latter computations are shown on DD Form 1861.

The following tables illustrate the computations of the cost of money factors and the contract facilities capital employed:

FORM CASB-CMF

FACILITIES CAPITAL
COST OF MONEY FACTORS COMPUTATION
("Regular" Method)

CONTRACTOR: ABC Corporation
BUSINESS UNIT: A Division
ADDRESS:

COST ACCOUNTING PERIOD: (Historical) Y.E. 12/31/75

	1. APPLICABLE COST OF MONEY RATE 8.0%	2. ACCUMULATION & DIRECT DISTRIBUTION OF N.B.V.	3. ALLOCATION OF UNDISTRIBUTED (BASIS OF ALLOCATION)	4. TOTAL NET BOOK VALUE (COLUMNS 2+3)	5. COST OF MONEY FOR THE COST ACCOUNTING PERIOD (COLUMNS 1X4)	6. ALLOCATION BASE FOR THE PERIOD (IN UNITS OF MEASURE)	7. FACILITIES CAPITAL COST OF MONEY FACTOR (COLUMNS 5÷6)
BUSINESS UNIT FACILITIES CAPITAL — RECORDED		8,270,000					
LEASED PROPERTY							
CORPORATE OR GROUP		450,000					
TOTAL		8,720,000					
UNDISTRIBUTED		3,450,000					
DISTRIBUTED		5,270,000					
OVERHEAD POOLS — Engineering		320,000	756,000	1,076,000	86,080	2,000,000	.04304
Manufacturing		4,500,000	2,250,000	6,750,000	540,000	3,000,000	.18000
Technical Computer			444,000	444,000	35,520	2,280 hr	15.57895
G&A EXPENSE POOLS — G&A Expense		450,000		450,000	36,000	36,700,000	.00098
TOTAL		5,270,000	3,450,000	8,720,000	697,600	////////	////////

CONTRACT FACILITIES CAPITAL and COST OF MONEY				
CONTRACTOR: ABC Corporation BUSINESS UNIT: A Division ADDRESS:			RFP/CONTRACT PIIN NO: PERFORMANCE PERIOD:	
1. OVERHEAD POOLS	2. COST ACCOUNTING PERIOD	3. CONTRACT OVERHEAD ALLOCATION BASE	FACILITIES CAPITAL COST OF MONEY	
			4. FACTORS	5. AMOUNT
Engineering (DL $)		330,000	.04304	14,203
Manufacturing (DL $)		1,210,000	.18000	217,800
Technical Computer (Hrs)		280	15.57895	4,362
G&A (Total Cost Input)		5,369,000	.00098	5,261
6. CONTRACT FACILITIES CAPITAL COST OF MONEY			241,626	
7. FACILITIES CAPITAL COST OF MONEY RATE			÷ .08	
8. CONTRACT FACILITIES CAPITAL EMPLOYED			3,020,325	

DD Form 1861

Circumstances Relating to Publication of CAS 414

Later in this chapter we shall discuss CAS 409, Depreciation of Tangible Capital Assets, and the stormy reception it received from both the private and public sectors, including the criticisms at congressional hearings. In its defense, the CASB, while acknowledging that inflation was eroding industry's profits and that CAS 409 might further hurt contractors' profits and cash flow, nevertheless asserted that its job was to promulgate standards reflecting good cost accounting and that the other problems were up to other governmental agencies.

While maintaining that it was interested only in good cost accounting, the CASB had its staff hard at work on what was ultimately to be CAS 414, which, while useful and necessary for the defense industry, could hardly be defended on the basis of good cost accounting. In addition, the Board and its staff were very busy on what was then slated to be CAS 413, Adjustment of Historical Cost for Inflation. The latter proposal, with little research and virtually no effort to obtain views from industry or governmental agencies, would have provided for an inflation-related adjustment for depreciation computed by using the annual average of the Gross National Product Implicit Price Deflator (GNP Deflator). Assets would be segregated into vintage groups by year of acquisition, and the GNP Deflator would be applied annually to the depreciation expense based on the historical cost for each vintage group.

In May of 1975, DOD emphasized as a major initiative the promulgation of a new profit policy ("Profit '76") to be effective June 30, 1976. The new policy was to create incentive for contractors to invest in cost-cutting machinery, as discussed in greater detail in Chapter XXV of this text. DOD received a commitment from the CASB that a standard on the Cost of Money as an Element of the Cost of Capital would be effective June 30, 1976, to dovetail with the new profit policy. However, as work proceeded on CAS 413 and 414, the Board and its staff encountered difficulties and delays. When word of these delays reached DOD, the Department officials urged the Board to meet its commitment. Whether because of its efforts to complete its work by June 30, 1976, or because of serious changes in its thinking, the CASB not only abandoned the standard on Adjustment of Historical Depreciation Costs for Inflation (the designation CAS 413 was subsequently given to the standard on Adjustment and Allocation of Pension Cost), but also eliminated any consideration of operating capital from CAS 414, retitling the standard as Cost of Money as an Element of the Cost of Facilities Capital. In announcing these decisions in the minutes of its February 1976 meeting, the CASB stated that it had "directed the staff to perform further research on the subject of Cost of Money Applicable to Operating Capital." As nearly as anyone can tell, no real effort in this direction was ever undertaken.

Rushing ahead on the truncated cost-of-money standard, the Board published it in the *Federal Register* within days of its meeting and allowed only 45 instead of the usual 60 days for comment. Despite opposition from OFPP and the civilian agencies, the CASB moved quickly and CAS 414 became effective October 1, 1976.

The problem surfacing in the late stages of this project was the discovery that allowing the cost of facilities capital might increase the cost of acquisition to the Department of Defense by as much as $200 million. Senator Proxmire became aware of this and initiated action with both CASB and DOD. The Board sought to avoid this problem by stating in its prefatory comments, without citing evidence, that: "The procurement agencies are now reconsidering their pricing policies and the Board expects the agencies in doing this to give appropriate recognition to this Standard." DOD, confronted by a direct request by Senator Proxmire to take CAS 414 into account, ultimately published its profit policy with the use of a factor to reduce the weight accorded to costs incurred. Thus some contractors received no benefit at all from CAS 414, although others, with heavy capital investments, did gain by it.

The OFPP, meanwhile, continued to view CAS 414 in a negative fashion and initiated its own profit study. The civilian agencies, without guidance from OFPP, looked to FPR, which ultimately offered five alternatives including the option not to adopt the standard. All elected not to adopt CAS 414. This divided government position continued until OFPP changed its position in its Policy Letter 80-7, effective January 9, 1981, making the imputed cost an allowable cost under contracts subject to the cost principles for commercial organizations. The General Services Administration (GSA) was required to implement this policy directive within 120 days of January 9, 1981, by revisions to the FPR.

GAO Defends CAS 414 from Congressional Criticisms

Some congressional critics of defense procurement policies and practices have alleged over the years that defense contractors were enjoying high profits. Some of these critics have never quite understood the mechanics of CAS 414 and seemed persuaded that this standard permitted contractors duplicate recovery. GAO, usually counted upon to join in any criticisms of DOD and the defense industry, finds itself in a complex position where cost accounting standards are concerned. The feasibility study that led to the enactment of P.L. 91-379 was a GAO product; the CAS Board chairman was the GAO chief; the CASB meetings were held in the GAO executive conference room; the executive secretary and a number of the staff members were former GAO employees; and the first CASB attorney is currently GAO's general counsel.

In connection with the 1984 legislative Appropriations Bill, the Chairman of the Subcommittee on Defense, House Committee on Appropriations, requested GAO to study CAS 414 and DOD's profit policy and to specifically address three issues:

1. Whether CAS 414 has continued relevance in light of current profit policy;

2. Whether DOD's profit policy, that permits the facilities investment value to be used twice in the computation of profit objectives, results in "double-dipping"; and

3. Whether CAS 414, in the context of DOD's profit policy, induces investment in cost-reducing facilities.

In its report dated March 14, 1986, GAO responded to the first two issues. As to whether CAS 414 induces investment in cost-reducing facilities, GAO reported that investment in facilities by defense contractors had increased since 1976 but that it had been unable to determine whether there had been a corresponding increase in productivity.

Most of this report addresses DOD profit policy and for that reason our major review thereof is contained in Chapter XXV of this text, Profit Limitation Under Government Contracts. As to CAS 414, GAO found that the standard had a continuing relevance and did not result in "double-dipping."

GAO reminded Congress that the watchdog agency had always looked favorably on the recognition of investment in arriving at contract profit objectives and that such recognition had, in part, been the objective of DOD's revised policy in 1976 and was made possible by CAS 414. GAO further stated:

> We believe that investment by a contractor should be a major consideration in determining the profit to be negotiated for each contract. CAS 414 is a device used by DOD to identify facilities capital with individual contracts. As such it is an integral part of DOD's profit policy. Therefore, the standard is relevant as a means for measuring the total cost of money associated with investments in facilities and to allocate this cost to individual contracts, and is necessary if investment continues to be a basis for developing profit objectives.

As to the second issue, GAO noted that the use of the facilities capital employed figure twice, once in costs and once on the profit objective, "raises the question of duplicate recovery or double dipping." It further noted, however:

> Using this figure twice does result in duplicate recovery, or profit, based on the same facilities, but for two distinct purposes. However, to prevent an increase in overall profit levels being negotiated at the time the new policy was put into effect, DOD developed an offset factor to reduce the profit objective based on estimated cost.

Most of this report, however, as reviewed in Chapter XXV, focused on criticisms of the DOD profit policy from 1976 to date for its alleged failure to provide a sufficient offset, as a result of which GAO asserted that profit objectives were negotiated at higher rates than they should have been.

CAS 417—Cost of Money as an Element of the Cost of Capital Assets Under Construction

From the time CAS 414 was in the formulation process, the Board was urged to expand the provision for imputed cost to include capital assets under construction. After resisting this recommendation for some time, the CASB finally promulgated the above-captioned standard, effective December 15, 1980, to be followed by each contractor on or after the start of its next cost accounting period beginning after the receipt of a contract to which this standard is applicable.

The Fundamental Requirements and Techniques for Application sections of CAS 417 are quoted below:

§ 417.40 Fundamental requirement.

The cost of money applicable to the investment in tangible and intangible capital assets being constructed, fabricated or developed for a contractor's own use shall be included in the capitalized acquisition cost of such assets.

§ 417.50 Techniques for application.

(a) The cost of money for an asset shall be calculated as follows:

(1) The cost of money rate used shall be based on interest rates determined by the Secretary of the Treasury pursuant to Public Law 92-41 (85 Stat. 97).

(2) A representative investment amount shall be determined each cost accounting period for each capital asset being constructed, fabricated or developed giving appropriate consideration to the rate at which costs of construction are incurred.

(3) Other methods for calculating the cost of money to be capitalized, such as the method used for financial accounting and reporting, may be used, provided the resulting amount does not differ materially from the amount calculated by use of paragraphs (a)(1) and (2), of this section.

(b) If substantially all the activities necessary to get the asset ready for its intended use are discontinued, cost of money shall not be capitalized for the period of discontinuance. However, if such discontinuance arises out of causes beyond the control and without the fault or negligence of the contractor, cessation of cost of money capitalization is not required.

DEPRECIATION

As in the case of Compensation for Personal Services, Depreciation is a complex and controversial contract cost principle, further complicated by CASB promulgations. The standards related to the depreciation cost principle are CAS 404—Capitalization of Tangible Assets and CAS 409—Depreciation of Tangible Capital Assets.

CAS 404—Capitalization of Tangible Assets

The CASB originally contemplated a single standard on depreciation but, after some research, concluded the subject was too broad. It then moved first to CAS 404 to establish criteria for capitalization of tangible assets. The original draft proposed that the costs constructed by the contractor would include all direct and indirect costs, including G&A expenses. This provision drew considerable opposition, and the Board retreated a bit. The final requirement, as set forth in CAS 404.50(b), states: "This requires the capitalization of general and administration expenses when such expenses are identifiable with the constructed asset and are material in amount (e.g., when the in-house construction effort requires planning, supervisory, or other significant effort by officers or other personnel whose salaries are regularly charged to general and administrative expenses). When the constructed assets are identical with or similar to the contractor's regular product, such assets shall be capitalized at amounts which include a full share of indirect costs."

CAS 404 may not win awards for the best treatment of this subject, but it does fairly well conform with GAAP except for its failure to address capitalized leases. This coverage is now provided in FAR 31.205-36.

Although the standard's requirement for capitalization of assets with life exceeding two years and cost exceeding $500 compared favorably with general practices, the dollar threshold came under increasing criticism as high inflation continued. After a considerable number of delays for research and study, the Board finally raised the dollar threshold to $1,000.

The text of the Fundamental Requirements and Techniques for Application sections of CAS 404 is quoted below:

§ 404.40 Fundamental requirement.

(a) The acquisition cost of tangible capital assets shall be capitalized. Capitalization shall be based upon a written policy that is reasonable and consistently applied.

(b) The contractor's policy shall designate economic and physical characteristics for capitalization of tangible assets.

(1) The contractor's policy shall designate a minimum service life criterion, which shall not exceed 2 years, but which may be a shorter period. The policy shall also designate a minimum acquisition cost criterion which shall not exceed $1,000, but which may be a smaller amount.

(2) The contractor's policy may designate other specific characteristics which are pertinent to his capitalization policy decisions (e.g., class of asset, physical size, identifiability and controllability, the extent of integration or independence of constituent units).

(3) The contractor's policy shall provide for identification of asset accountability units to the maximum extent practical.

(4) The contractor's policy may designate higher minimum dollar limitations for original complement of low cost equipment and for betterments and improvements than the limitation established in accordance with paragraph (b) (1) of this section, provided such higher limitations are reasonable in the contractor's circumstances.

(c) Tangible assets shall be capitalized when both of the criteria in the contractor's policy as required in paragraph (b) (1) of this section are met, except that assets described in paragraph (b) (4) of this section shall be capitalized in accordance with the criteria established in accordance with that paragraph.

(d) Costs incurred subsequent to the acquisition of a tangible capital asset which result in extending the life or increasing the productivity of that asset (e.g., betterments and improvements) and which meet the contractor's established criteria for capitalization shall be capitalized with appropriate accounting for replaced asset accountability units. However, costs incurred for repairs and maintenance to a tangible capital asset which either restore the asset to, or maintain it at, its normal or expected service life or production capacity shall be treated as costs of the current period.

§ 404.50 Techniques for application.

(a) The cost to acquire a tangible capital asset includes the purchase price of the asset and costs necessary to prepare the asset for use.

(1) The purchase price of an asset shall be adjusted to the extent practical by premiums and extra charges paid or discounts and credits received which properly reflect an adjustment in the purchase price.

(i) Purchase price is the consideration given in exchange for an asset and is determined by cash paid, or to the extent payment is not made in cash, in an amount equivalent to what would be the cash price basis. Where this amount is not available, the purchase price is determined by the current value of the consideration given in exchange for the asset. For example, current value for a credit instrument is the amount immediately required to settle the obligation or the amount of money which might have been raised directly through the use of the same instrument employed in making the credit purchase. The current value of an equity security is its market value. Market value is the current or prevailing price of the security as indicated by recent market quotations. If such values are unavailable or not appropriate (thin market, volatile price movement, etc.), an acceptable alternative is the fair value of the asset acquired.

(ii) Donated assets which, at the time of receipt, meet the contractor's criteria for capitalization shall be capitalized at their fair value at that time.

(2) Costs necessary to prepare the asset for use include the cost of placing the asset in location and bringing the asset to a condition necessary for normal or expected use. Where material in amount, such costs, including initial inspection and testing, installation and similar expenses, shall be capitalized.

(b) Tangible capital assets constructed or fabricated by a contractor for its own use shall be capitalized at amounts which include all indirect costs properly allocable to such assets. This requires the capitalization of general and administrative expenses when such expenses are identifiable with the constructed asset and are material in amount (e.g., when the in-house construction effort requires planning, supervisory, or other significant effort by officers or other personnel whose salaries are regularly charged to general and administrative expenses). When the constructed assets are identical with or similar to the contractor's regular product, such assets shall be capitalized at amounts which include a full share of indirect costs.

(c) In circumstances where the acquisition by purchase or donation of previously used tangible capital assets is not an arm's length transaction, acquisition cost shall be limited to the capitalized cost of the asset to the owner who last acquired the asset through an arm's-length transaction, reduced by depreciation charges from date of that acquisition to date of gift or sale.

(d) Under the "purchase method" of accounting for business combinations, acquired tangible capital assets shall be assigned a portion of the cost of the acquired company, not to exceed their fair value at date of acquisition. Where the fair value of identifiable acquired assets less liabilities assumed exceeds the purchase price of the acquired company in an acquisition under the "purchase method," the value otherwise assignable to tangible capital assets shall be reduced by a proportionate part of the excess.

(e) Under the "pooling of interest method" of accounting for business combinations, the values established for tangible capital assets for financial accounting shall be the values used for determining the cost of such assets.

(f) Asset accountability units shall be identified and separately capitalized at the time the assets are acquired. However, whether or not the contractor identifies and separately capitalizes a unit initially, the contractor shall remove the unit from the asset accounts when it is disposed of and, if replaced, its replacement shall be capitalized.

CAS 409—Depreciation of Tangible Capital Assets

While the reactions to CAS 404 were relatively mild, CAS 409 proved to be the most controversial standard issued to that time. Industry even mobilized, albeit too late, an organized protest to the Congress, and hearings were held.

A new proposal, considerably modified in some respects as compared with the more severe provisions of the earlier draft, did depart from the status quo. The prefatory comments plunged into the thick of the battle very early in expressing the view that "[c]ontractors often select depreciation lives and methods for contract costing purposes based on what is permitted by (income tax) regulations rather than on bases which are representative of the consumption of the service potential of the tangible capital asset." Having raised this basic issue early, the Board followed with the flat statement that "[i]n these circumstances many choices have resulted in unduly accelerating allocation of depreciation cost to earlier cost accounting periods and to final cost objectives within those earlier cost accounting periods."

Some of the essence of the standard is summarized in the following excerpt from the prefatory comments:

> The proposed Standard would establish the principle that for contract costing purposes the service lives established for tangible capital assets be the expected actual service lives at the date of acquisition. Accordingly, the proposed Standard would require that the service lives used shall be the estimates used for financial accounting purposes unless financial accounting lives are unrealistic, in which case the proposed Standard would require that more realistic estimated service lives be used. The proposed Standard also would require that the method of depreciation used for contract costing purposes approximate the expected consumption of asset services in each cost accounting period. The method of depreciation used for financial accounting purposes is satisfactory if reasonable in the circumstances.

The proposed standard included an Appendix A, which was derived from the IRS RP 71-25, Asset Guidelines Periods. These periods, under the proposed standard, would establish lower limits for estimated service lives that may be used for contract costing purposes "where contractors' accounting records do not support shorter lives."

As noted earlier, the provisions of this proposed standard reflected some movement from the more severe requirements of the earlier drafts. There remained, however, certain requirements that, predictably, were opposed by many of the associations and individuals who submitted comments to the Board.

For example, there was the insistence that estimated service lives for assets shall be their expected actual periods of usefulness and in no case shorter than the IRS asset guideline periods. The contractor desiring to use shorter estimated service lives was required to present support for such lives by records of past retirement or replacement experience. As to methods of depreciation, some of the earlier drafts made the use of any method other than the straight line almost impossible. Although the rigidity of the requirement was somewhat alleviated, the proposed standard continued the preference for the straight line method. The contractor's method must "reflect the expected consumption of services for the tangible capital asset. . . ." The standard recognized that an accelerated method might be acceptable, but only "where the consumption of asset services is significantly greater in early years of asset life."

Many of the objections to the prior versions of proposed standards on depreciation were reiterated. One of the basic points articulated by most industry associations (and incidentally agreed to by top DOD procurement officials) was that there was no need for a cost accounting standard on depreciation. For many years, this subject had been largely in the province of the Internal Revenue Service, which offered a rather wide range of options, particularly regarding methods to be used. The complexity of this subject, regarding lives and methods, and the controversies surrounding it, led the Department of Defense to substantially adopt the IRS ground rules so long as the amount does not exceed that used for book and statement purposes. Except for this reservation, DOD had not considered it useful to embark upon all of the research, investigation, and controversy that would necessarily be required if the Department were to consider issuing independent guidelines on depreciation. Many in industry had found the ASPR provisions reasonable, and if they did not find them so before, they certainly discovered them to be reasonable upon reading the proposed cost accounting standard.

Another major consideration offered in opposition to any standard that would restrict industry from depreciating fixed assets using lives as short as possible and methods as accelerated as possible was the matter of national policy. The CASB was accused of failing to recognize that national interests of technological development, defense, and overall economic progress are fostered and investments encouraged by permitting rapid writeoffs.

There was considerable concern generated by the earlier drafts, which required contractors to demonstrate support for and document the use of just about any method other than straight line. Some of the major problems were that such documentation was just not available, the record keeping is not otherwise needed by management, and this requirement would impose unnecessary financial burdens. The same arguments were made with respect to the final version.

Introduced into the debate on computing service lives was the point that it is inappropriate to compute the useful life of a tangible capital asset from the date of acquisition to the date of disposition. The industry Board member and other industry representatives emphasized that the real period of usefulness ends when these assets cease being in active use and are retained only for standby or incidental use (a consideration not addressed by ASPR).

The Board accepted this point, and CAS 409.50(e) was revised to state that "the estimate of the expected actual periods of usefulness need not include the additional period tangible capital assets are retained for standby or incidental use. . . ." But, to avoid including the standby period in the estimated useful life, this provision, which immediately follows the one quoted above, states that contractors may only do so "where adequate records are maintained which reflect the withdrawal from active use."

The CASB's recognition that the periods of usefulness of capital assets do not end when they are transferred from actual to standby use did not satisfy industry. The prefatory comments asserted that most contractors have records from which they could determine asset retention periods even though further analyses would be necessary. However, industry commentators were almost unanimous in contending that they did not have records reflecting the transfer of assets from active to standby use. Furthermore, industry generally contended that it would be very costly to develop such records.

The Board moved in three directions to address this point. The maintenance of records showing the transfer of assets from active to inactive use was made optional. This' provision could hardly be expected to evoke a warm reception because a contractor exercising its option not to maintain such records would be required to use a service life from date of acquisition to date of disposal.

In a more significant provision on this point, the Board sought to ease the pains of defense contractors by providing for a two-year period for the development of analyses of historical asset lives. In the prefatory comments, the Board expressed the opinion that the two-year period should provide adequate working time to develop such analyses.

The record keeping, analyses, etc., constituted one of the major sources of irritation and complaint on the part of industry. In the prefatory comments and in one of the illustrations, the Board suggested the use of sampling techniques to arrive at reasonable estimates, thus obviating the need for extensive record keeping for all of the capital assets.

The Board also provided for a temporary alternate procedure for estimating service lives. As stated in CAS 409.50(e)(4), for assets where the contractor has no available data or prior experience, the contractor may estimate service lives "based on a projection of the expected actual period of usefulness, but shall not be less than asset guideline periods (mid-range) established for asset guideline classes under the Revenue Procedure 72-10. . . ."

And finally, in this area, the Board recognized that there may be government-industry disagreements relating to the appropriate adjustments to be made. Here the Board encouraged the procurement agencies to provide written guidance for its field personnel. The Board offered the services of its staff to help.

Protests and criticisms related to CAS 409 continued, emanating from industry, DOD, and even within the CASB where one of the members of the Board wrote a very strong and lengthy dissent to the final promulgation. Critics of the standard appeared before the CASB on several occasions to present their views and, even after the standard became effective on March 25, 1979, the attacks continued, culminating in congressional hearings. These and other problems generated by CAS 409 have remained to plague both industry and DOD and have been aggravated by DCAA's periodic efforts to insist on overzealous strict application and by GAO's attacks on any effort to accommodate the provisions of this standard to the defense interest of this country.

The requirement to use the long lives to compute depreciation for contract costing and pricing purposes has always seemed illogical to many observers. To provide incentive for modernization of plant and equipment, some countries permit writing off the total capital expenditures in the years they are made. Even in this country, tax laws have increasingly recognized the need for such an incentive by significantly liberalizing the ground rules for selecting service lives for income tax purposes. CAS 409 stands alone, in the United States and indeed in the world, in illogically requiring companies to use the longer service lives for computing depreciation.

In an effort to find a solution to the problems caused by the disincentives for capital investment contained in this standard, DOD appointed an ad hoc committee to perform a study and submit suggestions.

A major consideration in the ad hoc committee's deliberations was the DOD Industrial Modernization Incentive Program (IMIP). One of the Carlucci (former Deputy Secretary of Defense) initiatives, IMIP was designed to improve the defense industrial base and to provide incentives for contractor capital investment. The committee noted that "IMIP inherently recognizes the use of economic technical useful service lives and is not limited to historical service lives." Its further studies concluded that the IMIP objectives could be achieved within the provisions of the standard by better use of CAS 409.50(e)(5), quoted below:

> The contracting parties may agree on the estimated service life of individual tangible capital assets where the unique purpose for which the equipment was acquired or other special circumstances warrant a shorter estimated service life than the life determined in accordance with the other provisions of this § 409.50(e) where the shorter life can be reasonably predicted.

Based on the committee report, the following letter was sent by the Under Secretary of Defense, Research & Engineering, December 20, 1982, to the Military Departments, DCAA, and DLA.

SUBJECT: Encouraging Capital Investment Within Cost Accounting Standard 409—Depreciation of Tangible Capital Assets

Encouraging contractor capital investment to enhance productivity is of vital importance to DOD, and policies that further that goal must be actively pursued. Cost Accounting Standard (CAS) 409 has been widely criticized as being counter to DOD policies which promote increased contractor productivity. We have reassessed CAS 409 and find that it may be administered in a manner which is consistent with our need to improve contractor productivity.

The Standard provides the latitude under CAS 409.50(e)(5) to enter into advance agreements with contractors on shorter depreciation periods for certain assets than would otherwise be determined by application of the standard. These shorter periods may be based on expected useful economic or technical lives. This allows the depreciation period for qualifying assets to match more closely their expected period of usefulness and thereby reduce contractors' investment risk. Such agreement supports DOD Acquisition Improvement Program Initiative Number 5, "Encouraging Capital Investment to Enhance Productivity."

All DOD components are encouraged to pursue the advance agreement flexibility within CAS 409, along with other programs now being implemented to provide incentives for industrial modernization.

Some of the committee's deliberations, as set forth in its report, are in consonance with the views of certain contractors whose contracts require the use of a significant amount of capital assets. These contractors have concluded that their interest in optimum cost recovery is better served by foregoing the use of any kind of accelerated depreciation or shorter lives because the allowance for cost of money under CAS 414, particularly in periods of high Treasury interest rates, provides a higher recovery than they would obtain by faster write-offs of the assets. Shorter depreciation lives result in higher depreciation charges, which reduce the net book value of the assets. Since the net book value is the basis for calculating cost of money, recovery under this allowance is reduced.

It has long been recognized that the advantages and disadvantages of shorter depreciation lives will vary with contractors and will depend on the extent of capital assets used. Providing a method for shorter depreciation periods is essential, according to the committee, mainly ". . . because it mitigates the contractor's concern with the stability of the government market to which the particular asset is directed.

The efforts of the Department of Defense to "live with" CAS 409 and at the same time mitigate the adverse impact of this standard on industry incentive to invest in new, more effective, cost-reducing plant and equipment were received with heavy hostility by GAO and certain congressional critics. One Senate and two House committees conducted hearings during 1983 in which representatives of the General Accounting Office and the DOD IG criticized the Defense Department efforts and predicted that their implementation would result in substantial additional costs to the government.

The congressional and other protests were futile, and, the sixty-day requirement having already elapsed, CAS 409 was in effect. The text of the Fundamental Requirements and Techniques for Application sections of the final version of the standard is cited below:

§ 409.40 Fundamental Requirement.

(a) The depreciable cost of a tangible capital asset (or group of assets) shall be assigned to cost accounting periods in accordance with the following criteria:

(1) The depreciable cost of a tangible capital asset shall be its capitalized cost less its estimated residual value.

(2) The estimated service life of a tangible capital asset (or group of assets) shall be used to determine the cost accounting periods to which the depreciable cost will be assigned.

(3) The method of depreciation selected for assigning the depreciable cost of a tangible capital asset (or group of assets) to the cost accounting periods representing its estimated service life shall reflect the pattern of consumption of services over the life of the asset.

(4) The gain or loss which is recognized upon disposition of a tangible capital asset shall be assigned to the cost accounting period in which the disposition occurs.

(b) The annual depreciation cost of a tangible capital asset (or group of assets) shall be allocated to cost objectives for which it provides service in accordance with the following criteria:

(1) Depreciation cost may be charged directly to cost objectives only if such charges are made on the basis of usage and only if depreciation costs of all like assets used for similar purposes are charged in the same manner.

(2) Where tangible capital assets are part of, or function as, an organizational unit whose costs are charged to other cost objectives based on measurement of the services provided by the organizational unit, the depreciation cost of such assets shall be included as part of the cost of the organizational unit.

(3) Depreciation costs which are not allocated in accordance with (b) (1) or (2) above shall be included in appropriate indirect cost pools.

(4) The gain or loss which is recognized upon disposition of a tangible capital asset, where material in amount, shall be allocated in the same manner as the depreciation cost of the asset has been or would have been allocated for the cost accounting period in which the disposition occurs. Where such gain or loss is not material, the amount may be included in an appropriate indirect cost pool.

§ 409.50 Techniques for application.

(a) Determination of the appropriate depreciation charges involves estimates both of service life and of the likely pattern of consumption of services in the cost accounting periods included in such life. In selecting service life estimates and in selecting depreciation methods many of the same physical and economic factors should be considered. The following are among the factors which may be taken into account: quantity and quality of expected output, and the timing thereof; costs of repair and maintenance, and the timing thereof; standby or incidental use and the timing thereof; and technical or economic obsolescence of the asset (or group of assets), or of the product or service it is involved in producing.

(b) Depreciation of a tangible capital asset shall begin when the asset and any others on which its effective use depends are ready for use in a normal or acceptable fashion. However, where partial utilization of a tangible capital asset is identified with a specific operation, depreciation shall commence on any portion of the asset which is substantially completed and used for that operation. Depreciable spare parts which are required for the operation of such tangible capital assets shall be accounted for over the service life of the assets.

(c) A consistent policy shall be followed in determining the depreciable cost to be assigned to the beginning and ending cost accounting periods of asset use. The policy may provide for any reasonable starting and ending dates in computing the first and last year depreciable cost.

(d) Tangible capital assets may be accounted for by treating each individual asset as an accounting unit, or by combining two or more assets as a single accounting unit, provided such treatment is consistently applied over the service life of the asset or group of assets.

(e) Estimated service lives initially established for tangible capital assets (or groups of assets) shall be reasonable approximations of their expected actual periods of usefulness, considering the factors mentioned in paragraph (a) of this section. The estimate of the expected actual periods of usefulness need not include the additional period tangible capital assets are retained for standby or incidental use where adequate records are maintained which reflect the withdrawal from active use.

(1) The expected actual periods of usefulness shall be those periods which are supported by records of either past retirement or, where available, withdrawal from active use (and retention for standby or incidental use) for like assets (or groups of assets) used in similar circumstances appropriately modified for specifically identified factors expected to influence future lives. The factors which can be used to modify past experience include:

(i) Changes in expected physical usefulness from that which has been experienced such as changes in the quantity and quality of expected output.

(ii) Changes in expected economic usefulness, such as changes in expected technical or economic obsolescence of the asset (or group of assets), or of the product or service produced.

(2) Supporting records shall be maintained which are adequate to show the age at retirement or, if the contractor so chooses, at withdrawal from active use (and retention for standby or incidental use) for a sample of assets for each significant category. Whether assets are accounted for individually or by groups, the basis for estimating service life shall be predicated on supporting records of experienced lives for either individual assets or any reasonable grouping of assets as long as that basis is consistently used. The burden shall be on the contractor to justify estimated service lives which are shorter than such experienced lives.

(3) The records required in paragraph (e)(1) and (2) of this section, if not available on the date when the requirements of this Standard must first be followed by a contractor, shall be developed from current and historical fixed asset records and be available following the second fiscal year after that date. They shall be used as a basis for estimates of service lives of tangible capital assets acquired thereafter. Estimated service lives used for financial accounting purposes (or other accounting purposes where depreciation is not recorded for financial accounting purposes for some non-commercial organizations), if not unreasonable under the criteria specified in paragraph (e) of this section, shall be used until adequate supporting records are available.

(4) Estimated service lives for tangible capital assets for which the contractor has no available data or no prior experience for similar assets shall be established based on a projection of the expected actual period of usefulness, but shall not be less than asset guideline periods (mid-range) established for asset guideline classes under the Revenue Procedure 72—10 published by the Internal Revenue Service, and any additions, supplements or revisions thereto, which are in effect as of the first day of the cost accounting period in which the assets are acquired. Use of this alternative procedure shall cease as soon as the contractor is able to develop estimates which are appropriately supported by his own experience.

(5) The contracting parties may agree on the estimated service life of individual tangible capital assets where the unique purpose for which the equipment was acquired or other special circumstances warrant a shorter estimated service life than the life determined in accordance with the other provisions of this § 409.50(e) and where the shorter life can be reasonably predicted.

(f)(1) The method of depreciation used for financial accounting purposes (or other accounting purposes where depreciation is not recorded for financial accounting purposes) shall be used for contract costing unless (i) such method does not reasonably reflect the expected consumption of services for the tangible capital asset (or group of assets) to which applied, or (ii) the method is unacceptable for Federal income tax purposes. If the contractor's method of depreciation used for financial accounting purposes (or other accounting purposes as provided above) does not reasonably reflect the expected consumption of services or is unacceptable for Federal income tax purposes, he shall establish a method of depreciation for contract costing which meets these criteria, in accordance with paragraph (f)(3) of this section.

(2) After the date of initial applicability of this Standard, selection of methods of depreciation for newly acquired tangible capital assets, which are different from the methods currently being used for like assets in similar circumstances, shall be supported by projections of the expected consumption of services of those assets (or groups of assets) to which the different methods of depreciation shall apply. Support in accordance with paragraph (f)(3) of this section shall be based on the expected consumption of services of either individual assets or any

reasonable grouping of assets as long as the basis selected for grouping assets is consistently used.

(3) The expected consumption of asset services over the estimated service life of a tangible capital asset (or group of assets) is influenced by the factors mentioned in paragraph (a) of this section which affect either potential activity or potential output of the asset (or group of assets). These factors may be measured by the expected activity or the expected physical output of the assets, as for example: Hours of operation, number of operations performed, number of units produced, or number of miles traveled. An acceptable surrogate for expected activity or output might be a monetary measure of that activity or output generated by use of tangible capital assets, such as estimated labor dollars, total cost incurred or total revenues, to the extent that such monetary measures can reasonably be related to the usage of specific tangible capital assets (or groups of assets). In the absence of reliable data for the measurement or estimation of the consumption of asset services by the techniques mentioned, the expected consumption of services may be represented by the passage of time. The appropriate method of depreciation should be selected as follows:

(i) An accelerated method of depreciation is appropriate where the expected consumption of asset services is significantly greater in early years of asset life.

(ii) The straight-line method of depreciation is appropriate where the expected consumption of asset services is reasonably level over the service life of the asset (or group of assets).

(g) The estimated service life and method of depreciation to be used for an original complement of low-cost equipment shall be based on the expected consumption of services over the expected useful life of the complement as a whole and shall not be based on the individual items which form the complement.

(h) Estimated residual values shall be determined for all tangible capital assets (or groups of assets). For tangible personal property, only estimated residual values which exceed ten percent of the capitalized cost of the asset (or group of assets) need be used in establishing depreciable costs. Where either the declining balance method of depreciation or the class life asset depreciation range system is used consistent with the provisions of this Standard, the residual value need not be deducted from capitalized cost to determine depreciable costs. No depreciation cost shall be charged which would significantly reduce book value of a tangible capital asset (or group of assets) below its residual value.

(i) Estimates of service life, consumption of services, and residual value shall be reexamined for tangible capital assets (or groups of assets) whenever circumstances change significantly. Where changes are made to the estimated service life, residual value, or method of depreciation during the life of a tangible capital asset, the remaining depreciable costs for cost accounting purposes shall be limited to the undepreciated cost of the assets and shall be assigned only to the cost accounting period in which the change is made and to subsequent periods.

(j)(1) Gains and losses on disposition of tangible capital assets shall be considered as adjustments of depreciation costs previously recognized and shall be assigned to the cost accounting period in which disposition occurs except as provided in paragraphs (j)(2) and (3) of this section. The gain or loss for each asset disposed of is the difference between the net amount realized, including insurance proceeds in the event of involuntary conversion, and its undepreciated balance. However, the gain to be recognized for contract costing purposes shall be limited to the difference between the original acquisition cost of the asset and its undepreciated balance.

(2) Gains and losses on the disposition of tangible capital assets shall not be recognized where: (i) Assets are grouped and such gains and losses are processed through the accumulated depreciation account, or, (ii) the asset is given in exchange as part of the purchase price of a similar asset and the gain or loss is included in computing the depreciable cost of the new asset. Where the disposition results from an involuntary conversion and the asset is replaced by a similar asset, gains and losses may either be recognized in the period of disposition or used to adjust the depreciable cost base of the new asset.

(3) The contracting parties may account for gains and losses arising from mass or extraordinary dispositions in a manner which will result in treatment equitable to all parties.

(4) Gains and losses on disposition of tangible capital assets transferred in other than an arms-length transaction and subsequently disposed of within 12 months from the date of transfer shall be assigned to the transferor.

(k) Where, in accordance with § 409.40 (b)(1), the depreciation costs of like tangible capital assets used for similar purposes are directly charged to cost objectives on the basis of usage, average charging rates based on cost shall be established for the use of such assets. Any variances between total depreciation cost charged to cost objectives and total depreciation cost for the cost accounting period shall be accounted for in accordance with the contractor's established practice for handling such variances.

(l) Practices for determining depreciation methods, estimated service lives and estimated residual values need not be changed for assets acquired prior to compliance with this Standard if otherwise acceptable under applicable procurement regulations. However, if changes are effected such changes must conform to the criteria established in this Standard and may be effected on a prospective basis to cover the undepreciated balance of cost by agreement between the contracting parties pursuant to negotiation under (a)(4)(B) or (C) of the Contract Clause set out at § 331.50 of the Board's regulations (4 CFR 331.50).

CAS 409 was born in controversy and still lives in controversy. The bookkeeping and related requirements are onerous and costly. A more deleterious problem is the requirement for longer periods to depreciate assets, which has resulted in a disincentive for contractors to invest in new cost-reducing facilities and equipment.

The current FAR text is cited below:

31.205-11 Depreciation.

(a) Depreciation is a charge to current operations which distributes the cost of a tangible capital asset, less estimated residual value, over the estimated useful life of the asset in a systematic and logical manner. It does not involve a process of valuation. Useful life refers to the prospective period of economic usefulness in a particular contractor's operations as distinguished from physical life; it is evidenced by the actual or estimated retirement and replacement practice of the contractor.

(b) Contractors having contracts subject to CAS 409, Depreciation of Tangible Capital Assets, must adhere to the requirement of that standard for all fully CAS-covered contracts and may elect to adopt the standard for all other contracts. All requirements of CAS 409 are applicable if the election is made, and its requirements supersede any conflicting requirements of this cost principle. Once electing to adopt CAS 409 for all contracts, contractors must continue to follow it until notification of final acceptance of all deliverable items on all open negotiated Government contracts. Paragraphs (c) through (e) below apply to contracts to which CAS 409 is not applied.

(c) Normal depreciation on a contractor's plant, equipment, and other capital facilities is an allowable contract cost, if the contractor is able to demonstrate that it is reasonable and allocable (but see paragraph (i) below).

(d) Depreciation shall be considered reasonable if the contractor follows policies and procedures that are—

(1) Consistent with those followed in the same cost center for business other than Government;

(2) Reflected in the contractor's books of accounts and financial statements; and

(3) Both used and acceptable for Federal income tax purposes.

(e) When the depreciation reflected on a contractor's books of accounts and financial statements differs from that used and acceptable for Federal income tax purposes, reimbursement shall be based on the asset cost amortized over the estimated useful life of the property using depreciation methods (straight line, sum of the years' digits, etc.) acceptable for income tax purposes. Allowable depreciation shall not exceed the amounts used for book and statement purposes and shall be determined in a manner consistent with the depreciation policies and procedures followed in the same cost center on non-Government business.

(f) Depreciation for reimbursement purposes in the case of tax-exempt organizations shall be determined on the basis described in paragraph (e) immediately above.

(g) Special considerations are required for assets acquired before the effective date of this cost principle if, on that date, the undepreciated balance of these assets resulting from depreciation policies and procedures used previously for Government contracts and subcontracts is different from the undepreciated balance on the books and financial statements. The undepreciated balance for contract cost purposes shall be depreciated over the remaining life using the methods and lives followed for book purposes. The aggregate depreciation of any asset allowable after the effective date of this 31.205-11 shall not exceed the cost basis of the asset less any depreciation allowed or allowable under prior acquisition regulations.

(h) Depreciation should usually be allocated to the contract and other work as an indirect cost. The amount of depreciation allowed in any accounting period may, consistent with the basic objectives in paragraph (a) above, vary with volume of production or use of multishift operations.

(i) In the case of emergency facilities covered by certificates of necessity, a contractor may elect to use normal depreciation without requesting a determination of "true depreciation," or may elect to use either normal or "true depreciation" after a determination of "true depreciation" has been made by an Emergency Facilities Depreciation Board (EFDB). The method elected must be followed consistently throughout the life of the emergency facility. When an election is made to use normal depreciation, the criteria in paragraphs (c), (d), (e), and (f) above shall apply for both the emergency period and the post-emergency period. When an election is made to use "true depreciation", the amount allowable as depreciation—

(1) With respect to the emergency period (five years), shall be computed in accordance with the determination of the EFDB and allocated rateably over the full five year emergency period; *provided* no other allowance is made which would duplicate the factors, such as extraordinary obsolescence, covered by the Board's determination; and

(2) After the end of the emergency period, shall be computed by distributing the remaining undepreciated portion of the cost of the emergency facility over the balance of its useful life provided the remaining undepreciated portion of such cost shall not include any amount of unrecovered "true depreciation."

(j) No depreciation, rental, or use charge shall be allowed on property acquired at no cost from the Government by the contractor or by any division, subsidiary, or affiliate of the contractor under common control.

(k) The depreciation on any item which meets the criteria for allowance at a "price" under 31.205-26(e) may be based on that price, provided the same policies and procedures are used for costing all business of the using division, subsidiary, or organization under common control.

(l) No depreciation or rental shall be allowed on property fully depreciated by the contractor or by any division, subsidiary, or affiliate of the contractor under common control. However, a reasonable charge for using fully depreciated property may be agreed upon and allowed (but see 31.109(h)(2)). In determining the charge, consideration shall be given to cost, total estimated useful life at the time of negotiations, effect of any increased maintenance charges or decreased efficiency due to age, and the amount of depreciation previously charged to Government contracts or subcontracts.

(m) CAS 404, Capitalization of Tangible Assets, applies to assets acquired by a "capital lease" as defined in Statement of Financial Accounting Standard No. 13 (FAS-13), Accounting for Leases, issued by the Financing Accounting Standards Board (FASB). Compliance with CAS 404 and FAS-13 requires that such leased assets (capital leases) be treated as purchased assets; i.e., be capitalized and the capitalized value of such assets be distributed over their useful lives as depreciation charges, or over the leased life as amortization charges as appropriate. Assets whose leases are classified as capital leases under FAS-13 are subject to the requirements of 31.205-11 while assets acquired under leases classified as operating leases are subject to the requirements on rental costs in 31.205-36. The standards of financial accounting and reporting prescribed by FAS-13 are incorporated into this principle and shall govern its application, except as provided in subparagraphs (1), (2), and (3) below.

(1) Rental costs under a sales and leaseback arrangement shall be allowable up to the amount that would have been allowed had the contractor retained title to the property.

(2) Capital leases, as defined in FAS-13, for all real and personal property, between any related parties are subject to the requirements of this subparagraph 31.205-11(m). If it is determined that the terms of the lease have been significantly affected by the fact that the lessee and lessor are related, depreciation charges shall not be allowed in excess of those which would have occurred if the lease contained terms consistent with those found in a lease between unrelated parties.

(3) Assets acquired under leases that the contractor must capitalize under FAS-13 shall not be treated as purchased assets for contract purposes if the leases are covered by 31.205-(b)(4).

ECONOMIC PLANNING COSTS

About two decades ago, as United States military expenditures began to rise, farsighted people with long memories began to accord increasing thought and attention to the need for reconversion planning—reconversion from defense to commercial business. Even at that time, at least for some, the need for economic planning assumed serious implications. Although industry in general experienced a surge of increasing military expenditures, many individual companies suffered as specific weapons systems were canceled or substantially reduced. In more recent years, of course, the subject of economic planning has assumed proportions of the gravest significance to many industrial segments in aerospace and elsewhere.

The entire subject of conversion and reconversion in regard to government contracts also includes a number of controversial cost problems. At one extreme, there is a school of thought (fortunately a very small one today) that holds that the government is required to pay only and specifically for the goods or services contracted for and that the contractor is responsible for any engaging or disengaging costs. This school not only applauds the disallowance of reconversion costs but also would like to disallow the costs of converting to government contracts. At the other extreme, there are those who believe firmly that the transitory and uncertain characteristics of government contracts require, in equity, that the government reimburse the contractor for all conversion or get-ready costs, then leave the contractor whole by reimbursing it for all costs necessary to place the firm back in position for commercial work.

Prior to the issuance of the 1959 comprehensive contract cost principles, defense procurement regulations were not very specific on this subject. As a matter of practice, conversion costs were generally allowed, but these matters were preferably treated as advance agreements to obviate subsequent controversies. Reconversion costs were generally not reimbursable.

As explained later in this chapter, the current cost principles formalized this practice, but the provisions now tend to be somewhat flexible. FAR 31.205-31 describes plant reconversion costs as "those incurred in the restoration or rehabilitation of the contractor's facilities to approximately the same condition existing immediately prior to commencement of the Government contract, fair wear and tear excepted." Such costs, says FAR, "are unallowable except for the cost of removing Government property and the restoration or rehabilitation costs caused by such removal." Strict adherence to this principle is recognized as being potentially inequitable under certain circumstances. Accordingly, FAR provides a degree of flexibility: "However, in special circumstances where equity so dictates, additional costs may be allowed to the extent agreed upon before the costs are incurred."

Early in 1964, DOD initially incorporated a provision into the ASPR contract cost principles to recognize the propriety, as a matter of fact, the wisdom, of economic planning. With minor modifications, this principle was set forth in DAR and is now incorporated in FAR.

31.205-12 Economic planning costs.

(a) This category includes costs of generalized long-range management planning that is concerned with the future overall development of the contractor's business and that may take into account the eventual possibility of economic dislocations or fundamental alterations in those markets in which the contractor currently does business. Economic planning costs do not include organization or reorganization costs covered by 31.205-27.

(b) Economic planning costs are allowable as indirect costs to be properly allocated.

(c) Research and development and engineering costs designed to lead to new products for sale to the general public are not allowable under this principle.

EMPLOYEE MORALE, HEALTH, WELFARE, FOOD SERVICE, DORMITORY COSTS AND CREDITS.

The text of FAR 31.205-13 is set forth below:

(a) Aggregate costs incurred on activities designed to improve working conditions, employer-employee relations, employee morale, and employee performance (less income generated by these activities) are allowable, except as limited by paragraph (b) immediately below, and to the extent that the net amount is reasonable. Some examples are house publications, health clinics, recreation, employee counseling services, and food and dormitory services, which include operating or furnishing facilities for cafeterias, dining rooms, canteens, lunch wagons, vending machines, living accommodations, or similar types of services for the contractor's employees at or near the contractor's facilities.

(b) Losses from operating food and dormitory services may be included as costs only if the contractor's objective is to operate such services on a break-even basis. Losses sustained because food services or lodging accommodations are furnished without charge or at prices or rates which would not be conducive to the accomplishment of the above objective are not allowable. A loss may be allowed, however, to the extent that the contractor can demonstrate that unusual circumstances exist (e.g., (1) Where the contractor must provide food or dormitory services at remote locations where adequate commercial facilities are not reasonably available, or (2) where charged but unproductive labor costs would be excessive but for the services provided or where cessation or reduction of food or dormitory operations will not otherwise yield net cost savings) such that even with efficient management, operating the services on a break-even basis would require charging inordinately high prices or prices, or rates higher than those charged by commercial establishments offering the same services in the same geographical areas. Costs of food and dormitory services shall include an allocable share of indirect expenses pertaining to these activities.

(c) When the contractor has an arrangement authorizing an employee association to provide or operate a service, such as vending machines in the contractor's plant, and retain the profits, such profits shall be treated in the same manner as if the contractor were providing the service (but see paragraph (d) immediately below).

(d) Contributions by the contractor to an employee organization, including funds from vending machine receipts or similar sources, may be included as costs incurred under paragraph (a) above only to the extent that the contractor demonstrates that an equivalent amount of the costs incurred by the employee organization would be allowable if directly incurred by the contractor.

These costs and credits, although not described in such comprehensive terms prior to 1959, were generally allowed in practice. To that extent, there was no change in the allowability of these items until 1965. Until then, the specific provisions of the cost principles were as follows:

Reasonable costs of health and welfare activities, such as house publication, health or first-aid clinics, recreational activities, and employee counseling services, incurred, in accordance with the contractor's established practice or custom in the industry or area, for the improvement of working conditions, employer-employee relations, employee morale, and employee performance, are allowable. Income generated from any of these activities shall be credited to the costs thereof unless such income has been irrevocably set over to employee welfare organizations.

The current lengthy and imposing title was also the caption for paragraph 15-205.10 of DAR and represents the current contract cost principles for these expenses unchanged since December 1965, except for extensive editorial changes reflected in FAR and the minor "clarification" in (b)(2).

Elsewhere in this text, we comment upon the congressional hearings before the Porter Hardy Committee, resulting from a GAO investigation into practices by defense contractors relative to these expenditures. The General Accounting Office asserted that there was a complete absence of uniformity among DOD contracting officers and auditors as to the basis for determining the reasonableness and allowability of employee expenses. The problems involved the nature of the expenses. Further, there were such specific problems as the treatment of losses from contractor-operated food and dormitory activities and the treatment of income from vending machines, etc., particularly when such income was turned over to the control of employee associations.

The current FAR provision states that all of the expenses included in the title, less income generated by such activities, are allowable if the net amount is reasonable, subject to certain limitations. One of the limitations relates to losses from operations of food and dormitory services. These losses shall be considered allowable "only if the contractor's objective is to operate such services on a break-even basis." In arriving at what the contractor's objective may be, government contracting officers and auditors must bear in mind that the "costs of food and dormitory services shall include an allocable share of indirect expenses pertaining to these activities." This provision establishes certain built-in difficulties in interpreting the term "break-even" and even greater problems in determining on an after-the-fact basis whether or not the contractor's objective was, in fact, to break even.

The requirement to allocate indirect expenses to such operations produces many additional complications. Many restaurants prepare sales and cost budgets based on the use of facilities for three meals per day, whereas plant restaurants and cafeterias must be geared to only one or sometimes two meals per day. In these circumstances, an allocation of indirect expenses on a strict mathematical-accounting basis would seldom yield equitable or meaningful data.

FAR 31.205-13(d) seems to be a rather roundabout way of saying that the government will be taking a hard look at the manner in which the employee association spends the funds it has thus received from the contractor. If the nature of the expenditures made by the employee association would have been considered allowable had they been made by the contractor, all is well; otherwise, the presumption is that it would be disallowed. Industry has objected to this provision on the grounds that the employer cannot be held responsible for the precise manner in which employee organizations dispose of the funds. Industry feels that, once it has given a reasonable amount of money to an employee association, pursuant to agreements between the two parties, the cost should be allowed without potential limitations based on the ultimate expenditures.

ENTERTAINMENT COSTS

The basis for exclusion of entertainment expenses in the instances of research and supply contracts with commercial organizations has been commented upon previously in this book. It was noted that entertainment of commercial customers is deemed applicable solely to commercial business and hence not related to performance of government contracts.

Entertainment of government personnel, of course, is contrary to public policy. It is that type of charge particularly to which armed services take exception. However, carrying the principle to what appears an unwarranted extreme, government auditors have at times disallowed everything designated as such, even if the expense represents picking up a lunch check for a supplier of critical materials. Inasmuch as such expenses are seldom sufficient to result in a substantial difference in contract cost calculations, little has been done to clarify the principle involved.

In one case, the Armed Services Board of Contract Appeals rejected a contracting officer's action in disallowing an entire account because it was captioned "entertainment." The board examined the contractor's details of the account, found that about one-half the expenditures were for "the cost of meals of other employees when paid by one employee while they were away from their office on the contractor's business," and allowed that portion. *Gar Wood Industries, Inc.,* 1956, ASBCA 2327-2330, 6 CCF par. 61,869.

FAR 31.205-14 provided that "[c]osts of amusement, diversion, social activities, and any directly associated costs such as tickets to shows or sports events, meals, lodging, rentals, transportation, and gratuities are unallowable (but see 31.205-13 and 31.205-43)."

Pursuant to P.L. 99-145 (see Chapter XVI of this text), the following was added to this cost principle: "Costs of membership in social, dining, or country clubs or other organizations having the same purposes are also unallowable, regardless of whether the cost is reported as taxable income to the employees." Also, the parenthetical references to other cost principles were changed to "31.205-1 and 31.205-13."

The appeal of *Lulejian and Associates,* ASBCA No. 20094, 76-1 BCA par. 11,880, included a dispute involving entertainment costs. Woven into this controversy were also recruitment costs and trade, business, technical, and professional activity costs.

The following is quoted from the decision:

> In the "Travel," "Recruitment" and "Professional Services" accounts the auditors questioned some costs incurred for meals on the ground they constituted unallowable "entertainment costs" under ASPR 15-205.11 . . . .
>
> *　*　*　*
>
> According to respondent's witness, the disallowed charges included lunches or dinners with appellant's attorney, accountant or consultants,

lunches at which business propositions reportedly were discussed, employee's share of a local lunch or dinner with a prospective recruit, and the unreasonable portion of any lunch or dinner expense of a person interviewed for a position or of an employee while in travel status. A lunch expense of $5.00 and a dinner expense of $10.00 were considered reasonable by the auditor in view of the government's $20 per diem at that time . . . .

In the opinion of appellant's expert witness meals associated with recruitment and business were not social activities but truly business expense. Their cost was deducted by appellant as business expense on Federal income tax returns.

No other evidence was introduced by either party regarding prices for lunches and dinners in localities where the charges were incurred, whether employees in travel status took their meals at hotels where they stayed or at some other place, or whether the charges included alcoholic refreshments. Appellant did not place in evidence either the company's internal instructions or other policy statements covering employee's travel expenses.

However, in a number of unsolicited proposals which later resulted in contract awards, appellant included the estimated cost of meals while an employee was on travel from California to Washington, DC, at a rate of $28.00 for a trip that included a 2-night stay at the destination. The number of meals was not shown but it would not be unreasonable to assume that the amount included was to cover at least 4-5 meals, including one dinner.

Although the amounts involved in this category were very small, the board's rulings are a matter of considerable concern.

The government relied heavily on ASPR 15-205.11, Entertainment Costs, and 15-205.43(c), Meetings and Conferences. The contractor's expert witness argued that these costs were not indicative of social activities, as alleged by the government, but represented business expense of the kind deductible for federal income tax purposes.

The board first disposed of the argument concerning the deductibility of the expenses for tax purposes: "Whether or not the IRS has recognized certain costs as deductible business expense for Federal income tax purpose is not necessarily determinative of their allowability under government cost-reimbursement type contracts where such costs fail to satisfy the ASPR allowability or reasonableness criteria."

The position taken by the board was to be expected and is not a cause of alarm. What does cause concern is the ruling that the cost of meals at business meetings was unallowable. These are the comments of the board:

We agree with respondent that lunches and dinners at which company officials, while not on travel, discussed business matters including new business ventures with business associates are rather "social activities" than business meetings within the meaning of ASPR 15-205.43. That the wife of the vice-president attended one of these dinners further emphasizes its social aspect. Cf. *Manuel M. Liodas, Trustee in Bankruptcy for*

Argus Industries, ASBCA No. 12829, 71-2 BCA par. 9015. Cost of such meals is properly excludable from the indirect expense pool. We place in the same category dinners and lunches at which appellant's executives met with attorneys to discuss company legal matters. These meetings were obviously scheduled in this manner for the convenience of the participants. The cost of these meals is disallowed. On the other hand, the cost of the dinner meeting of appellant's directors, in these circumstances is properly allowable as "other business expense" under ASPR 15-205.24.

In our opinion, the board evidenced either unfamiliarity with or disregard for sound, generally accepted and widely followed business practices. We would acknowledge that the costs of some lunches and dinners that find their way into corporate books of account are tinged with what might be described as social activities. On the other hand, it is widely accepted that very serious business matters are discussed over a lunch or dinner and significant business decisions made in those circumstances. We hope the board will ultimately recognize the facts of life and that the decision in this case will not become a precedent.

Similar issues were raised in connection with costs of luncheons and dinners relating to recruitment. Some of the expenses disallowed related to luncheons and dinners attended by the contractor's executives and wives and applicants and wives when out-of-town. Here the board ruled:

With respect to recruiting costs ASPR 15-205.33 provides in pertinent part:

"(a) (CWAS) Subject to (b), (c), and (d) below, and *provided* that the size of the staff recruited and maintained is in keeping with workload requirements, ... *travel costs of employees* while engaged in recruiting personnel, *travel costs of applicants* for interviews for prospective employment ... are allowable to the extent that such costs are incurred pursuant to a well managed recruitment program ..." (Italics added.)

Subparagraphs (b), (c) and (d) are not pertinent to matters under consideration.

Since allowable travel costs for both employees and applicants include cost of meals (ASPR 15-205.46), disallowance of these costs for appellant's executives while on travel in connection with recruitment and for out-of-town applicants was improper, provided they were reasonable. This criteria will be discussed below. Appellant's entitlement to reimbursement for cost of meals of its employees who treat prospective employees to lunches or dinners at company's expense at the location of their employment would depend on whether the meal was primarily for purposes of socializing, thus constituting an unallowable cost of social activity under ASPR 15-205.11, or was an integral part of the interviewing process. Obviously, the line between the two types of activities is vague and we would look to appellant to make a showing that socializing was not the primary purpose, especially where wives of appellant's executives were present. On this record we are not persuaded that the meals in question were of the type justifying the Government's sharing in their cost. Hence, the cost of the meals of the wives and local company employees is properly disallowed. There is no objection to including in the indirect expense pool the reasonable cost of meals of the prospective employees being interviewed.

FINES AND PENALTIES

FAR 31.205-15 provides that "costs of fines and penalties resulting from violations of, or failure of the contractor to comply with, Federal, State, or local laws and regulations, are unallowable except when incurred as a result of compliance with *specific* terms and conditions of the contract or *written* instructions from the *contracting* officer." Emphasis is added to call attention to the key words. Among the recent changes to the contract cost principles, the words "or foreign" were inserted after "local."

GAINS AND LOSSES ON DISPOSITION OF DEPRECIABLE PROPERTY OR OTHER CAPITAL ASSETS

The provisions of FAR 31.205-16 are quoted below:

(a) Gains and losses from the sale, retirement, or other disposition (but see 31.205-19) of depreciable property shall be included in the year in which they occur as credits or charges to the cost grouping(s) in which the depreciation or amortization applicable to those assets was included (but see paragraph (d) below).

(b) Gains and losses on disposition of tangible capital assets, including those acquired under capital leases (see 31.205-11(m)), shall be considered as adjustments of depreciation costs previously recognized. The gain or loss for each asset disposed of is the difference between the net amount realized, including insurance proceeds from involuntary conversions, and its undepreciated balance. The gain recognized for contract costing purposes shall be limited to the difference between the acquisition cost (or for assets acquired under a capital lease, the value at which the leased asset is capitalized) of the asset and its undepreciated balance (except see subdivisions (c)(2)(i) or (ii) below).

(c) Special considerations apply to an involuntary conversion which occurs when a contractor's property is destroyed by events over which the owner has no control, such as fire, windstorm, flood, accident, theft, etc., and an insurance award is recovered. The following govern involuntary conversions:

(1) When there is a cash award and the converted asset is not replaced, gain or loss shall be recognized in the period of disposition. The gain recognized for contract costing purposes shall be limited to the difference between the acquisition cost of the asset and its undepreciated balance.

(2) When the converted asset is replaced, the contractor shall either—

(i) Adjust the depreciable basis of the new asset by the amount of the total realized gain or loss; or

(ii) Recognize the gain or loss in the period of disposition, in which case the Government shall participate to the same extent as outlined in subparagraph (c)(1) above.

(d) Gains and losses on the disposition of depreciable property shall not be recognized as a separate charge or credit when—

(1) Gains and losses are processed through the depreciation reserve account and reflected in the depreciation allowable under 31.205-11; or

(2) The property is exchanged as part of the purchase price of a similar item, and the gain or loss is taken into consideration in the depreciation cost basis of the new item.

(e) Gains and losses arising from mass or extraordinary sales, retirements, or other disposition shall be considered on a case-by-case basis.

(f) Gains and losses of any nature arising from the sale or exchange of capital assets other than depreciable property shall be excluded in computing contract costs.

From time to time, a government procurement regulation sets forth a really new principle, a policy that represents a departure from the past. An illustration of a new or substantially different contract cost principle was reflected in Paragraph 15-205.32, incorporated into ASPR by Revision No. 4 dated August 29, 1969. For the first time, gains and losses on disposition of certain capital assets affected the costs of performing DOD contracts.

To indicate the extent to which that revision represented a departure from prior policies, we can go back to the "Green Book," published in April 1942, which included among inadmissible costs "losses from sales or exchanges of capital assets." Similarly, the original contract cost principles of 1949 included the following among examples of unallowable costs: "Losses from sales or exchanges of capital assets, including investments."

Moving to the more current regulations, immediately before the afore-mentioned Revision No. 4, ASPR 15-205.32 provided: "Profits or losses of any nature arising from the sale or exchange of plant, equipment, or other capital assets, including sale or exchange of either short or long term investments, shall be excluded in computing contract costs. . . ."

The origins of the move towards this major policy change are traceable in part to the increasing liberalization of depreciation regulations issued by the Internal Revenue Service. Over the years, elements within the Defense Department became concerned that the accelerated methods and short lives permitted by the IRS resulted in increasing profits when the capital assets were sold or otherwise disposed of. It was concluded that this matter was of greater consequence to the Defense Department since the contract cost principles, unlike the income tax regulations, contained no provision for reflecting the effects of profits and losses on these transactions. Certain studies made within the Defense Department intended to support the position of those who had been alleging that contractors' use of IRS depreciation provisions ultimately resulted in many more profits than losses upon sales or exchanges.

The first version of the ASPR provision relating to gains and losses was forwarded for coordination in the summer of 1967.

One of the major controversies involved the issue of depreciation recapture versus total gains recognition. Under the depreciation recapture concept, the gain on disposal to be recognized is limited to the total depreciation charged during those years in which government contracts have participated in such charges. The alternative concept would recognize all gains regardless of their origin on the reasoning that all losses would be recognized.

In May 1968, a revised version of the contract cost principles involving gains and losses on the disposition of depreciable property was sent out for coordination. One of the major changes established the government position as being in favor of requiring recognition of total rather than partial gains and losses.

Industry objected to the proposed revision in concept. For example, CODSIA stated that the proposed cost principle would be inappropriate because (1) it was unlikely there would be any relationship between the contracts that originally received the depreciation charges and those subsequently credited or charged with gains or losses on disposition and (2) DOD's sharing in gains and losses would make it a quasi-partner and bring about further intrusion into contractors' management decisions, etc. Objections were also raised to the considerable clerical effort that would be involved in implementing this procedure. On the apparent premise that some regulation in this area was forthcoming, industry submitted a number of suggestions that it hoped would be adopted if DOD persisted in its course.

DOD did persist in its course and adopted just a few industry suggestions. However, before the new ASPR 15-205.32 was formally issued in August 1969, some changes in principle were made, most important of which was the shift back from the total gain recognition to the depreciation recapture concept.

A major change in the DAR, which governed prior to FAR, limited the measurement of gains for contracting cost purposes to the difference between the acquisition cost of the asset and its undepreciated amount. This provision conforms to CAS 409.50(j)(1). It also provides the government with assurance against paying more than the contractor charged as depreciation while at the same time preventing the government from sharing in gains that the contractor may have derived from appreciation of the asset. No substantive changes were made in FAR.

IDLE FACILITIES AND IDLE CAPACITY COST

The notion that certain facilities are idle and excess to a contractor's needs, and hence unallowable, has been a source of controversy over many years. A number of the controversies have ended in disputes which required decisions by the Armed Services Board of Contract Appeals.

As initially promulgated in November 1959, the ASPR Contract Cost Principle provided: "Costs of maintaining, repairing, and housing idle and excess contractor-owned facilities, except those reasonably necessary for standby purposes, are unallowable. Any costs of excess plant capacity reserved for mobilization production which are to be paid for by the Government should be the subject of a separate contract."

The government-industry arguments centered on such questions as: When and under what circumstances is a facility idle or excess? How is a determination made that idle facilities are needed for standby purposes? There were, as might be expected, some rather extreme views expressed on both sides. Some overzealous contracting officers and auditors were difficult to convince that contractors cannot operate at a theoretical full capacity, and these government people sometimes tended to question costs of any facilities idle at a given point in time. On the other hand, there are those in industry who have contended that the retention or disposal of idle facilities is a management determination, based on various short-range and long-range considerations, and should not be challenged by the government.

As mentioned previously, this divergence of views led to controversies, some of which could not be worked out, that became subjects of unilateral determinations by contracting officers and ultimate appeals to the ASBCA. Three decisions by the board in this area are commented upon below.

AVCO Corporation, ASBCA No. 10858, 66-1 BCA par. 5360

The contractor appealed from a disallowance of manufacturing burden based on the government's contention that the costs involved were attributable to excess plant capacity. The governing ASPR provision then applicable held that "[c]osts of maintaining, repairing, and housing idle and excess contractor-owned facilities, except those reasonably necessary for standby purposes, are unallowable."

The contractor argued that the space referred to as excess represented only 13% of its total capacity. The resulting 87% operating rate was compared favorably to a 60% to 70% range that the contractor contended was normal for most organizations.

The government stated that the excess or idle space could not be considered as reasonably necessary for standby or potential expansion purposes. It pointed out that the particular space involved was not used but rented out to another firm during its peak year. Considering this fact and the point that the contractor's sales volume had since declined and future declines were forecast, the government concluded that the space must be considered excess and hence the related costs unallowable under the provisions of ASPR 15-205.12.

The board appeared to have little difficulty in deciding to deny the appeal. The pertinent portion of its decision is quoted below:

> We think the Government has made a prima facie case that the building space to which the disapproved costs apply was an idle and excess facility within the meaning of the regulation. It was idle and there is no showing that it constituted any part of the contractor's current operational requirements. While appellant has offered no evidence to support its contention that the normal operating rate for most organizations is somewhere in the 60% to 70% range, it is common enough knowledge to be officially noticed that many, if not most, firms do not operate at 100% capacity. But we do not think that helps appellant's case. In our view, the regulation is addressed to that very problem. It says to us that the Government will not bear a share of the costs of that excess capacity unless it is reasonably necessary for standby purposes. It

is not enough to say that a firm's operations are within a normal range, or are at an even higher than normal rate, at least in the absence of evidence that the only economic factor governing that range is a reasonable standby requirement.

Cook Electric Company, ASBCA No. 11100, 66-2 BCA par. 6039

The contractor's division involved in this appeal suffered a decline in its business for fiscal year 1964, which, according to the government, resulted in excess and idle facilities. The contractor argued against the government's position in total and also contested specific government estimates of the extent of excess and idle facilities in the various buildings. The text of the board's decision does not present a clear and comprehensive insight into the bases for its various determinations. However, we summarize some parts of this decision as an aid to government contractors and as information regarding the board's thinking.

There were several buildings involved, and in each case the Air Force auditor estimated the idle portions based on his visual observations. According to the decision, there appeared to be no precise measurements submitted by either party.

The auditor estimated that 25% of Building No. 1 was idle, on the basis that a portion of the building contained a drawing board section with desks that were not regularly occupied and never fully used during the year. The contractor admitted that some space may have been occupied by unused desks, but claimed that it was all occupied. In making his final determination, the contracting officer determined that a reasonable position was to reduce the auditor's estimate by one-half, and he determined that Building No. 1 was $12\frac{1}{2}\%$ idle. In its deliberations, the board concluded that there was some unused space and, lacking specific measurements and "in the absence of any other criterion," declared itself "satisfied that the contracting officer made a reasonable allowance." It accordingly found that Building No. 1 was $12\frac{1}{2}\%$ idle.

The government estimated that 20% of Building No. 2 was idle. The contractor contended that this idle area contained various items of machinery and tools for making models. The board was satisfied that this area was used off and on during the year although at a reduced rate. It reasoned, however, that "this usage of space and equipment is ancillary to the appellant's principal operations. It is not continuous, but the facilities must be maintained ready for use in order to allow the uninterrupted operation of the plant." On this basis, the board ruled for the contractor and found that there was no idle excess space in Building No. 2.

The auditor estimated that 75% of Building No. 4 was idle, but here again, the contracting officer reduced the estimate by one-half and determined that $37\frac{1}{2}\%$ of the building was idle. From the testimony presented, the board concluded that there was unused space and equipment, but found no basis for a precise determination. After weighing the various evidence presented, the board found that the contracting officer's $37\frac{1}{2}\%$ was reasonable.

The government contended that 15% of Building No. 5 was idle. The building consisted of test laboratories, all of which were apparently used, but at a reduced rate. Here the board found for the contractor on the following reasoning: "This is another instance where facilities must be maintained, even though they are not continuously used. In research and development work, and the manufacture of prototypes a certain amount of test work is required."

The government contended that 25% of Building No. 6 was idle. The decision does not explain the basis on which the 25% was estimated. However, from the information contained in the decision, it does appear that the building contained a carpenters' shop, residual inventories, an old wind tunnel not used during the year, a chemical laboratory, and various pieces of equipment. In ruling for the contractor the board stated: "We are furthermore, not convinced that there was any idle and excess space and equipment in Building No. 6. A plant of this size requires space for storage of maintenance equipment and other currently unused large machinery, whether it is mobile or permanently set up. The chemical laboratory was an integral part of the plant. The old wind tunnel may have outlived its usefulness, but it does not appear to have been a material item in relation to plant space and equipment, and we see no reason to disturb the judgment of the company management as to when to dispose of it."

The old ASPR Committee, predecessor to the DAR Council, worked for years on a cost principle governing the cost of idle facilities and idle capacity, and a substantive revision was published in February 1967. Although subjected to criticisms from both the private and public sectors, this cost principle has stood the test of time and governed DOD contracts prior to the promulgation of FAR, which effected editorial revisions but made no substantive change:

31.205-17 Idle facilities and idle capacity costs.

(a) "Costs of idle facilities or idle capacity," as used in this subsection, means costs such as maintenance, repair, housing, rent, and other related costs; e.g., property taxes, insurance, and depreciation.

"Facilities," as used in this subsection, means plant or any portion thereof (including land integral to the operation), equipment, individually or collectively, or any other tangible capital asset, wherever located, and whether owned or leased by the contractor.

"Idle capacity," as used in this subsection, means the unused capacity of partially used facilities. It is the difference between that which a facility could achieve under 100 percent operating time on a one-shift basis, less operating interruptions resulting from time lost for repairs, setups, unsatisfactory materials, and other normal delays, and the extent to which the facility was actually used to meet demands during the accounting period. A multiple-shift basis may be used in the calculation instead of a one-shift basis if it can be shown that this amount of usage could normally be expected for the type of facility involved.

"Idle facilities," as used in this subsection, means completely unused facilities that are excess to the contractor's current needs.

(b) The costs of idle facilities are unallowable unless the facilities—

(1) Are necessary to meet fluctuations in workload; or

(2) Were necessary when acquired and are now idle because of changes in requirements, production economies, reorganization, termination, or other causes which could not have been reasonably foreseen. (Costs of idle facilities are allowable for a reasonable period, ordinarily not to exceed 1 year, depending upon the initiative taken to use, lease, or dispose of the idle facilities (but see 31.205-42)).

(c) Costs of idle capacity are costs of doing business and are a factor in the normal fluctuations of usage or overhead rates from period to period. Such costs are allowable provided the capacity is necessary or was originally reasonable and is not subject to reduction or elimination by subletting, renting, or sale, in accordance with sound business, economics, or security practices. Widespread idle capacity throughout an entire plant or among a group of assets having substantially the same function may be idle facilities.

(d) Any costs to be paid directly by the Government for idle facilities or idle capacity reserved for defense mobilization production shall be the subject of a separate agreement.

Analyzing the current cost principle, we find that "idle facilities" are defined as "completely unused facilities that are excess to the contractor's current needs." This category of facilities shall be allowed when "necessary to meet fluctuations in workload" or where it is established that "they were necessary when acquired and are now idle because of changes in program requirements, contractor efforts to produce more economically, reorganization, termination, or other causes which could not have been reasonably foreseen." In the latter categories, FAR limits the allowability of costs of idle facilities "for a reasonable period of time, ordinarily not to exceed one year, depending upon the initiative taken to use, lease, or dispose of such facilities. . . ."

An insight in judicial thinking in this area is found in ASBCA. No. 12292, 68-2 BCA par. 7081, in the appeal of Stanley Aviation. The government had attempted to disallow significant amounts of indirect costs on various contentions, most of them involving the fact that the contractor had lost considerable business, as a result of which its overhead rates on the remaining government contracts were significantly higher than its previous experience. Many points were involved in this case, but we limit our discussion here to those relating to idle facilities. And here we cite an analysis of the board's conclusion as reflected in one of our monthly newsletters.

Another Government argument suggested that "The sharp increase in overhead rates during the period of low level operations . . . reflected the cost of excess and idle plant facilities." The board hit hard at this argument. It noted that ASPR 15-205.12, while making the costs of certain idle facilities unallowable, made a specific exception where facilities "were necessary when acquired and are now idle because of changes in program requirements . . . termination, or other causes which could not have been reasonably foreseen." In these circumstances, the cost of idle facilities may be allowed for a period of up to one year "depending upon the initiative taken to use, lease, or dispose." The board found that both the circumstances which the contractor experienced and the contractor's "extraordinary diligence and initiative in leasing and disposing of the facilities . . ." clearly precluded a basis for disallowance on the basis of ASPR 15-205.12.

Although it apparently had thus rejected this contention by the Government, the board devoted additional attention to the argument of idle facilities and appeared to be lecturing the Government officials on what to do and what not to do in ascertaining the existence of idle facilities or idle capacity. "The proper way for applying the standard of reasonableness to appellant's overhead costs," said the board, "is to examine them on an item by item basis and exclude from the allowable overhead pools the specific overhead cost items or parts of items found to be unreasonable under the prevailing circumstances." In the board's opinion, the Government had made no real attempt to establish "whether appellant in fact had idle capacity." The board also pointed up that "the Government has not cited a single instance of where appellant had idle facilities or capacity which it failed to dispose of within a reasonable time . . . (and) The Government has not cited a single cost item in the overhead pools as having been incurred unnecessarily or in a larger amount than was necessary under the circumstances." Quite the contrary, the board found that the contractor ". . . did everything it possibly could to eliminate and reduce overhead costs."

Another interesting decision by the Armed Services Board of Contract Appeals is set forth in ASBCA Nos. 12126, 12127, and 12128.

The contractor here involved had been operating substantially on government work, and its business fell drastically around the end of its fiscal year, ending September 1964. In arriving at overhead rates for the fiscal year ending September 30, 1965, the government industrial engineer and auditor concluded that the contractor's plant was used only to the extent of about 40%. Accordingly, it was recommended to the contracting officer that only about 40% of the rental expense be allowed and the balance eliminated as excess idle facilities. In his testimony, the contracting officer explained that he had raised the amount to 50% of the rental cost "in the interest of settling out these contracts."

The contractor's appeal included various objections to methods and calculations employed by the government's engineer and audit personnel.

A review of the board's decision suggests that the contractor fared better than anticipated or argued. While the contractor contested the various calculations by the government representatives, the ASBCA concluded that the government had not presented sufficient support to sustain any reduction of rent payments.

The contractor testified, and the board accepted the assertion "that some work was going on in the plant of a production nature during the period here involved." From this point, the board apparently felt that the burden was upon the government to prove the existence of idle facilities within the framework of the ASPR provisions. The board did not believe that the government had sustained this burden:

> There is no showing either way of the approximate minimum space necessary to carry on this production. There is no indication whatsoever

of what other facilities might have been available to appellant to carry on this production or what might have been its ability, or the cost to it, to be released from the balance of the leasehold period. The lease apparently had been renewed in 1964 for a 3-year period. The Government does not assert that this renewal was then unreasonable in view of the then present and anticipated workload or that the facilities were not then necessary (see ASPR 15-205.12(b)(ii)).

Although conceding that "the United States is not obliged to pay a contractor to maintain excess plant facilities," the board nevertheless sustained the appeal in these words:

> However, in view of the language and intent of the cited ASPR paragraph in the time period here involved in relation to . . . previous operations, sales, and workload, something more than is present in this record is necessary to support the reduction for purposes of their inclusion in an overhead pool for allocation on an otherwise proper basis to Government contracts of rent payments actually made.

INDEPENDENT RESEARCH AND DEVELOPMENT AND BID AND PROPOSAL COSTS

The contract cost principles for IR&D and B&P (FAR 31.205-18) and the related CAS 420 are reviewed in Chapter XIV of this text.

INSURANCE AND INDEMNIFICATION

The contract cost principles for insurance and indemnification have been revised extensively over the years, most recently to reflect the provisions of CAS 416—Accounting for Insurance Costs. The current text of FAR 31.205-19 is cited below:

> (a) Insurance by purchase or by self-insuring includes coverage the contractor is required to carry, or to have approved, under the terms of the contract and any other coverage the contractor maintains in connection with the general conduct of its business. Any contractor desiring to establish a program of self-insurance applicable to contracts that are not subject to CAS 416, Accounting for Insurance Costs, shall comply with the self-insurance requirements of that standard as well as with Part 28 of this Regulation. However, approval of a contractor's insurance program in accordance with Part 28 does not constitute a determination as to the allowability of the program's cost. The amount of insurance costs which may be allowed is subject to the cost limitations and exclusions in the following subparagraphs.

> (1) Costs of insurance required or approved, and maintained by the contractor pursuant to the contract, are allowable.

> (2) Costs of insurance maintained by the contractor in connection with the general conduct of its business are allowable, subject to the following limitations:

> (i) Types and extent of coverage shall follow sound business practice, and the rates and premiums must be reasonable.

(ii) Costs allowed for business interruption or other similar insurance must be limited to exclude coverage of profit.

(iii) The cost of property insurance premiums for insurance coverage in excess of the acquisition cost of the insured assets is allowable only when the contractor has a formal written policy assuring that in the event the insured property is involuntarily converted, the new asset shall be valued at the book value of the replaced asset plus or minus adjustments for differences between insurance proceeds and actual replacement cost. If the contractor does not have such a formal written policy, the cost of premiums for insurance coverage in excess of the acquisition cost of the insured asset is unallowable.

(iv) Costs of insurance for the risk of loss of or damage to Government property are allowable only to the extent that the contractor is liable for such loss or damage and such insurance does not cover loss or damage that results from willful misconduct or lack of good faith on the part of any of the contractor's directors or officers or other equivalent representatives.

(v) Contractors operating under a program of self-insurance must obtain approval of the program when required by 28.308(a).

(vi) Costs of insurance on the lives of officers, partners, or proprietors are allowable only to the extent that the insurance represents additional compensation (see 31.205-6).

(3) Actual losses are unallowable unless expressly provided for in the contract, except—

(i) Losses incurred under the nominal deductible provisions of purchased insurance, in keeping with sound business practice, are allowable for contracts not subject to CAS 416 and when the contractor did not establish a self-insurance program. Such contracts are not subject to the self-insurance requirements of CAS 416. For contracts subject to CAS 416, and for those made subject to the self-insurance requirements of that Standard as a result of the contractor's having established a self-insurance program (see paragraph (a) above), actual losses may be used as a basis for charges under a self-insurance program when the actual amount of losses will not differ significantly from the projected average losses for the accounting period (see 4 CFR 416.50(a)(2)(ii)). In those instances where an actual loss has occurred and the present value of the liability is determined under the provisions of CAS 416.50(a)(3)(ii), the allowable cost shall be limited to an amount computed using as a discount rate the interest rate determined by the Secretary of the Treasury pursuant to 50 U.S.C. App. 1215(b)(2) in effect at the time the loss is recognized. However, the full amount of a lump-sum settlement to be paid within a year of the date of settlement is allowable.

(ii) Minor losses, such as spoilage, breakage, and disappearance of small hand tools that occur in the ordinary course of doing business and that are not covered by insurance are allowable.

(4) The cost of insurance to protect the contractor against the costs of correcting its own defects in materials or workmanship is unallowable.

However, insurance costs to cover fortuitous or casualty losses resulting from defects in materials or workmanship are allowable as a normal business expense.

(5) Premiums for retroactive or backdated insurance written to cover occurred and known losses are unallowable.

(b) If purchased insurance is available, the charge for any self-insurance coverage plus insurance administration expenses shall not exceed the cost of comparable purchased insurance plus associated insurance administration expenses.

(c) Insurance provided by captive insurers (insurers owned by or under the control of the contractor) is considered self-insurance, and charges for it must comply with the self-insurance provisions of CAS 416. However, if the captive insurer also sells insurance to the general public in substantial quantities and it can be demonstrated that the charge to the contractor is based on competitive market forces, the insurance will be considered purchased insurance.

(d) The allowability of premiums for insurance purchased from fronting insurance companies (insurance companies not related to the contractor but who reinsure with a captive insurer of the contractor) shall not exceed the amount (plus reasonable fronting company charges for services rendered) which the contractor would have been allowed had it insured directly with the captive insurer.

(e) Self-insurance charges for risks of catastrophic losses are not allowable (see 28.308(e)).

(f) The Government is obligated to indemnify the contractor only to the extent authorized by law, as expressly provided for in the contract, except as provided in paragraph (a)(3) above.

(g) Late premium payment charges related to employee deferred compensation plan insurance incurred pursuant to Section 4007 (29 U.S.C. 1307) or Section 4023 (29 U.S.C. 1323) of the Employee Retirement Income Security Act of 1974 are unallowable.

CAS 416—Accounting for Insurance Costs

In the two years or more in which the CASB and its staff were developing this standard, one of the most frequently asked questions was why the Board was devoting its time to this subject. In the prefatory comments to CAS 416, the CASB alleged that it initiated research on accounting for insurance costs because of differences between ASPR and the CASB on self-insurance, disputes relating to insurance accounting and "knowledge of unresolved problems obtained by discussions with contractors and audit agencies." These kinds of reasons could justify a standard on just about any and every cost.

In addition to the wide consensus that the imposition of additional governmental regulations was not needed by searching out costs like insurance, the strongest opposition was voiced to the treatment of self-insurance, which, some commentators suggested, indicated that the CASB did not really understand the nature of self-insurance. Despite the protests, the standard was promulgated and its Fundamental Requirements and Techniques for Application are quoted below:

§ 416.40 Fundamental requirement.

(a) The amount of insurance cost to be assigned to a cost accounting period is the projected average loss for that period plus insurance administration expenses in that period.

(b) The allocation of insurance costs to cost objectives shall be based on the beneficial or causal relationship between the insurance costs and the benefiting or causing cost objectives.

§ 416.50 Techniques for application.

(a) Measurement of projected average loss.

(1) For exposure to risk of loss which is covered by the purchase of insurance or by payments to a trusteed fund, the premium or payment, adjusted in accordance with the following criteria, shall represent the projected average loss:

(i) The premium cost applicable to a given policy term shall be assigned pro rata among the cost accounting periods covered by the policy term, except as provided in subparagraphs (ii) through (vi) of this paragraph. A refund, dividend or additional assessment shall become an adjustment to the pro rata premium costs for the earliest cost accounting period in which the refund or dividend is actually or constructively received or in which the additional assessment is payable.

(ii) Where insurance is purchased specifically for, and directly allocated to, a single final cost objective, the premium need not be prorated among cost accounting periods.

(iii) Any part of a premium or payment to an insurer or trustee, or any part of a dividend or premium refund retained by an insurer or trustee which would be includable as a desposit in published financial statements prepared in accordance with generally accepted accounting principles shall be accounted for as a deposit for the purpose of determining insurance costs.

(iv) Any part of a premium or payment to an insurer or to a trustee, or any part of a dividend or premium refund retained by an insurer, for inclusion in a reserve or fund established and maintained on behalf of the insured or the policyholder or trustor, shall be accounted for as a deposit unless the following conditions are met: (A) The objectives of the reserve or fund are clearly stated in writing;

(B) Measurement of the amount required for the reserve or fund is actuarially determined and is consistent with the objectives of the reserve or fund;

(C) Payments and additions to the reserve or fund are made in a systematic and consistent manner; and

(D) If payments to accomplish the stated objectives of the reserve or fund are made from a source other than the reserve or fund, the payments into the reserve or fund are reduced accordingly.

(v) If an objective of an insurance program is to prefund insurance coverage on retired persons, then, in addition to the requirements imposed by subparagraph (iv) of this paragraph:

(A) Payments must be made to an insurer or trustee to establish and maintain a fund or reserve for that purpose;

(B) The policyholder or trustor must have no right of recapture of the reserve or fund so long as any active or retired participant in the program remains alive unless the interests of such remaining participants are satisfied through adequate reinsurance or otherwise; and

(C) The amount added to the reserve or fund in any cost accounting period must not be greater than an amount which would be required to apportion the cost of the insurance coverage fairly over the working lives of the active employees in the plan. If a contractor establishes a terminal-funded plan for retired persons or converts from a pay-as-you-go plan to a terminal-funded plan, the actuarial present value of benefits applicable to employees already retired shall be amortized over a period of 15 years.

(vi) The contractor may adopt and consistently follow a practice of determining insurance costs based on the estimated premium and assessments net of estimated refunds and dividends. If this practice is adopted, then any difference between an estimated and actual refund, dividend, or assessment shall become an adjustment to the pro rata net premium costs for the earliest cost accounting period in which the refund or dividend is actually or constructively received or in which the additional assessment is payable.

(2) For exposure to risk of loss which is not covered by the purchase of insurance or by payments to a trusteed fund, the contractor shall follow a program of self-insurance accounting according to the following criteria:

(i) Except as provided in paragraph (a)(2) (ii) and (iii) of this section actual losses shall not become a part of insurance costs. Instead, the contractor shall make a self-insurance charge for each period for each type of self-insured risk which shall represent the projected average loss for that period. If insurance could be purchased against the self-insured risk, the cost of such insurance may be used as an estimate of the projected average loss; if this method is used, the self-insurance charge plus insurance administration expenses may be equal to, but shall not exceed, the cost of comparable purchased insurance plus the associated insurance administration expenses. However, the contractor's actual loss experience shall be evaluated regularly, and self-insurance charges for subsequent periods shall reflect such experience in the same manner as would purchased insurance. If insurance could not be purchased against the self-insured risk, the amount of the self-insurance charge for each period shall be based on the contractor's experience, relevant industry experience, and anticipated conditions in accordance with accepted actuarial principles.

(ii) Where it is probable that the actual amount of losses which will occur in a cost accounting period will not differ significantly from the projected average loss for that period, the actual amount of losses in that period may be considered to represent the projected average loss for that period in lieu of a self-insurance charge.

(iii) Under self-insurance programs for retired persons, only actual losses shall be considered to represent the projected average loss unless a reserve or fund is established in accordance with § 416.50(a)(1)(v).

(iv) The self-insurance charge shall be determined in a manner which will give appropriate recognition to any indemnification agreement which exists between the contracting parties.

(3) In measuring actual losses under paragraph (a)(2) of this section:

(i) The amount of a loss shall be measured by (A) The actual cash value of property destroyed; (B) amounts paid or accrued to repair damage; (C) amounts paid or accrued to estates and beneficiaries; and (D) amounts paid or accrued to compensate claimants, including subrogation. Where the amount of a loss which is represented by a liability to a third party is uncertain, the estimate of the loss shall be the amount which would be includable as an accrued liability in financial statements prepared in accordance with generally accepted accounting principles.

(ii) If a loss has been incurred and the amount of the liability to a claimant is fixed or reasonably certain, but actual payment of the liability will not take place for more than 1 year after the loss is incurred, the amount of the loss to be recognized currently shall not exceed the present value of the future payments, determined by using a discount rate equal to that prescribed for settling such claims by the State having jurisdiction over the claim. If no such rate is prescribed by the State, then the rate shall be equal to the interest rate as determined by the Secretary of the Treasury pursuant to Pub. L. 92—41, 85 Stat. 97, in effect at the time the loss is recognized. Alternatively, where settlement will consist of a series of payments over an indefinite time period, as in worker's compensation, the contractor may follow a consistent policy of recognizing only the actual amounts paid in the period of payment.

(4) The contractor may elect to recognize immaterial amounts of self-insured losses or insurance administration expenses as part of other expense categories rather than as "insurance costs."

(b) Allocation of insurance costs:

(1) Where actual losses are recognized as an estimate of the projected average loss, in accordance with § 416.50(a)(2), or where actual loss experience is determined for the purpose of developing self-insurance charges by segment, a loss which is incurred in a given segment shall be identified with that segment. However, if the contractor's home office is, in effect, a reinsurer of its segments against catastrophic losses, a portion of such catastrophic losses shall be allocated to, or identified with, the home office.

(2) Insurance costs shall be allocated on the basis of the factors used to determine the premium, assessment, refund, dividend, or self-insurance charge, except that insurance costs incurred by a segment or allocated to

a segment from a home office may be combined with costs of other indirect cost pools if the resultant allocation to each final cost objective is substantially the same as it would have been if separately allocated under this provision.

(3) Insurance administration expenses which are material in relation to total insurance costs shall be allocated on the same basis as the related premium costs or self-insurance charge.

(c) Records. The contractor shall maintain such records as may be necessary to substantiate the amounts of premiums, refunds, dividends, losses, and self-insurance charges, paid or accrued, and the measurement and allocation of insurance costs. Memorandum records may be used to reflect any material differences between insurance costs as determined in accordance with this standard and as includable in financial statements prepared in accordance with generally accepted accounting principles.

Other Regulations Pertaining to Insurance

FAR Part 28 contains extensive coverage relating to bonds, insurance, and indemnification.

INTEREST AND OTHER FINANCIAL COSTS

FAR 31.205-20 provides:

Interest on borrowings (however represented), bond discounts, costs of financing and refinancing capital (net worth plus long-term liabilities), legal and professional fees paid in connection with preparing prospectuses, costs of preparing and issuing stock rights and directly associated costs are unallowable except for interest assessed by State or local taxing authorities under the conditions specified in 31.205-41 (but see 31.205-28).

A well-written but unsuccessful letter from an industry association to the Deputy Secretary of Defense some years ago is excerpted below:

The disallowance of interest on borrowings as a cost is inconsistent with the requirements of Federal Statutes applicable to contractors. For instance, interest is accepted as an allowable cost for tax purposes under Section 163 of the Internal Revenue Code of 1954. It is also recognized as a cost in Renegotiation under Section 103(f) of the Renegotiation Act of 1951. It should be noted that "reasonable interest, not in excess of 4%," is allowable as a cost under the VinsonTrammell Act when paid on indebtedness, the proceeds of which are used to acquire additional equipment and facilities for defense production or working capital to operate such equipment and facilities. See I. T. 3400, 1940-2 C. B. 415.

Interest on borrowings is also recognized as a cost under ASPR 8-402(b)(14) in settling terminations of fixed-price contracts and ASPR 8-512 authorizes its inclusion in settling the termination of cost-type contracts when not inconsistent with the reimbursement provisions of the particular contract. (Changed in November 1959.)

Allowance of interest as a cost has been expressly authorized by statute. The Judicial Code (28 U. S. Code Sec. 2516) provides that "interest on a claim against the United States shall be allowed in a judgment of the Court of Claims ... under a contract expressly providing for payment thereof." Under prior legislation which is essentially identical (as codified in the 1948 Judicial Code), the Supreme Court has construed such legislation as authorizing the payment of interest on sums due and owing by the United States under a contract expressly providing for such allowance. See also *U.S. v. Thayer-West Point Hotel Company,* 329 U.S. 585, 590 (1947); *U.S. v. Tillamooks,* 341 U.S. 48, 49 (1951); *Ramsey et al. v. U.S.,* 101 Supp. 353, 356 (Ct.Cls. 1951), *cert. den.* 343 U.S. 977 (1952).

The First War Powers Act permits the allowance of interest on borrowings as a cost without regard to the provisions of any other law, even if any other law which might be existent caused doubts. See 40 Ops. Atty. Gen. 225 (1942).

Interest as a cost has been allowed by the Armed Services Board of Contract Appeals. In *Hughes Aircraft Company,* 1954, ASBCA 1933, the Board allowed interest as a cost under a cost-type contract where ASPR Section XV was not incorporated by reference and, therefore, did not control. In *Hayward Woolen Co.,* 1955, ASBCA 1580, 6 CCF par. 61,733, the Board allowed interest on an RFC loan as provided by contractual agreement. Where there was nothing specific with respect to the disallowance of interest and interest was disallowed only because there was nothing in the record "which would serve as a proper basis for the allowance of interest." See *Edo Corp.,* 1951, ASBCA 670, 5 CCF par. 61,243.

Where specific departmental regulations, other than ASPR, Section XV, applicable to contracts have disallowed interest in repricing a fixed-price contract, the Board has followed such provisions. See *Rainier, Inc.,* 1948, Army BCA 1733, 4 CCF par. 60,519; *Swartzbaugh Mfg. Co.,* 1952, ASBCA 792, 6 CCF par. 61,479, motion for reconsideration denied, (1953). However, in a very recent decision of the *Wichita Engineering Co.,* 1955, ASBCA 2522, 6 CCF par. 61,804, the Board in setting forth the current policy of the Army (as set forth in Army Procurement Procedure par. 7-152, and in Department of Defense Instruction No. 4105.11 dated 23 November 1954, which applies to the administration of all "Price Redetermination" articles, stated: "We find no prohibition against the inclusion of interest as a cost for the purpose of pricing fixed-price contracts, including fixed-price contracts containing Price Redetermination articles, in current regulations (Armed Services Procurement Regulations and Army Procurement Procedure) and the Government has cited us to none. Thus to the extent that the decision in Rainier was based only upon policy as set forth in procurement regulations, it can be no longer relied upon to automatically exclude the allowance of interest." At another point in the decision, the Board stated, "we see nothing in the above statement of policy that requires that interest be disallowed, or permits it to be disallowed merely because it is interest."

The Several Facets of Interest as a Cost Under Government Contracts

There is no single principle or policy that has governed the recovery of interest under government contracts. In the ensuing brief summary, we shall attempt to establish a perspective for this subject in its several facets.

Interest as a Cost of Contract Performance

From the time of Treasury Decision 5000 and the "Green Book," interest expense has been enunciated as unallowable in determining contract costs. However, beginning with the period of late 1954-early 1955, DOD Directive 4105.11 was clearly and uniformly interpreted by judicial bodies as establishing that neither interest nor any other expense, in and of itself and absent other reasons, was unallowable under fixed-price contracts. From that time until Defense Procurement Circular No. 79, dated May 15, 1970, effective July 1, 1970, specifically extended ASPR Section XV to fixed-price contracts, boards of contract appeals and the Court of Claims rejected government efforts to disallow costs under fixed-price contracts where the sole reason for their identification as unallowable was ASPR Section XV. For DOD contracts awarded on and after July 1, 1970, ASPR Section XV was found to be generally applicable. As usual, the provisions of FPR were subsequently revised to conform to ASPR.

Imputed Interest as a Cost of Contract Performance

As discussed earlier in this chapter, the CASB promulgated CAS 414—Cost of Money as an Element of the Cost of Facilities Capital, and CAS 417—Cost of Money as an Element of the Cost of Capital Assets under Construction. These complex actions were intended to make some amends for the damages created by CAS 409—Depreciation of Tangible Capital Assets, but were diluted by the requirements imposed upon the Department of Defense to adjust its weighted guidelines formula to reduce the weight accorded to contractor performance and by the initial rejection of these standards by the civilian agencies. Although these factors have prevented many contractors from obtaining significant or any recognition for imputed interest, other contractors have derived real benefits, even though such benefits have not equaled those that would be available if the government recognized interest costs as allowable.

Interest as a Cost in Claims for Equitable Adjustments

This subject is discussed in Chapter VII of this text.

LABOR RELATIONS COSTS

FAR 31.205-21 provides that "costs incurred in maintaining satisfactory relations between the contractor and its employees, including costs of shop stewards, labor management committees, employee publications, and other related activities, are allowable."

LEGISLATIVE LOBBYING COSTS

As a result of congressional demands (P.L.99-145), the title of this cost principle (FAR 31.205-22) was changed by prefixing the word: legislative. The principle was further revised, effective July 30, 1987. As set forth later in this chapter, a new cost principle, FAR 31.205-50 Executive Lobbying Costs, was added. FAR 31.205-22 states:

(a) Costs associated with the following activities are unallowable:

(1) Attempts to influence the outcomes of any Federal, State, or local election, referendum, initiative, or similar procedure, through in kind or cash contributions, endorsements, publicity, or similar activities;

(2) Establishing, administering, contributing to, or paying the expenses of a political party, campaign, political action committee, or other organization established for the purpose of influencing the outcomes of elections;

(3) Any attempt to influence (i) the introduction of Federal or state legislation, or (ii) the enactment or modification of any pending Federal or state legislation through communication with any member or employee of the Congress or state legislature (including efforts to influence state or local officials to engage in similar lobbying activity), or with any government official or employee in connection with a decision to sign or veto enrolled legislation;

(4) Any attempt to influence (i) the introduction of Federal or state legislation, or (ii) the enactment or modification of any pending Federal or state legislation by preparing, distributing or using publicity or propaganda, or by urging members of the general public or any segment thereof to contribute to or participate in any mass demonstration, march, rally, fund raising drive, lobbying campaign or letter writing or telephone campaign; or

(5) Legislative liaison activities, including attendance at legislative sessions or committee hearings, gathering information regarding legislation, and analyzing the effect of legislation, when such activities are carried on in support of or in knowing preparation for an effort to engage in unallowable activities.

(b) The following activities are excepted from the coverage of (a) above:

(1) Providing a technical and factual presentation of information on a topic directly related to the performance of a contract through hearing testimony, statements or letters to the Congress or a state legislature, or subdivision, member, or cognizant staff member thereof, in response to a documented request (including a Congressional Record notice requesting testimony or statements for the record at a regularly scheduled hearing) made by the recipient member, legislative body or subdivision, or a cognizant staff member thereof; provided such information is readily obtainable and can be readily put in deliverable form; and further provided that costs under this section for transportation, lodging or meals are unallowable unless incurred for the purpose of offering testimony at a regularly scheduled Congressional hearing pursuant to a written request for such presentation made by the Chairman or Ranking Minority Member of the Committee or Subcommittee conducting such hearing.

(2) Any lobbying made unallowable by (a)(3) above to influence state legislation in order to directly reduce contract cost, or to avoid material impairment of the contractor's authority to perform the contract.

(3) Any activity specifically authorized by statute to be undertaken with funds from the contract.

(c) When a contractor seeks reimbursement for indirect costs, total lobbying costs shall be separately identified in the indirect cost rate proposal, and thereafter treated as other unallowable activity costs.

(d) Contractors shall submit as part of their annual indirect cost rate proposals a certification that the requirements and standards of this subsection have been complied with.

(e) Contractors shall maintain adequate records to demonstrate that the certification of costs as being allowable or unallowable pursuant to this subsection complies with the requirements of this subsection.

(f) Time logs, calendars, or similar records shall not be required to be created for purposes of complying with this subsection during any particular calendar month when—

(1) The employee engages in lobbying (as defined in paragraphs (a) and (b) of this subsection) 25 percent or less of the employee's compensated hours of employment during that calendar month; and

(2) Within the preceding 5-year period, the organization has not materially misstated allowable or unallowable costs of any nature, including legislative lobbying costs.

When the conditions of subparagraphs (f)(1) and (2) of this subsection are met, contractors are not required to establish records to support the allowability of claimed costs in addition to records already required or maintained. Also, when the conditions of subparagraphs (f)(1) and (2) of this subsection are met, the absence of time logs, calendars, or similar records will not serve as a basis for disallowing costs by contesting estimates of lobbying time spent by employees during a calendar month.

(g) Existing procedures should be utilized to resolve in advance any significant questions or disagreements concerning the interpretation or application of this subsection.

A significant change involving recordkeeping was made effective July 30, 1987. The following explanation was provided in FAC 84-26:

FAR 31.205-22, Legislative lobbying costs, paragraph (f), is rewritten to clarify that detailed activity records for an individual employee need not be maintained during any particular calendar month when *both:* (1) The employee engages in lobbying activities 25 percent or less of the employee's compensated hours of employment during that calendar month, *and* (2) within the preceding 5-year period the contractor has not materially misstated allowable or unallowable costs of any nature, including legislative lobbying costs.

The "25 percent" rule is an extraordinary waiver of only the special recordkeeping requirements. It is extended only to those contractors who have demonstrated that their cost representations are fair and accurate over an extended time period. Complaints have been received that some contractors have denied Government auditors access to records regularly maintained (e.g., time, attendance, and other payroll records), on the basis of the "25 percent" rule in FAR 31.205-22(f). Accordingly, paragraph (f) is revised to clarify its original intent that records usually maintained to demonstrate the allowability of costs must continue to be maintained and made available for audit.

Many government contract cost principles have lengthy histories. Lobbying costs is a relative newcomer, just about a decade old, but its history is one of the more turbulent and interesting ones. The origins may be traced back to 1975 when DCAA conducted a congressionally mandated series of special audits of defense contractors' offices in Washington, D.C. The audit reports accented "questioned costs" involving alleged entertainment of government officials, questionable payments abroad, illegal political expenditures—and lobbying costs. As many people in and out of the government observed at that time, lobbying costs were not identified as unallowable under ASPR, FPR, or other government regulations. Indeed, these costs were not even mentioned in any of the regulations addressing cost principles.

After considerable study involving procurement, legal, and audit officials, DOD initiated a project to define lobbying costs and distinguish between allowable and unallowable expenditures in this area. Some two years later, on December 12, 1977, the ASPR Committee offered for comment what was to be the first in a long series of attempts to formulate a cost principle relating to this complex area.

The December 1977 proposal, although not as severe as the later DAR or even OMB and FPR versions, was widely perceived as harsh and was challenged on numerous grounds, including equity and violation of the United States Constitution. Criticisms were so widespread and intense as to persuade DOD to withdraw the proposal for further review. Late in 1979, DOD tried again but its revised proposal was not considered much of an improvement over the initial effort. It was understood that final action on the 1979 proposal was suspended as a result of direction from high level officials before the Administration in office at the time departed the scene.

There followed a period of relative quiet until late 1981, when the Secretary of Defense personally directed a revision to DAR, which reflected the harshest provisions seen to that time. As ultimately issued (DAR 15-205.51), this cost principle was widely perceived as even more severe, declaring as unallowable costs of virtually any and every relationship between the citizenry represented by defense contractors and their legislative representatives, regardless of the nature and regardless of who initiated the action.

On January 20, 1983, the Office of Management and Budget issued proposed OMB Circular A—122, which set forth Cost Principles for Nonprofit Organizations. Borrowing from the Internal Revenue Code, 26 U.S.C. 4911, OMB introduced the term "political advocacy" and proposed to make unallowable a wide range of activities that might be construed by government auditors and contracting officers as efforts to influence government officials or the general public. This proposal assumed particular significance in view of indications that its applicability would extend beyond nonprofit organizations.

OMB's proposal, which was intended for incorporation into DAR, FPR, and NASA PR, generated a storm of protest. Although the protests from contractors, grantees, and related industry and professional associations were expected, something new was added—close attention by the news media, which rarely notice or comment upon government cost principles. A major national periodical contained an article titled "A Sneak Attack on Lobbying," which termed the proposal a political curiosity in that it was assailed by both liberal and conservative groups. A major newspaper, in an analysis in its general coverage rather than in the business section, stated that the proposed regulations ". . . have produced an unusual alignment of opposed groups: military contractors, such as Boeing and Lockheed, and environmentalists, Catholic Charities and Planned Parenthood, the Girl Scouts, the National Urban League, and others . . . ." The hue and cry was prominent in Congress, where three committees scheduled hearings on the proposal. At these hearings, committee members and witnesses raised many objections to the extension of unallowable "political advocacy" activities to appropriate liaisons with the legislative and executive branches of the government and to the senseless accounting rules under which total costs would be disallowed where only a minute portion of an individual's time or building space was devoted to what might be termed lobbying.

Under considerable pressure from both Congress and virtually every element in the private sector, OMB stepped back again for further review and study. The Department of Defense, however, continued to hang tough as it has in its increasing attacks on alleged fraud, waste, and abuse, harsh cost principles relating to compensation for personal services and good will, and other actions that increased DOD-industry adversarial relationships. Protests from CODSIA and other major industry associations seemed to fall on deaf ears in the Pentagon.

Nor was DOD moved when its attention was directed to President Reagan's Executive Order No. 12352, which stated, among other things:

> Present cost principles will be reviewed with the objective of allowing all normal and necessary costs of doing business. The cost principles will recognize that the disallowance of necessary costs erodes contractor profits. This in turn reduces competition. The only unallowable costs should be those which are against public policy.

What made the DOD position seem even more incredible was its insistence on harsher provisions than those adopted by the other executive agencies of the government, without any explanation as to why the Department of Defense should pursue more punitive rules. DOD's refusal to agree to a uniform cost principle continued even after FAR was promulgated with the issuance of the harsher cost principle in the DOD FAR Supplement. Indeed, it was not until July 1, 1984, that the government was able to persuade DOD to join the other agencies, and FAR 31.205-22, quoted earlier, was established as a uniform cost principle for application to government contracts and grants.

The provisions of the revised OMB Circular A-122 and related FAR 31.205-22 have generated complaints and rejections from wide-ranging opposition. However, any regulation restricting reimbursement of ordinary and necessary expenses meets with opposition, varying only in extent and intensity. We believe that, even with its objectionable features, the new principle represents a considerable improvement over the prior OMB efforts and over the harsh provisions promulgated by the Department of Defense.

The term "lobbying costs" was used in DAR and the DOD FAR Supplement, but the proposed OMB circulars first offered the newly coined "political advocacy" and then the equally broad and objectionable "lobbying and related activities." The latter appeared vague and ominous to many who were concerned that "related activities" might serve as a basis for expanding the unallowable category beyond the original intent. To allay these concerns, OMB struck this term.

LOSSES ON OTHER CONTRACTS

FAR 31.205-23 provides: "An excess of costs over income under any other contract (including the contractor's contributed portion under cost-sharing contracts) is unallowable."

MAINTENANCE AND REPAIR COSTS

FAR 31.205-24 provides:

(a) Costs necessary for the upkeep of property (including Government property, unless otherwise provided for) that neither add to the permanent value of the property nor appreciably prolong its intended life, but keep it in an efficient operating condition, are to be treated as follows (but see 31.205-11):

(1) Normal maintenance and repair costs are allowable.

(2) Extraordinary maintenance and repair costs are allowable, provided those costs are allocated to the applicable periods for purposes of determining contract costs (but see 31.109).

(b) Expenditures for plant and equipment, including rehabilitation which should be capitalized and subject to depreciation, according to generally accepted accounting principles as applied under the contractor's established policy or, when applicable, according to CAS 404, Capitalization of Tangible Assets, are allowable only on a depreciation basis.

According to this contract cost principle, normal maintenance and repair costs are straightaway allowable, but extraordinary maintenance and repair costs are allowable only if "allocated to the periods to which applicable for purposes of determining contract costs." One looks in vain for definitions distinguishing "normal" from "extraordinary." There is also a reference to advance agreements in FAR 31.109, but the only item that would appear applicable is "deferred maintenance costs."

We suggest CAS 404 (see text earlier in this chapter) as a useful guide for the kinds of costs government auditors accept as maintenance and repair costs vis-a-vis capital expenditures. For unusual circumstances, advance agreements are recommended.

MANUFACTURING AND PRODUCTION ENGINEERING COSTS

These selected costs and the significance of distinguishing them from IR&D costs are discussed in Chapter XIV of this text.

MATERIAL COSTS

These selected costs are discussed as part of the analysis of the broad subject of Accounting Methods and Controls for Material in Chapter X of this text.

ORGANIZATION COSTS

FAR 31.205-27 provides:

(a) Except as provided in paragraph (b) below, expenditures in connection with (1) planning or executing the organization or reorganization of the corporate structure of a business, including mergers and acquisitions, or (2) raising capital (net worth plus long-term liabilities), are unallowable. Such expenditures include but are not limited to incorporation fees and costs of attorneys, accountants, brokers, promoters and organizers, management consultants and investment counsellors, whether or not employees of the contractor. Unallowable "reorganization" costs include the cost of any change in the contractor's financial structure, excluding administrative costs of shortterm borrowings for working capital, resulting in alterations in the rights and interests of security holders whether or not additional capital is raised.

(b) The cost of activities primarily intended to provide compensation will not be considered organizational costs subject to this subsection, but will be governed by 31.205-6. These activities include acquiring stock for (1) executive bonuses, (2) employee savings plans, and (3) employee stock ownership plans.

We have referred previously to the government's unfortunate practice of revising its cost principles when a board of contract appeals or a court hands down a decision that some of the contract auditors and other hard-liners believe results in the allowance of costs intended to be categorized as unallowable. The decision in the appeal of *The Boeing Company*, ASBCA No. 14370, 73-2 BCA par. 10,325, reinstated substantial sums of monies disallowed by the government, and we have referred to this ruling under our discussion of advertising and other costs in Chapter XV. Changes were also made to assure that certain organization costs, disallowed by the government and reinstated by the ASBCA, would be clearly established as unallowable in the future.

DPC 76-9, dated August 30, 1977, contained the following summary on this subject:

"The changes to 15-205.23 are intended to clarify the principle that the costs of any corporate financial structure change resulting in alterations to the rights and interests of the security stockholders, are unallowable whether or not additional capital is raised. The changes to 15-205.17 and 15-205.41 clarify the references in those cost principles to the revised 15-205.23."

One could argue that many of the costs specified as unallowable under DAR 15-205.23 and carried forward into FAR 31.205-27 should be allowed under the allocability sections of the acquisition regulations, which provide that "a cost is allocable to a Government contract if it . . . is necessary to the overall operation of the business, although a direct relationship to any particular cost objective cannot be shown." Unfortunately, the government regulators frequently tend to ignore this sound, basic principle. In the case of organization costs, some expenditures are identified with financing and thus considered unallowable under FAR 31.205-20. The rationale advanced for disallowing other organization and reorganization costs is that the government entered into a contract with a specific entity considered competent to perform the work and should not reimburse the costs of corporate changes not incident to contract performance.

As discussed in greater detail in Chapter XVIII, congressional and media allegations that the government was allowing costs incident to corporate takeovers resulted in a proposed FAR revision specifically disallowing costs of "golden parachutes" and "golden handcuffs." A related proposal would revise FAR 31.205-27 (a) to read as follows:

> (a) Except as provided in paragraph (b) of this subsection, expenditures in connection with (1) planning or executing the organization or reorganization of the corporate structure of a business, including mergers and acquisitions, (2) *resisting or planning to resist the reorganization of the corporate structure of a business or a change in the controlling interest in the ownership of a business*, and (3) raising capital (net worth plus long-term liabilities), are unallowable. Such expenditures include but are not limited to incorporation fees and costs of attorneys, accountants, brokers, promoters and organizers, management consultants and investment counselors, whether or not employees of the contractor. Unallowable "reorganization" costs include the cost of any change in the contractor's financial structure, excluding administrative costs of short-term borrowings for working capital, resulting in alterations in the rights and interests of security holders, whether or not additional capital is raised. (Emphasis added to refer to change.)

OTHER BUSINESS EXPENSES

FAR 31.205-28 provides:

> The following types of recurring costs are allowable when allocated on an equitable basis:

> (a) Registry and transfer charges resulting from changes in ownership of securities issued by the contractor.

> (b) Cost of shareholders' meetings.

> (c) Normal proxy solicitations.

> (d) Preparing and publishing reports to shareholders.

(e) Preparing and submitting required reports and forms to taxing and other regulatory bodies.

(f) Incidental costs of directors' and committee meetings.

(g) Other similar costs.

What are the major distinctions between the unallowable organization costs and the allowable other business costs? We have commented above on the government's rationale for disallowing the costs in the former category. The key terms in the other business expenses classification seem to be "recurring," "normal," and "required." The disallowance of these costs, in our judgment, would be just about impossible to justify, and this selected cost was probably included to (1) try to distinguish these expenses from the so-called organization costs, and (2) deter overzealous auditors from questioning them.

PLANT PROTECTION COSTS

FAR 31.205.31 provides that "costs of items such as (a) wages, uniforms, and equipment of personnel engaged in plant protection, (b) depreciation on plant protection capital assets, and (c) necessary expenses to comply with military requirements, are allowable."

PATENT COSTS

FAR 31.205-30 provides:

(a) The following patent costs are allowable to the extent that they are incurred as requirements of a Government contract (but see 31.205-33):

(1) Costs of preparing invention disclosures, reports, and other documents.

(2) Costs for searching the art to the extent necessary to make the invention disclosures.

(3) Other costs in connection with the filing and prosecution of a United States patent application where title or royalty-free license is to be conveyed to the Government.

(b) General counseling services relating to patent matters, such as advice on patent laws, regulations, clauses, and employee agreements, are allowable (but see 31.205-33).

(c) Other than those for general counseling services, patent costs not required by the contract are unallowable. (See also 31.205-37.)

The 1949 cost principles provided that these expenses were allowable "to the extent expressly provided for elsewhere in the contract or otherwise authorized by the Government"; the cost of "prosecution of patent infringement litigation" was considered unallowable. In addition, patents, purchase designs, and royalties payments were listed as subjects requiring special consideration.

The 1959 cost principles treated the subjects of patent costs and royalty payments in more detail, and the provisions were more liberal. As to patent costs, the principles provided: "Costs of preparing disclosures, reports, and other documents required by the contract and of searching the art to the extent necessary to make such invention disclosures, are allowable. In accordance with the clauses of the contract relating to patents, costs of preparing documents and any other patent costs, in connection with the filing of a patent application where title is conveyed to the Government, are allowable."

Despite the inclusion of further details, the new cost principles were not successful in resolving problems and controversies regarding the allowability of patent costs. Some government contracting officers tended to view patent costs in a rather restrictive manner; auditors in the military departments, and their successors in DCAA, were generally more severe; and, as might be expected, the GAO representatives took the most rigid path of all.

An appeal from an audit disallowance of patent costs led to what is now a well-known and widely quoted decision by the Armed Services Board of Contract Appeals in the case of the *American Electronics Laboratories, Inc.,* ASBCA No. 9879, 65-2 BCA par. 5020. The government had disallowed certain indirect expenses on the basis that they represented "legal fees relating to . . . patent cases not allocable to the contracts." Under then-existing procedures under Navy contracts, the contractor appealed to the Navy Director of Contract Audit, who denied the appeal on the ground that legal fees in connection with patents were specifically unallowable under ASPR 15-205.26 unless required by the contract.

In overruling the government on this issue, the board made several significant statements. For example, it expressed the opinion that "ASPR 15-205.26 does not purport to cover all patent costs, nor does it state or imply that all patent costs not made specifically allowable therein are to be disallowed." In support of this contention, the board referred to related ASPR coverage in ASPR 15-205.31 (patent infringement litigation costs) and ASPR 15-205.36 (royalties). It also noted that ASPR 15-204 established that the individual selected items of cost are not intended to be all-inclusive "and that failure to treat an item of cost in ASPR 15-205 is not intended to imply that it is either allowable or unallowable."

The board found that the contractor had given "uncontroverted evidence" that the cost involved "was incurred in patent searches tending to benefit the appellant's business as a whole." The board also noted that the contractor had not contended that this type of expense was made specifically allowable by ASPR 15-205.26; however, the contractor did argue that the expenditure constituted a reasonable and necessary business expense and, as such, should be included in the G&A pool for allocation to all of its business.

The board concluded that the cost of patent searches "represents costs actually incurred by appellant and meets all the allowability tests specified by ASPR Section XV, Part 2 and is not made unallowable for inclusion in the G&A pool."

In July 1968, the board rendered another very significant decision, relating both to the specific question of allowability of patent costs under government contracts and, in a broader sense, dealing with the bigger subject of allocability. ASBCA No. 11499, 68-2 BCA par. 7117, dealt with the appeal by TRW, Inc., of the government's disallowance of certain patent costs. The disallowances were under cost-reimbursable contracts that incorporated Section XV contained in the 1960 edition of ASPR. The matters not in controversy included the facts that: (1) TRW had been engaged extensively in contracts for highly technical services and products for DOD, NASA, and AEC; (2) the contractor's IR&D and patent efforts and expenses were oriented towards those types of contracts and those customers; and (3) the costs in dispute were actually incurred and were not unreasonable. The items under dispute included appellant's filing and prosecution costs for U. S. patents to be issued in appellant's name; the portion of the costs of operating appellant's patent department, which the contracting officer prorated to nonsubject inventions (see ASPR 9-107.2), including awards to inventors, purchased patentability searches, and attorney analysis of disclosures; and appellant's costs for foreign patent applications and related filing fees. The government's disallowance and the contractor's appeal reflected a controversy as to whether such costs were allocable.

The arguments and the board's decision centered on the interpretation of the definition of allocability set forth in ASPR 15-201.4. The governing portions, as cited in the board's decision, follow: "A cost is allocable if it is assignable or chargeable to a particular cost objective, such as a contract, . . . class of customer or activity, in accordance with the relative benefits received or other equitable relationship. Subject to the foregoing, a cost is allocable to a Government contract if it— . . . (III) is necessary to the overall operation of the business, although a direct relationship to any particular cost objective cannot be shown."

The government stressed the words "relative benefits received." It argued that the phrase "necessary to the overall operation of the business" must be interpreted in the light of benefits to the government in the sense that such costs should be allocable and hence allowable only "if, but for such costs, the contractor's business operations would be adversely affected to a substantial extent, resulting in serious interference with performance of the existing Government contracts." The government would also have the term "operation" refer to "day-to-day activities being performed at the time of contracting" instead of anything having to do with the future.

The contractor argued that, for a cost to be allocable to a government contract, it was only necessary to establish its "necessity to the overall operation of a business" and that "benefit to the Government automatically follows from any necessary expenditure."

The board did not accept either argument in its entirety, but it ruled for the contractor and sustained the appeal (except for foreign patent costs, which are commented upon subsequently).

The board concluded that "[o]bviously, any expense which is so necessary that its payment is a *sine qua non* for doing business would automatically and without question, be held to benefit or bear an equitable relationship to Government contracts being performed by that business equity." On the other hand, it would not go as far as the contractor in viewing necessity of a cost as automatically establishing allocability. Here the board noted that "[w]hen considering expenses which are not necessary in the absolute sense, the element of 'benefit or other equitable relationship' becomes less automatic and thus more difficult to determine." It cited two Court of Claims decisions in an effort to distinguish the differences.

The first case was *Lockheed Aircraft Corp. v. United States*, 179 Ct.Cl. 545. The City of Burbank, Calif., imposed personal property taxes on Lockheed's commercial inventory, but not on its inventory of government contracts. The government held this tax unallowable on the grounds that it was not allocable to government contracts and because its allowance would in effect waive the immunity granted to the federal government by the City of Burbank. In ruling for Lockheed, the Court of Claims focused on ASPR 15-201.4 and concluded that government contracts, even though not directly taxed, benefited by the personal property taxes Lockheed paid on its commercial inventory.

In contrast, the board cited *Pressed Steel Car Co., Inc. v. United States*, 141 Ct.Cl. 318, 157 F. Supp. 950, *cert. denied*, 356 U. S. 967 (1958). Here the contractor was a Pennsylvania corporation, operating in both Pennsylvania and Illinois, with a CPFF contract performed entirely in the Illinois plant at issue. The controversy involved the contractor's allocation to the government contract of the Pennsylvania capital stock tax. The court found that the tax was based solely on activities and properties located in Pennsylvania and that no portion of it was incident to the performance of the government contract in Illinois and hence should not be allocated thereto.

Both the Court of Claims in the two aforementioned cases and the ASBCA in the *TRW* appeal under discussion found a relationship between the necessity of a cost for overall business operations and the allocability of that cost to government contracts; but they did not find that an absolute relationship existed, nor were they able to arrive at "any general rule or litmus paper test for allocability." In its *TRW* decision, the board set forth the following general proposition: "Expenses which are absolutely necessary for the operation of a business are, for that reason alone, beneficial to or bear an equitable relationship to Government contracts. As the absolute necessity decreases, the contractor's burden to show some benefit or other equitable relationship with Government contracts increases."

The board then considered the individual disallowed patent costs in the light of allocability principles discussed above.

For purposes of its decision, the board grouped the various items in dispute into two categories, costs for foreign patent applications and all others. As to the costs other than those relating to foreign patents, the contractor argued that the patent program was necessary to the overall operation of its business and hence benefited government contracts because it (1) stimulated inventions, (2) facilitated recruitment and retention of qualified personnel, (3) protected it from competition, and (4) protected it from claims of interference or infringement. The contractor's argument that the patent program enhanced its employees' morale was not heavily contested by the government; on the other hand, it argued that it would be important to the prestige of these people to have an article published in a scientific journal as distinguished from a patent.

The contractor argued strongly that the protection afforded by a patent protected its risk in such an investment. And, more importantly, patents provided significant protection against claims by others. The dangers of neglecting the patenting process were illustrated by various case studies submitted by the contractor's witnesses. The government was not persuaded by these arguments because it felt that "the patenting process is so slow that patent expenditures during any accounting period are not likely to benefit operations during that period." This was the government's "benefit to day-by-day operations" argument. It also contended that if it assumed a portion of these costs, it might "very likely someday be in the position of having paid a substantial part of the cost of obtaining a patent which will be used offensively against the Government."

The board found nothing in ASPR 15-201.4 to support the government's contention that allocability required a showing of benefit to day-by-day operations. It was no more favorably impressed with the government's apprehension that patents might be used offensively against it. Here the board noted that the same argument could be invoked against IR&D costs.

The board visualized what might be considered sound reasons to support the allocability of such patent costs, but it emphasized that "[t]he issue before this Board is whether ASPR permits allocation of certain patent costs to Government contracts and not whether ASPR should permit such allocation."

The appeal of *The Boeing Company* (ASBCA No. 12731, 70-1 BCA par. 8298; 69-2 BCA par. 7980) plowed most of the ground of *American Electronics* and *TRW, Inc.* The decision went beyond the one rendered in the appeal of *TRW,* however, to the extent that the board found that Boeing had extensive foreign operations; accordingly, costs incident to foreign patents were also allowed.

The decision noted that, "[i]n addition to its foreign commercial activity Boeing has sought to obtain business from foreign governments in their military and space programs . . . . Boeing regards its foreign patent activity as important to maintaining its position in foreign markets and thus necessary to Boeing's foreign business." The board was able to discern certain benefits that accrued to the government from the costs incurred by Boeing on foreign patents. Some of the board's comments in this area, including a comparison of its conclusions here with those it reached in the appeal of *TRW,* are cited below:

> The Board found that the Government did not derive similar benefits from TRW's foreign patent program since TRW, at the time of the hearing before the Board, did not have any foreign business which would have required the protection afforded by foreign patents. Noteworthy is the Board's rejection of the theory advanced by the Government in the present appeal, that in order for patent costs to be considered allocable to Government contracts under the ASPR 15-201.4 definition of allocability, they must be shown to relate directly to work performed under Government contracts. In *TRW* the Board held appellant's United States patent costs to be allocable to Government contracts, and, therefore, allowable on the basis of the overall equitable benefits received by the Government without regard to the quantum of patent office work performed with respect to particular Government contracts.

Except for their respective foreign operations, Boeing's activities relating to patents are similar to those described in the Board's TRW opinion. The business of both companies relies heavily on technological advancement, therefore requiring them to be afforded the protection and benefits of the United States patent system. The patent application work and defensive aspects of patenting are described similarly in the records of both appeals. The invention incentive program described in *TRW*, is similar to that of Boeing, and was regarded as a "necessary" cost for the purpose of determining allocability. However, unlike *TRW*, Boeing has extensive foreign operations which require a measure of protection afforded by foreign patent systems. We think, therefore, that both the domestic and foreign patent activities of Boeing satisfy the test of allocability applied by the Board in the *TRW* case.

The Board summed up its views on this point stating that: "Boeing's foreign operations were extensive, both in terms of commercial sales and in connection with foreign military and space programs. Thus, while *TRW*'s foreign patent costs were disallowed because of the lack of business requiring the protection of foreign patents, the rationale of the *TRW* decision warrants sustaining the allowability of Boeing's foreign patent costs as necessary to Boeing's over-all business and having an equitable relationship to the Government as a class of customer.

In summary, we find the cost principles relating to patent costs unduly restrictive if literally construed; however, the judicial decisions cited indicate that the Armed Services Board of Contract Appeals tended to take a broader and more equitable approach. The enactment of the Trade Agreements Act of 1979 (Public Law 96-39) and the ensuing Agreement on Government Procurement is broadening international contracting. With foreign and domestic suppliers given equal treatment and opportunity to compete for defense and other federal government supplies and services, it is certainly time to eliminate the regulations making unallowable the costs of filing and prosecuting foreign patent applications.

PLANT RECONVERSION COSTS

FAR 31.205-31 provides:

Plant reconversion costs are those incurred in restoring or rehabilitating the contractor's facilities to approximately the same condition existing immediately before the start of the Government contract, fair wear and tear excepted. Reconversion costs are unallowable except for the cost of removing Government property and the restoration or rehabilitation costs caused by such removal. However, in special circumstances where equity so dictates, additional costs may be allowed to the extent agreed upon before costs are incurred. Care should be exercised to avoid duplication through allowance as contingencies, additional profit or fee, or in other contracts.

This item was not specifically mentioned in the 1949 ASPR Section XV, except that "rearrangement or relocation of facilities or plan site" was included in the subjects requiring special consideration. Generally, the cost of converting the plant to government contracts was considered allowable, but the cost of reconverting it to commercial work *was* usually questioned.

The current cost principles formalized this practice, but the provisions are not rigid. According to the current principles, "reconversion costs are unallowable except for the cost of removing Government property and the restoration or rehabilitation costs caused by such removal." It is recognized, however, that this provision may be unfair in certain circumstances. Accordingly, the principles state that "where equity so dictates, additional costs may be allowed to the extent agreed upon before the costs are incurred."

PRECONTRACT COSTS

FAR 31.205-32 provides: "Precontract costs are those incurred before the effective date of the contract pursuant to the negotiation and in anticipation of the contract award when such incurrence is necessary to comply with the proposed contract delivery schedule. Such costs are allowable to the extent they would have been allowable if incurred after the date of the contract." (See 31.109).

PROFESSIONAL AND CONSULTANT SERVICE COSTS

FAR 31.205-33 provides:

(a) Costs of professional and consultant services rendered by persons who are members of a particular profession or possess a special skill and who are not officers or employees of the contractor are allowable subject to paragraphs (b), (c), (d), and (e) below when reasonable in relation to the services rendered and when not contingent upon recovery of the costs from the Government (but see 31.205-30).

(b) In determining the allowability of costs (including retainer fees) in a particular case, no single factor or any special combination of factors is necessarily determinative. However, the following factors, among others, should be considered:

(1) The nature and scope of the service rendered in relation to the service required.

(2) The necessity of contracting for the service, considering the contractor's capability in the particular area.

(3) The past pattern of such costs, particularly in the years prior to the award of Government contracts.

(4) The impact of Government contracts on the contractor's business.

(5) Whether the proportion of Government work to the contractor's total business is such as to influence the contractor in favor of incurring the cost, particularly when the services rendered are not of a continuing nature and have little relationship to work under Government contracts.

(6) Whether the service can be performed more economically by employment rather than by contracting.

(7) The qualifications of the individual or concern rendering the service and the customary fee charged, especially on non-government contracts.

(8) Adequacy of the contractual agreement for the service (e.g., description of the service; estimate of time required; rate of compensation; termination provisions).

(c) Retainer fees to be allowable must be supported by evidence that—

(1) The services covered by the retainer agreement are necessary and customary;

(2) The level of past services justifies the amount of the retainer fees (if no services were rendered, fees are not automatically unallowable); and

(3) The retainer fee is reasonable in comparison with maintaining an in-house capability to perform the covered services, when factors such as cost and level of expertise are considered.

(d) Costs of legal, accounting, and consulting services and directly associated costs incurred in connection with organization and reorganization (also see 31.205-27), defense of antitrust suits, defense against Government claims or appeals, or the prosecution of claims or appeals against the Government (see 33.201) are unallowable (but see 31.205-47). Such costs incurred in connection with patent infringement litigation are unallowable unless otherwise provided for in the contract.

(e) Except for retainers, fees for services rendered shall be allowable only when supported by evidence of the nature and scope of the service furnished. (Also see 31.205-38(c).)

(f) Costs of legal, accounting, and consulting services and directly associated costs incurred in connection with the defense or prosecution of lawsuits or appeals between contractors arising from either: (1) An agreement or contract concerning a teaming arrangement, a joint venture, or similar arrangement of shared interest; or (2) dual sourcing, co-production, or similar programs, are unallowable, except when: (i) Incurred as a result of compliance with specific terms and conditions of the contract or written instructions from the contracting officer, or (ii) when agreed to in writing by the contracting officer.

A careful reading of the contract cost principles for professional and consultant service costs, together with a tracing of the evolution of these provisions, indicates that they are among the most overregulated, overmanaged, and overaudited.

In discussing cost principles for DOD contracts, we have referred from time to time to the "Green Book," issued in 1942 to interpret T.D. 5000. The only unallowable costs in this area were set forth in paragraph 54(p): "Special legal and accounting fees incurred in connection with reorganizations, security issues, capital stock issues, patent infringement or antitrust litigation, and the prosecution of claims of any kind (including income tax matters) against the United States."

Let us compare these provisions with those included in the ASPR contract cost principles that preceded the 1959 version. The prior cost principles included as "Allowable Indirect Costs":

Legal, accounting, and consulting services and related expenses (but see paragraph 15-205(d) and (1)).

The following paragraphs were included as "Examples of Items of Unallowable Cost":

(d) Commissions and bonuses (under whatever name) in connection with obtaining or negotiating for a Government contract.

(1) Legal, accounting and consulting services and related expenses incurred in connection with organization or reorganization, prosecution of patent infringement litigation, defense of antitrust suits, and the prosecution of claims against the United States.

From these limited restrictions on professional and consultant service costs, the Defense Department (with the civilian agencies generally following and conforming) continued to revise this cost principle, adding further restrictions with each revision. FAR 31.205-33(b), which does not differ in substance from the DAR provisions in effect before April 1, 1984, sets forth eight factors that contract auditors and contracting officers are to consider in determining allowability. A careful reading of these factors suggests that a number of them are beyond the ability of most government representatives to properly evaluate.

When these factors were first included in the acquisition regulations, industry and professional associations expressed serious concern about the possibility that they would generate overzealous surveillance and administration and unnecessarily detailed tests. These problems have materialized to a significant degree as government representatives devote inordinate time to scrutinizing professional and consultant fees.

As a matter of sound business policy and practice, hard and fast rules are seldom established regarding the source of professional and consultant service. This type of service is obtained both from in-house capability and from outside specialists, based on several considerations. As a rather obvious illustration, a General Motors or a General Electric maintains staffs of attorneys, accountants, engineers, and other professionals. These types of firms, nevertheless, as a matter of good business, engage specialists when appropriate. Generally, the smaller the firm, the less will be its professional in-house capability and, therefore, the greater will be its need for outside specialists and experts. But there are no mathematical formulas here. Ultimate decisions involving the alternatives of in-house or outside specialists constitute essentially management determinations and involve many considerations including the nature and intricacies of the problem, capability and availability of in-house talent, etc.

From time to time, government personnel tend to substitute their own views for those of industrial managers in this area and question the allowability of professional service costs under government contracts. Many of the questions are based on allegations that these services (usually legal fees) involved the prosecution of claims against the government or that the rates charged were excessive. With respect to the latter area, we have found in numerous instances that government representatives tend to compare these outside professional fees with their own salaries. Of course, such comparison is highly unreasonable and inappropriate in the circumstances. If the contractors and professionals involved stand firm in their position, it will usually prevail with the contracting officer. In many disputes of this type, accounting and legal fees involving necessary actions required in support of negotiations with contracting officers have been held to be allowable. Of course, professional fees relating to the preparation and presentation of appeals to administrative boards and to courts from decisions of contracting officers have been held unallowable.

Baifield Industries, Division of A-T-O, ASBCA No. 20006, 76-2 BCA par. 12,203; 76-2 BCA par. 12,096

A default termination involving Baifield Industries, Division of A-T-O, Inc., was converted to a convenience termination in an earlier ASBCA decision. The termination settlement proposal was complex and controversial, and we deal here only with legal fees ($73,049) and accounting fees ($130,653).

By way of a quick monetary perspective, Baifield claimed approximately $1,700,000, and the contracting officer's final decision aggregated about $850,000. After the appeal was docketed, but before the hearing, the differences between the parties were reduced, mostly by government withdrawals. The amount remaining in dispute was some $320,000, which included the above-mentioned legal and accounting fees.

After the termination for default action, the contractor engaged a law firm and a firm of certified public accountants, both of which were known to have considerable experience in termination of government contracts and general dealings with the government. Both firms expended considerable effort in developing the accounting and legal bases for the contractor's contentions. Baifield's accounting department was headed by a CPA, "but neither he nor anyone else on his staff had substantial experience in dealing with termination of a Government contract." A-T-O headquarters had a small accounting staff, but it was not adequate to cope with a complex termination settlement. A-T-O headquarters had a legal department, but none of the attorneys had the requisite experience in government contract terminations. The contractor's testimony included the view that engaging "an independent accounting firm would add more credibility to statements of costs claimed."

As indicated earlier, this whole matter was complex and controversial, and, as indicated by the professional fees, the accountants and lawyers devoted considerable time and effort to it. As compared with the actual legal fees, the termination contracting officer (TCO) allowed $9,600, representing 160 hours at $60 per hour. He disallowed the remainder of the amount claimed as unreasonable. For accounting services, the TCO allowed $6,000, computed as 120 hours at $50 per hour. The remainder, as in the case of legal fees, was disallowed as unreasonable.

In addition to the reasonableness factor, the government offered other reasons for disallowing portions of the professional fees, including allegations that portions related to unallowable litigation costs. In this connection, the board established the following position:

> In determining whether to allow professional fees and expenses as part of a termination for convenience settlement, as distinguishable from unallowable litigation expenses, the Court of Claims and this Board have based the distinction on the purpose and character of the services rendered, not necessarily their timing. The expenses of efforts to settle the claim with the contracting officer are allowable; the expenses of litigating an appeal before the Board of Contract Appeals are not allowable. *Acme Process Equipment Co. v. U.S.* (10 CCF par. 73,065), 171 Ct.Cls. 251 (1965); *Sundstrand Turbo, A Division of Sundstrand Corp.,* ASBCA No. 9112, 65-1 BCA par. 4653. Thus the pendency of an appeal does not bar recovery of legal or accounting expenses incurred as part of a genuine effort to settle a termination for convenience claim with the contracting officer. *Acme Process Equipment Co. v. U.S., supra.* See also *Kamen Soap Products Co., Inc.,* ASBCA No. 2587, 57-2 BCA par. 1366; *Western States Painting Co.,* ASBCA No. 13843, 69-1 BCA par. 7616.

The government disallowed legal expenses beginning after default termination through July 1970 as costs related to litigation and unallowable under ASPR 15-205.31 as costs of prosecuting the claim against the government. The board found that the legal *efforts* were expended in an attempt to convince the government to convert the default termination to a convenience termination. It conceded the correctness of the government's allegation that the costs substantially related to the contractor's effort to establish the impropriety of the default termination. However, it did not see this factor as establishing a basis for disallowing the costs.

The government's contention that the legal fees were unreasonable included the allegations that much of the work done by the law firm should have been performed by Baifield's people and that the attorneys performed administrative and clerical work. The board cited its ruling in *Cryo-Sonics, Inc.,* ASBCA 13219, 70-1 BCA par. 8313. In that case, an outside attorney expended considerable time in connection with a contract termination. The board found in that instance that the case was very complex, that there was evidence of substantial government-contractor disagreement, and generally that the attorney's efforts were not inappropriate. The board said in *Cryo-Sonics:* "However, the Government has not pointed to any of the particular charges listed by Mr. Gubin as reflecting services not incident to legal advice or assistance reasonably sought of Mr. Gubin by appellant. And we cannot engage in the unrealistic exercise of attempting to determine whether, for example, a particular fifteen minutes of Mr. Gubin's time in fact required the use of expertise unique to him."

In reviewing the evidence of the legal efforts and the government's allegations in *Baifield Industries,* the board found the government's arguments unpersuasive. The board found the problems complex and thought it entirely reasonable that Baifield should "rely heavily on the experience and knowledge" of the law firm's people "for assistance, as well as guidance, in gathering and analyzing factual material relevant to support appellant's settlement problems." It found that the government's views on disallowance were "based on an unreasonably narrow view of the scope of legal services proper for use by a contractor when faced with a large, complex and thoroughly contested termination claim. . . ."

Many of the government's contentions were obviously of the nitpicking variety, such as questioning the time spent by the law firm's people in conferences at its own offices. The board found the need for consultations among the attorneys entirely reasonable. A similar item, but one which we think significant as a precedent, was the government's questioning of the travel time expended by the attorneys from their Washington offices. The board thought the charges for travel time appropriate. Also, the government challenged some of the legal expenses as inadequately substantiated. The board thought the government's arguments unreasonable and found that the contractor had *prima facie* established the allowability of the expenses.

The accounting fees received the same treatment by government auditors and the TCO. As indicated previously, the government would allow $6,000 for accounting expenses as compared with $130,653 in fees and expenses billed by the accounting firm. The government argued that Baifield had turned over an unreasonable portion of the accounting effort to its outside accountants and should have used its own personnel. The government also thought the outside accountants performed unreasonably excessive and detailed analyses. Finally, in similar nitpicking, the government questioned "the reliability of the evidence offered by appellant to show that the hours claimed represented work performed."

The board found no problems with the available support for the time spent by the independent accountants. There were contemporaneous time reports, although these records did not show the particular service. The latter information was acquired subsequently through analyses of work papers, interviews with authors, etc. The board concluded that "[t]here is no evidence challenging either the reliability of these estimates or the amounts of time recorded as having been charged to the Van Container job." As in the case of the arguments over the legal fees, the board seemed impatient with the government's contentions that the contractor's in-house accountants could have reasonably coped with such a large, complex termination. It also found that some of the accounting efforts resulted directly from demands for detailed support for items claimed in the termination settlement by DCAA auditors and other government people.

An interesting point from a professional outlook was the government's contention that, since the independent public accounting firm was also the contractor's regular auditing firm, it should have been quite familiar with its accounts and should not have found it necessary to spend the time analyzing and testing. The board found that the evaluation of A-T-O's periodic financial statements did not involve the independent public accounting firm "in a detailed inquiry into verification of costs incurred under a particular contract and determination of allocability sufficient to assure a professional judgment that the costs as stated on the termination settlement proposal were proper." The board found it entirely appropriate for the independent public accountants to have spent the time they did to verify and investigate the costs included in a termination settlement proposal on which they would express an opinion as certified public accountants.

The government argued that a substantial portion of the accounting firm's travel and per diem costs should be disallowed because the work could have been done by their Dallas office. Appearing as a witness, a representative of the accounting firm established that accountants experienced in such government matters as contract terminations are not numerous. In order to obtain the appropriate expertise, the firm had to seek appropriate personnel in whatever offices they were available.

Significantly, after obviously lengthy hearings (certainly the coverage in the decision is very comprehensive) the board allowed the full amount of both the legal and accounting fees. We do not suggest that professional fees should be treated entirely differently from any other expenses and should not be questioned for allocability, reasonableness, and other allowability factors. On the other hand, we think it extremely unfortunate and inappropriate that certain government personnel undertake to substitute their judgment for the judgment of contractors' management in these matters. The government fields its best available team in complex and substantial disputes; contractors cannot do less. The judgment as to whether the protection of corporate interests can be best achieved in-house or with the advice and assistance of outside experts is a judgment that management, not the government, which is in an adversary role, must make. Once a decision is made to retain the services of outside attorneys and accountants, the nature and extent of the professional services, we believe, should be initially determined by the consultants and made subject to the approval of the contractors' top management. We would reiterate that professional fees should not be beyond scrutiny and challenge by the government; however, we do think that the challenges should be based on careful and thoughtful judgment with full consideration to a contractor's prerogatives to support its interests.

In a motion for reconsideration, the government appealed a relatively smaller portion of the legal fees allowed by the board—approximately $10,000 in air fares and per diem costs incurred by Baifield's Washington, D.C.-based attorneys. The contractor was located in Dallas, Texas, and the government argued that it should not be required to pay the additional costs resulting from Baifield's decision to use counsel who had to travel a considerable distance. In this connection, the government urged the board to take official notice of the competence of several Dallas, Texas, law firms in public contract law.

The government's motion for reconsideration seemed surprising in several respects. The board had given short shrift to the substantial disallowance of accounting and legal fees, and we were puzzled by the decision of the government to return and insist on disallowance of a relatively small portion ($10,000 out of $200,000). We were surprised, too, by the government's failure to comprehend the basic and elementary principle that a contractor's management is entitled, and indeed obligated, to take every prudent action it considers appropriate to protect the company's interest. There appeared to be no basis for the government's argument that a contractor may not seek advice from whomever it considers most qualified to render it and instead must be forced to consult with professional firms in the same locality.

The board also failed to see any merit in the government's argument. It recognized that there were competent attorneys in Dallas and that there was no evidence that Baifield tried to retain any of them. On the other hand, the board found no evidence that, had Baifield attempted to seek this service in Dallas, "it would have been able to obtain the extensive and highly sophisticated legal services required at the time (the contractor) needed them." The board also noted that the travel expenses were a relatively small part of the total legal service costs claimed, and there was no showing that the overall cost would have been significantly lower had Baifield retained Dallas attorneys equivalent in competence to the Washington attorneys it did retain.

G.A. Karnavas Printing Company, ASBCA No. 22281, 78-2 BCA par. 13,312

A decision in the appeal of *G.A. Karnavas Painting Company* included, among other matters of dispute, certain attorneys' fees. The board's ruling is summed up as follows:

Allowed—amount incurred up to and including the date contractor's claim was directed to the contracting officer and acknowledged by the government as having been incurred by the contractor for the preparation and presentation of the termination claim to the contracting officer.

Denied—amount incurred for the prosecution of a prior appeal to the ASBCA. In support of its action, the board cited ASPR 15-205.31(d) which provided:

Costs of legal, accounting and consulting services, and related costs, incurred in connection with . . . prosecution of claims against the Government, are unallowable . . .

Hayes International Corp., ASBCA No. 18447, 75-1 BCA par. 11,076

A number of other significant decisions have been handed down relating to the type of legal, consultant, and accounting fees that were challenged by the government. In *Hayes International Corp.,* some of the costs at issue were incurred in connection with litigation filed by the Equal Employment Opportunity Commission following complaints by employees. The suit was brought under the provisions of the Civil Rights Act of 1964. The litigation continued over a period of years and was concluded by a Consent Decree issued by a U.S. District Court. The board noted that the record contained no finding by the court that appellant was in violation of the provisions of the Civil Rights Act.

The costs were questioned under the provisions of ASPR 15-205.31 as well as pertinent provisions of the Civil Rights Act.

The basis for the government's disallowance, in part, is described as follows:

The Government does not appear to contest the reasonableness of the amount of the legal fees, but rather seems to be arguing that the fees by their nature are unreasonable. According to the Government, while the defense against an unwarranted claim may be considered by some as an ordinary and necessary business expense, the defense against this claimed violation is not such an expense. The Government goes on to argue that although there is no direct finding of violation of law, the language of the consent decree and the circumstances surrounding the alleged violation leave an appearance or implication which would not warrant a finding of ordinary and necessary business expense. To support its position the Government cites *Dade Brothers, Inc. v. U.S.*, 163 Ct.Cls. 485 (1963) which held that a contractor could not recover costs incurred in defending against a suit brought by employees alleging a contractor-union conspiracy to deprive the suing employees of employment and seniority rights. In *Dade Brothers* the Appellate Division of the Superior Court of New Jersey found that "there was ample proof to warrant a finding by the jury that the employer (i.e., the contractor) and the union acted in concert in wilfully and maliciously interfering with plaintiff's right to employment under the collective bargaining agreement."

But the board was not persuaded and it found neither a court determination of willful or malicious conduct on the part of the appellant nor a factual basis to establish that Hayes was in violation of the Civil Rights Act. The board then reasoned that these costs were the kind that would have been incurred by an ordinarily prudent person and were ordinary and necessary for the conduct of the contractor's business.

Having concluded that these expenses were reasonable, the board addressed the government's objections based on considerations of allocability. ASPR 15-201.4 provided that a cost may be allocable to a government contract if it (i) is incurred specifically for the contract; (ii) benefits both the contract and other work; or (iii) is necessary to the overall operation of the business, although direct relationship to any particular cost objective cannot be shown. The board found the third criterion extremely broad, as it is, and it found that these fees were necessary for the overall operation of the contractor's business.

Having satisfied itself as to the reasonableness and allocability of these expenses, the board addressed the question as to whether they were specifically defined as unallowable costs under ASPR 15-205. And here, ASPR 15-205.31(a) and (d) were considered pertinent. The board found that the cited ASPR provision did not establish these expenses to be unallowable:

Section 15-205.31 specifies various categories of legal fees which are unallowable. It makes a clear distinction between the defense of a specific type of suit, i.e., antitrust suits, and other legal fees which could be incurred. The fees in question were not incurred in the defense of an antitrust suit nor were they incurred in connection with organization and reorganization, patent infringement litigation, or the prosecution of claims against the Government. Since the costs do not fall within any of these categories of unallowable costs, their recovery is not precluded by ASPR Section 15-205.

Other fees in dispute were described by the board as amounts paid to a law firm "for gathering data for the purpose of assisting appellant in responding to a Government allegation of defective pricing." The board found that the data assembled by the attorneys was not used for other purposes, that the attorneys made no personal appearances, and that the record had no indication that the defective pricing allegation was formalized as a contracting officer's decision.

The government argued that these expenses were incurred in the presentation of a claim against the government. Hayes contended that the fees were not incurred in anticipation of defending a defective pricing action, "but rather that the attorneys were engaged to review appellant's operating policies relative to these contracts and the administration of Public Law 87-653."

If the expenses were incurred in connection with prosecuting a claim against the government, they would be unallowable under the provisions of ASPR 15-205.31(d). But the board found that involved here was a claim of the government and not of the contractor, because it was the government that made a claim to reduce the contract price because of the alleged defective cost or pricing data.

As in the case of the legal fees incurred in connection with the Civil Rights Act suit, the fees on the defective pricing claim were also determined to be properly includable in appellant's G&A.

Hayes also instituted injunctive proceedings in the Federal District Court against the secretary of a military department in an effort to prevent execution of a contract award issued to another company. The government claimed that the expenses were unallowable because they were incurred in the prosecution of a claim against the government.

Hayes attempted to make a distinction between this type of lawsuit and the type that it considered would constitute a claim against the government. In support of this contention, the contractor cited a Supreme Court definition of the term "claim" as used in the False Claims Act. The Supreme Court ruled with respect to that Act that "A 'claim upon or against' the Government relates solely to the payment or approval of a claim for money or property to which a right is asserted against the government. . . ."

But the board decided not to recognize the narrow definition of a claim as used in the False Claims Act and instead used the broader definition "to mean a demand by one person upon another, to do or forbear to do some act or thing as a matter of duty." Using the broader definition, the board found the legal fees unallowable under the provisions of ASPR 15-205.31(d).

The chairman of the ASBCA dissented from this conclusion. He found that "[d]efining a 'claim' has always been a problem in government contracting . . ." and that "[n]o attempt has ever been made to define the term, and apparently this is the first Board case in which it has become critical to a result." He concluded that "[e]xclusions from allowable costs ought to be read narrowly. . . ." He further expressed the view that "[s]eeking an injunction to protect the integrity of the procurement process . . . does not fall within the definition."

Hirsch Tyler Company, ASBCA No. 20962, 76-2 BCA par. 12,075

The decision here is another illustration of the board's rejection of the government's efforts to take extremely narrow positions in classifying professional costs.

The contractor incurred and the government disallowed the following costs: (1) legal costs, principally attorneys' fees incurred by Hirsch Tyler in defending court litigation; and (2) the expenses of satisfying a judgment awarding back wages, court costs and attorney fees to the plaintiff in the litigation.

The alleged discriminatory employment practices that gave rise to the disputed costs emanated from a complaint by a female employee that she was not considered for a position because of her sex and, further, that she was subsequently discharged when the contractor became aware that she had filed the discrimination charges with the Equal Employment Opportunity Commission. The board noted that Hirsch Tyler "from its inception and throughout the proceedings ... kept (the Government) continuously informed about the progress of the litigation and apprised (the Government) concerning anticipated and actual legal expenses."

According to the ASBCA decision, it was established that the female employee had not actually applied for the position until it was filled. Although the district judge was apparently inclined to dismiss the complaint for that reason, he ultimately ruled for the employee because of a contemporaneous decision "that application for a position or showing that the plaintiff was the most qualified person to fill the job were not essential elements of proof in a case involving alleged discriminatory failure to promote." Before entry of judgment, Hirsch Tyler advised the ACO of the outcome and indicated it did not consider it worthwhile to appeal.

The contractor paid the costs as required by the court, and the government refused to reimburse them under the cost-type contract.

Under a cost-type contract, costs are allowable to the extent they are incurred, reasonable, allocable, and are not expressly excluded from payment by the terms of the contract itself or the cost principles incorporated therein by reference. The government would concede only that such costs were incurred, but the contracting officer found them unallowable in all other respects.

In challenging allocability, the government asserted that "the accounts giving rise to the disputed costs were not incidental to the proper performance of the contract (and) were of no benefit to the contractual effort. ...." The board disagreed and found the government's contention without merit. As the board saw it, the costs:

> ... would normally be treated as indirect costs, in which event the definition of allocability provided by ASPR 15-201.4 and the issue of "relative benefits received" would be germane. We observe that in determining the allocability of indirect costs a broad view is taken of the concept of "benefit." *Lockheed Aircraft Corp. v. U.S.* (12 CCF par. 80,039), 179 Ct.Cl. 545, 375 F.2d 786 (1967); *General Dynamics Corp., Electric Boat Division,* ASBCA No. 18503, 75-2 BCA par. 11,521. Were the legal expenses and costs of satisfying a judgment to be charged indirectly to contract 0390, we would follow our decision in *Hayes International Corporation,* ASBCA No. 18447, 75-1 BCA par. 11,076, to find that these costs were allocable.

*   *   *   *

But this appeal presents an *a fortiori* case as to allocability, since all costs arising out of the operation of the USAF Cadet Tailor Shop can be identified specifically with contract 0390. Pursuant to the terms of the contract. "The Tailor Shop will be a completely self sustained entity. No General and Administrative costs at the factory will be allowable or reimbursed hereunder." Therefore, the costs in dispute are direct costs in accordance with the contract and ASPR 15-202 and, if allowable, they are reimbursable only as direct costs incurred under contract 0390. The costs in question were incurred specifically for operation of the Tailor Shop, therefore for the contract and are allocable thereto under standards prescribed in ASPR 15-201.4.

All of the discussions up to this stage relate to the first of the category of costs involved as identified at the beginning of this analysis: "Legal costs, principally attorneys' fees, incurred by Hirsch Tyler in defending the litigation." At this point, the board took on the second category: "The expenses of satisfying a judgment awarding back wages, court costs and attorney fees to the plaintiff in the litigation." The board found this category of expenses to be quantitatively distinct from the first category and ruled that a determination of their allowability must be made on a case-by-case basis. Citing other board and court cases as precedent, the board ruled that the court had not found willful or malicious conduct on the part of Hirsch Tyler. Moreover, viewing the judgment standing alone, it found no basis to conclude that the contractor had intentionally discriminated against the employee or otherwise acted in bad faith. It also noted that, despite the contracting officer's decision that Hirsch Tyler had violated the provision of the Equal Opportunity clause of the contract, he did not invoke any of the penalties and sanctions authorized by that clause. In summary on this aspect of the appeal, the board said: "The back wages awarded represent a type of cost generally allowable under ASPR. (See ASPR 15-205.6) There being no provision of ASPR which compels disallowing the costs incurred in satisfying the judgment involved in this appeal, we conclude that they were allowable. Accordingly, the appeal is sustained."

John Doe Co., Inc., ASBCA No. 24576, 80-2 BCA par. 14,620

We consider this decision of particular significance in the light of the atmosphere in which government contractors have been operating in the 1980s.

The board's ruling in the appeal of the *John Doe Co., Inc.,* (contractor's name not identified in view of grand jury investigation of possible fraud), will be of considerable interest to contractors who are or may be involved in these or related unpleasant circumstances. As we have advised our readers elsewhere in this text, such events as the enactment of the Inspector General Act of 1978, continuing GAO reports of horror stories about fraud in government contracting, and efforts by some members of the Congress to achieve publicity through disclosure of established and alleged fraud have combined to make the Defense Contract Audit Agency (DCAA) and other government organizations increasingly sensitive to the possibility of fraudulent activities on the part of government contractors. In a number of instances, transactions that would have been considered unallowable costs are now considered in the category of fraud or suspicion of fraud in today's environment. In this atmosphere, allegations of fraud against government contractors have sharply increased and have resulted in considerable pain, discomfort, and financial damages to companies doing business with the government.

In the *John Doe Co., Inc.,* case, the government withheld approximately half a million dollars on several contracts based on a DCAA Form 1 that stated that its auditors had "detected a considerable number of alterations of employee semi-monthly time reports." Other alleged alterations to labor time records and distribution summaries were asserted to have taken place. DCAA stated it had not been able to determine the exact amount, although the Form 1 recommended the suspension of $498,143, "representing an approximation of the magnitude of unsupported labor and indirect expenses reimbursed to the contractor."

Omitting the details involved in the charges and countercharges, the contractor asserted that the corrections it had made of the time records involved a very small percentage of the recorded hours, and the manner in which many of the corrections were made failed to establish a basis for the allegation that it was attempting "to carefully obliterate uncorrected time sheet entries." The contractor further criticized DCAA's charges as particularly misleading since the company had been following the same procedures for a ten-year period during which no questions had been raised by DCAA.

The amount suspended by DCAA Form 1 was the subject of a previous appeal in which the government moved to suspend all further proceedings and to dismiss the appeal without prejudice pending the outcome of a criminal investigation plus grand jury deliberations and any resulting prosecutions or similar litigation. At that time, the ASBCA had directed the parties to discuss an arrangement for provisional payment upon appropriate security. The matter was ultimately settled by the government's agreement to release the funds provided John Doe posted a bond. The appeal was then withdrawn without prejudice to reinstatement if the government again questioned the costs.

The dispute now before the board concerns the allowability of legal fees and related costs incurred by John Doe in connection with the grand jury investigation. Based on the published decision, John Doe had incurred substantial legal and related expenses in connection with the audit and investigation, resulting in a significant increase in its G&A expense rate. The government refused to recognize the increased G&A expense rate, questioning the allowability of the legal fees and related costs.

The proceedings and investigations continued and so did the incurrence of legal and related costs by John Doe. However, the government continued to refuse to recognize for provisional billing purposes the increased G&A rates. The contractor appealed to the ASBCA, moving for summary judgment that the costs were allowable and should be reimbursed provisionally. The government argued that the appeal was premature since the contracting officer had not refused to issue a final decision regarding John Doe's proposed final G&A rates for 1979 or its proposed provisional rates for 1980, but was unable to do so until the audit by DCAA was completed.

John Doe argued that the government misrepresented the issue in that no audit could settle the fundamental question, which was the reimbursability of the aforementioned legal and related expenses. John Doe asserted that the real issue before the board could be found in the government's stated position:

> It is the position of the Government that the legal and related expenses can only satisfy the requirement that they are allocable costs if the direct labor costs, from which they arose are allocable. Stated in the converse, to the extent it is determined that the direct labor charges under criminal investigation are determined not to be incidental to the proper performance of the contract and of no benefit to the contractual effort (albeit because they were actually not incurred or tainted) they would not be allocable to the contract and therefore the legal and related expenses incurred by Appellant in defending the validity of such costs would not be allocable.

The board identified as the threshold question the allowability of the investigation-related costs, including the cost of photocopying the millions of documents provided to the grand jury, salaries of the company's in-house attorneys working to produce the grand jury materials, etc.

The board then reviewed the provisions of DAR 15-201.2, 15-201.3 (reasonableness), 15-201.4 (allocability), and 15-205.31(d). The board then took note of the board and court decisions cited by both parties concerning the reimbursement of legal fees under government contracts. It found that "none of them is precisely in point" and discussed only *Hayes International Corp.,* ASBCA No. 18477 (discussed earlier) and *Commissioner of Internal Revenue* v. *Tellier,* 383 U.S. 687, 86 S. Ct. 1118, 16 L.Ed. 2d 185 (1966).

In *Commissioner* v. *Tellier,* a taxpayer was brought to trial on a criminal indictment, found guilty, and sentenced to pay a fine and serve a prison term. At issue was the allowability of the legal expenses he incurred and paid in his unsuccessful defense of the criminal prosecution. The deduction was disallowed by IRS and the appeals carried right up to the Supreme Court, which held for the taxpayer. The Court found these costs to be ordinary business expenses, which should be disallowed only where their deduction would "frustrate sharply designed national or state policies proscribing particular types of conduct. . . ." The Court found that these expenses did not meet the criterion and stated: "No public policy is offended when a man faced with serious criminal charges employs a lawyer to help in his defense. That is not '*proscribed conduct*'. . . . In an adversary system of criminal justice, it is a basic of our public policy that a defendant in a criminal case have counsel to represent him. . . ."

The board's decision in *John Doe,* while definitely favorable to the contractor, was not as clear-cut as it might have been. It did decide that the appeal was not premature, the company having waited long enough. However, it stopped just short of a definitive ruling in favor of the contractor on its motion for summary judgment.

First, it definitely disagreed with the government's position that, if the labor costs were found to have been recorded fraudulently, "then unsuccessful litigation expenses related to such nonexistent or otherwise unallocable costs also may not be allocated to the contract." The board stated that "the allocability of indirect G&A expenses . . . does not depend on a direct relationship with a particular cost objective. (ASPR 15-201.4(iii)." It reiterated that expenses of defending the allowability of a mistakenly or fraudulently recorded cost are not "necessarily excluded from the G&A pool."

The board's disinclination to rule forthrightly in favor of the contractor is less definitive, and perhaps we would do best to cite the legalistic language verbatim:

> Appellant's argument on the other hand, although perhaps not so intended, can be construed to contend that the expenses of defending against criminal investigations or indictments must be allowable in nature, notwithstanding the circumstances in which incurred or the fraud that may have been committed. But the boundaries of fraud are indiscernible, and a corporation might be subjected to criminal prosecution in innumerable circumstances. See *19 C.J.S. Corporations, par. 1358-1371, Cf. In re Special September 1978 Grand Jury (II).* CA 7 (4/30/80), 48 U.S. Law Week No. 45. Pending completion of an investigation and possible prosecution, the Board has no assurance whether the retention of legal services and the expenditure of all costs related to alleged fraud are, in all respects, reasonable *in nature.*

> Accordingly, we may not conclude that the reasonableness in nature and allocability of such costs may not be made to depend in some cases on the ultimate outcome of an investigation and prosecution.

Concluding its opinion, however, the board said that, while it could not rule that the G&A expenses were allowable, "we do rule partially, that they may not be disallowed on the ground that the government has asserted. Unless the government has evidence of other grounds for disallowance, e.g., that the costs are otherwise unreasonable, they should be reimbursed provisionally."

Complex Issues of Allowability When Government Relations Are Breached

The captioned issue, at least from the layman's viewpoint, has not been fully resolved. We review here, however, a decision in the appeal of *Lear Siegler, Inc.,* ASBCA No. 20040, 79-1 BCA par. 13,687, affirming prior decisions on Reconsideration (76-1 BCA par. 11,897 and 78-1 BCA par. 13,110) as a case providing some clues to the answer to the perplexing problems. We consider this case particularly noteworthy not because it established precise criteria for allowability of legal fees, but because of the references to the various board and court cases on related controversies and the effort to place these decisions in perspective.

It may be useful to begin this review by citing the statutory prohibition against recovery of legal fees associated with the prosecution of a claim against the government (28 U.S.C. 2412 (1970)):

> Except as otherwise specifically provided by statute, a judgment for costs, as enumerated in Section 1920 of this Title, but not including the fees and expenses of attorneys, may be awarded to the prevailing party in any civil action brought by or against the United States . . . .

It would also appear appropriate to cite the then governing DAR 15-205.31, Professional and Consultant Service Costs, Legal, Engineering and Other, subparagraph (d), (same language contained in FPR 1-15.205-31(d)):

"Costs of legal, accounting and consulting services, and related costs incurred in connection with . . . the prosecution of claims against the government, are unallowable."

With this background, we proceed to the *Lear Siegler* case, in which the contractor was successful in having the board sustain its appeal from the government's claim for alleged defective pricing. However, the contractor's claim for legal fees paid for responding to the government's defective pricing claim was denied by the board.

Lear Siegler leaned on the decision in *Hayes International Corp., supra,* ASBCA No. 18447, 75-1 BCA par. 11,076. The board, however, asserted that there was a distinction between *Hayes* and the instant case, where legal fees were sought for defending against a defective pricing claim, and quoted its decision on this point in *Dewey Electronics Corporation,* ASBCA No. 17696, 76-2 BCA par. 12,146:

> In *Hayes* the issue was the allowability, under cost reimbursement contract provisions and the ASPR Section 15 cost principles, of including in G & A the legal expenses related to the defense of a defective pricing claim, where the attorneys gathered data to assist the appellant to respond to the Government's defective pricing allegations and made no personal appearance on appellant's behalf in connection with the claim. The record contained no indication that the defective pricing allegation was ever formalized as a contracting officer's decision from which an appeal could be taken to the Board.

The board further stated that Lear Siegler's Motion for Reconsideration displayed "a misunderstanding of the *Hayes* decision as did the appellant in the *Dewey* appeal." It thereupon sought to explain the distinction and began the explanation by referring to *Grumman Aerospace Corporation v. The United States* (Ct.Cl. 1978) [25 CCF par. 82,460] 579 F.2d 586.

Grumman incurred legal costs in connection with renegotiation proceedings, included such costs in its G&A expenses, and charged them to its government contracts. All of these legal costs were disallowed by the government. Grumman appealed, and its appeal was denied in NASA BCA No. 873-11, 75-2 BCA par. 11,627 and NASA BCA Nos. 873-11, 1073-15, 76-1 BCA par. 11,763. Grumman appealed to the Court of Claims.

The legal and accounting fees at issue could be divided into two categories. The Renegotiation Board made a finding of excessive profits, the contractor refused to accept the finding, the Renegotiation Board issued a unilateral order, and the parties ultimately reached a compromise settlement. Grumman was trying to recover the legal and accounting expenses involved with its appeal of the unilateral order to the Court of Claims. The contractor's contention was that, since the government initiated the renegotiation process by making a claim against Grumman, the appeal was not a claim against the government. However, the Court of Claims found that Grumman was contesting an order to make a payment to the government, and this characteristic aspect of renegotiation met the definition of a "claim against the Government." The Court found that the proceedings had gone beyond the Renegotiation Board and, having reached the Court of Claims, definitely constituted the prosecution of a claim.

The second aspect of this case involved legal costs incurred by Grumman in a suit under the Freedom of Information Act to obtain information used by the Renegotiation Board in determining that Grumman had earned excess profits. In this instance, the Court of Claims found the contractor's efforts did not constitute a claim for money or property, but sought information only, and hence the related expenses were allowable.

The board then included a lengthy rationale, citing various Court of Claims decisions as well as its own, and because Lear Siegler had made a particular point of Hayes International, the board included a lengthy analysis in which it sought to make a distinction between Lear Siegler and Hayes.

I. *General Rules*

Hayes is distinguishable from the long standing general rule that legal fees for litigation in the federal courts, whether for prosecution of a claim or its defense, may not be taxed to either party, and the general rule that legal fees for prosecuting or defending claims in contract appeal proceedings may not be awarded. Although these rules are influenced in part by the doctrine of sovereign immunity, they do not depend on it. As stated in *F.D. Rich Co. v. Industrial Lumber Co.* [20 CCF ¶ 83,070], 417 U.S. 116 (1974):

$$* \quad * \quad * \quad *$$

In addition to the general rule against the award of attorneys' fees for litigation in the federal courts, the rule that costs or expenses may not be taxed against the sovereign has long prevented such allowances. *United States v. Chemical Foundation,* 272 U.S. 1 (1926); *United States v. Worley,* 281 U.S. 339 (1930). That rule was codified in 28 U.S.C. § 2412, which, as amended in 1966, provides for the allowance of some costs to the prevailing party in actions brought by or against the United States, "but not including the fees and expenses of attorneys."

The rule is similar in proceedings before this Board. *Power Equipment Corp.,* ASBCA No. 5904, 1964 BCA ¶ 4025 and 4228. In *Drexel Dynamics Corporation,* ASBCA No. 9502 et al., 67-2 BCA ¶ 6410, the Board denied a claim for counsel fees and miscellaneous expenses of defending against government claims, stating:

"We can see no reason for making the defense of a Government claim an exception to the general rule prohibiting payment of attorney's fees."

$$* \quad * \quad * \quad *$$

In a Board proceeding, however, the issue normally is, as it was in *Hayes,* the proper interpretation of a provision of a contract or regulation, not the applicability of a general federal rule against taxing such costs or the doctrine of sovereign immunity. In *Reed & Prince Mfg. Co.,* ASBCA No. 3172, 59-1 BCA ¶ 2172, the Board construed provisions of ASPR concerning termination settlement expenses and claims prosecution costs, which were similar to those in force today. It stated:

"We are not disposed to interpret ASPR 8-302b(27), quoted above, to include expenses of litigation with the Government incurred before submissions of a convenience termination settlement proposal and indeed incurred for the purpose of securing the right to submit such a proposal. The ordinary meaning of the words used should not be so enlarged. We ought to presume that the drafters of these words were aware of the general rule against allowance of attorney fees in suits against the United States. If they had intended to carve out an exception in favor of successful litigation against default terminations they could have done so in plain words.

"So runs the argument against the appellant. Appellant seeks to avoid its thrust. Counsel for appellant urged that for appellant to resist successfully, as contrary to law, the Government's assertion against appellant of default costs and reprocurement costs is not the prosecution of a claim against the United States within the ASPR meaning.

"We must disagree. Suppose that appellant could have and actually did litigate the validity of the default action after, instead of before, it had paid the assessed default costs and reprocurement costs to the Government. Could it then urge that what it did was not the prosecution of a claim against the United States? We think not. In substance, except for bookkeeping, the two actions are the same."

*   *   *   *

"Furthermore, attorney's fees for prosecuting disputes before the administrative boards have been held to be not recoverable, because they were not incurred in performance of the contract . . . ."

But compare the recent comments of the Court of Claims in the *Singer Company Librascope Division v. United States* [24 CCF ¶ 81,914], 215 Ct.Cl. 281, 568 F.2d 695, 720 (1977):

"Claim Preparation Costs Including Attorneys' Fees

"[17] In this claim the contractor seeks recovery, by way of an equitable adjustment in contract price, for the attorneys' fees, technical consultants' fees, and in-house personnel costs that were incurred in connection with the preparation and documentation of the claims for equitable adjustment that it presented to the contracting officer. The Board denied this claim, saying:

"It is clear from the facts that the costs in question were not incidental to performance of work or alleged changes but were incidental to a claim. That the claim was to the contracting officer for an equitable adjustment rather than to this Board for the same relief is not significant." [73-2 BCA at 48,426.]

We agree with the Board's decision.

"The contractor does not dispute the proposition that legal fees associated with the prosecution of a claim before a contract board are not recoverable. Such fees fall within the statutory prohibition of 28 U.S.C. § 2412 (1970)."

*   *   *   *

II. Application in the *Hayes* Appeal

In *Hayes* the Board did not establish a precedent that departs from the general rules against the award of litigation costs or claims prosecution expenses. With respect to the costs of defense against defective pricing claims, the decision was a very narrow one. First, it was dealing with cost reimbursement provisions and a G&A expense pool, i.e., only a portion of the expenses would be recoverable if allowable and allocable. Second, the Board pointed out that at no time had the attorneys made personal appearances on behalf of appellant in connection with the claim, which was settled. In fact, the record did not even indicate a contracting officer's decision had been issued, much less that a dispute had been prosecuted before the Board. The costs in issue were those paid to a law firm for gathering data for the purpose of assisting the contractor to "respond" to a government allegation of defective pricing. Therefore, . . . the Board did not have to reach the question whether legal fees for prosecuting a dispute before the Board in defense of a defective pricing claim would be barred by the peculiar wording of the claims prosecution provisions of ASPR 15-205.31d.[1] [Footnote not reproduced—CCH.] Had such fees been in issue, the Board presumably would have allowed them in view of the comparable precedent it set in *Hayes* in connection with the legal fees for defense against the government's civil rights suit. However, such a precedent would only be for an interpretation of that ASPR provision, which so readily lends itself to the distinction the Board made between expenses of defending and prosecuting claims. On that point *Hayes* is distinguishable from *Reed & Prince Mfg. Co., supra,* in which the Board bolstered its above-quoted rationale by noting that defense of a default action is, or may be, an inseparable part of a maneuver to permit the prosecution of a termination for convenience claim against the government; a procedure not available upon a successful defense of a defective pricing claim, and one not noted in the opinion in *Grumman, supra.*

*   *   *   *

In the appeal of *Dynalectron,* ASBCA No. 16895, 73-1 BCA ¶ 9909, this Board decided that the contractor's costs of defending a lawsuit arising out of a guaranty of a commercial sales contract were not allocable as a part of appellant's G&A pool to its government cost contracts. The decision was not based on any general rule or ASPR provision against reimbursement of such legal expenses; rather, it was based on the accounting conclusion that the costs were not indirect expenses chargeable to government contracts, but were direct costs chargeable either to the cost objective of the commercial guaranty contract out of which they arose or to appellant's commercial business generally.

The contractor then sought relief in the Court of Claims. In *Dynalectron Corporation v. United States* [23 CCF ¶ 80,877], 212 Ct.Cl. 118, 545 F.2d 736 (1976), the court stated:

"The Board held, and defendant contends here, that the above ASPR provisions are decisive against the plaintiff, and we agree. The costs in dispute are not allocable to the Government contracts under subparagraph (i) of ASPR 15-201.4 because they were not incurred specifically for the contracts. They are not allocable to the contracts under subparagraph (ii) because they did not benefit the contracts; and they are not allocable to the contracts under subparagraph (iii) because they were not necessary to the overall operation of the business, but had a direct relationship to a particular cost objective, namely, the commercial guaranty venture.

* * * *

"Plaintiff cites the case of *Hayes International Corp.,* ASBCA No. 18447, 75-1 BCA para. 11076 as support for allowing legal expenses to be charged as indirect costs. That case is also distinguishable from our case. There the contractor was sued for racial discrimination of its employees. The contractor had cost reimbursable contracts with the Government. The Board held that the legal fees could be charged as indirect costs to the Government contracts, as there was no showing that the employees had worked only on commercial contracts. There appeared to be a relationship between the complaint of the employees and the performance of the Government contracts. The legal fees, accordingly, were proper indirect costs of the Government contracts under ASPR 15-201.4(iii). There is no such relationship between the legal fees and the Government contracts in the instant case."

In the review of this cost principle (as well as in connection with others), the author has presented analyses, including reviews of judicial and quasi-judicial decisions, from a layman's viewpoint. Consistent with avoiding legal interpretations, we shall not attempt to evaluate some of the decisions reviewed in the light of all of the changing statutes and regulations. We do wish to invite the reader's attention to the following points:

The term "claim" has been significant in some of the rulings and we should consider the definition of this word as it now appears in FAR 33.201:

"Claim," as used in this subpart, means a written demand or written assertion by one of the contracting parties seeking, as a matter of right, the payment of money in a sum certain, the adjustment or interpretation of contract terms, or other relief arising under or relating to the contract. A claim arising under a contract, unlike a claim relating to that contract, is a claim that can be resolved under a contract clause that provides for the relief sought by the claimant. However, a written demand or written assertion by the contractor seeking the payment of money exceeding $50,000 is not a claim under the Contract Disputes Act of 1978 until certified as required by the Act and 33.207. A voucher, invoice, or other routine request for payment that is not in dispute when submitted is not a claim. The submission may be converted to a claim, by written notice to the contracting officer as provided in 33.206(a), if it is disputed either as to liability or amount or is not acted upon in a reasonable time.

The second point to consider in viewing prior rulings in today's environment relates to some of the changes to regulations. For example, the expanded FAR 31.205-33(d) has added to unallowable costs: "defense against Government claims or appeals, or the prosecution of . . . appeals against the Government." Another very important change to the cost principles since some of the cited decisions were handed down, and one which bears on some of the rulings, was the promulgation of FAR 31.205-47, Defense of Fraud Proceedings, reviewed later in this chapter.

RECRUITMENT COSTS

FAR 31.205-34 provides:

(a) Subject to paragraphs (b) and (c) below, and provided that the size of the staff recruited and maintained is in keeping with workload requirements, the following costs are allowable:

(1) Costs of help-wanted advertising.

(2) Costs of operating an employment office needed to secure and maintain an adequate labor force.

(3) Costs of operating an aptitude and educational testing program.

(4) Travel costs of employees engaged in recruiting personnel.

(5) Travel costs of applicants for interviews.

(6) Costs for employment agencies, not in excess of standard commercial rates.

(b) Help-wanted advertising costs are unallowable if the advertising—

(1) Is for personnel other than those required to perform obligations under a Government contract;

(2) Does not describe specific positions or classes of positions;

(3) Is excessive relative to the number and importance of the positions or to the industry practices;

(4) Includes material that is not relevant for recruitment purposes, such as extensive illustrations or descriptions of the company's products or capabilities;

(5) Is designed to "pirate" personnel from another Government contractor; or

(6) Includes color (in publications).

(c) Excessive compensation costs offered to prospective employees to "pirate" them from another Government contractor are unallowable. Such excessive costs may include salaries, fringe benefits, or special emoluments which are in excess of standard industry practices or the contractor's customary compensation practices.

The contract cost principle on recruitment costs is another illustration of government efforts to overregulate and overmanage firms engaged in contracts where prices are based on costs. If subparagraph (b)(1) were to be taken literally, which it seldom is, such costs should be charged directly to the contracts involved. Whether the amount of help-wanted advertising "is excessive relative to the number and importance of the positions or to the industry practices" is a difficult question, one which few auditors or ACOs are really qualified to pass upon.

Similarly, judgments as to whether the help-wanted advertising "is designed to 'pirate' personnel from another Government contractor" are surely difficult to make.

Despite the complexities of this area, DCAA's Contract Audit Manual devotes considerable space (paragraph 7-1904) to furnishing guidance to its auditors on this sensitive area and advises: "Due care should accordingly be exercised to assure that the audit program and the audit attain the desired objective."

RELOCATION COSTS

FAR 31.205-35 provides:

(a) Relocation costs are costs incident to the permanent change of duty assignment (for an indefinite period or stated period, but in either event for not less than 12 months) of an existing employee or upon recruitment of a new employee. The following types of costs are allowable as noted, subject to paragraphs (b) through (f) below:

(1) Cost of travel of the employee and members of the immediate family (see 31.205-46) and transportation of the household and personal effects to the new location.

(2) Cost of finding a new home, such as advance trips by employees and spouses to locate living quarters, and temporary lodging during the transition periods not exceeding separate cumulative totals of 60 days for employees and 45 days for spouses and dependents, including advance trip time.

(3) Closing costs (i.e., brokerage fees, legal fees, appraisal fees, points, finance charges, etc.) incident to the disposition of actual residence owned by the employee when notified of transfer, except that these costs when added to the costs described in subparagraph (a)(4) below shall not exceed 14 percent of the sales price of the property sold.

(4) Continuing costs of ownership of the vacant former actual residence being sold, such as maintenance of building and grounds (exclusive of fixing up expenses), utilities, taxes, property insurance, mortgage interest, after settlement date or lease date of new permanent residence, except that these costs when added to the costs described in subparagraph (a)(3) above, shall not exceed 14 percent of the sales price of the property sold.

(5) Other necessary and reasonable expenses normally incident to relocation, such as disconnecting and connecting household appliances; automobile registration; driver's license and use taxes; cutting and fitting rugs, draperies, and curtains; forfeited utility fees and deposits; and purchase of insurance against damage to or loss of personal property while in transit.

(6) Costs incident to acquiring a home in a new location, except that (i) these costs will not be allowable for existing employees or newly recruited employees who, before the relocation, were not homeowners and

(ii) the total costs shall not exceed 5 percent of the purchase price of the new home.

(7) Mortgage interest differential payments, except that these costs are not allowable for existing or newly recruited employees who, before the relocation, were not homeowners and the total payments are limited to an amount determined as follows:

(i) The difference between the mortgage interest rates of the old and new residences times the current balance of the old mortgage times 3 years.

(ii) When mortgage differential payments are made on a lump sum basis and the employee leaves or is transferred again in less than 3 years, the amount initially recognized shall be proportionately adjusted to reflect payments only for the actual time of the relocation.

(8) Rental differential payments covering situations where relocated employees retain ownership of a vacated home in the old location and rent at the new location. The rented quarters at the new location must be comparable to those vacated, and the allowable differential payments may not exceed the actual rental costs for the new home, less the fair market rent for the vacated home times 3 years.

(9) Cost of canceling an unexpired lease.

(b) The costs described in paragraph (a) above must also meet the following criteria to be considered allowable:

(1) The move must be for the benefit of the employer.

(2) Reimbursement must be in accordance with an established policy or practice that is consistently followed by the employer and is designed to motivate employees to relocate promptly and economically.

(3) The costs must not otherwise be unallowable under Subpart 31.2.

(4) Amounts to be reimbursed shall not exceed the employee's actual expenses, except that for miscellaneous costs of the type discussed in subparagraph (a)(5) above, a flat amount, not to exceed $1,000, may be allowed in lieu of actual costs.

(c) The following types of costs are not allowable:

(1) Loss on sale of a home.

(2) Costs incident to acquiring a home in a new location as follows:

(i) Real estate brokers' fees and commissions.

(ii) Cost of litigation.

(iii) Real and personal property insurance against damage or loss of property.

(iv) Mortgage life insurance.

(v) Owner's title policy insurance when such insurance was not previously carried by the employee on the old residence (however, cost of a mortgage title policy is allowable).

(vi) Property taxes and operating or maintenance costs.

(3) Continuing mortgage principal payments on residence being sold.

(4) Payments for employee income or FICA (social security) taxes incident to reimbursed relocation costs.

(5) Payments for job counseling and placement assistance to employee spouses and dependents who were not employees of the contractor at the old location.

(6) Costs incident to furnishing equity or nonequity loans to employees or making arrangements with lenders for employees to obtain lower-than-market rate mortgage loans.

(d) If relocation costs for an employee have been allowed either as an allocable indirect or direct cost, and the employee resigns within 12 months for reasons within the employee's control, the contractor shall refund or credit the relocation costs to the Government.

(e) Subject to the requirements of paragraphs (a) through (d) above, the costs of family movements and of personnel movements of a special or mass nature are allowable. The cost, however, should be assigned on the basis of work (contracts) or time period benefited.

(f) Relocation costs (both outgoing and return) of employees who are hired for performance on specific contracts or long-term field projects are allowable if—

(1) The term of employment is not less than 12 months;

(2) The employment agreement specifically limits the duration of employment to the time spent on the contract or field project for which the employee is hired;

(3) The employment agreement provides for return relocation to the employee's permanent and principal home immediately prior to the outgoing relocation, or other location of equal or lesser cost; and

(4) The relocation costs are determined under the rules of paragraphs (a) through (d) above. However, the costs to return employees, who are released from employment upon completion of field assignments pursuant to their employment agreements, are not subject to the refund or credit requirement of paragraph (d).

FAC 84-25, effective July 1, 1987, revised FAR 31.205-35 by defining the time requirement for permanent change of duty assignment in paragraph (a) to make it clear that it must be for 12 months or more to qualify for coverage under the relocation cost principle. It also added a new paragraph (f), which clarified the allowability of the relocation costs of employees who are hired, relocated, and returned to their domiciles in connection with specific long-term field projects.

The history of this cost principle reflects efforts by companies to obtain the best qualified employees and the attendant need to reimburse them for the costs incurred incident to (1) disposing of, without loss, the homes they owned, (2) finding a home in the new location, and (3) acquiring and making the home livable without undue out-of-pocket cost. Our experience does not suggest major policy differences in this area between firms with substantial government contracts and those with a preponderance of commercial work. Government contractors, however, are severely regulated.

Among the reasons for the overregulation is the one that has been identified as at least a partial cause for the heavy restrictions on compensation, professional fees, travel, and other expenses—that is, a tendency to compare industry practices with those in the federal government and to view any benefits in excess of those available to government employees as excessive or unreasonable. For the last quarter of a century or so, the government has added restriction and limitation upon restriction and limitation. Industry has been largely unsuccessful in halting this tendency and the best it has been able to accomplish is to persuade the government to somewhat broaden the various allowances so as to approach industry practices outside the government contract market area.

RENTAL COSTS

FAR 31.205-36 provides:

(a) This subsection is applicable to the cost of renting or leasing real or personal property, except ADPE (see 31.205-2), acquired under "operating leases" as defined in Statement of Financial Accounting Standards No. 13 (FAS-13), Accounting for Leases. Compliance with 31.205-11(m) requires that assets acquired by means of capital leases, as defined in FAS-13, shall be treated as purchased assets; i.e., be capitalized and the capitalized value of assets be distributed over their useful lives as depreciation charges, or over the lease term as amortization charges, as appropriate (but see subparagraph (b)(4) below).

(b) The following costs are allowable:

(1) Rental costs under operating leases, to the extent that the rates are reasonable at the time of the lease decision, after consideration of (i) rental costs of comparable property, if any; (ii) market conditions in the area; (iii) the type, life expectancy, condition, and value of the property leased; (iv) alternatives available; and (v) other provisions of the agreement.

(2) Rental costs under a sale and leaseback arrangement only up to the amount the contractor would be allowed if the contractor retained title.

(3) Charges in the nature of rent for property between any divisions, subsidiaries, or organization under common control, to the extent that they do not exceed the normal costs of ownership, such as depreciation, taxes, insurance, facilities capital cost of money, and maintenance (excluding interest or other unallowable costs pursuant to Part 31), provided that no part of such costs shall duplicate any other allowed cost. Rental cost of personal property leased from any division, subsidiary, or affiliate of the contractor under common control, that has an established practice of leasing the same or similar property to unaffiliated lessees shall be allowed in accordance with subparagraph (b)(1) above.

(4) Rental costs under leases entered into before March 1, 1970 for the remaining term of the lease (excluding options not exercised before March 1, 1970) to the extent they would have been allowable under Defense Acquisition Regulation (Formerly ASPR) 15-205.34 or Federal Procurement Regulations section 1-15.205-34 in effect 1 January 1969.

(c) The allowability of rental costs under unexpired leases in connection with terminations is treated in 31.205.42(e).

Background and Case Studies—Rental Costs

Prior to the overhaul of ASPR XV in 1959, no specific ground rules for rental costs had been formally established by DOD. The 1959 principle, DAR 15-205.34, as our readers know, contained a rather lengthy discussion of this cost item. However, the inclusion of this elaborate write-up, with its many vague phrases, created more confusion and problems and accomplished little by way of clarification.

The following decade witnessed considerable attention to this area, including strong and adverse positions by DOD auditors, particularly where the transactions suggested possible sale and leaseback or intracompany transactions. The General Accounting Office, which at that time performed many audits of, and issued reports on, individual defense contractors, raised many questions regarding the reasonableness of rental costs, even where no sale and leaseback or intracompany transactions were involved.

The 1963 ASPR cost principle stated that rental costs were allowable if reasonable except that the *excess* of such costs over ownership costs was unallowable where the transactions were between affiliates or under sale and leaseback agreements. ASPR 15-205.34(a) also contained a sentence which created considerable controversy and which was subject to many different interpretations: "Application of these factors, in situations where rentals are extensively used, may involve, among other things, comparison of rental costs with the amount which the contractor would have received had he owned the facilities." This statement did not apply to intracompany or sale and leaseback situations. It therefore appeared to be in direct contradiction to the general rule stated in the same paragraph that rental costs are allowable if reasonable "in light of such factors as rental costs of comparable facilities and market conditions in the area. . . ."

GAO's efforts were probably climaxed in the Comptroller General's report to Congress No. B-156818, issued in October, 1968, entitled: "Increased Costs to the Government Attributed to Leasing Rather Than Purchasing Land and Buildings by Department of Defense Contractors." The General Accounting Office reported on some seventeen major contractors and concluded that, under the leasing arrangements for land and buildings, the government was incurring substantially higher costs than it would have if the contractors had purchased those assets. According to GAO, "By the end of the initial leases at the locations reviewed, the additional cost to the Government could amount to about $55.8 million. Furthermore, if all renewal options are exercised, additional costs could amount to as much as $99.3 million." GAO did not have a specific suggestion to take care of all these problems; however, it did recommend to DOD that "[i]n negotiating profits and fees, consideration be given to the methods used by the contractor to acquire real property for use under Government contracts."

In January 1969, capping many years of deliberations, DOD finally arrived at a proposed revision to ASPR 15-205.34. As summarized in the transmittal letter from the Chairman of the ASPR Committee, the revised provision "generally allows the costs of short-term leasing. Short-term leasing is defined as being two years or less for personal property and five years or less for real property. Any leases extended beyond these terms will be treated as long-term as of the date of the extension. The allowability of long-term leasing costs would generally be subject to the same criteria now applicable to ADPE under ASPR 15-205.48."

The proposed revision met with strong industry opposition. CODSIA identified the DOD proposal as essentially adding up to a new criterion— "least cost to the Government"—as forming the basis for acceptability of rental costs. CODSIA saw a disregard for concepts of reasonableness and feared that the proposal "would precipitate a drastic imbalance in the present rather delicate financial equilibrium of cost recovery, profits, and capital investment. . . ." CODSIA noted that its member organizations had submitted various detailed objections to the proposal; however, it thought that the fundamental impropriety and unfairness of the proposal overshadowed them all. Accordingly, it concluded by urging that DOD forget the whole idea and retain ASPR 15-205.34 as it was in January 1969.

Other industry associations, the American Institute of Certified Public Accountants, and the Financial Executives Institute also opposed the revision in whole or in part. All of these comments, together with those submitted from within the government (generally favorable), were received in the spring of 1969 and subjected to detailed study and analysis by the ASPR Committee. As a result of this analysis, certain clarifying editorial and other relatively minor revisions were made; however, the language was not changed in any substantial manner. The weight and extensiveness of the opposition to the change further delayed its issuance, although the final answer was a foregone conclusion.

The revised cost principle was effective March 1, 1970, and the "Notes Regarding Substantive Changes" contained the following summary description of the change:

A revised 15-205.34 generally allows rental costs under short-term leases. Rental costs under long-term leases are limited to the amount the contractor would be allowed had he purchased the property unless he can demonstrate that long-term leasing will result in less cost to the Government under the anticipated useful life of the property. Short-term leasing is defined as leasing where the cumulative term of the use or occupancy (initial term plus additional terms whether or not pursuant to a renewal option) is two years or less for personal property and five years or less for real property. Conversely, long-term leasing means leasing where the cumulative term is more than two years or five years, respectively.

The revised ASPR 15-205.34 represented an extremely significant development in government contract cost principles. By way of a brief summary, the above citation from "Notes Regarding Substantive Changes" will serve an introductory purpose. A few other points should be added.

As to short-term leases, allowability required the determination that they were reasonable in terms of rates and that they did not "give rise to a material equity in the facilities."

As to long-term leases, there are a number of factors that require consideration in demonstrating that they will result in less cost to the government. For one thing, the two factors mentioned above with regard to short-term leases will be involved. Another point here is the more specific spelling out of the costs to be considered in determining ownership costs (for comparison with rental costs). As DOD has done in the past where certain officials were unhappy with ASBCA decisions, this revision included language that was intended to overcome some of the ASBCA decisions where interest on mortgage was considered an allowable cost under certain circumstances. The revision specifically stated that "[f]or the purposes of this comparison, the costs of property . . . exclude interest. . . ."

The provisions governing rental charges between organizations under common control were expanded and included a tie-in with ASPR 15-205.22(a), which governs allowances for supplies and services sold or transferred between affiliated organizations.

In DPC 76-17 dated September 1, 1978, significant revisions were made to DAR 15-205.9, 15-205.32, 15.205.34, and 15-205.48 to conform DAR with the provisions of applicable cost accounting standards. A major change was incorporating into DAR the requirement for contractors to follow the provisions of Standard No. 13 promulgated by the Financial Accounting Standards Board (FASB).

Subparagraphs (j), (j)(1), and (j)(2) were added to DAR 15-205.9. As revised, DAR included as tangible assets any asset acquired by means of a "capital lease" as defined in FAS-13. FAS-13, Accounting for Leases, dated November 1976, established the following criteria for classifying a lease as a capital lease:

a. The lease transfers ownership of the property to the lessee by the end of the lease term.

b. The lease contains a bargain purchase option.

c. The lease . . . is equal to 75% or more of the estimated economic life of the leased property.

d. The present value at the beginning of the lease term of the minimum lease payments (with certain exclusions) equals or exceeds 90% of the fair value of the leased property . . . to the lessor at the inception of the lease over any related investment tax credit retained by the lessor and expected to be realized by him.

Leased assets thus capitalized were subject to provisions for depreciation (15-205.9) rather than rental costs (15-205.34).

Comparable changes of significance were made to DAR 15-205.34 and 15-205.48. With assets acquired under capital leases required to be capitalized and treated as tangible assets subject to depreciation, rental costs in DAR

15-205.34 became applicable only to property acquired under "operating leases" as defined in FAS-13. The four criteria established by FAS-13 for capital leases were summarized above. If a lease does not meet one or more of those criteria, it shall be classified as an operating lease.

Rental costs under operating leases are allowable under the same criteria formally established in DAR for rental costs under short-term leasing. Limitations on rental costs under sale and leaseback arrangements and in the cases of charges between organizations under common control remained substantially unchanged.

FAR 31.205-36 adopted the provisions of DAR in all substantive respects.

ROYALTIES AND OTHER COSTS FOR USE OF PATENTS

FAR 31.205-37 provides:

(a) Royalties on a patent or amortization of the cost of purchasing a patent or patent rights necessary for the proper performance of the contract and applicable to contract products or processes are allowable unless—

(1) The Government has a license or the right to a free use of the patent;

(2) The patent has been adjudicated to be invalid, or has been administratively determined to be invalid;

(3) The patent is considered to be unenforceable; or

(4) The patent is expired.

(b) Care should be exercised in determining reasonableness when the royalties may have been arrived at as a result of less-than-arm's-length bargaining; e.g., royalties—

(1) Paid to persons, including corporations, affiliated with the contractor;

(2) Paid to unaffiliated parties, including corporations, under an agreement entered into in contemplation that a Government contract would be awarded; or

(3) Paid under an agreement entered into after the contract award.

(c) In any case involving a patent formerly owned by the contractor, the royalty amount allowed should not exceed the cost which would have been allowed had the contractor retained title.

(d) See 31.109 regarding advance agreements.

The contract cost principle has remained pretty much unchanged over the years. Established as unallowable are payments where the government already has a license or the right to free use of the patent, or where the patent is invalid, unenforceable, or expired.

SELLING COSTS

Selling costs are covered in Chapter XV of this text.

SERVICE AND WARRANTY COSTS

FAR 31.205-39 provides:

Service and warranty costs include those arising from fulfillment of any contractual obligation of a contractor to provide services such as installation, training, correcting defects in the products, replacing defective parts, making refunds in the case of inadequate performance. When not inconsistent with the terms of the contract, such service and warranty costs are allowable. However, care should be exercised to avoid duplication of the allowance as an element of both estimated product cost and risk.

Although grouped together, service costs illustrated in the cost principle on installation and training differ in important respects from costs relating to warranties, such as correcting defects, replacing defective parts, and making refunds in the case of inadequate performance. Those in the first category are obviously easier to project. Those in the second category must nevertheless be provided for in pricing proposals in a clear manner.

SPECIAL TOOLING AND SPECIAL TEST EQUIPMENT COSTS

FAR 31.205-40 provides:

(a) The terms "special tooling" and "special test equipment" are defined in 45.101.

(b) The cost of special tooling and special test equipment used in performing one or more Government contracts is allowable and shall be allocated to the specific Government contract or contracts for which acquired, except that the cost of (1) items acquired by the contractor before the effective date of the contract (or replacement of such items), whether or not altered or adapted for use in performing the contract, and (2) items which the contract schedule specifically excludes, shall be allowable only as depreciation or amortization.

(c) When items are disqualified as special tooling or special test equipment because with relatively minor expense they can be made suitable for general purpose use and have a value as such commensurate with their value as special tooling or special test equipment, the cost of adapting the items for use under the contract and the cost of returning them to their prior configuration are allowable.

Further discussions relating to methods of charging and financing special tooling and special test equipment are contained in Chapter XII of this text, Accounting Methods and Controls for Other Direct Charges to Government Contracts.

TAXES

FAR 31.205-41 provides:

(a) The following types of costs are allowable:

(1) Federal, State, and local taxes (see Part 29), except as otherwise provided in paragraph (b) below that are required to be and are paid or

accrued in accordance with generally accepted accounting principles. Fines and penalties are not considered taxes.

(2) Taxes otherwise allowable under subparagraph (a)(1) above, but upon which a claim of illegality or erroneous assessment exists; provided the contractor, before paying such taxes—

(i) Promptly requests instructions from the contracting officer concerning such taxes; and

(ii) Takes all action directed by the contracting officer arising out of subparagraph (2)(i) above or an independent decision of the Government as to the existence of a claim of illegality or erroneous assessment, to (A) determine the legality of the assessment or (B) secure a refund of such taxes.

(3) Pursuant to subparagraph (a)(2) above, the reasonable costs of any action taken by the contractor at the direction or with the concurrence of the contracting officer. Interest or penalties incurred by the contractor for non-payment of any tax at the direction of the contracting officer or by reason of the failure of the contracting officer to ensure timely direction after a prompt request.

(b) The following types of costs are not allowable:

(1) Federal income and excess profits taxes.

(2) Taxes in connection with financing, refinancing, refunding operations, or reorganizations (see 31.205-20 and 31.205-27).

(3) Taxes from which exemptions are available to the contractor directly, or available to the contractor based on an exemption afforded the Government, except when the contracting officer determines that the administrative burden incident to obtaining the exemption outweighs the corresponding benefits accruing to the Government. When partial exemption from a tax is attributable to Government contract activity, taxes charged to such work in excess of that amount resulting from application of the preferential treatment are unallowable. These provisions intend that tax preference attributable to Government contract activity be realized by the Government. The term "exemption" means freedom from taxation in whole or in part and includes a tax abatement or reduction resulting from mode of assessment, method of calculation, or otherwise.

(4) Special assessments on land that represent capital improvements.

(5) Taxes (including excises) on real or personal property, or on the value, use, possession or sale thereof, which is used solely in connection with work other than on Government contracts (see paragraph (c) below).

(6) Taxes on accumulated funding deficiencies of, or prohibited transactions involving, employee deferred compensation plans pursuant to Section 4971 or Section 4975 of the Internal Revenue Code of 1954, as amended.

(7) Income tax accruals designed to account for the tax effects of differences between taxable income and pretax income as reflected by the books of account and financial statements.

(c) Taxes on property (see subparagraph (b)(5) above) used solely in connection with either non-Government or Government work should be considered directly applicable to the respective category of work unless the amounts involved are insignificant or comparable results would otherwise be obtained; e.g., taxes on contractor-owned work-in-process which is used solely in connection with non-Government work should be allocated to such work; taxes on contractor-owned work-in-process inventory (and Government-owned work-in-process inventory when taxed) used solely in connection with Government work should be charged to such work. The cost of taxes incurred on property used in both Government and non-Government work shall be apportioned to all such work based upon the use of such property on the respective final cost objectives.

(d) Any taxes, interest, or penalties that were allowed as contract costs and are refunded to the contractor shall be credited or paid to the Government in the manner it directs. However, any interest actually paid or credited to a contractor incident to a refund of tax, interest, or penalty shall be paid or credited to the Government only to the extent that such interest accrued over the period during which the contractor had been reimbursed by the Government for the taxes, interest, or penalties.

Except for editorial changes, this FAR cost principle substantially reflected the ground rules set forth in DAR 15-205.41.

Controversies and Regulation Changes Involving Taxes Contract Cost Principle

Many of the revisions made to this cost principle over the years were attributable to controversies that led to litigation before the ASBCA and the Court of Claims, including personal property taxes on property used exclusively on commercial work, income tax accruals to account for differences between taxable and pretax income, and establishing the fiscal year to which tax credits or refunds are applicable.

Personal Property Taxes—The *Lockheed* and *Boeing* Cases

In September 1969, the Armed Services Board of Contract Appeals handed down decision No. 11866, 70-1 BCA par. 8298; 69-2 BCA par. 7898, in the appeal of *The Boeing Company*. A major point here involved the government's disallowance of the contractor's allocation to government cost-reimbursement contracts of "personal property taxes assessed against and paid by Boeing, which was measured by the value of special tooling and work-in-process used by Boeing solely or principally for production under non-Governmental contracts (identified as 'commercial inventory') . . . ."

The subject of California personal property taxes has been a complicated and controversial one. Few isolated cost items have generated this degree of concerted attention from industry. The unusual attention may be attributed to two factors: (1) basic accounting and pricing principles involved, including "benefit" theory, allocation methods and equity, and (2) the number of defense contractors and subcontractors located in California. This matter is steeped in considerable history, which may be summarized as follows:

The personal property tax is levied by local political subdivisions of California on tangible personal property, and the proceeds are used for various community services such as fire and police protection, water and sewage service, schools, parks, recreation, health, justice, etc. Originally imposed on contractor-owned property, the tax began to be levied on government-owned property beginning in 1953. The federal government entered into litigation, and, in 1958, the California Supreme Court held that the tax on government-owned property was invalid. Thereafter, beginning in 1959, DOD disallowed personal property taxes because the costs related solely to the contractor's commercial inventory and was not incident to the performance of government contracts. But for the commercial work, or if only government work were being performed, argued the contracting officer, the personal property tax would not be payable.

An early major challenge to DOD's position came in the form of an appeal by the Lockheed Aircraft Corp. from a contracting officer's unilateral decision disallowing the personal property taxes on contractor-owned inventory (ASBCA Nos. 6196, 6197 and 6386, 1964 BCA par. 4056). Lockheed offered several arguments, the major one involving the "benefit" concept. The contractor contended that the community services for which personal property taxes were paid (fire and police protection, water and sewage service, etc.) benefited all of its operations, commercial and government, and all operations should, therefore, bear a proportionate allocation. Lockheed also argued that similar services in other states are paid for by franchise taxes, which are considered allowable, and hence California contractors were being discriminated against.

The ASBCA ruled for the government, finding that "nothing really equitable appears from the suggestion that the Government should bear taxes neither assessed upon its property nor incurred in respect of its contracts." The board was also impressed by the fact that the federal government had successfully litigated against the imposition of the tax on its inventories and that to share in the tax imposed on commercial inventories "would be simply to defeat by indirection the tax immunity of Government-owned property."

Lockheed appealed to the Court of Claims and, in decision No. 179 Ct.Cl. 545, handed down in April 1967, the court overruled the ASBCA and held for Lockheed.

The court appeared somewhat cautious about accepting the contractor's emphasis on the benefit argument. It found "benefit" to be "an extremely slippery concept" and "the requirement of benefit may have a more or less general scope depending on the type of expense." In this case, however, the court found that "benefit has a general scope and that sufficient benefit has been shown." In ruling for Lockheed, the court was persuaded that government contracts benefited from the tax in two ways: first, by the fact that the contractor was meeting its responsibilities as a corporate citizen of the community; and second, and specifically, by the services provided by the community.

But for government contractors the court decision amounted to "winning a battle but losing the war" because, in the interim, the Defense Department amended its regulations by adding paragraph ASPR 15-205.41(a)(v), which made unallowable "taxes on any category of property which is used solely in connection with work other than on Government contracts."

As mentioned earlier, in September 1969, the ASBCA issued its decision No. 11866 in the appeal of *The Boeing Company,* where one of the major issues was the allocability to government contracts of personal property taxes levied by local governments. Over 140 cost reimbursement contracts were involved in this appeal, broken down by the board chronologically as: (1) subject to ASPR 15 prior to November 1959; (2) subject to ASPR 16 between November 1959 and September 1962, the date of the aforementioned addition of 15-205.41(a)(v); and (3) subject to ASPR 15 thereafter. The board ruled for Boeing with regard to the first and second periods; it ruled for the government with regard to the period during which the ASPR provision 15-205.41(a)(v) was in effect. The board's denial of Boeing's arguments with respect to the latter period are summarized below.

Boeing's argument, using the "benefit" concept as distilled from ASPR 15-201 and 15-203, was countered by the introduction of the restrictions in 15-201.2, which list among factors affecting allowability of costs "any limitations or exclusions set forth in this Part 2." A salient limitation in this case since September 1962, according to the board, has been ASPR 15-205. 41(a)(v), which specifically prohibits the allowance of "taxes on any category of property which is used solely in conjunction with work other than on Government contracts." Quoting further from this ASPR provision, the board established it as specifically prohibiting allowing this tax and added, in passing, that "[t]he application of this limitation was understood by industry generally and the appellant in particular, from its inception."

Accruals for Tax Effects of Differences Between Taxable Income and Pretax Income

An ASPR revision in August 1969 added a new provision, paragraph 15-205.41(b), which established that "[i]ncome tax accruals designed to account for the tax effects of differences between taxable income and pre-tax income, as reflected by the books of account and financial statement, are unallowable as a contract cost." Inasmuch as federal income taxes have traditionally and consistently been considered unallowable (ASPR 15-205.41(a)(i)), this change is directed to state and local income taxes.

The origin of this ASPR change is traceable to the publication of Accounting Principles Board (APB) Opinion No. 11 by the American Institute of CPA's (AICPA) titled: Accounting For Income Taxes, in December 1967.

When this opinion was reviewed and digested in the Department of Defense, the Defense Contract Audit Agency voiced the concern that APB No. 11 established hypothetical income taxes on the differences between accounting income and tax income as a "generally accepted accounting principle." This would establish the so-called hypothetical tax as an allocable cost under government contracts. A special revision to 15-205.41 to assure that this type of hypothetical charge would not be considered allowable was therefore proposed and approved by the ASPR Committee.

The proposed ASPR revision encountered severe criticism from some sources, particularly from the major industry spokesman, the Council of Defense and Space Industry Associations (CODSIA).

CODSIA's main argument here was that ASPR referred to and accepted generally accepted accounting principles as a criterion for establishing allowability of costs. As we have indicated elsewhere, the validity and even the meaning of generally accepted accounting principles have been controversial matters. Without belaboring this point now, it is sufficient to note that, while an APB opinion does not carry statutory or regulatory weight, it was about the closest authoritative source for generally accepted accounting principles. In this vein, CODSIA protested strongly that the proposed ASPR revision not only disregarded "the major reasons for the establishment of these principles," but it failed to consider the very clear applicability of these principles to costs of government contracts. The argument did seem to have merit because ASPR Section XV frequently referred to generally accepted accounting principles as bearing on the acceptability of costs for contract purposes. And the CODSIA letter to the chairman of the ASPR committee, written in August 1968, was careful and diligent in making this point.

Apart from this general point of principle, the industry position was that the proposed revision "would prevent the distribution of tax expense to the period to which the tax expense is applicable and over the cost objective (base) which generated the taxable income; therefore, the wrong contracts and the wrong business would be charged with a tax expense created in the prior year.
. . ."

The AICPA, which, unfortunately, does not always seem to expend enough time and effort in commenting on accounting aspects of ASPR/DAR changes, felt it necessary to do so here because its very own Accounting Principles Board was being challenged. The AICPA joined industry in opposing the proposed revision. On the other hand, government departments and agencies included in the DOD coordination were just about unanimous in their concurrence.

The Defense Department's ultimate determination to go with this change appeared to establish several points of interest for government, industry, and accounting people concerned with costing and pricing aspects of defense contracts. One point is certainly clear, and that is that conformance with generally accepted accounting principles is not sufficient in and of itself for an accounting method to be accepted as a government contract cost principle. We predicted then that it would become increasingly evident in government, industry, and the accounting profession that the term "generally accepted accounting principle" is not substantial enough to withstand storms or even strong winds of controversy when specific points, such as the income tax accruals here, are concerned.

Another very significant factor in this ASPR change was the government's consideration that this income tax accrual did not really represent a definite liability and might perhaps even be thought of in the light of a contingent cost which DOD will seldom accept on a historical basis.

State Tax Refund—Period to Which Applicable

In a major dispute on this subject, the Grumman Corporation carried its appeal to the ASBCA and then to the U.S. Court of Claims, but the judicial ruling was that, by application of ASPR 15-205.41(c) and the contract language, the carryback of a net operating loss from 1971 to 1968 was appropriate because the credit represented a refund of Grumman's tax liability for 1968. This case is summarized in Chapter XVI of this text.

Allocation of State Income and Franchise Taxes

The 50 states levy a myriad of taxes, including those categorized as income taxes and franchise taxes. The precise distinctions between these two latter categories are difficult for many reasons, including the fact that the basis of calculating a tax is not necessarily indicative of its objective. Thus it has been alleged that some state taxes are computed on the basis of income whereas their purpose is mainly to have business concerns pay for the privilege of doing business (franchise tax).

Problems and controversies in this area are aggravated by the same difficulty that exists throughout the entire area of cost accounting—the absence of authoritative principles or ground rules, and the concommitant opportunity for each side to argue that its position is the right one and/or is in accordance with generally accepted accounting principles governing the allocation of state income and franchise taxes among divisions or cost objectives. Accordingly, no one can prove that his method is in accord with these mythical principles; on the other hand, it is also difficult for anyone to demonstrate conclusively that any method is contrary to such principles.

In previous editions of this text we discussed the ramifications of this question, the different opinions held regarding the proper method of allocating state income and franchise taxes, and the lack of an authoritative professional or regulatory determination. We also reviewed major ASBCA decisions in this area and the apparently different judgments reached by the board within one year. Although the historical background is of interest to scholars of cost accounting for government contracts and of cost accounting in general, the question became moot when the Armed Services Board of Contract Appeals ruled on the interpretation of CAS 403 in the *Lockheed, McDonnell Douglas,* and *Grumman* appeals in 1980 and 1982. These decisions are reviewed in Chapter XV of this text.

Change in Cost Accounting Practice for State Income and Franchise Taxes as a Result of Change of Method of Reporting Income from Long-Term Contracts.—On February 10, 1981, the Department of Defense CAS Steering Committee issued Interim Guidance W.G. 81-25 on this subject. As we have mentioned previously in this text, the Interim Guidance releases, while directive on all DOD contracting officers and auditors, do not have any statutory, regulatory or contractual force. At this writing, there is considerable debate in the private sector regarding the correctness of this guidance.

W. G. 81-25 is quoted below:

BACKGROUND

State tax regulations usually permit a taxpayer to initially select one of several acceptable methods of stating the elements that determine taxable income and later, under specified conditions, to change from the initial selection to another acceptable method. Some elements for which alternate acceptable methods are allowed are (1) income from long-term contracts, (2) inventory pricing, and (3) depreciation methods.

According to CAS Board regulation 331.20(h), a "cost accounting practice" is any accounting method or technique which is used for measurement of costs, assignment of costs to cost accounting periods, or allocation of cost to cost objectives. According to § 331.20(i), a "change to either a disclosed cost accounting practice or an established cost accounting practice" is any alteration in a cost accounting practice, as defined in paragraph (h).

A number of major defense contractors recently changed their method of reporting income from long-term contracts for State tax purposes from a percent of completion method (PCM) to a completed contract method (CCM). Under PCM, the net income or loss for a contract is reported for each tax year by relating cost incurred to estimated revenue based on the percentage a contract is determined to be complete. Under CCM, the total net income or loss for a contract is reported in the year of completion.

Contractors typically have changed when CCM will eliminate or reduce their tax cost in the year of the change and the years shortly thereafter. When this occurs, the amount of state tax cost allocated to contracts will generally be lower than the amount projected to be allocated to the contracts at the time they were negotiated.

DISCUSSION

In order to establish that a change in cost accounting practice for State tax costs has occurred, it is necessary to identify the nature of the practice prior to the presumed change. The best evidence of the prior practice is the State tax cost previously estimated and recorded for defense contract purposes. In most cases, the practice prior to the change was to estimate and record based on the actual tax payment, or the amount for which a current liability exists. This is the position DAR 15-205.41 requires in terms of cost allowability; however, the same principles apply in terms of CAS allocability. Consequently, when a contractor changes the method of determining its actual tax liability, such as by changing from PCM to CCM of reporting contract income, it changes its cost accounting practice for State tax costs. The fact that a contractor does not change its financial accounting practice at the same time has no particular significance. Differences occur between cost and financial accounting because the defense acquisition process requires accurate costing and pricing of individual contracts while financial accounting is concerned with a contractor's total operations over an extended period.

It is clear that a change in method of reporting income from long-term contracts alters the measurement of the State tax cost for a period by assigning taxable income or loss to other cost accounting periods. Because measurement and assignment of cost is involved, the change in determining contract income is a change in accounting practice as described in § 331.20(h) and is not a "determination of the amount paid—for a unit of good services" as also described in that paragraph. Changing the contract income method is comparable to the change in the actuarial cost method for computing pension costs, which is cited as an illustration of a change in § 331.20(j)(2).

To summarize, a contractor's cost accounting practice for measuring and assigning State tax costs to periods should be the same as the accounting practice used to prepare the State tax return filed for an accounting period. The determination of income or loss for long-term contracts is a material component of the cost accounting practice for State tax costs.

GUIDANCE

A change from PCM to CCM of reporting income from long-term contracts is a change in cost accounting practice because it alters the measurement and assignment of State tax costs. Consequently, if the cost impact is material, contract prices should be adjusted in accordance with provisions of the contract CAS clause prescribed in § 331.50.

TERMINATION COSTS

A comprehensive coverage of termination of government contracts is contained in Chapter XXI of this text.

TRADE, BUSINESS, TECHNICAL AND PROFESSIONAL ACTIVITY COSTS

FAR 31.205-43 provides:

The following types of costs are allowable:

(a) Memberships in trade, business, technical, and professional organizations.

(b) Subscriptions to trade, business, professional, or other technical periodicals.

(c) Meetings and conferences, including meals, transportation, rental of meeting facilities and other incidental costs when the primary purpose of the incurrence of the costs is the dissemination of technical information or stimulation of production.

In mid-1987, the DAR and CAA Councils concluded that a revision to this cost principle was required. The basis for this conclusion, as set forth in the background information accompanying the proposal, and the proposed revision are quoted below:

SUPPLEMENTARY INFORMATION:

A. Background

There has been a proliferation of non-Federal Government sponsored symposia resulting in possibly unreasonable costs being charged against Government contracts. In addition, Government contracting officers and auditors have found that the present cost principle does not address the attendance of company employees at such activities, it does not describe the circumstances in which the cost of attendance by noncontractor employees might be allowable, and it does not distinguish between setting up or sponsoring meetings, conferences, symposia, and seminars and attending those events. This proposed rule was necessitated by a need to control costs, to clearly state the policy of the Government with respect to these costs, and to describe more specifically the nature of costs which are allowable. The proposed changes do not reflect or result from a change in allowability policy.

(c) When the principal purpose of a meeting, conference, symposium, or seminar is the dissemination of trade, business, technical or professional information, or the stimulation of production or improved productivity:

(1) Costs of organizing, setting up and sponsoring the meetings, symposia, etc., including rental of meeting facilities, transportation, subsistence, and incidental and directly associated costs.

(2) Costs of attendance by contractor employees, including travel costs (see 31.205-46).

(3) Costs of attendance by noncontractor personnel provided (i) such costs are not also reimbursed to the individual by the employing company or organization, and (ii) the individual's attendance is essential to achieve the purpose of the conference, meeting, symposium, etc.

A review of the above cost principle would suggest to most readers that these kinds of memberships, subscriptions, and meetings are recognized as useful activities by the government. As a matter of fact, government officials frequently participate, including serving as speakers and panelists at the meetings and conferences. However, DCAA, which seems to have not enough to do with its vital conventional work, plus its operations audits, plus its increased alertness to possible fraud, waste, and abuse, published special guidance to its field auditors on this subject in Revision 3 to its Contract Audit Manual, September 1980. As many contractors view this guidance, DCAA auditors were encouraged to extend their checking to include further detail and literally "nickel and dime" the contractors in this area.

The text of the current DCAA guidance is cited below:

7-1103 Professional Activity Costs

General. Paragraph (c) of FAR 31.205-43, Trade, Business, Technical and Professional Activity Costs states that the cost of technical or professional meetings and conferences includes the cost of meals, transportation, rental of facilities for meetings, and related incidental costs. Such costs are allowable when the primary purpose of the meeting is the dissemination of technical information or the stimulation of production, provided the costs meet the other requirements controlling allowability (FAR 31.201-2).

7-1103.1 Conference Costs versus Entertainment Costs

The term business meetings and conferences refers to both contractor and trade association hosted activities of a purely business nature. Determinations as to whether or not expenses associated with a particular meeting or conference represent allowable business expense under FAR 31.205-43(c) provisions or unallowable social activity under FAR 31.205-14 (Entertainment Costs) should be made on a case-by-case basis, based on all pertinent facts.

7-1103.2 Documentation

a. Determination of allowability requires knowledge concerning the purpose and nature of activity at the meeting or conference. The contractor should maintain adequate records supplying the following information on properly prepared travel vouchers or expense records supported by copies of paid invoices, receipts, charge slips, etc.

(1) Date and location of meeting including the name of the establishment.

(2) Names of employees and guests in attendance.

(3) Purpose of meeting.

(4) Cost of the meeting, by item.

b. The above guidelines closely parallel the current record-keeping requirements in Section 274 of the Internal Revenue Code for entertainment costs as a tax deductible expense. Where satisfactory support assuring the claimed costs are allowable conference expenses is not furnished, the claimed conference/meal costs and directly associated costs (see 8-405.1d. for description) should be questioned.

c. *Meal Expense.* Expenses for meals of contractor personnel, not in travel status, who act as hosts at contractor-sponsored business luncheons or dinners are allowable if it is determined that the activity constitutes a business meeting or conference associated with the active conduct of the contractor's business and not a social function.

7-1103.3 Standards of Conduct—Federal Employees

Guest expenses for meals or other incidentals applicable to Federal employees should normally be questioned as unnecessary, and hence unreasonable costs, except under limited circumstances, since they are prohibited from accepting gratuities by Executive Order 11222 of 1965, Title 5 CFR 735(c), and various departmental implementing directives (e.g., DoDD 5500.7, "Standards of Conduct").

TRAINING AND EDUCATION COSTS

FAR 31.205-44 provides:

(a) *Allowable costs.* Training and education costs are allowable to the extent indicated below.

(b) *Vocational training.* Costs of preparing and maintaining a non-college level program of instruction, including but not limited to on-the-job, classroom, and apprenticeship training, designed to increase the vocational effectiveness of employees are allowable. These costs include (1) salaries or wages of trainees (excluding overtime compensation), (2) salaries of the director of training and staff when the training program is conducted by the contractor, (3) tuition and fees when the training is in an institution not operated by the contractor, and/or (4) training materials and textbooks.

(c) *Part-time college level education.* Allowable costs of part-time college education at an undergraduate or postgraduate level, including that provided at the contractor's own facilities, are limited to—

(1) Fees and tuition charged by the educational institution, or, instead of tuition, instructors' salaries and the related share of indirect cost of the educational institution, to the extent that the sum thereof is not in excess of the tuition that would have been paid to the participating educational institution;

(2) Salaries and related costs of instructors who are employees of the contractor;

(3) Training materials and textbooks; and

(4) Straight-time compensation of each employee for time spent attending classes during working hours not in excess of 156 hours per year where circumstances do not permit the operation of classes or attendance at classes after regular working hours. In unusual cases, the period may be extended (see paragraph (h) below).

(d) *Full-time education.* Costs of tuition, fees, training materials and textbooks (but not subsistence, salary, or any other emoluments) in connection with full-time education, including that provided at the contractor's own facilities, at a postgraduate but not undergraduate college level, are allowable only when the course or degree pursued is related to the field in which the employee is working or may reasonably be expected to work and are limited to a total period not to exceed 2 school years or the length of the degree program, whichever is less, for each employee so trained.

(e) *Specialized programs.* Costs of attendance of up to 16 weeks per employee per year at specialized programs specifically designed to enhance the effectiveness of managers or to prepare employees for such positions are allowable. Such costs include enrollment fees and related charges and employees' salaries, subsistence, training materials, textbooks, and travel. Costs allowable under this paragraph do not include costs for courses that are part of a degree-oriented curriculum, which are only allowable pursuant to paragraphs (c) and (d) of this subsection.

(f) *Other expenses.* Maintenance expense and normal depreciation or fair rental on facilities owned or leased by the contractor for training purposes are allowable in accordance with 31.205-17, 31.205-24, and 31.205-36.

(g) *Grants.* Grants to educational or training institutions, including the donation of facilities or other properties, scholarships, and fellowships are considered contributions and are unallowable.

(h) *Advance agreements.* (1) Training and education costs in excess of those otherwise allowable under (c) and (d) of this subsection, including subsistence, salaries, or any other emoluments, may be allowed to the extent set forth in an advance agreement negotiated under 31.109. To be considered for an advance agreement, the contractor must demonstrate that the costs are consistently incurred under an established managerial, engineering, or scientific training and education program, and that the course or degree pursued is related to the field in which employees are now working or may reasonably be expected to work. Before entering into the advance agreement, the contracting officer shall give consideration to such factors as—

(i) The length of employees' service with the contractor;

(ii) Employees' past performance and potential;

(iii) Whether employees are in formal development programs; and

(iv) The total number of participating employees.

(2) Any advance agreement must include a provision requiring the contractor to refund to the Government training and education costs for employees who resign within 12 months of completion of such training or education for reasons within an employee's control.

(i) *Training or education costs for other than bona-fide employees.* Costs of tuition, fees, textbooks, and similar or related benefits provided for other than bona-fide employees are unallowable, except that the costs incurred for educating employee dependents (primary and secondary level studies) when the employee is working in a foreign country where public education is not available and where suitable private education is inordinately expensive may be included in overseas differential.

(j) *Employee dependent education plans.* Costs of college plans for employee dependents are unallowable.

FAC 84-15, effective July 1, 1987, revised FAR 31.205-44 to clarify the allowability of training materials and textbook costs and to increase the one-year full-time education limitation to two years. The revision also provided that an advance agreement may be negotiated to allow certain costs in excess of those otherwise allowable for part-time college-level education and full-time education. Any advance agreement must provide for the contractor to reimburse the government for such costs for employees who resign within 12 months of completing such education for reasons within an employee's control. FAR 31.109, Advance Agreements, was also amended by adding training and education costs as an item for which advance agreements are recommended.

In Chapter XVI of this text, we discussed the concepts underlying principles for determining allowable and unallowable costs under government contracts. One of the categories of unallowable costs consisted of those asserted to be unreasonable in nature or amount. We noted that, in some instances, the provisions of FAR 31.205, Selected Costs, contain specific limitations on costs to be allowed, many of them based on government concepts of reasonableness.

It has always been difficult for those in the private sector, and indeed for many in the public sector, to understand why the government, spearheaded by the Department of Defense, would place limitations on training and educational costs incurred by contractors when there seems to be such a wide consensus that this country's national interests would be best served by providing maximum opportunities for increased training and education.

This category of expense had not been specifically cited in the past. However, it was the general practice to allow these costs, subject only to review for general considerations of reasonableness. The comprehensive contract cost principles promulgated in November 1959 for the first time set forth policy and procedures governing the treatment of these costs.

The Defense Department, generally, believed that the 1959 cost principles set forth appropriate and liberal guidelines relating to the nature and extent of training and educational expenses that the government would share in through allocation to its contracts. Many in industry, however, did not share this view and believed that the new guidelines resulted in a restriction rather than a liberalization of past practices. Finally, on May 8, 1967, the Aerospace Industries Association of America, Inc., (AIA) wrote the Chairman of the ASPR Committee that: "The knowledge explosion now enveloping the world has made such startling changes in the training and education requirements of contractors and the manners of meeting them as to render the present ASPR 15-205.44 basically out of step with the realities of the present needs." The AIA asserted that the ASPR provision "is not in consonance with national education objectives and is actually a potential detriment to the national security responsibilities of the Department of Defense." The lengthy and learned letter, however, ended with a less than specific recommendation to revise ASPR "in a manner which will (1) allow the contracting officer to apply an appropriate measure of judgment in determining the reasonableness of the contractor's training and education program expenditures . . . and (2) free the contractor to manage prudently . . . without being constrained by inapplicable quantified criteria." The DOD consensus was that AIA wished only to eliminate all restrictions and controls, and the ASPR Committee asked the Association to suggest specific language, together with supporting rationale. Nothing productive developed from the ensuing AIA-DOD correspondence.

In May 1969, CODSIA took up the cudgel in a lengthy letter to the ASPR Committee, supported by two substantial attachments. Again, the industry thrust was that the 1959 ASPR revision was restrictive, rather than liberal, out of step with national goals and viewpoints of leading educators, and should be modified. Again, the attitude in DOD was that industry proposed relaxation of all controls without presenting a basis for such action.

During this period, suggestions for revisions of ASPR 15-205.44 also surfaced from DOD sources, including requests for clarification from DCAA and what has become an increasingly frequent occurrence—an ASBCA decision that motivated DOD to revise ASPR so as to obviate the board's more liberal views. We refer here to, and shall reproduce below the pertinent portions of, ASBCA No. 12731, 70-1 BCA par. 8132; 69-2 BCA par. 7980, a decision in the appeal of *The Boeing Company,* handed down in October 1969, and the motion for reconsideration, ruled upon in February 1970.

Involved in this decision are costs incurred by Boeing for participation of certain of its employees in a Sloan Fellowship program, including tuition, salaries, and expenses for one-year enrollments. The course of study included subjects relating to business management, economics, political science, and the humanities. The contracting officer disallowed these costs "as neither meeting the tests of allocability" stated in ASPR 15-201.4, nor allowable under ASPR Section 15-205.44. The following is quoted from the board's original decision:

It appears from the contracting officer's testimony that he regarded the Sloan Fellowship program as outside the normal training and education programs contemplated by ASPR 15-205.44, that the benefits were primarily for the individual, to help him advance, and that the benefit to the Government was limited to the individual's association with Government programs (Tr. 217). Boeing concedes that the Sloan Fellowship costs are not rendered allowable as training as education costs within the scope of ASPR 15-205.44. However, Boeing contends that these costs meet the test of allocability in ASPR 15-201.4, that ASPR 15-205.44 does not preclude their allowability, and that the general requirements of ASPR 15-204(a) regarding allowable costs are satisfied.

The Government does not contend that the costs incurred by Boeing in sponsoring Sloan Fellows in 1962 and 1963 were unreasonable. Nor are there any specific limitations in ASPR which preclude the allowability of such costs. ASPR 15-205.44 is inapplicable, since there was no necessary relationship between the course of study pursued by Sloan Fellows and their occupations at Boeing upon their return. Although Boeing sponsored scientific and engineering employees as Sloan Fellows, any specific technical knowlege acquired by them during their course of study was incidental to the broad educational experience. However, like ASPR 15-205.26 pertaining to certain allowable patent costs, ASPR 15-205.44 is merely an example of certain types of costs considered allowable by ASPR and does not proscribe the allowability of educational costs under general provisions of ASPR Section XV, Part 2.

The Government's principal contention is that the Sloan Fellowship costs are not allocable to Government contracts under the tests prescribed by ASPR 15-201.4. Specifically, the Government contends that any benefits to the Government derived from the Sloan Fellowship experience of a few Boeing employees is so remote as to be nonexistent. In determining whether these costs are allocable to Government contracts, we think that the analysis of ASPR 15-201.4 applied by the Board in *TRW Systems Group of TRW, Inc., supra,* to determine the allocability of certain patent costs is equally applicable to determining the allocability of the Sloan Fellowship costs. Thus, these costs would be allowable as necessary to the over-all operation of Boeing's business if assignable to particular cost objectives in accordance with the relative benefits or other equitable relationship and taking account of whether these costs bear an equitable relationship to Government contracts or the Government as a class of customer.

We find that these requirements are satisfied in this instance. As indicated by the uncontroverted testimony of Boeing witnesses, the costs of sponsoring Boeing employees as Sloan Fellows were incurred principally for the benefit of Boeing, with a view to the eventual promotion of these employees to top management positions. As indicated by the broad representation from industry and Government, it is evident that the program is recognized as a valuable experience for top management candidates to undertake. At the time of the hearing in this appeal, several previous Sloan Fellows had succeeded to high managerial posts in Boeing. The Government did not take issue with the Boeing testimony that the Sloan Fellowship experience did have a beneficial effect on performance, albeit difficult to measure. Although it cannot be concluded from the record that Boeing's operations would have seriously suffered had the Sloan Fellowship program not been available, we do find that the managerial competence of Boeing was enhanced by the program through an educational experience widely recognized in industry and Government as valuable for this purpose.

The Government has not taken issue with Boeing's accounting method of accumulating these costs in corporate or divisional overhead pools and distributing them over all of Boeing's business, both Government and non-Government. As for whether Boeing's allocation of these costs bears an equitable relationship to Government contracts or to the Government as a class of customer, we find that the Government has benefited intangibly, and that the benefits derived by the Government were not so remote as to be nonexistent. To the extent that participation by Boeing employees in the Sloan Fellowship program enhanced Boeing's top management capability for the conduct of all of its business, the capability with which Boeing performed its work under Government contracts was proportionately increased. It is not possible to measure this increased capability in any finite way. But merely because the additional benefit cannot be quantified does not mean that the cost thereof is not allocable under ASPR 15-201.4. Boeing's appeal from the contracting officer's disallowance of the cost of sponsoring Boeing employees under the Sloan Fellowship program is, therefore, sustained.

In the years since that decision, the cost principle governing training and educational costs was revised on a number of occasions and the present FAR reflects, with editorial changes, the substance of DAR 15-205.44 prior to April 1, 1984. On several occasions, industry associations importuned the Defense Department to eliminate the detailed quantitative criteria and restrictions and confine tests of allowability to the question of whether the instruction was designed to increase the employee's effectiveness. DOD was urged repeatedly to adopt the liberal and enlightened views of the ASBCA; however, these pleas were not persuasive, and the current FAR provisions reflect numerous arbitrary restrictions. Additionally, the opening sentence of this cost principle establishes that such costs shall be considered allowable "to the extent indicated" therein.

Some flexibility (with restrictions) is provided in 31.205-44(h).

TRANSPORTATION COSTS

FAR 31.205-45 provides:

Allowable transportation costs include freight, express, cartage, and postage charges relating to goods purchased, in process, or delivered. When these costs can be identified with the items involved, they may be directly costed as transportation costs or added to the cost of such items. When identification with the materials received cannot be made, inbound transportation costs may be charged to the appropriate indirect cost accounts if the contractor follows a consistent and equitable procedure. Outbound freight, if reimbursable under the terms of the contract, shall be treated as a direct cost.

TRAVEL COSTS

FAR 31.205-46 provides:

(a)(1) Costs for transportation, lodging, meals, and incidental expenses incurred by contractor personnel on official company business are allowable subject to paragraphs (b) through (f) of this subsection. Costs for transportation may be based on mileage rates, actual costs incurred, or on a combination thereof provided the method used results in a reasonable charge. Costs for lodging, meals, and incidental expenses may be based on per diem, actual expenses, or a combination thereof, provided the method used results in a reasonable charge.

(2) Except as provided in subparagraph (a)(3) of this subsection, costs incurred for lodging, meals, and incidental expenses (as defined in the regulations cited in (a)(2)(i) through (iii) of this subparagraph) shall be considered to be reasonable and allowable only to the extent that they do not exceed on a daily basis the maximum per diem rates in effect at the time of travel as set forth in the—

(i) Federal Travel Regulations, prescribed by the General Services Administration, for travel in the conterminous 48 United States, available on a subcription basis from the Superintendent of Documents, U.S. Government Printing Office, Washington, DC 20402, Stock No. 022-001-81003-7;

(ii) Joint Travel Regulations, Volume 2, DoD Civilian Personnel, Appendix A, prescribed by the Department of Defense, for travel in Alaska, Hawaii, The Commonwealth of Puerto Rico, and territories and possessions of the United States, available on a subscription basis from the Superintendent of Documents, U.S. Government Printing Office, Washington, DC 20402, Stock No. 908-010-00000-1; or

(iii) Standardized Regulations (Government Civilians, Foreign Areas), section 925, "Maximum Travel Per Diem Allowances of Foreign Areas," prescribed by the Department of State, for travel in areas not covered in (a)(2)(i) and (ii) of this paragraph, available on a subscription basis from the Superintendent of Documents, U.S. Government Printing Office, Washington, DC 20402, Stock No. 744-088-00000-0.

(3) In special or unusual situations, actual costs in excess of the above-referenced maximum per diem rates are allowable provided that such amounts do not exceed the higher amounts authorized for Federal civilian employees as permitted in the regulations referenced in (a)(2)(i), (ii), or (iii) or this subsection. For such higher amounts to be allowable, all of the following conditions must be met:

(i) One of the conditions warranting approval of the actual expense method, as set forth in the regulations referred in (a)(2)(i), (ii), or (iii) of this subsection must exist.

(ii) A written justification for use of the higher amounts must be approved by an officer of the contractor's organization or designee to ensure that the authority is properly administered and controlled to prevent abuse.

(iii) If it becomes necessary to exercise the authority to use the higher actual expense method repetitively or on a continuing basis in a particular area, the contractor must obtain advance approval from the contracting officer.

(iv) Documentation to support actual costs incurred shall be in accordance with the contractor's established practices provided that a receipt is required for each expenditure in excess of $25.00. The approved justification required by (a)(3)(ii) and, if applicable, (a)(3)(iii) of this subparagraph must be retained.

(4) Subparagraphs (a)(2) and (a)(3) of this subsection do not incorporate the regulations cited in (a)(2)(i), (ii), and (iii) in their entirety. Only the coverage in the referenced regulations dealing with special or unusual situations, the maximum per diem rates, and definitions of lodging, meals and incidental expenses are incorporated herein.

(5) An advance agreement (see 31.109) with respect to compliance with subparagraphs (a)(2) and (a)(3) of this subsection may be useful and desirable.

(b) Travel costs incurred in the normal course of overall administration of the business are allowable and shall be treated as indirect costs.

(c) Travel costs directly attributable to specific contract performance are allowable and may be charged to the contract under 31.202.

(d) Airfare costs in excess of the lowest customary standard, coach, or equivalent airfare offered during normal business hours are unallowable except when such accommodations require circuitous routing, require travel during unreasonable hours, excessively prolong travel, result in increased cost that would offset transportation savings, are not reasonably adequate for the physical or medical needs of the traveler, or are not reasonably available to meet mission requirements. However, in order for airfare costs in excess of the above standard airfare to be allowable, the applicable condition(s) set forth in this paragraph must be documented and justified.

(e)(1) "Cost of travel by contractor-owned, -leased, or -chartered aircraft," as used in this subparagraph, includes the cost of lease, charter, operation (including personnel), maintenance, depreciation, insurance, and other related costs.

(2) The costs of travel by contractor-owned, -leased or -chartered aircraft are limited to the standard airfare described in paragraph (d) of this subsection for the flight destination unless travel by such aircraft is specifically required by contract specification, term, or condition, or a higher amount is approved by the contracting officer. A higher amount may be agreed to when one or more of the circumstances for justifying higher than standard airfare listed in paragraph (d) of this subsection are applicable or when an advance agreement under subparagraph (e)(3) of this subsection has been executed. In all cases, travel by contractor-owned -leased, or -chartered aircraft must be fully documented and justified. For each contractor-owned, -leased, or -chartered aircraft used for any business purpose which is charged or allocated directly or indirectly, to a Government contract, the contractor must maintain and make available manifest/logs for all flights on such company aircraft. As a minimum, the manifest/log shall indicate—

(i) Date, time, and points of departure;

(ii) Destination, date, and time of arrival;

(iii) Name of each passenger and relationship to the contractor;

(iv) Authorization for trip; and

(v) Purpose of trip.

(3) Where an advance agreement is proposed (see 31.109), consideration may be given to the following:

(i) Whether scheduled commercial airlines or other suitable, less costly, travel facilities are available at reasonable times, with reasonable frequency, and serve the required destinations conveniently.

(ii) Whether increased flexibility in scheduling results in time savings and more effective use of personnel that would outweigh additional travel costs.

(f) Costs of contractor-owned or -leased automobiles, as used in this paragraph, include the costs of lease, operation (including personnel), maintenance, depreciation, insurance, etc. These costs are allowable, if reasonable, to the extent that the automobiles are used for company business. That portion of the cost of company-furnished automobiles that relates to personal use by employees (including transportation to and from work) is compensation for personal services and is unallowable as stated in 31.205-6(m)(2).

Recent Changes to Cost Principles Relating to Travel

This cost principle has undergone extensive revisions as the FAR authors and certain members of Congress have vigorously competed in effecting punitive changes. The changes have one consideration in common—all further restrict contractors' opportunities to recover normal business expenses.

Air Travel

Wilbur and Orville Wright flew their heavier-than-air craft about 85 years ago and Charles Lindbergh spanned the Atlantic Ocean solo some 60 years back. Progress in air travel, including the Voyager's nonstop flight around the world at the close of 1986, has been one of the technological wonders of this century. Concomitant benefits have been realized in vast improvements to business management, operations and controls. Many of the larger firms, with widely dispersed plants and field operations, have found they can maximize their effectiveness by supplementing available commercial airlines with company-owned or -leased aircraft. For these major corporations, the judicious use of both public and private aircraft is fully understood and accepted as sound business practice. For cost and price considerations under government contracts, however, we depart the real world and enter a heavily overregulated planet with arcane and unreasonable rules and regulations aimed at micromanagement of government contractors.

Led by GAO, and closely followed by congressional defense critics and DCAA, contractor air travel cost recovery was attacked in two respects. In the early 1960s, GAO embarked on a crusade against first class travel. The watchdog agency apparently viewed first class travel as a major ill in this nation and, with the support of its congressional allies, succeeded in forcing regulations that made it virtually impossible for most federal employees to use higher than coach accommodations. Not satisfied with this achievement, GAO went after the private sector. Unable to completely prohibit higher than coach air travel, it succeeded in forcing the promulgation of regulations that required contractors to submit considerable documentation to justify first class travel, absent which the difference in cost between first class and less than first class fare was disallowed.

Although the current provision (FAR 31.205-46(d)) does not reflect any change in concept, it does include additional language designed to make it more difficult for contractors to recover air fare costs "in excess of the lowest customary standard, coach, or equivalent . . ."

The other avenue of attack by GAO and DCAA against contractor recovery of air travel costs has been directed at cost of travel by contractor-owned, -leased, or -chartered aircraft. The major thrust of the auditors is to disallow such costs to the extent they exceed the costs that would have been incurred had the contractor traveled at the lowest commercial airline fare. Regulations initially emphasized the conditions under which other than commercial airlines could be used and each change increased the nature and amount of documentation the contractor was required to submit to recover the higher costs of company-owned or -leased aircraft.

A proposed FAR revision, initially floated in February 1985, continued in this direction and added the further extreme restriction that allowed costs would be limited to standard airline fares "unless travel by such aircraft is specifically required by contract specification, term, or condition, or a higher amount is approved by the contracting officer." FAR 31.205-46(d)(2). Between the increasing restrictions in the regulations and the aggressive efforts of DCAA auditors, contractors are experiencing great difficulties in recovering such costs even when travel is made to sites not included   in commercial airline schedules. A congressional investigation team, staffed by GAO and DCAA auditors (see Chapter XVI of this text), sharply criticized contracting officer allowances of costs questioned by DCAA auditors. Cost of travel by company-owned or -chartered aircraft was one of the expenses highlighted, assuring that, absent a contractual provision or advance agreement, chances of recovering such costs are poor indeed.

Transportation, Lodging, Meals, etc.

A move that ultimately resulted in a regulation that has been described as another step to the nationalization of government contractors may have had its origins in an August 1985 Navy directive instructing that department's contracting officers to use the government's Joint Travel Regulations (JTR) "to determine the maximum reasonable per diem cost to reimburse contractors." JTR applies to DOD civilian employees and at that time, prescribed maximum per diem reimbursement of $50 a day except for $75 a day in designated "high cost areas." The Assistant Secretary of the Navy (Shipbuilding and Logistics), previously identified with other punitive measures against contractors, sought to justify his directive by arguing that: "Government employees and Contractor employees working under Government contracts are all reimbursed for official travel expenses with taxpayer's money, and there is no reason why either group should have higher reimbursement entitlements than the other."

Although many observers have long recognized that defense contractors constitute members of a highly regulated industry, few believed that placing private sector and government employees in the same category would be tried in a non-socialistic society.

Widespread protests against the Navy directive included a CODSIA letter to the Navy Assistant Secretary pointing out that, among other things, the FAR system did not permit a military department to effect such deviation from existing regulations without authorization by the Secretary of Defense. The Navy official ignored industry protests and also a recommendation from the Assistant Secretary of Defense (A&L), but was finally forced to withdraw the directive at the instruction of the Deputy Secretary of Defense who, however, stated that this latest attack on contractor cost recovery would be studied for a possible FAR revision.

The promised study was eagerly led by DCAA, which submitted a proposed change in September 1985 that would substantially comply with the Navy objective. Whether the subject is compensation, accounting fees, or a number of other expenses, some contract auditors are apparently unhappy to find industry at times more generous than the government even though few contractors offer the security of employment or the generous retirement and annual sick and holiday leave benefits available in the government. As incorporated hastily in the DOD FAR Supplement, the revision essentially stated that costs of lodging, subsistence, and incidental expenses in excess of the amounts determined for federal employees "shall be considered to be not reasonable and unallowable."

While the DOD revision was being considered for incorporation into FAR, amid widespread opposition from industry, congressional critics of defense contractors joined in the attack and enacted P.L. 99-234 on January 2, 1986. Title I of this law required action to increase the obsolete and unreasonably low per diem rates for federal employees, an action generating few objections. Title II of the law, however, stated that contractor travel expenses shall be considered reasonable and allowable only to the extent they do not exceed those established for federal civilian employees.

During the progress of this statute through Congress and after its enactment, representatives of industry associations and individual contractors made strong but unsuccessful efforts to explain its inequities and to obtain some reasonable flexibility in its implementation, or at least to mitigate the discriminatory provisions. Virtually all lodging places provide special "government rates" and many private sector employees simply cannot obtain comparable discounts. In these instances contractors would have only two options: (1) direct employees to pay the excess of actual costs over government per diem rates out of their own pockets, or (2) reimburse their employees for actual costs, in which event the excess over government per diem rates would be disallowed and come out of contractors' profits or net worth.

The proposed statutory implementations were published in the *Federal Register* on May 30, 1986. They included amendments to the Federal Travel Regulations (FTR), FPMR 101-7, to implement Title I of the law, and the proposed FAR revision to implement Title II. As reflected in FAR 31.205-46(a), quoted earlier, the punitive measure is ameliorated only by permitting reimbursement of actual costs under tightly specified conditions and with extensive documentation. If actual costs are required on a repetitive basis, advance approval must be obtained from the contracting officer.

Contractor-Owned or -Leased Automobiles

Limitations on contractor cost recovery have continued in every conceivable category, involving both major matters and those of nitpick variety. A new FAR 31.205-46(f) reiterates a provision also included under compensation for personal services:

> That portion of the cost of company-furnished automobiles that relates to personal use by employees (including transportation to and from work) is compensation for personal services and is unallowable as stated in 31.205-6(m)(2).

DCAA Guidance on Auditing Travel Costs

Although DCAA's Contract Audit Manual does not direct the automatic questioning of the excess cost of travel by company-owned aircraft over commercial airline coach travel, the guidance in CAM 7-1004, cited below, clearly indicates the hardline approach of this audit agency to such costs. We have also quoted CAM 7-1002, which instructs DCAA auditors to demand increasing proof to support any kind of travel and points out to its field people that "more extensive documentation" is now required by the Internal Revenue Service, suggesting that such documentation should be obtained.

7-1003 Travel Costs, Contractor-Owned, -Leased, or -Chartered Aircraft

7-1003.1 General Audit Considerations

a. FAR 31.205-46(e) sets forth principles and criteria for determining the allowability of costs incurred in the operation and maintenance of contractor-owned, -leased, or -chartered aircraft (collectively referred to as private aircraft).

b. The use of such aircraft generally results in higher costs than travel by commercial airlines or other modes of transportation. The increased use by contractors of jet in lieu of propeller driven aircraft has tended to accentuate the cost difference.

c. As a general rule, travel costs via private aircraft in excess of the standard commercial airfare are unallowable. Exceptions to this general rule are described in 7-1003.2.

7-1003.2 Conditions for Allowability of Contractor-Owned, - Leased, or -Chartered Aircraft

a. As a prerequisite to allowability, the contractor must maintain and make available to the government full documentation in support of the costs including the manifest/log for all flights (see 7-1003.6). If the contractor fails to maintain required documentation or refuses to provide such documentation, the auditor should disallow costs in excess of otherwise allowable standard commercial airfare.

b. Travel costs via private aircraft in excess of the standard commercial airfare are allowable in two situations: (1) when travel by such aircraft is specifically required by contract specification, term, or condition; or (2) when a higher amount is approved by the contracting officer.

c. All or part of excess costs incurred for operating private aircraft may be approved by the contracting officer: (1) when one or more of the conditions described in FAR 31.205-46(d) are present that would justify costs in excess of the lowest standard commercial airfare, such as requiring circuitous routing, travel during unreasonable hours, excessively prolonged travel, etc.; or (2) when an advance agreement has been executed.

7-1003.3 Use of Advance Agreements

a. When the contractor proposes an advance agreement with respect to the costs of company aircraft, the auditor should evaluate the contractor's proposal and provide audit findings and recommendations to assist the contracting officer in establishing the negotiation objective. The auditor should request technical assistance in areas such as the size, type and number of aircraft, safety factors, and other technical requirements of aircraft.

b. In evaluating the contractor's proposal, the auditor should consider major financial and non-financial factors. Generally, the contractor must demonstrate that scheduled commercial airline service is not readily available at reasonable times to accommodate the company's air travel requirements. Proximity of commercial airline terminals to the contractor's location as compared with private air fields which are used, or intended to be used, is also a factor in conjunction with any time savings of key personnel. Increased flexibility in scheduling flights may result in time savings and more effective use of personnel. However, the auditor should be mindful that a contractor in the normal course of conducting its business seldom needs corporate aircraft and that the convenience of corporate aircraft should not substitute for the economy of commercial flights. While there may be critical or emergency situations that cannot be effectively handled by commercial flights, such situations generally occur so infrequently that they justify the long-term use of corporate aircraft. It is the contractor's responsibility to justify and demonstrate that the need for corporate aircraft truly outweighs cost savings arising from the use of commercial airlines.

c. In situations where the contractor's proposal includes acquisition of an aircraft, either through purchase or capital lease, the auditor should carefully review the feasibility studies the contractor has made in advance of acquiring the aircraft, justification presented to the approving authorities within the company, the contractor's decision and the implementing procedures adopted. Since corporate aircraft costs, once the purchase or capital lease is made, are very much like sunk costs and cannot be rapidly altered by management decisions, it is particularly important for the auditor to recommend that the contracting officer not approve the proposed acquisition of the aircraft unless the contractor can demonstrate the cost-effectiveness of corporate aircraft.

7-1003.4 Reasonableness of Contractor-Owned, -Leased, or - Chartered Aircraft Costs

a. In situations where all or part of travel costs via private aircraft in excess of the standard commercial airfare are approved by the contracting officer (see 7-1003.3), such costs are subject to the determination of reasonableness and allocability. Costs of private aircraft include costs of lease, charter, depreciation, operation (including personnel), maintenance, repair, insurance, and all other related costs.

b. A corporate aircraft is sometimes used for nonbusiness or otherwise unallowable activities. The contractor is required under CAS 405 and FAR 31.201-6 to identify all unallowable costs. However, the auditor should review the flight manifest/log to determine whether the contractor has excluded the amount allocable to any travel for nonbusiness or otherwise unallowable activities.

c. The size, type, and number of aircraft maintained or chartered are major considerations in evaluating the reasonableness of the costs involved. The auditor should also review the flight manifest/log and other available documentation to determine whether optimum use is made of such aircraft to the extent that they are used for all suitable trips except where the variable costs involved in their use would exceed the trip cost by commercial airline.

d. Depreciation often represents the major item of contractor-owned aircraft costs. In evaluating it, the auditor should ensure that the allowable amount is determined in accordance with the provisions of FAR 31.205-11. Supplemental audit guidance on depreciation is at 7-400.

Costs of aircraft overhaul and major component replacement, and their accounting treatment, also merit close audit scrutiny. If such costs are not capitalized and amortized by the contractor but are expensed in the period they are incurred, the auditor should assure that the procedure does not result in distorting the total aircraft costs for the period involved. Any gain or loss on the disposition of contractor-owned aircraft should be accounted for as provided in FAR 31.205-16.

e. Audit of private aircraft costs should include the evaluation of the propriety of the method used for their assignment or allocation to government contracts. Where an aircraft is used exclusively by a particular organizational element; e.g., home office, division, or plant, the costs of the aircraft should be charged to that entity. Where use is broader based, the aircraft should be distributed equitably to all of the user units. Some contracts may provide for travel costs as direct charges. In these cases, the auditor should assure that similar type costs are not duplicated as part of the allocation of aircraft costs to these contracts through overhead. Aircraft may also be used for nontravel purposes; e.g., instrument testing. Applicable costs should be charged directly to the benefiting projects.

7-1003.5 Contractor Responsibility

FAR 31.205-46(e)(2) specifically requires that the contractor must maintain documentation of all travel via private aircraft as a prerequisite of consideration for allowability of such costs. The contractor has the responsibility to support and justify the cost of aircraft usage. This responsibility includes: (1) identification of all costs associated with private aircraft, (2) submission of a comparative analysis of costs of private aircraft and standard commercial airfares, and (3) maintenance of a flight manifest/log. Costs that are unsupported as a result of a contractor's inability or unwillingness to furnish the required documentation should be disallowed.

7-1003.6 Maintenance of a Flight Manifest/Log by Contractor

The flight manifest/log which the contractor is required to maintain, plus other necessary backup data, should be in sufficient detail to serve as a source of support for its proposed costs. At least the following information for each flight should be provided:

(1) Date, time, and point of departure (airport).

(2) Date and time of arrival, and destination (airport).

(3) Names of pilot and crew.

(4) For each passenger aboard:

(a) Name.

(b) Name of company or organization represented.

(c) Position held in company or organization.

(d) Authorization for trip.

(e) Purpose of trip.

7-1002 Employee Travel Costs.

7-1002.1 General Considerations.

Audits of travel cost (see FAR 31.205-46) should include appropriate examination of the contractor's travel policies and procedures as well as the selective review of individual trips made by contractor personnel. Coverage of this area should thus include a determination that the contractor's travel authorization procedures provide for documented justification and approval of the official necessity of each trip, its duration and the number of travelers involved. The contractor's procedures should provide for advance planning of travel to assure that (1) wherever feasible and economically practical, required visits to locations in the same geographical area are combined into a single trip, (2) maximum use is made of the lowest customary standard, coach, or equivalent airfare accommodations available during normal business hours, and (3) coordination between organizational elements is effected to minimize the number of trips to the same location. Individual trips should be reviewed to determine whether they were undertaken in conformity with the contractor's procedures with respect to essentiality and minimization of travel costs. In addition, the auditor should review the contractor's accounting procedures to determine whether or not they provide adequate controls in segregating unallowable per diem and airfare costs.

7-1002.2 Documentation Required by the Internal Revenue Service.

Section 274 of the Internal Revenue Code (IRC) requires more extensive documentation of travel and entertainment expense in order for these costs to be deductible for income tax purposes. The following documentation, which companies are required to maintain in order for the expense to be deductible, may provide additional information for audits of travel costs: (1) the amount of the expenditure, (2) time and place of the expenses, (3) business purpose of the expenditure, and (4) business relationship to taxpayer of person(s) entertained. This information must be maintained in a book, diary, account book, or similar records. Cancelled checks, credit card receipts, hotel bills, etc. are to be maintained as corroboration for expenses, but without the diary, book, etc., they may not be sufficient support for deductibility.

DEFENSE OF FRAUD PROCEEDINGS

FAR 31.205-47 provides:

(a) *Definitions.* "Costs," as used in this subsection, include, but are not limited to, administrative and clerical expenses; the cost of legal services, whether performed by in-house or private counsel; the costs of the services of accountants, consultants, or others retained by the contractor to assist it; the salaries and wages of employees, officers, and directors; and any of the foregoing costs incurred before commencing the formal judicial or administrative proceedings which bear a direct relationship to the proceedings.

"Fraud," as used in this subsection, means (1) acts of fraud or corruption or attempts to defraud the Government or to corrupt its agents, (2) acts which constitute a cause for debarment or suspension under 9.406-2(a) and 9.407-2(a) and (3) acts which violate the False Claims Act, 31 U.S.C., sections 3729-3731, or the Anti-Kickback Act, 41 U.S.C., sections 51 and 54.

(b) Costs incurred in connection with defense of any: (1) criminal or civil investigation, grand jury proceeding or prosecution; (2) civil litigation; or (3) administrative proceedings, such as suspension or debarment, or any combination of the foregoing, brought by the Government against a contractor, its agents or employees, are unallowable when the charges, which are the subject of the investigation, proceedings, or prosecution, involve fraud or similar offenses (including filing of a false certification) on the part of the contractor, its agents or employees, and result in conviction (including conviction entered on a plea of nolo contendere), judgment against the contractor, its agent or employees, or decision to debar or suspend, or are resolved by consent or compromise.

(c) In circumstances where the charges of fraud are resolved by consent or compromise, the parties may agree as to the extent of allowability of such costs as a part of such resolution.

(d) Costs which may be unallowable under 31.205-47, including directly associated costs, shall be differentiated and accounted for by the contractor so as to be separately identifiable. During the pendency of any proceeding or investigation covered by paragraph (b) of this subsection, the contracting officer should generally withhold payment of such costs. However, the contracting officer may in appropriate circumstances provide for conditional payment upon provision of adequate security, or other adequate assurance, and agreement by the contractor to repay all unallowable costs, plus interest, if a conviction or judgment is rendered against it.

On March 22, 1983, DOD promulgated DAR 15-205.52, Defense of Fraud Proceedings, criticized by industry officials and their legal advisors as punitive and unconstitutional. With some editorial revisions but no substantive changes, this cost principle was incorporated into FAR, as cited above.

The only harsher position conceivable was reflected in DOD's initial proposal, June 29, 1982, which would have made unallowable all costs incurred by contractors in defending themselves against these various allegations, even where such allegations were ultimately proven to be unfounded and the contractors prevailed. The author joined industry and professional commentators in vigorously opposing this proposal and citing judicial decisions that established contrary positions. See, for example, our comments on *Commissioner of Internal Revenue v. Tellier* earlier in this chapter in the review of FAR 31.205-33, Professional and Consultant Service Costs. Questions were also raised as to which was the greater threat to our country's defense and our way of life—the relatively few instances of fraud related to government procurement or the unrealistically aggressive practices by some government officials to shout fraud whenever they discover a contractor's mistake, to convert contract auditors into investigators, and to add one punitive regulation upon another on companies that are expected to provide the goods and services required by the government.

CODSIA, commenting on the initial proposal, pointed out that contractors and their employees have a right under the Sixth Amendment of the United States Constitution to defend themselves and to seek counsel or other assistance for this purpose. "Contractors are entitled," wrote the highly respected industry group, "to be free of undue government interference without infringement upon the full and uncompromised exercise of these rights."

Convinced that the proposal was unconstitutional, CODSIA recommended that DOD use the "reasonable man test," that is, judge such costs by what a reasonable man would incur to defend himself. The Association also expressed concern for the potential abuse of such provisions where government auditors and procurement officials might use the threat of alleging fraud as a lever to coerce contractors to agree to disallowance of otherwise allowable costs.

DOD ultimately concluded that a provision disallowing costs of defense against fraud and related allegations by the government, even when the contractor prevailed, would likely be found illegal and unconstitutional. The Department accordingly backed off from the provision; however, the cost principle as finally published in DAR and adopted by FAR remains, in the unanimous judgment of the government contractors and their legal advisors, harsh, extreme, and of questionable legality.

DEFERRED RESEARCH AND DEVELOPMENT COSTS

FAR 31.205-48 provides:

"Research and development," as used in this subsection, means the type of technical effort which is described in 31.205-18 but which is sponsored by, or required in performance of, a contract or grant. Research and development costs (including amounts capitalized) that were incurred before the award of a particular contract are unallowable except when allowable as precontract costs. In addition, when costs are incurred in excess of either the price of a contract or amount of a grant for research and development effort, such excess may not be allocated as a cost to any other Government contract.

GOODWILL

Defense Acquisition Circular (DAC) 76-48, January 25, 1984, added DAR 15-205.53 Goodwill:

Goodwill, an unidentifiable intangible asset, originates under the purchase method of accounting for a business combination when the price paid by the acquiring company exceeds the sum of the identifiable individual assets acquired less liabilities assumed, based upon their fair market values. The excess is commonly referred to as goodwill. Goodwill may arise from the acquisition of a company as a whole or a portion thereof. Any costs for amortization, expensing, write-off, or write-down of goodwill (however represented) are unallowable.

The background of this cost principle reflects the familiar story of an ASBCA decision in favor of a contractor and DOD's immediate reaction to undermine the ruling by revising its regulations.

In a comprehensive, carefully researched decision, the Armed Services Board of Contract Appeals ruled that goodwill acquired upon a merger of two firms, when recorded and amortized in accordance with generally accepted accounting principles (GAAP), is includable as an element of facilities capital for computing cost of money under CAS 414. In these circumstances, the amortization is an allowable contract cost. Because the contractor failed to amortize goodwill, however, the board found it failed to meet the requirements of CAS 414 that this asset should be stated at the same values that are used to generate depreciation or amortization. Accordingly, goodwill in these circumstances was not permitted to be included in facilities capital except for the periods during which no exception was taken by the government. The board allowed the inclusion for these periods, holding the government was estopped from challenging it.

Those who take the time and make the effort to study carefully the ruling in *Gould Defense Systems, Inc.*, ASBCA No. 24881, June 10, 1983, 83-2 BCA par. 16,676, will be rewarded by an erudite dissertation on the accounting and regulatory aspects of goodwill. It totally overwhelms and demolishes the effort of DCAA in that Agency's Audit Guidance Paper No. 157, dated March 14, 1980, which concluded that goodwill, whatever its origin and treatment, could not be included in the base for cost of money under CAS 414 and that goodwill amortization was not an allowable contract cost. The DCAA's Guidance Paper was flawed by a selective citation of authorities and an apparent bias reflected in what appeared to be an objective to make a case against allowing goodwill. In contrast, the *Gould* decision contains a full account of GAAP, DAR, and CAS provisions that relate to this subject and accords full attention to the arguments on both sides of this issue.

Inclusion of Goodwill Generally in Facilities Capital

The parties in *Gould* stipulated that goodwill is an intangible asset within the meaning of CAS 414. The government argued, however, that goodwill may not be included in the base for cost of money because it does not meet the CAS 414 requirements that (1) it be subject to amortization and (2) its value(s) not be used to generate amortization that is allowed for government contract costing purposes. The board disagreed to the extent that GAAP required goodwill to be amortized. Further, the board found that the issue of including goodwill must have been considered by the CASB because it had been raised by commentators when the standard was being developed. The CASB therefore was on notice that this was a question, and, because it failed to specify its exclusion, was held to have concluded that goodwill should be included in the base.

The board found irrelevant the fact that internally generated goodwill could not be objectively measured or amortized, because the issue in this dispute was purchased goodwill.

The board further found in its research of DAR that goodwill was nowhere excluded. On the other hand, DAR recognized acceptability under

GAAP as a criterion for cost allowability, and GAAP establishes goodwill amortization as an acceptable cost. The board also pointed out that the government in CAS 404 and 409 established depreciation on stepped-up assets following a purchase combination to be allowable, and found goodwill amortization to be analogous.

Inclusion of Goodwill in the CAS 414 Computation in This Appeal

Having found that goodwill may be included in the base for computing cost of money and that amortization of goodwill may be considered as an allowable cost, the board emphasized its conclusion by striking down various objections raised by the government and its expert witnesses. A theoretical interpretation of a footnote to Gould's financial statement, which suggested goodwill might not be diminished, was rejected on the grounds that treatment for external financial reporting purposes does not control determination of allowability for government contract costing purposes. Similarly rejected was the government's argument that goodwill amortization was not acceptable for federal income tax purposes. DCAA and other government agencies were quick to argue that neither the treatment for financial reporting nor the treatment for income tax purposes represents criteria for allowing costs under a contract.

However, in the only aspect of this decision with which we are unable to agree (a separate concurring opinion by one of the administrative judges also expressed doubts on this point), the board held that goodwill could not be included in the CAS 414 base in this appeal because the contractor failed to satisfy the provisions in CAS 414, Appendix A, that "... facilities capital values should be the same values that are used to generate appreciation or amortization that is allowed for Federal Government contract costing purposes . . . ." The board emphasized that "since we have found the includability of assets under CAS 414 to be controlled substantially by the current and allowable amortization of the related intangible asset, those assets automatically are includable once amortization commences." Gould had not recorded, either in its books of account or in any form of memorandum records, such amortization or its allocation from the corporate home office to the segments.

Gould had made no claim for goodwill amortization as a contract cost, a claim that the board found the contractor could have made. However, the board found that the record of amortization should have been available even if Gould had elected, for whatever reason, not to claim such amortization as a cost of government contracts.

The government could find no authoritative statute or regulation denying the allowability of goodwill amortization as a cost or the unamortized portion as includable in the base for calculating cost of money. The only paper on this subject was in the form of guidance from DCAA, which, of course, directed its minions to disallow goodwill. A number of contractors noted that the guidance paper was flawed by a selective citation of authorities and an apparent bias reflected in what appeared to be a predetermined objective to make a case against allowing goodwill. More importantly, DCAA guidance papers have no regulatory or other authority.

As most observers predicted, DOD, which usually takes considerable time in developing cost principles and at that time had its people heavily involved in final touches on FAR and the DOD FAR Supplement, nevertheless and with unseemly haste published on September 7, 1983, a proposed cost principle declaring costs for amortization of goodwill to be unallowable. Of course, no rationale was provided for this effort to reverse the ASBCA decision. Although at least 60 days are usually allowed for comments, only 30 days were provided in this case.

Working rapidly to comply with the unreasonable time limit, CODSIA nevertheless prepared a well reasoned response in the form of a letter with a scholarly attachment containing the Association's analysis and observations on the proposed cost principle. Excerpts of the CODSIA letter are cited below:

We believe that Government contract cost principles should consist of broad criteria such as those used by a prudent person in the decision making process during the conduct of a competitive business. To be effective, these cost principles must promote and protect the best interests of both Government and industry, and should allow recovery of all reasonable ordinary and necessary expenses. Accordingly, we believe it is inequitable for those with regulatory authority to reverse reasoned and wellfounded decisions of the Armed Services Board of Contract Appeals. While the Government may believe that such an approach works to its advantage, in the long run it cannot help but weaken the defense industrial base, as contractors are required to write off against profits more and more of the normal costs of doing business. Contractors will inevitably be forced to decline to make the investments necessary to ensure the continued viability of the underlying industrial base.

The proposed cost principle on the amortization of goodwill should be withdrawn. No public interest is served by promulgating regulations which discourage needed investment. The recoverability of goodwill amortization is not contrary to any fundamental or congressionally-expressed policy. To the contrary, the proposed cost principle ignores economic reality and will contravene long standing DOD profit policy. Further, by attempting to indirectly disallow the reimbursement of a portion of a contractor's cost of money on facilities capital, the proposed cost principle will frustrate the principal purpose of Cost Accounting Standard 414, Cost of Money as an Element of the Cost of Facilities Capital, which was designed to encourage valuable investment in defense facilities by recognizing the real cost of capital investments committed to Government Contracts.

CODSIA's letter forwarded a brief treatise on goodwill, which was submitted because industry saw the proposed cost principle as an improper reaction to the ASBCA decision. "Workable acquisition regulations," wrote CODSIA, "must flow from a clear understanding of basic issues. It is our purpose to develop such an understanding in this paper." After explaining just "what is goodwill" the industry association explained the difference between "internally generated goodwill" and "purchased goodwill," a distinction effectively developed in the ASBCA decision, and explained that purchased goodwill, under generally accepted accounting principles, is properly recorded as an asset and amortized over a period not to exceed 40 years. Focusing on the case for allowing amortization of purchased goodwill as a contract cost, the CODSIA paper stated:

> The recovery of the amortization of purchased goodwill is not contrary to any fundamental or congressionally-expressed policy. The Government's acceptance of purchase accounting for business combinations is established in law (Cost Accounting Standard 404). The reasonableness of the amount of purchased goodwill is established by arms-length transaction in the marketplace. Under generally accepted accounting principles, the cost basis of goodwill is objectively measurable only when purchased. The cost basis of goodwill should not be treated any differently than other assets. The proposed DAR provision is inconsistent with Cost Accounting Standard 404. It would be anomalous for the Government to mandate the use of purchase accounting for business combinations on the one hand and preclude recovery of real costs arising from such use on the other.

> Amortization of goodwill meets the general requirements of DAR 15-201.1 that costs be determined in accordance with a generally accepted method. Goodwill amortization is an ordinary and necessary cost of doing business. Amortization of goodwill is allowable once the DAR allocability criteria are settled.

Although the proposal to disallow amortization of goodwill was published on September 7, 1983, with an unusually short 30 days permitted for industry response, DOD would not even await this period before striking at the ASBCA and at industry. In a hastily prepared memorandum dated September 14, 1983, and signed by the Deputy Under Secretary of Defense (Acquisition Management) to the military departments, DCAA, and DLA, the Defense Department in effect admitted that the disallowance of goodwill amortization had been predetermined and that the request for views from the private sector was a sham. The memorandum directed the exclusion of goodwill "in proposals for new contracts, or in billing rates, bid rates, facilities capital cost of money rate, or financial overhead rate submissions." In the case of existing contracts, the DOD memorandum asserted that the ASBCA decision in *Gould Defense Systems, Inc.,* "involved a particular fact situation which may not exist elsewhere" and directed contracting officers to "seek appropriate technical and legal advice prior to making a final decision as to the allowability of any costs associated with goodwill."

As expected, the cognizant DOD people persuaded the civilian agencies to agree to FAR revisions under which goodwill becomes unallowable for inclusion in the base for computing cost of money, and amortization of goodwill becomes unallowable as a cost. The FAR revisions were included in Federal Acquisition Circular (FAC) 84-3, appearing in the *Federal Register* of June 20, 1984, with an effective date of "October 1, 1984, but may be observed sooner."

The first change was effected by adding paragraph 31.205-10(a)(5):

> The cost of money resulting from including goodwill (however represented) in the facilities capital employed base is unallowable.

The second change was made by adding paragraph 31.205-49:

Goodwill, an unidentifiable intangible asset, originates under the purchase method of accounting for a business combination when the price paid by the acquiring company exceeds the sum of the identifiable individual assets acquired less liabilities assumed, based upon their fair values. The excess is commonly referred to as goodwill. Goodwill may arise from the acquisition of a company as a whole or a portion thereof. Any costs for amortization, expensing, write-off or write-down of goodwill (however represented) are unallowable.

These revisions represented a victory for certain DOD personnel who thus succeeded in rebuffing and overcoming the accounting profession and its generally accepted accounting principles, industry, and the Armed Services Board of Contract Appeals, all of whom expressed contrary views regarding goodwill. FAC 84-3 offered no rationale for the revisions but neither had the Department of Defense when it published DAC 76-48 on January 25, 1984, adding DAR 15-205.53, which FAR 31.205-49 quoted almost verbatim.

EXECUTIVE LOBBYING COSTS

As noted earlier, P.L. 99-145 cited 16 expense categories with respect to which the Secretary of Defense was required to issue regulations clarifying their allowability. Included was "Actions to influence (directly or indirectly) executive branch action on regulatory and contract matters (other than cost incurred in regard to contract proposals pursuant to solicited or unsolicited bids)."

In compliance with the statute, FAR was revised by retitling FAR 31.205-22 from "Lobbying Costs" to "Legislative Lobbying Costs," and a new FAR 31.205-50 was added with the above caption:

Costs incurred in attempting to improperly influence (see FAR 3.401), either directly or indirectly, an employee or officer of the executive branch of the Federal Government to give consideration or to act regarding a regulatory or contract matter are unallowable.

FAR 3.401, referred to in this cost principle, defines "improper influence" as "any influence that induces or tends to induce a Government employee or officer to give consideration or to act regarding a Government contract on any basis other than the merits of the matter."

COSTS OF ALCOHOLIC BEVERAGES

In accordance with a specific provision of P.L. 99-145, an additional cost principle, FAR 31.205-51 was added:

Costs of alcoholic beverages are unallowable.

Chapter XVIII

Application of Government Contract Cost Principles to Specific Costs and Expenses— Compensation for Personal Services

In our discussion of the application of Government Contract Cost Principles to Specific Costs and Expenses in Chapter XVII of this text, we noted that regulations governing compensation for personal services are among the lengthiest and most complex and controversial. Contributing factors include the CASB promulgations of four standards relating directly to this broad area, a major revision of this cost principle by the Department of Defense, which was subsequently incorporated into FAR without substantive change, and subsequent FAR revisions and judicial rulings. For all of these reasons, we concluded that this subject should be treated separately and have devoted this Chapter XVIII to it.

PRIOR COST PRINCIPLES

For coverage of this area in the 1949 cost principles, reference had to be made to eleven different and separate paragraphs: ASPR 15-204(c), 15-204(e), 15-204(n), 15-204(p), 15-204(t), 15-204(x), 15-205(p), 15-502(h), 15-502(u), 15-601 and 15-603. The first six referenced paragraphs cited conditions under which compensation is allowable. For example, compensation paid to or set aside for officers and executives including, under certain circumstances, retirement benefits, etc., were allowable except that the total compensation of an individual may be limited in consideration of the relationship of such total compensation to the services rendered. Directors and executive committee fees were cited as allowable. The allowability of overtime compensation was limited "to the extent expressly provided for elsewhere in the contract or otherwise authorized by the Government." The 1949 ASPR provision also allowed "vacation, holiday and severance pay, sick leave and military leave . . . to the extent required by law, by employer-employee agreement, or by the contractor's established policy . . . ." Premiums for insurance on the lives of directors, officers, proprietors or other persons, where the contractor is the beneficiary either directly or indirectly, were specifically cited as an unallowable cost. ASPR 15-601 of the 1949 cost principles contained a lengthy interpretation of pension and retirement plan costs. In summary, such costs were considered allowable if (1) they were approved by the Internal Revenue Service and (2) the total compensation, including pension and retirement provision, was reasonable. A cost interpretation was also issued with regard to supplemental employment benefit plans, which provided that payments to funds established for that purpose would be allowed when:

(i) Made to an irrevocable fund or trust for the exclusive benefit of the contractor's employees as a result of an arm's-length agreement between the employer and his employees;

(ii) Accepted by the Internal Revenue Service as deductible for federal income tax purposes;

(iii) Equitably allocated between defense and nondefense business at the plant or division level, whichever is lower, for which payments are calculated, provided the maximum funding has not been reached for such activity.

The 1959 cost principles grouped most of the considerations relating to compensation for personal services within a single section. The additions or changes included the limitation on total compensation of individual employees to the amounts "allowable by the Internal Revenue Code and regulations thereunder."

Whereas the 1949 regulations merely listed wages or salaries of partners or sole proprietors as an item requiring special consideration, the 1959 principles suggested that such compensation, as well as compensation to owners of closely held corporations, would be considered allowable upon the determination "that such compensation is reasonable for the actual personal services rendered rather than a distribution of profits." The 1959 cost principles also suggested that special attention be accorded by the government where salaries are substantially increased concurrently with an increase in the ratio of government contracts to other business or in circumstances where "a contractor's business is such that his compensation levels are not subject to the restraints normally occurring in the conduct of competitive business."

The subject of bonuses and other incentive compensation was treated at considerable length in the 1959 cost principles. All such compensation was considered allowable provided it was "based on production, cost reduction, or efficient performance . . . to the extent that the overall compensation is determined to be reasonable and such costs are paid or accrued pursuant to an agreement entered into in good faith between the contractor and the employees before the services were rendered, or pursuant to an established plan followed by the contractor so consistently as to imply, in effect, an agreement to make such a payment." An addition in this area set forth the method for placing evaluation on compensation where payment was in stock, i.e., "fair market value at the time of transfer, determined upon the most objective basis available." The cost of stock options, however, remained unallowable.

MAJOR CHANGES IN COST PRINCIPLES: 1959-Present

A comparison of the 1959 and current cost principles governing compensation for personal services reveals that, while some of the provisions have withstood the test of time for over two decades, a number of major changes have been made. We have quoted below the full text of FAR 31.205-6 current at this writing. The analysis that follows includes comments on the major changes.

31.205-6 Compensation for Personal Services

(a) *General.* Compensation for personal services includes all remuneration paid currently or accrued, in whatever form and whether paid immediately or deferred, for services rendered by employees to the contractor during the period of contract performance (except as otherwise provided for severance pay costs in paragraph (g) below and for pension costs in paragraph (j) below). It includes, but is not limited to, salaries; wages; directors' and executive committee members' fees; bonuses (including stock bonuses); incentive awards; employee stock options, stock appreciation rights, and stock ownership plans; employee insurance; fringe benefits; contributions to pension, annuity, and management employee incentive compensation plans; and allowances for off-site pay, incentive pay, location allowances, hardship pay, severance pay, and cost of living differential. Compensation for personal services is allowable subject to the following general criteria and additional requirements contained in other parts of this cost principle:

(1) Compensation for personal services must be for work performed by the employee in the current year and must not represent a retroactive adjustment of prior years' salaries or wages (but see 31.205-6(g), (h), (j), (k), and (m) below).

(2) The compensation in total must be reasonable for the work performed; however, specific restrictions on individual compensation elements must be observed where they are prescribed.

(3) The compensation must be based upon and conform to the terms and conditions of the contractor's established compensation plan or practice followed so consistently as to imply, in effect, an agreement to make the payment.

(4) No presumption of allowability will exist where the contractor introduces major revisions of existing compensation plans or new plans and the contractor—

(i) Has not notified the cognizant ACO of the changes either before their implementation or within a reasonable period after their implementation, and

(ii) Has not provided the Government, either before implementation or within a reasonable period after it, an opportunity to review the allowability of the changes.

(5) Costs that are unallowable under other paragraphs of this Subpart 31.2 shall not be allowable under this subsection 31.205-6 solely on the basis that they constitute compensation for personal services. (See 31.205-34(c).)

(b) *Reasonableness.* (1) The compensation for personal services paid or accrued to each employee must be reasonable for the work performed. Compensation will be considered reasonable if each of the allowable elements making up the employee's compensation package is reasonable. In determining the reasonableness of individual elements for particular employees or classes of employees, consideration should be given to all potentially relevant facts. Facts which may be relevant include general conformity with the compensation practices of other firms of the same size, compensation practices of other firms in the same industry, the compensation practices of other firms in the same geographic area, the compensation practices of firms engaged in predominantly non-Government work, and the cost of comparable services obtainable from outside sources. While all of the above factors, as well as any other relevant ones, should be considered, their relative significance will vary according to circumstances. For example, in the case of secretarial salaries, conformity with the compensation paid by other firms in the same geographic area would likely be a more significant criterion than conformity with compensation paid by other firms in the same industry wherever located. In administering this principle, it is recognized that not every compensation case need be subjected in detail to the above or other tests. The tests need be applied only when a general review reveals amounts or types of compensation that appear unreasonable or unjustified. Based on an initial review of the facts, contracting officers or their representatives may challenge the reasonableness of any individual element or the sum of the individual elements of compensation paid or accrued to particular employees or classes of employees. In such cases, there is no presumption of reasonableness and, upon challenge, the contractor must demonstrate the reasonableness of the compensation item in question. In doing so, the contractor may introduce, and the contracting officer will consider, not only any circumstances surrounding the compensation item challenged, but also the magnitude of other compensation elements which may be lower than would be considered reasonable in themselves. For example, a contractor, if challenged on the amount of base salaries for management, could counter by showing lower than normal end-of-year management bonuses. However, the contractor's right to introduce offsetting compensation elements into consideration is subject to the following limitations:

(i) Offsets will be considered only between the allowable elements of an employee's (or a class of employees') compensation package. For example, excessive management salaries cannot be offset against lower than normal secretarial salaries.

(ii) Offsets will be considered only between the allowable portion of the following compensation elements of employees or classes of employees:

(A) Wages and salaries.

(B) Incentive bonuses.

(C) Deferred compensation.

(D) Pension and savings plan benefits.

(E) Health insurance benefits.

(F) Life insurance benefits.

(G) Compensated personal absence benefits.

However, any of the above elements or portions thereof, whose amount is not measurable, shall not be introduced or considered as an offset item.

(iii) In considering offsets, the magnitude of the compensation elements in question must be taken into account. An executive bonus that is excessive by $100,000 is not fully offset by a base salary that is low by only $25,000. In determining the magnitude of compensation elements, the timing of receipt by the employee must be considered. For example, a bonus of $100,000 in the current period will be considered as of greater value than a deferred compensation arrangement to make the same payment in some future period.

(2) Compensation costs under certain conditions give rise to the need for special consideration. Among such conditions are the following:

(i) Compensation to (A) owners of closely held corporations, partners, sole proprietors, or members of the immediate families, or (B) persons who are contractually committed to acquire a substantial financial interest in the contractor's enterprise. Determination should be made that salaries are reasonable for the personal services rendered rather than being a distribution of profits. Compensation in lieu of salary for services rendered by partners and sole proprietors will be allowed to the extent that it is reasonable and does not constitute a distribution of profits. For closely held corporations, compensation costs covered by this subdivision shall not be recognized in amounts exceeding those costs that are deductible as compensation under the Internal Revenue Code and regulations under it.

(ii) Any change in a contractor's compensation policy that results in a substantial increase in the contractor's level of compensation, particularly when it was concurrent with an increase in the ratio of Government contracts to other business, or any change in the treatment of allowability of specific types of compensation due to changes in Government policy. Contracting officers or their representatives should normally challenge increased costs where major revisions of existing compensation plans or new plans are introduced by the contractor, and the contractor—

(A) Has not notified the cognizant ACO of the changes either before their implementation or within a reasonable period after their implementation; and

(B) Has not provided the Government, either before implementation or within a reasonable period after it, an opportunity to review the reasonableness of the changes.

(iii) The contractor's business is such that its compensation levels are not subject to the restraints that normally occur in the conduct of competitive business.

(iv) The contractor incurs costs for compensation in excess of the amounts which are deductible under the Internal Revenue Code and regulations issued under it.

(c) *Labor-management agreements.* Notwithstanding any other requirements of this subsection 31.205-6, costs of compensation are not allowable to the extent that they result from provisions of labor-management agreements that, as applied to work in performing Government contracts, are determined to be unreasonable because they are either unwarranted by the character and circumstances of the work or discriminatory against the Government. The application of the provisions of a labor-management agreement designed to apply to a given set of circumstances and conditions of employment (e.g., work involving extremely hazardous activities or work not requiring recurrent use of overtime) is unwarranted when applied to a Government contract involving significantly different circumstances and conditions of employment (e.g., work involving less hazardous activities or work continually requiring use of overtime). It is discriminatory against the Government if it results in employee compensation (in whatever form or name) in excess of that being paid for similar non-Government work under comparable circumstances. Disallowance of costs will not be made under this paragraph (c) unless—

(1) The contractor has been permitted an opportunity to justify the costs; and

(2) Due consideration has been given to whether unusual conditions pertain to Government contract work, imposing burdens, hardships, or hazards on the contractor's employees, for which compensation that might otherwise appear unreasonable is required to attract and hold necessary personnel.

(d) *Salaries and wages.* Salaries and wages for current services include gross compensation paid to employees in the form of cash, stock (see subparagraph (f)(2) below regarding valuation), products, or services, and are allowable.

(e) *Domestic and foreign differential pay.* (1) When personal services are performed in a foreign country, compensation may also include a differential that may properly consider all expenses associated with foreign employment such as housing, cost of living adjustments, transportation, bonuses, additional Federal, State, local or foreign income taxes resulting from foreign assignment, and other related expenses.

(2) Although the additional taxes in subparagraph (1) above may be considered in establishing foreign overseas differential, any increased compensation calculated directly on the basis of an employee's specific increase in income taxes is unallowable. Differential allowances for additional Federal, State, or local income taxes resulting from domestic assignments are unallowable.

(f) *Bonuses and incentive compensation.* (1) Incentive compensation for management employees, cash bonuses, suggestion awards, safety awards, and incentive compensation based on production, cost reduction, or efficient performance are allowable provided the awards are paid or accrued under an agreement entered into in good faith between the contractor and the employees before the services are rendered or pursuant to an established plan or policy followed by the contractor so consistently as to imply, in effect, an agreement to make such payment and the basis for the award is supported.

(2) When the costs of bonuses and incentive compensation are paid in the stock of the contractor or of an affiliate, the following additional restrictions apply:

(i) Valuation placed on the stock shall be the fair market value on the measurement date (i.e., the first date the number of shares awarded is known) determined upon the most objective basis available; and

(ii) Accruals for the cost of stock before issuing the stock to the employees shall be subject to adjustment according to the possibilities that the employees will not receive the stock and that their interest in the accruals will be forfeited.

(3) When the bonus and incentive compensation payments are deferred, the costs are subject to the requirements of subparagraph (f)(1) above and of paragraph (k) below.

(g) *Severance pay.* (1) Severance pay, also commonly referred to as dismissal wages, is a payment in addition to regular salaries and wages by contractors to workers whose employment is being involuntarily terminated. Payments for early retirement incentive plans are covered in subparagraph (j)(6) below.

(2) Severance pay to be allowable must meet the general allowability criteria in subdivision (g)(2)(i) below, and, depending upon whether the severance is normal or abnormal, criteria in subdivision (g)(2)(ii) for normal severance pay or subdivision (g)(2)(iii) for abnormal severance pay also apply.

(i) Severance pay is allowable only to the extent that, in each case, it is required by (A) law, (B) employer-employee agreement, (C) established policy that constitutes, in effect, an implied agreement on the contractor's part, or (D) circumstances of the particular employment. Payments made in the event of employment with a replacement contractor where continuity of employment with credit for prior length of service is preserved under substantially equal conditions of employment, or continued employment by the contractor at another facility, subsidiary, affiliate, or parent company of the contractor are not severance pay and are unallowable. Severance payments, or amounts paid in lieu thereof, are not allowable when paid to employees in addition to early or normal retirement payments.

(ii) Actual normal turnover severance payments shall be allocated to all work performed in the contractor's plant, or where the contractor provides for accrual of pay for normal severances, that method will be acceptable if the amount of the accrual is reasonable in light of payments actually made for normal severances over a representative past period and if amounts accrued are allocated to all work performed in the contractor's plant.

(iii) Abnormal or mass severance pay is of such a conjectural nature that measurement of costs by means of an accrual will not achieve equity to both parties. Thus, accruals for this purpose are not allowable. However, the Government recognizes its obligation to participate, to the extent of its fair share, in any specific payment. Thus, allowability will be considered on a case-by-case basis.

(h) *Backpay.* (1) *Backpay resulting from violations of Federal labor laws or the Civil Rights Act of 1964.* Backpay may result from a negotiated settlement, order, or court decree that resolves a violation of Federal labor laws or the Civil Rights Act of 1964. Such backpay falls into two categories: one requiring the contractor to pay employees additional compensation for work performed for which they were underpaid, and the other resulting from other violations, such as when the employee was improperly discharged, discriminated against, or other circumstances for which the backpay was not additional compensation for work performed. Backpay resulting from underpaid work is compensation for the work performed and is allowable. All other backpay resulting from violation of Federal labor laws or the Civil Rights Act of 1964 is unallowable.

(2) *Other backpay.* Backpay may also result from payments to union employees (union and non-union) for the difference in their past and current wage rates for working without a contract or labor agreement during labor management negotiations. Such backpay is allowable. Backpay to nonunion employees based upon results of union agreement negotiations is allowable only if (i) a formal agreement or understanding exists between management and the employees concerning these payments, or (ii) an established policy or practice exists and is followed by the contractor so consistently as to imply, in effect, an agreement to make such payment.

(i) *Stock options, stock appreciation rights, phantom stock plans, and junior stock conversions.*

(1) The cost of stock options awarded to employees to purchase stock of the contractor or of an affiliate will be treated as deferred compensation and must comply with the requirements of paragraph (k) of this subsection. The allowable cost of stock options is limited to the difference between the option price and the market price on the first date on which the option price and the number of shares are known. Accordingly, when the stock option price is equal to or greater than the market price on that date, then no costs are allowable for contract costing purposes.

(2) Stock appreciation rights are rights granted to employees by contractors to receive the increase in value, or appreciation, of company stock even though the employee neither purchases the stock nor receives title to it. Stock appreciation rights will be treated as deferred compensation and must comply with the requirements of paragraph (k) of this subsection. The allowable cost of stock appreciation rights is limited to the difference between the stock-appreciation-right base price from which appreciation will be measured and the market price on the first date on which both the number of shares and the stock-appreciation-right base price are known. Accordingly, when the stock-appreciation-right base price is equal to or greater than the market price on that date, then no costs are allowable for contract costing purposes.

(3) In phantom-stock-type plans, contractors assign or attribute contingent shares of stock to employees as if the employees own the stock, even though the employees neither purchase the stock nor receive title to it. Under these plans, an employee's account may be increased by the equivalent of dividends paid and any appreciation in the market price of the stock over the price of the stock on the first date on which the number of shares awarded is known. Such increases in employee accounts for dividend equivalents and market price appreciation are unallowable.

(4) Junior stock is a class of equity stock that (i) is sold to employees at a price below that of the contractor's common stock, (ii) carries reduced dividend and voting rights, and (iii) is convertible to common stock upon the attainment of specified corporate goals. Costs associated with the conversion of junior stock into common stock are not allowable, whether or not they are accounted for as compensation costs.

(j) *Pension costs.* (1) A pension plan is a deferred compensation plan that is established and maintained by one or more employers to provide systematically for paying benefits to plan participants after their retirement, provided that the benefits are paid for life or are payable for life at the option of the employee. Additional benefits such as permanent and total disability and death payments and survivorship payments to beneficiaries of deceased employees may be treated as pension costs, provided the benefits are an integral part of the pension plan and meet all the criteria pertaining to pension costs.

(2) Pension plans are normally segregated into two types of plans: defined benefit or defined contribution pension plans. The cost of all defined benefit pension plans shall be measured, allocated, and accounted for in compliance with the provisions of CAS 412, Composition and Measurement of Pension Costs, and CAS 413, Adjustment and Allocation of Pension Cost. The costs of all defined contribution pension plans shall be measured, allocated, and accounted for in accordance with the provisions of CAS 412. Pension costs are allowable subject to the referenced standards and the cost limitations and exclusions set forth below in this subparagraph and in subparagraphs (j)(3), (4), (5), (6), and (7) below.

(i) To be allowable in the current year, pension costs must be funded by the time set for filing the Federal income tax return or any extension thereof. Pension costs assigned to the current year, but not funded by the tax return time, shall not be allowable in any subsequent year.

(ii) Pension payments must be reasonable in amount and be paid pursuant to (A) an agreement entered into in good faith between the contractor and employees before the work or services are performed and (B) the terms and conditions of the established plan. The cost of changes in pension plans which are discriminatory to the Government or are not intended to be applied consistently for all employees under similar circumstances in the future are not allowable.

(iii) Except as provided for early retirement benefits in subparagraph (j)(6) below, one-time-only pension supplements not available to all participants of the basic plan are not allowable as pension costs unless the supplemental benefits represent a separate pension plan and the benefits are payable for life at the option of the employee.

(iv) Increases in payments to previously retired plan participants covering cost-of-living adjustments are allowable if paid in accordance with a policy or practice consistently followed.

(3) *Defined benefit pension plans.* This subparagraph covers pension plans in which the benefits to be paid or the basis for determining such benefits are established in advance and the contributions are intended to provide the stated benefits. The cost limitations and exclusions pertaining to defined benefit plans are as follows:

(i) Normal costs of pension plans not funded in the year incurred, and all other components of pension costs (see CAS 412.40(a)(1)) assignable to the current accounting period but not funded during it, shall not be allowable in subsequent years (except that a payment made to a fund by the time set for filing the Federal income tax return or any extension thereof is considered to have been made during such taxable year). However, any part of a pension cost that is computed for a cost accounting period that is deferred pursuant to a waiver granted under the provisions of the Employee's Retirement Income Security Act of 1974 (ERISA) (see CAS 412.50(c)(3)), will be allowable in those future accounting periods in which the funding does occur. The allowability of these deferred contributions will be limited to the amounts that would have been allowed had the funding occurred in the year the costs would have been assigned except for the waiver.

(ii) Any amount paid or funded before the time it becomes assignable and allowable shall be applied to future years, in order of time, as if actually paid and deductible in those years. The interest earned on such premature funding, based on the valuation rate of return, may be excluded from future years' computations of pension costs in accordance with CAS 412.50(a)(7).

(iii) Increased pension costs caused by delay in funding beyond 30 days after each quarter of the year to which they are assignable are unallowable. If a composite rate is used for allocating pension costs between the segments of a company and if, because of differences in the timing of the funding by the segments, an inequity exists, allowable pension costs for each segment will be limited to that particular segment's calculation of pension costs as provided for in CAS 413.50(c)(5). Determination of unallowable costs shall be made in accordance with the actuarial method used in calculating pension costs.

(iv) Allowability of the cost of indemnifying the Pension Benefit Guaranty Corporation (PBGC) under ERISA Section 4062 or 4064 arising from terminating an employee deferred compensation plan will be considered on a case-by-case basis; provided that if insurance was required by the PBGC under ERISA Section 4023, it was so obtained and the indemnification payment is not recoverable under the insurance. Consideration under the foregoing circumstances will be primarily for the purpose of appraising the extent to which the indemnification payment is allocable to Government work. If a beneficial or other equitable relationship exists, the Government will participate, despite the requirements of 31.205-19(a)(3) and (b), in the indemnification payment to the extent of its fair share.

(4) *Defined contribution pension plans.* This subparagraph covers those pension plans in which the contributions to be made are established in advance and the level of benefits is determined by the contributions made. It also covers profit sharing, savings plans, and other such plans provided the plans fall within the definition of a pension plan in subparagraph (j)(1) above.

(i) The pension cost assignable to a cost accounting period is the net contribution required to be made for that period after taking into account dividends and other credits, where applicable. However, any portion of pension cost computed for a cost accounting period that is deferred pursuant to a waiver granted under the provisions of ERISA (see CAS 412.50(c)(3)) will be allowable in those future accounting periods when the funding does occur. The allowability of these deferred contributions will be limited to the amounts that would have been allowed had the funding been made in the year the costs would have been assigned except for the waiver.

(ii) Any amount paid or funded to the trust before the time it becomes assignable and allowable shall be applied to future years, in order of time, as if actually paid and deductible in such years.

(iii) The provisions of subdivision (j)(3)(iv) above concerning payments to PBGC apply to defined contribution plans.

(5) *Pension plans using pay-as-you-go methods.* A pension plan using pay-as-you-go methods is a plan in which the contractor recognizes pension cost only when benefits are paid to retired employees or their beneficiaries. Regardless of whether the payment of pension benefits contribution can or cannot be compelled, allowable costs for these types of plans shall not exceed an amount computed as follows:

(i) Compute, by using an actuarial cost method, the plan's actuarial liability for benefits earned by plan participants. This entire liability is always unfunded for a pay-as-you-go plan.

(ii) Compute a level amount which, including an interest equivalent, would amortize the unfunded actuarial liability over a period of no less than 10 or more than 40 years from the inception of the liability.

(iii) Compute, by using an actuarial cost method, a normal cost for the period.

(iv) The sum of (ii) and (iii) above represents the amount of pension costs assignable to the current period. This amount, however, is limited to the amount paid in the year.

(v) For purposes of determining contract cost where a pay-as-you-go plan is initiated as either a supplemental plan or an additional but separate plan to a basic funded plan, the plans will be treated as one plan; e.g., the actuarial cost method, past service amortization period, etc., of the basic plan will be used on the supplemental or additional pay-as-you-go plan in determining the proper costs assignable to the current period. Any costs in excess of those determined by using the actuarial cost method and assumptions of the basic plan are unallowable. However, where assumption for salary progressions, mortality rates of the participants, and so forth are significantly different, the assumptions used for the basic and supplemental plan may be different.

(vi) The requirements of subdivisions (j)(3)(i) through (iv) above are also applicable to pay-as-you-go plans.

(6) *Early retirement incentive plans.* An early retirement incentive plan is a plan under which employees receive a bonus or incentive, over and above the requirement of the basic pension plan, to retire early. These plans normally are not applicable to all participants of the basic plan and do not represent life income settlements, and as such would not qualify as pension costs. However, for contract costing purposes, early retirement incentive payments are allowable subject to the pension cost criteria contained in subdivisions (j)(3)(i) through (iv) provided—

(i) The costs are accounted for and allocated in accordance with the contractor's system of accounting for pension costs (see subdivision (j)(5)(v) above for supplemental pension benefits);

(ii) The payments are made in accordance with the terms and conditions of the contractor's plan;

(iii) The plan is applied only to active employees. The cost of extending the plan to employees who retired or were terminated before the adoption of the plan is unallowable; and

(iv) The total of the incentive payments to any employee may not exceed the amount of the employee's annual salary for the previous fiscal year before the employee's retirement.

(7) *Employee stock ownership plans (ESOP)* (i) An ESOP is an individual stock bonus plan designed specifically to invest in the stock of the employer corporation. The contractor's contributions to an Employee Stock Ownership Trust (ESOT) may be in the form of cash, stock, or property. Costs of ESOP's are allowable subject to the following conditions:

(A) Contributions by the contractor in any one year may not exceed 15 percent (25 percent when a money purchase plan is included) of salaries and wages of employees participating in the plan in any particular year.

(B) The contribution rate (ratio of contribution to salaries and wages of participating employees) may not exceed the last approved contribution rate except when approved by the contracting officer based upon justification provided by the contractor. When no contribution was made in the previous year for an existing ESOP, or when a new ESOP is first established, and the contractor proposes to make a contribution in the current year, the contribution rate shall be subject to the contracting officer's approval.

(C) When a plan or agreement exists wherein the liability for the contribution can be compelled for a specific year, the expense associated with that liability is assignable only to that period. Any portion of the contribution not funded by the time set for filing of the Federal income tax return for that year or any extension thereof shall not be allowable in subsequent years.

(D) When a plan or agreement exists wherein the liability for the contribution cannot be compelled, the amount contributed for any year is assignable to that year provided the amount is funded by the time set for filing of the Federal income tax return for that year.

(E) When the contribution is in the form of stock, the value of the stock contribution shall be limited to the fair market value of the stock on the date that title is effectively transferred to the trust. Cash contributions shall be allowable only when the contractor furnishes evidence satisfactory to the contracting officer demonstrating that stock purchases by the ESOT are or will be at a fair market price; e.g., makes arrangments with the trust permitting the contracting officer to examine purchases of stock by the trust to determine that prices paid are at fair market value. When excessive prices are paid, the amount of the excess will be credited to the same indirect cost pools that were charged for the ESOP contributions in the year in which the stock purchase occurs. However, when the trust purchases the stock with borrowed funds which will be repaid over a period of years by cash contributions from the contractor to the trust, the excess price over fair market value shall be credited to the indirect cost pools pro rata over the period of years during which the contractor contributes the cash used by the trust to repay the loan. When the fair market value of unissued stock or stock of a closely held corporation is not readily determinable, the valuation will be made on a case-by-case basis taking into consideration the guidelines for valuation used by the IRS.

(ii) Amounts contributed to an ESOP arising from either (A) an additional investment tax credit (see 1975 Tax Reduction Act— TRASOP's); or (B) a payroll-based tax credit (see Economic Recovery Tax Act of 1981) are unallowable.

(iii) The requirements of subdivision (j)(3)(ii) above are applicable to Employee Stock Ownership Plans.

(k) *Deferred compensation.* (1) Deferred compensation is an award given by an employer to compensate an employee in a future cost accounting period or periods for services rendered in one or more cost accounting periods before the date of receipt of compensation by the employee. Deferred compensation does not include the amount of year-end accruals for salaries, wages, or bonuses that are paid within a reasonable period of time after the end of a cost accounting period. Subject to 31.205-6(a), deferred awards are allowable when they are based on current or future services. Awards made in periods subsequent to the period when the work being remunerated was performed are not allowable.

(2) The costs of deferred awards shall be measured, allocated, and accounted for in compliance with the provisions of CAS 415, Accounting for the Cost of Deferred Compensation.

(3) Deferred compensation payments to employees under awards made before the effective date of CAS 415 are allowable to the extent they would have been allowable under prior acquisition regulations.

(l) (Proposed) *Compensation incidental to business acquisitions.* The following costs are unallowable:

(1) Payments to employees under agreements in which they receive special compensation, in excess of the contractor's normal severance pay practice, if their employment terminates following a change in the management control over, or ownership of, the contractor or a substantial portion of its assets. These arrangements are commonly known as "golden parachutes."

(2) Payments to employees under plans introduced in connection with a change (whether actual or prospective) in the management control over, or ownership of, the contractor or a substantial portion of its assets in which those employees receive special compensation, in addition to their normal pay, provided that they remain with the contractor for a specified period of time. These arrangements are commonly known as "golden handcuffs."

(m) *Fringe benefits.* (1) Fringe benefits are allowances and services provided by the contractor to its employees as compensation in addition to regular wages and salaries. Fringe benefits include, but are not limited to, the cost of vacations, sick leave, holidays, military leave, employee insurance, and supplemental unemployment benefit plans. Except as provided elsewhere in Subpart 31.2, the costs of fringe benefits are allowable to the extent that they are reasonable and are required by law, employer-employee agreement, or an established policy of the contractor.

(2) That portion of the cost of company-furnished automobiles that relates to personal use by employees (including transportation to and from work) is unallowable regardless of whether the cost is reported as taxable income to the employees (see 31.205-46(f)).

(n) *Employee rebate and purchase discount plans.* Rebates and purchase discounts, in whatever form, granted to employees on products or services produced by the contractor or affiliates are unallowable.

Fragmentation of Elements of Compensation to Determine Reasonableness

For at least a quarter of a century, the Defense Department had recognized that its many contractors have different policies relating to compensation, including the portions established as basic salary and the portions assigned to various types of incentive pay. It had been clearly understood and accepted that the government was interested in the reasonableness of the total compensation but would not intrude upon individual management prerogatives as to what portion of the compensation might consist of the basic salary and whatever various bonus, incentive, and fringe benefit plans individual contractors would establish. Abruptly, and without any explanation, the proposed revision (DAR 15-205.6(a)(2)) provided that criteria for allowability would include as one of the requirements: "The compensation in total and each element thereof must be reasonable for the effort or work performed."

This requirement was repeated in proposed 15-205.6(b):

> Compensation for personal services will be considered reasonable if the total and each element thereof conforms generally to the compensation paid by other firms of the same size, in the same industry, or in the same geographic area, for similar services or work performed.

The following excerpt from the CODSIA comments is to the point:

> The words "and each element thereof" must be deleted. Reasonableness of total compensation can be judged only on the total, not the constituent elements. Some companies pay lower basic salaries and wages, coupled with larger end-of-year bonus payments. Others pay a higher salary or wage with no bonuses. The total compensation in both cases may be the same. However, the first condition could result in disallowance of some part of the bonuses, while the latter situation risks disallowance of some part of the salary or wage—an unfair result in either case. This position ignores differences between compensation problems of different contractors and will result in inequitable treatment of compensation costs. Some contractors place a very strong emphasis on performance evaluation and may calculate a high percentage of total compensation for a certain class of employees on performance which is compensated in the form of a bonus. Such employees may receive salaries below industry averages so that the total compensation does not exceed industry averages. Under these conditions, a DOD auditor following the proposed DAR would disallow appropriation of the bonus as unreasonable. This is unfair and inequitable. Concern should be only with respect to reasonableness of total compensation cost. The manner in which the total cost is distributed among elements of compensation is based on a myriad of influencing factors (e.g., employer or employee preferences, collective bargaining, funding assumptions, etc.). Contractors must necessarily keep total cost within reasonable, competitive limits. To impose a test of reasonableness on each element of compensation usurps contractor prerogatives and imposes additional administrative burdens on all contractors.

Industry continued to appeal to DOD officials, inasmuch as the Defense Department was responsible for the notion that elements of compensation should be fragmented in determining reasonableness. Finally, in December 1985, a proposed change to FAR 31.205-6(b) was published. Despite the negative reactions, the proposed change in all essential respects was ultimately promulgated.

Considering all of the time and effort devoted to this cost principle, the proposed revision was considered extremely disappointing. Many editorial changes were introduced and the language expanded. The most important change provided a contractor an opportunity to introduce offsetting compensation elements into consideration when the reasonableness of any individual element of compensation is challenged. However, as discussed below, the limitations imposed to any such offsets are so severe as to cast doubts on the sincerity of the officials who had indicated a measure of agreement with industry's opposition to the concept that individual elements of compensation could be disallowed as unreasonable even where the total compensation was considered reasonable.

The proposed revision contained language even stronger than in the existing regulation with respect to the government's right to challenge individual elements of the total compensation: "Contracting officers or their representatives may challenge the reasonableness of any individual element or the sum of the individual elements of compensation paid or accrued to particular employees or classes of employees. In such cases, there is no presumption of reasonableness and, upon challenge, the contractor must demonstrate the reasonableness of the compensation item in question."

The first limitation imposed on consideration of offsets when one element of the total compensation is challenged is that it must be "between allowable elements of an employee's (or class of employees') compensation package." This language leaves unclear one of the major points in controversy. Can the government deny offset between, say, base salary and bonus of an individual if a contracting officer or contract auditor concludes in his own mind that one of the offsetting elements is unreasonable? In paragraph (b)(1)(iii), an illustration is provided that "an executive bonus that is excessive by $100,000 is not fully offset by a base salary that is low by only $25,000."

The above illustration appears to open the door to increased arguments over exact amounts of reasonableness levels for each cost element of the total compensation and it still does not appear to answer the question as to whether an offset would be permitted automatically if the amount by which one element was alleged to be "excessive" was approximately the same as the element considered "low."

Paragraph (b)(1)(ii) provides that offsets will be considered among specified compensation elements but any of such elements or portions thereof "whose amount is not measurable, shall not be introduced or considered as an offset item." This language should be clarified by an illustration or otherwise to avoid arguments.

Another limitation on offsets concerns timing of the receipt by the employee. In the example provided, "a bonus of $100,000 in the current period will be considered as of greater value than a deferred compensation arrangement to make the same payment in some future period." The obvious question is how much greater value will the government official assign to the current bonus than to the deferred compensation.

No changes in substance were made regarding compensation costs requiring "special consideration." These categories include owners of closely held corporations, partners, sole proprietors, etc., and government representatives are admonished to be sure that the amounts are reasonable and do not constitute a distribution of profits. Some elaboration here would have been appropriate. As we have written on a number of occasions in these pages, there have been wide differences of opinion and approach in this area on the parts of contracting officers, contract auditors, boards of contract appeals and federal courts.

All too often, various government officials erroneously conclude that owners and officers of small contractors somehow should be satisfied if the companies perform at a profit. These profits have been considered as adequate total compensation. We have emphasized frequently that owners are entitled to profits for return on invested capital, risk and management. They are separately entitled to compensation in terms of salaries for specific work performed.

All in all, the results of years of consideration and debate appear quite unsatisfactory. There is the recognition of offsets but that window seems to have been closed, at least in part, as soon as it was opened. The view is widely held that the offsets concept should be extended so that, except in very unusual circumstances, where the total compensation is found to be reasonable by the various comparisons with other firms, the individual elements should generally not be challenged.

With the publication of FAC 84-15, effective April 7, 1986, industry was disappointed, although close observers were not surprised, to find that all efforts to persuade the regulators to adopt a rule of reason had proven futile, and indications from high Pentagon levels that favorable consideration was being accorded to cogent points offered had proven false; the final language remained harsh and inequitable. Indeed, the final language went from bad to worse. With respect to changes in compensation policy that result in a substantial increase in the contractor's level of compensation, the proposal provided that such circumstances required special consideration and, if the government had not been notified in advance or within a reasonable period of such changes, "no presumption of reasonableness will exist." In response to complaints about the unfairness of this provision, the final language was more punitive, stating that in such circumstances "contracting officers or their representatives should normally challenge the increased costs."

The DOD 1986 Authorization Act included the cost of company-furnished automobiles as one of the expenses for which the Secretary of Defense was to provide clarification regarding allowability. Several alternative positions could have been taken; however, in conformance with the prevailing hardline approach, FAC 84-15 reflects the harshest: "That portion of the cost of company-furnished automobiles that relates to personal use by employees (including transportation to and from work) is unallowable regardless of whether the cost is reported as taxable income to the employees. . . ." In other cost principles, and indeed in 31.205-6, the government contract cost regulators selectively accept provisions of the IRC as guidelines to allowability. Why the punitive approach here? If the cost of the personal use of company-owned cars plus all other forms of compensation to an individual do not exceed an amount found reasonable in toto, what is the justification for this provision?

Requirement for Total Compensation to Conform to Plan

Because of the substantial changes in sequence and language, a comparison of the existing and revised provisions was sometimes difficult. The prior cost principles stated that, to be allowable, cash bonuses and other incentive compensation must meet certain requirements including that the costs be incurred pursuant to an agreement or an established plan followed so consistently as to imply, in effect, an agreement. This provision was restructured so that a requirement for conforming to a contractor's established plan applied to the total compensation, including all of its elements. This provision appeared unnecessarily restrictive and, as a matter of fact, is entirely impracticable for small business and indeed for many medium-sized concerns that do not have a written plan to submit if one is demanded by an over-zealous contract auditor or contract administrator. It appeared that the prior regulations had sufficient restrictions and imposed enough demands of this kind to make this requirement unnecessary. It seemed doubtful that this provision would accomplish anything but to generate government-industry controversies.

ALLOWABILITY OF PENSION COSTS WHEN CAS AND COST PRINCIPLES CONFLICT

A significant dispute that advanced to a board of contract appeals and the federal courts involved the allowability of accrued but unfunded pension costs. *The Boeing Company,* ASBCA No. 28342, 85-3 BCA par. 18,435. The issues involved were of wide interest to defense contractors, and amicus curiae briefs were filed by Westinghouse and Lockheed. The decision is among the lengthiest issued by the board and includes a joint stipulation of facts by the parties that contains a most comprehensive and informative history of contract cost principles and cost accounting standards relating to pensions and deferred compensation. A review of this ruling is recommended for instructional purposes.

As analyzed below, a DAR provision was involved, but the ruling has continuing interest because this provision was carried over into FAR.

At issue was the allowability, under Boeing's Supplemental Executive Retirement Plan (SERP) for designated executives, of costs that were accrued annually on an actuarial basis, recorded as an expense and liability, but not funded.

There was no apparent dispute that Boeing's SERP was a defined-benefit plan and that the contractor accounted for it pursuant to the applicable provisions of CAS 412, which provide for the use of an actuarial cost method reflecting an accrual basis. The substantial disallowance by the government was based on the application of DAR 15-205.6(f)(2)(ii)(B), as identified in February 1981, which limited the amount allowed to the *actual payment made,* consistent with the provisions of the Internal Revenue Code.

Boeing contended that CAS and DAR were in conflict and that the provisions of CAS must prevail because (1) DOD is required to use the CAS accounting rules, which thereby supersede any conflicting rules, (2) the CAS provisions are the more specific of the two, and (3) both clauses having been drafted by the government, the conflict must be construed against the government.

The government argued that the relevant CAS and DAR provisions were not in conflict. Essentially, the government's position was that the cost accounting standards were clearly understood to apply to *allocability* whereas *allowability* was governed by DAR's contract cost principles.

The lengthy decision surfaced a number of additional contentions by the parties and the contractors filing the amicus briefs. However, although a number of cogent arguments were advanced and considered, together with regulatory and legislative history and case law, it appeared that the issue essentially centered on the arguments noted above. Although Boeing was in compliance with CAS, if the amount charged to DOD contracts was subject to further limitation on the grounds that DAR governed allowability, the disallowance would prevail.

The board found that the cost accounting standards, whether based on their own official standing or on the basis of incorporation into DAR, had the force and effect of law. It also found that the DAR contract cost principles, having been promulgated under the general statutory authority of 10 U.S.C. 2202, also had the force and effect of law.

The board's review of the term "allowability," as used in DAR, led it to the conclusion that the meaning was considerably broader than the government suggested in its motion for summary judgment, and included allocability, reasonableness, conformance with CAS, where applicable, or GAAP (generally accepted accounting principles), and provisions relating to "selected costs." Where the pertinent DAR and CAS 412 provisions both prescribe rules for allocability and the rules differ, there is, contrary to the government's argument, a conflict between the two.

A study of the pertinent IRC provisions that limit deductibility of contributions to pension and other funds to amounts paid in a taxable year persuaded the board that the limitation related to the measurement and assignment of costs, i.e., allocability, and in that sense, when incorporated into DAR, represented a clear-cut conflict with CAS 412.

It would appear that the board drew a clear distinction relating to circumstances where a cost allocated in accordance with DAR might nevertheless be limited by DAR allowability considerations. Such limitations are appropriate where "the allowability or unallowability of such costs is based on policy considerations independent of the cost accounting considerations of proper assignment and allocation of costs." It might have cited such expenses as entertainment and contributions, which have been mandated to be unallowable in these terms. In the case of pensions, however, the board found that their allowability under DAR 15-205.6 "is based on their measurement, assignment, and allocation in accordance with paragraph 404(a) of the Internal Revenue Code rather than in accordance with CAS 412."

The board concluded that "the tax liability criterion of DAR 15-205.6(f)(2)(ii)(B) addresses, in substance, the same matters of assignment of pension cost to an accounting period as addressed in CAS 412 and that the two standards of assignment of costs are in conflict with each other." The board also stated that the Allowable Cost, Fixed Fee and Payment Clause, and the CAS clause of the contract, incorporate both the pertinent DAR provisions and CAS 412 as contract terms, "thereby imposing contradictory cost accounting requirements on a contractor for measuring, assigning and allocating pension costs."

In the circumstances involved, the board found that CAS 412 was controlling with respect to the determination, measurement, assignment and allocation of Boeing's SERP costs, and that the DAR tax deductibility provisions "cannot impose a limitation on appellant's recovery of its SERP costs to the extent that they are determined, measured, assigned and allocated pursuant to CAS 412 and CAS 413 and are otherwise allowable under the contract.

The board noted that Boeing had not cross-moved for summary judgment, but that its brief opposing the government's motion clearly indicated its views that material facts were in dispute and its wish for evidentiary hearings to establish the existence of a conflict between the pertinent DAR and CAS provisions. The government maintained that there were no material facts in dispute and the board agreed. However, the board's substantive conclusion was opposite to the government's, the latter maintaining that DAR and CAS were not in conflict and the board finding that a clear conflict existed. Accordingly, even though Boeing had not cross-moved for summary judgment, the board found the contractor was entitled to such judgment. The appeal was sustained and remanded to the contracting officer for a determination of quantum of SERP costs to be allowed consistent with this decision.

The government appealed and the court affirmed the board's decision. *U.S. v. The Boeing Company,* CA FC, No. 86-927 [33 CCF par. 74,612].

Summarizing the positions of the parties, the court stated:

The government asserted before the Board, and asserts on this appeal, that the clear language of DAR 15-205-7(f)(2)(ii)(B) (the DAR) limits allowability of pension costs only to those costs which are tax deductible in the tax year contemporaneous with recordation. The government contends that the DAR is a procurement regulation which governs *allowability* of costs, and is consistent with CAS 412, which governs only *allocability* of costs. Boeing contended before the Board, and maintains its position on this appeal, that the DAR is, in effect, an allocability provision requiring cash basis accounting, and is in impermissible conflict with the CAS which requires accrual basis accounting.

The Air Force moved for summary judgment. After concluding there were no genuine issues of material fact in dispute, the Board held that Boeing was entitled to reimbursement of the accrued unfunded costs of its SERP. The Board held that since (1) CAS 412 has the force and effect of law, (2) both CAS 412 and the DAR address the same matter of *allocability* of pension costs and (3) CAS 412 controls, the DAR cannot limit Boeing's reimbursement of its SERP costs because Boeing measures, assigns and allocates those costs pursuant to CAS 412.

Thereafter it succinctly stated the issues as follows:

(1) Whether the Board correctly held that the contracts at issue in this appeal contain provisions—the DAR and CAS 412—which are in conflict with each other.

(2) Whether the Board, having determined that there was a conflict between the two provisions, correctly held that the provisions of CAS 412 prevail.

As did the board, the court agreed "as general propositions" with the government's contentions that costs may be assignable and allocable under CAS but nevertheless unallowable under acquisition regulations. For example, the court opined that DOD had the legal authority to make all pension costs unallowable if it chose to do so. It also had the authority to declare certain types of pensions unallowable or even to limit or place ceilings on the amounts it would allow. In these instances, however, the limitations or ceilings must be based on some formula such as percentage of cost. When the limitation of allowability determination is based on the use of cost measurement, allocation or assignment, the cost principle comes into conflict with CAS.

Where CAS 412 establishes the appropriate period as the one in which the cost was accrued, while the cost principle prescribes allowability based on the period in which paid, the conflict is obvious. Agreeing with the ASBCA, the court found that by adopting CAS 412 and the provision in DAR 15-205.6(f)(2)(ii)(B), DOD had imposed *contradictory* cost requirements on Boeing. For a resolution of this problem, the court referred to an ASPR Subcommittee report in a 1975 memorandum, which stated that "(s)hould there be a conflict with respect to allocability between the ASPR and the CAS, the former regulation will be superseded."

The court found that "(r)esolving the conflict in this manner comports with the authority of DOD to promulgate rational procurement policies. To hold otherwise would force this court to sanction DOD exercising its procurement authority in an arbitrary and capricious manner by completely ignoring a particular cost accounting standard. That is not the law of this court."

EMPLOYEE STOCK DISCOUNT COSTS IN CONNECTION WITH ESOP RULED ALLOWABLE

DOD's continuing efforts to expand areas of cost disallowances were set back again as the Armed Services Board of Contract Appeals granted the contractor's motion for summary judgment in *Honeywell, Inc.*, ASBCA Nos. 28814, 29140, 84-3 BCA par. 17,690.

For many years Honeywell's collective bargaining agreements had required the contractor to provide its employees with HESOP or comparable benefits, under which participants in the plan were provided an opportunity, through regular payroll savings, to acquire the company's stock at a discount from market price. Under the terms of the annual HESOPs, the employees were entitled to elect to have from 3% to 12% of their wages deducted for deposit in the plan. Employees could withdraw from the plan at any time prior to September 30th of each year, with full refund of their contributions.

Honeywell promised to set aside a fixed number of its shares of stock for employee purchase, such purchases being effective as of the last working day in September in the year in which the plan ended. The price paid for the stock purchased on behalf of the participants was the lower of (1) 85% of the highest price of the stock on the N.Y. Stock Exchange on the first working day of October in which the plan began, or (2) 85% of the highest price of the stock on the last working day in September in the year in which the plan ended. In each year, Honeywell calculated the difference between the highest and lowest market price of a share of its stock on the effective date of purchase, and the amount paid for each share of stock by employees who participated in the HESOP for that year. The difference was considered the discount realized by the employees for each share of stock purchased in that year.

Honeywell reported such discount as taxable income of the employees for their income tax purposes and claimed the same amount as deduction on its own income tax returns. The tax treatment of the discounts was accepted by the IRS after audit.

Honeywell allocated the discount costs to its divisions, the amount earned by each employee being assigned to the division in which he worked. However, the difference between the purchase price paid by the employees and the market value of the stock was not reported as an expense for third party financial reporting purposes, the transactions being recorded as adjustments to equity on Honeywell's balance sheet.

Prior to 1978, at the government's insistence, Honeywell had treated the costs of the HESOPs as unallowable stock option costs. However, after the decision in *Singer Co. v. United States* [28 CCF par. 80,741], 225 Ct.Cl. 637 (1980), the contractor amended its indirect cost submissions for the open years to claim the HESOP costs. 1978 was the earliest open year.

In disallowing these costs, the contracting officer asserted that the HESOPs were noncompensatory under Section 423 (26 USC 423) of the Internal Revenue Code. In its response to the conractor's motion for summary judgment, however, the government admitted that the HESOPs did not meet all of the requirements of 26 USC 423 and thus were not qualifying transfers under 26 USC 421. In opposing the contractor's motion, the government then questioned whether the discount was a cost and whether the average price on the N.Y. Stock Exchange on the issue dates accurately measured the amount for which Honeywell could have sold its treasury stock to the public, the contractor having met some of its obligations in certain years by purchasing treasury stock. The board ruled that this was a question of law and had been ruled upon by the Court of Claims in *Singer, supra,* where the government had argued that payments under the Singer plan constituted stock options, unallowable under DAR, but the court had agreed with Singer's contention to the contrary.

In *The Singer Co.,* ASBCA No. 18857, 82-1 BCA par. 15,684, the government also had raised the issue of the cost of financing a stock issue, and the board in *Honeywell* cited its conclusions on this point:

> The Government also argues that recovery by appellant is precluded under DAR 15-205.17 which provides:

> "*Interest and Other Financial Costs.* Interest on borrowings (however represented), bond discounts, costs of financing and refinancing operations, legal and professional fees paid in connection with the preparation of prospectuses, costs of preparation and issuance of stock rights, and costs related thereto, are unallowable except for interest assessed by State or local taxing authorities under the conditions set forth in 15-205.41."

> We are not impressed with the Government's argument in the instant case. While both the dollar amount and the percentage increase in corporate equity are noteworthy, this, alone, is insufficient to bring the item under the above-cited DAR provision. Every stock plan for employees increases the equity of a corporation; and, in a corporation as

extensive as that of appellant it can result in large figures. The finite dollar amount in and of itself is not the determining factor. The Government's argument that the employees did not receive compensation or that the Board should allocate some portion to compensation and some portion to cost of financing is contrary to the facts in this appeal. Not allowing the discount as a reimbursement cost would be contrary to the provisions of DAR 15-205.6. This was a voluntary plan. The employees need not have subscribed to the plan. Here, it is clear that the purpose for the employee stock purchase plan was an inducement and incentive for retaining its employees.

We, therefore, conclude that appellant is not precluded from recovery under DAR 15-205.17 under the Government's cost of financing capital theory.

The government then argued that Honeywell differed from Singer, the latter selling the stock for 80% of the average price on the N.Y. Stock Exchange, compared to Honeywell's 85%, and Singer having distributed its discount to the operating divisions whereas Honeywell did not. The argument relating to the difference in percentages was disposed of by the board as follows:

We agree that 15 percent is different from 20 percent. However, we do not accept the Government's reasoning that follows from this difference. Since 15 percent is the same percentage figure appearing in 26 U.S.C. 423, which provides for deferred taxation of the difference between the fair market value and the amount paid for the stock, if all nine conditions set out in 26 U.S.C. 423 are met, the Government contends that the appellant's plan is noncompensatory. The Government has admitted, and we have found, that appellant's plan does not meet all requisite conditions to qualify under 26 U.S.C. 423. We conclude that the fact that appellant's plan provides for a 15 percent discount does not distinguish it from *Singer* on this basis.

The government offered APB Opinion No. 25, issued by the American Institute of Certified Public Accountants (AICPA), in support of the argument that the Honeywell plan was noncompensatory. The board noted, however, that APB 25 cites as an example of a noncompensatory plan, the "statutory employee stock purchase plan that qualifies under Section 423 [26 U.S.C. 423] of the Internal Revenue Code." In the board's opinion, the HESOP does not qualify under the cited IRC section and hence the government's position is not supported by APB 25.

The arguments concerning the manner in which the discounts were recorded in the records and shown in financial statements were similar to those raised by the government in the *Singer* dispute. The board's disposition of this argument and its conclusions leading to the granting of Honeywell's motion for summary judgment and the remanding to the contracting officer to determine quantum, are instructive and are quoted below:

"The Government further argues that by not charging income in its accounting treatment of its consolidated financial statements for shareholders, appellant treated the Plan as non-compensatory. We do not agree. The record establishes that the Plan did not qualify for income deferral for federal income tax purposes. Thus, the employee was required to treat the discount as compensation subject to federal income tax in the taxable year the restriction was removed and the appellant was entitled to a deduction in that year from its income tax. The Government argues that treatment for tax purposes is not germaine [sic] since the Internal Revenue Code does not follow generally accepted accounting principles. While treatment of items for tax purposes has been held to be of no import in considering cost reimbursement under Government contracts, here we have the question of whether an item constitutes compensation to the employee. Treatment for tax purposes, thus, becomes extremely relevant in the appeal before us. We have not been cited to any precedent for the proposition propounded by the Government that a plan would be compensatory for federal income tax purposes but not for Government contract purposes. We, therefore, conclude that appellant's plan was compensatory.

"Having concluded that the Plan was compensatory and reimbursement was not precluded under 15-205.6(e) or is violating generally accepted accounting principles, we conclude that recovery of these costs is not precluded under the Government's inconsistent accounting theory."

We conclude that the HESOPs are compensatory. The stock discount costs are allowable costs. We see no basis for distinguishing *Singer* and find that it is controlling in these appeals.

ALLOWABILITY REQUIREMENTS FOR BONUSES

The unsuccessful appeal of Petroleum Operations and Support Services, Inc. (POSSI), EBCA No. 291-6-83, April 3, 1985, 85-2 BCA par. 18,037, represents a sad illustration of a contractor's inability to recover fair, reasonable and appropriate expenses where the government demonstrated that the company had not complied with the letter of the applicable procurement regulation.

POSSI entered into a cost-plus-award fee (CPAF) contract for certain support services for the Department of Energy (DOE) Strategic Petroleum Reserve project. The payment clause included the provision that allowable costs would be determined in accordance with FPR Subpart 1-15.2.

Under the incentive provisions of the contract, DOE evaluated POSSI's performance for a quarterly period and rated it "outstanding," leading to recognition in the award fee. Following this award, POSSI developed a bonus plan for all eligible employees and paid such bonuses in accordance with the plan. When the bonuses were submitted for reimbursement on a public voucher, the amount was suspended by the contracting officer, who requested additional information concerning the bonus payments. POSSI's response contained the following explanations:

1. The bonus plan was based on employee contributions to optimization of contract performance;

2. The nominal amounts of the awards in no instance caused otherwise reasonable compensation to employees prior to bonus awards to become unreasonable;

3. The bonuses were paid pursuant to a plan the contractor had established, the estimated cost of which had been included in its proposal.

The contracting officer requested DCAA to conduct an audit of the bonus payments. The auditor visited the project site and was apparently permitted to interview the contractor's employees. According to the decision, the auditor asked each employee two questions:

1. Did you recently receive a cash bonus from POSSI?

2. Was the bonus paid to you pursuant to an agreement entered into, in good faith, with POSSI?

According to the DCAA audit report, of the 113 employees, 69 or 61% advised the auditor there was no agreement to get a bonus, most of them stating they were surprised to receive the bonus. The remaining 44 or 39% were reported as saying that they were informed of a bonus program prior to their employment but none was promised a bonus. Based on these interviews, the DCAA auditor concluded that the bonus payments were unallowable under FPR 1-15.205-6(c). The contracting officer then denied reimbursement for these payments and POSSI appealed.

The referenced FPR provisions state that bonus and incentive compensation are allowable "[p]rovided the awards are paid or accrued under an agreement entered into in good faith between the contractor and the employees before the services are rendered, or under an established plan or policy followed so consistently as to imply, in effect, an agreement to make such payment, and the basis for the award is supported." The current provision of FAR 31.205-6(f) is identical.

POSSI was represented by a leading law firm experienced in government contracts, and a number of arguments were presented in an attempt to support the allowability of the payments. However, despite these arguments and the fact that such costs should have been considered acceptable by the application of almost any reasonable criteria, the board found them unallowable by reference to the specific FPR provision quoted above.

POSSI argued that "if a bonus plan represents sound business judgment, is in fact intended as a bonus to recognize or motivate employee performance, is entered into before a substantial portion of the services are rendered, and is not unfair to either the employees or the government, then the requirement of a good faith agreement is met." The points are logical and persuasive; however, the contractor ran afoul of the specific language of the regulation and the government prevailed by showing that there was never any prior specific corporate commitment or agreement to a bonus plan.

Arguments that POSSI had understandings with its employees concerning bonus payments based on overall performance similarly did not prevail when evidence to the contrary was presented, and the board concluded that "the evidence does not support a general and clear understanding by employees of a company commitment to a specific plan for bonuses."

POSSI argued that if the bonus payments were not allowed under FPR 1-15.205-6(c), they should be allowed under the other provisions of this principle as additional salary. This argument failed when the board found that the parties had stipulated that these costs were bonuses and it found "nothing in the record that would persuade this Board to disturb this stipulation."

In our experience, government people, particularly contract auditors, take a very keen interest in bonuses (as well as all other aspects of compensation for personal services). The specific requirements relating to bonuses, as mentioned earlier, were carried into FAR from FPR and DAR. Contractors would be well advised to study, and conform closely to, these provisions.

STOCK OPTIONS, APPRECIATION RIGHTS, PURCHASE PLANS

For a great many years, government procurement regulations cited stock options as an unallowable cost without furnishing any explanation. Industry had almost given up its efforts to persuade the Department of Defense to allow such costs when CAS 415—Accounting for the Cost of Deferred Compensation was promulgated. Inasmuch as this standard recognized stock options as an allocable cost, DOD was asked to reconsider its views, which many felt had no real basis. However, DOD remained firm and reminded industry that, while the CASB addresses the aspect of allocability, it is the executive departments and agencies that decide allowability. And stock options have remained unallowable. As a matter of fact, DOD seemed to be going further and seeking to describe other plans as stock options to provide a basis for disallowing the related costs.

In *Singer Company, Kearfott Division,* ASBCA No. 18857, 75-1 BCA par. 11,185, the contractor appealed the disallowance of the cost of its stock purchase plan on the basis that it represented a stock option plan. The board ruled in favor of the government, perhaps influenced by the fact that the contractor's records referred to the plan as stock options.

Singer was successful, however, in its appeal to the U.S. Court of Claims, No. 381-79C, 10/3/80. As described by the court, Singer's plan provided for the following:

> All regular employees on the United States payrolls of Singer were eligible to enter the Plan if they had one year of continuous service and were at least 21 years of age. Enrollment consisted of filing a form with the payroll department authorizing regular payroll deductions of not less than $20.00 per month nor more than 10% of compensation. A stock purchase account was maintained for each participating employee. On a fixed date each month as many whole shares were purchased for each employee as the funds in his account would permit. The shares were obtained directly from Singer at 80 per cent of their current market value, the 20 per cent discount representing compensation to the employee—and cost to Singer. The remainder of funds left after making each month's purchase would be held for the next month's transaction.

DCAA concluded that this plan constituted a stock option and was therefore unallowable under ASPR 15-205.6(e), which provided that "the cost of stock options to employees to purchase stock of the contractor or of an affiliate is unallowable." The contracting officer accepted the audit opinion and disallowed the cost, and Singer appealed. ASBCA ruled in favor of the government, and Singer sought review by the court.

The court observed that the ASBCA based its decision on the definition of a stock option set forth in Webster's Third New International Dictionary (unabridged): "stock option n: an option giving to the holder the right to purchase a specified number of shares of stock from a corporation at a stated price and by a stated date and constituting a device used to provide supplementary compensation to corporation officers and employees."

The court could not agree with the board's rationale and, in fact, saw the controversy in a diametrically different way. We believe the court's deliberations and conclusion extremely significant and have included them verbatim for careful study of our readers:

> The Singer Plan in no way satisfies the essentials of the above definition. It does not confer a right to purchase a "specified number of shares." Rather, the number of shares purchased upon each monthly purchase date will vary with the monthly earnings of the participant and the current market value of the stock. The Plan does not create a right to purchase "at a stated price." Instead, the price changes as the market rate changes. Finally, the Plan does not involve a "stated (expiration) date." Rather, the Plan is an ongoing activity, involving automatic purchases of whole shares on each monthly purchase date to the extent the accumulated funds in an individual's account permit.

> Second—and more importantly—the Singer Plan falls outside the original reason for the disallowance of stock options. The reason was the concern of the draftsmen that companies could "game" the time between grant and exercise of the stock option to coincide with a period of major performance of Government cost-type contracts. In other words, where the option could be exercised over a variable time, it could be possible to select the time most advantageous in terms of Government contracts. See, *Singer Company,* ASBCA No. 18857 (March 17, 1975). It is easy to see how stock options in the Webster's Dictionary sense create such an opportunity for manipulation. The Singer Plan, however, provides no such opportunity. Under the Plan, the timing of stock purchases is not subject to manipulation. Rather, purchases are made according to a fixed, predetermined formula: if, on the monthly purchase date, an individual's account aggregates sufficient funds to cover the cost of a single share, stock is bought.

For many government contractors, there are obviously lessons to be learned from this decision. Although some government auditors and even contracting officers tend to almost automatically peer extra closely at most forms of incentive compensation, it has been fairly well established that such compensation is allowable provided the total pay to an individual or group is reasonable, the incentive compensation is based on the contractor's established policies and practices, and amounts computed are in accordance with applicable cost accounting standards. As stated in DAR 15-205.6(e) and FPR 1-15.205-6(e), however: "The cost of options to employees to purchase stock of the contractor or of an affiliate is unallowable." The precise meaning of stock options is not set forth in the procurement regulations, and some government officials tend to view almost any incentive plan involving stock with suspicion. The Court of Claims ruling in this case establishes the need to assure that such plans are structured in a manner to preclude their inclusion in the category of stock options.

FAR 31.205-6(i), following the DAR provisions as revised in March 1983, contains the expanded treatment for stock options, stock appreciation rights, and phantom stock plans described earlier in this chapter.

In what appeared to be a relentless effort to disallow all compensation costs associated in any manner with payments in company stock, the government disallowed the costs associated with Stock Appreciation Rights (SARs), declaring them to be stock options (*The Boeing Company,* ASBCA No. 24089, 81-1 BCA par. 14,864).

The summary of Boeing's SARs plan as provided in the board's decision follows:

#1. The only persons eligible to receive SARs were those individuals who were Boeing Option holders and who were deemed to be "insiders" under Section 16 of the Securities Act.

#2. The grant of SARs meant that instead of being required to purchase stock in order to exercise an option, the option holder could be paid in cash or stock at the Option Committee's discretion, an amount equal to the appreciation of the stock in market value over its option price at the time of exercise.

#3. The Option Committee (composed exclusively of individuals not eligible to receive options) retained the sole discretion to determine (a) whether or not to grant SARs, (b) whether the SARs should extend to all, or a portion of the shares covered by an individual's options, and (c) whether (if a grant of the SARs is made) payments would be made in cash, stock, or a combination thereof.

#4. No SARs could be exercised until the underlying option became exercisable, or the expiration of at least six months, after the date of the grant of the SARs whichever occurred last.

#5. SARs could be granted at any time after 1 January 1979, until 6 months prior to the expiration date of the options to which they related.

#6. Upon payment of a SAR the applicable portion of the related option must be surrendered and shall not thereafter be exercisable.

SARs granted under the amended 1969 Plan were evidenced by amendments to the existing stock option agreements between the eligible employees and Boeing. SARs granted under the 1979 Plan were evidenced by separate Agreements.

In each instance where a SAR was granted, Boeing entered into a written agreement with the employee which provided *inter alia* that the SAR was granted to induce the employee to continue his employment with Boeing, that the SAR could not be exercised prior to the expiration of a period of employment set forth in the agreement, and that (except for death, disability, or retirement) the SAR would terminate upon the termination of the employee's employment at Boeing. The agreements also provide that SARs must be exercised between the 3rd and 12th business day following public release by Boeing of its quarterly financial information, and that for each SAR exercised, the employee will be paid in cash or stock, the difference between the price of Boeing stock on the date the SAR is granted and the day that notice of exercise is received by Boeing.

The board's statement of the government's contentions:

First, the Government contends that SARs are simply another variant of stock options and therefore are not allowable under DAR Section 15-205.6(e) which states that the cost of options is unallowable. In support of this position, the Government argues that Boeing's SARs are directly related to options because an employee must be eligible to receive a stock option before he can be granted a SAR. Its expert witness reasoned that since SARs "cannot be divorced from stock options" and since the costs of options are unallowable, "it follows that the cost of SARs are also unallowable." In his view, option costs are not allowable because the market price of a share of stock does not necessarily have any relationship to the value of the services rendered by the holder of an option for that share since "market prices are a function of a great many variables—rational as well as irrational."

Another reason for holding option costs unallowable is "the opportunity for the contractor to select the period in which the option cost is assigned." That is, according to the Government's theory, a contractor could "game" its SAR costs by granting SARs that are exercisable during an accounting period where the Government's participation in its indirect cost pools is greater than normal. No evidence of "gaming" on the part of Boeing was presented by the Government.

Next, the Government argues that the SARs costs do not qualify as allowable under DAR Section 15.205.6(c) or 15.205.6(d) to the extent that payment is made in stock, because they are not (1) incentive compensation based on production, cost reduction, or efficient performance, or (2) "paid or accrued pursuant to an agreement entered into in good faith . . . before services were rendered, or pursuant to an established plan followed . . . so consistently as to imply, in effect, an agreement to make such payment." In this regard, the Government's expert concluded that since the SARs program was not initiated at Boeing until the amendment of its 1969 Stock Option Plan "there was no established plan with regard to pre-existing options and the portion of the cost principles dealing with an established plan is not appropriate" for determining the SARs allowability. He also contended, since Boeing's Stock Option Committee has the sole discretion regarding (a) whether or not to grant SARs, (b) whether the SARs will cover all or only a portion of an individual's options, and (c) whether Boeing's payment will be made in cash, or stock or a combination of the two, that no mutual "agreement" to make SAR payments existed. Another Government witness commenting on the agreement's lack of mutuality, stated that the SARs program placed employees "at the mercy of what the Company chose to do in the future."

The Government also argues that, with regard to the SARs attached to pre-existing exercisable options, any market appreciation which had already occurred "relates to something in the past," and therefore did not comply with the general mandate of DAR Section 15.205.6(a)(1) "Compensation For Personal Services" that compensation be paid for services rendered "during the period of contract performance."

No evidence was offered of the market price of Boeing's stock during any of the applicable time periods.

Finally, the Government contends that the costs are unallowable under the provisions of DAR Section 15.204(d) residual clause which provides that "with respect to all items, whether or not specifically covered, determination of allowability shall be based on the principles and standards set forth in this part and, where appropriate, the treatment of similar or related selected issues." According to the Government the most closely related selected cost item to a SAR is an option and "therefore, SARs do not have to be specifically mentioned since 15.204(d) provides the necessary coverage."

The board summarized Boeing's rebuttal:

Boeing argues first that SARs are a form of compensation separate and distinct from stock options and thus not affected by the unallowability of option costs under DAR 15.205.6(e). One of Boeing's experts enumerated a number of dissimilarities between SARs and options. He noted that under the SAR program, an employee was not obligated to actually purchase shares of stock as he would under an option program. This avoids the necessity for the employee to raise capital with which to exercise an option and it also enables him to minimize his exposure to potential liability for short term profits under the S.E.C. "insider" rules.

Boeing also argues that from an accounting point of view, SARs and options are not alike. The issuance of stock upon the exercise of an option involves a capital transaction on Boeing's books. There is, however, no capital transaction involved in a cash payment of a SAR, or in the cash payment of an employee incentive award, the cost in both these instances is treated as a cost. As recited in the parties joint stipulation Boeing states that "a SAR payment is a cost, which in accordance with generally accepted accounting principles must be recorded on the books of the company as a charge against earnings. Stock options in contrast do not require a payment by the company to the employee, and do not require the company to record any cost on its books of account or any charge against earnings". Boeing's comptroller commented that "that's the difference between day and night in accounting treatment. . . . of all the incentive plans, the stock option is the most dissimilar to a SAR in the accounting treatment." Boeing's accounting practices in this instance are consistent with the treatment set out in Accounting Principles Board Opinion 25 (APB 25) and Financial Accounting Standards Board Interpretation 28 (FASB 28).

Boeing also contends that the SARs program has been initiated under a "good faith agreement" and that services of at least six months must be performed prior to their exercise. In any event, argues Boeing, it issued SARs to each option holder under the 1969 and 1979 Plans to the full extent of all options held by such individuals and therefore it complied with the DAR Section 15.205.6(c) test that payments be made pursuant to a consistently followed plan that implied an agreement to make such payments. Boeing thus contends that the SARs program qualifies as a management employee incentive compensation plan under the DAR Section 15.205.6(a)(1).

Because of the importance attached to this decision, we have cited at some length the nature of Boeing's SARs plan, the government's contentions, and the contractor's rebuttal. Before similarly proceeding with the board's decision, it may be well to summarize the government's arguments: (1) SARs are just a variant of stock options and hence unallowable under DAR 15-205.6(e); (2) SARs are unallowable under DAR 15.205.6(c) and (d) because they are not "paid or accrued pursuant to an agreement entered into in good faith ... before services were rendered, or pursuant to an established plan followed ... so consistently as to imply, in effect, an agreement to make such payment"; (3) as to SARs attached to pre-existing exercisable options, any market appreciation already occurred relates to the past and does not comply with DAR 15.205.6(a)(1), which requires compensation to be paid for services rendered during the period of contract performance in order to be allowable; and (4) costs associated with SARs are unallowable under 15.204(d), which states that costs not specifically identified shall be treated based, "where appropriate, (on) the treatment of similar or related selected items and the most closely related selected cost item to a SAR is a stock option."

The board disagreed with all of the government's arguments:

First, we do not believe that SARs are "options" and thus unallowable under paragraph 15.205.6(e). While we acknowledge that common characteristics are indeed present, it is clear to us that SARs are far more readily described not as "options" but as "bonuses (including stock bonuses)" as that term is used in paragraph 15.205.6(a)(1). The dictionary definition of the terms bears this out. *Webster's Third New International Dictionary* defines a "bonus" *inter alia* as "money or an equivalent given in addition to the usual compensation." Certainly SARs, whether paid for in cash or stock, fit easily within that definition. On the other hand, it is equally evident that SARs are distinct from the *Webster's* definition of "options" relied upon recently by the Court of Claims in *Singer Co. v United States,* Ct.Cls. Order No. 581-79C (Oct. 3, 1980). *Singer* cites the definition which characterizes a stock option as "an option giving to the holder the right to purchase a specified number of shares of stock from a corporation at a stated date ...." Here again the distinctions between options and the Boeing SARs are obvious. Exercise of a SAR does not involve a purchase of anything, the employee is the recipient of either cash or stock; the amount of cash or stock received is not fixed, it varies depending on the market price of the stock on the date of notice to exercise; and the exercise date, although confined to certain quarterly "windows", is also not fixed, it is variable depending on the employee's own inclinations. The differences between SARs and options are further highlighted in a recent article on the topic of SARs. In Cohn, *Stock Appreciation Rights,* 79 Columbia Law 67 (January 1979), Professor Cohn notes that:

"Unlike stock options, however, the exercise of an SAR requires no payment by the grantee to obtain the value of the market spread. . . . At no time is there a purchase or sale by the grantee (as such transactions are commonly regarded) of any of the underlying traded securities to which the SAR relates . . . ."

All this compels us to conclude that SARs cannot be considered the equivalent of options for purposes of the regulation which declares the costs of options unallowable.

Since we have found SARs are not "options", the next question for consideration is whether the costs of SARs are so similar or related to option costs that the two should be identically treated as provided in Section 15.204(d). Here again, particularly within the context of the intent of Section 15.205.6 to find compensation costs allowable, if they are reasonable, we must conclude that the inclusion of SARs as the equivalent of options for purposes of the residual language of Section 15.204(d) is not appropriate. On the contrary, we believe that it would be correct to apply the residual language to equate SARs with cash or stock bonuses and to test their allowability on that basis.

Paragraphs 15.205(c) and (d) deal positively and specifically with cash and stock bonuses, provides that they are potentially allowable and distinguishes their cost treatment from that accorded options. If the Government had intended to render SAR costs unallowable it is logical to assume that it would have done so (as required by the Section's language) specifically, and in the body of Section 15.205.6. Indeed we are aware of the DAR Council's currently pending amendments to Section 15.205.6(e), which would provide, among other things, for identical cost treatment for both SARs and options. It is true that the Boeing SARs are attached to outstanding options, and in that general sense are related to those options. This relationship, however, is only superficial and not one of substance. There is no requirement under the S.E.C.'s amended Rule 16b-3 that SARs be attached to options, nor was any persuasive evidence presented to indicate that this was done by Boeing for any purpose other than convenience. We will not, therefore, ascribe any particular significance to this aspect of the SARs question. Accordingly, we are of the view that treating SARs as options on the basis of Section 15.204(d) would be giving an interpretation to that Section which is far beyond that warranted by its language or by the language of Section 15.205.6. This we decline to do.

Having determined that the Boeing SARs are, or are "most similar" to, cash or stock bonuses, we will decide their allowability within the context of the specific criteria set out for these costs in paragraphs 15.205.6(c) and (d). These provisions require that, in order to be allowable, the overall compensation paid to the employee must be reasonable (since the parties have stipulated that reasonableness is not being contested here, we will not discuss this element further) and the bonus must be paid either pursuant to a good faith agreement entered into before the employee's service were rendered, or pursuant to an established consistently followed contractor plan.

With respect to the requirement of a "good faith" agreement, the government makes much of the fact that Boeing's Stock Option Committee has the sole discretion regarding whether to grant SARs, how many to grant, and how payments will be made, and argues that, therefore, no real agreement exists in the context of Section 15,206.6(c), presumably because there are no mutual rights on the part of Boeing's employees, and because Boeing is not contractually bound to grant SARs to anyone. In our opinion, this position represents a misconception of the basic purpose of a bonus program such as that represented by Boeing's SARs. As noted in *Freedman v. Barrow,* 427 F.Supp. 1129 (1976),

> "To understand these incentive programs, their effect and purpose, some general observations may be helpful. The larger, more profitable American corporations which have achieved their success against overwhelming international competition have done so through the efforts of highly skilled, experienced managerial and executive personnel who generally have little or no ownership of the business and no share in the customary rewards of shareholders. Keeping the high level of motivation of these employees, retaining their loyalty in the future, and protecting their skills, experience and specialized knowledge from raids by competitors or others is the biggest single responsibility of top management, which naturally is also interested in its own compensation."

Thus, in our view, it would be self defeating for a corporation such as Boeing to enter into employee incentive arrangements with its key officials while at the same time, as the government seems to suggest, arbitrarily depriving them of their rights. Boeing and other large public governmental contractors are faced with a difficult task when they initiate an incentive program such as SARs and begin the preparation of the various agreements and other documentation that are required for its implementation. They must comply with a wide range of regulations that have been initiated for varying, perhaps even inconsistent, purposes. In the instant case Boeing no doubt considered the requirements of the Internal Revenue Service and the Securities and Exchange Commission as well as those of Section XV in devising and operating the SARs program. For example, the SARs program provides for a minimum six month holding period, and for a disinterested SAR administering Board with sole discretion to decide whether payments will be made in cash or stock, are required for compliance with Rule 16b-3 and have no relationship to the allowability of SARs costs. Thus, we are of the opinion that to the extent that the SARs agreements contain provisions which the Government apparently believes are one-sided and deprive them of their mutuality, they are simply a reflection of these varied regulatory mandates and not an attempt to unfairly penalize Boeing executives. To conclude otherwise would simply reflect an unawareness of modern business practices. Moreover, there was no evidence offered to indicate that the Agreement's supposedly one-sided nature has had an adverse impact on any of Boeing's SAR participants. On this basis, we conclude that the SARs program was initiated pursuant to "an agreement entered into in good faith." as that phrase is used in DAR paragraph 15.205.6(c).

Moreover, since the SAR participants must remain in Boeing's employ for a minimum of six months prior to exercise of a SAR, we believe that the paragraph 15.205.6(c) requirement that the agreement be entered into "before the services were rendered" is also satisfied. As was the case in *Martin-Marietta Corp.,* ASBCA No. 12143, 69-1 BCA par. 7506, while the amount of the bonus (i.e. the number of SARs to be granted) may be based, in part, on services previously rendered, entitlement to that bonus is based upon services to be rendered thereafter. We have also considered, and we similarly reject, the Government's argument that because the earlier SARs granted under the Boeing program were attached to pre-existing options which may already have increased in market price they involve consideration for past, not future, services. No evidence was offered to support this theory, and in any event, market appreciation subsequent to attachment of those SARs could also constitute compliance with this aspect of paragraph 15.205.6(c).

Nor are we persuaded by the contention that Boeing might gain some unfair cost advantage in its dealings with the government through "gaming"; that is, through selectively choosing the accounting periods during which it charges the costs of its SARs program. This aspect of the problem was emphasized in *Singer, supra;* however, the potential for gaming is minimized here because the decision to exercise a SAR rests solely with the employee and not with Boeing, and is confined (by Rule 16b-3) to three ten-day periods each year. Thus, the flexibility to engage in gaming which apparently concerned the original drafters of the ASPR Option Provision, is not present in Boeing's SARs program. Moreover, as stated in our findings, there was no evidence offered to support a conclusion that Boeing has engaged in practices of this sort. If such indications should appear in the future, the Government's proper recourse would be to challenge the allowability of the suspect costs on the basis of their reasonableness or their allocability. We do not believe that a disallowance based upon the mere suspicion that certain activities might take place at some indeterminate future time is proper or permissible under Section XV. As noted in *Bell Aerospace, Bell Helicopter Division,* ASBCA Nos. 9625 and 10193, 65-1 BCA par. 4865, "the logical or mathematical possibility of abuse is no basis for government objection . . . ." That conclusion is equally applicable here.

In summary, we believe that the costs of Boeing's SARs program must be treated as cash or stock bonuses, that they meet the requirements of Section XV, and that they are therefore allowable.

Deferred Compensation

Several major changes were made affecting this cost, but those initiated by government procurement officials were dwarfed by three cost accounting standards directly applicable to pensions and other deferred compensation. Following the new DAR 15-205.6, FAR 31.205-6 incorporates the applicable standards for contracts covered by CAS and provides somewhat different requirements for noncovered contracts. This provision requires close review to assure that the appropriate ground rules are applied. The cost accounting standards involved are:

CAS 412 Composition and Measurement of Pension Costs

CAS 413 Adjustment and Allocation of Pension Costs

CAS 415 Accounting for the Cost of Deferred Compensation

The Fundamental Requirements and Techniques for Application sections of each of the above standards, together with any additional comments considered appropriate, are set forth below.

CAS 412 Composition and Measurement of Pension Costs.—

§ 412.40 Fundamental requirement.

(a) *Components of pension cost.* (1) For defined-benefit pension plans, the components of pension cost for a cost accounting period are (i) the normal cost of the period, (ii) a part of any unfunded actuarial liability, (iii) an interest equivalent on the unamortized portion of any unfunded actuarial liability, and (iv) an adjustment for any actuarial gains and losses.

(2) For defined-contribution pension plans, the pension cost for a cost accounting period is the net contribution required to be made for that period, after taking into account dividends and other credits, where applicable.

(b) *Measurement of pension cost.* (1) For defined-benefit pension plans, the amount of pension cost of a cost accounting period shall be determined by use of an actuarial cost method which measures separately each of the components of pension cost set forth in paragraph (a)(1) of this section, or which meets the requirements set forth in § 412.50(b)(2).

(2) Each actuarial assumption used to measure pension cost shall be separately identified and shall represent the contractor's best estimates of anticipated experience under the plan, taking into account past experience and reasonable expectations. The validity of the assumptions used may be evaluated on an aggregate, rather than on an assumption-by-assumption, basis.

(c) *Assignment of pension cost.* The amount of pension cost computed for a cost accounting period is assignable only to that period. Except for pay-as-you-go plans, the cost assignable to a period is allocable to cost objectives of that period to the extent that liquidation of the liability for such cost can be compelled or liquidation is actually effected in that period. For pay-as-you-go plans, the entire cost assignable to a period is allocable to cost objectives of that period only if the payment of benefits earned by plan participants can be compelled. If such payment is optional with the company, the amount of assignable costs allocable to cost objectives of that period is limited to the amount of benefits actually paid to retirees or beneficiaries in that period.

§ 412.50 Techniques for application.

(a) *Components of pension cost.* (1) Any portion of an unfunded actuarial liability included as a separately identified part of the pension cost of a cost accounting period shall be included in equal annual installments. Each installment shall consist of an amortized portion of the unfunded actuarial liability plus an interest equivalent on the unamortized portion of such liability. The period of amortization shall be established as follows:

(i) If amortization of an unfunded actuarial liability has begun prior to the date this Standard first becomes applicable to a contractor, no change in the amortization period is required by this Standard.

(ii) If amortization of an unfunded actuarial liability has not begun prior to the date this Standard first becomes applicable to a contractor, the amortization period shall begin with the period in which the Standard becomes applicable and shall be no more than 30 years nor less than 10 years. However, if the plan was in existence as of January 1, 1974, the amortization period shall be no more than 40 years nor less than 10 years.

(iii) Each unfunded actuarial liability resulting from the institution of new pension plans or from adoption of improvements to pension plans subsequent to the date this Standard first becomes applicable to a contractor shall be amortized over no more than 30 years nor less than 10 years.

(2) Pension costs applicable to prior years that were specifically unallowable in accordance with then existing Government contractual provisions shall be separately identified and eliminated from any unfunded actuarial liability being amortized pursuant to the provision of paragraph (a)(1) of this section, or from future normal costs if the actuarial cost method in use does not separately develop an unfunded actuarial liability. Interest earned on funded unallowable pension costs, based on the valuation rate of return, need not be included by contractors as a reduction of future years' computations of pension costs made pursuant to this Standard.

(3) A contractor shall establish and consistently follow a policy for selecting specific amortization periods for unfunded actuarial liabilities, if any, that are developed under the actuarial cost method in use. Such policy may give consideration to factors such as the size and nature of unfunded actuarial liabilities.

(4) Actuarial assumptions used in calculating the amount of an unfunded actuarial liability shall be the same as those used for other components of pension cost. If any assumptions are changed during an amortization period, the resulting increase or decrease in an unfunded actuarial liability shall be separately amortized over no more than 30 years nor less than 10 years.

(5) Actuarial gains and losses shall be identified separately from unfunded actuarial liabilities that are being amortized pursuant to the provisions of this Standard. The accounting treatment to be afforded to such gains and losses shall be consistently applied for each pension plan.

(6) An excise tax assessed pursuant to a law or regulation because of inadequate or delayed funding of a pension plan is not a component of pension cost.

(7) If any portion of the pension cost computed for a cost accounting period is not funded in that period, no amount for interest on the portion not funded in that period shall be a component of pension cost of any future cost accounting period. Conversely, if a contractor prematurely funds pension costs in a current cost accounting period, the interest earned on such premature funding, based on the valuation rate of return, may be excluded from future years' computations of pension cost made pursuant to this Standard.

(8) For purposes of this Standard, defined-benefit pension plans funded exclusively by the purchase of individual or group permanent insurance or annuity contracts shall be treated as defined-contribution pension plans. However, all other defined-benefit pension plans administered wholly or in part through insurance company contracts shall be subject to the provisions of this Standard relative to defined-benefit pension plans.

(9) If a pension plan is supplemented by a separately-funded plan which provides retirement benefits to all of the participants in the basic plan, the two plans shall be considered as a single plan for purposes of this Standard. If the effect of the combined plans is to provide defined-benefits for the plan participants, the combined plan shall be treated as a defined-benefit plan for purposes of this Standard.

(10) A multiemployer pension plan established pursuant to the terms of a collective bargaining agreement shall be considered to be a defined-contribution pension plan for purposes of this Standard.

(11) A pension plan applicable to colleges and universities that is part of a State pension plan shall be considered to be a defined-contribution pension plan for purposes of this Standard.

(b) *Measurement of pension cost.* (1) The amount of pension cost assignable to cost accounting periods shall be measured by the accrued benefit cost method or by a projected benefit cost method which identifies separately normal costs, any unfunded actuarial liability, and periodic determinations of actuarial gains and losses, except as provided in paragraph (b)(2) of this section.

(2) Any other projected benefit cost method may be used, provided that:

(i) The method is used by the contractor in measuring pension costs for financial accounting purposes;

(ii) The amount of pension cost assigned to a cost accounting period computed under such method is reduced by the excess, if any, of the value of the assets of the pension fund over the actuarial liability of the plan as determined by a projected benefit cost method set forth in paragraph (b)(1) of this section;

(iii) The contractor accumulates supplementary information identifying the actuarial gains and losses (and, separately, gains or losses resulting from changed actuarial assumptions) that have occurred since the last determination of gains and losses and the extent to which such gains and losses have been amortized through subsequent pension contributions or offset by gains and losses in subsequent cost accounting periods, and

(iv) The cost of future pension benefits is spread over the remaining average working lives of the work force.

(3) Irrespective of the projected benefit cost method used, the calculation of normal cost shall be based on a percentage of payroll for plans where the pension benefit is a function of salaries and wages and on employee service for plans where the pension benefit is not a function of salaries and wages.

(4) The cost of benefits under a pay-as-you-go pension plan shall be measured in the same manner as are the costs of defined-benefit plans whose benefits are provided through a funding agency.

(5) Actuarial assumptions should reflect long-term trends.so as to avoid distortions caused by short-term fluctuations.

(6) Pension cost shall be based on provisions of existing pension plans. This shall not preclude contractors from making salary projections for plans whose benefits are based on salaries and wages, or from considering improved benefits for plans which provide that such improved benefits must be made.

(7) If the evaluation of the validity of actuarial assumptions shows that, in the aggregate, the assumptions were not reasonable, the contractor shall (i) identify the major causes for the resultant actuarial gains or losses and (ii) provide information as to the basis and rationale used for retaining or revising such assumptions for use in the ensuing cost accounting period(s).

(c) *Assignment of pension cost.* (1) Amounts funded in excess of the pension cost computed for a cost accounting period pursuant to the provisions of this Standard shall be applied to pension costs of future cost accounting periods.

(2) Evidence that the liquidation of a liability for pension cost can be compelled includes (i) provisions of law such as the funding provisions of the Employee Retirement Income Security Act of 1974, except as provided in paragraph (c)(3) of this section, (ii) a contractual agreement which requires liquidation of the liability, or (iii) the existence of rights by a third party to require liquidation of the liability.

(3) Any portion of pension cost computed for a cost accounting period that is deferred to future periods pursuant to a waiver granted under provisions of the Employee Retirement Income Security Act of 1974, shall not be assigned to the current period. Rather, such costs shall be assigned to the cost accounting period(s) in which the funding takes place.

(4) A liability for pension cost for a cost accounting period (or, for pay-as-you-go plans, for payments to retirees or beneficiaries for a period) shall be considered to be liquidated in the period if funding is effected by the date established for filing a Federal income tax return (including

authorized extensions). For contractors not required to file Federal income tax returns, the date shall be that established for filing Federal corporation income tax returns.

The increasing costs of pension plans and the amounts being allocated to defense procurements made the promulgation of cost accounting standards in this area predictable. However, there were many who believed that the guidance contained in Accounting Principles Board (APB) Opinion No. 8 and the Employee Retirement Income Security Act of 1974 (ERISA), added to the DAR and FPR cost principles, provided ample guidance on this subject and that further promulgations by the CASB would serve to confuse rather than to clarify the requirements for CAS-covered contracts. However, as in other instances, the CASB found that ERISA and APB No. 8 were promulgated for specific purposes not particularly directed to determining contract costs.

Finding the subject too large and complex to deal with in a single standard, the Board promulgated CAS 412 to establish the composition of pension costs, the basis of measurement, and the criteria for assigning pension costs to cost accounting periods. The accounting treatment of actuarial gains and losses and the allocation of pension costs to segments of an organization are covered in CAS 413. The pension standards incorporate some of the concepts of ERISA and APB No. 8 but also reflect specific differences.

CAS 412 recognizes pension costs measured by either the accrued benefit cost method or the projected benefit cost method. The first provides benefits to retirees according to the amount of the fixed contribution to be made by a contractor, while in the second the contributions to be made by the contractor are calculated actuarially to provide preestablished benefits.

Under the defined contribution plan, the pension cost of a cost accounting period is the net contribution required to be made, after adjustment for dividends and other credits. For a defined benefit plan, the pension cost for a period may consist of four elements: (1) normal annual cost, (2) amortization of unfunded actuarial liability, (3) interest equivalent on the unfunded actuarial liability and actuarial gains or losses being amortized, and (4) adjustment for the differences between the forecast assumptions of actuarial gains and losses and the actual experience.

The unfunded actuarial liability is to be amortized over a period of not less than ten and not more than thirty years (forty years if the plan predates January 1, 1974).

By recognizing the interest equivalent, as mentioned above, CAS 412 (as do some of the other standards) allows interest despite the prohibitions in the cost principles.

The following guidance is provided DCAA auditors in the Agency's Contract Audit Manual, paragraph 8-412.1 d-o.

d. During the compliance review, the auditor should determine that these requirements are compatible with the block checked on item 7.1.6— "Amortization of the Past Service Costs" of the contractor's Disclosure Statement. Item 7.1.6 should be reviewed to determine that any changes in amortization periods which are required by the standard are properly reflected in the Disclosure Statement. CAS 412.50(a)(3) requires a contractor to establish and consistently follow a policy for selecting specific amortization periods for unfunded actuarial liabilities. An acceptable pension amortization plan does not necessarily have to result in a straight line writeoff of past service pension costs. Under the contractor's procedure, the number of years to be considered in determining the annual amortized amount may vary from year to year. As an example, a contractor may maintain a variable amortization schedule in which (1) the amortization period is based on the ratio of pension assets to pension liabilities and (2) the determination of the amortization period is made annually based on the ratio of pension assets to pension liabilities in that year. In this situation, the change in amortization period is not considered a change in accounting practice since it is in accordance with an established policy. The contractor should describe in writing the practice for setting the amortization period. Auditors reviewing variable amortization plans should be alert to situations reflecting a deviation from established procedures governing the variable aspects of the plan. Ideally, forces that are largely external to the contractor's operations, such as market conditions, general business and employment levels, etc., should trigger those factors that determine the amortization period. Of primary importance for the auditor is to ascertain whether the plan is applied consistently. Unauthorized deviation from the established plan should be cited as a noncompliance.

e. Pension costs applicable to prior periods which were specifically unallowable under then-existing contractual provisions should be separately identified and excluded from an amortization of unfunded liability or from future normal costs if the unfunded liability is not identified. Also excludable from pension costs are excise taxes and interest costs incurred as a result of inadequate or delayed funding.

f. Actuarial methods used by contractors include the accrued benefit cost method and five principal projected benefit cost methods: entry age normal, attained age normal, individual level premium, frozen initial liability, and aggregate. A major difference between methods is that, under the accrued benefit cost method, costs are based on units of future benefits which have been accrued to employees to the present date; whereas, under the various projected benefit methods, costs are based on benefits which will accrue over the entire expected period of credited service of the individuals involved. Projected benefit cost methods are subdivided into individual and aggregate methods. An individual benefit method develops an annual cost accrual based on a summation of the amounts computed for each plan participant. The aggregate cost method, however, develops an annual cost based on averages of accruals for all participants. The standard does not require the use of a specific actuarial cost method; however, the method selected by the contractor must provide for separate measurement of the pension cost elements listed in paragraph b. above. The cost elements are identified under the accrued benefit method and some of the projected benefit cost methods. They are not identified under certain methods, which neither disclose actuarial gains and losses nor develop the amount of unfunded liability. If the projected benefit cost method used does not separately measure the cost elements, FASB No. 87, Employers Accounting for Pensions, does not permit its use for financial accounting purposes and it would not be acceptable under CAS 412.50(b)(2)(i). The effective dates for FASB No. 87 are (i) fiscal years beginning after 15 December 1986 for most contractors, or (ii) fiscal years beginning after 15 December 1988 for certain foreign concerns and for defined benefit plans of employers that are nonpublic, enterprises and sponsor no defined benefit plans with more than 100 participants. Until the contractor with plans that do not separately identify the cost elements is required to change its accounting practice to comply with FASB No. 87, the method will be considered acceptable only if:

(1) The method is used for financial accounting.

(2) An alternative computation is made (under a projected benefit cost method—i.e., entry age normal—which separately identifies normal costs, unfunded actuarial liabilities, and actuarial gains and losses) to disclose the funding status of the plan and pension costs assigned to the cost accounting period are reduced by any excess funding. The plan is excessively funded if the value of the pension fund assets exceed the actuarial liability.

(3) Supplementary records are maintained to identify actuarial gains and losses and show their disposition.

(4) The cost of future benefits is spread over the remaining average working lives of the work force.

g. The auditor's compliance review should identify the actuarial method used by the contractor for each plan in effect. The auditor should review actuarial reports and statements, as well as accounting records. If projected benefit methods are used which do not separately identify the pension cost elements, the auditor should review the contractor's proposed procedure for developing the supplementary records and the computations made thereunder until the contractor is required to comply with FASB No. 87. (See f. above.) Indications that the contractor may not be able to develop the supplementary data on a timely basis should be promptly reported to the ACO. If the contractor has previously filed a Disclosure Statement, the auditor should determine that the block checked for items 7.1.3—"Actuarial Cost Methods" complies with the provisions of the standard. Blocks "B" through "G" of item 7.1.3 represent variants of projected cost methods which will trigger the visibility requirements in CAS 412.50(b). If response "B—Aggregate," "C—Attained Age—Initial Liability Frozen," "E—Entry Age—Initial Liability Frozen," and "G—Individual Level Premium" are checked, the alternative computation and supplementary information requirements of CAS 412.50(b)(2) will be applicable. The auditor should determine what accounting practice changes the contractor will make to comply with FASB No. 87.

h. The normal costs computed under the accrued benefits cost method are the present value of future benefits earned by employees during the year. The projected benefits cost methods shall base normal costs on a percentage of payroll where the benefits are a function of salaries and wages; otherwise, normal costs shall be based on employee service or headcount.

i. While pension costs must be based on the provisions of existing plans, contractors may consider (1) salary projections for plans whose benefits are based on salaries and wages and (2) improved benefit projections for plans specifically providing for such improvements.

j. Actuarial assumptions are related to (1) interest or return on funds invested and (2) other projected factors such as future compensation levels, inflation, mortality, retirement age, turnover, and projected social security benefits. Each actuarial assumption used by the contractor in calculating pension costs must be identified separately. The assumptions should represent the contractor's estimated future experience based on long-term trends to avoid short-term fluctuations. The validity or the reasonableness of the actuarial assumptions can be measured in the aggregate of gains and losses rather than by a separate gain or loss analysis for each assumption. However, if the assumptions prove to be unreasonable in total; that is, the total gain or loss is significant, the contractor must be able to identify the major causes and give reasons for either retaining or revising the assumptions. If the actuarial assumptions are revised, any resulting increase or decrease in the unfunded actuarial liability will be amortized over not less than 10 or more than 30 years. Support for each actuarial assumption used by the contractor should be critically examined by the auditor. The compliance review should include steps to identify and evaluate the reasonableness of the assumptions and to monitor actuarial gains and losses to assure that the assumptions remain valid.

k. Pension costs computed for a cost accounting period are assignable to that period only, except when a payment deferral has been granted under the provisions of ERISA. ERISA permits a contractor which has received a funding deficiency waiver for a particular year to amortize related pension costs over the immediately succeeding 15 years. Pension costs deferred to future periods under this provision must be assigned to the periods in which the funding actually takes place. However, in accordance with the first sentence of FAR 31.205-6(j)(3)(iii) and CAS 412.50(a)(7), the interest equivalent on the unfunded actuarial liability which results from this delayed funding would be unallowable.

l. Except for pay-as-you-go plans, the cost assignable to a period is allocable to cost objectives of that period if (1) costs are funded in the period or (2) funding can be compelled. Costs will be considered funded for a period if payment is made by the Federal income tax return due date, including any extension. Funding provisions in ERISA, contractual funding agreements, or existence of third-party rights to required funding would constitute evidence that funding can be compelled. Excess funding is considered applicable to future periods.

m. Pay-as-you-go plans are different from trusteed or insured plans in that they are not funded. Therefore, the cost of benefits under a pay-as-you-go plan shall be measured the same as costs of defined benefit plans whose benefits are funded. Costs assignable to a period under a pay-as-you-go plan are allocable to the cost objectives of the period only if the payment of benefits is made in that period or can be compelled. If payment is optional with the contractor, costs allocable to cost objectives of the period are the lesser of the amount of benefits actually paid to beneficiaries in that period or the amount computed as assignable to that period.

n. FAR has retained the requirement that pension contributions be deductible for IRS purposes in order to be allowable. Therefore, even though the standard provides criteria for measurement and assignment of pension costs, the auditor will continue to establish the allowability of pension costs in accordance with FAR requirements.

o. In accordance with FAR 52.230-4, a contractor is required to describe to the ACO the kind of changes made because of the new standard. The description should be submitted 60 days after the award of a contract to which the standard is applicable. This should be done whether or not the contractor has filed a Disclosure Statement. If it appears that accounting changes will be required as a result of CAS 412, and the contractor has not submitted the description on time, the auditor should advise the ACO.

CAS 413 Adjustment and Allocation of Pension Costs.—

§ 413.40 Fundamental requirement.

(a) *Assignment of actuarial gains and losses.* Actuarial gains and losses shall be calculated annually and shall be assigned to the cost accounting period for which the actuarial valuation is made and subsequent periods.

(b) *Valuation of the assets of a pension fund.* The value of all pension fund assets shall be determined under an asset valuation method which takes into account unrealized appreciation and depreciation of pension fund assets, and shall be used in measuring the components of pension cost.

(c) *Allocation of pension cost to segments.* Contractors shall allocate pension cost to each segment having participants in a pension plan. A separate calculation of pension cost for a segment is required when the conditions set forth in § 413.50 (c) (2) and (3) are present. When these conditions are not present, allocations may be made by calculating a composite pension cost for two or more segments and allocating this cost to these segments by means of an allocation base.

§ 413.50 Techniques for application.

(a) *Assignment of actuarial gains and losses.* (1) In accordance with the provisions of 4 CFR Part 412, actuarial gains and losses shall be identified separately from unfunded actuarial liabilities being amortized.

(2) Actuarial gains and losses determined under a pension plan whose costs are measured by an immediate-gain actuarial cost method shall be amortized over a 15-year period in equal annual installments, beginning with the date as of which the actuarial valuation is made. The installment for a cost accounting period shall consist of an element for

amortization of the gain or loss and an element for interest on the unamortized balance at the beginning of the period. If the actuarial gain or loss determined for a cost accounting period is not material, the entire gain or loss may be included as a component of the current or ensuing year's pension cost.

(3) Actuarial gains and losses applicable to a pension plan whose costs are measured by a spread-gain actuarial cost method shall be included as part of current and future normal cost and spread over the remaining average working lives of the work force.

(b) *Valuation of the assets of a pension fund.* (1) The actuarial value of the assets of a pension fund shall be used (i) in measuring actuarial gains and losses, and (ii) for purposes of measuring other components of pension cost.

(2) The actuarial value of the assets of a pension fund may be determined by the use of any recognized asset valuation method which provides equivalent recognition of appreciation and depreciation of pension fund assets. However, the total asset value produced by the method used shall fall within a corridor from 80 to 120 percent of the market value of the assets, determined as of the valuation date. If the method produces a value that falls outside the corridor, the value of the assets shall be adjusted to equal the nearest boundary of the corridor.

(3) The method selected for valuing pension fund assets shall be consistently applied from year to year within each plan.

(4) The provisions of paragraphs (b) (1) through (3) of this section are not applicable to plans that are funded with insurance companies under contracts where the insurance company guarantees benefit payments.

(c) *Allocation of pension cost to segments.* (1) For contractors who compute a composite pension cost covering plan participants in two or more segments, the base to be used for allocating such costs shall be representative of the factors which the pension benefits are based. For example, a base consisting of salaries and wages shall be used for pension costs that are calculated as a percentage of salaries and wages; a base consisting of the number of employees shall be used for pension costs that are calculated as an amount per employee.

(2) Separate pension cost for a segment shall be calculated whenever any of the following conditions exist for that segment, provided that such condition(s) materially affect the amount of pension cost allocated to the segment: (i) There is a material termination gain or loss attributable to the segment, (ii) The level of benefits, eligibility for benefits, or age distribution is materially different for the segment than for the average of all segments, or (iii) The appropriate assumptions relating to termination, retirement age, or salary scale are, in the aggregate, materially different for the segment than for the average of all segments. Calculations of termination gains or losses shall give consideration to factors such as unexpected early retirements, benefits becoming fully vested, and

reinstatements or transfers without loss of benefits. An amount may be estimated for future reemployments.

(3) Pension cost shall also be separately calculated for a segment under circumstances where (i) The pension plan for that segment becomes merged with that of another segment, and (ii) The ratios of assets to actuarial liabilities for each of the merged plans are materially different from one another after applying the benefits in effect after the merger.

(4) Whenever the pension cost of a segment is required to be calculated separately pursuant to paragraphs (c) (2) and (3) of this section, such calculations shall be prospective only; pension costs need not be redetermined for prior years.

(5) For a segment whose pension costs are required to be calculated separately pursuant to paragraph (c)(2) of this section, there shall be an initial allocation of a share in the undivided pension fund assets to that segment, as follows: (i) If the necessary data are readily determinable, the amount of assets to be allocated to the segment shall be the amount of funds contributed by, or on behalf of, the segment, increased by income received on such funds, and decreased by benefits and expenses paid from such funds; (ii) if the data specified in subdivision (i) of this subparagraph, are not readily determinable, the actuarial value of the pension fund's assets shall be allocated to the segment in a manner consistent with the actuarial cost method or methods used to compute pension cost. For a segment whose pension costs are required to be calculated separately pursuant to paragraph (c)(3) of this section, the initial allocation of assets to the segment shall be the market value of the segment's assets as of the date of the merger.

(6) If prior to the time a contractor is required to use this Standard, it has been calculating pension cost separately for individual segments, the amount of assets previously allocated to those segments need not be changed.

(8) If plan participants transfer among segments, contractors need not transfer assets or liabilities unless a transfer is sufficiently large to distort the segments' ratio of fund assets to actuarial liabilities.

(9) Contractors who separately calculate the pension cost of one or more segments may calculate such cost either for all pension plan participants assignable to the segment(s) of for only the active participants of the segment(s). If costs are calculated only for active participants, a separate segment shall be created for all of the inactive participants of the pension plan and the cost thereof shall be calculated. When a contractor makes such an election, assets shall be allocated to the segment for inactive participants in accordance with paragraphs (c) (5), (6), and (7) of this section. When an employee of a segment becomes inactive, assets shall be transferred from that segment to the segment established to accumulate the assets and actuarial liabilities for the inactive plan participants. The amount of funds transferred shall be that portion of the actuarial liabilities for these inactive participants that have been funded. If inactive participants become active funds and liabilities shall similarly be transferred to the segments to which the participants are assigned.

Such transfers need be made only as of the last day of a cost accounting period. The total annual pension cost for a segment having active lives shall be the amount calculated for the segment plus an allocated portion of the pension cost calculated for the inactive participants. Such an allocation shall be on the same basis as that set forth in paragraph (c)(1) of this section.

(10) Where pension cost is separately calculated for one or more segments, the actuarial cost method used for a plan shall be the same for all segments, as required by 4 CFR 412.50(b). Unless a separate calculation of pension cost for a segment is made because of a condition set forth in paragraph (c)(2)(iii) of this section, the same actuarial assumptions may be used for all segments covered by a plan.

(11) If a pension plan has participants in the home office of a company, the home office shall be treated as a segment for purposes of allocating the cost of the pension plan. Pension cost allocated to a home office shall be a part of the costs to be allocated in accordance with the appropriate requirements of 4 CFR Part 403.

(12) If a segment is closed, the contractor shall determine the difference between the actuarial liability for the segment and the market value of the assets allocated to the segment, irrespective of whether or not the pension plan is terminated. The determination of the actuarial liability shall give consideration to any requirements imposed by agencies of the United States Government. In computing the market value of assets for the segment, if the contractor has not already allocated assets to the segment, such an allocation shall be made in accordance with the requirements of paragraph (c)(5) (i) and (ii) of this section. The market value of the assets allocated to the segment shall be the segment's proportionate share of the total market value of the assets of the pension fund. The calculation of the difference between the market value of the assets and the actuarial liability shall be made as of the date of the event (e.g., contract termination) that caused the closing of the segment. If such a date cannot be readily determined, or if its use can result in an inequitable calculation, the contracting parties shall agree on an appropriate date. The difference between the market value of the assets and the actuarial liability for the segment represents an adjustment of previously determined pension costs.

As noted earlier, CAS 412 established the composition of pension costs, the basis of measurement, and the criteria for assigning pension costs to a cost accounting period. The purpose of CAS 413 is to provide guidance for adjusting pension costs by measuring actuarial gains and losses and assigning them to cost accounting periods. CAS 413 also provides the bases on which pension costs are to be allocated to segments of an organization.

CAS 413 requires that actuarial gains and losses be calculated and assigned annually based on specific criteria. The standard does not require the use of any specific valuation method; however, if the method used by the contractor results in a value outside a corridor of 80% to 120% of market value, the value must be adjusted to the closer limit.

The subject of pensions is a very complex one, and, with a growing portion of this nation's wealth involved in the various plans, the author advises, where the amounts are significant, the engagement of outside consultants, in both the pension and accounting fields.

Portions of the guidance, regarding this aspect, furnished DCAA auditors in the Agency's Contract Audit Manual are excerpted below (8-413.1):

c. Except where certain significant disparities in actuarial factors exist between segments, contractors have the option to calculate pension costs either separately for segments or on a composite basis for allocation to segments on a base which represents the factors used in computing pension benefits. Separate calculations of pension costs for each segment are acceptable. CAS 413.50(c)(2) and (3) provide that pension costs must be separately calculated for a segment (on a prospective basis) when the pension costs at the segment are materially affected by any of the following conditions:

(1) The segment experiences material termination gains or losses.

(2) The level of benefits, eligibility for benefits, or age distribution is materially different for the segment than for the average of all segments.

(3) The aggregate of actuarial assumptions for termination, retirement age, or salary scale is materially different for the segment than for the average of the segments.

(4) The ratios of assets to actuarial liabilities for merged segments are different from one another after applying the benefits in effect after the merger. Differences between segments as to level of benefits and eligibility of benefits should be obtainable from the provisions of the pension plan. Segment data for termination experience, age distribution, and actuarial assumptions for termination, retirement age or salary scale will generally not be included in actuarial reports, CPA reports, Schedule B to IRS Form 5500 or other pension source documents. Thus, the auditor should attempt to gain an understanding at the onset of the pension review as to the segment data to be provided by the contractor which are necessary for audit determination of compliance with CAS 413.50(c)(2) and (3).

d. When separate pension fund calculations are required because of disparities in termination gains or losses, level of or eligibility for benefits, or actuarial assumptions for termination, retirement age or salary scale, undivided pension fund assets must be initially allocated to the segment for which the separate calculation is being made. The value of the pension fund assets allocated shall equal the segment's pension fund contributions, adjusted for earned interest and paid benefits/expenses, if such information is determinable; if not, the assets can be allocated among segments on any ratio which is consistent with the actuarial cost method(s) used to compute pension costs. The initial allocation of assets to merged segments must be the market value of the segment's pension fund assets when the merger occurred.

e. Employees participating in a multisegment pension plan occasionally transfer between segments. However, the applicable pension fund assets and liabilities need not follow the employees from one segment to the other unless the transfers involve such a large number of employees that a segment's ratio of fund assets to actuarial liabilities would be distorted.

f. Contractors who separately calculate pension costs for one or more segments have the option of establishing a separate segment for inactive participants (e.g., retirees). If this action is taken, the pension fund assets and actuarial liabilities should be transferred to the inactive segment when employees participating in the pension plan become inactive. The funds transferred are to reflect the funded portion of the inactive participants' actuarial liability. CAS 413.50(c)(1) and 413.50(c)(9) provide that inactive segment costs shall be allocated to the segments with active lives on a basis representative of the factors upon which pension costs are based. Thus, pension cost calculated for the inactive participants should be allocated to the segments with active lives on a basis which is relatively comparable to the amounts that would have been computed if a separate segment for inactives had never been established.

g. When a segment is closed, the contractor must determine the difference between the actuarial liability for the segment and the market value of the assets allocated to the segment as of the closure date. Although this difference represents an adjustment of previously determined pension costs, it is to be allocated to existing contracts in the cost accounting period of closure, not prior cost accounting periods. Because of the complex nature of plant terminations, audit actions related to such closures should be coordinated with Headquarters, Attention PAD.

Spread Gain Actuarial Pension Cost Method Phased Out

CAS 412.50(b)(2)(i) permits the use of the spread gain actuarial cost method to measure pension cost for cost accounting purposes provided contractors are also using this method for financial accounting. In December 1985, the Financial Accounting Standards Board (FASB) issued Statement of Financial Accounting Standards No. 87 (FAS 87), a 132-page treatment of Employers' Accounting for Pensions. Under FAS 87, companies are not permitted to use the spread gain method for financial accounting purposes because they are required to measure pension cost using only the projected unit cost credit method or the unit credit method, depending on the type of plan. FAS 87 is applicable to company fiscal years beginning after December 15, 1986.

Based on FAS 87, companies will no longer have the option of using the spread gain method for financial accounting and, therefore, will not be able to use this method for cost or pricing government contracts.

Both the FASB and FAR recognized that a number of companies will encounter time problems in changing to an acceptable actuarial cost method. Contractors subject to full CAS coverage will be unable to effect timely recomputations for forward pricing purposes to cover periods after the application of FAS 87. The government recognized that these circumstances could impede the negotiation process and provide DCAA with the opportunity of issuing an inordinate number of reports alleging noncompliance with CAS during the period contractors are transitioning to the new method. To avoid these circumstances and facilitate the transition, FAC 84-20, effective August 20, 1986, instructed contracting officers to proceed as follows:

a. When a contractor, which currently is using the spread gain actuarial cost method, can demonstrate to the satisfaction of the contracting officer that it is unable to change to another actuarial cost method acceptable under CAS 412 (as impacted by FAS 87) and is unable to make the computations necessary for forward pricing purposes to cover contractor fiscal years beginning after December 15, 1986, the following applies:

i. Contract negotiations will be conducted using the actuarial cost method currently employed by the contractor.

ii. A specific date will be established for the contractor to make the necessary changes to its estimating, accumulating, and reporting systems, to incorporate an acceptable actuarial cost method under CAS 412.

iii. An advance agreement or savings clauses will be used to provide for a price adjustment to reflect the cost impact of changing from the spread gain actuarial cost method to an acceptable method under CAS 412, retroactive to the applicability date of FAS 87 to the contractor's accounting system. The advance agreement or savings clauses will include a requirement for interest on overpayments assessed at the rate specified in Pub. L. 92-41 (85 Stat. 97).

b. When the above procedures are followed, the Government will not issue CAS noncompliance reports concerning CAS 412.50(b)(2)(i) unless the contractor fails to meet the specific date referred to in paragraph (a)(ii) above.

Administrative Contracting Officers, who have cognizance over contractors that are currently using the spread gain actuarial cost method and cannot timely change to another acceptable method under CAS 412, should negotiate with those contractors to implement procedures set out in paragraphs 2(a) and 2(b) of this Federal Acquisition Circular information notice.

Government Demands Share in Excess Pension Fund Assets When Contractors Terminate Overfunded Defined Benefit Pension Plans

As a result of increases in equity values in recent years, a number of contractors found themselves in the happy position of having overfunded defined benefit pension plans. Some have withdrawn the excess funds and others have terminated the funds and used the excess pension plan assets for other company purposes. After some time of casting covetous eyes on the excess funds, DOD initiated efforts to obtain advance agreements with such companies that would provide that DOD would receive a credit or refund for "its equitable share" of the proceeds.

In related circumstances, the pension plan asset values of some companies exceeded the full funding limitation established by the Internal Revenue Code. Some companies stopped further contributions until the overfunding was eliminated while others continued funding because otherwise the amounts would be unallowable under CAS. In the latter case, the excess is not deductible for federal income tax purposes. Here, too, DOD decided it was entitled to benefit and would do so under advance agreements that would be effective pending revisions to FAR and CAS. Directions to seek these advance agreements were contained in memoranda from the Assistant Secretary of Defense (A&L) to the Secretaries of the Military Departments and Directors of DLA and DCAA in September 1986.

NASA, dealing to a large extent with companies who perform on DOD contracts, thought well of the DOD initiatives, distributed the memoranda and proposed advance agreements to its contracting officers, and directed them to support DOD where that Department had cognizance and to reach similar agreements at locations where NASA had cognizance.

Some contractors entered into these advance agreements while others resisted on the grounds that the government has no vested right in the disposal of company assets and liabilities and, further, because the government had not indicated it would pay the increased costs if the pension investments were to decline.

On February 9, 1987, a proposed FAR revision was published that would formalize the government demands to share in any benefits to companies whose pension plan investments had increased and that would provide rules for determining the amount of the government's "equitable share." The background information to this proposed revision states that "(c)harges for pension costs have been accepted on Government contracts on the basis that funding was irrevocable and therefore that the Government would participate in all gains and losses incurred by pension plans." Noting the reversion of excess plan assets in some instances recently, the further assertion is made that "(s)uch proceeds represent an adjustment of prior period's pension costs. If the actual cost had been known, the prices the Government previously paid would have been reduced commensurately."

The major part of the revision is to FAR 31.205-6(j), Pension Costs, and the text of the proposal is quoted below.

> Section 31.205-6 is amended by revising the fourth sentence in paragraph (j)(2); by removing in paragraph (j)(2)(iii) the reference "(j)(6) below" and inserting in its place the reference "(j)(7) of this paragraph"; by removing paragraph (j)(3)(iv); by adding a new paragraph (j)(4); by redesignating existing paragraphs (j)(4) through (j)(7) as new paragraphs (j)(5) through (j)(8); by revising new paragraphs (j)(5)(iii); by revising (j)(6)(vi); by revising the third sentence in new paragraph (j)(7); and by revising new paragraph (j)(7)(i) to read as follows:

> **31.205-6 Compensation costs.**

> * * * *

> (j) * * *

> (2) * * * Pension costs are allowable subject to the referenced standards and the cost limitations and exclusions set forth below in this subparagraph and in paragraphs (j)(3) through (8) of this section.

> * * * *

(4) *Termination of defined benefit pension plans.* Termination of a defined benefit pension plan refers to a transaction in which pension benefit obligations (i.e., liabilities for vested benefits) of the plan are irrevocably settled, such as by purchasing paid-up annuity contracts or by making lump-sum cash payments to plan participants in exchange for their rights to vested benefits. Because of the unique manner in which pension costs for an accounting period are determined (i.e., the actuarial methods and techniques employed), Government recognition of such costs has always been on a basis that funding is irrevocable and that the Government will fully participate, to the extent of its fair share, in gains and losses incurred by the plan. When a pension plan is terminated, the termination value of the liabilities of the plan, based on employee service and/or earnings through the date of termination, shall be the lesser of the amount determined under the Pension Benefit Guaranty Corporation (PBGC) valuation method, or the amount paid for an annuity contract(s) purchased to settle the plan's liabilities. When the market value of the assets exceeds the termination value of the liabilities, the residual assets are generally refunded to the contractor upon settlement of all liabilities. When the termination value of the liabilities exceeds the market value of the assets, additional funding may be required. For contract costing purposes, the funding change which results from termination of a defined benefit pension plan shall be treated in the current year as an adjustment of pension costs for accounting periods preceding the date of plan termination. Government participation in such adjustments of prior periods' pension costs shall be determined in accordance with paragraphs (j)(4)(i) through (vi) of this section.

(i) When CAS 413.50(c) requires that separate pension costs be calculated for a segment(s), or that segmented pension records be maintained, the amount of the adjustment of prior periods' pension costs shall be apportioned initially to segments based on the market value of the assets and the termination value of the liabilities applicable to each segment, and on a basis consistent with the actuarial method(s) used to compute pension costs and the accounting procedures used to allocate such costs to final objectives.

(ii) The Government's share of the adjustment of prior periods' pension costs, calculated for each segment in accordance with paragraph (j)(4)(i) of this section, shall be the product of such adjustment (net of any amount prefunded) and the ratio of pension expense absorbed by all Government contracts and subcontracts (including Foreign Military Sales) to total pension costs incurred during the 10-year period preceding the date of plan termination, or the period from the inception date of the plan being terminated, whichever is shorter. If this ratio cannot be determined readily, a surrogate for it may be used provided the contracting officer determines that it achieves an equitable result.

(iii) In order to determine the total amount of the Government's share of the adjustment of prior periods' pension costs, the share calculated in accordance with paragraph (j)(4)(ii) of this section, shall be further adjusted as follows:

(A) It shall give effect to any unallowable costs included in the segment's pension liabilities immediately before termination.

(B) It shall give effect to the consequence of any delayed funding, such as when the Government vs. non-Government portions of pension plan contributions have not been funded on the same schedule, or funding has been deferred under a waiver granted under the requirements of ERISA (see paragraph (j)(3)(i) of this section).

(iv) When a participating annuity contract is used to settle pension plan liabilities, the Government's share of dividends paid to the contractor under the annuity contract in future periods shall be the product of the ratio determined in paragraph (j)(4)(ii) of this section and the dividends paid.

(v) The cost of indemnifying the PBGC under ERISA section 4062 or 4064 is allowable, provided that if insurance was required by the PBGC under section 4023, it was so purchased and the indemnification payment is not recoverable under the insurance. The Government will participate, notwithstanding the requirements of 31.205-19(f), in the contractor's indemnification payment to the PBGC to the extent of its fair share determined in accordance with paragraph (j)(4)(iii) of this section.

(vi) The contracting officer shall determine whether the amount due to the Government shall be received by refund or by credit to specific contracts. Any amount due to the Government shall be payable in full on the date of plan termination, or for dividends declared under participating annuity contracts, on the date the dividends are payable to the contractor. Interest at the rate specified by the Secretary of Treasury pursuant to 50 U.S.C. App. 1215(B)(2) shall be assessed on the amount due for the period from the date payable until the date of receipt by the Government.

(5) * * *

(iii) The provisions of paragraph (j)(4)(v) of this section concerning payments to PBGC apply to defined contribution plans.

(6) * * *

(vi) The requirements of paragraph (j)(3) of this section are also applicable to pay-as-you-go plans.

(7) * * * However, for contract costing purposes, early retirement incentive payments are allowable subject to the pension cost criteria contained in paragraph (j)(3) of this section provided—

(i) The costs are accounted for and allocated in accordance with the contractor's system of accounting for pension costs (see paragraph (j)(6)(v) of this section for supplemental pension benefits);

* * * *

The proposed revision would also add a new clause, FAR 52.215-27, Termination of Defined Benefit Pension Plans.

The Contractor shall notify the Contracting Officer in writing when it determines that it will terminate a defined benefit pension plan. If pension fund assets revert to the Contractor under any such termination, the Contractor shall make a refund or credit to the Government for an equitable share determined in accordance with FAR 31.205-6(j)(4). If indemnification payments must be made to the Pension Benefit Guaranty Corporation (PBGC) under any such termination, the Government's share of such payments shall be determined in accordance with FAR 31.205-6(j)(4)(v). The Contractor shall include the substance of this clause in all subcontracts under this contract, except for those types of contracts specified in FAR 15.804-8(e).

CAS 415 Accounting for the Cost of Deferred Compensation.—

§ 415.40 Fundamental requirement.

(a) The cost of deferred compensation shall be assigned to the cost accounting period in which the contractor incurs an obligation to compensate the employee. In the event no obligation is incurred prior to payment, the cost of deferred compensation shall be the amount paid and shall be assigned to the cost accounting period in which the payment is made.

(b) The measurement of the amount of the cost of deferred compensation shall be the present value of the future benefits to be paid by the contractor.

(c) The cost of each award of deferred compensation shall be considered separately for purposes of measurement and assignment of such costs to cost accounting periods. However, if the cost of deferred compensation for the employees covered by a deferred compensation plan can be measured with reasonable accuracy on a group basis, separate computations for each employee are not required.

§ 415.50 Techniques for application.

(a) The contractor shall be deemed to have incurred an obligation for the cost of deferred compensation when all of the following conditions have been met. However, for awards which require that the employee perform future service in order to receive the benefits, the obligation is deemed to have been incurred as the future service is performed for that part of the award attributable to such future service.

(1) There is a requirement to make the future payment(s) which the contractor cannot unilaterally avoid.

(2) The deferred compensation award is to be satisfied by a future payment of money, other assets, or shares of stock of the contractor.

(3) The amount of the future payment can be measured with reasonable accuracy.

(4) The recipient of the award is known.

(5) If the terms of the award require that certain events must occur before an employees is entitled to receive the benefits, there is a reasonable probability that such events will occur.

(6) For stock options, there must be a reasonable probability that the options ultimately will be exercised.

(b) If any of the conditions in § 415.50(a) is not met, the cost of deferred compensation shall be assignable only to the cost accounting period or periods in which the compensation is paid to the employee.

(c) If the cost of deferred compensation can be estimated with reasonable accuracy on a group basis, including consideration of probable forfeitures, such estimate may be used as the basis for measuring and assigning the present value of future benefits.

(d) The following provisions are applicable for plans that meet the conditions of § 415.50(a) and the compensation is to be paid in money.

(1) If the deferred compensation award provides that the amount to be paid shall include the principal of the award plus interest at a rate fixed at the date of award, such interest shall be included in the computation of the amount of the future benefit. If no interest is included in the award, the amount of the future benefit is the amount of the award.

(2) If the deferred compensation award provides for payment of principal plus interest at a rate not fixed at the time of award but based on a specified index which is determinable in each applicable cost accounting period, e.g., a published corporate bond rate, such interest shall be included in the computation of the amount of future benefit. The interest rate to be used shall be the rate in effect at the close of the period in which the cost of deferred compensation is assignable. Since that interest rate is likely to vary from the actual rates in future periods, adjustments shall be made in any such future period in which the variation in rates materially affects the cost of deferred compensation.

(3) If the deferred compensation award provides for payment of principal plus interest at a rate not based on a specified index or not determinable in each applicable year:

(i) The cost of deferred compensation for the principal of the award shall be measured by the present value of the future benefits of the principal and shall be assigned to the cost accounting period in which the employer incurs an obligation to compensate the employee and

(ii) The interest on such awards shall be assigned to the cost accounting period(s) in which the payment of the deferred compensation is made.

(4) If the terms of the award require that the employee perform future service in order to receive benefits, the cost of the deferred compensation shall be appropriately assigned to the periods of current and future service based on the facts and circumstances of the award. The cost of deferred compensation for each cost accounting period shall be the present value of the future benefits of the deferred compensation calculated as of the end of each such period to which such cost is assigned.

(5) In computing the present value of the future benefits, the discount rate shall be equal to the interest rate as determined by the Secretary of the Treasury pursuant to Pub. L. 92—41, 85 Stat. 97, at the time the cost is assignable.

(6) If the award is made under a plan which requires irrevocable funding for payment to the employee in a future cost accounting period together with all interest earned thereon, the amount assignable to the period of award shall be the amount irrevocably funded.

(7) In computing the assignable cost for a cost accounting period, any forfeitures which reduce the employer's obligation for payment of deferred compensation shall be a reduction of contract costs in the period in which the forfeiture occurred. The amount of the reduction for a forfeiture shall be the amount of the award that was assigned to a prior period, plus interest compounded annually, using the same Treasury rate that was used as the discount rate at the time the cost was assigned. For irrevocably funded plans, pursuant to § 415.50(d)(6), the amount of the reduction for a forfeiture shall be the amount initially funded plus or minus a pro rata share of the gains and losses of the fund.

(8) If the cost of deferred compensation for group plans measured in accordance with § 415.50(c) is determined to be greater than the amounts initially assigned because the forfeiture was overestimated, the additional cost shall be assignable to the cost accounting period in which such cost is ascertainable.

(e) The following provisions are applicable for plans that meet the conditions of § 415.50(a) and the compensation is received by the employee in other than money. The measurements set forth herein constitute the present value of future benefits for awards made in other than money and, therefore, shall be deemed to be a reasonable measure of the amount of the future payment.

(1) If the award is made in the stock of the contractor, the cost of deferred compensation for such awards shall be based on the market value of the stock on the measurement date, i.e., the first date the number of shares awarded is known. Market value is the current or prevailing price of the security as indicated by market quotations. If such values are unavailable or not appropriate (thin market, volatile price movement, etc.) an acceptable alternative is the fair value of the stock.

(2) If an award is made in the form of options to employees to purchase stock of the contractor, the cost of deferred compensation of such award shall be the amount by which the market value of the stock exceeds the option price multiplied by the number of shares awarded on the measurement date, i.e., the first date on which both the option price and the number of shares is known. If the option price on the measurement date is equal to or greater than the market value of the stock, no cost shall be deemed to have been incurred for contract costing purposes.

(3) If the terms of an award of stock or stock option require that the employee perform future service in order to receive the stock or to exercise the option, the cost of the deferred compensation shall be appropriately assigned to the periods of current and future service based on the facts and circumstances of the award. The cost to be assigned shall be the value of the stock or stock option at the measurement date as prescribed in § 415.50(e)(1) or (e)(2).

(4) If an award is made in the form of an asset other than cash, the cost of deferred compensation for such award shall be based on the market value of the asset at the time the award is made. If a market value is not available, the fair value of the asset shall be used.

(5) If the terms of an award, made in the form of an asset other than cash, require that the employee perform future service in order to receive the asset, the cost of the deferred compensation shall be appropriately assigned to the periods of current and future service based on the facts and circumstances of the award. The cost to be assigned shall be the value of the asset at the time of award as prescribed in § 415.50(e)(4).

(6) In computing the assignable cost for a cost accounting period, any forfeitures which reduce the employer's obligation for payment of deferred compensation shall be a reduction of contract costs in the period in which the forfeiture occurred. The amount of the reduction shall be equal to the amount of the award that was assigned to a prior period, plus interest compounded annually, using the Treasury rate (see § 415.50(d) (5)) that was in effect at the time the cost was assigned. If the recipient of the award of stock options voluntarily fails to exercise such options, such failure shall not constitute a forfeiture under provisions of this Standard.

(7) Stock option awards or any other form of stock purchase plans containing all of the following characteristics shall be considered noncompensatory and not covered by this Standard:

(i) Substantially all full-time employees meeting limited employment qualifications may participate,

(ii) Stock is offered to eligible employees equally or based on a uniform percentage of salary or wages,

(iii) An option or a purchase right must be exercisable within a reasonable period, and

(iv) The discount from the market price of the stock is no greater than would be reasonable in an offer of stock to stockholders or others.

CAS 415 was designed to provide criteria for the measurement of the cost of deferred compensation, other than pensions covered in CAS 412 and 413, and the assignment of such cost to cost accounting periods. The standard covers deferred compensation regardless of the form in which it is made and thus includes cash, stock, stock options, etc. It addresses payments to employees in future periods for services rendered prior to receipt of compensation, but excludes normal salaries and bonus accruals.

Deferred compensation is measured by the present value of future benefits to be paid and is assigned to the cost accounting period in which the employee earns the deferred compensation. If the contractor does not incur an obligation prior to payment, the cost must be assigned to the period in which the payment is made.

Some further insights into the manner in which the standard is intended to operate and be supported are contained in the DCAA Contract Audit Manual, quoted below (8-415.1f):

(f) The auditor's review should:

(1) Identify all deferred compensation awards currently provided to employees.

(2) Determine what accounting changes, if any, are contemplated as a result of the standard. (According to DAR 7-104.83(b), the contractor is required to describe to the ACO the kind of changes required by the standard.) If the contractor previously utilized a cash basis of accounting for deferred compensation costs on Government contracts, a change from a cash to an accrual basis will be required for all new awards made after the applicability date of the standard.

(3) Verify, through examination of the award provisions, that all applicable conditions for establishing the obligation for compensation have been met for those awards in which the entire cost is recognized in the year of award.

(4) Review the present-value calculations to determine that the treasury rate specified in the standard has been used correctly.

(5) Review costs for proper credit of estimated forfeitures, based on past experience and future expectations, where deferred compensation costs are accounted for on a group basis.

(g) Interest cost will be included in computing future benefits for all deferred compensation cash awards which provide for the payment of interest. The allowability of such interest cost will be determined in accordance with applicable procurement regulations, if determined in accordance with applicable procurement regulations. If the award stipulates a fixed interest rate, the interest cost is assigned at the fixed rate to the cost accounting period in which the contractor is obligated to compensate the employee. Some deferred compensation awards provide for the payment of interest at variable rates from the date of the award until payment. When the variable rate is based on specified index which is determinable by cost accounting period, the interest cost is assigned to the applicable period at the actual rate for the index at the close of the period. Since that rate may vary from the actual rates in future periods, adjustments will be made in any future period in which the variable rate materially affects the cost of deferred compensation. When the variable rate is not based on a specified index and is not determinable by year, the total interest cost will be assigned to the period of payment. The auditor should review each deferred compensation plan which provides for a cash award, to determine whether the payment of interest is required. For each plan which provides for interest, the auditor should check the contractor's annual interest cost calculation to ascertain that only interest costs for which the rates are fixed or based on specific indices have been accrued.

(h) If a deferred compensation plan for a cash award requires irrevocable funding (including interest) of future payments to employees, the amount irrevocably funded will be assigned to the cost accounting period in which the funding occurs.

(i) The deferred compensation cost of an award of contractor stock will be based on the current or prevailing market value of the stock (as indicated by market quotations) on the date the number of shares awarded becomes known. It should be noted that the standard does not provide for present value discounting of the market price for stock. Since the market price is presumed to reflect future expectations, further discounting would not be appropriate.

(j) While the standard provides criteria for the measurement and assignment of stock option costs, it should be noted that stock options are unallowable costs under existing procurement regulations. The CAS Board has emphasized in its prefatory remarks that the provisions of the standard deal with *allocability* and that the use of cost accounting standards has no bearing on *allowability* determinations. The auditor should continue to establish the allowability of stock options according to applicable procurement regulations.

(k) The cost of an award of an asset other than cash, will be based on the market value of the asset when the award is made. If the market value is not available, a fair value of the asset will be established. The auditor should verify that the claimed market value of the asset is supported by a valid appraisal obtained from an outside source.

(l) If the terms of an award of either cash, other assets, or stock require than an employee perform future service to receive benefits, the deferred compensation cost will be assigned on a pro rata basis to those applicable periods of current and future service. The standard does not specify the method or proration but provides that the proration be based on the circumstances of the award. The requirement of the standard conforms with Accounting Principles Board Opinion No. 12 which states that only the portion applicable to the current period should be accrued if elements of both current and future services are present. The auditor should determine the basis on which the contractor prorates costs between current and future periods. Where deferred compensation plans do not clearly establish a basis for prorating costs between accounting periods, the contractor will be required to support the prorations. In most instances the contractor, because of the ease of computation, will prorate the costs evenly over the number of years of additional service required before exercise of the award. For example, a contractor, declaring a year-end cash award to key employees under a plan requiring three additional years of service before payment, prorates the cost evenly over the following three years (excluding adjustment for present value factors). The contractor's proration would be accepted by the auditor unless the circumstances of the award clearly indicated that the award was related in total, or in part, to past services rendered.

(m) Any forfeitures which reduce the contractor's obligation for payment of deferred compensation will be credited to contract costs in the period the forfeiture occurs. The reduction will be the amount of the award assigned to the prior period(s), plus interest compounded annually at the Public Law 92-41 treasury rate. For irrevocably funded plans, the reduction will be the amount initially funded, adjusted for a pro rata share of fund gains or losses. The voluntary failure of a recipient to exercise a stock option is not considered a forfeiture. If the cost of a cash award for a group deferred compensation plan is later determined to be greater than the amount initially assigned due to an overestimate of forfeitures, the additional cost attributable to the incorrect estimate will be assigned to the cost accounting period in which the revised cost becomes known.

CAS 408 Accounting for Costs of Compensated Personal Absence.—The Fundamental Requirement and Techniques for Application sections of CAS 408 are quoted below:

§ 408.40 Fundamental requirement.

(a) The costs of compensated personal absence shall be assigned to the cost accounting period or periods in which the entitlement was earned.

(b) The costs of compensated personal absence for an entire cost accounting period shall be allocated pro-rata on an annual basis among the final cost objectives of that period.

§ 408.50 Techniques for application.

(a) *Determinations.* Each plan or custom for compensated personal absence shall be considered separately in determining when entitlement is earned. If a plan or custom is changed or a new plan or custom is adopted, then a new determination shall be made beginning with the first cost accounting period to which such new or changed plan or custom applies.

(b) *Measurement of entitlement.* (1) For purposes of compliance with § 408.40(a), compensated personal absence is earned at the same time and in the same amount as the employer becomes liable to compensate the employee for such absence if the employer terminates the employee's employment for lack of work or other reasons not involing disciplinary action, in accordance with a plan or custom of the employer. Where a new employee must complete a probationary period before the employer becomes liable, the employer may nonetheless treat such service as creating entitlement in any computations required by this Standard, provided that he does so consistently.

(2) Where a plan or custom provides for entitlement to be determined as of the first calendar day or the first business day of a cost accounting period based on service in the preceding cost accounting period, the entitlement shall be considered to have been earned, and the employer's liability to have arisen, as of the close of the preceding cost accounting period.

(3) In the absence of a determinable liability, in accordance with paragraph (b)(1) of this section, compensated personal absence will be considered to be earned only in the cost accounting period in which it is paid.

(c) *Determination of employer's liability.* In computing the cost of compensated personal absence, the computation shall give effect to the employer's liability in accordance with the following paragraphs:

(1) The estimated liability shall include all earned entitlement to compensated personal absence which exists at the time the liability is determined, in accordance with paragraph (b) of this section.

(2) The estimated liability shall be reduced to allow for anticipated nonutilization, if material.

(3) The liability shall be estimated consistently either in terms of current or of anticipated wage rates. Estimates may be made with respect to individual employees, but such individual estimates shall not be required if the total cost with respect to all employees in the plan can be estimated with reasonable accuracy by the use of sample data, experience or other appropriate means.

(d) *Adjustments.* (1) The estimate of the employer's liability for compensated personal absence at the beginning of the first cost accounting period for which a contractor must comply with this Standard shall be based on the contractor's plan or custom applicable to that period, notwithstanding that some part of that liability has not previously been recognized for contract costing purposes. Any excess of the amount of the liability as determined in accordance with paragraph (c) of this section over the corresponding amount of the liability as determined in accordance with the contractor's previous practice shall be held in suspense and accounted for as described in subparagraph (3) of this paragraph.

(2) If a plan or custom is changed or a new plan or custom is adopted, and the new determination made in accordance with paragraph (a) of this section results in an increase in the estimate of the employer's liability for compensated personal absence at the beginning of the first cost accounting period for which the new plan is effective over the estimate made in accordance with the contractor's prior practice, then the amount of such increase shall be held in suspense and accounted for as described in subparagraph (3) of this paragraph.

(3) At the close of each cost accounting period, the amount held in suspense shall be reduced by the excess of the amount held in suspense at the beginning of the cost accounting period over the employer's liability (as estimated in accordance with paragraph (c) of this section) at the end of that cost accounting period. The cost of compensated personal absence assigned to that cost accounting period shall be increased by the amount of the excess.

(e) *Allocations.* Except where the use of a longer or shorter period is permitted by the provisions of the Cost Accounting Standard on Cost Accounting Period (Part 406 of this chapter), the costs of compensated personal absence shall be allocated to cost objectives on a pro-rata basis which reflects the total of such costs and the total of the allocation base for the entire cost accounting period. However, this provision shall not preclude revisions to an allocation rate during a cost accounting period based on revised estimates of period totals.

CAS 408 was promulgated to provide uniformity in the measurement of the costs of vacation, sick leave, holiday, and other compensated personal absence for a cost accounting period. As in the case of a number of other standards, questions were raised as to the need for CAS 408 and whether there were any benefits to match the costs some contractors would be required to incur to change their practices to conform to the requirements. We heard of no "horror cases" suggesting that contractors were manipulating these costs to burden unfairly their government contracts.

On the other hand, there was no denying the lack of uniformity. Some companies recorded these costs when paid (cash basis) while others recorded them when the employee's entitlement was determined (accrual basis). And there were also variances in practices among the companies that accounted for these costs on an accrual basis.

As noted in the very first paragraph of CAS 408.40(a), the standard requires, specifically and definitively, that the accrual basis be used, i.e., that the cost be assigned to the cost accounting period in which the entitlement was earned.

The term "compensated personal absence" includes a number of payroll-related fringe benefits, and government auditors are required to review each plan individually to determine when entitlement is earned by the employee and the liability assumed by the contractor. Plans may and do vary so that a given contractor may be required to use the accrual basis for some plans (where the employee obtains entitlement as time passes) and the cash basis for other plans where there is no liability established on the part of the employer.

As described elsewhere in this text, certain members of the Senate Committee on Governmental Affairs have used a series of hearings in 1983-84, featuring critical GAO testimonies and reports, to attack DOD on a broad scale, including: implementation of P.L. 87-653, Truth in Negotiations Act; application of CAS 409, lowering thresholds for requiring certificates of cost or pricing data; and progress payment policies. One of the topics apparently suggested by the committee staff was the implementation of CAS 408, which resulted in inappropriate government financing of contractors subject to CAS.

The Senate committee wrote to the Comptroller General requesting his views about the so-called "premature reimbursement" resulting from DOD's recognition and reimbursement of these expenses when accrued while contractors do not actually pay out these monies until a later date. The Comptroller General's views were requested about a proposal to amend contract payment clauses so that contractors would not be reimbursed for these costs until they had paid them. What the committee appeared to be proposing, in effect, was a nullification of CAS 408 by effectively changing the practice from an accrual to a cash basis.

Although GAO can usually be counted upon to join (or initiate) criticisms of DOD on a wide range of subjects, this inquiry presented a problem in that agreement with the committee could not be expressed without a concomitant derogation of CAS 408. And, the GAO could not readily criticize a standard in view of the frequent statements by the Comptroller General and his staff that all of the Board's promulgations were characterized by accounting expertise, independence, etc. In this light, the Comptroller General replied: "Since the amount of the accrual is determined in accordance with the standard and paid as an accrual pursuant to DOD policy, we cannot call this reimbursement premature."

The committee was further advised that the CASB files on this standard revealed that contractors generally did not have plans for unlimited accrual and "the overwhelming majority of plans had an accrual plan of less than or equal to one year." While suggesting there was no need for any action in view of the fact that the period between the accrual and the payment would seldom exceed 12 months, the GAO chief seized this opportunity to make another argument for the reestablishment of a CASB function: "It has been almost 8 years since the standard became effective and over 10 years since the research was initiated on the subject. The procurement environment has changed and it is possible that new issues related to vacation pay expense may have surfaced." He did not explain how a change in the "procurement environment," whatever this means, could be related to possible "new issues related to vacation expense."

The Comptroller General was not in favor of amending the contract payment clauses but stated his belief that "the extent of the problem you pose has not yet been fully developed" and suggested further studies.

Although finding no support on its proposal from GAO, the committee did strike a respondent chord in the DOD Office of Inspector General whose representatives appeared to be competing with GAO in criticizing the Department of Defense. See for example testimony by the Deputy IG on DOD implementation of the Truth in Negotiations Act, Chapter XXII.

While accepting the use of accrual accounting for compensated personal absence, the DOD Deputy Inspector General expressed concern regarding cases "when the contractor accrues the costs but doesn't pay them until much later." The Deputy IG, frequent critic of DOD's procurement and financial practices, further stated:

> It often takes 18 months between the initial accrual of vacation costs and the contractors' actual payment for them. No one, to my knowledge, has analytically quantified the amounts of accrued vacation costs, but we can estimate that it approaches $2 billion annually. With large accrued vacation costs and the current high rates* of progress payments under fixed price contracts, it is possible that current progress payments to contractors could exceed their actual outlays of cash. This could also be true for cost-type contracts. *If this is true, the government could be providing some contractors with interest-free loans. The U.S. Treasury would be paying significant interest costs for what are, in effect, cash advances.* (Emphasis in original.)

The Deputy IG gave no clue as to how he arrived at his estimate that accrued vacation costs "approach $2 billion," neither did he explain his statement that "it often takes 18 months between the initial accrual of vacation costs and the contractors' actual payment for them." In this connection, even the GAO chief expressed the opinion that the period between the accrual and the actual payment "would seldom exceed 12 months."

The OIG representative let it be known that '[i]n June 1982, I proposed to the Under Secretary of Defense that he consider limiting contract payments for vacation expense to the amounts actually paid by contractors." He reported that the Under Secretary did not agree and that the correspondence between the OIG and other offices on this subject had been provided to the committee.

REASONABLENESS OF COMPENSATION FOR PERSONAL SERVICES

The entire subject of reasonableness, as discussed in Chapter XVI of this text, is a complex one. Costs are disallowed as unreasonable mainly where they are accrued or otherwise projected. When costs are actually incurred (paid), unless they are specifically designated as unallowable or limited by a provision in FAR 31.205, the government formerly carried a heavy burden in seeking to disallow them. The burden of proof was generally upon the government to establish that such costs were unreasonable.

As noted in several other analyses in this text, the DOD 1986 Authorization Act included considerable coverage inimical to firms doing business with the Department of Defense, such as adding a number of business expenses to the growing list of costs established as unallowable. One of the other provisions, implemented in FAR, overturned many years of consistent judicial precedent by mandating that when costs are challenged as to reasonableness, the burden of proof shall be upon the contractor to establish that such costs are reasonable.

The judicial precedent is fair and logical and certainly had not deterred the government from challenging the reasonableness of incurred costs and, at times, prevailing. Shifting the burden of proof to the contractor has been explained by most observers by the hostile congressional attitude toward companies providing goods and services for the nation's defense during this period of fraud, waste, and abuse allegations. Where the government representatives, without specific contractual, regulatory, or statutory support, assert a cost is unreasonable, the contractor is now required to marshall documentation and data to persuade these representatives to the contrary.

The change loomed as a major problem in view of DCAA auditors' proclivity to "question" costs submitted by contractors, and the undue pressure upon contracting officers to acquiesce in the auditors' "recommendations" as a result of DOD Directive 7640.2 and congressional criticisms. The problems were exacerbated when DOD transferred the authority for establishing final indirect cost rates and billing rates from the contracting officer to the contract auditor.

With respect to compensation for personal services, there have been significant differences in the government approach depending upon the size of the contractor's operations. For example, compensation of executives of major contractors have seldom been questioned in terms of reasonableness where the individual amounts were in the six- and seven-figure range. On the other hand, government representatives, especially contract auditors, have been known to devote considerable time and effort in challenging the reasonableness of modest compensation paid the executives or owners of small firms.

Challenging total compensation to individuals has presented problems to the government because of the absence of generally accepted levels with consideration to nature of business, geographical location, and a host of other factors. GAO has recently reported to the Congress, based on incomplete testing, that salaries of aerospace executives of companies heavily involved in defense work were generally higher than averages. GAO had been requested by Congressman Brooks to review the reasonableness of salaries paid in such firms. In accordance with its usual practice, GAO avoided original and positive conclusions, preferring to criticize the efforts of others. The congressional watchdog persuaded Mr. Brooks to pare down his request so that GAO would review compensation at only 12 aerospace companies and limit its findings to comparing such compensation with averages for similar positions surveyed by the Bureau of Labor Statistics (BLS) and the American Management Association (AMA).

GAO reported that the 12 contractors "on the average, paid executives and clerical, technical, and factory employees more than the average pay for similar positions surveyed by ... BLS and ... AMA. Professional salaries (mostly engineers) were slightly below BLS averages." GAO noted that there were wide pay variations but asserted that "employee earnings have increased faster for those contractors than in the general economy ..."

Eschewing substantive reporting in favor of its hindsight approach, GAO stated (NSIAD-85-1, October 12, 1984):

> These comparisons in themselves do not allow GAO to draw conclusions about whether the level of compensation is reasonable, but they do suggest a need for defense contracting officials to examine compensation carefully during negotiations, and a need to find a workable means of assessing the reasonableness of compensation—generally one of the largest cost items in contracts.

A more extensive study of executive compensation by the Department of Defense Inspector General is reviewed in Chapter XXVI of this text.

Prior to the recent statute and implementing regulation relating to burden of proof as to reasonableness, boards of contract appeals tended to reject government positions that compensation of company executives was unreasonable in amount unless the government could make a clear-cut case to the contrary. However, a review of some of the decisions reveals a most disturbing attitude by boards and courts with respect to compensation of owners in failing to recognize that contractor-owners of small companies are entitled to be reimbursed for work performed as well as for profit, i.e., return on investment and reward for risk. These decisions conflicted with, and were harsher than, the prevailing acquisition regulations. In the following pages we have reviewed a number of decisions involving disputes over compensation to small companies.

An early decision was handed down in ASBCA Nos. 12126, 12127 and 12128, *Vare Industries, Inc.,* 68-2 BCA par. 7120. The contractor's president had drawn an annual salary of $30,000 for a number of years and no objection thereto had been made by the government auditors or contracting officers in an environment where virtually all of the company's business was in government contracts. Beginning with the year the contractor's business fell dramatically, however, the government decided that the president's efforts on the government work were no longer worth $30,000 and reduced the amount to about one-half. The contracting officer, according to the board's decision, "felt that for the salary to be charged indirectly to these government contracts, there had to be a clear showing of direct benefit thereto by activities of the president." The board further described the contracting officer's position as follows:

> ... He said that he would take into account the overall value to the company of the president in arriving at a proper salary to be paid to him, but at the same time, he indicated that he would not consider what value the president might be to the company's commercial business ... In effect, he conceded that he was not viewing the president's salary as an overhead item in the usual sense but wanted a showing of direct benefits to the Government contracts, as would be the case with direct charges thereto.

The contractor argued that the president was both an engineer and executive and, during the period in question, was giving guidance to two engineers whose annual salaries were $21,000 and $18,000 respectively. The contractor also stated that the president was actively engaged in running the corporation during this time. The contractor's representative conceded, however (for reasons that are difficult for us to fathom), that "[i]n view of the company's then financial difficulties and declining sales, some reduction in the $30,000 salary claimed by the president would perhaps be in order, but that it should in no sense be the 50% reduction made by the government. . . . He felt that a cut of 10% to 15% from past years' salaries might be in order." We have, then, the contractor volunteering to accept a reduction of from $3,000 to $4,500, leaving a net claimed salary of between $27,000 and $25,500.

Based on reasoning not clearly explained, the board established a reasonable annual salary for the period involved at $25,500. It is difficult to say what reduction, if any, the board would have made to the $30,000 if the contractor had not volunteered a cut of 10% to 15%.

In *Lulejian and Associates,* ASBCA No. 20094, 76-1 BCA par. 11,880, the government argued that the salaries and bonuses were unreasonably high when compared to what comparable firms and the industry in general paid to persons in similar positions. As a basis for its disallowances, the government used the rates deemed acceptable by the ACO in the 1970 overhead negotiations and concurred in by the contractor, updated by addition of the same percentage of annual increases the contractor had granted these individuals in 1971 and 1972. Before reaching the issue of just how to fix reasonable amounts, the board addressed a point that is extremely important and must always be kept in mind by government contractors:

> Before we reach the issue of reasonableness of these salaries and bonuses, we need to consider respondent's argument that the FY 1970 overhead rate agreement established what was reasonable compensation for appellant's key personnel in that year and these rates should therefore be used "as a basis for determining the reasonableness of salaries and benefits in succeeding years realizing that circumstances and business conditions could change". Accordingly, respondent specifically claims that the FY 1971 and 1972 salaries and bonuses, computed on the basis of the rates included in the FY 1970 agreement, are reasonable. Inconsistent with this position, however, respondent does not consider itself bound by

this agreement with respect to allowing in FY 1971 and 1972 appellant's contributions to the profit sharing plan which it accepted in FY 1970.

This argument is without merit. With the exception of the matter of legal fees and the related travel expense, there is nothing in the ACO's letter of 16 August 1972 to indicate that the proposed agreement was intended to cover succeeding fiscal years. This was confirmed by the statement in appellant's letter of 28 September 1972, transmitting concurrence in the proposed agreement, that the agreed on settlement "applies only to FY 1970 and is not meant to establish a precedent". Being thus on notice of appellant's position, the Government carried out the terms of the agreement by reimbursing appellant fror its FY 1970 overhead costs at the agreed on rate. It cannot now place a different interpretation on this agreement. *Fairchild Industries, Inc. (formerly Fairchild Hiller Corporation)*, ASBCA Nos. 16302, 166413, 74-1 BCA par. 10,567. Hence, we agree with appellant that the FY 1970 overhead rate agreement is not binding with respect to determining the reasonableness of various cost items in FY 1971 and 1972.

We cannot be certain about which way the board would have ruled if the contractor had not written specifically that the 1970 agreement was "not meant to establish a precedent." However, it is clear from the above excerpt that the contractor's letter assured the board's rejection of the government's precedent argument.

Addressing the reasonableness issue, the board reviewed the government's contentions, including various studies used by its compensation experts, and found them wanting in several respects. First, it noted that ASPR 15-205.6(a)(2) required comparison with individuals in comparable positions "by other firms of the same size, in the same industry, or in the same geographic area." The board concluded that the government had little evidence of this kind relating to the years in dispute, most of its data involving prior and subsequent periods. The board also found faulty several other aspects of the government data. This finding pointed up the importance of contractors taking a hard look at any government data asserting the establishment of reasonable compensation levels.

The contracting officer had also disallowed portions of executive employees' fringe benefits, which he considered unreasonable. These benefits included contributions to a pension fund and a profit-sharing plan and group life insurance premiums. The government offered two arguments for its action. First, it alleged that the benefits paid to the key employees were unreasonably high when compared to the average fringe benefit cost of companies included in a Chamber of Commerce survey. The second argument held that the combined retirement benefits from the pension and profit plans were unreasonably high, and hence the costs of the plans were unreasonable.

As in the case of salaries and bonuses, the board found the government's contentions faulty and deficient in some respects and unpersuasive in others. As an illustration, it found that the government-introduced Chamber of Commerce study showed only industry averages, which the government sought to relate to Lulejian's data for executives. The board concluded that the government had produced no data showing fringe benefits available to executives in similar positions in comparable companies and therefore failed to prove its case.

FAR 31.205-6(b)(1), cited earlier in this chapter, incorporated the provisions of DAR and FPR that admonished that special consideration should be accorded in determining the reasonableness of compensation to "owners of closely held corporations, partners or sole proprietors, or members of their immediate families . . . ." This has proven to be a difficult area for small businesses, which are frequently subject to what we believe to be unfair treatment.

The appeal of *Paul E. McCollum, Sr.,* ASBCA No. 23269, 81-2 BCA par. 15,311, involved disputes over the number of hours devoted by Mr. McCollum and a fair hourly rate for his time. As to the latter, the auditor had allowed only $95 per day, less than $12 per hour for an eight hour day, which was the salary paid to a supervisor who had been replaced by the owner. The contractor testified that the going rate for an engineer doing the same kind of work under this contract was $50 per hour. The $25 per hour rate included in the termination proposal in dispute, according to the contractor's independent certified public accountant, represented Mr. McCollum's "annualized average income."

The board's position was even harsher than the auditor's:

Appellant-owner is a single proprietorship and, as such, derives salary from the profits of the business. The owner has not shown that he drew a regular salary or had set up any account from which to make regular withdrawals as a form of salary. The owner attempted to prove a rate of pay by comparison to the "going rate for an engineer doing that kind of work." We found no evidence to show that the owner had been paid a salary nor could we find any recorded liability for payment of the owner's salary. We were confronted with similar facts in *Norman M. Giller & Associates,* ASBCA No. 14696, 73-1 BCA par 10,016, later affirmed by the United States Court of Claims in *Norman M. Giller & Associates v. U.S.* (22 CCF par 80,240, 210 Ct.Cl. 80, 535 F.2d 37 (1976)). The contractor in that case was a sole proprietorship performing architectural services under a cost-plus-fixed-fee contract. Following expiration of the contract an audit was conducted of appellant's direct and indirect costs. Neither the owner nor his wife, who performed administrative work, drew any salary nor were accruals for such services entered on the contractor's books. In seeking recovery of amounts due following completion of the contract, the contractor claimed constructive salaries for the owner and his wife, with the amounts based on an ex post facto canvassing of salaries for comparable positions. There was neither allegation nor evidence of outstanding company indebtedness for salary. The Board held that the constructive compensation sought was unallowable ". . . as representing nothing actually paid nor any company obligation charged or incurred." The Court of Claims agreed, concluding that the contractors-proprietors ". . . considered themselves satisfactorily compensated for their administrative duties from the onset of their multi-year contract by the contract's fixed fee, and that the instant claim amounts to a contrived attempt to recover from defendant an imaginary cost."

Note the harshness of the board's views and those of the Court of Claims, which upheld similar views in the appeal of *Norman M. Giller & Associates.* It seems to us quite obvious that there is compensation for labor, in the form of salaries and wages, and there is compensation for capital invested, risks assumed, etc., in the form of profit. The boards and courts have few problems in accepting this basic principle when different persons perform the labor and invest the capital. However, if one and the same person does both, and if the contractor's financial condition prohibits concurrent compensation, the boards and courts seem to develop blind spots and become overly involved in theories of "constructive" salaries. We fail to see any logic or equity in demanding that a "contractor-owner" should provide the government gratis either his time and effort or his capital investment and risk.

Despite the unfavorable precedence, McCollum appealed the board's decision, which had limited his compensation to $11.88 per hour solely because this amount was not contested by the government. In *Paul E. McCollum, Sr. v. U.S.,* Cl. Ct. No. 346-82C (1984) [32 CCF par. 73,013], the court concluded McCollum's profits from his business over the past two years averaged only $4 per hour rather than the $25 average testified to by the independent accountant. With blatant non sequitur, the court said: "In the light of this evidence, the Board's award is generous. It is not precisely clear what [McCollum's] actual rate of compensation should be, but he was awarded a higher rate than he had earned in the period preceding this contract. [The government] has not challenged the Board's award, so it will not now be reduced. But there is no reason to increase it."

Seven Science Industries, ASBCA No. 23337, 80-2 BCA par. 14,518.

The contractor was much more successful in this case. Again we have a small company (although a corporation instead of a sole proprietorship), with a firm fixed-price contract terminated for default and, on the basis of a prior ruling (ASBCA No. 21079, 77-2 BCA par. 12,730), converted into a termination for the convenience of the government.

The corporation appeared to have only two full time employees, both of whom performed direct labor under this contract and whose compensation constituted the major portion of the termination settlement proposal. Mr. Linker was the president and owned 70% of the stock. Mr. Azar was a full-time employee and owned 20% of the stock. The remaining 10% was owned by a third individual.

Mr. Linker testified that he was owed a salary of $10,000 per year "based on oral agreement of the shareholders," and this testimony was corroborated by the contractor's independent accountant. Mr. Linker was never actually paid any salary, nor was any salary accrued for him on the contractor's accounting records nor shown on his federal income tax returns. The accountant testified that the shareholders had agreed that Mr. Linker would be paid when the company was in a position to do so. In explaining the absence of any documents reflecting any corporate indebtedness for Mr. Linker's salary, Mr. Linker explained that, since he was the majority shareholder, there was no point in executing the note. The accountant testified, however, that the accrued salaries for Linker and Azar were legal debts of the corporation.

Mr. Linker and the accountant testified that there was an oral agreement between the shareholders that Mr. Azar was to earn $17,000 per year during the performance of the contract but he was only paid half his salary during that period, with the remainder reflected as a loan to the company.

The above facts were noted in a report prepared by DCAA, which stated, however, that the salary levels for Linker and Azar were considered "reasonable considering the skills, education and experience of the two employees." Additionally, prior to the trial, there did not appear to be any evidence that the government was questioning the fact that the unpaid salaries to Linker and Azar represented corporate indebtedness. The board accordingly stated:

> On the record presented we find that the salaries of Messrs. Linker and Azar were established at annual rates of $18,000 and $17,000, respectively during the period between contract award and termination. We further find that none of Mr. Linker's salary was paid and that only half of Mr. Azar's salary was paid. We find that the unpaid salaries were owed to Messrs. Linker and Azar and thus constituted corporate debts of appellant. In making these findings we have taken into account the paucity of written documentation supporting the existence of corporate indebtedness, particularly in the case of Mr. Linker's salary. However, the sworn testimony of Mr. Linker as to the corporate indebtedness for his salary is uncontradicted and is corroborated by the testimony of appellant's independent accountant. The salary rates for Messrs. Linker and Azar, included in appellant's redesign proposal, are evidence that these individuals were salaried employees. Neither DCAA nor the contracting officer prior to the hearing in this appeal, questioned the status of Messrs. Linker and Azar as salaried employees. Finally, as indicated by the stipulation, there is no dispute over the reasonableness of the salary rates claimed for Messrs. Linker and Azar.

At the trial, however, the government contended that Linker and Azar worked on contingencies, and the amounts said to be salaries were therefore unallowable under ASPR (DAR) 15-205.7. The government would recognize only the $4,250 actually paid to Mr. Azar, about half of his salary for six months. The government further contended that Linker and Azar were "[a]ppellant's owners who were willing to work for an indefinite period of time without compensation so that appellant might survive and prosper."

Inasmuch as the government was not, at this point, addressing the number of hours that were devoted to the terminated contract, its contention appears to be a demand that private individuals provide services to the government without cost.

The government's contentions drew the board's attention to decisions handed down in *Norman M. Giller & Associates,* discussed above in connection with the *Paul E. McCollum, Sr.* appeal. The government also referred to other decisions, DOD and IRS regulations, etc., in a most tenacious effort to persuade the board to deny the allowance of any salaries except for the above-mentioned amount actually paid to Mr. Azar. The board's analysis is informative and instructive and reflects a much more understanding attitude than it displayed in the appeal of *Paul E. McCollum, Sr.* We believe this portion of the decision is of sufficient interest to cite verbatim:

Absence of a bona fide accrual or obligation to pay salaries of corporate officials was also found in *Space Dynamics Corporation,* ASBCA No. 19118, 78-1 BCA par. 12,885, where salaries shown as having been accrued on earlier financial statements remained unpaid and were not carried forward to later statements. The absence of the carry-forward was not explained. The corporate books were prepared by the contractor's secretary-treasurer, not an independent accountant.

ASPR 15-201.1 provides that to be allowable the cost must be "incurred or to be incurred." We have carefully scrutinized the evidence to ascertain whether appellant incurred a bona fide indebtedness for Mr. Linker's salary and the unpaid portion of Mr. Azar's salary. As distinguished from *Giller* and *Space Dynamics,* Linker and Azar constituted appellant's productive labor force; they were not merely administrative officers of a sort, who might reasonably be expected to be compensated out of corporate profits. We note that in *Space Dynamics, supra,* amounts were allowed for the direct labor efforts of the two corporate officers whose administrative salaries were disallowed. Appellant here was a closely held corporation whose management kept poor records and relied on oral understandings on matters which should ordinarily have been reflected in writing. Nevertheless we are persuaded by the sworn testimony of Mr. Linker and the accountant that a bona fide indebtedness for the unpaid Linker and Azar salaries has been established. See *C&H Construction Co.,* ASBCA No. 22193, 79-2 BCA par. 13,950; *Fred Schwartz,* ASBCA No. 23183, 80-1 BCA par. 14,272. The amounts of such salaries recoverable under the Termination for Convenience clause are determinable as of the time of the termination. The incurrence of appellant's indebtedness for those salaries was not contingent upon future events and the direct labor amounts are not unallowable contingencies.

The Government contends in the alternative that the unpaid Linker and Azar salaries should not be allowed under a provision of ASPR (DAR) 15-205.6(a)(i) which provides:

"Except as otherwise specifically provided in this 15-205.6, such costs are allowable to the extent that the total compensation of individual employees is reasonable for the services rendered and they are not in excess of those costs which are allowable by the Internal Revenue Code and regulations thereunder."

ASPR (DAR) 15-205.6(a)(i) deals generally with the allowability of compensation for personal services. In the case of Linker's salary the Government cites Section 267 of the Internal Revenue Code (26 U.S.C.A. par 267), which *inter alia,* prohibits deductions from corporate income of expenses, otherwise deductible, where the expense is owed to a person owning more than 50% of the outstanding stock and the expense is unpaid $2\frac{1}{2}$ months after the close of the corporation's taxable year. One might question the propriety of appellant's failure to show Mr. Linker's salary on its tax return. However, there was clearly no income from which amounts owed to Linker could be paid or deducted. ASPR (DAR) 15-205.6(a)(i) generally allows reasonable compensation for services rendered by employees of the contractor. Linker's salary was so treated by the DCAA auditor who questioned only the number of hours claimed, not the existence of an owed salary. As concluded in our earlier decision the Government was responsible for the deterioration of appellant's financial condition and ultimate failure. Under these circumstances we cannot find that appellant's inability to pay Linker's salary within $2\frac{1}{2}$ months of the close of the taxable year operates as a bar to allowability of the cost.

In the case of Azar's salary the Government cites Treasury Regulation 1.461-1(a)(2) (26 C.F.R. § 1.461-1(a)(2) (1970) which provides:

"Under an accrual of accounting, an expense is deductible for the taxable year in which all the events have occurred which determine the fact of the liability and the amount thereof can be determined with reasonable accuracy."

The "all events" test is explained in *Putoma Corp. v. Commissioner of Internal Revenue*, 601 F.2d 734 (5th Cir. 1979). Essentially it means that an expense cannot properly be accrued if it is contingent. We have concluded above that Mr. Azar's salary was not contingent. Consequently, the Treasury regulation cited by the Government is inapplicable.

Space Dynamics Corporation, ASBCA No. 19118, 78-1 BCA par. 12,885

The next case we shall be discussing in this analysis of compensation to owners of small, closely held corporations, partnerships, and sole proprietorships involved a complex appeal including a prior decision in which a default termination was also converted into one for the convenience of the government, and the above-captioned decision, which encompassed both termination and equitable adjustment claims. Our analysis, however, is limited to the subject of compensation.

The contractor was a small business corporation wholly owned by three shareholders: Dr. Maden L. Ghai owned about 80 percent; Delores Yackle, Dr. Ghai's wife, owned 10 percent; and the balance was owned by a shareholder who was not apparently actively involved in the day-to-day activities of the business as an officer. Dr. Ghai was the president of the corporation and its chief engineer, holding four advanced degrees and enjoying an excellent reputation. Ms. Yackle was described in the decision as the secretary/treasurer and also acted as a contracting officer for SDC. In addition, she did most of the corporation's bookkeeping and accounting.

The story that appears to emerge from the text of the decision is another instance of a small company with significant efforts expended by the officer-principal shareholders, a company in financial difficulties caused at least in part by government actions, with the officer-principal shareholders unable to draw their authorized salaries because of the financial difficulties. Add to this mix inappropriate accounting practices and a hardline government attitude, and the result is another example of the government's denying appropriate reimbursement by resorting to technicalities.

The board was apparently furnished evidence of corporate resolutions for salaries to be paid to Dr. Ghai and Ms. Yackle during the years involved. Their salaries were allocated among the direct labor, overhead, and general and administrative expense categories. The contractor's accounting records, however, as described in the decision, were confusing. The decision presented annual summaries of salaries for Dr. Ghai and Ms. Yackle, with columns for "gross," "paid," "accrued," and "not recorded." Reviewing the years 1967-1974 did not reveal a consistent pattern. The reader might assume that the "gross" column represents the salaries authorized. There were money amounts in this column for all of the years. Explanations for the other three columns were not given. In some years, portions of the salaries were paid; in others, there were no payments. Accruals were shown for some years but not for others. And even the "not recorded" column failed to produce balancing figures for some of the years.

The board seemed to have given up on searching for an equitable answer amidst this confusion. The pertinent portions of its ruling on the compensation to the two officers are quoted below:

> The provisions of the Changes clause of the contract allow an equitable adjustment for any increased costs incurred in connection with performance of changed work.

> In determining the costs appellant incurred in connection with performance of changed work we examine the expense claimed for officers' salaries. The appellant corporation exhibits a long-standing custom of neither paying nor accruing significant portions of its officers' salaries. (See, e.g., FYs 1964, 1965, 1966 and 1967 which was the first year of performance of the instant contracts.) We therefore do not find the salaries authorized by corporate resolution to be an accurate representation of the amounts which the appellant corporation was in fact obligated to pay.

> Some of the salaries which were recorded on individual ledgers during a fiscal year were not carried forward in the end-of-year financial statements or balance sheets. (See, e.g., 1967, 1969 during which years the instant contracts were performed, where significant amounts of $24,450 and $30,900 were not recorded.) We therefore do not find that the salaries represented on individual ledger sheets represent accurately the amounts which the appellant corporation was obligated to pay.

> Finally, the salaries recorded as "accrued" on certain end-of-year financial statements, i.e. 1967 and 1968, were not carried forward on the 1969 financial statements, which was the last year of performance under the instant contracts. The absence of any carryforward is not explained by any corresponding entry, such as transfer to stockholders' equity, officers' loans, accounts payable, or any other account. There is indeed no explanation whatever for the absence of such carryforward, and there is no reserve fund, contingency fund, or other indicia of an outstanding obligation as of the end of FY 1969, some eight and one half years ago. The absence of such carryforward, without explanation or corresponding entry, cannot be found to be in accord with generally accepted accounting principles unless interpreted to mean the absence of an outstanding obligation on the part of the corporate appellant to pay any salaries over and above those paid contemporaneously.

> We therefore find, based on the particular facts presented here, that the "accrual" of officers' salaries, to the extent such accruals appear on

appellant's financial statements for FYs 1967 and 1968, does not represent a bona fide obligation to pay the amounts stated as "accrued". We do not here decide the effect of an accrual of officers' salaries during years of contract performance in accordance with accepted accounting principles, which accrual is subsequently extinguished also in accord with accepted accounting principles. We conclude that in this appeal, the only costs incurred by appellant which can be considered in rendering an equitable adjustment are the amounts of salaries actually paid, not those "accrued".

In view of our finding above, we need not discuss here the Government's further contention that the "accrued" salaries constitute an unallowable cost under the provisions of ASPR 15-205.6.

We are cognizant of appellant's contention that the only reason the corporate officers' salaries were in fact not paid was because of wrongful Government action causing the increase of expenses without corresponding revenues. We need not discuss this contention in detail here. As the basis for our finding we do not concentrate on the dichotomy between actually "paid" and "nonpaid" or accrued salaries and hence the proffered explanation for appellant's failure actually to pay the salaries is of no import to our decision. We concentrate instead on the absence of a bona fide accrual of obligation to pay salaries at any time, present or future. We have found on the particular facts herein that the appellant corporation has not established the incurrence of a bona fide accrual or of an obligation to pay these salaries sufficient to warrant our inclusion of these items as a cost incurred.

Given the absence of such a bona fide accrual or obligation to pay the salaries, our disallowance of the claimed costs thereof is consistent with the principle espoused in *Norman M. Giller & Associates,* ASBCA No. 14696, 73-1 BCA par. 10,016; 210 Ct.Cl. 80, 535 F.2d 37 (1976) in connection with constructive or "imaginary" salaries (under admittedly different factual circumstances and involving a cost-plus contract).

Accordingly, in this case the amounts of salaries which were actually paid during FYs 1967, 1968, should be computed with respect to entries of direct labor, overhead and G&A. Further, the statement of expenses incurred in connection with the Tee contracts' changes in issue here should be revised to include only those portions of the Ghai and Yackle salaries which we find were actually paid and properly included.

The decision proved too much for one of the administrative judges who dissented in respect of the majority's treatment of accrued salaries in connection with the equitable adjustment computation:

The majority refuses to allow appellant to recover for the accrued salaries of appellant's president and secretary-treasurer. These accrued wages are shown in appellant's books and records for fiscal years 1967 and 1968. The wages are a bona fide accrued expense of the corporation and are not challenged on the basis of reasonableness or allocability. Moreover, in computing an equitable adjustment as part of the termination claim, the contracting officer recognized that the accrued wages of these individuals were an allowable cost to be included in calculating amounts due and owing appellant. We should do likewise in our computation of the equitable adjustments. By failing to allow recovery for the accrued wages, the majority has compensated appellant for the time spent on the changed work by its president and secretary-treasurer, at an hourly rate below that of the corporation's nonsupervisory personnel. The majority has not shown that this result is supported by the contract or applicable regulations.

Burt Associates, Inc., ASBCA No. 25884, 82-1 BCA par. 15,764

Small business concerns comprise the large majority of companies doing business with the government even though, in terms of dollars, the preponderance of contracts are awarded to the larger firms. As indicated earlier, small business firms encounter many problems, such as appropriate reimbursement for their owners or officers, and such firms generally cannot afford the expertise available to major contractors. For this reason, we have devoted considerable attention to the disputes involving compensation for personal services of small, closely held corporations, partnerships, and sole proprietorships.

The contractor was a small research and consultant firm with a substantial portion of its business consisting of government CPFF contracts. Dr. M.R. Burt, president of the corporation, and his wife, J.L. Burt, each owned 50% of the stock and with Mr. A.B. Eddy constituted the three-member board of directors. Dr. B. Sowder was the corporate vice president in the year under dispute.

Testimony demonstrated that the board of directors met during late June or July of each year (fiscal year ended June 30) to review the performance of the company, its officers, and employees, to review projections for the following year, and to approve salary increases and bonuses. For the year in question (1977), the salary for Dr. Burt was $53,000, the maximum bonus voted for him was $20,000, and the actual bonus received totaled $18,000, of which $10,000 was charged to overhead and the balance was not charged against government contracts. Dr. Sower's salary was $32,860, the maximum bonus voted was $3,000, of which $2,000 was paid and charged to overhead. The revenue for that year aggregated $409,000, which yielded a net profit of $4,000.

According to the decision, the contractor's criteria for determining what bonus if any was to be paid to each officer were: (1) whether or not the company had a good year from a profit standpoint, (2) whether the efforts of the individual officers had been instrumental in achieving the successful results, and (3) whether the company's overhead structure could absorb bonus payments while remaining competitive. The amounts depended on the judgment of the board.

The $12,000 in bonuses charged to overhead were disallowed by the government, which alleged they were unreasonable, represented a distribution of profits, were not paid or accrued pursuant to an established plan followed so consistently as to imply, in effect, an agreement to make such payments. FPR 1-15.205-6 was cited in support of the disallowance action.

On the issue of the reasonableness of the total compensation, Burt Associates presented a publication by Dietrich Associates, Inc., titled "Executive Compensation Analysis of Professional Service Firms," which established that, for firms doing the volume of business experienced by the contractor, the total compensation and the bonuses were within the range generally with regard to executives owning 50% of their companies' stock.

The government then questioned "the necessity of awarding incentive bonuses to owners of closely held corporations since the owners' self interest in making the corporation profitable is more than adequate incentive for superior performance. Moreover, 'owners should not be allowed to use incentive bonuses as a guise for channelling profits into their own pockets.' " The government further alleged that the bonuses were not paid in good faith because they were paid as a way to recover part of the overhead payments made at a provisional rate that was higher than the actual rate and that the bonuses were in reality a distribution of profits, which is not allowable as an indirect cost.

The government's arguments closely parallel those offered in the other disputes discussed earlier and appeared to reflect a harsh and discriminatory attitude toward owners of small closely held corporations, partners, and sole proprietors. Compensation that would go unchallenged in the case of larger corporations is frequently questioned when paid by the category of organizations under discussion. The argument that there is no "necessity" for awarding bonuses to owners of closely held corporations since the owners' self interest in making their corporation profitable is more than adequate incentive for superior performance seems particularly illogical and borders on the unconscionable. Once the reasonableness of the compensation is established, we would think no distinction should be made by the type of organization making the payment. As we have discussed in analyses of other disputes in this area, the government consistently confuses compensation for work performed and entitlement for capital employed and risk in the form of profit.

The board gave short shrift to this government argument, noting that "the applicable regulations neither prohibit or condemn the payment of bonuses to owner-officers of corporations and, in fact, the payment of bonuses to such individuals appears to be a common practice." This view was supported by Executive Compensation Analysis cited earlier. The board also admonished the government that "the 'necessity' for paying a bonus to spur incentive is not the test for allowability of bonus payments."

The government then argued that an analysis of several years revealed payment of dividends in 1975 but not thereafter as indicative that the bonuses were, in reality, a distribution of profits. This argument, too, was not persuasive to the board, which noted that the year 1975 was the most profitable of the years in the analysis and both dividends and bonuses were paid in that year. On the other hand, in other years within this period, neither dividends nor bonuses were paid. The board observed:

> ... On this bare record we are unwilling to conclude that a failure to declare dividends, which may be attributable to many reasons in addition to unprofitability, is indicative that a bonus payment in a year that dividends are not paid is a distribution of profits. More than mere surmise or speculation is required to sustain such a conclusion.

A review of the significant contributions made by Dr. Burt and Dr. Sowder was totally persuasive of the reasonableness of their compensation and the board turned to the remaining government argument that bonus payments "were 'sporadic' and thus were not followed so consistently as to imply, in effect, an agreement to make payments." This argument, too, was rejected. The board observed that, in the six years in which the bonus plan was in effect, the contractor made bonus payments in four of those years while in the other two years bonuses were authorized but not paid because the contractor's plan was dependent upon, among other things, contingencies or profit realization.

In terms of lessons learned, it is essential that the corporation adopt a plan or agreement under which bonuses would be paid and follow such plan. Where reasonableness of the compensation is challenged, contractors should avail themselves of studies of compensation structure and levels in the same or similar industrial category. Efforts by the government to obtain free services by the wholly improper theory that profits should suffice as compensation for corporate owner-officers, partners, and sole proprietors should be strongly contested.

Walber Construction Company, Inc., HUD BCA No. 80-445-C2, 83-2 BCA par. 16,885

This appeal involved several disputes incident to a contract termination for the convenience of the government, but this analysis will focus on the claim for the time spent on the contract by the "owner-operator," Pauline Walber. This portion of the decision is quoted below and our observations follow.

> . . . Compensation for personal services to sole proprietors such as Pauline Walber are only allowable if such compensation is normally made in the course of business by either a salary, draw, or deferred compensation for actual personal services and is not a distribution of profits. FPR 1-15.205(a)(2). While we do not doubt that Pauline Walber invested her personal time in preparing for work on the contract prior to its termination, because she is recompensated solely out of profits and pays herself no salary, takes no draw, and allocates herself no deferred compensation apart from profits, her time spent on the contract is not an allowable cost. *Walber Construction Co., supra;* FPR 1-15.205(a)(2).

The board's view appears to unreasonably stretch an ultra legalistic interpretation to deny the contractor compensation for the fruits of her labor.

Elementary economic and business principles clearly distinguish between compensation for efforts expended as labor on the one hand and a fair profit for return on capital, risk, and other factors on the other. Given this well recognized distinction, given the board's recognition of the proprietor's labor ("we do not doubt that Pauline Walber invested her personal time . . ."), and given that the United States is a free capitalist economy that recognizes profit, it would appear that the board strained to establish a technicality to deny this portion of the claim.

The FPR provision cited by the board does not assert that compensation for a sole proprietor is unallowable. Indeed, the regulation does not even demand a salary payment or drawing as prerequisite to the allowability of compensation to a sole proprietor. FPR does caution that there are "certain conditions (which) give rise to the need for special consideration and possible limitation as to allowability for contract cost purposes where amounts appear excessive."

One of the conditions referred to in FPR is compensation to sole proprietors. We can understand that, in these and other illustrations cited in that section, as the regulation suggests, "[d]etermination should be made that such compensation is reasonable for the actual personal services rendered rather than a distribution of profits." We cannot understand the flat disallowance of the entire salary charge in the absence of any stated question as to its reasonableness.

The FPR provisions were closely similar to those in DAR and the same reasoning was adopted in FAR 31.205-6(b)(1), which further states: "Compensation in lieu of salary for services rendered by partners and sole proprietors will be allowed to the extent that it is reasonable and does not constitute a distribution of profits." Inasmuch as the reasonableness of Pauline Walber's claim for compensation was not challenged and the board conceded she "invested her personal time," we cannot equate the claim with a distribution of profits.

The ruling also took comfort and accepted as a precedent a prior decision that involved the same contractor with similar disputes concerning a convenience termination of another contract (*Walber Construction Co.,* HUD BCA No. 79-421-C40, July 1, 1983, 83-2 BCA 16,641). In this ruling, the same administrative judges used somewhat different language and waffled a bit, but ultimately came to the same conclusion.

> Walber requested $1,000.00 for time she spent "involved with the contract." Walber is compensated solely out of profits and is paid no salary or other form of compensation. On a termination claim, a contractor is entitled only to the unreimbursed *costs* of performance plus a reasonable profit on those incurred costs. 41 C.F.R. § 1-8.703(e). If a contractor incurs no costs, it cannot recover profit on those costs. *Shin Enterprises, Inc.,* ASBCA No. 16542, 72-1 BCA ¶ 9391. Appellant incurred no costs for Walber's time because Walber was not compensated for the time she spent on the contract preparations. While compensation to sole proprietors may be a recoverable cost under certain limited circumstances, the compensation must be for actual personal services rendered rather than a distribution of profits. 41 C.F.R. § 1-15.205-6(2)(i) and (3); 41 C.F.R. § 1-15.403-7(c). In the absence of a specific provision in the contract, "constructive" compensation of an unsalaried proprietor is not allowed. *Norman M. Giller & Associates v. United States,* 210 Ct.Cl. 80, 535 F.2d 37 (1976).

We believe it is completely unrealistic to argue that a proprietor "is compensated solely out of profits" in light of the government's consistent assertions that it seeks to pay a fair and reasonable price for the goods and services it purchases. Such price, in our judgment, must reimburse a contractor for the costs of performance, regardless of whether performance was by a sole proprietor, partner, corporation officer, or employee, plus a profit or fee.

H&H Reforestation, AGBCA No. 84-311-3, 85-3 BCA par. 18,255

One of the issues involved was the claim for labor performed by the company's two partners. Although the decision contains no indication that the amounts were considered unreasonable, the claim was denied because the salaries were not actually paid to the partners.

The board found that the two partners "were not paid a salary, but instead worked on a percentage basis . . . . No salary was paid during performance of the contract and it was not until after its termination did Appellant decide to claim an amount for salaries or wages of these two partners."

The board conceded that the FPR cost principles governing this contract (substantially incorporated into FAR 31.205-6(b)(1)) provide that "(c)ompensation in lieu of salary for services rendered by partners . . . will be allowed to the extent that it is reasonable and does not constitute a distribution of profits." The board concluded, however, that "it appears to be a distribution of profits in this case." The board further stated:

> Moreover, cases interpreting and applying this language do not allow it absent either actual payment or an accrual or a *bona fide* obligation to pay. *Norman M. Giller & Associates v. United States* [22 CCF ¶ 80,290], 210 Ct.Cl. 80, 535 F.2d 37 (1976); *Space Dynamics Corp.,* ASBCA No. 19118, 78-1 BCA ¶ 12,885. The contract here in question reimburses for costs actually incurred, i.e., costs expensed or paid.

> There is no evidence introduced of the partnership's business records which showed an intention to pay these two partners a salary for their work on this contract, i.e., no accrual was proven . . . Rather, the testimony [of one of the partners] is clear that had the contract been completed, [the partners] would have received as their compensation a proportionate share of the profits achieved . . . . [cited cases omitted].

Hoyer Construction Company, Inc., ASBCA No. 31241, 86-1 BCA par. 18,619

A more recent ruling reveals that the ASBCA position in this area remains unchanged. Although other issues were also involved in this dispute, our review focuses on the compensation to the "principals" of the company.

The principals were the construction manager, project manager, and secretary, and the contractor was apparently unable to provide auditable support for the hours or the hourly rates claimed for the work of these individuals on the modification in dispute. In the unilateral determination, the contracting officer allowed a lesser amount than claimed, based on some estimates for time spent and hourly rates. The manner in which the contracting officer arrived at these estimates is not explained in the decision of the board. The contracting officer's determination also included allowances of 15% for overhead and 10% for profit.

The salient portion of the decision on the subject under review is quoted below:

> We have found that the three aforementioned individuals are the principals in the firm and that they do not draw a salary but share in the profit or loss. Under appellant's accounting system the "compensation"

for the three individuals would be covered under the overhead and profit figures, and not as a separate hourly wage. *J.M.T. Machine Company, Inc.,* ASBCA Nos. 23928, 24298, 24536, 85-1 BCA 17,820. *Spruill Realty/Construction Company,* ASBCA No. 28650, 85-3 BCA 18,395 30 August 1985. Accordingly, the claim for a separate hourly wage for the construction manager, project manager and secretary is denied.

Where the contracting officer had made some allowances for the compensation of these individuals, the board ruled that, since the proceedings before it are *de novo,* it could and did set aside such allowances. This is another illustration where the ASBCA has demonstrated that, with regard to compensation to owners of closely held corporations, partners and sole proprietors, it takes a more severe and punitive approach than contracting officers and even DCAA auditiors.

In the *J.M.T. Machine Co., Inc.* appeal, referred to in the above quote, the contractor's claim for an equitable adjustment included compensation for the firm's engineer who, it was established, devoted considerable time to the solution of the problems created by the government's defective specifications. This individual was also a corporate officer whose salary, under J.M.T.'s accounting classification, was included in a category analagous to G&A expenses. The DCAA auditor, upheld by the contracting officer, refused to accept the contractor's reclassification of this individual's time spent on the contract to direct engineering labor. The board, in accordance with the perverse reasoning it applies for closely held corporations, upheld the government on the grounds that the individual continued to perform his duties as the corporate officer. "Nobody was hired to replace him, he was not paid more for the work on [the contract], and his salary did not increase the cost to J.M.T. of producing the [contract item].

The important cost accounting point of charging costs directly where they can be related to specific cost objectives was of no concern to the auditor, contracting officer, or the board. The ASBCA, as it does frequently, found comfort and support in a previous decision of its own (*Kurz & Root Company, Inc.,* ASBCA Nos. 11436, 11698, 68-1 BCA par. 6916). In that instance the board refused to accept as a direct charge, the time devoted by the chief engineer specifically to a contract. "We are not here concerned," the board curiously asserted, "with an exercise in costing." An odd statement indeed, it occurred to us. The board's reasoning was that the chief engineer's salary remained the same despite his work relating to the government's defective specifications, and hence the overall cost to the contract did not increase. Although we are still not persuaded that accounting matters in disputes can be severed from other controversies and assigned to an "accounting court," as some have suggested, statements by the ASBCA that it is not "concerned with an exercise in costing," make us wonder whether such a court might merit some consideration.

In *Spruill, supra,* the contractor's claim for increased costs arising from a contract change order included an amount for the time spent by the owner, a sole proprietor, based on a very low rate of $13.25 per hour, computed by dividing the owner's withdrawals for the year by 2,080 hours (52 weeks × 40 hours per week). But even this modest amount ($2,213) was denied by the board. The basis for this punitive action was that the contractor "has shown no payment of salary or other compensation to the owner . . ." In the board's consistent position in this area, the allowance of overhead and profit was somehow sufficient to include all ownership costs plus the direct efforts of the owner.

As precedent follows upon precedent, it is unfortunately clear that recognition of compensation to owners of closely held corporations, partners and sole proprietors is extremely difficult to obtain. In the absence of formal arrangements establishing that such salaries were paid, reimbursement is just about impossible. No matter how grievous and obvious the inequity, the ASBCA falls back on its previous, unjust decisions for precedence.

Regardless of how one may view the legality and equity of judicial rulings in this area, there appears to be no basis for expecting any significant changes for the future. Accordingly, the important point is to "light a candle rather than curse the darkness," i.e., understand the thinking of government contracting and audit officials, and appeals boards and courts, with respect to compensation of sole proprietors, partners, and officers of small closely held corporations, and take action to optimize the opportunities of achieving fair and reasonable recoveries.

Focusing first on efforts expended by such owners directly on contract performance, it must be recognized that, when salaries or any portions of such salaries are charged directly to contracts, such charges are frequently suspect. This reaction is based, among other things, on the frequent absence of adequate supporting documentation. Whereas contractor employees whose time is charged directly must maintain time cards or other records, and such records are required to contain some indication of supervisory approval, owners and officers frequently maintain no time records or their records are not subject to the normal kind of internal controls. Recognizing that direct labor charges may be viewed with some suspicion, owners and officers should exercise care to maintain careful, contemporaneous records of time spent directly on government contracts. While these officials should not be expected to have their time records reviewed and approved by subordinate employees, they should try to make their time records as far as practicable a part of the total company time keeping process, related to specific government contract operations.

Where the number of hours devoted directly to contract performance can be reasonably supported, contractors must then establish the appropriate hourly rate. The first step is to establish, through corporate minutes or other company documents, the salaries of the owners or corporate officers. Many studies and other data are available through trade associations and other sources which compile average salary structures by industry, further broken down by company size in terms of sales volume, etc. However, such averages may not apply in every instance. For example, some owners and officials devote considerably more time to the business than others and have special skills that have been recognized by the government in selecting the contractor for award. In these instances, a well documented paper can support salary structures at higher levels than those that obtain in similar companies in the same industry.

It is essential that such data be accumulated and presented to contract auditors, contracting officers and, where disputes occur, appeals boards and courts for, otherwise, government representatives may assign arbitrary low salary levels, which the contractor may have difficulties in overturning.

As indicated in most of the cases discussed in this analysis, small businesses with modest or inadequate financial means face major problems not encountered by the major, well financed contractors. One of the most difficult circumstances is that of a sole proprietor, partner, or corporate official of a small business who expends considerable time on direct contract performance and, in addition, substantial efforts on overall company management, but whose struggling company lacks the money to pay his or her salary in the same manner it is required to meet the regular employee payroll. Although there is probably no practice that will assure against government challenge based on the distorted thinking that somehow whatever small profit can be made from the contract should cover both the personal labor and compensation for use of capital and risk taking, some methods have been much more successful than others.

Ideally, the sole proprietor, partner, or corporate officer should draw the established salary currently. Where the company is in dire need of funds, which are not reasonably available from outside sources, the owner or officer may make a loan to the company. Such loans should be executed under formal business procedures and should be evidenced by appropriate documentation of indebtedness. It is preferable by far that the notes be interest-bearing although the interest rates may be lower than those that would be paid to commercial banks or other sources. This text does not offer suggestions for actions of questionable propriety to be taken to obtain reimbursement of costs to which a contractor is not fully entitled. The drawing of a reasonable salary, charging applicable portions directly to contracts, and making loans to companies, in our judgment, represent appropriate transactions and sound business practice. It should be noted, however, that this suggested practice must be characterized by realism. If a sole proprietor (or partner or officer of a closely held corporation) is paid regularly and in the normal course of business events and makes periodic interest-bearing loans to the company, which loans are duly recorded on the company's records, but the company makes no payment for interest or principal over the years, questions may still be raised.

To the above suggestions, we should add a recommendation, which appears obvious to most and yet has been ignored in some instances. Salaries received by corporate officers must, of course, be reported as such for federal income tax purposes.

Where the process of owners, partners, and corporate officers receiving their stipulated salaries and loaning portions back to the companies may not be feasible, such salaries may of course be accrued. Normal accruals represent business indebtedness of a company and the related costs should be acceptable. However, care should be taken to assure that the transactions are recorded in accordance with generally accepted accounting principles. Furthermore, some evidence is needed that such accruals will be extinguished.

These problems are complex and are made much more difficult because they are encountered by small businesses, which sometimes do not have the requisite expertise relating to government contracting and accounting and business practices. In these instances, it would certainly appear prudent for such companies to engage consultants who do have expertise in these matters. Although the cost of an outside consultant may in and of itself pose a financial difficulty to the company, the alternative may be the failure to recover significant amounts to which the contractor is entitled.

Chapter XIX

Government Cost Principles for Special Contracts and Grants

CLASSIFICATION OF GOVERNMENT COST PRINCIPLES

In terms of dollar volume, the preponderance of government transactions involving prices where costs are a factor is found in negotiated supply, service, experimental, developmental, and research contracts with commercial organizations. Accordingly, the major portion of this text is focused on such contracts. However, the government acquires other goods and services from different categories of organizations. This chapter reviews the cost principles for special contracts and grants and with entities other than commercial organizations as included in the sections of the FAR cited below. Although a number of differences will be noted, many of the fundamentals are identical or similar. A thorough grasp of the other parts of this text, especially Chapters IX through XVIII, will facilitate the understanding of the special contracts and grants discussed in this chapter.

Cost Principles for Educational Institutions, Office of Management and Budget (OMB) Circular No. A-21; FAR 31.104, Subpart 31.3.

Cost Principles for Construction and Architect-Engineer Contracts, FAR 31.105.

Cost Principles for Facilities Contracts, FAR 31.106.

Cost Principles for Contracts with State and Local Governments, OMB Circular No. A-87; FAR 31.107, Subpart 31.6.

Cost Principles for Nonprofit Organizations, OMB Circular No. A-122; FAR 31.108, Subpart 31.7.

SEQUENCE OF DISCUSSION

The numerical order of the various cost principles in FAR Part 31 appears to be based more on historical development than a considered design. To facilitate the understanding of the government cost principles for special contracts and grants, we have selected what we believe to be a more logical sequence. To continue with cost principles for commercial organizations, we shall discuss Construction and Architect-Engineer Contracts; Contracts for Industrial Facilities; and Grants, Contracts and Other Agreements with Nonprofit Organizations. We shall then proceed to awards to Educational Institutions and, finally, to State and Local Governments.

CONSTRUCTION AND ARCHITECT-ENGINEER CONTRACTS—FAR 31.105

The provisions of FAR 31.105 are set forth in Chapter XVI of this text.

The term "construction" relates to real property and, as set forth in FAR 36.102, "does not include the manufacture, production, furnishing, construction, alteration, repair, processing, or assembling of vessels, aircraft, or other kinds of personal property." Most of the cost principles applicable to supply and service contracts, contained in FAR Subpart 31.2, are applicable here as well. There are, however, a number of major differences, and they generate problems when audits are performed by contract auditors whose prior experience focused on production or R&D work. Some of the problems also surfaced in cost accounting standards developed by a Board and staff that had little exposure to construction activities. Special factors affecting the allowability of costs under construction and A-E contracts are described in FAR 31.105(d).

Jobsite Costs

In one sense, cost accounting for construction contracts is less complex than for production and R&D contracts. Usually, most of the costs are incurred at a location at which only a single contract is performed. In these instances, all of the costs incurred at that location are direct contract costs. This eliminates the complex cost accounting problems involved in allocating manufacturing, engineering, and other costs incurred at a factory in which a number of production or R&D contracts are being performed.

Construction Plant and Equipment Costs

Although incurred at the jobsite, depreciation of construction plant and equipment is treated separately in FAR 31.105(d)(2) because this cost is significant and the actual amount applicable to individual government contracts is impracticable to determine. As has been pointed out, these difficulties are compounded by the problem of allocating accurately the cost of overhaul or repairs applicable to an individual contract since the period of incidence of such cost may not correspond with the period of benefit derived therefrom. To illustrate, very costly construction equipment owned by the contractor may require extensive repairs during the life of a government contract. Assuming the equipment had a life of ten years, charging the total amount to the government during a one-year contract period would not be appropriate. On the other hand, major and expensive equipment repairs may be made prior or subsequent to the government contract period. These costs may substantially exceed an annual depreciation charge. In this instance, normal depreciation accounting would be inequitable to the contractor.

As provided in FAR 31.105(d)(2)(i), when actual cost data for both ownership and operating costs of construction equipment cannot be determined, the contract may specify a schedule of predetermined rates. FAR cites, as an example of a predetermined schedule of construction equipment use rates, the Construction Equipment Ownership and Operating Expense Schedule, published by the U.S. Army Corps of Engineers.

Central (Home) or Branch Office Expenses

Construction contract cost principles contained in DAR and FPR, especially as implemented by DCAA and other contract auditors, reflected the illogical concept that virtually the total costs incurred on such contracts were generated at the jobsite, and the minor or incidental contributions of the contractor's home or branch office were compensated for in the fee or profit. The operation of a major construction contractor's home office is a very costly one, covering all normal management, accounting, financial, legal, engineering, and many other expenses. It is unrealistic and inequitable, in our judgment, to suggest that such costs should not be allocated to *all* of the contractor's work, including government contracts. Additionally, there is no indication in CAS 403, Allocation of Home Office Expenses to Segments, or CAS 410, Allocation of Business Unit General and Administrative Expenses to Final Cost Objectives, that construction and A-E contracts should not bear their full pro rata share of central and branch office expenses.

The arguments advanced by some government representatives that a major construction project is entirely self-sufficient at a jobsite and receives no benefit from the home office accords no consideration to the years of experience and technical know-how that permits certain construction companies to undertake the major projects. We see no difference between the allocation of home office expenses under CAS 403 to a multidefense contractor's manufacturing plant and the allocation of home office expenses to contracts performed at various jobsites.

The arguments that most G&A and other management expenses are usually performed at the jobsite makes no more sense for construction projects than for manufacturing contracts. The point is that all home office expenses, unless made unallowable by specific regulations, should be charged to and recovered under all of the contractor's work, including government contracts. The failure to allow such costs results in their inappropriate allocation to commercial work.

The clear recognition of the allocability of home office overhead to construction contracts is emphasized in the numerous decisions by boards of contract appeals and federal courts on contractor claims for equitable price adjustment where performance is delayed or disrupted by actions or nonactions of the government. The amount of the equitable adjustment established in these rulings includes an allocable portion of home office overhead, frequently computed by the Eichleay formula, as described in Chapter VII of this text.

We should consider here the arguments sometimes advanced that whatever services are provided by the central or branch office "are considered to be compensated for in the fixed fee." If the fixed fee is indeed sufficient to provide for a fair allocation of central and branch office expenses and a reasonable profit margin, the contractor would suffer no damage. In our experience, this sufficiency is usually not the case; rather, the fixed fee provides a very small and inadequate amount to cover central and branch office expenses. We have found, too, that the construction industry does not appear to be as effectively organized to articulate its positions with respect to government regulations as are the aerospace, electronics, and other industry groups.

Some prime and subcontracts do provide for allocation of applicable central and branch office expenses. But in these instances, too, many problems are encountered because both the contract cost principles and cost accounting standards are oriented to manufacturing and R&D contracts. A clear illustration of the irrelevance of cost accounting standards is found in the application of CAS 410 to construction contracts. DCAA auditors generally insist on the total cost input base despite the wide differences in the nature of the work performed. For example, in some instances, commercial customers may provide some or a large part of the material used. In other instances, the contractor will provide only the specifications and the customer will acquire the material. Frequently, the central and branch offices have very little to do with the acquisition of material; in other cases, material specialists and engineers in the home office have a large role in material acquisition. In all of these diverse circumstances, the construction contractor usually records the total materials as both sales and cost of sales.

The inclusion of all labor in the cost input base also raises a number of questions. Some government contract auditors and other officials are unable to understand or refuse to acknowledge the distinction between the contractor's permanent staff, including professional construction engineers, and the temporary laborers hired at union halls for the specific project.

We have yet to see or hear a reasoned approach by the government to the allocation of central and branch office expenses to construction contracts. We recommend that construction contractors make every effort to recover all of their central and branch office expenses allocable to government contracts on a pro rata basis.

The authors of FAR adopted a more reasonable and logical approach to this subject than DAR and FPR and this Regulation does not contain the restrictive provisions that enabled contract auditors to disallow or reduce allocations of home office and branch office expenses. Essentially, FAR identifies this cost as one where advance agreements are particularly important ". . . to express the parties' understanding and avoid possible subsequent disputes or disallowances."

FACILITIES CONTRACTS—FAR 31.106

FAR Part 45—Government Property sets forth policies and procedures for government property in possession of contractors, whether furnished by the government or acquired by the contractor for the government's account. Contractors bidding or performing on facilities contracts should become familiar with this Part.

Contract cost principles for facilities contracts, FAR 31.106, are cited in full in Chapter XVI of this text. While recognizing that such contracts frequently differ from contractors' normal operations and accordingly require modified accounting treatment, these principles do not contain the volume of detailed and rigid requirements as was contained in DAR and FPR. Rather, these differences are noted and contracting officers are encouraged to work out contract terms and advance agreements to accommodate them.

Allocation of General and Administrative Expenses to Facilities Contracts

As we discussed in some detail in Chapter XV of this text, the allocation of G&A expenses to government contracts has been a matter of considerable controversy over the years, and the promulgation by the Cost Accounting Standards Board (CAS 410) resolved some controversies but generated new ones. This standard failed to address facilities contracts.

The Department of Defense encountered serious problems in this area. While following DCAA's lead in its early insistence on the total cost input base for allocating G&A expenses, it would not permit the use of such base on facilities contracts, particularly when a major portion consisted of purchases of equipment. The value-added cost input base, so vigorously opposed under other circumstances, found favor and was insisted upon by some DOD components.

The various controversies relating to the allocation of G&A expenses to facilities contracts resulted in a decision by DOD to publish interim guidance establishing the policy that G&A expenses should not be applied to the purchase price of facilities. The Department requested the approval of the CASB staff for the proposed policy and, in conjunction therewith, recommended that CAS 410.50(j) be revised by adding the following: "Costs associated with the acquisition of tangible assets, whether for capitalization by the business unit or use under one or more Government facilities contracts shall be treated as a particular final cost objective and, if appropriate, be accounted for by a special allocation from the G&A expense pool."

The CASB executive secretary disagreed with the Defense Department's view that work performed under facilities contracts is similar to that performed in connection with self-constructed tangible assets as required to be accounted for under CAS 404.

The DOD letter had particularly complained about the restrictive aspects of CAS 410.50(j) "in that it permits a special allocation for only a single final cost objective. If a contractor has two or more similar final cost objectives, both of which would receive a disproportionate G&A allocation, Part 410.50(j) cannot be used to effect a special allocation."

Although this construction of CAS 410.50(j) had been strongly endorsed by the CASB staff in the past, the executive secretary's letter of August 29, 1978, denied any intention of restricting CAS 410.50(j) to a single final cost objective. As the CASB staff saw it then: "Rather the purpose of that sentence in 410.50(j) is to provide a means for accounting for occasional occurrences, aberrations that could involve more than one final cost objective."

Although the above-cited excerpt opened the door to a broader and more intelligent use of CAS 410.50(j), the executive secretary hastily narrowed the opening: "CAS 410.50(j) is not to be applied to products or services which are or are likely to become part of the continuing operations of a contractor."

The letter to DOD concluded with the views (1) that it was unnecessary to revise CAS 410.50(j) and (2) that the Guidance Paper should be revised to interpret CAS 410.50(j) as the CASB staff saw it rather than deal solely with facilities contracts.

After considerable rethinking, the Defense Department adopted a middle-of-the-road position: it accepted the CASB staff's interpretation of CAS 410.50(j) and used it in W.G. 79-24, but restricted this Guidance Paper to facilities contracts. The essence of the guidance is to alert DOD personnel that facilities contracts will usually "receive significantly less benefit from G&A expense than other contracts," and, accordingly, a special G&A allocation under CAS 410.50(j) shall be required.

The salient portions of W.G. 79-24 are quoted below:

DISCUSSION

Contractors' normal operations consist of the production of goods and services, such as aircraft or weapons systems. Contractors may, however, also receive Government facilities contracts which require the acquisition of significant amounts of facilities. These purchases are made at the direction of the Government, and no profit is granted to the contractor for making the acquisitions.

Facilities acquisition contracts normally do not require the same level of contractor risk and associated management attention as contracts which provide for the delivery of regular goods and services. As a result, a full allocation of a contractor's management or G&A expense to such contracts would generally not be equitable. An exception to this would be the rare circumstances when the preponderance of the contractor's activity is acquiring facilities as a service for the Government.

Government-funded facilities, when needed by a contractor to meet production contract requirements, are usually provided under a single facilities contract. However, in some instances contractors are awarded two or more concurrent contracts for the acquisition of facilities. The dollar magnitude of facilities acquisition under these contracts may be substantial when compared with contractors' normal business activities. However, because these acquisitions are generally not part of the normal business activity, this dollar magnitude is probably not a valid indicator of the proportion of G&A expense related to the facilities contracts.

In the case of consolidated facilities contracts (i.e., those contracts which provide for both facilities acquisition and facilities maintenance), a special allocation of G&A expense would be applied to the acquisition portion of the contracts. The maintenance portion would remain in the base and would receive the normal allocation G&A expense.

GUIDANCE

When a contractor has one or more facilities contracts, such contracts should be reviewed to ascertain whether they receive significantly less benefit from G&A expense than other contracts. This is usually the case.

When it is determined that facilities acquisition contracts will not receive an appropriate allocation of G&A expense by participating in the contractor's selected G&A expense allocation base, a special G&A expense allocation under the provisions of CAS 410.50(j) shall be required.

FAR 31.106 does not accord detailed treatment to G&A expenses but notes that such expenses should be considered for advance agreements.

GRANTS, CONTRACTS AND OTHER AGREEMENTS WITH NONPROFIT ORGANIZATIONS—OMB CIRCULAR A-122

On June 27, 1980, OMB published Circular A-122, effective immediately with implementation to be phased in by incorporating the provisions of the circular into new awards made after the start of the organization's next fiscal year. Provisions are also included for earlier or later implementation upon mutual agreement between an organization and the cognizant federal agency.

Circular A-122 establishes uniform cost principles for determining costs of grants, contracts, and other agreements with nonprofit organizations. Prior to the issuance of the circular, considerable confusion existed with respect to (1) the definition of a nonprofit organization, (2) the determination of which organizations should be included in this category, and (3) the various and differing cost principles used by individual federal departments and agencies. Circular A-122 was several years in the making, and its development included considerable coordination by OMB with nonprofit organizations, federal agencies, and others. Readers whose organizations are governed by the cost principles set forth in Circular A-122 may wish to obtain copies from the Office of Management and Budget, Washington, DC 20503. The text of this circular is also contained in the CCH GOVERNMENT CONTRACTS REPORTER, Volume 2 at par. 18,810.

To establish the applicability of the Circular A-122 cost principles, we should cite the definition of a nonprofit organization:

> Any corporation, trust, association, cooperative, or other organization which (1) is operated primarily for scientific, educational, service, charitable, or similar purposes in the public interest; (2) is not organized primarily for profit; and (3) uses its net proceeds to maintain, improve, and/or expand its operations. For this purpose, the term "nonprofit organization" excludes (i) colleges and universities; (ii) hospitals; (iii) State, local and federally recognized Indian tribal governments; and (iv) those nonprofit organizations which are excluded from coverage of this Circular . . . .

As to nonprofit organizations that are specifically excluded from coverage of Circular A-122, the circular asserts that "[s]ome nonprofit organizations, because of their size and nature of operations, can be considered to be similar to commercial concerns for purposes of applicability of cost principles." Attachment C to this circular identifies over 30 specific nonprofit organizations that are not subject to these cost principles, including nonprofit insurance companies such as Blue Cross and Blue Shield organizations, Aerospace Corporation, Battelle Memorial Institute, Mitre Corporation, Rand Corporation, SRI International.

In formulating the cost principles for nonprofit corporations, OMB could have looked to the cost principles for commercial organizations set forth in the Defense Acquisition Regulation, Federal Procurement Regulations, the individual cost principles established by federal agencies for nonprofit organizations, and the cost principles for educational institutions and state and local governments. According to the supplementary information set forth as prefatory comments to this circular, OMB followed the suggestion of GAO to conform the nonprofit cost principles as closely as possible to those of educational institutions and state and local governments. However, a review of the General Principles (Attachment A of this circular) and Selected Items of Cost (Attachment B) suggests that the cost principles more nearly resemble a regulation containing pieces of cost principles for commercial organizations as well, including occasional language taken almost verbatim from promulgated cost accounting standards, although the prefatory comments state that the awards covered by the circular would generally not be large enough to be covered by promulgations of the CASB. (The prefatory comments also state that "in the event that they do, however, the regulations of the CASB would apply.")

Circular A-122, Attachment A—General Principles

Paragraph A is entitled "Basic Considerations" and includes: Composition of Total Costs, Factors Affecting Allowability of Costs, Reasonable Costs, Allocable Costs, Applicable Credits and Advance Understandings. Although the language is not identical with the provisions of cost principles for contracts with commercial organizations or those with educational institutions, we found few requirements of consequence that would differentiate Circular A-122 from the other cost principles. One of the exceptions relates to reasonable costs and states: "The question of the reasonableness of specific costs must be scrutinized with particular care in connection with organizations or separate divisions thereof which receive the preponderance of their support from awards made by Federal Agencies."

Paragraph B covers direct costs. The basic concepts in this circular resemble those established for commercial organizations in FAR. Additionally, this paragraph provides that the costs of certain activities are not allowable as charges to federal awards, but must be nevertheless treated as direct costs for purposes of determining indirect cost rates. Costs of activities that must be treated as direct costs and to which indirect costs must be allocated include maintenance of membership rolls, subscriptions and publications; providing services and information to members, legislative or administrative bodies or the public; promotion, lobbying, and other forms of public relations; meetings and conferences except those held to conduct the general administration of the organization.

Paragraph C covers indirect costs, and the provisions are similar to both cost principles for commercial organizations and those for educational institutions.

As in the case of direct costs, the provisions embody the basic principles of CAS 401 and 402 without specifically referring to those standards.

Paragraph D prescribes procedures for allocation of indirect costs and determination of indirect cost rates. In a departure from many of the other cost principles, the circular permits the use of a simplified allocation method where a nonprofit organization has only one major function or where all its major functions benefit from its direct costs to approximately the same degree. Essentially, the simplified allocation method is a single rate determined by dividing the total allowable indirect costs by the base, which consists of direct costs.

As a matter of interest in connection with the simplified allocation method, the circular permits the use of total direct costs, direct salaries and wages, or other base which results in an equitable distribution. Importantly, it provides that the total direct cost base, if used, must exclude capital expenditures "and other distorting items, such as major subcontracts or subgrants." Our readers will recognize the logic of this provision and its sharp difference from the previous Department of Defense and CASB position in insisting that G&A expenses for commercial organizations be computed on a total cost input base including the distorting items referred to in this circular.

Where the conditions permitting the use of a simplified allocation method are not present, allocation of indirect costs are effected through the use of separate cost groupings. With regard to a base period, the circular leans toward the provisions of FAR in expressing a preference for the organization's fiscal year, but stops short of the inflexible requirements of CAS 406 for the mandatory use of the fiscal year.

Where the multiple allocation base method must be used, the circular provides guidance that, in essence, does not differ in any substantial manner from those guides provided for commercial organizations in FAR.

Paragraph E addresses the negotiation and approval of indirect cost rates. These actions are the responsibility of the "cognizant agency," the federal agency responsible by virtue of having the largest dollar volume of awards with the organization.

We find here certain procedures in terms that are not used in indirect cost determinations with commercial organizations but that resemble more closely the procedures in use for educational institutions. For example, where there is reasonable assurance that a rate for use on awards is not likely to exceed the rate based on the organization's actual costs, a predetermined rate may be negotiated. This is described as "an indirect cost rate, applicable to a specified current or future period . . . based on an estimate of the costs to be incurred during the period. A predetermined rate is not subject to adjustment." Another procedure not found in contracts with commercial organizations is the use of a fixed rate, described as "an indirect cost rate which has the same characteristics as a predetermined rate, except that the difference between the estimated costs and the actual costs of the period covered by the rate is carried forward as an adjustment to the rate computation of a subsequent period."

Where neither predetermined nor fixed rates are considered appropriate, the circular provides for the negotiation of provisional and final rates as these terms are generally understood in contracts with commercial organizations.

Circular A-122, Attachment B—Selected Items of Cost

Attachment B covers 51 selected items of cost, most of which do not differ substantially from those provided for contracts with commercial organizations and awards to educational institutions. One of the surprising aspects of Attachment B is its failure to address Bid and Proposal costs and Independent Research and Development. These costs are listed as numbers 3 and 17, respectively, within the 51 selected items, but are followed only by the parenthetical word "reserved." Despite the many years of experience by the Department of Defense and the civilian departments and agencies, differences of views continue to exist.

FAR 31.205-18 achieved a reasonable degree of uniformity for profit organizations although the DOD FAR Supplement 31.205-18 further limits "the total amount of IR&D/B&P costs allocated to DOD contracts . . . [to] the total expenditures for IR&D/B&P projects with a potential relationship to a military function or operation." Also, despite the many years in which these costs have been discussed and studied by the executive and legislative branches of the government and by the private sector, and despite the promulgation of CAS 420 on this subject and the continuing studies by OFPP and other groups within OMB, the Financial Management Branch of the Office of Management and Budget, responsible for Circular A-122, was apparently not ready to bite the bullet.

The provisions regarding compensation for personal services address the requirements for support of salaries and wages, a subject similarly covered in the cost principles for the educational institutions, but not referred to in the cost principles for commercial organizations. In the case of educational institutions, the government has long recognized the difficulties of precisely measuring the interrelated activities of professorial and professional employees. OMB Circular A-21 permits the distribution of direct salaries and wages based on the so-called monitored work-load system, which reflects budgeted or assigned work load updated to reflect any significant changes in work-load distribution. In contrast, Circular A-122 requires that direct labor costs be supported by reports that "reflect an after-the-fact determination of the actual activity of each employee. Budget estimates (i.e., estimates determined before the services are performed) do not qualify as support for charges to awards." Personnel activity reports are required, but may be waived when a substitute system has been approved in writing by the cognizant agency.

The provisions relating to depreciation resemble the cost principles for educational institutions much more closely than those for commercial organizations. Where the depreciation method is followed by the organization, the straight-line method is perceived to be the appropriate method "in the absence of clear evidence indicating that the expected consumption of the asset will be significantly greater or lesser in the early portions of its useful life than in the later portions."

The allowance method is provided for in rates established for categories of assets like buildings and equipment.

The circular addresses donations. The value of donated or volunteer services is not allowable either as a direct or indirect cost, but the value of such services when used in the performance of a direct activity must be included in the base for indirect cost rate calculations. Similar provisions apply to donated goods and space.

Unallowable costs are governed by provisions that resemble closely the cost principles for both educational institutions and commercial organizations. Thus most advertising, bad debts, contributions, entertainment, interest, organization costs, etc., are unallowable. Somewhat greater flexibility is provided in that organization costs and other expenses may be allowable when approved in writing by the awarding agency.

A major effort was made in the private sector to have interest recognized as an allowable cost. The cost principles for state and local governments provide a partial recognition of interest in that rental rates for publicly owned buildings may be based on actual costs, including depreciation, interest, etc. In the prefatory comments to Circular A-122, OMB stated that this provision for state and local governments had been extensively studied before its promulgation. For reasons not explained, OMB stated that it had not yet studied this problem as it relates to nonprofit organizations.

Early in 1983, OMB and its Circular No. A-122 achieved unusual and widespread prominence when that agency stepped into the complex controversy initiated by DOD with respect to providing a cost principle on lobbying costs. The account of OMB's efforts and the problems it generated with Congress and the various elements in both the executive agencies and the private sector are contained in Chapter XVII of this text.

References to contracts with nonprofit organizations are contained in FAR 31.108, Subpart 31.7, limited largely to establishing that cost for such organizations shall be determined in accordance with OMB Circular A-122.

GRANTS, CONTRACTS AND OTHER AGREEMENTS WITH EDUCATIONAL INSTITUTIONS—OMB CIRCULAR A-21; FAR 31.104, SUBPART 31.3

Background

There are many differences between principles for determining costs applicable to contracts and grants with educational institutions and those applicable to other contracts. Some are well-founded; others are doubtful. Different principles may be traced as far back as the 1940s to the publication of a "Blue Book" for nonprofit organizations, especially educational institutions, as a counterpart to the "Green Book," which elaborated on TD 5000 and provided guidelines for determining costs under contracts with commercial organizations. The 1949 edition of ASPR Section XV contained a Part 3, titled Research Contracts with Nonprofit Institutions. Consistent with the rest of the cost principles in the 1949 edition of ASPR, Part 3 was a terse statement relating mainly to listings of allowable and unallowable costs. (The Federal Procurement Regulations did not come into being until March 1959.)

The 1949 ASPR Section XV, Part 3, did not provide suitable accounting and auditing guidance, and many DOD personnel continued to look to the unofficial "Blue Book." Beginning with the 1959 Edition of ASPR, Part 3 was expanded to provide a basis for the current cost principles for educational institutions.

The interest in research contracts and grants with educational institutions has been government-wide, and, as a matter of fact, some of the other departments and agencies equaled or exceeded the volume of these awards by DOD. As a result of the interest in this matter by the Office of Management and Budget (OMB), that agency published the cost principles applicable to educational institutions as OMB Circular A-21, republished with changes as

Federal Management Circular (FMC) 73-8 in December 1973 by GSA and then revised and reissued under its original designation, OMB Circular A-21, February 26, 1979, amended and reissued effective August 3, 1982. These circulars were published for government-wide use and were incorporated into ASPR/DAR and FPR. The coverage in FAR is terse and serves mainly to refer readers to the OMB circular.

Some of the basic principles for determining costs of contracts with commercial organizations will be found in provisions for educational institutions, although even in these instances the language is frequently not identical. In part, the language changes are due to the fact that the educational institutions succeeded in obtaining a full exemption from the requirements to comply with CASB standards and regulations. In other instances, the principles for determining both direct and indirect costs vary substantially from those promulgated for contracts with commercial organizations.

Logical Reasons for Different Cost Principles for Educational Institutions

In discussing logical reasons for developing separate cost principles for educational institutions, many observers believe that these reasons do not apply to the Federally Funded Research and Development Centers operated by such institutions. The laboratories or similar operations, it is contended, operate much closer to such operations in the commercial world than educational institutions. We note, in this regard, that the CASB exemption for educational institutions specifically excluded FFRDCs.

When the work is performed on campus and the people involved are primarily those whose principal duties entail instruction, a number of circumstances combine to make contracting with educational institutions substantially different from contracting with commercial organizations:

1. The major mission and activity are instruction. Many of the other operations and related administration are related to instruction.

2. Many people engaged in performing federally sponsored research are primarily involved in instructional activities.

3. A considerable portion of the buildings and other facilities of some educational institutions, ranging in age up to 200 years or more, would have been fully depreciated and/or replaced under commercial organization operations. Additionally, funds for many facilities were donated in whole or in part.

4. OMB Circular A-21 states: "Provision for profit or other increment above cost is outside the scope of this chapter." Despite the apparent neutrality voiced by OMB, contracts and grants to educational institutions are generally on a cost basis, without provision for fee.

5. Colleges and universities are involved in numerous activities peculiar to those institutions, many of them not found in commercial or industrial organizations, or not found to the same extent.

Other Reasons for Different Cost Principles for Educational Institutions

Cost principles for educational institutions vary from those for commercial organizations for a number of other reasons, the logic of some of which has been questioned.

1. The basis and documentation for allocating salaries and wages directly to government contracts and grants are considerably less demanding than for similar work performed at commercial organizations. It is recognized that the variety of duties of the faculty, including efforts on the government work, the basic responsibility of instruction, related institutional duties, research and writing involved in the "publish or perish" requirement, and other activities sometimes overflow one into the other and that precise timekeeping is difficult. On the other hand, government auditors and others have complained about what they believe is a lack of discipline on the part of the faculty and a disinclination or inability of the institutions' administrators to enforce greater care in accounting for time. This area of problems with accountability is particularly noticed when university professors leave the campuses to work for commercial organizations and continue the same kind of research and development activities they had been engaged in at the educational institutions. The rules of the game change abruptly, and the allowable direct salaries for professors while on campus are found by the government to lack appropriate documentation and are either disallowed or at times become the subject of contract auditors' suspicion-of-fraud reports.

2. We mentioned earlier that educational institutions, except for the Federally Funded Research & Development Centers (FFRDCs) operated by these institutions, became exempt from all CASB regulations and standards in an amendment to Section 331.30(b)(3) published on June 8, 1978. From the earliest days of the CASB, colleges and universities and their business organizations had urged that they be granted full exemption because their operations and accounting systems varied so greatly from those of commercial organizations. The CASB and its staff were well known for their hard-line opposition to any exemptions or waivers, and they resisted these requests for many years. In our judgment, this resistence was wrong. We equally question, however, whether full exemption was appropriate. It can be argued that many standards, e.g., 401, 402, 405, 406, 411, 412 and 413, are no more inappropriate for educational institutions than for commercial organizations. Additionally, CAS 404 and 409, when applied to newly purchased equipment, may be as applicable here as in the case of commercial organizations.

Indirect Costs

The major categories of indirect costs at educational institutions are: depreciation and use allowances, operation and maintenance expenses, general administration and general expenses, departmental administration expenses, sponsored projects administration, library expenses, and student administration and services. The nature of these cost categories, the individual expenses included therein and the allocation methods are explained in OMB Circular A-21.

Depreciation and Use Allowances

These expenses should generally be identifiable with specific buildings or other capital equipment, and the charges would then be allocated to such facilities. Where the buildings are used for more than one function, this expense should be allocated to the individual functions on the basis of usable square feet of space or salaries and wages applicable to the joint function.

Operation and Maintenance Expenses

Where such expenses can be identified with cost objectives, either directly or through cost analyses, these would constitute the preferable bases for allocation. In the absence of such alternatives, operation and maintenance expense should be allocated on the same basis as described above for depreciation.

General Administration and General Expenses

Where allocation by specific identification of cost analysis is not feasible, these costs should be allocated to the benefited functions on the basis of modified total cost (salaries and wages, fringe benefits, materials and supplies, services, travel, and subgrants and subcontracts up to $25,000 each). As an aside here, the author invites attention to the significant difference between this allocation base and the requirements of CAS 410. We also invite the reader's attention to OMB Circular A-122, discussed earlier in this chapter, which states that the distribution base should exclude "other distorting items such as major subcontracts and subgrants . . . ."

Departmental Administration Expenses

These expenses, plus the department's appropriate share of general administration and general expenses and depreciation and/or use allowances, should be allocated on a modified total cost basis (described above) if a direct distribution is not feasible.

Sponsored Projects Administration

These expenses, plus an appropriate share of general administration and general expenses, operation and maintenance expenses, and depreciation and/or use allowances, should be allocated on a modified total-cost-of-sponsored-projects basis.

Library Expenses

The total library expenses should first be allocated on the basis of primary categories of users, including students, faculty members and other professional employees, and other users. In the next step, (1) the amount in the student category should be assigned to the instruction function, (2) the amount in the professional employee category should be assigned to the major functions of the institution on the basis of salaries and wages of the professional employees applicable to these functions, and (3) the amount in the other users category should be assigned to the other institutional activities function of the institution.

Student Administration and Services

The expenses in this category should be allocated to the instruction function and subsequently to sponsored agreements in that function.

Allocation of Indirect Costs

The distributions described above will, in most instances, result in a cost of the major functions of the institution. The allocation of the indirect costs of the major function in which the contract or grant is performed should be allocated thereto on the basis of modified total direct cost, previously explained.

Negotiated Lump Sum for Indirect Costs

Where work is performed as self-contained, off-campus activities and indirect costs cannot be readily determined, the parties may negotiate a fixed amount or lump sum.

Predetermined Fixed Rates for Indirect Costs

To simplify the administration of cost-type R&D contracts and grants with educational institutions, P.L. 87-638 authorizes the use of predetermined fixed rates in determining indirect costs. The OMB Circular notes the potential advantages of this procedure and suggests it be considered "where the cost experience and other pertinent facts available are deemed sufficient to enable the parties to reach an informed judgment as to the probable level of indirect costs during the ensuing accounting period."

Negotiated Fixed Rates and Carry-Forward Provisions

Where a fixed rate is negotiated in advance, the over- or underrecovery for that year may be included as an adjustment to the indirect cost for the next rate negotiation.

Simplified Method for Small Institutions

Where the total direct cost work of federally sponsored contracts and grants does not exceed $3 million in a fiscal year, and the results of this method do not appear to be inequitable to the government, a simplified method may be used from data developed from the institution's most recent annual financial report with supplementary information concerning salaries and wages. A single rate is developed by lumping all of the indirect expenses and using direct salaries and wages as the allocation base.

Selected Costs

OMB Circular A-21 contains 44 selected costs, including those established as allowable, unallowable, and qualified and limited as to their admissibility. Many are similar to those described at some length in Chapters X through XVII of this text, relating to contracts with commercial organizations, and will not be reiterated here. We shall focus instead on those that differ significantly from the ground rules provided in other government cost principles.

Compensation for Personal Services

Accounting and documentation for salaries and wages charged directly to federal contracts and agreements by educational institutions reflect probably the greatest difference as compared with contracts with commercial organizations or even contracts and grants awarded to nonprofit organizations (OMB Circular A-122). The basic rationale for the government's acceptance of estimates prepared in advance is that "because of the nature of work involved in academic institutions, the various and often interrelated activities of the professorial and professional employees frequently cannot be measured with a high degree of precision, . . . reliance must be placed on reasonably accurate approximations, and that acceptance of a degree of tolerance in measurement is appropriate." The text of the provision contained in OMB Circular A-21 is cited below:

J6. Compensation for Personal Services.

a. General

Compensation for personal services covers all amounts paid currently or accrued by the institution for services rendered during the period or performance under government sponsored agreements. Such amounts include salaries, wages, and fringe benefits (See section J15). These costs are allowable to the extent that the total compensation to individual employees conforms to the established policy of the institution, consistently applied, and provided that the charges for work performed directly on sponsored agreements and for other work allocable as indirect costs are determined and supported as provided below. Charges to sponsored agreements may include reasonable amounts for activities contributing and intimately related to work under the agreements, such as delivering special lectures about specific aspects of the ongoing activity, writing reports and articles, participating in appropriate seminars, consulting with colleagues and graduate students, and attending meetings and conferences. Incidental work (that in excess of normal for the individual), for which supplemental compensation is paid by an institution under institutional policy, need not be included in the payroll distribution systems described below, provided such work and compensation are separately identified and documented in the financial management system of the institution.

b. Payroll Distribution

(1) *General Principles.* (a) The distribution of salaries and wages whether treated as direct or indirect costs, will be based on payrolls documented in accordance with the generally accepted practices of colleges and universities. Institutions may include in a residual category all activities that are not directly charged to sponsored agreements, and that need not be distributed to more than one activity for purposes of identifying indirect costs and the functions to which they are allocable. The components of the residual category are not required to be separately documented.

(b) The apportionment of employee's salaries and wages which are chargeable to more than one sponsored agreement or other cost objective will be accomplished by methods which will (1) be in accordance with Sections A-2 and C above, (2) produce an equitable distribution of charges for employee's activities, and (3) distinguish the employees' direct activities from their indirect activities.

(c) In the use of any methods for apportioning salaries, it is recognized that, in an academic setting, teaching, research, service, and administration are often inextricably intermingled. A precise assessment of factors that contribute to costs is not always feasible, nor is it expected. Reliance, therefore, is placed on estimates in which a degree of tolerance is appropriate.

(d) There is no single best method for documenting the distribution of charges for personal services.

Methods for apportioning salaries and wages, however, must meet the criteria specified in J.6.b.(2) below. Examples of acceptable methods are contained in J.6.c. below. Other methods which meet the criteria specified in J.6.b.(2) below also shall be deemed acceptable, if a mutually satisfactory alternative agreement is reached.

(2) *Criteria for Acceptable Methods.* (a) The payroll distribution system will (i) be incorporated into the official records of the institution, (ii) reasonably reflect the activity for which the employee is compensated by the institution, and (iii) encompass both sponsored and all other activities on an integrated basis, but may include the use of subsidiary records. (Compensation for incidental work described in J.6.a. need not be included.)

(b) The method must recognize the principle of after-the-fact confirmation or determination so that costs distributed represent actual costs, unless a mutually satisfactory alternative agreement is reached. Direct cost activities and indirect cost activities may be confirmed by responsible persons with suitable means of verification that the work was performed. Confirmation by the employee is not a requirement for either direct or indirect cost activities if other responsible persons make appropriate confirmations.

(c) The payroll distribution system will allow confirmation of activity allocable to each sponsored agreement and each of the categories of activity needed to identify indirect costs and the functions to which they are allocable. The activities chargeable to indirect cost categories or the major functions of the institution for employees whose salaries must be apportioned (see J.6.b.1.(b) above), if not initially identified as separate categories, may be subsequently distributed by any reasonable method mutually agreed to, including, but not limited to, suitably conducted surveys, statistical sampling procedures, or the application of negotiated fixed rates.

(d) Practices vary among institutions and within institutions as to the activity constituting a full workload. Therefore, the payroll distribution system may reflect categories of activities expressed as a percentage distribution of total activities.

(e) Direct and indirect charges may be made initially to sponsored agreements on the basis of estimates made before services are performed. When such estimates are used, significant changes in the corresponding work activity must be identified and entered into the payroll distribution system. Short-term (such as one or two months) fluctuation between workload categories need not be considered as long as the distribution of salaries and wages is reasonable over the longer term, such as an academic period.

(f) The system will provide for independent internal evaluations to ensure the system's effectiveness and compliance with the above standards.

(g) For systems which meet these standards, the institution will not be required to provide additional support or documentation for the effort actually performed.

c. Examples of Acceptable Methods for Payroll Distribution:

1. *Plan—Confirmation:* Under this method, the distribution of salaries and wages of professorial or professional staff applicable to sponsored agreements is based on budgeted, planned, or assigned work activity, updated to reflect any significant changes in work distribution. A plan-confirmation system used for salaries and wages charged directly or indirectly to sponsored agreements will meet the following standards:

(a) A system of budgeted, planned, or assigned work activity will be incorporated into the official records of the institution and encompass both sponsored and all other activities on an integrated basis. The system may include the use of subsidiary records.

(b) The system will reasonably reflect only the activity for which the employee is compensated by the institution (compensation for incidental work described in J.6.a. need not be included). Practices vary among institutions and within institutions as to the activity constituting a full workload. Hence, the system will reflect categories of activities expressed as a percentage distribution of total activities. (But see Section H for treatment of indirect costs under the simplified method for small institutions).

(c) The system will reflect activity applicable to each sponsored agreement and to each category needed to identify indirect costs and the functions to which they are allocable. The system may treat indirect cost activities initially within a residual category and subsequently determine them by alternate methods as discussed in J.6.b.(2)(c).

(d) The system will provide for modification of an individual's salary or salary distribution commensurate with a significant change in the employee's work activity. Short-term (such as one or two months) fluctuation between workload categories need not be considered as long as the distribution of salaries and wages is reasonable over the longer term such as an academic period. Whenever it is apparent that a significant change in work activity which is directly or indirectly charged to sponsored agreements will occur or has occurred, the change will be documented over the signature of a responsible official and entered into the system.

(e) At least annually a statement will be signed by the employee, principal investigator, or responsible official(s) using suitable means of verification that the work was performed, stating that salaries and wages charged to sponsored agreements as direct charges, and to residual, indirect cost or other categories are reasonable in relation to work performed.

(f) The system will provide for independent internal evaluation to ensure the system's integrity and compliance with the above standards.

(g) In the use of this method, an institution shall not be required to provide additional support or documentation for the effort actually performed.

2. *After-the-fact Activity Records:* Under this system the distribution of salaries and wages by the institution will be supported by activity reports as prescribed below.

(a) Activity reports will reflect the distribution of activity expended by employees covered by the system (compensation for incidental work as described in J.6.a. need not be included).

(b) These reports will reflect an after-the-fact reporting of the percentage distribution of activity of employees. Charges may be made initially on the basis of estimates made before the services are performed, provided that such charges are promptly adjusted if significant differences are indicated by activity records.

(c) Reports will reasonably reflect the activities for which employees are compensated by the institution. To confirm that the distribution of activity represents a reasonable estimate of the work performed by the employee during the period, the reports will be signed by the employee, principal investigator, or responsible official(s) using suitable means of verification that the work was performed.

(d) The system will reflect activity applicable to each sponsored agreement and to each category needed to identify indirect costs and the functions to which they are allocable. The system may treat indirect cost activities initially within a residual category and subsequently determine them by alternate methods as discussed in J.6.b.(2)(c).

(e) For professorial and professional staff, the reports will be prepared each academic term, but no less frequently than every six months. For other employees, unless alternate arrangements are agreed to, the reports will be prepared no less frequently than monthly and will coincide with one or more pay periods.

(f) Where the institution uses time cards or other forms of after-the-fact payroll documents as original documentation for payroll and payroll charges, such documents shall qualify as records for this purpose provided that they meet the requirements in (a) through (e) above.

3. *Multiple Confirmation Records:* Under this system the distribution of salaries and wages of professorial and professional staff will be supported by records which certify separately for direct and indirect cost activities as prescribed below.

(a) For employees covered by the system, there will be direct cost records to reflect the distribution of that activity expended which is to be allocable as direct cost to each sponsored agreement. There will also be indirect cost records to reflect the distribution of that activity to indirect costs. These records may be kept jointly or separately (but are to be certified separately, see below).

(b) Salary and wage charges may be made initially on the basis of estimates made before the services are performed provided that such charges are promptly adjusted if significant differences occur.

(c) Institutional records will reasonably reflect only the activity for which employees are compensated by the institution (compensation for incidental work as described in J.6.a. need not be included).

(d) The system will reflect activity applicable to each sponsored agreement and to each category needed to identify indirect costs and the functions to which they are allocable.

(e) To confirm that distribution of activity represents a reasonable estimate of the work performed by the employee during the period, the record for each employee will include:

(1) The signature of the employee or of a person having direct knowledge of the work, confirming that the record or activities allocable as direct costs of each sponsored agreement is appropriate.

(2) The record of indirect costs will include the signature of responsible person(s) who use suitable means of verification that the work was performed and is consistent with the overall distribution of the employee's compensated activities.

These signatures may all be on the same document.

(f) The reports will be prepared each academic term, but no less frequently than every six months.

(g) Where the institution uses time cards or other forms of after-the-fact payroll documents as original documentation for payroll and payroll charges, such documents shall qualify as records for this purpose provided they meet the requirements in (a) through (f) above.

d. Salary Rates for Faculty Members

(1) Salary Rates for the Academic Year. Charges for work performed on sponsored agreements by faculty members during the academic year will be based on the individual faculty member's regular compensation for the continuous period which, under the policy of the institution concerned, constitutes the basis of his salary. Charges for work performed on sponsored agreements during all or any portion of such period are allowable at the base salary rate. In no event will charges to sponsored agreements, irrespective of the basis of computation, exceed the proportionate share of the base salary for that period. This principle applies to all members of the faculty at an institution. Since intra-university consulting is assumed to be undertaken as a university obligation requiring no compensation in addition to full-time base salary, the principle also applies to faculty members who function as consultants or otherwise

contribute to a sponsored agreement conducted by another faculty member of the same institution. However, in unusual cases where consultation is across departmental lines or involves a separate or remote operation, and the work performed by the consultant is in addition to his regular departmental load, any charges for such work representing extra compensation above the base salary are allowable provided that such consulting arrangements are specifically provided for in the agreement or approved in writing by the sponsored agency.

(2) Periods Outside the Academic Year.

a. Except as otherwise specified for teaching activity in b below, charges for work performed by faculty members on sponsored agreements during the summer months or other period not included in the base salary period will be determined for each faculty member at a rate not in excess of the base salary divided by the period to which the base salary relates, and will be limited to charges made in accordance with other parts of this section. The base salary period used in computing charges for work performed during the summer months will be the number of months covered by the faculty member's official academic year appointment.

b. Charges for teaching activities performed by faculty members on sponsored agreements during the summer months or other periods not included in the base salary period will be based on the normal policy of the institution governing compensation to faculty members for teaching assignments during such periods.

(3) Part-Time Faculty. Charges for work performed on sponsored agreements by faculty members having only part-time appointments will be determined at a rate not in excess of that regularly paid for the part-time assignments: e.g., an institution pays $5,000 to a faculty member for half-time teaching during the academic year. He devoted one-half of his remaining time to a sponsored agreement. Thus, his additional compensation, chargeable by the institution to the agreement, would be one-half of $5,000, or $2,500.

e. Noninstitutional professional activities

Unless an arrangement is specifically authorized by a Federal sponsoring agency, an institution must follow its institution-wide policies and practices concerning the permissible extent of professional services that can be provided outside the institution for noninstitutional compensation. Where such institution-wide policies do not exist or do not adequately define the permissible extent of consulting or other noninstitutional activities undertaken for extra outside pay, the Government may require that the effort of professional staff working on sponsored agreements be allocated between (i) institutional activities, and (ii) noninstitutional professional activities. If the sponsoring agency considers the extent of noninstitutional professional effort excessive, appropriate arrangements governing compensation will be negotiated on a case-by-case basis.

Washington University, **IBCA No. 1228-11-78, 80-1 BCA par. 14,297.**—Despite the less rigid requirements for documentation supporting charges for direct salaries and wages asserted to have been incurred by colleges and universities on government contracts, such costs are disallowed from time to time.

In the above-cited dispute, salaries and associated burden were disallowed based on the auditor's finding that they had been charged to other contracts and grants and subsequently transferred to the instant contract without sufficient documentation. The audit report also referred to a prior audit that criticized the university for deficiencies in charging salaries to projects on the basis of budget estimates rather than on the basis of the actual effort expended and for the common practice of making payroll transfers without sufficient review and justification.

The contractor argued that the contract was satisfactorily performed and that the government had not presented any evidence to indicate that the persons named in the salary transfers did not actually perform work on the contract. The university also asserted that there was ample after-the-fact justification to establish that the compensation claimed was reasonable and necessary for the performance of the contract. Finally, the university project director affirmed that, to the best of his recollection, he had verbally requested the salary transfers to be made contemporaneously but, upon learning that his verbal instructions had not been carried out, made the request again in a subsequent period. All of these procedures were alleged to be reasonable, especially since the contract allegedly contained no express provision concerning applicable cost accounting standards for educational institutions.

In rebuttal, while agreeing that the promulgations of the CASB were not applicable to colleges and universities, the government pointed to the provisions of FPR Subpart 1-15.3, which was incorporated in the contract. Additionally, the Audit and Records clause of the contract required the contractor to "maintain books, records, documents, and other evidence and accounting procedures and practices, sufficient to reflect properly all direct and indirect costs of whatever nature claimed to have been incurred and anticipated to be incurred for the performance of this contract."

The board found that FPR Subpart 1-15.3 did in fact apply to this contract by specific reference thereto in one of the clauses. The board then cited the following FPR provision regarding payroll systems of educational institutions:

> ... [I]nstitution payroll systems must be supported by either (1) an adequate appointment and workload distribution system accompanied by monthly reviews performed by responsible officials and a reporting of any significant changes in workload distribution of each professor or professional staff member, or (2) a monthly after-the-fact certification system which will require the individual investigators, deans, departmental chairman, or supervisors having firsthand knowledge of the services performed on each research agreement to report the distribution of effort.

The contractor's contention that the contract was fully and satisfactorily completed was given short shrift by the board, which pointed to the fact that it was a cost-reimbursable contract and that reimbursement had to be determined on the basis of allowable costs rather than contract completion.

Turning to the university's contention that the government had offered no evidence that the persons involved in the salary transfers did not work on the contract, the board observed that the university was seeking "a reversal of roles between the contractor and the government. It is the contractor's responsibility to maintain records in compliance with the contract requirements which show that the persons involved in the salary transfers did actually work on the contract."

Washington University's major support consisted of an affidavit from the director of the contract effort. The board noted that this individual's affidavit was "based entirely on his recollection of events five years past and no reference is made to any notes or memoranda in aid of his memory." Such evidence was not available from departmental officials closer to the contract project; nor were affidavits obtained from them; nor were they called to testify. In denying the contractor's claim, the board concluded:

> We find that appellant failed to maintain the contract cost records as required by the contract. The cost records that were maintained do not show that the disputed costs were actually incurred in performance of the contract. The absence of a contemporaneous justification of the tardy salary transfers cannot be overcome solely by an affidavit 5 years later by the project director relying totally on his recollection. There is no evidence in the record other than the affidavit to show that the transferred salary costs were incurred in performance of the contract.

Depreciation and Use Allowances

The guidance relating to these costs is extensive and differs from the cost principles for commercial organizations mainly in providing educational institutions with the option of use allowances, understandable in view of the fact that some buildings may be older than 200 years. Depreciation or use allowance may be charged on assets donated by a third party, with their fair market value at the time of the donation considered as the acquisition cost. Generally, a combination of the depreciation and use allowance methods may not be used, in like circumstances, for a single class of assets.

Profits and Losses on Disposition of Plant, Equipment, or Other Capital Assets

Neither profits nor losses on sale or exchange of capital assets may be considered in computing costs of federally sponsored agreements. This provision contrasts with both the cost principles for contracts with commercial organizations and those for nonprofit organizations where gains and losses are considered in the years in which they occur, with gains limited to the difference between the net amounts realized and the undepreciated balances.

Rental Costs

These provisions have not (as yet) adopted the provisions of FAS-13, which are set forth for commercial organizations in FAR 31.205-36; however, the provisions of J33 are not dissimilar.

Sabbatical Leave Costs

This allowable cost, for which no counterpart exists in any other government cost principles, consists of "leave of absence to employees for performance of graduate work or sabbatical study, travel or research, provided the institution has a uniform policy on sabbatical leave for persons engaged in research."

Reconversion Costs

These costs are allowable in awards to educational institutions and also to nonprofit organizations (OMB Circular A-122) when incurred to restore the facilities "to approximately the same condition existing prior to commencement of the sponsored agreement, fair wear and tear excepted."

Specialized Service Facilities

These cost principles address what are described as the costs "involving the use of highly complex or specialized facilities such as electronic computers, wind tunnels, and reactors," an area into which none of the other government cost principles have ventured. These costs are allowable provided the charge meets the following conditions from J38:

(b) The cost of each service normally shall consist of both its direct costs and its allocable share of indirect costs with deductions for appropriate income or Federal financing as described in Section C5.

(c) The cost of such institutional services when material in amount will be charged directly to users, including sponsored agreements based on actual use of the services and a schedule of rates that does not discriminate between federally and nonfederally supported activities of the institution, including those used by the institution for internal purposes. Charges for the use of specialized facilities should be designed to recover not more than the aggregate cost of the services over a long-term period agreed to by the institution and the cognizant Federal agency. Accordingly, it is not necessary that the rates charged for services be equal to the cost of providing those services during any one fiscal year as long as rates are reviewed periodically for consistency with the long-term plan and adjusted if necessary.

(d) Where the costs incurred for such institutional services are not material, they may be allocated as indirect costs. Such arrangements must be agreed to by the institution and the cognizant Federal Agency.

(e) Where it is in the best interest of the Government and the institution to establish alternative costing arrangements, such arrangements may be worked out with the cognizant Federal agency.

GRANTS AND CONTRACTS WITH STATE AND LOCAL GOVERNMENTS—OMB CIRCULAR No. A-87; FAR 31.6

These specialized cost principles differ from other cost principles we have been discussing, particularly those used in contracts with commercial organizations, in that they are much more restrictive. For example, one of the key "Factors Affecting Allowability of Costs," states that allowable costs must be "[n]ecessary and reasonable for proper and efficient administration of the grant program, be allocable thereto under these principles, and, except as specifically provided herein, not be a general expense required to carry out the overall responsibilities of State or local governments." As amplified in other provisions of these cost principles, the federal government intends to make full reimbursement for properly supported direct salaries, wages, and other direct costs but to sharply narrow the area of reimbursable indirect costs.

The principles reflected throughout establish that the federal government will reimburse a pro rata share of the indirect expenses of the departments in which the contracts or grants are performed, but will not assume any share of the overall cost of operating the state or local government.

Limitation of Cost Provisions of Government Cost-Reimbursement Type Contracts—Policies, Practices, and Case Law

Among the many mandatory clauses in government contracts, this Chapter XX and the following Chapters XXI and XXII focus on four that, with the exception of the Changes clause, have probably generated the largest volume of litigation. Chapter XXI addresses the Termination for Default and Termination for the Convenience of the Government clauses, and Chapter XXII analyzes at length the Price Reduction for Defective Pricing clause.

We should note one of the important distinctions. In the case of the Price Reduction for Defective Pricing clause, determinations as to if, when, and to what extent the contractor's cost or pricing data were defective were framed by a series of decisions by boards of contract appeals and the U. S. Court of Claims. As we shall see in Chapter XXII, ASPR/DAR and FPR were revised substantially to incorporate the judicial rulings into these regulations and these revisions were carried over to FAR. In contrast, despite the fact that the issue of unabsorbed overhead resulted in numerous disputes on which decisions were handed down by judicial bodies, government procurement regulations were, and continue to be, completely silent on this subject. Accordingly, as this issue continues to surface, we find the incongruous circumstance where neither party can find support for its position in official regulations and must turn for guidance to judicial decisions.

This chapter cites a large number of selected cases involving the basic dispute as to whether a contractor is entitled to reimbursement for costs incurred in excess of the total cost set forth in the contract schedule where the contractor is unable to demonstrate that it gave appropriate notice to the government and where the contracting officer, in turn, has notified the contractor that the estimated cost has been increased. Although the great preponderance of judicial decisions have been adverse to contractors, a number of appeals resulted in favorable rulings. Despite the plethora of litigation in this area, including what appeared to be inconsistent rulings in similar circumstances, neither DAR nor FPR in the past nor FAR today has ever undertaken to provide any guidance to which contracting officers and contractors could refer. As in the case of unabsorbed overhead in termination for the convenience of the government, the arguments of both parties must rest on judicial rulings.

THE LIMITATION OF COST CLAUSE (April 1984)

We begin with a full citation of the provisions of this clause as the required background and reference point for our review of the government's policies and practices and some of the leading decisions by boards of contract appeals and the U. S. Court of Claims.

FAR 52.232-20 provides:

(a) The parties estimate that performance of this contract, exclusive of any fee, will not cost the Government more than (1) the estimated cost specified in the Schedule or, (2) if this is a cost-sharing contract, the Government's share of the estimated cost specified in the Schedule. The Contractor agrees to use its best efforts to perform the work specified in the Schedule and all obligations under this contract within the estimated cost, which, if this is a cost-sharing contract, includes both the Government's and the Contractor's share of the cost.

(b) The Contractor shall notify the Contracting Officer in writing whenever it has reason to believe that—

(1) The costs the contractor expects to incur under this contract in the next 60 days, when added to all costs previously incurred, will exceed 75 percent of the estimated cost specified in the Schedule; or

(2) The total cost for the performance of this contract, exclusive of any fee, will be either greater or substantially less than had been previously estimated.

(c) As part of the notification, the Contractor shall provide the Contracting Officer a revised estimate of the total cost of performing this contract.

(d) Except as required by other provisions of this contract, specifically citing and stated to be an exception to this clause—

(1) The Government is not obligated to reimburse the Contractor for costs incurred in excess of (i) the estimated cost specified in the Schedule or, (ii) if this is a cost-sharing contract, the estimated cost to the Government specified in the Schedule; and

(2) The Contractor is not obligated to continue performance under this contract (including actions under the Termination clause of this contract) or otherwise incur costs in excess of the estimated cost specified in the Schedule, until the Contracting Officer (i) notifies the Contractor in writing that the estimated cost has been increased and (ii) provides a revised estimated total cost of performing this contract. If this is a cost-sharing contract, the increase shall be allocated in accordance with the formula specified in the Schedule.

(e) No notice, communication, or representation in any form other than that specified in subparagraph (d)(2) above, or from any person other than the Contracting Officer, shall affect this contract's estimated cost to the Government. In the absence of the specified notice, the Government is not obligated to reimburse the Contractor for any costs in excess of the estimated cost or, if this is a cost-sharing contract, for any costs in excess of the estimated cost to the Government specified in the

Schedule, whether those excess costs were incurred during the course of the contract or as a result of termination.

(f) If the estimated cost specified in the Schedule is increased, any costs the Contractor incurs before the increase that are in excess of the previously estimated cost shall be allowable to the same extent as if incurred afterward, unless the Contracting Officer issues a termination or other notice directing that the increase is solely to cover termination or other specified expenses.

(g) Change orders shall not be considered an authorization to exceed the estimated cost to the Government specified in the Schedule, unless they contain a statement increasing the estimated cost.

(h) If this contract is terminated or the estimated cost is not increased, the Government and the Contractor shall negotiate an equitable distribution of all property produced or purchased under the contract, based upon the share of costs incurred by each.

The basic provisions of the Limitation of Cost clause (LOCC) seem reasonably clear. Essentially, the contractor is required to notify the contracting officer if the contractor has reason to believe that (1) the costs that it expects to incur in the performance of the contract in the next succeeding 60 days, when added to all costs previously incurred, will exceed 75% of the total estimated cost, or (2) the total cost to the government, exclusive of any fee, will be greater or substantially less than the estimated cost thereof. Unless specifically overcome by other contract provisions, the government is not obligated to reimburse the contractor for any costs in excess of the estimated total, and the contractor is not obligated to continue performance under the contract without a written notification from the contracting officer of the increased estimate. Despite the apparently clear-cut provisions, companies performing under cost-reimbursement type contracts have frequently exceeded the estimated cost without the contracting officer's agreement to increase the contract amount and have resorted to litigation when the contracting officer refused to modify the contract.

In describing the cost-reimbursement type contract, FAR 16.301-1 states that it provides for payment of allowable incurred costs to the extent prescribed in the contract. These contracts establish an estimate of total cost for the purpose of (i) obligation of funds, and (ii) establishing a ceiling which the contractor may not exceed without the approval of the contracting officer.

The basic reason for this clause is to provide the government an option for the action to be taken when notified that it will be required to furnish the contractor funds in excess of the original estimate in order to obtain the completed work. In exercising the option, the government takes several matters into consideration. An important consideration is whether additional funds are available to obligate for this project. If no additional funds are available or can be transferred from other programs, the contracting officer has no option but to direct the contractor to stop all work and turn over what it has accomplished to date. Actual practice in these instances does not always conform to policy. Frequently, government representatives advise contractors that, while no additional funds are available, they are extremely interested in obtaining the final report or other end item and informally urge the contractor to complete the contract without reimbursement for the overrun. This situation presents difficult management decisions as contractors weigh the pros and cons of incurring losses against the potential advantages of favorable relations with government procuring activities and possible future awards. Government officials encouraging continuation of work must be aware that FAR 32.702 states: "No officer or employee of the Government may create or authorize an obligation in excess of the funds available, or in advance of appropriations (AntiDeficiency Act, 31 U.S.C. 1341), unless otherwise authorized by law . . . ."

The contracting officer may refuse to increase the contract price in these instances for other reasons as well. For example, the government technical people may advise that there is little if any likelihood that providing additional funds will yield anything of value to the government and that, in effect, there is no point "in throwing good money after bad." Another illustration may be where the government has lost interest in the work being performed in view of advances achieved by other contractors in the particular field.

The contractor's dilemma when it becomes aware of an actual or potential overrun and the government refuses to increase the contract amount has many facets. In addition to desiring to maintain good relations and place itself in a favorable position for future awards, as mentioned above, the contractor may be persuaded that the project, if completed, may be very useful to its commercial work as well as to government work, while, if all activity is terminated abruptly, it will have very little value. Here again, a management decision is required as to whether the contractor should continue to incur the costs or exercise its contractual rights and cease work when it has reached the total contract cost.

Apart from conscious contractor management decisions where knowledge of impending overruns is available, controversies involving the LOCC include a number of different circumstances, some of which seem to be the major causes of the substantial volume of litigation in this area. Definitive knowledge of overruns is often difficult to come by. This difficulty is true not only for the smaller companies without sophisticated accounting and administrative controls, but indeed for some of the largest government contractors. Many of the disputes we shall be discussing in the balance of this chapter involve contractors' assertions that they were not aware that the costs incurred under the contract were reaching the point where notification was required under the provisions of the LOCC. Litigation centers on whether the contractor knew or should have known. Another common problem relates to instances where contractors, over the years, exceed the costs of cost-reimbursement type contracts, but are ultimately, and at times routinely, reimbursed after contracting officers increase the contract amount. Is this practice a basis to rely upon?

These problems, modifications thereof, and different difficulties are reflected in the decisions by boards of contract appeals and the courts. On balance, a review of these decisions establishes that contractors have compiled an extremely low batting average, but nevertheless appeals are taken even though the circumstances are just about identical to those which suffered adverse rulings. Among the many losers there are a few winners, and these merit a closer study as a source of guidance to contractors facing these circumstances. Sometimes the differences between the winners and losers are clear; other times, the analysis is made more difficult because the differences are not readily apparent.

BCA AND COURT DECISIONS RELATING TO LOCC

There are several ways in which the major LOCC disputes can be arrayed. We have elected to discuss them, generally, in a chronological order to permit tracing of any trends in these decisions and also to add ease and logic in following the precedents cited by the boards and courts.

Acme Precision Products, ASBCA No. 6824, 61-1 BCA par. 3051

The contractor asserted that the overrun was attributable to certain shortcomings of its personnel and accounting system. The board dismissed the appeal and we cite the following from its decision:

> This (Limitation of Cost) clause is designed to give the Government unilaterally an effective tool to prevent the over expenditure of appropriated funds. . . . The clause established the estimated cost as the limit to the Government's obligation to make payment and as a ceiling beyond which the contractor cannot make expenditures except at his own risk, and it provides a method whereby the Government may at its election, increase the estimated cost and thereby authorize the contractor to continue performance and incur costs up to the limit of the revised estimated costs. . . . The clause is designed to give Government officials charged with such responsibilities an opportunity to determine before the exhaustion of funds whether there are additional funds which can and should be made available for the continuation of the project and, where the answer is in the affirmative, to make such additional funds available in ample time to prevent the cessation of work under the contract . . . .

> When appellant entered into the contract it assumed the responsibility of maintaining the necessary cost records and keeping the Government informed as to the status of expenditures under the contract. The contract provided safeguards to protect the contractor against incurring costs for which it could not be reimbursed. . . . A contractor cannot create an obligation against public funds by neglecting to inform the contracting officer that the allotment of funds has been exhausted in violation of the terms of the contract and continuing to incur costs in excess of the contract ceiling. The alleged shortcomings of appellant's own personnel and accounting system are no excuse for appellant's failure to comply with the obligations which it assumed when it entered into the contract . . . .

Emerson Electric Manufacturing Co., ASBCA No. 8788, 1964 BCA par. 4070

This case was one of the few successful appeals, with the added twist of involving a CPFF prime contract and a subcontract thereunder, both containing the standard ASPR Limitation of Cost provision. On several occasions, the subcontractor notified the prime contractor of an impending overrun. Although the notifications were timely, it appeared that none of the parties was aware that the ultimate overrun would be higher than that estimated by the subcontractor.

While the prime contractor did not formally authorize the overrun, it appeared clear from the record that the prime contractor, by its actions, encouraged the subcontractor to proceed with the work. The prime contractor also accepted delivery of the items required to be furnished under the subcontract.

Approximately three months after the completion of the subcontract, the prime contractor notified the government of the subcontractor's overrun, although the ultimate amount was still not known. The prime contractor testified that, prior to the time it notified the government, it was under the impression that sufficient money was available under the prime contract to take care of the overrun.

The contracting officer denied the prime contractor's claim for an increase in the contract price in the amount of the subcontractor's overrun on the grounds that:

(a) the prime contractor's overrun had not been approved in writing by the government;

(b) the government had not given prior approval of the subcontractor's overrun.

The board first considered whether the subcontractor had a valid claim against the prime contractor. In this regard, it found that the prime contractor had timely notice of the overrun and had made it clear to the subcontractor that it desired complete deliveries. Finally, it accepted delivery of the contract items. The board noted that, in previous instances of this kind, "we have held that the Government cannot avoid payment of costs exceeding the cost limitation when the contracting officer, after being notified of the overrun, constructively directed a contractor to proceed in spite of the cost limitation and accepted delivery of the full quantity of the items delivered under that contract." Precedents cited included *Clevite Ordnance, Division of Clevite,* ASBCA No. 5726, 1962 BCA par. 3330, and *Thiokol Chemical Corporation,* ASBCA No. 5859, 60-2 BCA par. 2852. Referring directly to the subcontract here involved, the board stated that "we see no reason why these principles should not be equally applicable to the subcontract . . . ."

Addressing itself next to the prime contractor's right to reimbursement, the board noted that, while the government was correct in its contention that the prime contractor did not notify the government of the subcontractor's overrun until after the fact, it found no clause in either the prime or subcontract that obligated the prime contractor to give the government such notice. The prime contract obligated the prime contractor to notify the government if the costs of the prime contractor (including of course any subcontracts) were likely to exceed the cost limitation. This, the board found, the prime contractor did by promptly notifying the government when it first ascertained that it could not absorb the subcontractor's overrun without an increase in the cost limitation of the prime contract.

In a further analysis of the evidence, the board noted that the government took no action available to it upon receiving the notification of the overrun from the prime contractor; on the contrary, there was every evidence that the government expected the prime contractor to continue.

In concluding its opinion that the prime contractor was entitled to reimbursement, the board made the following points:

> The purpose of the cost limitation clause is obviously to provide a means whereby the Government can avoid spending more money than it is willing to spend and whereby a contractor can stop work when it becomes obvious that the cost limitation will be exceeded.

> It is not intended, however, to enable the Government to avoid paying a fair and just amount for supplies or services delivered to the Government ... We do not think the cost limitation clause can reasonably be invoked by the Government where, as here, the Government's actions amounted to constructive direction (to the prime) to proceed with the work and where the Government accepted deliveries under the contract.

ITT-Kellogg Division, ASBCA No. 9108, 65-1 BCA par. 4635

This unsuccessful appeal involved an overrun due to the fact that actual overhead rates exceeded those used for billing purposes.

Despite the fact that the contractor's book rates were higher than those used for billing purposes, the contractor requested no change in the billing rates. It did, however, submit billings in which overhead was shown in excess of provisional rates, but these excess amounts were shown as suspended on DD Form 396 (predecessor to DCAA Form 1).

During the performance of the contract, technical difficulties and delivery schedule extensions were experienced. As a result, government representatives raised the question several times as to whether an overrun might occur. In each instance, the contractor, orally and in writing, informed the government that there would be no cost overrun. After the contract was substantially completed, and with no advance notice that the contract amount might be exceeded, the contractor submitted its final reimbursement voucher in an amount that brought the total billings in excess of the estimated cost of the contract.

The testimony indicated that the overrun was occasioned by the application of overhead rates in excess of those used for billing purposes. It was stipulated that the actual overhead data were available to the contractor during the contract performance; however, the overhead rates for the years in which the contract was performed had not been negotiated with the government. The contractor claimed, therefore, that it could have had no knowledge of the actual negotiated rates.

The contractor argued that the government was liable because it knew that an overrun was going to occur and concurred in it by establishing burden reimbursement rates that resulted in the overrun and by negotiating the *post facto* redetermination of the rates. But the board did not see it this way. It found that the contractor's difficulties arose from using rates that were lower than those indicated by its accounting records. The board particularly noted that the government made repeated inquiry as to the possibility of an overrun and that, in each instance, the contractor advised that there would be no overrun.

The contractor cited the opinion of the Comptroller General (No. B-137343, dated August 12, 1964) in *Arthur D. Little, Inc.* In this opinion, the Comptroller General stated in part:

> The making of an equitable adjustment at this time for overhead costs, which exceeded allowances to the Arthur D. Little Company at the provisional rates might be proper since this Office has allowed similar claims where it appeared that contract limitations were exceeded solely because of the contractor's inability to ascertain during contract perform- ance whether the specified provisional overhead rates in their contracts were sufficient to cover all allowable types of overhead costs.

The contractor also cited two other Comptroller General decisions (B-143892, dated October 31, 1960, and B-127863, dated June 6, 1956) which granted relief because of the inability of the contractor, in one case, and a subcontractor, in the other case, to ascertain costs during the performance of the contract.

The board saw the three cited Comptroller General decisions as having a common denominator—an inability to ascertain costs during contract per- formance. It expressed the opinion that it was this inability rather than the inability to negotiate overhead rates that made it impossible for the contrac- tors involved to ascertain their costs in order to comply with the Limitation of Costs clause. In the case of *ITT*, the board concluded that the contractor was able to ascertain its costs during contract performance.

As a final argument, the contractor urged on the board that the Limita- tion of Costs and Negotiated Overhead Rates clauses raised an ambiguity which should be construed against the government. But the board did not find any ambiguity since the Limitation of Costs clause limited the total costs and the Negotiated Overhead Rates clause provided that the allowability of costs shall be determined in accordance with ASPR Section XV, which in turn provided that among the factors to be considered in determining the allowabil- ity of individual items of cost is any limitation included in the contract as to type or amount of cost items. Moreover, the board saw the Limitation of Costs clause as a limitation applicable to all cost items considered collectively.

Scherr and McDermott, Inc. v. U.S., 11 CCF par. 80,439, 175 Ct.Cls. 440, 360 F.2d 966 (1966)

This was a different case, decided in a different arena, with a different test and a different conclusion. Under a CPFF contract with ICA (later AID), the contractor was to be reimbursed directly for certain costs and overhead at a provisional rate of 65%. This provisional rate was "subject to revision as at the end of the contractor's fiscal year to a rate which would reimburse the contractor for the actual overhead costs allocable to this contract on the basis of such annual or other audits as ICA (or other appropriate U.S. Government agency) may make. Promptly following establishment of an actual overhead rate by any such audit, an appropriate adjustment will be made in the billings for the period covered by the audit, and the rates so established shall become the provisional rate for the ensuing fiscal year. The provisional rate and payments and subsequent fiscal years shall be computed and adjusted accordingly."

The cost limitation provisions of the contract stated that the government's obligation would not exceed a specified amount "without prior approval of ICA." The first audit of the contract was performed by the government after the contract was completed. It revealed that the contractor's actual overhead costs exceeded the amounts reimbursed to it through the provisional billing rates. ICA then paid the contractor an amount that brought the total contract payments up to the maximum amount set forth in the contract. The balance was disallowed on the grounds that the contractor had exceeded the contract amount without prior written approval.

The contractor's appeal to the AID Board of Contract Appeals was denied, and suit was subsequently brought into the U. S. Court of Claims.

The government moved for summary judgment on the basis of the cost limitations provision of the contract and cited, in support of its position, *Greenfield Tap & Die Corp. v. U.S.,* 68 Ct.Cls. 61 (1929) *cert. denied,* 281 U.S. 737 (1930). But the court found the two cases clearly distinguishable. The Greenfield CPFF contract clause stated that in no event should payments to the contractor exceed a stipulated amount, and the court considered this express agreement of the parties as absolute. In comparison, the Scherr and McDermott contract stated that the government's obligation would not exceed the specified amount "without prior written approval of ICA." The court found this language not as unconditional as the language in the Greenfield contract since here the possibility of increasing the maximum price under certain circumstances was envisioned.

The burden of the contractor's argument was that the government had a contractual duty to audit its books at least once each year. ICA contended, on the other hand, that it had complete discretion as to the timing of its audit and in this view was upheld by the AID Board. The court agreed with the contractor and saw the contractual terms (quoted previously) as unmistakably showing that the government was to determine actual overhead costs each year and make appropriate adjustments. The court further found that this question was one of law, rather than of fact; accordingly, the court considered its rejection of the AID Board's holding as consistent with the requirements of the Wunderlich Act.

The court found that the government's failure to audit resulted in the contractor's inability to determine actual overhead; consequently, the contractor was deprived of the opportunity to make a timely request for increasing the maximum amount payable and should, therefore, be excused from the requirement of obtaining the prior approval of ICA for an increase in the cost limitation.

The government asserted that nothing prevented the contractor from examining its books and determining whether its actual overhead exceeded the provisional rate. In this regard, the AID Board stated that "the contractor was in the best position to know whether the cost of its services did result in charges beyond the maximum obligation. . . ." The court rejected this view. It cited the following explanation of overhead as contained in the contract: "The reimbursement for overhead . . . is intended to cover those items which are normally included by the contractor in indirect cost in accordance with generally accepted accounting principles, and such items of cost shall not be billed directly under other provisions of the contract, nor shall such costs include items of expenditures which are inadmissable as overhead costs under standard Government practices."

Contract Amendment No. 6 made the clause more specific by incorporating a detailed statement of cost principles.

In the opinion of the court, it could not be assumed that the contractor was in a position to make a reasonable determination of actual overhead, and it was not self-evident that the contractor could determine the extent to which its various indirect expenses were allowable under government standards. As a case in point here, the court cited the contractor's testimony that ultimately the government auditor applied two different overhead rates, one regarding the home staff, the other regarding the field staff.

The court noted that administrative bodies have recognized that, in some instances, a contractor may be unable to ascertain its overhead. On this point, the court's decision contains the following as Footnote No. 10 to the body of the text:

> Plaintiff cites *ITT-Kellogg Division,* ASBCA No. 9108, 65-1 BCA par. 4653. In this case, the Armed Services Board of Contract Appeals denied recovery (of costs which were in excess of the stated limit), having found that the contractor had been able, during performance of the contract, to determine its costs. The Board distinguished situations in which the Comptroller General decisions were based upon the fact that the contractor's failure to notify the Government of an impending over-run was caused by inability to ascertain (overhead) costs during performance.

> One of the Comptroller General decisions, B-137343 (Aug. 12, 1964), related to a claim of Arthur D. Little, Inc., arising out of a contract with ICA, the predecessor of AID. The Comptroller General asked AID, which had denied the claim, to reconsider the matter with a view toward settlement. The basis for this request was explained, in part, as follows:

>> The making of an equitable adjustment at this time for overhead costs which exceeded allowances to the Arthur D. Little Company at the provisional rates might be proper since this Office has allowed similar claims where it appeared that contract cost limitations were exceeded solely because of the contractor's inability to ascertain during contract performance whether the specified provisional overhead rates in their contracts were sufficient to cover all allowable types of overhead costs.

> Clearly, the Comptroller General considered with regard to a contract similar to that involved in the present case, that the contractor might have been unable to determine actual overhead.

The court's ruling for the contractor illustrates the tendencies of federal courts to hand down more reasonable and realistic decisions in this area than the majority of the rulings by the ASBCA and certain other (but not all) boards of contract appeals.

Bechman & Whitley, Inc., ASBCA No. 9904, 65-2 BCA par. 5246

The contractor was unexpectedly and extensively involved in another government contract, which delayed the beginning and progress on the contract involved in this appeal. The contractor negotiated for an extension of time. However, it lost some of its top engineers and was forced to assign the work to an inexperienced engineer.

On May 3, 1962, the contractor advised the government that the equipment could not be built in accordance with the contract and suggested certain revisions. The government approved the proposed changes and instructed the contractor to present them to the contracting officer for incorporation into the contract. This the contractor failed to do; instead, it proceeded on a crash basis to develop and build the equipment.

In an effort to complete the contract by the required date, the contractor assigned a substantial number of personnel to work on an overtime basis. The equipment was shipped on July 3. On July 6, the contractor advised the contracting officer that, with its invoice of May 25, its costs had exceeded 75% of the contract estimate. On July 16, the contractor advised the contracting officer that there had been an overrun and that additional costs would be required to complete the contract.

Bechman & Whitley ultimately submitted a request for the overrun costs, the request was denied by the contracting officer, and the contractor appealed.

One of the contractor's arguments was that the government had waived the cost limitations provision by its insistence on the original delivery date, necessitating the expedited work. The board conceded that, where the government knew about the cost overrun and still insisted upon continued performance in an urgent program, it had waived the limitation. *Thiokol Chemical Corporation,* ASBCA No. 5726, 61-1 BCA par. 3011; 60-2 BCA par. 2852 and *Consolidated Electrodynamics Corp.,* ASBCA No. 6732, 1963 BCA par. 3806. However, in this case, the board held that the government did not know, and had no reason to know, of the overrun until after the money had been spent and the equipment delivered. In this connection, the board clearly and emphatically stated: "The very essence of the cost limitation clause is to give the Government an option as to whether it will provide additional funds or modify or abandon the program. It is deprived of this right if it is not notified when the contractor knows, or should know, the estimated cost may be exceeded, and most certainly when they have been reached."

Finally, the contractor pleaded that its failure to provide notice of the cost overrun was due to its accounting system. To this point, the board said that the "appellant's accounting system is its own responsibility and it must bear the consequences of any inadequacies therein." As reference, the board cited its decision in *PRD Electronics, Inc.,* ASBCA No. 7713, 1962 BCA par. 3832.

Baird-Atomic, Inc., ASBCA No. 10824, 66-1 BCA par. 5616

In this instance, the contractor fared much better, with the board ruling that (1) a supplemental agreement had modified the LOCC and (2) termination costs were not governed by the provisions of the LOCC.

The overrun costs claimed by the contractor and denied by the government consisted of two distinct types. One related to overhead increases arising out of finally negotiated rates for the year being higher than the billing rates used by the contractor throughout the life of the contract. Here, the contractor alleged that actual costs could not be computed with exactness because final overhead rates were to be computed after performance. The other type of overrun costs pertained to termination settlement expenses, incurred as a result of partial termination. The government claimed that the Limitation of Cost clause barred the contractor's recovery under both claims.

With respect to overrun costs resulting from increased overhead costs, the government argued that the contractor could not recover under precedents established in ASBCA decisions in *ITT-Kellogg Division*, No. 9108, 65-1 BCA par. 4635; *Ion Physics Corporation*, No. 10493 (65-2 BCA par. 5245); and *PRD Electronics*, No. 7713, 1962 BCA par. 3282. The board acknowledged that these cases were similar to the one in dispute and that it had held that the contractor knew or should have known its actual overhead costs during performance and was, therefore, precluded from recovering costs that the government had failed to approve. However, the instant case involved circumstances that differed materially from the others, to the extent of persuading the board that BairdAtomic was clearly entitled to recover these overrun costs.

The big difference here was the execution of a supplemental agreement that provided that the contractor was to be reimbursed under the contract in accordance with overhead rates as negotiated. The supplemental agreement stated, in part: "By superseding subject contracts to the extent conflicting herewith, all previous provisions as to the reimbursement of overhead costs by the addition . . . of the following: All previous provisions to the contrary notwithstanding, the contractor shall be reimbursed for indirect costs incurred in the performance of this contract in accordance with the clause hereof entitled 'Negotiated Overhead Rates,' at the fixed rates indicated below, for the period . . . ."

The government contended that the contractor was nevertheless not entitled to recover because the Limitation of Cost clause prevailed. However, the board found for the contractor. It observed that the supplemental agreement was executed by both parties with full knowledge of the overrun and that the language clearly stated that the contractor would be reimbursed at the fixed rates indicated. The board was not impressed by the failure of the supplemental agreement to expressly include an additional obligation of funds because "it does include all the information required to fund the performance of the contract and an agreement to reimburse the contractor in accordance with the formula contained therein." Finally, the decision found that the language of the agreement, "by implication, if not expressly, modified the Limitation of Cost clause and that the Government thereby became obligated to reimburse the appellant for the overrun."

The other issue in this case was the contractor's claim for termination settlement expenses, and, here again, the board ruled for the contractor:

> The Limitation of Cost clause expressly relates to costs of performance of the contract. The portion of costs cognizable here under the Termination clause is that amount reasonably incurred after performance

had ceased and is clearly differentiated from contract performance costs. The Board accordingly, finds that appellant's entitlement to such settlement costs, as delineated in the Termination clause, is not governed by the Limitation of Cost clause.

The Marquardt Corporation, ASBCA No. 10154, 66-1 BCA par. 5576

Although the contractor's appeal was denied, this decision is cited at length because of the extensive references to previous, important decisions relating to LOCC. These citations, together with the board's commentary and rationale, should be useful and instructive to all firms engaged in government cost-reimbursement-type contracts. It should also be helpful as a base point in connection with studying other ASBCA cases and other problems involving limitations of costs.

Decision

Our decision concerning the cost overrun matters here in question will relate to (a) a line of Board decisions reflecting the general rule barring reimbursement on appeal of cost overruns incurred in violation of CPFF limitation of cost articles when not funded by discretionary action of the contracting officer; and (b) other decisions reflecting areas of exception to that rule on various special grounds. The cited decisions number about twenty-six in all.

General Rule

The general rule was recognized in early published decisions in the appeals of *Sterling Precision Corporation,* ASBCA No. 4646, 12 October 1959; *American Hydromath Corporation,* ASBCA No. 4505, 3 December 1959; and *General Electric Co.,* ASBCA No. 5897, 28 April 1961. Thereafter it was stated and explained as follows in the appeal of *Acme Precision Products, Inc.,* ASBCA No. 6824, 22 May 1961, (citing *American Hydromath* above):

> The Limitation of Cost clause of appellant's contract is a standard contract clause prescribed by paragraph 7-203.3 of the Armed Services Procurement Regulation as a mandatory clause for inclusion in all cost-reimbursement contracts of the Department of Defense. This clause is designed to give the Government unilaterally an effective tool to prevent the overexpenditure of appropriated funds. Navy Contract Law, Second Edition (1959). The clause established the estimated cost as the limit of the Government's obligation to make payment and as a ceiling beyond which the contractor cannot make expenditures except at his own risk, and it provides a method whereby the Government may at its election increase the estimated cost and thereby authorize the contractor to continue performance and incur costs up to the limit of the revised estimated cost. See ST 27-153, U.S. Army Procurement Law—Special Text of the Judge Advocate General's School (1956), p. 614. The effect of 41 U.S.C. and 31 U.S.C. is to prohibit involvement of the Government in any contract or obligation (unless otherwise specifically authorized by law) beyond the extent and availability of appropriations, and when the contractor complies with the advance notification

requirement of the Limitation of Cost clause this provides timely information to enable the contracting officer to avoid subjecting the Government to any obligation or commitment under the contract in excess of the funds which have been allotted for the performance of the contract. Notwithstanding the availability of additional funds which could be allotted to the contract, Government officials charged with responsibility for deciding whether additional funds should be allocated to the project may in their discretion decide that the expenditure of additional funds on the project is not warranted. The clause is designed to give Government officials charged with such responsibility an opportunity to determine before the exhaustion of funds whether there are additional funds which can and should be made available for the continuation of the project and, where the answer is in the affirmative, to make such additional funds available in ample time to prevent a cessation of work under the contract.

When appellant entered into the contract it assumed the responsibility of maintaining the necessary cost records and keeping the Government informed as to the status of expenditures under the contract. The contract provided safeguards to protect the contractor against incurring costs for which it could not be reimbursed. The contractor was responsible for knowing and informing the Government when the allotment of funds was nearing exhaustion and was under no duty to continue performance after it had incurred costs up to the ceiling. A contractor cannot create an obligation against public funds by neglecting to inform the contracting officer that the allotment of funds has been exhausted in violation of the terms of the contract and continuing to incur costs in excess of the contract ceiling. The alleged shortcomings of appellant's own personnel and accounting system are no excuses for appellant's failure to comply with the obligations which it assumed when it entered into the contract.

There is no evidence that appellant was asked to continue performance by any Government representative who knew or had reason to know that contract funds were exhausted. A different case would be presented if a Government official acting within the scope of his authority had asked the contractor to continue performance after being informed that the contractor had incurred costs up to the ceiling specified in the contracts." (Citing *Thiokol* and *Ryan*.)

The same proposition was stated as follows in *PRD Electronics, Inc.*, ASBCA No. 7713, 30 January 1962.

... The terms of the Limitation of Cost clause are quite plain. Appellant had a duty to notify the Government when it reached the 85% figure (and 30 days) named in the contract (here 75% and 60 days), and as a matter of prudent business it must have known or should have known what its actual situation was cost-wise at all times during performance. Under the terms of the contract appellant was not obligated to continue performance or incur costs in excess of the costs estimated beforehand and stipulated in the contract. The effect of this kind of contract generally, if the Government does not provide additional funds, is to excuse the contractor from failure to perform pending the decision to add the necessary funds. . . .

No less than twelve later Board decisions have recognized this rule in denying claims for cost overruns under generally comparable circumstances, also sometimes distinguishing the exceptional types of cases next discussed.

Respondent's brief also cites, to the same effect, M. S. (unpublished) decision of the Comptroller General B-152408 dated December 17, 1963, which includes the following statements of principle germane to the present issues:

It is well settled that the purpose of a cost limitation provision—Article 2 of the subject contract—is to afford the contracting agency an opportunity to determine whether a particular project warrants additional funds and to protect the Government against obligation in excess of available funds if the project does not warrant them. Notice to and approval by the Government of additional costs are conditions precedent to liability for reimbursement and, in Government contracts, conditions precedent are rigidly enforced. *U.S. v. Plumley,* 266 U.S. 545; *Hawkins v. U.S.,* 96 U.S. 689. According to the administrative report in the matter, your course of conduct demonstrated a clear laxity on your part in keeping account of costs incurred under the contract and in keeping the Government advised thereof in accordance with the requirements of Article 2(a) of the contract. Whatever the faults of the Government may have been, you have not established that the Government knew or should have known of the impending cost overrun, or that your failure to anticipate and report the overrun was due to any action on the part of the Government.

Exceptions to Rule

An early decision in 1961 granted relief for a cost overrun after finding that the contracting officer had given an adequate written notice of increased funding in the form of a proposed supplemental agreement. Also, in 1961 the *Acme* decision above distinguished two earlier decisions as involving the exceptional case where "a Government official acting within the scope of his authority asked the contractor to continue performance after being informed that the contractor had incurred costs up to the ceiling specified in the contract." Other decisions have turned in addition upon the general proposition, sometimes related to termination inventory situations, that "When the Government takes and uses contract-general material or services it is obligated to pay for them".

Additional decisions have discussed different and more specific grounds for possible relief from cost overruns, in terms of the particular facts and circumstances present, based upon the relationship between the Limitation of Cost article and standard CPFF contract articles concerning termination, changes, inspection-correction, and negotiated overhead rates. These and other related questions presently are under administrative consideration within the Department of Defense. To the extent relevant, the above suggested exceptions to the general rule are considered in the remaining decision.

Final Report Costs

Consistent with the above *Acme* and *PRD* quotations and other decisions, appellant correctly exercised its right to refuse completion of the final report at prospective additional expense of about $800 after giving notice of an overrun condition if new funding should not be provided, and respondent in turn exercised its right not to furnish such funding, for the unperformed and uncompensated residual work, electing instead to perform it at Government expense. We find on the entire record that when appellant subsequently chose to complete the final report work with no reservation of claim for whatever residual uncompensated costs may then have been involved, it abandoned its position and its right not to perform and proceeded in its own apparent interest as a volunteer. Accordingly the appeal will be denied as to any final report costs which may be included in the present residual claim of about $60,000.

Overhead Cost of Overruns

The actual overhead cost overrun as to which appellant gave written notice on 1 April 1963 in terms of nearly $150,000 was not caused or excused by any fact or circumstance like those upon which the several recognized exceptions to the above general rule were based. It was not caused by any Government action increasing the work completed before 28 September 1962 beyond its previously defined scope. The contracting officer was not informed or aware of the overhead overrun condition until about five months after appellant was aware of it, and several months after appellant's restricted and apparently final notice of the subcontract material cost overrun in late December 1962; and by March 1963 he clearly had made fiscal plans and arrangements inconsistent with those possibly available to him in early October 1962.

Under the attendant circumstances appellant had the sole responsibility of maintaining cost records sufficient to permit compliance with the requirement of the limitation of cost article or of assuming the risks attendant either upon an accounting failure of overrun disclosure or upon a management failure to give early notice of a known prospective or actual cost overrun. Accordingly, as of 1 April 1963 we find no bar to the contracting officer's exercise of discretion in refusing additional funding of the work completed by 28 September 1962.

U.S. Shoe Machinery Corp., ASBCA No. 11936, 68-2 BCA par. 7328

The *U. S. Shoe Machinery Corp.* decision is another important one in this area, both because of the nature of the circumstances involved and because the decision presents a well-rounded, comprehensive picture of limitation of cost matters through citation of preceding decisions, both its own and those of the courts.

Summarizing the board's decision, the overrun apparently was due to the fact that the contractor's overhead rates as negotiated were in excess of those used for provisional billing purposes. When the effect of the excess of the negotiated rates over the provisional rates became known, the contractor billed the government for this difference, the contracting officer refused to amend the contract to provide the additional funds, thus denying the request, and the contractor appealed from the contracting officer's decision. Pertinent portions of the board's decision are quoted below:

> The Limitation of Cost article is designed to permit the procuring agency to decide whether or not it will expend funds on a contract in excess of its initial funding. The CPFF contractor may cease work when the scheduled amount is reached, but is not entitled to further payment, as a matter of contractual right, if it continues work after the estimated ceiling is reached. Whether it will pay an overrun is discretionary with the agency. See discussion in *The Marquardt Corporation*, ASBCA No. 10154, 66-1 BCA par. 5576.

> The appellant contends that this case presents an exception to the above-stated general rule, and falls within several of the areas in which we have previously allowed payment of cost overruns. Its principal argument is that the overhead and G&A rates negotiated by the sponsor agency are binding upon the contracting officer. ASPR 3.706 is, it says, a mandatory direction that the contract be modified to incorporate the negotiated rates . . . . Further, it contends, this is merely a ministerial act which the contracting officer must perform and, where he fails to do so, the Board should order it done. Appellant then concludes that when the contract is amended to include the negotiated rates, the appellant would be entitled to payment of the overrun representing the difference between provisional and negotiated rates. In this it relies upon *Baird-Atomic, Inc.*, ASBCA No. 10824, 66-1 BCA par. 5616. We can agree that the rates are binding. *Raytheon Co.*, ASBCA Nos. 6984 and 6985, 1964 BCA par. 4284. The wording of the regulation is certainly directive. We do not agree that amendment of the contract to incorporate the negotiated rates would override the Limitation of Cost article. The Board has held in a number of appeals that the contractor may not recover cost overruns created, as here, by the negotiation of indirect cost rates higher than provisional rates. *The Marquardt Corporation, supra; ITT-Kellogg Division*, ASBCA No. 9108, 65-1 BCA par. 4635. The incorporation of the negotiated rates by contract modification would add nothing unless the funding was increased. Such rates would be on a par with all other allowable costs in the contract, reimbursable only up to the cost ceiling.

Baird-Atomic, Inc., supra, did not turn upon the mere fact that the negotiated rates were added by contract modification. Reimbursement was allowed because the board found that the wording of the particular supplemental agreement indicated an intention to modify the Limitation of Cost article to permit such payment. The procuring agency showed no such intention in this case.

Appellant next says that it is entitled to the overrun because its accounting system, approved by the Government, was known by the Government to be incapable of producing current overhead rate information, and was capable of producing such information. It argues that, where the cost limitations were exceeded because of the contractor's inability to ascertain during contract performance whether the provisional rates were sufficient to cover all allowable costs, overruns would be allowed. Citing Comp. Gen. Decs. B-137343, B-143892, and B-127863; *ITT-Kellogg Division, supra.* All three of the Comptroller General decisions cited were unpublished advisory opinions to the contracting agencies, which had requested advice as to whether overruns caused by adjustment in overhead rates might be properly funded. The Comptroller General replied that, since in those cases the contractor could not ascertain that the final rates would result in an overrun, payment might be properly made. There is no doubt that here payment might be properly made, but that is not the issue involved. The question before us is whether the appellant is contractually entitled to such payment, and the aforementioned decisions do not dictate the affirmative. *ITT-Kellogg Division* merely distinguishes the cited Comptroller General decisions on the facts.

Appellant further contends that the Court of Claims, in *Scherr & McDermott, Inc.,* 175 Ct.Cls. 440 (1966), put the burden of proof that the contractor knew his overhead costs on the Government and directed payment of the overruns where it failed to carry this burden. The contract involved in *Scherr & McDermott, Inc.,* stated that the contractor would be reimbursed for actual overhead costs on the basis of audits performed by the contracting agency. The agency delayed audit until after contract performance. Under those circumstances the court placed the burden of knowledge on the Government. It then found that the failure to audit prevented the contractor from making timely request for an increase in the ceiling price.

Under this contract the initial burden is upon the appellant. Negotiations of final overhead rates were to be initiated by the appellant's proposal. The Limitation of Cost article imposes duties of notice, and a consequent duty to maintain such accounting and internal financial reporting system as will enable it to report when costs near or reach the maximum allocated funds. *Beckman & Whitley, Inc.,* ASBCA No. 9904, 65-2 BCA par. 5246; *PRD Electronics, Inc.,* ASBCA No. 7713, 1962 BCA par. 3282. The contractor is not relieved of this responsibility by Government approval of its accounting system for billings under cost-reimbursement type contracts.

We have found that the appellant's accounting and financial reporting system did not advise management of actual overhead rates as they were incurred, thus in the instant case appellant was not aware when the cost ceiling was reached. The information was available, however, from which sufficient data could have been developed to permit appellant to comply with the notice requirements of the Limitation of Cost article. With the development of its proposed overhead and G&A rates for FY 1962, appellant actually knew that the rates experienced exceeded the provisional rates, but continued to bill the latter. Since compliance with the Limitation of Cost article was not impossible the overrun is not required to be funded. *General Electric Company,* ASBCA No. 11990, 67-1 BCA par. 6377.

Appellant next contends that the uniformly-followed practice of the Government of funding overruns created by final rate negotiations requires, under all of the facts of this case, the following of the practice here. Citing *Clevite Ordnance, Division of Clevite Corp.,* ASBCA No. 5859, 1962 BCA par. 3330; *The Bendix Corporation,* ASBCA No. 8761, 65-1 BCA par. 4773. Appellant did establish that its overruns under cost-reimbursement type contracts and subcontracts had been regularly funded and paid for a number of years.

In *Clevite* the pattern of reimbursing overruns had been on the same contract and its predecessors in the same development program; the parties were aware of the overrun in costs as they were incurred; the same persons were involved for both parties; the authorized representative of the contracting officer had assured the contractor that the overrun which led to dispute would be funded, while urging that the contractor continue performance. The contractor, in reliance thereon, did continue performance. Under these essential elements of estoppel the Board ordered the overruns paid. In the instant case the parties were not aware of the overrun during contract performance. The same persons were not involved in funding overruns on other contracts. And there was neither assurance from the Government that overruns would be paid, nor reliance by the appellant upon past funding of overruns to induce continued performance.

In *The Bendix Corporation, supra,* the history of funding past overruns was only one of the factors which led the Board to conclude that the Government had actually agreed to fund the overrun and that the actual dispute was over the reimbursable amount thereof. In *General Electric Company, supra,* the facts were similar to those in the present appeal. There had been a history of funding past overruns, some of them involving the same persons who had denied the overrun under dispute. The Board held that the fact that other contracts had been funded had no effect upon the Limitation of Cost clause in the contract in question. To the extent that some language in *Bendix* and similar cases might indicate that the mere fact that overruns in past instances were paid dictates payment of all such overruns, they must be considered as effectively overruled by *General Electric Company.*

The appellant must bear the burden of an accounting and financial reporting system which did not permit it to comply with the requirements of the Limitation of Cost article, or to protect it from the consequences thereof.

Ling-Temco-Vought, Inc., ASBCA No. 12312, 69-2 BCA par. 7810

The board concluded that the contractor exceeded the cost limitation without government approval and that the contracting officer appropriately refused to fund the overrun. We considered particularly interesting and useful a brief summation by the board rejecting the applicability of certain decisions cited by the contractor in support of its appeal:

> The cases relied on by appellant involved facts materially different from the facts in this case. For example: In *Thiokol*[1] there was a great urgency for the rocket engines and the Government stressed the absolute necessity that Thiokol meet the delivery schedules. The Board found that Thiokol did not in fact have the option to stop performance and would not have been permitted to do so. Here appellant could have discontinued performance. In *Ryan*[2] services were involved, and after it knew that the estimated costs had been exceeded the Government continued to place calls for services, which calls it did not fund. Ryan had not volunteered to fill such calls at its own expense. Here appellant had volunteered to complete the contract at its expense and the Government did fund all orders placed thereafter. In *Republic*[3] the contractor, unlike appellant here, did stop work; was asked to resume work; and was told, unlike appellant here, that action had been taken to get additional funding. The funding was in fact made available to the contracting officer and the contractor was so told—but the contracting officer did not actually add it to the contract. In *Clevite*[4] the Government added work which it did not fund after it knew the estimated costs had been exceeded, and repeatedly assured the contractor that additional funds would be forthcoming. Here the Government specifically told appellant it would not fund any overrun. In *Consolidated*[5] the contractor had not volunteered to fund the overrun, had specifically asked for an increase in the funding, and the Government insisted that the contractor continue performance and was told that its request for funds was being processed and that every effort was being made to get the funding. In *Emerson,*[6] as in *Thiokol,* there was a direction to proceed in spite of the overrun. Without discussing specifically other Board cases holding the appellants to be entitled to recover under the contracts, suffice it to say that none of them involved the factual situation present here—*viz.,* a flat statement that an overrun would not be funded and that the contract would instead be terminated, and a promise by appellant to complete it at its own expense.

Hoffman Electronics Corp., ASBCA No. 11352, 68-1 BCA par. 6794

One of the matters in dispute was the contractor's allegation that it could not ascertain its engineering overhead and G&A expense prior to audits and determination of negotiated rates for the years involved. Inasmuch as the audits were not completed for years afterward, the ultimate rates could not be known by either party. The board concluded "that the proposition fails in its premise of the asserted impossibility of knowing current costs." A footnote on this point in the decision is of interest:

---

[1] *Thiokol Chemical Corp.,* ASBCA No. 5726, 16 November 1960, 60-2 BCA par. 2852; M/R denied 19 April 1961, 61-1 BCA par. 3011.

[2] *Ryan Aeronautical Co.,* ASBCA No. 6244, 23 January 1961, 61-1 BCA par. 2911.

[3] *Republic Aviation Corp.,* ASBCA No. 5729, 6 February 1961, 61 1 BCA par. 2950.

[4] *Clevite Ordnance,* ASBCA No. 5859, 26 March 1962, 1962 BCA par. 3330.

[5] *Consolidated Electrodynamics Corp.,* ASBCA No. 6732, 18 July 1963, 1963 BCA par. 3806.

[6] *Emerson Electric Manufacturing Co.,* ASBCA No. 8788, 29 January 1964, 1964 BCA par. 4070.

Appellant relies principally upon the appeal of *ITT-Kellogg Division*, ASBCA No. 9108, 26 January 1965, 65-1 BCA par. 4635 and three earlier unpublished Comptroller General opinions cited therein; and upon *Scherr and McDermott, Inc. v. U.S.*, 175 Ct.Cls. 440 (1966) which in turn discusses *ITT-Kellogg* at page 449, note 10. It states incorrectly that this Board in *ITT-Kellogg* allowed claims similar to appellant's, where the contractor was unable to ascertain the final actual allowable and allocable overhead during performance. Recovery of a cost overrun was denied in that case with the express finding, applicable here, that the contractor was able to ascertain its costs during performance. Similarly, relief was denied in *PRD Electronics, Inc.*, ASBCA No. 7713, 30 January 1962, 1962 BCA par. 3282, a negotiated overhead rate case, on findings that the contractor as a matter of prudent business must have known or should have known what its actual situation was costwise at all times during performance. This also is applicable here. In *BairdAtomic, Inc.*, another negotiated overhead rate case, these general rules were reaffirmed but distinguished on grounds that the particular supplemental agreement establishing final rates, with knowledge of an existing overrun, by its express wording modified the LOC clause and made reimbursable all costs generated by the adoption of the final rates. The *Scherr and McDermott* decision found grounds for relief in specified Government fault not present here.

Andrew Alford, ASBCA No. 12032, 67-2 BCA par. 6716; 67-2 BCA par. 6541

The extreme difficulties of recovering cost overruns where all of the requirements of the LOC clause are not followed and the general complexities of this area are illustrated in a split decision by the Armed Services Board of Contract Appeals.

The contract ran over many years, considerably beyond the originally contemplated date, for reasons not explained. Similarly, the estimated costs were revised upward on several occasions and the contract price formally changed. In the dispute under appeal, the final overrun (relatively small amount) appeared to be known to the contractor and, as a matter of fact, to the government as well. However, the contractor did not comply with the Limitation of Cost clause. It appeared that the contractor was motivated by the desire to get the job done. It also appeared that he may have been reluctant to take the necessary action for other reasons. In any case, he officially notified the government of the overrun after it had been incurred.

The salient portion of the board's decision is quoted below:

> In view of appellant's statement, he must at that time already have been in an overrun position. The Government was apparently more aware of, at least, "the possibility" of an overrun than was appellant. It is a virtual certainty that if appellant had (previously) advised the Government concerning the relatively small overrun . . . the Government would not have permitted almost $400,000 to go down the drain at that point, and appellant would have been instructed to complete the work. On the other hand, appellant's mood at that time was commendably such as to impel him to complete the work whether or not he would receive addi-

tional funds. The Government gave appellant every opportunity to comply with the contract notice provisions. Appellant understood completely that the contracting officer was not master of the funding fate.

In view of the fact that a highly reputable and prominent accounting firm was allegedly conducting a survey of appellant's books of accounts during the period critical to this case, it is not understood why a special audit could not have been conducted at that time to obtain better awareness of appellant's fiscal position on this contract. It is clear that the Government pushed completion of the contract work. However, it is not clear that this was done with actual or constructive knowledge of an impending overrun. The Government's efficient speculation that an overrun was a possibility is not the equivalent of actual or constructive knowledge. To equate the two would probably put the Government in the awkward position of constructive knowledge of overruns relative to most cost-reimbursement type contracts.

Morally and equitably, perhaps the conclusion should be reached that the agencies controlling the purse strings should, under similar circumstances, have funded the work retroactively, as the Cost Limitation clause permits. However, this is predicated upon actual availability of RDT&E funds, which, as is commonly known, are strictly controlled. In any event, this Board possesses no jurisdiction to decide cases on this basis, and we find that the contracting officer's actions were appropriate in every respect.

Under the foregoing circumstances, but one decision can be reached by this Board, and that is to deny the appeal.

In contrast to the foregoing, apparently there was more than "but one decision," as evidenced by the following dissenting opinion:

Notwithstanding the "Limitation of Cost" clause, appellant should be reimbursed for all of his costs incurred up to the date of delivery if such costs were otherwise reimbursable under this CPFF type contract. After nearly six years of performance, and after three supplemental agreements had added separate increments of money to the estimated cost of the contract to balance previous cost overruns, the parties, by their conduct, had given the Cost Limitation clause new meaning. Although appellant may not be learned in the law, his feeling that, above all, the Army wanted this equipment, and wanted it in transit cases, and would hold still for a modest cost overrun, was truly a more accurate interpretation of what this contract had come to mean than were the bare letters of a clause inserted nearly six years before. Moreover, why should the Government, whose project engineer was in close touch with the situation, withhold reimbursement from a contractor who correctly judged that military need combined with economics to require that this particular investment of some $400,000 should not be wasted by abandonment?

General Electric Company, ASBCA No. 12466, 69-2 BCA par. 7863; 69-1 BCA par. 7708; 16 CCF par. 80,284, 194 Ct.Cls. 678 (1971)

The facts in the case, as stated in the ASBCA decisions, do not appear to be so unique or substantially different from those encountered in various other disputes involving the LOC contract clause (suggesting, incidentally, questions as to the possible outcome of appeals by other contractors had they elected to carry them forward to the courts). Involved here is a CPIF R&D contract where the contractor incurred costs in excess of the contract ceiling without compliance with the requirements of the LOC clause. The overrun was based on the excess of overhead costs computed through rates negotiated with the DOD Tri-Services Coordinating Committee over the provisional billing rates which G.E. had been using.

The government's major contention involved the LOC article's requirement for the contractor to notify the government of any substantial overrun or underrun it had reason to believe it would incur and the contractor's failure to do so until long after the contract completion, thus depriving the government of its prerogative to determine whether or not to fund the overrun. The contractor responded that it was unable to give the required advance notice because at contract completion its records showed that actual costs were within the total contract estimated cost. At this point, the board made a comment that was to loom significantly in the ultimate reversal by the Court of Claims: "The accounting evidence of record is generally consistent with this response."

The contractor explained that the overrun came about because of increased overhead rates during the latter part of the year and after substantial completion of the contract. This increase, resulting from a reduction in operations, led to higher annual overhead rates than were indicated at the time of contract completion. In the circumstances, a question was raised regarding the contractor's capability to decide whether to discontinue further performance. LOCC provides reciprocal rights—of the government to refrain from further funding and of the contractor to discontinue additional work. Absent information of an overrun, not only the government, but the contractor as well was deprived of its rights. In response to this line of argument, the board first quoted its decision in *Hoffman Electronics Corporation* (ASBCA No. 11352, 68-1 BCA par. 6794) and then applied that ruling to the instant case:

> Absent either Government fault or intervention causing an inability of the contractor to know its current cost position, or another contract provision to the contrary, the risk of such inability clearly is the contractor's. This agreed allocation of risk is consistent with the knowledge of both parties that the contract funding is in fact limited to the obligated amounts defined therein . . .

In the instant appeal, assuming without deciding the relevant circumstances to be as asserted by appellant, the resulting new question of interpretation is whether the Government's reserved right under LOC article paragraph (b) to refrain from additional funding remains in effect when the contractor's right to discontinue performance within current funding cannot be exercised during a performance period ending within the contractor's accounting year, and applicable overhead costs in excess of the then current funding are caused by later reductions in the contractor's other business which cause substantial decreases in the direct cost bases that form one factor of the overhead cost ratios.

In paraphrase of the above quotation, we conclude that absent either Government fault or intervention causing post-performance overhead rate increases within the contractor's accounting period, the risk of such increases in overhead cost ratios, whether or not foreseeable during performance, clearly must be the contractor's whether such overhead costs are to be determined on an "actual cost" basis by annual audits of all contract costs, or by the negotiated final overhead rate procedure as specified in the subject contract. This allocation of risk is consistent with the contractor's establishment of its own fiscal accounting period; the contractor's general responsibility for and control of its other business lost or attained during all of that period; and the knowledge of both parties that the contract funding is limited to the obligated funds stated therein.

Court of Claims Decision

On April 16, 1971, in what some have termed a landmark decision, the U.S. Court of Claims reversed the ASBCA and ruled for the contractor. The court recognized the government's basic contention that, when G.E. failed to give notice of the possibility of an overrun, it "did thereby deprive the Government of its prerogative to prevent and avoid a cost overrun." Its rationale for finding in favor of the contractor is very significant, and pertinent portions are cited on the following pages to afford an opportunity for careful study.

> The contracting officer erred in assuming that plaintiff was required to give timely notice of the overrun before it was incurred. By its own terms, paragraph (a) of the LOCC relieved General Electric of the notice requirement. Paragraph (a) provides that "(i)f at any time the Contractor has reason to believe" that a cost overrun is imminent the contractor is required to so notify the contracting officer. If the contractor has no reason to believe that an overrun is imminent, he is not required to give notice. As pointed out below, at no time during performance of the contract did General Electric have reason to know of its overrun. It was, therefore, excused from the notice requirement.

> In *General Elec. Co. v. U.S.*, 188 Ct.Cls. 620, 412 F.2d 1215 (1969), this court dealt with the LOCC and the role of the contracting officer. In that case the court, citing board decisions, stated that under the clause "although the Government is not compelled to fund an overrun in the absence of proper notice, it is within the discretionary authority of the contracting officer to allow the additional costs." Id. at 627, 412 F.2d at 1220. See *United Shoe Mach. Corp.*, 68-2 BCA par. 7328, at 34,091 (ASBCA 1968); *The Marquardt Corp.*, 66-1 BCA par. 5576, at 26,069 (ASBCA 1966). As we view it, the question in this case is whether the contracting officer abused his discretion in refusing to allow the additional costs incurred by General Electric.

Of the facts of this particular case, we are of the opinion the contracting officer abused his discretion under the LOCC and that the board erred in supporting his decision.

As noted briefly above, the LOCC does not require the contracting officer to deny additional funding, where the contractor incurs a cost overrun, without first obtaining the contracting officer's approval. The clause appears to anticipate that in some circumstances where advance authorization is not given it would be inequitable for the Government to refuse additional funding. For example, in *Scherr & McDermott, Inc. v. U.S.*, 175 Ct.Cls. 440, 360 F.2d 966 (1966), it was held that the contractor was relieved of the requirement of obtaining prior approval for an increase in the contract's cost limitation where the contractor's inability to determine actual overhead was traceable to the Government's failure to audit.

In the present case it is not argued that plaintiff's failure to timely seek advance authorization for the overrun is in any way attributable to fault on the Government's part. It is contended, however, and supported by the board's opinion, that General Electric, through no fault or inadequacy of its own, had no notice itself of the overrun until well after completion of its performance. The board stated that the accounting evidence was generally consistent with plaintiff's contention that:

> ... at the completion date of 31 May 1964 and at the time the supplement to the final report was made in July-August 1964, its current cumulative expenditures and commitments, based in part upon its then cumulative year-to-date actual overhead rates, were within the total estimated costs of the contract and therefore there was no revised estimate of the total estimated cost which could then be given.

69-1 BCA par. 7708, at 35,779. In effect, the board agreed with plaintiff's argument that obtaining advance approval for the overrun in this case was impossible . . . .

* * * *

With respect to defendant's contention that the board made no findings as to plaintiff's knowledge of the overrun before it was incurred, we need only refer to the board's statement (to which reference has already been made) that the accounting evidence was generally consistent with plaintiff's contention that it had no advance notice of the overrun. Although the board may not have made a finding of fact, in the technical sense of the term, relating to plaintiff's knowledge or lack of knowledge of its overrun during contract performance, the board did state as a fact that the accounting evidence generally supports the plaintiff's position. Although this statement is perhaps not as conclusive as it might be, it represents the board's considered appraisal of all the accounting evidence. Moreover, defendant has not called our attention to any "substantial" evidence that plaintiff did indeed have advance knowledge of the overrun.

* * * *

Notwithstanding its above-quoted statement, the board sustained the contracting officer's decision. It did so on the ground that "absent either Government fault or intervention causing post-performance overhead rate increases within the contractor's accounting period, the risk of such increases in overhead cost ratio, whether or not foreseeable during performance, clearly must be the contractor's . . . ." 69-1 BCA par. 7708, at 35,780. This allocation of risk by the board was erroneous—it totally ignores the discretion of the contracting officer in allowing or denying additional funding for cost overruns. Clearly, where the contracting officer possesses such discretion it can scarcely be said that the contractor assumes the risk of a cost overrun incurred without prior authorization.

As stated above, it is our opinion that the contracting officer in the present case abused his discretion under the LOCC in refusing to fund the overrun. The board found that General Electric could not have known of the overrun in time to notify the contracting officer and receive the latter's approval for an increase in funding. Moreover, there is no claim that General Electric was in any way to blame for its lack of timely knowledge of the overrun or that its accounting procedures were inadequate. Furthermore, there is no evidence in the record that the Government was displeased with General Electric's performance under the contract. Under these circumstances we hold that the contracting officer did not have discretion to refuse additional funding.

In so holding, we are comforted by the Comptroller General who stated as follows in a 1964 opinion:

> The making of an equitable adjustment at this time for overhead costs which exceeded allowances to the *Arthur D. Little Company* at the provisional rates might be proper since this Office has allowed similar claims where it appeared that contract cost limitations were exceeded solely because of the contractors' inability to ascertain during contract performance whether the specified provisional overhead rates in their contracts were sufficient to cover all allowable types of overhead costs.

B-137343 (Aug. 12, 1964) (unpublished). See also B-127863 (June 6, 1956) (unpublished).

We would stress that our decision in this case is not intended to encourage contractors to utilize less than fully acceptable accounting procedures. Where a contractor fails to obtain advance approval for an overrun and later claims that the giving of timely notice was impossible, the contractor's accounting methods and procedures should be a matter for the contracting officer's first concern.

In summary, we hold that a contracting officer abuses his discretion under paragraph (b) of the Limitation of Cost clause if he refuses to fund a cost overrun where the contractor, through no fault or inadequacy on its part, has no reason to believe, during performance, that a cost overrun will occur and the sole ground for the contracting officer's refusal is the contractor's failure to give proper notice of the overrun.

Stanwick Corporation, ASBCA No. 14905, 71-2 BCA par. 9115; 71-1 BCA par. 8777

In the appeal of *Stanwick,* the board found that the contractor did not notify the government of the overrun until contract performance had been completed. The board agreed that the overrun was attributable to the fact that final overhead rates established by audit exceeded provisional overhead rates used for billing purposes; however, it did not view with favor Stanwick's argument that it could not have possibly known the actual indirect costs until the end of its fiscal year and after completion of the government (DCAA) audit. In denying the appeal, the board quoted with approval its ruling in the *General Electric Co.* appeal, ASBCA No. 12466, *supra:*

> ... the agreements on provisional billing rates for overhead and G&A and for post fiscal year audit of indirect costs were necessarily determined by appellant's own method of accounting for these costs. An audit after the end of appellant's fiscal year was thus required in order to determine appellant's allowable contract costs. We can find nothing in the contract or in the other materials submitted for the record which would provide a basis for finding that appellant was relieved of its obligation to evaluate properly the internal financial data relating to its operations for the purpose of compliance with the notice requirement of Paragraph (a) of the Limitation of Cost Clause, or for the purpose of determining whether it was entitled to stop work under Paragraph (b). *Bionetics Research Laboratories, Inc.,* ASBCA No. 13984, 70-1 BCA par. 8221. In this regard we have considered various cases cited by appellant in support of the proposition which it seeks to establish, including *Scherr and McDermott, Inc.* v. *U.S.,* 175 Ct.Cls. 440 (1966). In that case the Court of Claims held that cost limitation and audit provisions similar to those involved here did not operate to deny the contractor recovery of an overrun, but the Court's decision was predicated on a finding that the Government breached a contractual duty to audit the contractor's books at least once per year. In the present appeal we can find no such breach of a Government obligation. As we stated in *General Electric Company,* ASBCA No. 12466, 69-1 BCA par. 7708 at p. 35,780:

> > Absent either Government fault or intervention causing post-performance overhead rate increases within the contractor's accounting period, the risk of such increases in overhead cost ratio, whether or not foreseeable during performance, clearly must be the contractor's, whether such overhead costs are to be determined on an 'actual cost' basis by annual audits of all contract costs, or by the negotiated final overhead rate procedure as specified in the subject contract. This allocation of risk is consistent with the contractor's establishment of its own fiscal accounting period; the contractor's responsibility for and control of its other business lost or attained during all of that period; and the knowledge of both parties that the contract funding is limited to the obligated funds stated therein. (It should be noted that the board's extreme position that the risk of overruns is the contractor's "whether or not foreseeable during performance" was overruled by the U.S. Court of Claims when the cited GE decision was reversed, *supra.*)

TMC Systems & Power Corporation, ASBCA No. 15211, 72-1 BCA par. 9209

We have included this dispute in our selection because it addresses a different facet of the LOCC problems. Here the board ruled that the government's failure to provide the contractor with a timely response to its request for additional funds resulted in a contract termination for convenience.

Under the Limitation of Cost clause, the contractor notified the government in July 1967 that 75% of the estimated cost would be reached within 60 days. In November 1967, TMC advised that over 75% of the funds had been obligated and requested additional funding. In December 1967, the contractor requested authority to overspend, without which the work would be stopped. The first government response was in January 1968, denying authority to overspend and requesting an estimate of the additional costs that would be required by stoppage and restart of work if requested funds were not made available. TMC replied to the government request and, throughout 1968, sent a series of letters containing estimates, requests, etc., without answer by the government until December 1968, at which time TMC was informed that no further funds would be made available and that the contract would be permitted to expire under its terms. The contractor contended that a termination for convenience had occurred; the contention was denied; and the appeal was made.

The board ruled for the contractor, and the salient portions of the decision are quoted below:

> Appellant's position on this issue is that the Government terminated the contract for convenience and that the Board has held on several occasions that termination costs in excess of the estimated costs are recoverable. The Government, on the other hand, argues that the contract expired under the terms of the Limitation of Cost clause and on that basis the Board cases cited by appellant are not applicable.

> Under appropriate circumstances a CPFF contract containing a Limitation of Cost clause can be permitted to expire under the terms of that clause. In order for this to occur the Government must provide a contractor with reasonably prompt notice that it intends to permit the contract to expire by its terms and provide the contractor with guidance as to the steps to be taken to close out the contract. What is reasonably prompt notice depends on the facts and circumstances of each case.

*   *   *   *

> The Government waited until the cost ceiling had been reached before responding to appellant's request for additional funds. Instead of immediately notifying appellant that the contract had expired by its terms and initiating close out procedures, the Government requested information on the cost of resuming work. On these facts the Government did not provide appellant with reasonably prompt notice of its intention to permit the contract to expire by its terms.

> Having failed to provide such notice, the Government, in effect, terminated the contract for convenience as to any work remaining to be performed under the contract, see *North American Rockwell Corporation,*

ASBCA No. 14329, 71-2 BCA, par. 9207, and, where such exist, appellant is entitled to recover its termination settlement costs in excess of the estimated cost. *Electro Nuclear Systems Corporation,* ASBCA No. 10092, 67-1 BCA par. 6111; *Douglas Aircraft Company, Inc.,* ASBCA No. 10495, 66-2 BCA par. 6049; *Baird-Atomic, Inc.,* ASBCA No. 10824, 66-1 BCA par. 5616; *General Electric Laboratories, Inc.,* ASBCA No. 8097, 1963 BCA par. 3921.

ARINC Research Corp., ASBCA No. 15861, 72-2 BCA par. 9721

The decision in *General Electric Company,* 194 Ct.Cls. 678 (1971), provided considerable hope in the private sector that the government would thereafter display a more reasonable attitude in implementing the LOC clause. However, this decision has remained unpopular with both government procurement officials and the ASBCA, and the hard line has been pursued, although, at times, as in *ARINC,* the ASBCA has grudgingly followed the court's ruling.

The contractor's overrun resulted from an increase in overhead not fully calculable until the end of its calendar year, and the contractor argued that the LOCC should not be a bar to payment because these excess costs were due to an unforeseen loss of business. The contractor's case was based entirely on the aforementioned Court of Claims ruling in *General Electric Company.*

The board ultimately ruled for the contractor, stating that "[w]hile we do not entirely agree with, we nevertheless accept the Court of Claims implicit ruling in *General Electric* that the Government's right to refuse funding of an overrun under paragraph (b) of the LOC clause is, in great measure, dependent upon the ability of the contractor to comply with the notice requirements of paragraph (a) of the clause."

The board's decision devoted some space to making the above point and to explaining that the result reached by the court in *GE* was correct, but should have been achieved on the basis of "more appropriate grounds." The board quoted with approval a paper written by one of its members (Shedd) and expressed the view that recovery in these types of cases cannot be properly premised upon a finding that the contracting officer's refusal to fund a cost overrun was an abuse of discretion. It found that such funding decisions rest with fiscal or fund control officials rather than with contracting officers. The board further stated: "We believe that the concept of 'abuse of discretion' has no valid application to an exercise by one of the parties to a contract of a specifically reserved right, as is the right reserved to the Government in paragraph (b) of the LOC clause."

It seems to us important for contractors to understand the thinking of the ASBCA in controversies arising from the administration of the LOC clause. It is not a legal splitting of hairs since, as our readers know, our reviews of judicial and quasi-judicial positions are limited to a layman's view. The point is that appeals resulting from disputes in these areas are usually first directed to the board, and contractors should obviously orient the preparation of their cases to the board's thinking. An excerpt from the board's closing comments is cited below, and we believe that a careful reading of these conclusions would be beneficial to government contractors.

In our view of this case, the real question is not one involving the scope of the contracting officer's discretion but, rather, the consequences (i.e., allocation of risk) attendant upon legal impossibility to comply with a contractual requirement. While we do not entirely agree with, we nevertheless accept, the Court of Claims' implicit ruling in *General Electric* that the Government's right to refuse funding of an overrun under paragraph (b) of the LOC clause is, in great measure, dependent upon the ability of the contractor to comply with the notice requirements of paragraph (a) of the clause. In light of the courts' ruling and the similarity of the controlling facts, there is but one result that can be reached here.

General Provision 4 of ARINC's contract provides that for performance of the contract the Government shall pay the cost thereof determined by the contracting officer to be allowable in accordance with Part 2, Section XV of ASPR and with the terms of the contract. The Government does not question under ASPR either the allowability or allocability of the overhead costs here involved. The only impediment to payment of the overrun is the LOC clause and, as we have seen, it was impossible for the appellant to comply with it. Having set up the contractual condition with which it was impossible to comply, the Government assumes the risk of the impossibility. In such a case the LOC clause is not available as a defense to funding an overrun. The payment clause of the contract is, thus, freely operable and it requires payment for all otherwise allowable and allocable costs such as the overhead costs here claimed.

The Bissett-Berman Corporation, NASA BCA No. 1270-19, 73-2 BCA par. 10,346; 71-2 BCA par. 9054

The contractor's request for NASA to fund an overrun was denied by the contracting officer because Bissett failed to provide notice as required by the LOCC. The contractor argued that the overrun resulted from costs incurred after contract performance, that the contractor could not have anticipated the overrun, and, therefore, that it was not required to provide the notice.

As the board saw it, "[t]he threshold question is whether Appellant could have reasonably foreseen the increase in its overhead during performance of contract and given the contracting officer the notice required by the LOC clause. The burden is on Appellant to establish its position." The board then identified the question requiring an answer before a determination could be made as being whether the criteria here fit those of the *General Electric* case where the contractor was successful:

The thrust of the Court of Claims decision in *General Electric, supra,* was that the Contracting Officer's right to deny funding of a cost overrun depended on the circumstances experienced by a contractor attending its reasons for not giving notice under paragraph (a) of the LOC clause. If Contractor could have reasonably forseen during performance of the contract that it was going to experience a cost overrun, then it should have given notice, if it could not, then the overrun should have been funded.

In *General Electric, supra,* the Contractor completed contract performance within the funds then obligated on the contract, hence up to that point there was not cost overrun. In the present case the evidence is clear, and the parties have stipulated, that up to October 31, 1967, the end of the contract performance period, Appellant was not in a cost overrun position. However, to bring the present case within the *General Electric* criteria, the question remains whether Appellant had reasonable cause to believe, during contract performance, that there would be a cost overrun and should have given Respondent notice thereof under the LOC clause.

The board cited *Cosmic, Inc.,* ASBCA 15078, 72-1 BCA par. 9278, where it believed the facts paralleled *Bisset.* In *Cosmic,* the board decided that no useful purpose would have been served by giving the LOC notice because the contract performance had already been completed and the funds expended: "Under these circumstances, notice to the Government would have been nugatory. The law does not require the doing of useless acts, and Appellant consequently should not be substantially penalized because it failed to take an action which, though required by the contract, was useless to the Government."

"We likewise conclude," said the board, "that Appellant (Bissett) should not be faulted for not giving LOC notice and further that Appellant could not give such notice under the wording of the clause."

The government argued that Bissett assumed the risk by keeping on the engineers and cited *Astrosystems International, Inc.,* ASBCA 12466, 70-2 BCA par. 8420, in support of its argument. But the board distinguished between *Astrosystems* and *Bissett:*

While it is true the Board in *Astrosystems* placed the responsibility for an overrun on the contractor when hopes for business did not materialize, we consider the facts in the present case to materially differ. In *Astrosystems* the contractor knew its overhead was running higher than its estimates throughout the year and during all that time it hoped for more business. Therefore, it had reasonable cause to foresee it would suffer an overrun. In the present case Appellant's overhead was within budget and it was not until the contract was nearly completed, that it was faced with the possible need for additional business which it immediately tried to secure.

The government cited a number of other decisions to support its action, but the board ruled in each case that there were sufficient differences between the circumstances there and in the instant case. For example, the government offered *Data Dynamics, Inc.,* where the contractor completed the contract within the estimated cost, but later filed a claim for a cost overrun due to an excess in its overhead expense over its provisional billings. Here again, the board pointed up that Data Dynamics had reasonable cause during contract performance to believe an overrun would occur; in contrast, Bissett was operating within its established rates "and the overrun was attributed entirely to overhead costs which accrued after completion of the work. . . ."

The board found that the ASBCA decision in *Arinc Research Corp.* and the Court of Claims decision in *General Electric* were cases in point:

Arinc, in summary, held that a contractor's right to be funded for a cost overrun was based on whether its actual overhead rates could be reasonably foreseen during performance and the Government's right to refuse such funding depended on the circumstances attending the contractor's duty to give notice under the LOC clause. The cause of Arinc's overrun was an increase in its overhead resulting in part from its failure to obtain a follow-on contract and the costs accrued after performance. Arinc did not give the LOC notice. The Board decided the facts did not require Arinc to give notice and it was entitled to be funded for its overrun.

The decision stated in part:

"Since *Arinc* knew that its loss of the follow-on contract would cause its overhead rates to increase, is it now foreclosed from recovering for the cost overrun? We think not.

*   *   *   *

An awareness of a probable overhead rate increase, however, cannot be equated with foresight of an actual overrun.

*   *   *   *

An accurate forecast of actual overhead rates nine months in advance could only be attributable to just plain luck or to the possession of clairvoyance of magnitude which we are unwilling to say *Arinc* should have possessed.

The facts of the present appeal lead us to the same conclusion in this appeal as the Court of Claims found in *General Electric v. U.S., supra.* We consider Appellant has carried its burden of proof.

John L. Thompson Company, ASBCA No. 17462, 74-1 BCA par. 10,412

After a "breather" for the NASA Board's decision on *Bissett-Berman,* we return to the hard-line position of the ASBCA in the unsuccessful appeal of *John L. Thompson Company.* Forty-five single-spaced pages were devoted to chastising the contractor before denying its request for overrun in the amount of some $17,000.

The board found that Thompson did not give notice of an overrun until after the contract was completed and that neither the contractor's failure to report the overrun nor the overrun itself was the fault of the government. The contracting officer alleged that Thompson knew or should have known about the overrun before it occurred and that the notice could and should have been given. The contractor contended, and the board accepted the contention, that Thompson did not know it was incurring overrun costs while they were being incurred and did not know there had been an overrun until the completion of the contract and the close of the appellant's fiscal year. This, according to the board, was not the issue. Rather, and with reference to the LOCC and the 1971 Court of Claims decision in the *GE* case, "the question is not as to what appellant actually knew and actually believed but is as to whether appellant, as stated in the contract article, had reason to believe that there would be an overrun. In the Board's opinion there is an important distinction between what one actually does or does not know or believe and what one, on the basis of available information, should know or have reason to believe."

This outlook established the board's posture and it governed all of its considerations and its ultimate decision. No evidence being available to indicate that Thompson had any knowledge of the overrun, the government went to great lengths to justify the denial on the basis that somehow, through almost ideal accounting and reporting procedures, Thompson could have and hence should have known and, therefore, should have reported the overrun. Failing that, the contractor was not entitled to receive the additional funds.

The board noted that it did render a favorable ruling in the *ARINC* *(supra)* case because the contractor had proven that it was impossible for it to have known about the overrun. It also emphasized that it was very conscious of the court's *GE* ruling, which turned on the fact that the contractor's records were satisfactory. Yet, GE had no reason to believe there would be an overrun; it was impossible for it to know there would be an overrun. And so the board had since paid very close attention to the accounting methods and procedures ("have been a matter of the board's first concern"). In this manner, the board was able to deny some dozen appeals because it was "unable to find that the appellants had no reason to believe during the performance that there would be an overrun and/or that it was impossible to give notice of a prospective overrun before it was incurred and has instead found that appellants, during performance of the contract, did have reason to believe that there would be an overrun and could have give notice. . . ."

The decision gave extensive coverage to the contractor's accounting system, the reporting of the information it developed, and management's monitoring and control of contract cost data. The objective seemed to be to establish that it was not impossible for Thompson to have known and reported the potential overrun. The board even faulted Thompson for relying on labor data that did not reach management until ten days after the end of a month; it thought Thompson "could and should have begun to keep a more current record of direct labor hours worked and direct labor costs incurred. . . ." We wonder about the reasonableness of this imposition had the contractor somehow managed to obtain more current direct labor data. (Would the board have insisted on daily input?) The board found that Thompson "could have known when the total direct labor costs incurred would reach the total estimated direct labor costs and could have discontinued performance under the contract."

The board ignored the contractor's arguments that it had been involved in this or similar programs for some 15 years and that neither it nor the Navy would have wanted an arbitrary cut-off.

Turning to overhead, the board found that these costs had also been overrun, and it was "unable to find that prior to the completion of the contract and before overrun costs were incurred appellant had no reason to believe there would be a cost overrun." Instead the board found that appellant "did have reason to believe there would be an overrun." (This kind of double emphasis pervades the decision.) Referring again to the *GE* court decision, the board found that Thompson's accounting methods and procedures "were not fully acceptable." Reports from the computer section used estimated instead of actual overhead rates. This use is certainly usual; few companies indeed would consider determining actual overhead monthly and allocating it to jobs in process. We suppose, however, that when the contractor was close to the total estimated cost, it might have calculated the actual rates for this contract. This calculation would have been particularly appropriate in view of the fact that the rates were increasing.

The board criticized the contractor for not properly and timely using the cost data available in its cost accounting system. In this connection, it took Thompson to task for the 15-20 day period between the end of a period and the reporting of overhead and G&A expenses. With all of the emphasis on monthly overhead and G&A rates, we wonder how this case would have come out if Cost Accounting Standard 406, providing that rates must be computed for the full fiscal period, had been in effect.

General Time Corp., ASBCA No. 18962, 75-2 BCA par. 11,462

This appeal involved essentially two issues:

1. Whether the government was estopped to deny payment of the overrun by its prior conduct in funding such overruns after final audit determination of overhead rates.

2. Whether the contractor should be excused from the notice requirement under the LOC clause since the burden rates were not determined until after performance was completed and the funds for the contract work had been expended.

In support of the first issue, General Time referenced a number of its contracts where the government in fact did fund overruns after final audit determination of burden rates, leading the contractor to believe that the same procedure would be followed on the contract in dispute. The contractor contended that it relied on this conduct by the government and refrained from giving the required notice.

The board recognized the principle of equitable estoppel but concluded this principle was not applicable to the instant case:

> ... we do not consider that the facts are sufficient to bring this case within the ambit of the estoppel doctrine. It suffices to point out that the record is devoid of any indication that appellant relied on the Picatinny Arsenal's funding of overruns caused by after-the-fact burden rate determinations as inducing it to incur the overrun or to believe that similar overruns on Department of the Navy contracts would likewise be funded. *United Shoe Machinery Corporation*, ASBCA No. 11936, 68-2 BCA ¶ 7328. Further, this Board has consistently held that the fact the contracting officer funded one particular overrun does not operate as a waiver of the Government's right to refuse to fund later reported overruns. Each claim for funding must stand on its own feet. *North American Rockwell Corporation*, ASBCA No. 14329, 72-1 BCA ¶ 9207 .... *A fortiori*, the NOL contracting officer should be even less bound by actions of the contracting officer at the Picatinny Arsenal. We accordingly conclude that the Government was not estopped from denying the overrun.

General Time also contended it should be excused from the notice requirement because the overrun was due to increases in burden rates that were not determined by the DCAA audit until after the time for giving notice had passed. General Time argued that:

> [I]t would be an abuse of the contracting officer's discretion not to fund the overrun in these circumstances, citing *Scherr & McDermott, Inc. v. United States* [11 CCF par. 80,439], 175 Ct.Cl. 440 (1966); *J.J. Henry Company, Inc.*, ASBCA No. 13835 et al., 71-1 BCA par. 8898; *General Electric Company v. United States* [16 CCF par. 80,284], 194 Ct.Cl. 678 (1971). It also argued that since audit determination of burden rates occurred after funds on the contract had been spent and performance had been completed, notice of overrun would have been a useless act for which appellant should not be penalized. *Cosmic, Inc.*, ASBCA No. 15078, 72-1 BCA par. 9278.

The government in its rebuttal contended that the contractor is charged with monitoring its own costs and is not entitled to delay of notice determined by DCAA audits. The government further charged that General Time had actual knowledge of increasing overhead rates prior to the time at which the overrun occurred.

The board was unsympathetic to the contractor's arguments and, consistent with the preponderance of its decisions involving LOCC disputes, brushed quickly by the GE Court of Claims decision and found greater satisfaction in citing its own decisions, most of which denied the contractor's appeals. As reflected in the ensuing excerpt, the board stressed the heavy burden that the contractor must bear of showing that it could not have reasonably foreseen the increase in the costs that caused the overrun. As to the obvious impossibility of forecasting the burden rates until the year end, the board leaned on its own prior decisions where it had ruled that the contractor must give notice under the LOCC when it "has reason to believe" that a possible overrun will occur and that there is no requirement that the overrun be known with exactness or accuracy.

> Since the Court of Claims held in *General Electric Company. v. United States., [supra],* 194 Ct.Cl. 678 (1971), that the contracting officer cannot refuse to fund a cost overrun where the contractor through no fault or inadequacy on its part has no reason to believe during performance that a cost overrun will occur and the contracting officer's refusal is based solely on lack of notice, the rule has been well established starting with *ARINC Research Corporation,* ASBCA No. 15861, 72-2 BCA par. 9721, that the Board must consider whether an overrun could have been reasonably foreseen by the contractor. As the Board stated in *Kaman Science Corporation,* ASBCA No. 18072, 74-1 BCA par. 10,604 (p. 50,285):
>
> > "One may argue about the merits of placing the risk of such fluctuations [of indirect and direct cost rates] on contractors, fixed price or cost type. However, we have little doubt but that the standard Limitation of Cost clause has that effect except where there is no reasonable foreseeability, even with appropriate accounting controls, that an overrun will occur."

We are unable to accept appellant's broad proposition that in situations where post-determined overhead rates are used to determine the reimbursable costs to which the contractor is entitled under the contract, and overrun cannot be computed until the final rates are established by the DCAA. Stated in another way, appellant would have us find that there are no circumstances, prior to the determination of final overhead rates, when an overrun is foreseeable. This position has no contractual basis and the cases appellant cites do not support the proposition. The notice requirement in the LOC clause operates independently of the determination of final overhead rates, which by definition must occur after completion of contract work, and requires notice of possible overrun during contract performance so as to permit the Government to stop work under the contract and so to avoid the expenditure of more funds that have been allocated for the contract work. *Cosmic, Inc., supra; University of Colorado,* ASBCA No. 18750, 75-1 BCA par. 11,288.

Thus we reach the central issue whether appellant was in a position, prior to completion of the work, which admittedly and for all practical purposes happened by the end of October 1971, where it could have reasonably foreseen that an overrun would occur or could have forecast increases in the burden rates which would result in a cost overrun. In order to avoid the consequences flowing from noncompliance with the notice requirement, appellant must bear the burden of showing that it could not have reasonably foreseen the increase in the costs that caused the overrun. *J.J. Henry Company, Inc.,* ASBCA No. 15473, 72-2 BCA par. 9641 . . . .

We do not see any merit in appellant's contention that it was unable to determine the effect of burden rate increases, of which it was aware, with any precision and this it was impossible to give "effective and meaningful" notice until final DCAA determination of the burden rates for FY 1972. The LOC clause only requires that the contractor give notice when it "has reason to believe" that the total cost for the performance of the contract will be "greater" than the estimated cost. There is no requirement that the overrun be known with exactness or accuracy. *Optonetics, Inc.,* ASBCA Nos. 17074, 17834, 73-2 BCA par. 10,174; *Industrial Technological Associates, Inc., supra, Data Dynamics, Inc.,* ASBCA No. 15468, 73-1 BCA par. 9774.

The board concluded that the contractor had sufficient, if not precise, knowledge during contract performance that an overrun was occurring, and to that extent distinguished this appeal from the *General Electric* case. (With reference, to the court's ruling in *RMI, Inc. v. U.S.,* discussed later in this chapter, we wonder how General Time would have fared had it appealed the board's decision.)

California Earth Sciences Corporation, IBCA No. 1138-12-76, 77-1 BCA par. 12,541

We have selected this case to indicate the more reasoned approach of the Interior Board of Contract Appeals to disputes involving the LOCC. The essence of the initial IBCA decision is contained in the following excerpt:

The board finds that this appeal is prematurely before us for consideration because the contracting officer has not yet made the necessary determinations as to whether appellant's failure to give advance notice of the overrun was excusable so that in the exercise of a sound discretion the overrun should or should not be allowed. See *J. J. Henry Company, Inc.,* ASBCA No. 15473 (August 16, 1972), 72-2 BCA par. 9641 at 45,022. In the case of *General Electric Company v. U.S.* (16 CCF par. 80,284) 194 Ct.Cl. 678 (1971), the Court stated at page 687:

> In summary we hold that a contracting officer abuses his discretion under paragraph (b) of the Limitation of Cost clause if he refuses to fund a cost overrun where the contractor, through no fault or inadequacy on its part, has no reason to believe during performance, that a cost overrun will occur and the sole ground for the contracting officer's refusal is the contractor's failure to give proper notice of the overrun.

The IBCA stated that:

> In the wake of the *GE* decision, the provision of the LOCC has had to be interpreted in the context of the particular case. The central issue in such cases has been whether assuming the adequacy of appellant's accounting system, the appellant was in a position to have reasonably foreseen that an overrun would occur or had "reason to believe" that forecasted increases in burden rates would result in a cost overrun. The burden remains on appellant to show that it could not have reasonably foreseen the overrun in order to avoid the consequences of the failure to give advance notice. See *J. J. Henry Company, Inc., supra.* Nor is it necessary that the imminent overrun be foreseeable with any precision in order to charge the contractor with the obligation to give advance notice of an overrun.

The board's conclusion is instructive:

> The appeal is dismissed and remanded to the contracting officer for a determination by him, in the exercise of his discretion, as to whether or not the overrun in question should be funded based on findings covering whether or not (i) the contractor's accounting system was considered adequate by the government, (ii) the appellant could have reasonably foreseen the overrun, and (iii) the appellant had reason to believe that the forecasted increase in burden rates would result in a cost overrun.

In accordance with the board's order, the contracting officer issued the final decision, and the board handed down its ruling in favor of the contractor (78-1 BCA par. 13,045). We cite the salient portions of the IBCA's decision with the observation that, based on the limited information presented in this and other BCA decisions, it would appear that a number of contractors whose appeals were denied by the ASBCA would have enjoyed a more favorable, equitable and reasonable result from other boards of contract appeals.

By letter dated November 4, 1977, the contracting officer issued the final decision denying the request for the overrun on the grounds that the audit had confirmed:

1. The contractor's accounting system was considered adequate during the performance period of the contract;

2. The contractor had foreseen the possibility of a cost overrun approximately four months prior to completion of the contract; and,

3. The cost overrun is primarily the result of the contractor's failure to book direct labor costs on a timely basis.

Appellant reinstated this appeal by letter dated November 28, 1977, contending that:

1. The auditor found the accounting system to be adequate;

2. The auditor would have been equally correct had he stated that the contractor could have foreseen an *underrun* four months before the contract completion, and,

3. The failure to timely book direct labor costs was not previously in issue; but, rather the question was whether the appellant could reasonably have foreseen the overrun attributed to a 22 percent increase in overhead rates in the last six months of the contract.

The Government's disregard for timely compliance with the Board's Orders would suffice to sanction an adverse ruling on the question of notice. However, the brief audit report dated October 20, 1977, provides information helpful to resolution of the appeal. Although attributing the overrun to the appellant's failure to timely record (certain) direct labor costs during the last four months of the contract, the audit report confirms that the contractor was billing overhead at the rate of 105 percent of direct labor and was unaware during the last 6 months of the contract that the overhead rate would increase 22 percent from the billing rates. This knowledge would not become apparent to appellant until a post-contract audit was completed over 5 months after contract completion.

The audit report also states that "the contractor is a small business concern and does not maintain a financial management staff to provide timely financial data." Therefore, the auditor's conclusion—underlying the contracting officer's decision denying the overrun—that the contractor's accounting system was considered adequate falls short of the necessary determination that the accounting system was adequate enough to enable the contractor to foresee the overrun. To the contrary, the auditor finds an adequate accounting system for a cost-type contract which did not make the contractor aware of a significant increase in overhead rates during the contract period.

The Government's argument that the overrun was caused by tardy posting of direct labor late in the contract performance period deals more with which dollars expended exceeded the contract amount rather than the true cause of the overrun and its foreseeability.

The unforeseen 22 percent increase in overhead during the last 6 months of the contract would have a far greater impact, when applied to all direct labor, than the tardy posting of direct costs.

Appellant contends that the auditor could have stated correctly that appellant foresaw an underrun rather than an overrun. In the final months of the contract, a saving of . . . was realized on subcontracting (appellant's letter, September 22, 1976). Considering the unsophisticated accounting system of the contractor described by the auditor, it is reasonable to conclude that without knowledge of an increase in the actual overhead rate the contractor had no reason to believe that an overrun was imminent.

We find that the cost overrun involved in this appeal occurred without the fault or inadequacy of the appellant and was attributed to an unforeseeable increase in overhead rates during the last 6 months of contract performance.

Kirschner Associates, Inc., ASBCA No. 24958, 81-1 BCA par. 14,834

The contractor elected to use the accelerated procedures and to waive its brief and rely upon earlier correspondence and other documents of record. We cannot say with certainty whether the results would have been different had Kirschner elected a hearing and engaged counsel and expert witnesses.

Essentially, the facts appeared to be that Kirschner failed to give the required notice under the LOCC and the contracting officer refused to fund the overrun. The contractor stated that the overrun was essentially caused by an unexpected increase in the overhead rate, the extent of which it did not learn until after the contract was completed because its fiscal year ended three months after contract completion. The contractor pointed to the government's delay and termination of another contract. This occurrence, plus other government procurement curtailments, reduced the base for overhead allocation while increasing the overhead expenses as Kirschner sharply stepped up its bid and proposal activities in an effort to reduce the lost business.

In denying the appeal, the board referred on several occasions to the fact that Kirschner was ". . . an experienced Government cost-type contractor and the record does not indicate that its accounting system was not adequate to apprise it of increasing costs during performance of the contract." In our judgment, these are not meaningful observations because (1) the same circumstances obtained in the previously mentioned *General Electric* cases and (2) in other decisions, the board refused to accept as extenuating circumstances either a contractor's lack of experience or the inadequacy of a cost accounting system.

The board then leaned, as it frequently does, on its own prior decisions and elected to follow them. In this connection, it repeated that a contractor need not have knowledge of the precise amount of the overrun to give notice under the LOCC but merely "reason to believe." From the documents presented to it, the board concluded that somehow Kirschner ". . . already knew or should have known that efforts to obtain additional Government contracts to maintain or reduce the level of its fiscal year 1978 overhead would not be successful. Indeed the record shows that the Government had already awarded all of its contracts for which appellant had submitted proposals." It is difficult to comment on this conclusion, inasmuch as we are not aware of what the records showed or whether the contractor's contracts were limited to one procuring office.

Metametrics, Inc., IBCA No. 1552-2-82, 82-2 BCA par. 16,095.

In another significant decision marking a departure from the ASBCA approach, the Interior Board of Contract Appeals sustained the appeal of Metametrics in its claim for overrun costs, advance notice of which had not been provided to the contracting officer.

When the contract was completed on March 31, there appeared to be a small underrun. However, after the close of the fiscal year, it turned out there was an overrun, mainly because the actual overhead and G&A rates unexpectedly exceeded the provisional rates. This development was attributable to Metametrics' failure to obtain new business as ongoing contracts were completed.

The government argued that Metametrics should have foreseen the increase in overhead and G&A rates and given appropriate notice to permit the government to discontinue performance rather than fund the overrun. In this connection, it noted that it had repeatedly advised Metametrics there were no additional funds available for the contract.

There appeared to be no disagreement as to the adequacy of the contractor's accounting system for reflecting contract costs as incurred; the issue was joined on the question of the adequacy of the contractor's "business acquisition procedures" to forecast the future volume of business and the related future overhead. The government argued that the fall-off of business was predictable and that the contractor's failure to make such a prediction entitled the government to refuse to fund the overrun (*Stanwick Corp.*, ASBCA No. 14905, 71-2 BCA par. 9115). *Stanwick* was also cited by the government to argue in the alternative that the costs were unreasonable because, as its contracts were expiring without replacement, Metametrics assigned its direct labor personnel to overhead. This latter argument was rejected by the IBCA when the contractor demonstrated that it had taken appropriate action to reduce its expenses. The board further stated: "The suggestion of the government that he was obliged to reduce overhead costs consistent with his reduced business must be tempered by the obvious necessity that he continue in business to meet these commitments."

The contractor cited *The Bissett-Berman Corp.*, NASA BCA No. 1270-19, November 19, 1973, 73-2 BCA par. 10,346, *supra*. The circumstances were similar to those in *Metametrics*, and NASA BCA ruled in favor of the contractor on the finding that Bissett-Berman could not foresee a cost overrun during contract performance. The board ruled that the retention of skilled workers at the expense of overhead increases was considered a reasonable exercise of management prerogative.

Metametrics' major citation of judicial precedent was *General Electric Co. v. United States* (16 CCF 80,284), 194 Ct.Cl. 678, April 16, 1971, *supra*. At the time this decision was handed down overruling the ASBCA's denial of the contractor's appeal, we thought it represented a landmark ruling and one that would reverse the line of rigid ASBCA decisions in this area. Essentially, the court found that the contracting officer abused his discretion in refusing to fund an overrun of postperformance indirect costs due to increased overhead rates "where the contractor through no fault or inadequacy on its part, has no reason to believe during performance, that a cost overrun will occur and the sole ground for the contracting officer's refusal is the contractor's failure to give proper notice of the overrun."

As the IBCA pointed out, this reversal of its decision did not sit well with the ASBCA. In some of its subsequent decisions, it questioned the "abuse of discretion" doctrine but finally agreed that funding the overrun would be appropriate where timely notice in compliance with LOCC requirements could be proved an impossibility. Our close review of ASBCA decisions thereafter reveals few instances indeed where the ASBCA ruled that the government's right to refuse funding of overruns was dependent on the contractor's ability to comply with the LOCC notice requirements. In most instances where this issue surfaced, the ASBCA has not been persuaded that a contractor was unable to comply with this clause and hence has denied the appeal.

In ruling for Metametrics, the IBCA addressed the *General Electric* case at some length and set forth its departure from boards of contract appeals decisions that have not followed the court ruling. We believe the IBCA comments are appropriate and instructive, and quote them for study by our readers.

It is obvious that the reliability of overhead rate projection is dependent upon the timely acquisition of expected new business. An adequate accounting system is necessary to accurately project the effect that future business will have on the overhead rates. In fact, the *General Electric* holding is bottomed on the necessity of maintaining an adequate accounting system, and the failure to have an adequate system places fault on the contractor for the failure to give timely notice of overruns. The more difficult problem involved in these cases is the lack of any standards by which to measure the adequacy of the contractor's new business projections. Including the *General Electric* case, the cause of the postperformance overruns is rooted in the failure to secure new business equal to projections on which the provisional overhead rates are based. The court did not discuss or impute fault to General Electric for failure to secure new business in accordance with its overhead rate projections. However, subsequent Board of Contract Appeals' decisions denying the overruns have indicated a great degree of contractor responsibility to foresee that hoped for new business will not materialize. We consider that the *General Electric* holding must necessarily embrace the contractor's new business acquisition system as well as his accounting system. Otherwise, the court's ruling is nullified by a finding that the contractor should have anticipated that he would not secure the business on which his overhead rates were projected. After the expected business has been lost with the resultant increase in overhead rates and a postperformance overrun, the conclusion is easily reached that the contractor should have known business would be lost many months before, when it was time to give notice of an overrun. Procurement and award procedures do not support this conclusion. These procedures often stretch over many months or years. Lengthy interfaces between the Government and contractors often precede the actual bidding or proposal effort. Evaluation and award after receipt of bids or proposals may involve extended periods. In actual practice, contractors rarely discontinue marketing efforts and expenditures until the expected business is awarded to another or a decision not to procure is announced. Under such circumstances, the placement of an unreasonable burden on the contractor to foresee the failure to secure expected business many months before the opportunity its actually lost results in reestablishing the total risk on the contractor to foresee and give notice of postperformance overhead-induced overruns.

In this view of the rule of the *General Electric* case, the postperformance overhead-induced overrun should be funded where the contractor, through no fault or inadequacy in its accounting or business acquisition procedures, has no reason to foresee that a cost overrun will occur and the sole reason for refusal to pay the overrun is the contractor's failure to give proper notice. In the case before us, the parties agree on the adequacy of appellant's accounting system. The record discloses no basis on which appellant should have known, at the time that a notice of overrun should have been provided, that he would be markedly unsuccessful in acquiring new business. Exhibit 20 shows a sustained marketing effort throughout the year, even though at a reduced rate in the last half when it became necessary to reduce all overhead expenditures. We find no fault or inadequacy in appellant's accounting or business acquisition procedures and that it was not possible for appellant to comply with the notice requirement of the LOCC because the contract funds were adequate to complete contract performance.

OAO Corporation, DOT CAB No. 1280, 83-1 BCA par. 16,298

In another appeal to a board of contract appeals other than the ASBCA, a contractor was less fortunate then Metametrics. However, although denying the contractor's appeal, the views of the Transportation Board appeared to be considerably more moderate and balanced than those reflected in many ASBCA decisions.

This appeal involved two decisions. The first, February 18, 1983, 83-1 BCA par. 16,298, provided a much needed reminder to government contracting officials regarding the discretionary aspects of a contracting officer's decision as to whether to fund overrun costs.

In refusing to fund the overrun under a CPFF contract, the contracting officer stated:

> Since the Limitation of Cost Clause provisions must be exercised in a timely manner during contract performance, your delayed notification cannot be favorably considered. It is my conclusion that the possibility of the overrun was foreseeable to OAO and that the proper notice should have been given. Therefore I cannot fund the overrun.

The board found that the contracting officer had interpreted the provisions of the clause as requiring a denial of the contractor's request for an upward adjustment in the contract ceiling absent the timely notice provided in the LOC clause. On this point the board said: "In this interpretation of law, the Contracting Officer was in error. The ... clause ... does not preclude a Contracting Officer from increasing the contract ceiling if timely notice is not received. In fact. . . there is nothing in the clause which sets forth any results which must follow if notice is not given in a timely manner . . . ."

In the further discussion of its decision the board quoted approvingly from *General Electric Co. v. U.S.* [13 CCF par. 82,881], 188 Ct.Cl. 620, 412 F.2d 1215 (1969), and the preceding board ruling, ASBCA No. 11990, 67-2, BCA par. 6565; 67-1 BCA par. 6377. The salient portion of the board's decision to suspend the proceedings for 20 days to permit the contracting officer to exercise her discretion and determine whether or not to fund the overrun "free from any belief that this exercise is precluded by the purported failure of appellant to give timely notice" is quoted below:

> The decision to increase a contract ceiling, or to hold to the existing ceiling, is vested in the Contracting Officer to be rendered in his or her personal exercise of discretion, and this authority is in no way affected by a contractor's failure to give timely notice under the Limitation of Cost clause. "[A]though the Government is not compelled to fund an overrun in the absence of proper notice, it is within the discretionary authority of the contracting officer to allow the additional costs." *General Electric Co. v. United States* . . . .

> Since the sole reason given by the Contracting Officer for denial is the statement in the final decision that she could not fund all or any portion of the overrun because of the failure to give timely notice of overrun, it must be concluded that she did not realize that she had the discretionary authority to either fund or decline to fund the overrun. To the extent that the result she reached was based upon a mistaken belief as to the requirements of the law, the decision not to fund the overrun was not a result of the exercise of the discretion vested in the Contracting Officer. What is necessary is to have the unfettered opinion of the person vested with the discretion. *Ibid.,* at page 629. This discretion is not restricted to granting only that to which a contractor may be legally entitled. *Ibid.,* page 627.

> We view *General Electric* as giving a contractor a right to have the Contracting Officer exercise her discretion in the matter of funding the overrun. Inasmuch as the Contracting Officer had discretionary authority which she failed to recognize and did not exercise, the appellant has been deprived of its right to have the Contracting Officer exercise this discretion. We believe that it would be inappropriate for us to consider whether appellant does have a legal right to obtain funding of the overrun until the Contracting Officer has had an opportunity to exercise the discretion vested in her to fund or not to fund the overrun, as she sees fit.

In a subsequent letter, the contracting officer, in her discretion, declined to fund the overrun, and the board then proceeded to consider the appeal on the merits, 83-1 BCA par. 16,379. OAO elected to proceed on the record pursuant to Rule 11 and it is difficult to state with certainty what the outcome of the appeal might have been had full hearings been held. The facts appear to be that OAO did not comply with the notice requirements of the LOC clause and the board found that, acting within her discretion, the contracting officer properly exercised the government's option to deny funding the overrun.

Delays in finalizing the contract resulted in compressing the time available for performance within the chronological constraints but the board found that OAO was aware of these circumstances prior to signing the contract and hence could not assert the accelerated work schedule as a reason for an overrun which the government was obliged to fund. Further, a review of the proposed and actual costs revealed that OAO had underrun almost each cost but overran subcontract costs in an amount which exceeded the total proposed for all of the other direct costs. The board concluded that at the time OAO entered into two subcontracts beyond those initially anticipated, it knew or should have known that the costs involved would result in a contract overrun.

Portions of the DOT CAB decision are excerpted below because we believe they provide a useful summary of considerations involved in funding overruns and demonstrate a balanced approach to this subject. We also believe that these excerpts contain citations to a number of court and board rulings, a study of which should provide a good overall picture of this continually controversial area.

The general rule is that the Government is not obligated to fund an overrun, although the Contracting Officer may elect to do so. *General Electric Co. v. United States* [13 CCF par. 82,881] 188 Ct.Cl. 620, 412 F.2d 1215 (1969). As will be discussed below, there are some exceptions to the general rule.

Conversely, a contractor is not obligated to continue performance if to do so will cause incurrence of costs beyond the contract ceiling. *Systems Associates, Inc.*, DOT CAB No. 72-40, 74-1 BCA par. 10,403; see also the Limitation of Cost clause of the contract General Provisions. If it does so, it is at its own risk absent the existence of one of these exceptions.

The Contracting Officer has elected not to waive the ceiling and fund the overrun. Such being her discretionary act, the issue we now have before us is whether as a matter of legal obligation, rather than of discretions, the respondent must fund the overrun.

The cases in which the courts or contract appeal boards have carved out exceptions to the general rule are generally situations in which:

(i) the cause of the overrun was a Government failure to conduct timely audits required by the contract. *Scherr & McDermott v. United States* [11 CCF par. 80,439], 175 Ct.Cl. 440, 360 F.2d 966 (1966).

(ii) the Government, knowing of an overrun, constructively directs a contractor to continue performance and therefore accepts full delivery of the work called for by a contract. *Consolidated Electrodynamics Corp.*, ASBCA No. 6732, 1963 BCA par. 3806; *Emerson Electric Manufacturing Co.*, ASBCA No. 8788, 1964 BCA par. 4070.

(iii) when there has been a change to the contract work. *Airtech Services, Inc.*, DOT CAB No. 68-19, 68-2 BCA par. 7290; *Electra-Optical Systems, Inc.*, ASBCA No. 9521, 65-1 BCA par. 4732; *Ryan Aeronautical Co.* ASBCA No. 6244, 61-1 BCA par. 2911.

(iv) the Contracting Officer waives the contract ceiling. *Wind Ship Development Corporation*, DOT CAB No. 1215, 83-1 BCA par. 16,135; *Air Repair, G.M.B.H.*, ASBCA No. 10288, 67-1 BCA par. 6,115.

(v) the contractor had no reason to know of, and could not know of, imminent overrun. *General Electric Company. v. United States.* [16 CCF par. 80,284], 194 Ct.Cl. 678, 440 F.2d 420 (1971).

If a contractor believes that one of these exceptions is applicable to its contract performance, then it has the burden of proof in that regard. *Airtech Services, supra; Datex, Inc.*, ASBCA No. 24,794, 81-1 BCA par. 15,060; *Planer Corporation*, ASBCA No. 21060, 77-1 BCA par. 12,269.

In the instant case, it would appear that the exceptions we have numbered (iii) and (v) are the basis for appellant's claim. According to appellant, the respondent caused it to accelerate performance, and during the short period during which performance took place, billings from overseas subcontactors could not be received in time to form a basis for the notice required by the Limitation of Cost clause.

When the Government directs a change to contract work, including a change to the period of performance, it becomes liable for any reasonable and allocable additional costs for that work. Under the adjustment provision of the Changes clause, a mandatory increase in the cost limit is one of the modes of relief promised for a change having the effects described in the clause. *Electro-Optical Systems, Inc., supra.*

However, in the instant case, the board concluded that "the change, if any, did not occur subsequent to the award, and was known to [OAO] at the time of execution." Although the contractor contended that the acceleration was not known until after the negotiations, the board stated that OAO should have informed the contracting officer that the negotiations would have to be reopened if accelerated performance was desired. Apparently it did not do so and the board concluded that "there was no change in the contract which would create in [the government] a legal obligation to fund the overrun."

The board then addressed the second possible basis, i.e., that OAO had no reason to know of, and could not know of, the imminent overrun, and ruled that the contractor had failed to carry the burden of proof in this regard:

It is a contractor's obligation to maintain reasonable records and expend reasonable effort in monitoring performance, to be able to ascertain when a contract ceiling will be reached. See *Systems Associates, supra; General Time Corporation*, ASBCA No. 18962, 75-2 BCA par. 11,462.

On July 24, a week after award, when appellant entered into the two additional subcontracts, it knew, or reasonably should have known, that one result of the action it was taking was that performance within the contract cost ceiling was factually impossible ... Such knowledge of the impending overrun forecloses any application of the doctrine of impossibility set out in *General Electric v. United States*, 194 Ct.Cl. 678 (1971), *supra.*

We have determined that appellant failed to heed the restrictions of the Limitation of Cost clause on the respondent's liability to fund overruns and, despite actual or constructive knowledge that its actions would cause an overrun, continued to incur costs. Therefore, appellant is not entitled as a matter of law to reimbursement of costs incurred in excess of the contract ceiling. We do not need to reach the questions of whether timely notice was given and, if not, what would be the effect of a failure to give timely notice.

RMI, Inc. v. The United States, CA FC No. 86-659 [33 CCF par. 74,556], Vacating ASBCA No. 28831, 85-3 BCA par. 18,231

This next case selected for an in-depth review again suggests that in controversies relating to the LOC clause, the ASBCA tends to take a hardline approach and, where circumstances and financial impact warrant, relief may be obtained by carrying the appeal to the courts.

RMI was one of two contractors selected to compete for developing system designs for an advanced marine vehicle. Upon completion of these contracts, RMI was selected and was awarded a production contract in June 1980 with a scheduled completion date of November 1981. In June 1981, RMI's contract was terminated for convenience and the follow-on production contract was awarded to the other contractor.

RMI subsequently submitted a termination settlement proposal that included contract costs, termination expenses and contract fees, including a cost overrun which was attributed to unexpected and unforseeable increases in engineering and business overhead rates which were not discovered until after the termination of the contract.

DCAA conducted a termination audit and generally found the contractor's submission acceptable, but questioned the portion representing the overrun because RMI failed to comply with the LOC clause. RMI and the Termination Contracting Officer (TCO) agreed that DCAA would perform a supplemental audit to examine RMI's claim that it had no reason to believe prior to the termination that its actual overhead expenses would exceed its estimates. However, prior to the completion of the supplemental audit, the TCO advised RMI that he had neither the funding nor the authority to recognize and negotiate the cost overrun and then made a unilateral determination that RMI's overrun payment request was without merit because the contractor had failed to notify the government in advance of the overrun pursuant to the provisions of the LOCC.

RMI appealed and stated that the TCO had failed to consider whether RMI knew or should have known that a cost overrun would occur at the yearend. The government in the appeal conceded that it had no specific information as to whether RMI knew or should have known of a cost overrun but argued RMI should have reasonably foreseen the overrun.

The ASBCA, citing with favor some of its own previous decisions in LOCC disputes which were adverse to the contractors involved, declared that "[t]he burden of proof is on the contractor to prove that it reasonably could not have foreseen the overrun" and concluded that RMI failed to carry its burden of proof. Without providing details in its decision, the board stated that information concerning a cost overrun "was available to [RMI] months before termination of the contract and award of the follow on contract."

In other disputes, the ASBCA has dealt harshly with contractors' excuses, especially those by small business concerns, that their accounting systems were inadequate in notifying management of impending overruns. In the case of RMI, the contractor noted that DCAA reported that its system was "acceptable for recording actual performance costs under cost type contracts." Here, however, the ASBCA ruled that the adequacy of the system was not germane to the dispute but rather RMI had the information of the impending overrun but "simply did not choose to use or realistically assess information reported by the system (and available to it prior to completion) and take into consideration the possibility that it might not be awarded the follow-on . . . contract." A heavy burden indeed to impose on the contractor.

RMI appealed ASBCA's adverse decision to the United States Court of Appeals for the Federal Circuit.

Citing the Court of Claims ruling in *General Electric, supra,* the court pointed out that the LOCC requires the contractor to notify the contracting officer if at any time he has reason to believe a cost overrun is imminent. "Conversely, '[i]f the contractor has no reason to believe that an overrun is imminent, he is not required to give notice.' *Id.* Therefore if a 'contractor, through no fault or inadequacy on its part, has no reason to believe, during performance, that a cost overrun will occur and the sole ground for the contracting officer's refusal [to fund a cost overrun] is the contractor's failure to give proper notice of the overrun' the contractor is entitled to have the overrun funded."

The court agreed that the board properly placed the burden of proof on RMI to show that the cost overrun was not reasonably foreseeable but noted that such proof related only to "the time of performance of the contract . . . and therefore before performance is completed or the contract terminated." The court also stated that "the LOCC affords the government an opportunity to stop work under the contract before the funds then obligated to the contract are exhausted. Here the agency terminated the contract . . . . The requirement for a post-termination notice under the LOCC would be nugatory."

"The crux of the matter," established by the court, was "whether RMI knew or should have known *prior to June 1, 1981,* the contract termination date, that there would be a total cost overrun at year-end."

In reviewing the board's conclusion that RMI "failed to prove the overrun in question was not reasonably foreseeable," the court found that information relied upon by the board was not all that clear or convincing, and some of the data relied upon was inconsistent with other information cited in the decision. The court also observed that the board seemed to give considerable weight to the conclusion that information to the effect that a cost overrun would occur "was available to (RMI) months before the termination of the contract and award of the follow on contract," but found no support for this conclusion in the board's findings of fact.

Decisions of boards of contract appeals are freely reviewable by the courts on points of law; findings of fact, however, are accepted unless found to be arbitrary and capricious, and in this instance the court did find that "the decision cannot stand [because] it is arbitrary, capricious, and based on less than substantial evidence." The court accordingly vacated the board's decision and remanded the case for a hearing "at which the board can and should take additional evidence, particularly the testimony of experts in the accounting field."

JRS Industries, Inc., ASBCA No. 33871, 87-2 BCA par. 19,796

The implementation of paragraph (d), now (h) under FAR, of the Limitation of Cost clause has always generated an interest as to the ultimate conclusion and disposition of the services rendered or property generated by virtue of a cost-type contract containing an LOC clause that was overrun without the authorization of the cognizant contracting officer. It obviously raises the question of the government's obtaining access to services or property generated from such services without compensation therefor.

In seeking a resolution to the above question as regards unreimbursed overrun costs in the appeal of *JRS Industries,* the board representative immediately homed in on a recent decision thereon involving the *Breed Corp.,* ASBCA Nos. 14523 and 15163, 86-3 BCA par. 19,086:

> We do not determine here that appellant's proposal that certain software be returned is the proper disposition of this claim. We determine only that the parties are required to negotiate and they are referred to the *Breed* decision for guidance.

> The appeal is sustained to the extent that the parties are directed to negotiate an equitable distribution of property pursuant to paragraph (d) of the Limitation of Cost clause . . . .

Thereafter, it was pointed out in *JRS* that the contracting officer was mistaken in his interpretation of the (d) segment of the LOC clause regarding the disposition of the property attributable to the overrun costs.

> Paragraph (d) provides for an "equitable" distribution of all property produced under the contract based on the share of costs incurred by each. The Government's offer of a copy of the software cannot be considered such an equitable distribution. Nor can the return of appellant's final report.

In the discussion phase in *JRS,* it was highlighted that the government had no obligation to reimburse the contractor for overrun costs but, on the other hand, if the contractor had stopped work at this juncture, the government would not have received the final product it obtained and used.

> The system was delivered in late June 1985 and the Government learned of the cost overrun almost immediately thereafter from appellant's voucher dated 3 July 1985. It refused to pay the cost overrun which was within its rights. However, it also refused to return any part of the software on the basis that this would make the entire system unusable. This is a record submittal and we infer from the Government's refusal to return any portion of the software developed by appellant because that would make the system unusable, that the Government used and has continued to use the software developed under the contract.

The government's contention was that the contractor incurred the excess costs in the interest of making a contribution to the government's benefit. The board member evaluated the aforegoing situation in the following manner:

> It could have returned the portion of the software, which would have made the rest of the product useless, or it could have paid appellant the value of appellant's share of the property. The choice was the Government's. The one thing the Government could not do, in light of paragraph (d) of the Limitation of Cost clause as interpreted in *Breed Corporation, supra*, was retain the property and not reimburse the appellant for the value of appellant's share of the property which it was using.

Inasmuch as the concerned parties were not able to negotiate a resolution of the disposition of the property in accordance with paragraph (d) of the LOC clause, the board awarded the reimbursement of the overrun costs of $37,003.30, plus interest, which allowed the government to retain title to the subject property. The above is an interesting explanation and evaluation of the implementation of the (d) paragraph of the LOC clause that responds to organizations faced with similar situations.

Summary

The provisions of the Limitation of Cost clause are relatively clear and straightforward. Under cost-reimbursement type contracts, the contractor is required to notify the contracting officer of the cost progress in relation to the estimated cost, particularly "whenever it has reason to believe" that the total cost will exceed the estimated amount in the contract schedule, and to obtain a change order increasing the estimated cost. The government exercises its option of funding the anticipated overrun or not. If it decides not to, "it is not obligated to reimburse the contractor for costs incurred in excess of the estimated cost." On the other hand, if the contracting officer does not issue the change order, "the contractor is not obligated to continue performance under the contract."

ASPR/DAR and FPR in the past, and FAR at this time, offer virtually no guidance to contractors or contracting officers as to the administration of this clause. Accordingly, when controversies arise, both sides must study the case law—decisions by federal courts, boards of contract appeals, and the General Accounting Office—to reach a judgment regarding the relative rights and responsibilities of the parties in the specific circumstances. A study of the case law, however, reveals that this area is extremely complex, especially where a contractor has failed to comply with the notification provisions of the LOCC, incurred costs in excess of the schedule, and the contracting officer has refused to provide funds for such excess.

In the preponderance of its rulings, the ASBCA stresses that the LOCC is designed to protect the government by offering it the options to fund or not to fund amounts beyond the contract estimate. Contractors' arguments that they did not have "reason to believe" they would overrun the contract are seldom acceptable to this board, which appears to have established extremely high, and what at times appear to be unreasonable, standards for contractors' accounting and management information systems. In our review of ASBCA decisions in this chapter, we have selected the few where that board did rule in the contractors' favor and some in which appeals were denied. It is important for the reader to be aware of the fact that the ASBCA decisions described here are not indicative of the heavy preponderance of ASBCA adverse rulings. Because that board tends to justify what appears to us to be a hard-line approach by repetitiously citing its own prior decisions, we have omitted analyses of a number of rulings, presented in the prior editions of this text, that denied contractors' appeals. Brief summaries of some of these decisions are included below.

In *Ion Physics Corp.,* ASBCA No. 10493, 65-2 BCA par. 5245, the contractor was unsuccessful in arguing (1) that the costs in excess of the estimate were incurred in anticipation of a contract award that did not materialize because the government lacked the funds and (2) that the work performed benefited the government.

In *Hittman Associates, Inc.,* ASBCA No. 14638, 71-1 BCA par. 8706, the contractor asserted that it had received authority to continue work beyond the contract completion date and had obtained agreement that costs incurred thereafter would be reimbursed. The board turned down the appeal when the government denied it had authorized expenditures beyond the contract estimate and Hittman could not prove that such authority emanated from the contracting officer or other authorized official.

In *The Stanwick Corporation,* ASBCA No. 14905, 71-2 BCA par. 9115; 71-1 BCA par. 8777, the board rejected the contractor's argument that it could *not have* known of the overrun attributable to actual overhead rates in excess of provisional rates until the completion of the DCAA audit. It distinguished this appeal from the court's ruling in *Scherr and McDermott, Inc., supra,* where the government's failure to audit timely breached a contractual duty. Such contractual requirement was not included in Stanwick's (and most other) contract.

In *Industrial Technological Associates, Inc.,* ASBCA No. 16075, 72-2 BCA par. 9531, the contractor's arguments included the assertion that its circumstances were similar to those of the General Electric Company where a Court of Claims in 1971 ruled that the contracting officer abused his discretion by refusing to fund the cost overrun where a contractor, through no fault on its part, had no reason to believe during performance that a cost overrun would occur. Here the board ruled against the contractor on the basis that the facts were different in that Industrial's accounting system was not adequate to apprise it of a possible overrun.

In *The J.J. Henry Company, Inc.,* appeals, ASBCA Nos. 13835-7, 13839, and 13881, 71-1 BCA par. 8898; ASBCA No. 15168, 72-1 BCA par. 9362; and ASBCA No. 15473, 72-2 BCA par. 9641, the contractor presented several arguments but none was acceptable to the board. Detailed management reports to the government were not considered "the specified notice required by the" LOCC. Henry's use of higher overhead rates for proposals for additional work, and the government's acceptance of such rates for substantial contract modifications were not accepted as "a constructive directive by the government for Henry to proceed regardless of the original limitation." With regard to both of these arguments, the board further noted that notice by the contractor alone does not "constitute a license" for it to incur costs since the contracting officer will not necessarily decide to fund them. Henry also argued, in line with the 1971 *General Electric Company* Court of Claims decision, that the contracting officer had failed to exercise his discretion regarding the funding of the overruns. However, never enthusiastic about this court ruling, the ASBCA asserted that Henry's circumstances were different and that Henry did indeed have reason to believe that a cost overrun would be incurred.

In *Data Dynamics, Inc.,* ASBCA No. 15468, 73-1 BCA par. 9774, a contractor again tried to cite the *GE* decision and argued that, since it had no reason to know it would incur an overrun, it was not obliged to notify the government. The board ruled, however, that the contractor's records were adequate to furnish the requisite information to forecast overhead rates.

Systems Research Corporation (SRC), ASBCA No. 16907, 73-1 BCA par. 9931, represented another Armed Services Board of Contract Appeals denial of a contractor's appeal, but the contractor's arguments differed from those in the preceding cases. SRC argued (1) at the time the contract was awarded the Navy indicated that the program would represent a long-term relationship; (2) DCAA audits establish its costs and bases for recoveries; and (3) under a similar contract the overrun was funded. The board swept aside these arguments: (1) Navy had furnished no guarantees to SRC regarding long-term relationships; (2) DCAA audits do not relieve contractors of the obligation of complying with the provisions of the LOCC; and (3) experiences on prior contracts do not establish precedents.

In *The Optonetics, Inc.,* ASBCA Nos. 17074 and 17834, 73-2 BCA par. 10,174; ASBCA No. 17015, 73-2 BCA par. 10,173, the board was not impressed by the fact that the contractor was a small business firm whose work was 100% on government contracts, and who went bankrupt while trying to perform on its remaining contracts and to conform to the government accounting and reporting requirements. It turned a deaf ear to the contractor's arguments that it had been unable to afford a bookkeeper, that it was preoccupied with its financial problems, and that the overrun resulted when actual overhead exceeded the provisional overhead rates.

In *Research Triangle Institute,* ASBCA Nos. 18757 and 18875, 74-1 BCA par. 10,613, one of the issues was the alleged ambiguity between the LOCC and the Negotiated Overhead Rates (NOR) clause, an issue that had surfaced in a number of other disputes. The rulings in these instances have held that the NOR clause limits recovery to the extent of excluding unallowable costs and that the costs that exceed the contract estimate without contracting officer approval are unallowable. On other arguments presented by Research, the board said it "need not reach the issues of appellant's anticipated decline in overhead, expectations for new business, whether the contracting officers abused their discretion in refusing to fund overruns, or the relevance of such overruns having been funded on many other similar contracts." The board's reason for turning away from these significant defenses was its conclusion that Research "knew or should have known it would have a cost overrun . . . ."

Looking beyond the Armed Services Board of Contract Appeals, however, we find a number of authorities with a more even-handed outlook on the appropriate and equitable application of the LOCC. GAO, for example, which certainly is not known for an overly kind disposition to government contractors, has handed down several opinions, cited earlier in this chapter, where it concluded overruns should be funded because of the inability of contractors to ascertain costs during contract performance.

More significant in terms of practical considerations today have been the rulings of the U.S. Court of Claims, particularly the cited 1971 decision in *General Electric Company* in which the court said the ASBCA finding "was erroneous—it totally ignores the discretion of the contracting officer in allowing or denying additional funding for overruns." Citing the ASBCA's own findings of fact, the court said that General Electric was not to blame for its lack of timely knowledge of the overrun nor were its accounting procedures inadequate. "Under the circumstances we hold that the contracting officer did not have discretion to refuse additional funding."

Other significant differences between the views of the court and the ASBCA include the latter's extremely high, and what at times appear to be quite unreasonable, standards for contractors' accounting and management information systems. In contrast, although the court stressed its interest in "fully acceptable accounting procedures," it has not demanded the perfection and unrealistic timeliness of data flow insisted upon by the ASBCA.

Reference is also made to the 1986 ruling by the Court of Appeals for the Federal Circuit, vacating the ASBCA's adverse ruling in *RMI, Inc.* on the basis that it was "arbitrary, capricious, and based on less than substantial evidence." The board's ruling on the remand is not available at this writing. It will be interesting to see whether the board tries to justify its original ruling or if it takes this opportunity to undergo an agonizing reappraisal of its position on disputes relating to the LOC clause.

Even a number of its sister boards of contract appeals display a more reasonable approach to this complex area. In *The Bissett-Berman Corporation, supra,* the NASA Board of Contract Appeals sustained the contractor's appeal finding it could not have anticipated the overrun and, therefore, was not required to provide the notice required under the LOCC. The NASA BCA decision was based, in part, on the court's 1971 *General Electric* ruling. In *California Earth Sciences Corporation, supra,* the Interior Board of Contract Appeals, also guided by the aforementioned court ruling, concluded that the cost overrun "occurred without the fault or inadequacy of the appellant and was attributed to an unforeseeable increase in overhead rates during the last 6 months of contract performance." And finally, in *Metametrics, Inc., supra,* the Interior Board of Contract Appeals again elected to follow the reasonable and even-handed views of the Court of Claims rather than those of the ASBCA in finding for the contractor. The IBCA found that the contractor had no reason to foresee the cost overrun—it could not have anticipated the loss of business and its inability to replace it. Interestingly, the Interior Board chided the ASBCA for not gracefully accepting and following the Court of Claims and found that ASBCA decisions "have indicated a great degree (compared with that of the Court) of contractor responsibility to foresee that hoped-for new business will not materialize."

To reiterate the basic considerations in the LOC clause, the contractor is required to give appropriate notice of cost status and assumes a very real risk if it incurs costs in excess of the contract estimate without a change order that provides funding for such additional costs. All of the boards of contract appeals and the Court of Claims agree that a contractor under a cost-reimbursement type contract is responsible for "fully acceptable accounting procedures." Accordingly, a contractor who failed to comply with the LOCC and cannot demonstrate acceptable accounting procedures and appropriate estimating procedures, where a contracting officer refuses to fund the overrun, will likely fail in litigation. The contractor cannot expect any relief based on the facts that the government funded overruns in the past or that the procurement agency's technical people urged continuation of the work. Each contract stands on its own and authority to proceed must emanate from the contracting officer.

There are circumstances, however, where cost overruns cannot be foreseen despite an adequate accounting system. For example, as demonstrated by some of the cases reviewed in this chapter, there may not be an overrun at the completion of the contract; however, where the contract is completed before the end of the contractor's fiscal year, and an unpredictable loss of business results in a higher-than-anticipated overhead rate for the year, the final costing of the contract may reflect an overrun. In these circumstances, a favorable decision may be expected from the courts and some of the boards of contract appeals while more difficulties would probably be encountered if the company does business with the Department of Defense or another agency from which appeals flow to the ASBCA.

Where a contractor has been denied an overrun funding by the contracting officer and an appeal under the Disputes clause is under consideration, the final decision on whether to expend the time and expense of litigation should be based on the views of the company's legal and accounting advisors as to whether the circumstances parallel those of the contractors who prevailed in the appeals described in this chapter. Special consideration is required before appealing to the ASBCA in view of that board's unusual and at times unrealistic conceptions as to the near-perfection expected in contractors' accounting and estimating systems in disputes arising under the LOC clause.

Chapter XXI

Termination of Government Contracts

SCOPE OF CHAPTER

Virtually all government contracts for supplies and services contain two termination clauses: termination for the convenience of the government and termination for default. We shall address the regulations, policies, and practices related to both types of termination. However, the major attention will be accorded to convenience terminations because they present most of the accounting and financial management problems. Default terminations are usually more disastrous, but they entail technical and legal matters to a greater extent.

DAR Section VIII and Section XV, Part 2, paragraph 15-205.42, and FPR Part 1-8 and Subpart 1-15.2, paragraph 1-25.205-42, set forth the basic government procurement regulations governing termination of contracts awarded as a result of solicitations dated prior to April 1, 1984. As in many other areas, FPR has tended to play follow-the-leader to DAR. The two regulations are identical in most respects and substantially similar in others. FAR, of course, is the significant regulation at this writing and for the future and will be cited in this chapter for regulatory references. Coverage will also be accorded to certain additional provisions of the DOD FAR Supplement.

At the opening of Chapter XX of this text, Limitation of Cost Provisions of Government Cost-Reimbursement Type Contracts—Policies, Practices and Case Law, we noted three areas where accounting and related principles have been established essentially through judicial decisions: Limitation of Cost clause, Price Reduction for Defective Pricing, and continuing costs under contracts terminated for the convenience of the government. Accordingly, this chapter will contain reviews and analyses of decisions by the federal courts and boards of contract appeals that have provided the framework for establishing the allowability of continuing costs arising from convenience terminations.

TERMINATION FOR DEFAULT v. TERMINATION FOR CONVENIENCE OF THE GOVERNMENT

We shall discuss in some detail some of the financial, economic, and other differences between the two types of contract termination actions by the government. In these introductory comments, we wish to note that, in many respects, the concepts and procedures underlying default terminations have their counterparts in transactions in the private sector. A seller agrees to provide goods or services meeting certain specifications at a specified date or

803

dates. The contract will generally provide that, where the seller is unable or unwilling to perform under the agreed-upon terms, the buyer may cancel or terminate the contract. There will also be provisions requiring the seller to compensate the buyer for the damages the latter suffers by reason of the default.

The termination for convenience has no real counterpart in commercial practice in which a buyer's decision to cancel may well result in requirements for the buyer to reimburse the seller for large costs that may include the total price of the original contract and, in some instances, additional amounts for various financial damages suffered by the seller. In sharp contrast, the government as a buyer plays two roles: one parallels that of the commercial buyer, and the second, more importantly, parallels the role of the sovereign. It is in the role of the sovereign that principles governing government convenience terminations must be understood.

More than 100 years ago, the U.S. Supreme Court ruled that the federal government had the right to terminate a contract even though the contract did not contain a termination clause. The Court reasoned that the government must enter into numerous contracts for the public service and must have the capability to terminate any of them when the goods or services are no longer required. In more recent times, in *G.L. Christian and Associates v. U.S.* (312 F.2d 408) Ct.Cls. 1963, the Court of Claims enunciated the so-called "Christian Doctrine," which provides, in effect, that any clause required to be included in a contract shall be considered to be included even if it was omitted. In any case, however, today's contracts for goods and services do contain a convenience termination clause.

When the previous editions of this text were written, the government's sovereign role was disturbing, frequently overshadowing its role as a party to a contract. In recent years, however, as described later in this chapter, major court decisions in *A. Tornecello* and *Soledad Enterprises, Inc.,* and *Vibra-Tech Engineers, Inc.,* appeared to restore a more reasonable sense of balance and justice to government-contractor relationships where the government terminates contracts for its convenience.

COMPLETE v. PARTIAL TERMINATIONS FOR CONVENIENCE OF THE GOVERNMENT

Although the terms are self-explanatory, the accounting, economic, and legal differences are very significant. As we shall describe later in this chapter, judicial rulings have generated severe economic consequences as a result of complete terminations to contractors because of the limitations imposed on recovery of continuing costs beyond the contractors' control. In contrast, in the case of partial terminations, these consequences can be mitigated to the extent that claims may be filed for equitable price adjustments for the unterminated portion of the contract.

Assume a contractor has a contract for 1,000 widgets, has shipped 100, and is notified that, under a partial termination, the total quantity is reduced to 500. In these circumstances, it should prepare two claims: one for the costs incident to the 500 widgets terminated, and the second, and frequently more important, for the increased unit price of the 400 widgets to be delivered.

When a contractor has planned for space, equipment, and people to produce a quantity of 1,000, the manufacture of half this quantity will inevitably result in much higher unit costs.

TERMINATIONS FOR CONVENIENCE OF THE GOVERNMENT

Duties of Parties After Notice of Termination

In some circumstances, the contractor receives advance indications that its contract will be terminated. At other times, the first notification and related shock is in the form of a telegram, closely followed by a letter sent by certified mail with a return receipt requested. These notifications contain standardized instructions. The required actions by the contractor and contracting officer set forth below are extracted from FAR.

49.104 Duties of prime contractor after receipt of notice of termination.

After receipt of the notice of termination, the contractor shall comply with the notice and the termination clause of the contract, except as otherwise directed by the TCO. The notice and clause applicable to convenience terminations generally require that the contractor—

(a) Stop work immediately on the terminated portion of the contract and stop placing subcontracts thereunder;

(b) Terminate all subcontracts related to the terminated portion of the prime contract;

(c) Immediately advise the TCO of any special circumstances precluding the stoppage of work;

(d) Perform the continued portion of the contract and submit promptly any request for an equitable adjustment of price for the continued portion, supported by evidence of any increase in the cost, if the termination is partial;

(e) Take necessary or directed action to protect and preserve property in the contractor's possession in which the Government has or may acquire an interest and, as directed by the TCO, deliver the property to the Government;

(f) Promptly notify the TCO in writing of any legal proceedings growing out of any subcontract or other commitment related to the terminated portion of the contract;

(g) Settle outstanding liabilities and proposals arising out of termination of subcontracts, obtaining any approvals or ratifications required by the TCO;

(h) Promptly submit the contractor's own settlement proposal, supported by appropriate schedules; and

(i) Dispose of termination inventory, as directed or authorized by the TCO.

49.105 Duties of termination contracting officer after issuance of notice of termination.

(a) Consistent with the termination clause and the notice of termination, the TCO shall—

(1) Direct the action required of the prime contractor;

(2) Examine the settlement proposal of the prime contractor and, when appropriate, the settlement proposals of subcontractors;

(3) Promptly negotiate settlement with the contractor and enter into a settlement agreement; and

(4) Promptly settle the contractor's settlement proposal by determination for the elements that cannot be agreed on, if unable to negotiate a complete settlement.

(b) To expedite settlement, the TCO may request specially qualified personnel to—

(1) Assist in dealings with the contractor;

(2) Advise on legal and contractual matters;

(3) Conduct accounting reviews and advise and assist on accounting matters; and

(4) Perform the following functions regarding termination inventory (see Subpart 45.6):

(i) Verify its existence.

(ii) Determine qualitative and quantitative allocability.

(iii) Make recommendations concerning serviceability.

(iv) Undertake necessary screening and redistribution.

(v) Assist the contractor in accomplishing other disposition.

(c) The TCO should promptly hold a conference with the contractor to develop a definite program for effecting the settlement. When appropriate in the judgment of the TCO, after consulting with the contractor, principal subcontractors should be requested to attend. Topics that should be discussed at the conference and documented include—

(1) General principles relating to the settlement of any settlement proposal, including obligations of the contractor under the termination clause of the contract;

(2) Extent of the termination, point at which work is stopped, and status of any plans, drawings, and information that would have been delivered had the contract been complete;

(3) Status of any continuing work;

(4) Obligation of the contractor to terminate subcontracts and general principles to be followed in settling subcontractor settlement proposals;

(5) Names of subcontractors involved and the dates termination notices were issued to them;

(6) Contractor personnel handling review and settlement of subcontractor settlement proposals and the methods being used;

(7) Arrangements for transfer of title and delivery to the Government of any material required by the Government;

(8) General principles and procedures to be followed in the protection, preservation, and disposition of the contractor's and subcontractors' termination inventories, including the preparation of termination inventory schedules;

(9) Contractor accounting practices and preparation of SF 1439 (Schedule of Accounting Information (49.602-3));

(10) Form in which to submit settlement proposals;

(11) Accounting review of settlement proposals;

(12) Any requirement for interim financing in the nature of partial payments;

(13) Tentative time schedule for negotiation of the settlement, including submission by the contractor and subcontractors of settlement proposals, termination inventory schedules, and accounting information schedules;

(14) Actions taken by the contractor to minimize impact upon employees affected adversely by the termination (see paragraph (g) of the letter notice in 49.601-2); and

(15) Obligation of the contractor to furnish accurate, complete, and current cost or pricing data, and to certify to that effect in accordance with 15.804-4(h) when the amount of a termination settlement agreement, or a partial termination settlement agreement plus the estimate to complete the continued portion of the contract exceeds the threshold in 15.804.

Administrative and Accounting Problems Relating to Contract Terminations

Some of the principal problems are generated by the very nature of a contract termination, which creates administrative and accounting circumstances substantially different from those contractors are accustomed to in the day-to-day affairs of a going concern. The very first step, based on the recognition that different circumstances will be encountered, should be the establishment of plans and procedures, including organizational accommodations.

As provided in FAR 49.105(b), the termination contracting officer (TCO) is advised to "request specially qualified personnel" within the government to assist in the legal, accounting, administrative and technical matters surfacing as a result of the termination.

A company whose contract has been terminated cannot afford to do less, and it is the failure to effectively organize for the settlement that has caused many of the problems that prevented contractors from obtaining equitable recovery resulting from the government's action. In the author's extensive experience in contract terminations of almost four decades, he has urged his clients, as the initial step in terminations that are likely to involve large sums of money and other significant consequences, to appoint a "termination project leader," a counterpart to the TCO, to charge the termination project leader with coordinating all of the contracting technical, legal, accounting, and other matters, and to give the project leader the authority to organize a team of experts in each of these fields.

Among the initial actions, the termination project leader should assure compliance with the duties and requirements of the termination notice (see FAR 49.104). If all work is not stopped immediately, the contractor risks incurring costs that will not be reimbursed. On the other hand, both the contractor's and the government's interests are often best served when the cessation of all work is not immediate. Sometimes, as a matter of fact, the abrupt stoppage of assembly lines and other activities is impractical. It is most important to raise this subject promptly with the PCO and arrange, where possible, to obtain approval for work stoppage at an appropriate subsequent point rather than immediately.

Termination of Subcontracts and Settlement of Subcontractors' Claims

The contractor's termination project leader, or someone designated by the project leader, should move promptly to terminate all subcontracts relating to the terminated portion of the prime contract and to settle subcontractors' claims. The designated individual should become familiar with the provisions of FAR 49.108.

It is important for prime contractors unfamiliar with termination settlement proposals to understand that there is usually no privity of contract between the subcontractor and the government and that the prime contractor is responsible for the settlement of termination claims of immediate subcontractors. Each immediate subcontractor, in turn, is responsible for settlements with the next lower-tier subcontractor.

A provision for termination for convenience is one of the flow-down clauses that companies should incorporate in their subcontracts. Suggested subcontract termination clauses are discussed and referenced in FAR 49.502(e).

Subcontract Settlement Procedures

Generally, settlements with subcontractors should be made in conformity with the policies and principles relating to settlements of prime contracts with the government, and guidance in this area is provided in FAR 49.108-3 and subsequent sections. Subcontract settlements are sensitive actions because they will be examined by the TCO, and, where significant, the TCO will request the contract audit agency to perform accounting reviews of these settlements. If the government finds the subcontract settlement inappropriate, it may disapprove it in whole or in part and disallow the amounts considered improper or unreasonable. The prime contractor has then the option of either seeking recovery of the disallowed amounts from its subcontractor or bearing the costs itself.

Despite the responsibilities of the prime contractor, audit reviews of subcontractors' settlement proposals submitted by companies under audit by government contract auditors may be referred to the government.

In large terminations there may be substantial terminated subcontracts to settle, and, if the TCO is satisfied with the adequacy of the prime contractor's procedures, the TCO may approve a written request authorizing the prime contractor to conclude settlement of subcontract claims of $10,000 or less.

Settlement of Contractor's Termination Claim

Under the provisions of the convenience termination clauses, the contractor must submit its termination claim within a year, unless extensions are granted, and the claim must be submitted in the form and with the certifications provided by the TCO. Terminations for convenience of the government are disruptive in many respects, and contractors are understandably interested in concluding the settlements as expeditiously as possible in order to obtain reimbursement for the costs to which they are entitled, to dispose of the terminated contract inventories (unless they enter into agreements to retain any of such inventories), and to otherwise move to get the entire unpleasant experience behind them. While these objectives can be easily understood, contractors are cautioned to move with considerable thought and care to assure that they have obtained full recovery.

Termination for Convenience Contract Clause

FAR 52.249-2 prescribes the following contract clause covering termination for the convenience of the government in fixed-price contracts over $100,000 except in contracts for (a) dismantling and demolition, (b) research and development work with educational or nonprofit institutions on a no-profit basis, or (c) architect-engineer services. Because the clause contains so much instructive information regarding the actions the contractor must take upon receiving the termination notice and thereafter, the time for submitting the termination settlement proposal, the payments to be made by the government in the absence of an agreement, and other important matters, we have quoted the clause in its entirety.

TERMINATION FOR CONVENIENCE OF THE GOVERNMENT (FIXED-PRICE) (APR 1984)

(a) The Government may terminate performance of work under this contract in whole or, from time to time, in part if the Contracting Officer determines that a termination is in the Government's interest. The Contracting Officer shall terminate by delivering to the Contractor a Notice of Termination specifying the extent of termination and the effective date.

(b) After receipt of a Notice of Termination, and except as directed by the Contracting Officer, the Contractor shall immediately proceed with the following obligations, regardless of any delay in determining or adjusting any amounts due under this clause:

(1) Stop work as specified in the notice.

(2) Place no further subcontracts or orders (referred to as subcontracts in this clause) for materials, services, or facilities, except as necessary to complete the continued portion of the contract.

(3) Terminate all subcontracts to the extent they relate to the work terminated.

(4) Assign to the Government, as directed by the Contracting Officer, all right, title, and interest of the Contractor under the subcontracts terminated, in which case the Government shall have the right to settle or to pay any termination settlement proposal arising out of those terminations.

(5) With approval or ratification to the extent required by the Contracting Officer, settle all outstanding liabilities and termination settlement proposals arising from the termination of subcontracts; the approval or ratification will be final for purposes of this clause.

(6) As directed by the Contracting Officer, transfer title and deliver to the Government (i) the fabricated or unfabricated parts, work in process, completed work, supplies, and other material produced or acquired for the work terminated, and (ii) the completed or partially completed plans, drawings, information, and other property that, if the contract had been completed, would be required to be furnished to the Government.

(7) Complete performance of the work not terminated.

(8) Take any action that may be necessary, or that the Contracting Officer may direct, for the protection and preservation of the property related to this contract that is in the possession of the Contractor and in which the Government has or may acquire an interest.

(9) Use its best efforts to sell, as directed or authorized by the Contracting Officer, any property of the types referred to in subparagraph (6) above; *provided,* however, that the Contractor (i) is not required to extend credit to any purchaser and (ii) may acquire the property under the conditions prescribed by, and at prices approved by, the Contracting Officer. The proceeds of any transfer or disposition will be applied to reduce any payments to be made by the Government under this contract, credited to the price or cost of the work, or paid in any other manner directed by the Contracting Officer.

(c) After expiration of the plant clearance period as defined in Subpart 45.6 of the Federal Acquisition Regulation, the Contractor may submit to the Contracting Officer a list, certified as to quantity and quality, of termination inventory not previously disposed of, excluding items authorized for disposition by the Contracting Officer. The Contractor may request the Government to remove those items or enter into an agreement for their storage. Within 15 days, the Government will accept title to those items and remove them or enter into a storage agreement. The Contracting Officer may verify the list upon removal of the items, or if stored, within 45 days from submission of the list, and shall correct the list, as necessary, before final settlement.

(d) After termination, the Contractor shall submit a final termination settlement proposal to the Contracting Officer in the form and with the certification prescribed by the Contracting Officer. The Contractor shall submit the proposal promptly, but no later than 1 year from the effective date of termination, unless extended in writing by the Contracting Officer upon written request of the Contractor within this 1-year period. However, if the Contracting Officer determines that the facts justify it, a termination settlement proposal may be received and acted on after 1 year or any extension. If the Contractor fails to submit the proposal within the time allowed, the Contracting Officer may determine, on the basis of information available, the amount, if any, due the Contractor because of the termination and shall pay the amount determined.

(e) Subject to paragraph (d) above, the Contractor and the Contracting Officer may agree upon the whole or any part of the amount to be paid because of the termination. The amount may include a reasonable allowance for profit on work done. However, the agreed amount, whether under this paragraph (e) or paragraph (f) below, exclusive of costs shown in subparagraph (f)(3) below, may not exceed the total contract price as reduced by (a) the amount of payments previously made and (2) the contract price of work not terminated. The contract shall be amended, and the Contractor paid the agreed amount. Paragraph (f) below shall not limit, restrict, or affect the amount that may be agreed upon to be paid under this paragraph.

(f) If the Contractor and the Contracting Officer fail to agree on the whole amount to be paid because of the termination of work, the Contracting Officer shall pay the Contractor the amounts determined by the Contracting Officer as follows, but without duplication of any amounts agreed on under paragraph (e) above:

(1) The contract price for completed supplies or services accepted by the Government (or sold or acquired under subparagraph (b)(9) above) not previously paid for, adjusted for any saving of freight and other charges.

(2) The total of—

(i) The cost incurred in the performance of the work terminated, including initial costs and preparatory expenses allocable thereto, but excluding any costs attributable to supplies or services paid or to be paid under subparagraph (f)(1) above;

(ii) The cost of settling and paying termination settlement proposals under terminated subcontracts that are properly chargeable to the terminated portion of the contract if not included in subdivision (i) above; and

(iii) A sum, as profit on subdivision (i) above, determined by the Contracting Officer under 49.202 of the Federal Acquisition Regulation, in effect on the date of this contract, to be fair and reasonable; however, if it appears that the Contractor would have sustained a loss on the entire contract had it been completed, the Contracting Officer shall allow no profit under this subdivision (iii) and shall reduce the settlement to reflect the indicated rate of loss.

(3) The reasonable costs of settlement of the work terminated, including—

(i) Accounting, legal, clerical, and other expenses reasonably necessary for the preparation of termination settlement proposals and supporting data;

(ii) The termination and settlement of subcontracts (excluding the amounts of such settlements); and

(iii) Storage, transportation, and other costs incurred, reasonably necessary for the preservation, protection, or disposition of the termination inventory.

(g) Except for normal spoilage, and except to the extent that the Government expressly assumed the risk of loss, the Contracting Officer shall exclude from the amounts payable to the Contractor under paragraph (f) above, the fair value, as determined by the Contracting Officer, of property that is destroyed, lost, stolen, or damaged so as to become undeliverable to the Government or to a buyer.

(h) The cost principles and procedures of Part 31 of the Federal Acquisition Regulation, in effect on the date of this contract, shall govern all costs claimed, agreed to, or determined under this clause.

(i) The Contractor shall have the right of appeal, under the Disputes clause, from any determination made by the Contracting Officer under paragraph (d), (f), or (k), except that if the Contractor failed to submit the termination settlement proposal within the time provided in paragraph (d) or (k), and failed to request a time extension, there is no right of appeal. If the Contracting Officer has made a determination of the amount due under paragraph (d), (f), or (k), the Government shall pay the Contractor (1) the amount determined by the Contracting Officer if there is no right of appeal or if no timely appeal has been taken, or (2) the amount finally determined on an appeal.

(j) In arriving at the amount due the Contractor under this clause, there shall be deducted—

(1) All unliquidated advance or other payments to the Contractor under the terminated portion of this contract;

(2) Any claim which the Government has against the Contractor under this contract; and

(3) The agreed price for, or the proceeds of sale of, materials, supplies, or other things acquired by the Contractor or sold under the provisions of this clause and not recovered by or credited to the Government.

(k) If the termination is partial, the Contractor may file a proposal with the Contracting Officer for an equitable adjustment of the price(s) of the continued portion of the contract. The Contracting Officer shall make any equitable adjustment agreed upon. Any proposal by the Contractor for an equitable adjustment under this clause shall be requested within 90 days from the effective date of termination unless extended in writing by the Contracting Officer.

(*l*)(1) The Government may, under the terms and conditions it prescribes, make partial payments and payments against costs incurred by the Contractor for the terminated portion of the contract, if the Contracting Officer believes the total of these payments will not exceed the amount to which the Contractor will be entitled.

(2) If the total payments exceed the amount finally determined to be due, the Contractor shall repay the excess to the Government upon demand, together with interest computed at the rate established by the Secretary of the Treasury under 50 U.S.C. App. 1215(b)(2). Interest shall be computed for the period from the date the excess payment is received by the Contractor to the date the excess is repaid. Interest shall not be charged on any excess payment due to a reduction in the Contractor's termination settlement proposal because of retention or other disposition of termination inventory until 10 days after the date of the retention or disposition, or a later date determined by the Contracting Officer because of the circumstances.

(m) Unless otherwise provided in this contract or by statute, the Contractor shall maintain all records and documents relating to the terminated portion of this contract for 3 years after final settlement. This includes all books and other evidence bearing on the Contractor's costs and expenses under this contract. The Contractor shall make these records and documents available to the Government, at the Contractor's office, at all reasonable times, without any direct charge. If approved by the Contracting Officer, photographs, microphotographs, or other authentic reproductions may be maintained instead of original records and documents.

No-Cost Settlement

Although government procurement regulations direct the TCO to effect fair and reasonable settlements, it is not uncommon for the government to seek no-cost settlements under which the contractor unconditionally waives any claim against the government by reason of the termination actions. Although there are circumstances under which no-cost settlements may be appropriate, it is obvious that such agreements should not be executed until the contractor has made a thorough review of all of the circumstances and is satisfied that it has incurred no cost or that the effort and expense of preparing and negotiating a settlement proposal will exceed the funds that may be recoverable.

Partial Settlements and Partial Payments Upon Termination

The government is reluctant to make partial settlements covering particular items of the prime contractor's settlement proposal, preferring to effect the settlement in one agreement. However, as provided in FAR 49.109-5, the TCO is authorized to enter into partial settlement agreements when (1) a complete settlement cannot be achieved promptly, (2) the issues involved are clearly severable from other issues, and (3) the interests of the government with respect to the balance of the claim will not be prejudiced.

For some contract terminations, it may take years before the settlement is negotiated and final payment is made. When final settlement is likely to be prolonged, the contractor should arrange for partial payments on its own work as well as payments on subcontractors' claims. Salient provisions regarding partial payments (FAR 49.112-1) are cited below:

(a) *General.* If the contract authorizes partial payments on settlement proposals before settlement, a prime contractor may request them on the form prescribed in 49.602-4 at any time after submission of interim or final settlement proposals. The Government will process applications for partial payments promptly. A subcontractor shall submit its application through the prime contractor which shall attach its own invoice and recommendations to the subcontractor's application. Partial payments to a subcontractor shall be made only through the prime contractor and only after the prime contractor has submitted its interim or final settlement proposal. Except for undelivered acceptable finished products, partial payments shall not be made for profit or fee claimed under the terminated portion of the contract. In exercising discretion on the extent of partial payments to be made, the TCO shall consider the diligence of the contractor in settling with subcontractors and in preparing its own settlement proposal.

(b) *Amount of partial payment.* Before approving any partial payment, the TCO shall obtain any desired accounting, engineering, or other specialized reviews of the data submitted in support of the contractor's settlement proposal. If the reviews and the TCO's examination of the data indicate that the requested partial payment is proper, reasonable payments may be authorized in the discretion of the TCO up to—

(1) 100 percent of the contract price, adjusted for undelivered acceptable items completed before the termination date, or later completed with the approval of the TCO (see 49.205);

(2) 100 percent of the amount of any subcontract settlement paid by the prime contractor if the settlement was approved or ratified by the TCO under 49.108-3(c) or was authorized under 49.108-4;

(3) 90 percent of the direct cost of termination inventory, including costs of raw materials, purchased parts, supplies, and direct labor;

(4) 90 percent of other allowable costs (including settlement expense and manufacturing and administrative indirect costs) allocable to the terminated portion of the contract and not included in subparagraphs (1), (2), or (3) above; and

(5) 100 percent of partial payments made to subcontractors under this section.

Bases for Settlement Proposals

The regulation provides that, in the termination of fixed-price contracts, the termination settlement proposal may be prepared on either the Inventory

Basis or Total Cost Basis. A description of each is contained in FAR 49.206-2, quoted below:

49.206-2 Bases for settlement proposals.

(a) *Inventory basis.* (1) Use of the inventory basis for settlement proposals is preferred. Under this basis, the contractor may propose only costs allocable to the terminated portion of the contract, and the settlement proposal must itemize separately—

(i) Metals, raw materials, purchased parts, work in process, finished parts, components, dies, jigs, fixtures, and tooling, at purchase or manufacturing cost;

(ii) Charges such as engineering costs, initial costs, and general administrative costs;

(iii) Costs of settlements with subcontractors;

(iv) Settlement expenses; and

(v) Other proper charges.

(2) An allowance for profit (49.202) or adjustment for loss (49.203(b)) must be made to complete the gross settlement proposal. All unliquidated advance and progress payments and all disposal and other credits known when the proposal is submitted must then be deducted.

(3) This inventory basis is also appropriate for use under the following circumstances:

(i) The partial termination of a construction or related professional services contract.

(ii) The partial or complete termination of supply orders under any terminated construction contract.

(iii) The complete termination of a unit-price (as distinguished from a lump-sum) professional services contract.

(b) *Total cost basis.* (1) When use of the inventory basis is not practicable or will unduly delay settlement, the total-cost basis (SF-1436) may be used if approved in advance by the TCO as in the following examples:

(i) If production has not commenced and the accumulated costs represent planning and preproduction or "get ready" expenses.

(ii) If, under the contractor's accounting system, unit costs for work in process and finished products cannot readily be established.

(iii) If the contract does not specify unit prices.

(iv) If the termination is complete and involves a letter contract.

(2) When the total-cost basis is used under a complete termination, the contractor must itemize all costs incurred under the contract up to the effective date of termination. The costs of settlements with subcontractors and applicable settlement expenses must also be added. An allowance for profit (49.202) or adjustment for loss (49.203(c)) must be made. The contract price for all end items delivered or to be delivered

and accepted must be deducted. All unliquidated advance and progress payments and disposal and other credits known when the proposal is submitted must also be deducted.

(3) When the total-cost basis is used under a partial termination, the settlement proposal shall not be submitted until completion of the continued portion of the contract. The settlement proposal must be prepared as in subparagraph (2) above, except that all costs incurred to the date of completion of the continued portion of the contract must be included.

(4) If a construction contract or a lump-sum professional services contract is completely terminated, the contractor shall—

(i) Use the total-cost basis of settlement;

(ii) Omit Line 10 "Deduct-Finished Product Invoiced or to be Invoiced" from Section II of Standard Form-1436 Settlement Proposal (Total Cost Basis); and

(iii) Reduce the gross amount of the settlement by the total of all progress and other payments.

(c) *Other basis.* Settlement proposals may not be submitted on any basis other than paragraph (a) or (b) above without the prior approval of the chief of the contracting or contract administration office.

Inventory Basis

The government prefers the inventory basis on the assumption that, by limiting the submission to the costs directly attributable to the terminated portion of the contract, a clearer picture of the termination costs can be obtained and a "cleaner" settlement can be achieved.

In theory, the inventory basis is sound. In practice, this basis presents problems and risks. For one thing, the use of the inventory basis requires a well-developed cost accounting system that accurately segregates the costs of work in process and finished goods. It is important to remember here, as mentioned previously, that accounting systems are developed on a going-concern basis and are not specifically oriented towards the unusual and disruptive complications resulting from contract terminations. Additionally, the use of the inventory basis presents the possibility of omitting certain costs, a danger minimized under the total cost basis.

A termination settlement proposal on an inventory basis may be advantageous where the contractor's cost accounting methods readily provide the required information and the dangers of omitting costs are minimized. Another point for consideration is the indicated profit on the contract items that have been completed and shipped. Where the record suggests that the experienced profit was higher than contemplated in the initial contract negotiations, the use of the inventory basis is advantageous because, as explained below, the government may seek to recover some of the higher-than-negotiated profit where the settlement proposal is prepared on a total cost basis.

Total Cost Basis

FAR 49.206-2(b)(1) cites examples of situations where the total cost basis may be permitted by the TCO, and it is important to remember that the

TCO's approval is required for the use of this method. In view of the accounting system demands for the inventory basis, contractors frequently find it necessary to resort to the total cost basis, and the TCO's approval is generally not difficult to obtain. However, contractors should be aware of the guidance DCAA furnishes its auditors (Defense Contract Audit Manual, 12-302.2a):

> When requested by the contracting officer, the auditor should render an opinion on the feasibility of using the inventory basis. The opinion should be based on a limited office or on-site review, of the information contained in the preliminary conference. If no request is received but the auditor, based on his review of the contractor's records, is of the opinion that the inventory rather than the total cost cost basis should be used, the contracting officer should be promptly advised.

COST PRINCIPLES APPLICABLE TO CONTRACT TERMINATION SETTLEMENTS

In the preparation of contract termination settlement proposals, the contractor is required to adhere to many of the standard contract cost principles set forth in FAR Part 31. For example, in reviewing the cost of both the completed and partially completed portions of the contract, the audit of direct material, direct labor, other direct costs, and indirect costs will be based on the respective provisions of FAR in much the same manner as for contracts that were not terminated. In addition, then, there are the cost aspects peculiar to terminations.

As to contract cost principles that are generally applicable, extensive coverage to which the reader may refer is found in this text in Chapters IX through XIX. Our discussion here will focus on cost principles applicable specifically to terminated contracts.

FAR Subpart 49.2 contains further provisions in this area, covering costs, profit and loss, and other matters. The comments on cost and profit are quoted below:

49.201 General.

(a) A settlement should compensate the contractor fairly for the work done and the preparations made for the terminated portions of the contract, including a reasonable allowance for profit. Fair compensation is a matter of judgment and cannot be measured exactly. In a given case, various methods may be equally appropriate for arriving at fair compensation. The use of business judgment, as distinguished from strict accounting principles, is the heart of a settlement.

(b) The primary objective is to negotiate a settlement by agreement. The parties may agree upon a total amount to be paid the contractor without agreeing on or segregating the particular elements of costs or profit comprising this amount.

(c) Cost and accounting data may provide guides, but are not rigid measures, for ascertaining fair compensation. In appropriate cases, costs may be estimated, differences compromised, and doubtful questions settled by agreement. Other types of data, criteria, or standards may furnish equally reliable guides to fair compensation. The amount of recordkeeping, reporting, and accounting related to the settlement of terminated contracts should be kept to a minimum compatible with the reasonable protection of the public interest.

Distinctions in Application of Contract Cost Principles

The principles set forth in FAR 49.201, above, essentially carried over from DAR and FPR, establish quite clearly for most people that there are definite differences in applying contract cost principles to terminated fixed-price contracts, as compared with applying such principles to ongoing or completed fixed-price contracts. These differences are disliked, and at times ignored, by representatives of such agencies as DCAA and GAO, which favor strict formula approaches to termination settlement proposals, based on auditor determination of allowability. The pressure by these agencies, together with such things as DOD Directive 7640.2 and congressional criticisms, at times inhibits contracting officers from appropriately considering and applying the principles of FAR 49.201.

Codex Corporation v. United States, U.S. Court of Claims, No. 371-77, [28 CCF par. 81,099], 2/24/81, previously before the Armed Services Board of Contract Appeals, ASBCA No. 17983, 74-2 BCA par. 10,827; 75-2 BCA par. 11,554.

In the brief comments on this and another ruling discussed below, it is necessary to emphasize a cautionary note involving revisions to cost principles between the 1970s when these disputes occurred and the present. These changes may somewhat dilute the basic point but they do not eliminate it.

The contractor had previously produced an electronic equipment that became unsalable. Subsequently, the Air Force became interested in this device in its mobile communications operations. At its own expense, but with the encouragement of the Air Force, Codex developed its device to include a field case specifically designed for mobile operations. The Air Force then awarded Codex a contract for seven of these items at a total cost approximating $92,600; however, before any deliveries were made, the contract was terminated for convenience.

Codex submitted a termination settlement proposal approximating $78,100, consisting primarily of the costs of its electronic devices and the field cases. The contracting officer denied substantially the entire claim on the basis that these costs were unallowable under ASPR 15-205.30, now substantially incorporated into FAR 31.205-32, which made precontract costs unallowable except to the extent required to meet delivery schedules, etc. The board upheld the contracting officer and rejected the contractor's arguments that it was entitled to recovery under the provisions of then ASPR 8.301, which identified fairness as a major consideration in negotiating termination settlement proposals.

Codex was equally unsuccessful in its motion for reconsideration and thereafter appealed to the U.S. Court of Claims where the trial judge upheld the disallowance of the cost of the electronic item but set aside the board's rejection of the cost of the carrying case, finding it allowable under the fairness concept of ASPR 8-301.

The court remanded the case to the ASBCA, noting that a reconciliation was required between the provisions of ASPR 8.301 and 15.205-30 with respect to the allowability of the cost of the carrying cases. The court said that its "holding is not that section 8.301 governs the plaintiff's claim for the field case costs, but that the application of the cost principles in part 2 of section 15 to that claim must be made 'subject to the general policies set forth' in section 8.301." The case was remanded to the ASBCA "to make that determination."

General Electric Company, ASBCA No. 24111, 82-1 BCA par. 15,725

General Electric (GE) terminated a subcontract for production of missile system components with Solar Division, International Harvester Company (Solar). As a result of its review of the negotiated settlement agreement between GE and Solar, the government disallowed $116,000, representing certain employee severance costs and post-termination costs incurred by Solar and allowed in negotiations by GE.

Although the precise allowability of the disputed items did not appear to be clearly established under cost principles applicable to ongoing or completed contracts, the board found that GE had performed an effective, hard bargaining negotiation of the subcontractor's proposal. The board allowed the entire amount questioned by the government, finding that "[i]t does not seem proper to hold a prime contractor who successfully negotiates a settlement by agreement with its subcontractor, in accordance with the general policies set forth in ASPR 8.301, to a higher standard of reasonableness than that imposed by ASPR 8-209.5 with respect to judgments."

The board referred to the U.S. Court of Claims ruling in *Codex,* discussed above, noting that the court had expressed the view that "the 'proper reconciliation of the strict standard of allowable costs' in ASPR Section XV and the 'fairness concept' in section 8-301 'is a matter primarily within the discretion of the Board.' " The board thought that, actually, this discretion should have been exercised by the government's Settlement Review Board (SRB) but the SRB had apparently failed to do so, accepting instead the views of DCAA and the TCO, which were based solely on the strict standards of the then ASPR Section XV cost principles.

49.202 Profit.

(a) The TCO shall allow profit on preparations made and work done by the contractor for the terminated portion of the contract but not on the settlement expenses. Anticipatory profits and consequential damages shall not be allowed (but see 49.108-5). Profit for the contractor's efforts in settling subcontractor proposals shall not be based on the dollar amount of the subcontract settlement agreements but the contractor's efforts will be considered in determining the overall rate of profit allowed the contractor. Profit shall not be allowed the contractor for material or services that, as of the effective date of termination, have not been delivered by a subcontractor, regardless of the percentage of completion. The TCO may use any reasonable method to arrive at a fair profit.

(b) In negotiating or determining profit, factors to be considered include—

(1) Extent and difficulty of the work done by the contractor as compared with the total work required by the contract (engineering estimates of the percentage of completion ordinarily should not be required, but if available should be considered);

(2) Engineering work, production scheduling, planning, technical study and supervision, and other necessary services;

(3) Efficiency of the contractor, with particular regard to—

(i) Attainment of quantity and quality production;

(ii) Reduction of costs;

(iii) Economic use of materials, facilities, and manpower; and

(iv) Disposition of termination inventory;

(4) Amount and source of capital and extent of risk assumed;

(5) Inventive and developmental contributions, and cooperation with the Government and other contractors in supplying technical assistance;

(6) Character of the business, including the source and nature of materials and the complexity of manufacturing techniques;

(7) The rate of profit that the contractor would have earned had the contract been completed;

(8) The rate of profit both parties contemplated at the time the contract was negotiated; and

(9) Character and difficulty of subcontracting, including selection, placement, and management of subcontracts, and effort in negotiating settlements of terminated subcontracts.

(c) When computing profit on the terminated portion of a construction contract, the contracting officer shall—

(1) Comply with paragraphs (a) and (b) above;

(2) Allow profit on the prime contractor's settlements with construction subcontractors for actual work in place at the job site; and

(3) Exclude profit on the prime contractor's settlements with construction subcontractors for materials on hand and for preparations made to complete the work.

31.205-42 Termination costs.

Contract terminations generally give rise to the incurrence of costs or the need for special treatment of costs that would not have arisen had the contract not been terminated. The following cost principles peculiar to termination situations are to be used in conjunction with the other cost principles in Subpart 31.2:

(a) *Common items.* The costs of items reasonably usable on the contractor's other work shall not be allowable unless the contractor submits evidence that the items could not be retained at cost without sustaining a loss. The contracting officer should consider the contractor's plans and orders for current and planned production when determining if items can reasonably be used on other work of the contractor. Contemporaneous purchases of common items by the contractor shall be regarded as evidence that such items are reasonably usable on the contractor's other work. Any acceptance of common items as allocable to the terminated portion of the contract should be limited to the extent that the quantities of such items on hand, in transit, and on order are in excess of the reasonable quantitative requirements of other work.

(b) *Costs continuing after termination.* Despite all reasonable efforts by the contractor, costs which cannot be discontinued immediately after the effective date of termination are generally allowable. However, any costs continuing after the effective date of the termination due to the negligent or willful failure of the contractor to discontinue the costs shall be unallowable.

(c) *Initial costs.* Initial costs (see 15.804-6(f)), including starting load and preparatory costs, are allowable as follows:

(1) Starting load costs not fully absorbed because of termination are nonrecurring labor, material, and related overhead costs incurred in the early part of production and result from factors such as—

(i) Excessive spoilage due to inexperienced labor;

(ii) Idle time and subnormal production due to testing and changing production methods;

(iii) Training; and

(iv) Lack of familiarity or experience with the product, materials, or manufacturing processes.

(2) Preparatory costs incurred in preparing to perform the terminated contract include such costs as those incurred for initial plant rearrangement and alterations, management and personnel organization, and production planning. They do not include special machinery and equipment and starting load costs.

(3) When initial costs are included in the settlement proposal as a direct charge, such costs shall not also be included in overhead. Initial costs attributable to only one contract shall not be allocated to other contracts.

(4) If initial costs are claimed and have not been segregated on the contractor's books, they shall be segregated for settlement purposes from cost reports and schedules reflecting that high unit cost incurred during the early stages of the contract.

(5) If the settlement proposal is on the inventory basis, initial costs should normally be allocated on the basis of total end items called for by the contract immediately before termination; however, if the contract includes end items of a diverse nature, some other equitable basis may be used, such as machine or labor hours.

(d) *Loss of useful value.* Loss of useful value of special tooling, and special machinery and equipment is generally allowable, provided—

(1) The special tooling, or special machinery and equipment is not reasonably capable of use in the other work of the contractor;

(2) The Government's interest is protected by transfer of title or by other means deemed appropriate by the contracting officer; and

(3) The loss of useful value for any one terminated contract is limited to that portion of the acquisition cost which bears the same ratio to the total acquisition cost as the terminated portion of the contract bears to the entire terminated contract and other Government contracts for which the special tooling or special machinery and equipment was acquired.

(e) *Rental under unexpired leases.* Rental costs under unexpired leases, less the residual value of such leases, are generally allowable when shown to have been reasonably necessary for the performance of the terminated contract, if—

(1) The amount of rental claimed does not exceed the reasonable use value of the property leased for the period of the contract and such further period as may be reasonable; and

(2) The contractor makes all reasonable efforts to terminate, assign, settle, or otherwise reduce the cost of such lease.

(f) *Alterations of leased property.* The cost of alterations and reasonable restorations required by the lease may be allowed when the alterations were necessary for performing the contract.

(g) *Settlement expenses.* (1) Settlement expenses, including the following, are generally allowable:

(i) Accounting, legal, clerical, and similar costs reasonably necessary for—

(A) The preparation and presentation, including supporting data, of settlement claims to the contracting officer; and

(B) The termination and settlement of subcontracts.

(ii) Reasonable costs for the storage, transportation, protection, and disposition of property acquired or produced for the contract.

(iii) Indirect costs related to salary and wages incurred as settlement expenses in (i) and (ii); normally, such indirect costs shall be limited to payroll taxes, fringe benefits, occupancy costs, and immediate supervision costs.

(2) If settlement expenses are significant, a cost account or work order shall be established to separately identify and accumulate them.

(h) *Subcontractor claims.* Subcontractor claims, including the allocable portion of the claims common to the contract and to other work of the contractor, are generally allowable. An appropriate share of the contractor's indirect expense may be allocated to the amount of settlements with subcontractors; provided, that the amount allocated is reasonably proportionate to the relative benefits received and is otherwise consistent with 31.201-4 and 31.203(c). The indirect expense so allocated shall exclude the same and similar costs claimed directly or indirectly as settlement expenses.

Interest on Settlement Proposals

A "cost principle" is also set forth in FAR 49.112-2(d), which provides that "[t]he Government shall not pay interest on the amount due under a settlement agreement or a settlement by determination." There were few challenges to this provision until a dispute that led to a recent adverse (at least initially) ruling against a contractor who claimed this cost.

A 3-2 decision by the Armed Services Board of Contract Appeals ruled that interest on an amount agreed upon to settle the amount due the contractor in a termination for the convenience of the government was not allowable. *Mayfair Construction Co.,* ASBCA No. 30800, 87-1 BCA par. 19,542. The majority and minority opinions rely heavily on laws and regulations having the force of law and, accordingly, a detailed analysis is more appropriate for a legal journal. However, the substantial interest in this matter to managers and contract administrators and the closely divided ruling both suggest the possibility that this subject will soon be considered by the federal courts in the light of previous affirmative decisions in this area, which *Mayfair* upset.

The issue was whether Mayfair could recover interest under the Contract Disputes Act of 1978 (CDA) on the amount agreed upon as settlement for the convenience termination. The contractor contended it was due interest from the time it certified the settlement proposal and labeled it a claim under the CDA. The government argued that interest was not payable, among other reasons, because (1) the termination settlement proposal was not a claim under the CDA since the amount was not disputed, and (2) termination settlement proposals traditionally have not been considered as claims, and FAR and previous DAR provisions support this position. Certain other issues were involved but they are not addressed because they did not appear pertinent to the major question.

Mayfair submitted a certified settlement proposal and, after government audit and review, submitted a revised proposal that included interest in the amount of $146,600. The parties agreed to a settlement based on the revised proposal with the exception of interest. This amount was subsequently denied in a contracting officer's final decision, based on the contention that a settlement proposal is not a claim as defined in FAR 33.001 but is a routine request for payment under the termination for convenience clause, and therefore interest is not payable.

Mayfair pointed out that the termination for convenience clause refers to the contractor's submission as a claim. The government countered with an excerpt from DAR 8-213.2(c), substantially incorporated into FAR 49.112-2(d), which states specifically that interest shall not be paid "on the amount due under a settlement agreement or a settlement by determination." The FAR provision goes on to provide that interest may be paid "on a successful contractor appeal from a contracting officer's determination under the Disputes clause . . . ."

The Contract Disputes Act requires payment of interest on contractors' claims but does not define the word "claim," and efforts at definition have continued for years, participated in by OFPP and the DAR and CAA Councils.

The majority cited some of the board's prior rulings, e.g., *Raquette River Construction, Inc.*, ASBCA No. 26486, 82-1 BCA par. 15,769, wherein it denied interest on a settlement proposal during the time it was considered "a written request . . . for payment of money." However, it allowed interest for the period beginning with unsuccessful settlement negotiations that led to the contractor's request that a contracting officer's final decision be issued, at which time the board decided that the contractor's proposal had ripened into a claim.

Concluding that the CDA does not plainly authorize "payment of interest while the government and contractor are in a pre-dispute negotiation posture," and emphasizing the DAR and FAR provisions that prohibit such interest, the board denied Mayfair's claim for interest, noting that it "must respectfully disagree with the contrary views of the Engineer Board (*R.G. Beer Corporation*, ENG BCA No. 4885, 85-2 BCA ¶ 18,162; *Barter Engineering Corporation*, Eng BCA Nos. 4754, 4791, 85-3 BCA ¶ 18,342)."

The dissenting opinion stated that the CDA requires payment of interest on contractor claims and asserted:

> The Government cannot contravene the plain meaning of a statute by enforcing a contrary regulation or utilizing a Disputes clause that denies payment of interest by stretching the meaning of the word claim beyond the commonly accepted definition without the clear support of legislative history.

This opinion noted the extensive case law on this subject and that "disagreement exists between and within the tribunals regarding the requirement for the existence of an antecedent dispute in order to have a 'claim' under the CDA." However, it found the statute clear and that "claim" has the plain meaning contained in *Webster's New World Dictionary* (1968 ed.)—"a demand for something rightfully or allegedly due; assertion of one's right to something." It found no common or legal usage applying the "requirement of a dispute to the meaning of the word claim."

The dissent reiterated the legislative history of the CDA and stated that the board would have to find in such history a congressional intent to give the term a special meaning other than the common one cited above, an intent it did not find. To the contrary, it read the accompanying Senate Report to explain that the allowance of interest on claims was designed to reduce contractor financial burden and encourage government agencies to avoid interest payments by expediting settlements.

Delving further into the language of the statute and legislative history, the dissent emphasized the absence of specific language limiting interest to instances where a dispute preceded. To the contrary, it cited the preamble to the CDA (P.L. 95-563) which identified it as an Act "to provide for the resolution of *claims and disputes* relating to Government contracts awarded by executive agencies."(Emphasis in dissenting opinion.) It also cited other sections of the Act in which the words "claim" and "dispute" were separated by the disjunctive "or."

Finding no ambiguity in the CDA, the dissent objected to the creation of any and insisted that the plain meaning of "claim" should govern. As to the acquisition regulation prohibiting interest on termination for convenience settlements, the dissent opined that such regulation "contravenes the statute and does not apply." The only instances where the dissenting opinion found an exception to interest payment were "routine payment requests under the contract payments clause, such as progress payments, and not to requests for extraordinary payments, including termination for convenience settlement proposals."

In view of the current *Mayfair* environment, it is suggested that in the processing of termination settlement proposal costs being submitted, those elements not susceptible to controversy be processed in an expeditious manner, including immediate requests for partial payments and attempting a final resolution thereof without waiving any rights to the other areas that may be subject to dispute. These latter items may be treated separately by the Termination Contracting Officer (TCO) pending subsequent resolution or the possibility of the need to issue a final decision generating access to the appeals board or applicable court having appropriate jurisdiction. When an item enters the aforementioned dispute category, the filing of the proper certificate at the outset or when it approaches that stage would initiate the running of interest until a final settlement and payment thereon is made.

Termination Costs

Common Items

It does not appear unreasonable for the government to decline to accept and pay for materials that the contractor can reasonably use in the normal course of its work. It is important to note, however, that the contractor is not expected to retain common items acquired for the contract if the quantities on hand and on order exceed its reasonable requirements. Government technical and audit personnel will be seeking to eliminate from the termination settlement proposal any material that appears to represent "common items." The contractor's technical people should be at least equally scrupulous in reviewing normal requirements to assure that the company is not left with quantities of so-called common items in excess of the amount that can be used in a reasonable period of time.

DCAA auditors are instructed to examine closely into this area as indicated by paragraph 12-304.6 of the Agency's Contract Audit Manual:

12-304.6 *Common Items.*

a. Common items are items of material which are common in nature to both the terminated contract and other work of the contractor. FAR 45.606-2 states that, except for property, delivery of which has been required by the Government, and except for Government-furnished property, the contractor's inventory schedules should not include any items reasonably usable without loss to the contractor on its other work. Cost principles in FAR 31.205-42(a) state that the cost of items reasonably usable on the contractor's other work shall not be allowable unless the contractor submits evidence that the items could not be retained without sustaining a loss. In determining whether common items are reasonably usable by the contractor on other work, the auditor should review the contractor's plans and orders for current and scheduled production and for current purchases of such common items. The auditor can also determine whether inventory items are properly classified as common items by reviewing stock record cards to ascertain whether the items are being used for other work and by reviewing bills of material and procurement scheduled for products similar to those included in the termination inventory. Acceptance of common items as part of termination inventory should be limited to the quantities on hand, in transit, and on order which are in excess of the reasonable quantities required by the contractor for work on other than the terminated contract. In determining whether the inventory contains common items, the total available quantity (inventory on hand, in transit, and on order) should be first allocated to continuing or anticipated Government or commercial production and the remainder, if any, allocated to the terminated contract. The contractor should assign to the terminated contract (1) the least processed inventory, and (2) those purchase commitments which may be terminated at the least cost.

b. Under certain circumstances, complex or specialized items may qualify as common items. For example, the compressor unit of a military jet engine might qualify as a common item if the contractor also uses the unit in the production of commercial jet engines; or the memory unit of a computer might qualify if the unit is also used in a commercial computer. The test is whether the item can be diverted to other work without loss to the contractor.

c. Common items need not be so classified by the contractor if the contractor can demonstrate that the elimination of the item from termination inventory would cause financial hardship. For example, when raw materials are common to the contractor's other work but the amount resulting from the termination would be equal to a year's supply, an amount largely in excess of the contractor's usual inventory, the retention of the material might adversely affect the contractor's cash or working capital position and result in a financial hardship. The retention of a large inventory by the contractor does not in itself, however, entitle the contractor to claim an amount for excess inventory. When the inventory can be used within a reasonable period, regardless of size, the excess inventory claim would not be allowable.

d. If subsequent to the submission of the termination settlement proposal, the contractor is awarded other contracts or receives commercial orders on which the items of the termination inventory can be used, the contractor should withdraw items to be used on the new work, (except for Government property or other items reserved by the contracting officer), adjust the claim accordingly, and so notify the contracting officer.

e. Reworkable rejects in the termination inventory which can be diverted to other work of the contractor provided the contractor is allowed the cost of reworking the items should be brought to the attention of the contracting officer. The contracting officer may find it in the interest of the Government to allow the reworking costs in order to obtain credit for items reworked and diverted.

Costs Continuing After Termination

FAR 31.205-42(b) recognizes that there may be circumstances under which, "despite all reasonable efforts by the contractor, costs cannot be discontinued immediately after the effective date of termination." This paragraph states that such costs are generally allowable unless they are "due to the negligence or willful failure of the contractor to discontinue such costs." The procurement regulations cite no examples in this paragraph, but FAR 31.205-42(e) addresses rental costs under unexpired leases. Such costs, plus related alterations necessary for the performance of the contract and reasonable restoration required by the lease, are allowable for a reasonable period if the contractor makes all reasonable efforts to terminate or otherwise reduce the cost of the lease.

The treatment of costs continuing after termination represents one of the most controversial aspects of contract terminations, and, even though neither DAR, FPR, nor FAR thereafter has addressed the subject directly, decisions by judicial bodies have resulted in an inequitable and illogical treatment of companies whose contracts have been fully terminated for the convenience of the government.

DCAA's Contract Audit Manual, paragraph 12-305.7b, states flatly that "[a]mounts claimed as unabsorbed overhead, under whatever name, representing that overhead or parts of it which would have been absorbed by the contract if not terminated, will be questioned." It is interesting that DCAA makes no effort to provide any accounting or other rationale for questioning these costs. Instead, it leans on two ASBCA decisions and a reference to the manual published by the Defense Logistics Agency (DLA). The reference to the DLA manual is particularly curious inasmuch as DCAA holds itself out as the sole professional contract audit organization in the Department of Defense and, to our knowledge, has never quoted DLA as an accounting authority in any other circumstances. The DLA manual, like the DCAA manual, of course has no authoritative basis.

Those of us who can remember the mass contract terminations of World War II find it difficult to understand the basis for questioning continuing costs, including unabsorbed overhead, to the extent that they are reasonable and traceable to the termination. Few questions were raised about this cost in principle at that time, and the Joint Termination Regulation (JTR) specifically recognized that some costs and expenses just could not be discontinued immediately, and, where reasonable attempts had been made in this direction, they "should not be denied merely because they were incurred after the effective date of termination."

Some twenty years later, noting the absence of existing authoritative DOD regulations on this subject, the Defense Industry Advisory Council (DIAC, predecessor to IAC) specifically recommended an addition to ASPR to recognize continuing fixed overhead expense after termination for the convenience of the government. The ASPR Committee refused to take any action on this recommendation in July and December 1965. While it evaded the issue and suggested that perhaps a problem really did not exist, the ASPR Committee gave no indication as to whether it was for or against allowing unabsorbed overhead. Ever mindful of the pitfalls in government contracting, industry continued from time to time to seek a forthright recognition of the allowability of unabsorbed overhead and other continuing costs. In July 1971, in a report prepared by CODSIA and forwarded to the Government Procurement Commission, industry again requested that formal recognition be given to continuing costs under convenience terminations, including "[u]nabsorbed ongoing fixed overhead which would have to be unfairly absorbed against other business of the contractor, if not allowed on the termination claim."

Meanwhile, DOD hard-liners moved to counter this pressure. In February 1971 the Defense Supply Agency (DSA) proposed a revision to ASPR to provide that "the cost of idle facilities and idle capacity or any form of unabsorbed overhead is not allowable as a direct charge to a terminated contract." As the ASPR Committee people studied this proposal, they found little in the way of definitive, authoritative precedent. Specific, clear-cut BCA or court cases at that time were difficult to come by, and the study group grudgingly quoted the views expressed in the author's text (5th Edition) that unabsorbed overhead claims tend to be negotiated between the contractor and the contracting officer without resort to formal appeals. The study group expressed concern about what it thought were signs of increasing claims for unabsorbed overhead and its own inability to identify policy pronouncement allowing or disallowing unabsorbed overhead as a termination cost.

The DSA offered the view that the increasing claims for unabsorbed overhead might be attributable to the ASPR revision to DAR 15-205.12 in May 1967. This ASPR paragraph previously contained sharp limitations on the allowability of costs of idle facilities and idle capacity. The aforementioned revision described these costs as including "maintenance, repair, housing, rent, and other related costs, e.g., property taxes, insurance, and depreciation," and stated that they would be allowable under a number of circumstances, including where *"they were necessary when acquired and are now idle because of . . . termination. . . ."* (Emphasis added.)

After some deliberation, an ASPR subcommittee led by DCAA concluded that the regulation should be revised to specifically provide that unabsorbed overhead was unallowable. The reasoning appeared to be that the traumatic, unexpected effect of termination was no different from the conditions experienced after a contract completion. The lack of logic and equity that characterizes this conclusion is so obvious as to make further discussion futile. More importantly, the ASPR Committee rejected the subcommittee's recommendation. In our judgment, the rejection should have included: (1) a forthright statement that the recommendation was completely incorrect, and (2) a direction to the group to return to their desks to write an ASPR revision that would clearly proclaim the propriety of all reasonable continuing costs resulting from terminations for the government's convenience. Unfortunately, the Committee again refused to meet the problem headon, and the case was closed with standard bureaucratic jargon that can mean all things to all people. In essence, the Committee concluded that the existing ASPR provisions were clear and doubted whether any additional language or refinement would be helpful. As a matter of fact, the Committee expressed the concern that a revision might even "cause uncertainty in termination settlements where none currently exists."

When the Department of Defense refused to address this problem, its follower, FPR, also looked away, leaving a regulatory vacuum into which the boards of contract appeals and the courts moved. We initially believed that the judicial bodies could have nevertheless found the regulatory language necessary to establish the allowability of reasonable continuing costs, including the so-called unabsorbed overhead. When the ASPR Committee refused to address this subject directly, it seemed that the following regulatory provisions were sufficiently significant and persuasive:

> 15-205.42(b) Costs Continuing After Termination. If in a particular case, despite all reasonable efforts by the contractor, certain costs cannot be discontinued immediately after the effective date of termination, such costs are generally allowable within the limitations set forth in this Part, except that any such costs continuing after termination due to the negligent or willful failure of the contractor to discontinue such costs shall be considered unallowable.

> 15-205.42(e) Rental costs under unexpired leases are generally allowable where clearly shown to have been reasonably necessary for the performance of the terminated contract . . .

> 15-205.12(b) The costs of idle facilities are unallowable except to the extent that . . . (ii) they were necessary when acquired and are now idle because of . . . termination.

Unfortunately, the judicial bodies were not persuaded.

Nolan Brothers v. U.S., 16 CCF par. 80,119, 194 Ct.Cls. 1 (1971).—A construction contract was terminated for the convenience of the government, and the many issues in dispute were appealed to the ASBCA and then carried further by the contractor to the U. S. Court of Claims. Although Nolan was successful on some of the issues, its claim for home office expenses was rejected and the ruling by the court on this point, although the parallel to subsequent ASBCA decisions that cited this case is doubtful, seemed to mark the beginning of a hard-line attitude by boards of contract appeals that have rejected claims for unabsorbed overhead when they were presented as such. As we shall see in discussing some of the major BCA decisions on this subject, the use of this term, or a claim that can be identified with this term, has been sufficient to assure denials of contractors' claims.

In *Nolan*, the contractor's claim included home office expenses for the 16-month period from contract termination to the date the contracting officer made his unilateral determination. The board upheld the contracting officer's disallowance of this item, noting that Nolan "has cited no authority or precedent for allowing post termination G&A as such, and we know of none. . . ." Nolan argued that the charge was proper pursuant to the contract termination article that permitted "reasonable cost of the preservation and protection of property . . . and any other reasonable costs incidental to termination of work under this contract. . . ." The court, however, reasoned that home office expense subsequent to termination "related to (Nolan's) existence as an ongoing organization, and was not 'incidental to termination of work under this contract.' " Although it rejected this charge, it noted that the board had properly allowed salaries and other expenses of home office employees who had been "directly involved in the termination and settlement of the contract."

The *Nolan* case was unfortunate in several respects. The court overruled the BCA decision on a number of items. For example, Nolan claimed a substantial termination cost for what it considered a reasonable period of 2.6 months for the removal of the equipment from the job-site following the contract cancellation. The board cited regulations that "charges for equipment stop when the contract is completed." The court's thinking as expressed in overriding the board is very significant for all government contractors and far transcends construction work:

> Paragraph (e) of clause 23 of the contract provided that the plaintiff should be reimbursed for "any . . . reasonable costs incidental to termination of work under this contract . . ." (emphasis supplied). When the contracting officer terminated the work under the contract on March 27, 1964, the result was the valuable equipment which the plaintiff had brought to the job site in order to build jetties under the contract suddenly became idle and useless, at least for a temporary period. In considering a somewhat similar situation, this court said in *Brand Investment Co. v. U.S.*, 2 CCF 826, 102 Ct.Cls. 40, 45, 58 F.Supp. 749, 751 (1944), cert. denied, 324 U.S. 850 (1945):

>> . . . [W]hen the Government, . . . in effect condemns a contractor's valuable and useful machines to a period of idleness and usefulness, we think that it should make compensation comparable to what would be required if it took the machines for use for a temporary period, but did not in fact use them. As a jury verdict, we allow the proved rental value, discounted by one-half because of the absence of actual use with its resulting wear and tear. . . .

> It is believed, therefore, that the plaintiff's equipment ownership expense during the standby period immediately following the termination of the contract should properly be regarded as coming within the category of "reasonable costs incidental to termination of work under this contract," and that the Board erred in wholly rejecting the plaintiff's claim based upon this item of expense.

On the claim for home office allocation for a 16-month period, however, the court affirmed the board's disallowance, and this one point has served over the years as justification for boards of contract appeals to disallow continuing costs. Without passing judgment on the merits of the claim and decision, we would note that a 16-month period might be challenged on the basis of reasonableness, but BCAs have used this decision to support denials of virtually every claim of this kind even when the periods claimed were much shorter and the basis more supportable. Future BCA decisions have also been invariably incomplete in failing to state that the court had allowed reimbursement for salaries and expenses of home office employees who had been "directly involved in the termination and settlement of the contract." The term "directly" has grown in importance as the author's advice to his clients to identify direct payroll and related costs as costs continuing after termination has proven acceptable, whereas claims for lump sum unabsorbed overhead or the like have been rejected.

In the Sixth Edition of this text, published by Commerce Clearing House, Inc., in June 1971, we noted the absence of regulatory prohibition against costs continuing after termination, when properly presented for reasonable periods of time. In the years that followed, the government has still not published any official regulations on this subject (DCAA and DLA manuals lack statutory, regulatory, or contractual authority). The government has been able to evade the issue by leaning on BCA decisions, some of which we have found inequitable, unjustifiable, and unreasonable. In our Sixth Edition, referring to DAR and FPR provisions, we asked:

> ... [W]hat logic supports allowing rental costs under unexpired leases but not allowing depreciation, taxes and other ownership costs? It seems to us that ASPR 15-205.42(e) clearly expresses the government's recognition of its responsibility to absorb a reasonable amount of continuing occupancy costs (including costs of alterations) where it terminates a contract for its convenience. This obligation, in our opinion, continues until the contractor finds other work to perform or for a period otherwise agreed upon as reasonable in the circumstances. We find no basis for assuming a different position where the property is owned by the contractor, and we believe that the burden of proof is properly on any government representative who espouses such distinction.

In the time since, we have heard no logical argument to the contrary; however, the executive agency acquisition policy makers continue to evade the issue, and it was not addressed in FAR.

The terms "continuing costs" and "unabsorbed overhead" have several connotations in accounting and business. In discussing this cost in connection with termination settlement proposals, we refer to that portion of indirect costs which would have been absorbed by, or charged to, a specific contract but for the termination for the government's convenience. The termination action results in unabsorbed overhead, and disposition of this cost must be determined. Logically, inasmuch as the unabsorbed overhead is the direct result of the government's action in terminating the contract for its convenience, it should be paid (absorbed) by the government as a cost of the terminated contract. Where the government has defaulted in assuming this obligation, this overhead cost must be charged against other work which neither caused it nor benefited in any way therefrom. In effect, of course, the BCA decisions result in this cost unfairly coming out of the contractor's profit. Why should the contractor's profit on unrelated work be reduced by an action taken by the government for its own convenience?

Fairchild Stratos Corporation, **ASBCA No. 9169, 68-1 BCA par. 7053; 67-1 BCA par. 6225.**—The Navy partially terminated an engine contract, and several months later the Air Force completely terminated all of its contracts. The latter action, leading to the ultimate shutdown of the contractor's plant, understandably occupied most of the contractor's attention. The Fairchild Air Force termination settlement, which did not go to dispute, apparently included an assumption by the government of a considerable portion of the continuing costs. A similar procedure with the Navy, however, could not be agreed upon and became the basis for this appeal.

It is important to note that the board's views on the financial consequences of the termination are subject to various interpretations. It framed a question as to whether Fairchild was entitled to an equitable adjustment because of the partial termination. In effect, it seemed to be considering the effect of the continuing costs, including unabsorbed overhead, on the remaining portion. The board's answer to its own question was: "If, by a rational means, a method is found for calculating the monetary effect upon appellant of the partial termination of the contract, and if the application of that method shows an increase in cost, then appellant is entitled to an equitable adjustment."

We find here an obvious parallel to the problem of unabsorbed overhead under a contract terminated in its entirety. In the case of the partial termination, the board found no pain in compensating the contractor by an upward adjustment in price for the remaining engines. In the case of a complete termination, the only comparable financial relief is through reimbursement of the costs that could not be absorbed because of the termination.

The board made a number of statements in the same vein. At one point it offered its view of an equitable adjustment in the case of a partial termination as an adjustment that "should give appellant a price for the units produced equivalent to what would reasonably have been agreed upon had the parties known that the total number of engines to be manufactured under the contract was the unterminated quantity rather than the original quantity."

It is essential to bear in mind that in the *Fairchild* decision, the board was preoccupied with the financial problems generated by the plant-wide Air Force termination action, including the attendent distortions of the data necessary to compute an appropriate termination settlement in dispute. It was critical of the contractor's methods and also in disagreement with its contention that the Navy's action should be consistent with the reasonable Air Force approach. As to the principle involved, however, we find the board saying, for example: "*We think that there may be instances where allowance of unearned or unabsorbed dollar overhead would be appropriate.* But the unabsorbed overhead which the appellant now seeks was not arrived at by determining what plant, equipment, etc., would go directly* into the performance of this contract . . ." (Emphasis added).

*Note reference to direct costing-type computation that the author has recommended over the years.

Technology, Inc., ASBCA No. 14083, 72-1 BCA par. 9281; 71-2 BCA par. 8956.—According to the board, the contractor claimed "entitlement to the entire continuing overhead, from the date of termination until the contemplated date of completion, the amount of which is $84,733. The TCO disallowed in its entirety appellant's claim for unabsorbed overhead but determined that certain indirect expenses could not be immediately discontinued and allowed appellant $9588." As explained in a footnote to the decision, "This figure was computed by the TCO using appellant's unabsorbed overhead figure . . . ." We found both the basic statement and the related footnote unclear. The results of our further research into this case are set forth in subsequent portions of this analysis.

Portions of the board's decision with respect to unabsorbed overhead are quoted below:

> Before reaching the question posed by the parties, we must determine whether unabsorbed overhead is a continuing cost reimbursable under the contract. Our research has uncovered no cases in which the question of unabsorbed overhead has been considered under a termination for convenience clause of the type included in this contract. In connection with the partial termination for convenience of a fixed price supply contract, this Board has refused to allow recovery of unabsorbed overhead. . . . *Fairchild Stratos Corporation,* ASBCA No. 9169, on Motion for Reconsideration, 68-1 BCA par. 7053 (Recon. den.).

The Court of Claims took a similar position in *Nolan Brothers, Inc.,* Ct.Cl. No. 371-67 Slip Op. (Feb 19, 1971). In that case appellant claimed entitlement to post termination G&A expense as part of a termination for convenience settlement under a fixed price construction contract . . . The Court, discussing the nature of the claimed costs, stated:

> The plaintiff's home-office overhead, after the work under the contract has been terminated on March 27, 1967, related to the plaintiff's existence as an ongoing organization, and was not "incidental to termination of work under this contract . . . ."

The unabsorbed overhead which appellant is claiming here is likewise related to appellant's existence as an ongoing organization and not a continuing cost of the terminated contract. It is true that because of the termination appellant's direct labor pool was reduced for some months and not at the level anticipated during several of the months, and thus appellant was required to charge the overhead that would have been absorbed by the direct labor under this contract against the direct labor expended under other contracts. However, to hold as appellant would have us, that all of the unabsorbed overhead is chargeable against the terminated contract would place the Government in the position of a guarantor of appellant's overhead. We do not believe this result was intended by the language of the termination clause.

Even if we were to determine that appellant is entitled to unabsorbed overhead as a continuing cost we would have difficulty finding for appellant on the record presented. Appellant has shown the difference between the actual overhead rates and the rates that would have been chargeable had the contract not been terminated. Appellant has not shown, however, the overhead rates used in computing bids on contracts either bid or executed during the period when appellant contemplated that this contract would remain in effect. *The most persuasive evidence of the incurrence of unabsorbed overhead would be the overhead rates actually used by appellant during this period of time. This is particularly true where the direct labor pool has increased to its pretermination level within a short period of time following termination. Lacking the establishment of this fact appelant's claim for unabsorbed overhead would have to be denied.* (Emphasis added.)

Zealous elements in the Defense Department hailed this decision. The Defense Contract Audit Agency (DCAA), in the monthly bulletin distributed to its staff in August 1971, headlined its satisfaction in this manner: GOVERNMENT SCORES ON QUESTION OF UNABSORBED OVERHEAD. The DCAA bulletin quoted the next-to-the-last paragraph we cited above, beginning with "The unabsorbed overhead . . . ." However, it omitted the immediately following paragraph from the board's decision (see above), which reopens basic questions. This is the one in which the board begins "Even if we were to determine that appellant is entitled to unabsorbed overhead as a continuing cost. . . ." Does this paragraph suggest that perhaps nonacceptability of unabsorbed overhead is not that all-definitive? Could it be interpreted that all or some portion of this element of the contractor's claim might have been accepted had the contractor presented evidence regarding the overhead rates used by the contractor in bidding or executing contracts during the period the contract under discussion would have been in production if not for the termination? And was the board influenced by the fact that the direct labor apparently increased to its pretermination level shortly after the termination?

We noted earlier that the explanation in the board's decision concerning an amount of $9,588 allowed by the TCO was not clear. Further research disclosed that the TCO testified as follows: "In deciding the amount of money to allow the contractor for the continuing indirect costs I used the contractor's settlement proposal of $57,000, approximately, for the fiscal year 1967, and I divided that by $1/6$ *allowing approximately $9,500 in total settlement for the contractor's claim of unabsorbed overhead,* or continuing indirect costs as indicated in my unilateral decision." (Emphasis added.)

***Chamberlain Manufacturing Corp.,* ASBCA No. 16877, 73-2 BCA par. 10,139.**—This decision establishes rather conclusively that government contractors must use more direct methods to obtain equitable compensation for unabsorbed burden costs arising out of contracts terminated for the government's convenience. The term "unabsorbed overhead" is a red flag to the board when reviewing and evaluating submittals of this nature.

At issue in the *Chamberlain* case was a claim for "continuing overhead costs following the termination" (unabsorbed burden). The contractor computed the amounts by comparing the overhead rates in the four months following the termination and the three months preceding it. The increase in the rates in the posttermination period was applied to the actual direct labor in that period. The contractor selected the four-month period because the contract was scheduled for completion in that period. The three-month pretermination period was considered by Chamberlain to be representative, and the average monthly production during that time approximated the rate required to complete the contract.

This is a very significant and frequently cited decision, and we have quoted widely from the official text. We recommend a careful review by our readers, beginning with the board's summary of the parties' contentions:

> Appellant's primary contention is that the termination caused a decrease in production which resulted in a decrease in labor dollars which thereby increased its overhead rates. It urges us, in keeping with equity

and fairness, to regard the increase in its overhead rates as, in effect, a continuing cost after termination and thus allowable under ASPR 15-205-42(b) which provides as follows:

* * * *

"(b) Costs Continuing After Termination. If in a particular case, despite all reasonable efforts by the contractor, certain costs cannot be discontinued immediately after the effective date of termination, such costs are generally allowable within the limitations set forth in this Part, except that any such costs continuing after termination due to the negligent or willful failure of the contractor to discontinue such costs shall be considered unallowable."

Appellant sees no just or logical distinction between the continuing overhead costs and rental cost under unexpired leases which is generally allowable.

Not unmindful of the Board's past denials of unabsorbed overhead claims (*Technology, Incorporated,* ASBCA No. 14083, 71-2 BCA par. 8956, Motion for Reconsideration denied 72-1 BCA par. 9281; *Fairchild Stratos Corporation,* ASBCA No. 9169, 67-1 BCA par. 6225, Motion for Reconsideration denied 68-1 BCA par. 7053), appellant also asserts that the special requirements imposed by the termination notice concerning the maintenance of termination inventory and Government-owned tooling in a readily accessible condition, which requirements continued for a protracted period, distinguish this case from the cited decisions and buttress its claim.

The Government contends that the claimed costs were not occasioned by the termination but relate to appellant's existence as an ongoing organization, *Nolan Brothers* v. *U.S.,* 194 Ct.Cls. 1 (1971). . . .

The government also challenged the contractor's claim on the basis of various technical aspects that we do not comment upon because they did not enter into the board's decision.

A verbatim account of the salient portions of the board's decision follows:

The measure of recovery for the exclusive remedy afforded by the termination for convenience clause is costs incurred plus a reasonable profit on work performed. *William Green Construction Company, Inc. et. al.* v. *U.S.,* Ct.Cls. No. 124-72, decided 11 May 1973. The claimed post-termination overhead costs were neither incurred as a result of the work performed on the contract nor generated directly by the termination action. [See author's note (a), below.] The termination action merely reduced the direct labor base against which appellant's overhead could be applied. In essence, appellant's plea is that fairness and equity require the Government to reimburse a terminated contractor who has been unable to recover its overhead by the acquisition of sufficient new business to generate enough labor to compensate for the labor lost because of the termination. However, its arguments and analogies are not persuasive.

Just as anticipatory profits are not allowable, so a loss of business, whether in the guise of post-termination G&A or otherwise, is not recoverable in a termination claim. See *Golden State Construction* ASBCA No. 11727, 67-1 BCA par. 6192; and *Nolan Brothers v. U.S., supra.* The continuing costs to which ASPR 15-205.42 refers clearly are only those costs directly related to the terminated contract which cannot reasonably be shut off immediately upon termination. It is obvious that appellant's overhead is a cost which will continue so long as appellant continues to exist as an ongoing organization and is thus not directly related to the terminated contract. Neither are allowable rental costs analogous to appellant's overhead since ASPR 15-205.42 (e) manifestly requires that in order for those costs to be allowable they must be clearly and directly related to performance of the terminated contract although they cannot be immediately stopped. Moreover, the continuation of overhead after a termination is a common occurrence and if the drafters of the regulation had intended to allow such costs they could have done so simply and clearly as they did for rental costs. [See author's note (b), below.]

In thus circumscribing those continuing costs which are allowable, the regulation is neither unfair nor inequitable. In practical effect, if claims such as presented by appellant were allowed the Government would be guaranteeing a contractor's overhead costs, without receiving any benefit therefrom, as a "penalty" for exercising its contractual rights. See *Technology, Incorporated, supra;* cf. *Fred D. Wright Co. Inc.* ASBCA No. 7211, 1962 BCA par. 3432. In *Technology Incorporated* we faced the identical issue presented here in deciding that unabsorbed overhead was not a continuing cost of the terminated contract, although we said that certain specific indirect costs might be allowable. In *Fairchild Stratos Corporation, supra,* we allowed an increased allocation of overhead to unterminated items in determining a proper equitable adjustment in the price of those unterminated items following a partial termination, but refused to allow recovery of unabsorbed overhead as a cost of termination, thus foreshadowing our decision in *Technology Incorporated.* (68-1 BCA par. 7053 at p. 32,599) In *Nolan Brothers, supra,* the Court of Claims distinguished between ownership expenses incidental to the termination and ongoing, unrelated home office expenses.

*   *   *   *

Thus, following the clear precedents cited, we hold that appellant's increased overhead rates do not constitute costs caused by or incidental to the termination and that its continuing overhead expenses are not continuing costs of the terminated contract.

Our decision makes it unnecessary to make detailed findings in the light of conflicting evidence as to what extent, if any, the increase in overhead rates resulted from the termination. . . .

Author's notes: (a) If not generated by the termination action, what caused these costs? (b) Regulations never cited continuation of overhead costs as unallowable.

The *Chamberlain* decision referred to the board's rulings in *Technology, Inc.* and *Fairchild Stratos Corp.* and to the judicial ruling in *Nolan Brothers v.*

U.S. These decisions were analyzed earlier, except that we did not previously comment on the board's opinion on the Motion for Reconsideration in the appeal of Technology, Inc. With respect to unabsorbed overhead, the ASBCA said:

> In connection with the Board's disallowance of unabsorbed overhead, appellant has cited *Pamco Corporation,* ASBCA No. 3114, 57-2 BCA par. 1489; *Lowell O. West Lumber Sales,* ASBCA No. 10879, 67-1 BCA par. 6101; and *Sundstrand Turbo, A Division of Sundstrand Corporation v. U.S.* (12 CCF par. 81,589), 182 Ct.Cls. 31 (1968) for the proposition that this Board and the Court of Claims have recognized the allowability of various unabsorbed fixed overhead costs. In all three cases where relief was granted it was on the basis that the facilities or buildings had been built or leased specifically for the terminated contracts and the claimed costs were treated as direct costs and not as overhead. Thus the cited cases hold that direct costs which continue for a reasonable time are includable in a termination settlement. They do not stand for the proposition that unabsorbed overhead is a continuing cost to be reimbursed as part of a termination for convenience settlement. We do not disagree with the holdings of the cited cases. Neither do we read these cases as controlling the question of unabsorbed overhead as it confronts us in this appeal.

> Appellant argues that *Fairchild Stratos Corporation* ASBCA No. 9169, on Motion for Reconsideration, 68-1 BCA par. 7053 and *Nolan Brothers, Inc. v. U.S.* (16 CCF par. 80,119), Ct.Cls. No. 371-67 Slip Op. (Feb. 19, 1971), which were cited by the Board as cases which have denied claims for unabsorbed overhead, are distinguishable and should not have been relied upon by the Board in this appeal. The Board fully recognized the factual differences between the cited cases and this appeal, and in its decision pointed out certain of these distinctions. Although factual distinctions do exist these cases denied the allowance of unabsorbed overhead and in Nolan the Court characterized unabsorbed G&A as a cost of the contractor's existence as an ongoing corporation. We take a similar view of appellant's unabsorbed overhead in this appeal. Appellant has not persuaded us that our conclusion is incorrect.

Readers of the previous editions of this text and of our monthly newsletters are familiar with our views on this subject. Without unduly replowing old ground, we would make these few summary comments regarding the board's rulings.

First, in our judgment, the ASBCA opinions have failed to accord consideration to basic principles of equity. A company must deploy required space, facilities, and people to perform a government contract or be subject to all of the penalties and other hardships involved in a default termination. Having done so, and having been suddenly confronted with a unilateral decision by the government to terminate at the government's convenience, just what can the company do? Obviously it cannot swing into production on new business the day after the abrupt government action. So, indirect expenses continue— indirect expenses in the form of space, depreciation, and other unabsorbed burden caused by and directly attributable to the government action. In our judgment, it is both inequitable and unreasonable for the board to say to the contractor in effect: "Eat the unabsorbed burden or take it out of profits, if there be any, or out of equity."

Second, the ASBCA decision dictates an accounting monstrosity. Virtually all of industry and the accounting profession today conform to the full absorption theory whereby all costs incurred are charged or allocated to specific cost objectives. In the case of unabsorbed burden attributable to the abrupt, unilateral termination action by the government, consideration should be addressed to the question of which cost objective(s) should bear this burden. Assuming, hypothetically, that the termination leaves a half of a plant and its facilities idle for six months before new business is obtained, should these costs be charged to the remaining, ongoing business?

Assuming the remaining work was commercial, the government would not be disturbed if the contractor inflated the cost thereof. What if conditions were reversed? What if the company had 50% government and 50% commercial work, and all of the commercial work were suddenly cancelled and the company were unable to recover the unabsorbed burden from its commercial customer? Would the government consider allowing the unabsorbed burden on its contracts? In the past (especially on DOD work) contract auditors and contracting officers have time and again adopted the position that such unabsorbed burden was not allocable to the defense work. And yet, the board's decision suggests that the contractor pursue one of two alternatives with regard to unabsorbed burden resulting from contract termination by the government: (1) incorrectly inflate the cost of the remaining work or (2) charge the costs against the company's profits or equity.

In the above *Chamberlain* ruling, the board strains to make a fine, hairsplitting distinction. It would allow "only those costs directly related to the terminated contract which cannot be reasonably shut off immediately upon termination." As to unabsorbed burden, the board makes the following prognostication: "It is obvious that appellant's overhead is a cost which *will continue so long as appellant continues to exist as an ongoing organization* and is thus not directly related to the terminated contract." (Emphasis added.)

Obviously the foregoing comment is a specious observation. The contractor did not claim all of its overhead for all time, but only the portion that, for a short period of time (four months), could not be absorbed by other work because of the usual abruptness of the government's termination action.

The board's argument is also flawed when it states that ASPR does provide for allowing certain continuing costs (rental cost under unexpired leases) and that "if the drafters of the regulation had intended to allow such costs (continuation of overhead) they could have done so simply and clearly as they did for rental costs." This statement seems to be contrary to the numerous opinions by the ASBCA that emphasized that, where ASPR identifies specific costs as allowable, there is no implication that "costs not made specifically allowable therein are to be disallowed."

It further seems to us that the board might have inquired into the reasons for the fact that unabsorbed burden is not now and, to the best of our recollection, never was specifically covered in ASPR. The board would have learned that this subject has proven too controversial for DOD to reach a position and that, today, some contracting officers understand and appreciate the equity and propriety of compensating contractors for reasonable continuing overhead costs and, where possible, do make allowances in whole or in part on such costs.

The author has advised his clients that "unabsorbed overhead" costs should not be calculated on a lump sum basis and presented in this manner, and has suggested that such costs should be broken down into direct cost-associated categories flowing directly from the terminated contract. As a reaffirmation of this approach, it is pertinent to quote from previous editions of this text:

"In the past few years, the author has had much additional experience with this particular situation in the presentation and negotiation of termination settlement proposals. The method of submission has been changed to reflect a direct costing approach, for a reasonable period of four to twelve months subsequent to termination date, and the balance as a lump sum amount of unabsorbed overhead. In direct costing, the items are broken down as to:

(a) Fixed overhead costs, in the form of space and related overhead, set aside for the terminated portion of the contract and which cannot be used on other work for a reasonable period of time. The author's definition of a reasonable period of time has been four to twelve months, however, this could vary with the individual circumstances.

(b) Semi-Variable overhead, set aside for the terminated contract, for a reasonable period of time, wherein it cannot be absorbed by other work and that would have been absorbed by the contract terminated.

(c) Variable overhead for a reasonable period after termination date."

The costs that cannot be discontinued immediately after the effective date of termination, despite all reasonable efforts by the contractor, are computed in the same manner as suggested for direct costs on early terminations elsewhere in this chapter. This approach is analogous to devoting a total plant and its capacity to one contract that has been terminated. In this event, the government would have no objection to paying for all the costs, for a reasonable period of time, until the facility is cleaned out or diverted to other work. The same condition would hold true for unexpired leased space obtained specifically for the terminated contract performance. Related costs of this latter type of item are allowable items of cost without question. Why should there be a difference in concept between leased space and companyowned space and facilities made idle by the termination?

In the light of the above presentation, the author has been successful, in many instances, in obtaining a substantial portion of those costs computed on a direct basis for that reasonable period of time subsequent to termination. The remainder of the unabsorbed overhead amount has been a negotiating factor in the overall settlement.

KDI Precision Products, Inc., **ASBCA No. 21522, 79-1 BCA par. 13,640.**—This is another decision that highlights the inequities suffered by contractors as the government literally as well as figuratively turns its back on costs that it caused to be incurred because of its action in terminating a contract for its own convenience.

KDI was awarded a firm fixed-price contract for the production of fuze rockets. The contract included a provision under which the government could require KDI to convert the fuze type and an option under which the government could increase the quantity. Some 14 months after award, the contract was partially terminated for the convenience of the government. The same modification converted some of the terminated rockets into a different fuze type.

KDI contended that the contract modification accomplished six separate things: (1) termination for the convenience of the government; (2) the addition of a new item (the converted fuze type rocket); (3) suspension of work; (4) a stop-work order; (5) delay in production schedule; and (6) invocation of the Changes clause, which provides an equitable adjustment for all costs in dispute. The board agreed that the modification had accomplished some of the things KDI alleged, but denied that it had invoked the Changes clause to allow an equitable adjustment. In this regard, too, the board pointed out that KDI, in signing the modification, had agreed to the unit cost for the revised fuze-type rocket and to the delivery schedules for that type as well as for the number of original fuze rockets which had not been terminated. Important in the board's consideration was the fact that KDI had not requested an equitable adjustment for the unterminated units of the original fuze rocket. If this were so, it certainly was a sad error on the contractor's part inasmuch as this request is the major step toward recovering unabsorbed overhead caused by partial terminations.

This decision contains considerable details about KDI's original and revised proposals, DCAA audits, etc., which we have omitted in the interest of focusing on the major issue—the claim for unabsorbed overhead, or, as KDI termed it, excessive overhead. The excessive overhead claim "is premised upon the allegation that the partial termination reduced the direct labor base against which its overhead could be applied." Interestingly but sadly, the board offered the gratuitous comment that KDI did not allege that such costs were "generated directly by the termination action." If the termination did not create the unabsorbed overhead, what did? Surely the culprit was not the ongoing work on other jobs.

The board's decision establishes that KDI's claim for excessive overhead is based on the fact that, due to the partial termination, it did not perform on this contract for a period of time and the excessive overhead was incurred in that period. In completely rejecting this part of the claim, the board cited as precedents its own prior decisions in similar circumstances. We have excerpted a portion of this decision so that the board's thinking and references might be available for our readers' study and files:

> We were faced with a similar situation in *Henry Spen & Company,* Inc., ASBCA No. 20766, 77-2 BCA par. 12,784. A contract for the manufacture of trailers was partially terminated for the convenience of

the Government. The contractor claimed the costs of continuing (excessive) overhead. We held at page 62,183 that:

"... We are allowing no continuing overhead as part of the termination claim itself, in keeping with our previous decisions on claims arising from complete terminations for convenience, see *Chamberlain Manufacturing Corporation,* ASBCA No. 16877, 73-2 BCA par. 10,139; *Technology, Inc.,* ASBCA No. 14083, 72-1 BCA par. 9281, and on attempts to recover continuing overhead on the basis of the terminated portion of the contract. See *Fairfield Stratos Corporation,* ASBCA No. 9169, 68-1 BCA par. 7053. ..."

Chamberlain Manufacturing Corporation, supra, concerned a manufacturing contract which was terminated for the convenience of the Government. The contractor sought to recover for overhead for the period following the termination for convenience. The contractor computed its claim by comparing the overhead rates with the direct labor costs prior to and after the termination, as the appellant has done in the instant case. We said at page 47,679:

"Just as anticipatory profits are not allowable, so a loss of business, whether in the guise of post-termination G&A or otherwise, is not recoverable in a termination claim. ... It is obvious that appellant's overhead is a cost which will continue so long as appellant continues to exist as an ongoing organization and is thus not directly related to the terminated contract. ... In practical effect, if claims such as presented by appellant were allowed the Government would be guaranteeing a contractor's overhead costs, without receiving any benefit therefrom, as a 'penalty' for exercising its contractual rights."

Appellant in its post-hearing brief has cited eight appeals decided by this Board in support of its excessive overhead claim. *Robert McMullan & Son, Inc.,* ASBCA No. 19023, 76-1 BCA par. 11,728 involved the Suspension of Work clause. *Fairchild Stratos Corporation,* ASBCA No. 9169, 67-1 BCA par. 6225 concerned an equitable adjustment for the unterminated items. *Allied Materials and Equipment Co., Inc.,* ASBCA No. 17318, 75-1 BCA par. 11,150 denied a claim for overhead for the period after the termination, citing with approval *Chamberlain Manufacturing Corporation, supra. Kurz & Root Company, Inc.,* ASBCA No. 14665, 72-2 BCA par. 9552 involved a claim for defective specifications and a resultant period of disruption and delay. *Eichleay Corp.,* ASBCA No. 5183, 60-2 BCA par. 2688 concerned a claim involving the Suspension of Work clause. *Therm-Air Manufacturing Co., Inc.,* ASBCA Nos. 15842, 17143, 74-2 BCA par. 10,818 involved a claim for delay arising out of defective specifications. We also note the Board denied a claim for unabsorbed overhead on an allegation of a delay in production in this case. In *American Electric, Inc.,* ASBCA No. 16635, 76-2 BCA par. 12,151 we found that the claim did not concern overhead. *Switlik Parachute Company, Inc.,* ASBCA No. 18024, 75-2 BCA par. 11,434 at page 54,445, to which appellant refers in its brief, discusses the measure of damages in a delay claim. We do not find any support for appellant's claim for excessive overhead in the cases cited by appellant and discussed above.

Pioneer Recovery Systems, Inc., ASBCA No. 24658, 81-1 BCA par. 15,059

This dispute and the one following have been included in this analysis to demonstrate that in the 1980s, no changes have been discerned in the judicial hardline rulings relating to continuing costs in total terminations for the convenience of the government.

Approximately 98% of Pioneer's business consisted of manufacturing parachutes and related equipment to government specifications. Accordingly, when a large contract was suddenly terminated for the government's convenience, it was obviously impossible for the company to immediately replace the planned work with other business. As the contractor pointed out, if the government failed to reimburse it for the unabsorbed overhead directly attributable to the termination, this additional cost would have to be borne by other contracts "which were priced based on forecasts which utilized workload data of the terminated contract."

It should have been obvious to the contracting officer and to the ASBCA that inasmuch as such costs could not be recovered under the other contracts, denial thereof under the terminated contract would be inequitable. Additionally, from an accounting viewpoint, it would be incorrect to charge to ongoing contracts, expenses that were caused by the terminated contract. Unfortunately, the government did not concern itself with equity or accounting logic. Instead, leaning on prior ASBCA decisions, the contracting officer disallowed the claim for unabsorbed overhead.

The ASBCA, which finds much comfort and authority in its decisions, devoted a major portion of its opinion to quoting its ruling in *Chamberlain Manufacturing Corporation, supra,* based on which it denied Pioneer's claim. Some of its comments seem inappropriate. For example:

> ... the risk of unabsorbed overhead in termination cases is essentially no different than in cases of a contractor's failure to obtain other business which it anticipates obtaining during the accounting period.

We find this observation illogical. It is certainly the responsibility of a company's management to plan ahead and to seek sufficient business to replace orders scheduled for completion. And it is understandable that companies which are unsuccessful in the circumstances must suffer the economic consequences. But surely, such circumstances cannot be reasonably compared with those that result from an unexpected telegram announcing, at times without the slightest advance warning, that the government decided, solely for its own convenience, to terminate a major portion of the work that the contractor had every reason to believe he would complete.

In the penultimate paragraph of this decision, the board finally recognized the point we have been advancing over the years: "... *in individual instances the impact of a termination on overhead absorption may be practically indistinguishable from the impact of a comparable suspension of work, where unabsorbed overhead may be recoverable.*" (Emphasis added.) Unfortunately, however, the board walked away from this valid point with the observation that "in view of the long standing precedent, construing ASPR 15-205.42, any change in the rule should be a matter for regulatory consideration." Here the board was referring to its comments in other appeals that if the writers of government procurement regulations intended to allow unabsorbed overhead they would have specifically stated so.

ASPR 15-204(d), governing at that time (see comparable current provision in FAR 31.204(c)) stated:

> Selected items of cost are treated in 15-205. However, 15-205 does not cover every element of cost and every situation that may arise in a particular case. *Failure to treat any item of cost in 15-205 is not intended to imply that it is either allowable or unallowable.* With respect to all items, whether or not specifically covered, determination of allowability shall be based on the principles and standards set forth in this Part and, where appropriate, the treatment of similar or related items. (Emphasis added.)

The board, of course, was well aware of the above provision and has cited it in decisions involving other matters. A review of this paragraph, or the current FAR 31.204(c), has suggested to many observers that (1) the absence of a specific reference to unabsorbed overhead does not, per se, make it unallowable in complete terminations, and (2) unabsorbed overhead here may well be considered comparable to the selected items in 15-205.42(b) (currently FAR 31.205-42(b), Costs Continuing after Termination), and 15-205.42(e) (currently FAR 31.205-42(e) Rental under Unexpired Leases).

As to any possible FAR revision to specifically spell out circumstances under which unabsorbed overhead would be allowable in complete contract terminations, the chances in today's environment must be considered nonexistent. They were in this category even in periods of lesser hostility to defense contractors and, it is pertinent to note, while unabsorbed overhead in delay and disruption situations is recognized by boards of contract appeals and courts, this recognition is not reflected in current acquisition regulations.

Metadure Corporation, ASBCA No. 21183, 83-1 BCA par. 16,208

The company's contract was completely terminated for the convenience of the government and its unabsorbed overhead claim was a modest one, being limited to "fixed and continuing" costs for a seven-month period in which the contractor stated it was unable to obtain other work to absorb such costs.

As noted earlier in this analysis, the ASBCA finds much comfort in citing its own previous decisions. Here it cited its decision in *Pioneer* in which, in turn, it had quoted its decision in *Chamberlain*. Inasmuch as companies continually enter the government procurement arena for the first time, we thought it would be useful for such firms, as well as to provide a review for experienced contractors, to quote a portion of the board's decision in *Metadure,* quoting *Pioneer,* quoting *Chamberlain,* to provide a comprehensive account of the board's views on unabsorbed overhead under complete contract terminations for the convenience of the government:

> We have had occasion to construe ASPR 15-205.42 recently in *Pioneer Recovery Systems, Inc.,* ASBCA No. 24658, 81-1 BCA ¶ 15,059. In *Pioneer* we were faced with a termination for the convenience of the

Government. The contractor requested recovery for unabsorbed overhead in its termination settlement proposal. We said at 74,493 and 74,494:

[I]n our opinion, established precedent precludes appellant's recovery. We follow the Board's decision in *Chamberlain Manufacturing Corporation,* ASBCA No. 16877, 73-2 BCA ¶ 10,139, from which the following discussion is quoted:

"The measure of recovery for the exclusive remedy afforded by the termination for convenience clause is costs incurred plus a reasonable profit on work performed. *William Green Construction Company, Inc. et al. v. United States* [18 CCF ¶ 82,234], Ct.Cl. No. 124-72, decided 11 May 1973. The claimed post-termination overhead costs were neither incurred as a result of the work performed on the contract nor generated directly by the termination action. The termination action merely reduced the direct labor base against which appellant's overhead could be applied. In essence, appellant's plea is that fairness and equity require the Government to reimburse a terminated contractor who has been unable to recover its overhead by the acquisition of sufficient new business to generate enough labor to compensate for the labor lost because of the termination. However, its arguments and analogies are not persuasive.

"Just as anticipatory profits are not allowable, so a loss of business, whether in the guise of post-termination G&A or otherwise, is not recoverable in a termination claim. See *Golden State Construction,* ASBCA No. 11727, 67-1 BCA ¶ 6192; and *Nolan Brothers v. United States, supra.* The continuing costs to which ASPR 15-205.42 refers clearly are only those costs directly related to the terminated contract which cannot reasonably be shut off immediately upon termination. It is obvious that appellant's overhead is a cost which will continue so long as appellant continues to exist as an ongoing organization and is thus not directly related to the terminated contract. Neither are allowable rental costs analogous to appellant's overhead since ASPR 15-205.42(e) manifestly requires that in order for those costs to be allowable they must be clearly and directly related to performance of the terminated contract although they cannot be immediately stopped. Moreover, the continuation of overhead after a termination is a common occurrence and if the drafters of the regulation had intended to allow such costs they could have done so simply and clearly as they did for rental costs.

"In thus circumscribing those continuing costs which are allowable, the regulation is neither unfair nor inequitable. In practical effect, if claims such as presented by appellant were allowed the Government would be guaranteeing contractor's overhead costs, without receiving any benefit therefrom, as a "penalty" for exercising its contractual rights. See *Technology, Incorporated, supra;* cf: *Fred D. Wright Co., Inc.,* ASBCA No. 7211, 192 BCA ¶ 3432. In *Technology Incorporated* we faced the identical issue presented here in deciding that unabsorbed overhead was not a continuing cost of the terminated contract, although we said that certain specific indirect costs might be allowable. In *Fairchild Stratos Corporation, supra,* we allowed an increased allocation of overhead to unterminated items in determining a proper equitable adjustment in the price of those unterminated items following a partial termination, but refused to allow recovery of unabsorbed overhead as a cost of termination, thus foreshadowing our decision in *Technology Incorporated.* (68-1 BCA ¶ 7053 at 32,599) In *Nolan Brothers, supra,* the Court of Claims distinguished between ownership expenses incidental to the termination and ongoing, unrelated home office expenses."

"Notwithstanding such precedent, appellant's main contention appears to be that it is inequitable for the Government not to compensate for the occurrence of a termination by allowing unabsorbed overhead because appellant was not allowed to include this contingency in its proposals for new Government business. But a contractor must decide for itself whether its negotiated prices and business forecasts warrant accepting the risk of such contingencies; and, in doing so, will necessarily have to consider the fact that the potential contract, to the extent not terminated, will absorb some overhead with which its other business would otherwise be burdened. Although convenience terminations are relatively rare, the risk of unabsorbed overhead in termination cases is essentially no different than in cases of a contractor's failure to obtain other business which it anticipates obtaining during the accounting period.

"The Board recognizes that in individual instances the impact of a termination on overhead absorption may be practically indistinguishable from the impact of a comparable suspension of work, where unabsorbed overhead may be recoverable. But, in view of the innumerable circumstances in which delays or terminations may result in under absorption, or even "over absorption" (*e.g.,* opportunity for other more profitable business), and in view of the long standing precedent, constructing ASPR 15-205.42, any change in the rule should be a matter for regulatory consideration."

It is discouraging to read BCA decisions where the board cites with approval what many observers believe to be illogical, inequitable, and otherwise inappropriate prior decisions of its own. These decisions seem to indicate that some administrative judges do not really understand the nature of overhead and its causes and simply reiterate what was written by their predecessors. How can it be said that unabsorbed overhead clearly and specifically resulting from the government's action in terminating the contract is "not directly related to the terminated contract"? The fact that overhead will continue as long as a company remains in business is completely irrelevant to the basic issue of accounting and equity: What generated this overhead?

The ASBCA's theorizing of the government "guaranteeing a contractor's overhead costs, without receiving any benefit therefrom, as a 'penalty' for exercising its contractual rights" also suggests the lack of real understanding as well as the lack of interest in providing equity to a government contractor.

We all understand that, within certain limitations, the government has a contractual right to terminate a contract for its convenience for any reason or for no reason at all. However, it is difficult to see how that unilateral right, which is inserted in contracts, should be a basis for refusing equitable treatment to contractors. Obviously, one could not argue that unabsorbed overhead should be paid for indefinite periods of time. On the other hand, it seems to us that, assuming a contractor makes diligent efforts to fill the void left by the termination by securing other business, the government should permit the recovery of properly computed unabsorbed overhead for some reasonable period of time. The term of such a reasonable period of time might be incorporated in regulations, but we believe it would be preferable for the regulations to establish the principle and then allow the parties to arrive at a period considered reasonable in the particular circumstances. We think it is specious for the ASBCA to speak of the government not receiving any benefit from unabsorbed overhead costs. Certainly, the company whose contract has been terminated does not receive any benefits from such costs. The ongoing business receives no benefits from such costs. The facts are clearly and simply that these costs bear an obvious and precise causal relationship to the government's action in terminating the contract for its convenience. From a cost accounting viewpoint, there is no basis to charge such costs to any cost objective other than the terminated contract. From an equity viewpoint, we just cannot understand how the government feels justified in turning its back on, and refusing to compensate for, the costs it caused a contractor to incur.

Initial Costs, Including Starting Load and Preparatory Costs

FAR 31.205-42(c) states that the above costs are allowable. The major problem is to locate them and to be sure they are properly included and supported in the termination settlement proposal.

One of the problems in this area is caused by the fact that recognized accounting texts and dictionaries differ in their definitions of these terms. This problem is not too serious and may best be solved by using the definitions provided in FAR 31.205-42(c), quoted earlier in this chapter. By far the larger problem involves locating all of the initial costs. For example, FAR 31.205-42(c)(2) states that preparatory costs "are costs incurred in preparing to perform the terminated contract, including costs of initial plant rearrangement and alterations, management and personnel organization, production planning and similar activities. . . ." If most of these expenses are generally charged to overhead accounts, without segregation by contract, there may be considerable difficulty in finding and supporting their applicability to the satisfaction of government auditors. Somewhat similar problems obtain with respect to starting-load costs, that is, the after-the-fact identification of early excessive spoilage, subnormal production, and so on. As we shall see in the guidance DCAA furnishes its auditors, quoted below, the Agency plants a suspicion in their minds that "high initial costs may be an indication that a loss would have occurred had the contract gone to completion."

12-305.1 Initial Costs.

a. Initial costs include starting load costs and preparatory costs. The criteria for the allowability of initial costs are provided in FAR 31.205-42(c).

b. There are basically two major areas of consideration involved in the contractor's determination and the auditor's review of initial costs, namely, (1) the identification in terms of total dollars, and (2) the allocation of these dollars to the terminated portion of the contract. Regarding identification, FAR 31.205-42(c)(4) provides that "if initial costs are claimed and have not been segregated on the contractor's books, segregation for settlement purposes shall be made from cost reports and schedules which reflect the high unit cost incurred during the early stages of the contract." To be considered, the contractor must, therefore, submit the claim for initial costs and be able to support it with meaningful data taken from formal or informal records. Contractors rarely segregate initial costs in the formal records or books of account, and claims can normally be expected to involve informal records, cost reports, production data, etc., as well as estimates developed from the foregoing on the basis of the contractor's judgments. The auditor will, of course, be required to evaluate the supporting documentation, the reasonableness of the total amount claimed to represent initial costs, and the allocation to the terminated work.

c. One area which can usually be identified with initial costs is the rate of production loss in the early stages of production. The contractor should have scrap reports, efficiency reports, spoilage tickets, etc., which can be used to develop and support a claim for a high initial production loss. Another cost often readily identifiable is initial plant rearrangement and alterations. Generally, a work order or service order is required to perform work of this nature and costs are accumulated against the work order. The costs of management and personnel organization and production planning may be difficult to evaluate; if claimed, such costs will probably be based on estimates and the assistance of technical personnel will normally be necessary. The remaining elements of initial costs are defined in FAR 31.205-42(c)(1). They include such items as idle time, subnormal production, employee training, and unfamiliarity or lack of experience with the product, materials or processes involved. Although the FAR states that these costs are nonrecurring in nature, they may occur to some degree throughout the life of the contract. However, as production continues and learning takes effect, these costs should diminsh. This learning process may be expressed in the improvement curve which is discussed in considerable detail in Appendix F. Generally, it is difficult to distinguish between normal production labor and that portion of labor attributable to idle time, subnormal production, employee training, or lack of experience; however, many contractors maintain data on these factors in a collective manner in the form of efficiency reports, equivalent units produced, etc., and it is often found to be acceptable as support for starting load costs.

d. After identification, the next consideration is that of allocating the initial costs to the terminated and nonterminated portions of the contract. Usually initial costs can be allocated to delivered and terminated units on a basis proportionate to the respective quantities. Initial costs which cannot be directly identified but which constitute those types of diminishing costs discussed earlier can be allocated through the use of an improvement curve. (See Appendix F.) In the case of direct labor, for instance, the learning curve technique can be used to project total direct labor hours if the contract had been completed. Average direct labor hours per unit can then be determined and applied to the delivered units. The quantity so allocated would then be deducted from the total labor hours required to produce the delivered items. The difference can then be costed using historical labor and indirect cost rates, to determine the initial costs allocable to the terminated portion of the contract.

e. It will be necessary to determine if initial costs are reasonable; this determination involves analysis of the causes of initial costs as well as a comparison of such costs to those experienced on similar programs. Further, high initial costs may be an indication that a loss would have occurred had the contract gone to completion.

Loss of Useful Value of Special Tooling, Special Machinery, and Equipment

FAR 31.204-42(d) establishes these costs as allowable providing the assets are really special, i.e., not usable for other work, the government's interests are protected by transfer of title or other means agreed upon with the contracting officer, and, if applicable to two or more government contracts, the cost is appropriately prorated. We would also invite the reader's attention to Chapter XVII of this text, where we discussed in considerable detail, including citation of BCA cases, FAR 31.205-17, Idle Facilities and Idle Capacity Costs. Subparagraph (b)(2) provides that such costs are allowable where these facilities have become idle because of various reasons, including termination.

Loss of useful value of special tooling, special machinery, and equipment is a normal cost incident to contract termination and, unlike the initial costs discussed earlier, is usually easier to identify. Here again, companies that experience contract termination will find it useful to study the guidance furnished DCAA auditors regarding the audit and other steps to be taken before recommending costs for acceptance by the contracting officer. The instructions below from the Audit Agency's Contract Audit Manual also indicate the reviews that may be performed by government technical personnel:

12-304.14 *Special Tooling.*

a. The auditor should determine that the items which the contractor claims as special tooling comply with the definition of special tooling in FAR 45.101. When tooling can be used on the contractor's other work, it does not qualify as special tooling, and the costs are not allocable to the terminated portion of the contract. In many cases it may be desirable to obtain a technical determination as to whether claimed special tooling meets the definition criteria contained in FAR.

b. The contractual intent of the Government and the contractor as to reimbursement of special tooling costs affects the allowability of these costs. When it is determined that there was an intent to reimburse the contractor for special tooling, reimbursement may have been contemplated as part of the product price or as a separate contract line item.

(1) When there is no indication as to the method of reimbursing special tooling costs, the auditor should assume that reimbursement was made through the product price and thus the costs are allocable to both the terminated and unterminated portion of the contract.

(2) If special tooling was negotiated as a separate, nondeliverable contract line item, tooling costs may be claimed only if the contractor has not previously received payment for the tooling at its line item price. In this case, regardless of the amount expended on tooling, recovery in the termination claim would be limited to the line item price less any payments previously received for tooling.

(3) When special tooling is a deliverable item of the contract, the contractor will be paid the contract price only if the tooling is available. If portions of the tooling have been consumed, lost, or are otherwise unavailable, the contract price of the tooling will be reduced for these circumstances as well as for previous payments.

c. Before accepting special tooling costs, the auditor should determine that:

(1) the special tooling was not acquired prior to the date of the contract, or as a replacement of items so acquired.

(2) the special tooling claimed is not consumable small tools or items which could be classified as capital goods.

(3) the special tooling does not exceed the requirements of the contract. For example, when the contract is for the design and production of a prototype unit and only a few experimental parts are needed, the contractor should normally not purchase special tooling intended for mass production. The contractor may have exceeded requirements on the basis of the expectation of future contracts.

d. Special tooling may have been worn out and its usefulness expended in the production of the finished and delivered units. No part of such tooling costs would be allocable to the terminated portion of the contract. All or a portion of the special tooling required for production of the terminated portion of the contract may not yet have been constructed or purchased and therefore all or most of the tooling cost incurred to the date of termination may equitably be allocable to the completed portion of the contract.

12-304.15 *Special Machinery and Equipment.*

a. General. The audit of special machinery and equipment costs included in termination claims is similar to the audit of special tooling costs. The determination that a particular item of machinery or equipment is "special" is usually a technical matter. It may also involve a legal determination as to the intent of the contracting parties. To qualify as "special," the equipment or machinery must be of a type that is not generally used in the contractor's industry, but is peculiar to the needs of the Government. Machinery or equipment should not be considered "special" when it is (1) ordinary or normal-type equipment in the contractor's industry, (2) similar to other facilities owned by a contractor, or (3) usable on other work without loss to the contractor.

b. Loss of Useful Value. Allowability of loss on special machinery or equipment is dependent upon the original intentions of the contracting parties. When a contract contemplates or requires that a contractor purchase certain special machinery or equipment in order to perform the contract, and the cost is considered in establishing the price for the contract, the contractor is entitled to recover the loss of useful value of the special equipment at termination. The maximum allowance for loss of useful life should not exceed the portion of the cost of the equipment considered in establishing the contract price which is applicable to the terminated units. When the purchase of special equipment was not specifically considered in the course of the contract negotiations, reimbursement for loss of its useful value is not automatically disregarded, though it may raise a question as to the "special" nature of the equipment. A usual consideration in granting a contract is that the contractor be equipped to do the work required and meet delivery schedules. The auditor may have a valid basis to question the cost when, for example, (1) the contractor continues to use the "special" machinery on other work, (2) the special machinery was owned by the contractor prior to the contract date, or (3) the contractor is unwilling to transfer title to the Government if the transfer is required upon honoring the termination claim. When a firm audit position is not possible because of insufficient information, the auditor should solicit the assistance of technical personnel.

Rental Costs Under Unexpired Leases

DAR, FPR, and now FAR recognize that, if the contractor was required to lease property for the performance of the contract, suffered a termination for the government's convenience, and was unsuccessful in terminating, assigning, or otherwise settling the lease, the rental costs under the unexpired lease should be considered allowable costs. Allowable, too, are any costs of alterations necessary for contract performance as well as restoration of the premises required by the provisions of the lease.

Settlement Expenses

Government regulations establish that settlement expenses as described in FAR 31.205-42 are allowable. However, the inclusion of the words "reasonably" and "reasonable" have generated many controversies, some of which have moved to litigation. Reference is made here to Chapter XVII of this text for our discussion of Professional and Consultant Service Costs, particularly regarding the inclination of government auditors and some contracting officers to question charges for outside legal and accounting fees incurred in connection with preparing the termination settlement proposal. The government's batting average in this area is extremely low, as it is generally in connection with any payments actually made in arm's-length transactions that are questioned on the basis of reasonableness.

Despite the government's almost invariable defeats when such costs are alleged to be unreasonable and the contractor appeals the decisions to a board of contract appeals or to the courts, these controversies continue to surface. The following excerpts from DCAA's Contract Audit Manual, paragraph 12-309, reflect the kind of guidance that encourages the auditors to make evaluations and arrive at judgments that at times they may not be technically competent to make:

g. Costs in excess of those which the auditor deems are reasonably appropriate to the termination settlement such as for unnecessary work, unrealistic professional fees, etc., should be questioned. Where questions concerning the reasonableness of an amount cannot be resolved, the auditor should refer the amount to the contracting officer as unresolved cost, furnishing factual information and comments which may be useful to the contracting officer in making a determination on the acceptability of the costs.

h. It may be necessary for a contractor to obtain professional accounting services in order to facilitate settlement proceedings. The costs of such services, including preparation of the settlement proposal, may be reimbursed to the contractor. The auditor should evaluate the reasonableness of the charge for accounting service by considering the relative complexity of the proposal in relation to the number of staff-days represented by the amount of the fee.

i. Where legal expenses are claimed, the auditor should appraise their reasonableness on the basis of the time expended, the nature of the services rendered, and the proportionate relationship of the legal expenses to the total amount of the termination settlement proposal. Appropriate comments should be included in the audit report. In cases of contingent fee arrangements, i.e. where the legal fee is based on the amount of the negotiated terminal settlement, the nature of the arrangement should be clearly described. Legal expenses or other costs incident to an appeal from a settlement determination by the contracting officer are not allowable.

Clary Corporation, **ASBCA No. 19274, 74-2 BCA par. 10,947.**—We referred to the special problems generated by contract terminations arising from the fact that companies' books and records are maintained on a going-concern basis. The precise documentation demanded by DCAA, unless accumulated from the day the notice of termination is received, is extremely difficult to compile.

Clary's settlement expenses included selling expense; processing purchase order and in-house orders; recording, scheduling, and releasing inventory to stock room; preparing in kits and recording all back orders; recording schedule changes and canceling releases; restocking and rerouting components to other jobs; canceling/distributing in-house orders; processing settlement proposal; and restocking charges from vendors. The proposal was audited by DCAA. The auditor was apparently satisfied with the claim for restock charges for vendors. As to the other items, he took no exception to the labor rates used by the contractor in estimating each item. However, he was unable to evaluate the reasonableness of the hours estimated in each category and recommended that the contracting officer obtain a technical evaluation. The audit report stated that the proposed labor hours "are estimates only and are not supported by time cards."

On receiving the audit report, the contracting officer advised Clary that he intended to render a unilateral determination, noted the areas of disagreement related to the estimated hours, and invited the presentation of any additional evidence the contractor might wish to present.

According to the published decision, the contractor replied that the "costs were estimated by personnel who have been associated with manufacturing and production control of this product for a period of eight years. The costs closely agree with those used in the bidding and award of subject contract." Clary further advised that the necessary activities "were accurately depicted . . ., are valid costs of the contract, and represent a reasonable and equitable settlement."

The contracting officer disallowed selling expenses because they were "indirect type costs and allocability, propriety and reasonableness thereof was not substantiated." As to the next six items (see listing earlier), the contracting officer said: "These costs are considered indirect expenses claimed directly and constitute a claim for unabsorbed overhead which cannot be allowed. Further, practical support for this claimed activity was not supportable by your accounting records."

The contracting officer then addressed the claim for processing the settlement proposal and concluded that the estimated hours "to prepare a relatively simple proposal is considered unsupported, unnecessary and unreasonable." He then allowed about 20% of the hours estimated by Clary.

The board upheld the contracting officer's unilateral determination. Its closing comments are of interest:

Although it may have been legitimate for the appellant to have estimated its costs of performance where those costs were not shown on its accounting records, it was still necessary to demonstrate the bases and accuracy of those estimates. No such showing was made to the Audit Agency, or the Contracting Officer and it has not been made to this Board on this submitted record. We said in appeal of *Herbert R. Button and Winfield & Frances Beesley, a Joint Venture,* ASBCA No. 17281, 73-1 BCA par. 9780, "Appellant has the burden of proving by a preponderance of the evidence that it is entitled to a greater settlement allowance than determined by the contracting officer. *Atlas Fabricators, Inc.,* ASBCA No. 16426, On Mot. for Recon., 72-1 BCA par. 9446. It is well settled that such burden is not carried by unsupported allegations."

Western States Painting Co., **ASBCA No. 13843, 69-1 BCA par. 7616.**—Chapter XVII of this text includes several judicial decisions that found legal, accounting, and other professional fees allowable after hard-line government actions culminated in their disallowance and contractors' appeals. The above-captioned case is another instance.

A termination settlement proposal under a contract ruled to have been terminated for the convenience of the government included legal and other professional service costs, all of which were declared unallowable by the government. The rationale employed by the ASBCA in support of its mixed ruling provides a good reference for defense contractors who may be involved in contract terminations.

To begin with, the board would not accept the government's wholesale disallowance, which was predicated on the contracting officer's conclusion that these costs were incurred in connection with the prosecution of claims against the government. Instead, it performed a chronological analysis of these costs on the basis that "the circumstance of chronological concurrence with formal claim proceedings does not exclude the costs of an attorney's services shown to have been employed for settlement negotiations with the contracting officer. *Acme Process Equipment Co., etc. v. U.S.,* 10 CCF par. 73,065, 171 Ct.Cls. 251, 262 (1965). ..." On this basis, however, the board found that, while claiming proceedings before it and the court for a specified period did not represent conclusive circumstances, "the expenses claimed for that period cannot be allowed by the Board because there is no showing that they reflect any settlement negotiations with the contracting officer. See *Reed & Prince Mfg. Co.,* ASBCA No. 3172, 59-1 BCA par. 2172; *Typo-Machine Company,* ASBCA No. 5083, 59-2 BCA par. 2435; *Bolinders Company, Inc.,* ASBCA No. 5740, 60-2 BCA par. 2746; *Q.V.S. Inc.,* ASBCA No. 7513, 1963 BCA par. 3699."

The period for which such expenses were disallowed by the board ran from November 16, 1961, the date of termination, to about October 1, 1968, when the Court of Claims ruled that the termination should be considered for the convenience of the government instead of for default.

Further settlement expenses for legal and other professional services covered the period continuing to February 17, 1969. The contracting officer disallowed expenses incurred between October 1 and 8, 1968, and, subsequently, to January 9, 1969, "on the grounds that such expenses related to the prosecution of the present appeal rather than to settlement negotiations."

The board ruled against the government regarding the allowability of expenses during the period October 1-8 on the ground that no action by the parties was required during that period. Inasmuch as it could see no action taken by the contractor to pursue its claim through judicial or quasi-judicial bodies, the ASBCA saw "no ground for inferring that claimed expenses in (that) period ... related to anything but presentation of a termination claim to the contracting officer."

Regarding the settlement expenses incurred after January 9, the date of the contracting officer's unilateral decision, the board found evidence of continuing negotiations by telephone between the contractor and the contracting officer up until January 23, 1969. Accordingly, with the exclusion of certain specific items, it reversed the government and allowed the professional service costs through that date.

The Boeing Company, ASBCA No. 12685, 69-2 BCA par. 7795.— Many controversies and disputes relating to settlement costs under contracts terminated for convenience involve overhead allocations to such costs. The above-captioned decision in this area is of interest.

Involved here was a very large termination settlement proposal, exceeding $200 million, with negotiations proceeding smoothly except for Boeing's claim of an overhead allowance approximating $400,000. This amount represents 22.6% of termination settlement labor dollars, and a few words must be said about the manner in which this percentage was computed. Without discussing Boeing's overhead structure in detail, we would note that certain expenses are included in so-called "secondary pools" and ultimately distributed to "primary pools" (manufacturing and engineeering). Before the secondary pools are distributed to the primary pools, credits are made for overhead considered allocable to "special service work orders." These are activities that may be performed either by indirect personnel or by direct and indirect personnel and/or are of such nature that the contractor would be unduly burdened by applying the full book overhead rate. Accordingly, based on certain mathematical and accounting manipulations, special overhead rates, considerably lower than book rates, are computed for these special activities or projects. Boeing included termination settlement activities among these special activities or projects and, accordingly, applied the 22.6% special rate thereto.

The government claimed that the sum, $400,000, thus allocated represented expenses that (1) were unrelated to the termination settlement activities or (2) bore only a minor relationship to such activities. It was further contended that the other amounts claimed and allowed Boeing adequately compensated the contractor for its termination settlement costs and that this additional claim duplicated many costs already allowed.

Boeing's main contention was that the use of the special overhead rate for special service work orders and projects had been computed and applied consistently for a number of years and had been consistently accepted by the government for all contract cost determinations including termination settlements. The contractor particularly pointed out that the overhead charged to the terminated contract had been taken out of its regular overhead. Accordingly, if it were now disallowed on a retroactive basis, Boeing could not recover it against any other business.

Taking up the government's contention that the contractor had already been adequately compensated, the board queried a DCAA auditor. This auditor acknowledged that the government had been accepting Boeing's procedure through the years and that "there was possibly an assumption that it (the approved limited service order overhead rate) was suitable for terminations also, although I am not sure that consideration was even given to that point." He further testified "that he had spent considerable time analyzing the accounts . . . but he found it 'very difficult to make an analysis of these costs and say they are either good for termination or they are not good.'" The board concluded that "[a] fair summary of this witness's testimony is that he could not say positively that there were any improper charges but there might have been."

A DCAA supervisory auditor, in answer to the question as to whether the overhead charge should be considered allowable or unallowable as termination settlement expense, stated: "I did not come to any definite determination. I felt that this sort of thing would have to be prepared by the contractor after we had understood certain ground rules and then we could evaluate which items were allowable and which were not, but just looking at a mere listing would not just give you the answer."

It would appear that the sense of the auditors' statements was that, having completed the audit, they did not know whether or not these overhead charges were appropriate. We wonder if these audit remarks were cleared with their headquarters, since, in effect, they could be viewed as representing DCAA audit policy before the ASBCA. But the government's position grew even worse with the testimony of a Settlement Review Board Chairman. He testified that ASPR 15-205.42(f) provides that the contractor shall be reimbursed primarily on a direct basis for termination settlement activities. He further stated: "We have never allowed an overhead type of cost in settlement expense. We have allowed costs of a similar nature but we have never identified it as overhead. In other words, we have recognized that the contractor incurs certain expenses which it is not practicable for the contractor to identify and accumulate and charge directly, so contracting officers have negotiated sums which they have allowed contractors for such things as supervision, occupancy, clerical help. . . ."

When asked an opinion as to what portion of the contractor's costs should be allowed, this government representative suggested 5%, but added that, "[w]hether or not this would be considered reasonable by the contractor I don't know, I doubt it." He then suggested that, if the 5% were unacceptable, "I have a feeling that perhaps something in the neighborhood of a hundred thousand dollars . . ." would be.

As might be expected, the board asked: "From what is this feeling based on that a hundred thousand dollars would be about right?" The answer was: "The only experience we have is on other types of terminations. We have been running between 3 and 5%. Perhaps in a termination this large 5% would not be sufficient. I don't know."

The Chairman of the Review Board was then asked whether "all contractors have uniform accounting procedures in regard to what labor they charge directly." The amazing answer was: "I don't know anything about contractors' accounting systems."

It would be just as well to spare the reader the other portions of the government's testimony. Turning to the contractor's testimony again, Boeing's representatives included its controller and a certified public accountant. Their testimony was effective in establishing the consistencies of the contractor's procedures and the inequity that would result from a government disallowance. It appeared somewhat weaker in establishing the accounting accuracy and validity of the method employed, and at one point the Boeing controller conceded that "[t]he secondary pools from which costs are allocated to termination settlement activities obviously contained costs which did not pertain to termination." However, he testified that the inclusion of those costs did not violate good accounting principles.

While allowing the full amount of the claim, the board closed its decision by reiterating the emphasis it accorded to the inequity that would have resulted from a retroactive rejection of a method previously and consistently approved. Said the board: "We think it appropriate to state that this decision does not reach the question of the Government's right to disapprove Boeing's system of allocating overhead expenses to contract termination on a prospective basis."

New York Shipbuilding Company, ASBCA No. 15443, 73-1 BCA par. 9852.—A contract for the construction of a submarine was terminated for the convenience of the government before completion, and the job of finishing the work was awarded to another contractor. During the work performed by the second contractor, certain deficiencies were found and a claim was made by the government as a counter to the contractor's termination settlement proposal.

There were several factors involved in this appeal, but our analysis is limited to what we consider the most significant one, the conclusion of the board "that the termination for convenience precludes the Government from recovering the amounts paid for correcting the alleged deficiencies, even if the existence of such deficiencies were proved and the Government's cost to correct them were established."

The following excerpt from the board's decision, which includes citation of several of its prior decisions, merits attention.

> In several previous cases we have held that where a contract is terminated for convenience of the Government, the contractor is entitled to recover its reasonable, allocable, and allowable costs incurred with respect to termination inventory even if such inventory did not comply in all respects with specification requirements. *The Douglas Corporation,* ASBCA No. 5550, 60-1 BCA par. 2531; *Atlas Can Corp.,* ASBCA No. 3381, 60-1 BCA par. 2651; *Caskel Forge, Inc.,* ASBCA No. 7638, 1962 BCA par. 3318; *Remsel Industries, Inc.,* ASBCA No. 8462, 1963 BCA par. 3918; *Best Lumber Sales,* ASBCA No. 16737, 72-2 BCA par. 9661. The rationale for this holding was set forth in *Caskel Forge, supra,* in which we stated that the general effect of a termination for convenience of a fixed price contract is to convert the terminated portion of the contract into a cost reimbursement contract and to provide for the reimbursement of allowable costs incurred in the performance of the terminated portion of the contract. We stated that:

>> 'Costs of producing defective work are normally reimbursable under a cost reimbursement contract, unless it is established that the defective production resulted from 'the contractor's own fault or folly' or 'careless conduct of the work or other disregard of his contractual duties.'

> We further stated in effect that while a fixed price contractor is not entitled to be paid for items which do not comply with specification requirements, the termination for convenience deprives the contractor of the opportunity to recoup expenses associated with defective work incurred in the early stages of performance.

The government disputed the applicability of the cases cited above and emphasized that the instant controversy involved a government counterclaim for the government's costs of correcting deficiencies, not with a claimed disallowance of costs incurred by the contractor. However, the board reviewed its rulings in *Western States Painting Co.,* ASBCA 13843, 69-1 BCA par. 7616, and *J.D. Shotwell Company,* ASBCA 8961, 65-2 BCA par. 5243, which "stand for the principle that upon terminating a contract for convenience the government loses whatever right it might have possessed to hold the contractor responsible for correcting deficiencies in the work included in the terminated portion of the contract."

Switlik Parachute Co., Inc., ASBCA No. 18024, 75-1 BCA par. 11,434.—One of the issues in this appeal concerned entitlement to costs of production line teardown. The teardown costs covered (1) cleaning and restorage of sewing machines and (2) moving of tables. The amounts involved were small, but the principles are interesting for defense contractors.

The government's disallowance was based on three grounds: "*First*, that this is an overhead item that should not be set up on a direct-charge basis; *second*, that these costs constitute "plant reconversion cost," unallowable under the cost principle in ASPR 15-205.29; and *third*, that these costs should be charged as set-up costs on the next contract, not to this contract, and hence presumably they are not allocable to this contract."

Switlik's position:

> Appellant argues, *first*, that when the contract is terminated for convenience and the contractor is not paid in full contract price, these costs which ordinarily would be absorbed within the price cannot be recovered except as a direct charge; *second*, that the ASPR 15-205.29 prohibition only applies to a situation where a contract is complete and all the costs of the contract can be amortized throughout the contract; and *third*, that ASPR 15-205.42(f)(2), allowing reasonable costs for disposition of property produced for the contract, is applicable in that the setting up of the line in effect constituted space and equipment properly produced and made available for the anticipated contract production; and *fourth;* that tear-down costs are of the same nature as facility and equipment lease costs which ordinarily are allowable post-termination costs.

The board first rejected the government's argument that this must be an overhead item and could not be charged directly:

> There is nothing objectionable about charging any cost directly, provided it is properly allocable to the contract, and other costs of the same character are excluded from indirect pools charged to the contract, in order to avoid "double screening" or duplicate charging. See ASPR 15-202. In particular, in a termination for convenience situation, it is common to remove some or all types of indirect costs from overhead or G&A and to charge them directly in order to achieve equitable allocation.

The board also rejected the contractor's argument that ASPR 15-205.42(f)(2) applied: "That cost principle on its face applies only to 'property acquired or produced for the contract,' and so is patently inapplicable to space or equipment made available for production. We similarly reject appellant's attempted analogy between tear-down costs and facility and equipment lease costs continuing after termination."

The issues upon which the allowability of these costs turned, in the opinion of the board, were plant reconversion principle and allocability. As to allocability, the board found no difficulty in establishing that the cost of putting the sewing machines back in storage was allocable to the terminated contract. Using reasoning that we have urged both the board and government to apply to unabsorbed overhead, the ASBCA said: "There would be no basis for allocating this cost to any other contract, where there was not another job for which the machines could be used immediately and it was this contract which necessitated taking the machines out of storage in the first place."

Addressing ASPR 15-205.29, which made reconversion costs unallowable except when related to government property, the board found the cost principle inapplicable. It found that the cost was for taking the sewing machines off the line, cleaning them, etc., and putting them back on the shelf, and it construed this cost as "more in the nature of standard maintenance and preservation work than restoration or rehabilitation within the apparent meaning of the cost principle. . . ." The board decided that these costs fit more closely to the normal maintenance and repair costs made allowable by ASPR 15-205.20(a).

The contractor was less fortunate with the claim for the cost of moving the tables after the termination, which the board could not see as a necessary part of winding up the contract: "Unlike the situation with the sewing machines, appellant has shown no reason why the tables could not stay where they were until either they or the space was needed for another contract, at which time the cost of moving the tables would have been allocable to that other contract. We conclude that the cost of moving tables is not allocable to this contract and is therefore unallowable."

ACCOUNTING FOR TERMINATED CONTRACTS AND THE CASB

As we discussed earlier, certain aspects of government regulations on accounting for contracts terminated for the convenience of the government have resulted in inequitable and illogical consequences to contractors. Perhaps more than the precise language of the regulations, the major problems are attributable to judicial precedents developed over the years through case law in decisions by courts and boards of contract appeals.

One of the most inequitable judicial determinations has been the requirement imposed upon the contractor to bear the costs of unabsorbed overhead, expenses continuing after and as a direct result of the government's action in terminating a contract for its convenience. Where unabsorbed overhead is caused by the government's action in delaying or disrupting contract performance, the costs are allowed without question. There is yet to appear a logical rationale for not reimbursing the same costs, also caused by government action, where the action is full termination as contrasted with partial termination, delay, etc.

Some years ago, the existence of problems in accounting for terminated contracts was recognized by the now-defunct Cost Accounting Standards (CAS) Board's staff, which established, with the Board's approval, a project that was supposed to lead to the promulgation of a standard dealing with this matter. Unfortunately, the history of the project was a sad one. The CASB staff project director did not appear to display an overabundance of interest, finally taking the very unusual step of asking an industry association to prepare a draft standard. A subcommittee, acting without appropriate checks and balances by the association, fell into a trap. It proposed an extreme regulation, which the CASB staff rejected out of hand.

The ball seemed now to be in the CASB's court, but for various reasons the staff, although always on the lookout for new projects, was reluctant to pursue this one. Finally, the staff seemed to have decided that, if unabsorbed overhead was a problem, it should deal with the subject wherever it arose—terminations, delays, disruptions, etc. As near as we were able to follow the course of events, this revised approach met with the same lack of interest as the original project on accounting for terminated contracts. What ultimately developed was a staff issues paper on Accounting for Capacity-Related Costs. As part of its action in formally disassociating itself from any responsibility for a standard on accounting for terminated contracts, the CASB Executive Secretary wrote to the DAR Council on November 6, 1978, advising the staff had concluded "an extensive inquiry" into this subject, determined that the problems "involve allowability and reasonableness . . . rather than allocability," and was therefore suspending further work. Although we agreed with the widely held view that the CASB should not be encouraged to issue additional standards, we could not help but wonder how the Board's staff concluded that accounting for contract terminations did not involve allocability.

When the government terminates the contract for its convenience, a contractor is left with a void that results in continuing overhead costs until new business can be acquired to absorb them. From an accounting viewpoint it does not appear appropriate to allocate the unabsorbed overhead cost to the ongoing business because this business neither caused the unabsorbed overhead nor benefited by it. Certainly, it would not be debated that unabsorbed overhead is a cost. Where then should this cost be allocated? It has always seemed clear to us that unabsorbed overhead was caused by the government's action in the convenience termination, and therefore the cost must be allocated to the terminated contract. If the CASB staff took serious issue with this accounting rationale, it seems to us it would have at least recognized the existence of a problem—and a major part of the problem is, indeed, allocability.

Returning to the staff's letter to DOD of November 6, 1978, after ascertaining that there are no questions of allocability and deciding that it would do nothing further in this area, the staff offered DOD some advice on what it might do to clarify the DAR provisions on terminations.

The first matter considered significant by the CASB staff was that whatever research it had performed led it to the view that "[n]ot all contractors establish separate work orders for the identification of termination-related costs." As a major contribution to accounting for contract terminations, the CASB staff suggested that DAR be revised to provide "a requirement to account for costs related to a contract termination in a separate final cost objective established for such costs . . . ."

The letter did recognize in an offhand manner that there was a question about unabsorbed overhead attributable to contract terminations. However, the furthest the staff would go was to advise DOD about its project on capacity-related costs and comment vaguely that "[a]t *some future time* we may have a proposal which will be applicable both to delays and to terminations." (Emphasis added.)

The third subject on which the CASB staff offered suggestions to DOD was settlement expenses. In the opinion of the staff, the provision of DAR 15-205.42(f)(3) was too broad and "leaves room for difference of opinion on application." It suggested that the provision be made more explicit to obtain uniform treatment in allocating indirect costs as settlement expenses. The staff saw a similar problem in DAR 15-205.42(g), which provided for allocating indirect expenses to the cost of settlements with subcontractors. The staff thought this provision, too, should be sharpened.

It is curious that, having concluded that accounting for contract terminations does not involve allocability, the CASB staff's advice to DOD was directed specifically to matters of allocability but addressed only minor matters.

The ultimate action taken by DOD in response to these suggestions (DAC 76-26, December 15, 1980) was a revision to DAR 15-205.42, the essential change being a requirement to establish separate cost account(s) or work order(s) when termination settlement expenses are significant. The total impact on cost principles related to terminated contracts attributable to the CAS Board are contained in this short sentence in FAR 31.205-42(g)(2): "If settlement expenses are significant, a cost account or work order shall be established to separately identify and accumulate them."

Prior to concluding the aspect of the treatment of settlement expenses, it would appear of interest to point up several controversial items in this area that were recently decided favorably to the contractor by the ASBCA in *Celesco Industries, Inc.,* ASBCA No. 22460, 84-2, BCA par. 17295, concerning the following:

1. Direct labor charges—The parties agreed with the direct labor charges made directly to the aforementioned termination project account. However, DCAA recommended the application of a fringe overhead rate of 16.2 percent, which was concurred in by the cognizant Termination Contracting Officer (TCO). The board used a normal full factory overhead rate of 180.09 percent on the principle that such labor was no different than any other labor, citing *Condec Corp.,* ASBCA No. 14324, 73-1 BCA par. 9808 at 45,844.

2. The TCO also denied indirect type costs charged direct as settlement expenses inasmuch as such costs were recovered through the allocation of the overhead during the period incurred. The board's response to this posture by the TCO is cited below:

> A more appropriate approach when significant duplicate recovery could occur otherwise, and one we have employed frequently, is that used in *Amplitronics, Inc.,* ASBCA No. 20545, 76-1 BCA par. 11,760. There conversion of indirect charges to direct charges was made with the provision that these charges be removed from the overhead or G&A expense pool and that other charges of the indirect personnel for their work on other contracts are deleted from indirect cost pools as well. Id at 56, 120, 56, 122. See also *Condec Corp.,* ASBCA No. 14123, 73-1 BCA par. 9808; *Baifield Industries,* Divn. of ATO, Inc., ASBCA No. 20006, 76-2 BCA par. 12,096, on motion for reconsid. par. 12,203. (Emphasis added)

*   *   *   *

> We also will allow as direct charges the remaining indirectly charged settlement expenses. However, to minimize the effect of any possible duplicate recovery, we will remove these costs from the 1972 G&A

expenses allocable to the cost of purchased parts and work-in-process. We believe that this treatment of the indirectly charged costs is in conformance with the teaching of *Codex Corp. v. United States, supra,* and ASPR 8-301(a) and "necessary in arriving at fair compensation" for appellant's termination settlement efforts. *Agrinautics,* ASBCA Nos. 21512, 21608, 21609, 79-2 BCA par. 14,149 at 69,650.

3. With respect to the often-highlighted aspect of the reasonableness of the total settlement expenses being claimed representing 33 percent in the subject instance, the Administrative Judge pointed out that in *Contract Maintenance Inc.,* ASBCA No. 20689, 77-1 BCA par. 12,446, the total settlement expenses constituted 85 percent of the claimed costs and the ultimate decision was directed toward an analysis of the specific expenses being claimed with reasonableness being a factor in the final adjudication process.

4. A final item often challenged by the government people consists of the outside professional fees expended in the preparation and processing of the settlement proposal termination claim as being unreasonable in the light of the degree of complexity of the matter. In this instance also, the board differed and determined that the very nature of preparing a termination claim was complex and approved the total time being claimed by an attorney and the hourly rates of $60.00 in the early period and $90.00 in the later stages.

Indirect Costs—Special Problems Incident to Contracts Terminated in Early Stages

Where considerable work has been completed under a contract, costs may be reasonably determined through the use of the contractor's usual accounting procedures. For example, the cost of work in process in late stages may be costed with material, labor, and manufacturing overhead as a percentage of direct labor and general and administrative expense as a percentage of total factory cost. However, where termination occurs in the early stages, the normal costing procedures will not yield reasonable approximations of termination costs. For example, if most of the material has been purchased and received, and little direct labor applied, and if purchasing and receiving expenses are in the manufacturing overhead pool, it is obvious that an allocation of factory overhead as a percentage of direct labor will not produce an equitable apportionment of such costs to the terminated contract. The circumstances of early termination described above is quite common. When it is encountered, appropriate and equitable costing demands a departure from the contractor's usual accounting procedures. The justification is obvious. The usual procedures that have been employed are suitable for the usual operations of the firm. A contract terminated in an early stage presents an unusual situation and, therefore, requires a different (tailored) accounting solution.

But the solution is considerably more difficult than the mere recognition of the problem. Once the contractor departs from his usual procedures, some government auditors and administrators tend to become suspicious and alarmed. It becomes essential, therefore, not only to devise accounting solutions that will achieve fair and reasonable recoveries, but also to present, support, and document them in a manner acceptable to the government. The author of this text has been among the pioneers in establishing techniques for determining costs of contracts terminated in their early stages. We have devoted many years to the solution of these and other accounting and administrative problems incident to government contracts. Many of our experiences, analyses of judicial and quasi-judicial decisions, etc., have been recorded and reviewed in our monthly newsletter, which we have been publishing since 1954. Summaries of some of the more significant items are discussed below. They elaborate on the accounting concepts of early terminations and illustrate the related practical applications.

Illustration No. 1.—The difficulties in effecting fair and equitable recoveries under terminated government contracts are multiplied where the cancellation is at an early stage. As an illustration, we were requested to review a claim about to be submitted on a contract terminated for the convenience of the government. The tentative amount of the claim was nominal, as computed by the firm in accordance with its normal accounting procedures. However, we found that very substantial costs had been incurred that were determinable only through direct costing and not by the use of normal accounting methods.

As a case in point, substantial engineering effort had been expended up to the termination date. Inasmuch as all of the contractor's engineering salaries and related expenses were normally included in the overhead category, only the salaries of the engineering personnel had been claimed. A review of the organization and expenses of the engineering department revealed that the ratio of engineering overhead (indirect salaries, light, heat, depreciation, maintenance, etc.) to engineering direct salaries was about 100%. The application of this engineering overhead rate doubled that portion of the termination claim. This was further increased by the application of the G&A factor.

A close review of the history of this contract also revealed substantial salaries and expenses of executive, purchasing, selling, and other personnel. Many of the costs involved had not been identified and claimed because they were included in overhead accounts under the contractor's normal accounting methods.

There were many other factors involved that converted the nominal claim into a significant amount. It is important to note that all of the additions to the claim represented appropriate determinations of actual costs incurred under the terminated contract. The essential point involved is the need for careful analysis and direct costing procedures, with applicable overhead, where contracts are terminated before substantial production has occurred.

Illustration No. 2.—A contractor was engaged in a production-run contract requiring prototype delivery three months after date of contract, with production units to be completed seven months thereafter, for a total contract span of ten months. Purchasing and production were authorized, but finished units were not to be accepted until completion of the prototype and acceptance thereof by the agency. The contractor's accounting system provided for one overhead pool of expenses for manufacturing and engineering burden prorated on a basis of direct labor dollars. General and administrative expenses were allocated on a cost-incurred basis.

Subsequent to delivery and testing of the prototype, the agency decided to terminate the contract for convenience. At this point, approximately 15% of the total direct labor costs, including engineering, was expended on the contract as compared to costs that would have been incurred had the contract gone to completion.

Obviously, in order to comply with the tight delivery schedule, all phases of overhead effort had to be generated at a rate much in excess of the 15% absorption percentage. Engineering and purchasing for all practical purposes were almost complete. Machinery and electrical assembly were far in excess of 15%. The final assembly area was set aside in preparation for this assignment. The financial and administrative obstacles had been overcome, thus allowing the contract to proceed in an orderly manner.

We suggested that subsidiary cost centers be created and allocated on a basis that more closely associated the overhead as shown on the books with that expended on the terminated contract. For instance, purchasing overhead effort was allocated to total purchases and purchase orders let on the subject contract. Engineering overhead was prorated on a basis of total engineering and engineering completed on the terminated contract during the contract period.

Depreciation and related fixed costs were applied on the basis of the total machine hours set aside for the subject contract as compared to total machine hours available in the period. Assembly area space allocated to the terminated contract was charged on a direct basis, after computation of a square footage rate. These same principles and procedures were adhered to with respect to production planning and control, contract administration, and executive administration.

Implementation of the aforementioned accounting procedures resulted in a recovery of three to four times the overhead amount that would have been recouped had the contractor remained with its normal accounting system.

ADJUSTMENT FOR LOSS

If the government concludes that the contract it terminated would have been completed at a loss, not only will no profit be allowed, but the amount paid to the contractor will be reduced to reflect an adjustment for such loss. These provisions are contained in FAR 49.203, quoted below:

49.203 Adjustment for loss.

(a) In the negotiation or determination of any settlement, the TCO shall not allow profit if it appears that the contractor would have incurred a loss had the entire contract been completed. The TCO shall negotiate or determine the amount of loss and make an adjustment in the amount of settlement as specified in paragraph (b) or (c) below. In estimating the cost to complete, the TCO shall consider expected production efficiencies and other factors affecting the cost to complete.

(b) If the settlement is on an inventory basis (see 49.206-2(a)), the contractor shall not be paid more than the total of the amounts in subparagraphs (1), (2), and (3) below, less all disposal credits and all unliquidated advance and progress payments previously made under the contract:

(1) The amount negotiated or determined for settlement expenses.

(2) The contract price, as adjusted, for acceptable completed end items (see 49.205).

(3) The remainder of the settlement amount otherwise agreed upon or determined (including the allocable portion of initial costs (see 31.205-42(c)), reduced by multiplying the remainder by the ratio of (i) the total contract price to (ii) the total cost incurred before termination plus the estimated cost to complete the entire contract.

(c) If the settlement is on a total cost basis (see 49.206-2(b)), the contractor shall not be paid more than the total of the amounts in subparagraphs (1) and (2) below, less all disposal and other credits, all advance and progress payments, and all other amounts previously paid under the contract:

(1) The amount negotiated or determined for settlement expenses.

(2) The remainder of the total settlement amount otherwise agreed upon or determined (lines 7 and 14 of SF 1436, Settlement Proposal (Total Cost Basis)) reduced by multiplying the remainder by the ratio of (i) the total contract price to (ii) the remainder plus the estimated cost to complete the entire contract.

The Defense Contract Audit Agency devotes considerable attention to the possibility that a terminated contract, had it been completed, would have reflected a loss, because this loss would have permitted the auditor to recommend a reduction in the termination claim by the prorata portion of any such loss. The Contract Audit Manual, even though not binding on anyone outside of DCAA, contains probably the clearest and most comprehensive illustration of how the adjustment for loss would be computed.

12-308 Adjustment for Loss Contracts.

(a) The auditor should determine whether a contract that has been terminated would have resulted in a loss if it had been completed. This determination is significant because (i) no profit is allowable if it appears that the contractor would have incurred a loss had the contract been completed, and additionally, (ii) the termination claim must be reduced by an amount equal to the pro rata portion of any loss that would have been sustained had the contract been completed. For terminated "loss" contracts, DAR 8-304(b) and (c) set forth the methods for determining the maximum to be paid on inventory and total cost settlements. Fundamentally, the methods are intended to adjust the contractor's termination claim by applying to the amount claimed the percentage which the total contract price bears to the total estimated cost which would have been incurred had the contract been completed. The following examples illustrate the loss adjustment under the inventory basis and the total cost basis.

(1) Assume a termination having the following conditions:

Total contract price (50 units @ $2,400 each)	$120,000
Total amount invoiced for completed units	$ 84,000
Total costs incurred under the contract	$135,000
Estimate of cost to complete contract, including $10,000 subcontract settled for $5,000	$ 15,000

Settlement with subcontractor	$	5,000
Settlement expenses	$	1,000
Disposal credits	$	5,000
Units completed and delivered prior to termination		35
Units completed and on hand and not to be delivered		5
Units terminated		10

(2) Assume also that the contractor has submitted a settlement proposal on the inventory basis as follows:

Finished components	$ 7,000	
Work in process	3,250	
Dies, jigs, fixtures, and special tools	2,000	
General and administrative expenses	1,000	
Other costs	3,000	$ 16,250
Profit		2,000
Settlement expenses		1,000
Settlements with subcontractors		5,000
Acceptable finished product (adjusted for freight and packing savings)		11,000
Disposal credit		(5,000)
Net payment requested		$ 30,250

The amount recommended for settlement, assuming all claimed costs are otherwise acceptable, would be computed as follows based on ASPR 8-304(b):

Settlement expenses	$ 1,000
Contract price, as adjusted, for acceptable completed end items	11,000
Total settlement amount otherwise agreed to or determined, adjusted for estimated loss	17,000*
Less disposal credit	(5,000)
Recommended settlement amount	$24,000

* Computed by multiplying the sum of the contractor's own costs of $16,250 plus settlements with subcontractors of $5,000 by the ratio of the total contract price of $120,000 to the total indicated cost of $150,000. Total indicated cost is composed of the total cost of $135,000 incurred prior to termination plus the estimated cost of $15,000 to complete the entire contract:

$$\$21,250 \times \frac{\$120,000}{\$150,000} \text{ OR } \$21,250 \times 80\% = \$17,000$$

(3) Assume that the contractor has submitted a proposal on the total cost basis as follows:

Direct material	$24,000	
Direct labor	30,000	
Indirect factory expense	50,000	
Dies, jigs, fixtures, and special tools	10,000	
Other costs	15,000	
General and administrative expenses	6,000	$135,000
Finished product invoiced or to be invoiced		84,000 $ 51,000
Profit		
Settlement expenses		1,000
Settlement with subcontractors		5,000
Disposal and other credits		(5,000)
Advance, progress and partial payments		(0)
Net payment requested		$ 52,000

The amount recommended for settlement, assuming all claimed costs are otherwise acceptable, would be computed as follows based on ASPR 8-304(c):

Settlement expenses	$ 1,000
The total settlement amount otherwise agreed to or determined, adjusted for estimated loss	112,000 [2]
Less disposal credit	(5,000)
Less amount previously paid contractor	(84,000)
Recommended settlement amount	$ 24,000

[1] No claim for profit made by contractor because the contract price has been exceeded.

[2] Computed by multiplying the sum of the contractor's own costs of $135,000 plus settlements with subcontractors of $5,000 by the ratio of the total contract price of $120,000 to the total indicated costs of $150,000. Total indicated cost is composed of the total costs of $135,000 incurred prior to termination plus the estimated cost of $15,000 to complete the entire contract:

$$\$140,000 \times \frac{\$120,000}{\$150,000} \text{ OR } \$140,000 \times 80\% = \$112,000$$

(b) When there are unpriced changes existing at the time of the accounting review, the auditor should advise the contracting officer that the loss adjustment is tentative and will require recomputation if the changes result in upward or downward revisions of the total contract price. Similarly, where estimates are used for subcontract settlement amounts, the auditor should advise the contracting officer that the loss adjustment will require recomputation if the settlements as finally negotiated differ from the estimated amounts.

Experience indicates that DCAA auditors tend to be the most zealous in searching for possible loss situations and in going to great lengths to compute and project the loss factors. These computations entail projections of the estimated costs that would have been necessary to expend in order to complete the contract had it not been terminated. The projections are frequently very complex, requiring intimate knowledge of production methods and processes, not to mention a good crystal ball. Inasmuch as few individuals possess either of these, it is essential that contractors accord careful consideration to any estimates compiled, compute their own projections, and correct any misconceptions before they are carried too far. Unless this is done, loss projections, even where later demonstrated to be incorrect, may become negotiating factors for the government and sometimes lead to costly, time-consuming disputes and appeals.

ASBCA No. 4143 is a case in point, and the following facts are pertinent:

1. The appellant was a subcontractor holding a price redeterminable subcontract under a price redeterminable prime contract.

2. The subcontract was awarded originally for 50,000 units, terminated for alleged default, and reinstated as to 30,000 units. It was subsequently terminated after 13,000 units had been delivered because of the termination of the prime contract.

3. Pursuant to agreement of all parties, proceedings regarding the subcontract termination settlement were conducted directly between the appellant and the government. Based on a DOD audit, the contracting

officer determined that this was a "loss contract" and otherwise substantially reduced the subcontractor's claim.

4. Agreement could not be reached on the termination settlement, and the contracting officer's unilateral determination was appealed by the subcontractor.

5. For purposes of determining cost to complete, the board based the cost on 30,000 units. (The subcontractor's claim that the original 50,000 quantity should be used was denied.)

The board of contract appeals reviewed the calculations and other determinations of the government auditors and found that their calculations concerning the loss contract were substantially in error.

1. The auditors used the target selling price whereas the board found the price that should have been used was the target price plus 10% (amount of upward price revision for the subcontract).

2. The auditors were unable to explain fully a substantial difference in the unit cost that they used for castings. Certain spoilage factors added by the auditors were refuted by the subcontractor on the ground that the spoilage experience used for the computation was based on the early production under the subcontract, at which time spoilage ran high. The subcontractor was able to satisfy the board that, at the time of the termination, production efficiency had increased to the point where the amount of rejects was negligible. The auditors' contention that transportation charges should be added to material cost was rebutted on the ground that, during the subcontract production, the subcontractor had started using its own trucks for transportation. The related expenses were charged to overhead and, hence, were not properly included in direct material costs.

3. The auditors' projection of direct labor costs for completing the terminated portion of the subcontract was sharply challenged by the board. For one thing, the auditors' estimate was based on production during a holiday season. This usually unsettled period was further complicated by the impending termination of the contract. It was also found that the auditors' projected labor cost for the completion of the subcontract turned out to be much higher than the average cost actually experienced on the completed portion. The board found this projection completely unrealistic in view of the fact that the completed portion included all of the starting load costs and other high costs of semiautomatic equipment, whereas at the termination date fully automatic equipment was in use.

Although a totally precise determination could not be made, the board ruled that "everything considered . . . it would not be equitable to treat the terminated portion as a losing contract." The remaining comments deal with some of the board's rulings on the disallowance of subcontractors' claims for termination inventory and unamortized preproduction expense.

The auditors' disallowance of the claim for termination inventory involved the number of units that should be included. During the examination, the auditors noticed certain defective units. As a result, the inventory was reinstated by the procurement officer and the acceptable number was reduced by 27 for incorrect count and by 570 for rejects. The board reversed the disallowance for the rejects and stated: "work in process is not supposed to be in acceptable condition, and there is no substantial evidence that the rejects, or any of them, were nonrepairable. We do not believe that appellant has the burden of proving that defective work in process was repairable when it was not discovered until a second inspection several months after termination."

In regard to the claim for unamortized preproduction expense, the auditors noted that some $4,000 of the tooling costs was not sufficiently supported to meet audit criteria and then questioned the total amount claimed on the basis that the termination contract was a loss contract. Since the board had already dispensed with this latter contention, it turned to the actual cost computations. The board examined the subcontractor's list of tooling and concluded: "we are unable to find any valid reason to question the substantial accuracy of the costs claimed." Accordingly, the unamortized preproduction costs, claimed by the subcontractor and disallowed by the government, were reinstated by the board, although the amount was reduced on the ground that the calculation should have been made on the basis of 30,000 units rather than on the subcontractor's claim of 50,000 units.

The author has encountered a number of instances where DOD auditors have projected a loss on a terminated contract. The extensive starting load costs, normally associated with many defense contracts, can often lead to such a conclusion. In order to avoid spending time and money in extensive negotiations, appeals, etc., defense contractors' representatives should prepare comprehensive analyses and cost data in connection with termination settlement proposals. These data should isolate the heavier cost experience of the early portions of the contract, establish the cost experience at the time of contract termination, and project the costs needed to complete. In this latter connection, care should be taken to give effect to any expected continuing improvement in efficiency that would result from training and experience of the labor officers and addition of laborsaving machinery. We suggest that the contractor's officials who best know the circumstances, or an outside expert consultant, supervise the preparation of the data and the submission and explanation of it to government auditors and contracting officers.

Another very interesting case involves an adjustment for loss where the termination was attributed to the government's defective specifications. In ASBCA No. 7954, the board held that termination for default was appropriate. Thereafter, the U.S. Court of Claims (No. 194—164) ruled that the contractor's failure to complete the contract was due to causes beyond its control and, more specifically, resulted from defective government specifications. The court ruled that the termination be considered one for the convenience of the government and that the amount due the contractor be determined through administrative proceedings.

The ASBCA then remanded the question of the amount due the parties.

The contractor filed its termination claim and indicated that the work was 75% complete at the time of termination. The contracting officer accepted this figure, computed the estimated percentage of completion and projected the cost for 100% completion. After other adjustments, the allowable costs agreed upon were reduced by an amount constituting an adjustment for loss.

The contractor appealed, arguing that the contract should not be found in a loss position because the failure to complete (including the improper default termination) was caused by the government's defective specifications. The ASBCA (*Western States Painting Co.*, No. 13843) agreed with the contractor's contention, noting that it "has held that the adjustment for loss provision cannot be construed to include a loss caused by Government action in a contractual capacity. *The Douglas Corporation*, ASBCA No. 8566, 69-1 BCA par. 7578; *R.H.J. Corporation*, ASBCA No. 12404, 69-1 BCA par. 7587." The board further ruled that the contractor was entitled to profit determined in accordance with the termination-for-convenience clause.

ALLOWANCE FOR PROFIT

FAR 49.202 provides certain vague guidance to the contracting officer in negotiating an allowance for profit on contracts terminated for the convenience of the government:

49.202 Profit.

(a) The TCO shall allow profit on preparations made and work done by the contractor for the terminated portion of the contract but not on the settlement expenses. Anticipatory profits and consequential damages shall not be allowed (but see 49.108-5). Profit for the contractor's efforts in settling subcontractor proposals shall not be based on the dollar amount of the subcontract settlement agreements but the contractor's efforts will be considered in determining the overall rate of profit allowed the contractor. Profit shall not be allowed the contractor for material or services that, as of the effective date of termination, have not been delivered by a subcontractor, regardless of the percentage of completion. The TCO may use any reasonable method to arrive at a fair profit.

(b) In negotiating or determining profit, factors to be considered include—

(1) Extent and difficulty of the work done by the contractor as compared with the total work required by the contract (engineering estimates of the percentage of completion ordinarily should not be required, but if available should be considered);

(2) Engineering work, production scheduling, planning, technical study and supervision, and other necessary services;

(3) Efficiency of the contractor, with particular regard to—

(i) Attainment of quantity and quality production;

(ii) Reduction of costs;

(iii) Economic use of materials, facilities, and manpower; and

(iv) Disposition of termination inventory;

(4) Amount and source of capital and extent of risk assumed;

(5) Inventive and developmental contributions, and cooperation with the Government and other contractors in supplying technical assistance;

(6) Character of the business, including the source and nature of materials and the complexity of manufacturing techniques;

(7) The rate of profit that the contractor would have earned had the contract been completed;

(8) The rate of profit both parties contemplated at the time the contract was negotiated; and

(9) Character and difficulty of subcontracting, including selection, placement, and management of subcontracts, and effort in negotiating settlements of terminated subcontracts.

(c) When computing profit on the terminated portion of a construction contract, the contracting officer shall—

(1) Comply with paragraphs (a) and (b) above;

(2) Allow profit on the prime contractor's settlements with construction subcontractors for actual work in place at the job site; and

(3) Exclude profit on the prime contractor's settlements with construction subcontractors for materials on hand and for preparations made to complete the work.

The large and complex subject of profit is discussed in Chapter XXV of this text. For our purposes here, we would emphasize that some government officials display a hard-nosed approach in this area with a view toward minimizing profits on terminated contracts. They appear to not recognize the significant extent of high-level company effort that enters into the initial contract stages as well as to those incident to the termination action. In most instances, the rate of profit on terminations should be no less than that which was contemplated at the time of negotiation.

TERMINATION OF COST-REIMBURSEMENT TYPE CONTRACTS

Additional principles for cost-reimbursement type contracts are contained in FAR Subpart 49.3.

Discontinuance of Vouchers

When a cost-reimbursement type contract has been completely terminated, the contractor has an option to continue seeking reimbursement by the use of Standard Form (SF) 1034 for a period not to exceed six months. Within a year after the date of termination, unless a longer period has been approved, the contractor must submit a settlement proposal covering the unvouchered costs and fee.

AUDIT OF PRIME CONTRACT SETTLEMENT PROPOSALS AND SUBCONTRACT SETTLEMENTS

As in all other matters relating to contract negotiations where costs are a factor, the role of the government contract auditor has assumed increasing influence. The role of DCAA and other federal government contract audit organizations is covered in depth in Chapter II of this text. Special attention to audit in connection with prime and subcontract settlement proposals is set forth in FAR 49.107:

(a) The TCO shall refer each prime contractor settlement proposal of $25,000 or more to the appropriate audit agency for review and recommendations. The TCO may submit settlement proposals of less than $25,000 to the audit agency. Referrals shall indicate any specific information or data that the TCO desires and shall include facts and circumstances that will assist the audit agency in performing its function. The audit agency shall develop requested information and may make any further accounting reviews it considers appropriate. After its review, the audit agency shall submit written comments and recommendations to the TCO. When a formal examination of settlement proposals under $25,000 is not warranted, the TCO will perform or have performed a desk review and include a written summary of the review in the termination case file.

(b) The TCO shall refer subcontract settlements received for approval or ratification to the appropriate audit agency for review and recommendations when (1) the amount exceeds $50,000 or (2) the TCO wants a complete or partial accounting review. The audit agency shall submit written comments and recommendations to the TCO. The review by the audit agency does not relieve the prime contractor or higher tier subcontractor of the responsibility for performing an accounting review.

(c)(1) The responsibility of the prime contractor and of each subcontractor (see 49.108) includes performance of accounting reviews and any necessary field audits. However, the TCO should request the Government audit agency to perform the accounting review of a subcontractor's settlement proposal when—

(i) A subcontractor objects, for competitive reasons, to an accounting review of its records by an upper tier contractor;

(ii) The Government audit agency is currently performing audit work at the subcontractor's plant, or can perform the audit more economically or efficiently;

(iii) Audit by the Government is necessary for consistent audit treatment and orderly administration; or

(iv) The contractor has a substantial or controlling financial interest in the subcontractor.

(2) The audit agency should avoid duplication of accounting reviews performed by the upper tier contractor on subcontractor settlement proposals. However, this should not preclude the Government from making additional reviews when appropriate. When the contractor is performing accounting reviews according to this section, the TCO should request the audit agency to periodically examine the contractor's accounting review procedures and preformance, and to make appropriate comments and recommendations to the TCO.

(d) The audit report is advisory only, and is for the TCO to use in negotiating a settlement or issuing a unilateral determination. Government personnel handling audit reports must be careful not to reveal privileged information or information that will jeopardize the negotiation position of the Government, the prime contractor, or a higher tier subcontractor. Consistent with this, and when in the Government's interest, the TCO may furnish audit reports under paragraph (c) above to prime and higher tier subcontractors for their use in settling subcontract settlement proposals.

WHEN IS TERMINATION FOR CONVENIENCE OF THE GOVERNMENT A BREACH OF CONTRACT?

A much discussed and cited June 1982 decision by the United States Court of Claims, *Ronald A. Torncello and Soledad Enterprises, Inc. v. United States* [30 CCF par. 70,005], 231 Ct.Cl. 20, 681 F.2d 756, generated considerable interest in the significance and limitations of the standard termination for convenience clauses incorporated into federal government contracts. Many officials of the Department of Justice and other executive agencies view these clauses as essential to government operations and believe they should not be challenged absent a showing that a temination was not in the best interests of the government or that the contracting officer did not act in good faith.

The private sector has argued that this overly broad interpretation enabled the government to effect termination for convenience for exculpation and permitted breach of contract without appropriate compensation. In finding for the contractor, the *Torncello* court stated that "the government may not use the standard termination for convenience clause to dishonor, with impunity, its contractual obligations." These stirring words gave considerable hope to government contractors, a hope which turned cloudy upon a close reading of the decision itself and particularly of the qualifying language of the concurring opinions of three of the judges. Further questions have surfaced as a result of court and board of contract appeals decisions handed down since then.

The following comments represent a layman's summary of some historical aspects of this question and current case law.

A unilateral termination of a commercial contract between two parties in the private sector by the buyer generally permits the seller to prevail in a suit for breach of contract. In contrast, since the very early days of this nation, it was recognized that different circumstances should be considered when the federal government was one of the contracting parties. The Act of April 30, 1798, Ch. 35.1 Stat. 533, permitted the government to suspend contract performance if the public interest so required.

This law was relied upon by the Supreme Court in *United States v. Corliss Steam Engine Co.*, 91 U.S. 321 (1876), which affirmed the ruling of the lower tribunal establishing as basic law and policy that procuring agencies must have the power to settle contracts that "have been subjected to great changes in expectations." The settlement agreement between the Navy and Corliss concerned termination of certain contracts that remained uncompleted when the Civil War ended and the need for the supplies no longer existed.

The *Corliss* doctrine was greatly expanded during World War I, with statutes and judicial rulings responding to the need for the government not to remain committed for items ordered during the war and made obsolete upon its conclusion or not to continue to stockpile unneeded items at the war's end. In World War II, this doctrine was further extended and embodied in a mandatory termination clause, the direct predecessor to the modern Termination for Convenience clause, with broad authority for the government to terminate contracts in whole or in part.

A major development in 1974, which greatly disturbed companies doing business with the federal government, was the ruling in *Colonial Metals v. United States*, [20 CCF par. 82,973], 204 Ct. Cl. 320, 494 F.2d 1355.

Colonial was awarded a supply contract at a price higher than would have been charged by a primary source supplier, quotations for which regularly appeared in trade papers. Before any deliveries were made, the government terminated the contract for convenience and made the award to the primary source supplier. Although recognizing that "the government terminated to get a better price from another source, a price which the government throughout knew or ought to have known was readily available," the court denied the contractor's appeal and, as observed by the *Torncello* court, "made a clean break with all of the prior law on the subject." The objection by this court and others centered on the following ruling in *Colonial Metals*:

> Termination to buy elsewhere at a cheaper price is essentially such a termination as has repeatedly been approved. The added element that the contracting officer knew of the better price elsewhere when he awarded the contract to [Colonial] . . . means only that the contract was awarded improvidently and does not narrow the right to terminate.

> Termination for convenience is as available for contracts improvident in their origin as for contracts which supervening events show to be onerous or unprofitable for the Government.

We turn to *Torncello*, where the contractor was awarded a 12-item maintenance requirements contract, including a call item for pest control. The per-call charge was high and the Navy concluded that it only needed a lesser service, which it was able to obtain from a competing bidder on the original solicitation who had submitted a lower bid for pest control. On discovering his company was not receiving any calls for pest control, Torncello offered to reduce the per-call charge. However, the Navy ignored the offer and contracted with the other firm for all of this work. Torncello's company, Soledad Enterprises, Inc., went into bankruptcy.

Torncello's claim for breach of contract was denied by the Navy contracting officer and he lost his appeal to the board of contract appeals, *Soledad Enterprise, Inc.*, ASBCA No. 20376, 20423 to 20426, 77-2 BCA par. 12,552. As the *Torncello* court summarized the board's ruling:

> Although the ASBCA cursorily accepted that the government may have committed a breach, it viewed that issue as unimportant because of the overriding availability to the government of constructive termination for convenience.

The board had noted that the contract included the short form termination for convenience clause under which the government was liable only for payment for services rendered prior to the effective date of termination and, since no pest control services were furnished and no costs incurred, the contractor was not entitled to any compensation.

On appeal to the court, Torncello argued that the practical effect of the board's decision was "to exculpate the government completely. The government was allowed to walk away from plaintiff's contract with impunity."

The board had placed principal reliance on *Nesbitt v. United States*, 170 Ct. Cl. 666, 345 F.2d 583 (1965), cert. denied 383 U.S. 926 (1966). The court, however, found *Nesbitt* inapplicable because there the "contractor who had agreed to service the government's needs .... after the contract award, refused to meet them." The court distinguished Nesbitt from Torncello, the latter remaining at all times ready and willing to perform as per its agreement.

The constructive use of termination for convenience "to allow the government to walk away from all of its contractual obligations" concerned the court, which stated at this point:

> We note as one of the most elementary propositions of contract law that a party may not reserve to itself a method of unlimited exculpation without rendering its promises illusory and the contract void, and we question if the government's termination for convenience clause should be construed that broadly.

A comment by the *Torncello* court that perhaps did not originally attract sufficient attention because it appeared overwhelmed by the final conclusion of the judge who wrote the decision was that the ASBCA considered the contract was not of the requirements type but rather only for an indefinite quantity and, therefore, the diversion of work to the other company was allowed. "This," said the court, "would mean that there was no breach, and it would render unnecessary any consideration of the ASBCA's resort to constructive termination for convenience to justify the diversion." In any event, the court found that the law, contract terms, and circumstances surrounding the award all clearly established that this indeed was a requirements contract.

The court then recognized the impact of legislation on government contracts in that specific statutes may permit the government to abrogate common law contract doctrines. Absent such specific statutory authority, however, the court asserted that the "government contracts as does a private person, under the broad dictates of the common law."

Looking at the termination clause in light of its conclusions that the Navy was obligated to give all of its pest control requirements to Torncello and gave it none, the court raised the question whether, at the time the Navy gave pest control work to the other company, it could have had a convenience termination of that item under the clause in Torncello's contract, and answered in the negative. Turning then to *Colonial Metals*, the court stated that the ruling:

> ... marked a dramatic departure from the development of convenience termination as a method of risk allocation. It established a new reading of the clause, convenience termination for exculpation, and it is this reading that the government contends for in the case now before us. It is the only decision of this court in which a plaintiff was denied

recovery after convenience termination that was based on knowledge acquired before the contract was awarded.

The court ruled that it is the very essence of a requirements contract, such as in this case, that the buyer agrees to turn to the supplier for *all* of its needs. If it was implicit in the termination clause that the government could give the contractor none, there would be "no promise at all. The contract would thus fail."

The government argued that convenience termination was appropriate so long as the contracting officer determines in good faith that such action would be in the best interest of the government. The court dismissed the first point by characterizing it as the government merely "promising only to do whatever suits it." As to the second point, the court noted the extreme difficulty involved in proving that a government action is not in good faith. It cited the well-known *Knotts v. United States*, 121 F. Supp. 630,631, 128 Ct. Cl. 489, 492 (1954):

> It requires "well-nigh irrefragable proof" to induce the court to abandon the presumption of good faith dealing.

In its concluding comments, the court recognized that the termination for convenience clause is a valuable and important aspect of federal procurement but emphasized "that the government may not use [it] ... to dishonor, with impunity, its contractual obligations." When the Navy called on another company to do the work it had contracted for Torncello to do, "there were no changes from the circumstances of the bargain between [the parties], or in their expectations." Accordingly, the court found that the ASBCA had erred, termination for convenience was not available to the Navy, and the Navy's breach of the contract was unexcused.

As mentioned earlier, three of the six judges submitted separate concurring opinions. One stated he joined in the opinion based on his understanding that "the court holds only that when the government enters into a requirements contract, knowing that it can obtain an item the contract covers for less than the contract price and intending to do so, there cannot be a constructive termination for convenience of the government when the government follows that course."

Another wrote that he fully concurred in the opinion "that a convenience termination clause could not be properly used to end this requirements contract where the Government knew, at the time it entered into the agreement, that it could obtain a better price from another person." He also agreed, among other things, that *Colonial Metals* should be overruled. However, he expressed the view that the opinion was unnecessarily broad and contained statements with which he could not agree. He seemed particularly concerned that the decision suggested that the termination clause could not be used even when a better price appears after the contract is awarded. This judge would have wished that the ruling had been limited to the narrow issues of this particular case.

The third judge, also agreeing with the decision, likewise expressed concern about the "needlessly sweeping dicta."

Three months later, in September 1982, the General Services Board of Contract Appeals handed down a decision that appeared to broaden the *Torncello* court ruling. *S&W Tire Services, Inc.*, GSBCA No. 6376, 82-2 BCA par. 16,048.

This case involved numerous facets and side streets that are not addressed here because they are either not pertinent to the main issue under analysis or because, while unusual, the board did not deem that they affected the decision. Essentially, the contractor was awarded a standard GSA mandatory requirements-type term contract for tire recapping at a number of locations, including Robins Air Force Base. Before the term was completed, the Air Force awarded a contract to another company for total vehicle operations and maintenance (including tire recapping) at several locations, including Robins AFB. When S&W found it was no longer receiving tire recapping calls, it looked into the matter, discovered the recapping was included in the terms of the operations and maintenance contract and performed by that contractor, and submitted a claim for loss of profits on the work provided for in its contract but performed by the other company. The claim was denied and S&W appealed.

The board found that the government "wrongfully diverted its requirements for tire recapping and service by having a motor pool contractor do that work even though it was covered by [S&W's] contract." Tracing past BCA decisions, it concluded that various remedies had been decided upon in the past because, prior to the enactment of the Contract Disputes Act, the boards were not authorized to consider contract breaches and therefore looked for other contract provisions to award damages where appropriate. Now that the boards had the same jurisdiction in such matters as the federal courts, "we can award damages to appellant without resort to either [the termination or changes] contract clause. We might as well stop being coy and use the correct term. What we have here . . . is a breach."

Having concluded that the government breached the contract and that it had jurisdiction to consider this matter, the board turned to *Torncello*. In one sense, it found that ruling broad, overruling *Colonial Metals* as allowing "termination for convenience for exculpation." In another sense, according to the board, "particularly in light of the three concurring opinions, the precise holding of *Torncello* is quite narrow."

The board recognized certain differences between this case and *Torncello* but found it close enough to the latter "to permit us to follow it, and we do so. To hold that the parties intended the Termination for Convenience clause to apply to this situation would do violence to their entire agreement." The board stated further:

> We hold that the Government may not treat its breach of appellant's contract as a termination of that contract for convenience, actual or constructive, and that the proper measure of appellant's damages is its lost profits, as permitted at common law . . . .

While some of the views in *Torncello* referred to the use of the short-form convenience termination clause, which cuts off not only lost profits but also any other sort of settlement to take into account the reduction in quantity of work performed, the board here was not sure whether the result in *Torncello* "was colored by the presence" of that clause. In any case, concluded the board, "[o]ur result would have been no different, in view of *Torncello,* if appellant's contract had contained the standard long-form clause." And finally:

> We think *Torncello,* despite the narrowness of its specific holding, reflects a recognition by the Court of Claims that Government contracts are not as different from private commercial contracts as those of us who call ourselves specialists in Government contract law like to think. Granted, the Government has its unique attributes and its unique imperatives, but the right to commit flagrant breaches of contract with impunity is not one of them.

A positive recognition of *Torncello* was also indicated in a district court ruling in July 1983. *Vibra-Tech Engineers, Inc. v. United States of America, U.S. Dept. of Interior, U.S. Bureau of Mines, and R.J. Simonich,* U.S. District Court for the District of Colorado, Civil Action No. 83-C-186 [31 CCF par. 71,375].

The government issued an RFP for a study of the extent to which geological factors transmit vibrations from surface mine blasting. Vibra-Tech and STS Consultants, Ltd., were among companies responding, and the technical evaluation narrowed to these two firms with Vibra-Tech outscoring STS by a considerable margin. Despite this difference the evaluation committee stated that scores were "technically equivalent" and recommended award to STS because its proposal was lower in price.

The contracting officer found there was no rational basis for the determination that the proposals were technically equal, a finding necessary for the award to STS, and awarded the contract to Vibra-Tech. Four months later, the contract was suddenly terminated for convenience and awarded to STS. This award was affirmed by GAO for reasons not provided in the court's decision, and Vibra-Tech appealed, claiming the action was arbitrary and capricious.

"Sovereign power" and other explanations have been given for the government's authority to terminate contracts for convenience. However, according to the decision, "[t]he courts . . . consistently have recognized limitations on the government's right to invoke this extraordinary doctrine." Citing *Torncello* and other precedents, the court said:

> "[T]he government may not use the standard termination for convenience clause to dishonor, with impunity, its contractual obligations . . . . We cannot condone termination based on knowledge of a lower cost when that knowledge preceded award of the contract." *Torncello v. United States [supra]* . . . *National Factors, Inc. v. United States* [19 CCF ¶ 82,909], 492 F.2d 1383 (Ct.Cl. 1974); *Henry Spen & Co., Inc. v. Laird* [18 CCF ¶ 82,054], 354 F.Supp. 586, 558 (D.D.C. 1973).

The court found the contracting officer's initial decision to award the contract to Vibra-Tech appropriate and in full accord with the government's procedures, and the decision to terminate to be arbitrary and capricious.

Turning to the question of remedy, Vibra-Tech sought termination of the STS contract and reinstatement of its own. The government opposed, arguing Vibra-Tech had an exclusive and adequate remedy at law—damages for termination or breach of contract—and thus the remedy of the injunction could not be granted. The court rejected the government's argument:

> An award of damages, however, would compensate the plaintiff only for a small percentage of its anticipated profit. Additionally, if Vibra-Tech had been allowed to complete the contract it would have increased ... Vibra-Tech's prestige in the scientific and business community, thus enhancing its ability to obtain future contracts. On the other hand, the abrupt, arbitrary and unexplained termination of its contract in midstream by a prestigious client such as the federal government certainly damages Vibra-Tech's business reputation in a manner and to an extent not precisely measurable in money damages. For these reasons, I find and conclude that Vibra-Tech has no adequate remedy at law and declaratory and injunctive relief are appropriate.

The court ordered the government to terminate the STS contract and reinstate the contract as originally awarded to Vibra-Tech.

The uncertainty in this area, however, was reflected in a later decision by the General Services Board of Contract Appeals, *Drain-A-Way Systems,* GSBCA No. 7022, 84-1 BCA par. 16,929, November 16, 1983. Drain-A-Way entered into a contract for grass-cutting services upon the premise that services would be provided over one growing season. During such season, grass cutting is performed more often, which results in greater profits to the contractor. As a result of a convenience termination, the contractor did not perform during the profitable season and submitted a claim for loss of anticipatory profits. The claim was denied by the contracting officer.

The board observed that the termination for convenience clause prohibits recovery of anticipatory profits and consequential damages. In the case of partial terminations, the clause provides for an equitable adjustment of price specified in the contract related to the continued portion of the contract. It appeared that the board considered it had two options: (1) to provide such equitable adjustments or (2) consider that the government's prior actions (failure to pay for services it had contracted) constituted a breach, ". . . then appellant may recover the full panoply of common law damages, including recovery of anticipatory profits." (citation omitted.) The board elected the first option.

The board observed that all termination for convenience clauses, especially the short form, are exculpatory devices, and their use is particularly unfair when "invoked not because of a change in the circumstances of the bargain or in the expectations of the parties, but rather as a device to limit the damages to be recovered after a material breach by the Government." It then referred to *Torncello* and its own *S&W Tire Services* decisions. It also cited several U.S. Claims Court decisions in surplus sales contracts that declined to enforce exculpatory provisions of the contracts because limiting government liability to a refund of the purchase prices would "permit the Government to rescind the contract at will and without penalty."

On the other hand, the board also cited court rulings that enforced contract terms and declined to award recovery of anticipatory profits, and noted that it had taken just such action in *Adams Manufacturing Co.,* GSBCA No. 5747, 82-1 BCA par. 15,740, where the government terminated a small parts storage cabinets contract. The board found that the government had breached that contract but concluded that adequate recovery was available under the termination for convenience clause, which could enable Adams (board ruled only on entitlement) to recover all costs incurred to date of termination plus profit of such costs.

The *Adams* March 1982 decision preceded the June *Torncello* court ruling. However, the board cited an unpublished opinion of the United States Court of Appeals for the Federal Circuit, issued in May 1983, which upheld the board's ruling in *Adams*. Adams had appealed to the court for recovery for anticipatory profits upon the authority of *Torncello* but the appeal had been denied by the court on the basis that *Torncello* was limited to its facts. This is all the decision tells us about the unpublished opinion but further comments suggest that both the board and court held that exculpatory provisions are to be upheld if they do not operate to deny an effective remedy to the contractor.

The conclusion in *Drain-A-Way* was that an equitable adjustment which would increase the profit the contractor would have earned if the rate enjoyed by work in the grass-growing seasons represented adequate recovery in this partial termination situation and denied the claim for anticipatory profit.

A favorable decision under *Torncello* was indicated in *Municipal Leasing Corporation v. United States,* [32 CCF par. 73,129], 7 Ct.Cl. 43, decided December 1984. This appeal was formerly before the court [30 CCF par. 70,909], 1 Ct.Cl. 771, and the court's March 1983 decision denied the government's motion for summary judgment because material facts were in issue.

Under a contract with the Air Force involving "lease to ownership," Municipal was to provide ten Intercolor desk top computer terminals. The contract period was two months plus two option years. The option years were based on availability of funds and the contract also provided that the "Air Force shall use its best efforts to obtain appropriations of the necessary funds to meet its obligations and to continue this contract in force."

On September 8, 1981, the contracting officer advised Municipal that the contract would be terminated on September 30. On July 1, 1982, the contractor's claim was denied, the Air Force pointing to the contractual provisions making renewals subject to availability of funds. As to using its best efforts to obtain additional funds, the contracting officer stated, in part:

> Despite our efforts, when the United States Government determines that Air Force requirements no longer exist, it will not appropriate funds
> . . . .

> Consequently, due to the non-availability of appropriated funds, the contract expired on 30 September 1981 without legal liability on the part of Government for payment or performance . . . .

Omitting other issues, the hearing developed that the Air Force in fact did not use its best efforts to obtain appropriated funds to continue the contract but rather determined that the contract was necessary and did not seek funds to renew it. The government defended its action, arguing it constituted a constructive termination for convenience, the decision not to seek appropriations resulting from a changed condition. The court saw the central issue as "whether the circumstances were changed such as to warrant the application of the termination for convenience clause."

The court held that contract provisions must be read as a whole and an "interpretation which gives a reasonable meaning to all [the clauses] will be preferred to one which leaves [one or more clauses] useless . . . meaningless or superfluous; nor should any [clause] be construed as being in conflict with another unless no other reasonable interpretation is possible . . . Applying these principles to this instance, the termination for convenience clause must be read to be limited by the best efforts clause."

The court found that, before contracting with Municipal for the terminals, the Air Force had considered purchasing replacement chips for the existing Hazeltine equipment from another company but had rejected this approach. Later, it decided to pursue this option. "To this end," said the court, "it did not renew Municipal's contract." The court found that this action directly contravened the best efforts provision.

Citing *Torncello,* the court said that "[t]he termination for convenience clause can appropriately be invoked only in the event of some kind of change from the circumstances of the bargain or in the expectations of the parties." The Air Force had promised it would not replace Municipal's Intercolor terminals. Repairing the existing Hazeltines resulted, in effect, in replacing the Intercolor terminals with the Hazeltines. Additionally, and importantly, the "Hazeltine repair was considered as an alternative prior to contracting with Municipal." The court concluded:

> The termination for convenience clause will not act as a constructive shield to protect [the government] from the consequences of its decision to follow an option considered but rejected before contracting with [Municipal].

A narrower interpretation of *Torncello,* one considered much closer to the views expressed in the separate concurring opinions than in the basic decision, was reflected in an opinion of a Department of Transportation Board of Contract Appeals administrative judge, *Automated Services, Inc.,* DOT BCA No. 1753, 87-1 BCA par. 19,459, November 25, 1986.

Automated Services (ASI) entered into a subcontract (Small Business Administration—prime) with the Department of Justice (DOJ) to provide automated data processing support services. Upon a DOJ request, ASI submitted a work plan that, after revision, was considered unacceptable by the Department's Project Management Section, which concluded that ASI did "not possess the qualified personnel or the required experience" and requested the contract be terminated for convenience. This action was taken without any call having been made for ASI's services.

ASI filed a claim asserting the termination was an invalid attempt by DOJ to circumvent its obligations and liabilities under the contract and amounted to a breach of contract. The contracting officer denied the claim and ASI appealed to the board. The government moved for summary judgment, contending ASI failed to state a claim upon which relief could be granted, and ASI filed a cross-motion, arguing that the "termination for convenience of its contract was undertaken in bad faith, constituted an abuse of discretion, and was otherwise invalid due to the absence of any changes in the parties' bargain or expectations."

The government argued that the only limit upon the contracting officer's authority to terminate for convenience is that such authority be exercised in good faith and without a clear abuse of discretion. Alternatively, the government contended that if a reason were necessary, termination for convenience was appropriate because ASI was unable to perform the initial task and DOJ had no further requirements that could be satisfied under the terms of the contract.

ASI argued that genuine issues of material fact existed as to whether DOJ in fact had any requirements under the contract; whether ASI was qualified to perform the contract; and whether the government acted in bad faith by neglecting to issue task orders to ASI. The contractor also disputed the government's contention that bad faith or abuse of discretion constituted the limits on the government's ability to terminate for convenience. Citing *Torncello,* the contractor argued that, in a requirements contract, that clause could be appropriately invoked only where a change has occurred in the circumstances of the bargain or in the expectations of the parties, neither of which prevailed here.

The administrative judge ruled that the contract was one of indefinite quantity rather than requirements, reaching this conclusion by a review of the contract, which appeared to identify it specifically as an indefinite quantity one. Under this type of contract, as contrasted with a requirements-type, the buyer is not obligated to purchase from the seller even if he has the need. However, this contract also obligated the government to purchase from ASI services equalling the minimum number of hours per labor category specified in the contract for the one-year contract period.

Citing court decisions that defined indefinite quantity contracts, the administrative judge stated that "the Government's guarantee to purchase a minimum level of services is the element that ensures mutuality of obligation of the parties' respective promises to purchase and sell. Without that element, the Government's promise to purchase services from ASI would be illusory and render the contract unenforceable." However, the administrative judge ruled that "merely because the Government's promise to purchase a minimum amount of services from ASI is couched in the terms of a guarantee, that promise does not supersede the terms of the convenience termination clause." In support of this conclusion, the decision cited other case law and legal authorities that opined that termination for convenience in such instances, even where the minimum has not been reached, "does not render the bargained for consideration illusory . . ." "[T]he basic purpose of requiring changed circumstances is to assure that the Government has entered into a real, not illusory, obligation at the time of contract award." (Citations omitted.)

ASI apparently leaned heavily on *Torncello,* but the administrative judge viewed that decision very narrowly:

> But [ASI] argues further that *Torncello* holds that bad faith or abuse of discretion, as urged by the Government, are no longer the limits on the Contracting Officer's use of the termination for convenience procedures,

but that those procedures must now be predicated upon a change in the circumstances of the bargain or in the expectations of the parties. We do not interpret the court's holding as going that far.

Conceding that the *Torncello* court "employed a broad rationale in reaching its decision," the administrative judge decided that a careful reading of the decision and the concurring opinions establishes "that the holding of the case is much narrower than the rationale would suggest and that the opinion should be limited to the specific facts of the case as found by the court." The administrative judge cited a number of board and court decisions that, in his opinion, "have shown a similar reluctance to apply the holding in *Torncello* beyond the scope of the specific fact situation of that case."

It has proven difficult for specialists in federal government contract law to establish, with certainty, how broadly *Torncello* was intended to apply. Although the administrative judge's opinion that *Torncello* had not "abandoned forever the standard of bad faith or abuse of discretion as basis for invoking the convenience termination clause" has been well supported, there seems to be far less consensus as to how narrow the court's ruling should be considered, i.e., whether its applicability should be limited *solely* to the circumstances in that case. However, the administrative judge asserted:

> . . . we read *Torncello* as allowing the Government to continue to invoke the termination for convenience clause in supply contracts to limit its liability . . . except where it terminates the contract, without any change in the parties' conditions or expectations, solely to obtain a better price from a different source that it was fully aware of at the time of contracting.

Indeed a narrow reading of *Torncello*.

The administrative judge concluded that the termination was valid "absent a showing of bad faith or some other indication of Government wrongdoing or illegality." In this respect the government denied any bad faith and cited the well-know holdings that it takes "well-nigh irrefragable proof" to overcome the presumption of good faith in government administrative actions.

Although the administrative judge, to his satisfaction, restricted *Torncello* to not much more than an overruling of *Colonial Metals,* the latter having been interpreted as virtually eliminating any limits to the government's right to terminate for convenience, absent the "well-nigh irrefragable proof" or bad faith, it stopped short of denying ASI's claim. The contractor's other arguments included the existence of material issues of fact as to whether certain services DOJ obtained from other contractors during the period of the ASI contract were identical to those ASI contracted to provide and whether the government had pre-existing knowledge of such services "within the narrowest interpretation and strictest construction of the *Torncello* doctrine." On this basis the government's motion for summary judgment was denied and the parties were ordered to proceed with discovery and agree upon a hearing date.

The last word on the meaning and application of the "*Torncello* doctrine" has not been heard.

TERMINATION FOR DEFAULT

There are substantial differences between terminations for default of cost-reimbursement type contracts and fixed-price contracts. In the latter instance, the contractor is reimbursed for its costs and is penalized only for an adjustment in the fee and the unallowability of costs of preparing the settlement proposal. Unlike the significant problems involved in default termination of fixed-price contracts, cost-reimbursement type contracts do not contain any provision for recovery of excess costs of reprocurement.

Termination of Fixed-Price Contracts for Default

FAR Subpart 49.4 sets forth the regulation for default termination of fixed-price contracts. The many problems caused by termination for convenience are often clearly outweighed by the traumas and controversies of default terminations. Indeed, an analysis of the ASBCA annual decisions indicates that from 25% to 33⅓% of the appeals involve terminations for default.

In addition to all of the other problems, under a contract terminated for default, the contractor is paid only for the completed and accepted items and receives no payment for any raw materials or work in process. Additionally, the government may repurchase the supplies and services if it still needs them and charge the contractor in default any resulting differences in price.

Unlike a termination for convenience, which may come as a bolt from the blue, a notice of termination for default is usually not all that unexpected. The contractor will have received early indications through such means as a Show Cause Notice or Cure Notice, etc. These notices generally spell out the contractor's requirements and deficiencies and request explanations for failure to perform in accordance with the terms of the contract. Where the contractor is a small business firm, a copy of the Cure Notice or Show Cause Letter is usually furnished to the Small Business Administration regional office where the contractor is located.

There are many defenses to a termination for default action. They all require careful technical documentation, and many of them lead to litigation. The author's constant reiteration of the importance of effective contract administrative controls is probably as significant in this area as any.

Contractors frequently have been successful before boards of contract appeals in establishing that their failure to perform was attributable in whole or in part to actions or inactions on the part of the government. In such instances, the initial appeal seeks a ruling that the termination should be established as one for the government's convenience rather than for default. If successful in this action, the contractor should submit an additional appeal to recover all of the costs and profit allowable under convenience terminations.

Success in persuading judicial bodies to convert default terminations into terminations for convenience frequently depends on careful observations and documentation regarding such matters as government-furnished property or materials received late or in defective condition, constructive changes by various government personnel, imposition of more arduous inspection criteria, etc. At the earliest indication of government dissatisfaction with the quality of the product or compliance with delivery schedules, contractors should immediately seek the root causes of the problems, correct them if it is within their control, or furnish prompt advice when the problems are attributable to the government.

The author has been involved with companies whose contracts were terminated for default despite the fact that the product could not be produced based on the government-furnished specifications. Some of the default terminations concern determinations of impossibility. The point to be reiterated is the essentiality of taking prompt action at the earliest sign of government dissatisfaction. If the contractor can establish that its failure to perform arose from causes beyond its control and without its fault or negligence, and the government is nevertheless determined to terminate the contract, the action must be a termination for convenience rather than default.

As an overall summary, contractors have been successful in persuading boards of contract appeals to convert default terminations to terminations for the convenience of the government when they were able to demonstrate that:

1. The government's actions or inactions caused or contributed to the non-performance;

2. The defects used as a basis for the default action were "minor";

3. Defects could be cured within a reasonable time, which time was not granted by the contracting officer;

4. The government's actions indicated its intent that the contractor continue with performance; and

5. The failure to perform was due to causes beyond the control and without the negligence of the contractor.

Judicial Decisions on Appeal from Terminations for Default

Government contractors are early made aware of the significance and potential difficulties relating to the standard termination-for-default clause, inserted as a routine "boiler plate" provision in each government contract. Our experience suggests that the government generally hesitates to invoke this clause, preferring a less harsh solution. However, many contracts are terminated for default, and these occasions frequently create substantial financial and other troubles.

In a number of instances, default terminations are appealed to the boards of contract appeals. Although many instances may be cited where the contractor has been successful in its appeal, studies indicate that in recent years denials have far outweighed cases where contractors have prevailed. To provide a general acquaintance and understanding of this area, and without seeking to provide any legal commentaries or opinions, we offer digests of a number of board and court decisions dealing with terminations for default. Many of these have been commented upon in the author's monthly *Administrative and Accounting Guide for Defense Contracts* and are compiled here to provide an overall focus and perspective on this area.

ASBCA Nos. 4025 and 4123.—In ASBCA Nos. 4025 and 4123, the contractor appealed from the contracting officer's determination to terminate a contract for default and assess substantial excess costs of reprocurement.

This was a contract set-aside for small business in accordance with a request from the Small Business Administration. The invitation to bid was answered by only one firm other than the successful bidder (appellant in this case). The appellant's bid was considerably lower than that of the other firm.

Upon receipt of the invitation to bid, which indicated an urgent need for the item, the appellant quickly contacted responsible suppliers and received quotations on the parts and components that had to be purchased. These quotations were used as a basis for the bid. After the contract was signed, however, several of the suppliers repudiated their earlier quotations, and their higher demands resulted in contract costs substantially higher than the contractor had estimated.

The government knew at the time of the bid that the contractor's key officials were reliable and experienced in this line of work. The government also knew of the contractor's very modest net worth. The contractor attempted to find other sources of supply but was not successful. Accordingly, it could not perform the contract because of the substantial loss that it would incur. The government then reprocured the items and assessed the excess costs against the contractor.

The board found that the contractor could not have made the necessary financial arrangements to perform the contract. The board stated that, while financial inability at the time of the bid does not excuse failure to perform, the financial inability, if it arises later, if it is not due to the contractor's fault, and if it makes performance impossible, is an excusable cause for nonperformance under the default article.

The board, accordingly, ruled for the contractor and held that the termination was for the convenience of the government. The contractor in its brief requested a no-cost termination settlement, and this was accepted by the board. We are not aware of the reasons for the contractor's voluntary offer of a no-cost settlement or what would have been the views of the board if the contractor had not offered this stipulation. Certainly, based on the board's ruling, the contractor had nothing to gain but something to lose from this voluntary offer.

As an additional word of caution, the history of appeals against default terminations that are based on financial difficulties indicates a very low percentage of success for contractors.

ASBCA No. 4987.—An illustration from the author's experience deals with a research and development contract for an item that had not been previously produced, or at least not in the degree of sophisticated design required. The contractor had apparently been somewhat too enthusiastic in agreeing to a tight delivery schedule. To expedite the solution of the complex technical problems, the contractor launched a dual engineering program, simultaneous development work being accomplished both by an outside engineering firm and by the contractor's own staff. Two months later (original delivery due in three months), the design of the outside firm was considered superior, and the contract was entered into with that firm with delivery within six to eight weeks. The government was apprised of these developments.

Despite the prime contractor's urgings, the item was not delivered by the subcontractor until more than four months later. Extensive tests made by the prime contractor revealed that the item did not meet the very stringent specifications, and the government was so advised. Finally, the delivery schedule was extended to a date some six months after the initial delivery target.

Omitting many of the details, we can summarize events as follows: the item was rejected by the government, and another one, subsequently engineered and delivered the following month, was likewise rejected. At this point, the contractor consulted with two leading companies in this field. Both advised that the contractor's basic approach was sound but that certain changes in design were necessary, which would require four additional months. These facts were made known to the government, which, however, terminated the contract for default.

Shortly thereafter the government awarded a contract to one of the firms that had advised our client about the need for four additional months for engineering work. This firm produced an acceptable item six months thereafter, including two months for testing by an independent laboratory.

Although no assessment for excess costs had been made against our client at this time, the termination for default was nevertheless appealed to the Armed Services Board of Contract Appeals. In reviewing the details surrounding the facts summarized above, the board came to the conclusion that the initially established period for contract deliveries was utterly unrealistic. This view was supported by the experience of a major contractor in this area, which had spent five years of experimentation on the item involved and had not at that time achieved success. The board noted that the time limitation, as unrealistic as it was, could have been insisted upon by the government if it had chosen to demand strict compliance. However, this strict compliance was not enforced, and, therefore, the board held that the government was thereupon obligated to set up a new and reasonable delivery schedule. In the opinion of the board, the government had not done so. In this regard, the board noted that the additional four months last requested by the contractor, upon the advice of the two major firms in this area, coincided with the time required by the successor contractor (excluding the period for laboratory testing). The board also brought into the case the facts that the past record of our client had always been creditable and that none of its contracts theretofore had been terminated for default.

The board ruled that the termination of the contract must be regarded to have been for the convenience of the government.

A major factor involved in the decision favorable to the contractor was the government's waiver of the original delivery schedule. The determination as to whether there occurred, in fact, a waiver, is frequently a difficult matter to determine. Where the waiver can be established, however, a default action is difficult to sustain.

ASBCA No. 4255.—The possibility of termination of contracts by the government always represents a source of potential danger and problems to the defense contractor. In view of the substantial interest generated by this subject, our monthly *Guide* and this text devote considerable coverage to its various aspects, including what sometimes appears to be a very thin line separating termination for default from termination for the convenience of the government.

Another dispute, asserting impossibility of performance, was ruled upon by the board in ASBCA No. 4255. Involved here was the government's desire for a special automatic data processing system. The government's design for this system was considered impractical by most of the industrial firms that were considered as prospective bidders. The appellant in this case submitted an alternative proposal, which was ultimately accepted by the government, and a contract was entered into. Ultimately, the contractor was unable to develop the system in accordance with the very advanced requirements, and the government terminated the contract for default.

In the appeal from the contracting officer's decision, the contractor argued that its failure was due to impossibility of performance in that the system contracted for was beyond the state of the art. The contractor further argued that its obligation required it to exercise the skill and competence of ordinary prudent and skillful engineers engaged in a similar field of enterprise. This, stated the contractor, it had done.

The board's decision referred to *E. L. Cournand & Co. Inc.,* ASBCA No. 2955, 60-2 BCA par. 2840, where the government was responsible for the design of an item to be manufactured and where the contractor neither knew nor had reason to know that the design was inadequate to produce an item that would perform as required by the contract. In this case, termination for default was inappropriate.

On the other hand, the board also referred to the decision in ASBCA No. 4129 where the contractor knew, or should have known at the time of contracting, that it was obligating itself to make a scientific breakthrough and to produce beyond the existing state of the art, and where it was familiar with the risk that it was assuming. In this latter case, the board held that the contractor's obligation went beyond the mere duty to exercise ordinary skill; its obligation would not stop until performance had been reached, and, if the task was impossible, it must bear the cost attributable to nonperformance.

In the instant case, the board noted that the design upon which the contract was based was the contractor's own and that the contractor had or should have had full knowledge that it was being confronted with perilous scientific development and with hazardous manufacturing achievement.

Since the contractor assumed the risk, the failure to perform justified termination for default.

ASBCA No. 6936.—As most readers know, there are numerous factors that lead to contract termination for the convenience of the government, such as changes in programs, changes in policies, technological breakthroughs, etc. Although the contractor faces the hazard of unexpected idle plant and facilities in these instances, there is at least a basis for recovery of the costs incurred. In the case of termination for default, the government not only may fail to pay for the costs of undelivered work, but may further require the contractor to pay the cost incurred by the government in repurchasing the supplies from another company. This entire area is tremendously complicated by the fact that there is often a very fine distinction between termination for default and termination for the convenience of the government. In this regard, we have frequently advised our readers of instances where a careful analysis has revealed that a contract terminated for reasons of alleged default by the contractor actually involved the fault of the government. We have also cited various decisions by the Armed Services Board of Contract Appeals that directed contracting officers to rescind their decisions to terminate contracts for default and, instead, revise the actions to terminations for the convenience of the government. Frequently, decisions of this type have come about where certain actions by the government, including delays in furnishing the required government property, or furnishing unsuitable government property, were established as the causative factors of the contractor's inability to comply with the contractual terms. The importance of this facet of contract termination warrants continual attention. Accordingly, we present a summary of another decision by the Armed Services Board of Contract Appeals (ASBCA No. 6936).

A firm was a successful bidder on a supply contract that provided that certain special tooling, the property of the government, was available for use by the successful bidder. The contractor telephoned the procurement office and requested information as to when the tools would be delivered. Upon being advised that a formal request would have to be made for those tools, the contractor made this request in writing. The tooling was delivered to the contractor's plant approximately 30 days after the oral request and 25 days after the government had received the formal written request. The contractor failed to meet the prescribed delivery schedule, and the contract was terminated for default.

In its appeal to ASBCA, the contractor contended that the government should have delivered the tooling either automatically upon the award of the contract or immediately after the oral request. In this connection, the contractor pointed out that its bid had reflected its intention to use the government-owned tooling and, further, that it had advised the government in writing, before the award of the contract, that it would require the use of the tooling if it obtained the contract.

The government argued that, under the type of contract involved, tools are not furnished until the contractor asks for them. The government also contended (denied by the contractor) that the contractor was informed before the award of the contract that it would have to make a request to the government for the tools.

The board ruled for the contractor and directed negotiation in accordance with the Termination for the Convenience of the Government article of the contract. Portions of the board's decision are of general interest and are quoted below.

> Appellant requested that the notice of termination for default issued under the contract "Default" article be deemed a termination for the convenience of the Government. To grant such a request, on this record, we must, in accordance with the "Default" article of the contract, find either (1) that the appellant did not fail to make delivery of the supplies within the time specified in the contract; or (2) that if such failure did

occur it arose out of causes beyond the control and without the fault or negligence of appellant.

... We find that appellant did fail to make delivery of the supplies within the time specified in the contract ... and under ... "Default" article the Government acquired the right to terminate for default; subject, of course, to the possibility that it might later be determined that the failure was due to causes beyond the control and without the fault or negligence of appellant, in which case ... such termination for default would be deemed a termination for the convenience of the Government. ...

When an appellant raises an issue as to the Government's right to terminate a contract for default, the Government has the burden of proving the contractor's default. The excusability of the contractor's failure to deliver in accordance with the contract delivery schedule is an affirmative defense, and this Board has held repeatedly that the contractor has the burden of proof as to the excusability of his delay in performance or failure to perform ... in the instant appeal the contractor has offered in support of his burden of proof on excusability, evidence to the effect that its failure to perform in accordance with the contract delivery schedule was caused by the Government's failure to make timely delivery of the Government-owned tools.

We are persuaded by the evidence that the contractor has succeeded in sustaining that burden. There is no requirement in the contract that the appellant make a formal request for the tooling, and even if such a requirement did exist the Government's delay of 25 days in making the tooling available after receipt of the formal request is clearly excessive by at least 10 days.

This decision establishes that one of the most potent weapons in an appeal against a default termination is the ability to show that failure to perform is attributable to the government, including such matters as failure to furnish specifications, tooling, property, etc., and failure in terms of quality or timeliness.

Johnson Electronics, Inc., ASBCA No. 9366, 65-1 BCA par. 4628.—
Involved was an Air Force contract for a transistorized power supply for use in government-owned radios, awarded pursuant to an advertised invitation for bids restricted to small business concerns. Johnson was second low bidder out of 58 received after the low bidder was found not to qualify as a small business concern. While the facts in the case and the board's decision are lengthy and complex, it appears there was a government attempt to purchase an item through formal advertising, restricted to small business, which item had never been previously manufactured so as to meet all required specifications and tests. Further, the government had accumulated a considerable amount of knowledge and experience concerning this item, which became dissipated as a result of its personnel actions and organizational adjustments.

The contractor made a very substantial effort to produce the item, but was unable to do so. The contract was ultimately terminated for default.

In its argument before the board, the contractor recognized that it had to produce under a performance specification and that some development work might normally be expected. On the other hand, it felt that it could assume from the type of procurement that the item could be fabricated by putting together readily available components without the expenditure of substantial design and engineering effort. It argued further that the short period of delivery supported a reasonable conclusion that the government was not expecting a requirement for research and development. It concluded that, in the circumstances, performance was impossible because it required work beyond the state of the art.

The board doubted that a case could be made for literal impossibility of performance, that is, that no one in any circumstances could have performed to this contract's specifications. On the other hand, the board cited legal authority in support of the proposition that there can be legal impossibility without literal impossibility. Further, it stated that "a workable definition of practical impossibility would be to say that it means not possible within the basic objectives contemplated by the parties as evidenced by the contract itself and the surrounding circumstances."

Viewed in these circumstances, the board considered that the type of contract, the small business set-aside feature, the 90-day period for producing the first item, and other circumstances could not have reasonably contemplated the extended research and design effort that the item turned out to require. It agreed with the contractor that the contract called for "a major design effort, virtually if not actually a breakthrough in the existing state of the art." Further, it saw no evidence of fault in the technical competence of Johnson or in its approaches and efforts under the contract. It concluded that Johnson had "made out a case of practical legal impossibility of performance of this contract."

The board found that the government had failed to highlight to the prospective bidders some of the past problems with this item and that the nature of the contract and restricted solicitation could be construed as misleading the bidders "into a task, the proportions of which it [they] could not reasonably have anticipated." The board's ruling in the *Midvale-Heppenstall Company* case, ASBCA No. 7525, handed down in December 1964, and the Court of Claims case No. 251-56, involving the *Helene Curtis Industries, Inc.,* were cited in this connection.

The decision concluded that the contractor's failure to perform the contract was for causes beyond its control and without its fault or negligence and was caused by acts of the government. Accordingly, the contracting officer's termination of the contract for default was not proper, and the default should have been deemed effected for the convenience of the government.

In contrast to the majority opinion, the dissenting opinion stated that "the contractor assumes the risk of impossibility when the specifications are of the performance type."

ITT Kellogg, Division of International Telephone and Telegraph, ASBCA No. 5980, 65-2 BCA par. 5077; 65-1 BCA par. 4675.—In the motion for reconsideration, the contractor complained that the board had erred in its initial decision that the contract was not impossible to perform, that it had not done all the work required to prove that it was impossible, and that it had, in effect, abandoned the contract. It further argued that the board did not properly consider its own decisions in two similar cases.

The board reiterated its original position. First, it observed that it had not ruled, nor did it need to establish, that performance was not impossible; rather, the contractor had to prove that performance was impossible, and this it had failed to do.

The record falls short of establishing that appellant could not have fully performed the contract if it had tried to do so or that other concerns would have found it impossible to do so. With respect to the words, "perform all the work," it may well be that in all cases it would not be necessary to do "work" in order to establish impossibility and that impossibility could be established by technical, scientific, or professional evidence showing why the performance called for would be impossible. There is no such evidence in this case.

In referring to other cases allegedly considered not proper by the board, the contractor cited *Johnson Electronics, Inc.*, ASBCA No. 9366, 65-1 BCA par. 4628, December 31, 1964, and *Midvale-Heppenstall Co.*, ASBCA No. 7525, 65-1 BCA par. 4629, December 31, 1964. The board found that these decisions did not support the contractor's position. The reasoning is interesting because of the additional light it sheds on the board's thinking in this area.

In *Johnson* the Government had studied the problem concerned for several years, knew previous manufacturers had been unable to meet the specifications, and knew extensive research and development efforts would be required before production of the unit could be successfully undertaken. Johnson did not know these facts. In *Midvale-Heppenstall* the Government had studied the problem for several years, knew that meeting the specified mechanical requirements had never been attempted in a production contract, had actual knowledge of the difficulty presented by the specifications, and knew that the steel appellant proposed to use was unsatisfactory. Midvale did not know these facts. In both cases the Government, because of its studies and prior experience, possessed knowledge of the difficulties that could be expected in performance that was superior to that of the industry concerned. Knowing, or at least having every reason to believe, that bidders generally—including the appellants concerned—were unaware of such difficulties the Government did not disclose its special knowledge to prospective bidders. It should be clear from the decisions that the above facts were important and indeed essential to the result reached. No similar facts are present in the instant case. There is no evidence that the Government had knowledge superior to that of the industry concerned or that it failed to disclose anything it should have disclosed.

Another significant aspect involved in proving impossibility of performance relates to the nature of the specifications furnished by the government. It is generally considered that the government assumes the risk of impossibility where it furnishes detailed design specifications. On the other hand, this risk may well be on the contractor where the specifications are more nearly in the nature of performance goals or objectives. In this case, the contractor characterized the specifications as "highly descriptive, restrictive and definitive." The board acknowledged that "the government did go to some length in describing and defining the performance requirements to be met," but saw nothing in that which would excuse the contractor from performance. It further noted:

> This is not a case where the Government furnished detailed drawings containing errors so that performance was impossible; or specified methods or processes which would not produce the required results; or specified the material to be used and such material would not meet requirements. This is a case where the Government specified its performance requirements. It has not been shown that they were impossible to meet, that the specifications were defective, or that they misrepresented the difficulty involved in performing the contract.

The concept of impossibility as a defense against nonperformance can be traced to early common law. The lawyers tell us that the courts originally construed the word "impossibility" in a very strict manner. It was thought of in terms of "actual impossibility," which meant that it was necessary to prove that it was physically impossible to perform. With the development of trade and commerce, a more liberal and practical alternative was developed— "practical impossibility." This more modern and liberal view recognizes impossibility where performance would involve unusual or extremely difficult efforts and costs over and beyond those contemplated by either party to the contract.

In the case under discussion, the contractor argued that practical impossibility had been established but not recognized by the board. The contractor further attributed the board's failure to recognize this point on its acceptance of certain "offhand comments by Government engineers." The board said that its conclusion "was based not so much on the testimony of Government witnesses as it was on the testimony of appellant's witnesses which was unpersuasive. The burden was not on the Government to disprove the appellant's allegations. The appellant has to prove performance was impossible. . . ."

Superior Products Co., ASBCA No. 9808, 67-1 BCA par. 6227; 66-2 BCA par. 6054.—The board's decision (reaffirmed in motion for reconsideration) includes the following principles of impossibility of performance: (a) the government assumes risk when it provides detailed design specifications and (b) occasional performance success by another contractor is not adequate proof of feasibility.

The contract was awarded to Superior by RMK, a joint venture that was authorized to procure materials, supplies, and equipment as the government's agent and to deal with the vendors. However, these vendors or subcontractors were permitted to appeal decisions by contracting officers to the ASBCA.

The specifications included certain materials that were invented and on which a patent was secured by a representative of the government procuring office involved. For a brief time, the NEJ Company acted as this individual's licensee, and it was to the NEJ Company that Superior turned to perform the contract at issue. Ultimately, the product failed to meet the government's requirements, and the contract was terminated for default.

An award was subsequently made to the ARR Company, and its product was accepted, based on testing by a private laboratory. Although it did not conform to the government specifications, it was found suitable for the purpose.

Superior objected to the default termination on the ground that it was impossible in the state of the art to meet the contract requirements. The government argued that ARR Company's performance demonstrated that the requirements could be met; however, as the board noted, it had been established that ARR's product similarly failed to conform to the government specifications. The board's specific comments leading to its ultimate decision are of interest.

Respondent has not countered the foregoing evidence in any way by demonstrating through appropriate testimony, for instance, that there were practical ways of obtaining the disputed specification requirements. Such evidence of this kind, as was adduced, related to achieving a uniform asphalt content and appears to us more to put the finger on the problem than to disclose technical processes for resolving it. We may also accept that the private laboratory tests up to 19 February 1963 show that at times recovery of original thickness was successfully retarded. But such occasional success is not adequate proof of feasibility of performance. *Electro-Nuclear Laboratories, Inc.,* ASBCA No. 9863, 65-1 BCA par. 4682, at p. 22,363; *Midvale-Heppenstall Co.,* ASBCA No. 7525, 65-1 BCA par. 4629, at p. 22,115.

The preponderance of the evidence here compels, therefore, the conclusion that the feasibility of the uniform asphalt content and the 5 minute recovery test specified in P. O. 201 and P. O. 202 has not been proven. On the contrary, the record convinces us that these requirements had never been adequately met either in prior experimentation, test application or manufacture and that as a practical matter they could not be met.

But demonstration of impossibility of performance is not sufficient for appellant to prevail. As we pointed out in *Electro-Nuclear Laboratories, Inc., supra,* at p. 22, 364, the Government is relieved of liability arising from the fact that it is objectively impossible to perform as specified in the contract, where the contractor has knowingly assumed the risk of impossibility: For instance, where he has taken his chance on successful performance and the advantages which it may bring, where he has relied on highly advanced but unproved manufacturing techniques, which he may be anxious to try out or perfect, though the chances of success are unknown to the contracting parties. Such situations may involve "space age novelties," as appellant's counsel suggests, but they may also be presented in homelier guise as here. We fail to find, however, in the record anything which would indicate that P. O. 201 was presented to bidders in any way as an aleatory undertaking. There was no discussion of the specifications with bidders, no prebid conference with interested parties, no indication that technical problems of manufacture were unresolved or that in fact the product with the specific asphalt content and 5 minute recovery parameters was a heretofore unknown application of polyurethane foam.

Nor was it appellant who suggested the use of the product. Rather, it appears, respondent and RMK considered its use to result in a substantial saving of costs and hence desirable.

There is thus nothing in the record which would shift the risk of impossibility of performance from the Government to appellant. P. O. 201 was presented to appellant and other bidders as a simple production undertaking which involved no problem not readily capable of solution. *Robbins Mills, Inc.,* ASBCA No. 2255, 6 CCF par. 61,799 (1955); *E. L. Cournand & Company, Inc.,* ASBCA No. 2955, 60-2 BCA par. 2840; *Utah-Manhattan-Sundt,* ASBCA No. 8991, 1963 BCA par. 3839; *Advance Industries, Inc.,* ASBCA No. 7402, id. par. 3774. Accordingly, the appeal is allowed.

We, therefore, see no reason for excepting the present appeal from the principle long adhered to by the courts and this and other Contract Appeals Boards that "where the Government authors the specifications, it warrants that, if they are complied with, satisfactory performance will result. *U.S. v. Spearin,* 248 U.S. 132 (1918); *R. M. Hollingshead Corp. v. U.S.,* 124 Ct.Cls. 681, 111 F.Supp. 285 (1953)." *Natus Corporation v. U.S.,* Ct.Cls. No. 166-61, dec. 20 January 1967, Slip Op. p. 6, upholding the Board's decision in *National U. S. Radiator Corp.,* ASBCA No. 3972, 59-2 BCA par. 2386." There, affirmative, though not uncontradicted, evidence offered by the Government demonstrated the possibility of manufacturing the product involved and appellant's own evidence did not show absolute impossibility. Such evidence is altogether lacking here and the overwhelming weight of the evidence in the record points in the direction of impossibility and supports our finding.

Valor Electronics, **ASBCA No. 10056, 67-1 BCA par. 6320.**—This is another default termination and reprocurement cost assessment from which the contractor appealed. On considerations in some ways similar to those of *Superior Products Co.,* ASBCA No. 9808, discussed above, the board found that the government had provided detailed specifications on which the contractor could reasonably be expected to rely. When contract performance proved impossible under these specifications, the responsibility was attributed to the government, and the board ordered that the default termination be converted to one for the convenience of the government. This case involved the additional factor referred to previously—the distinction between actual and practical impossibility.

The contract was for certain types of transformers and inductors, and Valor is described as an experienced manufacturer of these items. The drawings provided by the government "basically indicated exactly what was described, and spelled out in detail the materials, and fabricating procedures" with certain exceptions. Further, Valor "had little discretion with respect to materials except where brand name or equal was specified or where a military spec listed a product which was manufactured by more than one firm." As a result, Valor regarded this as a production contract.

Very early, Valor began to encounter significant difficulties. When mass production began, relatively few items proved satisfactory to Valor, and most of those that were shipped to the government were rejected. After unsuccessful attempts at obtaining a no-cause cancellation, the contractor finally gave up; the contract was terminated for default, and the government entered into reprocurement with the Milwaukee Transformer Co.

Milwaukee encountered similar substantial difficulty with the reprocurement contract, according to the board's opinion, including experiencing a 60% in-plant rejection rate as compared with its normal 5% rate on similar work. The board also stated that Milwaukee was permitted to deviate from certain specifications. The contentions of the two parties are succinctly summarized by the board as follows:

> It is appellant's contention that the contract, which is the subject matter of this dispute, is a supply contract and as such the Government impliedly warranted the efficacy of its specifications; that the specifications were impossible and impractical to perform and the Government assumed the risk of such impossibility because the procuring activity failed to divulge that the items had not been manufactured previously. Therefore, appellant's failure to deliver in accordance with the delivery schedule was not a default and appellant is entitled to a recharacterization of the termination for default to one for convenience of the Government, as well as an equitable adjustment based on its costs in attempting to perform under the defective and impossible specifications.

> The respondent contends that the specifications cannot be defective, for appellant did in fact deliver acceptable quantities of each line item; that appellant did not possess the skills and technical knowledge necessary for successful fabrication of the contract items. Appellant has not shown impossibility and Modification No. 2 of the contract constitutes an accord and satisfaction on the question of specification deficiencies. Additionally, appellant has failed to show cause for excusable delay, and this appeal should therefore be denied.

Salient excerpts from the board's conclusions and decision, together with references to leading court and board cases and legal references, are cited below:

> The Government warrants the adequacy of its plans and specifications. *U.S. v. Spearin,* 248 U.S. 32 (1918). Appellant, in proper contemplation of a production task, was entitled to rely upon the contract plans as correct representations of good and sufficient engineering skill and ability. When the Government, through one of its important agencies, orders the production of specified items by specified means, it would be a rare instance when the supplier could reasonably be expected to conduct independent research to determine whether compliance with the specifications would, in fact, produce the desired result. *R. M. Hollingshead Corp. v. U.S.,* 124 Ct.Cls. 681 (1953). The fact that appellant and later the reprocurement contractor each effected a number of deliveries is without consequence. The magnitude of appellant's production efforts to make a small number of acceptable items is convincing on point of commercial impracticability ... With respect to reprocurement deliv-

eries, we find substantial evidence of material deviations from the contract drawings of which the procuring activity may or may not have been cognizant.

In addition to demonstrating the impossibility of performing this contract, appellant has shown that the respondent failed to divulge to bidders that the contract end items had not previously been procured. There was no discussion of the specifications with bidders, no prebid conference with interested parties and no indication of technical problems. The Invitation for Bid was presented to appellant and other bidders as a simple production undertaking for items previously manufactured. This was not the case. *Superior Products Company,* ASBCA No. 9808, . . . and cases therein cited . . . Appellant, not having knowledge of any deficiencies inherent in this procurement, could not knowingly have assumed any risk of impossibility and there is nothing otherwise in the record which would warrant the transfer of such risk from the respondent to the appellant. We, therefore, conclude appellant's default termination was in error and it is hereby converted to one for convenience of the Government in accordance with contract provisions.

Our result on the termination does not impair appellant's right to a price adjustment for appellant's extra production efforts attributable to the defective specifications. We conclude he is so entitled. Allowance of proper costs as part of a general convenience termination settlement would normally account for those costs as well.

Ryan Aeronautical Company, ASBCA No. 13366, 70-1 BCA par. 8287.—Another case study in this series involves an appeal from a contracting officer's decision to terminate a contract for default. Ryan contended that the appropriate action should be a termination for the convenience of the government because the contract was impossible to perform and because Ryan had not assumed the risk of impossibility.

The contract required the development of a precision drop glider (P.D.G.) system and "included both design and performance requirements and, in addition, required the contractor to incorporate a command control and guidance subsystem provided by the Government." The default action was taken after the P.D.G. system prototype fabricated by the contractor failed to meet certain performance requirements. The contractor conceded that it had failed to meet some of the performance requirements, but argued that it was technically impossible to do so in the circumstances. Accordingly, if performance requirements were impossible, the contractor's failure to perform should be excused. The government had raised the point that the contractor should have done whatever redesigning was necessary to meet the performance requirements; however, the contractor rebutted "that it had performed a substantial amount of work above and beyond its original expectations." In leading up to its ultimate decision, the board observed that "the adequacy of this extra work is in issue, but we conclude that if the performance requirements were technically impossible, as alleged by appellant, its failure to redesign would also be excusable." It then stated the issues to be whether the "requirement was technically possible, and, if so, whether appellant had assumed the risk of the impossibility."

The board then took up the question of assumption of the risk of impossibility. Here it made the following observations:

> We have recently held that if the Government asks a contractor to perform a task which is technically impossible, the contractor is entitled to a convenience termination settlement if he fails to perform and the contract is terminated by the Government for that reason. *Kinn Electronics Corporation,* ASBCA No. 13526, 69-2 BCA par. 8061, and cases cited. This general rule would be inapplicable in this case, however, if we were to find that the appellant had assumed the risk of the impossibility.

The board's review of the technical requirements led it to the conclusion that the government's requirement as to accuracy—Circular Error Probability (CEP)—"was technically impossible of attainment." It found unrebutted evidence that the contractor was unaware of this fact when it entered into the contract. Although the contractor did not thereafter review the performance requirement, the board concluded that it "cannot be considered to have assumed the risk of impossibility on this account" and cited *The Austin Company v. U.S.,* 161 Ct.Cls. 76 (1963); cert. denied, 375 U.S. 380 (1963).

General Comments.—We have offered certain observations regarding the concepts of contractual impossibility of performance and have reviewed here several ASBCA decisions on this subject. We would caution our readers against drawing any inferences from the fact that some board cases cited culminated in favorable rulings for contractors. In practice, impossibility of performance is quite difficult to sustain before the boards and courts after adverse decisions by contracting officers. Actual or at least practical (commercial) impossibility must be established, but this is not sufficient. The contractor must further prove that it was not the contractor, but the government, who assumed the risk of impossibility.

It is also essential to understand that a contractor's personal or subjective problem is not sufficient. In other words, if the contractor is to establish impossibility, it must prove that "this cannot be done" rather than "we cannot do it."

REPURCHASE AGAINST CONTRACTOR'S ACCOUNT

The default termination action per se does not end the troubles in these circumstances. There is also the possibility that the government will repurchase.

FAR 49.402-6 provides:

(a) When the supplies or services are still required after termination, the contracting officer shall repurchase the same or similar supplies or services against the contractor's account as soon as practicable. The contracting officer shall repurchase at as reasonable a price as practicable, considering the quality and delivery requirements. The contracting officer may repurchase a quantity in excess of the undelivered quantity terminated for default when the excess quantity is needed, but excess cost may not be charged against the defaulting contractor for more than the undelivered quantity terminated for default (including variations in quantity permitted by the terminated contract). Generally, the contracting officer will make a decision whether or not to repurchase before issuing the termination notice.

(b) If the repurchase is for a quantity not over the undelivered quantity terminated for default, the Default clause authorizes the contracting officer to use any terms and acquisition method deemed appropriate for the repurchase. However, the contracting officer shall obtain competition to the maximum extent practicable for the repurchase. The contracting officer shall cite the Default clause as the authority. If the repurchase is for a quantity over the undelivered quantity terminated for default, the contracting officer shall treat the entire quantity as a new acquisition.

(c) If repurchase is made at a price over the price of the supplies or services terminated, the contracting officer shall, after completion and final payment of the repurchase contract, make a written demand on the contractor for the total amount of the excess, giving consideration to any increases or decreases in other costs such as transportation, discounts, etc. If the contractor fails to make payment, the contracting officer shall follow the procedures in Subpart 32.6 for collecting contract debts due the Government.

It is to be noted that the method of repurchasing does not have to be consistent with that used in the original procurement. Due to the exigencies of the situation, it may even be sole source.

OTHER DAMAGES

Whether or not a default termination action is taken, the government may also take certain additional measures.

FAR 49.402-7 provides:

(a) If a contract is terminated for default or if a course of action in lieu of termination for default is followed (see 49.402-4), the contracting officer shall promptly ascertain and make demand for any liquidated damages to which the Government is entitled under the contract. Under the contract clauses for liquidated damages at 52.212-4, these damages are in addition to any excess repurchase costs.

(b) If the Government has suffered any other ascertainable damages as a result of the contractor's default, the contracting officer shall on the basis of legal advice, take appropriate action as prescribed in Subpart 32.6 to assert the Government's demand for the damages.

Chapter XXII

Contract Price Reduction for Defective Cost or Pricing Data (Public Law 87-653)

INTRODUCTION

This is the third subject on which, in varying degrees, the government's procurement agencies appear to have abdicated their responsibilities and permitted the judicial branch to establish procurement policies and procedures. In Chapter XX of this text, we explained how the Department of Defense and the civilian agencies promulgated the Limitation of Cost clause and then did little to provide guidance for its procurement, contract administration, and audit personnel to implement the provisions of this clause in the many and varied circumstances under which government-contractor controversies arise. Over the years, as many controversies moved to formal disputes and litigation, it has been the administrative boards of contract appeals and the federal courts that have really implemented this clause through case law. And today, despite the numerous judicial rulings handed down on this subject, government acquisition regulations writers have made no real effort to translate these decisions into regulations. Accordingly, when controversies surface, both government and industry people must look to case law for guidance. Chapter XX, therefore, presents analyses of major judicial decisions which interpret and explain circumstances under which the provisions of the LOCC apply.

The procurement agencies of the government have accomplished considerably more in providing ground rules involving termination of contracts. However, as detailed in Chapter XXI of this text, and despite the huge volume of contract terminations, the executive agencies have yet to speak clearly on the important subject of recovery of unabsorbed overhead. Here again, the procurement and contract administration authorities have abdicated to the judiciary and, with apparently little regard for accounting principles, logic, or equity, the boards of contract appeals and federal courts have virtually established that such costs, when so labeled, are not to be allowed.

This discussion brings us to the Price Reduction for Defective Cost or Pricing clause, reviewed in this chapter. On this subject, the writers of procurement regulations have accomplished much more than in the other two areas, but the similarity enters in that virtually all of the policies and procedures resulted from judicial rulings.

This chapter presents a comprehensive account of the origins and development of, and the present government regulations and their implementation concerning, defective cost or pricing data and related penalties. Our review includes the origins of the Truth in Negotiations Act, Public Law 87-653, legislative changes, regulatory implementation, and DCAA activity, continually prodded by GAO and DOD IG. In view of the significant influence of judicial rulings on the development of contract price reduction for defective cost or pricing data, a substantial portion of this chapter is devoted to analyses of major decisions by boards of contract appeals and federal courts.

Events Leading to Enactment of P.L. 87-653

As noted in Chapter XXVIII of this text, Joseph Campbell's appointment as Comptroller General in December 1954 has been identified as the beginning of GAO's emphasis on examinations into pricing of defense contracts. In the succeeding years, GAO issued an increasing volume of reports alleging overpricing attributable to a large degree to the contractors' failure to submit, or the Defense Department's failure to obtain accurate, complete and current cost data upon which to establish prices. In some instances, GAO succeeded in establishing its conclusions; others were vigorously contested. Both categories of reports, however, tended to produce a snowballing effect on some members of Congress, as well as the press, the public, and DOD officials. The latter became increasingly defensive as the criticisms from Congress and elsewhere mounted.

In August 1958, the Air Force issued procurement instructions requiring contractors to submit certifications of their cost data under specified circumstances. In October 1959 (effective January 1960), a similar requirement was promulgated as an ASPR revision, applicable defense-wide. It should be noted, however, that these early moves included no provision for audit by DOD to ascertain whether, in fact, the submissions conformed to the certifications.

At about this time, some congressmen were becoming disenchanted with the incentive contract, which was becoming increasingly popular, especially with the Air Force. It was contended that some contractors were padding their estimated costs, with the result that some of their ultimate profits were directly attributable to incorrect cost data rather than efficiency. These suspicions, fanned by the continuing stream of GAO reports on overpricing, ultimately resulted in the enactment of P.L. 87-653 on September 10, 1962, effective December 1, 1962. (To assure that an incorrect impression is not obtained from this brief account, it should be noted that the legislation was not enacted quickly or without opposition. The initial statutory proposal was introduced in the House in May 1960, and its endorsement was limited to GAO. Objections were raised by industry, the Defense Department and many members of Congress. DOD continued to object to this legislation and issued various ASPR revisions to support its contention that legislation was unnecessary. Ultimately, however, congressional critics of defense procurement, with GAO assistance, prevailed. DOD procurement officials then collaborated in the framing of the final draft and succeeded in injecting exemptions for such contracts as those based on price competition, etc.)

Provisions of Public Law 87-653 as Originally Enacted

P.L. 87-653 is an amendment to the Armed Forces Procurement Act of 1947. It established several objectives that Congress wished DOD to strive for, including increase in formal advertising, decrease in negotiated contracts, and increase in bargaining when negotiated contracts were used. Its main feature, and the one of interest to us here, however, is Section 2306(f), which provides for prime contractors and subcontractors, under certain circumstances, to submit and certify cost or pricing data and for the contract price to be adjusted when such data are found to be inaccurate, incomplete, or non-current. The full text of this section is quoted below:

A prime contractor or any subcontractor shall be required to submit cost or pricing data under the circumstances listed below, and shall be required to certify that, to the best of his knowledge and belief, the cost or pricing data he submitted was accurate, complete and current—

(1) Prior to the award of any negotiated prime contract under this title where the price is expected to exceed $100,000;

(2) Prior to the pricing of any contract change or modification for which the price adjustment is expected to exceed $100,000, or such lesser amount as may be prescribed by the head of the agency;

(3) Prior to the award of a subcontract at any tier, where the prime contractor and each higher tier subcontractor have been required to furnish such a certificate, if the price of such subcontract is expected to exceed $100,000; or

(4) Prior to the pricing of any contract change or modification to a subcontract covered by (3) above, for which the price adjustment is expected to exceed $100,000, or such lesser amount as may be prescribed by the head of the agency.

Any prime contract or change or modification thereto under which such certificate is required shall contain a provision that the price to the Government, including profit or fee, shall be adjusted to exclude any significant sums by which it may be determined by the head of the agency that such price was increased because the contractor or any subcontractor required to furnish such a certificate, furnished cost or pricing data which, as of a date agreed upon between the parties (which data shall be as close to the date of agreement on the negotiated price as is practicable), was inaccurate, incomplete, or noncurrent; Provided, that the requirements of this subsection need not be applied to contracts or subcontracts where the price negotiated is based on adequate price competition, established catalog or market prices of commercial items sold in substantial quantities to the general public, prices set by law or regulation or, in exceptional cases where the head of the agency determines that the requirements of this subsection may be waived and states in writing his reasons for such determination.

GAO Report on Need for Postaward Audits, B-158193, February 1966

The passage of the Truth in Negotiations Act and the implementing changes to ASPR did little to satisfy certain DOD procurement critics, especially the General Accounting Office. GAO continued to issue reports alleging overpricing on government contracts because of the contractors' failure to furnish accurate, complete, and current pricing data and DOD's failure to discover these conditions. Finally, and perhaps because it grew discouraged at the lack of attention accorded to these reports, the GAO compiled several old cases wherein it had previously alleged defective pricing, consolidated them into one report, and used this report as the basis for a concerted attack on DOD's failure to implement P.L. 87-653.

Essentially, GAO reiterated its allegations that contractors were submitting cost estimates that proved excessive in the light of information available at the time of negotiation and award; however, for a variety of reasons— because the contractors failed to disclose the proper information, because preaward audits were not made, or because preaward audits were not effective because of time limitations and other circumstances—the defective cost or pricing data were not disclosed and excessive profits resulted. GAO further claimed that there were frequently lengthy time spans between the completion of the preaward audit and the completion of negotiations and award and that significant information concerning occurrences in that period were not disclosed by contractors.

The General Accounting Office asserted that these and a variety of other situations that adversely affected the government's interests were discovered as a result of postaward audits performed by GAO. It was alleged, in effect, that for the most part postaward audits represented the only hope for the government to uncover defective submissions by contractors. In contrast, the report alleged that the Defense Department was performing few, if any, postaward audits. This type of examination did not tend to be requested by procurement officials. In this connection, the report noted that ASPR contained no policy for the guidance of contracting officers as to their responsibility for requesting postaward audits when appropriate. As to the then newly established Defense Contract Audit Agency (DCAA), GAO noted that its audit manual provided for only general surveillance of this area and not for regularly scheduled, selective postaward reviews. Further, GAO noted that a contractual right for postaward audits of this kind was available for certain flexibly priced contracts; however, negotiated firm-fixed-price contracts contained no provision permitting DOD personnel to audit incurred costs.

GAO made the following recommendations:

1. DCAA should establish a program for regularly scheduled postaward reviews of selected contracts.

2. Contracting officers should evaluate the need for post-award audits and specifically request DCAA to perform them where appropriate.

3. ASPR should be revised to permit the government to audit all books and records generated during the contract period for all negotiated contracts in excess of $100,000 except those exempted by P.L. 87-653.

The Defense Department concurred in the first two recommendations. The GAO suggestion for the ASPR revision affecting certain negotiated firm fixed-price contracts was referred to the ASPR Committee for its consideration.

JUDICIAL DECISIONS AND OTHER DEVELOPMENTS

As mentioned earlier, this chapter includes reviews and analyses of the major decisions by boards of contract appeals and federal courts, which placed the meat on the bare bones of the provisions of P.L. 87-653. The vagueness and terseness of the Act created problems for the judicial authorities who were forced to delve into the legislative history for congressional intent and, as in the case of offsets, arrive at conclusions that even then admittedly lacked conclusive statutory guidance.

There have been other considerably briefer written efforts to provide guidance in the implementation of the Truth in Negotiations Act. For example, we have seen some of the major issues (such as what constitutes adequate cost or pricing data, time when such data would be reasonably available to the contractor, and whether they should be submitted or made available) briefly explained and a single judicial ruling cited in an effort to provide the required illustration. The problem with these short-cuts has been the inability to provide the numerous nuances related to each issue. In our practice and in our instruction courses, we have found that a real understanding of some of the major issues can be gained only by studying several judicial rulings to see how the principles have been applied in differing conditions. This more extensive study also brings to the surface what appear to be remaining pockets of inconsistencies. For example, one decision held that submission of the data required a reasonable effort to assure that the government official saw the data and realized its significance. In another case, however, the ruling held that the contractor was not required "to lead the auditor by the hand."

American Bosch Arma Corporation, ASBCA No. 10305, 65-2 BCA par. 5280; 66-2 BCA par. 5747; Natural and Probable Consequences of Nondisclosure; Significant Effect on Price

American Bosch Arma was probably the first major ruling relating to defective cost or pricing data, and the board addressed several significant and precedent-setting issues. The most important one was attributable to the fact that the final contract price was negotiated on a total cost basis. Not uncommonly then or now, the parties discussed the various cost elements and profit, but reached no formal agreement except as to the total price. The alleged overstatement related to material costs.

The board noted that "[t]his case illustrates the difficulties of establishing that non-disclosure of pricing data concerning a specific cost element caused an increase in the negotiated total price when there was no agreement or understanding with respect to specific cost elements."

Wrestling with this problem, the board observed that this type of situation (in the absence of agreements of specific cost elements) was typical of contracts containing the Price Reduction clause. It further stated:

Not only was the general absence of agreement on specific cost elements known to DOD, representatives of industry and members of the Senate and House Armed Services Committees at the time of promulgation of ASPR provisions requiring the inclusion of the Price Reduction Clause in the contract, but both appellant and the Government negotiators knew that there was no agreement on the amount of the materials cost included in the target price at the time the contract was negotiated.

Notwithstanding this point, the board said: "We do not think that the absence of any understanding or agreement on amount of materials cost operates to defeat the effectiveness of the Price Reduction clause when both parties knew such to be the situation when they included the Price Reduction clause in the contract." In these circumstances and without any specific evidence as to the effect of the nondisclosure on the negotiated target cost, the board concluded that it must "adopt the natural and probable consequences of the disclosure as representing its effect." It, therefore, held that the negotiated target price was overstated in the amount of the material overestimates not disclosed plus the related G&A allowance. It then computed the price reduction by the application of appropriate profit factors to the total estimate thus computed.

The board found the overstatement to be $21,000, and a question arose as to whether this amount was significant in relation to the $15 million contract. However, here and in future decisions, the board appeared to disregard practical consideration of what may be significant in terms of percentages. Instead, the board found that, in amount, $21,000 represented significant pricing data.

FMC Corporation, ASBCA Nos. 10095 and 11113, 66-1 BCA par. 5483; Natural and Probable Consequences of Nondisclosure; Failure to Disclose Reasonably Available Data; Significance of Nondisclosed Data on Price; Facts v. Judgments

While the circumstances in this dispute differed considerably, some of the major issues and findings were similar to those in *American Bosch Arma.* First, the board reiterated its position that negotiation on the basis of total price would not in itself serve to defeat the intent of the Price Reduction clause. An important addition to the case law was the board's conclusion that "cost or pricing data consist of all facts which can reasonably be expected to contribute to sound estimates of future cost as well as to the validity of costs already incurred." As to the estimates of future costs, however, the board found that, while the contractor "does not make representations as to the accuracy of the contractor's judgment as to the estimated portion of future cost of projections," the certificate "does, however, apply to the data upon which the contractor's judgment is based."

The data submitted indicated that FMC would purchase certain components, but, in the performance of the contract, it manufactured them in-house at a lower cost. The government asserted that FMC knew but failed to disclose that it could manufacture these components cheaper than it could buy them. After reviewing the facts, the board found that, although FMC was engaged in experiments that ultimately led the company to manufacture the components, the results of these experiments were not reasonably available to the contractor as of the cutoff date and concluded that FMC "did not fail to disclose cost or pricing data within the definition of that term." (The board's decisions in some of the later cases analyzed in this chapter raise questions as to the manner in which the board would rule in these circumstances today.)

Another issue involved the government's contention that the prices FMC disclosed it would receive for aluminum scrap were lower than the amounts ultimately received and that this information was known to FMC and should have been disclosed. FMC argued that government representatives had as much knowledge of aluminum scrap price prospects as the contractor. The government conceded this knowledge, but contended it would have insisted on an Escalation clause if all of the information on the realization from scrap had been available. The major point in the board's decision on this issue was what appeared to be a departure from its ruling in *American Bosch Arma*. It expressed doubts as to whether the government would have actually moved to something other than a firm-fixed-price contract to accommodate a factor of 16/100ths of 1% of the contract price, particularly in view of its previous awards of similar vehicles amounting to more than $50 million on a firm-fixed-price basis. Referring to its decision in *American Bosch Arma*, the board stated that "while we have said that 'significance' within the meaning of the Price Reduction clause does not bear any relationship to percentage of the total contract price, it seems to us that such percentages do affect significance of negotiations for contract price."

Defense Electronics, Inc., ASBCA No. 11127, 66-1 BCA par. 5688; 66-1 BCA par. 5604; Natural and Probable Consequence of Nondisclosure; Facts v. Judgments

In the third major case involving assertions of defective pricing, the board was again confronted with the issue of whether the natural and probable consequence of nondisclosure would have had any practicable effect on price negotiations, and it followed the path of its ruling in *FMC Corporation* rather than in *American Bosch Arma*.

The government's claim for price reduction was based on its allegation that the contractor did not furnish complete, accurate, and current data with respect to the pricing of a major subcontract and on other factors.

In addressing itself generally to the government's position, the board stated:

> In order for the Government to have any valid claim, it must be established (1) that the contractor furnished inaccurate, incomplete or non-current pricing data in connection with the negotiation of the price adjustment for the change order, (2) that the inaccurate, incomplete or noncurrent pricing data caused the price adjustment for the change order to be increased, and (3) the dollar amount by which the price adjustment for the change order was increased as a result thereof. The Government has the burden of proving every element in the chain of proof necessary to substantiate its claim . . . it is incumbent on the Government to show that the change order price adjustment was overstated *because* of the contractor's failure to disclose or its improper disclosure of data . . . (Italics in original.) . . .

> When the contractor made data available to the Government auditor for his use in auditing the contractor's change order proposal, that was a

sufficient furnishing of such data for the purpose of the Price Reduction clause, and the contractor was under no obligation to furnish to the contracting officer personally data not requested by the contracting officer which the contractor had already made available to the auditor and which the auditor had used and referred to in the audit report which was furnished to the contracting officer.

The board found that the cost and pricing data furnished to the government auditor was complete, accurate, and current as of the date the auditor completed his audit. However, the government contended that the prime contractor's negotiations with its subcontractor as of that date were not firm and were continuing. It further argued that the contractor was obligated to disclose further information as to contract costs, including the subcontract, at or prior to the negotiation of the change order.

In addressing itself to this contention, the board stated:

> For the purpose of the defective pricing data statute and negotiations, "cost or pricing data" is defined by ASPR 3-807.3(e) as "that portion of the contractor's submission which is factual." The duty to disclose is satisfied when all facts reasonably available to the contractor which might reasonably be expected to affect the negotiated price are accurately disclosed. ASPR 3.807.1(e). Cost or pricing data includes such factual matters as vendor quotations and "all facts which can reasonably be expected to contribute to sound estimates of future costs." It does not apply to or make representations as to the accuracy of the contractor's judgment in estimating future costs. A clear distinction is drawn between "facts" and "judgment."

The board found that some of the information concerning the contractor's negotiations with its subcontractor had, in fact, been made available to the government. There was other information in this connection, including correspondence, which the board determined constituted pricing data that the contractor should have but did not disclose. However, in the opinion of the board, a disclosure of these data "with full factual explanation would not have disclosed to the Government negotiation team anything appellant had not already disclosed . . . ." The board further concluded that "[i]t is unlikely that this information would have had any effect on the change order price negotiations . . . ."

The board proceeded further and concluded that, even if the contractor had made a full disclosure based on circumstances known at the time the change order was being negotiated, this would not have justified any reduction in the amount of the change order price adjustment. It was not convinced that the price adjustment was increased because of any failure of the contractor to disclose information available to it at the time of the negotiation. The board continued:

> This is not a case where the natural and probable effect of the non-disclosure was to increase the negotiated price adjustment. *American Bosch Arma Corp., supra.* Instead, it is like the situation presented in *FMC Corp., supra,* where the Board held that the non-disclosed data concerning the price of aluminum scrap was not significant for the reason that it would not have had any practicable effect on price negotiations.

Lockheed Aircraft, Lockheed-Georgia (Midwestern Instruments, Subcontractor), ASBCA No. 10453, 67-1 BCA par. 6356; Availability v. Disclosure; Offsets

Although the appeal was filed in the name of Lockheed, the real party in interest was Midwestern, whose data were alleged to be defective based on a detailed GAO audit performed in 1963.

This decision included an issue that was to continue to surface in many future defective pricing disputes: requirement to disclose versus making available. A major amount involved in the defective pricing allegation concerned material costs, and the government asserted that more current lower cost data had not been made available to it. Midwestern contended that these records had not been denied to the government and hence had been available to it. But the board concluded that Midwestern had "failed to fulfill its duty to disclose . . . ." It said that, if the subcontractor had disclosed the information and the government had failed to review or otherwise take advantage of it, it would have concluded that the disclosure requirements had been met.

The board continued along these lines:

> Here, however, the subcontractor did not inform Lockheed or later the Air Force that it had already obtained firm prices on a substantial amount of materials. In no other way did the subcontractor make the other parties aware of the existence of this significant information. It is wholly unreasonable to say that the other parties had this data available. The gesture allegedly made to Lockheed or to the Air Force that all records were available was practically meaningless absent any inkling that such specific, significant data was in reality present and available.

The board sought to distinguish its position here from those it took in *American Bosch Arma* and *Defense Electronics.* In those cases the board said that significant, accurate, complete, and current data available to the contractor had actually been made available to the government and had been examined, or was subject to examination, by the government. The ASBCA emphasized "that the issue here is not the 'availability' of records to the Government auditors, but whether in fact there was disclosure to the Government of pertinent pricing information that was reasonably available to Midwestern." It held that the government was "bound by its examination of the limited records . . . because there was disclosure to that extent."

Another significant point in this decision involved offsets (i.e., the netting of the over- and understatements.) In *American Bosch Arma* it appeared that both the GAO and the contracting officer applied offsets and hence this matter had not become an issue. In *Lockheed* the subcontractor claimed that it had overlooked certain development and royalty costs in its submission. Upon being faced with a price reduction for defective pricing, Midwestern then requested that these items be offset against the overstatements alleged by the government. Although the board denied the claim for offsets, its ruling was directed to certain peculiarities of the case as cited below, and hence this decision was not considered a precedent.

> It is obvious to us that these two cost items were only remotely related to the "material costs" in issue. Besides, they were known to

Midwestern long before the culmination of the negotiations. Lockheed was not made aware of these items during the negotiations prior to 6 June 1962, nor was the respondent made aware of them during the discussions in September, 1962. The obvious answer to the offsetting suggestion is that the equitable reduction permitted under the clause is intended to cover solely the cost items concerning which the pricing data was [were] defective. To permit unrelated offsets would be tantamount to repricing the entire contract, which is not within the contemplation of the clause.

Cutler-Hammer, Inc., ASBCA No. 10900, 67-2 BCA par. 6432; Offsets; Nature of Data to Be Disclosed

A substantial portion of this decision relates to the arguments for and against offsets and the board's rationale for denying offsets except with respect to identical components. The rationale was at the time a matter of considerable interest, but is not presented here in view of the action of the U.S. Court of Claims in overruling this decision. We might make two observations here. First, the board's long study of appeals under P.L. 87-653 and its legislative history failed to surface "absolute conclusive evidence of Congressional purpose . . . ." The board was also prescient in its conclusion: "We are therefore constrained to adopt a literal interpretation of the statute, and if we err, it is for others, be it the Congress or the courts, to set the matter right."

It is also of interest to note that, at the time, the board's decision reflected the broad consensus within the Department of Defense.

The second major issue decided in *Cutler-Hammer* related to the nature of information that the contractor was required to disclose. This is another issue which was to prove extremely controversial and surface repeatedly in future decisions by boards and courts.

To acquire an important component (lens) of the end item, the contractor issued an RFQ to five vendors. Only one of the five submitted a bid, and this company alone had produced this lens in the past. The vendor's price compared favorably with the contractor's own independent study and was included in its price proposal to the government. Dates play an important role in this interesting story, and close attention should be directed thereto.

11/8/63	Government issued RFQ to prime.
12/2/63	Prime submitted pricing proposal.
1/13/64—2/13/64	Government order and price analysis of prime's proposal.
2/13/64—2/19/64	Contract price negotiations.
2/26/64	Prime signed certificate of current cost or pricing data certifying that complete data, current as of 1/13/64, had been submitted to the government; that all significant changes occurring therein through 2/19/64 had similarly been submitted; and that no more recent significant changes had occurred in such data to the knowledge of the signer thereof as of 2/26/64.

With the above chronology in mind, we can turn to the disclosure that "sometime during the early part of January 1964" Vendor T learned of the contractor's RFQ for the lens and asked for one. The prime contractor forwarded the RFQ on 1/16/64, sent the specifications on 1/20/64, and set a proposal closing date for 1/31/64. A price proposal, in an amount considerably less than that of the original vendor, was received from Vendor T on 2/10/64. The contractor requested technical data and received it on 2/24/64. At the time the prime contract price negotiations were concluded, the contractor was exploring Vendor T's proposal but had not obtained any technical data from that company. The contractor's negotiating people conceded having knowledge of Vendor T's quotation during the negotiations. They defended their decision not to disclose this knowledge to the government on the ground that Vendor T's proposal seemed ridiculously low, was not supported by technical information, and hence was not susceptible to evaluation.

At the time the company's treasurer signed the Certificate (2/26/64), Vendor T's technical proposal had been received and preliminarily studied; but the treasurer testified that he had no knowledge of this matter.

Negotiations and discussions with Vendor T continued, and a purchase order for a limited quantity was issued on 4/9/64. Additional purchase orders were awarded to Vendor T over the next year as the contractor's confidence in that vendor increased.

After considering these circumstances, the board concluded that as of the date of the execution of the defective pricing certificate, although Vendor T's quotation was far from being data upon which a firm price reduction could have been reached, it is also inescapable that the information was significant from the standpoint of overall contract negotiation. The board thus decided that information regarding Vendor T should have been disclosed to the government and faced the next problem, which was that "the very fact of its nondisclosure to the government leads us to conjecture as to what precise effect a full disclosure might have had on these negotiations." At this point, the board made a significant comment in establishing that the consequence of the failure to disclose must be borne by the contractor rather than by the government.

The board conceded that, in *Defense Electronics, Inc.* (ASBCA No. 11127), it had imposed on the government "the burden of proving that causal relationship between significant, nondisclosed, pricing data and the resulting contract price reduction." The rationale for what some believe to be a substantial if not a complete reversal of this position was given in these words: "However, we did not then, nor do we here, intend that that burden be an unreasonably heavy one."

In contemplating what might have happened if Vendor T's quotation had been disclosed, the government argued that it might have either (1) delayed the execution of the prime contract until more information was available or (2) excluded the lens from the contract price and reserved it for further negotiation. The board doubted that the execution of the contract would have been delayed, but was persuaded that the government would have selected the latter alternative of excluding the lens from the contract price and reserving it for further negotiation.

The board then addressed itself to the question "as to when and in what amount this outstanding cost item would have been definitized." The board concluded that it had no basis upon which to answer these questions and that any attempt on its part to do so would be purely conjecture. Accordingly, the board remanded this portion of the appeal for negotiations between the government and the contractor.

Sparton, Sparton Electronics Division, ASBCA No. 11363, 67-2 BCA par. 6539; MFR Denied 68-1 BCA par. 6730; Nature of Data to Be Disclosed

One of the major issues in *Sparton* involved the contractor's obligation to disclose a quotation of the low vendor, and it seemed that the board moved away from its position in *Cutler-Hammer* without a really clear-cut explanation.

Sparton had previously purchased its circuit boards from Vendor M, a sole source, and had used the average cost of such purchases in its proposal to the government. The government contended that at the time of its proposal Sparton knew of a considerably lower quotation for circuit boards from Vendor P, but had not disclosed this information, and that the failure to disclose such cost and pricing data resulted in a defective pricing situation.

The board, however, was favorably inclined to Sparton's position that the circuit boards were critical parts, that they could not be purchased from untried vendors, that Vendor P's capability had not been evaluated as of the date of the proposal, and hence that the Vendor P quotation did not constitute data that were required to be submitted. The board noted that in its *FMC* decision it had "stated that vendors' quotations are considered to be cost and pricing data which should be disclosed, but this is qualified by the caveat that such data would 'reasonably be expected to have a significant bearing on costs under the proposed contract'." At this point, the board made a significant and apparently contradictory statement when it held that "[u]nless specifically asked to do so under the contract clause of this case, a prospective contractor is not required to list each and every quote received from prospective vendors whose responsibility had not previously been evaluated and where the quote concerns a part deemed to be critical .... Under the facts stated, the Government does not prove its case unless it shows that the contractor, at the time the data is submitted, did not intend to deal with the vendor listed, but did intend to do business with the lower cost vendor. Such proof is lacking here." With an unusual display of unanimity, DOD and industry commentators alike found the board's ruling contradictory to its decision in the *Cutler-Hammer* case.

The government lost little time in moving for reconsideration of the board's decision in the *Sparton* case. It viewed with alarm the serious impact that this decision might have on P.L. 87-653. The government's major contentions otherwise were to the effect that the *Sparton* decision contradicted the *Cutler-Hammer* ruling.

In its Motion for Reconsideration, the government first addressed the definition of "data" and the circumstances under which data must be disclosed to the government. In *Cutler-Hammer,* the board ruled that negotiations with a virtually unknown vendor in circumstances where the possibility of an ultimate award appeared remote nevertheless had to be disclosed. The government saw an identical situation in *Sparton* and challenged the board's decision that the contractor was not obliged to advise the government.

But the board ruled that the component involved in *Cutler-Hammer* "required resolution of 'state of the art production difficulties,'" whereas in *Sparton* "evaluation of the product required a production run and testing of first production articles." Second, in *Cutler-Hammer,* the contractor's evaluation of the vendor's item "was commenced before execution of the prime contract." In *Sparton,* "the prime contractor was not shown to have been in contact with the proposed supplier for about eight months after the proposal was received—more than three months after the prime contractor's proposal was made to the Government and more than $2\frac{1}{2}$ months after contract execution." Third, the components in *Cutler-Hammer* were small-quantity, high-dollar items, with the difference between the amount submitted by the prime contractor and the amount ultimately paid to the vendor amounting to $300,000. In *Sparton,* in contrast, large quantities of the component were required and the unit price was low. Further, the total difference was only $8,500. Fourth, *Cutler-Hammer* involved an incentive type contract while the Sparton contract was firm-fixed-price. In this latter case, the board was not persuaded that DOD's stated preference for firm-fixed-price contracts would have been significantly affected even if the government had known about the possibility of a reduced vendor price, especially where the amount was "miniscule as compared to the total contract price."

Bell and Howell Co., ASBCA No. 11999, 68-1 BCA par. 6993; What Constitutes Cost or Pricing Data; Effect of Nondisclosure on Negotiated Contract Price

The issues are familiar, but the differences in circumstances and the board's conclusions are sufficient to make this case of interest.

The case originated with a GAO audit that asserted that Bell & Howell had available to it lower quotations on certain components than it reflected in its proposal and that the failure to use such lower quotations resulted in increasing the contract price by approximately $389,000 over what it would have been had the contractor made the required disclosures. The contracting officer agreed with the GAO and, after failing to reach agreement with Bell & Howell, handed down a unilateral determination from which the contractor appealed.

What Constitutes Cost or Pricing Data?

Bell apparently did not deny that it was aware of lower quotations than the prices used in its proposal to the government. One of its arguments in the appeal was that these lower quotations did not constitute cost or pricing data as contemplated by ASPR. The rationale and reasons offered by the contractor are illustrated below:

1. The low bidder "had indicated some reservation about delivery," and Bell concluded that the quotation of this bidder would be "too risky to use. . . ."

2. Negotiations had not been concluded with the vendor supplying the lowest quote, and the higher price quoted by another vendor was used because "a contingency was necessary. . . ."

3. The vendor offering the lowest quotation was new to the contractor, and Bell had had "sad experience" on this component. Bell justified non-use of the lowest quote on this basis, because of "the rising brass market and the fact that (the vendor) had not made the part during the previous ten years."

These and similar arguments were made by the contractor in support of its contention that the quotation involved did not constitute cost or pricing data. But Bell's arguments were not favorably considered by the board, and the ASBCA commented as follows:

We find no merit in the contractor's contention that the six undisclosed low quotes were not "cost or pricing data" as defined in ASPR 3-807.3(e), which defines cost or pricing data as including such factual matters as vendors' quotations. The vendor quotations themselves were cost or pricing data; the contractor's judgmental decision not to base its proposed price on such quotations was not cost or pricing data. Appellant could have complied with the Truth in Negotiation Act by submitting the same proposed price that it did, but disclosing the low quotes and explaining why it was not using them for pricing purposes.

Included in the definition of cost or pricing data made by ASPR 3-807.3(e) is the concept that the factual data be such as "might reasonably be expected to affect the price negotiations." Citing the Board's decision in *Sparton Corporation (Sparton Electronics Division)*, ASBCA No. 11363, 67-2 BCA par. 6539, appellant argues that the undisclosed low quotes do not meet the test of being data "which might reasonably be expected to affect the price negotiations." *A simple factual answer to this argument is that a full disclosure of the facts pertaining to the low quotes at the time of negotiation of Modification No. 1 would have disclosed that appellant was actively and vigorously engaged in negotiating with and making plant surveys of the vendors who had submitted the low quotes and that it was probable that appellant would place orders for the purchase parts with the six low quote vendors.* Under the circumstances, it is unrealistic to say that knowledge of these facts could not reasonably be expected to affect price negotiations. The low quotes in the instant appeal are more analogous to the undisclosed quotation in *Cutler-Hammer, Inc.*, ASBCA No. 10900, 67-2 BCA par. 6432, and *Lockheed Aircraft Corporation, Lockheed-Georgia Company Division*, ASBCA No. 10453, 67-1 BCA par. 6356, than they are to the undisclosed low quotation in *Sparton Corporation, supra*. See the Board's decision on Motion for Reconsideration in *Sparton Corporation (Sparton Electronics Division)*, ASBCA No. 11363, 68-1 BCA par. 6730.

Effect of Nondisclosure on Negotiated Contract Price

We now reach a new and quite interesting aspect of this decision and the ASBCA views on P.L. 87-653. The board found:

The Government has sustained its burden of proving the nondisclosure . . . and we have found that a price . . . computed on the basis of the low quotes would have been $389,000 lower than a price based on the vendor quotations that were in fact disclosed by appellant. It does not necessarily follow, however, that the nondisclosure of such cost and pricing data caused the negotiated price to be increased by $389,000 or any other amount, and the Government has the burden of proving that the nondisclosure caused the negotiated price to be increased and the amount of such increase.

The board here noted Bell's contention "that the disclosure of the low quotes would not have resulted in any reduction of the price below what was agreed to. ..." The board also noted that the government negotiator "conceded at the hearing that, if he had known about the low quotes, he would not have refused to consider the explanation given by the contractor for not basing its price on the low quotes and demanded a further price reduction ...."

After mulling over this situation further, the board concluded that, on the one hand, the knowledge of the low quotes would not have enabled the government to negotiate a reduction in the firm fixed price in the amount of the difference between the vendor quotes used by the contractor and the lower quotes not disclosed "or any comparable amount." On the other hand, the board was equally convinced that, "if the Government had any knowledge of the low quotes, it would not have entered into the firm fixed-price specified in the contract modification ... or any comparable figure. ..."

The board found that the government had moved toward a firm-fixed-price contract because its evaluation of the contractor's proposal led it to believe that the contractor had realistic firm prices on the purchase parts. The disclosure of the low quotes, in the board's opinion, and the probable discussion of the risks attending such quotes would have persuaded the government to conclude that there were still too many risks and contingencies to shift to a firm-fixed-price basis.

And now we reach the interesting portion of the board's decision. Concluding (1) that low quotes were not disclosed, (2) that the total indicated effect was $389,000, and (3) that had the low quotes been disclosed the parties would not have been able to agree upon a firm fixed price, the board decided that the government and Bell would have likely negotiated a fixed-price-incentive contract on the same 60/40 sharing arrangement on cost underruns as had been provided for in the original contract. On this assumption, the board ruled that the contract price should be reduced by 60% of the $389,000.

Public Law 90-512, September 1968

As mentioned earlier in this chapter, the GAO report issued in February 1966 included a recommendation that DOD obtain contractual rights to audit performance costs of firm-fixed-price contracts, and ASPR was revised accordingly in November 1967. Despite this action, Congress concluded that legislation was needed, and P.L. 90-512 was enacted to provide:

> For the purpose of evaluating the accuracy, completeness, and currency of cost or pricing data required to be submitted by this subsection, any authorized representative of the head of the agency who is an employee of the United States Government shall have the right, until the expiration of three years after final payment under the contract or subcontract, to examine all books, records, documents, and other data of the contractor or subcontractor related to the negotiation, pricing, or performance of the contract or subcontract.

Aerojet-General Corporation, **ASBCA No. 12873, 69-1 BCA par. 7585;**
  What Constitutes Cost or Pricing Data; Disclosure v. Making
  Available; Effect of Nondisclosure on Negotiated Price

The now familiar issue of what constitutes cost or pricing data involved
the contractor's alleged failure to disclose a lower quote from a subcontractor
whose delivery schedule was not responsive to Aerojet's requirements. Subsequent to the award of the prime contract, Aerojet conducted further negotiations with the subcontractor, who agreed to conform delivery schedules to
Aerojet's requirements and, further, reduced its originally proposed price.

The contractor's major point, that the lower quote did not constitute data
because the proposal was nonresponsive as to delivery factors, was not viewed
as meritorious by the board. It conceded that "such factors . . . might in some
instances render the quotation for a particular item so meaningless or unreliable that no 'prudent buyers and sellers would reasonably expect (the quotation) to have a significant effect on the price negotiations.' (ASPR
3-807.3(e))." In this case, however, the board thought that the lower offer
"should reasonably have been expected to affect the price negotiations."

The board was similarly unimpressed with the argument that the lower
quote was, in one way or another, available to the government. It found that
the government's knowledge of the contractor's system, its interest in the
subcontractor who submitted the lower quote, and the possibility that this
subject may have been mentioned in the negotiations "are not substitutes for a
submission by appellant of complete, accurate and current cost or pricing
data." The board referred here to its decisions in the appeals of *Bell & Howell*
(ASBCA No. 11999) and *Lockheed* (ASBCA No. 10453).

The final matter for discussion in this decision involves the board's
determination of the amount by which the price should be reduced. The
contractor's contention that an overstatement could not be proven because the
negotiations were conducted on a total cost basis was rejected by the board.
However, neither did the board accept the government's contention that the
price should be reduced by the full effect of the nondisclosure, although this
might have been contended on the "natural and probable consequence of
defective data" theory, originally introduced by the board in *American Bosch
Arma, supra.* In this case, the board conjectured that if the contractor had
submitted the lower quote, the government would have reduced its target cost
figure for negotiation purposes. On the other hand, it also conjectured that, in
the circumstances, Aerojet would not have reduced its proposal to reflect the
difference between the quote it submitted and the lower, nonresponsive
quotation.

Having backed itself into a corner with these conjectures, the board
proceeded to extricate itself with neat arithmetical maneuvering. Its analysis
of the offers and counteroffers between the parties during the negotiations
revealed that the increase between the government's initial proposal and the
ultimate target cost represented 49.05% "of the difference between the parties' first offers." The board then reduced the government's initial target cost
by the effect of the undisclosed lower quote. Finally, it applied the 49.05%
split to the difference between Aerojet's initially proposed target cost and the
adjusted Air Force initial target cost.

Aerojet-General Corporation, **ASBCA No. 12264, 69-1 BCA par. 7664; What Constitutes Cost or Pricing Data; Disclosure v. Making Available**

The main issue centered on a sizeable subcontract with Straza, included in Aerojet's proposal. According to the decision, during Aerojet's negotiations with the government, including negotiations on the data on which agreement was reached regarding the prime contract price, engineering analyses by Aerojet had concluded that Straza's proposal was substantially overstated and negotiations were under way between the prime contractor and subcontractor, which ultimately led to a substantial reduction in the subcontract price. The board further concluded that, as of the date Aerojet executed its certificate, it had reached agreement with Straza on substantially reduced amounts for material and labor costs and the subcontractor was reconsidering its proposal for overhead. Aerojet argued that, as of the date of its certificate, agreement had not been reached for the price reduction with Straza and, further, that the government was aware of the negotiations. The salient portions of the board's ruling in favor of the government are cited below.

The above argument misses the point. The appellant's obligation under the contract was to furnish accurate, complete and current cost and pricing data. This the appellant did not do. Appellant's engineering analyses, cost estimates or other data which revealed that some elements of Straza's quotation were significantly overstated are in themselves significant cost and pricing data, which appellant relied on in its negotiations with Straza. We hold that the failure to disclose these analyses, cost estimates or other data was sufficient to justify a finding, which we hereby make, that the appellant did not furnish accurate, complete and current cost or pricing data.

We have found that both the appellant's and respondent's negotiators conducted the negotiations upon the assumption that the cost or pricing data furnished in relation to the nozzles was accurate, complete and current. It follows, and we find, that any change in the subcontract price of the nozzles, based on the inaccuracy, incompleteness or noncurrency of the cost or pricing data at the time of the execution of the certificate, would have a direct dollar-for-dollar effect upon the target cost of the prime contract. This effect would, in turn, influence other elements in the contract pricing formula.

The fact that neither the appellant's negotiators nor the person who signed the certificate was aware of appellant's engineering analyses, estimates or other data is not material. The information was reasonably available because some of appellant's personnel at management level, including negotiators of the Straza subcontract, were aware of the fact that Straza's quotation for some of the changes were significantly excessive. The appellant is obligated to furnish accurate, complete and current cost and pricing data to the extent that the data are significant and reasonably available. This obligation cannot be reduced either by the lack of administrative effort to see that all significant data are gathered and furnished the Government, or by the subjective lack of knowledge of such data on the part of appellant's negotiators or the person who signed the certificate.

Cutler-Hammer, Inc. v. U.S., 189 Ct.Cls. 76, 416 F.2d 1306 (1969); Offsets; Meaning of Data

In the two major issues decided in ASBCA No. 10900, the court overruled the board on offsets, but upheld it on meaning of data.

The matter of offsets, while clear when viewed in terms of equity and logic, is extremely difficult if the decision is to be based strictly on the law and legislative history because neither furnish definitive guidance. This point was emphasized by the split decision of the court. A portion of the court's rationale is cited below:

> It is clear that when only overstatements are included in estimates, the Government has the right to reduce the contract price. In such a situation, a downward revision of the price is mandated. Whether offsets in favor of the contractor are to be allowed presents a more difficult question, the answer to which is not so readily apparent. The legislative history of the Act does indicate that efforts were made to have the language of P.L. 87-653 cover situations where errors in favor of the Government would cancel out errors in favor of the contractor, but these efforts were to no avail. . . . Plaintiff contends that the literal language of the statute allows setoffs; defendant argues that the language of the statute in the legislative history dictates against allowing understatements to be set off against overstatements. In our view, neither the statute nor the legislative history is clear cut. In the absence of concise guidelines, we must resort to finding the legislative intent.

> It is argued that since the statute talks in terms of "reducing" the contract price, and the contract clause speaks in terms of "excluding" defective prices, there can only be a downward revision of price. With this we agree, but we interpret these words to mean that where overstatements exceed understatements, the price is not raised.

The second major issue found the ASBCA upheld by the Court of Claims.

As previously described, the Cutler-Hammer proposal with respect to a major component (lens) included a quotation from the only vendor originally responding to its RFQ—the only company that had produced this lens in the past. Sometime thereafter, but before the negotiation of the contract price, Cutler-Hammer was advised of an interest by another firm in manufacturing this component—and at a considerably lower price. Cutler-Hammer looked into the technical and other aspects of this proposal, but did not disclose it to the government on the grounds that it was considered "ridiculously low," was not supported by technical information, and hence was not susceptible to evaluation. Ultimately, as it turned out, Cutler-Hammer did award the purchase order to this newcomer (Transco). The government alleged defective pricing on the grounds that Cutler-Hammer failed to submit information about Transco's bid. The ASBCA concluded that Cutler-Hammer should have disclosed this information to the government, and having failed to do so, its data were not accurate, complete, and current.

The Court of Claims acknowledged that "when a contractor issues a Request for Quotations, he is not required to divulge to the Government every proposal he receives." However, the court concluded that "Transco was not just another bidder ... whose bid had been considered ... and disregarded. Plaintiff was interested enough in Transco's bid, even at a later date, to follow it up with the request for a technical proposal. Since Cutler-Hammer saw Transco as a possible supplier, it should have informed the Government that a lower price on the antenna may have been obtainable. Although no firm agreement had been reached with Transco until after the Certificate was filed, the fact that its proposal was being considered at this time indicates that the cost and pricing data submitted by plaintiff were less than complete or current."

The court further elaborated on its views and emphasized that it was not alleging that Cutler-Hammer had predetermined that it would use Transco. On the other hand, said the court: "In our view, P.L. 87-653 could lose much of its effectiveness if contractors could argue that they did not disclose a quotation because they did not consider it 'cost or pricing data', although they later took advantage of it to the detriment of the Government." The court further rejected Cutler-Hammer's contention that cost or pricing data should be defined as data upon which a reasonable businessman would rely in negotiating a contract. "This definition," said the court, "begs the question; 'cost and pricing data' is made up of costs which may or will make up part of the total cost of a contract and which should therefore be divulged in negotiating a contract."

Aerojet-General Corporation, ASBCA No. 12264, MFR Denied 70-1 BCA par. 8140; What Constitutes Cost or Pricing Data

The board's finding that Aerojet's cost or pricing data were defective because it knew, based on its engineering analyses, cost estimates, etc., that Straza's quotation was "grossly inflated" was discussed earlier in this chapter. In its motion for reconsideration, Aerojet contended that no causal relationship had been established between whatever might have been the incompleteness of the data furnished to the government and any overstatement of the prime contract price. The board rejected this argument for the reasons and rationale cited below:

Even if we assume the facts to be as stated in appellant's argument, we do not reach the result for which it contends. Indeed, we think that it is immaterial whether the Government's negotiators know the nature of the defect in a contractor's certified cost or pricing data in a case of this sort. What is material is whether the cost or pricing data furnished by a contractor are complete, accurate and current, as certified, and, if not, whether the Government relied on the incomplete, inaccurate or noncurrent data in agreeing to a price that was overstated as a result.

In our decision in this appeal, we have found that the Straza price quotation furnished by appellant to respondent on 10 October 1962 as part of its proposal for pricing the prime contract was not complete or current on 4 December 1962, when appellant certified its cost or pricing data. Our basis for this finding was that appellant had made certain studies, analyses, factual investigations, and the like in preparation for negotiating a definitive price for the Straza subcontract, and based on these cost data appellant knew, before 4 December 1962, that the original Straza price quotation was significantly overstated. Since the amount of the overstatement was by agreement of the parties, not in issue at the hearing, it was unnecessary for us to go further than this in our findings. Despite this knowledge, appellant failed to furnish the cost data to respondent during the negotiation of the prime contract, and the latter's negotiators continued, throughout the negotiations, to rely on the original Straza price quotation. This failure, we concluded, caused an overstatement in the price of the prime contract.

Sylvania Electric Products, Inc., ASBCA No. 13622, 70-2 BCA par. 8387; Availability v. Disclosure; Reliance on Submission; "Natural and Normal Consequences" of Defective Data

The review of the pricing proposal was made by a military department price analyst, and the decision indicates that he did not devote significant attention to the material portion of the submission. Some three years later, the GAO performed a postaward review alleging that the contract price had been overstated by some $250,000 because the contractor had failed to furnish accurate, complete and current data. The military department ordered the price reduced in this amount, and Sylvania appealed.

The contractor argued that "by furnishing the government data (documents) from which the government could have discovered the materials cost errors in the proposal, by checking the data furnished against documents in the proposal, it thereby disclosed the materials cost errors, even though the government did not check such data against the proposal and hence did not in fact discover the materials cost errors in the proposal." Although it considered the evidence as to what documents were furnished not very satisfactory, the board proceeded on the assumption that the contractor did furnish the price analyst with the documents it contended it had. However, reasoned the board, this was not sufficient because none of the documents "actually showed that the material costs in the proposal were in error. . . ." The board then focused on the basic issue of "disclosure v. availability" in the following very specific and emphatic terms:

> In order that there be effective disclosure of cost and pricing data by the prospective contractor either the Government must be clearly advised of the relevant cost and pricing data or it must have actual (rather than imputed) knowledge thereof. It does not suffice to make available or physically hand over for Government inspection files which, if examined, would disclose differences between proposal costs and lower historical costs. It is also necessary in order to make a disclosure, to advise the Government representatives involved in the proposed procurement, of the kind and content of the cost or pricing data and their bearing on the prospective contractor's proposal which examination of the files would disclose. Our decisions in *McDonnell Douglas Corp., supra, Lambert Engineering Company,* ASBCA No. 13338, 69-1 BCA par. 7663, and *Aerojet-General Corp., supra,* and ASBCA No. 12264, 69-1 BCA par. 7664, point in this direction. The decision herein follows the path which they blazed. In this light, even if appellant's exhibits had all been

disclosed to the price analyst or any other cognizant Government representative, such mere transmission of documents without informing the
Government representatives of the current cost or pricing data which
they contain is not a "disclosure" within the meaning of GP 48 and the
underlying statute (10 USC 2306(f)).

Appellant also argues that these considerations are overridden by
what it characterizes as respondent's negligent failure to protect itself by
scrutinizing all aspects of the proposal and all related data, however they
came into its hands. The Board's prior decisions, already cited, negate
this argument. Appellant was required to make an actual disclosure of
accurate, current, and complete cost and pricing data and did not do so as
the prices of materials stated in its proposal contained unreported errors.
Respondent was not required to audit each and every aspect of the
proposal to enjoy the contractual protection of the contract and statute or
to protect appellant from its own failure to make full disclosure.

The contractor's third argument was that, even if it had failed to disclose
accurate, current, and complete cost and pricing data, the government had not
relied on its data in the contract negotiations. This argument was rejected by
the board, which found that the government had performed considerable work
on the labor, engineering, and overhead costs, but had "accepted the material
costs unquestioned. . . ." And it was the category of material costs that was
declared to be defective data.

Another issue involved the "normal consequences" or the actual effect
that defective data would have had on the contract price. The board saw it
this way:

> In the nature of things any conclusion reached by the Board must
> contain an element of speculation and hypothesis. *Lambert Engineering
> Company, supra.* But in negotiating a fixed price contract the normal
> consequences of an initial overstatement of the price by one party on the
> order of $250,000 is that, after disclosure, negotiations would have
> started from that lower figure. In other words the amount of the over-
> statement would be eliminated from their mutual offers absent any other
> factor. *Bell & Howell Company,* ASBCA No. 11999, 68-1 BCA par. 6993.
> In that case and in *Aerojet-General Corp.,* ASBCA No. 12873, 69-1 BCA
> par. 7585, cited by appellant, the Board had to consider the effect of a
> price overstatement on incentive pricing and cost sharing and found
> appropriate a more complex form of price adjustment involving applica-
> tion of a cost-sharing formula to the amount of the price overstatement.
> Here no such problem nor any other reason for a different result is
> presented. No evidence was offered that in the light of this disclosure of
> the price overstatement appellant would not have agreed to a price of
> about $4,360,000. Respondent is, therefore, entitled to a price reduction
> equal to the amount of the price overstatement as the most likely result
> to flow from its disclosure.

Lockheed Aircraft, Lockheed-Georgia (Midwestern Instruments, Subcontractor) v. U.S., 15 CCF par. 84,015, 193 Ct.Cls. 86, 432 F.2d 801 (1970); Offsets; Availability v. Disclosure

The U.S. Court of Claims had ruled in favor of offsets in denying the *Cutler-Hammer* appeal described earlier in this chapter. The court reaffirmed its decision in the instant case, and we have cited salient excerpts of its decision.

The reason we allowed offsets to the extent of overstatements in *Cutler-Hammer,* was that including both understatements and overstatements in a price proposal negated any attempt on the part of the contractor at creating "artificial savings." This allows them to cancel each other out, at least to the extent of the overstatements, and means that only savings which were brought about through "demonstrated performance of the work" would be available as added profit. This means that the savings were the product of efficiencies of production, and not through the use of inflated cost estimates. In a fixed-price contract, as in an FPIF contract, costs are estimated, and a profit figure is added. If the contractor produces the product for less than his negotiated price, he keeps all the savings (absent any possible renegotiation or other contingency which would limit his profit). Thus, the same manipulation of costs which led to inflating costs in FPIF contracts is possible with a fixed-price contract. Similarly, allowing the offsetting of understatements against overstatements in a fixed-price contract, limited to the extent of the overstatements, leaves only those savings which are the result of "demonstrated performance of the work."

The allowance of offsets does not give the contractor a windfall, nor does it penalize the Government. In both the *Cutler-Hammer* situation and the one which prevails here, allowing offsets according to our formula merely allows the setting of the negotiated price in an amount which reflects the true costs. If overstatements exceed understatements, the Government is still allowed to reduce the contract price by the amount of the excess. No raising of the price is allowed, however.

As discussed earlier in this chapter, the *Lockheed/Midwestern* appeal in ASBCA No. 10453 also included the issue of availability v. disclosure. Pertinent portions of the court's ruling in upholding the board of contract appeals are cited below.

The Board found that shortly after submitting its proposal to Lockheed in February 1962, Midwestern began to make substantial purchases of materials for use in fabricating the recorders, and that by June 1 or June 6, 1962 Midwestern had purchased in excess of 90 percent of the materials needed. The negotiated materials costs in June 1962 and September 1962 were found to exceed the costs gotten from reasonably available data.

Plaintiff argues that Midwestern satisfied the requirements of the Defective Pricing Clause when it allowed the Air Force pricing team to inspect its Kardex file. This is an accounting system in which the price of each item of material ordered is recorded on a card which also contains the prices paid in previous purchases of the item. The material costs are thus segregated by item and not by end-product.

Since it was not possible for the Air Force price team to accurately audit Midwestern through use of the Kardex file, a member of the team asked for a bill of materials on the 813LQ recorder. He was told that this was not available, but that it could be prepared within two weeks. Due to the shortness of time which the team had, this offer was unacceptable, and the bill of materials was not prepared.

Had the team been given a bill of materials on the 813LQ recorder during its two-day investigation, it is fair to say that it would have found evidence of cost overstatements. The information which it was afforded, i.e., the Kardex file, did not clearly indicate the overstatements. It is true that the actual costs may have been contained on the Kardex files; however, so were many other prices for the same items, and it was impossible for the team to separate out the costs attributable to other products with which they were not concerned.

Plaintiff also contends that there was no available evidence which was withheld from the Air Force, and that Air Force could have inspected the purchase orders to ascertain relevant costs. Such an examination may have been informative, but merely looking at the Kardex file, which did not indicate to what use the various items were put, would not have put the Air Force on notice that there were purchase orders relating to the 813LQ recorder.

When the Kardex file was supplied to the Air Force team, Midwestern knew that it had already obtained firm prices on much of its materials. The Air Force may have seen recent prices listed; but they could not know that these prices related to the 813LQ recorder.

Assuming, however, that there were indicia in the Kardex file as to what the true material costs were, we still are of the opinion that there is a duty on the part of the subcontractor to completely disclose this information. We stated as much in *Cutler-Hammer,* Inc., supra:

> ... If a cost is known when the contract price is being negotiated, it must be furnished accurately, completely, and on a current-price basis. If the contractor purchases components from a subcontractor, these costs are also subject to the Defective Pricing Clause. 189 Ct.Cls. 84, 416 F.2d 1311.

We reiterate that proposition here. This is especially true in the factual context presented here, where the Kardex file, itself a cumbersome accounting system, contained over 600 line items for a component of the larger MADREC system.

Luzon Stevedoring Corporation, ASBCA No. 14851, 71-1 BCA par. 8745; Contract Price Not Necessarily Affected by Nondisclosure

The government solicited a proposal from Luzon on a sole source basis for the rental of tubs and barges, the procurement being urgent because of ongoing Vietnam operations. Luzon was asked to submit a DD Form 633 and a Certificate of Current Cost or Pricing Data. The contractor did so, but also asked the government to advise promptly whether it would accept or decline the offer as presented "in view of alternate towage commitments." The contract performance began December 1968, and the contract was executed January 1969, effective November 1968. DCAA issued an audit report in April 1969 questioning various elements in Luzon's proposal. The auditor's position was upheld by the contracting officer, who sought to reduce the price under the Price Reduction for Defective Cost or Pricing Data clause. Luzon appealed from the contracting officer's unilateral determination.

The board found that the auditors had used the latest actual data recorded in Luzon's books to reconstruct its initial proposal. The board agreed with Luzon that the government was attempting to use the Defective Pricing clause as a contract repricing device and admonished the government that P.L. 87-653 was not designed for this purpose.

The board found that some of the data, viewed in the light of the date submitted, appeared to be accurate, complete, and current, but some were not. However, the board was more impressed by the unusual circumstances involved in the negotiations and concluded "that the rental price was not increased because of the failure to disclose, or the incompleteness of the data." It further found that "no amount of negotiation would have convinced Luzon to lower its price."

The board was further impressed by the fact that the same contracting officer had entered into a similar contract for the same price on May 16 despite the fact that he had had possession of the audit report since April 30. Although the government argued that this action was irrelevant, the board disagreed:

> In our opinion, it shows conclusively that if Luzon had disclosed all of the information found by the auditors, the rental rates for the subject contract would have remained immutable. The "Natural and probable consequence" doctrine announced in *American Bosch Arma Corporation* ASBCA No. 10305, 65-2 BCA par. 5280, has a limitation. We wrote there that:

>> In the absence of any more specific evidence tending to show what effect the nondisclosure of the pricing data had on the negotiated target cost, we are of the opinion that we should adopt the natural and probable consequence of the nondisclosure as representing its effect.

> In the case now before us, there is specific evidence not only tending to show that the nondisclosure would not have affected the price, but actually showing this fact. See *FMC Corporation,* ASBCA Nos. 10095 & 11113, 66-1 BCA par. 5483.

M-R-S Manufacturing Company, ASBCA No. 14825, 71-1 BCA par. 8821; Submission v. Making Available

According to the decision, the contractor's accounting system accumulated cost information by parts, both cumulatively and by individual production runs. In submitting its proposal, the contractor apparently used the unit costs from the highest cost production runs. The proposal was examined, and although the data by individual production runs were available to the auditor, the contractor did not submit them nor did the audit disclose this information. A subsequent audit, however, by a different auditor did unearth this data, and the related report constituted the basis for the contracting officer's determination of defective pricing.

There were two contracts involved. With respect to the first one, the proposal was reviewed (and it was here that the contractor argued that it had submitted complete and current cost data) and its argument rejected by the board.

We disagree. The data which appellant furnished were neither complete nor current. At the time when the priced bill of materials was given the auditor other production orders representing production runs with significantly lower labor costs occurring at a later date than the one cited and furnished were in possession of appellant. These data were not furnished or otherwise disclosed to representatives of the Government. But appellant views the facts as establishing that all cost and pricing data were actually and physically submitted to the Government together with advice and information as to variances in and between costs proposed and other experienced costs, since a complete audit could be performed from the priced bill of materials and the data referenced in the bill of materials to which the auditor had access. Appellant thus argues that under decisions of this Board and the Court of Claims the appellant made, as it was required to do, a full disclosure of all pertinent cost and pricing data, citing *Lockheed Aircraft Corporation, Lockheed Georgia Co. Div. v. United States,* Ct.Cl. No. 250-67, 432 F.2d 801 (1970); see also *Sylvania Electric Products, Inc.,* ASBCA No. 13622, 70-2 BCA par. 8387 (1970) and cases cited therein. These cases do not support appellant's position under the facts of this appeal. We think appellant misconstrues its obligations with respect to the furnishing of data. Whether the auditor was familiar with appellant's accounting system or not, or whether a complete price analysis could have been conducted from the materials furnished the auditor together with the other materials the auditor had at hand, makes little difference. Appellant may quote its prices on any basis it wishes, it may formulate its profit factor on any basis it wishes and it may use any fair accounting system it wishes. However, when it chooses to furnish cost factors on which to base its prices it must also disclose variances it knows it has currently experienced in the application of those same factors when the costs quoted are, in relation to the other currently experienced costs, significantly overstated. If a cost is known when the contract price is being negotiated it must be furnished accurately, completely and on a current cost basis. *Lockheed Aircraft Corp., supra.*

In *Lockheed,* the Court observed that, if the Government is furnished with a clear set of costs and then does not make any use thereof, it cannot be heard to complain. The Court also pointed out, however, that a contractor bears the affirmative burden of meeting the contractual disclosure requirement and of making such a full disclosure of all relevant data. We do not believe that appellant discharged that obligation here. . . .

* * * *

Significant cost differences among production runs were known to appellant at the time the contract was negotiated. This information was readily extractable from its accounting records. Appellant did not disclose this cost and pricing data to the Government by calling to anyone's attention the cost variances in the production runs or by physically handing over to the auditor, as it might easily have done, other material production order documents. *Lambert Engineering Company,* ASBCA No. 13338, 69-1 BCA par. 7663. We find, therefore that the Government was not furnished complete and current cost and pricing data pertaining to the four manufactured parts and the lack of such data resulted in a significant overstatement of the contract price.

Chu Associates, Inc., ASBCA No. 15004, 73-1 BCA par. 9906; MFR Denied 73-2 BCA par. 10,120; What Constitutes Cost or Pricing Data

The decisions reviewed in this chapter include a number where the board or court ruled that certain quotations constituted cost or pricing data despite the assertions of the contractors involved that, at the time they submitted the certificate, they had not anticipated awarding subcontracts to the companies in question. In some of the decisions, the judicial bodies seemed to have unduly extended this concept, which made the ruling in *Chu Associates* extremely welcome. Essentially, the board ruled that a subcontractor's quotation, received before the Certificate of Current Cost or Pricing Data was signed by the prime contractor, but not at that time intended to be used, did not constitute cost or pricing data and hence the prime contractor's failure to disclose it did not subject the contractor to price reduction for defective data.

Chu had manufactured this contract item in the past and had employed the same firm (Columbia Products) to produce one of the important components. In connection with the contract under dispute, Chu had secured several quotations, but had every intention to deal with Columbia Products as in the past until the close of the negotiation, when the government inserted a Liquidated Damages clause for late deliveries.

Subsequent discussions with Columbia established that this company could not guarantee timely delivery of the component, nor would it accept any portion of the liquidated damages.

The board found that, at the date Chu executed its Certificate of Current Cost or Pricing Data, it had not negotiated with or seriously considered Geonautics. The component involved was a critical one and "Geonautics was a new and untried supplier." Throughout the negotiations, Chu had planned to use Columbia and had not even made any investigation of Geonautics capability.

In ruling for Chu, the board distinguished the circumstances in *Cutler-Hammer.*

This case represents a variation of the Luneberg Lens issue decided by the Court of Claims in *Cutler-Hammer, Inc. v. United States,* 189 Ct.Cls. 76 (1969). In that case the contractor failed to disclose a quotation it had received from a potential supplier. Although that contractor regarded the non-disclosed quotation as being unreasonably low, and hence not to be taken seriously, it was interested enough to follow it up with a request for a technical proposal, which it received two days before it executed its Certificate of Current Cost or Pricing Data. The Court held that such a quotation, which was under active consideration prior to the date on which the Certificate was executed, was cost or pricing data that should have been disclosed. By contrast, although appellant here received the Geonautics, quote well before the date on which it executed its Certificate of Current Cost or Pricing Data, it gave no consideration before that date to the use of Geonautics as a source of supply, nor did it make so much as a casual investigation of its capabilities of performing the work. Under such circumstances, we conclude that the cost or pricing data furnished by appellant were accurate, complete and current as of 5 May 1966 when its Certificate was executed.

LTV Electrosystems, Inc., ASBCA No. 16802, 73-1 BCA par. 9957; MFR Denied 74-1 BCA par. 10,380; The Time When Cost or Pricing Data Were Reasonably Available to the Contractor

On November 3, 1967, LTV was asked to submit a proposal for items urgently required for Vietnam and did so within twenty-four hours. According to the decision, no further action was taken until December 8, when the government issued a Letter Contract, executed by the contractor on the same day. On December 16, the contractor submitted a DD Form 633 and supporting papers, including a priced-out bill of materials. The government audited the proposal starting immediately after receipt, and the audit report was issued on January 2, 1968. On January 4, the parties negotiated a contract price and the contractor filed a Certificate of Current Cost or Pricing Data. The definitive contract was signed on January 22.

During the preaward audit, in response to the auditor's request, LTV furnished vendor's quotations that were obtained almost a year prior to the date of the certificate. On further request, LTV furnished current purchase orders for 11 of the 650 parts that comprised the Bill of Materials. There was apparently no dispute over the fact that more current data were not furnished to the government even though during the period between March 1967 and January 1968 the contractor was purchasing additional parts and obtaining vendor quotations. As the board concluded, "It appears that appellant's priced bill of materials was neither complete nor current on the date of certification . . . ." The board noted, however, that "[w]e do not find it necessary to rule on this point since we base our decision on other grounds . . . ." And these "other grounds" were that, although the contractor had more current data on the date of its certification than that it furnished the government, "[t]he Government has not shown that the more complete and current data in appellant's possession were reasonably available or that it knew, or should have known, the actual material costs based thereon."

The principle of "reasonably available" is one of considerable importance and one that should be clearly understood by government contractors. For this reason, we have excerpted portions of the decision section of the board's opinion so that precise language and citations might be studied and serve as a point of reference to the reader.

Availability of Complete, Accurate and Current Cost or Pricing Data. Notwithstanding the apparent incompleteness and noncurrency of the priced bill of materials supplied by appellant in support of its direct material cost, the Government may not recover on its claim unless it can show, by a preponderance of the evidence, that more accurate, complete and current cost or pricing data were reasonably available to appellant on the date of certification under the prevailing circumstances. *American Bosch Arma Corp.*, ASBCA No. 10305, 65-2 BCA par. 5280. On the present record, we conclude that the Government has not sustained this burden.

*   *   *   *

Witnesses for appellant have testified that the time required to update its priced bill of materials would have been 3 to 6 months ... Furthermore, the buy card system, which would have simplified the process by making such purchase order and quotation data more readily retrievable, was at that time incomplete and hence unusable. Even with a complete buy card system, the post-award audit, which sampled purchase order data for only 381 or 650 parts, consumed 43 man-days and would have consumed roughly twice that amount of time, by the auditor's own estimate, had he checked such data for all of the parts.

Under these circumstances, we conclude that appellant has convincingly demonstrated that its failure to produce more complete and more current cost or pricing data was not the result of a failure to make the necessary administrative effort to obtain them, but rather, that such data were simply not reasonably available within the time allowed. On this point, we do not have to determine the length of time that would have been required to reprice the bill of materials in order to establish a reasonable cut-off date, as we did in *American Bosch Arma Corp., supra.* It is enought here that we find that the period from 8 December 1967 to 4 January 1968 was not reasonably sufficient to permit appellant to reprice its bill of materials. The Government has not introduced any evidence to the contrary. *Cf. Sylvania Electric Products, Inc.,* ASBCA No. 13622, 70-2 BCA par. 8387 and *Lambert Engineering Co.,* ASBCA No. 13338, 69-1 BCA par. 7663, in each of which the data in question were readily available to the contractor's negotiators but not made known to them or to the Government at the price negotiations simply because of the contractor's lack of effort or inadequate internal procedures.

Sylvania Electric Products, Inc. v. U.S., 18 CCF par. 82,334, 202 Ct.Cls. 16, 479 F.2d 1342 (1973); Availability v. Disclosure; Reliance on Data

Sylvania variously argued that the data were either not reasonably available in time to disclose to the government or had, in effect, been made available or submitted to various government representatives. The court found that the contractor did have the time and opportunity to disclose the required data. As to submission v. disclosure, the court said:

In general, as to all of the above items, plaintiff has argued that mere submission of data satisfied the requirement of disclosure. We do not agree. In order that there be effective disclosure of cost and pricing data by the prospective contractor the Government must be clearly advised of the relevant cost and pricing data. This is particularly true after the Government has analyzed the data and the contractor then receives reduced quotations from its suppliers.

If the Truth in Negotiations Act is to have any force and effect then the Government must be clearly and fully informed. This can only be achieved by complete disclosure of the item or items in question.

In its appeal before the ASBCA, Sylvania argued that, even if it had failed to disclose accurate, complete, and current cost or pricing data, the government had not relied on such data in contract negotiations. Sylvania also challenged the government to prove that the price would have been lower had the data been available. The board ruled against Sylvania on the grounds that "in negotiating a fixed price contract the normal consequences of an initial overstatement of the price of one party on the order of $250,000 is that, after disclosure, negotiations would have started from that lower figure." Nor was Sylvania any more fortunate when it carried this argument to the Court of Claims, which stated:

Plaintiff argues finally that the Board adopted a new and erroneous standard of burden of proof on the issue of reliance. Such is not the case. This burden was clearly discussed by the Board in a previous case, *American Bosch Arma Corp.,* 65-2 BCA par. 5280. While that Board recognized that the responsibility of proving nondisclosures or use of inaccurate and noncurrent data falls upon the Government, it held that once this burden has been satisfied it would be the natural and probable consequence that such nondisclosure would result in an overstated negotiated contract price. This is a logical presumption, for it is reasonable to assume that the government negotiators relied upon the data supplied by the contractor and that this data affected the negotiations.

Thus although the Government has the burden of proof as to the issue of nondisclosed data, which it met in this case, the burden of persuasion on the issue of relying upon that data has shifted to the contractor. He must show nonreliance on behalf of the Government in order to rebut the natural and probable consequences of the existence of the nondisclosed or inaccurate data. This the contractor has not done in this case. Accordingly the presumption stands and there was a casual relationship between the disputed data and the final negotiated price.

Levinson Steel Co., Inc., ASBCA No. 16520, 73-2 BCA par. 10,116; Disclosure v. Making Available; Effect of Nondisclosure on Negotiated Price

At issue here is the manner in which Levinson presented and the government relied upon projections of certain vendor credits for steel found to be defective and chargeable back against the respective steel mill vendors. To brief a rather lengthy story, Levinson had recently instituted a program under which it charged the mills for defective steel. The reactions varied. In some instances, the contractor received credit for the exact amounts, in other instances for various percentages of the charge-backs. In summary, Levinson had no precise fix on the potential contract cost impact of these credits in the future. The amount it reflected in its proposal was $.0215 per unit. Although a new item in the contractor's proposals, this amount not examined or challenged by DOD auditors, analysts or negotiators during the preaward period.

In the postaward audit, the auditor found that the credit was based on Levinson's experience in its 13th accounting period of 1968. Using the experience for the entire year, with updating for the period January 1—March 29, 1969 (the latter date was the one on which agreement on price was reached), resulted in an amount of $.12 per unit. The difference between $.12 and $.0215 per unit, multiplied by the number of ammunition, constituted the alleged effect of defective cost or pricing data.

Levinson argued that all of its records were made available to DOD auditors, including the historical data on total credits received. Additionally, the credit it included was clearly identified in schedules and working papers submitted to the government. In the contractor's view, there was appropriate disclosure in terms of the statute, the contract clause and related regulations.

The board's conclusions were that, first, there was no disclosure under the law and regulations, and second, the nondisclosures had no effect on the negotiated contract price; accordingly, the "Government has failed to sustain its burden of showing that the non-disclosures resulted in an increased contract price." Pertinent excerpts of the decision leading to these conclusions are cited below:

> No one questions that the entry on Schedule A constituted a judgment by the contractor. Essentially, therefore, we must decide whether appellant disclosed that the $.0215 figure was a result of its judgment and disclosed complete, accurate and current facts upon which its judgment was made. *Aerojet-General Corporation,* ASBCA No. 12264, 69-1 BCA par. 7664 (April 29, 1969); *Lambert Engineering Company,* ASBCA No. 13338, 69-1 BCA par. 7663 (April 30, 1969).

> There is no basis for a price reduction for defective pricing resulting from erroneous judgment if full disclosure of facts has been made. *Sylvania Electric Products, Inc.,* ASBCA No. 13622, 70-2 BCA par. 8387 (July 14, 1970). Therefore, one issue presented is whether Schedule A and the applicable portions of the supporting workpapers given to the Government during its pre-award audit constituted complete, accurate and current data.

> The workpapers ... included the various credits during its thirteenth accounting period. The Government argues this was not sufficient and that appellant should have disclosed in the workpapers a complete list of all credits up to that time rather than just those of the thirteenth accounting period. Certainly the workpapers disclosed that appellant's vendor credits entry on Schedule A was a "judgment" amount and that the percentage of actual credits to debits exceeded that used in computing the $.0215. The workpapers set forth facts upon which this judgment was based.

> While the workpapers might have disclosed all the facts upon which appellant based its judgment we feel, and so hold, that this was not

complete and accurate cost or pricing data. The appellant had the responsibility to disclose all the facts which would have put the Government in an equal position with the contractor to make its own judgment. *Lockheed Aircraft Corporation* v. *United States,* 193 Ct.Cl. 86 (1970). It failed to do so when it did not include all the credits received from August 1968 to the time it submitted the revised price proposal. The data was, in our opinion, significant. It was also readily available. . . .

However, despite the fact that the disclosures and certificate were not complete, accurate and current, the government by its own admissions has clearly failed to sustain its recognized burden of proving that the negotiated price was increased by any significant sums as a result thereof. Despite the fact that the term "vendor credit" used on Schedule A was a term never before seen by the government auditors or other negotiators, no question was ever asked about it prior to or during negotiations. The workpapers setting forth the computation were never even studied by any government personnel. This $.0215 entry on the schedule was not challenged by the government. We are not persuaded by the government's bootstrap argument that not questioning this item and affirmatively accepting it was sufficient proof. Why ever audit if such is the case? ASPR Sec. 3-807.7 specifically states that a certificate of current cost or pricing data is not a substitute for examination and analysis of the contractor's proposal.

The government has admitted that Levinson was always most cooperative and readily supplied any requested information. We have also found that the usual government audit procedure at the Hays Plant was to ask for what it wanted, not to encourage help or advice from the Levinson personnel on what it should examine. The government negotiating personnel have also admitted that had they looked at the workpapers they would have "asked questions"—the very questions which were asked during the post performance audit and resulted in the immediate receipt of the appropriate Levinson files. Most significant has been the recognition by the Government that if every credit received up until the date of submittal of the revised price proposal had been set forth, there would have been no question of failure to disclose, but that this information would not have been seen and the Government would have been 'down the drain' concerning any possible defective pricing claim.

In some situations we have expressed the opinion that to give the statute and its implementing regulations the intended effect, the natural and probable consequence of the non-disclosure should represent its effect. See *American Bosch Arma Corporation,* ASBCA No. 10305, 65-2 BCA par. 5280. As found above appellant failed to disclose significant data. However, as stated previously, the Government has the ultimate burden of proving a causal connection between the non-disclosure and an increased contract price. This appeal presents an unusual situation where the Government's own witnesses have testified that they would not have seen or used the information had it been disclosed. In view of this weighty evidence that the Government would not have relied on the undisclosed data had it been revealed, we are unable to find that the Government has sustained its burden of proving a cause-effect relationship between the failure to disclose and the increased price. We are not persuaded otherwise by the Government's argument that appellant had an affirmative duty to call the credits to the Government's attention.

Public Law 87-653 and the related claims and regulations call for reasonable disclosure prior to or during negotiations. They do not provide a substitute for renegotiation or return of excess profits but are intended to assure equality in negotiations where there is no effective price completion. *Sparton Corporation,* ASBCA No. 11363, 67-2 BCA par. 6539 affd. on recon., 68-1 BCA par. 6730.

Our decision in *Sylvania Electric Products, Inc.,* supra, is clearly distinguishable. There the defect involved costs of material which were erroneously stated in the pricing proposal. The Government could have discovered it by checking certain submitted supporting data but did not do so. The contractor discovered the error prior to the date agreement as to price was reached and deliberately chose not to disclose it during negotiations on the ground the Government could have discovered it by checking. Here, we have a judgment determination, the workpapers showed how it had been derived and showed further the percent figure used was less than the actual one experienced during the thirteenth accounting period—an entirely different factual situation.

Lockheed Aircraft, Lockheed-Georgia (Midwestern Instruments, Subcontractor) v. U.S., 19 CCF par. 82,586, Ct.Cls. 250-67 (1973); Offsets

This litigation is characterized by an unusually lengthy history. We first referred to it early in this chapter because a 1967 ruling in ASBCA No. 10453 failed to address the subject of offsets head-on. Instead, the board denied the claim for offsets on the ground that the initially unclaimed development and royalty costs now offered as offsets were "only remotely related to the material costs . . . (and) to permit unrelated offsets would be tantamount to repricing the entire contract which is not within the contemplation of the clause."

We next discussed this dispute in connection with a ruling by the Court of Claims in 1970. Following its decision in the previous year in *Cutler-Hammer,* the court ruled that Lockheed (hence Midwestern) was entitled to offset the royalty and development costs that the subcontractor "had overlooked and excluded . . . ."

We encounter the dispute for the third time in the 1972 ASBCA No. 10453 decision. Here the board was faced with a problem. It had initially referred to the royalty and development costs as having been "overlooked and excluded," and the Court of Claims subsequently used comparable language when it directed that offset of such costs be permitted. The board then addressed the question of whether these costs had actually been overlooked and inadvertently excluded or whether their omission was intentional and deliberate. The board's deliberations led it to the conclusion that the omission was intentional, and it once again denied offsets.

This chain of events brings us to the final episode, the Court of Claims decision after Lockheed appealed the board's ruling under the provisions of the Wunderlich Act. The contractor argued that, under the prior court decision in

Cutler-Hammer, an understatement of costs may qualify as a setoff whether it is inadvertent or intentional. The government argued that the court had not previously addressed the issue of intentional understatements and that P.L. 87-653 should be interpreted as permitting only unintentional understatements to be set off against overstatements.

This line of argument seemed to clearly identify an interesting issue for resolution: specifically, whether intentional understatements are eligible for offsets. Unfortunately, the court elected not to address this issue and, instead, arrived at its decision based on a number of errors that it concluded the ASBCA had made.

The court found that the board had "arbitrarily and capriciously cast upon plaintiff the burden of proof that the understatement of royalty costs was unintentional." In the opinion of the court, and with reference to its decision in *Sylvania Electric Products, Inc.* (June 20, 1973), "the Government has the burden of proving its entitlement to a price reduction under the Defective Pricing Clause."

In the judgment of the court, "[i]f the government seeks to enlarge the net price reduction allowed by urging that certain non-disclosed data were intentionally withheld and therefore should not be considered in set off, it bears the burden of proof on the issue of intentional non-disclosure." The court further stated that there did not exist "substantial evidence to support the board's conclusion that the understatement of royalty costs was intentional."

As we observed in our initial analysis of this decision and in the prior editions of this text, the court's decision not to address the subject of intentional understatements left this subject unresolved and deferred its consideration to other disputes and other tribunals, and ultimately to legislative action.

American Machine & Foundry Co., ASBCA No. 15037, 74-1 BCA par. 10,409; Effect of Nondisclosure on Negotiated Price

The government argued that American had submitted defective data by naming only two suppliers for one of the component parts, whereas the contractor was allegedly aware that it (1) would be purchasing a substantial number of these components from a third (unnamed) supplier and (2) would be canceling its order from the supplier who had quoted the highest unit price. The facts in the case appeared to be murky and in controversy, but the board concluded that the contractor had failed to meet its disclosure requirements. The more complex issue centered on the effect of the nondisclosure.

The board described the government's position as contending that it is automatically entitled to a price reduction once an overstatement has been established. The board disagreed and found that this could not have been the intent of Congress:

> It is crystal clear that the statute does not expressly provide for an automatic price reduction measured by the amount of any overstatement of the cost of a component part of the end item, plus the percentages that the Government chooses to use for G&A and profit. Nor can it reasonably be said that the act does so by necessary implication. Rather, the remedy clearly envisaged by the statute where an overstatement in the cost of a component part has been established is an adjustment in the contract

price of the end item "to exclude any significant sums by which it may be determined . . . . that such price was increased because the contractor or any subcontractor . . . . furnished cost or pricing data which . . . . was inaccurate, incomplete, or noncurrent." In other words, the statute, rather than requiring an automatic price reduction in the end item equal to the amount of the dollar and cents overstatement of a component part, plus G&A and profit, as advocated by the Government, requires that first, as a *sine qua non,* there exist a causal connection between any inaccurate, incomplete or noncurrent data with respect to a component part, on the one hand, and any increase of the contract price of the end item, on the other hand. Further, even if the existence of such a causal relationship is established, the statute requires that, before a price reduction may be effected, the "significant sums by which . . . . such price (for the end item) was increased because the contractor or any subcontractor . . . furnished cost or pricing data (with respect to a component part) which . . . . was inaccurate, incomplete, or noncurrent" must be determined, because such "significant sums, and no other, may be excluded from the contract price for the end item because of the defective pricing data furnished with respect to the component part.

Having concluded that the law does not provide for an automatic price reduction, the board examined the government's computation. It found a wide array of assumptions and conjectures, which yielded different results by government auditors, price analysts, and cost analysts. The board recognized a "rebuttable presumption that the natural and probable consequences of non-disclosure would be an increase in the contract price . . . in an amount equal to the overstatement . . . ." However, it ruled that "before such a presumption can arise, the Government must prove by a preponderance of the evidence that the cost to the appellant of a component part was overstated by the appellant in a *specific amount.*" (Emphasis added.) Acknowledging the difficulty in this case, the board said: "Nevertheless, this difficulty does not excuse the Government from its aforesaid evidentiary obligation." And in this instance, the board reiterated its conclusion that the "Government has utterly failed to sustain such a burden."

M-R-S Mfg. Co. v. U.S., 203 Ct.Cls. 551, 492 F.2d 835 (1974); Submission v. Making Available; P.L. 87-653 and Price Reduction Operative Even if Data Were Not Submitted; Duty to Furnish Data Imposed on Contractors by Statute and Cannot Be Waived by Government Agent

The details of this dispute were set forth earlier in this chapter in our analysis of the contractor's unsuccessful appeal, ASBCA No. 14825, 71-1 BCA par. 8821. In our review of the decision by the Court of Claims, we shall refer to the first contract as C976 and the second as C8006.

With respect to contract C8006, M-R-S argued that the government could claim defective pricing only if data referenced in the Certificate of Current Cost or Pricing Data were defective, whereas M-R-S had submitted no data in support of C8006. The court found that the M-R-S argument contained several flaws, "any one of which would be fatal, even if it stood alone." First, it agreed with the ASBCA that the "DD Form 633 submitted with plaintiff's proposal constituted cost or pricing data." Several sets of DD Form 633 were submitted, and one of them referred to "cost records." This reference supported the court's view that the DD Form 633 constituted data. In any case, even if there were questions as to whether the DD Form 633 and the reference to the cost records constituted data, the court found persuasive and held against M-R-S its transmittal letter, which stated that its DD Form 633 (attached) utilized the exact costs audited and negotiated for C976.

The court found another flaw in the M-R-S argument that data must be submitted in support of a proposal before the Defective Pricing clause will allow a price reduction. The court conjectured that this argument might have merit if only contractual provisions, and not a statutory directive, were involved. However, since the clause and certificate exist pursuant to P. L. 87-653, said the court, "The scope of these items turns on the scope of the Act":

> As this court has said on several occasions, the Truth in Negotiations Act imposes a duty on Government contractors to completely disclose cost and pricing information. *Sylvania Elec. Prods., Inc. v. United States,* 202 Ct.Cl. 16, 479 F.2d 1342 (1973); *Lockheed Aircraft Corp. v. United States,* 193 Ct.Cl. 86, 432 F.2d 801 (1970); *Cutler-Hammer, Inc. v. United States,* 189 Ct.Cl. 76, 416 F.2d 1306 (1969). The information so disclosed must be, in the words of the Act, accurate, complete, and current. The Act grants to the Government the right to adjust the contract price when the price is increased because the contractor did not meet his duty to furnish accurate, complete, and current data. Therefore, even if, as the plaintiff asserts, no data were submitted "in support" of the proposal for Contract 8006, the plaintiff still did not meet the requirements imposed by the Act. But regardless of what the situation would have been if the plaintiff had submitted no data, we must still deal with the plaintiff's assertions concerning the Contract C976 data since we approve the Board's finding that the same data were submitted for Contract 8006.

Another argument presented by M-R-S was that its objection to furnishing accurate, complete, and current data was waived by the government because it had used only the data for C976 and did not review any data developed since then. But the court found that "The duty to furnish accurate, complete, and current data is a duty imposed on Government contractors by a statute, and therefore, that duty cannot be waived by a Government agent. *United States v. Stewart,* 311 U.S. 60 (1940); *Utah Power & Light Co. v. United States,* 243 U.S. 389 (1917); see *Federal Crop Ins. Corp. v. Merrill,* 332 U.S. 380 (1947); *Montilla v. United States,* 198 Ct.Cl. 48, 457 F.2d 978 (1972)."

As to the question of submission versus making available, it appears undisputed that "the data physically delivered to the auditor, i.e., the bill of materials, the inventory cards and the production cards for only one run per part, were not accurate, complete, and current. Production cards not physically delivered reflected the costs of other production runs, all of which were lower, and some of which were more current, than the costs shown in the delivered cost or pricing data." The board identified the issue as whether M-R-

S submitted all of the data "or stated in another way, what must a Government contractor do to submit data to the Government within the meaning of the Truth in Negotiations Act."

In reaching its conclusion, the court cited its decision in *Sylvania Electric Products, Inc., v. U.S.,* 18 CCF par. 82,334, 202 Ct.Cls. 16, where it concluded that to achieve "effective disclosure of cost and pricing data .... the Government must be clearly advised of the relevant cost and pricing data. ... If the Truth in Negotiations Act is to have any force and effect then the Government must be clearly and fully informed. This can only be achieved by complete disclosure. ....." The court then elaborated and further clarified its views on this issue:

> We fully recognize that words such as "clearly advised" and "complete disclosure" do not automatically resolve difficult questions. We do believe, however, that such language adequately shows the intent and purpose of the Truth in Negotiations Act and how it should be interpreted. A proper consideration of the Act's purpose, as stated above, is of great help in applying its provisions to cases such as the one before us.

> Situations wherein accurate, complete, and current information is known to the contractor and not known to the Government can certainly be avoided if such information is physically delivered to the Government and the information's significance to the negotiation process is made known to the Government by the contractor. We do not hold that both of these conditions must always be met before a contractor can be said to have submitted the required information to the Government. We conclude, however, that if a contractor possesses accurate, complete, and current information that is relevant to negotiations with the Government, and he neither physically delivers the data to the Government, nor makes the Government aware of the informations' significance to the negotiation process, then he has not fulfilled his duty under the Act to furnish such information to the Government.

Conrac Corp., ASBCA No. 15964, 74-1 BCA par. 10,605; Submission v. Making Available; Time When Cost or Pricing Data Were Reasonably Available to the Contractor; Government Reliance on Defective Data

A summary of some of the facts involved is essential to an understanding of the decision. This was a sole source urgent procurement. The RFP was made by telephone, and the proposal was requested by the end of the week. The negotiations, all of them by telephone, were concluded in three weeks.

Conrac's written proposal included material costs based on a priced bill of materials prepared in June 1965 and bearing that date on its face. It appeared that the government was aware that the bill of materials was 14 months old. It was further aware that the bill of materials was priced for quantities smaller than those required by this contract. In consideration of these two factors, the government's negotiator proposed a reduction of 4% and ultimately negotiated a reduction of 2% of the materials cost proposed by the contractor.

There were some 500 components involved, but the government's allegation of defective pricing was limited to 15 of the higher-valued items as set forth in a subsequent DCAA audit report. These 15 items were listed on Conrac's purchase history cards, and the government's negotiator testified that neither the cards nor the data listed thereon were disclosed to him. Conrac contended that the government knew or should have known that there was procurement activity and therefore should have requested the contractor to furnish such data.

The board turned to the question of whether Conrac submitted complete, accurate, and current data to the government. As mentioned previously, it was established that the bill of materials was 14 months old. The question needing resolution was whether the intervening data that were available to Conrac were cost or pricing data within the meaning of the Act or clause.

The board reviewed the definition of cost or pricing data as contained in ASPR 3-807.1 at that time (not different in any significant way from the current definition). It concluded that the data originating in the 14-month period as set forth in Conrac's purchasing history records and presented in the audit report were cost or pricing data within the meaning of the Act. It referred to its decision in *Norris Industries, Inc.*, ASBCA 15442, 74-1 BCA par. 10,482, and concluded, referring to the ASPR definition of that time: "These data are factual. They can reasonably be expected to contribute to sound estimates of future costs. They are susceptible to verification. It is undisputed that they were not furnished to the Government negotiator."

The second question was directed to whether the purchase history card data for the 14-month period was reasonably available to Conrac at the time of price negotiation. The board concluded that the contractor knew or should have known of the existence of these data.

In its defense, the contractor reminded the board of the urgency of the procurement, and its representative testified that it would require four to six weeks to update the priced bill of materials. A question was also raised regarding the relevance of another decision by the board in similar circumstances where the ruling had gone in favor of the contractor. The board's comment is of interest.

In *LTV Electrosystems, Inc.*, ASBCA No. 16802, 73-1 BCA par. 9957, aff'd on recons., 74-1 BCA par. 10,380, we held, in similar circumstances, that the appellant there was under no duty to update its priced bill of materials because of the urgency of the procurement and limited time available in which to do so. That case is distinguishable from this in that LTV did not have a buy card or purchase history card system in effect at the time of the price negotiations. Here, appellant had a purchase history card system in effect and the raw or unevaluated data in question were readily retrievable therefrom.

The board reasoned that, while time did not permit the use of the purchase history cards to update the bill of materials, it would have been feasible for the contractor to reproduce those 500 cards and submit them to the government so that the parties would have been on an equal footing. The board conceded that time limitations would not have permitted consideration of all of the 500 items; however, the board thought the government negotiators might have evaluated the high-dollar-value items and thus found the price overstatement on the 15 items brought to issue through the audit report.

The nub of the present case is that appellant had the purchase history cards in its possession and could have made the kind of evaluation mentioned above; the government did not have that opportunity, because it did not have the data.

The board then considered the contractor's contention that the government negotiator knew or should have known of the purchasing activity during the 14-month period. The board concluded that the government negotiator in fact did not have this knowledge. As to whether he should have known, the board found that the Act, regulation, clause, and certificate "placed the burden of effective disclosure of cost and pricing data on the prospective contractor. *Sylvania Electric Products, Inc. v. United States,* 18 CCF par. 82,334, 202 Ct.Cl. 16, 479 F.2d 1342 (1973)."

The next question was whether the government had relied to its detriment on the defective data and whether it might not be held to have waived the submission of better data. As mentioned previously, the record seemed to show that the parties discussed both the age and quantity of the contractor's materials cost proposal and negotiated a reduction of 2% to compensate for those deficiencies. The contractor contended that the negotiation was predicated on the bill of materials and that the bargain made by the parties to resolve the contingencies in such cost data should be allowed to stand. The board rejected this contention:

> If this were a case in which the Government's negotiator knew of appellant's available purchase history card data but rejected them as having no significant effect on the price negotiations, appellant's argument would have merit. *Lockheed Aircraft Corp. v. United States,* 193 Ct.Cl. 86 (1970). Since we have found that the Government's negotiator had no such knowledge, he was not able to make a conscious decision in the matter, for which reason the argument necessarily fails.

> Moreover, even if the parties had deliberately agreed in advance upon a cut-off date that would have relieved appellant of any duty to submit the data that became available after June 1965, during the 14 months between the date of the bill of materials and the date of certification, such an agreement would have been unreasonable and in practical effect a waiver of the statute. In *M-R-S Manufacturing Co., supra,* the Court held that the duty of contractors to furnish the Government accurate, complete and current data is imposed by statute and cannot be waived by a Government agent. On the other hand, an advance agreement on a reasonable cut-off date to establish the availability of specific categories of data would not be a waiver of the statute, and, indeed, such agreements are now expressly provided for by ASPR 3-807.5 (a)(1).

E-Systems, ASBCA No. 17557, 74-2 BCA par. 10, 782; Affirmed on MFR 74-2 BCA par. 10, 943; Is a Contractor's Profit Plan Cost or Pricing Data?

The essence of the controversies is succinctly stated in the opening paragraph of the decision:

> This dispute involves a Government action to recover $445,684 because of claimed defects in the cost and pricing data submitted by the

appellant during the negotiation of a contract. The alleged defective data consists of a "profit plan" which admittedly was not provided to the Government by the appellant. It is the Government's position that the profit plan included information concerning future work which justified projecting substantially lower overhead rates than those accepted by the Government on the basis of other data provided by the appellant.

Based on DCAA audits and reviews by DCAS analysts and other members of the negotiating team, the government accepted the overhead rates proposed by the contractor, which were based on current experience. Some two years later, in a defective pricing review, DCAA learned that E-Systems had a profit plan in being at the date the contract was negotiated in February 1968. This profit plan, which was not disclosed to any of the government representatives, included overhead rates considerably lower than those proposed by the contractor and accepted by the government. After unsuccessful attempts to negotiate a reduction in the contract price, the contracting officer issued a final determination, finding "that the underlying data, included in the 1968 Profit Plan and upon which that document was based, constituted such factual matter as would 'reasonably be expected to contribute to sound estimates of future costs. . . .' "

There were several major facets to this controversy. In the words of the board, "[f]undamental to this dispute is a question of whether a 'profit plan' in itself is documentation that should be submitted . . . as part of . . . cost or pricing data." The decision indicates that the board obtained testimony on this subject and also performed its own research. The board ultimately concluded that profit plans differ and their relationship to cost or pricing data must be determined on a case-by-case basis. Because this conclusion is significant, we have excerpted the following portion from the decision so that the reader can study the specific language used by the board.

We conclude that the term "profit plan" includes a wide variety of fiscal projections that may serve various purposes. For example, many profit plans apparently are used by firms as budgets with profit projections. In contrast, other profit plans are apparently used by various corporations for the purpose of motivating personnel to achieve higher standards or goals. If a profit plan were to include higher than normal sales or lower than normal overhead rates, and personnel had their performance evaluated against such standards, presumably the personnel would strive to achieve higher sales and lower operating expenses.

In contrast, if a corporation desired to appear to have an outstanding management organization, it could intentionally establish low sales, high overhead rates, or similar features and at the end of a reporting period show that its dynamic management had far exceeded all of the projected goals.

Profit plans possess no magic formula and similar to other projections and statistical analysis, their accuracy is directly dependent upon the reliability of the data used and the skill and expertise of the personnel applying and interpreting it. Some profit plans may be very accurate and reliable and others may serve no useful purpose.

We find that profit plans, as a group, cannot reasonably be classified. Their relationship to cost or pricing data submitted by contractors in connection with the negotiation of a contract must be examined and evaluated on a case by case basis.

The board's review of the profit plan here involved, as used by the E-Systems subsidiary that was awarded the contract, resulted in a conclusion that the plan did not constitute cost or pricing data. Although the board pointed out deficiencies in the plan that made its reliability questionable, it took the further step of specifically adding the point that the profit plan was not cost or pricing data "under the implementation of Public Law 87-653 in effect at that time. . . ." The ruling was made further complex by the board's insistence that the government had the same information on future business as did the contractor. A summary of the board's conclusions regarding the profit plan is excerpted below.

1. The basic underlying firm data upon which the appellant's 1968 profit plan was based were known by the Government auditors and negotiators;

2. The appellant's profit plan included inaccuracies because it was not prepared in accordance with the appellant's normal accounting methods. Specifically, the profit plan did not indicate the high and low volume overhead rates or research and engineering charges;

3. The plan included an arbitrary addition of $3,000,000 of forecast future work;

4. The plan was prepared primarily for training purposes and was not used by the management as the basis for any significant management decisions;

5. The exact definition as to what constituted cost or pricing data, at the time of the preparation of the appellant's proposal and the negotiation of this contract, was unclear and the information provided by the appellant with regard to its overhead rates was essentially the same as that indicated in the example in DPC 55.

On the basis of the foregoing, it was concluded that, at the time this contract was negotiated, and under the implementation of Public Law 87-653 in effect at that time, the appellant's 1968 profit plan was not cost or pricing data and the failure of the appellant to furnish a copy of the plan to the negotiation team was not contrary to the requirements of P.L. 87-653 and the implementation of that statute.

In its motion for reconsideration, the government contended that the board had erred in a number of respects:

1. It failed to address the Government's ultimate claim which was based on the original profit plan and was described as reflecting business which was 90% firm at the date of contract negotiation.

2. It was mistaken in its assumption that the data underlying the 1968 profit plan were known by the Government auditors and negotiators.

3. It erred in concluding that the plan was unreliable for pricing purposes.

4. It erred in finding the ASPR definition of cost or pricing data as not sufficiently clear at date of contract negotiations to require submittal of the profit plan data.

5. It erred in concluding that the Government would not have negotiated the lower contract price had the profit plan been made available.

6. It ignored legal precedents to the effect that the contractor's duty to disclose cost or pricing data is imposed by statute and so cannot be waived.

The motion for reconsideration was not persuasive to the board in any respect. It reiterated that there was evidence that the government negotiation team was aware of the additional work, which would increase the contractor's operations and could reduce its overhead rates.

The motion for reconsideration stressed precedent rulings by the ASBCA and the Court of Claims that mere acceptance or availability does not constitute a valid submittal of cost data. The government accordingly argued that the contractor had a duty to either furnish the plan or inform the government as to the significance of the additional work. In support of its contention, the government referred to numerous rulings, placing particular reliance on *Sylvania Electric Products, Inc.,* ASBCA 13622, 70-2 BCA 8387, and *M-R-S Manufacturing Company v. United States,* 492 F.2d 835, February 20, 1974.

The cited cases (and there are others) clearly establish the contractor's responsibility for submitting cost data as contrasted with establishing that it was available. However, the board found that "these decisions are predicated on the basis that the government did not have actual knowledge of the data in question." To support its point, the board quoted from the aforementioned *MRS* decision: "This Court has stated that the purpose of the Truth in Negotiations Act was to avoid excessive contract cost that result from a contractor having in his possession accurate, complete and current information *when the Government does not possess* the same data." (Emphasis added.)

The board also reiterated the view expressed in its original decision that the government had sufficient information but did not use it. It continually stressed that the contractor must disclose relevant factual data, but only that "which was unknown to the government."

Muncie Gear Works, Inc., ASBCA No. 18184, 75-2 BCA par. 11, 380; Government Not Permitted to Sustain Defective Cost or Price Allegation When It Relied on Incomplete Data It Unilaterally Selected

In this dispute, some of the circumstances were unusual and complex, which made the decision somewhat difficult to follow. However, there are several important points here that make this decision worthy of review and analysis.

For one thing, the government accepted DD Forms 633, which were incomplete and one of which was not responsive to the request for the proposal. For another thing, according to the decision, the government auditor did not request the contractor to furnish data in support of its proposal. The proposal was based on standard labor costs, and the data requested by the government auditor led him to believe that Muncie's proposal was understated. He did not discuss this belief with the contractor or include it in his audit report to the contracting officer. The auditor's unilateral action was to prove fatal to the government's case.

In introducing its conclusions regarding the alleged defective labor data, the board referred to its decision in *Norris Industries:*

> In recent years the law with regard to the issues in this appeal has been analyzed, theorized and summarized. In *Norris Industries, Inc.,* ASBCA No. 15442, 74-1 BCA par. 10,482, we stated:
>
>> Under the Truth in Negotiations Act the Contractor is obliged to disclose all the facts necessary to place the Government in a position equal to that of the contractor with respect to making judgments on pricing. *Lockheed Aircraft Corporation v. United States,* ... (193 Ct.Cl. 86 (1970) *Levinson Steel Company,* ASBCA No. 16520, 73-2 BCA par. 10,116. This disclosure obligation is satisfied if the Government personnel who participated in the proposal evaluation or contract negotiations were clearly advised of the relevant cost or pricing data or, if they were not so advised, nevertheless had actual knowledge thereof. *McDonnell Douglas Corporation,* ASBCA No. 12786, 69-2 BCA par. 7897; *Sylvania Electric Products, Inc.,* ASBCA No. 13622, 70-2 BCA par. 8387. Where there is a dispute over whether this obligation was satisfied, as is the case here, the Government has the overall burden of persuading the deciding tribunal that it was not clearly advised of the relevant data and that it lacked knowledge of the cost or pricing data which it contends the contractor failed to disclose. *Sylvania Electric Products, Inc. v. United States* ... (Ct.Cl. No. 378-70), 479 F.2d 1342 (1973); *American Bosch Arma Corp.,* ASBCA No. 10305, 65-2 BCA par. 5280.
>
> *   *   *   *
>
>> ... [T]he natural and probable consequence of appellant's failure to disclose and more current cost data for paint solvent, etc. was an overstated contract price. *American Bosch Arma Corp., supra, Sylvania Electric Products Corp. v. United States, supra.* This presumption is subject to rebuttal, but appellant has the burden of persuading us that the more current cost data would have been of no consequence even if it had been disclosed. *Sylvania Electric Products Corp. v. United States, supra.* In some cases particularly persuasive evidence has indicated that indeed there would have been no reliance on more current or accurate cost or pricing data for the purpose of negotiating the contract price. Under such circumstances, the record did not adequately establish a causal relationship between the undisclosed data and an overstated contract price. *Luzon Stevedoring*

Corporation, ASBCA No. 14851, 71-1 BCA par. 8745; *Levinson Steel Company, supra . . . .*

Applying the principles set forth in these precedents, the board found that the "actual negotiations were not conducted on the basis of the claimed defective data . . . (and) this was not due to a failure to supply data but because of an independent judgment made by the government auditor without the knowledge of the appellant. In resolving the conflict without consulting appellant, the government assumed the risk of an erroneous judgment."

The board further concluded that, had the auditor been provided with more current data, he would have disregarded it as he had the data initially provided. The board also was of the opinion that, had the auditor discussed the matter with Muncie, the contractor would have provided an acceptable explanation. This portion of the decision was summed up: "If the Government is to recover it must rely on defective data provided by the appellant in support of its proposal. Here the Government relied only on the data it unilaterally selected. Therefore, it is not entitled to recover the labor price adjustment. . . ."

The Singer Co., Librascope Division, ASBCA No. 17604, 75-2 BCA par. 11, 401; aff'd on MFR 76-1 BCA par. 11,819; Contractor Assumes Heavy Burdens for Submission Requirements

The government's demand for price reduction because of defective cost or pricing data (not current) was upheld by the board even though Singer did submit such data in connection with actions other than the pricing proposal in dispute.

A brief explanation of the contractor's estimating system is essential to the understanding of the appeal and the decision. (As a digression, when reading descriptions of contractors' estimating and accounting systems in boards of appeals and court decisions, we often wonder about the incongruity between the unrestricted, open disclosure contained in such decisions and the great concern by contractors over the confidentiality of the same or similar information when presented in Disclosure Statements under regulations of the CAS Board.) Briefly, Singer estimated manufacturing labor by taking standard times for parts assembled or fabricated at its plant and adjusting them by the use of multipliers known as combined performance factors and support factors. Weighted factors included consideration of actual hours used in the machine, assembly, and circuit board shops as well as supervision, scrap, rework, etc. A weighted monthly performance factor, referred to as direct labor factors (DLF), was prepared for use in estimating. The report reflecting these factors, which is the center of this dispute, is also referred to throughout the decision as DLF.

The contractor's pricing proposal was submitted on October 27, 1967, and its documentation included DLF dated October 11, 1967, reflecting data compiled through the month of August 1967. Negotiations took place in April 1968, and the contractor's certification was dated May 3, both based on the October 11 DLF.

In August 1967, a new DCAA resident auditor performed an Estimating System Survey, became familiar with the contractor's procedures, and arranged to be placed on regular distribution for the DLFs beginning in November 1967. During his survey, the auditor did not relate the DLFs to the pricing proposal in dispute. He did plot the DLFs and, noting a downward trend, selected two specific proposals for postaward review against the current data. In the case of the proposal at issue, using updated DLFs, the auditor found and reported an overstatement of over 20,000 manufacturing hours.

Singer argued that the government was completely aware of its system, particularly the fact that, once a DLF was submitted with a proposal, it was not thereafter revised. This information, according to the contractor, was known not only to the DCAA auditor, but to the DCAS Administrative Contracting Officer (ACO), who received a copy of the latest available DLF with each of the contractor's proposals, estimated at 30 to 40 monthly. Thus, Singer contended that it had met its responsibility for submitting current data but that the government had elected not to use it. The contractor further asserted that it had a tacit agreement with the government that updating of the DLF was not required. The decision provided no details on the latter point except for the board's statement that it found no evidence of such agreement.

The contractor's arguments were unavailing as the board found that P.L. 87-653:

> ... with its implementing regulations, clearly places the onus of disclosure squarely on the contractor. *Conrac Corporation*, ASBCA No. 15964, 74-1 BCA par. 10,605, *Sylvania Electric Products, Inc. v. United States*, 202 Ct.Cl. 16 (1973). The Act makes no provision for waiver of the disclosure requirement by any Government agent. *M-R-S Manufacturing Co. v. United States*, Ct.Cl. 95-72, decided 20 February 1974. Consequently, appellant's argument that the Government was aware that its DLF data was not current, as it was not updated after it was submitted with the proposal, must fail. *Conrac Corporation, supra.* Appellant had the duty to update its data to the date of its certificate. See *Lambert Engineering Co.,* ASBCA No. 13338, 69-1 BCA par. 7663.

The board then specifically addressed Singer's arguments that current DLFs had, in fact, been submitted to government representatives and found unacceptable.

> The duty to disclose in this case was not satisfied by a general submission of more current data for an unrelated estimating system survey or by a submission of more current data on other and later proposals. We have held that it does not suffice merely to make available or physically hand over data for Government inspection which, if examined, would disclose differences between proposal costs and lower historical costs. It is also necessary to advise the Government representatives involved in the proposed procurement of the kind and content of the cost or pricing data and their bearing on the prospective contractor's proposal which examination of the files would disclose. *Sylvania Electric Products, Inc.,* ASBCA No. 13622, 70-2 BCA par. 8387. As it is necessary to advise the Government of the import of the data, it follows that the data must be clearly identified with the specific proposal to which the data in question relates. Appellant argues this case differs from the *Sylvania* cases, *supra,* since it had provided more recent data to the same

ACO who reviewed proposal BF.* We cannot agree as this more recent data was provided on other proposals, unrelated to BF, which came in at the rate of 30 to 40 a month. Further, the significance of the updated DLF was ultimately learned by a Government representative who did not review any of the labor portion of proposal BF.

* Designation used to refer to pricing proposal in controversy.

Hardie-Tynes Manufacturing Co., ASBCA No. 20717, 76-2 BCA par. 12,121; Nature of Cost or Pricing Data; Requirement to Disclose; Natural and Probable Consequence of Nondisclosure

This decision encompassed several basic aspects of disclosure requirements under P.L. 87-653 and the related Price Reduction for Defective Cost or Pricing Data contract clause. In each instance, the dispute involved proposed materal costs, a common occurrence in government allegations of defective pricing. DCAA performed a preaward audit and accepted the material costs as proposed except for minor amounts relating to errors in computation and vendor discounts not passed along to the government. The dispute here arose from a subsequent DCAA defective pricing audit and the contracting officer's acceptance of the auditor's revised recommendations.

The first issue involved the amount proposed for weldments, with Fab-Rite shown as the probable vendor. Prior to the solicitation, Hardie understood that the contract would call for 75 modification kits and so obtained a quotation from Fab-Rite for 75 weldments. However, the solicitation called for 33 kits for delivery in fiscal year 1971 and 42 additional kits in fiscal year 1973. Hardie solicited new, separate quotations for the 33 and 42 units. Fab-Rite's quotation specified the same prices for the 33 and 42 units as had been quoted earlier for the 75. In both cases the quotation specified that the prices were for acceptance within 30 days.

In its proposal, Hardie showed one amount for weldments modification kits. However, in its bill of materials, Hardie showed the costs for weldments for 33 units based on the Fab-Rite quotation, but indicated a 5% higher cost for the 42 units.

According to the decision, the board could not establish which Fab-Rite quotation the preaward auditors saw. In any case, the auditor did not object to the higher unit prices for 42 units as shown on the bill of materials, recommending only that the proposed cost be reduced to reflect the 1% discount offered by Fab-Rite.

Hardie explained its 5% increase as being based on its conviction that the prices quoted in April 1971 would not hold for deliveries in fiscal year 1973. It considered a 5% increase a reasonable prediction, and the wholesale price index actually increased about 5.7% between fiscal year 1971 and fiscal year 1973.

As it turned out, Hardie ultimately fabricated its own weldments. It testified that, as of the date of its proposal, it had no fabricating facilities and no employees experienced in fabricating weldments. Hardie had been discussing the possibility of fabricating its own weldments with the Navy for some years to avoid untimely deliveries and other problems with weldment manufacturers. Hardie received the contract in June 1971 and decided to fabricate its own weldments in October of the same year.

As a result of the defective pricing audit, DCAA recommended a price reduction based on Hardie's failure to disclose the second Fab-Rite quotation to the preaward auditor. DCAA thought that the 5% escalation by Hardie was improper inasmuch as FabRite had not changed its price. The auditor found nothing to either substantiate or refute Hardie's contention that the decision to make the weldments was not arrived at until after contract negotiations were completed.

On this issue, the board found for the contractor, deciding that the 5% escalation was reasonable and that "even if (Hardie) failed in its obligation to disclose the second Fab-Rite quotation, we conclude that the agreed price for the weldments would not have been less if that quotation had been known to the auditor."

The second issue in this appeal involved the purchase of gears and pinions. The proposal was based on a quotation from Brad Foote Gear Works (Brad). The lowest quote was from Cincinnati Gear Company (Cincinnati), but Hardie did not use it in the proposal because of substantial doubts as to Cincinnati's ability to make the parts. After further discussions between Hardie and Cincinnati, the contractor concluded Cincinnati could make the parts successfully and gave it the order.

The defective pricing auditor concluded that Hardie had not disclosed the Cincinnati quote to the government and recommended a price reduction accordingly. He testified that it was DCAA policy to note a contractor's justification for not using a low quote in the notes of the preaward audit and that the absence of such notation was the basis for his conclusion as to the nondisclosure. The preaward auditor testified that he could not recall whether he had seen the Cincinnati quote, but said he would have made the appropriate notation if he had seen it. Hardie's president testified that the Cincinnati quote should have been in a separate folder on gears and pinions, which was furnished to the preaward auditor.

The board found "on the basis of the entire record" (no further explanation furnished) that the Cincinnati quote was in the folder furnished to the auditor and concluded that Hardie had "adequately submitted that quotation to the auditor."

The board stated further:

> The Cincinnati Gear quote was not "hidden in a mass of information," but was in folder containing only two other quotes and three replies indicating "no quote." See *Plessey Industries, Inc.*, ASBCA No. 16720, 74-1 BCA par. 10,603.

> The absence of a notation on the pre-award auditor's work sheet as to why the Cincinnati Gear quote was not being used could indicate a failure of the auditor to realize that the quote was low or a failure in this instance to follow the prescribed policy of making such notations. In any event, the absence of a notation is not conclusive evidence of a nondisclosure. See *American Machine & Foundry Company, supra.*

Under these particular circumstances, we do not believe appellant was obligated to "lead the auditor by the hand" by pointing out to him that the Cincinnati Gear quote was low but was not being used for the reasons indicated. See *American Machine & Foundry Company, supra.*

The third issue, also relating to disclosure, involved bushings. These were not major cost items and Hardie did not solicit quotes, both for that reason and because "its design . . . was not sufficiently firm to ask vendors to quote thereon." The unit costs used in the proposal were $10 and $25 and were described as a " 'top of the head' guess by appellant's purchasing agent." Hardie furnished no data in support of its proposal for bushings, and the preaward auditor did not include this item in his spot check of the less significant components.

During the defective pricing audit, the DCAA auditor found that Hardie had purchased 888 similar bushings on five different prior occasions during the period 1966—1968. He applied an escalation factor in recognition of the three-year period since the last purchase to arrive at a unit cost of $3.47. The difference between this and the $10 and $25 proposed was recommended for a downward price adjustment. The unit cost computed by the auditor was close to the actual amount paid by Hardie based on a subsequent quote from the same vendor from whom he had purchased bushings in the 1966—68 period.

Hardie's rebuttal included the assertion that the bushings required for this contract had different engineering details and were not similar to those previously purchased. The contractor further contended "that the figures used in the proposal obviously were pure estimates and thus not cost or pricing data, and that, in any event, the prior bushing purchases cannot be considered cost or pricing data because those purchases were 'too minimal to constitute a basis for violation of pricing data requirements.' "

The issue here and the related background are not uncommon. They are quite important, and, with this in mind, we have quoted a substantial portion of the ruling in this area:

We have held previously that the test of whether an offeror has complied with its obligations to make disclosure is an objective one. See *Hardie-Tynes Manufacturing Company,* ASBCA Nos. 20367 and 20387, 76-1 BCA par. 11,827. Thus, even if appellant's purchasing agent did not consider the prior purchases of bushings in arriving at his "guess" as to what bushings for this contract would cost, we must decide whether a prudent offeror should have considered those purchases and based the proposal prices thereon.

Appellant was free to estimate the cost of bushings in preparing its proposal. However, it was obliged to make available to the government all facts which reasonably could be expected "to have a significant effect on the price negotiations." The government was entitled to such information so it could independently determine the reasonableness of appellant's estimates. See *Aerojet-General Corporation,* ASBCA No. 16988, 73-2 BCA par. 10,242. Although pure estimates are not "cost and pricing data" the facts reasonably relating thereto most assuredly are. See *E-Systems, Inc.,* ASBCA No. 17557, (on mot. for recon.), 74-2 BCA par. 10,943.

We are persuaded that, in the absence of more relevant data, the prior purchases of bushings should have been considered by appellant in arriving at its estimated costs and made available to the pre-award auditor. Although the previously-purchased bushings were not identical to the bushings being designed for this contract, the degree of dissimilarity has not been shown. In any event, the prices paid for them were the best evidence available as to what the new bushings would cost. The previous prices certainly were a sound basis for projecting bushing costs, and should not reasonably have been ignored by appellant.

Therefore, we hold that appellant breached its duty to disclose accurate, complete and current cost and pricing data. Accordingly, appellant has the burden of showing that the information would have been of no consequence even if it had been disclosed. *Sylvania Electric Products Corp. v. U.S.* (18 CCF par. 82,334), 202 Ct.Cl. 16(1973).

The likelihood is that the pre-award auditor would have questioned the great disparity between the proposed costs for bushings and the prices paid previously if those prior purchases had been brought to his attention. With those figures before him, he surely would have included bushings in his spot check. Appellant has not shown otherwise. Although bushings were not a "major" item, the difference between previous costs and the "estimated" costs was a "significant sum" within the meaning of the statute and contract clause. See *Hardie-Tynes Manufacturing Company, supra; Sylvania Electric Products, Inc.,* ASBCA No. 13622, 70-2 BCA par. 8387.

The price used by the defective pricing auditor is reasonable, as confirmed by the price actually paid under the contract by appellant. We reject appellant's contention that the previous purchases were "minimal" as clearly without merit. The total quantities purchased previously substantially exceeded the quantity required for this contract, and 5 separate purchases were made.

The fourth issue was Hardie's proposal for the cost of bimetallic thermometers, quoted in the proposal at $24.48 and $21.76 for two types required. The basis for these amounts was described as an oral estimate from Weston. The preaward auditor's work sheet noted that the proposed price was based on a Weston quote (apparently in reliance on advice from Hardie's purchasing agent) and that a lower quote from another firm was not being used because the thermometers did not meet the specifications.

The auditor performing the defective pricing audit "was unable to determine the basis for (Hardie's) prices for bimetallic thermometers since he did not find any written quotations predating price negotiations." He did find prior purchases of this component from American Standard at $8.90 per unit in 1968. Applying an escalation factor, the auditor computed a cost of $9.70 and considered the differences between that and the amounts shown in the proposal as an overstatement warranting a price reduction for defective pricing. Actually, Hardie had ultimately purchased the thermometers from a Weksler Instrument Corp. at a unit price of $8.51. The board found that Hardie had never heard of Weksler until that firm was mentioned as a possible source by Navy people sometime after the contract award.

Although Hardie had not disclosed the prior American Standard experience to the government, its officials believed it not necessary because it had had previous unsatisfactory experience with that vendor. Further, American informally advised Hardie that it no longer manufactured those thermometers, but would specially fabricate them if desired at $100 per unit.

The board ruled for Hardie on the following reasoning:

> Under the circumstances, appellant made a reasonable attempt to determine a realistic price for these small dollar volume items, and reasonably ignored the prior purchases from American Standard as not a viable indication of what the thermometers would cost. In light of the contemporaneous, if informal response from American Standard that it would charge $100 each for the thermometers, appellant justifiably regarded the procurement history from American Standard as a dead letter. That history no longer constituted cost or pricing data. The cost estimates from Weston were the best current information appellant had as to what the thermometers would cost.

> Accordingly, the Government has failed to show a failure by appellant to disclose cost or pricing data relating to bimetallic thermometers.

The final issue was a valve for which Hardie proposed a unit price of $37.82, based on a telephonic quotation by Air and Hydraulic Engineering for a stainless steel valve. After the conclusion of the preaward audit but prior to the date the Certificate of Current Cost or Pricing Data was signed, Air submitted separate written quotations for brass and stainless steel valves, the former at a unit price of $16.50. This information was not disclosed to the government, and Hardie ultimately purchased the brass valves from Air for $16.50.

On the defective pricing audit, the auditor recommended a price reduction for the difference. Hardie argued that, at the time Air's written proposal was received, it was not definite which valve would be used. As a matter of fact, it was reasonable to assume that it would be the stainless steel one since it was for a stainless steel connection. Finally, Hardie asserted that the decision to use the brass valve was not made until August 1971; however, this assertion was unsupported.

In this instance, the board found for the government:

> The duty of disclosure of material quotations has been held to extend not only to quotes a contractor knows he will use but also to quotes he may use. *Cutler-Hammer, Inc. v. U.S., supra.* The record indicates that, as of the date of appellant's certification of cost and pricing data on 2 June 1971, use of the brass valve was a definite possibility. Therefore, appellant was under a duty to inform the Government of the quotation on the brass valve and that it might obtain a lower price for the valves by ordering brass rather than stainless steel valves. *Cutler-Hammer, Inc. v. U.S., supra.*

> We conclude that appellant failed to disclose current cost and pricing data on the valves to the Government. Accordingly, appellant has the burden of showing that the quote on the brass valve would have been

of no consequence even if it had been disclosed. *Sylvania Electric Products v. U.S., supra.* No such showing has been made by appellant.

Summary

Although this appeal did not entail substantial sums of money, the board devoted considerable time, effort, and space to the decision, and we did likewise in our analysis. The reason for this attention is the significance and pervasiveness of the principles involved. Of the five issues, the board ruled favorably for Hardie on three.

The issue on weldments has two aspects. As we read the decision, it seems evident that Hardie had not disclosed its addition of a 5% increase over the vendor's quotation as an estimate of the probable price increase in the future period. However, the board said that it was persuaded "that the escalation action was reasonable and would have been accepted by the auditor." Quoting the board again: "even if appellant failed in its obligation to disclose . . . we conclude that the agreed price for the weldments would not have been less if the quotation had been known to the auditor." The second aspect relating to weldments was the board's finding that the in-house fabrication of weldments was not a definite possibility as of the date of the certification of cost and pricing data.

In the case of the gears and pinions, unfortunately the decision does not provide sufficient detail to establish precisely how the board became convinced that the folder containing the Cincinnati quotation was furnished to the auditor. However, having arrived at this conclusion, the board used a term that might be well remembered for use where appropriate: "we do not believe appellant was obligated to 'lead the auditor by the hand' . . . ." This is an important point especially in light of the many other decisions where the board had found that, while the contractor had made available certain data to the government, he had not actually submitted it.

The board also found for Hardie with respect to the dispute over the thermometers. Here, based on the information available in the written decision, it would seem obvious that American Standard's letter referring to the $100 per unit charge was, as the board described it, a "dead letter."

The board ruled against Hardie in the case of the bushings. The basic point here is that, while a contractor is free to use estimates in its proposal, it is "obliged to make available to the government all facts which reasonably could be expected 'to have a significant effect on the price negotiations.' " The board saw the information on prior bushings purchases as that kind of fact and then established that Hardie had "the burden of showing that the information would have been of no consequence even if it had been disclosed." The board concluded that Hardie had not successfully carried such burden.

The final issue centered on valves and was also resolved adversely to the contractor. The board said that "the duty of disclosure of material quotations has been held to extend not only to quotes a contractor knows he will use but also to quotes he may use," and found that the use of brass valves was a definite possibility at the date of Hardie's certification. It concluded that Hardie had failed to disclose current data (brass valve quotes) and could not demonstrate that such disclosure "would have been of no consequence even if it had been disclosed."

Baldwin Electronics, Inc., ASBCA No. 19683, 76-2 BCA par. 12,199; Offsets

This dispute involved several issues but we have elected to limit our review to the contractor's successful claim that offsets, represented by understatements, exceeded the government's claims for price reduction. As a result, the board concluded that "the Government's dollar recovery is nullified."

The major and most interesting aspect of the contractor's offset claim involved an amount of almost $160,000 "for erroneously computing and forecasting the G&A rate" for the contract in contention.

In July 1968, Baldwin received a partial termination notice for a concurrent contract to be effective January 1969. Although the partial termination removed some 40% of the projected sales base used by Baldwin in computing the G&A rate for the price proposal under discussion, the contractor's proposal in October 1968 failed to exclude the effect of the termination from the sales base. A recomputation based on the exclusion of the terminated portion of the contract would have increased the G&A rate from 12% to 18%. This error resulted in underpricing the contract by some $160,000.

The government contested the proposed offset on the grounds that the G&A forecast was "a judgmental estimate and not within the accepted definition of cost or pricing set forth in ASPR 3-807.3(h)." We found the government's argument curious. We are persuaded that if the contractor had failed to include additional business that it knew it was going to get in January 1969 from the base for allocating G&A expenses, the government would not have thought in terms of a "judgmental estimate." The board was of a similar view: "We think the Government has failed to distinguish fact from judgment .... The loss of this business was a fact not an estimate. The estimate of future business may not be cost or pricing data but factual datum in the estimate is. See: Appeal of *E-Systems, Inc.*, Appeal No. 17557, 74-2 BCA par. 10,782."

Conrac Corp. v. U.S., 23 CCF par. 81,510, Ct.Cl. No. 368-74 (1977); Impact of Nondisclosure; Submission v. Making Available; Time When Cost or Pricing Data Were Reasonably Available to the Contractor

Earlier in this chapter we discussed the results of Conrac's appeal in ASBCA No. 15964, 74-1 BCA par. 10,605. While agreeing with the government that the contract was overpriced because of defective data, the board reduced the amount of the refund due the government from the price reduction asserted by the contracting officer.

The trial judge recommended reversal of the board's finding, concluding that Conrac owed nothing to the government because its disclosure had been adequate and, independently, because the sum determined by the board was too small to be made the subject of a mandatory refund under the Act and the contract. The court, however, rejected the view of its trial judge and sustained the ruling of the ASBCA.

In its appeal before the Court of Claims, Conrac again cited the *Lockheed* decision, 15 CCF par. 84,015, 193 Ct.Cls. 86, 432 F.2d 801 (1970), and argued that the Act's disclosure requirements are not met by the furnishing of data in undigested form, meaning the purchase history cards rather than an updated bill of materials. But the court saw a major difference in the circumstances here as compared to *Lockheed,* where raw purchase history data in a Kardex file was furnished to government negotiators. In that case, the Court of Claims held "that such disclosure was not sufficient to inform the negotiators of the component prices, and thus inadequate to comply with the Act's strictures. It is clear from the opinion that the Kardex file presented information to the negotiators that was, in the court's view, so difficult to isolate and understand as to be, in essence, worthless."

In contrast, in the *Conrac* appeal, the court accepted the ASBCA's "presumptively correct fact-finding and its expertise in dealing with such matters" when it concluded that, had Conrac disclosed the purchase history cards, the government would have at least evaluated the high dollar items and would have considered the overstatements and taken them into consideration in the negotiations.

Responding further to Conrac's arguments, the court drew a careful line between these circumstances and those at Lockheed, and its commentary on a contractor's duty to disclose information under the Act is significant:

> The second answer to plaintiff's relevance contention is that the *Lockheed* decision does not absolve a contractor from disclosure of whatever information he possesses, simply because there is not sufficient time, as in this case, to create a formal, updated BOM. Lockheed pronounced the data submission in that case inadequate in view of the fact that there had been time to assemble the component price information in a more readily usable form than the Kardex file, though the contractor did not do so. Such time, it is true, was not present in *Lockheed* before the pre-contract auditors reviewed the contractor's cost data, but it did exist thereafter, and it is evident from the court's thinking that a BOM compilation during the time that was available would have been useful in finalizing the pricing arrangements.

> Where, however, there was not time enough to prepare a BOM, in light of the urgency of the procurement, Lockheed does not say that less accessible but nonetheless useful price information need not be disclosed. To say otherwise would be to eliminate the Act effectively from operation precisely when it is needed the most, when information is difficult to come by. The rule in *Lockheed* is that the best price data must be furnished, not that data in less than prime form, because of time or other constraints, may handily be hidden from the Government. *Lockheed* thus cannot be relied on in this case to relieve the contractor from a duty to disclose the information on its purchase history cards simply because there was insufficient time to assemble that information in BOM form.

Conrac Corp., ASBCA No. 19507, 78-1 BCA par. 12,985; Impact of Defective Data on Negotiated Price

In another Conrac dispute relating to P.L. 87-653, the company's appeal was sustained. The dispute was complicated by the fact that six years had passed since the contract negotiations, and the memories of the participants were not very sharp any more. In any case, there appeared to be no question but that the data presented by the contractor for the negotiations were not accurate. Conrac's position, however, was "that the data in its proposals were updated in the negotiations and the Government negotiator was specifically informed . . . ." Conrac further argued that updated data were confirmed in its letter forwarding its Certificate of Current Cost or Pricing Data.

Directing itself to the essence of the dispute, the board said: "Under the Act the contractor has a duty to disclose completely cost and pricing information, but in the case of a dispute over whether this obligation was satisfied, the Government has the overall burden of persuasion that it was not clearly advised of the relevant data and lacked knowledge of the claimed undisclosed cost or pricing data."

Moving further, the board made these cogent comments:

Even if we were to assume that the Government has satisfied its burden with respect to nondisclosure, there still must be a finding that the contract price was overstated as a result of appellant's failure to disclose the data in question. As a matter of law, once nondisclosure of data has been proved, it would be the natural and probable consequence that such nondisclosure would result in an overstated negotiated contract price. At this point the burden of persuasion falls upon the contractor to show nonreliance on behalf of the Government on the inaccurate or incomplete data in order to rebut the natural and probable consequences of nondisclosure. *Sylvania Electric Products, Inc. v. U.S.* (18 CCF par. 82,334), 202 Ct.Cl. 16, 27-28 (1973). The ultimate burden of showing the causal connection between the incomplete or inaccurate data and an overstated contract price remains however with the Government. In our opinion the Government in the instant case has not met this burden.

Without pursuing the details of the arguments, the board noted that the aforementioned letter forwarding the certificate should have prompted the government negotiator to make an inquiry. The fact that he filed the letter "without making inquiry would support an inference that the continued availability of combined material purchases was not new information to him or was no longer regarded as significant . . . ." In sustaining Conrac's appeal, the board concluded:

We are unable to conclude that, had the same information been brought to his attention during negotiations, it would have had any practical effect on the negotiated price of $42,000 per unit. *American Machine & Foundry Company*, ASBCA No. 15037, 74-1 BCA par. 10,409; *Hardie-Tynes Mfg. Co.*, ASBCA No. 20717, 76-2 BCA par. 12,121.

*   *   *   *

In our opinion these circumstances are sufficient to rebut the presumption of the natural and probable consequences of the alleged nondisclosure. Since no evidence was adduced to overcome this rebuttal, we conclude that respondent failed to carry its ultimate burden of showing that the contract price was overstated because of appellant's failure to correct inaccurate data. *The Levinson Steel Co.,* ASBCA No. 16520, 73-2 BCA par. 10,116. Hence, there is no basis for reducing the contract price on account of the savings the contractor may have realized by combining the material purchases for the ASO and Grumman orders.

The Singer Company, Librascope Division v. U.S., 24 CCF par. 81,695, Ct.Cls. 257-76, 576 F.2d 905 (1978); Requirements and Criteria for Disclosure of Cost or Pricing Data

The government asserted that the contract price should be reduced because Singer had failed to adequately disclose current cost or pricing data. As we have discussed earlier in this chapter, Singer had appealed the contracting officer's decision and the appeal was denied by the ASBCA, with the board affirming its denial on Singer's motion for reconsideration. The data involved in this dispute concerned Singer's Direct Labor Factor Report, referred to hereinafter as DLF.

There seemed to be no question but that current DLF reports were available to government personnel resident at the Singer plant, but the labor data current as of the date of the certificate were not made available to the PCO who negotiated the contract.

The controversy was joined when a newly assigned DCAA auditor, as a result of performing an estimating system survey, became aware that there had been downward labor trends but that Singer had a practice of not updating the DLF. In a subsequent defective pricing audit report, the DCAA auditor stated that the contractor knew but did not disclose that the labor costs at the time the certificate was signed were lower and that the trend indicated further reduction. The DCAA auditor testified that this information came to his attention only after the conclusion of the price negotiations. Although both the ACO and the DCAS price analyst were aware of the DLFs, they apparently made no review or analysis that would have warned them of the downward trend.

The court ruled that Singer was required to "physically deliver the information to the Government and make the information's significance to the negotiation process known. *M-R-S Manufacturing Co. v. U.S.,* 492 F.2d 835, 203 Ct.Cls. 551 (1974). Under the facts of this case, it is concluded that the plaintiff could have accomplished appropriate disclosure by disclosing to any one of the four Government employees involved."

Singer argued that, when the three government employees at the plant were given the later-developed DLF, they became aware or should have become aware of the significance of the downward trend in DLFs and therefore it was unnecessary to point out the significance to them. With respect to the DCAA auditor, Singer noted that he had become aware of the significance of the DLF and it was therefore incumbent upon him to relate the significance to the proposal at issue. The court did not see it this way: "But that is not what the law quoted above directs. Furthermore, it shifts the affirmative duty of disclosure from the plaintiff to the Government."

The court found that the information concerning the DLFs was submitted to the government people "in another context, for another purpose unconnected with the BF proposal negotiation, without an explanatory word from the plaintiff." In the words of the trial judge, adopted by the court:

> I therefore agree with the defendant's contention that mere submission of DLFs to these gentlemen in these contexts was not enough to substitute disclosure of the facts in this case. In the light of their relative isolation from the contract negotiations and preoccupation with other tasks, plaintiff could not reasonably expect these gentlemen to independently identify and transmit the pricing data to (the PCO and negotiator). The affirmative duty to disclose the appropriate information remained with the plaintiff.

UNIVERSAL RESTORATION, INC.—AN ADVENTURE IN DEFECTIVE PRICING

The vagaries of the Truth in Negotiations Act and the judicial process after numerous decisions extending over many years were illustrated in the strange story of Universal Restoration, Inc. The chronology of the litigation is summarized below:

ASBCA No. 22833, 82-1 BCA par. 15,762, April 9, 1982. In a 3-2 decision, the board ruled that Universal had submitted defective data but the government could not assert a price reduction, because it had not relied on such data.

ASBCA No. 22833, 83-1 BCA par. 16,265, February 2, 1983. The government filed a motion for reconsideration and the board reversed its original ruling, finding for the government 3-2. One of the judges who had originally voted with the majority for Universal had resigned in the meantime and the administrative judge appointed to the panel in his place voted in favor of the government. The other four judges did not modify their original positions.

ASBCA No. 22833, 84-1 BCA par. 16,918, October 7, 1983. Universal moved to vacate the decision on the motion for reconsideration as arbitrary and capricious, noting that no new facts had been presented and the reversal of the original decision was attributable solely to the change in the composition of the panel. Universal's motion was denied, with the board defending its procedural practices and not addressing the substantive issues of the dispute.

Universal Restoration, Inc. v. U.S., Cl.Ct. 77-84C [32 CCF par. 73,704], August 9, 1985. The court upheld the board's decision in favor of the government, ruling that the contractor had not supported his contention that the government did not rely on the defective data.

Universal Restoration, Inc. v. U.S., CA FC No. 85-2662 [33 CCF par. 74,555], August 22, 1986. The U.S. Court of Appeals for the Federal Circuit reversed the lower court and ruled for Universal, finding that the initial board decision had properly stated the facts and conclusions and there was no basis for any ruling inconsistent therewith.

The contract involved the repair and restoration of the ceiling and clerestory vaults of the National War College, a National landmark at Fort McNair, Washington, D.C., and generated considerable publicity in the news media when the initial contract amount of $65,000 increased to over $1 million. This publicity was a factor in the performance of six audits by the government, of which four related to cost and pricing data and overhead expense.

Universal was initially awarded the $65,000 contract on a time and materials basis, predicated on the company's proposal, which was deemed fair and reasonable when compared with the government's own estimate. The contracting officer also concluded that Universal was the only source available to do this work and accepted the offer, which included an overhead rate of 115% and profit of 10% based upon direct labor costs. The decision states that these percentages represented "standard company add-ons and the appellant, as a matter of company policy, would accept nothing less than its established markups on any of its contracts."

Between the date the contract was signed in May 1974 and the last modification in March 1975, all of the changes for enlarging the scope or providing for additional work reflected the 115% overhead rate on estimated direct labor. Three different contracting officers were assigned successive responsibility for this contract and each one, in each instance, apparently found the overhead rate to be reasonable. The decision states that the contracting officers' decisions were approved by the Board of Awards. It was also determined, as the work progressed, "that it would be impracticable to allow another contractor to perform any of the contract work."

One of the DCAA postaward audits found that as the scope of the work under the contract increased, the overhead rate had decreased and that Universal's continuing submission of 115% rates constituted defective data. The contracting officer concurred and issued a unilateral decision demanding price reduction; the contractor appealed.

In the original decision, the board agreed that the 115% overhead rate submitted constituted defective data, and this conclusion was concurred in throughout the lengthy litigation process.

Having established nondisclosure, the board said, "... it would be the natural and probable consequence that an overstated contract price had resulted." The second, and in this case vital, question was whether the government had relied on the defective data. Here the board reasoned: "The burden of persuasion is with the appellant to establish nonreliance on the part of the Government on the inaccurate data in order to rebut the natural and probable consequences of the nondisclosure. *Sylvania Electric Products, Inc., v. United States,* 202 Ct.Cl. 16, 27-28 (1973), 479 F.2d 1342. The ultimate burden of showing the causal connection between the inaccurate data and an overstated contract price, however, remains with the Government. In our opinion the Government has not satisfied this burden."

The board further cited precedents establishing exceptions to the principle that the natural and probable consequence of nondisclosure is an overstated contract price:

> The exception to this principle (evidence to the contrary) has been applied to situations where the Government, by exhibiting a complete disinterest in the contractor's cost proposal, evidenced an independent price analysis based upon prevailing market conditions. *Luzon Stevedor-*

ing Corporation, ASBCA No. 14851, 71-1 BCA par 8745. The exception also has been applied to situations where it was reasonable to assume that because of contractor's superior bargaining position the Government had no alternative but to accept a contractor's stated price. *American Machine & Foundry Company,* ASBCA No. 15037, 74-1 BCA par 10,409.

Thus, to establish a basis for price reduction, (a) the data must have been defective and (b) the government must have relied upon it in negotiating the price. Here, the board found this reliance was lacking:

> Inasmuch as the record presented establishes that each contract pricing action was determined to be fair and reasonable independent of any negotiation or discussion with the appellant, we find that the contracting officers involved did not rely on the appellant's pricing data and thus were not misled by the appellant's failure to disclose its actual overhead rate.

The board traced the history of the several contract modifications and concluded that the three contracting officers involved had never questioned or challenged the price proposals, which contained the same 115% overhead rate identified as the contractor's established add-on or markup. It accordingly assumed that the proposals were accepted either because they were justified by independent government estimates or because of the "appellant's superior bargaining position due to its unique and sole source status." The board concluded:

> We are unable to conclude from the record before us that even if the fact of the appellant's declining overhead had been brought to the contracting officer's attention it would have had any practical effect on the price of any one of the contract modifications. The record establishes that the appellant would accept nothing less than its stated overhead rate leaving the Government to take it or leave it. There is no question in our mind but that the Government would have taken it in view of its obvious and proven reluctance to question any of the appellant's several price proposals.

> In our opinion, these circumstances are sufficient to rebut the presumption of the natural and probable consequence of the nondisclosure. Inasmuch as no evidence was presented to overcome this rebuttal, we are unable to find that the Government satisfied its ultimate burden of establishing that the contract price was overstated because of the appellant's failure to reveal its actual as opposed to its policy overhead. Hence, there is no basis for reducing the contract price because of the variance between the appellant's actual as opposed to its established policy overhead. cf. *CONRAC Corporation,* ASBCA No. 19507, 78-1 BCA ¶ 12,985 . . . .

The two dissenting judges believed that the cases cited by the majority were distinguishable, but neither appeared to directly address the contractor's stated position that he would not have accepted anything less than the standard 115% "add-on" for overhead.

In its motion for reconsideration, the government specifically objected to several findings of the board, particularly:

23. Each of the three contracting officers assigned to this contract appeared as Government witnesses at the hearing of this appeal. None of them testified that if they had known of the appellant's actual overhead they would have refused to accept the appellant's various price proposals.

24. Inasmuch as the record presented established that each contract pricing action was determined to be fair and reasonable independent of any negotiation or discussion with the appellant, we find that the contracting officers involved did not rely on the appellant's pricing data and thus were not misled by the appellant's failure to disclose its actual overhead rate.

On reconsideration, the board agreed with the government and found the findings cited above misleading or in error. We do not wish to detract from efforts of the government counsel, yet it would be difficult indeed to suggest that it was their presentation of the case that caused the sharp reversal. Rather, the two judges who dissented from the original decision now found themselves in the majority. Indeed, the judge who wrote the major dissenting opinion in the original decision now wrote the majority opinion in the motion for reconsideration. The essence of the reversal is cited below:

> On reconsideration, we find the last sentence of finding 23 misleading without a further finding that: "Neither did they testify that they would have accepted appellant's proposed prices even if the current overhead rate had been disclosed." We reject the argument that lack of testimony by the contracting officers as to what they would have done had proper disclosure been made requires the conclusion that the agreed price was unaffected by the nondisclosure. There is a legal presumption that the nondisclosure did affect the price. *American Bosch Arma Corporation*, ASBCA No. 10305, 65-2 BCA ¶ 5280. Government counsel was not required to elicit testimony to the same effect to establish the Government's *prima facie* case. It was incumbent on appellant to rebut the presumption. *Sylvania Electric Products, Inc. v. United States* [18 CCF ¶ 82,334], 202 Ct.Cl. 16, 27-28, 479 F.2d 1342, 1349 (1973). If the contracting officers had testified that they would have agreed to the same price even if the current overhead rate had been disclosed, then the presumption would have been rebutted. But appellant's counsel did not elicit such testimony from them.

> We also find error in our finding 24. The absence of price discussions does not support a finding of nonreliance by the contracting officer on the disclosed costs. Since those costs supported the proposed prices, the contracting officers had no reason to discuss or negotiate those prices. Neither do the contracting officers' determinations that the prices were fair and reasonable support the conclusion that they would have agreed to those prices regardless of appellant's actual costs. Moreover, there is no exception in the Truth in Negotiations Act for fair and reasonable prices.

We now address the views of the dissenting minority, the two judges who were part of the majority in the original decision. Rejecting the government's argument that the finding that the contractor had failed to discharge its duty of disclosure renders irrelevant the board's finding of fact 23, the dissenting view reiterates that "the Government has the ultimate burden of showing the causal connection between the inaccurate data and an alleged overstated contract price."

As to finding of fact 24, the dissenting opinion noted that Universal's financial vice president testified that the company's overhead rate was based not on calculations but rather on company policy and that he would not negotiate less than the policy rate. The point is emphasized that this testimony was unrebutted. The dissenting opinion further states:

> The fact that appellant continued to submit its historical company policy rate for each of the contract modifications as opposed to its monthly overhead calculations is not per se a basis for recovery. Appellant's overhead rate reduction resulted from the broadened base of labor hours needed to perform the effort added by the contract modifications. The impact of these additional labor hours on appellant's overhead rates was a natural and predictable occurrence. The contracting officer, under the facts of this appeal, including the size and nature of appellant's business, either knew or should have known that appellant's rates would be decreasing. The contracting officers ignored this obvious fluctuation and instead for each and every modification chose to rely on prices it found to be fair and reasonable based on independent pricing.

> Having found no evidence that the withholding of the monthly estimates increased the negotiated contract price our decision of 9 April 1982 should be affirmed.

The judges holding for Universal appeared to take a less extreme position with regard to the contractor's need to prove the government was aware of the defective data. In the circumstances surrounding Universal, they found it must or should have been obvious to the contracting officers that a small contractor with a $65,000 time and material contract increasing to well over $1 million within a short period, with overhead computed as a percentage of direct labor, would experience a reduction in its overhead rate. Finding that this knowledge was available to the contracting officers, the judges holding for the contractor said in the original decision:

> ... Since both the expanding labor base and charged overhead rate were known to the contracting officer, we consider this to be further evidence that the contracting officer could care less what the appellant was charging. Since such knowledge is at least chargeable to the contracting officer, he or she was in parity so far as negotiation was concerned if that official had done his or her duty.

In its motion to vacate the decision on the MFR, Universal argued that such decision "was not based on any new evidence or new point of law, but on a reconsideration of previously submitted evidence ..." The contractor further contended that the participation of the new judge in the second decision "was improper because, in the absence of new evidence or new argument or a change of mind by one of the judges participating in the original decision, the change in result occurred solely because of the change in personnel, was unrelated to the merits of the case, and was therefore arbitrary and capricious."

Although these points appear persuasive, particularly to a layman, the board denied the motion to vacate, asserting it had followed its established administrative procedures and perceived "no unfairness or impropriety" in its actions.

In the hearings and briefs before the Claims Court, both sides cited case law in which, in other judicial forums, court members who did not participate in previous decisions by a court could or could not participate in any reconsideration of the previous decision. Although Universal argued that "[i]t . . . [was] gross procedural error to permit a new division member to take part in the decision on reconsideration and operate as a 'swing vote' or a 'tie-breaker' " and that this "converted the process of rational decision-making into a gambling transaction dependent on the vagaries of personnel changes," the Claims Court was more impressed by the arguments on the other side. It cited instances where courts ruled that parties to litigation "have no right, constitutional or otherwise, to a decision by any particular judge or group of judges." In ruling against Universal, the court also noted that the ASBCA action was in consonance with its established procedure.

As to the substantive issues relating to price reduction for defective pricing, Universal offered a number of arguments but all of them were rejected by the court. The most consequential, it seems to us, related to whether the contractor had met the burden of rebutting the presumption that the natural and probable consequence of submitting defective cost or pricing data is an overstated contract price.

This issue had been similarly identified by the ASBCA, which, in its original decision, had found that the contractor indeed met this burden, but reversed itself with a new judge in the MFR and concluded that Universal had failed to meet this burden. It is a most crucial issue, for ample case law supports the position that the government cannot assert a reduction in a contract price for defective data when it did not rely on such data. Here the question seemed one of fact rather than law and, as we read the ASBCA decisions and the court ruling, it appeared to us that the contracting officers' failures to question or ask for contemporaneous audits of the overhead rates, and the contractor's contention that it would not accept a price for a contract or modification without its standard markup, strongly suggest that the government did not rely on the original cost or pricing data.

However, the court found in its view of the administrative record that "it can be reasonably inferred that government personnel at all times was relying on the cost and pricing data set out in [Universal's] letter of May 28, 1974, as being accurate, complete, and current as to the various contract modifications." Acceptance of this contention, it would appear to us, requires a conviction that the three contracting officers involved, together with whatever cost and pricing advisors who assisted them, believed that a small business firm with a sudden and extremely large increase in its work would have continued to experience the same overhead rate.

Although the administrative record may have failed to establish with certainty whether or not the contracting officers relied on the 115% in the original $65,000 contract as representing the overhead experience when the work during the year of performance skyrocketed to well over $1 million, one must surely question how government personnel could have made such an assumption. And, if they made no such assumption, but simply accepted the 115% markup because they believed the contractor would not have agreed to any other data, then reliance does not appear to have been established.

In an admirable display of perseverance, Universal carried its legal struggles to the United States Court of Appeals for the Federal Circuit where, in what most observers believe should be the concluding chapter to this long story, the higher court reversed the Claims Court and ruled in favor of Universal. It found that the initial board decision had properly stated the facts and conclusions and that there was no basis for departing from them or ruling inconsistent therewith. Emphasis was placed on the facts that Universal would not accept any overhead rate less than its standard add-on and that this contractor was the only company that could complete the work required by the contract. Thus, Universal had successfully rebutted the presumption that the price was increased because of government reliance on defective data.

The essence of the court's ruling, including the appropriate rejection of the specious contention that the contracting officers had never actually testified that they would have accepted the 115% standard add-on had they known the actual rates were lower, is quoted below:

> In its first decision, the ASBCA explicitly found that the overhead rate was a standard company add-on; that Universal would accept nothing less than its established markups on any of its contracts; that Universal was "the only source available to perform the necessary emergency repair work"; and "that it would be impracticable to allow another contractor to perform any of the contract work." 82-1 BCA at 77,995, 77,997. These explicit findings were never set aside and are wholly inconsistent with the board's conclusion on reconsideration that Universal failed to overcome the presumption that nondisclosure resulted in an overstated contract price. Accord *Luzon Stevedoring Corp.,* 71-1 BCA par. 8745 (ASBCA 1971) (contractor's proof of a take it or leave it offer rebuts presumption of natural and probable consequences); *American Machine & Foundry Co.,* 74-1 BCA par. 10, 409 (ASBCA 1973) (contractor's superior bargaining position resulting in part from status as sole source supplier rebuts presumption).

> Accepting as correct that Universal's overhead rate was in fact lower than 115% we agree that Universal's nondisclosure of that fact would give rise to a presumption that the nondisclosure affected the government's agreement to the price. We further agree that no testimony from the government contracting officers to the effect that they would not have agreed to the price but for the nondisclosure is necessary to establish the government's *prima facie* case. By the same token, it cannot be required that the contractor obtain an admission from the contracting officers that they would have agreed to the price had they known the true rate of current overhead. The issue would not be before the board if the contracting officers were of that mind. One cannot expect that by skillful cross-examination Universal's counsel would have obtained statements from the government's witness that would explicitly negate the government's claim. Had counsel asked the suggested questions, the answer one

would expect is, "Yes, it would have made a difference." That is basic to the government's claim in seeking a reduction in the price. Counsel cannot be faulted for not asking a question to which the answer is self-evident and would buttress the government's case. Moreover, the board's view that Universal was required to elicit testimony from the government admitting nonreliance effectively makes the presumption irrebuttable. An irrebuttable presumption of fact violates due process. *Vlandis v. Kline,* 412 U.S. 441, 453 (1973).

The key finding here was that Universal would not accept less than 115% markup for overhead. If Universal would accept no less, as the board found, there would have been no contract, not a contract at a lower price. The conclusion is inescapable that nondisclosure of actual overhead—a cost Universal did not ever actually calculate in its regular business—did not affect the agreed-upon contract price.

Because the government relied solely on the presumption that nondisclosure resulted in an overstated contract price, our holding that Universal rebutted the presumption ends our inquiry. In the terms of our standard of review, the board's decision is unsupported by substantial evidence.

Sperry Univac Division, Sperry Rand Corporation, DOT CAB No. 1144, 82-2 BCA par. 15,812; Government Reliance on Contractor Submissions

The initial ASBCA decision in *Universal Restoration* was handed down on April 9, 1982, and shortly thereafter, on May 24, 1982, the Department of Transportation Contract Appeals Board issued its ruling in *Sperry.* Paralleling the initial decision in *Universal Restoration,* the DOT CAB found that the data submitted by Sperry were defective but ruled in favor of the contractor on the grounds that the government did not rely on such data.

The board ruled that Sperry did not disclose all of the cost or pricing data available to it. The data not furnished involved a reconfiguring of components, which made it possible to combine purchases on this and another potential contract so as to obtain quantity discounts from a subcontractor. Sperry asserted it had made this information available to the government during the negotiation discussions in connection with controversies over the amount of proposed labor costs. But the board said that, assuming the contractor's representative did make this disclosure, (denied by the government), ". . . it ordinarily owes the Government clearer disclosure than an offhand comment during a break . . . . When a contractor does furnish cost or pricing data to the Government, he cannot furnish it in an obfuscated manner; rather, it must be presented in such a manner that the Government personnel may in the exercise of reasonable care grasp its significance. *M-R-S Manufacturing Company v. United States* (19 CCF 82,862) 203 Ct.Cl. 551, 564, 492 F.2d 835 (1974)."

The board further ruled that the Certificate of Current Cost or Pricing Data specifically states that the data must be submitted or identified in writing, whereas any information that may have been made relating to the availability of the quantity discount was made orally.

To this point the board answered the first question in the affirmative; it then proceeded to the second question:

A failure to furnish current, complete, and accurate cost or pricing data will ordinarily mean that the resulting negotiable price was higher than it would otherwise have been, for that is a natural and probable consequence of a failure to disclose. *Sylvania Electric Products v. United States, supra,* at p. 27. Therefore, once the respondent has shown that data was not disclosed, a so-called "burden of persuasion" falls upon an appellant to show that the nondisclosure did not result in a higher negotiated price, even though the respondent retains the overall burden of proof. *Cf. Ibid.* at p. 28. If an appellant can "persuade" a tribunal that, for some reason, the failure to disclose did not result in a higher price, then despite the failure to disclose there will be no adjustment of the contract price under the clause. *Conrac Corp.* ASBCA No. 19507, 78-1 BCA par. 12,985.

The government's negotiator testified that, if he had known of the possible quantity discount, ". . . he would have obtained a lower contract price with a contingency clause under which FAA would pay any cancellation charge if the contemplated subsequent buy never materialized." Based on all of the facts, however, the board did not believe that the negotiated price of $2,400,000 would have been reduced by the $44,125 involved in the subcontractor's quantity discount.

As indicated in the decision, conclusive supporting data were scarce on both sides. However, the contractor's negotiator testified, and produced his contemporaneous notes showing, that FAA had made an offer of some $2.3 million, and when Sperry turned that offer down, the notes showed successive offers of $2,304,575, $2,330,000, $2,390,000, and $2,400,000. The board found the "evidence, buttressed as it is by a contemporaneous memorandum, to be more convincing, and therefore (found) that respondent . . . did make (a) successively increasing series of offers, that there were no revelations concerning the basis for pricing, and that the only reduction offered by Univac was to $2,400,000, based upon the FAA's offer to provide labor to assist with cable pulling." The negotiation was on a total price basis and the available records did not disclose any agreements on individual cost elements or profits.

The board found other circumstances as well that suggested that the FAA would have agreed to the $2,400,000 price even if it knew that the proposed subcontract price would have been $44,125 lower. The FAA Administrator had instituted a crash program, promising publicly that within one year all commercial aircraft would be equipped with devices to warn pilots when they are below the minimum safe altitude. This followed the crash of an aircraft on Mount Weather, west of Dulles International Airport. Because of certain technological developments, Sperry was in a sole source position, which suggested to the board the probability that FAA had indeed made a series of increasing offers to the contractor and that the latter would stand on its position. All in all, the board concluded that ". . . the record clearly shows that the contract price was the best which respondent (the government) would have obtained even had it known the actual details of the subcontract pricing."

We should emphasize that the great preponderance of judicial rulings in this area finds that cost overstatements resulting from defective cost or pricing data constitute natural and probable causes of higher negotiated contract prices. To state this in another manner, higher negotiated contract prices are generally found to be the natural and probable consequences of defective data and become a basis for reduction in the contract price. A number of instances, however, stand out as exceptions to this rule. These exceptions occur when a contractor such as Sperry in this instance or Conrac or Luzon or Universal can persuade a board of contract appeals or court that the defective data did not result in a higher contract price because the government did not rely on the contractor's submission.

Central Navigation and Trading Company, S.A., ASBCA No. 23946, September 30, 1982, 82-2 BCA par. 16,074; Time When Data Were Reasonably Available to the Contractor

The contract was to perform stevedoring and terminal services in Vietnam in March 1974 during the hostilities in that country. Neither the original contract, nor supplemental agreements that extended its term, were based on certified cost or pricing data, for reasons not explained in the record. On June 29, 1974, the government advised Central Navigation that it wished to extend the contract for an additional three months but that certified cost or pricing data would have to be submitted for the negotiation. The board found that this was the first indication the contractor had of this requirement. The negotiations were conducted in the contractor's Saigon offices on June 29 and 30, and certified cost or pricing data were submitted on June 30, 1974.

During August and September 1974, DCAA performed a postaward audit and recommended a price reduction alleging that the data were defective, mainly because they were not current.

Facts bearing on this case included the contractor's testimony that the data were used due to "the press of time" and that more current data could not be extracted from its files "fast enough" in the light of the June 30 expiration of the contract. The board also stated that it could find no indication in the record of where the records and documents relied upon by the DCAA auditors were physically located at the time of the modification or how accessible they were at that time. Company records, which were maintained in Vietnam, were abandoned when Central Navigation was forced by enemy action to leave Vietnam.

In the main, the contractor did not contest the cost figures developed by DCAA; its main argument, however, was that more current cost or pricing data were not reasonably available under the severe time limitations and war conditions with which it was faced.

In finding for the contractor, the board quoted at some length from its decision in *LTV Electrosystems, Inc., Memcor Division*, ASBCA No. 16802, 73-1 BCA 9957, aff'd. on recon. 74-1 BCA 10,380. Although the circumstances in *LTV* differed, the governing principle was the same, i.e., the time made available to the contractors was inadequate. As it stated in *LTV*, "notwithstanding the apparent incompleteness and noncurrency . . . the Government may not recover on its claim unless it can show, by a preponderance of the evidence, that more accurate, complete and current cost or pricing data were reasonably available to appellant on the date of the certification under the prevailing circumstances."

The board pointed out that Central Navigation was allowed less than two days on a weekend in an area in which a war was going on to develop certified cost or pricing data. It further found, contrary to the government's contentions, that the contractor had no reason to suspect that certified cost or pricing data would be required until June 29, the day before the contract was to expire.

Citing *LTV* again, the board said the government must allow a contractor a reasonable amount of time to prepare the certified cost or pricing data. "If the urgency of the procurement prevents the Government from doing so, the Government may not be heard to complain if the data submitted and certified by the contractor do not meet standards of accuracy, completeness and currency that would otherwise be applicable . . . ." Turning to Central Navigation, the board said that the government had failed to meet its burden of proving that more current data were reasonably available in the circumstances.

Rogerson Aircraft Controls, ASBCA No. 27954, 85-1 BCA par. 17,725; aff'd *U.S. v. Rogerson Aircraft Controls* [33 CCF par. 74,262], CA FC No. 85-2058, March 6, 1986; Availability of Intentional Understatements for Offsets

After more than a quarter of a century and extensive attention by the judicial, executive and legislative branches of the government, unresolved issues continue to surface in disputes over the interpretation of P.L. 87-653.

In our analysis of case law, we have reviewed several disputes that included contractor claims for offsets, and the differing views appeared to have been resolved in *Cutler-Hammer, supra,* when a 1969 ruling by the U.S. Court of Claims, after finding that "neither the statute nor the legislative history is clear cut," concluded that (1) the total contract price could only be reduced, i.e., offsets could not be used to increase the price, but (2) understatements up to the amounts of the overstatements were permissible because "where overstatements exceed understatements, the price is not raised."

But the subject of offsets surfaced again in the lengthy and complex *Lockheed Aircraft, Lockheed-Georgia (Midwestern Instruments, Subcontractor), supra,* dispute, which bounced up and back between the ASBCA and the Court of Claims. On a remand from the court, the board denied the appeal for offsets on the grounds that the costs involved had been omitted intentionally. When the dispute returned to the court, that tribunal had an opportunity to address the availability of intentional understatements as offsets but refused to do so. Instead, it faulted the board for imposing the burden of proof on the contractor to demonstrate that the understatement was not intentional whereas the court concluded that the government should bear the burden of proof on this issue. The court further stated, in ruling again for the contractor, that there did not exist "substantial evidence to support the board's conclusion that the understatement . . . was intentional."

We now reach Rogerson's dispute before the ASBCA where the complexities of this subject were illustrated by the closely divided (3-2) ruling for the contractor, which included four separate opinions: two judges voting to sustain, one joining them but presenting a separate concurring opinion, one dissenting opinion, and one joining in the dissent but presenting a somewhat different viewpoint.

The DCAA audit found that the raw material cost submitted by the contractor was overstated, and the contracting officer demanded a reduction in the contract price. Rogerson agreed in the overstatement but argued that the contract price should not be reduced because the submitted overhead rates were substantially understated and the application of the correct rates would more than offset the overstatement in the material costs.

The contractor usually submitted his proposals using indirect expense rates that prevailed in the year preceding the submission. At the time of the submission in controversy, late in 1980, indirect expense rate information was also available for the first nine months of 1980. Both the latter and former rates were much higher than those included in the proposal. According to the decision, this fact was known to Rogerson's controller, the government auditor, and the government negotiator when oral price negotiations began. The controller told the auditor, and the auditor told the negotiator, that the lower rates were based on "management estimates." The government argued that the contractor's understatement was a mistake of judgment, not fact, and that mistakes of judgment are, as a matter of law, not eligible for set-off.

In approaching the dispute, the board began by speculating "what the parties would have done if the undisclosed raw material cost had been disclosed during negotiation of the contract price. *American Machine & Foundry Co.,* ASBCA No. 15037, 74-1 BCA ¶ 10,409." Then, citing *Sylvania Electric Products, Inc. v. United States,* [18 CCF ¶ 82,334], 202 Ct.Cl. 16, 479 F.2d 1342 (1973), the board said: "There is a rebuttable presumption in defective pricing cases that an overstated cost causes an increase in the final negotiated contract price in the amount of the overstatement." And, in this case, the board said: "we find that presumption rebutted." While the government negotiator relied upon the overstatement in the raw material cost, both parties at the negotiation knew that the proposed price was based on a lower manufacturing overhead rate than experienced in either the prior full year or the first nine months of the current full year. Applying either rate would increase the proposed price by more than it was overstated by the raw material error.

The board then reasoned that "the natural and probable consequence of disclosure of the undisclosed raw material cost, and a Government proposal for a further . . . price reduction, would have been a counter-proposal by Rogerson citing the most recent manufacturing labor overhead as more than offsetting the material cost reduction." Citing other considerations, including the fact that Rogerson was the only source known for the contract item, the board concluded "it more likely than not that the most recent manufacturing labor overhead rate would also have been accepted by the Government, with the result being no substantial change in the final negotiated price."

The government argued that since the burden rates "were management estimates and were intentionally lower than its most recent actual rates, it [Rogerson] would have stuck with those lower rates no matter what further reduction in the bottom line price would have been proposed by the Government as a result of disclosure of the lower raw material cost." The board found this argument faulty in that it "fails to recognize that price is a function of customer acceptance as well as a function of cost." "A seller," the board continued, "may accept a certain level of cost risk, by bidding below historic costs, in order to maintain a competitive price or one acceptable to its customer. But usually, a seller will not knowingly agree to a price that is substantially below both historic cost *and* market. "

The board also noted that the unit price of this item in a recent Rogerson contract had been $909, which was the same as the contractor's initial proposal in the current contract. "It is unrealistic to assume," the board decided, "that Rogerson would have acquiesced in a further and more substantial price reduction below the final agreed price of $859.46 on the basis of raw material cost reduction when it had at hand a justifiable cost offset in a greater amount which would maintain its total price closer to what it reasonably perceived to be a level acceptable to its customer."

The board then addressed the government's argument that Rogerson's understatement was a mistake of judgment, not fact, and that mistakes of judgment are, as a matter of law, not eligible for set-off. Inasmuch as this was the significant issue, and perhaps reflective of a ruling of first impression, we cite this portion of the board's reasoning in full:

> We do not agree that the fact/judgment distinction referred to in *Baldwin Electronics, Inc.,* ASBCA No. 19683, 76-2 BCA par. 12,199, is applicable to Rogerson's case. That distinction is properly applied in cases such as *Hardie Tynes Manufacturing Co.,* ASBCA No. 20387, 76-1 BCA par. 11,827, where there is no contrary factual data at the time of negotiation which might lead the contractor to revise his estimating judgment and assert the understated cost as an offset to a proposed reduction. In Rogerson's case, however, there was a fact at the time of the negotiation—namely the nine month FY 1980 manufacturing labor overhead rate—which was contrary to the contractor's estimating judgment, and which was as much a fact as the accounting error in *Baldwin.*

> In *Cutler-Hammer, Inc. v. United States* [14 CCF par. 83,124], 189 Ct.Cl. 76, 416 F.2d 1306 (1969), where the Court first allowed the set-off of understatements in a defective pricing action, it made no distinction between intentional and unintentional understatements when it rejected the argument that allowance of set-offs would encourage "buying-in". The Court's discussion of "buying-in" was unnecessary if it believed that intentional understatements should not be eligible for set-off. See 189 Ct.Cl. at 86-87, 416 F.2d at 1312-1313. Moreover, in subsequently reversing on factual grounds the Board's decision in *Lockheed Aircraft Corp.,* ASBCA No. 10453, 72-1 BCA par. 9370, that an intentional understatement was not eligible for set-off, the Court expressed skepticism as to the Board's legal conclusion. *Lockheed Aircraft Corp. v. United States* [19 CCF par. 82,586], 202 Ct.Cl. 787, 790-91, 485 F.2d 584, 586 (1973).

We hold that the intentional nature of an understatement does not, as a matter of law, disqualify that understatement as a set-off against an overstatement. Whether an intentional understatement would have been raised as a set-off in a negotiation depends on the particular facts of each case. On the facts of Rogerson's case we have found that the understatement would have been raised, and that the price would not have been reduced.

The government appealed the board's ruling to the U.S. Court of Appeals for the Federal Circuit and, while the tribunal affirmed the board's decision, it elected to confine its ruling to a very narrow issue, leaving the status of intentional understatements under other circumstances unresolved.

Essentially, the government argued that *Cutler-Hammer* did not address intentional understatements and asked the court "to decide directly and broadly that all intentional errors of understatement fall outside the *Cutler-Hammer* rule*." The government asked the court to rule, in effect, that "an intentional understatement of costs automatically disqualifies that understatement as an offset."

The court refused to address intentional offsets "directly and broadly."

We cannot, however, take that general position in this case because, on the facts found below (which are not challenged), the Government's contracting agencies were fully aware (at all relevant times) of the understated errors and their extent—and, assuming that the contractor made those errors "intentionally," we hold that such "intentional" errors of which the Government knew full well are not excluded from the *Cutler-Hammer* holding. Accordingly, we affirm the ASBCA, leaving still undecided by this court the issue whether a deliberate, deceptive (or misleading) understatement (i.e., an intentional understatement which is unknown to the Government) can be offset in a "defective pricing" case.

The court's decision, as the board's before it, emphasized that the government representatives—contract auditors, negotiators, etc.—were fully aware of the understatements. The court then reasoned that "[I]n the technical sense that they were deliberate rather than inadvertent, or due to neglect, or to pure mistake, the Rogerson understatements . . . . can be denominated as intentionally made. But at the time of the contract negotiations those understatements were not at all in the class of intentional understatements that are designed to mislead or confuse the Government." The court further stated that it would be wrong to punish a contractor "for understatements which had and could have no impact on the Government's action in entering into this contract."

The court recognized the broader ramifications of intentional understatements but refused to rule on them where they extended beyond the circumstances in Rogerson:

Assuming without deciding that there are some intentional understatements that are barred as offsets, we cannot conclude the understatements in this case within that rule.

*   *   *   *

.... we do not answer the broad question the Government has presented. That issue must await another day and a different case appropriately raising the qualification as offsets of intentional under-statements designed to mislead or confuse the Government, or having that effect.

As we have noted from time to time, in our layman reviews and analyses of board and court rulings, there is a strong judicial inclination to decide disputes on narrow issues where possible and avoid expressing opinions on matters that are not considered necessary to settle the dispute. Although, as in *Rogerson,* this practice deliberately leaves issues for further disputes and litigation, boards and courts prefer to await the presentation of the other issues and rule on the basis of the particular facts involved.

The Boeing Company, ASBCA No. 20875, 85-3 BCA par 18,351; What Constitutes Cost or Pricing Data; Reasonable Availability of Data

A DCAA postaward review of a contract awarded by Boeing to Resalab, Inc., in an amount approximating $1 million, concluded that the prime contract should be reduced by over $330,000 as a result of Boeing's acceptance of allegedly defective data submitted by the subcontractor. The ACO adopted the auditor's report as his final determination and issued a demand for price reduction from which decision Boeing appealed.

Although our analysis focuses on the defective pricing issue, it is appropriate to note some of the board's criticisms of the DCAA audit because its deficiencies contributed significantly to the government's assertion of defective pricing, an assertion decisively rejected by the board. For example, in connection with certain testing costs questioned by the auditor, which Boeing successfully contested, the board stated:

> The auditor testified, however, that he was not an engineer, did not have any professional degree in science, technology, or engineering related areas, did not have academic or experience related background in cost estimating and that he did not review the specifications in Resalab's subcontract to determine if EMI and environmental tests were required for the system to be delivered under that subcontract. ... Moreover, in performing his audit, he did not consult any of [the government's] technical representatives ...

The above comment was typical of a number of criticisms the board directed at the audit in sustaining each and every Boeing appeal of costs questioned.

During the negotiations in mid-June, Resalab did not submit its actual labor costs for the period from April to the date of negotiations. The auditor used these costs to project what he believed should have been the proposed direct labor costs and asserted the excess represented defective pricing. Boeing was well aware that Resalab had been performing some preliminary work during this early period but the prime contractor's technical people concluded:

> ... that actual labor cost data would not have a significant impact on negotiations because this period was of short duration as compared with the total performance period, they were incurred before the design of the AWIS was complete and finalized, they were at the beginning of a

mobilization and manpower build-up period and that the funding limitation of $300,000.00 contained in [Boeing's] purchase order of intent to Resalab would affect the number of actual hours incurred by Resalab prior to the definitization of the purchase order. Therefore, [Boeing's] negotiator testified that even if Resalab had disclosed the raw data of actual labor costs, he would not have ascribed any significance to that data or conducted the negotiations differently. This opinion was also supported by one of [the government's] price analysts who had served as a contracting officer on this program and was a member of [the government's] negotiation team for the definitization of the prime contract with [Boeing].

In these circumstances, the board found that the raw labor costs for the preliminary period could not "reasonably be expected to contribute to sound estimates of future costs." The board said it was further "unable to conclude ... that it was of such a nature that prudent buyers and sellers would reasonably expect that information to have a significant effect on price negotiations as would bring it within the scope of the definition of cost or pricing data."

Although the above conclusions seemed to be the major ones on which the decision turned, the board also concluded that "the auditor's method of computation and computations are fatally flawed and based on invalid assumptions."

Resalab's accounting records did not segregate actual labor hours for each labor category and classification. The auditor could not determine what tasks were represented by the incurred labor hours and whether the incurred labor hours to perform specific tasks were greater than or less than projected on the monthly manloading schedules. There were inconsistencies and discrepancies in the auditor's work papers that could not be reconciled. Furthermore, the actual direct labor costs for the entire period of mid-April to mid-June 1970 were not reasonably available to Resalab at the time of negotiation of the definitized purchase order because direct labor costs were not accumulated by Resalab by labor category and classification for each task and could not be distributed from payroll records to obtain a cost breakdown for a job until three to four weeks after the close of a payroll period.

Grumman Aerospace Corporation, ASBCA No. 27476, 86-3 BCA par. 19,091; Failure to Disclose All Cost or Pricing Data Does Not Necessarily Result in Overstated Contract Price

A recent decision established that the nondisclosure of all cost or pricing data did not result in an overstated contract price and, while the government established defective cost or pricing data, it failed to make a case for contract price reduction. The firm fixed-price retrofit contract in the amount of $10.9 million included a major subcontract of $6.2 million to the General Electric Company for the Advanced Radar Processing System (ARPS). GE, in turn, obtained an item called a shift register from Hughes Aircraft Company, and it was the volatile production and cost experience of this item which seemed to have generated many of the pricing and negotiating problems and contributed to the government's unsuccessful demand for reduction in the prime contract price.

The dispute centered on Grumman's Cost Analysis Report (CAR) analyzing GE's cost proposal. The government contended that had Grumman furnished this report, which contained a bottom line of $5.8 million for the subcontract, it would have had an impact upon the negotiations and the prime contract price negotiated, which included $6.2 million for this subcontract. After Grumman add-ons for indirect expenses, etc., and profit, the government alleged a contract price overstatement and concurrently demanded a price reduction approximating $550,000.

Grumman's defense focused on the facts that it had provided the government with more current and accurate information than was contained in the CAR and that, in any event, the basic contents of this report had been conveyed orally to the government during the contract negotiations.

Before discussing the board's decision, we thought it would be instructive and useful to include a brief but cogent excerpt from the ruling that places the issue involved in perspective:

> In an action based upon alleged defective pricing the Government bears the burden of proving that the contractor failed to disclose accurate, complete and current pricing data. *Sylvania Electric Products, Inc. v. United States* [18 CCF ¶ 82,334], 479 F.2d 1342 (1973). In the determination of whether that burden has been met, an objective test, whether the undisclosed data would be reasonably expected to have a significant effect upon price negotiations, is applied. *Plessy Industries, Inc.,* ASBCA No. 16720, 74-1 BCA ¶ 10,603. A further burden borne by the Government is the requirement to demonstrate that the defective data resulted in a significant overstatement of the contract price. The weight of meeting this burden is somewhat alleviated by a rebuttable presumption that the natural and probable consequence of nondisclosure is an increase in the contract price. The burden of persuasion at that point is shifted to the contractor, who must show that the defective data was not relied upon, or that the undisclosed data would not have been relied upon even if complete disclosure had been made. *Sylvania Electric Products, Inc., supra.* This latter burden is met by the application of subjective criteria and thereby differs from the objective test which enters into the threshold determination of whether the document or information in question constitutes cost and pricing data. The ultimate burden of showing the causal connection between incomplete or inaccurate data and an overstated contract price remains with the Government. *Conrac Corporation,* ASBCA No. 19507, 78-1 BCA ¶ 12,985.

The board concluded that Grumman did advise the government of many of the figures contained in the CAR, but found the record unclear as to whether all of the major categories were provided. However, there was no dispute that the report's bottom line and narrative were not provided. Even though portions of the narrative contained judgment as distinguished from factual data, the board found that overall the narrative added meaning to the raw figures and must be considered as data.

Having determined that the CAR constituted cost or pricing data and was available, the board addressed the crucial issue as to whether the undisclosed data would have been relied upon by the government if full disclosure had been made. The DCAA report that initiated the government's demand for contract price reduction somehow concluded that the government negotiators would have acted differently than they did had this report been disclosed.

As noted earlier, many of the pricing and negotiating problems relating to the GE subcontract centered on the shift register obtained from Hughes, originally priced at $24 per unit in accordance with a blanket purchase agreement. Hughes experienced problems early on with this component and advised GE and Grumman that the price would be substantially increased. The decision indicates that the CAR included the original $24 figure, but the narrative included a caveat, based on later information, that the price was estimated to increase to $50.

During the period preceding the prime contract negotiations, "a wide variety of information was received by GE, [Grumman], and by the Government itself, from Hughes directly and from Government audit sources, to the effect that the shift register price would be increasing to a range of $50-$70 per unit." Based on these facts, the board concluded that "[t]he information upon which the note in the cost analysis report was based was certainly no more authoritative than were the other sources from which anticipated shift register price estimates were emanating."

There were other items of lesser importance in the CAR, but the board found that the government had been informed about them during negotiations.

The board concluded that, although the entire CAR constituted cost or pricing data and should have been disclosed, "the nondisclosure ... in this case, given [Grumman's] disclosure of more current information and the Government's independent knowledge, did not result in an overstated contract price."

LEGISLATIVE AND REGULATORY DEVELOPMENTS

Public Law 98-369

The voluminous Deficit Reduction Act of 1984 provided Congressmen an opportunity to add various favorite projects and provisions, including important measures affecting government procurement, such as efforts to increase competition, increasing GAO authority in bid protests, and applying the "Truth in Negotiations" Act provisions to civilian as well as military procurements, with a common threshold of $100,000 for submission of certified cost or pricing data. (Effective with solicitations issued April 1, 1985, and thereafter.)

The $100,000 threshold was originally included in P.L. 87-653, enacted in 1962, and the inflation during the period of over two decades since then made this amount obviously obsolete. As a basis for postaward audits by DCAA in search of defective cost or pricing data, this threshold likewise made little sense because the audit agency had for many years used its postaward audit resources on major contracts and accorded very little attention to contracts where the cost or pricing data fell below $500,000. Offering these and other cogent reasons, DOD persuaded Congress to increase the threshold to $500,000 in P.L. 97-86. As testified to by a high ranking DOD acquisition official, this change resulted in a 79% decrease in paperwork requirements while providing coverage to over 92% of the expenditures involved.

Instead of commendations for cost effectiveness, DOD received considerable criticism on the matter from Senator Roth and some members of the Senate Committee on Governmental Affairs and, of course, the GAO and the DOD Inspector General, all of whom, in common, appear to hold a strong distrust for those involved in the DOD acquisition process, both in the government and in the private sector. As part of the current scene, which seems to highlight attacks on contractors, contracting officers, and others, sufficient support was gathered in the Senate for such an amendment and this proposal was sold to the House conferees.

As to the application of requirements for submission of cost or pricing data on civilian procurements and making such procurements subject to price reduction for defective data, this had already been accomplished by regulation, first in FPR and now in FAR. Although the law seems merely to add statutory underpinning to an established requirement, a decision by the General Services Board of Contract Appeals, *Inter-Con Security Systems, Inc.,* GSBCA No. 6682, 84-2 BCA par. 17,274, suggests further significance to this provision.

Several issues were involved in the appeal of *Inter-Con* from a contracting officer's decision demanding reduction of the contract price as a result of defective cost or pricing data. The point applicable to this discussion is the government's agreement that P.L. 87-653 did not apply to GSA procurements but its contention that the requirement to submit certified cost or pricing data had been imposed on the civilian agencies by regulation. The board agreed but concluded that the regulation "*. . . . imposes no such requirement upon contractors; rather it imposes the requirement on contracting officers.*"

Federal Acquisition Regulation, Subpart 15.8

The salient FAR provisions as amended through P.L. 98-369 are set forth below.

15.602 Policy.

(a) 10 U.S.C. 2306(f) and 41 U.S.C. 254(d) provide that all executive agencies shall require a prime contractor or any subcontractor to submit and certify cost or pricing data under certain circumstances. The Acts also require inclusion of contract clauses that provide for reduction of the contract price by any significant amounts that such price was increased because of submission of contractor or subcontractor defective cost or pricing data.

* * * *

15.804-2 Requiring certified cost or pricing data.

(a)(1) Except as provided in 15.804-3, certified cost or pricing data are required before accomplishing any of the following actions:

(i) The award of any negotiated contract (except for unpriced actions such as letter contracts) expected to exceed $100,000.

(ii) The modifications of any sealed bid or negotiated contract (whether or not cost or pricing data were initially required) when the modification involves a price adjustment expected to exceed $100,000. (For example, a $30,000 modification resulting from a reduction of $70,000 and an increase of $40,000 is a pricing adjustment exceeding $100,000). This requirement does not apply when unrelated and separately priced changes for which cost or pricing data would not otherwise be required are included for administrative convenience in the same modification.

(iii) The award of a subcontract at any tier, if the contractor and each higher tier subcontractor have been required to furnish certified cost or pricing data, when the subcontract is expected to exceed $100,000.

(iv) The modification of any subcontract covered by subdivision (iii) above, when the price adjustment (see subdivision (ii) above) is expected to exceed $100,000.

(2) If cost or pricing data are needed for pricing actions over $25,000 and not in excess of $100,000, certified cost or pricing data may be obtained. There should be relatively few instances where certified cost or pricing data and inclusion of defective pricing clauses would be justified in awards between $25,000 and $100,000. The amount of data required to be submitted should be limited to that data necessary to allow the contracting officer to determine the reasonableness of the price. Whenever certified cost or pricing data are required for pricing actions of $100,000 or less, the contracting officer shall document the file to justify the requirement. When awarding a contract of $25,000 or less, the contracting officer shall not require certified cost or pricing data.

(b) When certified cost or pricing data are required, the contracting officer shall require the contractor or prospective contractor to submit to the contracting officer (and to have any subcontractor or prospective subcontractor submit to the prime contractor or appropriate subcontractor tier) the following in support of any proposal:

(1) The cost or pricing data.

(2) A certificate of current cost or pricing data, in the format specified in 15.804-4, certifying that to the best of its knowledge and belief, the cost or pricing data were accurate, complete, and current as of the date of final agreement on price.

15.804-3 Exemptions from or waiver of submission of certified cost or pricing data.

(a) *General.* Except as provided in paragraphs (b) and (c) below, the contracting officer shall not require submission or certification of cost or pricing data when the contracting officer determines that prices are—

(1) Based on adequate price competition (see paragraph (b) below);

(2) Based on established catalog or market prices of commercial items sold in substantial quantities to the general public (see paragraph (c) below); or

(3) Set by law or regulation (see paragraph (d) below).

(b) *Adequate price competition.* (1) Price competition exists if—

(i) Offers are solicited;

(ii) Two or more responsible offerors that can satisfy the Government's requirements submit priced offers responsive to the solicitation's expressed requirements; and

(iii) These offerors compete independently for a contract to be awarded to the responsible offeror submitting the lowest evaluated price.

(2) If price competition exists, the contracting officer shall presume that it is adequate unless—

(i) The solicitation is made under conditions that unreasonably deny to one or more known and qualified offerors an opportunity to compete;

(ii) The low offeror has such a decided advantage that it is practically immune from competition; or

(iii) There is a finding, supported by a statement of the facts and approved at a level above the contracting officer, that the lowest price is unreasonable.

(3) A price is "based on" adequate price competition if it results directly from price competition or if price analysis alone clearly demonstrates that the proposed price is reasonable in comparison with current or recent prices for the same or substantially the same items purchased in comparable quantities, terms, and conditions under contracts that resulted from adequate price competition.

(c) *Established catalog or market prices.* A proposal is exempt from the requirement for submission of certified cost or pricing data if the prices are, or are based on, established catalog or established market prices of commercial items sold in substantial quantities to the general public. In order to qualify for this exemption, the terms of the proposed purchase, such as quantity and delivery requirements, should be sufficiently similar to those of the commercial sales that the catalog or market price will be fair and reasonable.

(1) "Established catalog prices" must be recorded in a form regularly maintained by the manufacturer or vendor. This form may be a catalog, price list, schedule, or other verifiable and established record. The record must (i) be published or otherwise available for customer inspection and (ii) state current or last sales price to a significant number of buyers constituting the general public (see subparagraph (5) below).

(2) "Established market prices" are current prices that (i) are established in the course of ordinary and usual trade between buyers and sellers free to bargain and (ii) can be substantiated by data from sources independent of the manufacturer or vendor.

(3) "Commercial items" are supplies or services regularly used for other than Government purposes and sold or traded to the general public in the course of normal business operations.

(4) An item is "sold in substantial quantities" only when the quantities regularly sold are sufficient to constitute a real commercial market. Nominal quantities, such as models, samples, prototypes, or experimental units, do not meet this requirement. For services to be sold in substantial quantities, they must be customarily provided by the offeror, using personnel regularly employed and equipment (if any necessary) regularly maintained solely or principally to provide the services.

(5) The "general public" is a significant number of buyers other than the Government or affiliates of the offeror; the item involved must not be for Government end use. For the purpose of this subsection 15.804-3, items acquired for "Government end use" include items acquired for foreign military sales.

(6) A price is "based on" a catalog or market price only if the item being purchased is sufficiently similar to the catalog- or market-priced commercial item to ensure that any difference in prices can be identified and justified without resort to cost analysis.

(7) If an item is substantially similar to a commercial item for which there is an established catalog or market price at which substantial quantities are sold to the general public, but the price proposed is not *based on* this catalog or market price (see subparagraph (6) above), the contracting officer may, if doing so will result in a fair and reasonable price, limit any requirement for cost or pricing data to those data that pertain to the differences between the items. When the differences between the catalog or market price of an item or items and the proposed total contract price is $100,000 or more, the contracting officer shall require submission of certified cost or pricing data to identify and justify that difference unless an exemption or waiver is granted.

(8) Even though there is an established catalog or market price of commercial items sold in substantial quantities to the general public, the contracting officer may require cost or pricing data if (i) the contracting officer makes a written finding that the price is not reasonable, including the facts upon which the finding is based, and (ii) the finding is approved at a level above the contracting officer.

(d) *Prices set by law or regulation.* A price set by law or regulation is exempt from the requirement for submission of certified cost or pricing data.

Pronouncements in the form of periodic rulings, reviews, or similar actions of a governmental body, or embodied in the laws, are sufficient to establish the price.

(e) *Claiming and granting exemption.* To receive an exemption under paragraph (c) or (d) above, the offeror must ordinarily claim it on Standard Form 1412, Claim for Exemption from Submission of Certified Cost or Pricing Data, when the total proposed amount exceeds $100,000 and more than one catalog item for which an exemption is claimed exceeds $25,000. When an exemption is claimed for more than one item in a proposal, a separate SF 1412 is required for each such item exceeding $25,000 except as otherwise provided in the solicitation. The contracting officer may grant an exemption and need not require the submission of SF 1412 when—

(1) The Government has acted favorably on an exemption claim for the same item or similar items within the past year. In that case, except as otherwise directed by the contracting officer, the offeror may furnish a copy of the prior claim and related Government action. The offeror must also submit a statement to the effect that to its knowledge since the prior submission, except as expressly set forth in the statement, there have been no changes in the catalog price or discounts, volume of actual sales, or the ratio of sales for Government end use to sales in other categories which would cause a cumulative change in price exceeding $25,000;

(2) Special arrangements for the submission of exemption claims have been made in anticipation of repetitive acquisitions of catalog items; or

(3) There is evidence, before solicitation, that the item has an acceptable established catalog or market price or a price set by law or regulation. Evidence may include (i) recent submissions by offerors or (ii) the contracting officer's knowledge of market conditions, prevailing prices, or sources.

(f) *Verification.* (1) When a prospective contractor requests exemption from submission of certified cost or pricing data, the contracting officer shall ensure that applicable criteria in either paragraph (c) or (d) above, as appropriate, are satisfied before issuing the exemption.

(2) SF 1412 lists three categories of sales related to the established catalog price of a commercial item sold in substantial quantities to the general public: A, Sales to the U.S. Government or to contractors for U.S. Government use; B, Sales at catalog price to the general public; and C, Sales to the general public at other than catalog prices. Although "substantial quantities" cannot be precisely defined (see subparagraph (c)(4) above), the following guidelines are provided for determining whether exemption claims submitted under the catalog price provision of SF 1412 meet the "substantial quantities" criterion:

(i) Sales to the general public are normally regarded as substantial if (A) Category B and C sales are not negligible in themselves and comprise at least 55 percent of total sales of the item and (B) Category B sales comprise at least 75 percent of the total of Category B and C sales.

(ii) Sales to the general public are rarely considered substantial enough to grant an exemption if (A) Category B and C sales comprise less than 35 percent of total sales of the item or (B) Category B sales comprise less than 55 percent of the total of Category B and C sales.

(iii) When percentages fall between those above, the contracting officer should analyze the individual situation in order to determine whether or not an exemption is justified.

(3) The contracting officer may verify or obtain verification (including audit or contract administration assistance) of the submitted data pertaining to catalog or market prices or prices set by law or regulation. Access to the prospective contractor's records is limited to access to the facts bearing directly on the exemption claimed. It does not extend to cost, profit, or other data relevant solely to the reasonableness of the catalog or proposed price.

(g) *Individual or class exemptions.* The chief of the contracting office may authorize individual or class exemptions for exceptional cases when the contracting officer recommends that an exemption should be made, even though the case does not strictly meet all the criteria for catalog- or market-price exemption. The quantity and prices of actual commercial sales compared with prices offered to the Government, and price relationships as influenced by prevailing trade practices, are the important factors for consideration. The Government's need and the prospective contractor's resistance are not appropriate considerations.

(h) *Price analysis.* Even though an item qualifies for exemption from the requirement for submission of certified cost or pricing data, the contracting officer shall make a price analysis to determine the reasonableness of the price and any need for further negotiation. Unless information is available from Government sources, it may be necessary to obtain from the prospective contractor information such as that regarding—

(1) The supplier's marketing system (e.g., use of jobbers, brokers, sales agencies, or distributors);

(2) The services normally provided commercial purchasers (e.g., engineering, financing, or advertising or promotion);

(3) Normal quantity per order; and

(4) Annual volume of sales to largest customers.

(i) *Waiver for exceptional cases.* The agency head (or, if the contract is with a foreign government or agency, the head of the contracting activity) may, in exceptional cases, waive the requirement for submission of certified cost or pricing data. The authorization for the waiver and the reasons for granting it shall be in writing. The agency head may delegate this authority.

15.804-4 Certificate of Current Cost or Pricing Data.

(a) When certified cost or pricing data are required under 15.804-2, the contracting officer shall require the contractor to execute a Certificate of Current Cost or Pricing Data, shown below, and shall include the executed certificate in the contract file. The certificate states that the cost or pricing data are accurate, complete, and current as of the date the contractor and the Government agreed on a price. Only one certificate shall be required; the contractor shall submit it as soon as practicable after price agreement is reached.

CERTIFICATE OF CURRENT COST OR PRICING DATA

This is to certify that, to the best of my knowledge and belief, the cost or pricing data (as defined in section 15.801 of the Federal Acquisition Regulation (FAR) and required under FAR subsection 15.804-2) submitted, either actually or by specific identification in writing, to the contracting officer or to the contracting officer's representative in support of ....* are accurate, complete, and current as of ....**. This certification includes the cost or pricing data supporting any advance agreements and forward pricing rate agreements between the offeror and the Government that are part of the proposal.

Firm ....

Name ....

Title ....

Date of execution*** ....

* Identify the proposal, quotation, request for price adjustment, or other submission involved, giving the appropriate identifying number (e.g., RFP No.).

** Insert the day, month, and year when price negotiations were concluded and price agreement was reached.

*** Insert the day, month, and year of signing, which should be as close as practicable to the date when the price negotiations were concluded and the contract price was agreed to.

(End of certificate)

(b) The certificate does not constitute a representation as to the accuracy of the contractor's judgment on the estimate of future costs or projections. It does apply to the data upon which the judgment or estimate was based. This distinction between fact and judgment should be clearly understood. If the contractor had information reasonably available at the time of agreement showing that the negotiated price was not based on accurate, complete, and current data, the contractor's responsibility is not limited by any lack of personal knowledge of the information on the part of its negotiators.

(c) Closing or cutoff dates should be included as part of the data submitted with the proposal. Certain data may not be reasonably available before normal periodic closing dates (e.g., actual indirect costs). Before agreement on price, the contractor shall update all data as of the latest dates for which information is reasonably available. Data within the contractor's or a subcontractor's organization on matters significant to contractor management and to the Government will be treated as reasonably available. What is significant depends upon the circumstances of each acquisition.

(d) Possession of a Certificate of Current Cost or Pricing Data is not a substitute for examining and analyzing the contractor's proposal.

(e) Even though the solicitation may have requested cost or pricing data, the contracting officer shall not require a Certificate of Current Cost or Pricing Data when the resulting award is based on adequate price competition, established catalog or market prices of commercial items sold in substantial quantities to the general public, or prices set by law or regulation (see 15.804-3(a) through (d)).

(f) The exercise of an option at the price established in the initial negotiation in which certified cost or pricing data were used does not require recertification.

(g) Contracting officers shall not require certification at the time of agreement for data supplied in support of forward pricing rate agreements (see 15.809) or other advance agreements. When a forward pricing rate agreement or other advance agreement is used in partial support of a later contractual action that requires a certificate, the price proposal certificate shall cover (1) the data originally supplied to support the forward pricing rate agreement or other advance agreement and (2) all data required to update the price proposal to the time of agreement on contract price.

(h) Negotiated final pricing actions (such as termination settlements and total final price agreements for fixed-price incentive and redeterminable contracts) are contract modifications requiring certified cost or pricing data if (1) the total final price agreement for such settlements or agreements exceeds $100,000 or (2) the partial termination settlement plus the estimate to complete the continued portion of the contract exceeds $100,000 (see 49.105(c)(15)).

15.804-5 Reserved.

15.804-6 Procedural requirements.

(a) The contracting officer shall specify (1) whether or not cost or pricing data are required, (2) whether or not certification will be required, (3) the extent of cost or pricing data required if complete data are not necessary, and (4) the form (see paragraph (b) below) in which the cost or pricing data shall be submitted. Even if the solicitation does not so specify, however, the contracting officer is not precluded from requesting such data if they are later found necessary.

(b)(1) Cost or pricing data shall be submitted on Standard Form 1411 (SF 1411), Contract Pricing Proposal Cover Sheet, unless required to be submitted on one of the termination forms specified in Subpart 49.6. Data supporting forward pricing rate agreements or final indirect cost proposals shall be submitted in a format acceptable to the contracting officer.

(2) Contract pricing proposals submitted on SF 1411 with supporting attachments shall be prepared to satisfy the instructions and appropriate format of Table 15-2.

TABLE 15-2 INSTRUCTIONS FOR SUBMISSION OF A CONTRACT PRICING PROPOSAL

1. SF 1411 provides a vehicle for the offeror to submit to the Government a pricing proposal of estimated and/or incurred costs by contract line item with supporting information, adequately cross-referenced, suitable for detailed analysis. A cost-element breakdown, using the applicable format prescribed in 7A, B, or C below, shall be attached for

each proposed line item and must reflect any specific requirements established by the contracting officer. Supporting breakdowns must be furnished for each cost element, consistent with offeror's cost accounting system. When more than one contract line item is proposed, summary total amounts covering all line items must be furnished for each cost element. If agreement has been reached with Government representatives on use of forward pricing rates/factors, identify the agreement, include a copy, and describe its nature. Depending on offeror's system, breakdowns shall be provided for the following basic elements of cost, as applicable:

Materials—Provide a consolidated priced summary of individual material quantities included in the various tasks, orders, or contract line items being proposed and the basis for pricing (vendor quotes, invoice prices, etc.).

Subcontracted Items—Include parts, components, assemblies, and services that are to be produced or performed by others in accordance with offeror's design, specifications, or direction and that are applicable only to the prime contract. For each subcontract over $100,000 the support should provide a listing by source, item, quantity, price, type of subcontract, degree of competition, and basis for establishing source and reasonableness of price, as well as the results of review and evaluation of subcontract proposals when required by FAR 15.806.

Standard Commercial Items—Consists of items that offeror normally fabricates, in whole or in part, and that are generally stocked in inventory. Provide an appropriate explanation of the basis for pricing. If price is based on cost, provide a cost breakdown; if priced at other than cost, provide justification for exemption from submission of cost or pricing data, as required by FAR 15.804-3(e).

Interorganizational Transfer (at other than cost)—Explain pricing method used. (See FAR 31.205-26).

Raw Material—Consists of material in a form or state that requires further processing. Provide priced quantities of items required for the proposal.

Purchased Parts—Includes material items not covered above. Provide priced quantities of items required for the proposal.

Interorganizational Transfer (at cost)—Include separate breakdown of cost by element.

Direct Labor—Provide a time-phased (e.g., monthly, quarterly, etc.) breakdown of labor hours, rates, and cost by appropriate category, and furnish bases for estimates.

Indirect Costs—Indicate how offeror has computed and applied offeror's indirect costs, including cost breakdowns, and showing trends and budgetary data, to provide a basis for evaluating the reasonableness of proposed rates. Indicate the rates used and provide an appropriate explanation.

Other Costs—List all other costs not otherwise included in the categories described above (e.g., special tooling, travel, computer and consultant services, preservation, packaging and packing, spoilage and rework, and Federal excise tax on finished articles) and provide bases for pricing.

Royalties—If more than $250, provide the following information on a separate page for each separate royalty or license fee: name and address of licensor; date of license agreement; patent numbers, patent application serial numbers, or other basis on which the royalty is payable; brief description (including any part or model numbers of each contract item or component on which the royalty is payable); percentage or dollar rate of royalty per unit; unit price of contract item; number of units; and total dollar amount of royalties. In addition, if specifically requested by the contracting officer, provide a copy of the current license agreement and identification of applicable claims of specific patents. (See FAR 27.204 and 31.205-37).

Facilities Capital Cost of Money—When the offeror elects to claim facilities capital cost of money as an allowable cost, the offeror must submit Form CASB-CMF and show the calculation of the proposed amount (see FAR 31.205-10).

2. As part of the specific information required, the offeror must submit with offeror's proposal, and clearly identify as such, cost or pricing data (that is, data that are verifiable and factual and otherwise as defined at FAR 15801). In addition, submit with offeror's proposal any information reasonably required to explain offeror's estimating process, including—

a. The judgmental factors applied and the mathematical or other methods used in the estimate, including those used in projecting from known data; and

b. The nature and amount of any contingencies included in the proposed price.

3. There is a clear distinction between submitting cost or pricing data and merely making available books, records, and other documents without identification. The requirement for submission of cost or pricing data is met when all accurate cost or pricing data reasonably available to the offeror have been submitted, either actually or by specific identification, to the contracting officer or an authorized representative. As later information comes into the offeror's possession, it should be promptly submitted to the contracting officer. The requirement for submission of cost or pricing data continues up to the time of final agreement on price.

4. In submitting offeror's proposal, offeror must include an index, appropriately referenced, of all the cost or pricing data and information accompanying or identified in the proposal. In addition, any future additions and/or revisions, up to the date of agreement on price, must be annotated on a supplemental index.

5. By submitting offeror's proposal, the offeror, if selected for negotiation, grants the contracting officer or an authorized representative the right to examine those books, records, documents, and other supporting

data that will permit adequate evaluation of the proposed price. This right may be exercised at any time before award.

6. As soon as practicable after final agreement on price, but before the award resulting from the proposal, the offeror shall, under the conditions stated in FAR 15.804-4, submit a Certificate of Current Cost or Pricing Data.

7. HEADINGS FOR SUBMISSION OF LINE-ITEM SUMMARIES:

A. New Contracts (including Letter contracts).

Cost elements (1)	Proposed Contract Estimate—Total Cost (2)	Proposed Contract Estimate—Unit Cost (3)	Reference (4)

Under Column (1)—Enter appropriate cost elements.

Under Column (2)—Enter those necessary and reasonable costs that in offeror's judgment will properly be incurred in efficient contract performance. When any of the costs in this column have already been incurred (e.g., under a letter contract or unpriced order) describe them on an attached supporting schedule. When preproduction or startup costs are significant, or when specifially requested to do so by the contracting officer, provide a full identification and explanation of them.

Under Column (3)—Optional, unless required by the contracting officer.

Under Column (4)—Identify the attachment in which the information supporting the specific cost element may be found. Attach separate pages as necessary.

B. Change Orders (modifications).

Cost Elements (1)	Estimated Cost of All Work Deleted (2)	Cost of Deleted Work Already Performed (3)	Net Cost to Be Deleted (4)	Cost of Work Added (5)	Net Cost of Change (6)	Reference (7)

Under Column (1)—Enter appropriate cost elements.

Under Column (2)—Include (i) current estimates of what the cost would have been to complete deleted work not yet performed, and (ii) the cost of deleted work already performed.

Under Column (3)—Include the incurred cost of deleted work already performed, actually computed if possible, or estimated in the contractor's accounting records. Attach a detailed inventory of work, materials, parts, components, and hardware already purchased, manufactured, or performed and deleted by the change, indicating the cost and proposed disposition of each line item. Also, if offeror desires to retain these items or any portion of them, indicate the amount offered for them.

Under Column (4)—Enter the net cost to be deleted which is the estimated cost of all deleted work less the cost of deleted work already performed. Column (2) less Column (3) = Column (4).

Under Column (5)—Enter the offeror's estimate for cost of work added by the change. When nonrecurring costs are significant, or when specifically requested to do so by the contracting officer, provide a full identification and explanation of them.

Under Column (6)—Enter the net cost of change which is the cost of work added, less the net cost to be deleted. When this result is negative, place the amount in parentheses. Column (4) less Column (5) = Column (6).

Under Column (7)—Identify the attachment in which the information supporting the specific cost element may be found. Attach separate pages as necessary.

C. Price Revision/Redetermination.

Cutoff Date (1)	Number of Units Completed (2)	Number of Units to Be Completed (3)	Contract Amount (4)	Redetermination Proposal Amount (5)	Difference (6)

Cost Elements (7)	Incurred Cost— Preproduction (8)	Incurred Cost— Completed Units (9)	Incurred Cost— Work in Process (10)	Total Incurred Cost (11)	Estimated Cost to Complete (12)	Estimated Total Cost (13)	Reference (14)

Under Column (1)—Enter the cutoff date required by the contract, if applicable.

Under Column (2)—Enter the number of units completed during the period for which experienced costs of production are being submitted.

Under Column (3)—Enter the number of units remaining to be completed under the contract.

Under Column (4)—Enter the cumulative contract amount.

Under Column (5)—Enter the offeror's redetermination proposal amount.

Under Column (6)—Enter the difference between the contract amount and the redetermination proposal amount. When this result is negative, place the amount in parentheses. Column (4) less Column (5) = Column (6).

Under Column (7)—Enter appropriate cost elements. When residual inventory exists, the final costs established under fixed-price-incentive and fixed-price-redeterminable arrangements should be net of the fair market value of such inventory. In support of subcontract costs, submit a listing of all subcontracts subject to repricing action, annotated as to their status.

Under Column (8)—Enter all costs incurred under the contract before starting production and other nonrecurring costs (usually referred to as startup costs) from offeror's books and records as of the cutoff date. These include such costs as preproduction engineering, special plant rearrangement, training program, and any identifiable nonrecurring costs such as initial rework, spoilage, pilot runs, etc. In the event the amounts are not segregated in or otherwise available from offeror's records, enter in this column offeror's best estimates. Explain the basis for each estimate and how the costs are charged on offeror's accounting records (e.g., included in production costs as direct engineering labor, charged to manufacturing overhead, etc.). Also show how the costs would be allocated to the units at their various stages of contract completion.

Under Columns (9) and (10)—Enter in Column (9) the production costs from offeror's books and records (exclusive of preproduction costs reported in Column (8)) of the units completed as of the cutoff date. Enter in Column (10) the costs of work in process as determined from offeror's records or inventories at the cutoff date. When the amounts for work in process are not available in contractor's records but reliable estimates for them can be made, enter the estimated amounts in Column (10) and enter in Column (9) the differences between the total incurred costs (exclusive of preproduction costs) as of the cutoff date and these estimates. Explain the basis for the estimates, including identification of any provision for experienced or anticipated allowances, such as shrinkage, rework, design changes, etc. Furnish experienced unit or lot costs (or labor hours) from inception of contract to the cutoff date, improvement curves, and any other available production cost history pertaining to the item(s) to which offeror's proposal relates.

Under Column (11)—Enter total incurred costs (Total of Columns (8), (9), and (10)).

Under Column (12)—Enter those necessary and reasonable costs that in contractor's judgment will properly be incurred in completing the remaining work to be performed under the contract with respect to the item(s) to which contractor's proposal relates.

Under Column (13)—Enter total estimated cost (Total of Columns (11) and (12)).

Under Column (14)—Identify the attachment in which the information supporting the specific cost element may be found. Attach separate pages as necessary.

(c) Closing or cutoff dates should be included as part of the data submitted with the proposal. If possible, the contracting officer and offeror should reach a prior understanding on criteria for establishing closing or cutoff dates (see 15.804-4(c)).

(d) The requirement for submission of cost or pricing data is met if all cost or pricing data reasonably available to the offeror are either submitted or identified in writing by the time of agreement on price. However, there is a clear distinction between submitting cost or pricing data and merely making available books, records, and other documents without identification. The latter does not constitute "submission" of cost or pricing data.

(e) If cost or pricing data and information required to explain the estimating process are required and the offeror initially refuses to provide necessary data, or the contracting officer determines that the data provided is so deficient as to preclude adequate analysis and evaluation, the contracting officer shall again attempt to secure the data and/or elicit corrective action. If the offeror still persists in refusing to provide the needed data or to take corrective action, the contracting officer shall withhold the award or price adjustment and refer the contract action to higher authority, including details of the attempts made to resolve the matter and a statement of the practicability of obtaining the supplies or services from another source.

(f) Preproduction and startup costs include costs such as preproduction engineering, special tooling, special plant rearrangement, training programs, and such nonrecurring costs as initial rework, initial spoilage, and pilot runs. When these costs may be a significant cost factor in an acquisition, the contracting officer shall require in the solicitation that the offeror provide (1) an estimate of total preproduction and startup costs, (2) the extent to which these costs are included in the proposed price, and (3) the intent to absorb, or plan for recovery of, any remaining costs. If a successful offeror has indicated an intent to absorb any portion of these costs, the contract shall expressly provide that such portion will not be charged to the Government in any future noncompetitive pricing action.

(g)(1) The requirement for contractors to obtain cost or pricing data from prospective subcontractors is prescribed at 15.806. However, these data do not have to be submitted to the Government unless called for under subparagraph (2) below.

(2) The contracting officer shall require a contractor that is required to submit certified cost or pricing data also to submit to the Government (or cause the submission of) accurate, complete, and current cost or pricing data from prospective subcontractors in support of each subcontract cost estimate that is (i) $1,000,000 or more, (ii) both more than $100,000 and more than 10 percent of the prime contractor's proposed price, or (iii) considered to be necessary for adequately pricing the prime contract.

(3) If the prospective contractor satisfies the contracting officer that a subcontract will be priced on the basis of one of the exemptions in 15.804-3, the contracting officer normally shall not require submission of subcontractor cost or pricing data to the Government in that case. If the subcontract estimate is based upon the cost or pricing data of the prospective subcontractor most likely to be awarded the subcontract, the

contracting officer shall not require submission to the Government of data from more than one proposed subcontractor for that subcontract.

(4) The contracting officer shall require the prospective contractor to support subcontractor cost estimates below the threshold in 15.806(b) with any data or information (including other subcontractor quotations) needed to establish a reasonable price.

(h) Subcontractor cost or pricing data shall be accurate, complete, and current as of the date of final price agreement given on the contractor's Certificate of Current Cost or Pricing Data. The prospective contractor shall be responsible for updating a prospective subcontractor's data.

(i) When the prospective contractor has generally complied with subcontract cost or pricing data requirements, the contracting officer may, in exceptional cases, excuse failure to do so for particular subcontracts and award the prime contract. Each such excuse, unless limited to allowing additional time, requires approval by the chief of the contracting office. For each subcontract involved, the contractor remains obligated to obtain prospective subcontractor costs or pricing data before actual award of that subcontract. For each such subcontract, the contracting officer shall—

(1) Allow additional time for submission of data up to the date of agreement upon the prime contract price;

(2) Withdraw the requirement if data submitted are adequate to support the subcontract estimate;

(3) Reserve the subcontract item for future pricing;

(4) Consider another contract type; or

(5) Make other arrangements to provide an adequate basis for price agreement.

15.804-7 Defective cost or pricing data.

(a) If, before agreement on price, the contracting officer learns that any cost or pricing data submitted are inaccurate, incomplete, or noncurrent, the contracting officer shall immediately bring the matter to the attention of the prospective contractor, whether the defective data increase or decrease the contract price. The contracting officer shall negotiate, using any new data submitted or making satisfactory allowance for the incorrect data. The price negotiation memorandum shall reflect the revised facts.

(b) If, after award, cost or pricing data are found to be inaccurate, incomplete, or noncurrent as of the date of final agreement on price given on the contractor's or subcontractor's Certificate of Current Cost or Pricing Data, the Government is entitled to a price adjustment, including profit or fee, of any significant amount by which the price was increased because of the defective data. This entitlement is ensured by including in the contract one of the clauses prescribed in 15.804-8 and set forth at 52.215-22, Price Reduction for Defective Cost or Pricing Data, and 52.215-23, Price Reduction for Defective Cost or Pricing Data—Modifications. The clauses give the Government the right to a price adjustment for defects in cost or pricing data submitted by the contractor, a prospective subcontractor, or an actual subcontractor. In arriving at a price adjustment under the clause, the contracting officer shall consider—

(1) The time by which the cost or pricing data became reasonably available to the contractor.

(2) The extent to which the Government relied upon the defective data; and

(3) Any understated cost or pricing data submitted in support of price negotiations, up to the amount of the Government's claim for overstated pricing data arising out of the same pricing action (for example, the initial pricing of the same contract or the pricing of the same change order). Such offsets need not be in the same cost groupings (e.g., material, direct labor, or indirect costs).

(c) If, after award, the contracting officer learns or suspects that the data furnished were not accurate, complete, and current, or were not adequately verified by the contractor as of the time of negotiation, the contracting officer shall request an audit to evaluate the accuracy, completeness, and currency of the data. Only if the audit reveals that the data certified by the contractor were defective may the Government evaluate the profit-cost relationships. The contracting officer shall not reprice the contract solely because the profit was greater than forecast or because some contingency specified in the submission failed to materialize.

(d) For each advisory audit received based on a postaward review which indicates defective pricing, the contracting officer shall make a determination as to whether or not the data submitted were defective and relied upon. Before making such a determination, the contracting officer should give the contractor an opportunity to support the accuracy, completeness, and currency of the data in question. The contracting officer shall prepare a memorandum indicating (1) the contracting officer determination as to whether or not the submitted data were accurate, complete, and current as of the certified date and whether or not the Government relied on the data, and (2) the results of any contractual action taken. The contracting officer shall send one copy of this memorandum to the auditor and, if the contract has been assigned for administration, one copy to the administrative contracting officer (ACO). The contracting officer shall notify the contractor by copy of this memorandum, or otherwise, of the determination.

(e) If (1) both contractor and subcontractor submitted and (2) the contractor certified cost or pricing data, the Government has the right, under the clauses at 52.215-22, Price Reduction for Defective Cost or Pricing Data, and 52.215-23, Price Reduction for Defective Cost or Pricing Data—Modifications, to reduce the prime contract price if it was significantly increased because a subcontractor submitted defective data. This right applies whether these data supported subcontract cost estimates or supported firm agreements between subcontractor and contractor.

(f) If Government audit discloses defective subcontractor cost or pricing data, the information necessary to support a reduction in prime contract and subcontract prices may be available only from the Government. To the extent necessary to secure a prime contract price reduction, the contracting officer should make this information available to the prime contractor or appropriate subcontractors upon request. If release of the information would compromise Government security or disclose trade secrets or confidential business information, the contracting officer shall release it only under conditions that will protect it from improper disclosure. Information made available under this paragraph shall be limited to that used as the basis for the prime contract price reduction. In order to afford an opportunity for corrective action, the contracting officer should give the prime contractor reasonable advance notice before determining to reduce the prime contract price.

(1) When a prime contractor includes defective subcontract data in arriving at the price but later awards the subcontract to a lower priced subcontractor (or does not subcontract for the work), any adjustment in the prime contract price due to defective subcontract data is limited to the difference (plus applicable indirect cost and profit markups) between (i) the subcontract price used for pricing the prime contract and (ii) either the actual subcontract price or the actual cost to the contractor, if not subcontracted, provided the data on which the actual subcontract price is based are not themselves defective.

(2) Under cost-reimbursement contracts and under all fixed-price contracts except (i) firm-fixed-price contracts and (ii) contracts with economic price adjustment, payments to subcontractors that are higher than they would be had there been no defective subcontractor cost or pricing data shall be the basis for disallowance or nonrecognition of costs under the clauses prescribed in 15.804-8. The Government has a continuing and direct financial interest in such payments that is unaffected by the initial agreement on prime contract price.

Comments on FAR Provisions Regarding Cost or Pricing Data

The following comments highlight some of the major provisions of the current acquisition regulations. In every instance, these provisions originated in decisions by boards of contract appeals or federal courts.

Fact v. Judgment

FAR 15.804-4(b) states: "The certificate does not constitute a representation as to the accuracy of the contractor's judgment on the estimate of future costs or projections. It does apply to the data upon which the judgment or estimate was based. This distinction between fact and judgment should be clearly understood." Perhaps the distinction should be clearly understood; unfortunately, the subject is rather complex. For one thing, although price reduction for defective pricing cannot be asserted because the contractor's judgment was inaccurate, incomplete, or noncurrent, such assertion will prevail on a finding that the facts upon which the judgment was based were inaccurate, incomplete, or noncurrent.

In *Norris Industries, Inc.*, ASBCA No. 15442, 74-1 BCA par. 10,482, the government asserted that the contractor had forecast data indicating a lower G&A rate than proposed. Despite the contractor's protest that the forecast represented judgment and not factual data, the board held that there was defective pricing because Norris failed to disclose the facts upon which the forecast was based. In the same year, however, *E-Systems,* ASBCA No. 17557, 74-2 BCA par. 10,782, aff'd on MFR, 74-2 BCA par. 10,943, brought a different ruling. A DCAA postaward defective pricing audit revealed the existence, at the time of contract negotiations, of an E-Systems profit plan that forecast lower overhead rates than those submitted and that had not been disclosed by the contractor. The board ruled that the profit plan did not constitute cost or pricing data, and thus the contractor was under no obligation to disclose it.

Contractor's Responsibility for Information Available Within the Company

FAR 15.804-4(b) provides, with respect to readily available information, that "the contractor's responsibility is not limited by any lack of personal knowledge of the information on the part of its negotiators."

The board and court decisions discussed in this chapter include many illustrations where the government's assertion of contract price reduction was upheld on the basis that certain information, e.g., availability of a potential vendor who submitted a lower quote, was not disclosed. In some instances, the nondisclosure appeared attributable to a conscious decision by the company that, in the circumstances, such information did not constitute data and that, therefore, there was no requirement to disclose. In other instances, the nondisclosure appeared to be attributable to the fact that such information was known to the contractor's purchasing or engineering people but was not known by either the signatory to the certificate or the negotiator.

This provision emphasizes the point reiterated frequently by the author regarding the need for government contractors to assemble teams for all facets of government procurement and contract administration. These teams should include all of the required in-house talent available, plus outside consultants where desirable, under a coordinator, to match the government's contracting officer and the team of advisors. The company's official signing the Certificate of Current Cost or Pricing Data cannot possibly be aware of all the necessary information but can see to it that the support team has the data and will make it available on a timely basis.

Submitting v. Making Available

The distinction between "submitting" and "making available" has been made in many of the judicial rulings reviewed in this chapter, but this subject remains controversial. The boards and courts have emphasized over the years that it is not enough to grant access to books and records or even to submit the required records. Contractors have been charged with the additional burden of assuring that the government representatives understand the significance of such records for price negotiation purposes. On the other hand, judicial rulings have recognized some limitations with respect to this issue, as witnessed in *HardieTynes Manufacturing Co.,* ASBCA No. 20717, 76-2 BCA par. 12,121. A lower quote, which was not used in the proposal, was contained in a folder furnished the auditor. This folder had only two other quotes and three replies indicating "no quote." The board said: "Under these circumstances, we do not believe appellant was obligated to 'lead the auditor by the hand' by pointing out to him that the Cincinnati Gear quote was low but was not being used for the reasons indicated." Although this statement is somewhat reassuring, and a good reference point, we would caution the reader that most decisions by far appear to require a virtual "leading by the hand."

Closing or Cutoff Dates for Submission of Current Data

This subject is referred to in FAR 15.804-4(c), which provides:

Closing or cutoff dates should be included as part of the data submitted with the proposal. Certain data may not be reasonably available before normal periodic closing dates (e.g., actual indirect costs). Before agreement on price, the contractor shall update all data as of the latest dates for which information is reasonably available. Data within the contractor's or a subcontractor's organization on matters significant to contractor management and to the Government will be treated as reasonably available. What is significant depends upon the circumstances of each acquisition.

In the judicial rulings in which the time when cost or pricing data were reasonably available to the contractor was an issue, the board has generally appeared to look for pragmatic solutions. In *American Bosch Arma,* ASBCA No. 10305, 65-2 BCA par. 5280, for example, the board rejected the contentions of both parties and selected a cut-off date it considered reasonable after "(c)onsidering the time involved in the receipt of vendors' quotations, their posting or recording, and other procedures necessary to extract a new price or quotation. . . ." In *FMC Corporation,* ASBCA Nos. 10095 and 11113, 66-1 BCA par. 5483, the board held that the contractor's failure to disclose experiments as a result of which FMC ultimately manufactured certain components in-house at a lower cost than shown in quotations received from vendors did not constitute defective data because the results of such experiments were not reasonably available at the time of negotiations. As we cautioned in our analysis earlier in this chapter, we are not certain how the board would rule on similar circumstances today.

As one other illustration, in *LTV Electrosystems, Inc.,* ASBCA No. 16802, 73-1 BCA par. 9957, the board sustained the contractor's appeal from the contracting officer's decision that certain current data were not submitted. This was an urgent Vietnam-related procurement, and the board concluded that LTV did submit whatever data were reasonably available. However, it distinguished its decision from those in *Sylvania Electric Products, Inc.,* ASBCA No. 13622, 70-2 BCA par. 8387, and *Lambert Engineering Co.,* ASBCA No. 13338, 69-1 BCA par. 7663, in which, according to the board, "the data in question were readily available to the contractor's negotiators but not made known to them or to the government at the price negotiations simply because of the contractor's lack of effort or inadequate internal procedures."

What Data Must Be Disclosed?

We find little in FAR that offers guidance as to when certain information takes on data status and must be disclosed. The most that can be done is to review some of the judicial rulings in this area and to search for the one that most nearly parallels the actual circumstances under consideration.

In *Cutler-Hammer, supra,* the court upheld the ASBCA decision that ruled that a quote from a previously unknown company, without sufficient supporting technical information and at a "ridiculously low" price, should have been disclosed and that the failure to do so resulted in submission of defective data. The court acknowledged that a contractor is not required to divulge to the government every proposal it receives. In this case, however, the court found that Cutler-Hammer had continued to follow up the matter with this bidder and asked for a technical proposal, and, in fact, the proposal was still under consideration at the date of the contractor's certificate.

The ASBCA ruling in *Cutler-Hammer* was handed down in June 1967, but a few months later the board appeared to have reversed itself in *Sparton Corp.,* ASBCA No. 11363, 67-2 BCA par. 6539. The government filed a motion for reconsideration, asserting that circumstances in *Sparton* were identical to those in *Cutler-Hammer,* but the board did not find that Sparton's failure to disclose constituted defective pricing. The board rejected the government's motion for reconsideration for a number of reasons, one of which was that Cutler-Hammer was evaluating the undisclosed bid during contract negotiations while Sparton did not contact the proposed supplier for over two months after the prime contract was executed.

In *Aerojet-General Corp.,* ASBCA No. 12783, 69-1 BCA par. 7585, the contractor did not disclose the lower bid of a company whose proposed delivery schedule did not meet the needs of the prime contractor or the government. The board ruled that the lower bid, even though unresponsive as to delivery schedule, should have been disclosed. Here again, we have circumstances in which this company later agreed to meet the required schedule and was awarded the subcontract.

The board also ruled in favor of the contractor and denied the government's motion for reconsideration in *Chu Associates, Inc.,* ASBCA No. 15004, 73-1 BCA par. 9906; 73-2 BCA par. 10,120. Chu had manufactured this contract item in the past and had always employed Columbia Products as a subcontractor for one of the components. After the government inserted a Liquidated Damages clause for late deliveries and Columbia Products could not guarantee timely delivery and would not accept any portion of the liquidated damages, Chu looked elsewhere and ultimately awarded the subcontract to Geonautics, "a new and untried supplier." In ruling for the Chu company the board again distinguished the circumstances from *Cutler-Hammer* when it found that Chu had given no consideration to the use of Geonautics prior to the date it executed its certificate, "nor did it make so much as a casual investigation of its capabilities of performing the work." The board said that it found that the Geonautics award "was not in contemplation of appellant before the critical date on which appellant executed its certificate. . . ."

The issue of when information concerning the possibility of dealing with another vendor takes on the status of "data" and must be disclosed to the government appears in a number of other judicial rulings and has drawn a mixed reception. Quoting again from the Court of Claims decision in *Cutler-Hammer, supra,* we read, for example, that: "[t]o allow a contractor to submit data, arrive at a negotiated price, file a certificate, and then use a lower component cost, when that lower cost was a definite possibility during the negotiating stage, but was not then disclosed, would defeat the purpose of the statute and the contract clause."

The thinking in the above situation is understandable. The problems and uncertainties, however, do not generally arise when the award to a lower-cost subcontractor is a definite possibility. Rather, controversies surface when a lower-cost subcontractor is not under serious consideration at the time the certificate is signed by the prime contractor but does ultimately receive the award. As the board ruled in *Plessey Industries, Inc.,* ASBCA No. 16720, 74-1 BCA par. 10,603, implicit in determining whether vendor quotations constitute cost or pricing data "is the 'reasonable man's' test: would a prudent buyer and seller, under the particular circumstances, reasonably expect the undisclosed quotation to have a significant effect on the price negotiations?"

Government Reliance on Defective Data

The highly controversial aspects of this subject are illustrated by several cases in this chapter, and we invite particular attention to *Universal Restoration, Inc.* After five decisions by a board of contract appeals and two by federal courts, most of them closely divided, the contractor's appeal based on government nonreliance on its submitted cost or pricing data was sustained.

DCAA IMPLEMENTATION

As we noted earlier in this chapter, the enactment of P.L. 87-653 has been mainly attributable to GAO reports in the late 1950s and early 1960s alleging contract overpricing because of contractors' failure to submit, or DOD's failure to obtain, accurate, current, and complete cost data. Dissatisfaction in Congress with the increasingly popular incentive contracts helped provide a receptive mood for the so-called Truth in Negotiations Act.

It became evident early on that the existence of defective pricing could be discovered best through postaward audits. And in the early 1960s, most of the alleged instances of defective pricing were the results of postaward audits by the GAO.

When the GAO substantially reduced its postaward audits under P.L. 87-653, it continued to criticize the Department of Defense for not taking on this task, and a series of GAO reports persuaded DOD to direct the then newly established DCAA to move intensively into this area.

As DCAA increased its effort on these postaward audits, the number of alleged instances of defective pricing increased and so did the related litigation as many contractors appealed adverse decisions to the ASBCA and, in some instances, to the U.S. Court of Claims. The judicial rulings discussed in this chapter span approximately two decades beginning in 1965.

Throughout its history, DCAA has supported its annual requests for personnel and funds by pointing to the dollars it allegedly saved the taxpayers in relation to the cost of operating this agency. DCAA maintains an elaborate management information system that reflects the costs of its various audit endeavors and the related savings. DCAA's analyses revealed that the savings per audit man-year attributable to postaward reviews were continually decreasing.

There are a number of factors that have contributed to the reduced volume of defective pricing audit reports, including increased understanding of and attention to the requirements of P.L. 87-653 and DAR by government contractors, and improved DCAA preaward audits. For these and other reasons, the audit agency has gradually reduced the portion of its personnel resources devoted to this area, although not without continuing opposition and criticism from the GAO. DCAA's so-called matrix, the plan for selecting contracts for postaward review, has been modified to virtually exclude all but fixed-price and fixed-price incentive contracts of very high dollar volume.

The improvements in pricing proposal preparation and documentation by contractors and the decrease in DCAA postaward audit efforts are obvious causes of the significant decrease in litigation covering this area. Another significant factor that has served to reduce disputes involving defective pricing has been the increased tendency for contracting officers and contractors to negotiate price reductions where defective pricing is indicated, rather than to incur the costs involved in litigation. The decisions to negotiate rather than to litigate are largely based on the knowledge gained of the views of the boards and courts by both government and industry. The author has contributed to this understanding by including reviews, analyses, comparisons, and trends involved in defective pricing litigation in his monthly newsletter, the *Administrative and Accounting Guide for Defense Contracts*. The author hopes that all of the significant information on this subject contained in these monthly newsletters for almost two decades, together with additional information, analyses, and conclusions, compiled and presented in this chapter, will provide further assistance in alleviating the disputes and attendant costs and detrimental effects to government-industry relations created by Public Law 87-653.

Pertinent Provisions of DCAA Contract Audit Manual

Throughout this text we refer to the audit procedures of the Defense Contract Audit Agency. Although identified in FAR as an advisor to the contracting officer, with the latter possessing the sole authority for all contracting decisions including costing and pricing, DCAA has been a potent advisor indeed since its establishment in 1965. With the publication of DOD Directive 7640.2 on December 29, 1982, DCAA's position vis-à-vis the contracting officer was aggrandized. Indeed, many observers viewed this Directive as establishing the contract auditor's role beyond that of an advisor and diluting the authority of the contracting officer.

In accordance with the provisions of DODD 7640.2, the status of certain audit reports, including those on defective pricing reviews, must be tracked by DOD acquisition and contract administration organizations. Where the contracting officer's proposed disposition differs from the audit recommendations, the contracting officer's proposal disposition must be referred to a designated senior acquisition official (DISAO). This official shall review the proposed disposition and the audit report and "shall provide to the contracting officer a clear, written recommendation concerning all matters subject to review." This extremely controversial provision has influenced some contracting officers to lean in the direction of endorsing DCAA recommendations in preference to engaging in the paperwork necessary to refer the disagreement to higher levels and further risking the possibility that such higher level's recommendations may support the auditor's position.

"Defective Pricing Reviews" are addressed in CAM Chapter 14, Section 1. We have cited the following provisions (14-104) to provide an indication of the instructions furnished by DCAA headquarters to its auditors:

a. It is the policy of DoD that DCAA establish and conduct a program for performing regularly scheduled defective pricing reviews of selected contracts, subcontracts, and other eligible pricing actions. Based upon inter-agency agreements, contracts awarded by certain non-DoD agencies will be included in the program on the same basis as DoD contracts. In addition to the DCAA selected contracts and subcontracts, defective pricing reviews of individual contracts will be made upon the specific request of contracting officers or other authorized persons or activities.

b. The basic objective of an individual review is to determine if the contract or subcontract price, including fee or profit, was increased by a significant amount because the contractor or subcontractor furnished inaccurate, incomplete, or noncurrent cost or pricing data. As a generalization, this is done by examining and analyzing the records and data available to the contractor or subcontractor as of the date of prime contract final price agreement and comparing them with the submitted cost or pricing data.

c. Requests for defective pricing reviews of contracts awarded by non-DoD agencies will be considered in accordance with the criteria and procedures in 1-300.

d. Headquarters, OPD, will periodically issue guidance on program objectives.

e. Each DCAA branch office, suboffice, and resident office will perform defective pricing reviews in accordance with (1) selection plans issued by Headquarters and (2) specific requests received from contracting officers or other authorized persons or activities. Where field visits are made only for the purpose of defective pricing reviews, the contract administration activity should be notified before making the plant visit.

f. See 1-200 for the interface with GAO on defective pricing reviews.

GAO AND DOD IG CRITICIZE DOD AND DEFENSE CONTRACTORS AT CONGRESSIONAL HEARINGS FOR ALLEGEDLY FAILING TO IMPLEMENT LAW

During the mid-1980s, GAO and DOD IG representatives, at times joined by an Air Force trial attorney, unleashed a number of scathing attacks on contractors, contracting officers, ASBCA administrative judges and, at times, DCAA for allegedly failing to effectively implement the Truth in Negotiations Act. The sharpest attacks were made before Senator Roth's Committee on Governmental Affairs and Congressman Jack Brooks' Legislative and National Security Subcommittee of the House Committee on Government Operations.

Although accustomed to sharp criticisms from the above members of Congress and such officials as Assistant Comptroller General Conahan, Deputy DOD IG Vander Schaaf, and the Air Force trial attorney, many observers were astonished by the severity and harshness of the attacks and their one-sided nature wherein contractors and DOD officials were castigated without an opportunity for explanation and rebuttal. The allegations that the ASBCA was biased in favor of contractors even led to an investigation of the board by GAO, culminating in the board's complete vindication.

Although DCAA was also the subject of harsh criticism for allegedly failing to devote sufficient manpower resources to post-award audits in search of defective pricing, the then newly appointed agency director, William Reed, joined in the attacks. His promises to increase the agency's efforts in this area accompanied by complaints about insufficient personnel eventually were rewarded by congressional award of additional personnel authorization.

DOD 1987 AUTHORIZATION ACT

Although many recognized the extravagant, extreme and one-sided nature of the criticisms, the environment of this period, which reflected strong hostility toward defense contractors and the Department of Defense, inevitably led to legislation that eliminated many contractor defenses against government demands for price reduction for defective pricing that had been recognized by boards of contract appeals and federal courts. In the vigorous debates before congressional committees, it was the same critics, representatives of GAO, DOD IG, and the Air Force, who argued for the harshest possible provisions. The provisions ultimately enacted are quoted below.

SEC. 952. TRUTH-IN-NEGOTIATIONS ACT AMENDMENTS

(a) STRENGTHENING OF PREVENTION OF UNEARNED AND EXCESSIVE CONTRACTOR PROFITS.—Chapter 137 of title 10, United States Code, is amended by inserting after section 2306 the following new section:

§ 2306a. Cost or pricing data: truth in negotiations

(a) REQUIRED COST OR PRICING DATA AND CERTIFICATION.—(1) The head of an agency shall require offerors, contractors, and subcontractors to make cost or pricing data available as follows:

(A) An offeror for a prime contract under this chapter to be entered into using procedures other than sealed-bid procedures shall be required to submit cost or pricing data before the award of the contract if the price of the contract to the United States is expected to exceed $100,000.

(B) The contractor for a contract under this chapter shall be required to submit cost or pricing data before the pricing of a change or modification to the contract if the price adjustment is expected to exceed $100,000 (or such lesser amount as may be prescribed by the head of the agency).

(C) An offeror for a subcontract (at any tier) of a contract under this chapter shall be required to submit cost or pricing data before the award of the subcontract if—

(i) the price of the subcontract is expected to exceed $100,000; and

(ii) the prime contractor and each higher-tier subcontractor have been required to make available cost or pricing data under this section.

(D) The subcontractor for a subcontract covered by subparagraph (C) shall be required to submit cost or pricing data before the pricing of a change or modification to the subcontract if the price adjustment is expected to exceed $100,000 (or such lesser amount as may be prescribed by the head of the agency).

(2) A person required, as an offeror, contractor, or subcontractor, to submit cost or pricing data under paragraph (1) (or required by the head of the agency concerned to submit such data under subsection (c)) shall be required to certify that, to the best of the person's knowledge and belief, the cost or pricing data submitted are accurate, complete, and current.

(3) Cost or pricing data required to be submitted under paragraph (1) (or under subsection (c)), and a certification required to be submitted under paragraph (2), shall be submitted—

(A) in the case of a submission by a prime contractor (or an offeror for a prime contract), to the contracting officer for the contract (or to a designated representative of the contracting officer); or

(B) in the case of a submission by a subcontractor (or an offeror for a subcontract), to the prime contractor.

(4) Except as provided under subsection (b), this section applies to contracts covered into by the head of an agency on behalf of a foreign government.

(5) The head of the agency may waive the requirement under this subsection for a contractor, subcontractor, or offeror to submit cost or pricing data. For purposes of paragraph (1)(C)(ii), a contractor or subcontractor granted such a waiver shall be considered as having been required to make available cost or pricing data under this section.

(b) EXCEPTIONS.—This section need not be applied to a contract or subcontract—

(1) for which the price agreed upon is based on—

(A) adequate price competition;

(B) established catalog or market prices of commercial items sold in substantial quantities to the general public; or

(C) prices set by law or regulation; or

(2) in an exceptional case when the head of the agency determines that the requirements of this section may be waived and states in writing his reasons for such determination.

(c) AUTHORITY TO REQUIRE COST OR PRICING DATA.—When cost or pricing data are not required to be submitted by subsection (a), such data may nevertheless be required to be submitted by the head of the agency if the head of the agency determines that such data are necessary for the evaluation of the agency of the reasonableness of the price of the contract or subcontract.

(d) PRICE REDUCTIONS FOR DEFECTIVE COST OR PRICING DATA.— (1)(A) A prime contract (or change or modification to a prime contract) under which a certificate under subsection (a)(2) is required shall contain a provision that the price of the contract to the United States, including profit or fee, shall be adjusted to exclude any significant amount by which it may be determined by the head of the agency that such price was increased because the contractor (or any subcontractor required to make available such a certificate) submitted defective cost or pricing data.

(B) For the purposes of this section, defective cost or pricing data are cost or pricing data which, as of the date of agreement on the price of the contract (or another date agreed upon between the parties), were inaccurate, incomplete, or noncurrent. If for purposes of the preceding sentence the parties agree upon a date other than the date of agreement on the price of the contract, the date agreed upon by the parties shall be as close to the date of agreement on the price of the contract as is practicable.

(2) In determining for purposes of a contract price adjustment under a contract provision required by paragraph (1) whether, and to what extent, a contract price was increased because the contractor (or a subcontractor) submitted defective cost or pricing data, it shall be a defense that the United States did not rely on the defective data submitted by the contractor or subcontractor.

(3) It is not a defense to an adjustment of the price of a contract under a contract provision required by paragraph (1) that—

(A) the price of the contract would not have been modified even if accurate, complete, and current cost or pricing data had been submitted by the contractor or subcontractor because the contractor or subcontractor—

(i) was the sole source of the property or services procured; or

(ii) otherwise was in a superior bargaining position with respect to the property or services procured;

(B) the contracting officer should have known that the cost and pricing data in issue were defective even though the contractor or subcontractor took no affirmative action to bring the character of the data to the attention of the contracting officer;

(C) the contract was based on an agreement between the contractor and the United States about the total cost of the contract and there was no agreement about the cost of each item procured under such contract; or

(D) the prime contractor or subcontractor did not submit a certification of cost and pricing data relating to the contract as required under subsection (a)(2).

(4)(A) A contractor shall be allowed to offset an amount against the amount of a contract price adjustment under a contract provision required by paragraph (1) if—

(i) the contractor certifies to the contracting officer (or to a designated representative of the contracting officer) that, to the best of the contractor's knowledge and belief, the contractor is entitled to the offset; and

(ii) the contractor proves that the cost or pricing data were available before the date of agreement on the price of the contract (or price of the modification) and that the data were not submitted as specified in subsection (a)(3) before such date.

(B) A contractor shall not be allowed to offset an amount otherwise authorized to be offset under subparagraph (A) if—

(i) the certification under subsection (a)(2) with respect to the cost or pricing data involved was known to be false when signed; or

(ii) the United States proves that, had the cost or pricing data referred to in subparagraph (A)(ii) been submitted to the United States before the date of agreement on the price of the contract (or price of the modification), the submission of such cost or pricing data would not have resulted in an increase in that price in the amount to be offset.

(e) INTEREST AND PENALTIES FOR CERTAIN OVERPAYMENTS.—(1) If the United States makes an overpayment to a contractor under a contract with the Department of Defense subject to this section and the overpayment was due to the submission by the contractor of defective cost or pricing data, the contractor shall be liable to the United States—

(A) for interest on the amount of such overpayment, to be computed—

(i) for the period beginning on the date the overpayment was made to the contractor and ending on the date the contractor repays the amount of such overpayment to the United States; and

(ii) at the current rate prescribed by the Secretary of the Treasury under section 6621 of the Internal Revenue Code of 1954; and

(B) if the submission of such defective data was a knowing submission, for an additional amount equal to the amount of the overpayment.

(2) Except as provided under subsection (d), the liability of a contractor under this subsection shall not be affected by the contractor's refusal to submit a certification under subsection (a)(2) with respect to the cost or pricing data involved.

(f) RIGHT OF UNITED STATES TO EXAMINE CONTRACTOR RECORDS.— (1) For the purpose of evaluating the accuracy, completeness, and currency of cost or pricing data required to be submitted by this section with respect to a contract or subcontract, the head of the agency, acting through any authorized representative of the head of the agency who is an employee of the United States or a member of the armed forces, shall have the right to examine all records of the contractor or subcontractor related to—

(A) the proposal for the contract or subcontract;

(B) the discussions conducted on the proposal;

(C) pricing of the contract or subcontract; or

(D) performance of the contract or subcontract.

(2) the right of the head of an agency under paragraph (1) shall expire three years after final payment under the contract or subcontract.

(3) In this subsection, the term "records" includes books, documents, and other data.

(g) COST OR PRICING DATA DEFINED.—In this section, the term "cost or pricing data" means all information that is verifiable and that, as of the date of agreement on the price of a contract (or the price of a contract modification), a prudent buyer or seller would reasonably expect to affect price negotiations significantly. Such term does not include information that is judgmental, but does include the factual information from which a judgment was derived.

Some observers have complained that P.L. 87-653 contained only bare bones provisions and that the many ramifications involved in its implementation required decisions by boards of contract appeals and federal courts and subsequent revisions of ASPR/DAR, FPR and now FAR. Although some of the judicial decisions generated opposition in the private sector, the more knowledgeable observers recognized them as efforts to objectively interpret the terse law and probe the intent of the Congress through legislative history. There was no concerted effort by industry to persuade Congress to revise this statute because, particularly in recent years, this body has displayed an unusual hostility to contractors, particularly those supporting this country's defense efforts. It was therefore widely understood that any amendment to P.L. 87-653 would be punitive in nature.

However, instigated by critical reports and testimonies by GAO, DOD IG, and DCAA, Congress now has moved and a close reading of the aforegoing text will reveal many provisions which are, sometimes in the identical language, incorporated into FAR. The punitive additions identify circumstances in which the government did not rely on the cost or pricing data but which may nevertheless not be used as a defense against demands for price reduction, and prohibit offsets of intentional understatements in some instances. The amendment also provides for interest and penalties for submission of defective cost or pricing data.

The conference report on this Act also addresses the amendments to P.L. 87-653 and some of the House and Senate proposals considered and the decisions adopted will be of interest to those in both the private and public sectors who may become involved in defective pricing assertions:

Truth in Negotiations Act Amendments (Sec. 952).

The Senate bill contained a provision (Sec. 948) that would amend Section 2306(f) of title 10, United States Code, to state that cost or pricing data include only data that are factual and verifiable and do not include judgmental data. It would further provide that no judgmental or intentional understatement or cost or pricing data may be used as an offset to an adjustment under this section.

The House amendment contained a similar provision (Sec. 912), that would also define the term "cost and pricing" data to exclude information that is judgmental in nature, such as estimates of future productivity. Such data would, therefore, not be considered for purposes of determining whether defective pricing occurred or for purposes of determining whether a contractor may be entitled to an offset against an amount to be recovered for defective pricing.

The House amendment would also recognize for the first time in statute a contractor's right to offset against an amount that the government is entitled to recover, an amount that reflects cost or pricing data not revealed to the government that would have resulted in an increase in the agreed-to-price. This provision parallels that which authorizes the government to recover when the failure to provide accurate, complete and current data resulted in an increase in price. As in the case of a recovery by the government proof that information available to the contractor prior to the agreement on price establishes the right to recover that amount. The entitlement to recovery may be rebutted through proof by the government that, even if the required data had been provided, the government would not have agreed to a price increase. Finally, the section would restructure the existing Truth in Negotiations Act language to clarify its application.

The Senate recedes to the House with an amendment that would prohibit an offset, if the contractor intentionally withheld from the government information that would indicate a higher cost for an item or service and, thus, certified that the cost or pricing data it submitted was accurate, complete and current when, in fact, the contractor knew it to be false. The amendment would also clarify that a subcontractor may be required to provide cost or pricing data even though the requirement has been waived for the prime contractor or higher-tier subcontractor. The conferees acknowledge the practice of the Department of Defense to waive the requirement for certified cost or pricing data for universities under cost no-fee contracts but to require such data from subcontractors of the university.

The conferees were very concerned with clarifying the definition of cost or pricing data that a contractor is not required to provide and certify to data relating to judgments, business strategies, plans for the future or estimates. A contractor is required, on the other hand to disclose any information relating to execution or implementation of any such strategies or plans. For example, a corporate decision to attempt to negotiate a new labor wage rate structure with its employees union, although verifiable, is not cost or pricing data for purposes of this section. If the company has made an offer to the union, the fact that an offer has been made, and the details and status of the offer, on the other hand, is information that should be conveyed to the government. Finally, this provision was amended to clarify that it applies to contracts and modifications to contracts entered into after the effective date of this Act.

Thus, the provisions of this Act apply only as to information provided to support a new contract or the exercise of an option or modification of an existing contract but not to the cost or pricing data provided to support an existing contract entered into prior to the effective date.

FAR Implementation

The proposed FAR revision eliminates a number of contractor defenses against defective pricing assertions and limits the circumstances in which offsets are allowable.

The major change, eliminating certain contractor defenses against defective pricing allegations, is contained in a revised FAR 15.804-7(b)(3) and the related contract clauses, 52.214-27 and 52.215-22. The clauses provide that where a contracting officer determines that a price or cost reduction should be made because of defective data, "the Contractor agrees not to raise the following matters as a defense—"

(i) The Contractor or subcontractor was a sole source supplier or otherwise was in a superior bargaining position and thus the price of the contract would not have been modified even if accurate, complete, and current cost or pricing data had been submitted;

(ii) The Contracting Officer should have known that the cost or pricing data in issue were defective even though the Contractor or subcontractor took no affirmative action to bring the character of the data to the attention of the Contracting Officer;

(iii) The contract was based on an agreement about the total cost of the contract and there was no agreement about the cost of each item procured under the contract; or

(iv) The Contractor or subcontractor did not submit a Certificate of Current Cost or Pricing Data.

The same contract clauses would provide that unless prohibited by 52.214-27(d)(2)(ii) or 52.215-22(c)(2)(ii), offsets shall be allowed if:

(A) The Contractor certifies to the Contracting Officer that, to the best of the Contractor's knowledge and belief, the Contractor is entitled to the offset in the amount requested; and

(B) The Contractor proves that the cost or pricing data were available before the date of agreement on the price of the contract (or price of the modification) and that the data were not submitted before such date.

The cited exclusionary provisions state that an offset shall not be allowed if:

(A) The understated data was known by the Contractor to be understated when the Certificate of Current Cost or Pricing Data was signed; or

(B) The facts demonstrate that the contract price would not have increased in the amount to be offset even if the available data had been submitted before the date of agreement on price.

As to contractor defenses against allegations of defective pricing, hardliners in DOD IG, DCAA, and GAO would have also eliminated government reliance on defective data. After debate in Congress, this defense was specifically permitted in the Act and remains in FAR.

Another revision to FAR based on the statutory provision establishes that where a requirement for submission of cost or pricing data has been waived for a contractor under a contract, subcontracts thereunder in excess of $100,000, unless otherwise exempt, must submit certified cost or pricing data unless such requirement is specifically waived.

Chapter XXIII

Appeals and Litigation Arising from Disputes with the Government—Boards of Contract Appeals and Federal Courts

In contractual matters with the government, a company finds the government standing in two different positions: that of a contracting party and that of a sovereign. The government is represented by the contracting officer or such representatives to whom the contracting officer specifically delegates some portion of authority. Some government contracts generate a variety of controversies, such as those relating to compliance with specifications and delivery schedules, receipt of government-furnished material or other property in the condition and at the time specified, formal and constructive changes, terminations for default and convenience of the government, and costs and profits under variably priced contracts. By far the greatest number of controversies is settled between the contractor and contracting officer in a manner that at times is not dissimilar to commercial practices. Where the two parties cannot reach an agreement, the contracting officer exercises the government's sovereign power and makes a unilateral decision under the Disputes clause of the contract. This clause, as discussed later in this chapter, entitles the contractor to appeal from the contracting officer's decision.

BACKGROUND

Over the years, legislation and implementing regulations, further amplified by judicial interpretation, have established procedures under which contractors and would-be contractors can appeal from decisions by government officials. Although controversy and litigation continue to arise over questions of procedure, jurisdiction, and others, including constitutional issues, the basic ground rules have been well established and are familiar to the numerous attorneys and others in the public and private sectors who specialize in government procurement law.

The less experienced as well as the experts in this field have available information and authoritative publications to assist them in every aspect of the litigation that ensues when differences between contractors and government officials cannot otherwise be settled. The GOVERNMENT CONTRACTS REPORTER, published by Commerce Clearing House, Inc., contains a comprehensive and timely updated account of all aspects of disputes and remedies. In addition, CCH publishes the verbatim board of contract appeals decisions biweekly and, two or three times during the year, depending on the number of decisions, sets forth the texts of the decisions in cloth-bound form. The biweekly loose leaf publication is entitled CONTRACT APPEALS DECISIONS, and the cloth-bound volumes, BOARD OF CONTRACT APPEALS DECISIONS.

A particularly significant feature of these latter publications is that boards of contract appeals include the CCH references in citing their previous decisions for precedent or reference purposes.

CCH's GOVERNMENT CONTRACTS REPORTER also reports verbatim decisions in this area handed down by the U.S. Claims Court, the U.S. Court of Appeals for the Federal Circuit, and other federal courts as applicable.

Among other useful reference material is the *Manual for Practice Before Boards of Contract Appeals,* prepared by the Federal Bar Association.

The concept of contract disputes clauses and the establishment of administrative boards in the federal departments and agencies designed to provide a relatively inexpensive and expeditious way of resolving government-contractor controversies originated almost a century ago, and various adjustment boards were created and dissolved over the years. A formal and structured system, however, is traceable to the World War II period, with the creation of the War Department Board of Contract Appeals in 1942 and the Navy Board of Contract Appeals in 1944. In May 1949, the two boards merged into the Armed Services Board of Contract Appeals, the ASBCA.

As discussed later, boards of contract appeals (BCAs) were established by some of the other federal departments and agencies. The status of BCAs and their decisions was developed over the years by the U.S. Supreme Court and legislation. The 1954 Wunderlich Act, 41 U.S.C. 321, 322, was particularly significant in according finality to board factual findings absent a determination that such findings were fraudulent, capricious, arbitrary, so grossly erroneous as necessarily to imply bad faith, or not supported by substantial evidence. Neither that Act nor any subsequent legislation provides finality for board decisions on questions of law, a point requiring consideration in deciding whether to appeal board decisions to the federal courts.

CONTRACT DISPUTES ACT OF 1978, P.L. 95-563, NOVEMBER 1, 1978, EFFECTIVE MARCH 1, 1979

The Contract Disputes Act (CDA) was a significant development in the history of boards of contract appeals, providing statutory underpinning for the administrative resolution of contract disputes and prescribing procedures for establishing the boards, selecting their members, and expanding their jurisdiction.

The Act was designed to improve, and provide uniformity in, the resolution of claims and disputes relating to government contracts awarded by executive agencies. Some of the major changes included broadening the authority of the appeals boards to include matters "relating to" a contract as well as matters "arising under" a contract, providing the contractor an option to appeal from a contracting officer's decision to a board of contract appeals or directly to the court of claims (now the U.S. Claims Court), authorizing the executive agency to appeal from a board's adverse decision to the court of claims (now the U.S. Court of Appeals for the Federal Circuit), accelerating resolution of small claims, requiring contractors to certify their claims, and establishing contractors' liability for fraudulent claims. The latter two provisions were added during congressional hearings as a result of an allegation that some contractors were submitting unsupported and fraudulent claims.

Pertinent portions of this significant Act as originally enacted are cited below.

FRAUDULENT CLAIMS

SEC. 5. If a contractor is unable to support any part of his claim and it is determined that such inability is attributable to misrepresentation of fact or fraud on the part of the contractor, he shall be liable to the Government for an amount equal to such unsupported part of the claim in addition to all costs to the Government attributable to the cost of reviewing said part of his claim. Liability under this subsection shall be determined within six years of the commission of such misrepresentation of fact or fraud. [41 U.S. Code 604.]

DECISION BY THE CONTRACTING OFFICER

SEC. 6. (a) All claims by a contractor against the government relating to a contract shall be in writing and shall be submitted to the contracting officer for a decision. All claims by the government against a contractor relating to a contract shall be the subject of a decision by the contracting officer. The contracting officer shall issue his decisions in writing, and shall mail or otherwise furnish a copy of the decision to the contractor. The decision shall state the reasons for the decision reached, and shall inform the contractor of his rights as provided in this Act. Specific findings of fact are not required, but, if made, shall not be binding in any subsequent proceeding. The authority of this subsection shall not extend to a claim or dispute for penalties or forfeitures prescribed by statute or regulation which another Federal agency is specifically authorized to administer, settle, or determine. This section shall not authorize any agency head to settle, compromise, pay, or otherwise adjust any claim involving fraud.

(b) The contracting officer's decision on the claim shall be final and conclusive and not subject to review by any forum, tribunal, or Government agency, unless an appeal or suit is timely commenced as authorized by this Act. Nothing in this Act shall prohibit executive agencies from including a clause in government contracts requiring that pending final decision of an appeal, action, or final settlement, a contractor shall proceed diligently with performance of the contract in accordance with the contracting officer's decision.

(c)(1) A contracting officer shall issue a decision on any submitted claim of $50,000 or less within sixty days from his receipt of a written request from the contractor that a decision be rendered within that period. For claims of more than $50,000, the contractor shall certify that the claim is made in good faith, that the supporting data are accurate and complete to the best of his knowledge and belief, and that the amount requested accurately reflects the contract adjustment for which the contractor believes the government is liable.

(2) A contracting officer shall, within sixty days of receipt of a submitted certified claim over $50,000—

(A) issue a decision; or

(B) notify the contractor of the time within which a decision will be issued.

(3) The decision of a contracting officer on submitted claims shall be issued within a reasonable time, in accordance with regulations promulgated by the agency, taking into account such factors as the size and complexity of the claim and the adequacy of the information in support of the claim provided by the contractor.

(4) A contractor may request the agency board of contract appeals to direct a contracting officer to issue a decision in a specified period of time, as determined by the board, in the event of undue delay on the part of the contracting officer.

(5) Any failure by the contracting officer to issue a decision on a contract claim within the period required will be deemed to be a decision by the contracting officer denying the claim and will authorize the commencement of the appeal or suit on the claim as otherwise provided in this Act. However, in the event an appeal or suit is so commenced in the absence

of a prior decision by the contracting officer, the tribunal concerned may, at its option, stay the proceedings to obtain a decision on the claim by the contracting officer. [41 U.S. Code 605.]

CONTRACTOR'S RIGHT OF APPEAL TO BOARD OF CONTRACT APPEALS

SEC. 7. Within ninety days from the date of receipt of a contracting officer's decision under section 6, the contractor may appeal such decision to an agency board of contract appeals, as provided in section 8. [41 U.S. Code 606.]

* * * *

SEC. 8.

* * * *

(d) Each agency board shall have jurisdiction to decide any appeal from a decision of a contracting officer (1) relative to a contract made by its agency, and (2) relative to a contract made by any other agency when such agency or the Administrator has designated the agency board to decide the appeal. In exercising this jurisdiction, the agency board is authorized to grant any relief that would be available to a litigant asserting a contract claim in the Court of Claims.

* * * *

(f) The rules of each agency board shall include a procedure for the accelerated disposition of any appeal from a decision of a contracting officer where the amount in dispute is $50,000 or less. The accelerated procedure shall be applicable at the sole election of only the contractor. Appeals under the accelerated procedure shall be resolved, whenever possible, within one hundred and eighty days from the date the contractor elects to utilize such procedure.

(g)(1) The decision of an agency board of contract appeals shall be final, except that—

(A) A contractor may appeal such a decision to the Court of Claims within one hundred twenty days after the date of receipt of a copy of such decision, or

(B) the agency head, if he determines that an appeal should be taken, and with the prior approval of the Attorney General, transmits the decision of the board of contract appeals to the United States Court of Claims for judicial review, under section 2510 of title 28, United States Code, as amended herein, within one hundred and twenty days from the date of the agency's receipt of a copy of the board's decision.

* * * *

SMALL CLAIMS

SEC. 9. (a) The rules of each agency board shall include a procedure for the expedited disposition of any appeal from a decision of a contracting officer where the amount in dispute is $10,000 or less. The small claims procedure shall be applicable at the sole election of the contractor.

(b) The small claims procedure shall provide for simplified rules of procedure to facilitate the decision of any appeal thereunder. Such appeals may be decided by a single member of the agency board with such concurrences as may be approved by rule or regulation.

(c) Appeals under the small claims procedure shall be resolved, whenever possible, within one hundred twenty days from the date on which the contractor elects to utilize such procedure.

(d) A decision against the Government or the contractor reached under the small claims procedure shall be final and conclusive and shall not be set aside except in cases of fraud.

(e) Administrative determinations and final decisions under this section shall have no value as precedent for future cases under this Act.

* * * *

ACTIONS IN COURT; JUDICIAL REVIEW OF BOARD DECISIONS

SEC. 10. (a)(1). Except as provided in paragraph (2), and in lieu of appealing the decision of the contracting officer under section 6 to an agency board, a contractor may bring an action directly on the claim in the United States Court of Claims, notwithstanding any contract provision, regulation, or rule of law to the contrary.

*   *   *   *

(3) Any action under paragraph (1) or (2) shall be filed within twelve months from the date of the receipt by the contractor of the decision of the contracting officer concerning the claim, and shall proceed de novo in accordance with the rules of the appropriate court.

(b) In the event of an appeal by a contractor or the Government from a decision of any agency board pursuant to section 8, notwithstanding any contract provision, regulation, or rules of law to the contrary, the decision of the agency board on any question of law shall not be final or conclusive, but the decision on any question of fact shall be final and conclusive and shall not be set aside unless the decision is fraudulent, or arbitrary, or capricious, or so grossly erroneous as to necessarily imply bad faith, or is such decision is not supported by substantial evidence.

(c) In any appeal by a contractor or the Government from a decision of an agency board pursuant to section 8, the court may render an opinion and judgment and remand the case for further action by the agency board or by the executive agency as appropriate, with such direction as the court considers just and proper, or, in its discretion and in lieu of remand it may retain the case and take such additional evidence or action as may be necessary for final disposition of the case.

*   *   *   *

INTEREST

SEC. 12. Interest on amounts found due contractors on claims shall be paid to the contractor from the date the contracting officer receives the claim pursuant to section 6(a) from the contractor until payment thereof. The interest provided for in this section shall be paid at the rate established by the Secretary of the Treasury pursuant to Public Law 92-41 (85 Stat. 97) for the Renegotiation Board. [41 U.S. Code 611.]

*   *   *   *

EFFECTIVE DATE OF ACT

SEC. 16. This Act shall apply to contracts entered into one hundred twenty days after the date of enactment. Notwithstanding any provision in a contract made before the effective date of this Act, the contractor may elect to proceed under this Act with respect to any claim pending then before the contracting officer or initiated thereafter.

REGULATORY IMPLEMENTATION OF STATUTORY PROVISIONS GOVERNING CONTRACT DISPUTES

The basic regulatory implementation is contained in FAR Part 33—Protests, Disputes, and Appeals. However, as commented on elsewhere in this text, FAR does not provide complete coverage in a number of areas. Accordingly, it is necessary to review related coverage in the many FAR Supplements issued by the federal departments and agencies. Among the information contained in these supplements are the rules of practice for the various boards. Here again, a publication such as CCH's CONTRACT APPEALS DECISIONS is useful in that it includes the Final Uniform Rules of Procedure for Boards of Contract Appeals under the Contract Disputes Act of 1978, published by the Office of Management and Budget, and the Rules of Practice for each of the existing boards.

While a very few federal agencies have agreements for their disputes to be heard by a large board, such as the ASBCA, most federal departments and agencies have elected to establish their own appeals boards. At this writing, the following boards are in operation, varying greatly in case load and staffs:

Armed Services Board of Contract Appeals (ASBCA)

Department of Energy Board of Contract Appeals (EBCA)

Corps of Engineers Board of Contract Appeals (ENG BCA)

Department of Agriculture Board of Contract Appeals (AGBCA)

Department of the Interior Board of Contract Appeals (IBCA)

Department of Transportation Board of Contract Appeals (DOT BCA)

General Services Administration Board of Contract Appeals (GSBCA)

National Aeronautics and Space Administration Board of Contract Appeals (NASA BCA)

Postal Service Board of Contract Appeals (PSBCA)

Veterans Administration Board of Contract Appeals (VABCA)

Department of Labor Board of Contract Appeals (LBCA)

Department of Housing and Urban Development Board of Contract Appeals (HUD BCA)

FAR Part 33—Protests, Disputes and Appeals

Subject to specific deviations contained in the FAR Supplements, issued by federal departments and agencies, FAR Part 33 provides policies and practices relating to protests, disputes and appeals. As to protests, the statutory authority of the GSBCA with respect to protests involving most ADP procurements is described later in this chapter, and the policies and practices of GAO are reviewed in Chapter XXVIII of this text. Some of the pertinent provisions of FAR Part 33 related to the CDA are excerpted below:

33.205 Relationship of the Act to Public Law 85-804.

(a) Requests for relief under Public Law 85-804 (50 U.S.C. 1431-1435) are not claims within the Contract Disputes Act of 1978 or the Disputes clause at 52.233-1, Disputes, and shall be processed under Part 50, Extraordinary Contractual Actions. However, relief formerly available only under Public Law 85-804; i.e., legal entitlement to rescission or reformation for mutual mistake, is now available within the authority of the contracting officer under the Contract Disputes Act of 1978 and the Disputes clause. In case of a question whether the contracting officer has authority to settle or decide specific types of claims, the contracting officer should seek legal advice.

(b) A contractor's allegation that it is entitled to rescission or reformation of its contract in order to correct or mitigate the effect of a mistake shall be treated as a claim under the Act. A contract may be reformed or rescinded by the contracting officer if the contractor would be entitled to such remedy or relief under the law of Federal contracts. Due to the complex legal issues likely to be associated with allegations of legal entitlement, contracting officers shall make written decisions, prepared with the advice and assistance of legal counsel, either granting or denying relief in whole or in part.

(c) A claim that is either denied or not approved in its entirety under paragraph (b) above may be cognizable as a request for relief under Public Law 85-804 as implemented by Part 50. However, the claim must first be submitted to the contracting officer for consideration under the

Contract Disputes Act of 1978 because the claim is not cognizable under Public Law 85-804, as implemented by Part 50, unless other legal authority in the agency concerned is determined to be lacking or inadequate.

* * * *

33.208 Interest on claims.

The Government shall pay interest on a contractor's claim on the amount found due and unpaid from (a) the date the contracting officer receives the claim (property certified if required by 33.007(a)), or (b) the date payment otherwise would be due, if that date is later, until the date of payment. Simple interest on claims shall be paid at the rate, fixed by the Secretary of the Treasury as provided in the Act, which is applicable to the period during which the contracting officer receives the claim and then at the rate applicable for each 6-month period as fixed by the Treasury Secretary during the pendency of the claim. See 32.614 for the right of the Government to collect interest on its claims against a contractor.

* * * *

33.213 Obligation to continue performance.

(a) In general, before passage of the Act, the obligation to continue performance applied only to claims arising under a contract. However, Section 6(b) of the Act authorizes agencies to require a contractor to continue contract performance in accordance with the contracting officer's decision pending final decision on a claim relating to the contract. In recognition of this fact, an alternate paragraph is provided for paragraph (h) of the clause at 52.233-1, Disputes. This paragraph shall be used only as authorized by agency procedures.

(b) In all contracts that include the clause at 52.233-1, Disputes, with its Alternate I, in the event of a dispute not arising under, but relating to, the contract, the contracting officer shall consider providing, through appropriate agency procedures, financing of the continued performance; *provided,* that the Government's interest is properly secured.

The Disputes clause required by FAR is quoted below:

52.233-1 Disputes.

As prescribed in 33.014, insert the following clause in solicitations and contracts unless the conditions in 33.003 apply:

DISPUTES (APR 1984)

(a) This contract is subject to the Contract Disputes Act of 1978 (41 U.S.C. 601-613) (the Act).

(b) Except as provided in the Act, all disputes arising under or relating to this contract shall be resolved under this clause.

(c) "Claim," as used in this clause, means a written demand or written assertion by one of the contracting parties seeking, as a matter of right, the payment of money in a sum certain, the adjustment or interpretation of contract terms, or other relief arising under or relating to this contract. A claim arising under a contract, unlike a claim relating to that contract, is a claim that can be resolved under a contract clause that provides for the relief sought by the claimant. However, a written demand or written assertion by the Contractor seeking the payment of money exceeding $50,000 is not a claim under the Act until certified as required by subparagraph (d)(2) below. A voucher, invoice, or other routine request for payment that is not in dispute when submitted is not a claim under the Act. The submission may be converted to a claim under the Act, by complying with the submission and certification requirements of this clause, if it is disputed either as to liability or amount or is not acted upon in a reasonable time.

(d)(1) A claim by the Contractor shall be made in writing and submitted to the Contracting Officer for a written decision. A claim by the Government against the Contractor shall be subject to a written decision by the Contracting Officer.

(2) For Contractor claims exceeding $50,000, the Contractor shall submit with the claim a certification that—

(i) The claim is made in good faith;

(ii) Supporting data are accurate and complete to the best of the Contractor's knowledge and belief; and

(iii) The amount requested accurately reflects the contract adjustment for which the Contractor believes the Government is liable.

(3)(i) If the Contractor is an individual, the certification shall be executed by that individual.

(ii) If the Contractor is not an individual, the certification shall be executed by—

(A) A senior company official in charge at the Contractor's plant or location involved; or

(B) An officer or general partner of the Contractor having overall responsibility for the conduct of the Contractor's affairs.

(e) For Contractor claims of $50,000 or less the Contracting Officer must, if requested in writing by the Contractor, render a decision within 60 days of the request. For Contractor-certified claims over $50,000, the Contracting Officer must, within 60 days, decide the claim or notify the Contractor of the date by which the decision will be made.

(f) The Contracting Officer's decision shall be final unless the Contractor appeals or files a suit as provided in the Act.

(g) The Government shall pay interest on the amount found due and unpaid for (1) the date the Contracting Officer receives the claim (properly certified if required), or (2) the date payment otherwise would be due, if that date is later, until the date of payment. Simple interest on claims shall be paid at the rate, fixed by the Secretary of the Treasury as provided in the Act, which is applicable to the period during which the Contracting Officer receives the claim and then at the rate applicable for each 6-month period as fixed by the Treasury Secretary during the pendency of the claim.

(h) The Contractor shall proceed diligently with performance of this contract, pending final resolution of any request for relief, claim, appeal, or action arising under the contract, and comply with any decision of the Contracting Officer.

(End of clause)

(R 7-103.12 1980 JUN)

(R FPR Temporary Regulation 55-II 1980 JUN)

Alternate I (APR 1984). If it is determined under agency procedures, that continued performance is necessary pending resolution of any claim arising under or relating to the contract, substitute the following paragraph (h) for the paragraph (h) of the basic clause:

(h) The Contractor shall proceed diligently with performance of this contract, pending final resolution of any request for relief, claim, appeal, or action arising under or relating to the contract, and comply with any decision of the Contracting Officer.

JUDICIAL RULINGS RELATING TO CONTRACT DISPUTES ACT OF 1978

The agency BCAs and the federal courts found themselves involved at an early date in controversies relating to the Contract Disputes Act of 1978. The impact of this Act probably falls most heavily on the legal profession and secondarily on contract administrators. It is essentially in the latter sense that we summarize some of the decisions handed down to date.

Contract Disputes Act Does Not Permit Government to "Sit On" Contractors' Claims; *SCM Corporation v. U.S.*, 28 CCF par. 80,789, Ct.Cls. No. 576-79C, October 10, 1980

The author's involvement in government contracting matters for over thirty years has included providing guidance and advice to government contractors who are entitled to equitable contract price adjustments because of formal or constructive changes by the government. In some instances, contractors have been frustrated when they have filed appropriate claims under the Disputes clause and government officials have stalled or otherwise failed to take action.

The Contract Disputes Act of 1978 has been both praised and criticized by government contractors. One of its provisions that injected fairness, equity, and good judgment into the procurement process was illustrated in the above-captioned decision.

The SCM Corporation entered into a contract with the government in June 1970. On November 22, 1978, SCM submitted a request for an equitable adjustment, described in the court's decision as "in excess of ten million dollars." On May 7, 1979, SCM duly certified this claim in accordance with the requirements of the Contract Disputes Act of 1978 (hereinafter referred to as "Act"). After failing to obtain any action from the contracting officer, SCM filed for relief in the Court of Claims on December 20, 1979. The government filed for summary judgment, maintaining that the court was without jurisdiction to entertain SCM's claim under the Act because the contracting officer had not yet issued a final decision in the case. SCM contended "that such final decision is deemed to have been issued in the form of a denial by virtue of the contracting officer's having failed to issue the decision within the time period required by the Act." Accordingly, SCM argued that the jurisdictional prerequisite was satisfied.

The court's brief decision noted that the Act requires the contracting officer to issue a written decision within 60 days of receipt of a submitted certified claim. This time period can be extended if, within the 60 days, the contracting officer notifies the contractor of the additional time within which such a decision will be issued. Any such extension must be "reasonable." As the court pointed out, the Act further provides that "[a]ny failure by the contracting officer to issue a decision on a contract claim within the period required will be deemed to be a decision by the contracting officer denying the claim and will authorize the commencement of the appeal or suit on the claim . . . ."

The Act further provided that, once the contracting officer issues a decision or is deemed to have done so, the contractor has the option of appealing it to a board of contract appeals or directly to the U.S. Court of Claims.

With these provisions of the Act set out, the court found the decision to be clear. The contracting officer did not issue a decision within 60 days of receiving SCM's claim, nor did he formally notify SCM within that period that a specified time beyond 60 days would be required. Accordingly, "The contracting officer, therefore, is deemed to have issued a denial. This court now has jurisdiction."

Mistakes: Request for Relief for Damages Caused by Mistakes, Formerly Available Only Under P.L. 85-804, Now Available Through Appeals to BCAs or U.S. Claims Court

Section 8(d) of the Contract Disputes Act of 1978 states:

Each agency board shall have jurisdiction to decide any appeal from a decision of a contracting officer (1) relative to a contract made by its agency, and (2) relative to a contract made by any other agency when such agency or the Administrator has designated the agency board to decide the appeal. In exercising this jurisdiction, the agency board is authorized to grant any relief that would be available to a litigant asserting a contract claim in the United States Claims Court [originally, the Court of Claims].

Prior to the enactment of this law, a contractor's remedy to secure a contract amendment relating to mistakes was available essentially through a request for extraordinary relief under Public Law 85-804. DAR 17-204.3 and FPR 1-17.204.3, under the caption "Mistakes," provided the following examples under which a defense contract could be amended or modified to correct or mitigate the effect of a mistake:

(1) A mistake or ambiguity which consists of the failure to express or to express clearly in a written contract the agreement as both parties understood it;

(2) A mistake on the part of the contractor which is so obvious that it was or should have been apparent to the contracting officer; and

(3) A mutual mistake as to a material fact.

Both DAR and FPR provided that amending defense contracts "to correct mistakes with the least possible delay normally will facilitate the national defense by expediting the procurement program and by giving contractors proper assurance that such mistakes will be corrected expeditiously and fairly." These provisions were carried over into FAR 50.302-2.

Applied Devices Corporation, Navy Contract Adjustment Board, November 21, 1980

In a decision handed down on November 21, 1980, in an appeal by the Applied Devices Corporation for extraordinary contractual relief under P.L. 85-804, the Navy Contract Adjustment Board had apparently granted some relief for a mutual mistake but then rescinded the grant because Applied Devices had an adequate remedy under the Contract Disputes Act to seek contract modification on the grounds of a mutual mistake. In a rather complicated case, Applied Devices was successful in obtaining contract modification under the Contract Disputes Act. However, the case was returned to the Navy Contract Adjustment Board, which found that the relief under such modification was not sufficient to strengthen the contractor's weak financial condition. Whereupon the Navy CAB, acting under P.L. 85-804 on a basis not elsewhere available, further amended the contract without consideration to permit Applied Devices to furnish the equipment, which was considered vital to the government and which would facilitate the national defense.

Sperry Rand Corporation, Department of Transportation Contract Adjustment Board, December 23, 1980

Another decision in the same area was handed down by the Department of Transportation Contract Adjustment Board on December 23, 1980, in the appeal of Sperry Rand Corporation, Sperry Univac Division. The government and the contractor agreed that a mutual mistake had occurred, and extraordinary contractual relief was sought from the contract adjustment board under P.L. 85-804. However, the CAB declined jurisdiction on the grounds that the Contract Disputes Act and implementing OFPP Policy Letter 80-3 provided the appropriate channels for relief. The government argued that the OFPP Policy Letter guidance restricted relief available from a contracting officer to a "legal right" under the terms and conditions of the contract. However, inasmuch as boards of contract appeals were given the same authority as the court of claims under the Contract Disputes Act and since the court has the authority to grant equitable remedies, the matter may be heard on its merits by a contracting officer even if the relief under consideration would be "equitable" rather than "legal."

Paragon Energy Corporation v. U.S., Ct.Cls. No. 98-80C, April 8, 1981

After receiving an advertised construction contract, Paragon discovered a clerical error in its calculations. The contractor asserted that the contracting officer should have been aware of the mistake and, therefore, requested a price adjustment under P.L. 85-804 and DAR 17-204.3. The contracting officer denied the request; Paragon requested a contract reformation; and this too was denied, on the grounds that the contractor had waived this right by having first sought relief under P.L. 85-804. Paragon appealed the contracting officer's decision to the Court of Claims, requesting either contract reformation or adjustment under P.L. 85-804. The government asked the court to dismiss the appeal because the contracting officer had made no final appealable decision, lacking authority to do so. According to the government, the only relief available was under P.L. 85-804 because a unilateral bid mistake was involved.

"The threshold question" as framed by the court was whether Paragon had a cognizable claim under the Contract Disputes Act, and its position was that the contractor had a valid claim for contract reformation because the Contract Disputes Act extends to "all claims by a contractor against the government relating to a contract," but did not have a valid claim for reconsideration under P.L. 85-804.

In explaining and supporting its decision, the court dug deep into the legislative history, beginning with the recommendations of the Commission on Government Procurement in 1972 and moving to the House and Senate Reports accompanying the Contract Disputes Act of 1978, which "explicitly indicate that the new law was intended to implement . . ." the Commission's recommendation to "[e]mpower contracting agencies to settle and pay, and administrative forums to decide, all claims or disputes arising under or growing out of or in connection with the administration or performance of contracts entered into by the United States." (This decision contains an excellent historical analysis culminating in the conclusions regarding the intent of this Act.)

The court found full agreement on an "all disputes" clause, except for reservations by Admiral Rickover about the possibility that the Act might be construed as authorizing agencies to settle claims falling under the provisions of P.L. 85-804. The ultimate revisions and compromises eliminated the "all disputes" clause and provided that "the agency board is authorized to grant any relief that would be available to a litigant asserting a contract claim in the Court of Claims."

The essence of the decision seemed to turn on whether the claim was based on P.L. 85-804, as the government asserted, and hence was beyond the contracting officer's authority, or whether it involved contract reformation under the equitable principles recognized by the Court of Claims and hence, under the Act, was within the authority of the contracting officer. Excerpts of the court's decision denying the government's motion to dismiss Paragon's appeal and remanding it to the trial judge "for further appropriate proceedings respecting Paragon's claims for equitable reformation under the Contract Disputes Act" are contained below:

The singularity of contractual mistakes - unilateral and mutual is that they have been remedial both under Public Law 85-804 ("adjustment") and under the equitable principles recognized by this court ("reformation"). The Government asserts, in effect, that since unilateral bid mistakes have been remedial under Public Law 85-804, they fall by implication under the 85-804 "taint" irrespective of the fact that there has been a perfectly valid basis for remedying them independently of 85-804. We cannot find any merit to this view insofar as the separate legal basis is relied upon.

Congress could not have expressed itself more clearly to the effect that all contractor claims based upon a valid contractual theory fall within the procuring agencies' jurisdiction under the Contract Disputes Act. This was essential to Congress' design that all contract disputes be resolved according to the same set of procedures, beginning with the decision of the contracting officer. By implication - and also by express statement - equitable reformation to rectify bid mistakes is covered. There is no inconsistency here, because while procuring agencies will be affording a remedy previously available under 85-804, they will not be proceeding under the broadly discretionary "national defense" criterion of that law, but under the far more confining set of rules and principles which this court has evolved over a long string of reformation cases. Under these circumstances, the 85-804 "taint" is simply irrelevant.

DAR (ASPR) 1-314(f), 4 CCH Gov't. Contracts Rptr. par. 32,072, revised in light of the Contract Disputes Act, states that, "Requests for relief under Public Law 85-804 are not considered to be claims within the Contract Disputes Act, ... However, certain kinds of relief formerly available only under Public Law 85-804, i.e., legal entitlement rescission or reformation for mutual mistake, are now available within the authority of the contracting officer under the Act ... A contractor's allegation that it is entitled to rescission or reformation of its contract in order to correct or mitigate the effect of a mistake shall be treated as a claim under the Contract Disputes Act. ... A contract may be reformed or rescinded by the contracting officer if the contractor would be entitled to such remedy or relief under the law of Federal contracts." Accord, FPR 1-1.318-2, 7 CCH Gov't. Contracts Rptr. par. 66,046.

This court has stated that agency boards of contract appeals have authority under the Contract Disputes Act to grant equitable reformation. *Applied Devices Corp. v. United States,* 219 Ct.Cls. 109, 591 F.2d 635, 640 (1979). See also *Bromley Contracting Co., Inc. v. United States,* 219 Ct.Cls. 517, 596 F.2d 448, 449-451 (1979). The Armed Services Board of Contract Appeals recently held that, "it is too clear to require citation of authority that contracting officers and boards of contract appeals have authority under the Contracts Disputes Act to decide breach and reformation claims notwithstanding the fact that prior to the Act some such claims were cognizable within the executive departments only as extraordinary relief claims under P.L. 85-804". *Gentex Corp.,* 79-2 BCA par. 14,007, 68,777, 68,779 (1979). Accord, *Sperry Rand Corp., Sperry Univac Div.,* Dept of Transp. Contract Adj. Rd. No. 85-804-14 (December 23, 1980).

We thus hold that procuring agencies have authority under the Contract Disputes Act to reform contracts (and award proper monetary relief) to mitigate the effect of a unilateral bid mistake. A reformation claim for this purpose is cognizable before the contracting officer (and, by extension, agency boards of contract appeals).*

* The receipt of a negative decision under Public Law 85-804, as here, does not preclude the later initiation of a claim under the Contract Disputes Act. See *Embassy Moving & Storage Co. v. United States,* 191 Ct.Cl. 537, 545, 424 F.2d 602, 607 (1970). See also *Gentex Corp.,* 79-2 BCA par. 14,139, 69,569, 69,573 (1979).

DISPUTES INVOLVING BREACH OF CONTRACT

Prior to the enactment of the CDA, the jurisdiction of BCAs was limited to disputes arising under a contract. The 1978 Act expanded the jurisdiction of the boards in a number of respects such as correcting mistakes, amendments without consideration and including claims which relate to a contract. Under this broadened authority, BCAs are authorized to hear breach of contract claims. In this regard, reference is made to Chapter XXI of this text for a review and analysis of a number of court and BCA decisions on the complex subject of distinguishing between a termination for convenience and a breach of contract.

DISPUTES INVOLVING SUBCONTRACTORS

The government's contractual agreement is with the prime contractor. Absent a privity of contract between the subcontractor and the government, the subcontractor may not negotiate directly with the government, usually is not directly subject to a contracting officer's decision and, therefore, as a general rule, may not appeal decisions by contracting officers. The government's policy considers that the profit available to the prime contractor includes, among other things, the responsibility for total contract management, including relations with the subcontractors.

Succinct Commentaries on this subject are contained in CCH's *Government Contracts Reporter* at paragraphs 21,570 and 21, 580, quoted below.

¶ 21,570 Prime Contractors' Claims on Behalf of Subcontractors

Disputes arising under subcontracts of prime contracts with the government may not as a general proposition be pursued directly by the subcontractor at the contracting officer level or subsequently with a board of contract appeals. This is because there is no "privity" of contract between the subcontractor and the government. It is only the prime contractor who has a contract with the government. The legislative history of the Contract Disputes Act of 1978 indicates that subcontractors still will not be permitted to pursue relief directly and that the present "sponsorship" rules will remain in effect. (.05) Sponsorship refers to the practice of permitting the prime contractor to appeal on behalf of his subcontractor. The appeal is brought in the name of the prime and prosecuted with his approval even though the subcontractor is clearly the real party in interest. (.65) See ¶ 24,025 for further discussion of the Contract Disputes Act.

Severin Doctrine

In *Severin v. U.S.* (.80), the Court of Claims did not permit a prime contractor to recover from the government on behalf of his subcontractor in a breach of contract action because the prime was protected from liability to the subcontractor. To come under the *Severin* doctrine, however, the government must show, through some contractual term or a release, that the prime contractor is not liable to the subcontractor. An exculpatory clause relieving the prime contractor of liability for delay caused by the government did not preclude the prime contractor from recovering on behalf of his subcontractor because the prime was seeking not to recover delay damages, but only an equitable adjustment for additional expenses (.816). Conditioning the liability of the prime to the subcontractor, with respect to extra work, on whether or not the prime succeeds in receiving payment from the government does not bar recovery by the prime on behalf of the subcontractor (.85).

Contracting officers are prohibited from consenting to a provision in a subcontract purporting to give the subcontractor the right to obtain a direct decision of the contracting officer or the right of direct appeal to the ASBCA. The government, it is reasoned, is entitled to the management services of the prime contractor in adjusting disputes between himself and his subcontractors. Contracting officers are to act only in disputes arising under the prime contract, and then only with and through the prime contractor, even if a subcontractor is affected. Contracting officers may, however, consent to a subcontract containing a clause giving the subcontractor an indirect appeal to the ASBCA through prosecution of an appeal by the prime contractor on behalf of the subcontractor (.02).

¶ 21,580 Subcontractors' Claims Against the Government

Subcontractors have no contract with the government. Lacking privity of contract, they are generally not permitted to seek relief directly against the government. Subcontractors seeking relief must either proceed against the prime contractor or, if they think the government is responsible, ask the prime contractor to proceed against the government on their behalf.

Occasionally, however, a subcontractor may be permitted to appeal directly to a board of contract appeals or to assert a claim for relief before the General Accounting Office. An appeal taken directly by a subcontractor was permitted where the subcontract contained a clause authorizing appeals under the Disputes clause to the ASBCA, the subcontract was specifically approved by the contracting officer, and the dispute arose between the subcontractor and the government over the direct payment of certain claimed costs (.423). Mere government approval of the subcontract, however, does not in itself provide a contractual right for direct appeal by the subcontractor. (.425).

Contracting officers are instructed by FAR not to consent to a provision in a subcontract giving the subcontractor the right to appeal directly. Contracting officers are also instructed not to refuse consent to a provision in a subcontract giving the subcontractor an indirect appeal either through assertion of the prime's right to appeal or through prosecution of such an appeal by the prime on behalf of the subcontractor (.02).

Regulatory Provisions

FAR Part 44—Subcontracting Policies and Procedures covers the requirements for government consent to subcontracts and consent limitations and contractors' purchasing systems reviews.

Judicial Decisions Relating to Subcontractors' Appeal Rights

Although the government policy is well established, controversies and disputes continue to arise. The problems stem in part from a lack of a complete understanding of the government policy and contractual clauses. In addition, some government agencies under certain circumstances approve contractual provisions permitting subcontractors to appeal directly to the government.

The government also becomes intimately involved with subcontractors when such companies, because they are competitors of the prime contractors or for other reasons, deny the prime contractor access to the books and records. In these instances, reviews of pricing proposals, audits of costs incurred, reviews to determine compliance with cost accounting standards, etc., are performed by government auditors.

Remler Co., Ltd., ASBCA No. 5295, 59-2 BCA par. 2336; 60-1 BCA par. 2612

At issue was a cost-plus-a-fixed-fee subcontract under a cost-reimbursement prime contract with the Department of the Navy. The Changes clause incorporated in the subcontract provided that "[i]f the parties fail to agree upon the adjustment to be made, the dispute shall be determined as provided in paragraph 4 of Exhibit 'A' attached hereto." Exhibit "A" consisted of the standard General Provisions clause of the prime contract, and paragraph 4 was the standard Disputes clause. The Navy contracting officer approved the subcontract.

The subcontractor claimed certain costs under the Changes clause, which were denied by the prime contractor. The claim was informally referred by the prime contractor to the contracting officer, who refused to act favorably on it. At this point, apparently, the matter was dropped.

Some three years later, the prime contract having been long completed, the government was pressing the prime contractor for closing documents and the prime in turn sought similar papers from the subcontractor. At this time the latter requested direct review of its claim from the contracting officer. A meeting was held between the Navy contract administrator and the subcontractor's representative, and the latter was advised that the contracting officer would consider a direct submission. However, when the submission was forwarded, the contracting officer advised that the controversy was considered to be between the prime contractor and the subcontractor and that no basis existed for action by the government, whereupon the subcontractor appealed to the ASBCA. The government moved for dismissal on the grounds that the board lacked jurisdiction because the inclusion of the disputes clause was not ratified and hence there was no binding effect on the government to entertain a direct appeal from the subcontractor. The board decided to hear this motion before processing the appeal on its merits.

The subcontractor argued that the contracting officer's approval of the subcontract, which included the "Disputes" clause, constituted "force and effect to the terms and conditions of the subcontract" and, therefore, the government was bound to decide the dispute pursuant to the terms of the subcontract. The prime contractor testified that the inclusion of the General Provisions of the prime contract in the subcontract was effected only to inform the subcontractor of the prime contractor's obligation to the government and that there was no understanding that this action bound the contracting officer to accept a direct appeal by the subcontractor. The contracting officer was in agreement with the prime contractor's position and saw the subcontract as an independent contractual agreement between the prime contractor and subcontractor with full responsibility for administration on the prime contractor.

In the opinion of the board, the insertion of the standard Disputes clause in the subcontract without modification "was not intended to nor did it operate to give the subcontractor a right of direct appeal either to the Contracting Officer or to this board." The board further stated, "Unfortunately, we cannot agree that the mere fact of Government approval of the subcontract supports a contractual right by the subcontractor, as against the Government, for direct subcontractor appeal to the Contracting Officer or to this board." The board reasoned that "[t]he standard Disputes clause inserted in the subcontract requires modification (which was not done here) in order to make its terms applicable to a subcontract situation." The board also noted that, in the three years that had elapsed between the subcontractor's first effort to secure government intervention and its appeal, nothing was done by the government, the prime contractor, or the subcontractor to reflect the existence of the right of direct appeal. With regard to the Navy contract administrator's initial agreement to entertain a direct submission (subsequently reversed by the contracting officer), the board ruled that "[s]uch assent does not act to confer jurisdiction on this board." And so the board dismissed the appeal for lack of jurisdiction.

In the discussion of the facts in the case and its decision, the board made reference to several previous appeals involving this area:

1. The board conceded that in *Federal Telephone and Radio Co.,* ASBCA No. 4691, 59-1 BCA par. 2246, it did accept jurisdiction of a direct subcontractor appeal. However, the board noted that in this case the contracting officer's approval of the standard Disputes clause incorporated in the subcontract was specifically directed, inter alia, to subcontract amendment No. 1, which proposal made the context of the standard clauses applicable to a subcontract situation.

2. The board also took jurisdiction in *Grand Central Aircraft Co.,* ASBCA No. 1719, 6 CCF par. 61,525, where the subcontract Disputes clause was specifically worded to permit direct subcontractor appeals and the Contracting Officer had acted upon such a direct appeal.

3. Again, in ASBCA No. 3051, the decision that the board had jurisdiction of a direct subcontractor appeal was based on the subcontract Disputes clause which so provided. The ruling was similar in ASBCA No. 1238.

4. In contrast, in *Young and Smith Construction Co.,* IBCA No. 151, 58-1 BCA par. 1803, the board did not accept jurisdiction of a direct subcontractor appeal even though the subcontract, by its terms and by those of the prime contract, was made subject to all the terms of the prime contract, including a standard Disputes clause.

5. The board also refused jurisdiction in *Servil, Inc.,* ASBCA No. 8 (1950), where the subcontract Disputes clause named the Chief of Branch as the party to decide appeals; in *General Motors Corp. (Fischer Body Division),* WDBCA No. 174, 1 CCF 680 (1943), where no provision existed for direct subcontractor appeal but where the subcontract contained an arbitration clause; in Army BCA No. 1846, where neither the prime contract nor subcontract provided for direct subcontractor appeal; and in *Forest Box and Lumber Co., Inc.,* ASBCA No. 2916, 6 CCF par. 61,865, for the same reason as above.

In *Remler,* one of the three panel members forcefully dissented from the majority decision. He noted that the Changes clause specifically provided that a disagreement between the parties regarding price adjustments would be settled in accordance with the Disputes clause, and, in his opinion, this latter clause clearly permitted direct subcontractor appeal. The dissenting member found no ambiguity in the subcontract articles "which would justify a resort to parole evidence to determine what may have been subjectively in the minds of any of the parties as to their intended meaning." He was impressed too by the fact that the contracting officer had approved the subcontract on behalf of the government.

The dissenting member reasoned that the only conceivable defect in the subcontract was the use of the word "contractor" instead of "subcontractor" in the Disputes article. However, he stated that such criticism could only be considered "captious" because, reading in context, no one could have been misled. And finally, the dissenting member was of the opinion that this case did not differ from ASBCA No. 3051, where the board ruled that it had jurisdiction.

TRW, Inc., ASBCA No. 11373, 68-2 BCA par. 7099; 66-2 BCA par. 5882; 66-2 BCA par. 5847

A substantially different viewpoint and approach are evident in another decision by the board.

This appeal involved a claim by a cost-plus-fixed-fee subcontractor against a cost-plus-fixed-fee prime contractor. The subcontractor claimed as an allowable subcontract cost $326,404 of independent research and development expense (IR&D), but the prime contractor refused to pay on the ground that the IR&D was not an allowable cost. Between the government and the prime contractor, there was an issue as to whether, if the amount claimed by the subcontractor were held allowable and paid, the prime contractor would be barred by the Limitation of Cost clause of the prime contract from being reimbursed by the government for the amount paid the subcontractor. The subcontract contained a special provision that, if any cost claimed by the subcontractor were disallowed by either the prime contractor or the government, the subcontractor could appeal in the name of the prime contractor under the Disputes clause of the prime contract. After the government contracting officer refused to render a decision on the dispute between the subcontractor and the prime contractor, the subcontractor filed an appeal in the name of, and with the consent of, the prime contractor. The government filed a motion to dismiss the appeal on the ground that there was no dispute between the government and the prime contractor and, hence, no dispute cognizable under the Disputes clause of the prime contract. Both the prime contractor and the subcontractor opposed the government's motion to dismiss.

The board denied the government's motion to dismiss and ruled that it had jurisdiction to decide the appeal, but added that the matter it took jurisdiction of was the prime contractor's entitlement to be paid, which encompassed both the allowability of the subcontractor's claim and whether reimbursement of such costs otherwise allowable was barred by the cost limitation provision of the prime contract. In a decision on the government's motion to reconsider, the board said that, under circumstances where the government may ultimately be liable, the Disputes clause permits a prime contractor either to prosecute a claim on behalf of a subcontractor or to allow the subcontractor to prosecute the claim in the name of the prime contractor, regardless of whether the prime contractor agrees with the subcontractor as to the merits of the claim, except that, as a matter of legal ethics, the prime contractor must believe that the claim is being made in good faith.

The Boeing Company, ASBCA No. 10524, 67-2 BCA par. 6693; 67-1 BCA par. 6350

A significant quotation from this decision, which bears on subcontractors' rights to direct appeal, follows: "Entertainment of subcontract disputes in the name of a prime contractor on a derivative basis has long been recognized by this Board and the courts."

JUDICIAL INTERPRETATIONS OF THE EQUAL ACCESS TO JUSTICE ACT

The Equal Access to Justice Act, Public Law 96-481, was enacted with an effective date of October 1, 1981. Essentially, the law provides for the award of attorney fees and other expenses to eligible individuals and entities who prevail over the United States in certain civil actions brought by or against the federal government. This statute has been of some assistance to small business firms. However, the judicial interpretations to date have been disappointing and the benefits received by contractors have been less than expected.

Jurisdiction

An early question surfaced regarding the authority of boards of contract appeals under this Act. Views were expressed on both sides of this question and an expected policy statement by OFPP did not materialize. In the absence of an authoritative central policy enunciation, varying positions were articulated by the executive departments and agencies and in decisions by their boards of contract appeals.

On February 18, 1983, the U.S. Court of Appeals for the Federal Circuit ruled that BCAs did not have this authority (*Fidelity Construction Company v. U.S.,* CA FC 1983, 30 CCF 70,827). The decision covered other matters relating to the Equal Access to Justice Act, but the ruling regarding BCAs overshadowed them.

We do not find it appropriate to enter the complex legal controversies that have shown wide disagreement within the legal profession. We would note that the essential arguments for BCAs' authority, referred to as the derivative rationale, appeared to be well set out in *Brand S Roofing,* ASBCA No. 24688, 82-1 BCA par. 15,717, March 22, 1982. The board pointed to Section 8(d) of the Contract Disputes Act, which provided that boards are "authorized to grant any relief that would be available to a litigant asserting a contract claim in the Court of Claims." The board concluded that this "broad mandate encompasses the new remedies envisaged by the new Equal Access to Justice Act, since it specifically allows boards to grant 'any relief' available to Court of Claims litigants."

The court in *Fidelity* did not see it this way. It found no express language in the EAJA "granting the board of contract appeals the authority to award fees and expenses against the United States and no such authority will be implied." The court further stated:

> . . . Had Congress intended the board of contract appeals to independently award attorneys fees and expenses, it should have included statutory language expressly so providing to satisfy the strict construction standard.

The court further cited legislative history in support of its position. It found arguments to the effect that boards were authorized to grant any relief that would be available to a litigant asserting a contract claim in the Court of Claims. The court said, "although this argument is attractive and has been, in fact, successful in some board proceedings, we are not persuaded."

Jurisdiction of the U.S. Claims Court was also challenged (*Everett Plywood Corporation v. The United States,* No. 199-75, November 4, 1983, 31 CCF 71,733). This challenge was rejected. In this decision, the court ruled against Everett in the matter of the reasonableness of the hourly rates for attorney fees. The contractor had presented fees both in excess of the $75 maximum provided by the Act and below that amount, for an average hourly billing of $72.19. The court would not permit the averaging and denied the portion of the claim represented by the excess of individual billings over $75 per hour.

Time and Place of Substantial Justification

The Equal Access to Justice Act (EAJA) provides that eligible parties may recover attorney fees and costs unless "the position of the United States was substantially justified." The language of the Act was not specific as to whether "the position of the United States" included the government action preceding or precipitating the litigation or was limited to the "posture assumed by the government in litigation." In *Spencer v. NLRB,* 712 F.2d 539 (1983), the court interpreted the Act to apply to the government's position during litigation, not to governmental conduct prior to the initiation of legal proceedings.

The issue surfaced again in *Del Manufacturing Company v. The United States et al.,* No. 83-1094 (CA D.C. 1983), 31 CCF 71,935. Without going into the details, there appeared to be little question but that the government's actions preceding the litigation were extremely faulty. After Del finally overcame the problems generated by the SBA and Navy, particularly the former, the contractor sued for attorney fees and expenses and prevailed in the district court for the District of Columbia. The government appealed, citing the court's ruling in *Spencer* in support of its position.

The appeals court's decision is heavy with legal considerations, matters that this text does not confront in great depth. The major point was that the government's actions were extremely faulty but that, once Del filed suit, it obtained speedy relief. The court viewed the government's actions during litigation as entirely reasonable and, following the ruling in *Spencer,* decided that Del was not entitled to recover attorneys' fees. The complexity of this area is indicated by a split vote of the court in *Del.* However, from a layman's viewpoint, the dissent appeared to focus on the particular circumstances in this dispute and did not take issue with the basic conclusion that the position of the government that must be found substantially justified is the one in the litigation and not the conduct preceding the litigation.

Current Status of EAJA

On October 11, 1984, Congress passed H.R. 5479, to permanently reauthorize EAJA and give the boards of contract appeals authority to award attorneys' fees and costs. After hearing that a compromise version had been negotiated by the respective House and Senate committees, clarifying the "position of the U.S." to include underlying agency conduct, Administration officials objected to the bill and its present interpretation. The Department of Justice urged President Reagan not to approve legislation (H.R. 5479) extending the Equal Access to Justice Act because it defined the "position of the U.S." which must be substantially justified for the government to avoid paying attorneys' fees as including an agency's pre-litigation conduct. In addition, it would have required the government to pay interest on any awarded attorneys' fees not paid within 60 days after date of award, which was more favorable treatment than that afforded other groups entitled to interest. As a result, H.R. 5479 was pocket vetoed by the President on November 9, 1984.

Simultaneously with the foregoing pocket veto decision, the President issued a memorandum supporting his position and stressed the need for such legislation that hopefully would be passed in early 1985 and made retroactive to October 1, 1984. (The expiration date of the previous EAJA law was September 30, 1984.) In view of the explicit details of the aforementioned memorandum, indicating the President's reasons for the pocket veto and suggested implementing procedures thereafter, it is reproduced in full:

MEMORANDUM OF DISAPPROVAL

I am withholding my approval of H.R. 5479, a bill "to amend section 504 of title 5, United States Code, and section 2412 of title 28, United States Code, with respect to awards of expenses of certain agency and court proceedings, and for other purposes."

H.R. 5479 would permanently reauthorize and make a number of significant changes to the Equal Access to Justice Act. The Act allows the award of attorneys' fees to certain parties who successfully litigate against the government unless the government demonstrates that its position is substantially justified or that special circumstances exist that make a fee award unjust. Because the Equal Access to Justice Act expired on September 30, 1984, legislation is needed to reauthorize the Act.

I am firmly committed to the policies underlying the Equal Access to Justice Act and will make the permanent and retroactive reauthorization of the Act a high legislative priority of the Administration in the next Congress. Where the Federal government has taken a position in litigation that is not substantially justified, and thereby has caused a small business or individual to incur unnecessary attorneys' fees and legal costs, I believe it proper for the government to reimburse that small business or individual for those expenses. The Equal Access to Justice Act thus serves an important salutory purpose that should become a permanent part of our government. Unfortunately, H.R. 5479 makes certain changes to the Equal Access to Justice Act that do not further the Act's basic purposes and that are inconsistent with fundamental principles of good government. The most objectionable of these provisions is the change the bill would make in the definition of "position of the United States." Under this changed definition, the Act would no longer apply only to the government's position taken in the administrative or court litigation, but would extend to the underlying agency action. This would result in needless and wasteful litigation over what is supposed to be a subsidiary issue, the award of attorneys' fees, and would further burden the courts, which would have to hear the claims in each case not once, but twice. In addition, this change could also undermine the free exchange of ideas and positions within each agency that is essential for good government.

For example, this change would require courts in making fee determinations to examine the conduct of the agency even where that conduct is not at issue in the court's review of the merits of the case before it. This would mean that a fee proceeding could result in an entirely new and subsidiary inquiry into the circumstances that gave rise to the original lawsuit. This inquiry not only could lead to far lengthier proceedings than required if the court is merely to examine arguments made in court, but also could lead to extensive discovery of how the underlying agency position was formulated, and who advocated what position and for what reason at what time. In effect, every step of the agency decision-making process at whatever level, could become the subject of litigation discovery. Such extensive discovery could inhibit free discussion within an agency prior to any final agency policy decision or action for fear that any internal disagreements or reservations would be the subject of discovery and judicial inquiry.

In addition, H.R. 5479 contains a provision that would require the United States to pay interest on any awarded attorneys' fees not paid within 60 days after the date of the award. As noted by the Comptroller General of the United States, this provision would give lawyers who have received awards under the Act more favorable treatment than any other group entitled to interest payments from the United States. I agree with the Comptroller General that to the extent any interest should be paid under the Act, it should be paid on the same basis as other interest payments made by the government on court judgments.

The Department of Justice, the Office of Management and Budget, and other concerned agencies have repeatedly expressed to the Congress their serious reservations about these and other provisions of H.R. 5479. I wholly support the prompt reauthorization of the Equal Access to Justice Act and believe that the reauthorization should be retroactively effective to October 1, 1984. In light of the permanent nature of a reauthorization, such a reauthorization should include modifications and improvements in the Act, which the Administration is willing to explore with the Congress.

Concurrently with this memorandum, I am issuing a memorandum to all agency heads concerning the Equal Access to Justice Act. This memorandum reaffirms my strong commitment to the policies underlying the Act and instructs agency heads to review the procedures of their agencies to ensure that agency positions continue to be substantially justified. Special attention is to be given to those agency positions that affect small businesses. In addition, each agency is to accept and assist in the preparation of fee applications which can be considered once the Act is reauthorized.

I look forward to approving an acceptable reauthorization of the Equal Access to Justice Act early next year. For the reasons indicated, however, I am compelled to withhold my approval of H.R. 5479.

RONALD REAGAN

THE WHITE HOUSE

November 8, 1984

Revised EAJA Enacted into Law

On August 5, 1985, President Reagan signed Public Law 99-80, permanently reauthorizing the Equal Access to Justice Act (EAJA) and giving boards of contract appeals authority to award attorneys' fees and costs.

In signing the bill, the President emphasized that the revised definition of the term "position," one of the controversies which led to his prior veto, "limits the . . . fee inquiry to the agency action that is at issue in the litigation . . . and does not permit the examination of other agency conduct."

The original EAJA, P.L. 96-481 was enacted on October 21, 1982 with an effective date of October 1, 1981. Earlier we reviewed the major differences between the legislative and executive branches of the government that led to the President's veto. In the Memorandum of Disapproval, the President noted his agreement with other aspects of the law and suggested it be reauthorized upon return of Congress and made retroactively effective to October 1, 1984.

On June 24, 1985, the House passed H.R. 2378, permanently reauthorizing EAJA and retroactively extending coverage to cases pending on October 1, 1984. Inasmuch as the previous legislation had been interpreted as prohibiting boards of contract appeals from granting attorneys' fees, the House measure also retroactively extended coverage to requests for attorneys' fees that were pending before the boards of contract appeals on that date.

The bill also expanded the eligibility threshold to $2 million for individuals and $7 million for small businesses. The term "position of the United States" included underlying agency actions.

On July 24, 1985, the Senate approved H.R. 2378, both houses having coordinated the measure with administration officials and having been assured at the time that it would be signed by the President.

The language of the enacted legislation on the major controversial issue now states: "Whether or not the position of the agency was substantially justified shall be determined on the basis of the administrative record, as a whole, which is made in the adversary adjudication for which fees and other expenses are sought." (Section 504(a)(1)).

The provisions regarding fees and other expenses remain essentially unchanged, including:

> . . . the reasonable expenses of expert witnesses, the reasonable cost of any study, analysis, engineering report, test, or project which is found by the agency to be necessary for the preparation of the party's case, and reasonable attorney or agent fees (The amount of fees awarded under this section shall be based upon prevailing market rates for the kind and quality of the services furnished, except that (i) no expert witness shall be compensated at a rate in excess of the highest rate of compensation for expert witnesses paid by the agency involved, and (ii) attorney or agent fees shall not be awarded in excess of $75 per hour unless the agency determines by regulation that an increase in the cost of living or a special factor, such as the limited availability of qualified attorneys or agents for the proceedings involved, justifies a higher fee.)

*   *   *   *

> "[P]osition of the agency" means, in addition to the position taken by the agency in the adversary adjudication, the action or failure to act by the agency upon which the adversary adjudication is based; except that fees and other expenses may not be awarded to a party for any portion of the adversary adjudication in which the party has unreasonably protracted the proceedings.

The applicability of EAJA to board of contract appeals cases "shall apply to any adversary adjudication billing on or commenced on or after October 1, 1981, in which applications for fees and other expenses were timely filed or dismissed for lack of jurisdiction."

BOARDS OF CONTRACT APPEALS AND BID PROTESTS

A decision by the Veterans Administration Board of Contract Appeals reasserted the jurisdiction of the boards for hearing appeals of disappointed bidders in claims for bid preparation costs (*Le Prix Electrical Distributors, Ltd.,* VABCA No. 1642, 82-1 BCA par. 15,527, December 31, 1981).

The entire area of bid protests has been primarily associated with the Comptroller General of the United States, although the Court of Claims had accepted appeals and ruled on cases where a disappointed bidder claimed bid preparation costs. Contract appeals boards did not have jurisdiction over bid protests but acquired such authority under the Contract Disputes Act of 1978. This broadened area for remedies in bid protests is important for contractors to consider, and we have cited the salient sections of the decision in *Le Prix* and other cases to describe the authority and limitations of judicial actions in this area.

The response from Le Prix to a VA Request for Quotation (RFQ) was rejected, and the contract was awarded to another bidder. Le Prix contended that it was the low qualified bidder and that its bid was rejected erroneously and without justification. It requested the board to order the contracting officer to award it the contract, or, in the alternative, to award damages including bid preparation costs, profit, interest, etc.

The government filed a motion to dismiss the appeal for lack of jurisdiction, and the issue was identified as "whether, and to what extent, the board had jurisdiction to entertain an appeal of this nature."

A number of cases were cited in support of the motion to dismiss. In *James L. Jones,* PSBCA No. 778, 80-1 BCA par. 14,292, a bid protest was denied by the contracting officer and an appeal was filed with the Postal Service BCA. The government moved to dismiss the appeal on the grounds that contract appeals boards do not have jurisdiction over appeals filed by unsuccessful bidders against the award of contracts. The board agreed with the government's position and dismissed the appeal since it addressed matters outside the jurisdiction of the board.

In *Dakota Titles & Records, a Joint Venture,* IBCA No. 1420-1-81, 81-1 BCA par. 14,958, the disappointed bidder alleged that the contract was awarded to another company contrary to the evaluation procedures contained in the solicitation request. Prejudice on the part of the contracting officer was also alleged, and Dakota asked that the board order the contract to be awarded to it. The Interior BCA stated: "Jurisdiction over protests of an award has always been considered to lie with the Comptroller General. On many occasions in the past, this Board has held that the jurisdiction conferred by the Disputes Clause only extends to the resolution of disputes between the parties to the contract under which the appeal was taken . . . ." While acknowledging the expansion of jurisdiction of contract appeals boards by the Contract Disputes Act of 1978, the IBCA stated that "[t]he Act has been interpreted as not extending the jurisdiction of boards of contract appeals to protests of an award."

In *Ace Art Company, Inc.,* GSBCA No. 6032, 81-1 BCA par. 15,106, a similar decision was rendered by a contract appeals board. Ace Art Company requested the board to instruct GSA to award a contract to the company because its bid had been improperly rejected. The appeal was dismissed for lack of jurisdiction.

The cases referred to above addressed appeals to boards to order agencies to award contracts to disappointed bidders. In every instance, the board pointed out it lacked that jurisdiction, which seems to lie solely in the

Comptroller General. However, Le Prix had asked the board to order the contract be awarded to it, or, alternatively, to grant it bid preparation costs. In this latter area, the Court of Claims had accepted jurisdiction as reflected in a series of its decisions. Section 8(d) of the Contract Disputes Act authorized boards of contract appeals to grant any releif that would be available in the Court of Claims. A case in point was the decision in *Master Mechanics, Inc.*, GSBCA No. 5535, 80-2 BCA par. 14,584, discussed more fully later in this chapter.

The board denied the government's motion to dismiss for lack of jurisdiction, finding that jurisdiction for an appeal for bid preparation costs was clearly given to the contract appeals board by the Contract Disputes Act of 1978. The GSBCA, following precedents established by the Court of Claims, found that there was ". . . an implied contract made by the agency: a contract created when the implied offer contained in the invitation for bids was impliedly accepted by the appellant in submitting its bid." Noting that the Court of Claims had long accepted jurisdiction where the party appealing sought bid preparation costs, the board pointed out that it was authorized to grant any relief available in the Court of Claims.

The favorable (to the disappointed bidder) decision was limited to denying the government's Motion to Dismiss. As the GSBCA explained: "Acceptance of jurisdiction by this board does not *ipso facto* provide appellant with its bid preparation costs or any other relief that it seeks. It must still satisfy the criteria established by the Court of Claims for the successful presentation of claims of this nature."

As an illustration, in *Morgan Business Associates v. The United States,* Ct.Cl. No. 274-78, 27 CCF par. 80,313, April 2, 1980, the court set forth the following principles:

> . . . [W]hen the Government completely fails to consider a plaintiff's bid or proposal, the plaintiff may recover its bid preparation costs, if, under all the facts and circumstances, it is established that, if the bid or proposal had been considered, there was a substantial chance that the plaintiff would receive an award—that it was within the zone of active consideration. If there was no substantial chance that plaintiff's proposal would lead to an award, then the Government's breach of duty did not damage plaintiff. In that situation a plaintiff cannot rightfully recover its bid preparation expenses. This principle of liability vindicates the bidder's interest and right in having his bid considered while at the same time forestalling a windfall recovery for a bidder who was not in reality damaged.

Returning to the *Le Prix* decision, the VABCA concluded that it was "without jurisdiction or authority to order that the contract be awarded to *Le Prix* or to consider the other relief sought by the appellant except for its claim for recovery of bid preparation costs."

The VABCA cited a number of Court of Claims decisions including *Heyer Products Company, Inc. v. The United States,* 135 Ct.Cl. 63 (1956) and *KECO Industries, Inc. v. The United States,* 192 Ct.Cl. 773, 428 F.2d 1233, 15 CCF par. 83,778 (1970), wherein the principle was evolved "that the submission of a bid in response to a solicitation creates an implied contract obligating the Government to give fair and honest consideration to the bid proposal, and that if the contract is breached a bidder may recover the cost of preparing his bid."

The board made several references to *Master Mechanics, Inc.,* which we cited previously. One of the references to that case noted that the acceptance of jurisdiction by a board of contract appeals in these kinds of instances does not automatically entitle the appellant to recover its bid preparation costs.

The board concluded that the government's Motion to Dismiss should be denied and that its jurisdiction would be limited to considering the claim for bid preparation costs. To recover such costs, the board said Le Prix must satisfy the criteria established by the Court of Claims "for the successful presentation of claims of this nature as outlined in *KECO Industries, Inc. v. United States* [19 CCF par. 82,861], 203 Ct.Cl. 556, 492 F.2d 1200 (1974)." There the court stated that the ultimate standard is whether the government's conduct was arbitrary and capricious toward the bidder-claimant and set forth the general criteria to be satisfied.

Questions concerning whether boards of contract appeals have jurisdiction over bid protests, if so, the basis for this jurisdiction, and what the boards can and cannot do for disappointed bidders, surfaced again in *Longmire Coal Corporation,* EBCA No. 156-2-81, 82-2 BCA par. 15,813, decided May 13, 1982.

Longmire appealed a Department of Energy termination for default. The appeal included a claim for loss of profits in the amount of $90,000 for a contract it did not receive because DOE allegedly did not fairly consider its bid. Longmire asserted that it was low bidder but did not receive the contract because it was suspended on account of the default termination. The government asked the board to dismiss this portion of the complaint because the board had no jurisdiction to hear a bid protest where the company is seeking lost profits.

The government's motion to dismiss was granted because the board found it had no authority to award lost profits under the circumstances alleged. In the words of the board:

> Appellant is seeking lost profits under a procurement contract that was not awarded to it. Irrespective of the potential fact that the Government may have wrongfully suspended Appellant and such suspension caused it to lose the contract, the Court of Claims has consistently held that an unsuccessful bidder cannot recover the profit he would have made out of a contract because there is no contract until his bid is accepted. Thus, the measure of damages for breach of this type of implied contract has been limited to bid preparation costs. *Heyer Products Company v. U.S.,* 140 F.Supp. 409, 135 Ct.Cl. 63 (1956); *KECO Industries, Inc. v. U.S.* (15 CCF par. 83,778), 428 F.2d 1233, 192 Ct.Cl. 773 (1970); *Morgan Business Associates, Inc. v. U.S.* (27 CCF 80,313), 619 F.2d 892, 223 Ct.Cl. 317 (1980).
>
> Appellant has cited no legal precedent or other authority to show that the Government's breach of an implied contract to fairly and honestly consider its bid entitles it to lost profits.

The board found it unnecessary to decide whether an implied contract came into existence, because it concluded that, even if an implied contract did exist, it had no authority to award lost profits. However, it noted in passing that, under the Contract Disputes Act of 1978, boards of contract appeals have jurisdiction over express and implied contracts. It also noted that the Act authorized boards "to grant any relief that would be available to a litigant asserting a contract claim in the Court of Claims."

The board also noted Longmire's contention that an implied contract existed because "the solicitation of bids carries with it the implied condition that bids received will be honestly considered." However, the board noted, "the implied contract which may result from a bid submitted in response to a solicitation is independent of the procurement contract which ultimately results from an award." *Master Mechanics, Inc.*, GSBCA No. 5535, 80-2 BCA par. 14,584, was cited.

Master was the sole bidder of 13 companies solicited, which resulted in the contracting officer advising the company he was making no award because the sole bid received did not provide adequate competition to insure reasonable prices. Master appealed, and the government moved to dismiss because the board lacked jurisdiction. The government argued there was no express or implied contract and that the board's jurisdiction was limited to appeals from decisions by contracting officers arising under contracts. The contractor argued that an implied contract was in existence and that the board had jurisdiction and asked for bid preparation costs in addition to other relief.

The board ruled for Master, rejecting the government's motion to dismiss. It cited the Contract Disputes Act: "Each agency board shall have jurisdiction to decide any appeal from a decision of a contracting officer (1) relative to a contract made by its agency . . . ." and found that this jurisdictional section of the Act clearly and unambiguously vests jurisdiction for appeals of this nature in this board." The following significant portions of the decision are cited:

> In the instant case, we have a decision of a contracting officer from which an appeal has been taken. We too have an implied contract made by the agency; a contract created when the implied offer contained in the invitation for bids was impliedly accepted by the appellant in submitting its bid. Furthermore, this board is authorized, in exercising this jurisdiction, to grant any relief that would be available to a litigant asserting a contract claim in the Court of Claims. The Court of Claims has long accepted jurisdiction in situations where the party has sought bid preparation costs, as in the instant case. *Morgan Business Associates v. U.S.* (27 CCF par. 80,313), Ct.Cl. 274-78, April 2, 1980. Acceptance of jurisdiction by this Board does not *ipso facto* provide appellant with its bid preparation costs or any other relief that it seeks. It must still satisfy the criteria established by the Court of Claims for the successful presentation of claims of this nature. *Morgan Business Associates, supra.*

* * * *

It is our opinion that, in the instant case, we have "contracting parties." As the Court of Claims has repeatedly held, the Government's invitation for bids was an implied offer by the Government to act in good faith in dealing with bidders. The appellant accepted the Government's offer in timely fashion when it submitted its bid, thus creating an implied contract which is ancillary to and inextricable from the procurement contract sought here. An implied contract is clearly within the jurisdiction of this Board under the Contract Disputes Act of 1978. Our reading of the legislative history convinces us that the Congress fully intended that matters of this nature be heard by boards of contract appeals.

It is important to note the board's reference to the *Morgan Business Associates* decision. Here, the bidder appropriately submitted its proposal to ERDA (now a part of the Department of Energy). The proposal was received by that agency but was somehow thereafter lost, with the result that it was never considered and the awards were made to other proposers. Morgan sued for bid preparation costs.

At the suggestion of the Energy Research and Development Administration, Morgan submitted a copy of its proposal for informal evaluation after the awards had been made. An ERDA official reviewed the proposal under the evaluation criteria of the RFP and asserted that Morgan should not have been chosen for negotiation leading to an award, but the decision indicates that Morgan had cast doubts on the ERDA official's "qualifications and motivations."

The decision is packed with legal considerations and judicial citations relating to disappointed bidders and the circumstances under which they may and may not recover their bid or proposal costs. We would refer our readers to this case for a detailed exposition of the court's thinking. For our purpose here, we shall only recount that Morgan was not awarded its proposal costs, despite the government's admitted failure to consider its proposal, because the court was not persuaded that "if the bid or proposal had been considered, there was a substantial chance that the (bidder) would receive an award—that it was within the zone of active consideration." The court's conclusion is cited below:

> We hold, rather, that when the Government completely fails to consider a plaintiff's bid or proposal, the plaintiff may recover its bid preparation costs if, under all the facts and circumstances, it is established that, if the bid or proposal had been considered, there was a substantial chance that the plaintiff would receive an award—that it was within the zone of active consideration. If there was no substantial chance that plaintiff's proposal would lead to an award, then the Government's breach of duty did not damage plaintiff. In that situation a plaintiff cannot rightfully recover its bid preparation expenses. This principle of liability vindicates the bidder's interest and right in having his bid considered while at the same time forestalling a windfall recovery for a bidder who was not in reality damaged.

> Morgan has failed to show that it had a substantial chance of receiving an award. The only evidence in the stipulated record, Ms. Garbarini's opinion, indicates that plaintiff's chances for an award were not substantial. Plaintiff's arguments concerning Ms. Garbarini's qualifications and motivations go only to the weight we should give this evidence. In opposing the Government's motion for summary judgment, plaintiff must do more if we are to disregard the only evidence in the

record on the point. Morgan has failed to offer any rebuttal evidence or even to attempt to meet its burden of persuasion on the issue.

GSA BOARD OF CONTRACT APPEALS AUTHORIZED TO RESOLVE PROTESTS INVOLVING PROCUREMENT OF ADPE—P.L. 98-369, THE DEFICIT REDUCTION ACT OF 1984

The Summer of 1984 witnessed the enactment of a voluminous bill entitled "The Spending Reduction Act, Deficit Reduction Act of 1984." Before passage in each house and major changes/additions/deletions in conference, this measure contained proposals of many influential members of Congress, including a number that many observers believed would not have had much chance of enactment as separate proposals. Of major interest to government acquisition is Title VII, referred to as the Competition in Contracting Act of 1984. Aside from the major thrusts designed to achieve the continuous congressional objectives of maximizing competition in federal procurement, this Title also contained new provisions regarding protest and dispute procedures involving GAO and the GSA Board of Contract Appeals. Comments on provisions and related implementing procedures pertaining to the General Accounting Office are reviewed in Chapter XXVIII of this text. Those involving the GSBCA are commented upon below.

The following summary of the pertinent provisions is extracted by a paper published by the Office of Federal Procurement Policy (OFPP) to provide federal departments and agencies an overall view of the Act's salient provisions. (The abbreviation FPASA refers to the Federal Property and Administrative Services Act of 1949.)

B. Automated Data Processing (ADP) Dispute Resolution

1. The FPASA is amended to set up a three-year test program to allow the GSA Board of Contract Appeals to resolve protests involving procurement of ADP equipment under Public Law 89-306 (the Brooks Act).

2. The Board must hold an initial hearing within 10 days of the filing of a protest and issue a final decision within 45 days, unless the Chairman determines that specific and unique circumstances require a longer period of consideration.

3. If the protest is made before contract award, the Board must suspend the GSA Administrator's ADP procurement authority or his delegation of authority for the procurement at issue. No award can be made unless the agency establishes that urgent and compelling circumstances which significantly affect the United States' interests require award and that award is likely to occur within 30 days.

If the Board receives notice of a protest within 10 days after contract award, the Board must suspend the authority or delegation of authority and contract performance will be suspended, unless the agency finds that compelling circumstances exist.

4. If the Board sustains the protest, the Board may suspend, revoke, or revise the GSA Administrator's ADP procurement authority or his

delegation of that authority for the procurement at issue. The Board also may grant reimbursement of the costs of filing and pursuing the protest (including reasonable attorney's fees) and bid or proposal preparation costs.

C. GAO and ADP protest and dispute procedures will be applied as of January 15, 1985.

Further background on this statutory provision may be gleaned from the House/Senate Conference Report on this bill:

Section 2713—Automated Data Processing Dispute Resolution

Senate amendment

The Senate amendment contains no provision on automated data processing dispute resolution.

Conference substitute

The conference substitute amends Section 111 of the Federal Property and Administrative Services Act of 1949 to provide an alternate forum for resolving contractual disputes involving procurements of automated data processing (ADP) equipment and services conducted under Public Law 89-306 (the Brooks Act). This provision applies only to those automated data processing procurements conducted under the Brooks Act, and it does not apply to those ADP procurements exempted under the 1982 Department of Defense Authorization Act. ADP procurements conducted by DOD are exempt from the Brooks Act only if the equipment and services are primarily for functions involving intelligence, cryptology, command and control, weapon systems, or similar type systems. Protests over ADP procurements in those areas not covered by the Brooks Act will continue to be heard by the GAO or the courts, as under current practice.

The Brooks Act, enacted in 1965, provides the General Services Administration (GSA) with the sole authority to procure ADP equipment and services for federal agencies either by conducting the procurement on behalf of the agency, or by granting a delegation of procurement authority to the agency to conduct its own procurements. The Brooks Act has opened the federal marketplace to all responsible computer companies. However, due to the increasing number of computer procurements conducted every year, coupled with the complexity of the technology, the current informal process of resolving conflicts between the buying agency and the suppliers has become cumbersome and prolonged. Further, charges have been made by both the agencies and the contractors that GSA's current process does not provide an objective forum for dispute resolution. The conferees believe that it has become increasingly apparent that a new forum is needed to provide a fair, equitable and timely remedy in this area.

The conference substitute provides that remedy by authorizing the GSA Board of Contract Appeals to consider protest cases involving ADP procurements conducted under P.L. 89-306. The Board is well suited to hear protests of this nature. First, the Board can use already established procedures to hold hearings, compel production of documents, obtain testimony of witnesses, and conduct cross-examination under oath. Second, the Board can use the authority which GSA currently has under the Brooks Act to revoke, suspend or modify a delegation of procurement authority. Further, the Board is authorized to suspend any contract which was awarded pursuant to P.L. 89-306.

The conference substitute requires that an initial hearing be held by the Board within ten days of the filed protest, and that the Board then issue its final decision within 45 working days from the date of the protest unless its chairman determines that specific and unique circumstances require a longer period for consideration. Based upon the results of the initial hearing, the Board can suspend the delegation of procurement authority while the protest is pending. The suspension of a solicitation or contract performance shall not be ordered if the agency establishes that urgent and compelling circumstances exist. In addition, the conference substitute authorizes the Board to award the costs of pursuing a protest if such protest action is sustained by the Board.

The conferees recognize that these provisions provide a unique and innovative method of handling protests of a highly technical and complex nature. The conferees believe that the Board is well equipped to provide timely resolution of conflicts between the procuring agencies and the suppliers of computer products and services. To avoid disrupting legitimate procurements, and especially to prevent protest actions taken in bad faith from interrupting contract performance, the Board is authorized to dismiss at any point in the process any protest action that it determines to be frivolous or which, on its face, does not state a valid basis for the protest.

The conference substitute establishes a three-year sunset provision which should allow Congress to make a full and objective evaluation of the Board's operations in resolving ADP contractual disputes prior to the consideration of reauthorization.

The GSBCA has issued implementing procedures in the form of a restatement of its Rules of Practice, which are printed in full in various government and commercial publications, including the Commerce Clearing House, Inc. (CCH) CONTRACT APPEALS DECISIONS. The new bid protest procedures, both for GAO and GSBCA, are expected to increase the volume of bid protests because of the cost recovery and other provisions.

ARMED SERVICES BOARD OF CONTRACT APPEALS

As described earlier in this chapter, the ASBCA was established in 1949. It is by far the largest board in terms of activity and personnel. In view of the increasing interest in, and criticism of, the Department of Defense and defense contractors, the ASBCA has attracted congressional attention in recent years and has been subjected to criticisms, believed by many observers to be unwarranted.

Investigation by General Accounting Office

Harsh attacks on allegedly inadequate implementation of the so-called Truth in Negotiations Act have been made by defense critics in Congress, strongly supported by GAO and DOD IG. In Chapter XXII of this text we referred briefly to scathing attacks before Senate and House committees where the ASBCA was included among those subjected to vitriolic criticisms. According to witnesses from GAO, DOD IG and an Air Force trial attorney, some contracting officers were negotiating price reductions for defective pricing at small percentages of the amounts due the government, allegedly because of their concern that if the controversies resulted in contractors' appeals to the ASBCA, the government would recover even less, if anything.

Such accusations were considered irresponsible and incredible by most observers in both the public and private sectors and were found plausible by only a few of the harshest congressional critics of DOD and defense contractors.

One of the outcomes of these harsh hearings was an order by the Chairman of the Senate Committee on Governmental Affairs to the GAO to conduct an investigation of the ASBCA. As stated in its report, released September 23, 1985, the congressional watchdog was to address the following questions:

> Are there impairments to organizational and individual independence in the Board's charter, structure, and operating practices?

> Does the Board have sufficient knowledge and understanding of generally accepted accounting and cost principles?

> Are Board members selected, appointed, and removed in the manner prescribed for administrative law judges by the Administrative Procedure Act?

In addition, the chairman requested that GAO study the board's decisions to determine their effect, and the options available to the government and contractors to respond to the decisions.

The investigation and issuance of the final report took an unusually long time (even for GAO). As described in the eighth edition of this text, the ASBCA report on its proceedings for the fiscal year September 30, 1984, included the following comment by the board's chairman:

> The General Accounting Office conducted an investigation of the ASBCA during FY 1984 at the request of the Senate Committee on Governmental Affairs. A team of investigators spent some eight or nine months at the offices of the Board. Due to the shifting focus and voluminous detail, it was never quite clear what they were looking for. As this is written, I have not been furnished their preliminary report.

The preliminary or draft report was finally made available some months after that, but considerable additional time was to pass before the final, formal report was to be issued.

Observers believe that the lengthy investigation and even lengthier period required to issue the report was due at least in part to differences of views within GAO. There were the usual harsh critics whose inflammatory reports consistently berate government agencies and industry on every conceivable subject, and some of the legal and other GAO officials who understood the seriousness of this investigation and the fact that no basis existed for accusing the board of favoritism toward contractors. Even a valid effort to ascertain whether any favoritism was shown to any party would require detailed review and research of all of the factual, legal, technical and accounting issues, study of the texts of the proceedings and briefs filed, and so on. Of course, this kind of painstaking effort was not made by the ASBCA critics, nor could GAO actually undertake it and attempt second-guessing of both the board's and federal courts' decisions involved.

Responding to the questions posed by the Senate Committee, GAO found no impairment of the board's independence, the board's accounting knowledge adequate, and that sufficient options were available to all parties to the disputes to respond to the board's decisions. Significantly, and ironically, in the light of allegations that the board's decisions in defective pricing disputes tended to favor contractors, GAO found that the board members "are not fully insulated from agency control" and suggested that Congress consider legislation to further assure that BCA members "are insulated from agency control in their selection and removal."

With further references to the board's independence, in addition to reviewing its charter, other regulations, proceedings, etc., GAO reported it had "discussed the Board's independence with a number of attorneys and contracting officials, both government and private, and all believe the Board decided disputes independent of external pressure." This unanimous view coincides with our own experience and discussions with others. Many of us differ with various rulings of the board, but we know of no responsible person who has challenged the board's independence.

The question as to the board's knowledge of accounting, together with views expressed by a very few individuals concerning a possible "accounting board," merit little serious consideration by knowledgeable and responsible individuals. If an accounting court, why not also an engineering court, medical court, construction court, etc.? Among the many other arguments against this notion is the fact that hardly any dispute is without significant legal implications, which indicates that accountants on a court should also be attorneys. And further, if there is a need for separate accounting and other technical and professional BCAs, the same arguments presumably would obtain for federal courts.

Addressing the board's accounting knowledge in the digest of its report, GAO stated:

> During fiscal years 1980 through 1983, about 5 percent of the disputes disposed of by the board involved accounting principles. While expertise and experience in accounting are not requisite for Board membership, and it is debatable whether or not they should be, GAO found that six board members have some level of training or experience in accounting, and the chairman's legal advisor, who can hear appeals, is a certified public accountant.

GAO reported, as is well known, that a board decision is not the final step in the dispute process and that four options are available to either party: (1)

both can request the board to reconsider its decision; (2) both can appeal to a federal court; (3) the government can change its regulations; (4) both can request Congress to enact legislation. To add some realism to these options, the government, as we know, has indeed changed its regulations on a number of occasions to make unallowable a cost that the ASBCA ruled to be allowable. As to congressional action, especially in recent years, anti-industry legislation is enacted with or without government request. Industry views in this area tend to fall upon deaf ears in Congress.

Finally, and as mentioned most ironically in the light of the allegations that the board leaned in industry's direction, GAO reported that BCA members "are selected, appointed and . . . may be summarily removed by the agencies that are parties to contract disputes on which the boards issue decisions." Addressing this point, GAO stated:

> To assure that members of boards of contract appeals are insulated from agency control in their selection and removal, to the same degree as administrative law judges, Congress may want to . . . give the Office of Personnel Management and the Merit Systems Protection Board roles in these processes.

ASBCA Reports of Transactions and Proceedings

A five-year summary of the board's operations presents a striking and disturbing picture of the litigious environment in which defense procurement functions:

	1982	1983	1984	1985	1986
Cases pending beginning	1301	1594	1695	1729	2074
Docketed during year	1273	1256	1369	1638	1960
Total cases requiring attention	2574	2850	3064	3367	4034
Disposed of during year	980	1156	1335	1293	1938
Cases pending end	1594	1694	1729	2074	2096

The increasing activity and rising number of cases pending have been matters of concern to defense contractors and to the board's officials. This problem and the board's continuing requests for additional personnel were not addressed by GAO in its lengthy investigation.

The board engaged court management experts and, with their help, formulated a plan that was approved by Deputy Secretary of Defense Taft in June 1986, together with approval for additional authorization for administative judges and supporting staff. Chairman Paul Williams also reported that the judges' use of pre-trial methods to reduce records only to disputed facts resulted in the issuance of more summary judgment decisions, which limited hearing time as well as the quantity of permissible discovery, and resulted in the playing of a more active role in the settlement process. The increase in supporting staff is permitting the judges to spend more time on their primary responsibilities.

As a result of these and other efforts, the board in 1986 disposed of almost twice as many cases as in 1982. However, the board cannot reduce the number of cases docketed, which rose to an all time high of 1960 in 1986 and, despite a decrease in the average length of time on docket, cases pending at the end of fiscal year 1986 were slightly higher than the prior year.

The new management plan was to have taken into account the impact of expanded duties assigned to the board by legislation, but a 20% increase in cases docketed exceeded projections in the plan. Many observers believe that the basic problem is the continuing hostility between the government and contractors as the result of harsh criticisms by GAO, DOD IG, DCAA, and certain members of Congress, which discourage contracting officers from negotiating reasonable settlements with contractors lest such actions attract criticisms in investigative reports and congressional hearings.

FEDERAL COURTS IMPROVEMENT ACT OF 1982 (PUBLIC LAW 97-164)

This Act, enacted April 2, 1982 and effective October 1, 1982, resulted in the following major changes:

1. The U.S. Court of Claims and the U.S. Court of Customs and Patent Appeals were abolished and most of their functions were assigned to the newly created U.S. Court of Appeals for the Federal Circuit. This court is at the same level as the other circuit courts of appeals, except that its jurisdiction is based on subject matter rather than geographical considerations.

2. A new U.S. Claims Court was created to assume the trial jurisdiction of the U.S. Court of Claims that was exercised by the court's Trial Division Commissioners. A major difference is that the opinions of the commissioners were recommendations to the U.S. Court of Claims, could be accepted in whole or in part, or rejected, and had no precedential effect. The U.S Claims Court has equitable relief power on contract actions prior to award.

Chapter XXIV

Extraordinary Contractual Actions to Facilitate National Defense Under Public Law 85-804 and Executive Order No. 10789 as Amended

PUBLIC LAW 85-804, AUGUST 28, 1958, AS AMENDED NOVEMBER 16, 1973

The need for authority to permit the government to amend or modify contracts without regard to provisions of the law, wherever it was deemed that such action would facilitate the war effort, was recognized in Title II of the First War Powers Act of 1941. As amended and extended, Title II of the First War Powers Act expired June 30, 1958, as did its implementing Executive Order No. 10210. The successor Act, P.L. 85-804, was enacted in August 1958, and the successor implementation, Executive Order No. 10789, was signed in November 1958.

The essential provisions of the law are quoted below:

... the President may authorize any department or agency of the Government which exercises functions in connection with the national defense, acting in accordance with regulations prescribed by the President for the protection of the Government, to enter into contracts or into amendments or modifications of contracts heretofore or hereafter made and to make advance payments thereon, without regard to other provisions of law relating to the making, performance, amendment, or modification of contracts, whenever he deems that such action would facilitate the national defense. The authority conferred by this Section shall not be utilized to obligate the United States in an amount in excess of $50,000 without approval by an official at or above the level of an Assistant Secretary or his Deputy, or an assistant head or his deputy, of such department or agency, or by a Contract Adjustment Board established therein.

A 1973 amendment required that specified congressional committees be notified in advance when the proposed action would obligate the United States in any amount in excess of $25 million and when the action could be denied by the disapproval of either House of Congress within a 60-day period.

EXECUTIVE ORDER NO. 10789 AS AMENDED

The President authorized the Department of Defense, within the limits of the amounts appropriated and the contract authorization provided therefor, to implement the provisions of the law whenever in the judgment of either the Secretary of Defense, Army, Navy or Air Force "the national defense will be facilitated thereby."

The Executive Order was amended by No. 11610 in July 1971 to permit contractual provisions holding harmless and indemnifying contractors against unusually hazardous risks involving the performance of contracts in foreign countries or under unusual circumstances in the United States.

Part II of the Executive Order extended the same authority, when the action would facilitate the national defense, to the secretaries or heads of the following departments or agencies: Departments of the Treasury, Interior, Agriculture, Commerce, Transportation, and the Atomic Energy Commission, General Services Administration, National Aeronautics and Space Administration, Tennessee Valley Authority, and Government Printing Office.

REGULATORY IMPLEMENTATION—FAR Part 50

An unusual avenue for relief for companies doing business with a number of federal departments and agencies is provided through P.L. 85-804 and Executive Order No. 10789, as further implemented in FAR and Supplements of the agencies involved. A significant consideration in any contractual action under the law and executive order is that it must facilitate the national defense. One of the implications of this principle, as discussed later in this chapter, is that relief is frequently denied to contractors who cannot establish that their continued existence is essential to the national defense.

The following types of contract adjustments are available in appropriate circumstances.

50.302-1 *Amendments without consideration.*

(a) When an actual or threatened loss under a defense contract, however caused, will impair the productive ability of a contractor whose continued performance on any defense contract or whose continued operation as a source of supply is found to be essential to the national defense, the contract may be amended without consideration, but only to the extent necessary to avoid such impairment to the contractor's productive ability.

(b) When a contractor suffers a loss (not merely a decrease in anticipated profits) under a defense contract because of Government action, the character of the action will generally determine whether any adjustment in the contract will be made and its extent. When the Government directs its action primarily at the contractor and acts in its capacity as the other contracting party, the contract may be adjusted in the interest of fairness. Thus, when Government action, while not creating any liability on the Government's part, increases performance cost and results in a loss to the contractor, fairness may make some adjustment appropriate.

50.302-2 *Correcting mistakes.*

(a) A contract may be amended or modified to correct or mitigate the effect of a mistake. The following are examples of mistakes that may make such action appropriate:

(1) A mistake or ambiguity consisting of the failure to express, or express clearly, in a written contract, the agreement as both parties understood it.

(2) A contractor's mistake so obvious that it was or should have been apparent to the contracting officer.

(3) A mutual mistake as to a material fact.

(b) Amending contracts to correct mistakes with the least possible delay normally will facilitate the national defense by expediting the contracting program and assuring contractors that mistakes will be corrected expeditiously and fairly.

50.302-3 *Formalizing informal commitments.*

Under certain circumstances, informal commitments may be formalized to permit payment to persons who have taken action without a formal contract; for example, when a person, responding to an agency official's written or oral instructions and relying in good faith upon the official's apparent authority to issue them, has furnished or arranged to furnish supplies or services to the agency, or to a defense contractor or subcontractor, without formal contractual coverage. Formalizing commitments under such circumstances normally will facilitate the national defense by assuring such persons that they will be treated fairly and paid expeditiously.

Exercise of Authority Under Law and Executive Order

The authority to obligate the United States in an amount in excess of $50,000, as set forth in the statute, may not be delegated below the level "of an Assistant Secretary or his Deputy, or an assistant head or his deputy, of such department or agency, or by a Contract Adjustment Board...." In most instances, e.g., Army, Navy and Air Force, such boards have been established. Their decisions are not subject to appeal; however, the boards may reconsider and revise their own decisions.

The Contract Disputes Act of 1978 has extended the authority for amendments without consideration and for mistakes to boards of contract appeals and the appropriate federal courts. In some instances, contractors seeking relief for mistakes, etc., may consider submitting claims to both a board of contract appeals and a contract adjustment board.

Procedures in Requesting Relief

Inasmuch as this category is entitled "Extraordinary Contractual Action," it is not surprising to find that a very substantial amount of information and documentation must be submitted by contractors in order to merit consideration. Readers should review the provisions of FAR 50.303 and 50.304 to ascertain the requirements. Advice from legal and accounting experts in this area is usually extremely useful if not essential.

Residual Powers

This term relates to relief that may be available under the law and executive order other than amendments without consideration to correct mistakes, to formalize informal commitments and to make advance payments. A significant aspect of the residual powers applies to requests for indemnification contract clauses to cover unusually hazardous or nuclear risks. The procedures for submitting such requests are outlined in FAR 50.403-1 and the actions that government officials are required to take regarding such requests are set forth in FAR 50.403-2. When approved by the appropriate official, the following clause will be inserted in the contract (FAR 52.250-1):

INDEMNIFICATION UNDER PUBLIC LAW 85-804 (APR 1984)

(a) "Contractor's principal officials," as used in this clause, means directors, officers, managers, superintendents, or other representatives supervising or directing—

(1) All or substantially all of the Contractor's business;

(2) All or substantially all of the Contractor's operations at any one plant or separate location in which this contract is being performed; or

(3) A separate and complete major industrial operation in connection with the performance of this contract.

(b) Under Public Law 85-804 (50 U.S.C. 1431-1435) and Executive Order 10789, as amended, and regardless of any other provisions of this contract, the Government shall, subject to the limitations contained in the other paragraphs of this clause, indemnify the Contractor against—

(1) Claims (including reasonable expenses of litigation or settlement) by third persons (including employees of the Contractor) for death; personal injury; or loss of, damage to, or loss of use of property;

(2) Loss of, damage to, or loss of use of Contractor property, excluding loss of profit; and

(3) Loss of, damage to, or loss of use of Government property, excluding loss of profit.

(c) This indemnification applies only to the extent that the claim, loss, or damage (1) arises out of or results from a risk defined in this contract as unusually hazardous or nuclear and (2) is not compensated for by insurance or otherwise. Any such claim, loss, or damage, to the extent that it is within the deductible amounts of the Contractor's insurance, is not covered under this clause. If insurance coverage or other financial protection in effect on the date the approving official authorizes use of this clause is reduced, the Government's liability under this clause shall not increase as a result.

(d) When the claim, loss, or damage is caused by willful misconduct or lack of good faith on the part of any of the contractor's principal officials, the Contractor shall not be indemnified for—

(1) Government claims against the Contractor (other than those arising through subrogation); or

(2) Loss or damage affecting the Contractor's property.

(e) With the Contracting Officer's prior written approval, the Contractor may, in any subcontract under this contract, indemnify the subcontractor against any risk defined in this contract as unusually hazardous or nuclear. This indemnification shall provide, between the Contractor and the subcontractor, the same rights and duties, and the same provisions for notice, furnishing of evidence or proof, and Government settlement or defense of claims as this clause provides. The Contracting Officer may also approve indemnification of subcontractors at any lower tier, under the same terms and conditions. The Government shall indemnify the Contractor against liability to subcontractors incurred under subcontract provisions approved by the Contracting Officer.

(f) The rights and obligations of the parties under this clause shall survive this contract's termination, expiration, or completion. The Government shall make no payment under this clause unless the agency head determines that the amount is just and reasonable. The Government may pay the Contractor or subcontractors, or may directly pay parties to whom the Contractor or subcontractors may be liable.

(g) The Contractor shall—

(1) Promptly notify the Contracting Officer of any claim or action against, or any loss by, the Contractor or any subcontractors that may reasonably be expected to involve indemnification under this clause;

(2) Immediately furnish to the Government copies of all pertinent papers the Contractor receives;

(3) Furnish evidence or proof of any claim, loss, or damage covered by this clause in the manner and form the Government requires; and

(4) Comply with the Government's directions and execute any authorizations required in connection with settlement or defense of claims or actions.

(h) The Government may direct, control, or assist in settling or defending any claim or action that may involve indemnification under this clause.

(End of clause)

(R 7-303.62 1977 JAN)

Alternate I (APR 1984). In cost-reimbursement contracts, add the following paragraph (i) to the basic clause:

(i) The cost of insurance (including self-insurance programs) covering a risk defined in this contract as unusually hazardous or nuclear shall not be reimbursed except to the extent that the Contracting Officer has required or approved this insurance. The Government's obligations under this clause are—

(1) Excepted from the release required under this contract's clause relating to allowable cost; and

(2) Not affected by this contract's Limitation of Cost or Limitation of Funds clause.

CONTRACT ADJUSTMENT BOARD DECISIONS ON REQUESTS FOR RELIEF UNDER P.L. 85-804

Departments and agencies authorized to take action under P.L. 85-804 are required to submit annual reports to Congress of all actions taken annually. With respect to actions which involve actual or potential cost to the United States in excess of $50,000, the report must include the name of the contractor, the actual or estimated potential cost, property or services involved, and the circumstances justifying the action. Although all reports not classified for security reasons are available to the public, the Department of Defense reports reflect by far the most volume and they are most readily available. Accordingly, the actions summarized below are essentially those contained in some of the DOD annual reports. This means that more than $50,000 was involved and that the action of the Contract Adjustment Board was favorable. Some of the summaries are directly quoted from the DOD annual reports, while others are paraphrased. A review of these decisions should be informative as to the thinking of contract adjustment boards.

Mistakes

In response to an Invitation for Bid (IFB), the contractor submitted a bid which was substantially lower than those submitted by the other three bidders. However, after opening and prior to the award, the government determined that a revision in the drawing was necessary, and the IFB was cancelled. After this event, a representative of the contractor visited the procurement office and was advised that his bid appeared low in comparison to the other bids. Without being requested to recheck the data supporting the bid price, the contractor's representative stated that the bid price was based on analysis, that the item fit their other production work, and that the contractor's large business production facilities could cut costs below those of the other small business concerns bidding on the item.

About a month later, a new IFB was issued and bids were received from the same four companies. Again, this contractor's bid was much lower than those of the others. Although aware of disparity in bid prices, the contracting officer did not request verification because of the discussion with the contractor's representative in connection with the prior cancelled IFB and because the bid submitted on the current IFB was identical. The contract was ultimately awarded to the low bidder.

Two months later, the contractor advised the contracting officer that it had discovered omissions in its work sheets pertaining to machine operations which caused a mistake in the bid. In its request for relief, the contractor stated that the drawings on forgings for certain government parts were not available during the preparation of its bid. In this regard it was stated that, based on the fact that forging drawings were not available during the bidding stage, it was erroneously assumed that many dimensions would not be machined and would be left in the "as forged" condition. The contractor submitted certain work papers to show that a substantial number of milling operations were determined to be required after the receipt of the drawings.

The contractor, therefore, alleged that a mistake had occurred and requested a correction through an increase in the contract price.

The Army Contract Adjustment Board concluded that a mistake in bid had been made resulting from the omission of required milling operations. The board did not consider the contractor's prior explanation of its prior bid on the cancelled invitation as constituting verification and concluded that the contracting officer was under an obligation to request the bidder to recheck its computation of the bid, calling attention to any suspected mistake, and to verify the correctness of the price quoted.

Amendments Without Consideration

Continued deliveries were essential to meet requirements for the conflict in Southeast Asia. Failure to grant relief would almost certainly have resulted in serious financial damage to this company. If this occurred, the Army would not have been able to receive the items when required.

The contractor suffered losses under defense contracts which impaired its productive ability. Its continued operation for the performance of various Navy contracts was essential to the national defense.

Mistakes

The contracts were amended to provide for an additional amount to the contractor. This was to correct a mutual mistake.

The additional engineering services provided by the contractor resulted from changes made in the specifications after equipment had been delivered and installed. This required considerably more services than had been provided for in the contract.

Formalization of Informal Commitments

While a contract was being negotiated with the contractor the requirements were increased. Due to an urgent need for the services and further negotiation, the work was performed without a task order. Every effort was made to utilize normal procurement procedures but due to the urgency this was not practical.

Amendments Without Consideration

The Army approved $1.5 million to a contractor who had experienced difficulties in meeting contract specifications, had become delinquent on the delivery schedule, and as a result was incurring considerable losses. The Army needed the material and was unable to obtain it from another source without delay it could not afford and at a cost which would exceed the amount to be paid the original contractor. There was also the point that the contractor would have gone out of business without this assistance and this would have resulted in the Army's loss of the progress payments which it had made. As we described earlier, amendments without consideration may be made "[w]here an actual or threatened loss under a defense contract, however caused, will impair the productive capability of a contractor whose continued performance on any defense contracts or whose continued operation as a source of supply is found to be essential to the national defense. . . ."

The Navy awarded $500,000 to a contractor where it was determined that financial relief was required in order to provide for continued performance of a contract for "an essential communications element of the United States Navy Fleet." In this case the Navy concluded that obtaining another producer would result in delay which would be "detrimental to the National Defense."

Mistakes

The Army approved an action approximating $500,000 where, before the opening of the bid, the government had changed the specifications and failed to properly set forth the new requirements. The contractor bid on the basis of the original specifications, which required less costs.

The Defense Supply Agency (now Defense Logistics Agency) approved over $140,000 "to correct a mutual mistake in bid because of a misplaced decimal point in the unit price."

Amendments Without Consideration

An action by the Army involved a control set in a radio used in Southeast Asia and the relief granted amounted to $600,000. There were no questions about the requirements for this component, and the Army could not wait until other contractors could produce and ship this item. The relief was granted with the justification that "without this amendment the company would not have been able to complete its production and the required units would not have been delivered when needed."

Another contract contained an option which gave the government the right to negotiate for an extension on a yearly basis. The supplemental agreement establishing the firm labor rates for the first year was entered into subsequent to the renewal agreement, and the wording did not expressly provide that the firm labor rate agreed to would apply only to the first year of the contract. The contracting officer concluded that it established the labor rate for the duration of the contract.

Mistakes

The contractor submitted his bid on the basis that the item required was in production. He later discovered that his bid was in error and requested that the contract be cancelled. Because of need for the item, the contract was not cancelled, but it was ascertained that both the contractor and the government mistakenly believed that the contractor was currently producing the same item as required under the solicitation.

A subcontractor was to supply components for a projectile during the period January 1962 through January 1963. From the start of production through December 1962, samples of lots manufactured during the same period were tested, and it was found that the projectile did not meet the accuracy requirements desired by the government. It was mistakenly considered both by the subcontractor and the government, whose inspectors could not discover the reasons for the inaccuracy, that the fault was attributable to some error in manufacture. In early 1963, it was discovered that the specifications were inadequate. It has been determined that the contractor should be reimbursed for his losses due to inadequate specifications.

Amendments Without Consideration

"The Naval Electronics Systems Command has advised that the UHX-2 Facsimile Recorder is designated as critical and failure to receive that equipment would cause shipbuilding delays. That Command has also designated as critical the URM-47 Radio Interference Measurement Set and the CU-714 Antenna Coupler and estimates that reprocurement from other sources of all the equipment under their present contract with Decitron would entail delay of two and a half to three years. Should this company be forced to cease operations and default on these contracts the Navy stands to lose its advance payments of $715,000 plus unliquidated progress payments of approximately $2,028,373. In addition the estimated cost of reprocurement is $4,941,000."

Mistakes

"The contractor's bid price of $9.74 per unit included a price of $.213 quoted by a subcontractor for the housing materials instead of $2.13. The error was so obvious it should have alerted the Contracting Officer because of the vast difference in price from the other bids received."

"The contractor submitted his bid on the kit configuration 'E' ($32.67), which the Contracting Officer should have realized was far too low for the 'F' configuration that was being purchased. That configuration 'F' kit contains 244 parts as opposed to the 49 parts contained in configuration 'E', four types of which have a direct cost of over $20.00."

Amendments Without Consideration

Deruss had produced fuse lock cups under a contract with Frankford Arsenal under which specifications requiring the use of steel plate were changed to the much cheaper steel bar. Deruss had originally been advised of this by a Frankford Arsenal project engineer, who was neither a contracting officer nor a contracting officer's representative. Nevertheless, when Deruss received this award it noted that the specifications were officially changed as the project engineer had originally annotated.

While performing on this contract, Deruss (and eight other firms) were requested by Picatinny Arsenal to submit a proposal for another contract for fuse lock cups. As in the prior Frankford Arsenal solicitation, the one from Picatinny also specified steel plate. Before submitting its proposal, Deruss asked the Frankford project engineer whether a change to the cheaper steel bars would be authorized as in the case of the Frankford contract. Deruss understood from this conversation that such change would be authorized. Based upon this understanding, Deruss submitted its proposal based on the use of steel bars even though the solicitation specified steel plate.

The Deruss proposal was lowest and its facilities were the subject of a pre-award survey. The survey team included Picatinny Arsenal personnel and the Frankford Arsenal project engineer. The government personnel was shown the Deruss operations under which the Frankford Arsenal contract was being carried out with the use of steel bars. This change in specifications was discussed in some detail, and, according to Deruss, an understanding was reached that steel bars would be authorized.

Subsequently, the Picatinny Arsenal personnel reviewed Deruss's cost data, which showed material cost for steel bars rather than for steel plates. No question was raised and the cost data was approved.

After Deruss had received the award, it discussed the need to change the contract terms to specify the use of steel bars, and it ultimately submitted an engineering change proposal to this effect. It was then notified that this proposal would be denied, that steel plate would be required, and preproduction samples using steel bar were rejected. Deruss then used steel plate in lieu of defaulting on the contract. It contended that several actions by government personnel led it to believe that steel bars would be acceptable and that its proposal had been priced on this basis.

The review by the Army Contract Adjustment Board led it to the conclusion that the contentions of Deruss were correct. The change had been made under a previous contract; this change was evident to the pre-award survey team (especially since an entirely different production technique is required when steel bar is used); and, finally, the difference in cost between the plate and the bar was obvious. The Board concluded that the various "acts and omissions constitute government action for which consideration of fairness justify contractual action." The concluding paragraph of the Board's decision stated that "[t]he action authorized by this decision will facilitate the national defense."

Formalization of Informal Commitments

Another decision by the Army Contract Adjustment Board involved the appeal of the Trenton Textile Engineering & Manufacturing Company, Inc., handed down on February 11, 1970. Involved here was the formalization of informal commitments relied on in good faith by a contractor, together with related fair compensation. The case is notable, too, because of the extremely broad and liberal view taken by the government with respect to the requirement that a request for payment must be filed within six months (ASPR 17-205.1(d)).

The Procuring Contracting Officer (PCO) had been alerted to a large, urgent order for inert mines and advised to finalize procurement plans for early delivery. The urgency did not permit seeking competition, and Trenton was selected because of prior experience. After receipt of its acceptable price quotation and delivery schedule, the Army told Trenton that approvals had been received and that a letter contract would be executed. Thereupon, Trenton alerted its suppliers and ordered special machinery from a contractor. However, for reasons not explained in the decision, the requirement was later cancelled and Trenton was then advised that the proposed letter contract would not be executed.

Trenton contended that it had initially been advised of a specific contract number and told to begin work, which led to its awarding purchase orders and a subcontract. By the time it was notified of the cancellation, most of the supplies had already been delivered and the equipment manufactured by the subcontractor. It alleged that its P. L. 85-804 application had been filed timely, citing the numerous telephone inquiries and conversations as "sufficient notice to the government of its request for relief."

Based on these facts, the board concluded that (1) the initial advice by the government to Trenton did constitute a formal commitment for which relief was warranted under ASPR 17-204.4 and that (2) the contractor's various telephone and other conversations during the eleven-month period did constitute "a sufficient consideration of the six-month filing requirement."

Mistakes

"A requirement of the contract was for the contractor to submit provisioning data and a vendor list to the Procuring Officer. Collins Radio Co. submitted their bid with an asterisk by the price stating in a footnote that it did not include the cost of the vendor list. The contract was executed not taking this into consideration. The contractor was reimbursed to correct a mutual mistake."

On 6 December 1967, Continental was awarded a letter contract for the rebuilding of 3,000 engines with an option for the government to increase this amount by 100%. On 26 December 1967, Continental gave written confirmation that an error had been made in its offer in that the cost of pistons (6 per engine @ $24.25 each) had been omitted as a result of a clerical error. On 9 and 17 May 1968, the government exercised its option and increased the engines to 6,000. The contractor was granted relief in that the option had been exercised with full knowledge of the mistake.

Other

The Defense Fuel Supply Center awarded 153 contracts for residual fuel oil for delivery to 566 installations. Each contract contains a price escalation provision permitting escalation with the market up to 10% above the contract price, and each bidder certified that the bid price included no contingencies for price increase. The combination of increased demand, decreased supply, and an overloaded transportation system resulted in higher prices and all but one of the suppliers exceeded their maximum escalation under the contract. It was determined that the escalation ceiling should be removed from these contracts. The exact amount involved could not be determined as the contracts were for indefinite quantities, but six of these actions involved more than $50,000.

Amendments Without Consideration

"*Gap Instrument Corp.,* $1,091,329.—The company has asserted that it faces a financial crisis of such major proportions that without immediate relief it will be unable to continue operations. The MK-53 units, which constitute an integral portion of a shipboard underwater fire control system, are tightly scheduled for installation as government furnished equipment on two classes of Navy vessels presently under construction. A number of the remainder are for delivery to foreign governments. Although other companies have produced the console under prior contracts, none are currently in production. Should this company be forced to cease operations the Navy stands to lose its advance payments of approximately $2,265,000. In addition the estimated cost of reprocurement is approximately $6,000,000."

"*S.W. Electronics & Mfg. Co.,* $250,000.—The contractor is a small firm of approximately 60 employees and its financial distress was precipitated when it became unable to make delivery and receive payment under a contract for the government of Pakistan after the U. S. State Department imposed temporary restrictions upon the shipment of military supplies to that country in April 1971. The AN/ARR-69 radios are being purchased for use by both the Navy and the Air Force on F-4J, A-4B, TA-F4 and A-7E aircraft. Government inventories have been exhausted and equipment is not available for installation on operational aircraft. Introducing another source would entail a delay of from 12 to 18 months and a substantial increase in unit prices."

"*Lockheed Aircraft Corp.,* $500 Million.—In March 1970 the company submitted a letter to DOD citing its contractual and financial problems on several major defense programs, including programs involving the Cheyenne helicopter and the C-5A aircraft. The company asserted that "the unprecedented dollar magnitude of the claims and disputes" in which these programs among others were involved would "make it financially impossible for Lockheed to complete performance of these programs if we must await the outcome of litigation before receiving further financing from the Department of Defense." After a thorough review of this matter, the Deputy Secretary of Defense determined on 4 June 1971 that it was necessary to continue these essential defense programs as such action will thereby facilitate the national defense. Although such action will permit the company to continue operations its losses on these programs will be severe. In the case of the C-5A aircraft contract a fixed loss of $200 million was negotiated with the company."

"*Lockheed Aircraft Corp.,* $123 Million.—The actions taken with respect to the AH-56A Cheyenne basically involved a restructuring of the AH-56A research and development contract and the settlement of the claims of the corporation, then in litigation, relating to the AH-56A production contract which had been terminated for default. These actions were based on the authority of Public Law 85-804 and the authority to resolve disputes arising under the provisions of government contracts. The company's loss on the AH-56A contracts is estimated at $119 million. For further details, see comment above concerning the C-5A aircraft."

Formalization of Informal Commitments

"*Stromberg Datagraphix, Inc.,* $269.144.—General Services Administration placed a contract with Stromberg for the installation and rental of equipment at USARPAC overseas commands during FY 1969. During FY 1970 the government continued to use this equipment while a new contract was being negotiated. The resulting contract excluded these commands which should have been covered."

Mistakes

"*North Electric Co.,* $66,252.—The U.S. Army Electronics Command issued an RFQ for three Seventh Army Tactical Switching Systems with an option to purchase three more. The requirement to install, test and check the system was not set out as a separate item but appeared by way of a footnote. When the contract was awarded it required the contractor to furnish six systems instead of three. The contractor's bid covered the installation of only three systems instead of six."

"*Bendix Corp., $2,658,406.*—The original contract for 880 AN/APN-141 Radar Altimeters was a fixed price incentive contract permitting both fixed price or fixed price redeterminable purchases to be made. The pricing formula set the initial ceiling at 115% of target cost. Amendment #4 called for 450 additional units and excluded all reference to the ceiling. The effect of this modification was to increase the total final price permitted by the ceiling."

"*Lockheed Aircraft Corp., $98,182.*—On January 13, 1966 contract was awarded for 45 p-3B aircraft at a total fixed price. Shortly thereafter the contracting officer ordered various modifications to be made to 17 of the aircraft, which required extra work as well as partial termination of some work originally required on those planes. No provision was made at that time for the additional costs."

Other

"*Steuart Petroleum Co., $671,723.*—Steuart Petroleum Co. is the only supplier capable of supplying and distributing all #6 fuel oil requirements for the federal government in the Washington metropolitan area. There are over 200 separate delivery points within the area. Contractor would incur loss as a direct result of the ceiling on escalation under the contract. Ceiling did not forsee price rise due to shortages in both product and transportation."

Formalization of Informal Commitments

"*Alabama Forge & Machine, Inc., $235,000.*—The Army issued an RFP for procurement of 155m projectiles with the furnishing by the government of production facilities. The facilities project request required approval at the DOD level which had not been obtained prior to issuance of the RFP. While the approval was being sought the contractor was requested orally, several times, to extend the expiration date of its proposal which added up to approximately 13 months. During this time the contractor obtained a plant and approximately 40 personnel which it maintained from 1 October 1968 until the plant was finally closed in December 1969. The government was at fault for repeatedly asking Alabama Forge to extend its proposal and should share in the expenses incurred by the company."

Mistakes

"*General Electric Co., $87,123.*—On 30 September 1965 a letter contract was entered into which provided that the Value Engineering Incentive provision of ASPR 1-1707.2(b) would be incorporated into the definitized contract. GE submitted eight Value Engineering Change Proposals (VECPs) which were approved and applied under the contract prior to definitization. The total savings from the VECPs amounted to $174,246 of which 50% was due GE as its share. The definitized contract provision failed to increase the contract price to cover this cost."

Amendments Without Consideration

The Libby Welding Company.—Libby was awarded a three-year, multi-year, fixed-price type contract, with escalation applicable only to the second and third program years and a maximum upward limitation of 10%, resulting from two-step formal advertising procedures. It was a 100% small business set-aside. The contract was for certain generator sets which were to be used by the

Army, Navy, Air Force and Marine Corps. The generator sets were determined to be essential to DOD. It was further determined that if Libby went into bankruptcy, the DOD standardization program would be set back at least two years and would be detrimental to the mission responsibilities of the services.

There were delays involving reliability tests and for other reasons before Libby passed all first article test requirements and was ready to begin production. At that time, Libby's subcontractors stated that the long delays in ordering parts made it impossible for them to furnish the items at the quoted prices in view of the inflation which had taken place. The main subcontractors refused to furnish the items except at the cost-at-time-of-delivery basis. The additional amounts demanded by the subcontractors would force Libby into substantial losses which it could not afford and which would force it into bankruptcy.

Libby was awarded an amendment without consideration based on essentiality to the national defense and relief of a mutual mistake.

The West Electronic, Inc.—West received an advertised contract for communication hardware, most of which was to be provided to Grumman Aerospace Corporation as government-furnished equipment to be installed in certain Navy aircraft being manufactured by Grumman. The contracting officer and the Navy Contract Adjustment Board (NCAB) agreed that the aircraft could not be flown without this equipment, that present stocks were exhausted or about to become so, that procurement lead time did not permit use of other sources, and that West required up to $50,000 to permit contract completion. Without this relief, West would be forced into bankruptcy. The board authorized an amendment without consideration.

Amendments Without Consideration

"Allegheny Metal Stamping Co., Inc., $129,257.—Since award of the contracts, the price of steel and copper, major items of material used in the manufacture of the clips, has risen, and continues to rise. This increase has caused the contractor such a large loss under the contracts that it will be necessary to cease operations in the very near future without relief. These cartridge clips are for the M-16 Rifle which has been adopted as the basic small arm for the Armed Forces of the U.S. and several of its allies. There is only one contractor other than Allegheny currently in production of the clips. It is determined that the clips are an integral component of a critical procurement program and they are in urgent demand."

"Amron Corporation, $549,871.—On January 12, 1973, contract was awarded at a unit price of $0.2583 per case with a provision for an option procurement. During the performance of the contract, the market for brass incurred rapid increases in costs. The contractor in anticipation of the Government's exercise of the option requested that the option price be increased or allowed to expire. On October 15, 1973, the Government exercised its option but included no upward price escalation clause. It is found that adjustment is necessary for company to maintain its productive ability as a source of supply."

"Kisco Co., Inc., $6,077.779.—During the period October 16, 1970 through March 15, 1973 five contracts were awarded for various cartridge

cases and ammunition shipping and storage containers. Government furnished equipment, which was old and in constant need of repair proved costly and resulted in unanticipated maintenance, a high scrap rate and delays in delivery. Technical problems resulted due to production of large quantities and the lifting of price controls increased the costs of materials and labor. Company is now threatened with bankruptcy due to its losses. Company is the only planned mobilization base producer of M106mm M941B1 cartridge cases and the sole present source for the 57mm M30A1B3 cartridge case and the ammunition and storage container for the M61 Vulcan automatic weapon."

"*Optic-Electronic Corporation*, $2,082,039.—Eight contracts have been awarded for periscopes and telescopes but only 29% of the items have been delivered. Due to the contractor's underestimation of labor hours, failure to establish adequate financial controls as its business expanded, increased charges for materials and the decision to subcontract certain work at a higher cost in order to meet schedules, the company is in a precarious financial situation. All the items are necessary parts of the M60 tank program which carries a DX priority designating it as a program of highest national priority. There still exists an urgent requirement for these items and it would seriously impede the Army vehicle program if not continued."

"*Thompson Optical Engineering Company*, $501,474.—During March 1972 the contractor's facility was totally destroyed by fire. Original contract bids were based on fragmentary records salvaged from the fire which were overly conservative. The rising cost of inflation, inadequate tooling and a prolonged strike by a major subcontractor have put the company in a weak financial condition. An urgent requirement still exists for these items and procurement from any other source would take in excess of 12 months which would seriously hamper the Army's vehicle program."

"*Ashland Chemical Company*, $840,960.—The limited capacity for the production of malononitrile, a key component in CS materials, and its high domestic price resulted in dependence of the U.S. Government upon foreign countries. A decision was made to make the Army independent of foreign sources. Fisher's bid was based upon the Army's planning for large quantities during a five year period. In early 1970 the Army's future needs for CS was drastically reduced and future procurements never materialized. The contractor is entitled to unrealized amortization and depreciation because they were induced not to seek recovery of their capital costs over the original contract period, but instead over a 27 month period."

"*Kellett Corporation*, $358,032.—On July 22, 1973, Kellett filed bankruptcy. Company has exhausted, without success, all means of obtaining additional conventional financing to meet its current and projected cash flow needs and without relief it will have to close out its operations. To date, no other contractor has successfully manufactured this equipment though two have tried and failed. Continued performance is essential to the national defense."

"*Libby Welding Company*, $4,300,672.—Contractor was required to design, fabricate and test preproduction models which took approximately nine months. The subcontractors refused to furnish materials at the prices quoted at time of bid. The generator sets are utilized by all three Armed

Services and the aging inventory has been overhauled to the extent it is impractical to continue this practice. Procurement from another source would require at least two years or more."

"*Bowmar/Ali, Inc.,* $465,348.—The cancellation ceiling in a multi-year IFB was predicated on an unrealistic cost base. Later information indicated that the percentage should have been significantly higher. The contracting officer decided not to revise the solicitation before bid opening. It is found that the contracting officer's decision not to revise the original cancellation ceiling was unreasonable and resulted in the inclusion of unrealistic ceilings in the solicitation."

"*Alabama Industries, Inc.,* $4,314,180.—The Government furnished equipment being used for this contract is so aged, dilapidated, and undermaintained that the production rate stretched out the contractor's delivery period. This delay has caused an increase in the cost of materials, labor, overhead and other expenses. There are only two other producers making these shells and they are both producing at capacity. In addition to the requested relief, an additional amount has been authorized for repair of the equipment."

"*Environmental Systems Development, Inc.,* $561.704.—The contractor was a newly formed company and has suffered many problems during the performance of the contract. Progress payments of $747,846 would be lost if the company goes out of business. Procurement from another source would cost approximately $1,228,833 and would cause a delay of six months or more in the Navy's ASW program."

"*West Electronics, Inc.,* $50,000.—Most of the equipment is to be supplied to Grumman Aerospace Corp. as Government furnished equipment to be installed in E-2C and EA-6B Navy aircraft. Present stocks are either exhausted or about to become so and these aircraft cannot be flown without it. Other sources can supply these items but procurement lead time is such that delivery under new contracts would not begin until twelve months after award."

"*Engineering Research, Inc.,* $765,215.—During performance of the contract the supplier of bomb body castings ceased furnishing castings for this contract and procurement from other suppliers increased the price by 55%. These bombs are crucial to the Air Force's training requirements and there is a critical shortage of practice bombs."

Diamond Reo Trucks, Inc.—This case gives an example of a contractor who was not successful in his request to the Contract Adjustment Board.

Extraordinary contractual relief necessary to guarantee contract completion and to reestablish productive capacity was denied the only active supplier of M-602 Trucks and replacement parts because his company's continued existence was no longer essential to the national defense in view of a planned phase-out of the M-602 Truck series and the large inventory of replacement parts on hand. The board recognized that he would sustain a substantial loss on the subject contract, as he contended, but concluded that restorative relief was not justified because his continued existence as a viable producer was too speculative. The board also declined to grant relief on the grounds that a cessation of operations would have a substantially disruptive impact on the general economy. His withdrawal from the industrial marketplace would not leave an unabsorbable production inventory created by subcontractors totally dependent upon him for their continued existence.

Amendments Without Consideration

"*Kellett Corporation, $688,833.*—This contractor was granted relief in the amount of $358,032 . . . . The contractor contends that due to a miscalculation their request for needed funds was understated. It is determined that this contractor continues to be essential to the national defense."

"*Thompson Optical Engineer Co., $400,000.*—Thompson was granted relief in the amount of $501,474 . . . . The company's productive capability has been impaired as a result of losses suffered under several Army contracts. It is determined that continued performance under this contract is essential to the national defense."

"*G.C. Industries, Inc., $88,963.*—The contractor's original request for relief was based on mistake in bid preparation, which was denied. However, the distribution panels are urgently needed and reprocurement from another source would cause a lead time of at least thirteen months and an increase in price of at least $200 per unit."

"*Photronics, Corp., $159,512.*—There was such a disparity in the contractor's proposal and the government's estimate for this item that Photronics should have been notified. The company has suffered a heavy financial loss on this contract and their productive capability is impaired. Although there are other qualified sources for procurement of the telescopes it is economically impractical when the cost is compared to cost under this contract, including the relief required. Photronics is an important producer of other defense items, several of which are considered essential to weapons and missile systems."

"*American Gear & Pinion Corp., $409,634.*—The boosters were to be produced with Government Furnished Equipment which was, at the time of award, located in a defunct contractor's plant. Between the time of bid preparation and the time the GFE was removed from the plant it had been cannibalized and otherwise deteriorated to the point of being practically useless. The contractor was compensated for additional cost encountered through the period of delay caused by the faulty GFE but during the delay the cost of brass stock escalated sharply. The contractor is essential to the national defense as a producer of M125A1 boosters."

"*Medico Industries, Inc., $110,226.*—A letter contract was awarded with a ceiling price of $4.465 per unit and an option quantity at the same price. During the negotiations to definitize the letter contract the government was informed that as a result of rising costs a unit price of $4.7037 would be appropriate. However, the contract was definitized at the ceiling price contained in the letter contract. The government recognized at the time it exercised the option that the contractor would lose money on each unit produced, but felt there was no alternative in view of the option price in the contract as definitized."

"*Cincinnati Electronics Corp., $2,119,000.*—At the time of the IFB the present ownership of Cincinnati were employees of the Evandale Division of

AVCO and were negotiating to buy the business. This group bid on the contract even though their buy-out from AVCO was not complete. They requested the SBA to certify them as a small business concern, anticipating that, if they were low bidder on the non-set aside portion they could receive the entire award by achieving small business labor surplus area status. The SBA certified the company as a small business for the procurement. Cincinnati won the award but Sentinel Electronics which was next in line protested their small business status in view of their affiliation with AVCO. Cincinnati received the award for the non-set aside portion only even though they stated that their bid was premised upon award of the total quantity. The loss stems from the faulty premise in Cincinnati's bid and from sharp escalation in material costs during all of the delays. Cincinnati is considered essential as a producer under ongoing contracts and as a future source of supply for defense items."

"*G.W. Galloway Co.*, $321,053.—Almost immediately after award of the contract government price controls were lifted, causing a rapid increase in the cost of materials. To date half of the total quantity has been shipped and deliveries are ahead of schedule but the company's financial position has deteriorated to the point where it can no longer absorb losses engendered by the bridge contract and still have sufficient cash flow to remain in business. It is determined that Galloway's performance is essential to the national defense."

"*Intercontinental Mfg. Co.*, $1,400,000.—IMCO held contracts for both MK-82 and MK-84 bomb bodies. A dispute arose over the acceptability of the bombs and IMCO ceased production. The SPCC partially terminated the MK-82 contract but did not terminate the MK-84 contract because the bomb body is not obtainable from any source other than IMCO. SPCC has repurchased part of the MK-82 units pursuant to the default clause, and excessive reprocurement costs have placed IMCO in a weak financial condition. Without relief it would be impossible to continue the MK-84 contract. IMCO is and has been the sole producer of the MK-84 bomb body for many years and owns the only facility (including all the necessary plant equipment, tooling, etc.) capable of manufacturing the MK-84."

"*Simco, Inc.*, $162.215.—Contract was awarded in April 1974 for 646 NT-4 Universal Aircraft Towbars. In January 1975 (9 months later) the Government exercised its option for 592 additional units at *the basic contract price.* Simco is in a position where it cannot pay its suppliers for the additional materials required to complete the contract. The towbars have been in continuously short supply for several years and they are considered by type commanders to be one of the most critical items of ground support equipment. It is estimated that these units would cost considerably more if purchased from another source."

"*Hazeltine Corp.*, $2,500,000.—During the performance of its fixed-price contract for scan converter display systems, Hazeltine encountered technical performance problems which increased its cost of performance. The contractor then submitted a claim for equitable adjustment for asserted constructive changes which will be resolved under the disputes procedure. In conjunction with these developments, Hazeltine's main source of financing, Franklin

National Bank, failed, leaving the contractor in a critical cash flow posture. Hazeltine is considered an essential supplier for several defense systems, including the Maverick missile and AWACS. The amendment took the form of an increase in contract price accompanied by an agreement that if an equitable adjustment is approved the contract price will be reduced by the difference between the equitable adjustment and the $2.5 million price increase; if the equitable adjustment is not approved the contractor will refund the $2.5 million, plus interest."

"*Latsec, Inc.*, $400,000.—Latsec incurred substantial additional costs in performing its fixed price type contract. It was found that the financial failure of Latsec would result in the bankruptcy of Dr. Peter Toma, the company's founder and chief stockholder. The record evidences that in the event of this contingency Dr. Toma would be impelled to leave the U.S. to accept outstanding academic and commercial opportunities in Europe. Dr. Toma is the developer of unique innovations in the field of computerized foreign language translation including automated means of content and threat analysis, trend prediction and question answering. While there were alternate sources for the performance of this particular contract, it was found that Dr. Toma and his corporate retinue represent a source of technological contributions whose continued operation is considered essential to the national defense and that relief under the contract is justified."

"*Drexel Industries, Inc.*, $1,000,000.—In 1972 Drexel was awarded four contracts for a total of 621 trucks of which 320 remain undelivered. Production on these contracts was delayed several months by strikes. During this delay labor costs increased and the deterioration of the economy caused the company to incur substantial losses. Should these contracts be terminated for default, Drexel would be unable to pay the excess cost of reprocurement and, in all probability would be forced into bankruptcy. While Drexel is not the only source of supply for any type of forklift trucks used by the DOD, continuing spare parts support is and will be required for Drexel trucks currently in inventory. While many parts built into Drexel equipment are commercially available, detailed drawings, plans and diagrams would be required to permit alternate manufacture of parts distinctive to Drexel. Such drawings are not available to the Government."

Amendments Without Consideration

"*Champion Rubber Products, Inc.*, $101,065.—Cartridge cases used on 152mm rounds are susceptible to moisture damage which adversely affects their performance. The barrier bag is a protective device for 152mm ammunition and also protects the rounds from contamination or accidental ignition. This contractor represents the only procurement source for the barrier bags at this time and it would take approximately nine months to develop an alternative source. If this company were to discontinue production, it would result in a shutdown of the line at Iowa Ammunition Plant and place the line in a temporary inactive status."

Mistakes

"*Teledyne Continental Motors, General Products Division*, $106,516.—A letter contract was awarded for engine assemblies for the M60A1 tank on May 31, 1974, and, in October 1974, a price bill of materials was negotiated. As part of that negotiation, a price decrease for engineering changes was credited to the government. Subsequently, two modifications were effected, incorporating 30 engineering changes into the contract and extending to the government again the same decrease. The negotiators were not aware of the earlier October 1974 credits and the Army, in effect, has been receiving double credit for these engineering changes."

"*Velan Valve Corp.*, $56,696.—Velan was awarded a contract for twenty-five 6 inch gate valves on September 11, 1975 as a result of a formally advertised solicitation. Velan was the sole bidder and offered a unit price of $1,232. Although the only previous procurement of the item had been from Velan at a unit price of $3,500, and the government had estimated a unit price of $4,152, the contracting officer awarded the contract without seeking verification of the bid price. It appears that Velan made an error in its bid which should have been apparent to the contracting officer."

U.S. Forge, Inc.—A tank shoe contractor was denied a request for extraordinary contractual relief pursuant to P.L. 85-804, even though he claimed to be essential to the national defense as a continuing source for forged products, because there were seven forging suppliers capable of meeting the requirements. While the loss of the contractor, if forced to discontinue operations, could have resulted in a reduction of competition among DOD contractors producing forgings, the remaining producers had the capacity to meet both peacetime and mobilization requirements.

Amendments Without Consideration

"*Dixie Tool & Die Co., Inc. Gadsden AL*, $2,305,296.—A negotiated multiyear contract was awarded in July 1975 for seven components of the M-60 tank. The contractor immediately began having technical difficulties. The components being produced are necessary for the continued production of M-60 tanks. The Army Armament Material Readiness Command estimates that an average of 100 tanks per month will be manufactured over the next year. The costs associated with delay in production are estimated at $10,000 per tank. Without relief the contractor may fail and it will take approximately 10 to 12 months to reprocure these items. It is determined that continued performance of this contract is essential to the national defense."

"*Kellett Corp., Willow Grove, PA*, $667,235.—This contractor was granted relief in the amounts of $358,032 and $668,833 .... Payments authorized in September 1975 were suspended in November 1975 due to the fact that the appropriation involved was over obligated. Lacking sufficient funds, the contractor stopped work on Jan. 16, 1976. Another contractor has been found for the S-390 shelters but the unit price is excessive. Two other contractors who have been awarded a contract for the S-393 shelters have gone bankrupt attempting to perform. Apparently Kellet is the only contractor for these items. The ECOM Contract Adjustment Board concluded that the sole reason which caused Kellett to seek supplemental relief was the inability of the government to implement the decision of September 1975 in a timely manner. It is determined that the productive capability of the contractor has been and continues to be impaired as a consequence of losses experienced under these contracts."

"*Shuey Aircraft, Inc., Anaheim, CA,* $57,231.—Contract was awarded in June 1975 for 1,276 connecting rods at a unit cost of $41.26. Shuey has requested relief on the grounds of a mistake in submission of their bid as they failed to include the cost of tooling. There is no evidence of knowledge of the mistake on the part of the government. A balance of 349 pieces remain to be delivered. The average monthly demand for connecting rods for the past 25 months is 61. The lead time for procurement is 15 months. A new solicitation was opened in November 1976 and the bids ranged from $68 to $297 and delivery time 360 to 390 days. While Shuey's continued existence is not essential to the national defense, the continued performance of this contract, however, is essential."

"*Sysdyne, Inc., San Diego, CA,* $109,937.—In January 1974, a contract was awarded for engineeing support services for the Naval Undersea Center, Pasadena, CA. The contract estimated $409,000 worth of work during 1974 while actual orders totaled approximately $68,000. In 1975, the estimate was $126,000 with $57,000 actual. During this time, orders that should have been given to Sysdyne were placed elsewhere. The impact of the Navy estimate, and actual work performed was inexcusably deficient and little was done to minimize the impact on Sysdyne, a very small firm without the necessary capital to sustain the losses which resulted. It is the opinion of the Board that Sysdyne sustained a loss as a result of government action."

"*Vogue Instrument Corp., Richmond Hill, NY,* $783,097.—In July 1970, the Navy terminated Vogue for default on a page printer contract. The lengthy ASBCA appeal concluded in a decision in February 1974 that the termination for default be converted to a termination for convenience. This was followed by a protracted period during which a settlement was finally reached in January 1976. Vogue contends that the Navy's action in terminating them for default was a major contribution to their financial downfall. The Army's action in suspending funds owed as a part of the termination settlement caused an adverse impact on Vogue by inhibiting its ability to compete for and obtain business. In addition, there was evidence that Vogue's impaired financial condition contributed to its difficulties and losses sustained on the contracts in respect of which this relief was requested. Presently Vogue's financial situation is such that it cannot continue in business without a grant of relief. In the light of the extensive amount of additional information received, and after finding that Vogue has a history of successful manufacture of complex technology devices and that it would be desirable to retain Vogue as a viable second source for ballistic computers and distribution boxes, the Board determined that the circumstances warranted the grant of relief."

Amendments Without Consideration

"*Lynd Gear, Inc., Rochester, MI,* $645,190.—Lynd Gear is a small business which has been a manufacturer of gears for 27 years. The company filed for bankruptcy in Feb. 1977 contending that it sustained losses on three government contracts which impaired its productive capability. Lynd contends that if relief is granted it can complete the contracts in 10 months, otherwise it will be unable to do so. The gear sets are components of the M-48 and M-60 series tanks. While Lynd Gear's continued existence is not essential to the national defense, continued performance under these contracts is essential. The procurement lead time to obtain from another source could have an adverse impact on the tank program. It is determined that relief will facilitate the national defense."

"*Drexel Industries, Inc., Horsham, PA, $884,387.*—Production on Drexel's four contracts, awarded in 1972 for 621 trucks was delayed several months by strikes. During the delay, labor costs increased and coupled with the deterioration of the economy the company incurred substantial losses. Although relief was granted in 1975, Drexel was able to deliver only a portion of the trucks, ceased delivery, and requested additional funding. Two contracts were completed with no profit or fee. Following an extensive review, it is determined that if relief is not granted Drexel will enter into bankruptcy. Both DLA and Navy require the undelivered trucks. It will cost the Government approximately $1,750,000 to reprocure the 128 trucks remaining undelivered and the Government will lose most, if not all, of the $1,650,634 in unliquidated progress payments. This action was deemed necessary to facilitate the national defense."

"*Radionics Inc., Webster, NY, $50,000.*—The initial Radionics, Inc., request for interim financial relief of $150,000 from Navy was denied on the grounds that Radionics was not essential to the Navy. Sacramento Air Logistics Center (SMALC) advised the Navy that the Air Force considered Radionics essential to the Air Force and the contractor sought relief from the Air Force. The Board found that the VHF/AM antenna for the MRC 107/108 produced on a solesource basis by Radionics, is critical to the effective operation of the MRC 107-108 which is used for groundtoair communications and is a vital element of the tactical air control system. Without the VHF/AM antenna the Tactical Air Forces mission of closeair support cannot be accomplished. Also, the urgency of the mission for which the MRC 107/108 is used cannot withstand any delays incident to (1) Radionics prospective bankruptcy or (2) development of a new source of supply. There is now no alternate source or adequate substitute for these antennas. The Board considers continued uninterrupted production of the antenna and Radionics as the sole source essential to facilitate the national defense."

Mistakes

"*Varian Associates, Palo Alto, CA, $117,369.*—Varian Associates is the sole producer of the Hawk Klystron tube, and for many years has received contracts for the repair of these tubes. The company requested relief based on mutual mistakes made by the company and not noted by the contracting officer that analysis costs in the repair of tubes were not included in the total repair costs. The Board concurred that such a mistake was made by Varian and was so obvious that it should have been apparent to the contracting officer; it recommended that relief be granted. Such relief will result in equitable treatment of the contractor and in proper assurances to other contractors that mistakes will be corrected expeditiously and fairly."

"*Lockheed Aircraft Corp., Burbank, CA, $6,829,196.*—Request arose out of work Lockheed performed under four Navy contracts for S 3A aircraft. Each contract included several unpriced line items for the repair of government property for use in connection with these contracts. The contracting officer had the right to issue unilateral orders for the repair of the property after a price quotation from Lockheed for supplier prices which had been fully negotiated as of the date of the modification. There was no intent to bar Lockheed from the recovery of additional costs to which it may have been due as a result of work that was in the repair process and for which no vendor quotes had been received. The Board finds that the facts presented clearly indicate that a mistake was made by the parties' failure to express in the various executed modifications the agreements as both parties understood them."

"*Rockwell International Corp., Pittsburgh, PA, $976,724.*—A fixed-price incentive contract was awarded in fiscal year 1970 for production of missile-guidance sets, downstage control hardware, and supporting materials and services for the Minuteman III weapons systems and extended each year through fiscal year 1975. The contractor mistakenly omitted costs of certain components known as dialectrically isolated integrated circuits (DIIC's) when a fiscal year 1975 supplemental agreement had been decided upon instead of a new and separate fiscal year 1975 contract. This was not detected by the contracting officer who indicated that it was never his intent to omit the costs for DIIC's from the fiscal year 1975 supplemental agreement. The Board found that the failure of the parties to include the costs of the DIIC's in the finalized fiscal year 1975 supplemental agreement, when it was their intent to do so, constitutes a mutual mistake, and to correct this mistake would facilitate the national defense."

Formalization of Informal Commitments

"*Ampex Corp., Redwood City, CA, $145,659.*—Use of leased equipment by Ships Parts Control Center (SPCC) was continued beyond the contract expiration date. The contract expired on Sept. 23, 1976; SPCC retained the leased equipment until Feb. 17, 1977. Ampex was informed that a contract extension "was in the works," but the contract was not extended before its expiration date due to delays by the government. Therefore, the Navy's Automatic Data Processing Selection Office (ADPSO) was without authority to execute a contractual instrument otherwise legally permissible. The Board decided that the circumstances in this case depict an informal commitment by the government and formalization of this commitment will facilitate the national defense."

"*Sperry Rand Corp., Blue Bell, PA, $368,726.*—A contract with Sperry Rand for lease of ADP equipment to be used by the Naval Oceanographic Office expired Dec. 31, 1976. Though both parties were aware of the Dec. 31, 1976 expiration deadline, Navy continued the use of the equipment. The Navy Automatic Data Processing Selection Office, responsible for the contracting, informed the Board that there was informal guidance to Sperry-Univac to leave the equipment in place for further government use. The contractor relied on the apparent authority of government personnel. The Board found it was only an error on the part of government personnel that resulted in failure to submit a timely request for a delegation of procurement authority to GSA. Granting this relief will facilitate the national defense."

"*Vogue Instrument Corp., New York, NY, $270,000.*—Although by its 1977 action, the Board intended to provide sufficient funding to restore Vogue's viability as a business enterprise, the funds proved insufficient to maintain Vogue's viability. This was due to certain unforeseen circumstances such as the fact that additional projected business did not materialize. The Board at first denied additional relief but as the result of new information reconsidered. New information includes Navy's contention (1) that Vogue is now the only source from which Navy can obtain necessary torpedo actuators on a timely basis (other possible sources would require at least a year for first article), (2) that Vogue has the technical competence and capability to complete the actuator contract given the financial means, (3) Navy's desire to maintain Vogue as sole source for torpedo actuators, and (4) Navy is considering the purchase of a technical data package from Vogue for a substantial sum. However, without relief Vogue could not remain viable. This action will facilitate the national defense."

"General Dynamics Corp., St. Louis, MO, $359,000,000.—The Navy entered the 1970's with an urgent demand for a new class of nuclear attack submarines. On the basis of assumptions that history would later portray as overoptimistic, the SSN-688 program was considered to be merely an evolution from the SSN-637. In retrospect, significant misjudgments were made by both the Navy and industry. The attractiveness of the long-term business base provided by the SSN-688 class seemingly resulted in a willingness by the shipbuilder to accept contractual terms which would later prove unwise. Within a period of 35 months, General Dynamics was awarded a total of 18 SSN-668's. The company was forced by its contractual commitments into a dramatically rapid growth in its labor force, aggravated by the award of the 1st Trident, contract in July 1974. Delays were experienced in the receipt of government furnished information, materials were impacted by inflation, shortages of needed materials, and expanding business. Matters of utmost importance to the national defense are at stake. The Trident program with seven ships currently awarded and none delivered is a vital element of the Nation's figure strategic defense. The SSN-688 ships are an essential component of the attack submarine forces. This relief will facilitate the national defense."

"Litton Industries, Inc., Pascagoula, MISS, $182,000,000.—Contracts were awarded during 1969 and 1970 for five ships of the LHA class and 30 destroyers of the DD-963 class; 19 of which have not yet been delivered. The DOD adopted the total package procurement (TPP) for these contracts, and Litton was constructing a new shipyard in Pascagoula, Miss. Neither the concept of TPP nor the new yard, in the earlier stages, lived up to expectations. Given the complexities of shipbuilding, the Navy, contrary to an essential premise of TPP, became heavily involved in the design and construction process. The new yard and new construction techniques did not achieve expected efficiencies in production. Sufficient levels of skilled manpower proved unavailable, design problems emerged at the outset and persisted through significant stages of the program. Litigation has dominated the history of these programs for the last five years. The Board recognized the serious consequence of TPP, the essential need for amphibious ships and destroyers, and the importance to the national defense of the unique resources of the Ingalls shipyard."

"Tenneco, Inc., Newport News, VA, $23,200,000.—Starting in the late 1960's and early 1970's, Newport News was awarded contracts for construc-

tion of several classes of Navy vessels. These included nuclear-power guided-missile cruisers, nuclear-powered attack submarines, nuclear-powered aircraft carriers, and the SSN-688 lead ship nuclear-powered attack submarine. The number and complexity of ships ordered during this period required this shipbuilder to expand its work force. It was impossible to obtain skilled workers in the numbers required and the company was forced to dilute the skill level of its workforce and to convert competent journeymen into 1st-line supervisors. The effect of which was to decrease productivity of the yard and to stretch out the building periods of the ships under contract. This loss occurred during a period of double-digit inflation experienced in the mid-1970's and resulted in a severe financial impact of delay on the shipbuilder. At the same time, the Navy actions or inactions at critical stages during design and construction either delayed or increased the cost of construction and were, therefore, compensable under the terms of its contracts. Newport News is the largest shipbuilder in the free world and is the only private shipbuilder that currently has the capability to produce nuclear-powered surface ships. It is the only private shipbuilder in the United States capable of building aircraft carriers, whether nuclear or conventionally powered. The importance of Newport News to future Navy shipbuilding programs is self-evident. The Board determined that relief was essential to the resumption of a normal relationship with Newport News and that such action will facilitate the national defense."

Amendments Without Consideration

"*Daywood Products, Inc.*, $111,118.—Daywood Products, Inc., a small business firm and the sole producer of shipping containers for DRAGON anti-tank missiles, received three separate contracts to produce this item. The company has requested a modification of the first contract to cover the loss of $117,250 incurred because of the unpredicted, sustained and extraordinary inflationary costs of lumber, plywood, and labor. The company claims that because it was unable to obtain firm price commitments initially, there was no reasonable protection against inflation. Without recovery, bankruptcy and non-completion of the remaining contracts are imminent. All other producers of shipping containers have either defaulted on their contracts, have gone bankrupt, or have lost their facilities to fire. Based on audits and the repercussions associated with bankruptcy and default of a sole-source supplier, the DARCOM and MIRADCOM Boards concluded that continued operation is essential to the national defense. The Board agreed to this conclusion and authorized relief not to exceed $111,118 and to be paid out in installments to ensure completion of all remaining contracts with the company."

"*Davidson Optronics.* $750,000.—On June 15, 1978, the company requested that the Board's previous decision of September 14, 1977, be reconsidered and proposed a mutual waiver of any claims against the two Army contracts and a Government guaranteed loan of $750,000. The Air Force agreed to these terms and was willing to sponsor the loan guarantee. In a meeting with the Army board on March 21, 1979, Davidson proposed that (1) both the Army and the company waive their respective claims to both Army contracts; (2) the Air Force would guarantee the $750,000 loan; (3) the Army would hold Davidson's 15-year low interest subordinated note for $550,000; and (4) Davidson and United California Bank (UCB) renegotiate their settlement in terms of cash and company stock. Both the Army and Air Force contract adjustment boards granted relief based on the above proposal and found that this relief will facilitate the national defense."

"*Redifon Flight Simulator, Ltd.*, $321,993.—The contractor computed its offer on the exchange rate of $2.20 U.S. dollars to the British pound expecting the contract to be awarded on a dollar basis. The final contract at the Air Force's insistence called for payment in British pounds. However, during the life of the contract the exchange rate fell as low as $1.57 to the pound. Since a significant portion of the contractual effort required purchases in the U.S. and these purchases have resulted in substantial losses due to radical fluctuations in the currency exchange rate, fairness requires the granting of relief to this foreign contractor. The Board finds that the granting of relief will facilitate the national defense by strengthening the relationships underlying the reciprocal procurement agreements with our NATO countries."

Mistakes

"*Survival Technology, Inc.*, $436,550.—The contractor, a small business who manufactures medical equipment, was awarded a sole-source contract to ultimately provide 2,440,000 auto-injector "combo-pens" which they developed, to the Surgeon General. Initially, DOD had the responsibility for quality assurance; however, nine months into the contract DoD, through a contract modification, transferred this responsibility to the Food and Drug Administration (FDA) although this matter was not discussed with Survival during negotiations. Under DoD quality procedures, however, 800,000 units had been accepted and met contractual requirements including sterility. FDA, using the current Good Manufacturing Practice Regulations (GMPR's), issued a stop work order three months after assuming the quality assurance responsibility. The contract was adjusted to meet these costs. The order was in effect sixty (60) days before the contractor complied with the GMPR's incurring additional costs because of the stop work order. The company requests an additional $781,130 to meet compliance costs. The board found that the contractor suffered a loss on the contract because: (1) of their efforts to achieve compliance; and (2) the government changed quality assurance requirements. Through considerations of fairness, the Board directs that the contract price be amended not to exceed $436,559 in the interest of the national defense."

"*UTL Corp.*, $182,317.—An RFP received by UTL Corp. for the production of Quick Look II, which they developed, required that the AN/UYK-23 computer be provided by Sperry Univac Defense Systems as a sole-source subcontractor to UTL. During negotiations, the government reduced the amount of Sperry's subcontract by 23.8 percent based on a Defense Contract Audit Agency (DCAA) oral "should cost" report as part of a full audit of a similar computer. The Army and UTL later agreed to a 12.5 percent decrease. In February 1976, UTL provided 31 units from its inventory and awarded the subcontract to Sperry for 31 units for $2,335,000. The full written audit report questioned the costs by only 2.2 percent. The contractor contends that a mutual mistake of fact occurred when the Army and UTL relied on the oral audit. The contractor claimed $300,731 based on three components: (1) the difference ($120,790) between the prime contract price and the ultimate price negotiated with Sperry; (2) certain items not included in the prime contract, but negotiated with Sperry ($72,834); and (3) a claim for labor associated with UTL-furnished units ($14,462). The Board found that to facilitate the national defense the target price should be increased by no more than $182,317 ($120,790 plus add ons)."

"*Martin-Marietta Aerospace Corp., $202,799.*—A negotiated sole-source two-year contract for production of the Pershing PLA missile was awarded to Martin Marietta on October 31, 1977, who had supplied these items under a previous contract. The current contract called for 60 modification kits at a cost of $330,122 including contractor furnished "self destruct charges" which were government furnished equipment (GFE) under the previous contract. The contractor priced this item as GFE using the computer generated bill of materials derived from the previous contract which listed the item as GFE. As a result, the cost for the charges were omitted and the government failed to discover the mistake. The contractor discovered the error during a planning meeting on GFE availability, and notified the Board claiming $216,745 as additional payment. The Board ruled that both the contractor and the government were at fault but reduced the amount to $202,799, eliminating the contractor's profit and determined that this action will facilitate the national defense."

Amendments Without Consideration

"*Waltham Precision Instruments, Inc.* $400,000.—Waltham Precision Instruments is a small business which primarily manufactures mechanical clocks for aircrafts and is currently the only active U.S. producer using U.S. produced parts. The company has been established as a mobilization based producer of critical precision parts. A memorandum of understanding was concluded between the U.S. and Switzerland whereby DOD requirements in excess of an estimated quantity necessary to sustain Waltham were open for competition and awarded to Swiss firms. OSD determined that the minimum sustaining rate for Waltham was 300 clocks per month, but later found that 500 clocks per month was a more realistic figure.

"As a result of operating difficulties which led to losses in the last three years, attributable to errors in pricing, imprudent business ventures, and an inadequate accounting system, Waltham filed for bankruptcy in December, 1978, as a result, an advance payment of $150,000 was authorized. The Army recognized, however, that more extensive relief to make the company viable was necessary under P.L. 85-804.

"Waltham, working with DOD and the Army, effected changes in top management, improved the accounting system, and reduced overhead and G&A rates. The sustaining rate was increased to a profitable rate of 700 units per month. Based on the information submitted, the Board found that the continued viability of Waltham as a source of mechanical aircraft parts is essential to the national defense, and granted monetary relief not to exceed $400,000. Notwithstanding the recommendation of ARRCOM and DCAA for a lesser amount of $314,500."

"*Applied Devices, $1,149,293.*—The Naval Training Equipment Center (NTEC) awarded a fixed price incentive contract to Applied Devices Corp., (ADC) at a ceiling price of $3,123,728 for surface-to-air missiles radar training devices. ADC requested extraordinary relief because they had run out of time and money without completing the contract. An estimate of an additional $2,000,000 was made by ADC. NTEC recommended that the relief be granted because of a mutual mistake as to a material fact as described in the DAR and sought approval from the Naval Supply Systems Command to increase the ceiling by $4,142,206 to $7,250,707. The clearance was approved and ADC notified.

"A Navy review team investigated the facts leading to the new ceiling, did not conclude that a mutual mistake of material fact occurred, but that ADC could not complete the contract without additional funds because ADC's financial condition was so severe that a work stoppage was imminent. The Navy Contract Adjustment Board authorized an amendment without consideration to raise the contract ceiling price by $1,976,351 in order to satisfy ADC's incurred costs and to insure performance under the contract. ADC claimed this was a breach of contract since the contracting officer had legally raised the ceiling to $7,250,707. The Office of the General Counsel advised that the Navy would not be able to repudiate the contracting officer's agreement because he had authority to make the agreement and obtained the necessary clearance from higher authority. In addition, ADC relied on the contracting officer's representation that agreement had been reached.

"The Board rescinded its decision authorizing $1,976,351 and directed NTEC to settle ADC's claims for breach of contract by increasing the ceiling to $7,250,707. Based on technical and financial reviews of ADC's overall business base, the Board found that the eventual cost of the contract would reach an estimated $8.4M and authorized an immediate award of the difference or $1,149,193 thereby facilitating the national defense."

"*Cartwright Engineering, Inc.,* $348,000.—Cartwright Engineering, Inc. received three sole source contracts for the manufacture, test, and delivery of AN/DSQ-24A-DIGIDOP Scoring Sensors which are an integral part of the missile scoring systems for all Air Force aerial target drones. Cartwright based its request for relief on performance problems by its subcontractors. Cartwright subcontracted for a hybrid circuit with the MTS Corp. on a sole source basis. When MTS failed to meet delivery schedule and quality standards, Cartwright selected Environmental Communications, Inc. (ECI) as the new source for 100 units of the hybrid circuits at the same price as MTS.

"ECI also failed to meet performance criteria and Cartwright terminated the contract. However, Cartwright renegotiated the contract with ECI for the needed units at a considerably higher price. Cartwright sought relief of $486,213 based on ECI price increases which were caused by unanticipated technical and production difficulties. In the interim Cartwright stopped performance under the three contracts alleging that further performance would increase its losses to $531,743. The Air Force Logistics Command (AFLC) sustained that Cartwright's continued operation and performance under these contracts was essential to the national defense.

"The AN/DSQ-24A-DIGIDOP scoring sensor is an essential element of the missile scoring system and Cartwright is the only manufacturer and holder of proprietary rights to the AN/DSQ-24A-DIGIDOP. Development of a new source would cost an estimated $2-3.5 million and take at least two years.

"Based on the above recommendations by the Air Force and AFLC, the Board considered the scoring sensors and Cartwright as the sole producer to be essential to the national defense and that granting extraordinary contractual relief to Cartwright would facilitate the national defense. The board authorized the amendment of the existing contracts to provide for an increase in the unit price of the sensors of $1,665.11 and that Cartwright be paid a lump sum of $348,008 for 209 units already delivered with future payments of remaining units upon delivery."

Mistakes

Sperry Rand Corporation, Sperry Univac Division. The government and the contractor agreed that a mutual mistake had occurred, whereupon Sperry sought extraordinary contractual relief. However, the Department of Transportation Contract Adjustment Board declined jurisdiction on the grounds that the Contract Disputes Act and implementing OFPP Policy Letter provided that boards of contract appeals and the (then) court of claims had the authority to grant equitable relief in such circumstances.

In this same connection, reference is made to *Applied Devices Corporation,* discussed earlier. In a rather complicated case, it appeared that the Navy Contract Adjustment Board had granted some relief for a mutual mistake but then rescinded its decision because the contractor had adequate remedy under the Contract Disputes Act. The contractor then pursued this route, but the relief obtained was insufficient to strengthen the company's weak financial condition. The contractor then returned to the Navy Contract Adjustment Board, which, acting under P.L. 85-804 on a basis not elsewhere available, further amended the contract without consideration to permit the contractor to continue operations and furnish the equipment, which was considered vital to the national defense.

Formalization of Informal Commitments

"*Todd Shipyards Corp.* $310,850.—The Naval Sea Systems Command (NAVSEA) contracted with Todd Shipyards, Inc. (1,000) to lease three dry docks to them. Including the YFD-9, with options for renewal in 1976. Todd notified the Navy that it did not intend to exercise the option for the YFD-9 and requested that it be removed from their premises because of the vessel's poor condition and other cost factors. It remained at Todd for 3-1/2 years before it was sold and removed. NAVSEA and Todd agreed that berthing charges for the YFD-9 would be offset by the leasing charges of the remaining dry docks. It was later discovered that the statutory authorities for the lease, 10 U.S.C. 2667, did not authorize such offset, therefore, NAVSEA requested that the Board formalize what had become an informal contract. The Board decided that NAVSEA be authorized to formalize the committment in an amount not to exceed $310,850. Scheduled charges agreed to in the offsetting arrangement."

Amendment Without Consideration

The Wayne H. Colony Company, Inc. (Colony), a small business concern, had been awarded two contracts by the Air Force in 1981 and 1982 for container assemblies to store ammunition. Colony had provided these units since 1977 although actual production was largely subcontracted to Lawson

Industries, Inc. With the exception of Colony and Lawson, no other container suppliers had successfully completed first article qualifications.

In 1980, Lawson received an Air Force contract for 19,500 container assemblies, with an option for an additional 13,500 units at a unit price of $226.37. Colony submitted an unsolicited proposal for the 13,500 assemblies at a unit price of $230 and was subsequently awarded contract 0319 in April 1981 for 12,165 units. Lawson protested to the General Accounting Office, arguing that the option price was a part of the original competitive evaluation. The Comptroller General ruled in favor of Colony, but the contract award was delayed from June until October 1981. Colony received the award based on the best and final offers at a unit price of $214.14, submitted in September 1981.

In the request for relief, Colony insisted that during the four month delay in contract award, increased steel prices and vendor delivery schedule difficulties contributed to the company's loss position under 0319.

Colony submitted a bid on an Air Force proposal in April 1982 for 23,500 container assemblies; Colony was the low bidder and was awarded contract 0201 in June 1982 at a unit price of $212.99. Colony was unable to secure sufficient credit to continue operations and on August 13, 1982, filed for reorganization under Chapter 11 of the Bankruptcy Act. As of August 31, 1982, Colony had delivered 8,942 units under contract 0319 and made no deliveries under 0201.

On November 18, 1982, Colony and Davey Compressor Company reached an agreement for Davey to purchase, at its option, all of the issued and authorized shares of Colony in exchange for various payments and assumptions of existing indebtedness.

On September 1, 1982, Colony formally requested relief under the provisions of Public Law 85-804 in the amount of $1,821,257.90, an upward price adjustment of $50.45 per unit retroactive to include all delivered and deliverable units. The request for relief was premised upon the proposition that its continued operation is essential to the national defense.

Air Force Acquisition officials recommended to the board that Colony's request be given favorable consideration, primarily based on the avoidance of an estimated $8.6 million in reprocurement costs if Colony remained a viable government contractor. These reprocurement costs included those costs associated with twelve Colony contracts then pending and $3.2 million in unliquidated progress payments, which would have been unreasonable in the event of the company's demise.

The board believed that the circumstances warranted a finding that the national defense would be facilitated by an investment of the size requested for the purpose of avoiding the alternate reprocurement costs of $8.6 million and unestimable costs of other disruptions. To accomplish the interest of the Air Force, and to provide for Colony's various creditors, emergence of a new enterprise infused with a contribution of capital and management from the Davey Compressor Company had been prepared. Based on the November 18, 1982, purchase option agreement between Colony and Davey Compressor, financial data provided by the chairman of Davey Corporation, and on the basis of all available facts, the board was confident that the proposed acquisition plus the relief requested would permit Colony to be productive and meet its contractual commitments to the Air Force.

Advance Payments

Goldsworthy Engineering, Inc. was a subcontractor to Mason Chamberlain, Inc., the operating contractor to supply fiberglass wrap around machines for the Mississippi Army Ammunition Plant. Goldsworthy's request for extraordinary contractual relief was not considered by the Army Contract Adjustment Board to be "appropriate at that time." The board recommended to the Army acquisition officials that they "further examine the feasibility of alternative methods of obtaining the completion of the machines." The board further stated: "The request should not be resubmitted . . . unless extraordinary contractual relief is clearly the only acceptable solution available in the interest of national defense."

However, the board did approve the request to authorize advance progress payments by the prime contractor to the subcontractor, finding that "this action facilitated the national defense."

DOD Contractual Actions Under P.L. 85-804—Calendar Year 1986

A summary of the contractual actions taken in 1986 follows:

(Dollar Amounts in Thousands)

	No.	Actions Approved Requested	Approved	Actions Denied No.	Amount
Amendments without consideration	1	$9,290	$9,575	5	$4,018
Formalization of informal commitments	9	4,265	4,265	1	127
Other—government action	0	0	0	1	531
Contingent liabilities	52	0	0	0	0
Totals	62	$13,555	$13,840	7	$4,676

As noted earlier, the amendment to the Contract Disputes Act, which permitted boards of contract appeals to also have jurisdiction in requests for amendments without consideration and correction of mistakes, was a factor in reducing actions by the contract adjustment boards. The DOD low point was reached in 1984 when, except for contingent liabilities, only 13 actions were considered, 10 for amendments without consideration and three for correction of mistakes. The total amount approximated $29 million. One request for an amendment without consideration was approved, but it did not involve specific dollar costs. The other 12 requests were disapproved.

The major requests approved during 1986 were $9,574,732 to the Gila River Indian Community and $1,188,473 to the Government of Israel. These actions were characterized by unusual circumstances and their analyses would not be useful to the great majority of our readers.

Contractual actions for contingent liabilities do not vary extensively over the years. In 1986, the Army approved three, the Navy 33, and the Air Force 16, provisions to indemnify contractors against liabilities because of claims of death, injury or property damages arising from nuclear radiation, use of high energy propellants, or other risks not covered by the contractor's insurance program. The potential cost of the liabilities cannot be estimated since the liability to the government, if any, will depend upon the incurrence of an incident as described in the indemnification clause. Items procured are generally those associated with nuclear-powered vessels, nuclear-armed guided missiles, experimental work with nuclear energy, handling of explosives, or performance in hazardous areas.

DOD FAR Supplement

The full text of Public Law 85-804 and Executive Order 10789 is contained in DOD FAR Supplement, Subpart 50.70.

Chapter XXV

Profit Limitation Under Government Contracts

BACKGROUND AND SCOPE OF CHAPTER

Profit on government contracts has always been a matter of interest in both the private and public sectors. By far the major attention has focused on defense contracts, where allegations of excessive profits can be traced back to the Revolutionary War. The strident criticisms of defense expenditures combined with some instances of demonstrated excessive profits by some companies has generated a continuing stream of legislative and regulatory efforts at profit limitation. Some of these efforts have flowed into nondefense contracts but they have tended to lag far behind because of the preoccupation with defense. Accordingly, the chronology and current status of profit limitation under government contracts provided in this chapter necessarily emphasize contracts for goods and services required for this country's defense.

PROFIT LIMITATION LEGISLATION

Allegations of profiteering during World War I and its aftermath were contributing factors to the enactment of the Vinson-Trammell Act of 1934, which limited profits on military aircraft prime and subcontracts to 12% of the price, and on naval prime and subcontracts to 10% of the price. The latter limitation was also included in the Merchant Marine Act of 1936.

Shortly after the beginning of World War II, Congress enacted the first Renegotiation Act, providing for the elimination of profits on a contract-by-contract basis. Bases for determining reasonable and excessive profits on defense awards included such factors as contribution to the war effort, efficiency, extent of risk assumed, etc. The Renegotiation Act of 1943 abandoned the evaluation of excess profits on a contract-by-contract basis and substituted overall renegotiation of covered defense prime and subcontracts on a fiscal year basis. The 1943 Act was terminated in 1945 at the end of World War II but reenacted in 1948.

The aforementioned legislation was replaced by the Renegotiation Act of 1951, which transferred the administration of this statutory profit limitation from the War and Navy Departments to an independent Renegotiation Board. The 1951 Act included a termination or "sunset" provision but it was extended 13 times, the last extension expiring September 30, 1976.

The predecessor Vinson-Trammell Act had never been repealed and technically and automatically became effective upon the expiration of the Renegotiation Act. When it became apparent that the Renegotiation Act would not be extended, the Treasury Department and the Internal Revenue Service, responsible for the administration of the Vinson-Trammell Act, began the difficult task of modifying and adapting the 40-year old statute to the current environment. The considerable effort in both the public and private sectors came to naught when the Department of Defense Authorization Act, P.L. 97-86, mothballed Vinson-Trammell and provided for the President to issue profit limitation regulations in the event of war or national emergency. This Act was enacted on December 1, 1981.

Although sporadic congressional criticisms of defense profit policies continued, the major actions in the intervening years were taken by DOD in studies and regulations, as discussed in the following pages. The latest study at this writing was the Defense Financial and Investment Review (DFAIR), issued in 1985. Based in part on the recommendations of that study, DOD proposed substantial revisions to its existing profit policy in September 1986. While this proposal was undergoing review, its implementation, with some reservations, was mandated by the continuing appropriation resolution, enacted October 18, 1986, as P.L. 99-500. The statutory requirement is quoted below:

> Provided that for solicitations issued after the effective date of this Act which require price negotiation, contracts may only be awarded if such negotiation is based on new profit calculation procedures which provide for increased emphasis on facilities capital employed and contractor risk and which procedures do not provide an explicit fixed rate for working capital and which do not include profit based on specific individual elements of contract costs.

Comments of the House-Senate conferees regarding the above provision are set forth below:

> The conferees agree to the policy objectives stated by the Senate which place increased emphasis on facility capital employed and contractor risk and which provide a linking of profit and working capital requirements. The effect of this is to remove specific individual elements of contract cost as a determinant of profit objectives.

> The section describing the new profit policy for negotiated contracts has been clarified to reflect the consideration of working capital in profit calculations. This is the central feature in linking profit and financial risk. This also provides the Department of Defense another way in addition to changing progress payment rates for adjusting for changing financial conditions. The conferees understand that the allowance for financing (proposed as 2.5 percent of contract cost), and the interest rates used in adjusting profit objectives will be set administratively. This process merits the careful attention of the Committees and GAO as the new policy is implemented.

> Though the language indicates that the policy should place increased emphasis on capital investment and risk, the conferees recognize that some types of firms, such as professional and technical service firms, doing business with DOD inherently are called upon to make less capital investment and may participate in projects with less total risk.

It is the conferees' belief that, notwithstanding this modified emphasis, any profit policy must ensure that firms performing satisfactorily for the Department of Defense earn a reasonable profit.

The conferees also note that as a result of the Defense Financial and Investment Review, the Department published a new profit policy in the September 18, 1986 Federal Register. While a detailed review of the Department's new rules has not been made, it appears that these rules are generally consistent with the conferees' policy objectives. The conferees expect that all 1987 contracts will be awarded under these new rules which are designed to decrease the negotiated profit objective by one percentage point.

In supporting this new policy, the conferees agree to the across the board reductions proposed by the Senate totalling $700,000,000 as a result of the lower contract prices expected. The conferees acknowledge that permitting adjustments in profit for working capital will decrease the savings slightly, but feel that the $700,000,000 excess (one percent of $74 billion in negotiated contracts) is a reasonable adjustment.

PROFIT LIMITATION REGULATIONS AND STUDIES

The following commentary summarizes some of the major profit limitation studies and regulations over the past quarter of a century.

Weighted Guidelines (WGL)—The Structured Approach

While Congress and its GAO agents complained about profit policies, DOD performed a number of studies and revisions to its regulations, addressing a problem that appears to have no solution that could gain total acceptance in the public and private sectors. Many of the efforts have been faulted by experts, with 20-20 hindsight, who have shown little regard to the complexity of the problem.

Prior to 1964, all executive departments enunciated profit policies requiring contracting officers to consider various factors in arriving at profit objectives, such as degree of risk, nature of work to be performed, extent of government assistance, extent of contractor's investment, contractor's performance, and so on, not unlike the considerations employed by the Renegotiation Board. The policies generally failed to provide guidance as to the weight to be accorded to the various factors and the manner in which these considerations were to be translated into a profit objective.

In 1964, DOD revised its policy to reflect a "structured" approach. Major, and specific, weights were assigned to (1) the elements of the contractor's input to total performance and (2) the contractor's assumption of cost risk, essentially based on the type of contract. Lesser weights were assigned to certain "special" factors. Until required to move to a structured approach in 1981, the Federal Procurement Regulation (FPR) continued to provide for the unstructured approach for civilian agencies.

Increasing Consideration to Contractor Capital Investment

The WGL attracted early criticism for its heavy emphasis on estimated cost as a basis for establishing the profit objective and for the inadequate consideration given to the contractor's investment. The latter consideration drew considerable support as an incentive for contractors to invest in new equipment for defense production.

While DOD was trying to develop a revised policy to incorporate consideration to capital investment, Congress directed GAO to perform a study of defense profits. As discussed in Chapter XXVIII of this text, GAO was reluctant to relinquish its role as an after-the-fact critic but finally performed such study after the enactment of legislation requiring it to do so. Its report, following the tenor of the times, urged that the profit policy be revised to include greater consideration to capital investment, complexity of work, and other management and performance factors. Having formulated these broad policy objectives, GAO considered its task completed and recommended that the actual guidelines be developed by executive interagency action with the Office of Management and Budget (OMB) assuming the lead.

In December 1972, DOD issued its first effort at a contractor capital employed policy in Defense Procurement Circular (DPC) 107. Essentially this proposal provided that 50% of the profit objective would be based on the contractor's facilities and operating capital investment. DPC 107 was to be used only upon agreement by the government and contractor, was included in very few contracts, and was ultimately abandoned. Whether the methodology was too complex, or DOD support lacking, or whether it was a concept whose time had not yet come, the proposal was shelved for the time being but served as valuable background for future profit policy revisions and Cost Accounting Standard (CAS) 414.

Profit '76

DOD's concern with the need to strengthen the nation's competitive industrial base and provide an incentive for capital investment led to the comprehensive Profit '76 study, undoubtedly the major effort of its kind to that date. DOD was also spurred to action by the CAS Board's formulation of CAS 409, Depreciation of Tangible Capital Assets, which many observers believed served as a disincentive for capital investment. The study's conclusion led to the following revision in DOD's WGL:

	Before	After
Contractor effort (input to total performance)	65%	50%
Contractor assumption of cost risk	30	40
Contractor's capital investment	—	10
All other factors	5	—*
Totals	100%	100%

* Some of the factors, such as productivity, were not eliminated, but their precise weighting was indefinite.

The new policy recognized that the 10% weighting assigned to contractor's capital investment was too low and promised to effect a correction after further experience had been gained.

Although the CAS Board continued to defend its ill-conceived CAS 409, it felt the heat of the pervasive criticism. To make up for the disincentives to capital investment caused by CAS 409, the Board accelerated its work on CAS 413, Adjustment of Historical Depreciation Cost for Inflation, and CAS 414, Cost of Money as an Element of the Cost of Capital. The results of these activities failed to live up to the Board's promises. The proposed standard on Adjustment of Historical Depreciation Cost for Inflation was totally abandoned. As to CAS 414, the Board encountered difficulties in establishing criteria for operating capital, and the standard as ultimately promulgated was limited to facilities capital.

DOD profit policy, resulting from the Profit '76 study and incorporated into the Defense Acquisition Regulation by DAC 76-3, continued for a decade with few changes. The major revision, which was to become a subject of wide criticism, was promulgated in DAC 76-23, February 1980. The changes included an increase in the range of profit factors for facilities capital employed from 6%—10% to 16%—20%, increasing this factor's percentage of total profit from 10% to 17%. Among other major changes was the modification of the WGL to provide separate ranges for manufacturing, R&D, and service contracts. For the latter two contract categories, capital employed was eliminated and CAS 414 cost of money was required to be offset dollar for dollar.

Defense Financial and Investment Review (DFAIR)

As noted earlier, it would appear to be impossible to formulate a profit policy acceptable to all, and particularly to GAO, whose major mission appears to be after-the-fact criticism. The congressional "watchdog" agency sharply criticized the DOD profit policy, its recommendations including (1) substantially increasing the weight for facilities capital investment and reducing the portion based on estimated costs; (2) increasing the offset factor for CAS 414; (3) establishing more definitive criteria for contracting officers; and (4) developing "safeguards" to preclude negotiation of profits greater than government objectives.

DOD, too, was not satisfied with its profit policy. However, unlike the superficial review and broadbrush recommendations of the GAO, the Department initiated a "formal, full scale study effort . . . which shall have as its goal recommending changes to [DOD's] contract pricing, financing and profit policies." Taking full advantage of the lessons learned in the Profit '76 and other studies, DFAIR conducted the most comprehensive study ever attempted in this area, with selected government officials joined by representatives of the professions and industry associations involved, CPA firms, the Logistics Management Institute, and the Conference Board.

A significant and distinctive feature of the DFAIR report was its recognition of the interrelationships among profit, financing and other factors. Accordingly, the report was more far-reaching and reflected a more complete picture of this area. DFAIR's overall conclusion was that "current contract pricing, financing, and markup policies are balanced economically, are protecting the interests of the taxpayer, and are enabling U.S. industry to achieve an equitable return for its involvement in defense business." However, the study determined that a number of major actions were needed:

1. Progress payments should be tied in to current working capital financing requirements and revised as the requirements change.

2. Cost of facilities capital should be retained and WGL should take into account cost of operating capital, for which relatively simplified computation procedures were presented.

3. Profit policy should be simplified and better integrated with financing policy and length of contract performance. Overall, modifications should be made to yield results that average .5 to 1 point lower than results achieved under DAC 76-23.

4. Profit on facilities capital employed should recognize the differences among the assets and should be based on their productivity and risk.

5. Defense contractors had been making significant capital investments but factors other than DOD profit policy were driving such investments. Efforts to motivate contractors to make additional productivity changes should be pursued on an extracontractual, plant-wide basis.

6. Contractor investment should have provided an incentive and protection by government guarantee to purchase contractor-acquired equipment when the government cancels or fails to contract for the anticipated quantity of weapon systems.

Industry found many of the DFAIR conclusions and recommendations valid but strongly objected to the study's conclusion that profits should be reduced on the average by .5 to 1 point as unwarranted. On the contrary, with the continuing, significant identification of ordinary and business costs as unallowable, and such other actions as requiring contractors to fund 50% of special tooling and equipment costs, profits should be increased.

GAO, as further discussed in Chapter XXVIII of this text, criticized both the methodology and conclusions of the study. The perennial industry critics quarreled with DFAIR's efforts to provide comparability between government and commercial work by showing progress payments as liabilities. Inasmuch as DFAIR computed profits as a percentage of assets, GAO insisted that progress payments should be shown as reductions to assets, thus making it appear that the profit factors were higher than computed by the study.

CURRENT DOD PROFIT POLICY

As described earlier, DOD issued a revised profit policy, adopting many of the recommendations offered by DFAIR, on September 18, 1986. Although the proposal was not to be formally incorporated into DFARS until all of the comments had been considered, and revisions made where appropriate, its immediate adoption was mandated by P.L. 99-500 and DOD was directed to make certain additional changes before issuing its final rule. Such rule, in the form of a complete revision of DFARS Subpart 15.9, was issued on August 3, 1987, effective August 1, 1987, and its major provisions are set forth below.

* * * *

15.970-1 Procedures for establishing profit objectives.

(a) *Performance risk.* This profit factor addresses the contractor's risk in fulfilling the contractual requirements to provide the supplies or to perform the services being acquired.

(1) *Profit base.* The profit amount for performance risk is computed by multiplying a composite profit value assigned by the contracting officer times total contract costs, *excluding* general and administrative (G&A) expenses, contractor independent research and development/bid and proposal (IR&D/B&P) expenses, and facilities capital cost of money.

(2) *Normal values and designated ranges.—(i) Standard.* Except for limited cases as provided in 15.970-1(a)(2)(ii), the normal value and designated range for the performance risk profit factor are as shown below. It is expected that the standard will be used on most contracts.

	Normal value	Designated range
Performance Risk (Standard)	4%	2% to 6%

(ii) *Alternate.* It is DoD's intent to base a substantive portion of total profit on contractor investment in facilities capital. However, some research and development and service contractors require relatively low capital investment in buildings and equipment when compared to the defense industry overall. For such contractors, the contracting officer may use the alternate normal value and designated range shown below. If the alternate is used, the contractor may not be given any profit for facilities capital employed (15.970-1(c)).

	Normal value (percent)	Designated range (percent)
Performance Risk (Alternate)	6	4 to 8

(3) *Evaluation criteria.* Performance risk shall be evaluated using three criteria: technical, management and cost control. Each is an integral part of developing the composite profit value for performance risk. The contracting officer shall weight each criterion as judged appropriate for the supplies or services being acquired. The profit value assigned will vary according to the contractor's performance risk in providing the supplies or services required by the contract. While any value may be assigned within the designated range, it is expected that the maximum and minimum values will be restricted to cases where performance risk is substantially above or below normal. The following example demonstrates how a composite profit value for performance risk is calculated.

	Weight assigned (percent)	Value assigned (percent)	Weighted value (percent)
Technical............................	30	5.0	1.5
Management..........................	30	4.0	1.2
Cost Control	40	4.5	1.8
Composite Value......................			4.5

(i) *Technical.* This criterion focuses on the technical risk associated with providing the goods and services being acquired. The contracting officer's evaluation should address such factors as the technology being applied or developed by the contractor, technical complexity, program maturity, performance specifications and tolerances, and delivery schedule. The contracting officer is expected to carefully review the contract requirements and focus on the critical performance elements in the statement of work or specifications. The extent of a warranty or guarantee coverage should also be considered. Conditions which might justify higher or lower values are discussed below.

(A) *Above normal conditions.* The contracting officer may assign a higher than normal value in those cases where there is substantial technical risk. The following are indicators that such a condition may exist: the contractor is either developing or applying advanced technologies; items are being manufactured using specifications with stringent tolerance limits; the efforts require highly skilled personnel or require the use of state of the art machinery; the services and analytical efforts are of utmost importance to the Government and must be performed to exacting standards; the contractor's independent development and investment has reduced the Government's risk or cost; the contractor has accepted an accelerated delivery schedule to meet DoD requirements; the contractor has assumed additional risk through warranty provisions. A maximum value may be justified in the development or initial production of a new item, particularly if performance or quality specifications are tight, or if there is a high degree of development or production concurrency. Extremely complex, vital efforts to overcome difficult technical obstacles which require personnel with exceptional abilities, experience and professional credentials may also justify a value significantly above normal.

(B) *Below normal conditions.* The contracting officer may assign a lower than normal value in those cases where the technical risk is low. The following are indicators that such a condition may exist: off the shelf items are being acquired; relatively simple requirements are specified; there is little application of complex technology; efforts that do not require highly skilled personnel or which are relatively routine; mature programs; follow-on efforts and repetitive type procurements. A profit value significantly below normal may be justified for circumstances such as the following: routine services; production of simple items; rote entry or routine integration of government furnished information; simple operations within government owned facilities.

(ii) *Management.* This criterion considers the management effort involved on the part of the contractor to integrate the resources necessary to meet contract requirements. Resources include raw materials, labor, technology, information, and capital. The contracting officer should assess the contractor's management and internal control systems as well as the management involvement expected on the individual contract action. The contracting officer should consider the degree of cost mix as an indication of the types of resources applied and value-added by the contractor. The cost elements should not, themselves, be a basis for profit assignment. In evaluating management efforts, the contracting officer should use reviews made by the field contract administration office or other pertinent DoD field offices. The contracting officer should also give consideration to the contractor's support of federal socioeconomic programs, such as small business concerns, small business concerns owned and controlled by socially and economically disadvantaged individuals, handicapped sheltered workshops, labor surplus areas, and energy conservation. Conditions which might justify higher and lower values are discussed below.

(A) *Above normal conditions.* The contracting officer may assign a higher than normal value in those cases where the management effort is intense. The following are indicators that such a condition may exist: the value-added by the contractor is both considerable and reasonably difficult; the effort involves a high degree of integration or coordination; the contractor has a substantial record of active participation in federal socioeconomic programs. A maximum value for management may be justified under conditions such as the following: efforts requiring large scale integration of the most complex nature; major international activities requiring significant management coordination; or efforts with management milestones of critical importance.

(B) *Below normal conditions.* The contracting officer may assign a lower than normal value in those cases where the management effort is minimal. The following are indicators that such a condition may exist: a mature program where many end item deliveries have been made; the contractor adds minimum value to an item; routine efforts which require minimal supervision; the contractor provides poor quality, untimely proposals; the contractor fails to provide an adequate analysis of subcontractor costs; the contractor does not cooperate in the evaluation and negotiation of the proposal. A significantly below normal profit value may be justified if reviews performed by the field contract administration offices disclose unsatisfactory management and internal control systems (e.g., quality assurance, property control, safety, security) or if the effort requires an unusually low degree of management involvement.

(iii) *Cost control.* This criterion focuses on the contractor's efforts to reduce and control costs. The principal areas for evaluation are the expected reliability of cost estimates, cost reduction initiatives, and cost control management. Other factors which bear on the contractor's ability to meet the cost targets, such as foreign currency exchange rates and inflation rates, may also be considered. The contracting officer should assess the reliability of the contractor's estimating system and the extent of the contractor's cost reduction initiatives (e.g., competition advocacy programs, dual sourcing, spare parts pricing reforms, value engineering). In evaluating cost control management, the contracting officer should consider the adequacy of the contractor's management approach to the control of cost and schedule. Conditions which might justify higher or lower values are discussed below.

(A) *Above normal conditions.* The contracting officer may assign a higher than normal value if the contractor can demonstrate a highly effective cost control program. The following are indicators that such a condition may exist: the contractor provides fully documented and reliable cost estimates; the contractor has an aggressive cost reduction program that has demonstrable benefits; the contractor uses a high degree of subcontract competition (e.g., aggressive dual sourcing); the contractor has a proven record of cost tracking and control.

(B) *Below normal conditions.* The contracting officer may assign a lower than normal value if the contractor demonstrates minimal concern for cost control. The following are indicators that such a condition may exist: the contractor has a marginal cost estimating system; the contractor has made minimal effort to initiate cost reduction programs; the contractor's cost proposal is inadequate; or the contractor has a record of cost overruns or other indications of unreliable cost estimates and lack of cost control.

(b) *Contract type risk.* This factor focuses on the degree of cost risk accepted by the contractor under varying contract types.

(1) *Profit base.* The amount of profit for contract type risk is computed by multiplying the value assigned by the contracting officer times total allowable costs *excluding* G&A expenses, IR&D/B&P expenses, and facilities capital cost of money.

(2) *Normal values and designated ranges.* (i) The following normal values and designated ranges are applicable to contracts that contain no provisions or limited (first article financing) provisions for progress payments:

Contract type	Normal value (percent)	Designated range (percent)
Firm fixed-price	5	4 to 6
Fixed-price-incentive	3	2 to 4
Cost-plus-incentive-fee	1	0 to 2
Cost-plus-fixed-fee	.5	0 to 1

(ii) For fixed-price type contracts that contain provisions for progress payments, the normal value and designated ranges shown below shall be used. The value assigned by the contracting officer shall be further adjusted by adding an amount to recognize the contractor's investment in working capital, as described in 15.970-1(b)(4).

Contract type	Normal value[1] (percent)	Designated range[1] (percent)
Firm fixed-price	3	2 to 4
Fixed-price-incentive	1	0 to 2

[1] Add working capital adjustment to value assigned.

(iii) Time and material contracts; labor-hour contracts; overhaul contracts priced on a time and material basis; and firm fixed-price-level-of-effort-term contracts shall be considered to be cost-plus-fixed-fee contracts for the purpose of establishing a profit value for contract type risk and shall not receive the working capital adjustment described in 15.970-(b)(4). However, higher profit values within the designated range may be justified to the extent that portions of cost are fixed.

(iv) Fixed-price contracts with redeterminable provisions should be considered as a fixed-price-incentive contract with below normal conditions.

(v) In determining contract type risk, it is appropriate to consider additional risks associated with contracts for foreign military sales (FMS) which are not funded by United States appropriations. For example, a contract containing an offset arrangement with the foreign country may expose the contractor to additional risk. The contracting officer may recognize additional risk if the contractor can demonstrate that there are substantial risks above those normally present in DoD contracts for similar items. If an additional risk factor is recognized, the total profit factor for cost risk shall not exceed the designated range limits established for each contract type. The additional assigned value for contract type shall not apply to FMS sales made by United States Government inventories or stocks nor to acquisitions made under DoD cooperative logistics support arrangements.

(3) *Evaluation criteria.* (i) When assigning a profit value, the contracting officer should consider elements that affect contract type risk such as: length of contract; adequacy of cost data for projections; economic environment; nature and extent of subcontracted activity; protection provided to the contractor under contract provisions (e.g., Economic Price Adjustment clauses); the ceilings and share lines contained in incentive provisions. Conditions which might justify higher or lower values are discussed immediately below.

(A) *Above normal conditions.* The contracting officer may assign a higher than normal value in those cases where there is substantial contract type risk. The following are indicators that such a condition may exist: efforts where there is minimal cost history; long-term contracts without provisions protecting the contractor, particularly when there is considerable economic uncertainty; if the contract includes incentive provisions (e.g., cost and performance incentives) which place a high degree of risk on the contractor.

(B) *Below normal conditions.* The contracting officer may assign a lower than normal value in cases where contract type risk is low. The following are indicators that such conditions may exist: contracts involving a very mature product line with extensive cost history; relatively short-term contracts; contracts that contain provisions that substantially reduce the contractor's risk; the contract includes incentive provisions which place a low degree of risk on the contractor. Considerations regarding contract type risk on incurred costs are separately discussed below.

(ii) The contracting officer's assessment of contract type risk shall address the extent that costs have been incurred prior to definitization of the contract action (see also 17.7503(b)(8)). This assessment shall include any reduced contractor risk on both (A) the contract before definitization and (B) the remaining portion of the contract. The contracting officer should generally regard the contract type risk to be below normal within the designated range of the contract type. However, in cases where a substantial portion of the costs have been incurred prior to definitization, the contracting officer may assign a value as low as 0% for contract type risk, regardless of contract type. The contracting officer's risk assessment may consider the limitations placed on the contractor for the period prior to definitization.

(4) *Working capital adjustment (Maximum Value 4%).* For fixed-price type contracts that contain provisions for progress payments, the contracting officer shall calculate a working capital adjustment. This adjustment is added to the contract type risk and it shall not exceed 4% of contract costs. Although the working capital adjustment employs a formula approach, the intent is only to give general recognition to the contractor's cost of working capital under varying contract circumstances, financing policies and the economic environment. It is not intended to be an exact calculation of such costs.

The formula is discussed below:

Contract Costs

Multiply by Portion Financed by Contractor

Contract Costs Financed by Contractor

Multiply by Contract Length Factor

Working Capital Investment

Multiply by Interest Rate

Working Capital Adjustment

(i) *Contract costs.* This represents all allowable costs, *including* contractor G&A expenses and IR&D/B&P expenses (but not facilities capital cost of money). The contracting officer may adjust this amount where the contractor has a minimum cash investment (e.g., subcontractor progress payments liquidated late in period of performance). The contracting officer should also consider the degree which some costs are covered by special financing provisions, such as advance payments, and special funding arrangements on multi-year contracts.

(ii) *Portion financed by contractor.* The contractor's share of financing is generally the portion not covered by progress payments. Typically, this will be 100% minus the customary progress payment rate (32.501-1). For example, if the contract provides for progress payments at 75%, then the contractor's share of financing would be 25% (100% minus 75%). On contracts that provide progress payments to small businesses or flexible progress payments (52.232-7004), the contractor's share shall be computed using the customary progress payment rate for large businesses.

(iii) *Contract costs financed by contractor.* Multiply contract costs by portion financed by contractor.

(iv) *Contract length factor.* This factor represents the period of time that the contractor has a working capital investment in the contract. It is to be based on the time necessary for the contractor to complete the substantive portion of the work. The contract length factor is not necessarily the period of time between contract award and final delivery (or final payment), as periods of minimal effort should be excluded. It also should not include periods of performance contained in option provisions. The contracting officer should use the table below to establish the contract length factor. On contracts with multiple deliveries, the contracting officer should develop a weighted average contract length. Sampling techniques are permissible, so long as they provide a representative result.

Period to perform substantive portion	Factor
21 months or less	.40
22 to 27 months	.65
28 to 33 months	.90
34 to 39 months	1.15
40 to 45 months	1.40
46 to 51 months	1.65
52 to 57 months	1.90
58 to 63 months	2.15
64 to 69 months	2.40
70 to 75 months	2.65
76 months or more	2.90

(v) *Working capital investment.* Multiplying the contract costs financed by contractor by the contract length factor.

(vi) *Interest rate.* The contracting officer shall use the interest rate promulgated by the Secretary of the Treasury (30.7003(c)). No other interest rate is authorized.

(vii) *Working capital adjustment.* Multiply the working capital investment by the interest rate. The result is the working capital adjustment. It may not exceed 4% of contract costs.

*   *   *   *

(c) *Facilities capital employed.* The intent of this profit factor is to encourage and reward aggressive capital investment in facilities that benefit DoD. This factor recognizes both the facilities capital to be employed by the contractor in the performance of the contract and the contractor's commitment to improving productivity. The amount of recognition is differentiated among asset categories in proportion to the potential for productivity increases. In addition to the net book value of facilities capital employed, the contracting officer may consider facilities capital that is part of a formal investment plan if the contractor submits reasonable evidence that (i) achievable benefits to DoD will result from the investment, and (ii) the benefits of the investment are included in the forward pricing structure.

(1) *Profit base.* The profit amount for facilities capital employed is computed by multiplying the values assigned times the allocated facilities capital attributable to buildings and equipment, as derived in DD Form 1861, "Contract Facilities Capital Cost of Money" (see 30.7004).

(2) *Normal values and designated ranges.*

(i) Except as provided in 15.970-1(c)(2)(ii), the normal values and designated ranges for land, buildings, and equipment are as shown below:

Asset type	Normal value	Designated range
Land	0%	N/A
Buildings	15%	10% to 20%
Equipment	35%	20% to 50%

(ii) It is recognized that the method used to allocate facilities capital cost of money may produce disproportionate allocation of assets to research and development and services efforts which are being provided to the government by highly facilitized manufacturing firms. In such cases the contracting officer should use the alternate normal values and designated ranges shown below:

Asset type	Normal value	Designated range
Land	0%	N/A
Buildings	5%	0% to 10%
Equipment	20%	15% to 25%

(iii) If the contracting officer selected the alternate for performance risk (215.970-1(a)(2)(ii)), no profit for facilities capital employed may be assigned.

(3) *Evaluation criteria.* The contracting officer's assessment should relate the usefulness of the facilities capital to the goods or services being acquired under the individual contract action, as well as to the broader perspective of defense programs. The contracting officer may assign any appropriate profit value within the designated range. It is expected that the maximum values will be restricted to those cases where the benefits of the facilities capital investment are substantially above normal. The contracting officer should analyze the productivity improvements and other anticipated industrial base enhancing benefits resulting from the facilities capital investment. The assessment should consider the eco-

nomic value of the facilities capital, such as physical age, undepreciated value, idleness, and expected contribution to future defense needs. The contractor's level of investment in defense related facilities as compared with the portion of the contractor's business which is derived from DoD may be a useful indicator for the contracting officer in evaluating the contractor's commitment to improving the productivity of defense program efforts. The contracting officer should consider any special protection provisions that may be included in the contract which reduce the contractor's risk of investment recovery (termination protection clauses, capital investment indemnification, productivity savings rewards (15.872). Conditions which might justify higher or lower values are discussed below.

(i) *Above normal conditions.* The contracting officer may assign a higher than normal value if the facilities capital investment has direct and identifiable benefits which are considered exceptional. The following are indicators that such a condition may exist: new investments in state-of-the-art technology which reduce acquisition costs or yield other tangible benefits such as improved product quality or accelerated deliveries; investments in new equipment for research and development applications; or the contractor can demonstrate that the investments are over and above the normal capital investments necessary to support anticipated requirements of DoD programs. A value significantly above normal may be justified when there are direct and measurable benefits in efficiency and significantly reduced acquisition costs on the effort being priced.

(ii) *Below normal conditions.* The contracting officer may assign a lower than normal value if the facilities capital investment has little benefit to DoD. The following are indicators that such a condition may exist: allocations of capital which are predominantly applied to commercial product lines; furniture and fixtures, home or group level administrative offices, corporate aircraft and hangars, gymnasiums; old facilities or extensive idle facilities. A value significantly below normal may be justified when a significant portion of defense manufacturing is done in an environment characterized by outdated, inefficient, and labor-intensive capital equipment.

(iii) The contracting officer should ensure that increase in facilities capital investments are not merely asset revaluations attributable to mergers, stock transfers, take overs, sales of corporate entities, or similar actions.

* * * *

15.971 Alternate approaches to Weighted Guidelines Method.

As provided in 15.902(a) 1(ii) and (iii), alternate structured approaches may be used in lieu of the Weighted Guidelines Method. The contracting officer shall adhere to the provisions on profit factors and offset policy described below. See also guidance on cost-plus-award-fee contracts in 15.973.

15.971-1 Recognized profit factors.

The basic structure of the Weighted Guidelines Method establishes a uniform approach for examining the three components of profit: Performance risk, contract type risk (including working capital), and facilities capital employed. Alternate approaches should also consider these factors using the general principles described in 15.970.

15.971-2 Offset policy for facilities capital cost of money.

The values of the profit factors used in the Weighted Guidelines Method have been adjusted to recognize the shift in facilities capital cost of money from an element of profit to an element of contract cost (FAR 31.205-10). Reductions have been made directly to the profit factors for performance risk. In order to assure that this policy is applied to all DoD contracts which allow facilities capital cost of money, similar adjustments shall be made to contracts which use alternate structured approaches. Therefore, the contracting officer shall reduce the overall prenegotiation profit objective derived from alternate structured approaches by 1% of total cost or the amount of facilities capital cost of money, whichever is less.

* * * *

15.972 Modified Weighted Guidelines Method for nonprofit organizations.

15.972-1 Procedures for establishing fee objectives.

It is DoD's policy to establish the fee objective on defense contracts with nonprofit organizations in a manner that will stimulate efficient contract performance. To achieve this, the contracting officer shall use the Modified Weighted Guidelines Method described below. For purposes of applying this method, a nonprofit organization is a business entity which operates exclusively for charitable, scientific, or educational purposes; whose earnings do not benefit any private shareholder or individual; whose activities do not involve influencing legislation or political campaigning for any candidate for public office; and is exempted from Federal income taxation under section 501 of the Internal Revenue Code.

(a) The contracting officer shall use the guidelines described in 15.970 but make the following adjustments to the fee objective:

(1) If the standard performance risk factor is used (15.970-1(a)(2)(i)), the fee objective shall be reduced by an amount equal to 1% of total costs, *excluding* G&A expenses, IR&D/B&P expenses, and facilities capital cost of money. If the alternate performance risk factor is used (15.970-1(a)(2)(ii)), then the reduction shall be 2%.

(2) The designated range for the contract type risk shall be − 1% to 0% of total costs, *excluding* G&A expenses, IR&D/B&P expenses, facilities capital cost of money, for a cost-plus-fixed-fee contract with nonprofit organizations or elements that have been identified by the Secretary of Defense or Secretary of a Department, or their designees, as receiving sustaining support on a cost-plus-fixed-fee basis from a particular Department or Agency of the Department of Defense.

(b) In addition to the fee amounts computed in 15.972-1(a) above, the contracting officer shall consider the need for fee on contracts to be awarded to a nonprofit organization designated as a Federally Funded Research and Development Center (FFRDC). Such consideration shall include, the FFRDC's proportion of retained earnings as established under generally accepted accounting methods, that is relatable to DoD contracted effort. The need for fee may be based on the FFRDC's facilities capital acquisition plans working capital funding as assessed on operating cycle cash needs, contingency funding, and provision for funding unreimbursed costs deemed ordinary and necessary to the FFRDC.

As indicated at the outset, the foregoing was made effective August 1, 1987, and concludes the interim profit promulgations as delineated previously, with its concentration on the use of form DD-1547 for its implementation. The purpose of the aforementioned revisions was to increase the emphasis placed on facilities capital employed and contractor risk, give greater consideration to working capital requirements, and eliminate the profit computations predicated on individual cost elements. It is pertinent to note that the above structured approach is mandatory for use on negotiated contract actions exceeding $500,000 and optional between $100,000 and $500,000.

At first blush, the details and its respective computation instructions may appear overly complicated, but if one follows the form DD-1547 and devotes attention to each of the cited areas involved utilizing the aforegoing interim and final methods of computation, the end result should be similar to prior structured "weighted guideline" computations that have been in use over the years.

PROFIT POLICY—CIVILIAN AGENCIES

As described earlier, DOD formulated the first structured approach to establishing profit objectives with the issuance of the WGL in 1964 and conducted a number of subsequent studies leading to the WGL revisions, which decreased the weighting for estimated costs and increased the emphasis on facilities capital employed and contract cost risk. NASA and the Department of Energy (DOE), with missions that are related in part to military functions, engage some of the same contractors, and with some of their top officials having DOD backgrounds, adopted WGLs that were similar to, although not identical to, those promulgated by DOD. The other civilian agencies continued to be guided by the unstructured approach set forth in the Federal Procurement Regulation (FPR).

OFPP Policy Letter 80-7, December 9, 1980

Some years after Profit '76 and CAS 414, OFPP finally moved toward establishing a degree of uniformity through a structured approach for civilian agencies in the above-captioned Letter. Agencies that awarded over $50 million in noncompetitive contracts over $100,000 annually were required to adopt a structured approach. Those not meeting these criteria could also do so but were not required to. Agencies in the former category could adopt WGL formulated by DOD, NASA or DOE, or develop their own provided they incorporated logic or rationale similar to the aforementioned.

FAR Subpart 15.9 Profit

When FAR was published in 1984, it generally incorporated the intent of OFPP Policy Letter 80-7 relating to the requirements for most agencies to use a structured approach to determine profit objectives. Inasmuch as civilian agencies are authorized to adopt the WGL formulated by DOD, NASA or DOE, or formulate their own, FAR does not provide any specifics for WGL. The salient provisions of this Subpart are excerpted below.

15.901 General.

(a) Profit or fee prenegotiation objectives do not necessarily represent net income to contractors. Rather, they represent that element of the potential total remuneration that contractors *may* receive for contract performance over and above allowable costs. This potential remuneration element and the Government's estimate of allowable costs to be incurred in contract performance together equal the Government's total prenegotiation objective. Just as actual costs may vary from estimated costs, the contractor's actual realized profit or fee may vary from negotiated profit or fee, because of such factors as efficiency of performance, incurrence of costs the Government does not recognize as allowable, and contract type.

(b) It is in the Government's interest to offer contractors opportunities for financial rewards sufficient to (1) stimulate efficient contract performance, (2) attract the best capabilities of qualified large and small business concerns to Government contracts, and (3) maintain a viable industrial base.

(c) Both the Government and contractors should be concerned with profit as a motivator of efficient and effective contract performance. Negotiations aimed merely at reducing prices by reducing profit, without proper recognition of the function of profit, are not in the Government's interest. Negotiation of extremely low profits, use of historical averages, or automatic application of predetermined percentages to total estimated costs do not provide proper motivation for optimum contract performance. With the exception of statutory ceilings in 15.903(d) on profit and fee, agencies shall not (1) establish administrative ceilings or (2) create administrative procedures that could be represented to contractors as de facto ceilings.

*   *   *   *

15.903 Contracting officer responsibilities.

(a) When the price negotiation is not based on cost analysis, contracting officers are not required to analyze profit.

(b) When the price negotiation is based on cost analysis, contracting officers in agencies that have a structured approach shall use it to analyze profit. When not using a structured approach, contracting officers shall comply with 15.905-1 in developing profit or fee prenegotiation objectives.

(c) Contracting officers shall use the Government prenegotiation cost objective amounts as the basis for calculating the profit or fee prenegotiation objective. Before the allowability of facilities capital cost of money, this cost was included in profits or fees. Therefore, before applying profit or fee factors, the contracting officer shall exclude any facilities capital cost of money included in the cost objective amounts. If the prospective contractor fails to identify or propose facilities capital cost of money in a proposal for a contract that will be subject to the cost principles for contracts with commercial organizations (see Subpart 31.2), facilities capital cost of money will not be an allowable cost in any resulting contract (see 15.904).

* * * *

(e) The contracting officer shall not require any prospective contractor to submit details of its profit or fee objective but shall consider them if they are submitted voluntarily.

(f) If a change or modification (1) calls for essentially the same type and mix of work as the basic contract and (2) is of relatively small dollar value compared to the total contract value, the contracting officer may use the basic contract's profit or fee rate as the prenegotiation objective for that change or modification.

* * * *

15.905 Profit-analysis factors.

15.905-1 *Common factors.*

Unless it is clearly inappropriate or not applicable, each factor outlined in paragraphs (a) through (f) following shall be considered by agencies in developing their structured approaches and by contracting officers in analyzing profit whether or not using a structured approach.

(a) *Contractor effort.* This factor measures the complexity of the work and the resources required of the prospective contractor for contract performance. Greater profit opportunity should be provided under contracts requiring a high degree of professional and managerial skill and to prospective contractors whose skills, facilities, and technical assets can be expected to lead to efficient and economical contract performance. Subfactors (1) through (4) following shall be considered in determining contractor effort, but they may be modified in specific situations to accommodate differences in the categories used by prospective contractors for listing costs:

(1) *Material acquisition.* This subfactor measures the managerial and technical effort needed to obtain the required purchased parts and material, subcontracted items, and special tooling. Considerations include (i) the complexity of the items required, (ii) the number of purchase orders and subcontracts to be awarded and administered, (iii) whether established sources are available or new or second sources must be developed, and (iv) whether material will be obtained through routine purchase orders or through complex subcontracts requiring detailed specifications. Profit consideration should correspond to the managerial and technical effort involved.

(2) *Conversion direct labor.* This subfactor measures the contribution of direct engineering, manufacturing, and other labor to converting the raw materials, data, and subcontracted items into the contract items. Considerations include the diversity of engineering, scientific, and manufacturing labor skills required and the amount and quality of supervision and coordination needed to perform the contract task.

(3) *Conversion-related indirect costs.* This subfactor measures how much the indirect costs contribute to contract performance. The labor elements in the allocable indirect costs should be given the profit consideration they would receive if treated as direct labor. The other elements of indirect cost should be evaluated to determine whether they (i) merit only limited profit consideration because of their routine nature or (ii) are elements that contribute significantly to the proposed contract.

(4) *General management.* This subfactor measures the prospective contractor's other indirect costs and general and administrative (G&A) expense, their composition, and how much they contribute to contract performance. Considerations include (i) how labor in the overhead pools would be treated if it were direct labor, (ii) whether elements within the pools are routine expenses or instead are elements that contribute significantly to the proposed contract, and (iii) whether the elements require routine as opposed to unusual managerial effort and attention.

(b) *Contract cost risk.* (1) This factor measures the degree of cost responsibility and associated risk that the prospective contractor will assume (i) as a result of the contract type contemplated and (ii) considering the reliability of the cost estimate in relation to the complexity and duration of the contract task. Determination of contract type should be closely related to the risks involved in timely, cost-effective, and efficient performance. This factor should compensate contractors proportionately for assuming greater cost risks.

(2) The contractor assumes the greatest cost risk in a closely priced firm-fixed-price contract under which it agrees to perform a complex undertaking on time and at a predetermined price. Some firm-fixed-price contracts may entail substantially less cost risk than others because, for example, the contract task is less complex or many of the contractor's costs are known at the time of price agreement, in which case the risk factor should be reduced accordingly. The contractor assumes the least cost risk in a cost-plus-fixed-fee level-of-effort contract, under which it is reimbursed those costs determined to be allocable and allowable, plus the fixed fee.

(3) In evaluating assumption of cost risk, contracting officers shall, except in unusual circumstances, treat time-and-materials, labor-hour, and firm-fixed-price, level-of-effort terms contracts as cost-plus-fixed-fee contracts.

(c) *Federal socioeconomic programs.* This factor measures the degree of support given by the prospective contractor to Federal socioeconomic programs, such as those involving small business concerns, small business concerns owned and controlled by socially and economically disadvantaged individuals, handicapped sheltered workshops, labor surplus areas, and energy conservation. Greater profit opportunity should be provided contractors who have displayed unusual initiative in these programs.

(d) *Capital investments.* This factor takes into account the contribution of contractor investments to efficient and economical contract performance.

(e) *Cost-control and other past accomplishments.* This factor allows additional profit opportunities to a prospective contractor that has previously demonstrated its ability to perform similar tasks effectively and economically. In addition, consideration should be given to (1) measures taken by the prospective contractor that result in productivity improvements and (2) other cost-reduction accomplishments that will benefit the Government in follow-on contracts.

(f) *Independent development.* Under this factor, the contractor may be provided additional profit opportunities in recognition of independent development efforts relevant to the contract end item without Government assistance. The contracting officer should consider whether the development cost was recovered directly or indirectly from Government sources.

15.905-2 *Additional factors.*

In order to foster achievement of program objectives, each agency may include additional factors in its structured approach or take them into account in the profit analysis of individual contract actions.

Weighted Guidelines for Civilian Agencies

At this writing, neither FAR nor any individual civilian agency has yet adopted the concepts underlying the new DOD profit policy. Companies negotiating with civilian agencies should look for guidance relating to profit in the applicable agency FAR Supplement. For example, NASA profit policy is set forth in NASA FAR Supplement Subpart 18-15.9. Similarly, contractors should consult DOE FAR Supplement Subpart 915.9, GSA FAR Supplement Subpart 515.9, and Transportation Department (DOT) Subpart 1215.9, for contracts with those agencies. For other departments and agencies, contractors will need to ascertain whether those agencies have adopted the DOD, NASA, or DOE WGL or formulated their own.

It is expected that DOD's revised WGL, reflecting reduced weighting to estimated costs and increased weighting to facilities capital investment and contract cost risk, will ultimately be adopted by other departments and agencies, in whole or with some variations.

GAO PROPOSAL FOR PROFIT REPORTING LEGISLATION

As discussed in Chapter XXVIII of this text, GAO has faulted every profit study ever conducted and every profit policy that emanated from the various studies. Its own study, conducted in 1971, concluded with very broad recommendations that it suggested that an OFPP-led interagency group develop. Among GAO's criticisms of the various studies has been their failure to provide GAO with complete access to all of the contractors' records, as well as of the data developed by the individual CPA firms that attested to the validity of the contractors' profit reports and of the CPA firms that were selected to compile all of the information. These complaints continued despite the fact that contractors would not submit any data if they were subject to investigation by GAO.

After criticizing DFAIR and the profit policy revisions related to that study, GAO devised a plan that would make periodic profit reporting by major contractors required by statute, such legislation to include GAO access to any and all contractor and government records generated by the reports. The congressional watchdog, in this plan, would not be responsible for developing the reporting requirements or accomplishing or reporting the results. Rather, the legislation would grant GAO complete access to all plans and reports to enable it to engage in the activity it prefers, criticizing after the fact. At this writing the GAO-proposed legislation has met with just about unanimous opposition in both the public and private sectors. The future of this scheme will depend on GAO's ability to marshall the necessary support from congressional industry-bashers.

Chapter XXVI

Federal Inspectors General

An inspector general is generally considered to be ". . . the supervisor of a body of inspectors or a department or system of an inspector (of an army) . . . . also: an officer of a military corps of inspectors that investigates and reports on organizational matters (as discipline, morale, supply, accounts)." As the definition suggests, the origin of the term "Inspector General" is generally considered to be found in military organizations.

In contrast to the broad areas of interest of inspectors general, Webster defines an auditor as "one authorized to examine and verify accounts; one skilled in the technique of auditing." This requires reference to auditing, which is defined as "a branch of accounting that deals with examination and verification of accounts or books of account and with making the final reports." However, these modest definitions are eschewed by many auditors. The Defense Contract Audit Agency, for example, under the term "operations audits," has increasingly attempted to evaluate a wide variety of contractors' operations, moving into areas where its expertise has been strongly challenged. But even the expanding efforts of DCAA appear restrained and constrained indeed when compared to the seemingly limitless scope of examinations and investigations performed by the General Accounting Office. As discussed in Chapter XXVIII of this text, GAO apparently recognized that the competence of auditors to evaluate national policies of defense, health, energy, environment, etc., was subject to serious question. GAO's answer was to reclassify its auditors and give them the somewhat more impressive, if vague, title of "evaluators."

THE INSPECTOR GENERAL ACT OF 1978

Despite these efforts at self-aggrandizement, auditors continued to be viewed as "green eye shade" types by many people, including certain members of Congress. Accordingly, when a series of GAO reports, congressional studies, and exposes by the communications media alleged widespread fraud involving both government agencies and government contractors, congressional interest focused on establishing new organizations with the capability of ferreting out the fraud, waste, and abuse that some congressmen concluded abounded in the public and related private sectors.

After competitive hearings in both houses, Congress enacted the Inspector General Act of 1978, Public Law 95-452. Among the alleged inadequacies highlighted in congressional reports supporting this legislation were insufficient audit and investigative resources, organizational placement of audit and investigative components under the supervision of officials whose programs were being audited or investigated, absence of concerted programs to detect fraud and abuse, lack of a single high level official who could devote full time and attention to the overall direction of both audit and investigative activities and have an effective mechanism to keep the heads of executive agencies and Congress informed concerning fraud, waste, and other serious problems, and inadequate cooperation between the executive agencies and the Department of Justice in the prosecution of white collar crimes.

The IG Act established the position of Inspector General in twelve federal civilian agencies, to be appointed by the President of the United States and confirmed by the Senate. The IGs were given statutory responsibility and authority to provide policy direction and supervision for all audit and investigative activities within their departments and to keep the heads of their agencies and Congress informed concerning fraud and serious problems. Additionally, the IGs are required to prepare semiannual reports for the Congress describing the significant problems, abuses, and inefficiencies in administration of programs and operations within their departments, citing recommendations for corrective action, identifying previous significant recommendations in which corrective action has not been completed, preparing a summary of matters referred to prosecuting authorities, and citing prosecutions and convictions that have resulted.

Among the internal problems created by the Act were the prescribed relations between the head of the federal department or agency and the Inspector General. For example, the Act provides that where an IG discovers a particularly serious or flagrant abuse, he or she must immediately notify the head of the agency and the head of the agency must transmit such information to the Congress within seven calendar days. Additionally, the required semiannual reports by the IGs must be transmitted to the heads of the agencies and then, within thirty days, to the appropriate congressional committees. The head of an agency may attach his own comments to the IG's report, but may not prevent the report from being sent to Congress or alter or delete portions of the report. Further, within sixty days after the report is sent to Congress, the agency head must make copies of the report available to the public.

DEPARTMENT OF DEFENSE EFFORTS TO REMAIN EXEMPT FROM REQUIREMENTS OF THE INSPECTOR GENERAL BILL

Among the considerations confronting Congress in the enactment of the IG Act were the efforts of certain departments and agencies, principally Defense, State and Justice, to obtain exemptions. DOD officials testified that the size and complexities of its operations, the complicated relations between the Office of the Secretary of Defense and the military departments, and the numerous existing investigative and audit groups made the establishment of a single office of inspector general difficult and unnecessary. There were also controversies as to which of the existing groups should be included in the IG organization and which should remain independent in the event a DOD IG were established. In this connection, DCAA, which had successfully resisted a number of attempts to incorporate it into DOD contract administration operations, now bent its efforts to remain outside an IG organization if one were created.

As enacted, Public Law 95-452 excluded DOD but studies were mandated to permit Congress to arrive at a final judgment. In the meantime, DOD was directed to make semiannual reports to Congress concerning audits and inspections into fraud, waste, and abuse, as required by the IGs established by that Act. After resisting the establishment of an Office of Inspector General (OIG) for some four years, DOD was directed to do so by an amendment to the 1983 Defense Authorization Act.

During this period considerable debate within and outside of DOD continued regarding the status of DCAA, including total inclusion in the OIG, total exclusion, and a plan supported by GAO under which preaward audits would continue to be performed by DCAA but the postaward function would be transferred to OIG. DCAA's ultimately successful efforts to remain intact and outside of the OIG were to prove significant because the audit agency moved sharply in the 1978-82 period to increase its attention to fraud detection in an effort to persuade Congress and others that its incorporation into the OIG was not needed.

The statutory provisions relating to the DOD OIG and the status of DCAA are of considerable significance to defense contractors. For this reason, we have included an excerpt from the conference report on the 1983 DOD authorization bill pertaining to these matters.

The conferees agreed to provide an Inspector General for the Department of Defense appointed by the President and confirmed by the Senate. The Inspector General would work under the general supervision of the Secretary of Defense. The authority of the Secretary to supervise could be delegated only to the officer next in rank. With respect to audits or investigations that require information concerning sensitive operational plans, intelligence matters, counter-intelligence matters, ongoing criminal investigations of other administrative units of the Department of Defense related to military security, or other matters the disclosure of which would constitute a serious threat to national security, the conferees believe the Inspector General should be under the authority, direction and control of the Secretary of Defense. The Secretary could prohibit the Inspector General from initiating, carrying out, or completing any audit or investigation, or from issuing any subpenas with respect to the above-mentioned matters when the Secretary determines such prohibition is necessary to preserve the national security interests of the United States. The Secretary and the Inspector General would be required to report to the Committees on Armed Services and Governmental Affairs of the Senate and the Committees on Armed Services and Government Operations of the House of Representatives and to other appropriate committees and subcommittees of the Congress should the Secretary exercise his authority established by the amendment.

In addition to the transfers contained in both the House and Senate provisions, the conferees agreed that the Office of Inspector General of the Defense Logistics Agency should be transferred to the Office of Inspector General of the Department of Defense. The conferees agreed to direct the Secretary of Defense to transfer not less than 100 additional positions to the Office of Inspector General to be filled by the Inspector

General with persons trained to perform contract audits. The conferees believe that it is essential that the new Inspector General develop a significant capability in the highly technical area of contract audit. The conferees do not intend that these auditors advise Department of Defense contracting officers in the process of negotiating contracts, a function that the Defense Contract Audit Agency auditors perform. The conferees envision the contract audit capability in the Office of Inspector General to be used (1) to provide the manpower and technical expertise to oversee effectively and review the work of the Defense Contract Audit Agency, and (2) to provide the Inspector General flexibility and resources in situations where he deems it necessary or appropriate to look at entire procurements—the performance of defense contractors as well as the performance of defense personnel.

The conferees also agreed to impose duties and responsibilities on the Inspector General of the Department of Defense in addition to those contained in the 1978 Inspector General Act, including the following:

The Inspector General of the Department of Defense would—

(1) be the principal adviser to the Secretary of Defense for matters relating to the prevention and detection of fraud, waste and abuse in the programs and operations of the department;

(2) initiate, conduct, and supervise such audits and investigations in the Department of Defense (including the military departments) that the Inspector General deems appropriate;

(3) provide policy direction for audits and investigations relating to fraud, waste, and abuse and program effectiveness;

(4) investigate fraud, waste and abuse uncovered as a result of other contract and internal audits, as the Inspector General deems appropriate;

(5) develop policy, monitor and evaluate program performance, and provide guidance with respect to all department activities relating to criminal investigation programs;

(6) monitor and evaluate the adherence of department auditors to internal audit, contract audit, and internal review principles, policies and procedures;

(7) develop policy, evaluate program performance, and monitor actions taken by all components of the department in response to contract audits, internal audits, internal review reports, and audits conducted by the Comptroller General of the United States;

(8) request assistance as needed from other audit, inspection, and investigative units of the Department of Defense (including military departments); and

(9) give particular regard to the activities of the internal audit inspection and investigative units of the military department with a view toward avoiding duplication and ensuring effective coordination and cooperation.

DOD Office of Inspector General

Widely shared concerns about the role and activities of the DOD Office of Inspector General materialized early in the history of this new organization. The IG and his deputy soon became favorites of congressional critics of the Defense Department and defense contractors as they vied with GAO representatives in attacking various aspects of the acquisition process and activities. The OIG also issued numerous reports criticizing DOD organizations and activities, including DCAA, which it prodded to devote greater manpower to fraud detection and postaward audits in search of defective pricing, and to become tougher on contractors in demanding access to records.

The DOD IG on Defective Pricing

Chapter XXII of this text, addressing contract price reduction for defective cost or pricing data, referred to hard-hitting testimony by top DOD IG officials on this subject. Essentially, in that testimony and elsewhere, OIG officials have argued:

1. DCAA should increase the manpower devoted to postaward reviews to seek defective pricing.

2. Every defective pricing finding should be viewed as possible (or probable) fraud.

3. Contracting officers should be more diligent in pursuing contract price reductions when DCAA reports defective pricing.

4. P.L. 87-653 should be amended to remove just about all of the defenses then recognized by boards of contract appeals and courts.

In December 1986, the OIG issued a *Handbook on Scenarios of Potential Defective Pricing Fraud,* one of that office's "think fraud" publications. The handbook is excerpted as Appendix 4 of this text. Written as a guide for DCAA auditors and others, the handbook advises that once defective pricing is found, "it should be treated as an indicator of potential fraud. The auditor's suspicion must be raised when information which should have been known by the contracting officer before the award of a contract, was not disclosed." The handbook also directs: "The auditor should 'think fraud' when making a review. This awareness factor cannot be overemphasized." The handbook contains what it terms "scenarios" or "schemes" that "indicate the need for investigation for fraud."

The DOD IG on Progress Payments and CAS 408

In another congressional testimony, the Deputy DOD IG expressed concern that current progress payment rates were too high and decried the DOD implementation of CAS 408 because use of the accrual basis results in government payments to contractors before they make payments to their employees:

> With large accrued vacation costs and current high rates of progress payments under fixed price contracts, it is possible that current progress payments to contractors could exceed their actual outlays of cash. This would also be true for cost-type contracts. If this is true, the government could be providing some contractors with interest-free loans. The U.S.

Treasury would be paying significant interest costs for what are, in effect, cash advances.

The witness testified that he had written to the Under Secretary of Defense for Research and Engineering and recommended changes in DOD payment practices, but the Under Secretary had not agreed with him. The correspondence on this subject was made available to the committee.

The Deputy IG expressed concern about DOD's flexible progress payment procedure because it was widely used without audit to ascertain the accuracy of the flexible progress payment model. "Computer models," he said, "are notorious for the ways they can be 'gamed' to produce a desired outcome." He did not indicate who might have "gamed" this computer model, but his statement was recognized by most observers as having serious implications.

The witness advised the committee that he would not be as concerned about the reimbursement of accrued vacation expenses "if current progress payment rates were lowered to where they were a few years ago, 80 percent for a large business and 85 percent for a small business." In view of the decrease in inflation and interest rates, according to the witness, "I believe that it is time for DOD to reconsider its current progress payment rates to ensure that contractors are not provided additional profits through the interest-free use of government funds."

As in the case of a number of other standards promulgated by the defunct CASB, questions were raised regarding the need for a standard on Accounting for Costs of Compensated Personal Absence (CAS 408). Unlike the other costing areas, there were no allegations of contractors manipulating these costs to the disadvantage of the government or "horror cases." However, there was no denying a lack of uniformity, with some companies recording these costs when paid (cash basis) and others recording them when the employee's entitlement was established (accrual basis). And there were also variances in practice among the companies that accounted for these costs on an accrual basis. Essentially, CAS 408 (i) identified compensated personal absence as "any absence from work for reasons such as illness, vacation, holidays, jury duty or military training, or personal activities, for which an employer pays compensation directly to an employee in accordance with a plan or custom of the employer" and (ii) provided that such costs "shall be assigned to the cost accounting period or periods in which the entitlement was earned" (accrual basis).

The committee wrote to the Comptroller General requesting his views about the so-called "premature reimbursement" resulting from DOD's recognition and reimbursement of these expenses when accrued while contractors do not actually pay out these monies until a later date. The Comptroller General's views were requested about a proposal to amend contract payment clauses so that contractors would not be reimbursed for these costs until they had paid them. What the committee appeared to be proposing, in effect, was a nullification of CAS 408 by effectively changing the practice from an accrual to a cash basis.

Although GAO can usually be counted upon to join (or initiate) criticisms of DOD on a wide range of subjects, this inquiry presented a problem in that agreement with the committee could not be expressed without a concomitant derogation of CAS 408. And the GAO could not readily criticize a standard in view of the statements by the Comptroller General and others that all of the Board's promulgations were characterized by accounting expertise, independence, etc. In this light, the Comptroller General replied: "Since the amount of the accrual is determined in accordance with the standard and paid as an accrual pursuant to DOD policy, we cannot call this reimbursement premature."

While accepting the use of accrual accounting for compensated personal absence, the DOD Deputy Inspector General expressed concern "when the contractor accrues the costs but doesn't pay them until much later." He further stated:

> It often takes 18 months between the initial accrual of vacation costs and the contractors' actual payment for them. No one, to my knowledge, has analytically quantified the amounts of accrued vacation costs, but we can estimate that it approaches $2 billion annually. With large accrued vacation costs and the current high rates of progress payments under fixed price contracts, it is possible that current progress payments to contractors could exceed their actual outlays of cash. This could also be true for cost type contracts. If this is true, the government could be providing some contractors with interest-free loans. The U.S. Treasury would be paying significant interest costs for what are, in effect, cash advances.

The DOD Deputy IG did not explain how he arrived at his estimate that accrued vacation costs "approach $2 billion" nor did he explain his statement that "it often takes 18 months between the initial accrual of vacation costs and the contractors' actual payment for them." In this connection, even the GAO chief expressed the opinion that the period between the accrual and the actual payment "would seldom exceed 12 months."

The OIG representative let it be known that "[i]n June 1982, I proposed to the Under Secretary of Defense that he consider limiting contract payments for vacation expense to the amounts actually paid by contractors." He reported that the Under Secretary did not agree and that the correspondence between the OIG and other offices on this subject had been provided to the committee.

The DOD IG on the Defense System Acquisition Review Council

At a subsequent meeting before the House Budget Committee, a representative of the Committee apparently asked both GAO and DOD IG about a weapons system. Responding to this inquiry and speaking on other matters, Deputy DOD IG Vander Schaaf criticized the Defense System Acquisition Review Council (DSARC). This Council, composed of the top DOD officials concerned with acquisition, was said to require "increased discipline." He further alleged that DSARC information was not accurate and tended "to play up the good and play down the bad." He told the Committee that his "experts" found that decisions at the highest acquisition levels in DOD on whether or not to go ahead on production of weapons systems were based on deficient data.

Criticizing data made available to DSARC as "massaged" and asserting there was a "lack of credibility" in the decisions, the Deputy DOD IG assured the congressmen that his office was placing the entire DSARC process under a continuing review.

The IG official also stated that his office had made fifty recommendations to improve the handling of change orders under DOD construction contracts. He criticized DOD for failing to establish uniform policies among the Army Corps of Engineers and the Navy Facilities Engineering Command for determining profit.

Other criticisms by the DOD IG official included those levied at the Defense Logistics Agency (DLA) for lack of adequate controls over receipt of material and payments to contractors and for a wide failure to monitor overpayments to contractors under fixed price incentive contracts.

The DOD IG on Evaluations of Major Subcontractors' Pricing Proposals

In a lengthy report addressed to DOD officials but made public early in 1984, the DOD IG strongly criticized the Defense Department and prime contractors for failing to effectively evaluate pricing proposals submitted by major subcontractors. The following is an excerpt from this report:

We found that subcontractors' pricing proposals were not always promptly analyzed by either prime contractor or Government audit/technical agencies. Further, in those cases where analyses were made, the results were not always given appropriate consideration when negotiating prime contract prices. Generally, the DOD internal audit agencies had not audited contracts included in our review and, in fact, placed very little or no emphasis on evaluating subcontract management areas. As a result, potential savings are not being adequately identified and doubts will persist as to whether the DOD negotiated a fair and reasonable price for major weapon systems.

When issued in draft form, this report generated considerable controversy, and a top DOD acquisition official stated that it was so "replete with nonfactual data" and contained such "magnitude of errors" that it should be withdrawn. The OIG refused to do so but did make certain changes to correct erroneous allegations. The magnitude of the errors and the validity of the final "corrected" report remained in controversy.

In response to criticisms directed against them, the heads of the Army, Navy, and Air Force internal audit agencies stated that they would accord increased emphasis to the adequacy of the evaluation of subcontractors' proposals. It was not immediately clear whether DOD's internal audit agencies are expected to compete with DCAA and ACO staffs in reviewing subcontractors' pricing data and the evaluation of such data by prime contractors.

The Deputy DOD IG joined Assistant Comptroller General Frank C. Conahan, GAO's major critic of DOD and defense contractors, in another congressional appearance to discuss the related but broader areas of contractor estimating system surveys, their reviews of subcontractor proposals, and defective pricing. The two vied in criticizing contractors, contracting officers and contract auditors for failing to review estimating systems and take punitive action against contractors whose systems were considered inadequate. The criticisms included charges that contractors reduce subcontractor prices after the prime contract award, often without notifying the government.

The DOD IG on DCAA Access to Contractors' Records

The many contractors who have been disturbed over DCAA's growing demands for access to records, operations, and people, including demands that are widely considered as extending beyond the provisions of the pertinent contract clauses, were shocked to read a report prepared by the DOD IG on this subject, dated March 9, 1984 (No. APO 84-5).

The IG conceded that "DCAA field auditors were actively pursuing and generally receiving access to those contractor records required for audit accomplishment." However, this was far from satisfactory in the IG's opinion, as indicated by the following summary of the conclusions and recommendations resulting from its "oversight review":

The DCAA auditors were entitled, by law and contract terms, to the records denied by contractors. We concluded that more aggressive action and improved controls were required by DCAA in obtaining contractors' records required for audit functions. Actions recommended include (i) withholding of payments to contractors if requested records are not provided within 30 days; (ii) refusal by DCAA to issue audit reports when supporting data and records are not provided for contractors' proposals; (iii) strengthening of acquisition regulations to make the audit of all proposals in excess of $500,000 mandatory; (iv) increased support by DOD procurement officials in assisting DCAA auditors to resolve access problems with contractors; and (v) improved monitoring and oversight of access problems by DCAA Headquarters.

The major recommendation in this area was for DCAA to really toughen its position and actions when access to records was denied or delayed. The IG would have the DCAA Director provide instructions to the agency's field offices not to issue audit reports in such instances. Instead, these denials and/ or inadequate data should be promptly reported to the contracting officer *and* copies of such reports should be furnished to various top level Pentagon officials and the IG.

The IG was also dissatisfied with the matter of access to records in connection with DCAA audits of incurred costs: "The DCAA auditors were denied timely and full access by contractors to records needed for the effective accomplishment of incurred cost audits. While many of the access problems had been resolved at the time of our review, the procedures required to be followed by DCAA field auditors to resolve access disputes were cumbersome, time consuming and were not effectively monitored by DCAA Headquarters. Moreover, the ability of DCAA auditors to resolve disputes in a satisfactory and timely manner was hindered by the lack of any incentive for contractors to provide required records. These conditions result in a waste of audit resources and ineffective or untimely audit performance."

The IG reported that "access problems seldom occurred with small contractors" but such instances were found at thirteen of the 23 larger contractors visited. (This finding should not be considered a statistical indication of the extent of the problem inasmuch as the IG conceded that six of the 23 contractors were selected because of "suspected access problems.")

The thrust of the report is that DCAA auditors are too easy on such contractors and take too much time in trying to work out mutually satisfactory arrangements. Although the records are ultimately obtained by DCAA, the IG asserted that: "[t]he real issue is not that the access problem was resolved but the extended delays in resolving such access problems." The IG seemed impatient with the efforts expended by DCAA resident staffs and regional offices on these matters and believed that denials or delays should be elevated promptly to DCAA Headquarters which should either resolve the issues or elevate them to higher DOD levels.

A special point was made concerning denials of access to details of unallowable and/or unclaimed costs. DCAA auditors were criticized for frequently failing to obtain names of persons entertained or passengers riding on contractor-owned aircraft when the related costs were disallowed or not even claimed. The IG also faulted DCAA for failing to ferret out the names of government personnel where there may have been indications that such personnel had accepted gratuities from contractors.

And finally, the IG referred to its policy memorandum on the "Issuance of Inspector General Subpoenas in Audits and Investigations" and noted that DCAA and other activities had been encouraged to make "use of this valuable tool in all situations where access is not otherwise available." According to the report, "on October 27, 1983, DCAA forwarded the Inspector General policy memorandum to its regional directors advising them of availability of subpoenas to resolve access to records problems. The covering memorandum to the field advised the regional director that if a situation requiring the use of subpoenas is encountered they should submit a request to DCAA headquarters for processing."

In addition to the use of subpoenas, the IG recommended that DCAA revise its policy "to provide contractors 30 days notice from the date of the first denial that costs will be suspended if the records are not provided." To its credit, in our judgment, DCAA nonconcurred in this recommendation and, according to the IG report responded:

> We oppose an arbitrary 30-day delay period for suspending costs. If the access problem is related to costs being billed to the Government, it warrants immediate attention. On the other hand, if no current billings are affected by the access problem, imposing such a deadline may not allow adequate time to pursue informal resolution of the problem. It also tends to eliminate all judgment of the involved parties as to materiality of the impact, nature of the specific record requested, alternative sources of information, the types of audit and priority for completion, etc.

DCAA also advised the IG that its Manual (CAM 1-206.3) [now CAM 1-504.3] already provides for suspension of costs for denial of access to records and, "in view of the IG's concern, we are issuing a memorandum to our audit offices emphasizing the need for quick action on access problems."

The IG was not satisfied with DCAA's reply but agreed to compromise the matter if DCAA inserted the guidance contained in the aforementioned memorandum in CAM. Portions of the IG's comments on this matter and the cited DCAA memorandum are quoted below.

The strongest action available to DCAA auditors to force a resolution of access problems is the suspension of costs. This provides an incentive for the contractor to provide denied records. Under existing procedures and practices there appears to be a reluctance on the part of DCAA auditors and management to suspend costs in connection with access disputes. During our visits to DCAA field offices we found only one instance where costs were suspended because of an access to records issue.

On February 23, 1984, DCAA Headquarters issued the memorandum cited in their response to this recommendation (See Appendix E). This memorandum stated, in part, that:

As stated in CAM 1-206.3, [now CAM 1-504.3] auditors should promptly question and/or suspend cost amounts that are determined to be unsupported for lack of access to contractor records. There is no requirement that the contractor be given formal advance notice that costs are to be questioned or suspended, and no "waiting period" is appropriate after the auditor has determined the amounts of unsupported costs related to a denial.

We do not agree that the existing provisions of CAM 1-206.3 [now CAM 1-504.3] provide for the prompt suspension of costs. Only after the DCAA field office and regional office have exhausted all means to obtain such records will the regional director provide the field office with "guidance regarding the suspending or questioning of unsupported costs." If the guidance in the February 23, 1984 memorandum was inserted in the CAM to replace existing guidance we would consider that such an action was responsive to the intent of our recommendation.

* * * *

MEMORANDUM FOR REGIONAL DIRECTORS, DCAA

SUBJECT: Access to Contractors' Records

In a recent oversight review of DCAA, the DoD Inspector General raised concern about whether effective action is being taken to gain access to contractors' records. We have reviewed the CAM guidance on this subject and concluded that it is adequate. Nevertheless, a discussion of that guidance seems appropriate to assure that it is being given sufficient attention.

As stated in CAM 1-206.3 [now CAM 1-504.3], auditors should promptly question and/or suspend cost amounts that are determined to be unsupported for lack of access to contractor records. There is no requirement that the contractor be given formal advance notice that costs are to be questioned or suspended, and no "waiting period" is appropriate after the auditor has determined the amounts of unsupported costs related to a denial.

DCAA auditors are expected to exercise good judgment in deciding which contractor records are relevant to audit requirements for sufficient evidence to support conclusions and recommendations. If access to such records is denied, the procedures in CAM 1-206.3(e) [now CAM 1-504.3] become operative, i.e., all costs to which the records are relevant should be suspended if allocated to cost-reimbursement contracts, otherwise the costs should be questioned. Following that action, the procedural sequence in CAM 1-206.3(f) through (1) [now CAM 1-504.3] should be pursued.

If an audit report is required on costs affected by the access denial, and the costs are significant, an adverse summary opinion would be appropriate. For example, in a pricing proposal review, the summary opinion should state, "Therefore, we do not consider the proposal to be acceptable as a basis for negotiation of a price ..." (CAM 10-302.3(b)(10)) [now CAM 10-304.3].

Access to contractor records related to unclaimed costs arises as a requirement in the audit of compliance with Cost Accounting Standard 405, "Accounting for Unallowable Costs," which of course has been incorporated in all contracts subject to DAR Section 15, Part 2 [now FAR Part 31] cost principles. It is not possible to test compliance with provisions in this standard dealing with "directly associated costs" unless the auditor is permitted to examine at least a sample of unclaimed costs. Complete denial of those records should result in suspension or questioning of all costs which may be associated with unclaimed costs. For example, costs of accountants and attorneys claimed as overhead or G&A may be directly associated with expresssly unallowable organization costs. Thus, those costs may not be accepted for payment by the Government without sufficient evidence to assure the auditor that unclaimed costs do not represent organization costs in which the accountants and attorneys were directly involved. In requesting access to contractor records related to unclaimed costs, the auditor should emphasize that the records are required for tests of costs which are claimed.

Access to Records by Subpoena

As discussed in some detail in Chapter II of this text, DCAA had been auditing the Westinghouse Electric Corporation for almost 20 years, and its military department predecessor audit agency for many years before then, and examinations had apparently been adequately protecting the government's interests. In 1984, however, DCAA somehow concluded that it could not perform a satisfactory audit without access to all of the company's internal audit reports, working papers and related documents. When Westinghouse refused this extraordinary access demand, DCAA, although its officials had been assuring industry that it would never resort to this measure, requested the DOD IG to subpoena these records. Westinghouse contested this subpoena, but a court ruled that the DOD IG's subpoena authority was just about limitless and ruled in its favor.

DCAA used the threat of a DOD IG subpoena with other contractors until it obtained its own subpoena authority in P.L. 99-145. Thereafter it demanded and obtained access to internal audit reports and related documents, budgets, board of director minutes, federal and state income tax returns, and other data, regardless of their remoteness or applicability to contract costs, by the use of its own subpoena power or the threat to use it.

DCAA continued to invade contractors' privacy rights until it encountered a contractor strong enough to contest it. After the Westinghouse ruling, Newport News entered into an agreement with the DOD IG to submit its internal audit material for the years 1983-1985, which the DOD IG had demanded on behalf of DCAA. Flexing its muscles after obtaining its own subpoena authority, DCAA then demanded these documents prepared after January 1, 1986. The contractor refused, DCAA resorted to its subpoena power, which was likewise contested, and the Department of Justice stepped in to enforce it. At least for the time being, DCAA's unrestrained assault on contractors' records came to a grinding halt when a court found that the company's internal audit reports were proprietary, their disclosure would diminish the effectiveness of the internal audits, and DCAA's requirements were limited to data on the internal audit department's payroll and other expenses, which the contractor had already furnished. DCAA's subpoena power was seen as not as broad as the DOD IG's. *U.S. v. Newport News Shipbuilding and Dry Dock Co.*, DC EVA Misc. No. 87-5-NN, 3/20/87; *Newport News Shipbuilding and Dry Dock Co. v. William H. Reed et al.*, DC EVA CA No. 86-182-NN, 3/20/87 [34 CCF ¶ 75,294].

Although DCAA could have again requested DOD IG's help, it would have cast a deep shadow on the agency's prized "independence" and its own subpoena authority, and meant that the same kind of action would need to be repeated every time a contractor denied access to such records to DCAA. Accordingly, DCAA requested that the Department of Justice appeal the court's ruling and it consented.

The DOD IG on DCAA Reporting of Fraud

Among reports on oversight reviews of DCAA was one on Reporting of Fraud and Illegal Acts. The report was issued on March 9, 1984 (No. APO 84-4). The Inspector General was essentially pleased with DCAA's efforts in this area, noting:

> ... DCAA had undertaken some significant initiatives to increase the awareness of its auditors to contractor fraud. These initiatives included the preparation of a correspondence training course on fraud; assignment of a senior auditor on a full time basis to the Defense Procurement Fraud Unit; inclusion of articles on fraud in the DCAA monthly newsletter to its employees; and publication of fraud indicators for defective pricing audits. Also, DCAA plans to publish pamphlets on audit fraud cases that will describe the manner in which the fraud was committed and the audit techniques used to detect the fraud. Further, DCAA had entered into a memorandum of understanding with DoD investigative agencies on the referral of fraud cases and audit assistance for fraud investigations. *This increased emphasis on fraud awareness has undoubtedly contributed to an increase in fraud referrals.* During the last 6 months, DCAA referred 59 potential fraud cases to DoD investigative agencies. This compared with 46 cases for the preceding 12 months. (Emphasis added.)

Although generally satisfied, the IG made several recommendations which he believed would enable DCAA to do even better. The recommendations were directed at speeding up fraud referrals to investigative agencies and improving the reporting system "to control and monitor the processing of fraud reports" to assure that none fall through the cracks.

DOD IG HANDBOOKS ON FRAUD INDICATORS

In addition to its active schedule of investigations in all DOD operations, frequent testimonies before congressional committees, and meetings with DOD personnel at all levels, the OIG has published a wide range of formal and informal directives, memoranda, handbooks and other material. Its series of handbooks on fraud indicators in defense procurement has been of considerable interest, both within DOD and in the private sector, and has also generated considerable controversy.

Indicators of Fraud in Department of Defense Procurement

Initially published in June 1984, the above-titled handbook was revised and expanded in June 1987. Excerpts and analysis of this publication are contained in Appendix 1 of this text.

Handbook on Labor Fraud Indicators

The second handbook in this series, published in August 1985, is cited at length in Appendix 2 of this text.

Handbook on Fraud Indicators: Material

The third handbook, cited in Appendix 3 of this text, was published in July 1986.

Handbook on Scenarios of Potential Defective Pricing Fraud

Increasing its pace, the DOD IG published the fourth handbook in this series in December 1986. See Appendix 4 of this text.

All of the handbooks have been criticized for suggesting that most accounting, administrative, clerical and other errors committed by contractors should be considered as potential fraud. To the extent that these handbooks are closely followed by many DCAA auditors, observers have pointed out that the DOD OIG has been inappropriately transforming conventional contract auditing to investigating with an undue emphasis on fraud detection. As we have noted previously, these handbooks are from audit guides and are published, in their words, to encourage the contract auditors to "think fraud." The fact that so many contract auditors are strongly influenced by the guidance in these handbooks establishes the need for a knowledge of their contents by companies doing business with the government.

We advise our clients who perform on contracts with the government, particularly DOD and NASA, to incorporate all or appropriate sections of these handbooks into their own internal audit and administrative control publications, and to conduct training courses to assure that appropriate employees are fully familiar with their contents.

PRESIDENT'S COUNCIL ON INTEGRITY AND EFFICIENCY (PCIE)

Our comments regarding federal inspectors general have focused on the DOD OIG because it was created in controversy and has conducted its activities in controversy. This office has also been the most active of the OIGs and has achieved considerable publicity in the communications media through its allegations before congressional committees and in its reports. Some indications of the efforts of the other IGs can be gained by reviewing their individual semiannual reports or the semiannual summary reports prepared by the President's Council on Integrity and Efficiency.

The PCIE has a membership of 23, headed by the Deputy Director of the OMB and including the IGs of the Departments of Agriculture, Commerce, Defense, Education, Energy, Health and Human Services, Housing and Urban Development, Interior, State, Transportation and Treasury, and the following independent agencies: U.S. Agency for International Development, Environmental Protection Agency, General Services Administration, National Aeronautics and Space Administration, Office of Personnel Management, Small Business Administration and Veterans Administration. The Department of Justice is the only federal department that has not been required to establish an Office of Inspector General but it furnishes two members on the Council: Deputy Attorney General, and the Executive Assistant for Investigations, Federal Bureau of Investigation.

Each IG issues a semiannual report and the PCIE issues semiannual reports consolidating and presenting highlights of the individual IG reports. Additionally, as in 1987, the PCIE issues progress reports containing recapitulations and highlights of the accomplishments since its inception in April 1981. An excerpt from this report illustrates the activities of the PCIE, as distinguished from those of the individual IGs:

> The PCIE operates through its standing committees which represent the major emphases of the Inspector General community. Current committees include Audit, Computer, Inspections and Special Reviews, Investigations/Law Enforcement, Legislation, Prevention, Standards and Training. The Council initiates projects with Government-wide scope and application after extensive planning and review of past work of individual members, congressional interests, management initiatives and General Accounting Office reports. The Council also initiates special activities designed to increase professional quality and expertise and share information on proven tools and techniques. The Council is currently involved in over 30 projects in the priority areas of improved loan, cash and financial management systems; effective use of investigative techniques and civil fraud remedies; increased controls in automated information systems; and maintenance of trained and qualified professional staff.

Under highlights of OIG achievements for 1981-1986, the report lists:

> Extensive auditing and automation enhancements are being brought to bear on cash and financial management practices in the government.

Federal agencies are focusing resources on loan program collections and efficiencies.

Increased reliance by the government on civil remedies to sanction fraudulent contractors and others doing business with the government.

Increased use of information technology on the way the government runs its business.

Savings

The report asserts that savings of $84 billion is attributed to the work of the IGs, beginning with $5.5 billion in the six-month reporting period in 1981 and reaching a peak of $20 billion in fiscal year 1986. The $84 billion includes "9.6 billion in recoveries and restitutions arising from Inspector General findings, $.7 billion in investigative recoveries, and $73.7 billion in savings and avoidance of unnecessary expenditures." The latter amount was questioned by Congress and GAO when difficulties arose in tracing these amounts to actual budgetary savings or appropriation reductions. This is the same problem encountered in evaluating the "savings" asserted by DCAA each year, especially in its preaward audits.

Prosecutions

Successful civil and criminal prosecutions is another area where statistics are tabulated and the total, boasted as having been recommended by the IGs, working independently or with other agencies, is stated to be 18,601, beginning with 1,059 in 1981 and reaching the highest annual number of 4,094 in 1986.

Sanctions

The other major statistic trumpeted by this report asserts that 6,118 debarment and suspension actions have been taken against contractors or grantees who do business with the federal government. Here again, the numbers increase each year, beginning with 502 in 1982, the first year in which such data was accumulated, and totaling 2,047 in 1986.

Reported Accomplishments by Other OIGs

Department of Education estimated about $17 million in potential savings from better use of funds and program improvements as a result of education loan reviews.

Department of Commerce has obtained commitments to save $58 million in actions on defaulted business loans, suits against banks allegedly negligent in administering federal guaranteed loans, etc.

Improvements to the single family mortgage insurance program by HUD has resulted in cash recoveries of $3.4 million and additional potential savings of $4.6 million.

Department of Health and Human Services reports estimated savings of about $8 billion in various health programs.

Veterans Administration does not report an estimated savings figure but lists various actions resulting from its audits that have enhanced medical care to veterans.

Department of Health and Human Services recovered $27 million in fines and penalties against health providers involved in fraudulent activities during their participation in Medicare and Medicaid programs.

The DHHS OIG also estimated savings of about $240 million annually by improvements in the Social Security Administration's accounting and related methods under which SSA continued payments after death.

Department of Labor OIG disallowed $28 million in fraudulent and otherwise improper unemployment payments by states, of which $9 million was recovered to date and over 1,000 convictions obtained.

Department of Agriculture OIG investigations into the food stamp program over the past five years has resulted in 4,100 indictments, 3,500 convictions, and over $20 million in combined recoveries, savings, collections, fines and claims.

Potential savings of about $142 million were estimated by the Department of Energy OIG as a result of efficiencies recommended.

Department of Interior OIG audits identified over $131 million in additional gas and oil royalties owed the government, of which $47 million had been collected.

The Environmental Protection Agency IG believed that almost half a billion dollars were wasted on faulty projects in Puerto Rico.

OIG audits in the Small Business Administration resulted in $190 million in investment funds denied and recovered.

The Department of Labor OIG was instrumental in the collection of $270 million from job program closeouts.

The Department of Energy OIG concluded that more effective cash management could increase revenues by $245 million.

The DHHS OIG reported that cash management improvements in the Social Security Administration has increased the interest-earning potential of its trust funds by $1.33 billion annually.

IMPACT OF FEDERAL INSPECTORS GENERAL

There can be no valid objection to the federal government departments and agencies establishing effective administrative and accounting controls to enhance economy, efficiency, and integrity in carrying out their mission responsibilities. An essential feature of such controls is the provision of auditors, inspectors, investigators, and the like, who should conduct logically planned reviews of their agencies' policies, procedures, and practices to determine if, in fact, the operations are carried out in the manner intended.

There do not appear to be any activities of the kind mentioned above that were not being carried out prior to the enactment of the Inspector General Act of 1978; indeed, most of these activities had been routinely performed for many years prior to the enactment of this statute. Questions regarding the effectiveness with which such activities were carried out in the past do not yield uniform or easy answers, and one can conclude that it would depend on the quality of the people performing these functions, the adequacy of their staffs, and the degree of acceptance of and compliance with their legitimate recommendations. All of these factors will continue to influence the effectiveness of the audits, inspections, and investigations now largely consolidated in each agency under an inspector general whose top staff will generally include an assistant IG for audits and an assistant IG for investigations. Larger OIGs such as the one in the Defense Department have larger and more elaborate organizational arrangements.

Arguments as to whether the consolidation of each agency's audit, inspection, investigation and related activities would provide a more effective function are academic today in view of the enacted legislation. However, a very important problem identified by many observers is the extensive and intensive pressure upon the OIGs to report fraud, waste, and abuse, and take credit for criminal and civil prosecution, suspensions, debarments and monetary recoveries. Congressional and other critics who are convinced, or assert they are convinced, that these irregularities are rampant, have asserted that IGs who do not report such matters or who do not report such matters in sufficient volume may not be meeting their responsibilities. This attitude, unfortunately, tends to create an environment in which some of the IGs seem to be stretching to report fraud, waste, and abuse.

In this regard we found relevant an article in the October 1986 issue of the *Journal of Accountancy*, the official publication of the American Institute of Certified Public Accountants, by Arthur Lodge, from which the following is excerpted:

> Among the many ideas considered for the 1986 tax bill was one for establishing a multibillion dollar trust fund out of revenues to finance more intensive Internal Revenue Service enforcement activities. That one was rejected, much to the gratification of tax practitioners concerned about what the public perception of our tax system would be if there appeared to be a connection between the tax collector's zeal and his continued employment.
>
> The IRS, it would seem, has enough of a public relations problem without being looked upon as a bunch of bounty hunters. And, if the plan were to work for the tax collector, what would prevent other government agencies from helping to fund *their* operations by leaning on those in the private sector subject to their jurisdiction? (Emphasis in original.)

Unfortunately, the IRS has indeed been viewed as a bounty hunter as the Service's requests for larger appropriations and personnel authorizations have been supported by claims that each additional dollar appropriated for its operations will bring in X dollars of additional revenues by tax collections. But these claims are mild compared to the trumpeted "savings" by the IGs, together with prosecutions, suspensions, debarments, etc. These organizations, with the DOD IG far in front, have helped fund *their* operations "by leaning on those in the private (and public) sector(s) subject to their jurisdiction."

The IGs are certainly not alone. In its 1985 annual report, GAO boasted of alleged savings to the taxpayers of $11 billion, or $37 for each dollar of operating the agency. Although below DCAA's more creative assertion of saving taxpayers $60 for each dollar of operations, GAO's assertion, if valid, would be persuasive of the need to fund that agency, as are the claims of DCAA and the IGs to fund those agencies.

CHAPTER XXVII

FRAUD, WASTE, AND ABUSE

INTRODUCTION

It is a sad commentary indeed that a chapter on fraud, waste, and abuse has become a requirement in a text focusing essentially on accounting and administrative aspects of government contracts. We did refer to this ominous phrase in our Seventh Edition. However, the coverage accorded this subject was relatively brief, and in the six prior editions, the specific attention was insufficient to merit reference in the tables of content or indices. The prior (Eighth) edition was the first in which an entire chapter was devoted to this topic.

As discussed elsewhere in this text, most of the federal OIGs are organized with an assistant IG for audit and an assistant IG for investigations. The audit component, in turn, is divided into internal audit, with responsibility for reviewing the activities of the agency involved, and contract audit, responsible for examining the books and records of the agency's contractors and grantees. DOD alone departs from this organizational pattern in that its contract auditing is performed by DCAA, a separate organization reporting to the Assistant Secretary of Defense (Comptroller). As discussed in Chapter II, the question of whether DCAA should be incorporated into the DOD OIG surfaced early on and it was ultimately decided that it should remain outside that office. The relevant point of DCAA's organizational placement in terms of this chapter is the effect of these debates on that audit agency's attitude on fraud, waste, and abuse. Conscious and subconscious pressures, internal and external, continue to motivate the DOD contract auditors to devote increasing effort to detecting and reporting upon allegations of fraud in procurement.

As reviewed later in this chapter, on July 15, 1985, the President appointed a Blue Ribbon Commission on Defense Management, which became known as the "Packard Commission" after its chairman, David Packard. Operating with a broad charter, the Commission issued a series of reports beginning in February 1986.

One of the significant areas addressed by the Commission was "Industry Accountability: Contractor Self-Governance." While recognizing that charges of fraud in defense procurement were exaggerated, leading to distorted public perception, the Commission recommended that industry improve its accountability by self-governance in a number of ways described in their report. The Commission also recommended a program of voluntary disclosure of irregularities by defense contractors, provided the government offered some incentives for such disclosures and provided further that the heavy-handed and redundant government surveillance and oversight be restrained to permit contractors to accomplish this program.

DOD moved quickly to encourage voluntary disclosure but placed the term "voluntary" in some doubt by promulgating regulations and contract clauses requiring various disclosures. DOD and the Department of Justice were slower by far in formulating any incentives for voluntary disclosures such as modification of criminal prosecution. As to restraining the overzealous and duplicative surveillance and oversight of defense contractors, virtually no substantive action has been taken by DOD at this writing.

POPULARITY OF SUBJECT IN SEMINARS, MEETINGS, AND PERIODICALS

After a brief period in the White House, President John F. Kennedy was asked at a press conference what he thought of the press coverage of his administration. JFK replied: "I'm reading more and enjoying it less." His feelings may well describe the reactions of many in both the private and public sectors as we read (and hear) the increasing torrent of allegations and threats by certain government officials concerning the three words, frequently rolled into one: fraud, waste, and abuse. The stepped up rhetoric and activities have understandably generated considerable interest and concern, particularly among government contractors and their accounting and legal advisors, and propelled this subject to center stage.

Over the years, various topics have vied for attention at meetings of industry and professional associations whose members share an interest in government procurement. In the early 1980s, panel discussions and presentations on fraud, waste, and abuse have clearly predominated. This subject has been similarly featured in periodicals published by such associations. The intensification of this attention has been abetted by the ready availability of government officials to participate as speakers and panelists. Representatives of the Departments of Justice and Defense have been frequently heard and, of course, to provide a balance, program directors of the various associations invite attorneys and accountants from the private sector who are known to be actively engaged in these areas.

Such industry groups as the National Security Industrial Association (NSIA), Aerospace Industries Association (AIA), and Electronic Industries Association (EIA), and professional associations such as the National Contract Management Association, American Bar Association, Federal Bar Association, and Association of Government Accountants are but a few of the organizations which have devoted evenings and days to this subject. A joint effort by Fordham University School of Law and Legal Times developed a two-day seminar, given once on the east coast and once on the west coast, where some 25 speakers and panelists concentrated on fraud in government procurement. The participants included many of the well-known accountants and attorneys of the Departments of Defense and Justice, on the staffs of government contractors, and in private practice. Attendees received an 800-page volume containing presentations by the speakers and panelists, both during the two-day seminars and on prior occasions. The interest in this area was further manifested by an arrangement entered into by Totaltape Publishing under which the entire two-day proceedings were made available in cassette and printed form.

Despite the generally restrained commentaries by the government officials at the various meetings, many representatives of the private sector in attendance experience a chilling effect after hearing what appears to be a lack of perspective on the part of the government speakers in conjecturing on the proportions of the incidence of fraud in federal procurement, and in their belief that ever-increasing detection efforts and penalties and punishment are required. It is shocking, for example, to hear and read official opinions by highly placed government people that increased defense procurement *ipso facto* translates into increased fraud—it is there, they seem to be saying, and the job of the Justice Department lawyers and the Defense Department investigators, inspectors and auditors is to ferret it out and bring the perpetrators to trial.

The interest in, and concerns about, this subject continued but its high incidence as a topic in seminars, meetings, and periodicals was just about beginning to wane when the Packard Commission reports were issued in 1986, followed by DOD's vigorous efforts to persuade contractors to voluntarily disclose irregularities. The legal and other concerns over what began as a totally one-sided program, in effect involuntary voluntary disclosures, revived interest in this area in professional and industry meetings and periodicals.

THE ROLE OF THE JUSTICE DEPARTMENT

The disproportionate and sometimes seemingly irrational concentration on fraud in defense procurement has been a matter of much concern to everyone in the private sector involved in selling to the military departments. While GAO was forced to report that only a small percentage of alleged fraud it disclosed was in defense procurement, it emphasized that the increasing size of the defense budget in the early 1980s offered possibilities for large losses through fraud. This kind of thinking, unfortunately, was also voiced by DOD and DOJ officials to justify the increasing diversion of people to fraud detection and prosecution.

It is interesting to note, in this regard, that DOJ officials had made themselves increasingly available to participate in meetings of professional and business associations, as speakers and panelists. On February 4, 1983, for example, Assistant Attorney General Richard A. Sauber addressed the American Bar Association's Public Contract Law Section. His presentation was designed "to explain the background of the Department of Justice's interest in government procurement fraud including defense procurement, and the programs we have instituted at the Department of Justice to increase the Department's much needed sophistication and expertise to the complex problems of both investigation and prosecution in this area." Why were these programs being instituted and emphasized? Had DOJ uncovered many significant increases of fraud? No, the speaker noted that there had been a significant increase in defense related procurement and this trend was likely to continue, from which he concluded: "When overall government procurement—and defense procurement in particular—reaches these levels, the American public, and those of us with enforcement responsibilities, have a particular responsibility to focus on the potential for fraud." We thus find the DOJ official echoing GAO's non sequitur.

Let's consider further the Assistant Attorney General's comments:

It is a regrettable fact that the procurement process, despite the dedicated efforts of honorable and hardworking officials in the government and by representatives in the private sector, *is vulnerable to fraud and corruption.* As a consequence, even though the overwhelming majority of government contractors are honest, ethical and competent, it is also true that a very small number of wasteful or fraudulent transactions *are capable of inflicting enormous losses.* Moreover, because these losses can be measured in the millions of dollars, the American public demands that we assure them we are doing our best to eliminate fraud in defense procurement in general. (Emphasis added.)

In an effort to suggest that DOJ's concern with procurement fraud "is not a new phenomenon," he pointed to the I.G. Act of 1978, and congressional, GAO and media allegations of white collar crime. He then boasted that his department had secured 1,000 convictions in three years based on fraud in the housing industry uncovered by DOJ and HUD. He did not explain how these findings related to defense procurement.

With regard to the Defense Department, he believed the new DOD Office of Inspector General "will provide the necessary leadership that is critical to the detection and investigation of fraud and corruption which is tainting the procurement process and at times can frustrate the natural objectives in the defense area." He then addressed the DOD/DOJ Procurement Fraud Unit:

And what kind of a response does the new fraud unit represent? The Unit exists to insure that the Justice Department's response over the long term will be measured and consistent with a variety of enforcement and policy objectives of the United States. A major interest of the Unit is the successful detection, investigation, and prosecuting of matters which seriously obstruct the integrity of the procurement process—bidrigging, inflated claims, internal mischarging, inflated progress payments, falsified inspection reports, and the corruption of government personnel.

The Unit also exists to insure that the criminal process fits—that is, the allegation warrants use of the criminal remedy not because of any hoopla but because the conduct is criminal in nature. Cases will be continually reviewed when they are opened and as they are investigated and prosecuted to insure that other remedies designed to deal with contracting problems are not more suitable. To achieve this objective we have staffed the Unit not only with experienced prosecutors from the Criminal Division and the United States Attorneys Office in the Eastern District of Virginia but with lawyers from the Civil Division and from DOD—attorneys who are experienced in the civil and administrative processes as well as the broad range of the contract law and regulation issues that arise in these cases. We expect that this concentration of manpower and staffing of *experienced* government attorneys will set a higher standard within both Departments, a standard which demands that, given our limited resources, only the proper cases are investigated, with sensitivity to procurement practices and realities, and that we always consider civil and administrative implications and alternatives. (Emphasis in original).

Near the close of his prepared remarks, the speaker apparently thought it appropriate to recognize "the critical need for a partnership between the Defense Department and the procurement industry" but hastened to add that "some of the very arrangements which reflect the partnership relationship are those areas which in our view are the most susceptible to the public perception of the existence of fraud and corruption—imprecise definitions of allowable overhead and research and development reimbursement principles, self-certification of contract compliance, self-inspection procedures, fast payment programs and the like all designed with trust in the basic honesty of the contractor as a major premise, but subject to potential, and unfortunately in some cases actual abuse."

For another in the lengthy series of public appearances by DOJ officials to discuss the Department's preoccupation with fraud in procurement, we refer to an address in May 1984 by the Assistant Attorney General, Criminal Division, Stephen S. Trott, before a conference on government contracts sponsored by the Bureau of National Affairs and the Federal Bar Association in Washington, D.C.

The address contained the now-familiar references to the increases in defense-related procurement offered as a rational (or irrational) basis for intensified efforts by the Justice and Defense Departments to detect possible fraud. As an industry representative at that conference noted, however, although there have been no statistics furnished to demonstrate an increase in defense procurement fraud in the last five years, the manpower devoted by the government to detect such fraud has risen astronomically.

According to the DOJ official, it was about five years ago that his department became "concerned with the effectiveness of our procurement system and the coordination of criminal investigations." Congressional testimony by that department in those days asserted "that there were substantial problems in the Defense Department with the detection of criminal fraud matters and continuing difficulties with the referral of those cases to the Justice Department."

The speaker alleged that his department found "contracting officers and auditors who did not know what contract fraud was . . . . We found over 3,000 investigators and 5,000 auditors at the Department of Defense with little or no training in white collar crime investigation and no leadership within Defense to direct that otherwise sizeable resource." He noted that "at the same time, the Defense Department was complaining that the Department of Justice was not adequately supporting it through prosecution of cases referred." He was quite critical of DOD, alleging that, at that time, "except for the Defense Logistics Agency, (DOD procurement offices) had almost never debarred or suspended a contractor despite cases of substantial evidence of fraudulent conduct."

With considerable enthusiasm, the speaker asserted that "much progress has been made in the past five years, and we are literally in a new era with respect to our efforts against procurement fraud." He identified as significant events in this process the creation of the offices of inspectors general to train people and emphasize fraud detection, the "revitalization of the debarment and suspension remedy," which he alleged had been underutilized in the past, the creation of the DOD Fraud Procurement Unit in the Fraud Section of the Criminal Division, "a revamping of the enforcement relationships between" DOD and DOJ, and intensification of efforts in significant areas that he alleged were "heretofore ignored." Three examples of such areas identified by the speaker were mischarging, defective pricing ("even more recently discovered"), and "subtle abuses in the bidding process where control over certain defense contracts are used to intimidate small contractors from bidding against corporate giants."

As have other DOJ speakers, he claimed that "the people of the United States expect this emphasis on fraud detection." However, he tried to allay the apprehensions of many people involved in the procurement process about the overemphasis on fraud detection by asserting that the total personnel available for these efforts within the federal government is limited, culmination of successful prosecution is frequently a lengthy matter, only the relatively few "cases most deserving treatment" are selected, and Justice Department policies and procedures "require the prosecutor to conclude not just that probable cause exists to initiate a prosecution but that he be able to obtain and sustain a conviction."

Looking ahead, the speaker saw the solution for the predetermined but not demonstrated existence of rampant procurement fraud as a "balanced but aggressive use of all our resources and remedies." The "government response" should not be limited to criminal prosecution but should include "aggressive use of civil and administrative remedies," of which he emphasized increased use of suspension and debarment. He favored "making the contract auditor part of the Inspector General's office, arming the contract auditor with subpoena power, and criminal penalties for obstructing the audit." Inasmuch as all of the civilian departments' and agencies' contract auditors are already within their respective IG organizations, he could have reference only to incorporating DCAA into the DOD IG. This point was clarified in the speaker's response to a question from the floor regarding his views on the pros and cons of such action in DOD. He saw advantages of better training and communication emanating from the consolidation and no disadvantages.

The Department of Justice also has a major role in establishing incentives for contractor voluntary disclosure. This subject is more effectively addressed in its totality, which we have done later in this chapter.

Justice Department Economic Crime Council (ECC)

The ECC was established in 1983 as yet another activity dedicated to detection of white collar crime and initially identified defense procurement and health care benefits as the two areas requiring most attention. It concluded, apparently based on the extent of procurement fraud it believes to exist rather than on actual convictions, that defense procurement should be the major area for concentration. A widely circulated draft ECC report recommends that the Attorney General "reaffirm defense contracting as a top white collar crime priority, and enlist active cooperation from the FBI and Secretary of Defense."

The ECC points with pride to the Justice Department's own efforts, such as creating the Defense Procurement Fraud Unit (DPFU), which "provides significant leadership in this enforcement area." According to the ECC, "in addition to investigating and prosecuting highly complex cases, the Unit serves as a centralized case-screening mechanism, helps develop training programs, and provides case-handling expertise." Among the other results DOJ's Criminal Division boasts about is that "the U.S. Attorneys are receiving and handling an increasing number of referrals. Two United States Attorneys have established within their offices units devoted exclusively to prosecuting defense fraud."

The ECC notes the burgeoning activities in DOD and DOJ and believes that as a result of its efforts, the "overall level of criminal enforcement in defense contracting has increased significantly." However, far from being satisfied, it alleges that "because the current level of referrals appears to be miniscule in relation to the level of suspected criminal fraud, we wish to encourage DOD to continue to upgrade its ability to generate high-quality referrals."

Convinced, without offering proof of any basis for its conviction, that procurement fraud is rampant, ECC asserts that "the number of significant cases referred by the Defense Department to either the DPFU or the U.S. Attorneys remains alarmingly low."

Addressing DCAA, the Economic Crime Council begins with a mild pat on the back of the audit agency, noting that it has "increased its criminal referrals from 29 in 1982 to 119 in 1984." This quadruple increase, however, does little to satisfy the zealous DOJ officials. In what some observers believe to constitute ignorance on the part of the ECC relating to DCAA's operations, and others suspect it is simply distorting of data, the Council notes that DCAA issued 61,000 reports in 1984 and asserts that "119 referrals from 61,000 reports is still inadequate."

DCAA reports, of course, are issued as a result of a variety of audits and desk reviews. In many instances the nature and scope of review are limited to certain specific objectives, which would make fraud detection a virtual impossibility. In these circumstances, and in the light of its failure to demonstrate the existence of any great amount of undetected fraud, ECC's efforts to relate DCAA's fraud referrals to reports issued by the agency, and thereby seek to place additional pressure on the contract auditors to further efforts in this area have been widely deplored.

ECC's criticisms of DCAA is not limited to the "inadequate" number of referrals. "Moreover," carps the DOJ Unit, "quantity tells only part of the story. Historically, only a small portion of DCAA referrals have resulted in prosecutions, usually because the referrals lacked criminal potential." According to ECC then, DCAA does not refer enough cases of suspected fraud and most of the referrals made do not result in prosecutions. A conclusion could be logically drawn from these complaints that procurement fraud is not really rampant, but this is not the conclusion drawn by ECC. Having predetermined that considerable fraud exists and requires only better effort to detect it, the DOJ Unit has several suggestions.

Despite DCAA's established mission to provide accounting advice to contracting officers in the award, administration and settlement of contracts, the ECC, preoccupied with its single-minded thirst for fraud detection, would have the audit agency give priority "to auditing contracts with the greatest fraud potential." Does this mean that DCAA should reverse its emphasis and give priority to auditing costs incurred under a $100,000 contract where someone may suspect fraud over reviewing a $1 billion pricing proposal on an urgently needed major weapons system?

Another suggestion involving a revision of DCAA's mission would have "DOD upgrade its auditing capabilities by developing an elite corps of DCAA auditors, comparable to the IRS special agents, specifically trained to detect fraud." ECC does accord some recognition to the large number of people in the office of the DOD IG and the military services specifically assigned to this area. However, it apparently looks longingly at the large number of DCAA auditors continuously reviewing contractors' records and dreams how fraud detection might multiply if the contract auditors were better trained in, and developed more effort to, this area.

ECC is quite unhappy with the work of the Defense Criminal Investigation Service (DCIS), created to investigate large or complex cases, now a part of the DOD OIG, finding that "the limited number of referrals two years after DCIS's creation has been reason for concern." This view, of course, is based on the same presumption that procurement fraud is rampant and there would be more and "better" referrals if only the various DOD agencies assigned more people to this area and such people performed more effectively.

ECC is also unhappy about the the high cost of investigating and prosecuting fraud where even in instances when the government has been "successful," the costs sometimes exceed the amount of money recovered. This concerns the DOJ Unit because they fear it "may create a disincentive to thoroughly investigate and prosecute complex cases." But, ECC has suggestions in this area too, essentially by requiring contractors to foot the bill, regardless of whether they are proven innocent, guilty, or a compromise accord is reached. The extent of illogic and unfairness of this ECC Unit is reflected in its recommendation that FAR 31.105-47 be revised to disallow contractors' attorneys' fees and other costs generated as a result of a criminal investigation, *regardless of the outcome.*

We visualize a scenario where overzealous government people, prodded into a numbers game to demonstrate increasing fraud detections and prosecutions, allege fraud by a contractor without reasonable basis, and spend years in an unsuccessful effort to convict the company and/or its officials. After the contractor expends large sums of money in a successful defense against unreasonable government accusations, such expenditures would not even be considered necessary expenses and appropriately recoverable.

The ECC group has another suggestion to reduce government cost of prosecution to assure that such costs might not inhibit government people from vigorously pursuing prosecution. The DOJ suggested that either through FAR or statute, the government should be permitted to recover all of its investigation costs "in cases resulting in successful prosecution of a contractor." (Without regulatory or statutory provision, this practice is now generally followed.)

The need for greater consideration to punitive action available through the application of the False Claims Act is strongly urged by the ECC. It laments recent decisions by the U.S. Supreme Court which inhibit DOJ practices of passing leads among its civil and criminal attorneys but notes with hope the possibilities which may become available if a proposed "Procurement Fraud Enforcement Act of 1985" drafted by that Department is enacted. In the meantime, the Council recommends increased emphasis to the orientation and training of DOD criminal investigators in obtaining civil recoveries. ECC urges that no stone be left unturned to effect maximum coordination within the limitations established by the Supreme Court.

Concerned that small fraud recoveries are not pursued because the cost would exceed such recoveries, ECC recommends that DOJ support the creation of a civil money penalties remedy.

The ECC is pleased that the military departments have been more aggressive in recent years in pursuing suspension and debarment and supports governmentwide debarment. It cautions, however, that "an inflexible application of the automatic debarment policy may create a disincentive for major government contractors to negotiate settlements of their wrong-doings."

The ECC report closes by conceding some progress by DOD and DOJ "in their enforcement efforts against defense contracting fraud." However, it believes such efforts should be increased and "(a)bove all, expansion of these programs should not be hampered by lack of diversion of resources."

The one-upmanship efforts in this area feature the vigorous competition among federal agencies to report alleged fraud referrals to DOJ, controversies over the accuracy of the related statistics and over whether the many instances where accused companies are not convicted is attributable to the "quality" of the referrals or the inadequate actions by DOJ. One point stands out clearly: government contractors, particularly those supplying this country's defense capabilities, are squeezed in the middle of the bureaucratic competition for trumpeting fraud, competition further prodded by GAO and some congressional elements.

THE ROLE OF THE GENERAL ACCOUNTING OFFICE (GAO)

For a number of years GAO was the leading government agency in alleging fraud, waste, and abuse. Although it has not often uncovered substantial instances of fraud, it does accord prominence to those it encounters. In recent years, the executive department inspectors general and the Justice Department have concentrated their efforts so heavily in this area that there appears to be very little left for GAO to report. When this agency does find indications of fraud or potential fraud, the reports are frequently embellished by describing the findings as "just the tip of the iceberg," and warning that if the disclosures are in any way typical, total losses in the government could reach astronomical proportions.

In 1981, feeling a need to move beyond reporting on the occasional incidents of proven or alleged fraud it discovered, GAO embarked on a statistical analysis of over 77,000 cases of fraud and other illegal activities reported by 21 federal agencies during the two-and-a-half year period October 1, 1976 through March 31, 1979. The results of this analysis were published in three reports over a six-month period from May to November 1981, with the titles: "Fraud in Government Programs:—How Extensive Is It?—How Can It Be Controlled?"

A few of GAO's headline-type comments are quoted below:

"Fraud against Government programs is widespread. It undermines the integrity of Federal programs and makes people lose confidence in public institutions.

". . . controls over Federal programs are often inadequate, nonexistent, or ignored.

"Most fraud is undetected . . . The sad truth is that crime against the Government often *does* pay."

GAO sought to highlight its findings by statistically projecting total losses based on the cases it reviewed. Furthermore, wrote the congressional watchdog, "These losses are only what is attributable to *known* fraud and illegal activities investigated by the Federal agencies in this study."

As noted earlier, GAO has not found much in the way of fraud to report upon in recent years because of the intensive activities in this area by various executive agencies. However, under a caption "Fraud in Government Programs," GAO reports that it recommended that Congress enact legislation "to allow agencies to assess civil monetary penalties against persons who defraud federal programs." And under the caption "Taking the Profit Out of Crime," the agency reports on its recommendations that Congress amend the criminal forfeiture provisions of the "Racketeer Influenced and Corrupt Organizations" (RICO) and "Continuing Criminal Enterprise" (CCE) statutes to facilitate government actions to seize monies and other assets from firms accused of violating such statutes.

Reporting on its numerous audits/investigations of the Defense Department, GAO lists reports alleging that the military departments and defense agencies could operate more efficiently by doing things in the manner suggested by the congressional watchdog agency. However, the annual report contains no major disclosures of fraud in defense procurement.

THE ROLE OF CONGRESS

Allegations of fraud, waste, and abuse made by the legislative branch of the government began with this nation's first Congress and have continued without interruption for over 200 years. However, members of both houses have displayed keen interest in these areas regardless of their party affiliation. Whether motivated by fervent desires to enhance integrity and efficiency in government operations, or seeking favorable publicity to display to their constituents, there are always some Senators or Representatives sponsoring investigations either by their committee staffs or GAO. And these investigations generate a relentless pressure upon the officials of the executive departments and agencies who spend many hours testifying before the various committees.

THE DEPARTMENT OF DEFENSE

Secretary of Defense Weinberger's substantial emphasis on the prevention of waste and abuse is illustrated by his addresses to the International Investors' Conference in October 1982 and the Federal Procurement and Trade Conference in July 1984.

Criticizing the "old, inefficient way the Pentagon did business," he told his audience in October 1982 of DOD efforts to curb contractors from buying-in and "to assure that estimates are honest." He spoke about the DOD organization created "to investigate any and all reports of waste, fraud and mismanagement." He lauded DOD cost principles that disallow contractors' expenditures in defending themselves against accusations of fraud and in dealing with governmental officials in the legislative and executive branches and stated: "We have made a good beginning in ferreting out waste, fraud and inefficiency, but much remains to be done and we mean to continue working for reform." Further to this point, the Secretary told his audience:

> Our reforms will not result in miracles overnight. *Waste and mismanagement have been built into the defense budget over many years,* and only the most vigilant attention to our acquisition, auditing and contracting procedures will eliminate every unnecessary dollar. But, make no mistake—the reforms have begun and they will continue. (Emphasis added).

In his public address in July 1984, the Secretary again devoted almost all of his remarks to the same area. Telling his audience that he was "eager to speak" about management reforms within DOD, he stated:

> Shortly after arriving at the Pentagon three years ago, I began fighting the battle against waste, fraud and inefficiency in defense business. I am still fighting. I knew then that it would not be easy to change bureaucratic practice—practice that needlessly boosted the prices of military equipment. But I am determined to succeed . . .

> Let me outline three objectives of our management strategy:

> First, to identify sources of inefficiency and corruption in the defense marketplace.

> Second, to apply smart business sense to military procurement.

> Third, to revise and vastly improve the defense contracts we inherited—contracts that required us to use one supplier for spare parts, or to pay the price set by the seller.

His speech continued with reports about how DOD, through its auditors, inspectors and investigators, has been and is continuing to uncover inefficiency and fraud, the close working together of DOD and the Justice Department, and so on. He boasted of an increase of 80% in suspensions and debarments.

Addressing the spare parts problem which has drawn such considerable attention in the Congress and the press, he complained that the "horror stories" uncovered mainly had their origins in DOD reports but ". . . the press rarely give us credit for uncovering those problems ourselves."

When the head of an organization displays a strong interest in a subject, his subordinates usually follow suit. As an example, the then Assistant Secretary of Defense (Comptroller) Vincent Puritano whose responsibilities include the Defense Contract Audit Agency, attended its "managers' conference" in the Spring of 1983 and delivered several "initiatives" for that agency. One would have DCAA "reevaluate its approach to potential defective pricing reviews to identify conditions which might be indicative of intent to defraud the government." Another would have DCAA "coordinate closely with the DOD Inspector General and with the Department of Justice in such efforts which would demonstrate a commitment to the President's program against fraud and waste."

The DOD Inspector General

Chapter XXVI of this text contains a review and analysis of the origins and current acitivities of federal inspectors general, with particular emphasis on the DOD IG, the largest and most visible of these offices. The reader's attention is invited to that chapter for a commentary of the DOD IG's role in detection of fraud, waste and abuse. For our purpose here, we would reiterate that under the statute establishing that office he would . . . "be the principal advisor to the Secretary of Defense for matters relating to the prevention and detection of fraud, waste and abuse in the programs and operations of the department . . .; provide policy direction for audits and investigations in the Department of Defense (including the military departments) that the Inspector General deems appropriate; provide policy direction for audits and investigations relating to fraud, waste and abuse and program effectiveness; [and] investigate fraud, waste and abuse uncovered as a result of other contract and internal audits, as the Inspector General deems appropriate . . . ."

Defense Contract Audit Agency (DCAA)

The policies and practices of DCAA are covered in Chapter II of this text. DCAA's activities in detecting fraud, waste and abuse, however, are covered only briefly in that chapter. We concluded that a more comprehensive commentary on this score would be more appropriate at this location so that the subject could be better viewed in context.

As any other audit organization, in or out of the government, DCAA has always been aware of fraud possibilities. However, again as most audit organizations, DCAA formerly recognized that the detection of fraud was not its major mission. The DOD contract audit agency was established to review and make recommendations concerning contractors' cost representations submitted in connection with proposed, ongoing, terminated and completed contracts. The philosophy and goals during the first decade of the agency's life were to assure that unallocable, unreasonable, or otherwise unallowable costs contained in contractors' representations were not reimbursed or reflected in contract prices. Beginning in the late 1970s and expanding in the 1980s, however, some of the contract auditors moved increasingly to investigate costs they believed to be questionable not only to recommend their disallowance but to determine whether a basis also existed for reporting possible fraud, or at least waste or abuse.

In part, DCAA's increasing attention to fraud comes from considerable prodding from outside the Agency. GAO consistently looks over DCAA's shoulder, particularly critizing the DOD auditors for not spending more effort on postaward audits in search of defective pricing.

In 1981, GAO issued its revised Standards for Audit of Governmental Organizations, Programs, Activities, and Functions. Although designed primarily for internal audits within the federal government, this publication states that these standards ". . . must be followed by federal auditors for audits of . . . funds received by contractors . . . ." On the basis of this statement, DCAA has adopted the GAO ground rules, including one of the major additions to the "standards" from the 1972 and 1974 editions, the seventh standard for government economy and efficiency audits: "Auditors shall: (1) be alert to situations or transactions that could be indicative of fraud, waste and illegal acts, and (2) if such evidence exists, extend audit steps and procedures to identify the effect on the entity's operations and programs."

In the legislative debates preceding the enactment of the Inspector General Act of 1978, DOD succeeded in obtaining congressional approval for a temporary exclusion. Thereafter, the various DOD investigation and audit agencies, including DCAA, expended considerable effort to demonstrate their dedication to detecting fraud. The semi-annual reports required by Congress contained extensive data regarding activities in this area and it was hoped that these reports would convince the lawmakers that a formal IG organization as envisioned by the 1978 law would not be required for DOD.

When these efforts failed, and the establishment of an Office of Inspector General (OIG) in the Defense Department became a certainty, considerable debate arose as to whether DCAA, in whole or in part, should be included in this new organization. Ever valuing its "independence," DCAA again increased its efforts to detect and report upon alleged fraud by contractors to demonstrate its dedication to this objective and to persuade Congress that it could achieve it without becoming incorporated in the OIG. DCAA was successful, at least in substantial part. It remains at this writing, a separate agency; however, the OIG was given the authority to establish contract audit policy and oversee and review DCAA's work, especially with respect to its activities in connection with fraud, waste and abuse. Here again, DCAA must demonstrate that it is expending an appropriate degree of effort and skill in fraud detection lest the DOD Inspector General step in and direct its efforts.

The May 1983 issue of the Bulletin, DCAA's house organ, was devoted almost entirely to the results of a conference held the prior month, attended by the agency's headquarters staff and many of its field managers.

In an article entitled: "Executive Conferees Tackle Fraud, Waste and Abuse Problem," the Agency's Assistant Director, Operations, stated: "Because of the sensitivity generated by fraud, waste and abuse, a place was provided on the . . . agenda for participants in the Executive conference to devote some substantial time to applying creative problem solving to this sensitive area with expectations of identifying some possible new initiatives." Other excerpts from this article are quoted below:

> Several important conclusions came out of these discussions. Briefly, they are as follows:

—We are performing a substantial amount of work to identify and report instances of fraud, waste and abuse now.

—There is a need for clarification as to what should be reported under CAM 12-701.

—We should consider some type of "abuse report."

—A better defined means of obtaining corrective actions where inefficient government practices exist needs to be developed.

The teams identified a number of ways already being used to identify and report instances of fraud, waste and abuse. For example, the CAM 12-700 series addresses a number of improper practices, and our operations audits have identified numerous instances of waste and inefficiency. In addition, poor or abusive practices are often included in our audit reports on proposals and incurred costs.

Another item of interest in DCAA's May 1983 Bulletin is a listing of "initiatives" proposed by Vincent Puritano, then Assistant Secretary of Defense (Comptroller). As mentioned earlier, Mr. Puritano attended DCAA's "Managers' Conference" and delivered eight initiatives for the agency, some of which urged the agency to accord increased emphasis to fraud detection.

As we noted earlier, for the last several years DCAA has increasingly moved toward viewing some costs considered questionable by the auditors as potential fraudulent representations. Within this general philosophy, DCAA has also been scrutinizing alleged defective cost or pricing data for what might appear to the auditors as possible indications of fraud. In this respect, the audit agency found itself a step ahead of the Puritano initiative.

Although DCAA scarcely appears to require direction or encouragement to show greater zeal in its search for potential fraud and reporting thereon, under another Puritano initiative "DCAA would further systematize the collection of information from its field offices to better identify and report on conditions leading to contractor fraud or waste."

In speeches at meetings and symposia, some DCAA officials insist that the Agency is concentrating on conventional audits—business as usual—and deny increased emphasis on fraud. In light of the discussions at the agency's "Managers Conference," increased training and indoctrination provided its auditors at its Memphis facility and field offices, and actual behavior during some audits, it is easy to be unpersuaded by these statements and denials.

It is difficult indeed to understand how DCAA officials can continue to make public statements denying the agency's increasing emphasis on searching for fraud, waste and abuse while its internal publications contain statements to the contrary. In addition to the heavy emphasis in training and encouragement of reports for inclusion in DOD's semi-annual report to Congress compiled by the Office of Inspector General, there is the holding out of greater recognition to DCAA auditors whose reports may be included in releases by the President's Council on Integrity and Efficiency (PCIE). In an article in DCAA's July 1983 house organ, a headquarters official exhorts the auditors to produce reports in the areas of fraud, waste and mismanagement which are "unique, innovative and significant."

In the same issue of the agency's Bulletin, in the "Director's Message," the DCAA Chief asks, "What can we look forward to in the year to come?," and replies:

I feel that the American taxpayers, the Congress, and the news media will be expressing more and more concern with regard to fraud, waste and mismanagement. These buzz words have been around for several years but now they have developed more specific meaning among these groups. These concerns will result in higher visibility and an increased attention level being directed toward the agency. This can already be supported by our recent involvement in giving congressional testimonies relative to defective pricing, spare parts and labor mischarging issues.

The DCAA Director reminds the staff of the Assistant Secretary's "initiatives" mentioned earlier, and tells them "[o]ur success in implementing these initiatives will require input and cooperation from all levels within DCAA."

As another item in this review, we refer to the lead article in the August 1983 issue of DCAA's house organ, The Bulletin, headed by a large bold face caption: DCAA AIDS DOD IN FRAUD CASES. We quote this item verbatim below and invite attention to the apparent DCAA environment and attitude toward this subject as the author writes that the case "was brought to a successful conclusion when a defense contractor, its president and a former president, pleaded guilty to defrauding the government."

Since the inception of the Inspector General Act of 1978 (Public Law 95-452), the Defense Contract Audit Agency has referred over 180 suspected contractor irregularity cases to investigative agencies for appropriate action. In recent years, DCAA has assisted the Assistant United States Attorneys (AUSAs) as well as Department of Defense and other investigative agencies in the investigation, review, and prosecution of "fraud" cases.

One of the largest labor mischarging cases disclosed and referred by DCAA was brought to a successful conclusion recently when a defense contractor, its president and a former president, pleaded guilty to defrauding the government. In a plea bargaining agreement, the corporation will repay $750,000 to the government because it submitted false public vouchers which fraudulently inflated the hours charged to an Army contract. The government will withhold an additional $260,000 representing adjustments on other contracts. The officials face possible prison terms plus fines up to $10,000. The corporation also faces a $10,000 fine.

In June 1979 during an audit review of charges to a time and material contract, the following suspected irregularities were detected:

—Overtime labor hours were added to employees' weekly timecards after-the-fact for a full fiscal period.

—Cross-check of labor charges with employee travel vouchers revealed that labor charges were not consistent with either the travel voucher account number or the stated purpose of the respective trip.

—Indirect employees were recording their time as direct labor charges to the contract.

—Unusual labor charges of 15-20 hours per day for extended periods were charged to the contract by certain employees.

—Labor costs were overstated because employees were classified and billed at skill levels that they did not possess.

The Mountainside Branch Office furnished continuous and significant audit support for the investigation over a three-year period. In this case, the auditors assigned divorced themselves from the routine audit activity at this location, dispelling any appearance that routine audit activity and audit activity in support of an investigation could be commingled. This strict separation between the two audit activities was maintained from the outset of the grand jury investigation at the direction of the United States Attorney's Office. The corporation attempted to dismiss the charges, alleging abuse of the grand jury process. Corporate officials claimed that the same DCAA auditors had the responsibility for auditing the contract in which irregularities allegedly occurred and the successor contract. It was found that DCAA personnel who assisted the investigators were not involved in the ongoing audit of the successor contract. The corporation's motion to dismiss was denied.

The Agency is proud of the diligent efforts put forth by the branch manager and the auditors. They have all received letters of recognition from the Director.

DCAA's strong preoccupation with fraud detection and its eagerness to join forces with other government organizations involved in this area was illustrated in the agency's Bulletin of October 1983. The front page of this issue contained an article by the Chief of the Defense Procurement Fraud Unit for the Department of Justice headed: "How Would You Solve This Case?" He presented a "scenario illustrating the importance of a careful analysis of every potential CAM 4-702 case." We quote his illustration ending with a question to which he furnished his answer.

You are the auditor assigned to review the overhead accounts at World Corporation. Your have reviewed your own notes from the previous several years of auditing at World and have reviewed the previous auditors' notes as well. There are several sub-accounts to the overhead account including employee welfare and office supplies. Invariably the auditors have focused on the employee welfare account for their most detailed review and have systematically approved the office supply account without much detailed review.

You decide that this year you might want to look at the office supply account a little bit more closely and you ask the company representative for the backup data. In the data you find a charge of $300,000 that seems unexplainable and you ask the company rep for the file. It turns out that six months before your audit the company celebrated its most profitable year by bringing all of its managers to New York for a long weekend. The cost of the entire weekend, including first class airfare, entertainment and food, came to $300,000.

You question the company rep who tells you that though he does not know for sure, it's probably just a mistake that the $300,000 cost showed up in office supplies and that it should have been in the employee welfare account. In any event, he tells you, it does not matter since the DAR allows employee welfare costs so long as those costs are reasonable.

You also know from your knowledge of the DAR [now FAR] that employee welfare expenses are allowable under DOD contracts if they are reasonable expenses. You are uncertain at this point about whether the $300,000 is a "reasonable" expense.

Is this a matter which should be the subject of a 12-701 report? [4-702 in the CAM edition of December 1987.]

This is the answer provided by the DOD official:

If your answer to the puzzle on page one was that the matter should not be the subject of 12-701 report because the $300,000 could be an allowable reasonable expense, you are wrong. The issue in this case is not whether the cost is allowable but whether the company intentionally mislabeled the costs so as to sneak it by the auditor. Let us assume for the moment that the company knows that the employee welfare account is watched very closely whereas the office supply account is not. With this knowledge the company tries to sneak the $300,000 past you as an office supply expense, fearing that you would question the unreasonable part of the $300,000 if it showed up in the employee welfare account. The potential criminality involved in this is the intentional mislabeling of $300,000 by the company, even though had the costs been properly labeled, the reasonable portion would have been allowable.

Be aware of the difference between an allowability issue and a criminal issue. Allowability is generally irrelevant if the company is trying intentionally to disguise the real source of an expense.

The attorney's contribution illustrates forcefully our observation earlier in this analysis which pointed out that DCAA's mission from the day it was established until the late 1970s was to assist contracting officers to assure that unallocable, unreasonable or otherwise unallowable costs contained in contractors' representations were not reimbursed or included in contract prices. Beginning with the late 1970s, however, and despite denials by the agency's officials, the emphasis has increasingly shifted to detecting and reporting fraud. Note the DOD representative's specific guidance to the auditors: "The issue in this case is not whether the cost is allowable but whether the company intentionally mislabeled the cost so as to sneak it by the auditor."

The potential fraud, or "potential criminality" as the head of the DOD Procurement Fraud Unit refers to it, can move from the potential to actual if intent is proven. Inasmuch as DCAA auditors are admittedly not trained investigators, the guidance and encouragement to the auditors is to prepare a suspicion of fraud report. Such report may wind up in the office of DOD's IG or may be sent on to the Department of Justice where the FBI may be called in. Supposedly, trained investigators will descend on the contractor, whose sole sin may have been that an accounting employee erroneously coded this expenditure, and grill the employees and officials in an effort to establish whether fraud may have been involved.

As we understand the "scenario," the expenditure was not hidden from the auditors but charged to a wrong account in the same pool. But this possibility does not appear to be a matter of particular interest to the DOJ attorney. He does not raise the question or suggest that the auditor should explore the reasonableness of the expenditure. Rather, it would appear that the Justice official's sole interest is in the possibility that the contractor's accounting action could be established as fraud rather than error.

Of the many DCAA Bulletins reporting, with much fanfare, fraud detections in which the agency's auditors participated, and issues containing the Department of Justice views, not dissimilar from the DOD IG's "think fraud" admonitions, we have selected the following:

The November 1984 Bulletin featured a two-page spread with bold letter opening caption: "WHAT A DAY IT WAS !!!" A DCAA auditor appeared in three separate large pictures in connection with his receipt of the "Secretary of Defense Meritorious Civilian Service Award, for his exceptional contributions to the successful investigation and prosecution by the Department of Justice of fraudulent activities by a Defense contractor." Separate photographs of the broadly smiling auditor showed him with the DCAA Director, with the Secretary of Defense, and (most unusual) even with President Reagan, the latter picture having been arranged as this auditor was one of 12 DOD employees whose efforts were recognized by the President.

The continuing publicity and recognition of auditors identified with prosecution of fraudulent activities is obviously designed to encourage their colleagues to concentrate on this area.

The same issue of The Bulletin contained the second in a three part series, digesting an article titled: "MISCHARGING—A Contract Cost Dispute or a Criminal Fraud? " written by the Deputy Chief of the Fraud Section, Criminal Division, Department of Justice. The first of the series appeared in the August 1984 issue of DCAA's house organ, and the concluding one in the February 1985 issue. As might be readily imagined, the thrust of these articles was to impress upon the auditors that any instance of mischarging may well have criminal implications and guide them to look carefully and with suspicion on any mischarging.

The prefix "mis" refers to actions which prove to be incorrect or wrong, and there are numerous words beginning with this prefix. Thus, "misaddress" means that a communication was addressed erroneously; "miscalculate" refers to a wrong or erroneous calculation; "misfit" may refer to clothing which does not fit a person properly; the noun "mistake," according to *Webster's Third New International Dictionary,* is a "misunderstanding of the meaning or implication of something." But how does the DOJ official address this area for the benefit of the DCAA auditors? He begins by referring to mischarging as "the false description of costs in a government contractor's books and records." The implication and purpose of using this term is obvious especially when immediately followed by the statement that when mischarging is "accompanied by proof of intent to defraud, such activity appears to be a straightforward false claim or fraud on the government . . . ."

After seemingly complaining that this area is complicated by government rules relating to applicability of costs to a particular contract, the author thunders:

> Nonetheless, mischarging is a particularly suitable area in which to examine the distinctions between a contract disagreement and a criminal fraud. Although the number of criminal prosecutions for mischarging is not large, the impact on the public contracting community has been substantial. Every major contractor has been engaged in disputes which either could have been or were characterized as mischarging with criminal implications.

This certainly appears to be a most excessive, inflammatory and irresponsible statement, considering especially that the source is a high official in DOJ.

"Allocation of indirect costs among the various contracts," according to the author, "can also provide a vehicle whereby the contractor alters or otherwise falsifies the supporting records to conceal the true and proper nature of the costs." He apparently views it unfortunate that others do not find fraud in every instance of a mischarge, but "after review of the facts and circumstances, the courts and boards end up focusing on fairness and equitability." He also notes that IR&D costs, "by their very general and broad definition, become attractive means for contractors to recover costs otherwise not subject to recovery."

The author's continued equating of a mischarged cost with a false one is reflected in his reference to mischarges in entries on time cards, labor distribution forms and invoices as "false costs."

The author also seeks to impress DCAA auditors that mischarging by employees should not inhibit prosecuting the entire company, including upper management:

> In determining corporate responsibility, the investigation often reveals that the mischarging is accomplished by employees with no direct personal profit motive. In such cases, management's first response may be to use such employees as scapegoats, and to argue no involvement of upper level management. Such a maneuver, while sometimes preventing the prosecution of certain upper level management types, does not usually prevent the corporation from prosecution under standard agency theories. And, especially in small businesses, the involvement of the upper management in the day-to-day affairs of the company, when combined with their financial self-interest makes the use of this defense fairly unsuccessful.

Installment two of "MISCHARGING: A Contract Cost Dispute or a Criminal Fraud?" was published in the November 1984 issue of The Bulletin. Subcaptioned "Criminal Law Standards," the follow-on encouragement for the auditors to suspect possible criminal fraud in any case where they encounter what they believe to be mischarging cites several fraud statutes and comments on their application.

The first statute referred to is the False Statement/Concealment (18 U.S.C. 1001), explained as covering "false and fraudulent statements and representations, false writings and documents, and concealments by trick,

scheme or device, and is designed to protect the government from the evils
that may result from deceptive practices." The Justice official emphasized to
the auditors that the "statement or concealment need not actually be submitted to the United States or any agent of the United States, but may be made
in the corporate records which could be the subject of federal inspection. In the
cost accounting area, employees' time cards and other internal corporate
documents, if covered by the contract clause, for example, can be the vehicle
for a false statement prosecution of a contractor."

Pointing the DCAA auditors toward upper management officials of
defense contractors, he lamented that "(i)n some cases, proof of knowledge by
upper management (is) progressively more difficult." However, he instructed
his readers that such proof can be satisfied "by evidence of a reckless disregard
for the truthfulness of a statement coupled with a conscious effort to avoid
learning the truth." We wondered what DCAA people, laymen in legal
matters, will do with these comments.

The writer next addressed the False Claim Act (18 U.S.C. 287), and noted
that while it "is identical to 1001 in terms of the knowledge and intent
elements, its difference in scope can make it more effective in a mischarging
case." He explained:

> Although the government must prove the claim is false, fictitious, or
> fraudulent, the necessity of proving willfulness and materiality is in
> dispute among the Federal Circuit Courts. Proof of intent to defraud is
> not required, only proof that the defendant "had the specific intent to do
> something he knew the law forbade."

Under the caption "General Fraud Statutes," the DOJ official included
the mail and wire fraud statutes (18 U.S.C. 1341 and 18 U.S.C. 1343), and the
conspiracy statute (18 U.S.C. 371), and noted that the three generally apply
to mischarging cases. The following points were emphasized:

> The critical element in each statute is the definition of "defraud the
> United States." Proof that the United States has been defrauded does not
> require any showing of pecuniary or proprietary loss. The statutory
> language is not limited and the cases describe the conduct in broad terms.

> The most wide ranging aspect of the definition of defrauding the
> United States is the phrase "obstruct or impair legitimate government
> activity."

He then described for the auditors' benefit the various forms such type of
fraud might take.

The last installment of "MISCHARGING: A Contract Cost Dispute or a
Criminal Fraud?" appeared in the February 1985 issue of The Bulletin, and
consisted of brief digests of eight so-called "major mischarging cases filed to
date." With one exception, they "have been settled without a trial or any
appeals that would indicate a particular judicial acceptance or rejection of the
underlying legal issues." In the cases described, the contractors agreed to
plead guilty to various civil and/or criminal charges, and paid fines, interest,
and other charges. The settlements included various "corrective actions" by
the firms, including in several instances, agreements to strengthen their
internal audit procedures and make the results of such audits available for

review by DCAA. None of the firms were suspended or debarred. The DOJ official did not address the many cases where contractors prevailed.

PRESIDENT'S COUNCIL ON INTEGRITY AND EFFICIENCY (PCIE)

In Chapter XXVI of this text, we reviewed the composition of this council and one of its reports. The PCIE is of particular interest in demonstrating the interest in this area at the highest levels of the government.

The establishment of the PCIE was announced in an Executive Order signed by the President on March 26, 1981. The White House fact sheet described the Order as launching the President's "Government-wide anti-fraud and waste program" and as "a major step in fulfilling the President's promise to root out fraud and waste in federal government programs."

VIEWPOINTS FROM THE PRIVATE SECTOR

When the President of the United States promises "to root out fraud and waste in government programs," when high Department of Justice officials assert that the American public demands that they "eliminate fraud and corruption in government procurement," when the Secretary of Defense announces "we have made a good beginning in ferreting out waste, fraud and inefficiency, but much remains to be done," when DOD's Inspector General delivers public speeches entitled "Cracking Down on Fraud in Government Procurement," when the IG members of the PCIE seem to be in competition among themselves and with GAO and congressional committee staffs to detect and report on alleged fraud, waste, and abuse, and when DCAA continues increasing its emphasis in the same direction, government contractors are understandably concerned. The concern is further aggravated by increased efforts to suspend or debar contractors and to enact legislation designed to threaten government contractors and others with a wide range of additional criminal and civil penalties.

Contractors and their legal and accounting consultants increasingly confront situations where an auditor's suspicion of possible fraud moves secretly through the department's channels, finds its way to the Department of Justice, and the company is sudddenly confronted with FBI agents and grand jury investigations. These investigations have been known to last for years, during which the company and its employees are harassed by interrogations and demands for records and documents which literally can run into the millions. The ultimate outcome is frequently a finding that low-level company employees may have deviated from correct accounting for government contract costs for personal aggrandizement or to avoid criticisms. At other times, the government finds insufficient basis to prosecute and drops the case. In either event, however, the company and its officials are dragged through adverse publicity, huge expenses to supply the information demanded and to defend themselves, and frequent deterioration of market position.

Attorneys advise their clients to try to avoid the issuance of grand jury subpoenas and what one described as "the resulting momentum, often self-fulfilling, toward a criminal case." However, in light of the government approach where fraud is suspected, as described above, contractors frequently find it impossible to avail themselves of this good advice.

It has always been considered sound business practice for government contractors to assign responsible people to be aware at all times of what records the government auditor wishes to examine and what company employee he wishes to speak to. Although a cooperative attitude is to be encouraged, contractors must be aware of the insatiable interests some auditors display in records, employees and operations, even where the relationship to contract costs appears to be remote or nonexistent. Contractors have been advised to remember the judicial admonition that "auditors may not roam unrestricted through a contractor's plant." The need for care and caution in relations with DCAA auditors has increased substantially as that agency has become, in its own words, more "sensitive" and "alert" with regard to fraud.

The possibility of suspension or debarment has been recognized as a threat to the most scrupulous of contractors when such action is not taken in a responsible manner by government officials. The order of magnitude of this threat has increased because of current regulations which provide for debarment throughout the executive branch of government rather than only with respect to the debarring agency. The problem has also been aggravated by the increasing zeal and aggressiveness of some government officials involved in the procurement process.

In a report to the American Bar Association, Section of Public Contract Law, recommendations were made for debarment and suspension by an independent debarment and suspension board of administrative judges, for observance of uniform and fair standards and procedures, and for the separation of prosecutorial and adjudicative functions before the stigma of debarment and suspension may be imposed. The report recognized that legislation would be needed to achieve these goals.

Much concern has been expressed in the private sector over the controversial and seemingly punitive action by DOD, subsequently endorsed by incorporation into FAR, which makes unallowable the costs incurred by contractors incident to defense of fraud or related proceedings unless the contractor is clearly victorious. As described in Chapter XVII of this text, DOD's original proposal established costs of defending oneself against fraud accusations as unallowable even when the allegations proved unfounded and contractors ultimately prevailed. The storm of protest forced DOD to back down on the latter point.

The private sector also views with considerable alarm the efforts by some members of Congress to add to the growing list of statutes which provide civil and criminal penalties against companies doing business with the federal government. These proposals are invariably and aggressively championed by the DOD IG, General Accounting Office and the Justice Department. The continuing efforts to introduce new punitive legislation are particularly disturbing in view of the plethora of laws in this area already on the books and the harsh manner in which they are sometimes enforced or used as threats.

To effectively assist their clients who perform under contracts with the federal government, attorneys have been required to know and be able to apply the vast and complex conglomeration of laws, regulations, and judicial and quasijudicial decisions originating or related to something broadly termed contract law. In recent years, this knowledge has been found to be insufficient as these attorneys increasingly require criminal law expertise. Many major law firms specializing in contract law have augmented their staffs by attracting attorneys from the Justice Department and other sources to develop this criminal law capability.

A large majority of government contractors remain fortunate in that they have not been confronted by allegations that their actions have violated some law or regulation and that they may be subject to civil or criminal penalties. On the other hand, an increasing number are finding themselves in these positions, and it does not require much experience of this kind to make such companies extremely cautious in dealing with government representatives. For many contractors, the costs of legal and accounting services, both in-house and external, have been rising. Although prudent and responsible managements make every effort to control costs, experience persuades most of them that it would indeed be imprudent and irresponsible to fail to avail themselves of appropriate protection in today's environment of zealous government "sensitivity" and "alertness" to possible fraud, waste, and abuse.

FRAUD PREVENTION BY CONTRACTORS

We believe our extensive fraud coverage is fully justified by the attention accorded this subject in recent years and the serious consequences suffered by contractors who were unsuccessful in defending themselves against charges of criminal or civil wrongs. Indeed, severe damages have also been incurred by contractors against whom no wrong doings were proven but who suffered adverse publicity, personal anguish on the part of officials involved, and heavy costs in establishing their innocence.

Having deplored what we believe to be the distorted perception of government officials on this subject, and having cautioned those doing business with the government that the buyer may be simultaneously an investigator and prosecutor, a fact which demands the exercise of judgment and caution in opening doors and records to government representatives, we would leave this coverage incomplete without addressing the importance of fraud prevention on the part of contractors.

Much has been written about the important and interrelated subjects of fraud prevention and detection, internal and administrative controls, checks and balances, and the roles and responsibilities of management at all levels for efficiency and integrity in business conduct. The many facets of accounting for and administering government contracts precludes the type of concentrated, detailed coverage which would be required to deal satisfactorily with this area. However, in the following pages, we offer an overview that we believe should assist companies doing business with the government in establishing, reviewing and/or revising their control systems.

Most companies are concerned with the prevention of fraud. Generally speaking, the responsibility for accomplishing these objectives should be assigned to each and every employee of the companies. While this is an appropriate outlook, there is an immediate need to focus on one individual who will be identified internally and externally as the one with the ultimate responsibility.

Fraud has many legal ramifications, but fraud prevention is much too multi-faceted and complex a matter to assign to the company's legal counsel. Many forms of internal control are rooted in accounting and financial matters, but this subject goes beyond the normal scope of the controller or vice president-finance. Fraud necessarily involves people, but we would not recommend the vice president for personnel, nor, for that matter, anyone but the chief executive officer, the number one man of the company, whatever be its organization and whatever be his title. There are several cogent reasons for assigning this responsibility to such a high level. For one thing, the matter is of sufficient importance to warrant interest at the highest level. That individual, too, is the only one whose authority normally extends to *everyone* else in the company. Finally, and very importantly, it is essential that the company's commitment to integrity be clearly perceived internally and externally and that perception is best achieved when the commitment is articulated by the recognized head of the company.

Obviously, the task requires the coordinated utilization of all of the company's resources and talents: the legal, accounting, financial, and personnel officials mentioned earlier, as well as many others. The CEO is hardly expected to devote all of his time to this program; on the other hand, it is important that his interests and efforts be continuing and visible. If they appear to weaken, the major advantages of his initial participation will be lost.

Many firms have had difficulties in getting rid of the "it can't happen here" notion. Headed by officials of impeccable character who would not knowingly tolerate dishonesty, companies find it difficult to accept the possibility that fraud may be perpetrated within their walls. However, there are many factors which counsel strongly in favor of effective fraud prevention controls. There is the matter referred to on several occasions relating to the government's current zealous preoccupation with fraud, including the intense, microscopic examination of routine clerical errors for evidence of possible wrongdoing. The area of government acquisition/procurement is so broad and complex and permeated with so many laws, regulations, and other requirements that few individuals indeed can be expected to know and understand what should and should not be done.

Nor are good intentions and general honesty sufficient deterrents against fraud allegations. For example, in discussing the limitation of cost contractual provisions in Chapter XX of this text, we referred to situations in which companies notify the government that they are approaching the cost limitations and require additional funding to complete the project. In certain circumstances, government officials advise that they are very desirous of having the contract completed but simply have no additional funds to make available. The contractor can, of course, stop work. On the other hand, favorable relations with the procurement office are desired, and a decision must be made whether to use the company's own funds to complete the contract.

Or perhaps the hard-working, conscientious, ambitious project engineer decides on his own to achieve the best of both worlds and satisfy the government customer without the loss of company funds. He works this out by directing the employees working to complete the contract to charge their time to a different code number, perhaps one representing a firm fixed-price contract, or IR&D, or B&P. There are various ways in which almost any government auditor can detect such mischarging and, when he does, it may trigger a series of events that will cause the loss of infinitely more money than was possibly saved. Much worse, there could be criminal indictments, suspensions, or debarments, and so on.

The first step in a "clean company" program is a written statement by the CEO, delivered to *every* employee, stating in very specific terms that the company demands compliance with legal and moral codes of integrity. Thereafter, the company should mount an extensive educational campaign to educate employees in the "do's" and "don'ts" applicable to their jobs and to the company as a whole. The third major step in this triad is a continuous program to assure compliance with those policies and procedures. Although this program should be essentially operated by the company's own people, many companies find it useful to engage legal, accounting, and other outside consultants to assist in establishing such programs and to provide periodic checks to assure management that they are operating in the manner intended.

We observed that a fraud prevention program requires the use of virtually all of the company's resources. This point is emphasized by a report issued by the DOD Inspector General in June 1987, titled "Indicators of Fraud in Department of Defense Procurement." The DOD IG advises Defense Department personnel that potential for fraud exists in every stage of the procurement process and instructs them on how to detect it. The stages discussed in the report include the development of statements of work and specifications, presolicitation phase, solicitation phase, submission of bids and proposals, evaluation of bids and proposals, contract award, contract negotiation, defective pricing, collusive bidding and price-fixing, cost mischarging, product substitution, progress payment, fast pay, bribery, gratuities, and conflicts of interest. Each category has numerous subcategories, and we considered this IG document of sufficient interest to all government contractors to cite it virtually verbatim in Appendix I of this text.

A careful study of this report and the handbooks on Labor Fraud Indicators, Appendix 2, Fraud Indicators: Material (Appendix 3), and Potential Defective Pricing Fraud (Appendix 4), will illustrate how every facet of procurement requires measures designed to prevent possible fraud or the appearance thereof and will offer valuable guidance in the preparation of company fraud prevention programs.

THE PACKARD COMMISSION AND CONTRACTOR VOLUNTARY DISCLOSURE

What is widely considered one of the outstanding efforts in the review and analysis, and submission of cogent recommendations, with respect to the broad area of defense management was the series of reports by the President's Blue Ribbon Commission (Packard Commission) in 1986. A companion report to the overall "A Quest for Excellence" was titled "Conduct and Accountability," consisting of two major sections: I. Industry Accountability: Contractor

Self-Governance, and II. Government Accountability: DOD Auditing and Oversight, Standards of Conduct and Ethics. As stated in the opening of this report, the Commission concluded: "A study of defense management compels us to conclude that nothing merits greater concern than the increasingly troubled relationship between the defense industry and government."

The Commission's report was thoughtful and even-handed. It urged contractors, among other things, to have and adhere to written codes of conduct; train their employees in such codes; encourage employees to report violations of such codes, without fear of retribution; monitor compliance with laws incident to defense procurement; and adopt procedures for voluntary disclosure of violations and corrective action. It urged DOD to remove undesirable duplication of oversight and surveillance; administer standard codes of conduct for its personnel; and limit suspensions and debarments to instances where such action will protect the public interest, and eliminate automatic actions in this area and those used to coerce or threaten contractors in negotiations. As to voluntary disclosures, the Commission recommended that DOD and the Department of Justice (DOJ) should "jointly initiate a program encouraging the voluntary disclosure of irregularities by such contractors . . . . A voluntary disclosure will be more effective if there are inducements that assure skeptical contractors that they will not suffer greater sanctions by coming forward."

As discussed elsewhere in this text, DOD and DOJ were extremely slow in initiating any action which the Commission recommended them to take with regard to their own actions but quick to move out on matters such as voluntary disclosures by contractors. Initially, the Departments further seemed to ignore the Commission's suggestions of offering some inducements for contractors to adopt such policies.

In a letter of July 24, 1986, Deputy Secretary of Defense Taft encouraged major contractors to adopt a policy of voluntary disclosure of fraud and other irregularities. For contractors making full disclosure, providing government officials with complete access to all books and records, and otherwise cooperating in every way with DOD and, in criminal or fraud cases, with the Department of Justice (DOJ), Taft wrote: "We will consider such cooperation as an important factor in any decisions that the Department takes in the matter." Unlike certain federal and state income tax programs which promised no punitive action for taxpayers who voluntarily made payments of taxes that they should have paid previously, DOD offers only to expedite investigations and advise DOJ of these voluntary claims.

The text of this important kickoff letter and attachments thereto are quoted below.

During the past few years, public and congressional interest in the Department of Defense management of its programs and operations has remained intense. This is nowhere more true than in the acquisition area. These issues continue to command our personal attention and involvement. Many of the problems in the acquisition area came to light because of audits and investigations conducted by the Department of Defense. We are committed to detecting and eliminating inefficiency and improper practices in our acquisition process; we believe that most Defense contractors have institutional commitments to these same goals.

To demonstrate this commitment, a number of major Defense contractors have adopted a policy of voluntarily disclosing problems affecting their corporate contractual relationship with the Department of Defense. These disclosures are made by the contractor, without an advance agreement regarding possible Department of Defense resolution of the matter. The contractors understand the Department's view that early voluntary disclosure, coupled with full cooperation and complete access to necessary records, are strong indications of an attitude of contractor integrity even in the wake of disclosures of potential criminal liability. We will consider such cooperation as an important factor in any decisions that the Department takes in the matter.

I encourage you to consider adopting a policy of voluntary disclosure as a central part of your corporate integrity program. Matters not involving potential criminal issues should be presented to the appropriate contracting officer or Defense Contract Audit Agency auditor. Matters involving potential criminal or civil fraud issues should be directed to the Deputy Inspector General, Department of Defense.

A description of the Department of Defense program for voluntary disclosures is enclosed herewith for your consideration.

I believe that your corporate commitment to complete and timely disclosures of irregularities, regardless of their magnitude, is essential to increasing confidence in our ability to provide for the national defense effectively and efficiently.

Sincerely,

William H. Taft, IV

Enclosure

Department of Defense Program for Voluntary Disclosures of Possible Fraud by Defense Contractors

Background

Officials within the Department of Defense (DOD) have been approached by a number of contractors to determine the conditions and agreements that might be structured with the Government if a contractor sought to disclose voluntarily information that might expose the contractor to liability under Federal statutes relating to criminal and civil fraud. From the Department's perspective, the voluntary disclosure of information otherwise unknown to the Government and contractor cooperation in an ensuing investigation, offers a number of significant advantages:

The Government is likely to recoup losses of which it might otherwise be unaware;

Limited detection assets within the Government are augmented by contractor resources;

Consideration of appropriate remedies can be expedited by both DOD and Department of Justice when adversarial tensions are relaxed;

Voluntary disclosure and cooperation are indicators of contractor integrity; and

Contractors engaging in voluntary disclosure are more likely to institute corrective actions to prevent recurrence of disclosed problems.

Requirements on Contractors

Department of Defense recognition of a contractor as a "volunteer" will depend on four key factors:

1. The disclosure must not be triggered by the contractor's recognition that the underlying facts are about to be discovered by the Government through audit, investigation, or contract administration efforts or reported to the Government by third parties.

2. The disclosure must be on behalf of the business entity, in contrast to admissions by individual officials or employees.

3. Prompt and complete corrective action, including disciplinary action and restitution to the Government where appropriate, must be taken by the contractor in response to the matters disclosed.

4. After disclosure, the contractor must cooperate fully with the Government in any ensuing investigation or audit.

Defining DOD expectation of "cooperation" in any situation will depend on the individual facts or circumstances underlying the disclosure. However, DOD may enter into a written agreement with any contractor seeking to make a voluntary disclosure where such an agreement will facilitate follow-on action without improperly limiting the responsibilities of the Government. This agreement, which may be coordinated with the Department of Justice, will describe the types of documents and evidence to be provided to DOD and will resolve any issues related to interviews, privileges, or other legal concerns which may effect the DOD ability to obtain all relevant facts in a timely manner.

Department of Defense Actions

If a contractor is recognized as a "volunteer" based on the preceding criteria, the DOD is prepared to undertake the following:

1. Identify one of the Military Departments of the Defense Logistics Agency as the cognizant DOD component to represent DOD for suspension/debarment purposes, i.e., to assess contractor integrity in light of the disclosures. Early identification of the appropriate DOD component will permit relevant information relating to contractor integrity and management controls, e.g., internal controls, corrective measures, or disciplinary action taken as a result of the information disclosed.

2. The DOD, through the Office of the Inspector General and in cooperation with the Department of Justice, will seek to expedite the completion of any investigation and audit conducted in response to a voluntary disclosure, thereby minimizing the period of time necessary for identification of remedies deemed appropriate by the Government.

3. Advise the Department of Justice of the complete nature of the voluntary disclosure, the extent of the contractor cooperation and the

types of corrective action instituted by the contractor. As always, any determinations of appropriate criminal and civil fraud sanctions will be the ultimate prerogative of the Department of Justice.

Commencing a Voluntary Disclosure

Since initial judgments as to appropriate investigative and audit resources will be necessary in any voluntary disclosure involving possible fraud, the initial contact with the DOD on fraud-related disclosures should be with the Office of the Inspector General.

While the Office of the Inspector General will be the initial point of contact for fraud-related disclosures, other DOD components are expected to be advised or involved as circumstances warrant. Besides the Office of General Counsel, DOD and the appropriate suspension/debarment authority, other DOD components that expectedly would be advised, or involved, in voluntary disclosures are the Office of the Assistant Secretary of Defense (Acquisition and Logistics) and the Defense Contract Audit Agency.

The Office of the Inspector General that will serve as the initial point of contact is:

Assistant Inspector General for Criminal Investigations

Policy and Oversight

400 Army Navy Drive, Room 1037

Arlington, VA 22202

Key Elements in Contractor Voluntary Disclosures Related to Fraud

In order for a voluntary disclosure of improper or illegal practices to be truly effective, and in order for the contractor and DOD to be completely assured that these practices have been fully identified and rectified, it is essential that any internal examination undertaken by the contractor addresses certain important issues. The contractor should be prepared to share information regarding its resolution of these issues as part of its disclosure to DOD.

A. Nature of the Improper or Illegal Practice.

A full examination of the practice should be conducted to include:

1. Source of the practice (e.g. lack of internal controls; circumstances of corporate procedures or Government regulations).

2. Description of the practice to include:

   a. Corporate divisions affected.

   b. Government contracts affected.

   c. Detailed description as to how the practice arose and continued.

3. Identification of any potential fraud issues raised by the practice and relevant documentation.

4. Time period when the practice existed.

5. Identification of corporate officials and employees who knew of, encouraged or participated in the practice.

6. Estimate of the dollar impact of the practice on DOD and other Government agencies.

B. Contractor Response to the Improper or Illegal Practice

1. Description of how the practice was identified.

2. Description of contractor efforts to investigate and document the practice (e.g., use of internal or external legal and/or audit resources).

3. Description of actions by the contractor to halt the practice.

4. Description of contractor efforts to prevent a reoccurrence of the practice, (e.g., new accounting or internal control procedures, increased internal audit efforts, increased supervision by higher management, training).

5. Description of disciplinary action taken against corporate officials and employees who were viewed as culpable or negligent in the matter, or who were viewed as not having exercised proper management responsibility.

6. Description of appropriate notices, if applicable, provided to other Government agencies (e.g. Securities and Exchange Commission and Internal Revenue Service).

C. Conclusion

1. List and description of supporting investigative, audit and legal information to be provided to the Government as part of voluntary disclosure, including reports of interviews, audits and working papers.

2. Assurance that contractor is willing to reimburse Government for any damages suffered, including restitution and payment of Government costs to resolve the matters disclosed.

3. Assurance of contractor's full cooperation with Government audit/investigative efforts to resolve contractor's voluntary disclosure information, to include access to corporate records, premises and personnel.

Industry response to the Packard Commission's recommendations was rapid with some of the major industry associations and individual contractors endorsing the "commitment to integrity and high standard of ethics" and placing into effect a procedure for voluntary disclosure. Specifically, some major industry associations even required their company members to agree with the Defense Industry Initiative on Business Ethics as a condition of membership, and some of the companies entered into advance agreements regarding voluntary disclosures related to fraud.

Other defense contractors and law firms extensively involved in this area, however, were more cautious and questioned several aspects of DOD's detailed requirements, particularly in the light of the absence of the incentives recommended by the Commission. In late 1986, Deputy Secretary of Defense Taft participated in a seminar conducted by the National Security Industrial

Association (NSIA) to urge defense contractors to participate in DOD's voluntary disclosure program. Taft's comments generated little enthusiasm and several participants raised questions as to whether such advance agreements might negate attorney-client privilege and inhibit companies' own ability to uncover improper procurement practices. Questions were also raised about the propriety of contractors acting in effect as criminal investigators and the impact of this role on their employees' willingness to report irregularities.

Some observers concluded that DOD had rushed to select a portion of the Commission's report to assist it in uncovering fraud without thinking through the effects on the companies and their employees. Companies were to prominently display posters with special hotline numbers, but these were in competition with hotline numbers for GAO, DOD IG, DCAA, and others.

Taft's promise that voluntary disclosure would serve the mutual interests of the government and industry was not persuasive to many who saw the program as a one-way street. Among the big problems was the question of what happens after the voluntary disclosure. The DOD plan held out no assurance that a swarm of auditors, inspectors and investigators would not come down on the contractor and enlarge the investigation and widen the employees deemed involved with alleged fraud.

Later that year voluntary contractor disclosure was the focus of conferences conducted by the Bureau of National Affairs/Federal Bar Association, and another by the American Bar Association Section of Public Contract Law.

The major government speaker has been Michael Eberhardt, the DOD Assistant Inspector General for Criminal Investigations Policy and Oversight. Although private sector representatives acknowledged a broad commitment to voluntary disclosures, there were many questions as to the nature and extent of the disclosures and the nature of the "consideration" which would be accorded to those firms making these disclosures. Eberhardt's comments tended to be long on encouragement for voluntary disclosures, but short on the incentives to contractors to make such disclosures. He indicated that the firms making the voluntary disclosures would receive priority in attention and investigation, a point considered one of dubious advantage by industry. Although a specific assurance to this effect was not received, it did appear that voluntary disclosures could and should serve at least to avoid automatic suspension or debarment.

Questions were also raised concerning the allowability of costs incurred by contractors in the performance of compliance reviews and related actions leading to voluntary disclosures. Eberhardt thought that normal costs of these reviews would be allowable, but many contractors continued to express doubts on this point, especially in view of DCAA's hard line. The audit agency, without FAR or DFARS authority, directed its auditors to recommend disallowance of all contractor costs related to "extraordinary reviews" of unnegotiated overhead costs made for the purpose of identifying and excluding unallowable expenses. The warped thinking behind this punitive direction is that such reviews should have been made on a day-to-day basis. Accordingly, a contractor taking this extra step to exclude unallowable costs from overhead submissions would be penalized by disallowing the cost of such efforts.

There were also discussions of the allowability of other costs related to voluntary disclosures. Certain costs have been regulated as clearly unallowable (FAR 31.205-47 Defense of Fraud Proceeding). Subparagraph (b) of this cost principle states:

> Costs incurred in connection with defense of any: (1) Criminal or civil investigation, grand jury proceedings, or prosecution; (2) civil litigation; or (3) administrative proceedings such as suspension or debarment, or any combination of the foregoing, brought by the Government against a contractor, its agents or employees, are unallowable when the charges, which are the subject of the investigation, proceedings, or prosecution, involve fraud or similar offenses (including filing of a false certification) on the part of the contractor, its agents or employees, and result in conviction (including conviction entered on a plea of nolo contendere), judgment against the contractor, its agents or employees, or decision to debar or suspend, or are resolved by consent or compromise.

The above provision seems overwhelmingly all-inclusive but the DOD IG official was quoted as saying there are some differences of views within DOD as to the allowability of legal, accounting and other costs where fraud is surfaced in the compliance program. It would appear appropriate to allow such costs inasmuch as they do not fall within the "defense of fraud proceedings."

The matter of voluntary disclosure raises many additional questions to which acceptable answers are needed if this program is to continue successfully and serve and protect the interests of all concerned. The nature of the contractor's report to the DOD IG, in terms of general criteria, must be established, and very importantly, its confidentiality.

Numerous legal complications are involved in these reports, for example, an agreement by the DOD IG that the submission of the report specifically will not constitute a waiver of the attorney-client and work product privileges. In this latter regard, reference is made to DCAA guidance to its field offices, noting that "neither doctrine has been tested against DCAA's contractual or statutory rights to audit." The overzealous audit agency instructs its personnel to closely examine the attorney-client privilege or work product rule to assure that records are not being "laundered" through an attorney.

As DOD moved vigorously to enroll contractors into the voluntary disclosure program, one of the major problems continued to be the matter of inducements for contractors to agree to, in effect, serve as government agents in reporting fraud and other irregularities. It was understood that DOD, on its own, was limited as to the incentives it could offer and coordination and approval from DOJ was essential. Finally, Deputy Secretary Taft wrote to Justice on September 18, 1986, describing DOD's program. On February 5, 1987, a DOJ response over the signature of Deputy Attorney General Arnold I. Burns, advised Taft: "You have my assurance that the Department of Justice fully supports this program and will work with the Department of Defense for its successful implementation." In response to Taft's suggestion that DOJ guidance on voluntary disclosures would be helpful, Burns agreed and stated that such guidance would be prepared in the form of a supplement to the United States Attorneys Manual.

Addressing the criminal aspects of contractor irregularities, the DOJ official stated that his department would have a continuing interest in prosecuting offenders as a deterrent measure and to encourage contractors to conduct business in an honest manner. On the other hand, he stated that DOJ policy was "to take into consideration factors relating to the integrity of a company in assessing whether to bring charges." The letter further stated:

A voluntary corporate disclosure of wrongdoing is rarely the sole basis for a decision not to prosecute; however, it is one of a number of factors we view as relevant to the charging decision. Others include the strength of the evidence, indicia of scienter, level of employee or management involved, pervasiveness of the conduct, dollar impact on the taxpayers, the quality of cooperation during the investigation, the nature of the remedial actions taken in the wake of the discovery of misconduct, and the quality of the company's efforts to prevent misconduct in the first instance by a meaningful compliance program—implemented in fact, as well as recorded on paper.

Clearly, our objective is to bring prosecutions that will have a deterrent impact. At the same time we recognize the desirability of prosecutive judgments, whether at the charging stage, the plea stage or the sentencing stage of the criminal justice process, which will encourage contractors to initiate compliance programs.

In prosecuting corporations, particularly defense contractors, deterrence is a most significant factor. Through criminal prosecution and punishment, other contractors are put on notice as to the requirements of law and encouraged to modify their behavior to conduct business in an honest and non-criminal manner. Prosecutions of contractor corporations create an incentive for management to establish preventive measures and establish clear standards of right and wrong for their employees.

On the other hand, contractors that make serious and responsible efforts to comply with the law and promptly disclose misconduct should not be discouraged from those practices by inflexible prosecutive policies. In some self-disclosure situations, criminal prosecution of the self-disclosing contractor would undermine our law enforcement objectives and would therefore be inappropriate.

On the "civil side" Burns observed that the decision whether to pursue a False Claims Act case is governed by many of the same considerations that obtain with respect to the criminal side. He noted that the False Claims Act Amendments of 1986, P.L. 99-562, includes a provision to recover triple damages, which can be reduced to double damages if the offender makes full disclosure to investigating officials within 30 days and cooperates fully with them.

Burns closed by emphasizing the importance of DOD-DOJ close coordination in administering the voluntary disclosure program and stated that DOJ's Defense Procurement Fraud Unit in the Criminal Division would continue as the contact point and "will also have responsibility for making or reviewing prosecution decisions in cases involving voluntary disclosure by defense contractors."

DOD officials who have been proponents of the voluntary disclosure program have expressed their satisfaction with the DOJ response, as reflecting just about the most Justice could say in support of the program. Most responsible DOD officials are encouraged in that they see significant opportunities for reduction of fraud through contractors' self-governance and ethics programs and for reduction of GAO and congressional investigatory reports featured in the communications media through voluntary disclosures.

Industry officials and their legal and other consultants remain somewhat wary of this program, but a growing number of the major contractors are concluding that the adoption of the program by other companies makes it increasingly difficult for them not to follow.

With the Packard Commission's recommendations for industry accountability well implemented through contractor self-disclosure, one might believe that DOD would address its own responsibilities, including reduction of unnecessary duplication of contractor oversight and surveillance, discontinuance of the use of subpoenas to obtain every kind of contractor record, etc. Instead, the Department issued a proposed "Contractor Fraud, Waste, and Abuse Awareness Program" contract clause for incorporation into the DOD FAR Supplement (DFARS).

Under the proposed clause, which DFARS would require to be included in all defense prime and subcontracts, other than contracts using small purchase procedures or subcontracts less than $25,000, firms would be required to establish and actively maintain an employee awareness program. Essentially, employees are to be informed of the kind of actions that could subject them to fine or imprisonment and informed that no reprisal may be taken against them if they disclose any violation of law related to a defense contract to a member of Congress or an authorized official of the Departments of Defense or Justice. The full text of this clause is set forth below:

(a) The contractor agrees to maintain an employee fraud, waste and abuse awareness program. The purpose of this program is to inform employees of their duties, rights and responsibilities for preventing and reporting fraud, waste and abuse. The formality of the program and its scope shall be established as appropriate for the circumstances. However, the contractor agrees to include the following elements:

(1) Employee orientation that describes employee responsibilities for preventing and reporting fraud, waste and abuse. Employees shall be informed of the fines and penalties for false claims and false statements to the government; misappropriating properties purchased for use on government contracts; product substitution; collusive bids; and bribery, unlawful gratuities, mail fraud and wire fraud. Employees shall be informed that, pursuant to 10 USC 2409, they may not be discharged, demoted, or otherwise discriminated against as a reprisal for disclosing to a Member of Congress or an authorized official of the Department of Defense or the Department of Justice information relating to a substantial violation of law related to a defense contract. In addition, employees should be made aware of unethical practices reflecting an actual or apparent conflict of interest (e.g., subcontractor kickbacks, or vendor gratuities).

(2) Prominent display of posters that provide information on Government Inspector General Hotline procedures. Such posters shall be posted in conspicuous places that are available to employees and applicants for employment. Hotline posters are available from the government. If contractor-developed posters are used, they shall as a minimum, provide Hotline telephone numbers and state that government Hotline procedures assure employee anonymity.

(3) Informing employees of their responsibilities for assuring the accuracy of their time charges to government and, in turn, the integrity of the contractor's timekeeping system. Employees should be informed that willfully or knowingly mischarging their time may result in false claims or false statements to the government and may subject them to a fine and/or imprisonment.

(4) Periodic discussions with employees of their responsibilities and liabilities while working on government contracts to assure a continual awareness of the contractor's program for prevention of fraud, waste, and abuse.

(b) The contractor shall document employee orientations.

(c) The contractor shall include the substance of this clause, including this paragraph (c), in all subcontracts in excess of $25,000.

In a letter to the Under Secretary of Defense (Acquisition), CODSIA strongly opposed this proposal "because it impedes and undercuts companies' own efforts to implement individual corporate programs of self-governance." CODSIA quoted the Packard Commission report and Secretary of Defense Weinberger as favoring increased emphasis on contractor self-governance and added that "contractor effort to improve performance should not be impeded by DOD action; instead, DOD should foster effective contractor self-governance."

While recognizing DOD's responsibilities to impose fraud, waste, and abuse awareness programs, CODSIA urged that "the very strong industry commitment entered into voluntarily . . . be given a chance to work before mandating a competing effort directed and controlled by the Government." If company employees elect to use the government hotline rather than their company's, "the contractor loses the ability to take advantage of DOD's voluntary disclosure system because the employee rather than the company brought the matter to DOD's attention."

Among the many other cogent arguments advanced by CODSIA for the withdrawal of this ill-conceived proposal was the adverse impact of the requirements for predominantly commercial vendors and suppliers to participate. As the industry association explained, "This is another government imposed intrusion on a company's management prerogative in establishing and administering ethics and accountability programs, and will represent another in a growing list of disincentives to participate in government prime and subcontracts."

Continuing its efforts to further regulate the most overregulated industry, DOD issued another proposed DFARS revision, this time adding further demands and requirements that would make contractor voluntary actions in effect involuntary and imposing government detailed practices that some observers saw as making mockery of the term self-governance. Minimum requirements included written ethics codes and training employees in those codes, periodic reviews, hotlines, internal and external audits, program for disciplining improper conduct, timely disclosure of any improper action in connection with government contracts to the government, and full cooperation with government officials in all investigations. This proposal also contained, in detail, the various actions the contractor would be required to take to avoid suspension and debarment.

Once again industry complained that such proposals "impede and undercut companies' own efforts to implement individual corporate programs of self-governance." As CODSIA pointed out, the Packard Commission stated "Contractor effort to improve performance should not be impeded by DOD action; instead, DOD should foster effective contractor self-governance." With the emphasis on self-governance clearly enunciated by the Commission, CODSIA could not see how the heavy-handed and detailed requirements that DOD was proposing to impose were in consonance with the Commission's recommendations DOD was allegedly seeking to implement.

CODSIA further advised:

> We believe it is important that company-sponsored programs entered into voluntarily . . . be given a chance to work . . . . If they don't work, regulatory requirements can always be imposed later. But regulatory requirements now will only stifle industry initiation.

As noted earlier, the Packard Commission's findings and recommendations concerning "Conduct and Accountability" contained two major sections: I. Industry Accountability: Contractor Self-Governance, and II. Government Accountability: DOD Auditing and Oversight, Standards of Conduct and Ethics. To date, DOD has been totally preoccupied with industry accountability except that, losing sight of the basic premise, it has incessantly moved to regulate contractor governance making the term "self" almost a nullity. No action has been discerned with respect to the excessive and redundant DOD auditing and oversight. In this regard, the newly created Under Secretary of Defense for Acquisition has proved a disappointment. As the Commission observed in its July 1987 update assessment, the USD(A) had not been given adequate authority to achieve its recommendations.

Actually, observers have not detected any visible signs that the USD(A) has taken an interest in this area, leaving the field to the DOD IG. The hostility of this office to defense contractors offers little hope that heavy-handed, duplicative contractor oversight, or access to records through subpoenas, will be restrained.

CONTRACTOR MATERIAL REQUIREMENTS PLANNING (MRP) SYSTEMS

Horror stories alleging fraud, waste, and abuse in the procurement of spare parts had about ended as major subjects of interest for defense critics in Congress and the printed and electronic news media in the middle of 1987 when contractor MRP systems were injected to fill the void. DCAA, a prime mover in this field, emulated GAO's reporting technique by citing a limited experience in its investigations of these systems as a basis for trumpeting that the government may have been overcharged by hundreds of millions of dollars.

Without devoting too much space to details, MRP systems are described as a technique of managing production inventories that takes into account the specific timing of material requirements with the objective of minimizing the investment in inventory consistent with meeting given production plans. The Material Requirements System has been designated MRP-I. A more sophisticated version, featuring a higher degree of integration with cost accounting and other systems, is referred to as the Manufacturing Resource Planning System (MRP-II).

MRP systems are widely considered by industry and DOD as effective and efficient inventory control techniques that reduce the procurement of materials, the storing of excessive quantities, and the generating of obsolete and surplus stocks, and indeed many DOD procurement and contract administration officials have been quite familiar with their use. Inherent in the effective operation of these systems is the rapid movement of materials, as required, from contracts or cost objectives for which they were originally acquired to those where they are most urgently needed (instead of purchasing additional stocks while duplicate materials await movement into production).

DCAA audits concluded that these systems violated several cost accounting standards, progress payment clauses for fixed-price contracts, allowable cost and payment clauses for cost-type contracts, and so on. In some instances, the audit agency asserted there were violations of the Truth in Negotiations Act, overcharges and mischarges to government contracts, etc. One large contractor had been accused of fraud and the audit agency was confident it could find additional cases of fraud among the 300 major contractors it programmed to investigate.

This major investigation was coordinated with, and received the approval of, high level acquisition officials in the Pentagon, and contract administration field offices were directed to coordinate fully with DCAA's investigation and assist the agency in obtaining any and every kind of contractor record the auditors might conceive as somehow applicable.

The nationwide investigation was made public by DOD lest GAO or Congress learn of the fraud and related possibilities and move in before the Defense Department had an opportunity. However, this action in no way impeded congressional critics, who held a series of hearings, conjecturing on the possibilities of hundreds of millions in overcharging. Even DCAA, which had the major role in establishing this investigation, was criticized by some congressmen for not initiating this action earlier.

An opportunity to gain credit or otherwise become associated with a program that might disclose significant irregularities is not one for other government bounty hunters to pass up, and DOD IG jumped in to investigate some of the larger contractors, in full competition with DCAA. At this writing, there has been no official word about GAO and congressional staff investigators joining in competitive investigations. It is understood that GAO debated entering into the competition or awaiting until DCAA and DOD IG efforts ran their course and then criticizing these efforts.

At this writing, it seems likely that the investigation of the MRP systems will yield allegations of fraud, waste, abuse, etc. It is ironic in many respects because industry associations have long advised DOD officials that obtaining the economy, efficiency, and savings available from these systems, which are widely used in commercial work, could not be achieved within the letter of the numerous regulations. Industry officials had recommended that DOD-industry groups be established to study this matter to see if DOD were amenable to relax some of the regulations in order to obtain these savings. Unfortunately, DOD took no action on these recommendations at that time.

Chapter XXVIII

The General Accounting Office (GAO)

BACKGROUND, AUTHORITY, AND OPERATIONS

To state that the GAO and its head, the Comptroller General of the United States, represent unique phenomena in federal government would be a gross understatement. In the almost seventy years of its existence, the GAO has evolved into an awesome and powerful organization which has sought to extend the word "independent" beyond the limits conceived of by many people involved in the executive, legislative and judicial branches of the government and certainly by many in the private sector.

Near the conclusion of his fifteen-year tour as Comptroller General, Mr. Elmer Staats caused to be written *GAO 1966-1981: An Administrative History.* An appendix, described as a "previously unpublished paper [which] grew out of discussions between Comptroller General Staats and Assistant Comptroller General Morse," contains the following observations:

> Some have asserted that, as head of an agency in the legislative branch, the Comptroller General acts as an "agent of the Congress" and is a legislative officer. On the other hand, GAO has asserted, and the courts have confirmed, that the Comptroller General, while performing duties that are clearly an adjunct of the legislative process, *is an independent officer of the United States* who performs many of the legislative functions. Stated simply in Staats' words, *"He is an agent of Congress in the sense he functions on their behalf, but he does not do their bidding." Retaining this concept of independence requires that the Comptroller General remain a constitutional appointment made by the President.* (Italics added.)

GAO's ambitions for recognition as, in effect, an independent fourth branch of the federal government foundered on the provisions of the Gramm-Rudman-Hollings deficit reduction legislation, which gave the Comptroller General (CG) a key role in eliminating the national deficit. This Act provided that the Congressional Budget Office and the Office of Management and Budget were to issue a joint report to the CG specifying their estimates of federal expenditures and revenues and the extent to which the deficit would exceed ceilings established in the Act. The CG would then conduct an independent analysis and report his views to the President and Congress, and the President would be required to reduce expenditures in accordance with the CG's report.

The law was challenged by a number of interested parties, as well as the Department of Justice, asserting that the section of the law providing the CG with executive powers was unconstitutional because the CG was in the legislative branch. After considerable litigation, the controversy ended up in the Supreme Court, which affirmed the lower court decision that the CG is subservient to Congress because he may be removed by joint congressional resolution. Although the decision appeared appropriate, some observers believed that there were additional and significant reasons for ruling that GAO is an agent of Congress and a part of the legislative branch.

While alleging its independence, the record indicates that GAO performs many of its investigations, audits, and other work at the direct "requests" of congressional committees and individual congressmen. Observers experienced much difficulty in identifying any GAO investigations conducted at the request of the White House, and the records do not disclose substantive efforts on behalf of the executive departments and agencies. Additionally, in some of its congressionally directed investigations of executive agencies, GAO issues its reports directly to the legislative requesters, at times without even affording the investigated agency an opportunity to review and comment on the investigative conclusions before the report moves into the public domain by leaks to the press.

Efforts to establish GAO as some kind of independent fourth branch of the federal government were again challenged with respect to the role of the "legislative watchdog" in bid protests under the provisions of the Competition in Contracting Act (CICA), Public Law 98-369. The challenges related to the powers delegated to GAO under the Act to direct a "stay" of a contract award until the GAO considered any bid protest and handed down its opinion with respect thereto. At this writing, lower courts have not found these CICA provisions unconstitutional, on the technical and legal grounds that while GAO did enter the realm reserved for the executive branch, its mandatory authority was limited to delaying rather than overruling an action by the executive branch.

History

The GAO was established by the Budget and Accounting Act of 1921. The first Comptroller General, John R. McCarl, was a lawyer appointed by President Harding. He served the full fifteen-year tour, 1921-1936, and set the GAO's course as a watchdog that continually challenged and disputed actions proposed by the executive branch of the government. The post was not filled again until President Roosevelt appointed Fred H. Brown, a former senator, in 1939. Brown served only two years, retiring because of ill health and without having any significant effect on the GAO's development. President Roosevelt then appointed Lindsay C. Warren, who had enjoyed considerable experience and prestige in the House of Representatives. During Warren's term, 1940-1954, the agency's strength grew with the passage of the Budget and Procedures Act of 1950 and other significant legislation. Although Warren appeared to share many of McCarl's views concerning the GAO's responsibilities to serve as a watchdog over the federal establishment's expenditures, the accounts of those days invariably depict him as an individual sensitive to the importance of creating a favorable image for the GAO and reducing the hostility between the GAO and the executive branch.

When Warren was forced to leave before the end of his term because of poor health, President Eisenhower appointed Joseph C. Campbell, the first Comptroller General who was not a lawyer and did not have legislative experience. Campbell, too, failed to serve the entire fifteen-year term, retiring for health reasons in 1966. During his tour, however, he initiated many significant changes, some of which enhanced the professional accounting image of the agency and others which led to hostilities with a broad spectrum of people in both the public and private sectors. To his credit must be attributed, among other achievements, the GAO's move away from detailed voucher audits and into comprehensive management audits, the forerunners of today's audits for economy, efficiency and program results. In moving the GAO from voucher checkers to professional auditors, Campbell transferred a number of minor checking functions and the related personnel to executive agencies and recruited an increasing number of certified public accountants from public practice, industry and other government agencies.

The other side of the coin was the emergence of an increasing number of extremely critical and harsh reports directed at both government procurement agencies and government contractors. Some of the reports displayed little or no regard for appropriate tone and strongly indicated that some defense contractors were deliberately overpricing government contracts while the Defense Department officials lacked either the competence or zeal to prevent the overcharging. The reports included inflammatory titles and listed names of contractors and procurement officials involved. At times, these people were not given appropriate opportunity to state their side of the story.

These reports drew the interest of the press, which obtained frequent ready-made sensational headlines. The defenses and responses of government agencies and contractors, of course, seldom received the same attention. As matters worsened, congressional hearings were held at which, for probably the only time, the GAO was taken to task. Mr. Campbell resigned shortly thereafter and was replaced by Elmer B. Staats.

Elmer Staats had spent virtually his entire working career in the federal government, including service as deputy director of the Bureau of the Budget (predecessor of the Office of Management and Budget) under four presidents. He knew the federal and legislative establishments and many of their leaders and was astute politically. His academic background was in economics, and he continued and strengthened the GAO's movement from conventional accounting and auditing to evaluations of economy, efficiency and program results. During his fifteen-year tour, the GAO challenged the Department of Defense in matters relating to the selection and use of weapons systems; the old Department of Health, Education and Welfare over medical programs, education methods and philosophy, and welfare policies and practices; the Department of Agriculture on farming programs and subsidies, and so on. There was hardly an activity within the federal government, large or small, that did not come under the GAO's surveillance and criticism.

In recent years, disclosures (not by the GAO) identified incidences of what has come to be known as almost one word: fraud, waste and abuse. The

GAO immediately jumped in to proclaim that the reports to date represented only the tip of the iceberg and criticized all of the federal agencies for their failures to display greater vigilance in ferreting out and preventing the irregularities. Under Staats, the GAO has vigorously championed the internal audit organizations of the executive departments and agencies and chastized federal officials for not following up and taking action on the deficiencies alleged by their own internal auditors. All of the agencies are now required to maintain records of their auditors' findings and the actions taken on them.

In the early summer of 1981, President Reagan appointed Charles A. Bowsher, a partner in one of the leading CPA firms, to succeed Staats and admonished him to accord priority to rooting out fraud, waste and abuse. Apart from brief service as Assistant Secretary of the Navy for Financial Management, Bowsher's career has been in public accounting practice. Although he probably should have a better understanding of the private sector than any of his predecessors and although his public accounting background should have given him a deeper insight into how fraud, waste and abuse occur and can be deterred and how to distinguish among the three, the current Comptroller General has shown little evidence of providing new leadership or direction to GAO.

As mentioned earlier, the scope of the GAO's activities has expanded far beyond just about anybody's imagination. To list but a few, the GAO has reviewed and made recommendations concerning (1) the extent to which existing programs and activities achieve the objectives set forth in the Economic Opportunity Act and its successor antipoverty programs, (2) the defense acquisition process, including inquiries into the "deterioration of the expected performance characteristics of individual weapons systems . . .," (3) the ability of the Navy to "adequately defend critical sealanes against enemy attack. Were the carrier task forces composed of the appropriate ships and were they available on time and properly equipped?", (4) assessment of "cost, schedule and *performance* of major civil agency acquisitions [including the] Nation's first liquid metal fast breeder reactor, the Federal Aviation Administration's air control system, NASA's space shuttle, and METRO—the Washington, D.C. area's subway system," and (5) administration of nondiscrimination laws.

The above audits were mentioned in *GAO 1966-1981: An Administrative History,* prepared by the GAO staff and referred to earlier. The same publication lists with apparent pride the following examples of reports issued as a result of "reviews aimed directly at assessing program impact, or the results that programs were designed to achieve, and identifying causes that inhibit satisfactory performance":

> Early Childhood and Family Development Programs Improve the Quality of Life for Low Income Families
>
> War on Organized Crime Faltering—Federal Strike Forces Not Getting the Job Done
>
> The National School Lunch Program
>
> Handgun Control Effectiveness and Costs

In its 1986 annual report, GAO seemed concerned that the Supreme Court's decision relating to Gramm-Rudman might affect some of its other work, including bid protests, but noted that this authority had been upheld in the lower courts. As to deficit reduction, the report states that while GAO no longer has the statutory function of Gramm-Rudman, it is carrying out the same kinds of assessments it would have performed under the law—submitting advisory reports to Congress that contain forecasts of the deficits and calculating the across-the-board budget cut percentages.

In view of the major federal income tax action in 1986, the enactment of the Tax Reform Act of 1986, Public Law 99-514 (see Chapter XXIX of this text), GAO asserted that Congress required information to assist in evaluating whether the Act was having its intended effect, and it issued a series of studies to Congress on most of the major provisions of this law. As in prior years, GAO has devoted considerable attention to the Internal Revenue Service and alleged that its reports to Congress resulted in improving the policies and practices of the IRS.

GAO asserted that it had performed a number of studies that assessed the safety issues of nuclear energy. The annual report lays claim to extensive investigations into this area, including both commercial plants and Department of Energy (DOE) nuclear facilities. It has studied the Soviet Union's Chernobyl accident, and contrasted and compared safety and other characteristics of the Russian reactor and a DOE weapons material production reactor. The agency has been providing periodic reports to Congress regarding the safe deposit of nuclear waste, and evaluated the policies and practices of the Nuclear Regulatory Commission.

GAO also studied ways and means of promoting safer airways and has continued to emphasize this area as a result of actual and near accidents. It alleges that its investigations in this area and reviews of FAA's programs and operations have been of great help to Congress and the Department of Transportation in improving safety and efficiency.

There was hardly an activity of the government which the GAO did not audit, investigate or "evaluate." It explored the crisis in the farm credit system and concluded that "an underlying cause . . . is continued worldwide surplus." Its work on foreign aid expressed concern over the adequacy of the controls. It examined health programs and reported the "achieving high-quality care at an affordable cost is a key domestic issue and the underlying theme of our health work." It further criticized the lack of a coordinated national policy for the elderly. Evaluating overall financial management in the federal government, GAO concluded that "budgetary reform, improved accountability, and better financial management are necessary."

Boasting of its accomplishments, GAO stated it "continues to explore new ways to *help Congress* face future challenges." (Emphasis added.) It commented on its "unique audit and evaluation work" and its "equally unique . . . opportunity to affect government operations and budget decisions."

With further reference to discussions about GAO's "independence" and status as a "fourth branch of the government," it is interesting to study the concluding comments in GAO's 1986 annual report:

Assisting the Congress

GAO's primary goal is to serve Congress' need for accurate, objective, and timely information. More than 78 percent of the work done by GAO's audit and evaluation staff in fiscal year 1986 entailed responding to congressional committee and member requests and performing audit activities legislatively mandated by Congress. The rest of GAO's audit and evaluation work consisted mainly of assignments generated from GAO's planning process in close coordination with committees, members, and staff.

During the past year, GAO also responded to over 250 requests for legal opinions and advice from committees and members of Congress. For example, GAO provided Congress with an analysis of the legality of the Defense Department's activities in Honduras, alerted Congress to the constitutional issues raised by proposals to implement a drug testing program for federal employees, and testified on the legality of former Special Assistant to the President Michael Deaver's representation of Canada in the acid rain controversy.

GAO also assists Congress by assigning staff to work directly for House and Senate committees. In 1986 GAO staff assisted committees in such activities as investigating the pricing of spare parts by the military service, helping draft legislation for the new civil service retirement system, and researching various environmental issues. Details on GAO staff assigned to congressional committees during fiscal year 1986 are included in a separate appendix to this report that is available upon request.

In view of GAO's strong dedication to Congress, observers experience difficulty in accepting assertions that the agency is an independent fourth branch of the government.

Over 80% of GAO's professional staff consists of personnel with accounting academic backgrounds and questions have been raised as to their competence to evaluate the many technical, scientific and other complex programs of the government. Several years ago, GAO reclassified most of its accountants and auditors to "evaluators."

GAO AND GOVERNMENT CONTRACTING

GAO's report of its activities in 1986 states that nearly 30% of its resources was spent on defense-related work. The congressional watchdog asserted that its work in this area "resulted in about $10.3 billion in measurable benefits to the taxpayer." It also claimed its "evaluations of major items in Defense Department's budget led to potential budget reductions of about $15 billion." Although the agency's evaluations of Defense Department activities covered a wide range, including "problems that could lead to ineffective weapons and wasteful purchases," criticisms of specific major weapons systems, military compensation, etc., our review here is largely limited to costing and pricing matters.

GAO and Cost Accounting Standards

The promulgations of the Cost Accounting Standards Board (CASB) have had a profound influence on the many in the public and private sectors who award, administer, audit and perform CAS-covered contracts, and this text devotes considerable space thereto. We invite attention particularly to Chapter VIII, which traces the origins and demise of the CASB. It is interesting to note that the study concluding that cost accounting standards were feasible and desirable (P.L. 90-370) was conducted by GAO and that the enabling legislation in P.L. 91-379 specified that the Comptroller General would become the permanent chairman of the CASB. The first Executive Secretary was an ex-employee of GAO, as were a number of the staff members. It is interesting, too, to read the concession that the Board was never able to quantify the costs and benefits of its promulgations despite the statement included in the prefatory comments of each standard that its benefits would outweigh its costs. It was generally understood that there was no basis for these statements, but the CASB did not admit this fact until its twilight days.

One of Staats's infrequent congressional defeats came about in connection with his vigorous efforts to transfer the functions of the CASB to GAO or, failing that, to OMB. The fate of the CASB had already been sealed by the congressional decision to provide no funds for its operation after September 30, 1980, and Staats vainly tried to salvage some of its authority. When these efforts failed, he employed two members of the CASB staff on the rolls of the GAO and charged them to plan a GAO investigation into the manner in which the promulgations of the defunct Board were being implemented.

GAO continued its close interest in, and defense of, any and all promulgations of the Board headed by its ex-chief. In recent years, its main attention focused on legislative efforts to reconstitute the CASB. As reviewed in Chapter VIII of this text, it failed in these endeavors and in its vigorous efforts to prevent the incorporation of CAS into FAR.

Profit on Defense Contracts

It is far easier to criticize than to create and GAO's major contributions have been in finding fault with policies and practices of the executive departments and agencies. In contrast, it has displayed a strong reluctance toward positive and constructive action of its own. For example, after joining in criticisms of alleged excessive profits by defense contractors, GAO was requested by Congress to perform a study in this area. The agency offered various reasons why it could not or should not, and ultimately did perform a study but only after being directed to do so by law (P.L. 91-121). GAO ultimately reported that the rates of return on defense work in the late 1960s averaged the same or less than those on commercial work. It recommended the development (by others) of uniform guidelines for determining profit objectives on government contracts, a type of recommendation GAO has continued to advance.

Profit '76

President Theodore Roosevelt in a memorable observation stated:

> It is not the critic who counts, not the man who points out how the strong man stumbled or how the doer of deeds could have done them better. The credit belongs to the man who is actually in the arena ... who, at best, knows in the end the triumph of high achievement; and who, at the worst, if he fails, at least fails while daring greatly, so that his place shall never be with those cold timid souls who know neither victory nor defeat.

Without necessarily suggesting a direct analogy, it is a fact that DOD has continually explored profit policies and procedures, seeking concepts that would be fair to the government and also provide the necessary incentives for competent companies to seek defense work and perform the contracts efficiently. A brief history of these efforts is contained in Chapter XXV of this text.

As described in the above-mentioned chapter, Profit '76 represented one of the most extensive and intensive efforts to achieve these objectives. Some eight months after the new policy became effective, GAO issued a report on a "limited review" of the Profit '76 study. GAO was unhappy that DOD refused to provide the legislative watchdog with basic contractor financial data on which some of the study's conclusions were predicated. This refusal was well known in advance, for contractors would not have agreed to provide the data if it were made available to GAO, whose assurance of confidentiality had not impressed industry. GAO also expressed reservations concerning other matters, particularly doubting that the .7 adjustment factor to costs was sufficient to compensate for the increased recognition to capital employed.

In March 1979, GAO issued a more comprehensive report on Profit '76, concluding that the intended results of the new profit policy had not been achieved and, in fact, had increased the average profit negotiated with defense contractors.

Defense Financial and Investment Review (DFAIR)

Continuing its efforts to formulate an improved profit policy, DOD conducted a full-range study to include the interrelations of profit, pricing and financing. Among GAO criticisms of this study's conclusions was the effort to achieve a comparable basis for relating profits on defense contracts and commercial work by showing progress payments on the liability side of the balance sheet for reasons detailed in Chapter XXV of this text. GAO insisted in written comments and in congressional testimony that progress payments should be displayed as a reduction of assets. Thus, as profit markups were computed as a percentage of assets, the markups on defense work would be shown much higher than reported in DFAIR.

Profit and CAS 414

There was one occasion in which GAO supported DOD profit methodology. Some congressmen concluded that DOD's permitting facilities investment to be used twice in the computation of profit objectives resulted in "double-dipping." GAO was requested to review this matter and also provide answers to the questions as to whether CAS 414 had continued relevance in light of current profit policy and whether that standard, in the context of DOD's profit policy, induces investment in cost-reducing facilities.

As indicated earlier, GAO had consistently defended all aspects of the cost accounting standards issued by a board chaired by the then head of the GAO. It thus reported that there was no double-dipping because although the facilities investment value enters into the calculation twice, double-dipping was prevented by the offset factor. It took the occasion, however, to assert that profits had been increasing and attributed this to flaws in the offset design. GAO thus concluded that CAS 414 did have continuing relevance but reported it was not as yet in a position to state definitively whether DOD's profit policy had indeed induced increased investment in a cost-reducing policy.

GAO Proposal for Legislation Requiring Contractor Profit Reporting

For over two decades GAO either alleged defense contractors were reaping excessive profits or criticized DOD for failing to develop what the legislative watchdog considered an appropriate profit policy. As mentioned earlier, GAO did perform a profit study on its own, when directed by law in 1971, but its main contribution was a recommendation that some other organization develop a policy. It has been fairly consistent in recommending consideration to invested capital, a concept long shared by DOD and others. The problem was how to formulate the actual procedures, the methodology to be used, the distribution of weighting factors, and so on.

GAO also continued its attacks on every profit study performed by others because its demands for access to all records and data developed were not met. In both Profit '76 and DFAIR, the many major contractors who agreed to submit the considerable data required, much of it proprietary, participated in arrangements whereby such data were validated by independent certified public accountants and such validated data were then compiled by another CPA firm. The government was thus assured that it had obtained valid data from which to work, and contractors were assured of confidentiality. GAO, however, was unhappy that it was unable to gain access to all of such data.

In the summer of 1986, testifying at a congressional hearing, GAO representatives proposed legislation that would make it mandatory for contractors to submit extensive data relating to both government and commercial work, accompanied by certifications by independent CPA firms. This data would be turned over to some government agency (not GAO), which would develop an appropriate methodology for accumulating, evaluating and reporting on the results. A major feature of the plan is that while GAO would have no responsibility for accomplishing the work or evaluating the results, it would, by law, have access to all of the contractors' records, all of the working papers and reports prepared by the CPA firms, and all of the material used by the government agency that would compile and report on the results and make related recommendations—an ideal arrangement for the ultimate critic.

GAO's proposal found no support in the executive branch of the government and certainly none in the private sector. Undaunted, GAO continued to press its proposal, and did attract support among some congressional critics of this country's defense program. In congressional hearings, testimony unanimously opposed this scheme. GAO would not take on the task itself, it did not trust DOD to perform it, and its canvassing of other government agencies found none to be interested. Those turning down the GAO often included OFPP, Federal Trade Commission, Bureau of the Census, Bureau of Labor Statistics, SEC, Department of Commerce (Bureau of Economic Analysis), and DCAA.

At this writing legislation has been introduced to assign this chore to OFPP, together with some responsibility for CAS.

Unallowable Costs

Another major GAO interest during the past two decades has centered on unallowable costs. In numerous reports and testimonies at congressional hearings, GAO has hammered away at the following points.

The contract cost principles require "clarification." The ambiguity or lack of specificity enables contractors to recover costs that are intended to be unallowable.

"Bottom line" negotiations are an evil that permits contractors to recover portions of unallowable costs and continue to claim them in subsequent years.

Contracting officers allow costs that have been questioned by DCAA auditors without appropriate justification.

Reports replete with "horror stories" of contractors recovering patently inappropriate costs attracted the interest and attention of congressional defense critics, and a number of investigations were performed with teams comprised essentially of GAO and DCAA auditors. More horror stories presented at congressional hearings resulted in considerable legislation, described in Chapter XVI of this text, that specifically established certain costs as unallowable and directed the Secretary of Defense to "clarify" the allowability of a number of other costs. Other legislative provisions virtually eliminated bottom line negotiations of indirect costs, directed contracting officers not to resolve any costs questioned by auditors until they secured documentation and the auditors' opinions, provided penalties for contractors who submitted unallowable indirect costs, and so on.

Defective Cost or Pricing Data

As discussed in Chapter XXII of this text, GAO and the DOD OIG combined on a relentless campaign to "strengthen" P.L. 87-653. In fact these organizations, with DCAA assistance, succeeded in persuading Congress to enact legislation that stripped contractors of virtually all legitimate defenses that had been accepted by boards of contract appeals and federal courts for many years against government assertions of defective pricing.

Bid Protests

An important and interesting facet of GAO's activities relates to its adjudication of bid protests. Many members of the legal profession have questioned GAO's statutory authority for assuming this jurisdiction, and, in recent years, two attorneys general of the United States have formally challenged it. However, for many reasons more appropriate for comment in a legal text, including the inclination of federal courts to accept GAO decisions, perhaps to relieve their own overcrowded calendars, procurement bid protests are widely accepted as a GAO function.

History and Perspective as Viewed by the GAO

The following account is quoted from *GAO 1966-1981: An Administrative History:*

GAO receives the protest of an interested party to the award of a contract for procurement or sale by a Federal agency whose accounts are subject to settlement by the Office. From a historical and practical perspective, GAO has become the highest level of appeal within the Government to resolve bid protests. In recognition of GAO's expertise in this area, in recent years courts have often relied upon GAO decisions and advice in disposing of the bid protest cases brought before them.

During this period, GAO's legal role in Federal procurement has responded to external and internal developments that resulted in changes of approach designed to improve the resolution of protests and achieve more effectiveness and fairness. These changes reflected GAO's goal to maintain the delicate balance between a dissatisfied competitor's right to a full and fair hearing and the Government's necessity for the timely acquisition of supplies and services to satisfy minimum needs at the lowest cost. Some changes were made in response to recommendations of the Commission on Government Procurement issued in December 1972, which were designed to formalize and expedite the resolution of bid protests. The major changes basically concerned (1) formalizing of bid protest procedures, (2) developing administrative remedies, and (3) expanding of jurisdiction in the Federal grant area.

From 1921 to 1967, protests were handled without publicly announced procedures. Responding to increased congressional interest in this protest work and valid criticisms voiced at industry-Government symposiums on Government contracts, the first GAO bid protest procedures were issued in 1967 and 1968. These procedures permitted the contractors involved, either the protesters or the awardees, to request conferences with the OGC attorneys handling the cases. They also reserved GAO's right to disclose the protests publicly and provided for notice to the successful bidders if GAO sustains the protests.

In 1971 GAO announced extensive interim protest-handling guidelines that (1) provided for speedier disposition of protests by establishing specific time limits on all parties involved, including GAO, (2) prescribed strict timeframes within which protests were to be filed, (3) provided for inviting all interested parties to protest conferences, (4) assured automatic participation by all interested parties by prompt protest notifications and forwarding of relevant documents and (5) reduced the number of cases of awards made before decision. After 3 years experience under those procedures, detailed permanent procedures which generally tracked the interim procedures were issued in 1975. They continue in effect today.

Complementary measures and policies have been devised to resolve protests as fast as possible. These include summary denials where protests on their face have no merit and summary dismissals of matters which GAO does not have to decide.

One problem with bid protests has been finding a means to provide an effective remedy in the relatively small number of cases where GAO has decided that protesters were wrongfully denied contract awards. This is particularly difficult when the procuring agencies have already awarded the contracts and the contractors have commenced performance. Rather than require that the contracts be terminated, GAO for many years merely recommended that the agencies in the future not commit the improper practices disclosed by the protests.

In recent years, GAO began recommending termination of the improperly awarded contracts and award to the protesters in appropriate cases. Such recommendations are rare. Terminated contractors are made whole by being reimbursed for costs for performance, and the wronged protesters either obtain contracts or other opportunities to compete. In other cases, GAO recommends other remedies, such as nonexercise of contract options, resolicitation with a view toward termination if beneficial to the Government, and corrective action contingent on further agency analysis. Since 1970, these recommendations have been reported to specified congressional committees under procedures in the Legislative Reorganization Act of 1970 requiring that the agencies report to the Congress on the actions taken on GAO recommendations. Corrective action has generally followed GAO's report.

In addition, GAO began in 1975 to grant bid or proposal preparation costs—the protester's costs of competing for the contract—where remedial action is impractical but otherwise would have been warranted. Previously GAO had decided that these claims would not be settled until appropriate criteria and standards for recovery had been judicially established. The Court of Claims, in a decision announced in 1956 and subsequently refined by decisions through 1974, determined that recovery is permitted only if a bidder or proposer would have received an award but for arbitrary or capricious Government action. Following the court's lead, GAO has granted recovery in several cases in the last few years.

Extent of GAO Activity Relating to Bid Protests

The volume of this activity in the 1975-1979 period with respect to protests received and closed annually was in the 1100-1600 range. This activity increased in the 1980s, and in 1986, the first full year of bid protests under CICA, GAO reported total cases increased to 2,891, including 339 reconsideration requests, and total cases closed increased to 2,884, including 364 reconsideration requests.

One of the major and controversial questions over the years related to the chances of success as a result of filing a bid protest with GAO. In what has been heralded as an encouragement to file bid protests, GAO developed what it described as a "protester effectiveness rate" in 1985, a percentage of protests that resulted either in voluntary corrective actions by the contracting agency or in a GAO decision sustaining the protest. This percentage, based on withdrawals and dismissals resulting from corrective action, was 18.5% for 1985. For 1986, the Comptroller General trumpeted, it had increased to 24.3%.

On the other hand, statistics of protests decided by GAO on their merits reflected a different trend. For CICA cases in 1985, 18.7% were sustained, while in 1986, the percentage fell to 13.8%. The fact that the sustention rate "decreased somewhat" was explained by the Comptroller General as attributable "to an increase in the percentage of cases considered on their merits, and to greater willingness by contracting activities to voluntarily correct problems leading to protests." The inference is that the knowledge of GAO's existence in the bid protest process "encourages" contracting activities to heed complaints.

The 1985 bid protest activity report announced improvements in GAO's office of general counsel that enabled the agency to comply with CICA requirements to issue decisions within 90 days, or 45 calendar days in "express option" cases. The average number of days for closing CICA cases in 1985 was 22 days; for cases decided on their merits after full development, the average was 61. While keeping within CICA requirements, the comparable statistics for 1986 were 31.3 and 65.9 working days. These averages were well under those experienced prior to CICA. A significant factor in this decrease is attributable to the contracting agencies' compliance with CICA requirements to file reports within 25 days, unless extensions are granted. As compared to an average of 45.2 days for cases prior to CICA, the agencies averaged 21.9 working days in 1985 and 23.2 in 1986.

GAO's bid protest report for 1986 abounds with statistics of varying interest to companies doing business with the government and to government contracting agencies. The following is a summary of the disposition of initial protests closed in 1986:

Protests withdrawn:		
Due to corrective action taken	273	
For other known reasons	55	
For unknown reasons	208	
Total closed by withdrawal		536
Decided on merits:		
Denied	630	
Sustained	101	
Total decided on merits		731
Other protests closed:		
Due to corrective action taken	65	
Without known corrective action	1188	
Total other dispositions		1253
Total initial protests closed		2520

We noted earlier that the percentage of protests decided on their merits in 1986 and sustained was 13.8% and that the "protester effectiveness rate" was 24.3%. The experience of some of the major agencies with a significant volume of bid protests is tabulated below:

	% Sus.	Eff. Rate
Agriculture	5.3%	12.7%
Air Force	9.0	27.6
Army	10.7	25.1
DLA	12.5	38.1
GSA	16.7	17.0
Interior	14.3	16.0
Navy	14.3	29.6
Transportation	20.0	23.9
VA	20.0	12.3

An analysis of issue areas for bid protests revealed that the majority in both 1985 (24.2%) and 1986 (26.3%) was based on the allegation that the protester's offer was improperly rejected. Challenges that the solicitation was defective was the second most common issue involved in both years, 22.2% in 1985 and 17.7% in 1986. And the third issue area in both years was the claim that the awardee's offer was improperly accepted, 12.1% in 1985 and 16.4% in 1986. Other major issue areas included claims that the procurement was improperly sole-sourced, that the selection methodology was "otherwise" improper, that the protester was unjustifiably found to be nonresponsible, and that the awardee was not responsible.

Formal Bid Protest Procedures

GAO's authority was expanded and strengthened by the provisions of Public Law 98-369.

Salient excerpts of the provisions relating to the GAO authority on bid protests are set forth below:

(b)(1) In accordance with the procedures issued pursuant to subsection (d), the Comptroller General shall have authority to decide a protest submitted by an interested party or referred by an executive agency or a court of the United States.

(2) Except as provided in subsection (c)(1), the Comptroller General shall issue a final protest decision within 90 working days after the date of a protest unless the Comptroller General determines and states in writing the reasons that the specific circumstances of the protest require a longer period.

(3) The Comptroller General shall notify the executive agency within one working day after the date of the receipt of a protest and the executive agency shall submit a complete report (including all relevant documents) on the protested procurement to the Comptroller General within 25 working days after the agency's receipt of the notice of such protest, unless notified that the protest has been dismissed pursuant to subsection (c)(4) or unless the Comptroller General, upon a showing by such agency, determines and states in writing the reasons that the specific circumstances of the protest require a longer period. In a case determined by the Comptroller General to be suitable for the express option under subsection (c)(1), such report and documents shall be submitted within 10 working days after such receipt.

(4)(A) A contract may not be awarded on the basis of the protested procurement after the contracting officer has received notice of a protest to the Comptroller General and while the protest is pending.

(B) The head of the procurement activity responsible for award of the contract may authorize the award of a contract notwithstanding a protest of which the agency has notice under this paragraph—

(i) upon a written finding that urgent and compelling circumstances which significantly affect interests of the United States will not permit awaiting the decision of the Comptroller General; and

(ii) after the Comptroller General is advised of such finding.

(C) Before the award of a contract, a finding may not be made under subparagraph (B)(i) unless the award of the contract is otherwise likely to occur within 30 days.

(5)(A) If the contract has been awarded before the receipt of notice of a protest, contract performance shall be ceased or the contract shall be suspended upon receipt of such notice and while the protest is pending. This paragraph shall not apply when the protest is filed more than 10 days after award of the contract.

(B) The head of the procurement activity responsible for award of the contract may, after notifying the Comptroller General of his findings, authorize the performance of a contract notwithstanding a protest of which the agency has notice under this paragraph—

(i) upon a written finding that contract performance will be in the Government's best interests, except that if the head of the procurement activity makes such a finding, the Comptroller General shall make his determination of the appropriate recommended relief (if the protest is sustained) without regard to any costs or disruption from terminating, recompeting, or reawarding the contract; or

(ii) upon a written finding that urgent and compelling circumstances which significantly affect interests of the United States will not permit awaiting the decision of the Comptroller General.

(6) The authority of the head of the procuring activity to make findings and authorize award and performance of contracts under paragraphs (4) and (5) may not be delegated.

(7) The Comptroller General is authorized to determine whether a solicitation, proposed award, or award protested under this section complies with procurement statutes and regulations. If the Comptroller General determines that the solicitation, proposed award, or award does not comply with a procurement statute or regulation, or both, the Comptroller General shall recommend that the agency—

(A) refrain from exercising any of its options under the contract;

(B) recompete the contract immediately;

(C) issue a new solicitation;

(D) terminate the contract;

(E) award a contract consistent with the requirements of such statutes and regulations;

(F) comply with any combination of recommendations under clauses (A), (B), (C), (D), and (E); or

(G) comply with such other recommendations as the Comptroller General determines to be necessary in order to promote compliance with procurement statutes and regulations.

(c)(1) To the maximum extent practicable, the Comptroller General shall provide for the inexpensive and expeditious resolution of protests under this section. The Comptroller General shall establish an express option for deciding those protests which the Comptroller General determines suitable for resolution within 45 days from the date of protest. Within such deadlines as the Comptroller General prescribes, each executive agency shall provide to an interested party any document relevant to the protested procurement action (including the report required by subsection (b)(3)) that would not give such party a competitive advantage and that such party is otherwise authorized by law to receive.

* * * *

(5)(A) If the Comptroller General determines that a solicitation, proposed award, or award of a contract does not comply with a procurement statute or regulation, the Comptroller General may further declare an appropriate party to be entitled to the costs of—

(i) filing and pursuing the protest, including reasonable attorneys' fees; and

(ii) bid and proposal preparation.

(B) Monetary awards to which a party is declared to be entitled under subparagraph (A) shall be paid promptly by the executive agency concerned out of funds available to or for the use of such executive agency for the purpose of the procurement of property and services.

(d)(1) Within 180 days after the date of enactment of this subchapter, the Comptroller General shall establish such procedures, not inconsistent with this section, as may be necessary to the expeditious execution of the protest decision function, including procedures for accelerated resolution of the protest under the express option authorized by subsection (c)(1). Such procedures shall provide that the protest process shall not be delayed by the failure of a party to make a filing within the time provided or such filing.

* * * *

(e) An interested party adversely affected or aggrieved by the action, or the failure to act, of a Government agency with respect to a solicitation or award may obtain judicial review thereof to the extent provided by sections 702 through 706 of title 5, including determinations necessary to resolve disputed material facts or when otherwise appropriate.

(f) For purposes of this section—

(1) the term "protest" means a challenge to a solicitation or to the award or proposed award of a procurement contract; and

(2) the term "interested party", with respect to a contract, means an actual or prospective bidder or offeror whose direct economic interest would be affected by the award of or failure to award the contract. . . . .

As mentioned earlier, GAO's authority to adjudicate bid protests has been frequently questioned and, in recent years, even formally challenged by two attorneys general of the United States. The agency has asserted this power by virtue of the Budget and Accounting Act of 1921, which empowers it to determine the legality of federal government expenditures and to settle transactions between the federal government and its contractors. It is a fact that GAO has been active in this area for over 60 years and has built up considerable experience and expertise, which has influenced the federal courts, with their overcrowded dockets, to look favorably upon GAO's activity.

President Reagan signed H.R. 4170 on July 18, 1984, and stated that he vigorously objected to the "provisions that would unconstitutionally attempt to delegate to the Comptroller General of the United States, an officer of Congress, the power to perform duties and responsibilities that in our constitutional system may be performed only by officials of the Executive branch." His message further advised that he was "instructing the Attorney General to inform all executive branch agencies as soon as possible with respect to how they may comply with the provisions of the bill in a manner consistent with the Constitution." Lawyers active in federal government procurement waited with interest to see what kind of guidance the Department of Justice could issue that would be both responsive to the President's instructions and not violative of the legislation.

The position that GAO's close participation in the awarding of contracts is unconstitutional was formally expressed in a letter from the Justice Department to Congressman Brooks on April 20, 1984, in connection with his proposal, which at the time had been incorporated in H.R. 5184. The Justice Department asserted that the "Comptroller General is properly considered to be an officer of the legislative branch. As such, he cannot exercise executive or judicial authority without violating the doctrine of separation of powers . . . ." Congressman Brooks sent the lengthy Justice Department letter to GAO which, of course, disagreed with DOJ. We shall not attempt to discuss the differing interpretations of several leading cases in this area as viewed by GAO and DOJ, but note that GAO reiterated that it "has been deciding executive branch award protests for about 60 years . . . [and] has become the principal forum for resolving the protests of disappointed bidders."

With lawyers in both the private and public sectors divided on this issue, we certainly would not interject our views on this legal point. It does appear that H.R. 4170 significantly strengthens and expands GAO's authority in this area and provides the first specific legislation authorization for the activities it has been engaged in. For example, while a protest to the GAO is pending, a contract may not be awarded pending the GAO's decision unless the head of the procurement agency involved states in writing "that urgent and compelling circumstances which significantly affects interests of the United States will not permit awaiting the decision of the Comptroller General . . . ." A similar finding is necessary if a contract is to be continued where a notice of protest is received within ten days after contract award. In this regard, the House/Senate Conference Report contained the following comments:

If, when a protest is filed, the contract in question has not yet been awarded, an award may not be made unless the head of procuring activity responsible finds and reports to the Comptroller General that urgent and compelling circumstances which significantly affect the interests of the United States will not permit awaiting the Comptroller General decision. (This finding may be made only if the award is likely to occur within 30 calendar days.) If a protest is filed within 10 days after award of the contract, performance shall cease and all related activities which may result in additional obligations being incurred by the United States must be suspended, unless the head of the procuring activity informs the Comptroller General that urgent and compelling circumstances which significantly affect interests of the United States will not permit waiting for the Comptroller General's decision, or that performance of the contract is in the best interest of the United States.

Before notifying the Comptroller General that continued performance of a disputed contract is in the government's best interest, however, the head of the procuring activity should consider potential costs to the government from carrying out relief measures as may be recommended by the Comptroller General if the protest is subsequently sustained. This is to insure that if the Comptroller General sustains a protest, such forms of relief as termination, recompetition, or re-award of the contract will be fully considered for recommendation. Agencies in the past have resisted such recommendations on the grounds that the government's best interest would not be served by relief measures of this sort because of the added expenses involved. This provision is designed to preclude that argument in the future, and thus to avoid prejudicing those relief measures in the Comptroller General's review.

If the Comptroller General determined that a protested procurement action has involved government non-compliance with statutes or regulations, the Comptroller General is required to recommend corrective action to the executive agency responsible, and the head of the procuring activity involved must notify the Comptroller General if the agency has not implemented the recommendations within 60 calendar days. This provision does not preclude the Comptroller General from requesting the agencies to notify the GAO of the status of any other recommendation. An annual report of all notifications received by the Comptroller General, describing each instance of non-implementation, must be submitted to Congress.

PART 21 OF TITLE 4, CODE OF FEDERAL REGULATIONS (4 C.F.R. PART 21)

To implement this legislation, GAO published an amended 4 C.F.R. 21. After almost two years' experience with bid protests under CICA, GAO published revised procedures for comment on March 26, 1987. Two of the major revisions that generated strong criticisms from federal departments and agencies related to increased requirements for contracting agencies to furnish documents to requesters and expanded fact-finding conferences at which representatives of both parties would testify under oath before a GAO official.

Although the final rule was expected in the summer of 1987, the closing date for comments having been established as April 27, 1987, it was not printed in the *Federal Register* until December 8, 1987, with an effective date of January 15, 1988. The final rule contained very few changes of consequence from the March draft.

The full text of the GAO bid protest procedures effective January 15, 1988, is set forth below, as prepared by this agency. The underscored portions represent revisions or additions to the prior final rule.

§ 21.0 Definitions.

(a) "Interested party" for the purposes of filing a protest, means an actual or prospective bidder or offeror whose direct economic interest would be affected by the award of a contract or by the failure to award a contract.

(b) "Interested party" for the purpose of participation in a protest means an awardee if the award has been made, or if no award has been made, all bidders or offerors who appear to have a substantial prospect of receiving an award if the protest is denied.

(c) "Federal agency" means any executive department or independent establishment in the executive branch, including any wholly owned government corporation, and any establishment in the legislative or judicial branch, except the Senate, the House of Representatives and the Architect of the Capitol and any activities under his direction.

(d) "Contracting agency" means a federal agency which has awarded or proposes to award a contract under a protested procurement.

(e) All "days" referred to are deemed to be "working days" of the federal government except in § 21.4, where the statutory language is repeated. Except as otherwise provided, in computing a period of time prescribed by these regulations, the day from which the designated period of time begins to run shall not be counted, but the last day of the period shall be counted unless that day is not a working day of the federal government, in which event the period shall include the next working day. Time for filing any document or copy thereof with the General Accounting Office expires at 5:30 p.m. Eastern Standard Time or Eastern Daylight Savings Time as applicable on the last day on which such filing may be made.

(f) "Adverse agency action" is any action or inaction on the part of a contracting agency which is prejudicial to the position taken in a protest filed with the agency. It may include but is not limited to: a decision on the merits of a protest; a procurement action such as the opening of bids or receipt of proposals, the award of a contract, or the rejection of a bid despite the pendency of a protest; or contracting agency acquiescence in and active support of continued and substantial contract performance.

(g) The term "filed" regarding protests to the General Accounting Office means receipt of the protest and other submissions in the General Accounting Office.

§ 21.1 Filing of protest.

(a) An interested party may protest to the General Accounting Office a solicitation issued by or for a federal agency for the procurement of property or services, or the proposed award or the award of such a contract. After an interested party protests a particular procurement or proposed procurement of automated data processing equipment and services to the General Services Administration Board of Contract Appeals under section III(h) of the Federal Property and Administrative Services Act of 1949 (40 U.S.C. 759(h)) and while that protest is pending before the Board that procurement or proposed procurement may not be the subject of a protest to the General Accounting Office. An interested party who has filed a protest with the Board may not protest the same matter to the General Accounting Office.

(b) Protests must be in writing and addressed as follows: General Counsel, General Accounting Office, 441 G Street, NW., Washington, D.C. 20548, Attention: Procurement Law Control Group.

(c) A protest filed with the General Accounting Office shall:

(1) Include the name, address and telephone number of the protester,

(2) Include an original signed by the protester or its representative, and at least one copy,

(3) Identify the issuing agency and the solicitation and/or contract number,

(4) Set forth a detailed statement of the legal and factual grounds of protest including copies of relevant documents,

(5) Specifically request a ruling by the Comptroller General of the United States (Comptroller General), and

(6) State the form of relief requested.

(d) The protester shall furnish a copy of the protest (including relevant documents not issued by the contracting agency) to the individual or location designated by the contracting agency in the solicitation for receipt of protests. If there is no designation in the solicitation, the protester shall furnish a copy of the protest to the contracting officer. The designated individual or location, or if applicable, the contracting officer must receive a copy of the protest no later than 1 day after the protest is filed with the General Accounting Office. The protest document must indicate that a copy has been furnished or will be furnished within 1 day to the appropriate individual or location.

(e) No formal briefs or other technical forms of pleading or motion are required. Protest submissions should be concise, logically arranged, and clearly state legally sufficient grounds of protest. Protests of different procurements should be separately filed. If requested, the General

Accounting Office will time/date stamp and return a copy of the protest provided by the protester.

(f) A protest filed with the General Accounting Office may be dismissed for failure to comply with any of the requirements of this section. However, a protest shall not be dismissed for failure to comply with paragraph (d) of this section where the contracting officer has actual knowledge of the basis of protest or the agency, in the preparation of its report, is not otherwise prejudiced by the protester's noncompliance.

§ 21.2 Time for filing.

(a)(1) Protests based upon alleged improprieties in a solicitation which are apparent prior to bid opening or the closing date for receipt of initial proposals shall be filed prior to bid opening or the closing date for receipt of initial proposals. In procurements where proposals are requested, alleged improprieties which do not exist in the initial solicitation but which are subsequently incorporated into the solicitation must be protested not later than the next closing date for receipt of proposals following the incorporation.

(2) In cases other than those covered in paragraph (a)(1) of this section, protests shall be filed not later than 10 days after the basis of protest is known or should have been known, whichever is earlier.

(3) If a protest has been filed initially with the contracting agency, any subsequent protest to the General Accounting Office filed within 10 days of formal notification of or actual or constructive knowledge of initial adverse agency action will be considered, provided the initial protest to the agency was filed in accordance with the time limits prescribed in paragraph (a)(1) and (a)(2) of this section, unless the contracting agency imposes a more stringent time for filing, in which case the agency's time for filing will control. In cases where an alleged impropriety in a solicitation is timely protested to a contracting agency, any subsequent protest to the General Accounting Office must be filed within the 10-day period provided by this paragraph.

(b) The General Accounting Office, for good cause shown, or where it determines that a protest raises issues significant to the procurement system, may consider any protest which is not filed timely.

§ 21.3 Notice of protest, submission of agency report and time for filing of comments on report.

(a) The General Accounting Office shall notify the contracting agency by telephone within 1 day of the filing of a protest, and shall promptly mail confirmation of that notification to the contracting agency and also mail an acknowledgement of the protest to the protester. The contracting agency shall immediately give notice of the protest to the contractor if award has been made or, if no award has been made, to all bidders or offerors who appear to have a substantial and reasonable prospect of receiving an award if the protest is denied. The contracting agency shall furnish copies of the protest submissions to such parties with instructions to communicate further directly with the General Accounting Office. All parties shall furnish copies of any such communication to the contracting agency and to other participating interested parties.

(b) Material submitted by a protester will not be withheld from any interested party outside the government or from any federal agency which may be involved in the protest except to the extent that the withholding of information is permitted or required by law or regulation. If the protester considers that the protest contains material which should be withheld, a statement advising of this fact must be affixed to the front page of the protest submission and the allegedly protected information must be so identified wherever it appears.

(c) A protester may request in writing specific documents it considers relevant to its protest grounds, including but also in addition to the documents described in §21.3(i). The request must be filed with the General Accounting Office and with the individual or location referred to in §21.1(d) concurrent with the filing of the protest. A request that fails to meet one or more of the requirements of this paragraph may be dismissed.

(d) Where a request for documents is submitted pursuant to paragraph (c) of this section, those documents shall be furnished as follows:

(1) Except as provided below, the contracting agency shall furnish copies of the requested documents along with the copy of the agency report to the protester and to interested parties who have responded to the notice in §21.3(a).

(2) Requested documents that are not relevant to the protest or would give the protester or other interested party a competitive advantage or that the protester of the interested party is not otherwise authorized by law to receive shall not be furnished to the protester or to the interested party. Requested documents not furnished to the protester or the interested party shall be identified and the reason for not furnishing the documents stated. In any event, all requested documents shall be furnished to the General Accounting Office.

(e) The protester may subsequently request additional documents if the existence or relevance of such documents first becomes evident from the agency report. Any request for such documents must be filed with the General Accounting Office and with the contracting agency within 2 days of the protester's receipt of the agency report. The contracting agency must respond within 5 days by filing with the General Accounting Office the requested documents, and by identifying the documents not to be furnished to the protester or the interested party, and stating the reasons for not furnishing them.

(f) The General Accounting Office shall decide within 5 days of the receipt of the contracting agency's report under paragraph (d) of this section or its response under paragraph (e) of this section whether any documents withheld from the protester or other interested party shall be released to the protester or other interested party. If the General Accounting Office determines that withheld documents should be released, it will furnish the documents to the party or parties entitled to receive them or advise the agency to do so.

(g) When withheld documents are so released, protester's comments on the agency report shall be filed within 7 days of its receipt of the released documents. If the General Accounting Office determines that the documents were properly withheld, the protester's comments are due within 10 days of its receipt of the agency report as under § 21.3(k).

(h) In the event any contracting agency fails to comply with a decision that a document should be furnished to a protester or other interested party, the General Accounting Office may use any authority available under Chapter 7 of Title 31, United States Code, to provide the document to the protester or other interested party or may draw an inference regarding the content of the withheld document unfavorable to the contracting agency.

(i) The contracting agency shall file a complete report on the protest with the General Accounting Office within 25 days from the date of the telephone notice of the protest from the General Accounting Office. The report shall contain copies of all relevant documents including, as appropriate: the protest, the bid or proposal submitted by the protester, the bid or proposal of the firm which is being considered for award, or whose bid or proposal is being protested, the solicitation, including the specifications or portions relevant to the protest, the abstract of bids or offers or relevant portions, any other documents that are relevant to the protest, and the contracting officer's statement setting forth findings, actions, recommendations and any additional evidence or information deemed necessary in determining the validity of the protest. The statement shall be fully responsive to all allegations of the protest which the agency contests. Pursuant to section 3553(f) of the Competition in Contracting Act of 1984, 31 U.S.C. 3553(f) (Supp. III 1985) the contracting agency shall simultaneously furnish a copy of the report to the protester and interested parties who have responded to the notice given under paragraph (a) of this section. Copies of reports furnished to such parties shall include relevant documents that would not give the party a competitive advantage and that the party is otherwise authorized by law or regulation to receive. If documents are withheld from any of the parties, the agency must include in the report filed with the General Accounting Office and in the copies of the report provided to the protester and interested parties a list of the withheld documents. The copy of the report filed with the General Accounting Office shall also identify the parties who have been furnished copies of the report.

(j) The contracting agency may request, in writing, an extension of the 25-day report submission time period. The request shall set forth the reasons for which the extension is needed. The General Accounting Office will determine, in writing, whether the specific circumstances of the protest require a period longer than 25 days for the submission of the report and, if so, will set a new date for the submission of the report. Extensions are to be considered exceptional and will be granted sparingly. The agency should make its request for an extension as promptly as possible to permit it to submit a timely report should the General Accounting Office deny the request.

(k) Comments on the agency report shall be filed with the General Accounting Office within 10 days after receipt of the report, with a copy furnished by the commenting party to the contracting agency and other participating interested parties. Failure of the protester to file comments, or to file a written statement requesting that the case be decided on the existing record, or to request an extension under this section within the 10-day period will result in dismissal of the protest. The General Accounting Office will assume the protester received the agency report no later than the scheduled due date as specified in the acknowledgment of protest furnished by the General Accounting Office, unless otherwise advised by the protester. The General Accounting Office upon a showing that the specific circumstances of the protest require a period longer than 10 days for the submission of comments on the agency report, may set a new date for the submission of such comments. Extensions are to be considered exceptional and will be granted sparingly.

(l) The General Accounting Office may at its discretion permit the submission of additional statements by the parties, including the contracting agency, if the party requests to do so and the General Accounting Office determines such statements are necessary for the fair resolution of the protest. The General Accounting Office may at its discretion permit the submission of statements relevant to the protest from parties other than interested parties as defined in paragraphs (a) and (b) in § 21.0 such as federal agencies other than the contracting agency or trade associations.

(m) Notwithstanding any other provision of this section, when on its face a protest does not state a valid basis for protest or is untimely (unless the protest is to be considered pursuant to § 21.2(b)) or otherwise not for consideration by the General Accounting Office, it will summarily dismiss the protest without requiring the submission of an agency report. When the propriety of a dismissal becomes clear only after information is provided by the contracting agency or is otherwise obtained by the General Accounting Office, it will dismiss the protest at that time. If the General Accounting Office has dismissed the protest, it will notify the contracting agency that a report need not be submitted. Among the protests which may be dismissed without consideration of the merits are those concerning the following:

(1) Contract Administration. The administration of an existing contract is within the discretion of the contracting agency. Disputes between a contractor and the agency are resolved pursuant to the disputes clause of the contract and the Contract Disputes Act of 1978. 41 U.S.C. 601-13.

(2) Small Business Size Standards and Standard Industrial Classification. Challenges of established size standards or the size status of particular firms, and challenges of the selected standard industrial classification are for review solely by the Small Business Administration. 15 U.S.C. 637(b)(6); 13 CFR 121.3-6(1984).

(3) Small Business Certificate of Competency Program. Any referral made to the Small Business Administration pursuant to section 8(b)(7) of the Small Business Act, or any issuance of a certificate of competency or refusal to issue a certificate under such section is not reviewed by the General Accounting Office absent a showing of possible fraud or bad faith on the part of government officials.

(4) Procurements under section 8(a) of the Small Business Act. Since contracts are let under section 8(a) of the Small Business Act to the Small Business Administration at the contracting officer's discretion and on such terms as agreed upon by the procuring agency and the Small Business Administration, the decision to place or not to place a procurement under the 8(a) program and the award of an 8(a) subcontract are not subject to review absent a showing of possible fraud or bad faith on the part of government officials or that regulations may have been violated. 15 U.S.C. 637(a).

(5) Affirmative Determination of Responsibility by the Contracting Officer. Because a determination that a bidder or offeror is capable of performing a contract is based in large measure on subjective judgments which generally are not readily susceptible of reasoned review, an affirmative determination of responsibility will not be reviewed, absent a showing that such determination was made fraudulently or in bad faith or that definitive responsibility criteria in the solicitation were not met.

(6) Procurement Protested to the General Services Administration Board of Contract Appeals. Interested parties may protest a procurement or proposed procurement of automated data processing equipment and services to the General Services Administration Board of Contract Appeals. After a particular procurement or proposed procurement is protested to the Board, the procurement may not, while the protest is before the Board, be the subject of a protest to the General Accounting Office. An interested party who has filed a protest with the Board may not protest the same matter to the General Accounting Office. 40 U.S.C. 759(h), as amended by section 2713 of the Competition in Contracting Act of 1984, 40 U.S.C. 759(h) (Supp. III 1985).

(7) Protests not filed either in the General Accounting Office or the contracting agency within the time limits set forth in § 21.2.

(8) Procurements by Agencies Other Than Federal Agencies as Defined by Section 3 of the Federal Property and Administrative Services Act of 1949, 40 U.S.C. 472. Protests of procurements or proposed procurements by such agencies (e.g., U.S. Postal Service, Federal Deposit Insurance Corporation, nonappropriated fund activities) are beyond the General Accounting Office bid protest jurisdiction as established in section 2741 of the Competition in Contracting Act of 1984, 31 U.S.C. 3551-3556 (Supp. III 1985).

(9) Walsh-Healey Public Contracts Act. Challenges of the legal status of a firm as a regular dealer or manufacturer within the meaning of the Walsh-Healey Act is for determination solely by the procuring agency, the Small Business Administration (if a small business is involved) and the Secretary of Labor. 41 U.S.C. 35-45.

(10) Subcontractor Protests. The General Accounting Office will not consider subcontractor protests except where the subcontract is by or for the government.

(11) Judicial Proceedings. The General Accounting Office will not consider protests where the matter involved is the subject of litigation before a court of competent jurisdiction, unless the court requests a decision by the General Accounting Office. The General Accounting Office will not consider protests where the matter involved has been decided on the merits by a court of competent jurisdiction.

(n) A protest decision may not be delayed by the failure of a party to file a submission within the specified time limits. Consequently, the failure of any party or contracting agency to comply with the prescribed time limits may result in resolution of the protest without consideration of the untimely submission.

§ 21.4 Withholding of award and suspension of contract performance.

Sections 3553(c) and (d) of the Competition in Contracting Act of 1984, 31 U.S.C. 3553(c) and (d) (Supp. III 1985), set forth the following requirements regarding the withholding of award and suspension of contract performance when a protest is filed with the General Accounting Office. The requirements are included here for informational purposes.

(a) When the contracting agency receives notice of a protest from the General Accounting Office prior to award of a contract it may not award a contract under the protested procurement while the protest is pending unless the head of the procuring activity responsible for award of the contract determines in writings and reports to the General Accounting Office that urgent and compelling circumstances significantly affecting interests of the United States will not permit waiting for the General Accounting Office decision. This finding may be made only if the award is otherwise likely to occur within 30 days.

(b) When the contracting agency receives notice of a protest from the General Accounting Office after award of a contract, but within 10 days of the date of contract award, it shall immediately direct the contractor to cease contract performance and to suspend related activities that may result in additional obligations being incurred by the government under that contract while the protest is pending. The head of the procuring activity responsible for award of the contract may authorize contract performance notwithstanding the pending protest if he determines in writing and reports to the General Accounting Office that:

(1) Performance of the contract is in the government's best interest or

(2) Urgent and compelling circumstances significantly affecting interests of the United States will not permit waiting for the General Accounting Office's decision.

§ 21.5 Conferences.

(a) A conference on the merits of the protests may, at the sole discretion of the General Accounting Office, be held at the request of the protester, interested parties who have responded to the notice given under § 21.3(a), or the contracting agency. Requests for a conference should be made at the earliest possible time in the protest proceeding.

(1) Conferences will be held on a date set by the General Accounting Office as soon as practicable after receipt by the protester and participating interested parties of the agency report. All such interested parties shall be invited to attend. All parties should be represented by individuals who are knowledgeable about the subject matter of the protest. Ordinarily, only one conference will be held on a bid protest.

(2) If a conference is held, no separate comments under § 21.3(k) will be considered. The protester, all participating interested parties and the contracting agency may file comments on the conference and report as appropriate with the General Accounting Office, with copies furnished to the other parties, including the contracting agency, within 7 days of the date on which the conference was held.

(3) The General Accounting Office may request that a conference be held if at any time during the protest proceeding it decides that such a conference is needed to clarify material issues. If such a conference is held, the General Accounting Office shall make such adjustments in the submission deadlines as it determines to be fair to all parties.

(4) Failure of the protester to file comments, or to file a written statement requesting that the case be decided on the existing record, or to request an extension under this section within the 7-day period set forth in the paragraph (a)(2) of this section will result in dismissal of the protest. The General Accounting Office may set a new date for the submission of comments under the circumstances set forth in § 21.3(k).

(b) A fact finding conference may, at the sole discretion of the General Accounting Office, be held at the request of any party or on the initiative of the General Accounting Office. The fact finding conference may be held in order to resolve a specific factual dispute essential to the resolution of the protest which cannot be otherwise resolved on the written record.

(1) A fact finding conference may be held at any time during the protest proceeding. The General Accounting Office will notify all parties in writing at least 5 days before such a conference is scheduled and inform them of the factual issue or issues to be resolved and of any specific witness to be produced.

(2) The fact finding conference will be held at the General Accounting Office before a General Accounting Office official. Witnesses will testify under oath or affirmation, and a transcript of the proceeding will be made. Each party must pay for its copy of the transcript and will be given the opportunity to question the witnesses. Fact finding conferences shall be as informal as is reasonable and appropriate under the circum-

stances. Evidence shall be admitted in the sound discretion of the presiding General Accounting Office official.

(3) Each party may submit written comments to the General Accounting Office on the matter raised in the conference within 3 days of receipt of the transcript. Relevant findings of fact by the General Accounting Office hearing official shall be part of the bid protest decision.

(4) If any party refuses to attend such a conference, or a witness fails to attend or fails to answer a relevant question, the General Accounting Office may draw an inference unfavorable to the party refusing to cooperate.

§ 21.6 Remedies.

(a) If the General Accounting Office determines that a solicitation, proposed award, or award does not comply with statute or regulation, it shall recommend that the contracting agency implement any combination of the following remedies which it deems appropriate under the circumstances:

(1) Refrain from exercising options under the contract;

(2) Terminate the contract;

(3) Recompete the contract;

(4) Issue a new solicitation;

(5) Award a contract consistent with statute and regulation; or

(6) Such other recommendations as the General Accounting Office determines necessary to promote compliance.

(b) In determining the appropriate recommendation, the General Accounting Office, shall, except as specified in paragraph (c) of this section, consider all the circumstances surrounding the procurement or proposed procurement including, but not limited to, the seriousness of the procurement deficiency, the degree of prejudice to other interested parties or to the integrity of the competitive procurement system, the good faith of the parties, the extent of performance, cost to the government, the urgency of the procurement and the impact of the recommendation on the contracting agency's mission.

(c) If the head of the procuring activity makes the finding referred to in § 21.4(b)(1) that performance of the contract notwithstanding a pending protest is in the government's best interest, the General Accounting Office shall make its recommendation under the paragraph (a) of this section without regard to any cost or disruption from terminating, recompeting, or reawarding the contract.

(d) If the General Accounting Office determines that a solicitation, proposed award, or award does not comply with statute or regulation, it may declare the protester to be entitled to reasonable costs of:

(1) Filing and pursuing the protest, including attorney's fees; and

(2) Bid and proposal preparation.

(e) If the General Accounting Office decides that the protester is entitled to the recovery of such cost, the protester and the contracting agency shall attempt to reach agreement on the amount of the costs. If the protester and the contracting agency cannot reach agreement within a reasonable time, the General Accounting Office will determine the amount.

§ 21.7 Time for decision by the General Accounting Office.

(a) The General Accounting Office shall issue a decision on a protest within 90 days from the date the protest is filed with it.

(b) In those protests for which the General Accounting Office invokes the express option under § 21.8, the General Accounting Office shall issue a decision within 45 calendar days from the date the protest is filed with it.

(c) Under exceptional circumstances the General Accounting Office may extend the deadlines in paragraph (a) of this section on a case-by-case basis by stating in writing the reasons that the specific circumstances of the protest require a longer period.

§ 21.8 Express option.

(a) At the request of the protester, the contracting agency or an interested party for an expeditious decision, the General Accounting Office will consider the feasibility of using an express option.

(b) The express option will be invoked solely at the discretion of the General Accounting Office only in those cases suitable for resolution within 45 calendar days.

(c) Requests for the express option must be in writing and received in the General Accounting Office no later than 3 days after the protest is filed. The General Accounting Office will determine within 2 days of receipt of the request whether to invoke the express option and will notify the contracting agency, protester and interested parties who have responded to the notice under § 21.3(a).

(d) When the express option is used the filing deadlines in § 21.3 and the provisions of § 21.5 shall not apply and:

(1) The contracting agency shall file a complete report with the General Accounting Office on the protest within 10 days from the date it receives notice from the General Accounting Office that the express option will be used and furnish copies of the report to the protester and interested parties who have responded to the notice under § 21.3(a).

(2) Comments on the agency report shall be filed with the General Accounting Office within 5 days after receipt of the report with a copy furnished by the commenting party to the contracting agency and other participating interested parties.

(3) The General Accounting Office may arrange a conference to ascertain and clarify the material issues at any time deemed appropriate during the protest proceeding.

(4) The General Accounting Office shall issue its decision within 45 calendar days from the date the protest is filed with it.

(e) Where circumstances demonstrate that the case is no longer suitable for resolution within 45 calendar days, the General Accounting Office may establish new deadlines within the constraints established in § 21.7(a) and (c) regarding the issuance of a decision and in § 21.3(i) and (j) regarding the submission of the agency report.

§ 21.9 Effect of judicial proceedings.

(a) The General Accounting Office will dismiss any protest where the matter involved is the subject of litigation before a court of competent jurisdiction, unless the court requests a decision by the General Accounting Office. The General Accounting Office will dismiss any protest where the matter involved has been decided on the merits by a court of competent jurisdiction.

(b) Where the court requests a decision by the General Accounting Office, the times for filing the agency report (§ 21.3(i)), filing comments on the report (§ 21.3(k)), holding a conference and filing comments (§ 21.5), and issuing a decision (§ 21.7) may be changed if the court so orders.

§ 21.10 Signing and distribution of decisions.

Each bid protest decision shall be signed by the Comptroller General or a designee for that purpose. A copy of the decision shall be made available to all participating interested parties, the protester, the head of the contracting activity responsible for the protested procurement, the senior procurement executive of each federal agency involved, and any member of the public.

§ 21.11 Nonstatutory protests.

(a) The General Accounting Office may consider protests concerning sales by a federal agency or procurements by agencies of the government other than federal agencies as defined in § 21.0(b), if the agency involved has agreed in writing to have its protests decided by the General Accounting Office.

(b) All of the provisions of these Bid Protest Regulations shall apply to any nonstatutory protest decided by the General Accounting Office except for the provisions of § 21.6(d) pertaining to entitlement to reasonable costs of filing and pursuing the protest, including attorney's fees. Sections 3553 (c) and (d) of the Competition in Contracting Act of 1984, 31 U.S.C. 3553(c) and (d) (Supp. III 1985), pertaining to withholding of award and suspension of contract performance shall not apply.

§ 21.12 Request for reconsideration.

(a) Reconsideration of a decision of the General Accounting Office may be requested by the protester, any interested party who participated in the protest, and any federal agency involved in the protest. The General Accounting Office will not consider any request for reconsideration which does not contain a detailed statement of the factual and legal grounds upon which reversal or modification is deemed warranted, specifying any errors of law made or information not previously considered.

(b) Request for reconsideration of a decision of the General Accounting Office shall be filed, with copies to any federal agency and interested parties who participated in the protest, not later than 10 days after the basis for reconsideration is known or should have been known, whichever is earlier. The term "filed" as used in this section means receipts in the General Accounting Office.

(c) A request of reconsideration shall be subject to those bid protest regulations consistent with the need for prompt and fair resolution of the matter. The filing of a request for reconsideration will not invoke Section 3553 (c) or (d) of the Competition in Contracting Act of 1984, 31 U.S.C. 3553(c) and (d) (Supp. III 1985) relating to the withholding of award and the suspension of contract performance.

Requirement for Agencies to Produce Documents

The provisions of paragraphs 21.3(c) through (h) encountered strong opposition from the executive agencies. Essentially, the protester may request additional documents and, unless they are determined to be not relevant or would provide the protester or interested party "a competitive advantage [which that] party is not otherwise authorized by law to receive," the government must furnish the documents or explain to GAO its reason for not furnishing them. In any event, the government must furnish *all* requested documents to GAO, which will make the final decision as to whether the protester and/or interested parties are entitled to them. If GAO decides in favor of the requestor, it will furnish the documents to the party or advise the agency to do so.

Paragraph 21.3(h) indicates that if the agency refuses to furnish a requested document to GAO, and GAO is unable to obtain it through available statutory provisions, it "may draw an inference regarding the content of the withheld document unfavorable to the contracting agency."

The federal executive departments contend that GAO has no authority to release documents that a contracting agency believes are not appropriate to disclose or to draw negative inferences from such nondisclosures. They have argued that judicial rulings finding that GAO authority under CICA is not unconstitutional were based on the conclusion that, unlike in Gramm-Rudman, the Comptroller General was not granted final control over actions by executive departments. GAO's stay authority was considered more in the nature of oversight than control. The provision under which GAO could override an agency's determination and release a document the agency believed should not be disclosed, or draw a negative inference from the nondisclosure, was seen as "taking final control over a procurement decision" and, therefore, unconstitutional.

The executive agencies, in responding to these provisions in connection with the March 1987 draft, asserted that the head of the agency, not the GAO, had the final say over disclosure, subject only to the rights available under the Freedom of Information Act (FOIA).

Some of the industry commentators, on the other hand, believe that these provisions do not go far enough in providing meaningful discovery capability to protesters. If the new procedures require the protester to specifically designate the document needed, the protester would encounter problems in lacking precise identity of the relevant documents. At the time of the March draft, GAO was urged to expand these provisions to include the full range of discovery available in proceedings before boards of contract appeals and federal courts.

In the Supplementary Information accompanying the final rule for the revised procedures, GAO noted the objections of some of the contracting agencies to the new provisions relating to access to government documents, stated it did not agree, and set forth its position as follows:

> The authority to obtain documents and provide them to parties participating in a protest is contained in the Competition in Contracting Act of 1984 (CICA), 31 U.S.C. § § 3553(b)(2) and (f) and § § 3555(a) and (b) (Supp. III 1985). CICA requires that contracting agencies provide GAO with a protest report, including all relevant documents, and that the agencies provide parties to a protest with relevant documents, which the party is otherwise authorized by law to receive and would not give the party a competitive advantage (including the protest report) within such guidelines that GAO may set forth. CICA also establishes GAO's authority to prescribe necessary protest procedures and states that GAO may use its audit authority under chapter 7 of title 31 to verify parties' assertions. GAO believes that a reasonable reading of these portions of CICA provides the authority for GAO to establish a protest procedure whereby protesters and participating interested parties may obtain non-privileged documents which are relevant to the protest issues.

> GAO believes that this procedure is consistent with FOIA. CICA at 31 U.S.C. § 3553(f) states that any document provided to a party not give that party a competitive advantage and requires that the party would be otherwise authorized by law to receive the document to be released. New section 21.3(d)(2) reflects these restrictions. In GAO's view, 31 U.S.C. § 3553(f) restricts the release of documents to those that a particular party would be entitled to receive under FOIA. GAO intends to so limit parties' access to agency documents. In determining whether a party is entitled to specific documents, GAO will give due consideration to the agency's determination as to their releasability under FOIA. On the other hand, GAO believes that CICA envisions that those documents that would be releasable pursuant to FOIA would be made available to parties to a protest in accordance with GAO timeframes and procedures. GAO believes that there is no constitutional bar to the implementation of these procedures.

Fact Finding Conferences

An addition to paragraph 21.5(a)(1) requires that "All parties should be represented by individuals who are knowledgeable about the subject matter of the protest." Additionally, paragraphs 21.5(b) and (b)(1) through (4) were added to establish expanded fact finding conferences, all of which drew a number of objections at the time they appeared in the March 1987 draft. Contracting agencies argued that representation by "knowledgeable" individuals would be costly and inconvenient because such individuals are frequently not located in Washington, D.C. They also objected to the fact that this requirement in the March draft referred only to contracting agencies and not to protesters. GAO expanded this requirement to include "all parties."

Generally, contracting agencies disliked the expanded provisions and argued that GAO was moving away from the original concept of furnishing speedy, informal, and inexpensive forums for protests. Questions were raised in both the public and private sectors as to the ground rules under which these fact-finding conferences would be conducted, and some commenters questioned the qualifications of GAO officials to properly conduct them. A number of commenters recommended that the Federal Rules of Evidence be used for guidance. GAO agreed to use these rules for guidance but stated it would not necessarily be bound by them. In short, GAO maintained here as on other points that GAO and GAO alone would determine the conference procedures and the qualifications of its officials selected to preside over them.

There were questions as to the circumstances under which GAO would determine that such conferences should be held. The March 1987 draft contained a vague statement that such conferences "are considered exceptional and will be granted sparingly." Government contracting agencies in particular expressed concern over the possibility that they would become routine and result in the incurrence of time and cost in unnecessary circumstances. The final rule substituted the language in 21.5(b) that "The fact finding conference may be held in order to resolve a specific factual dispute essential to the resolution of the protest which cannot be otherwise resolved on the written record."

Recovery of Costs by Protester

Under the prior procedures, paragraph 21.6(e) specified circumstances under which protesters could recover attorneys' fees and bid and proposal costs. The revision deletes this paragraph, and what remains is the provision that where GAO decides that the protester is entitled to recover costs, and the protester and the contracting officer cannot reach agreement, GAO will determine the amount.

Contracting agencies recommended that the previous provisions be reinstated because they did indicate the circumstances under which protesters could recover costs, and the elimination of such standards could lead to the filing of frivolous protests. These commenters advised that if GAO refused to reinstate the previous provisions, it should adopt the standards provided for under the Equal Access to Justice Act (EAJA).

GAO refused to adopt these recommendations, insisting on its preference for decisions on a case-by-case basis. For the same reason it refused to adopt the EAJA standards adding, however: "This is not to say, on the other hand, that GAO will not refer to the Act for guidance in specific cases."

Summary

Although objections to the revised procedures were presented by representatives of both the public and private sectors, it seems quite evident that the greater dissatisfaction was expressed by the contracting agencies, which objected to what they believed to be GAO's unwarranted and unconstitutional expansion of its role in the bid protest area.

Bid Protests and Boards of Contract Appeals

Section 2713 of Public Law 98-369 also conferred upon the General Services Board of Contract Appeals (GSBCA) statutory authority to hear and decide protests involving procurements under 40 U.S.C. 759 for automatic data processing equipment (ADPE), software, maintenance and supplies.

The GSBCA implementation of this authority is contained in this Board's Rules of Practice, Title 48 CFR Chapter 6101.

From time to time questions surface as to whether the GSBCA's authority should be expanded to permit it to hear all bid protests. Also, after the Supreme Court found Gramm-Rudman unconstitutional because of the authority vested in the Comptroller General in establishing budget deficit estimates, the possibility was recognized that CICA's provisions granting the Comptroller General stay authority might also be declared unconstitutional.

Early in 1987 the ABA Public Contract Law Section debated various alternatives, including whether all boards of contract appeals should have bid protest authority similar to GSBCA's in ADPE protests, should this authority be vested in only the three largest boards (ASBCA, GSBCA and NASA BCA) or in all boards, should the boards have this authority instead of GAO, and should GAO's authority be preserved, minus the CICA stay provision, as an alternative for protesters opting for a simpler and less expensive forum. The lawyers were almost evenly divided on these questions, resulting in majority and minority 9-8 and 8-7 votes. By such close margins the majority reports recommended against further expanding the growing workload of boards of contract appeals and expressed concern about a loss of uniformity if all boards were given this authority. The majority further recommended changes in GAO's procedures including providing protesters expanded discovery rights and access to government records.

The minority believed that GAO had little capability to provide necessary discovery procedures while the boards had demonstrated such capability. This report would grant the ASBCA authority to hear all protests relating to defense contracts and extend the authority of the GSBCA to protests involving all civilian agency procurement.

When the GAO's draft revision was issued in March 1987, it reflected that agency's efforts to provide a limited type of discovery availability for protesters which, along with the fact-finding provisions, drew strong protests from executive agencies. Some industry spokesmen, on the other hand, asserted that the provisions did not go far enough in this respect and would grant protesters further discovery rights almost similar to those available before boards of contract appeals. As reflected in the text of the revised procedures cited earlier in this chapter, the final version much more closely approached the views of the private sector than those of the executive government agencies.

As the 100th Congress reached the midterm, discussions continued concerning legislation broadening the bid protest authority of the GSBCA and also extending this authority to the ASBCA. At this writing, sufficient experience has not been gained with GAO's revised procedures to ascertain what impact they may have on the views of those members of Congress who have been seeking to transfer this authority to the boards or establish the boards as an alternative forum.

FAR Part 33—Protests, Disputes and Appeals

Bid protests are covered in Subpart 33.1, quoted below. These procedures are current at this writing and are subject to future revision in recognition of the revised GAO bid protest procedures.

33.101 Definitions.

"Interested party," as used in this subpart, means an actual or prospective offeror whose direct economic interest would be affected by the award of or failure to award a particular contract.

"Protest," as used in this subpart, means a written objection by an interested party to a solicitation by an agency for offers for a proposed contract for the acquisition of supplies or services or a written objection by an interested party to a proposed award or the award of such a contract.

33.102 General.

(a) Contracting officers shall consider all protests, whether submitted before or after award and whether filed directly with the agency, the General Accounting Office (GAO), or for automatic data processing acquisitions under 40 U.S.C. 759 (hereinafter cited as "ADP contracts"), the General Services Board of Contract Appeals (GSBCA). The protester shall be notified in writing of the final decision of the protest. (See 19.302 for protests of small business status and 22.608-3 for protests involving eligibility under the Walsh-Healey Public Contracts Act.)

(b) An interested party wishing to protest—

(1) is encouraged to seek resolution within the agency (see 33.103) before filing a protest with the GAO or the GSBCA;

(2) May protest to the GAO in accordance with GAO regulations (4 CFR Part 21). An interested party who has filed a protest regarding an ADP contract with the GAO may not file a protest with the GSBCA with respect to that contract.

(3) May protest to the GSBCA regarding an award of an ADP contract in accordance with GSBCA Rules of Procedure (48 CFR Part 61). An interested party who has filed a protest regarding an ADP contract with GSBCA (40 U.S.C. 759(h)) may not file a protest with the GAO with respect to that contract.

33.103 Protests to the agency.

(a) When a protest is filed only with the agency, an award shall not be made until the matter is resolved unless the contracting officer or other designated official first determines that one of the following applies:

(1) The supplies or services to be contracted for are urgently required.

(2) Delivery or performance will be unduly delayed by failure to make award promptly.

(3) A prompt award will otherwise be advantageous to the Government.

(b)(1) When a protest against the making of an award is received and award will be withheld pending disposition of the protest, the offerors whose offers might become eligible for award should be informed of the protest. If appropriate, those offerors should be requested, before expiration of the time for acceptance of their offer, to extend the time for acceptance in accordance with 14.404-1(d) to avoid the need for resolicitation. In the event of failure to obtain such extensions of offers, consideration should be given to proceeding with award under (a) above.

(2) Protests received after award filed only with the agency shall be handled in accordance with agency procedures. The contracting officer need not suspend contract performance or terminate the awarded contract unless it appears likely that an award may be invalidated and a delay in receiving the supplies or services is not prejudicial to the Government's interest. In this event, the contracting officer should consider seeking a mutual agreement with the contractor to suspend performance on a no-cost basis.

33.104 Protests to GAO.

(a) *General.* (1) A protester shall furnish a copy of its complete protest to the official or location designated in the solicitation or, in the absence of such a designation, to the contracting officer, no later than one day after the protest is filed with the GAO. Failure to furnish a complete copy of the protest within one day may result in dismissal of the protest by GAO.

(2) When a protest, before or after award, has been lodged with the GAO, the agency shall prepare a report. The report should include a copy of—

(i) The protest;

(ii) The offer submitted by the protesting offeror and a copy of the offer which is being considered for award or which is being protested;

(iii) The solicitation, including the specifications or portions relevant to the protest;

(iv) The abstract of offers or relevant portions;

(v) Any other documents that are relevant to the protest; and

(vi) The contracting officer's signed statement setting forth findings, actions, and recommendations and any additional evidence or information deemed necessary in determining the validity of the protest. The statement shall be fully responsive to the allegation of the protest. If the contract action or contract performance continues after receipt of the protest, the report will include the determination(s) prescribed in paragraphs (b) or (c) below.

(3) Other persons, including offerors, involved in or affected by the protest shall be given notice of the protest and its basis in appropriate cases, within one work day after its receipt by the agency. The agency

shall give immediate notice of the protest to the contractor if the award has been made or, if no award has been made, to all parties who appear to have a reasonable prospect of receiving an award if the protest is denied. These persons shall also be advised that they may submit their views and relevant information directly to the GAO with a copy to the contracting officer within a specified period of time. Normally, the time specified will be 1 week.

(4) The agency shall submit a complete report (see (a)(2) above) to GAO within 25 work days after receipt from GAO of the telephonic notice of such protest, or within 10 work days after receipt from GAO of a determination to use the express options, unless—

(i) The GAO advises the agency that the protest has been dismissed; or

(ii) The agency advises GAO in writing that the specific circumstances of the protest require a longer period and GAO establishes a new date. Any new date shall be documented in the agency's protest file.

(5)(i) Timely action on protests is essential. Upon notice that a protest has been lodged with the GAO, the contracting officer shall immediately begin compiling the information necessary for a report to the GAO. To further expedite processing, when furnishing a copy of the report including relevant documents to the GAO, the agency shall simultaneously furnish a copy of the report including relevant documents to the protester and a copy of the report without relevant documents to other interested parties who have responded to the notice in (a)(3) above. Upon request the agency shall also provide to any interested party a relevant document contained in the report.

(A) Documents previously furnished to or prepared by a party (e.g., the solicitation or the party's own proposal) need not be furnished to that party.

(B) Classified or privileged information or information that would give a party a competitive advantage and other information that the Government determines under appropriate authority to withhold should be deleted from the copy of the report or relevant documents furnished to that party.

(ii) The protester and other interested parties shall be requested to furnish a copy of any comments on the report directly to the GAO as well as to the contracting officer.

(6) Agencies shall furnish the GAO with the name, title and telephone number of one or more officials (in both field and headquarters offices, if desired) whom the GAO may contact regarding protests. Each agency shall be responsible for promptly advising the GAO of any change in the designated officials.

(b) *Protests before award.* (1) When the agency has received notice from GAO of a protest filed directly with GAO, a contract may not be awarded unless authorized, in accordance with agency procedures, by the head of the contracting activity, on a nondelegable basis, upon a written finding that—

(i) Urgent and compelling circumstances which significantly affect the interests of the United States will not permit awaiting the decision of GAO; and

(ii) Award is likely to occur within 30 calendar days of the written finding.

(2) A contract award shall not be authorized until the agency has notified GAO of the above finding.

(3) When a protest against the making of an award is received the award will be withheld pending disposition of the protest, the offerors whose offers might become eligible for award should be informed of the protest. If appropriate, those offerors should be requested, before expiration of the time for acceptance of their offer, to extend the time for acceptance in accordance with 14.404-1(d) to avoid the need for resolicitation. In the event of failure to obtain such extensions of offers, consideration should be given to proceeding under paragraph (b)(1), above.

(c) *Protests after award.* (1) When the agency receives from GAO, within 10 calendar days after award, a notice of a protest filed directly with GAO, the contracting officer shall immediately suspend performance or terminate the awarded contract, except as provided in paragraphs (c)(2) and (3) below.

(2) In accordance with agency procedures, the head of the contracting activity may, on a nondelegable basis, authorize contract performance, notwithstanding the protest, upon a written finding that—

(i) Contract performance will be in the best interests of the United States; or

(ii) Urgent and compelling circumstances that significantly affect the interests of the United States will not permit waiting for the GAO's decision.

(3) Contract performance shall not be authorized until the agency has notified GAO of the above finding.

(4) When it is decided to suspend performance or terminate the awarded contract, the contracting officer should attempt to negotiate a mutual agreement on a no-cost basis.

(5) When the agency receives notice of a protest filed directly only with the GAO more than 10 calendar days after award of the protested acquisition, the contracting officer need not suspend contract performance or terminate the awarded contract unless the contracting officer believes that an award may be invalidated and a delay in receiving the supplies or services is not prejudicial to the Government's interest.

(d) *Findings and notice.* If the decision is to proceed with contract award, or continue contract performance under (b) or (c) above, the contracting officer shall include the written findings or other required documentation in the file. The contracting officer also shall give written notice of the decision to the protester and other interested parties.

(e) *GAO decision time.* GAO will issue its recommendation on a protest within 90 work days, or within 45 calendar days under the express option, unless GAO establishes a longer period of time.

(f) *Notice to GAO.* The head of the agency or a designee (not below the level of the head of the contracting activity) responsible for the solicitation, proposed award, or award of the contract shall report to the Comptroller General within 60 days of receipt of the GAO's recommendation if the agency has decided not to comply with the recommendation. The report shall explain the reasons why the GAO's recommendation will not be followed by the agency.

(g) *Award of protest costs.* (1) GAO may declare an appropriate interested party to be entitled to the costs of—

(i) Filing and pursuing the protest, including reasonable attorneys' fees; and

(ii) Bid and proposal preparation.

(2) Costs awarded under paragraph (g)(1) of this section shall be paid promptly by the agency out of funds available to or for the use of the agency for the acquisition of supplies or services.

33.105 Protests to GSBCA.

(a)(1) An interested party may protest an ADP acquisition conducted under Section 111 of the Federal Property and Administrative Services Act (40 U.S.C. 759) by filing a protest with the GSBCA. ADP acquisition protests not covered under this statute may not be heard by the GSBCA, but may be heard by the agency, the courts, or GAO. A protester shall furnish a copy of its complete protest to the official or location designated in the solicitation, or in the absence of such a designation to the contracting officer, on the same day the protest is filed with GSBCA. Any request for a hearing on either a suspension of procurement authority or on the merits shall be in the protest.

(2) The GSBCA procedures state that—

(i) Within one working day after receipt of a copy of the protest, the agency shall give either oral or written notice of the protest to all parties who were solicited or, if the solicitation has closed, only to those who submitted a sealed bid or offer; and

(ii) Written confirmation of notice and a listing of all persons and agencies receiving notice should be given to the Board within five working days after receipt of the protest.

(b) The GSBCA procedures state that within 10 work days after the filing of a protest, or such longer time as the GSBCA may establish, the agency shall file with the GSBCA and all other parties a protest file. Except where the agency determines under appropriate authority to withhold classified or privileged information or information that would give a competitive advantage, the protest file shall include the following:

(1) A contracting officer's decision, if any.

(2) The contract, if any.

(3) All relevant correspondence.

(4) Affidavits or statements of witnesses on the matter under protest.

(5) All documents relied upon by the contracting officer in taking the action protested.

(6) A copy of the solicitation, the protester's bid or proposal and, if bid opening has occurred and no contract has been awarded, a copy of any relevant bids and the bid abstract.

(7) In a negotiated acquisition, a copy of offers or proposals being considered for award and relevant to the protest should be included in the GSBCA file only, for *in camera* review by the Board. The agency shall serve all parties with a list of documents provided to the Board for *in camera* review.

(8) Any additional existing evidence or information necessary to determine the merits of the protest.

(9) Any information otherwise withheld, where it is appropriate for *in camera* review by the Board.

(c) The GSBCA procedures state that within 15 work days after the filing of the protest, or such longer time as the Board may establish, the agency shall submit its answer to the Board setting forth its defenses to the protest and its findings, actions, and recommendations in the matter.

(d)(1) If a protest contains a timely request for a suspension of procurement authority, a hearing will be held whenever practicable but no later than 10 calendar days after the filing of the protest. The Board shall suspend the procurement authority unless the agency establishes that—

(i) Absent suspension, the contract award is likely within 30 calendar days; and

(ii) Urgent and compelling circumstances which significantly affect interests of the United States will not permit waiting for the decision.

(2) Circumstances in (d)(1) above shall be established by a D&F executed by the agency head or designee.

(3) The Board's decision on suspension may be oral.

(e) A hearing on the merits, if requested, will be held within 25 work days after the filing of the protest and a GSBCA decision on the merits will be issued within 45 work days, unless the Board's chairman determines a longer period is required.

(f)(1) The GSBCA may declare an appropriate interested party to be entitled to the cost of—

(i) Filing and pursuing the protest, including reasonable attorney's fees; and

(ii) Bid and proposal preparation.

(2) Costs awarded under (f)(1) above shall be paid promptly by the agency out of funds available to or for the use of the acquisition of supplies or services.

(g) The GSBCA's final decision may be appealed by the agency or by any interested party, including any intervening interested parties, as set forth in Subpart 33.2.

GAO'S CONTINUING EFFORTS TO GAIN ACCESS TO CONTRACTORS' RECORDS

Earlier in this chapter we discussed GAO's proposals for legislation requiring periodic studies and reporting on defense contractor profits. A key provision of the legislation would mandate GAO access to virtually all of the contractors' records as well as those of the independent CPAs involved in certifying to the profit reporting and the records of the government agency that would be designated to accumulate and report on this data. This bold move to gain virtually unrestricted and total access to contractors' records, although shocking to some observers, should more logically be understood as another, albeit extreme, effort by that agency in this area, which has been a major goal of GAO for many years.

In this regard, GAO took the occasion to criticize and cast doubts on the major DOD profit studies, Profit '76 and DFAIR, because no provisions were made for GAO to examine all of the records of the contractors and the CPA firms involved.

This history must be kept in mind to understand the GAO's recent proposals for profit studies, featuring unlimited GAO access to any and all of the records available from the public and private sectors. This is not to suggest that GAO lacks authority to examine contractors' records. Over the years, whether at congressional requests or on its own initiative, the legislative watchdog has conducted continuing investigations of contractors' records and related records of government agencies in connection with defective pricing, treatment of costs the agency considered unallowable or doubtful, spare parts pricing, and many other areas, relating to cost and pricing and other subjects.

However, GAO's access to contractor records is not limitless and this has appeared to be a matter of dissatisfaction to the agency and has motivated its efforts to gain unrestricted access through legislation.

Except as dictated by statute, which could be construed as overcoming contractual provisions, GAO's access to records is governed by the following FAR clause:

52.215-1 Examination of Records by Comptroller General.

As prescibed in 15.106-1(b), insert the following clause:

EXAMINATION OF RECORDS BY

COMPTROLLER GENERAL (APR 1984)

(a) This clause applies if this contract exceeds $10,000 and was entered into by negotiation.

(b) The Comptroller General of the United States or a duly authorized representative from the General Accounting Office shall, until 3 years after final payment under this contract or for any shorter period specified in Federal Acquisition Regulation (FAR) Subpart 4.7, Contractor Records Retention, have access to and the right to examine any of the Contractor's directly pertinent books, documents, papers, or other records involving transactions related to this contract.

(c) The Contractor agrees to include in first-tier subcontracts under this contract a clause to the effect that the Comptroller General or a duly authorized representative from the General Accounting Office shall, until 3 years after final payment under the subcontract or for any shorter period specified in FAR Subpart 4.7, have access to and the right to examine any of the subcontractor's directly pertinent books, documents, papers, or other records involving transactions related to the subcontract. "Subcontract," as used in this clause, excludes (1) purchase orders not exceeding $10,000 and (2) subcontracts or purchase orders for public utility services at rates established to apply uniformly to the public, plus any applicable reasonable connection charge.

(d) The periods of access and examination in paragraphs (b) and (c) above for records relating to (1) appeals under the Disputes clause, (2) litigation or settlement of claims arising from the performance of this contract, or (3) costs and expenses of this contract to which the Comptroller General or a duly authorized representative from the General Accounting Office has taken exception shall continue until such appeals, litigation, claims, or exceptions are disposed of.

Attention is invited to the significant description (and limitation) of the GAO's access authority: "any *directly pertinent* books, documents, papers, and records of the Contractor *involving transactions related to this contract.*" (Italics added.) The emphasized terms have played an important role in the controversies and litigation.

A vigorous plea for what appeared to be unlimited access to contractors' records was made by ex-Comptroller General Campbell during his testimony before the Holifield Committee in 1965:

> In our opinion, the language of the act and the legislative history clearly establish that the basic purpose of the statutory provision was to make possible the close supervision and control over negotiated procurements, which the Congress regarded as necessary in the interest of the Government. This purpose requires that the act be interpreted to permit detailed examination of a contractor's records to insure the necessary degree of supervision and control. In other words, the clear intent of the statute is to provide for the examination by the General Accounting Office of such records of a contractor, to such an extent as will permit a meaningful examination of the reasonableness of the prices charged to the Government.

> It is our position that, under the statute and the contract clause, all books, documents, papers, and other records relating to the pricing and cost of performance of negotiated contracts are directly pertinent to the contracts and that such books, documents, records, et cetera, are not

limited to the formal cost-accounting records and their supporting data, but include all underlying data concerning contract activities and operations which afford the basis for contract pricing and the incurrence of costs by the contractor.

This position, reiterated and supported by Campbell's successors, Staats and Bowsher, finds substantial and sharp opposition outside the government. With specific regard to the clause contained in negotiated fixed-price type contracts, opinions have been expressed that no legal or logical basis exists for according the legal and contractual provisions any wider interpretation than reflected in the precise language employed. These opinions maintain that any other or broader intent could have been readily expressed by related language. As an illustration, it is argued that the words "directly pertinent" are patently restrictive and must so be interpreted. If it were intended that the GAO have carte blanche access to all of the records, the words "directly pertinent" would not have been employed.

The precise meaning of "directly pertinent," of course, is subject to a wide range of interpretation. Some have held that GAO access to records under negotiated fixed-price contracts should be limited to those relating to the negotiation and should not include those reflecting the actual costs of performance. A more widely held view would at least limit the GAO to specific books of account affecting contract costs, thereby excluding minutes of board of director meetings, budgetary data, internal audit reports and related confidential company communications, and reports to other government agencies such as income tax returns, etc. Another controversial point involves records of costs of items for which prices were accepted by the government based on catalog price of commercial items sold in substantial quantities to the public.

Hewlett-Packard Co. v. U.S., 385 F.2d 1013 (CA-9), Cert. Den. 390 U.S. 988 (1967)

A major court test of GAO authority to demand access to records, and the meaning of the words "directly pertinent," was involved in *U. S. v. Hewlett-Packard Co.,* argued before the U. S. District Court for the Northern District of California (San Francisco). The facts and issues of this case were summarized in the Comptroller General's testimony before the Holifield Committee:

Briefly, this case involves four contracts which were negotiated with Hewlett-Packard by the Department of the Air Force for certain electronic test and measuring equipment. The prices negotiated for the contracts were catalog prices established by the contractor less discounts ranging from 9 to 32 percent. In connection with our work, our auditors, conducting an examination at the Hewlett-Packard Co. requested cost records on the four contracts. This request was denied by Hewlett-Packard. After extensive correspondence with Hewlett-Packard and a hearing by the House Committee on Armed Services, we requested the Department of Justice to bring an action against Hewlett-Packard to require that the cost records be made available.

The basis for Hewelett-Packard's refusal is that production costs are not considered directly pertinent because costs were not a factor in the negotiation of the contracts involved. The firm contends that the use of the words "directly pertinent" in the contract clause and the underlying statute limit the application of the access-to-records clause to contracts where costs were a factor in the negotiation, where effective competition was not present, where standard catalog prices were not used as a basis for pricing, or where substantial quantities of the products involved were not sold to the general public. In brief, it is the position of Hewlett-Packard that the clause applies only to the type of records and information upon which price negotiations were conducted.

It is our position that the contract clause and the statute on which the clause is based gives us the right to examine the cost records of the contractor and other pertinent data that relate to the items included in the contract, in sufficient completeness and detail to permit us to examine into the reasonableness of the negotiated prices. We believe our position is supported by the statutory language and the contract provision and, to an even greater extent, by the legislative history of the statute.

Although *Hewlett-Packard* attracted considerable attention and the court's decision was awaited with much interest, it appeared doubtful that the decision in this case would be likely to have broad application. The Comptroller General had these doubts when he told the congressional committee that "we do not believe that the decision in the *Hewlett-Packard* case will answer all questions of interpretation of the contract clause." For example, a broad ruling by the court that the General Accounting Office had the right to examine Hewlett-Packard's cost records would not decide which records of the company were "directly pertinent."

We agree with the many observers who believe that considerable significance must be attached to the term "directly pertinent." At the very minimum, we would think that some unspecified restriction was intended. On this basis, we recommend to our clients that (1) cooperative and cordial relations be maintained with GAO auditors, but that (2) the GAO requests for records and other pertinent information be funneled through a single contact point within the company for review and consideration as to whether the data requested are appropriate and pertinent in the circumstances.

In any event, the district court handed down its decision in the summer of 1966 and supported the prediction of those who anticipated that it was not likely to furnish a conclusive or definitive precedent. In a rather unusual oral decision, and apparently displaying some unhappiness about the whole thing, the judge ruled for the government and upheld the right of the Comptroller General to examine Hewlett-Packard's cost records under the contracts involved. The judge granted the government's motion for summary judgment, but offered his own opinion that the examination of the disputed records by the GAO would not be in the interests of the government, the public, or the contractor. He also made clear his dissatisfaction with 10 U.S.C. 2313(b), the statute which establishes the authority for the GAO to examine contractor's records.

Hewlett-Packard appealed the ruling, and a decision (No. 21,323) thereon by the U. S. Court of Appeals for the Ninth Circuit was handed down on November 15, 1967. In essence, Hewlett-Packard argued again that emphasis

must be placed on the words "directly pertinent" and that costs of performance were not directly pertinent because they were not a factor in determining
the contract prices. Accordingly, such records were never intended by the
statute involved to be open to the government. The court agreed that the
statute intended placing a limitation on the government's right to examine
records; however, it also concluded that the GAO position, as upheld by the
lower court, was consistent therewith. For the lower court had not ordered the
contractor to make all of its records "without limitation" available to the
GAO, but had decided that the GAO could examine records relating to the cost
of producing the items contracted for. This, in the opinion of the Ninth Circuit
Court, gave full consideration to the statutory limitation.

A key point here is the difference of opinion as to the purpose for which
the GAO should be reviewing the records of contractors. Hewlett-Packard
contended that the sole purpose should be for the GAO to ascertain whether
the contracts had been performed in accordance with their terms and whether
the government had been defrauded or misled. The court found no such
limitation in the law or in the related legislative history and viewed the GAO
authority broad enough to inquire into whether the contract production costs
were "out of line with the contract price," in which case the GAO might
conclude that the government used an inappropriate contracting technique
and might recommend a different procedure for the future.

The pertinent concluding portions of the Circuit Court's decision are
quoted below:

> Hewlett-Packard argues that the decision of the district court have
> no effect to the words of limitation contained in 10 U. S. C. par. 2313(b),
> and reflected in clause 10 of each contract.

> The words of limitation to which the company refers limit the
> records which may be examined by the Comptroller General and his
> representatives to those of the contractor, or of any of his subcontractors,
> that directly pertain to, and involve transactions relating to, the contract
> or subcontract. Hewlett-Packard asserts that the district court has, in
> effect, placed a period after the word "subcontractors" in the quoted
> clause, and has thus given no practical effect to the words of limitation.

> A mere reading of the judgment indicates that this is an overstate-
> ment. If, in its decree, the district court had placed a period after the
> word "subcontractors," then the Comptroller General and his representa-
> tives would have been authorized to examine the books of the company
> without limitation. Instead, the court declared that the Comptroller could
> examine any such records "relating to the cost of producing the items
> furnished by Hewlett-Packard Company under the aforesaid contracts,
> including costs of direct material, direct labor and overhead costs. . . ."

> It is therefore clear that the district court sought to give effect to the
> words of limitation. The question is whether it gave full effect to those
> words. This depends upon the meaning to be attached to those words.

> The key word in the limitation clause is "contract." If that word is
> used in Section 2313(b) only with reference to the terms and conditions as
> were formulated, then the district court failed to give full effect to the

limitation clause. As Hewlett-Packard correctly points out, under the stipulated facts summarized above, production costs were not taken into consideration in arriving at the terms and conditions of the contracts in question. Thus data pertaining to production costs could not be said to directly pertain to, and involve transactions relating to, the contract, as so defined.

In our opinion, however, the word "contract," as used in this statute is intended to have a broader meaning, embracing not only the specific terms and conditions of the agreement, but also the general subject matter. The subject matter of these four contracts is the procurement of described property by the Government.

Production costs directly pertain to that subject matter, because if out of line with the contract price, the contract may have been an inappropriate means of meeting this particular procurement need of the Government. While this appraisal could not affect these particular contracts, it could lead to the use of other methods of meeting future procurement needs. Production costs involve transactions relating to the contract, because they encompass business arrangements made by the contractor in obtaining the materials, labor, facilities and the like required by it in fulfilling its commitment with reference to the subject matter of the contract.

Hewlett-Packard contends, in effect, that the sole purpose of the examination right accorded by Section 2313(b) and clause 10 of these contracts, is to enable the Comptroller General to find out whether the particular contracts which give rise to the examination had been performed in accordance with their terms and whether the contracting officer had been defrauded or misled in entering into the contract.

We find nothing in the words of the statute, its legislative history, or administrative interpretation, or in the impact of other statutes, which supports this view. On the contrary, it seems to us that if such a limited scope of examination had been intended by Congress it would have found the means to so indicate. The term "contract" could have been given a restricted meaning, or the scope of the permissible examination could have been specifically limited to lines of inquiry relevant to the legality and faithful performance of the particular contract giving rise to the examination.

Shortly thereafter, Hewlett-Packard announced its intention to carry its appeal to the United States Supreme Court. An appeal to the highest court in the land on a matter involving auditors' access to records appeared rather unusual; however, as Hewlett-Packard's Chairman of the Board of Directors stated, the matters here involved have "grave and far-reaching implications for the business community."

A point of primary interest involved a question of whether the Supreme Court would decide to rule on this case or not. To persuade the high court, Hewlett-Packard argued that its appeal was the first reported case to seek an interpretation of the government's rights under 10 U.S.C. 2313(b). Hewlett-Packard also contended that the Circuit Court's ruling confused or made this law inconsistent with 10 U.S.C. 2306(f), the Truth in Negotiations Act. P.L.

87-653 "would be completely inconsistent with the examination of records statute if the Comptroller General has unrestricted powers of examination, since the Congress would be saying on the one hand to the procurement agencies 'You do not need to rely on cost data in procurement negotiations for standard commercial catalog products,' and on the other hand 'We nevertheless expect the Comptroller General to audit and criticize the profit margin under these same contracts after the performance has been completed.' "

Hewlett-Packard also raised the point that the GAO's interpretation of its right to examination of records conflicts with or frustrates 18 U. S. C. 1905, which prohibits any officer or employee of the United States government from disclosing vital business data of a confidential nature. The Comptroller General, however, in the view of Hewlett-Packard, claimed that 18 U.S.C. 1905 does not apply to him and and that he, therefore, "is in a position to disclose publicly the results of his investigation and thereby frustrates the confidentiality afforded by Section 1905."

Several months later, on March 18, 1968, the hopes and plans of Hewlett-Packard (as well as of various industry and professional associations which were expected to file related briefs) were shattered when the Supreme Court announced that it would not review the ruling of the Circuit Court.

Eli Lilly & Co. v. Staats, 574 F.2d 904 (CA-7), Cert. Den., 439 U.S. 959 (1978), 24 CCF Par. 82,316

This case was the first of a series of controversies with drug manufacturers over GAO's access to records and the intent of the contract clause. Different decisions by different circuit courts and inconsistent positions taken by the U.S. Supreme Court prevented a clear-cut judicial ruling for a number of years.

The GAO reviews of the drug manufacturers were initiated by congressional interest in the reasonableness of the prices charged by the drug companies on contracts with the Veterans Administration and the Department of Defense. Lilly's contracts were awarded on the basis of catalog prices, and when the GAO tried to examine all of the records it considered necessary to determine the company's pricing practices, the district court granted Lilly's request for injunctive relief on the basis that the GAO's review was motivated by an improper purpose (study of pricing practices in the pharmaceutical industry) and that the records demanded by the GAO exceeded those Lilly was required to make available under the related statutory and contractural provisions. The district court concluded that the GAO's authority was limited "to determine whether the Government's purchase price was based on catalog prices of items sold in substantial quantities to the general public, and to determine whether the prices paid by the Government were equal or less than the catalog prices."

But GAO was successful in its appeal when the Seventh Circuit Court permitted the Agency access to the contractor's research and development and general and administrative expenses, even though the prices of the contracts involved were not based on costs. The Seventh Circuit Court handed down a similar ruling in *United States v. Abbott Laboratories,* 597 F.2d 672 (CA-7 1979), 26 CCF par. 83,496. The Second, Third, and District of Columbia

Circuits, however, have taken contrary positions and limited GAO's access to records of manufacturing costs, manufacturing overhead, royalty expenses, and delivery costs. See *Merck & Co., Inc., v. Staats, Comptroller General, U.S.,* No. 74-1447 (DC-DC 1977), 23 CCF par. 81,622, aff'd per curiam No. 79-1438 (CA-DC 1981), 29 CCF par. 81,872; *Bristol Laboratories Division of Bristol-Myers Co. v. Staats, Comptroller General, U.S.,* 428 F.Supp. 1388 (DC SD NY 1977), 23 CCF par. 81,243, aff'd per curiam, 620 F.2d 17 (CA-2 1980), aff'd by evenly divided court, 101 S.Ct. 2037 (1981) 28 CCF par. 81,339; *SmithKline Corp. v. Staats, Comptroller General, U.S.,* 688 F.2d 201 (CA-3 1981) 29 CCF par. 82,104.

The *Merck* Case: Appeal to the Supreme Court

Following in his predecessor's footsteps, Bowsher appealed the adverse ruling by the District of Columbia Circuit Court and petitioned the Supreme Court to settle this issue (*Bowsher, Comptroller General of the United States v. Merck & Co., Inc.,* S.Ct. Docket No. 81-1273, Jan. 7, 1982). Bowsher argued that Congress intended to give GAO broad authority for access to records under negotiated contracts and has not criticized GAO efforts to secure this broad access. However, complained the new Comptroller General, narrow judicial interpretations of the access provisions hamper GAO's ability to comply with its statutory mandate and contravene the legislative intent of the Congress in establishing the provision. Bowsher also asserted that the Supreme Court's failure to resolve the conflict among the circuit courts encourages contractors to shop for the most favorable forum because the construction of this contractual provision depends on the location of the contractor or the location of the lawsuit.

In its cross-petition, Merck & Co. opposed the GAO request for Supreme Court review. In addition, it requested of the Court that if it should review the issue raised by GAO, it should also consider certain other points raised in Merck's petition.

Merck first argued that there were really no cost records that might be considered as "directly pertinent" to the contracts involved in this case, all of them having been established by catalog, market, or other competitive pricing procedures. Inasmuch as the prices of the contracts were not based on costs, Merck asserted (as did others, see *SmithKline,* below) that no costs were directly pertinent and that the lower court was wrong in deciding that certain costs were in that category. In our judgment, Merck's point is particularly appropriate, and we believe the issue must be resolved by emphasis on accounting, business, and economic principles, rather than on legal principles. We see no merit in establishing arbitrary classifications of costs that GAO may or may not examine. We share the views of Merck and others that when costs are not a factor in contract pricing they should not be subject to review by any government agency. Exceptions may well be established, from a legal viewpoint, when fraud or other improprieties can be asserted in so strong a manner as to demonstrate the requirement for this kind of review.

In connection with the latter comment, Merck's cross-petition urged the Supreme Court to rule that the Comptroller General exceeded his statutory authority in demanding access to Merck's cost records, inasmuch as GAO had not alleged any improper, illegal, or irregular action or unfair profit.

Several factors should be considered to gain a perspective for that point in time.

The majority of Circuit Court decisions rendered to that date (2nd, 3rd and DC Circuits) were favorable to the contractors involved, those courts having refused to grant what appear to have been demands for unlimited access to all records of government contractors. GAO was successful before the 7th Circuit Court in *Eli Lilly & Co.* and *Abbott Laboratories.* However, footnote No. 7 in the *SmithKline Corp.* decision, reviewed below, states:

> We note that in *Abbott Laboratories* another panel of the Seventh Circuit addressed precisely the same issues as those addressed in *Lilly.* The district court had granted summary judgment to the Government on the basis of *Lilly,* and the circuit court affirmed. Two of the three judges, however, specifically expressed reluctance and concurred in the affirmance solely because they considered themselves bound by the earlier decision. See 597 F.2d at 674 (Pell, J., concurring); *id.* at 675 (Wood, J., concurring).

The second factor relates to the decision by the Ninth Circuit in the case of *Hewlett-Packard Co.* The government argued that in the 1967 decision the Ninth Circuit "sanctioned access to indirect overhead cost data." However, addressing that decision in its ruling in *SmithKline,* the U.S. Court of Appeals for the Third Circuit found the records to which access was sanctioned were limited to "costs of direct material, direct labor, and overhead costs." Uncertainty exists as to what the Ninth Circuit Court intended to "include as overhead." One might argue it intended limiting indirect expenses exposure to those included in a common definition of "overhead," i.e., manufacturing, factory, or production. If so, the Ninth Circuit's decision may parallel those of the Second, Third, and D.C. Circuit Courts.

The final factor to consider is the Supreme Court's action in the case of *Bristol Myers.* Here, the U.S. Court of Appeals for the Second Circuit had held that records relating to the contractor's research, development, promotion, distribution, and administration costs were not subject to examination by the GAO. The Supreme Court granted certiorari, and on April 29, 1981 (No. 80-264), affirmed this ruling in a four-to-four decision (Justice Potter Stewart not participating), without opinion.

SmithKline Corp. v. Staats, 688 F.2d 201 (CA-3 1981)

We referred several times to the ruling by the U.S. Court of Appeals for the Third Circuit in *SmithKline Corp.* Inasmuch as it accorded consideration to all of the previous case law, we thought a review of this decision would be informative for our readers.

During 1973 and 1974, SmithKline entered into negotiated contracts to supply drugs to the Veterans Administration and the Defense Supply Agency. The contracts are described in the decision as fixed price contracts where "the prices were established by reference either to catalog prices for ordinary commercial items sold in significant quantities to the general public or other evidence of competitive pricing." (One of the contractor's arguments was that cost data could not be directly pertinent to those contracts because the prices were not fixed by reference to costs but by catalog, market or competitive prices.)

Several years prior to these awards, GAO had launched a review of selected pharmaceutical firms, at the request of two U.S. Senators and their staff members, to ascertain and publicize cost and price data by individual company and product. GAO initially obtained the voluntary participation of drug manufacturers but encountered problems when it launched Phase II of the study, which was to cover all indirect expenses, including research, development, marketing, corporate expenses, etc. SmithKline was reluctant to furnish this data unless GAO guaranteed it would be kept confidential. Staats was prepared to give such guarantees, but the Senate staff members involved refused to sanction these arrangements. Thereupon, the Comptroller General abandoned the concept of a voluntary study and made formal written demands for access to those records.

The court pointedly observed that GAO had no reason to believe there were any improprieties, violations, or excess profits involved, and further, all of the contracts selected for review were fixed price with prices established on catalog or market prices or other evidence of a competitive price.

The district court ruled for the government and held that GAO could have access to all cost records the government contended were directly pertinent to the price of drugs sold under the contracts. On appeal to the U.S. Court of Appeals, SmithKline argued (1) that GAO sought the records for an improper purpose, and (2) the scope of GAO demands exceeded that allowed by the access to records provisions. The first argument centered on the premise that the access to records provisions were initially legislated because of the concern over suspected fraud, profiteering, etc., whereas they were being used for a general study of procurement techniques. Both sides cited statutes, legislative history, congressional debates, case law, and authoritative legal writings. To the many citations, the court added some of its own and, to a layman or to one learned in the law, it may appear that substantial cases had been made for both sides of the question. However, the U.S. Court of Appeals for the Third Circuit concluded that no real basis existed for establishing GAO's actions as improper, regardless of congressional prodding. It further endorsed a previous ruling (involving the Securities and Exchange Commission) in which a court said "we will not countenance judicial interference with agency decisions to conduct investigations, decisions that are committed entirely to agency discretion . . . ." Concluding on this facet of the dispute, the court said: "We have concluded . . . that, assuming GAO sought to conduct a broad economic study of the Pharmaceutical industry in order to provide cost and pricing data to individual senators, GAO did not invoke the access-to-records provisions for an improper purpose."

Probably of greater interest to most government contractors was whether GAO demands exceeded those allowed by the access to records provisions. On this substantive dispute, SmithKline won a significant although not total victory when the court ruled:

> SmithKline must allow GAO personnel to inspect its records with respect to manufacturing costs, manufacturing overhead, royalty expenses, and delivery costs. SmithKline need not produce data with

respect to research and development, marketing and promotion, distribution and administration, except to the extent that these costs may be included in the manufacturing costs.

The contractor's major arguments were previously framed, essentially that cost data cannot be "directly pertinent" to transactions related to contracts where the price is fixed not in reference to a standard of fairness in negotiating or to costs but to catalog, market, or competitive prices. The terms "directly pertinent" and "involving transactions related to this contract" as they apply to the nature of records that should be available to GAO form the basis for the major controversies over the GAO Examination of Records and Contract Clause.

The GAO Examination of Records Clause was based on 10 U.S.C. 2313(b) (1976) for defense and 41 U.S.C. 254(c) (1976) for nondefense contracts. Reviewing these statutes, the court concluded they "apply by their terms to negotiated contracts without qualification." The court further opined that if Congress had desired to exclude certain types of contracts, it could have explicitly done so as it did in the Truth in Negotiations and Renegotiation Acts. The court also observed that SmithKline had accepted this clause in the questioned contracts and had taken the further step of including it in subcontracts under such contracts.

The next significant issue was which records were directly pertinent to the contract in which the clause appears. Reaching back into legislative history again, the court noted that the governing legislation initially gave the Comptroller General access to pertinent records of the contractor. However, in debates preceding the enactment of the law, reservations and apprehensions were expressed by congressmen over possible GAO "snooping expeditions" and the fear that the original language would allow GAO "unlimited authority to go everywhere and snoop into everybody's business." Although the legislative history is not entirely definitive, and the government argued against interpretations of serious restrictions, the court found a strong congressional intent to prevent unlimited "snooping" and concluded the clause did not provide for unlimited access to the contractor's records.

Having concluded that the clause was operative in contracts where price was not affected by costs, but that the Congress intended to place some kind of limitations on the records to which GAO should have access, the court addressed probably the most difficult aspect of these disputes; the determination of which records were, and which were not, "directly pertinent" and hence available to GAO was cited earlier. While we are in full agreement that the words "directly pertinent" are significant and cannot be ignored, and therefore in agreement with the court's ruling that GAO's access to records must have limitations, we noted the court's failure to establish even reasonably clear guidelines as to how these key words could be identified with the related records. Essentially, the court adopted the language of the Second Circuit in Bristol Myers without really explaining why all of the costs identified in that decision, and only those costs, should be considered as "directly pertinent": "manufacturing costs (including raw and packaged materials, labor and fringe benefits, quality control and supervision); manufacturing overhead (including plant administration, production planning, warehousing, utilities, and security); royalty expenses; and delivery costs."

While not explaining its selection, the court criticized the government for failing to put forward an alternative definition. It noted that GAO had previously (in connection with its profit study) recognized its limitations in this area. The court also acknowledged that its limited definition might make some of GAO's investigations more difficult; however, it concluded that Congress appeared to prefer foregoing the prerequisite of obtaining all of the possible information GAO could discover if this information required a contractor to make virtually all of its records available.

Perhaps we have been overly critical of the court for failing to support the basis for distinguishing costs that are directly pertinent from costs that are not. In the interests of fairness, as well as of providing further information for our readers, we have cited below salient portions of the decision relating to this issue.

> When cost information is not allocated to specific contracts and their products, the Government's argument that generalized cost data are "directly pertinent" to any given contract is weakened. Like most manufacturing businesses, SmithKline divides its costs into a small category of direct manufacturing costs that can be readily assigned to a particular product and into other categories of cost, including research and development, distribution, marketing, advertising, and administrative costs, which are not assigned to any one product .... SmithKline maintains that this common practice reflects the lack of generally accepted accounting principles that permit accurate and meaningful allocation of these indirect costs.

> Obviously, however, these unassigned costs affect the price charged for the company's products, because the company must recover both the costs directly assigned and the unassigned pooled costs. Manufacturing and distribution costs of individual pharmaceutical products may constitute as little as nine percent of the products' sale price. By characterizing unallocated costs as "directly pertinent" to government procurement contracts, GAO would be able to demand access to all records of pooled costs whenever the price charged the government in the contracts at issue reflects costs attributable to the pool. GAO would thus have access to most, if not all, of SmithKline's pricing data.

> *   *   *   *

> In some industries, costs such as research and development have such a small impact that they arguably are not "directly pertinent" to the contract and its price. Whether a cost record is "directly pertinent" could vary from industry to industry. In some industries, direct costs are the predominant component of a product's price, and there would be no need to grant access to indirect cost information of those firms. But in the pharmaceutical industry, research and other costs not immediately attributable to one product form a large part of the costs of a pharmaceutical product. Each case could be decided on its facts by addressing one question: whether the records sought will show production costs and pricing of the contracts sufficient to determine why the contract price

was fixed as it was and whether "the contract may have been an inappropriate means of meeting this particular procurement need of the government." *Hewlett-Packard*, 385 F.2d at 1016. The judicial decision as to what records are necessary would thus be essentially an accounting problem which is not unlike those problems which are common in day-to-day discovery involving corporations.

Although it is tempting to take the opportunity to make the decision as equitably as possible in each case, we are not convinced that Congress intended for the interpretation of the access-to-records provision to depend on the facts of each case. The same provision appears in most Government contracts. We believe that Congress intended the words to acquire some common meaning so that the Government and the contracting firm could know within reason what they were contracting to perform. In contracts involving many millions of dollars, many firms, and many products, certainty is more important than deciding each case on its facts.

*   *   *   *

We therefore adopt the standard formulated in *Bristol,* which for the most part relies on the distinction between direct and indirect costs. We believe that it comports with Congress' intent to preclude GAO's scrutiny of nongovernmental contracts. Moreover, our distinction between information that is "directly pertinent" and that which is not follows the distinction drawn by every circuit to consider the issue with the exception of the Seventh Circuit . . . .

The Government argues that GAO's interpretation that the access-to-records provision provides for the access it seeks here has been well known and judicially established since the *Hewlett-Packard* decision in 1967. We do not believe, however, that the Ninth Circuit sanctioned access to all indirect overhead cost data. The Ninth Circuit held that GAO should have access to "production costs." 385 F.2d at 1016. Although the court never defined these costs, the district court's order, affirmed by the court of appeals, referred specifically to "costs of direct material, direct labor and overhead costs." *Id.* Our decision includes direct costs and some overhead within its definition of "directly pertinent." How much overhead the Ninth Circuit intended to include is uncertain. See *Merck,* slip op. at 23 n. 27 (Mikva, J., concurring in part and dissenting in part) ("Later decisions have disagreed over the *Hewlett-Packard* holding on this point."). Compare *Lilly,* 574 F.2d at 913, with *Bristol,* 428 F.Supp. at 1391. Thus, *Hewlett-Packard* does not necessarily suggest a result contrary to that in our case.

The *Merck* Case: Resolution in the Supreme Court

In what may have been the final shot fired in the judicial aspects of GAO's strivings for unlimited access to contractors' records, a divided U.S. Supreme Court ruled in *Merck* that GAO had no authority to examine contractors' indirect cost records where prices were based on the contractor's catalog prices (*Bowsher v. Merck & Co., Inc.,* Sup. Ct. No. 81-1273; *Merck & Co., Inc. v. Bowsher,* Sup. Ct. No. 81-1472, both decided April 19, 1983). The high court's decision ended GAO efforts extending over many years and involving the Hewlett-Packard Co. and several of the major American pharmaceutical firms. A ruling by the Supreme Court was particularly appropriate in view of the inconsistent positions taken by some of the lower courts.

Merck had entered into four negotiated firm fixed price contracts with the government for pharmaceutical products. These were standard commercial products sold by Merck in substantial quantities to the general public and the prices were based on the catalog prices at which Merck sold the items to the general public or were otherwise determined by adequate competition. All of the contracts contained the standard clause granting the Comptroller General the right to examine any directly pertinent records involving transactions related to the contract. Relying on these clauses, the Comptroller General issued a formal demand to Merck (and five other pharmaceutical firms) for access to the following:

> All books, documents, papers, and other records directly pertinent to contracts which include, but are not limited to, (1) records of experienced costs of direct materials, direct labor, overhead, and other pertinent corporate costs, (2) support for prices charged to the Government, and (3) such other information as may be necessary for use to review the reasonableness of the contract prices and the adequacy of the protection afforded the Government's interests.

Along with other pharmaceutical companies, Merck refused to comply with these GAO broad demands for wide-ranging data inasmuch as the contracts were not based on costs. The United States District Court for the District of Columbia ruled that the GAO could have access to records

> directly pertaining to the pricing and cost of producing items furnished by ... Merck under the ... contracts ..., including manufacturing costs, (including raw and packaging materials, labor, and fringe benefits, quality control and supervision), manufacturing overhead, (including plant administration, production planning, warehousing, utilities and security), royalty expenses and delivery costs.

The court barred access to records

> with respect to research and development, marketing and promotion, distribution, and administration, (except to the extent such data may be included in the cost items listed above.)

The district court's ruling was affirmed by the United States Court of Appeals for the District of Columbia, 655 F.2d 1236 (1981). The government appealed the ruling that certain of Merck's indirect expenses were not subject to GAO examination and Merck appealed the decision that any of its costs were "directly pertinent" in the circumstances. The Supreme Court ruling could have taken any of several directions: (1) affirmed the ruling of the lower courts, establishing GAO access to records as ruled by those courts (see above), (2) agreed with GAO that it was entitled to all of the records, or (3) agreed with Merck that, in the circumstances, GAO was not entitled to any of the records. It was interesting indeed to read that the high tribunal divided in all of the three directions. The majority of five justices affirmed the ruling of the lower courts. A separate opinion by two believed that GAO should have access to all of the records that had a "direct and substantial impact" on prices charged the government, subject only to the restriction of the Fourth Amendment to the U.S. Constitution.

The Fourth Amendment to the constitution provides: "The right of the people to be secure in their persons, houses, papers and effects, against unreasonable searches and seizures shall not be violated, and no warrants shall issue but upon probable cause, supported by oath or affirmation, and particularly describing the place to be searched, and the persons or things to be seized."

Another separate opinion by the remaining two justices stated that, inasmuch as the contract prices were not based on costs, GAO should not have access to any cost records.

The majority decision was bottomed on its interpretation of the legislative history of the bill now codified as 10 U.S.C. 2313(b) and 41 U.S.C. 254(c). As initially introduced, the bill provided access to "pertinent" records. After opposition arguing that it would permit "unnecessary snooping expeditions" and would allow GAO to "go into everybody's business and look it over if they just wanted to take a look at it", the language was revised to the more restrictive "directly pertinent." The Court was necessarily impressed that the change must have signified the intent to place limitations on GAO's access to contractor's records because the Congress "did not want unrestricted 'snooping' by the Comptroller General into the business records of a private contractor."

The Court also recognized that the sponsor of the legislation intended that the bill give the Comptroller General the tools to look for improprieties and waste in the negotiation of contracts. To this extent, the Court conceded that "broad access to cost records would enhance GAO's ability to evaluate the reasonableness of the price charged the Government and to identify areas of waste and inefficiency in procurement." On the other hand, there was the obvious restricting amendment which added the word "pertinent" and the Court said it had to "traverse uncharted seas" in arriving at a judgment which would appropriately "balance the public interest served by full GAO investigations against the private interest in freedom from officious governmental intermeddling in the contractor's private business affairs."

As a layman, we found little in the majority opinion that was clearly bottomed on any legislation or regulation. As stated in its closing comments, ". . . given the policy of protecting the privacy of contractors' business records also expressed in the statutory and legislative history, neither can we accept the Government's contention that it must be permitted access to *all* of Merck's cost records." (Emphasis in the original).

But what about Merck's contention that the only records directly pertinent to those contracts "are those necessary to verify that Merck actually had an established catalog price for the item procured, that it sold the items in substantial quantities to the general public at the catalog price, that it delivered the product specified, and that it received from the Government no more than the amount due under the contract?" The Court's rejection of Merck's argument was also based on legislative history, in this case the congressional intent to give GAO authority "to examine directly pertinent

records under individual procurement contracts in order to assess the reasonableness of the prices paid by the Government and to detect inefficiency and
wastefulness." The Court saw a congressional mandate to GAO "to detect
fraud, waste, inefficiency and extravagance . . . ."

Two of the justices, however, were favorably impressed with Merck's
argument. "The access to records statutes," according to this minority opinion, "were intended to permit inspection of cost records when the negotiation
of a particular contract depended on representations about the contractor's
costs, or when the contract price itself varied according to costs . . . . There is,
however, no indication that Congress intended to permit such inspection when
costs were not relevant to the contract's negotiation, its terms, or its performance."

This minority opinion quoted examples given by the sponsor of the
legislation and pointed out that all of them related to cost-based contracts, and
could not agree with the majority's approach of permitting access to direct
costs but not to indirect costs when none of the costs was relevant to the
contract price. It further stated:

> Merck's costs were thus irrelevant to the bargain reached by the
> parties. Because the Government chose not to make an issue during the
> negotiations, the terms of the contract would have been the same whether
> Merck's costs represented one percent, ten percent, or one hundred
> percent of the price the Government agreed to pay. The conclusion seems
> inescapable that Merck's costs, and consequently its cost records, are not
> pertinent to the agreements it entered into with the Government.

> *   *   *   *

> . . . . Cost records do not become "directly pertinent" to these contracts
> simply because the Government now wants information that did not
> concern it at the time of contracting.

As mentioned earlier, the Court divided into three opinions, with a
majority of five affirming the lower court's direct/indirect costs compromise, a
minority of two holding for Merck's arguments that no cost records were
"directly pertinent", and another minority of two believing that GAO's
request for direct and indirect cost records should be upheld ". . . but only to
the extent that: (1) the records sought by GAO related to costs that likely had
a direct and substantial impact on the prices charged to the Government
under the contracts; and (2) the request is reasonable in scope and would not
unduly burden Merck."

This minority view appears to minimize the nature of the contracts and
the manner in which the prices were arrived at to emphasize what the justice
perceived was a congressional intent to provide GAO with authority to
examine contractor's records "to detect waste, extravagance, and ineffective
procurement." Even this opinion, however, disagreed with the GAO claim that
"it has the right to examine records pertaining to every cost 'defrayed from
commingled general revenues that include the Government payments under
the contract.' " This GAO demand was viewed as "overbroad."

Finding difficulties, as did the majority, in establishing clear criteria
governing which records GAO could examine, this minority view was much

more sympathetic toward GAO so long as "GAO could bear the burden of proving the records are of costs that likely had a direct and substantial impact on the price charged to the Government under the contract." In addition, "the GAO's right of inspection is further circumscribed, and the contractors' right to privacy is further protected, by constitutional standards, such as the Fourth Amendment reasonableness requirement."

Venturing some layman's observations, we are favorably impressed with the uncluttered, clear-cut opinion of the minority which held that GAO had no right to access to any cost records of a contractor where "neither the contract price nor its performance was tied to costs in any respect." The writer of this opinion did not need to struggle with unprovable theories and try to rationalize compromises for which no real foundations could be laid.

As to the majority opinion, it is safe to say that it did not satisfy either party. Companies with contracts under which costs are irrelevant to prices must nevertheless tolerate GAO investigations. On the other hand, GAO's insatiable demands for access to books and records find little satisfaction from the right to examine costs which, in the case of the pharmaceutical companies, have been estimated to amount to about 9% of the total. Without any real support, it seems to us, the majority concluded: "In our view, the appropriate accommodation of the competing goals (GAO's mandate to investigate for waste and inefficient procurement practices v. its unwarranted intrusion into contractors' private affairs) reflected in the legislative history counsels us to draw the line precisely where both lower courts have drawn it."

Chapter XXIX

Income Tax Considerations Affecting Government Contractors

Income tax considerations of companies oriented toward government contracts, in a general sense, are similar to those of firms engaged in supplying goods and services in the commercial marketplace. The major problems confronting government contractors in recent years have centered on income recognition under long-term contracts and this chapter focuses mainly on this subject. We would emphasize that this text is directed essentially to government contract costing, pricing, and administration and, although we have attempted to address the major legislative and regulatory provisions of federal income tax provisions affecting government contractors, we would suggest consultations with federal income tax experts when confronted with significant decision-making requirements in this area.

THE RISE AND FALL OF THE COMPLETED CONTRACT METHOD (CCM)

CCM was initially authorized for income tax purposes to establish income recognition in 1918. Initially heralded as the practical answer to the problems involved in making annual estimates and determinations of profits or losses under long-term contracts under the percentage of completion method (PCM), and at one time highly favored by certain proponents of the Renegotiation Act who lacked confidence in the ability and integrity of contractors to arrive at appropriate estimates, CCM has come under increasing criticism during the 1980s from both the government and the accounting profession.

While many professional accountants have long leaned toward PCM as more nearly in consonance with the principles of matching income and costs, a practical recognition existed for many years that the use of this method required the existence of certain circumstances. Thus, the 1955 AICPA Accounting Research Bulletin (ARB) 45 stated:

> The Committee believes that, in general, when estimates of costs to complete and extent of progress toward completion of long-term contracts are reasonably dependable, the percentage-of-completion method is preferable. When lack of dependable estimates or inherent hazards cause forecasts to be doubtful, the completed-contract method is preferable.

In July 1981, the AICPA issued an Audit and Accounting Guide for Construction Contracts, prepared by the Institute's Construction Contractor Guide Committee, which included a Statement of Position on Accounting for Performance of Construction-Type and Certain Production-Type Contracts. Although this Position Statement does not have the status of FASB Statements or Interpretations, or AICPA APB publications, it has been considered as expressing a prevailing opinion of the majority of professional accountants.

Although the Position Statement continues to recognize that both the PCM and CCM, and some variations thereof, may be acceptable in certain circumstances, it emphasized that "the two methods should be used in specified circumstances and should not be used as acceptable alternatives for the same circumstances." Further, while agreeing that the use of PCM "depended on the ability to make estimates," the committee asserted its belief that PCM "is preferable as an accounting policy in circumstances in which reasonable dependable estimates can be made . . ." Its strong leaning toward PCM is further emphasized by the following comments:

> For entities engaged on a continuous basis in the production and delivery of goods and services under contractual arrangements and for whom contracting represents a significant part of operations, the presumption is that they have the ability to make estimates that are sufficiently dependable to justify the use of the percentage-of-completion method. Persuasive evidence to the contrary is necessary to overcome the presumption.

This concept is more readily acceptable in theory than in practice. The exact nature of "persuasive evidence" is not explained but this exception was apparently not considered significant by the framers of the Statement, who suggested, in effect, that where estimates are not dependable, management should take the necessary action to improve them rather than to use such deficiency as a basis for departing from what the writers believed to be the preferred method.

The impact of the changing views of the accounting profession may have had some influence on the 1982 and 1986 income tax legislation, but they certainly were not the major considerations. With regard to the Tax Equity and Fiscal Responsibility Act of 1982 (TEFRA), the major consideration was obviously the objective of constraining budgetary deficits by providing for certain "revenue enhancers," a euphemism for tax increases. Similar considerations and the increasing assertions that CCM was permitting long-term contractors to minimize or avoid payment of an appropriate amount of income taxes were the driving factors in the related revisions of the 1986 Tax Reform Act (TRA).

The TEFRA and TRA attacks on CCM were strongly opposed by a number of industry associations, which presented cogent arguments against some of the extreme provisions of the tax measures. However, except for certain considerations obtained by the construction industry and small business, the laws severely damaged CCM, first by drastically reducing the kinds of indirect expenses that could be charged off as period costs under such contracts, and then by the more drastic limitation on the use of this method regardless of the treatment accorded related costs and expenses.

For purposes of this discussion, we have traced the changes legislated for income recognition under long-term contracts, beginning with the IRS implementation of TEFRA and continuing through TRA and the regulatory implementation to this date.

TAX EQUITY AND FISCAL RESPONSIBILITY ACT OF 1982 (TEFRA)

Income from a long-term contract under TEFRA may be computed on either the PCM or CCM provided the method chosen, in the opinion of the Service, "clearly reflect(s) income." The "method chosen must be applied consistently to all long-term contracts of substantial duration in the same trade or business." However, contracts of less than substantial duration may be reported under a different, appropriate method.

A long-term contract is defined as a "building, installation, construction, or manufacturing contract which is not completed within the taxable year in which it is entered into." A manufacturing contract is considered a long-term contract "only if such contract involves the manufacturer of: (a) unique items of a type which is not normally carried in the finished goods inventory of the taxpayer, or (b) items which normally require more than 12 calendar months to complete (regardless of the length of the actual contract)."

Generally, "a long-term contract shall not be considered 'completed' until final completion and acceptance have occurred." The regulation cautions, however, that "a taxpayer may not delay the completion of a contract for the principal purpose of deferring Federal income tax." In determining "completion and acceptance" for Federal income tax purposes, IRS will consider such circumstances as "the manner in which the parties to the contract deal with each other and with the subject matter of the contract, the physical condition and state of readiness of the subject matter of the contract, and the nature of any work or costs remaining to be performed or incurred on the contract." Several examples are provided to illustrate the occurrence of different circumstances and the point at which final completion and acceptance occurs for tax purposes.

Where a long-term contract includes more than one subject matter, such as aircraft and training manuals and spare parts, the aircraft is determined as the "primary subject matter" of the contract and completion shall be determined without regard to the delivery of the other items. Where the other items of a long-term contract are not completed and accepted at the end of the fiscal year, the gross contract price and costs shall be separated from the long-term contract and accounted for under "a proper method of accounting," which would be a long-term contract method "if a separate contract for such other items would be a long-term contract . . . ."

Final completion and acceptance of a long-term contract shall be determined without regard to any additional compensation contingent upon the successful performance of the item or any obligation to assist or supervise in the installation or assembly of the item.

In the case of a subcontractor who completes his work on a long-term contract prior to the completion of the entire prime contract, the date of final completion and acceptance for the subcontractor shall be the date on which his work has been completed and accepted by the prime.

Extended period long-term contract. With exceptions noted below, the extended period long-term contract is "any long-term contract that the taxpayer estimates (at the time such contract is entered into) will not be completed .... within the 2-year period beginning on the first date .... that the taxpayer incurs any costs (other than costs such as bidding expenses, or expenses incurred in connection with negotiating the contract), allocable to such contract .... The preceding sentence shall be applied without regard to when costs allocable to a contract are recorded under the accounting procedures used by the taxpayer. In general, the contract commencement date will be the first date that any of the following activities occur: the taxpayer incurs design or engineering costs incurred solely for bidding for the contract; materials or equipment are shipped to the jobsite; or workers whose labor cost is treated as direct labor are sent to the jobsite. If the first date when any costs allocable to a contract are incurred is not determinable, the contract commencement date .... shall be the date such contract is entered into, unless the taxpayer establishes to the satisfaction of the district director that another date is a more appropriate commencement date. The contract commencement date shall not be earlier than the date the contract is entered into, unless the taxpayer delayed entering into the contract for the principal purpose of avoiding the rules of this section."

Certain construction contracts, as this term is defined in the regulations, are not included in the category of extended long-term contracts. These are contracts entered into by a taxpayer "(A) who estimates (at the time such contract is entered into) that such contract shall be completed within a 3-year period ... or (B) whose average annual gross receipts .... over the 3 taxable years preceding the taxable year the contract is entered into (or, if less, the number of preceding taxable years the taxpayer has been in existence) do not exceed $25 million."

Allocation of costs to long-term contracts. Allocation of direct material and direct labor costs conforms to general practices. The only difference that would be encountered by some contractors is that direct labor includes overtime pay, vacation and holiday pay, sick leave pay, shift differential, payroll taxes, and payments to a supplemental unemployment benefit plan on behalf of employees engaged in direct labor.

Indirect costs that must be allocated to long-term contracts include:

(A) Repair expenses of equipment or facilities used in the performance of particular long-term contracts,

(B) Maintenance of equipment or facilities used in the performance of particular long-term contracts,

(C) Utilities, such as heat, light, and power, relating to equipment or facilities used in the performance of particular long-term contracts,

(D) Rent of equipment or facilities used in the performance of particular long-term contracts,

(E) Indirect labor and contract supervisory wages, including basic compensation, overtime pay, vacation and holiday pay, sick leave pay (other than payments pursuant to a wage continuation plan under section 105(d) as it existed prior to its repeal in 1983), shift differential, payroll taxes, and contributions to a supplemental unemployment benefit plan incurred in the performance of particular long-term contracts,

(F) Indirect materials and supplies used in the performance of particular long-term contracts,

(G) Tools and equipment not capitalized used in the performance of particular long-term contracts,

(H) Costs of quality control and inspection incurred in the performance of particular long-term contracts,

(I) Taxes otherwise allowable as a deduction under section 164 (other than State and local, and foreign income taxes) to the extent such taxes are attributable to labor, materials, supplies, equipment or facilities used in the performance of particular long-term contracts,

(J) Depreciation, amortization and cost recovery allowances reported for the taxable year for financial purposes on equipment and facilities used in the performance of particular long-term contracts (but not in excess of the depreciation, amortization or cost recovery allowance allowable for the taxable year under Chapter 1 of the Code with respect to any item of equipment or facility),

(K) Cost depletion incurred in the performance of particular long-term contracts,

(L) Administrative costs incurred in the performance of particular long-term contracts (but not including any costs of selling or any return on capital),

(M) Compensation paid to officers attributable to services performed on particular long-term contracts (other than incidental or occasional services), and

(N) Costs of insurance incurred in the performance of particular long-term contracts, such as insurance on machinery and equipment used in the construction of the subject matter of a long-term contract.

Costs which are not required to be included in costs attributable to long-term contracts include:

(A) Marketing and selling expenses, including bidding expenses,

(B) Advertising expenses,

(C) Other distribution expenses,

(D) Interest,

(E) General and administrative expenses attributable to the performance of services which benefit the long-term contractor's activities as a whole (such as payroll expenses, legal and accounting expenses, etc.),

(F) Research and experimental expenses (described in section 174 and the regulations thereunder),

(G) Losses under section 165 and the regulations thereunder,

(H) Percentage of depletion in excess of cost depletion,

(I) Depreciation, amortization and cost recovery allowances on equipment and facilities that have been placed in service but are temporarily idle (for this purpose, an asset is not considered to be temporarily idle on non-working days, and an asset used in construction is considered to be idle when it is not en route to or not located at a jobsite), and depreciation, amortization and cost recovery allowances under Chapter 1 of the Code in excess of depreciation, amortization and cost recovery allowances reported by the taxpayer in the taxpayer's financial reports,

(J) Income taxes attributable to income received from long-term contracts,

(K) Contributions paid to or under a stock bonus, pension, profit-sharing or annuity plan or other plan deferring the receipt of compensation whether or not the plan qualifies under section 401(a), and other employee benefit expenses paid or accrued on behalf of labor, to the extent such contributions or expenses are otherwise allowable as deductions under Chapter 1 of the Code. "Other employee benefit expenses" include (but are not limited to): worker's compensation; amounts deductible or for whose payment reduction in earnings and profits is allowed under section 404A and the regulations thereunder; payments pursuant to a wage continuation plan under section 105(d) as it existed prior to its repeal in 1983; amounts includible in the gross income of employees under a method or arrangement of employer contributions or compensation which has the effect of a stock bonus, pension, profit-sharing, or annuity plan, or other plan deferring the receipt of compensation or providing deferred benefits; premiums on life and health insurance; and miscellaneous benefits provided for employees such as safety, medical treatment, recreational and eating facilities, membership dues, etc.,

(L) Cost attributable to strikes, rework labor, scrap and spoilage, and

(M) Compensation paid to officers attributable to the performance of services which benefit the long-term contractor's activities as a whole.

Allocation of costs to extended period long-term contracts. Requirements relating to direct material and direct labor generally conform to those established for long-term contracts. As to indirect costs, the provision for long-term contracts is prefixed by the description ".... which are incident to, and necessary for the performance...." The listing for extended period long-term contracts is somewhat more complex and refers to costs that directly benefit the performance of such contracts or are incurred by reason of performance thereof. The regulation further provides: "Certain types of costs may directly benefit, or be incurred by reason of the performance of extended period long-term contracts .... even though the same type of costs also benefits other activities of the taxpayer. Accordingly, such costs require a reasonable allocation...."

The listing of indirect costs which must be allocated to extended period long-term contracts generally follows that for long-term contracts, as above, through subparagraph (L). The differences begin with paragraph (M), as set forth below:

(M) Direct and indirect costs incurred by any administrative, service, or support function or department to the extent such costs are allocable to particular extended period long-term contracts pursuant to paragraph (d)(9) of this section,

(N) Compensation paid to officers attributable to services performed on particular extended period long-term contracts (but not including any cost of selling),

(O) Costs of insurance incurred in the performance of particular extended period long-term contracts, such as insurance on machinery and equipment used in the construction of the subject matter of an extended period long-term contract,

(P) Contributions paid to or under a stock bonus, pension, profit-sharing or annuity plan or other plan deferring the receipt of compensation whether or not the plan qualifies under section 401(a) (except for amounts described in paragraph (d)(6)(iii)(I) of this section), and other employee benefit expenses paid or accrued on behalf of labor, to the extent such contributions or expenses are otherwise allowable as deductions under Chapter 1 of the Code. "Other employee benefit expenses" include (but are not limited to): worker's compensation; amounts deductible or for whose payment reduction in earnings of profits is allowed under section 404A and the regulations thereunder; payments pursuant to a wage contribution plan under section 105(d) as it existed prior to its repeal in 1983; amounts includible in the gross income of employees under a method or arrangement of employer contributions or compensation which has the effect of a stock bonus, pension, profit-sharing, or annuity plan, or other plan deferring the receipt of compensation or providing deferred benefits; premiums on life and health insurance; and miscellaneous benefits provided for employees such as safety, medical treatment, recreational and eating facilities, membership dues, etc.,

(Q) Research and experimental expenses (described in section 174 and the regulations thereunder) directly attributable to particular extended period long-term contracts in existence at the time such expenses are incurred, or incurred under an agreement to perform research or experimentation,

(R) Rework labor, scrap and spoilage to the extent incurred in the performance of particular extended period long-term contracts, and

(S) Bidding expenses incurred in the solicitation of particular extended period long-term contracts ultimately awarded to the taxpayer. For purposes of this section, the term "bidding expenses" does not include any research and experimental expenses described in section 174 and the regulations thereunder. The taxpayer shall defer all bidding expenses paid or incurred in the solicitation of a particular extended period long-term contract until the contract is awarded. If the contract is awarded to the taxpayer, the bidding costs become part of the indirect costs assigned to the contract. If the contract is not awarded to the taxpayer, bidding costs become deductible in the taxable year the contract is awarded, or the taxable year the taxpayer is notified in writing that no contract will be awarded and that the contract (or similar or related contract) will not be re-bid, or in the taxable year that the taxpayer abandons its bid or proposal, whichever occurs first. Abandoning a bid does not include modifying, supplementing, or changing the original bid or proposal. If the taxpayer is awarded only part of the bid (for example, the taxpayer submitted one bid to build each of two different types of bridges and the taxpayer was awarded a contract to build only one of the two bridges), the taxpayer shall deduct the portion of the bidding expenses related to the portion of the bid not awarded to the taxpayer; in the case of a bid or proposal for a multi-unit contract, however, all the bidding expenses shall be allocated to a contract awarded to the taxpayer to produce any of such units (for example, where the taxpayer submitted one bid to produce three similar turbines and the taxpayer was awarded a contract to produce only two of the three turbines).

Costs which are not required to be included in costs attributable to extended long-term contracts include:

(A) Marketing, selling and advertising expenses,

(B) Bidding expenses incurred in the solicitation of contracts not awarded to the taxpayer (see paragraph (d)(6)(ii)(S) of this section),

(C) Interest,

(D) General and administrative expenses (but not including any cost described in paragraph (d)(6)(ii)(L) or (M) of this section) and compensation paid to officers attributable to the performance of services that do not directly benefit or are not incurred by reason of any extended period long-term contracts,

(E) Research and experimental expenses (described in section 174 and the regulations thereunder) neither directly attributable to particular extended period long-term contracts in existence at the time such expenses are incurred nor incurred under any agreement to perform research or experimentation,

(F) Losses under section 165 and the regulations thereunder,

(G) Depreciation, amortization and cost recovery allowances on equipment and facilities that have been placed in service but are temporarily idle (for this purpose, an asset is not considered to be temporarily idle on non-working days, and an asset used in construction is considered to be idle when it is not en route to or not located at a jobsite),

(H) Income taxes attributable to income received from extended period long-term contracts,

(I) Contributions paid to or under a pension or annuity plan allowable as a deduction under section 404 (and section 404A if applicable) to the extent such contributions represent past service costs, and

(J) Cost attributable to strikes.

As stated earlier, the regulations concerning accounting for long-term contracts and extended period long-term contracts are comprehensive and extensive, much too lengthy for additional review in this publication. Companies to which these regulations apply will wish to assure themselves that their in-house and outside consultants are thoroughly versed in the details and provide the information required to comply with all of the provisions while protecting the companies' interests. The TEFRA implementation relating to these contracts is found in 26 CFR Section 1.451-3.

While retaining the completed contract method of accounting, the law and implementing regulations have considerably diluted the essence of this accounting method through the requirement for allocating, in effect capitalizing, many indirect period expenses.

On January 17, 1986, GAO issued a report captioned: "Congress Should Further Restrict Use of the Completed Contract Method." In its usual manner, the watch-dog agency trumpeted that companies using CCM have been deriving great, unintended benefits and by far the greatest benefits had been derived by federal contractors. GAO concluded that CCM "should not be allowed for tax reporting purposes, except for those contractors who can satisfactorily demonstrate to IRS that they cannot obtain reasonably dependable estimates of costs to complete or the extent of progress toward completion of a particular contract." This conclusion was preceded by views that virtually all companies "either have or should be able to acquire the expertise needed to make reasonably dependable annual estimates of project costs or progress for tax purposes." GAO recommended related congressional action.

TAX REFORM ACT OF 1986 (TRA)—PUBLIC LAW 99-514

In the major change, contractors who do not use the percentage of completion method (PCM), for long-term contracts, *must use this method for 40% of the income and expenses and would be allowed to use the CCM for the remaining 60% of such contracts.* This provision and the requirement for the *"look-back method"* where the PCM is used are quoted below:

Sec. 804. MODIFICATIONS OF METHOD OF ACCOUNTING FOR LONG-TERM CONTRACTS

(a) General Rule—Subpart B of part II of subchapter E of Chapter 1 is amended by adding at the end thereof the following new section.

Sec. 460. Special Rules for Long-Term Contracts

(a) Percentage of Completion-Capitalized Cost Method.—

(1) In General.—In the case of any long-term contract.—

(A) 40 percent of the items with respect to such contract shall be taken into account under the percentage of completion method (as modified by subsection (b)), and

(B) 60 percent of the items with respect to such contract shall be taken into account under the taxpayer's normal method of accounting.

(2) 40 percent look-back method to apply.—Upon completion of any long-term contract, the taxpayer shall pay (or shall be entitled to receive) interest determined by applying the look-back method of subsection (b)(3) to 40 percent of the items with respect to the contract.

(b) Percentage of Completion Method.—

(1) Subsection (a) Not to Apply Where Percentage of Completion Method Used.—Subsection (a) shall not apply to any long-term contract with respect to which amounts includible in gross income are determined under the percentage of completion method.

(2) Requirements of Percentage of Completion Method.—In the case of any long-term contract with respect to which the percentage of completion method is used—

(A) the percentage of completion shall be determined by comparing costs allocated to the contract under subsection (c) and incurred before the close of the taxable year with the estimated total contract costs, and

(B) upon completion of the contract, the taxpayer shall pay (or shall be entitled to receive) interest computed under the look-back method of paragraph (3).

(3) Look-Back Method.—The interest computed under the look-back method of this subparagraph shall be determined by—

(A) first allocating income under the contract among taxable years before the year in which the contract is completed on the basis of the actual contract price and costs instead of the estimated contract price and costs,

(B) second, determining (solely for purposes of computing such interest) the overpayment or underpayment of tax for each taxable year referred to in paragraph (1) which would result solely from the application of paragraph (1), and

(C) then using the overpayment rate established by section 6621, compounded daily, on the overpayment or underpayment determined under paragraph (1).

It may be useful to study the House-Senate conference agreement on these provisions:

In General. The conference agreement adopts elements of both the House bill and the Senate amendment provisions. Under the conference agreement, taxpayers may elect to compute income from long-term contracts under one of two methods: (1) the "percentage of completion-capitalized cost method" (i.e., 40 percent PCM) described below or (2) the percentage of completion method. In general, percentage of completion is determined as provided in the House bill for purposes of both methods. Except in the case of certain real property construction contracts (i.e., those for which exceptions were provided under the House bill and Senate amendment), these are the exclusive methods under which long-term contracts may be reported. The conference agreement generally adopts the definition of a long-term contract in the Senate amendment. This definition is the same as present law.

The conference agreement also prescribes the treatment of independent research and development costs, effective for all open tax years.

Percentage of completion-capitalized cost method. In the case of any long-term contract not reported under the percentage of completion method, the taxpayer must take into account 40 percent of the items with respect to the contract under the percentage of completion method. Percentage of completion is determined by comparing the total contract costs incurred before the close of the taxable year with the estimated total contract costs. The contract costs taken into account in determining the percentage of completion are those for which capitalization is required under the Senate amendment in the case of long-term contracts ("capitalizable costs").

The remaining 60 percent of the items under the contract are to be taken into account under the taxpayer's normal method of accounting, capitalizing those costs as required under the Senate amendment. Thus, 60 percent of the gross contract income will be recognized, and 60 percent of the contract costs will be deducted, at the time required by the taxpayer's method. For example, if the taxpayer uses the completed contract method of accounting, these items would be taken into account upon completion of the contract. If the taxpayer uses an accrual method (e.g., an accrual shipment method), such contract items would be taken into account at the time of shipment.

Under the conference agreement, the look-back method provided in the House bill is to be applied to the 40-percent portion of the contract reported on the percentage of completion method. Thus, interest is paid to or by the taxpayer on the difference between the amount actually taken into account by the taxpayer for each year of the contract and the amount the taxpayer would have taken into account recomputing the 40-percent portion under the look-back method.

The provisions of the Act with respect to allocation of costs are quoted below and special attention is accorded to IR&D:

(c) Allocation of Costs to Contract.—

(1) Direct and Certain Indirect Costs.—In the case of a long-term contract, all costs (including research and experimental costs) which directly benefit, or are incurred by reason of, the long-term contract activities of the taxpayer shall be allocated to such contract in the same manner as costs are allocated to extended period long-term contracts under section 451 and the regulations thereunder.

(2) Costs Identified Under Cost-Plus and Certain Federal Contracts.—In the case of a cost-plus long-term contract or a Federal long-term contract, any cost not allocated to such contract under paragraph (1) shall be allocated to such contract if such cost is identified by the taxpayer (or a related person), pursuant to the contract or Federal, State, or local law or regulation, as being attributable to such contract.

(3) Allocation of Production Period Interest to Contract.—

(A) In General.—Except as provided in subparagraphs (B) and (C), in the case of a long-term contract, interest costs shall be allocated to the contract in the same manner as interest costs are allocated to property produced by the taxpayer under section 263A(f).

(B) Production Period.—In applying section 263A(f) for purposes of subparagraph (A), the production period shall be the period—

(i) beginning on the later of—

(I) the contract commencement date, or

(II) in the case of a taxpayer who uses an accrual method with respect to long-term contracts, the date by which at least 5 percent of the total estimated costs (including design and planning costs) under the contract have been incurred, and

(ii) ending on the contract completion date.

(C) Application of De Minimis Rule.—In applying section 263A(f) for purposes of subparagraph (A), paragraph (1)(B)(iii) of such section shall be applied on a contract-by-contract basis; except that, in the case of a taxpayer described in subparagraph (B)(i)(II) of this paragraph, paragraph (1)(B)(iii) of section 263A(f) shall be applied on a property-by-property basis.

(4) Certain Costs Not Included.—This subsection shall not apply to any—

(A) independent research and development expenses,

(B) expenses for unsuccessful bids and proposals, and

(C) marketing, selling, and advertising expenses.

(5) Independent Research and Development Expenses.—For purposes of paragraph (4), the term "independent research and development expenses" means any expenses incurred in the performance of research or development, except that such term shall not include—

(A) any expenses which are directly attributable to a long-term contract in existence when such expenses are incurred, or

(B) any expenses under an agreement to perform research or development.

* * * *

(1) In General—The amendments made by this section shall apply to any contract entered into after February 28, 1986.

(2) Clarification of Treatment of Independent Research and Development Expenses.—

(A) In General.—For periods before, on, or after the date of enactment of this Act—

(i) any independent research and development expenses taken into account in determining the total contract price shall not be severable from the contract, and

(ii) any independent research and development expenses shall not be treated as amounts chargeable to capital account.

(B) Independent Research and Development Expenses.—For purposes of subparagraph (A), the term "independent research and development expenses" has the meaning given to such term by section 263(A)(c)(5) of the Internal Revenue Code of 1986, as added by this section.

The conference agreement comments relating to IR&D are particularly significant in the light of IRS technical service memoranda to the contrary:

Independent Research and Development Costs

Under the conference agreement, independent research and development costs are expressly excepted from the category of capitalizable costs. Independent research and development costs for this purpose are defined as any expenses incurred in the performance of independent research and development other than (1) expenses directly attributable to a long-term contract in existence when the expenses are incurred, and (2) any expenses under an agreement to perform research and development.

In particular, the conferees intend that the contractual arrangement regarding IR&D and its allocation to the contract shall not be severed, for Federal income tax purposes, from the long-term contract in such a manner as to render IR&D ineligible for treatment as a cost of a long-term contract, or to accelerate the regulation of any income pertaining to IR&D in comparison to the recognition of income which would otherwise occur under the taxpayer's method of accounting.

The conferees are aware that the treatment of independent research and development (IR&D) is presently a subject of controversy between taxpayers and the Internal Revenue Service. Under the conference agreement, the position of the Internal Revenue Service in several recent technical advice memoranda is expressly overruled.

The foregoing 60-40 percentage allocation appears to be an arbitrary determination caused by budget constraints. It is difficult to comprehend the reasoning of our elected representatives when applying this decision-making process to finite cost accounting procedures for the ascertainment of taxable income on a PCM or CCM basis. A normal prudent accounting approach would be to go all the way with one method or another and not resort to a last minute flip-of-the-coin conclusion in such technical areas of determination.

IRS GUIDANCE ON ACCOUNTING FOR LONG-TERM CONTRACTS UNDER TRA

The Internal Revenue Service issued Advance Notice 87-81, subsequently published as Internal Revenue Bulletin No. 1987-38, dated September 21, 1987. The guidance relates to the procedures by which taxpayers may change their methods of accounting for long-term contracts for purposes of section 460 of the Internal Revenue Code of 1986. It also provides an elective, simplified method for determining the percentage of completion with respect to long-term contracts under sections 460 and 56 of the Code.

The text of the guidance is set forth below.

I. Background.

Section 460 provides that, in the case of a long-term contract, amounts are to be taken into account using (i) the percentage of completion—capitalized cost method, or (ii) the percentage of completion method (as modified by section 460). Section 460 is effective for long-term contracts entered into by the taxpayer after February 28, 1986, beginning with the taxpayer's first taxable year ending after such date. However, with the exception of the interest capitalization requirements of section 460(c)(3), section 460 does not apply to any contract for the construction of real property entered into by a taxpayer if (i) the taxpayer reasonably estimates (at the time the contract is entered into) that the contract will be completed within the 2-year period beginning on the contract's commencement date; and (ii) the taxpayer's average annual gross receipts for the 3 taxable years preceding the taxable year in which the contract is entered into do not exceed $10,000,000.

Under the percentage of completion method (as modified by section 460), the taxpayer is required to determine the percentage of completion with respect to each long-term contract under the "cost-to-cost" method. For purposes of the cost-to-cost method, the percentage of completion is determined by dividing the cumulative amount of contract costs incurred through the end of the taxable year by the total expected contract costs. (Contract costs are defined under section 460(c) as all costs which directly benefit or are incurred by reason of the long-term contract activities of the taxpayer). The cumulative amount of income earned under the contract through the end of the taxable year equals the percentage of the contract completed, multiplied by the expected contract price. The amount of income recognized for the taxable year is equal to the cumulative amount of income earned with respect to the contract through the end of the taxable year, decreased by the total amount of income with respect to the contract that was recognized by the taxpayer in previous taxable years. Moreover, under the percentage of completion method (as modified by section 460), the "look-back method" as described in section 460(b)(3) shall apply to all long-term contracts of the taxpayer to which section 460 applies.

For taxpayers using the percentage of completion—capitalized cost method of accounting for long-term contracts, 40 percent of the items with respect to each contract are to be taken into account using the percentage of completion method (as modified by section 460), and 60 percent of the items with respect to each contract are to be taken into account under the taxpayer's "normal" method of accounting for long-term contracts, subject to the requirements of section 460, including the cost allocation requirements of section 460(c). The cost allocation requirements of section 460(c) require the capitalization of costs that directly benefit or are incurred by reason of, the long-term contract activities of the taxpayer. For purposes of section 460, a taxpayer's normal method of accounting for long-term contracts is the method the taxpayer was using to account for long-term contracts immediately prior to the effective date of section 460.

II. Taxpayers Previously Using Percentage of Completion.

Any taxpayer previously reporting income from long-term contracts using the percentage of completion method immediately prior to the effective date of section 460 shall use the percentage of completion method (as modified by section 460) for all items under all long-term contracts entered into by the taxpayer after February 28, 1986, beginning with the taxpayer's first taxable year ending after such date. If, for example, a taxpayer was previously determining the percentage of the contract completed by comparing, as of the end of the taxable year, the work performed on the contract with the estimated total work to be performed (the "engineering cost method"), then such taxpayer shall use the percentage of completion method (as modified by section 460) for all contracts entered into after February 28, 1986. Thus, the taxpayer will be required to use the cost-to-cost method of determining the percentage of the contract completed for 100 percent of the items under each long-term contract, in addition to using the look-back method with respect to each contract.

Similarly, if a taxpayer was previously determining the percentage of the contract completed by using the cost-to-cost method allowed under prior law (see 1.451-3(c)(2)(ii) of the Regulations), then such taxpayer shall use the cost-to-cost method under section 460, utilizing, for example, the costs required to be allocated to the contract under section 460(c), and the look-back method. (However, see section VIII, relating to the simplified cost-to-cost method.)

Taxpayers described in this section II who are required to use the percentage of completion method (as modified by section 460) shall follow the notification procedures of section VI of this notice. Any taxpayer described in this section who desires to use a method other than the percentage of completion method (as modified by section 460), shall follow the provisions of section V of this notice.

III. Taxpayers Previously Using Methods Other Than Percentage of Completion.

Any taxpayer previously reporting income from long-term contracts immediately prior to the effective date of section 460 using a method of accounting other than the percentage of completion method is required to use the percentage of completion—capitalized cost method of accounting for all long-term contracts entered into by the taxpayer after February 28, 1986, beginning with the taxpayer's first taxable year ending after such date. (However, see section IV, relating to automatic changes to the percentage of completion method.) The requirements of this section shall apply regardless of whether the taxpayer's previous method of accounting for long-term contracts (i) was a correct method of accounting under the Code; or (ii) allocated more or fewer costs to long-term contracts than required under section 460(c). Thus, any taxpayer previously using the completed contract method to account for long-term contracts prior to the effective date of section 460 shall use the percentage of completion method (as modified by section 460) with respect to 40 percent of the items under each long-term contract, and the completed contract method (the taxpayer's "normal" method) with respect to 60 percent of the items under each long-term contract, subject to the cost allocation requirements of section 460(c). Moreover, such taxpayer shall be required to capitalize, under the completed contract method, the costs described in section 460(c) regardless of whether the taxpayer properly accounted for all costs required to be capitalized under the completed contract method of prior law.

Similarly, a taxpayer previously using an accrual method to account for long-term contracts immediately prior to the effective date of section 460 shall use the percentage of completion method (as modified by section 460) for 40 percent of the items under each contract, and the particular accrual method used by the taxpayer with respect to 60 percent of the items under each long-term contract, subject to the cost allocation requirements of section 460(c).

Finally, a taxpayer who was using the cash method of accounting to account for its long-term contracts immediately prior to the effective date of section 460 shall use the percentage of completion method (as modified by section 460) with respect to 40 percent of the items under each contract and the cash method with respect to 60 percent of the items under each long-term contract. (See section 448 of the Code which requires certain taxpayers to change from the cash method of accounting as their normal method of accounting for long-term contracts with respect to taxable years beginning after December 31, 1986).

Taxpayers described in this section III who are required to use the percentage of completion—capitalized cost method of accounting for long-term contracts shall follow the notification procedures of section VI of this notice.

IV. Automatic Change to Percentage of Completion for All Taxpayers.

For purposes of section 460, any taxpayer (*e.g.,* a taxpayer using the completed contract method of accounting or an accrual method of accounting as its normal method of accounting for long-term contracts) may automatically change its method of accounting to the percentage of completion method of accounting (as modified by section 460) for all items under all long-term contracts entered into by the taxpayer after February 28, 1986, beginning with the taxpayer's first taxable year ending after such date. Any such taxpayer shall follow the notification procedures of section VI of this notice.

V. Changes in Method of Accounting Requiring Commissioner's Consent.

Any taxpayer using the percentage of completion method of accounting for long-term contracts immediately prior to the effective date of section 460 who wishes to change to any method of accounting other than the percentage of completion method (as modified by section 460) will be required to obtain the consent of the Commissioner with respect to such change in method of accounting. In addition, any change in the taxpayer's "normal" method of accounting such as change from an accrual method to the completed contract method, from the completed contract method to an accrual method, or from one accrual method to another (*e.g.,* a change from accrual-shipment to accrual-delivery) for long-term contracts will constitute a change in method of accounting that requires the consent of the Commissioner.

Similarly, any taxpayer who, immediately prior to the effective date of section 460, accounted for contracts based on the position that such contracts were long-term contracts under section 1.451-3(b) of the Regulations, shall be required to account for such contracts (and any successor contracts) under section 460 unless such taxpayer obtains the consent of the Commissioner to change its method of accounting. The term successor contracts, as used in the preceding sentence, shall mean all contracts which, under the criteria and methods used by the taxpayer prior to the effective date of section 460 in determining whether a contract was a long-term contract under section 1.451-3(b), would be classified by such taxpayer as a long-term contract under section 1.451-3(b), regardless of whether such criteria and methods are correct.

Any taxpayer described in this section V who desires to change its method of accounting shall submit an application for change in accounting method under the administrative procedures applicable to taxpayers at the time of change, including the applicable procedures regarding the time and place of filing the application for change in method. However, with respect to any taxpayer described in this section who desires to change its method of accounting with respect to long-term contracts for any taxable year to which section 460 applies (including taxable years for which the taxpayer has previously filed a Federal income tax return), such taxpayer shall not be treated as filing the application for change in accounting method late if such application is filed with the National Office of the Internal Revenue Service on or before 180 days after the date that this notice is published in the Internal Revenue Bulletin. The taxpayer shall type or legibly print at the top of page 1 of the application for change in accounting method (Form 3115) the following statement: "Filed under Notice ___." In the case of a taxpayer receiving permission to change its methods of accounting for its first taxable year ending after February 28, 1986 under this section V, such change in method shall be effectuated by using a "cut-off" method with respect to contracts entered into after February 28, 1986, *i.e.,* the taxpayer shall not compute a section 481(a) adjustment with respect to its use of the new method of accounting. Taxpayers receiving permission to change their methods of accounting may be required, under appropriate circumstances, to file amended Federal income tax returns reflecting the new method of accounting for the year of change.

VI. Notification Procedures for Certain Methods of Accounting.

Any taxpayer described in section II, III, IV, or VIII of this notice shall complete and file a statement notifying the Service of its use of the various methods of accounting under this notice with the taxpayer's Federal income tax return (including amended returns) for the first taxable year ending after February 28, 1986, for which the taxpayer is required to account under section 460 for long-term contracts. The taxpayer shall type or legibly print the following language at the top of the statement required to be filed: Notification Procedures under Section

VI of Notice __ . Any amended return filed for the purpose, in whole or in part, of changing a taxpayer's method of accounting as described in sections IV or VIII of this notice must be filed on or before 180 days after the date that this notice is published in the Internal Revenue Bulletin.

Notwithstanding the requirements of the preceding paragraph, with respect to any taxpayer who has (i) filed a Federal income tax return for the first taxable year ending after February 28, 1986 for which the taxpayer is required to account under section 460 for long-term contracts, (ii) failed to file the statement described in the preceding paragraph with such return, and (iii) otherwise properly used the method of accounting as required or allowed under sections II, III, IV, or VIII of this notice, such taxpayer may file a statement indicating the use of its method of accounting under the following procedures. Such statement shall be attached to the taxpayer's first Federal income tax return filed subsequent to 90 days after the publication of this notice in the Internal Revenue Bulletin, for a taxable year subsequent to the first taxable year ending after February 28, 1986 for which the taxpayer is required to account under section 460 for long-term contracts. (A taxpayer, at its option, may attach such a statement with a return filed before the date described in the preceding sentence.) The taxpayer shall type or legibly print the following language at the top of the statement required to be filed: Notification Procedures under Section VI of Notice __ . Any use of a method of accounting described in this section VI shall be effectuated by using a "cut-off" method with respect to contracts entered into after February 28, 1986, *i.e.,* the taxpayer shall not compute a section 481(a) adjustment with respect to its use of the new method of accounting.

VII. General Requirement to Use Same Method of Accounting for All Long-Term Contracts.

Under section 1.451-3(a)(1) of the Regulations, taxpayers are generally required to use the same long-term contract method of accounting for all long-term contracts within the same trade or business. This general requirement to use the same long-term contract method for all long-term contracts shall be continued under section 460 of the Code, subject to the effective date provisions of section 460 which may require the use of different methods of accounting for long-term contracts depending on whether such contracts were entered into after February 28, 1986.

Under the current Regulations, however, an exception from this rule is provided for taxpayers who have certain long-term contracts of "substantial duration" and other long-term contracts of less than substantial duration. See section 1.451-3(a)(1) of the Regulations. Under the Regulations, taxpayers may report the income from the long-term contracts of substantial duration under the same long-term contract method, while reporting the income from the long-term contracts of less than substantial duration using another proper method of accounting (e.g., an inventory method). Under section 460, taxpayers may continue this practice and utilize two different methods of accounting as their "normal" methods of accounting for sixty percent of the items under each long-term contract, subject to the consistency provisions of the present Regulations and subject to section 460, including the cost allocation requirements of section 460(c).

Any taxpayer who used two different methods of accounting for long-term contracts immediately prior to the effective date of section 460 is required to obtain the consent of the Commissioner if the taxpayer desires to change to the use of only one method as its "normal" method of accounting for long-term contracts. Similarly, any taxpayer who wishes to change its method of accounting to the use of two methods as its "normal" method of accounting for long-term contracts is required to obtain the consent of the Commissioner to any such change. Any taxpayer described in this paragraph who desires to change its method of accounting may, at the taxpayer's option, submit an application for a change in method of accounting under the procedures and filing deadlines provided in section V of this notice.

VIII. Simplified Method for Determining Degree of Contract Completion.

For purposes of section 460, an elective, simplified method (the "simplified cost-to-cost method") is provided herein for determining the percentage of completion under the cost-to-cost method for taxpayers using the percentage of completion method (as modified by section 460) for all items under all long-term contracts. In addition to taxpayers using the percentage of completion method, taxpayers who are properly using the cash method of accounting as their normal method of accounting for long-term contracts may use the simplified cost-to-cost method for 40 percent of the items under each long-term contract. Any taxpayer properly using the cash method as its normal method of accounting for long-term contracts that uses the simplified cost-to-cost method as described herein, shall automatically change from the simplified cost-to-cost method to the cost-to-cost method under section 460 for the first taxable year that such taxpayer is required to change from the cash method of accounting under any section of the Code (including section 448). Such change shall take place under the transitional provisions of the particular section under which the taxpayer is required to change from the cash method of accounting.

Under the simplified cost-to-cost method, the following costs shall be used in determining the percentage of completion (i.e., contract costs incurred to date divided by total expected contract costs) attributable to a particular long-term contract:

(i) direct material costs and direct labor costs, as described in section 1.451-3(d)(6)(i) of the Regulations; and

(ii) depreciation, amortization and cost recovery allowances on equipment and facilities (to the extent allowable as deductions under Chapter 1 of the Code) directly used to construct or produce the subject matter of the long-term contract.

Thus, a taxpayer using the simplified cost-to-cost method shall utilize the costs described in clauses (i) and (ii) above in determining both the costs allocated to the contract and incurred before the close of the taxable year, and the estimated total contract costs. Moreover, such costs shall be used by any such taxpayer under the look-back method, as described in section 460(b)(3).

Any taxpayer described in this section VIII who desires to change its method of accounting to the simplified cost-to-cost method for its first taxable year ending after February 28, 1986, shall follow the notification procedures of section VI of this notice. If the taxpayer elects to change its method of accounting to the simplified method for a year subsequent to the taxable year described in the preceding sentence, then such taxpayer shall attach a statement describing the election to use the simplified cost-to-cost method to the taxpayer's Federal income tax return for the taxable year in issue. Any such election to use the simplified cost-to-cost method shall apply only to contracts entered into on or after the first day of the year of election. Such an election shall be treated as a method of accounting, and may not be revoked without obtaining the consent of the Commissioner.

IX. Alternative Minimum Tax.

Section 56(a)(3) of the Code provides that the percentage of completion method of accounting (as modified by section 460) shall be used in determining the alternative minimum taxable income ("AMTI") of a taxpayer for all long-term contracts entered into on or after March 1, 1986, with respect to taxable years beginning after December 31, 1986. The requirement to use the percentage of completion method of accounting under section 56(a)(3) applies to all long-term contracts of the taxpayer, including certain construction contracts with a duration of less than 2 years to which the provisions of section 460 do not otherwise apply.

Thus, in computing AMTI, taxpayers shall use the percentage of completion method (as modified by section 460) to account for all items under all applicable long-term contracts of the taxpayer. In addition, the cost-to-cost method under section 460 shall be used in determining the degree of completion, and the look-back method shall apply to the taxpayer's long-term contracts.

In determining the percentage of completion under the cost-to-cost method for purposes of determining AMTI, taxpayers may elect to determine their percentage of completion (i.e., cumulative contract costs incurred to date divided by total expected contract costs), using the methods of accounting and cost applied in computing regular tax ("regular methods" and "regular costs"). Thus, for example, with respect to equipment and facilities used in the performance of a particular long-term contract, a taxpayer making this election would determine the degree of completion of the contract for purposes of computing AMTI by taking into account depreciation deductions used in determining the regular tax ("regular depreciation") for both (i) the cumulative contract costs incurred through the end of the taxable year, and (ii) the total expected contract costs. In contrast, a taxpayer not electing to use this method would, in determining the degree of completion of a long-term contract for purposes of computing AMTI, calculate both cumulative contract costs incurred through the end of the taxable year, and total expected contract costs, using the depreciation methods described in section 56(a)(1) ("AMT depreciation"), including the alternative depreciation system of section 168(g).

Moreover, with respect to taxpayers having certain construction contracts with a duration of less than 2 years to which the provisions of section 460 do not otherwise apply, such taxpayers may elect to use the costs required to be capitalized under present law as it applies to such contracts in making the cost-to-cost calculations required under section 56(a)(3). In addition, taxpayers described in the preceding sentence who are properly using the cash method of accounting for long-term contracts may elect the use of the simplified cost-to-cost method as described in section VIII of this notice for purposes of section 56(a)(3).

Although taxpayers may elect to use regular methods and regular costs for purposes of calculating the degree of completion under section 56 for a long-term contract, the determination of AMTI shall be made under the provisions of section 55, including, for example, the adjustments provided in sections 56 and 58. Thus, for example, in determining AMTI with respect to a long-term contract, taxpayers shall determine their depreciation deductions using AMT depreciation under section 56(a)(1), although the degree of completion under the cost-to-cost method may have been determined using regular depreciation. The use of regular depreciation (and any other regular cost or method) for purposes of the alternative minimum tax is confined solely to the determination of the degree of completion of a long-term contract using the cost-to-cost method as described in section 460.

Taxpayers electing to use regular methods and regular costs in determining the degree of completion for long-term contracts under section 56 shall use whatever methods were used to determine the percentage of completion under section 460 for regular tax purposes. Thus, for example, an electing taxpayer shall use the simplified cost-to-cost method of determining its percentage of completion under section 56, if such taxpayer has used this method under section 460 in determining its regular tax. An electing taxpayer not using the simplified cost-to-cost method under section 460 shall use the costs described in section 460(c) in determining the degree of completion for long-term contracts under section 56.

Any taxpayer who elects to use regular methods and regular costs in determining the degree of completion for long-term contracts under section 56, shall note such election on the taxpayer's (i) is subject to the alternative minimum tax as amended by the Act, and (ii) computes income from a long-term contract under section 56 using the percentage of completion method. Such election shall be treated as a method of accounting, and shall not be revoked without obtaining the consent of the Commissioner.

Any taxpayer desiring to change to this method of accounting for a subsequent year shall submit an application for change in accounting method under the administrative procedures applicable to taxpayers at the time of change, including the applicable procedures regarding the time and place of filing the application for change in method.

COMPLETED CONTRACT METHOD—FURTHER LIMITATION LEGISLATED

The budget reconciliation act, P.L. 100-203, enacted December 22, 1987, provides a further attack on the completed contract method (CCM) of income recognition under long-term contracts. Under previous legislation, taxpayers using CCM were required to take into account 40% of the items under the contract using the percentage of completion method (PCM) and the remaining 60% using their normal method of accounting. Under P.L. 100-203, the percentage of long-term contracts that must be taken into account using PCM is increased to 70% and the portion for which CCM could be used is decreased to 30%.

The new provision is applicable to covered contracts entered into after October 13, 1987.

The House bill required all income under long-term contracts to be reported using PCM. The Senate bill did not address this subject, and the 70-30% represented the compromise in conference. The full text of the conference report on this subject is set forth below:

Completed contract method

Present law

Taxpayers engaged in the production of property under a long-term contract must compute income from the contract under the percentage of completion method or the percentage of completion-capitalized cost method. An exception is provided for certain small businesses with respect to construction contracts to be completed within two years.

Under the percentage of completion method, the taxpayer must include in gross income for the taxable year an amount based on the product of (1) the gross contract price and (2) the percentage of the contract completed during the taxable year. The percentage of a contract completed during the taxable year is determined by comparing costs incurred with respect to the contract during the year with the estimated total contract costs.

Under the percentage of completion-capitalized cost method, the taxpayer must take into account 40 percent of the items with respect to the contract under the percentage of completion method. The remaining 60 percent of the items under the contract must be taken into account under the taxpayer's normal method of accounting. For example, if the taxpayer's normal method of accounting is the completed contract method, income from a contract is included and contract costs are deducted upon final completion of the contract. All costs that directly benefit or are incurred by reason of a taxpayer's long-term contract activities must be allocated to its long-term contracts in a manner similar to that provided in Treasury regulations under section 451 for extended period long-term contracts.

House bill

Under the House bill, income from a long-term contract must be reported under the percentage of completion method. A long-term contract is defined in the same manner as under present law. The bill preserves the present-law exceptions for certain construction contracts.

The provision is effective for contracts entered into after October 13, 1987. An exception is provided for certain "qualified ship contracts." A "qualified ship contract" is a contract for the construction in the United States of not more than 5 ships that meet certain other requirements. Such ships must not be constructed (directly or indirectly) for the Federal Government and the taxpayer must reasonably expect to complete such contract within 5 years of the contract commencement date.

Senate amendment

No provision.

Conference agreement

The conference agreement changes the percentage of completion-capitalized cost method of computing income from long-term contracts. Seventy percent (versus 40 percent under present law) of items with respect to such a contract must be taken into account under the percentage of completion method. The remaining 30 percent (versus 60 percent under present law) are taken into account under the taxpayer's normal method of accounting. The look-back method of section 460(b)(3) is applied to the 70 percent taken into account under the percentage of completion method.

For this purpose, a taxpayer's normal method of accounting generally is considered to be the method of accounting it used for long-term contracts prior to February 28, 1986 (the effective date of the percentage of completion-capitalized cost method). Thus, any change in the taxpayer's normal method of accounting requires the consent of the Commissioner of Internal Revenue. It is anticipated that the criteria and methods used by the taxpayer, including those criteria and methods used to determine if an item is "unique," prior to February 28, 1986, in determining if a particular contract was a long-term contract will continue to be used by the taxpayer.

The provision of the conference agreement is effective for contracts entered into after October 13, 1987. The exception for certain "qualified ship contracts" in the House bill is included in the conference agreement.

IMPLICATIONS OF CONTRACT REPRICING

Government contracts may be repriced prospectively, retroactively, or both. Circumstances leading to repricing include the application of price redetermination or incentive clauses (Chapter III), equitable price adjustments as a result of contract changes (Chapter VII), changes involving application of the CAS clause (Chapter VIII), price reduction for defective cost or pricing data under P.L. 87-653 (Chapter XXII), and extraordinary contractual actions to facilitate the national defense under P.L. 85-804 (Chapter XXIV).

Prospective changes present no income tax problems because the increased or reduced price of future shipments will automatically be reflected in the periods of shipments. A retroactive price increase should be recognized as income in the year received. Retroactive price decreases may be treated in one of the following two ways: (1) filing an amended return and claiming a tax refund or adjustment for the years affected, or (2) if taxes were paid in the years affected by the decreases, the portion of taxes related to the reduction in income caused by these decreases could be taken as credits from the amounts due the procuring agency. The Internal Revenue Service addresses this point in Revenue Ruling 54-83, in connection with the application of Sections 3806 and 1481 of the 1939 and 1954 Codes to price redetermination refunds and upward price adjustments:

> Sections 3806 and 1481 of the 1939 and 1954 Internal Revenue Codes and Rev. Rul. 53, C.B. 1953-1, 479, do not apply to upward adjustments of income under price redetermination clauses embodied in Government contracts.

> Excessive profits on Government contracts, if made the subject of a credit memorandum or a definite commitment to reduce the contract price, preferably in writing, prior to the filing of the return, may be eliminated from income to be reported on the return. The adjustment for the excessive profits is, however, subject to the application of the credit provided for by Section 3806(b) of the Code (1954 Code Sec. 1481) as to any further downward price revision and to the restoration to income of the taxable year in which the amount of the commitment or credit was excluded, of any amount not included in the price redetermination as finally consummated.

Further explanation of this ruling is cited as follows:

> Ordinarily, to a taxpayer on the accrual basis, such upward adjustment to income in includible in gross income for the taxable year in which the contract is modified to provide for increased prices. As to downward adjustments only, Sections 3806 and 1481 of the 1939 and 1954 Codes require that such adjustments which represent excessive profits as defined in such section be related back to the year or years in which the original contract prices were included in gross income, unless permission is granted to adopt a different method of accounting under the provisions of Section 3806(a) (4) of the Code.

> The rules of accounting enforced upon a taxpayer by any regulatory body are not binding on the Internal Revenue Service, except as otherwise specifically provided for by statute, for the determination of tax liability under the Internal Revenue Code.

See *Old Colony Railroad Company v. Commissioner,* 284 U.S. 552, Ct. D. 456, C.B. XI-1, 274 (1932).

> With respect to the above, to the extent applicable to goods billed during the taxable year for which the income tax return has not yet been

filed, a credit memorandum issued by the taxpayer or a definite commitment to reduce the contract price made to the contracting officer, preferably in writing, prior to the filing of the return, may be considered as rendering the amount of such credit memorandum or commitment 'definitely determinable' so that the amount thereof which would otherwise be included in income may be eliminated therefrom in filing the return. Also, where excessive profits have been agreed upon with a local representative of a contracting agency and only the final approval thereof and repayment are necessary to give full effect to the redetermination, the amount agreed upon, to the extent applicable to goods billed during the taxable year, may be eliminated from income to be reported on the income tax return. However, where the taxpayer excludes the amount of such credit memorandum or commitment, a statement to that effect, including the amount and the contract involved, should be made on the return. When the price redetermination is finally consummated, if the amount thereof exceeds the amount of the credit memorandum or commitment which was excluded from income in filing the return, the credit provided for in Section 3806(b) is applicable but shall be applied only to such excess. If the amount of the price redetermination as finally consummated is less than the amount of the credit memorandum or commitment, the difference shall be restored to income for the year for which the amount of the credit memorandum or commitment was excluded.

Reference is also made to the decision by the U.S. Court of Appeals (6th Circuit, No. 20269), in *Gar Wood Industries, Inc. v. U.S.,* January 28, 1971, upholding the principle that income should not be recognized for federal income tax purposes until the taxpayer had a fixed right to the funds. In view of the importance of this decision, a summary is quoted below:

Amounts withheld from contract payments due an accrual basis contractor, pending final price redetermination, should have been excluded from his gross income during years prior to the final adjudication of the contract price because the taxpayer-contractor had no fixed right to the funds prior to the time of final price redetermination. Contracts for manufacturing crane shovels and related equipment executed in 1951 and 1952 contained standard Price Redetermination clauses which authorized contract price redetermination after partial performance, provided for settlement of new price disputes, and stated that until new prices went into effect upon redetermination, the government would pay for all deliveries at the rate of prices in force at the effective date of the contract revision subject to later revision. The government did not pay the full contract price, however, but, following a policy contained in an internal memorandum and not disclosed in the contract, it withheld 10% of the contract price when it appeared probable that the contract price would be renegotiated downward. Unilateral withholding by the government was a breach of contract and negated any right the contractor had to the amounts withheld until 1956 when his rights to the fund were established by final price redetermination. Since the test of includability in gross income is the accrual taxpayer's fixed right to funds, the amounts withheld were not properly includable until 1956.

ADVANCE PAYMENTS

Advance payments may be made by the government as provided in FAR Subpart 32.4 (see Chapter VI of this book) for the contractor's use in paying for material, labor, overhead, and other costs of performing the specified contract. The contract clause generally provides for liquidation of advance payments against payments due from the government for deliveries made. The operation of the Advance Payment clause confirms the recognition of a pro rata portion of the advance payment as income, as deliveries are made or services performed.

PROGRESS PAYMENTS

Provisions for progress payments are routinely included in government contracts that involve a long lead time or preparatory period between the beginning of work and the first production delivery (see FAR Part 32 and Chapter VI of this book). Progress payment clauses are also included in other types of contracts that require contractors to expend considerable funds before and between billable actions. The progress payment clauses provide formulas and procedures by which progress payments are liquidated against shipments made. It would thus appear logical for income to be recognized as earned when deliveries are made.

The progress payment clause provides that title to all inventories, tooling, equipment, etc., acquired for the contract and for which progress payments have been obtained, is acquired by the government. This provision has raised questions as to whether this transfer of title constitutes a sale both for financial statement and income tax purposes. In the author's judgment, the acquisition of title is effected in order to protect the government's interests and to permit it to take physical possession of the inventories in the event the contractor fails to perform satisfactorily or is unable to complete the contract for financial or other reasons. These precautionary measures are not intended to, and hence should not, be considered as a sale.

Title v. Security Interest in Progess Payments

The government's long-time assumption that it acquired title to the materials on which it made progress payments to contractors was shaken by the U.S. Court of Claims in *Marine Midland Bank v. The United States,* Ct.Cl. No. 308-81C, August 25, 1982 (30 CCF 70,265), which concluded that the progress payments gave the government a lien on the materials rather than title to them. This lien was ruled paramount to the liens of general creditors based "on the modern practice of giving priority to purchase money interests, as we consider purchase money to be closely analogous to the government's progress payments . . . ."

The government argued "that the plain meaning of its title vesting clause is that the government takes title in the traditional sense, that the government simply owns inventory subject to the operation of the clause." Midland argued that the clause and related regulations establish that "the government means only to take a security interest to secure its progress payments, and title in the traditional sense is not contemplated at all."

The court found Midland's position to be the correct one, with the progress payments representing "loans from the government ... to be repaid by withholding an appropriate amount of the contract price ultimately owing on full performance." The government's interest in the inventory as security in the interim, in the opinion of the court, "was far less than full ownership."

The controversy over this matter continues and surfaced in connection with the balance sheet presentation of progress payments in the DFAIR study, as described in Chapter XXV of this text.

COST-PLUS-A-FIXED-FEE CONTRACTS

As described in Chapter III of this book, CPFF contracts are essentially level-of-effort procurement. Assuming no changes are made during the period of performance, the contemplated negotiated dollar fee may be earned. This theoretical situation is not common inasmuch as (1) the estimated fee will be reduced to the extent that actual costs exceed the original estimates and (2) losses can be and have been incurred under CPFF contracts where actual costs incurred exceed the total of estimated costs plus the initially negotiated fixed fee and the contractor has failed to comply with the provision of the Limitation of Cost clause (see Chapter XX of this book).

CPFF contracts generally provide for retention of a portion of the fee until certain conditions are met and information furnished after the contract is completed. As noted earlier in this chapter, despite the IRS challenges to the contrary, arguments can be made that the retentions should not be included as income, particularly where it can be established that the contractor did not have a fixed right to the amounts retained, as decided in *Gar Wood Industries, Inc.*, cited previously in this chapter.

IRS generally will not permit any deferral of income for possible reductions due to disallowances of costs in audits performed by procuring agencies after contract completion. Where the estimated fee was reported as income in one fiscal period and the actual amount of income is decreased by audit disallowances of cost in the next period, the contractor should follow the procedures of Section 1481 of the 1954 Internal Revenue Code cited earlier.

INCENTIVE CONTRACTS

Under cost-plus-incentive-fee contracts (CPIF) and fixed-price-incentive contracts (FPIC), income recognition in each year should generally be based on a comparison of the target prices and costs incurred. When the prices are increased or decreased pursuant to the incentive provisions of the contract and are based on agreements reached between the two parties, the income should be adjusted in the year when the final prices are established or reasonably ascertainable.

TERMINATION OF GOVERNMENT CONTRACTS

Substantial experience with contract termination for the government's convenience was acquired during and immediately following World War II. The policies and procedures established as a result of this experience provide that a contractor must recognize income based on the contract receipts and allocable expenses in the period the contract was terminated. Inasmuch as the exact amount of settlement expenses the contractor will ultimately recover may not be known for some time thereafter, the contractor may include an estimate for these expenses for income tax purposes. Where actual recoveries differ substantially from the estimate, the income tax returns for the year in which the contract was terminated should be amended. Where the difference is not substantial, it would appear reasonable to increase or reduce the income for the year in which settlement is made.

The treatment of a default termination converted to a termination for the convenience of the government as the result of an appeal and a favorable decision by a board of contract appeals or a federal court will depend on the treatment initially accorded at the time the government terminated the contract for default. Where a contractor recorded the costs of the work in process on the defaulted contract as a loss and subsequently recovers those costs, plus settlement expenses, as a result of a judicial ruling that the termination should be treated as one for the convenience of the government, the recovery of those costs and expenses should be recognized as income in the year of the decision.

EXTRAORDINARY CONTRACTUAL ACTIONS UNDER PUBLIC LAW 85-804

As described in Chapter XXIV of this book, the government may amend contracts without consideration or take other actions to facilitate the national defense. Where a contractor submits a request for relief under this law and the relevant contract adjustment board hands down a favorable ruling, the amount of relief granted should be recognized as income in the year the decision is made.

Indicators of Fraud in Department of Defense Procurement (Excerpted from a Handbook by the DOD Inspector General, June 1987)

Introduction.

a. Fraud is characterized by acts of guile, deceit, trickery, concealment or breach of confidence which are used to gain some unfair or dishonest advantage. The objective may be to obtain money, property or services; to avoid the payment or loss of money, property or services; or to secure business or personal advantage. Fraud may occur at any stage of the Government contracting process. As discussed in Chapters 1 and 11, fraud may have criminal, civil, contractual, and administrative ramifications.

b. This chapter discusses factors which may indicate the presence of, or enhanced potential for, fraud at various stages in the procurement process. The indicators included in this chapter are not intended, each taken by themselves, to establish the existence of fraud. Rather, the presence of any of the indicators, when taken in the context of the particular procurement action being conducted, should cause DoD employees to be alert to the possibility of impropriety and take appropriate actions to ensure the integrity of the process. Three later chapters will discuss in more detail the concepts of (1) collusive bidding and price fixing; (2) defective pricing; and (3) bribery, gratuities and conflicts of interest. These activities are present in some of the indicators presented in this chapter and should be considered in light of the later explanations.

c. The motives and methods for fraud in the contract award process are varied. There are many instances where fraud is perpetrated to obtain a contract in order to create the opportunity to later engage in such activities as theft or embezzlement, product substitution, cost mischarging, fast pay or progress payment fraud. In some instances the fraud is perpetrated to obtain a contract at a higher price or with better terms than would have occurred in an award untainted by fraud. Still others commit fraud merely to obtain Government contracts because they need the business to keep their companies in operation when private sector activity is low.

d. Another factor to be considered is that frauds are sometimes committed by or with the help of DoD employees. The possibility should not be overlooked that a DoD employee has solicited or accepted bribes or gratuities or has a financial interest in a contractor. There have even been instances of DoD employees creating or participating in the ownership of outside businesses for the purpose of committing fraud through their ability to impact on or control the award process.

Chapter 1. Crimes Involved in Contract Fraud

1-1. Introduction.

When the Government and its programs have been defrauded or corrupted, Federal investigators and prosecutors will usually find that one or more Federal statutes have been violated. It is their job to develop conclusive evidence that each of the elements of a specific crime exists. This chapter discusses some of the most frequently violated statutes. The criminal penalties for violation of these statutes can result in up to 10 years imprisonment and a $1 million fine.

1-2. False Statements, 18 U.S.C. 1001.

a. This statute makes it illegal to engage in any of three types of activity in any matter within the jurisdiction of any department or agency of the United States.

(1) Falsifying, concealing, or covering up a material fact by any trick, scheme, or device;

(2) Making false, fictitious, or fraudulent statements or representations; or

(3) Making or using any false document or writing.

Any certification in a DoD contract which contains false, fictitious, or fraudulent information may be a violation of this statute.

b. The following is a typical scheme which resulted in convictions for violations of this statute. A contractor was required to provide test certifications to DoD for parts it supplied for use in the breach mechanism of a 105mm cannon. The test certifications provided by the contractor contained false representations because the tests had not been performed. The contractor was convicted of making false statements in violation of 18 U.S.C. 1001 for that conduct. It is significant to note that the contractor was prohibited from introducing evidence that the parts would have passed the tests if they were performed. The only relevant issue was whether the tests had been performed at the time the contractor made its certification. The crime is complete upon the submission of the statement to the Government. It is not necessary to prove that the Government relied on or was harmed by the false statement.

1-3. False Claims, 18 U.S.C. 287.

a. This statute makes it illegal to present or make any false, fictitious, or fraudulent claim against any agency or department of the United States. The crime is also complete when the claim is presented. Payment of the claim is not an element of the offense and need not be proven to obtain a conviction. (In a related civil statute, 31 U.S.C. 3729, the United States can recover treble damages, plus the cost of the civil action, plus a forfeiture of $5,000 to $10,000 per false claim for any false claims against the DoD.—See Chapter 11.)

b. The following scheme is typical of false claims violations which result in convictions. A contractor altered subcontractor invoices to show inflated prices on purchases made from a subcontractor. The inflated prices were then charged to the Government resulting in a monetary loss of over $1 million. The company paid a total of $3 million in fines, penalties, and restitution. The executive vice president was sentenced to five consecutive two year prison terms.

c. Any claim for a cost which has been declared unallowable by statute or regulation is a criminal and civil violation of the False Claims Act under the Defense Procurement Improvement Act of 1985 (10 U.S.C. 2324(i)) (See Chapter 11).

d. In addition, 18 U.S.C. 286 makes it a crime for two or more persons to agree or conspire to defraud the United States by obtaining or aiding in obtaining payment or allowance of any false, fictitious or fraudulent claim.

1-4. Mail Fraud, 18 U.S.C. 1341, and Wire Fraud, 18 U.S.C. 1343.

a. These statutes make it illegal to engage in any scheme to defraud in which the mails or wire communications are utilized. Utilization of the mails or wire communications includes sending or receiving any matter through the use of these mediums. As an example, they cover receiving payment from the Government which has been sent through the mail or by wire when such occurs in connection with a scheme to defraud.

b. A Virginia based contractor defrauded the Navy in performing a contract awarded and administered in California. The scheme to defraud involved the mailing of false claims (based on false and inflated costs for direct labor and employee benefits) to the Navy. The scheme also involved cost mischarging in an attempt to recover cost overruns on a fixed price contract by concealing the costs in later claims. The corporation and its president were convicted of violating the false claims, false statements, and mail fraud statutes. The president was sentenced to five years in prison on two charges and received a five year suspended sentence and five years probation on a third charge. In addition, the president was ordered to perform 2,500 hours of community service. The corporation was fined $22,000 and ordered to make restitution in the amount of $185,000.

1-5. Bribery, Gratuities, and Conflicts of Interest, Generally, 18 U.S.C. 201-208.

a. These statutes prohibit a broad range of activities which can be described generally as corruption. Such activities include giving or receiving a bribe or gratuity, as well as engaging in a conflict of interest. (See Chapter 9) (New authority delegated by the President in November 1983, under 18 U.S.C. 218, permits agencies to rescind any contract tainted by bribery, graft, or conflict of interest after conviction for such activity.—See Chapter 11.)

(1) Bribery includes giving a Government employee something of value for the purpose of influencing the performance of an official duty.

(2) Gratuities include giving a Government employee something of value because of his official position. There is no requirement for the Government to prove that the gratuity was given for the purpose of influencing any official act.

(3) Conflicts of interest include those situations where a Government employee engages in activities which create a conflict between his personal interests and his duty to protect and serve the interests of the Government.

b. The following schemes are typical of these violations:

(1) *Bribery*—A base laundry, dry cleaning and clothing repair contractor offered a quality assurance inspector (QAI) a bribe in return for approval of monthly service costs to the Air Force. The QAI notified the Air Force Office of Special Investigations (AFOSI) and cooperated in an undercover investigation during which the contractor provided money, food, hotel accommodations, liquor, and other gifts to the QAI. The contractor was found guilty on two counts of bribery and two counts of false claims. He was sentenced to three years in jail, given three years probation, and fined $3,000.

(2) *Gratuities*—A GS-12 contracting officer's technical representative (COTR) admitted soliciting and receiving gratuities from a contractor for which he had responsibility. The gratuities consisted of video equipment, meals, and use of an automobile and a beach condominium over the course of one year. There was no evidence that the COTR did anything in return for these gratuities. The COTR was convicted of receiving gratuities in violation of 18 U.S.C. 201(g), and was sentenced to one year in jail which was suspended and two years probation. He resigned from Federal service while removal action was pending.

(3) *Conflicts of Interest*—A military member used the authority of his position to direct the award of a contract to a subcontracting firm. The subcontractor, in turn, was to further subcontract to a firm which was wholly owned by the military member. The estimated loss to the Government was $43,500. The member pled guilty to two counts of bribery and one count of acts affecting personal financial interests (conflict of interest). He was sentenced to two years in prison on each of the three counts. He was confined for six months and received supervised probation for two years. He was also fined $2,000 for each count.

1-6. Trade Secrets Act, 18 U.S.C. 1905.

a. This statute prohibits unauthorized release of any information relating to trade secrets or confidential business data by a Federal employee who receives such information in the course of his employment. Such information includes advance procurement information, prices, technical proposals, proprietary information, income information, etc. (A conviction for violating this statute requires mandatory removal from employment.)

b. Criminal prosecutions under the statute are not brought frequently because it is only a misdemeanor; instead, prosecutors frequently choose to prosecute under the theft statute (see Section 1-7).

1-7. Theft, Embezzlement, or Destruction of Public Money, Property, or Records, 18 U.S.C. 641.

a. This statute prohibits intentional and unauthorized taking, destruction, or use of Government property or records. It also prohibits receiving or concealing such property or records.

b. The following is a typical case involving the theft of Government records pertaining to an upcoming solicitation. A quality assurance representative (QAR) solicited a bribe from a major electronics contractor and promised to return inside information on an upcoming bid solicitation. The QAR delivered the bid information in exchange for a $2,500 bribe. The QAR suggested a second transaction in exchange for payment of $30,000. A second meeting was scheduled and the QAR was arrested after asking for the payment again. The QAR was indicted on two counts of theft of Government property and two counts of bribery. The QAR pled guilty on the bribery counts in exchange for full cooperation with the prosecutor. The cooperation resulted in the indictment of a co-conspirator who was charged with theft of Government property and conspiracy. The QAR received a five year sentence, and the second defendant is awaiting trial.

1-8. Anti-kickback Act, 41 U.S.C. 54.

a. This Act makes it a crime for any person to provide, attempt to provide or offer any fee, commission, compensation, gift or gratuity to a prime contractor or any higher tier subcontractor, or an employee of one of these, for the purpose of improperly obtaining favorable treatment under a Government Contract.—(See Chapter 10).

b. A buyer for a major DoD contractor entered into an agreement with certain machine shops which provided that they would pay him an amount equal to five percent of the value on all contracts which he awarded to them. The Government identified $14,000 in such kickbacks to him. He was convicted on one count each of tax fraud, mail fraud, and violations of the Anti-kickback Act, and was sentenced to six months in jail and a $14,000 fine.

1-9. Sherman Antitrust Act, 15 U.S.C. 1.

a. This Act prohibits competitors from entering into any agreement to restrain trade in interstate commerce, including price fixing, bid rigging, and bid rotation schemes. (See Chapter 4)

b. The following is typical of the type of antitrust violations that can occur in connection with DoD contracts. A contractor entered into an agreement with a number of its competitors to divide the available Army Corps of Engineers dredging contracts between them. The scheme was carried out through meetings during which the competitors decided who among them would submit the low bid on any given solicitation. The president of the company was convicted for violating the Sherman Antitrust Act in connection with his activities in this regard, and was sentenced to three years in prison. The company was fined $325,000 and ordered to pay civil damages of $250,000.

1-10. Conspiracy, 18 U.S.C. 371.

a. This statute prohibits any agreement between two or more persons to defraud the United States or to violate any Federal law or regulation when at least one act is taken in furtherance of the agreement.

b. The president and vice president of a subcontractor conspired to provide defective aluminum castings for use by prime contractors in manufacturing the Navy Phoenix missile, the Air force mobile radio tower, and the cockpit display of the F-16. The officials agreed to and did make concerted efforts that the prime contractors and the Government were deceived regarding the defective nature of the parts. This involved instructing company employees who conducted random tests of the parts to test additional parts, whenever one or more of the originally selected parts failed, until the required number of parts passed the tests. In addition, the officials instructed shipping employees to conceal obviously defective parts by stacking conforming parts on top of them. The officials pled guilty to one count of conspiracy each after being charged with three counts of conspiracy and four counts of false claims. They were sentenced to imprisonment and required to pay substantial fines.

Chapter 2. Fraud in Government Contracts

2-1. Fraud in the identification of the Government's need for goods or services.

a. Normally, procurement actions are initiated after a formal or informal determination of general requirements. The requirements consist of a brief description of the types and amounts of goods and services needed together with a justification for the need. Fraud occurring during this stage of the procurement process may result in decisions to buy goods and services in excess of those actually needed or possibly not needed at all. As an example, need determinations for items that have scheduled disposal and reprocurement or reorder levels can be manipulated by including false information. In recent cases, this type of manipulation has resulted in excessive purchases of items such as drugs or auto parts. Further examination of the cases also disclosed indications of other criminal activity such as theft or diversion of the items.

b. With respect to fraud in defining requirements and stock levels, fraud indicators include:

(1) Requiring excessively high stock levels and inventory requirements to justify continued purchasing activity from certain contractors.

(2) Declaring items which are serviceable as excess or selling them as surplus while continuing to purchase similar items. (One documented scheme involved repurchasing the same items being sold as surplus on a recurring basis.)

(3) Purchasing items, services or research projects in response to aggressive marketing efforts (and possible favors, bribes or gratuities) by contractors rather than in response to valid requirements.

(4) Defining needs improperly in ways that can be met only by certain contractors.

(5) Failing to develop "second sources" for items, spare parts, and services being continually purchased from a single source.

c. In addition to the fraud indicators listed above certain types of activity create a greater vulnerability to fraud and may enhance the potential for fraud to occur.

(1) Such a situation can occur when a needs assessment is not adequately or accurately developed or when an agency continually changes its mind about what it wants. This provides an opportunity for the unscrupulous to try and recoup losses for which they could not otherwise be compensated by falsely characterizing them as increased costs due to Government mandated changes or defective specifications.

(2) Another situation that increases the potential for fraud exists when the Government identifies the need to purchase proprietary, trade secret or other technical information without making reasonable attempts to determine if that information is already owned by the Government.

2-2. Fraud in the pre-solicitation phase.

a. Bid specifications and statements of work detailing the types and amounts of goods or services to be provided are prepared to assist in the selection process. They are intended to provide both potential bidders and the selecting officials with a firm basis for making and accepting bids. A well-written contract will have specifications, standards and statements of work which make it clear what the Government is entitled to. Sloppy or carelessly written specifications make it easy for a contractor to claim that it is entitled to more money for what the Government defines as what it really wants. Sometimes, there is deliberate collusion between Government personnel and the contractor to write vague specifications. At other times there is an agreement to amend the contract to increase the price immediately after the award. One contractor actually developed a "cost enhancement plan," identifying all of the changes he would make in order to double the cost of the contract, before it was even signed.

b. Fraud indicators include:

(1) Placing any restrictions in the solicitation documents which would tend to restrict competition.

(a) Defining statements of work and specifications to fit the products or capabilities of a single contractor.

(b) Designing "prequalification" standards or specifications to exclude otherwise qualified contractors or their products.

(2) Unnecessary sole source/noncompetitive procurement justifications:

(a) Based on falsified statements.

(b) Which are signed by unauthorized officials.

(c) For which required levels of review were deliberately bypassed.

(3) Providing contractors any advice, advance information, or release of information concerning requirements or pending purchases on a preferential or

selective basis. (Applies equally, whether committed by Government personnel, consultants or contractors.)

(4) Using statements of work, specifications, or sole source justifications developed by or in consultation with a contractor who will be permitted to compete in the procurement. (Institutional conflict of interest.)

(5) Permitting contractors (architect engineers, design engineers, other firms or individuals) that participated in the development of statements of work, specifications or the preparation of the invitations for bids or request for proposals, to bid on or be involved with the prime contract or any subcontracts.

(6) Splitting requirements so that small purchase procedures can be utilized or to avoid required levels of review or approval, e.g., to keep each within the contracting authority of a particular person or activity.

c. Bid specifications or statements of work which are not consistent with the need determination, if unexplained, may indicate an attempt to steer a procurement to a preferred contractor.

(1) Splitting requirements so contractors each get a "fair share" may increase the potential for collusive bidding. (See Chapter 4)

(2) Vague specifications may inhibit the reasonable comparison of bids or proposals and facilitate steering a contract to a favored contractor.

2-3. Fraud in the solicitation phase.

a. Contractors are offered an opportunity to submit bids or proposals for the provision of goods or services that will meet the Government's needs as set forth in specifications or statements of work. This process is intended generally to maximize the use of competition and to ensure that the Government obtains goods and services which meet its needs at the best possible price.

b. Fraud indicators in this phase include:

(1) Procurements which are restricted to exclude or hamper any qualified contractor.

(2) Limiting the time for the submission of bids, thereby creating a situation where only those with advance information have an adequate time to prepare bids or proposals.

(3) Technical or contracting personnel revealing information about the procurement to one contractor which is not revealed to all. Examples of the types of information found to have been illegally disclosed in prior cases include competitor's cost or pricing data; competitor's trade secrets or proprietary information; the results of Government technical evaluations; and Government estimates.

(4) Failure to amend a solicitation to include necessary changes or clarifications. (Telling one contractor of changes that can be made afterward.)

(5) Bid solicitation which is vague as to time, place, or other requirements for submitting acceptable bids.

(6) Failure to assure that a sufficient number of potential competitors are aware of the solicitation. (Use of obscure publications, publishing in holiday seasons, providing a vague or inadequate synopsis to Commerce Business Daily, etc.)

(7) Special assistance to any contractor in preparing its bid or proposal.

(8) "Referring" a contractor to a specific subcontractor expert, or source of supply. (Express or implied that if you use the referred business, you will be more likely to get the contract.)

(9) Improper communication with contractors at trade or professional meetings or improper social contact with contractor representatives.

(10) Government personnel or their families acquiring stock or a financial interest in a contractor or subcontractor.

(11) Government personnel discussing possible employment with a contractor or subcontractor for themselves or a family member.

(12) Improper acceptance of a late bid.

(13) Falsification of documents or receipts to get a late bid accepted.

(14) Change in a bid after other bidders prices are known. This is sometimes done by mistakes deliberately "planted" in a bid.

(15) Withdrawal of the low bidder who later becomes a subcontractor to the higher bidder who gets the contract.

(16) Any indication of collusion or bid rigging between bidders. (See Chapter 4)

(17) False certifications by contractor.

(a) Small business certification.

(b) Minority business certification.

(c) Information provided to other agencies to support special status.

(d) Certification of independent price determination. (See Chapter 3)

(e) Buy American Act certification.

(18) Falsification of information concerning contractor qualifications, financial capability, facilities, ownership of equipment and supplies, qualifications of personnel and successful performance of previous jobs, etc.

2-4. Fraud in the award of the contract.

a. Government contracts are awarded based on the evaluation of contractor's bids and proposals. The evaluation process encompasses many factors, including price, responsiveness, and responsibility.

b. Fraud indicators during the evaluation and award process include:

(1) Deliberately discarding or "losing" the bid or proposal of an "outsider" who wants to participate. (May be part of a conspiracy between a Government official and a select contractor or group of contractors.)

(2) Improperly disqualifying the bid or proposal of a contractor.

(3) Disqualification of any qualified bidder.

(4) Accepting nonresponsive bids from preferred contractors.

(5) Seemingly unnecessary contacts with contractor personnel by persons other than the contracting officer during the solicitation, evaluation, and negotiation processes.

(6) Any unauthorized release of information to a contractor or other person.

(7) Any exercise of favoritism toward a particular contractor during the evaluation process.

(8) Using biased evaluation criteria or using biased individuals on the evaluation panel.

(9) Award of a contract to a contractor who is not the lowest responsible, responsive bidder.

(10) Allowing a low bidder to withdraw without justification.

(11) Failure to forfeit bid bonds when a contractor withdraws improperly.

(12) Material changes in the contract shortly after award.

(13) Awards made to contractors with an apparent history of poor performance.

(14) Awards made to the lowest of a very few bidders without readvertising considerations or without adequate publicity.

(15) Awards made that include items other than those contained in bid specifications.

(16) Awards made without adequate documentation of all preaward and postaward actions, including all understandings or oral agreements.

(17) Release of advance information concerning the award of a major contract. Such a release increases the potential illegal insider trading in the stock of both winning and losing contractors.

(18) Inadequate evaluation of contractor's present responsibility, including ignoring or failing to obtain information regarding a contractor's record of business ethics and integrity.

2-5. Fraud in the negotiation of a contract.

a. Negotiation occurs whenever the Government contracts without formal advertising. Negotiating permits bargaining and affords offerors an opportunity to revise their offers before award of a contract (Federal Acquisition Regulation (FAR) 15.102).

b. There are a number of abuses that can occur in the negotiation of a contract. The first stems from the assumption of many personnel that once it has been determined that negotiated procurement procedures can be used, that procurement on a sole source basis has also been justified. It is clear, however, that the FAR requires negotiated contracts to be awarded on a competitive basis unless less than full and open competition is authorized by an exception (FAR 6.301 and 15.105).

c. Fraud indicators involving negotiated contracts include:

(1) Back-dated or after-the-fact justifications in the contract file.

(2) Disclosure of information to one contractor which is not given to others, thereby giving that contractor an unfair competitive advantage.

(3) Improper release of information (e.g., prices, technical data, identity, or rank of competing proposals, proprietary data or trade secrets, or Government price estimates).

(4) Any indications that a contractor has provided false cost or pricing data. (See Chapter 3)

(5) Failure of Government personnel to obtain or rely on a Certificate of Current Cost or Pricing Data.

(6) Approval of less than full and open competition by an unauthorized person or for an improper reason (a reason other than one of the authorized exceptions to the requirement for full and open competition).

(7) Inadequate evaluation of contractor's present responsibility, including ignoring or failing to obtain information regarding a contractor's record of business ethics and integrity.

Chapter 3. Defective Pricing

3-1. Introduction: The Truth in Negotiations Act.

In the 1950s and early 1960s, the General Accounting Office (GAO) discovered numerous instances of "overpricing" by Government contractors on negotiated contracts. That is, costs quoted to the Government as those which would be incurred by the contractor in performing the work were found to be higher than the actual expenditures. At the time, however, the Government had no legal redress to reprice the contracts unless it could show fraud or deliberate misrepresentation by the contractor. In 1959, the DoD adopted regulations requiring the contractor to provide data reflecting the costs it would incur in performing the contract, called "cost and pricing data." However, GAO later found that the data were not being required or examined by the Military Departments. Consequently, in 1962, Congress passed the Truth in Negotiations Act. The Act required, among other things, submission of complete and current cost and pricing data to the Government during pre-award negotiations for all contracts valued at more than $100,000, and thereby ensured that the Government had the information necessary to determine the reasonableness of the contractor's bid price. The law also provided Government access to contractor records for purposes of assessing the costs of the contract. When a contractor's data submission is "defective," the Act permitted the Government to reduce contract payments by the amount attributable to the defective data.

3-2. Cost or Pricing Data Provision: 10 U.S.C. 2306(a).

a. The cost or pricing data provisions of the Truth in Negotiations Act are contained in 10 U.S.C. 2306(a). That section provides, in part, that a prime or subcontractor *shall* be required to submit cost or pricing data, and *shall* be required to certify that, to the best of his knowledge and belief, the data submitted is accurate, complete, and current, under the following circumstances:

(1) Prior to the award of any contract other than one using sealed-bid procedures where the price is expected to exceed $100,000.

(2) Prior to pricing a change or modification of *any* contract if the price adjustment is expected to exceed $100,000, or any lesser amount if so prescribed by the agency head.

(3) Prior to the award of a subcontract when the subcontract price is expected to exceed $100,000 *and* the prime contractor and each higher tier subcontractor was required, under the contract, to submit cost or pricing data.

(4) Prior to pricing a change or modification to a subcontract covered by paragraph (3), above, for which the price adjustment is expected to exceed $100,000, or any lesser amount if so prescribed by the agency head.

The certifications are to be made to the Government contracting officer in the case of prime contractors and to the prime contractor in the case of subcontractors. The exceptions to certification of data include contracts or subcontracts for which the price is based on "adequate price competition," "established catalog or market prices of commercial items sold in substantial quantities to the general public," "prices set by law or regulation," or, in exceptional cases, when waived by the head of the agency. Conversely, despite the above-noted provisions, the head of any agency can require submission of data if it is determined necessary for the evaluation of the reasonableness of the price of the contract or subcontract.

b. The Act also requires that each contract that falls under the Truth in Negotiations provisions contain a clause for allowing for a price reduction based on the amount of any overpricing due to defective data submissions by either the prime or any subcontractors. The reduction would include profits and fees. The Act does state, however, that if the contractor can show the Government did not rely on the data submitted, that fact can be a defense in any price reduction action.

c. As part of the 1986 Defense Authorization Act (PL 99-661), a penalty in an amount equal to the overpayment can be assessed against a contractor who knowingly submits defective cost data. In any case of overpricing, the Government is entitled to recover interest on the amount of the overpayment for the period beginning on the date of the overpayment until repayment of the sum owed (10 U.S.C. 2306a(e)—See Chapter 11).

3-3. Regulatory Requirements: Federal Acquisition Regulation (FAR).

a. Section 15.801 of the FAR defines costs or pricing data and specifies the form and language for the certificate of current cost or pricing data. Price reduction rights of the Government are found in clauses at FAR 52.214-27, 52.215-22, and 52.215-23.

b. Cost or pricing data are submitted to the DoD on DD633, Contracting Pricing Proposal Cover Sheet. Along with that form, the contractor (or offeror, if no contract award has yet been made) is required to provide a breakdown of his costs, and submit supporting documentation such as invoices or firm price quotes from his suppliers. In addition, the contractor must submit the certification as soon as practicable after agreement is reached on the contract or modification price. The certification references FAR 15.801 to specifically include vendor quotes as "cost or pricing data." A knowingly false or inaccurate certification by a contractor can lead to criminal prosecution for submission of false statements in violation of 18 U.S.C. 1001. A claim which is subsequently paid based on the false statement is a false claim which can be criminally prosecuted under 18 U.S.C. 287, and can result in civil liability under the civil False Claims Act (31 U.S.C. 3729). In addition, a false statement via certification can be penalized administratively under the Program Fraud Civil Remedies Act of 1986, Chapter 38 of Title 31, U.S.C. (See Chapter 11).

3-4. Defective Pricing Indicators.

a. In September 1983, the Director of the Defense Contract Audit Agency (DCAA) issued a memorandum to DCAA auditors stating guidance in the area of defective pricing where certain conditions exist which might indicate fraud. Auditors were instructed that when indications of fraud are found, the case will be referred to the proper investigative agency. Some of the most significant indicators include:

(1) Indications of falsification or alteration of supporting data.

(2) Failure to update cost or pricing data even though it is known that past activity showed that costs or prices have decreased.

(3) Failure to make complete disclosure of data known to responsible contractor personnel.

(4) Distortion of the overhead accounts or base line information by transferring changes or accounts that have a material impact on Government contracts.

(5) Failure to correct known system deficiencies which lead to defective pricing.

(6) Protracted delay in release of data to the Government to preclude possible price reductions.

(7) Repeated denial by the responsible contractor employees of the existence of historical records that are subsequently found.

b. As a result of increased emphasis on detection and referral of detective pricing cases, the Government, in 1986, prosecuted a major contractor and exacted the largest fraud penalty in DoD history. In July 1986, a Federal grand jury returned a 325 count indictment charging a major Defense contractor and two corporate officers, with engaging in a scheme to defraud the DoD of approximately $6,300,000 in connection with the bidding and award of 45 prime and subcontracts between 1975 and 1984. The charges, all relating to defective pricing, included concealing and covering up material facts, racketeering, mail fraud, conspiracy, and false statements. The indictment charged that the defendants submitted false and fraudulent cost and pricing data, representing to the DoD that the contractor would be paying more for material than the company would in fact pay. The inflated submissions became known as "chicken fat" among the conspirators and were accomplished by various means, including the use of blank quotation forms obtained from material vendors, and obtaining quotations at book or catalog prices which were higher than the actual costs known to the contractor. One defendant was also charged with failing to disclose to the Government the rebates the company received from vendors on purchases, and that he also lied to an auditor from the DCAA. The contractor agreed to plead guilty to all counts set forth in the indictment and to pay approximately $15 million to the Government in criminal and civil penalties and restitution. The individual defendants likewise pled guilty and were sentenced to imprisonment (suspended in one case), five years probation, and fines of $10,000 and $10,500.

c. The fraud indicators should be used by contracting officers as well as auditors and investigators. Particular note should be made of "intent" indicators in defective pricing cases. These are critical to a determination of whether a criminal act occurred. The deliberate concealment or misrepresentation of a single significant cost element could constitute a prosecutable crime.

Chapter 4. Antitrust Violations: Collusive Bidding and Price Fixing

4-1. Introduction.

a. Collusive bidding, price fixing, or bid rigging are commonly used interchargeable terms that describe many forms of illegal anticompetitive activity. The common thread throughout all of the anticompetitive activities is that they involve any agreements or informal arrangements among independent competitors which limit competition. Schemes that allocate contracts and limit competition can take many forms and are only limited by the imagination of the parties. Common schemes, which will be discussed in more detail later, include bid suppression or limiting, complementary bidding, bid rotation, and market division.

b. The essential elements of a criminal antitrust offense are (1) the formulation of a contract, combination, agreement, or conspiracy, and (2) the restraint of trade or commerce among the several states. With regard to the first element, the agreement must be between two or more real competitors. The evidence must establish that the competitors had a common plan, understanding, arrangement, or agreement to fix or stabilize prices, allocate customers, or allocate territories or markets. In regard to the second element, to satisfy the interstate commerce element of the offense, the evidence must establish that the conspiracy involved goods or funds traveling in the flow of interstate commerce, e.g., materials shipped by common carrier interstate, or affected interstate commerce, e.g., Federal funds involved in the procurement. There are certain agreements or business practices that by statute are *per se* violations. These agreements or practices, because of their previous effect on competition and lack of any redeeming virtue, are conclusively presumed to be unreasonable and thus illegal. These types of agreements among competitors which would violate the law include, but are not limited to, the following:

(1) Agreements to adhere to published price lists.

(2) Agreements to raise prices by a specified increment.

(3) Agreements to establish, adhere to, or eliminate discounts.

(4) Agreements not to advertise prices.

(5) Agreements to maintain specified price differentials based on quantity, type, or size of product.

c. The Antitrust Division, Department of Justice (DOJ), has primary prosecutive jurisdiction on all Federal antitrust violations. Responsible antitrust attorneys are located at the seven field office locations: Atlanta, Chicago,

Cleveland, Dallas, Philadelphia, New York City, and San Francisco. The Antitrust Division has successfully prosecuted defendants who have fixed prices or rigged bids in conjunction with the award of contracts for the following types of commodities and services widely used by DoD: asphalt paving; electrical equipment; shipment of household goods; wholesale produce; retail gasoline; waste disposal; bread; milk; dredging; roofing; lumber; cigarettes; coal; and building construction. Prosecution of Sherman Antitrust Act offenses present in Defense procurement is a high priority within the DOJ Antitrust Division.

4-2. Impact on the procurement process.

a. One of the cornerstones of the Federal procurement system is the requirement that Government contracts should be awarded, to the greatest extent possible, on the basis of free and open competition. The preference for competition in the procurement of goods or services on behalf of the United States was first set by statute in 1890. That preference still remains and has been specifically expressed in statutes concerning DoD purchases and contracts. Title 10, U.S. Code, Section 2304(a), sets forth a specific requirement that, "Purchase of and contracts for property and services covered by this chapter shall be made by formal advertising, and shall be awarded on a competitive bid basis to the lowest responsible bidder, in all cases in which the use of such method is feasible and practicable under existing conditions and circumstances." In addition, 10 U.S.C. 2304(g) requires that, except in certain limited circumstances, competition must also be obtained in negotiated procurements. The requirements are also contained in DoD policy regarding competition as outlined in FAR 14.103.

b. Further evidence of the importance of competition in the DoD procurement process is provided by the requirement for "Certification of Independent Price Determination," FAR 3.103-1. The regulation requires contractors to certify that they have not engaged in certain specific activities which constitute what can generally be described as collusive bidding or price fixing.

c. It should be obvious that collusive bidding or price fixing among competitors completely undermines the Government efforts to use competitive purchasing and contracting methods. The harm in this situation, however, is not limited to the mere circumvention of the important Government policies that encourage free and open competition. In fact, collusive bidding and price fixing result in increased costs, destroy public confidence in the country's economy, and undermine our system of free enterprise. To illustrate the impact of the activities on DoD procurement, consider just a few recent cases:

(1) A 1983 prosecution in the Southeastern United States resulted in the conviction and incarceration of an electrical subcontractor. Plea negotiations culminated with the defendant pleading guilty to a criminal information charging a violation of 15 U.S.C. 1 (Sherman Antitrust Act). The subcontractor was sentenced to a six and one-half month prison term for his part in a conspiracy to ". . . fix, raise, and maintain electrical subcontract work on a $455,049 Army Corps of Engineers contract . . . ."

(2) In 1983, two household goods moving and storage companies and their respective presidents, entered guilty pleas to charges of price fixing in a Federal district court in South Carolina. The contractors, serving the Army

base at Fort Jackson, South Carolina, were indicted for ". . . conspiring to fix, raise, maintain, and establish the rates charged for providing non-temporary storage of household goods owned by military personnel . . . ." The two companies received respective fines of $100,000 and $25,000, and were debarred from bidding on Government contracts. The individual defendants were each fined $25,000 and $5,000, and personally debarred.

(3) A 1985 prosecution in the Southeastern United States yielded the first of several significant convictions of Army Corps of Engineers dredging contractors for bid rigging. Following a guilty plea to a criminal information alleging a conspiracy to rig bids on a $1.4 million contract, a Virginia dredging company and its president received substantial sentences in a Federal district court. The company was ordered to pay a criminal fine of $200,000. The president received a two year suspended sentence and was ordered to pay a $50,000 fine. A separate administrative/civil settlement with the Army Corps of Engineers and the DOJ resulted in the payment of a $235,000 civil fine.

d. It has been demonstrated that collusive bidding and price fixing schemes cause the DoD to pay much more for goods or services than it would have if true competition existed. Even though this is the case, the bids may appear to be fair and reasonable because the Government estimate may be too high. The appearance of reasonable prices should therefore not mistakenly be construed as proof that collusive bidding and price fixing are not occurring or that a violation of law does not exist because the harm in terms of monetary loss is not apparent. In fact, when such conduct is criminally prosecuted, the defendants are prohibited from introducing any evidence to justify their conduct or to demonstrate its reasonableness.

4-3. Indicators of collusive bidding and price fixing.

a. The list of indicators below is intended to facilitate recognition of those situations which may involve collusive bidding or price fixing. In and of themselves these indicators will not prove that illegal anticompetitive activity is occurring. They are, however, sufficient to warrant referral to appropriate authorities for investigation. Use of indicators such as these to identify possible anticompetitive activity is important because schemes to restrict competition are by their very nature secret and their exact nature is not readily visible.

b. Practices or events that may evidence collusive bidding or price fixing are:

(1) Bidders who are qualified and capable of performing but who fail to bid, with no apparent reason. A situation where fewer competitors than normal submit bids typifies this situation. (This could indicate a deliberate scheme to withhold bids.)

(2) Certain contractors always bid against each other or, conversely, certain contractors do not bid against one another.

(3) The successful bidder repeatedly subcontracts work to companies that submitted higher bids or to companies that picked up bid packages and could have bid as prime contractors but did not.

(4) Different groups of contractors appear to specialize in Federal, state, or local jobs exclusively. (This might indicate a market division by class of customer.)

(5) There is an apparent pattern of low bids regularly recurring, such as corporation "x" always being the low bidder in a certain geographical area or in a fixed rotation with other bidders.

(6) Failure of original bidders to rebid, or an identical ranking of the same bidders upon rebidding, when original bids were rejected as being too far over the Government estimate.

(7) A certain company appears to be bidding substantially higher on some bids than on other bids with no logical cost difference to account for the increase, i.e., a local company is bidding higher prices for an item to be delivered locally than for delivery to points farther away.

(8) Bidders that ship their product a short distance bid more than those who must incur greater expense by shipping their product long distances.

(9) Identical bid amounts on a contract line item by two or more contractors. Some instances of identical line item bids are explainable, as suppliers often quote the same prices to several bidders. But a large number of identical bids on any service-related item should be viewed critically.

(10) Bidders frequently change prices at about the same time and to the same extent.

(11) Joint venture bids where either contractor could have bid individually as a prime. (Both had technical capability and production capacity.)

(12) Any incidents suggesting direct collusion among competitors, such as the appearance of identical calculation or spelling errors in two or more competitive bids, or the submission by one firm of bids for other firms.

(13) Competitors regularly socialize or appear to hold meetings, or otherwise get together in the vicinity of procurement offices shortly before bid filing deadlines.

(14) Assertions by employees, former employees, or competitors that an agreement to fix bids and prices or otherwise restrain trade exists.

(15) Bid prices appear to drop whenever a new or infrequent bidder submits a bid.

(16) Competitors exchange any form of price information among themselves. This may result from the existence of an "industry price list" or "price agreement" to which contractors refer in formulating their bids, or it may take other subtler forms such as discussions of the "right price."

(17) Any reference by bidders to "association price schedules," "industry price schedules," "industry suggested prices," "industry-wide prices," or "market-wide prices."

(18) A bidder's justification for a bid price or terms, offered because they follow the industry or industry leader's pricing or terms, may include a reference to following a named competitor's pricing or terms.

(19) Any statements by a representative of a contractor that his company "does not sell in a particular area" or that "only a particular firm sells in that area."

(20) Statements by a bidder that it is not their turn to receive a job or, conversely, that it is another bidder's turn.

4-4. Collusive bidding and price fixing examples.

Common collusive bidding and price fixing schemes that DoD personnel may be able to recognize are discussed below. The schemes relate to one another and overlap. Frequently, an agreement by competitors to rig bids will involve more than one of the schemes.

a. *Bid suppression or limiting.* In this type of scheme, one or more competitors agree with at least one other competitor to refrain from bidding or agrees to withdraw a previously submitted bid so that another competitor's bid will be accepted. Other forms of this activity involve agreements by competitors to fabricate bid protests or to coerce suppliers and subcontractors not to deal with nonconspirators who submit bids.

b. *Complementary bidding.* Complementary bidding (also known as "protective" or "shadow" bidding) occurs when competitors submit token bids that are too high to be accepted (or if competitive in price, then on special terms that will not be acceptable). Such bids are not intended to secure the buyer's acceptance, but are merely designed to give the appearance of genuine bidding.

c. *Bid rotation.* In bid rotation, all vendors participating in the scheme submit bids, but by agreement take turns being the low bidder. In its most basic form, bid rotation will consist of a cyclical pattern for submitting the low bid on certain contracts. The rotation may not be as obvious as might be expected if it is coupled with a scheme for awarding subcontracts to losing bidders, to take turns according to the size of the contract, or one of the other market division schemes explained below.

d. *Market division.* Market division schemes are agreements to refrain from competing in a designated portion of a market. Division of a market for this purpose may be accomplished based on the customer or geographic area involved. The result of such a division is that competing firms will not bid or will submit only complementary bids when a solicitation for bids is made by a customer or in an area not assigned to them.

Chapter 5. Cost Mischarging

5-1. Introduction.

a. One of the most common of abuses found in the procurement system is cost mischarging. This is due in large part to the fact that most high-dollar Government research and development and production contracts are awarded as cost type contracts. Because such contracts are paid on the basis of incurred costs, the contractor may increase profits by mischarging. It is important to recognize that the impact of such mischarging is almost always far greater than the basic costs which were falsified. For example, a single hour of labor which is mischarged may result in payments of as much as three times the labor hour rate due to indirect cost allowances which are added based on that hour.

b. Mischarging can occur in a number of situations, with a variety of results. It can involve charging labor hours from one contract to another, charging at higher than allowed rates, charging to indirect accounts those charges which should be direct, or viceversa, as well as other schemes. In all cases, mischarging is a serious matter. Even when unintentional or without a fraudulent motive, it undermines confidence in the contractor's accounting and control systems and should raise questions as to the validity of other submissions.

c. The issue of whether a mischarge was a "mistake" or a crime usually turns on the intent of the maker. Investigators should examine the issue of intent. Because intentional false submissions themselves are criminal, prosecutors may pursue those cases even though no substantial loss occurs, particularly where the contractor has actively sought to conceal costs. Additionally, to overlook situations such as mischarging from one Government contract to another on the theory that it is merely a case of "robbing Peter to pay Paul" is to ignore the serious consequences of such a scheme. Because cost estimates for future procurements rely in large part on accurate historical cost figures from similar work, the estimates for later work will be tainted by false accounting. Further, moving costs from a Government job which is tight on budget to one which is "fat" could prevent an overrun in the case of the former and thus make the contractor appear more efficient than he actually is. This could result in awarding incentive fees or follow-on contracts which would not be appropriate were the true costs known.

d. Under cost type contracts, the Government reimburses the contractor's costs which are allowable, allocable to the contract, and reasonable. Those types of contracts include cost plus fixed fee, cost plus incentive fee, cost plus award fee, cost reimbursable, and cost sharing contracts. In addition, contract changes and equitable adjustment to contracts are reimbursed on the basis of incurred costs even on fixed price contracts. Cost mischarging occurs whenever the contractor charges the Government for costs which are not allowable, not reasonable, or which cannot be directly or indirectly allocated to the contract.

5-2. Allowable Costs.

a. The FAR 31-205 identifies costs which are allowable and those which cannot be charged to Government contracts. Such costs may be direct costs, such as labor and materials used on one contract and no other, or indirect costs, which contribute to a number of different contracts. Indirect costs are placed in "cost pools" which are then allocated to contracts on some agreed basis (such as total cost or labor hours). Title 10, U.S.C., Section 2324, specifically identifies certain unallowable costs for covered DoD contracts and requires the Secretary of Defense to prescribe regulations to clarify the allowability for certain other costs. The statute also requires that a proposal for settlement of indirect costs applicable to a covered contract include a certification by a contractor official that, to the best of his knowledge, all indirect costs submitted are allowable.

b. Unallowable costs include:

(1) Advertising costs (except to obtain workers or scarce materials for a contract, or to sell surplus or byproduct materials).

(2) Bid and proposal costs in excess of a set limit.

(3) Stock options and some forms of deferred compensation.

(4) Contingencies.

(5) Contributions and donations.

(6) Entertainment costs.

(7) Costs of idle facilities except in limited circumstances.

(8) Interest.

(9) Losses on other contracts.

(10) Long-term leases of property or equipment and leases from related parties are limited to the costs of ownership.

(11) Independent research and development costs beyond set limits.

(12) Legal costs related to a contractor's defense of any civil or criminal fraud proceeding or similar proceeding (including false certifications) brought by the Government when the contractor is found liable or has pled nolocontendre.

(13) Payments of fines and penalties resulting from violations of, or failure to comply with, Federal, state, local, or foreign laws and regulations, except in cases where authorized in writing by the contracting officer or by adherence to contract specifications.

(14) Costs incurred to influence (directly or indirectly) legislative action on any matter pending before Congress or a state legislature.

(15) Costs of membership in any social, dining, or country club or organization.

(16) Costs of alcoholic beverages.

(17) Costs of promotional items and memorabilia, including models, gifts, and souvenirs.

(18) Costs for travel by commercial aircraft which exceed the amount of the standard commercial fare.

5-3. Accounting Mischarges.

a. The mischarging most frequently encountered by DCAA auditors is called an accounting mischarge. A fraudulent accounting mischarge involves knowingly charging unallowable costs to the Government, concealing or misrepresenting them as allowable costs, or hiding them in accounts (such as office supplies) which are not audited closely. Another common fraud variation involves intentionally charging types of costs which have reached their limits (such as bid and proposal costs or independent research and development costs) to other cost categories.

5-4. Material Cost Mischarges.

a. Material is physical inventory and component deliverables. Material includes raw material, purchased parts, as well as subcontractor and intercompany transfers. Like labor, material costs are sometimes mischarged, both as to their reasonableness and allocability. Numerous cases have been discovered where Government-owned material was used on a similar commercial contract but the material accountability records showed that the material was used on a Government contract. There have also been cases where Government-owned materials were stolen and the thefts were concealed by showing the materials as being issued to and used on Government contracts.

b. Mischarges of materials are usually confined to situations involving raw material or interchangeable parts. Specialized material, such as a certain type gyroscope, cannot be easily mischarged and go undetected due to its character. For example, a gyroscope for a C-130 aircraft just will not fit on a KC-135 aircraft and would be easily detected as an improper billing. An excellent guide to detecting material mischarges, *Handbook on Fraud Indicators: Material,* was published in July 1986 by the Office of the Inspector General, DoD, and is available through the Assistant Inspector General for Audit Policy and Oversight.

5-5. Labor Mischarges.

a. Labor costs are more susceptible to mischarging than material costs because employees' labor can be readily shifted to any contract with the stroke of a pen on their time cards. The only absolute way to assure that labor costs are charged to the correct contract is to observe the actual work of each employee to determine which contract he is working on and then determine from the accounting records that the employee's cost is charged to the proper contract.

b. Contractors have devised a number of ways to mischarge labor costs. As in the case of material cost fraud vulnerability, the Assistant Inspector General for Audit Policy and Oversight has available a guide on the subject, titled, *Handbook on Labor Fraud Indicators,* dated August 1985. Labor mischarging schemes range from very crude to very sophisticated. Some of the common methods of mischarging are set forth below:

(1) *Transfer of Labor Cost.* This mischarge is usually made after the contractor realizes that he has suffered a loss on a fixed priced contract. To eliminate the loss, a journal entry is made to remove the labor cost from the fixed priced contract and put it on the cost type contract. This type of mischarge is very easy to detect but is difficult to prove. The contractor will contend that the labor charges to the fixed price contract were in error and the journal entry, transferring the cost to the cost type contract, was made to correct that error. Frequently the dollar amount of the transfer is estimated.

(2) *Time and Charges Do Not Agree with Contractor Billing to the Government.*

(a) This accounting mischarge method is probably the easiest to detect and prove. It is a simple matter of totaling the time and hours expended on the cost type contract and comparing them to the hours billed. For example, the time cards may show that 1,000 hours have been expended on the cost type contract when, in fact, the contractor has billed the Government for 2,000 hours of labor. The difference is obvious and the accounting records (time cards) will not support the billings.

(b) Contractor labor billings to the Government are normally supported by two accounting records. The source record is the individual employee time card. The other record is the labor distribution. The labor distribution is usually a computer printout that summarizes by contract the individual time card entries. The contractor will commonly use the labor distribution to support his Government billings. It is relatively easy to falsify a labor distribution but it is necessary to corrupt the entire work force to falsify the time cards. Hence, the individual time cards should be totaled and reconciled to the labor distribution at least on a test basis.

(3) *Original Time Cards are Destroyed or Hidden and New Time Cards are Prepared for the Auditor's Benefit.* This is a very successful method of concealing a labor mischarge. Mischarges of this nature are very difficult to detect. They are detected when:

(a) The hidden time cards are inadvertently given to the auditor.

(b) All of the old time cards are not destroyed and the auditor finds them.

(c) Employee signatures on the time cards are carbon copies because the employee's original signature has been traced.

(d) Time card entries are compared to time records maintained by individual employees (copies of time cards, logs, etc.).

(4) *Changes are Made to Individual Time Cards.* A frequent labor fraud encountered by the DCAA auditor involves improper changes to the original contract charge numbers on employee time cards. Some of the charges are so well done that it is difficult to tell that a change has been made. In one instance, the change was made so expertly that the auditor could not tell that a change had been made just from looking at the time sheet. The auditor detected the change by running his finger across the entry and noticed a difference in the "feel." Under magnification, the "white out" material used to cover the original entry could be seen. The auditors used a "light box" to determine what the original charge had been, i.e., by placing a light underneath the time sheet the auditor could read through the "white out" to determine the original charge. Just because changes are made on time cards, it does not necessarily mean that a fraud is being perpetrated. Many times innocent errors are made and corrected. In determining the possibility of fraudulent activity, one should:

(a) Determine the magnitude of the changes. If only a few changes have been made then, in all probability, the changes were made to correct errors. However, if a significant percentage of the charges have been changed, the probability of fraudulent activity is increased.

(b) A comparison of the original charge number to the revised charge number should be made. If the net effect of the changes is to increase the charges to cost reimbursable contracts, the likelihood of fraud is further increased.

(c) Make a review of the sequence of events. For example, in one case the tail number of the aircraft that the employee worked on was posted to the time card in addition to the contract charge number. The following discrepancies were noted:

1. The original contract charge number corresponded to the contract for which work was to be accomplished on a specified aircraft. The changed contract charge number was for work on another contract for an entirely different type of aircraft, i.e., the original charge was to the C-130 aircraft and the tail number was a C-130 aircraft, but the new charge was made to the KC-135 aircraft.

2. Based on the changed charge numbers, a ridiculous number of employees were working on the same aircraft during the same labor shift.

(d) Identify the employee who made the changes, find out why the changes were made and what was the employee's source of information for the changed charge number.

(5) *Time Card Charges are Made by Supervisors.* One should be especially skeptical of timekeeping systems where time card labor charges are posted by supervisors. Management can exert pressure and influence on supervisors to accomplish certain goals. The pressure may influence the supervisor to falsify time charges in order to keep higher level management satisfied with his performance. An even more serious situation occurs when senior level management requires the supervisor to record time charges in a manner most profitable to the company. Management might even go so far as to provide supervisors with "budgets" of how to charge the time for each job. However, if individual employees post their time cards it would be difficult to corrupt the entire work force.

(6) *Impact of Labor Mischarges.* When a labor cost is mischarged, so is the associated overhead and general and administrative (G&A) expenses. Overhead costs are allocated to labor costs based on an overhead rate or percentage. Overhead costs usually exceed 100 percent of the labor cost. Therefore, any mischarging on labor rates also impacts on overhead charges, which ultimately results in a greater than double loss to the Government. The same is true for G&A rates. In computing the dollar amount of the fraud, one must add the overhead and G&A cost because applied overhead and G&A will probably be more than the labor cost involved.

5-6. Cost Mischarging Examples.

a. An overhead audit conducted by DCAA disclosed substantial cost mischarging by a DoD accoustical research contractor. The mischarging principally involved shifting costs on both commercial and DoD contracts to the overhead category and then allocating the overhead to those contracts (principally DoD) which provided the best overhead rate. A thorough review of the audit work papers disclosed numerous examples of time sheets which had been altered by whiteouts. As a result of the audit and investigation, two senior company vice presidents were found guilty of violations of the Federal conspiracy statute and making false statements. Furthermore, the company was fined $706,000 and ordered to make restitution of approximately $2 million; the two senior vice presidents were fined $20,000 each and given six month sentences.

b. A major DoD contractor was found to have improperly shifted individual research and development costs (IR&D) to cost type contracts. The corporation was convicted and fined $30,000. An accompanying civil and administrative settlement resulted in the company paying an additional $720,000 to DoD. The corporation also agreed to major revisions in corporate contracting practices and to increased DoD audit access to contractor records. Additionally, $300,000 in legal costs were disallowed.

c. A company contracted by the Army to rewrite military technical manuals was convicted, as well as its president and vice president, of conspiracy to defraud and of submitting false statements after a seven-day jury trial which found the defendants had mischarged labor costs. The charges stemmed from a scheme where the company, whose contract with the Army was on a time and material basis of cost reimbursement, charged over $140,000 of commercial expenses against the DoD contract. The corporation was fined, and the officers were fined and sentenced to work-release and probation terms.

d. Based on information initially supplied by a Defense Logistics Agency employee who became suspicious of a price quote submitted by an Air Force parts supplier, a contractor was convicted of material mischarging and paid fines and recoveries amounting to $3 million. The contractor had altered documents to reflect greatly inflated costs of products of which it was then able to further inflate by adding on a percentage-of-cost overhead rate.

Chapter 6. Product Substitution

6-1. Introduction.

a. The term product substitution generally refers to attempts by contractors to deliver to the Government goods or services which do not conform to contract requirements, without informing the Government of the deficiency, while seeking reimbursement based on alleged delivery of conforming products or services. It is the policy of the DoD that goods and services acquired must conform to the quality and quantity required in the contract. Goods or services which do not conform in all respects to contractual requirements are to be rejected. It is essential that this policy be strictly adhered to, as failure to do so can result in providing substandard, untested, and possibly defective material to our Armed Forces. Defective material can have a serious and detrimental impact on the safety of DoD personnel, as well as the accomplishment of important missions.

b. When a contract calls for delivery of an item produced by the original equipment manufacturer (OEM), then the contractor must furnish that item. The rule excludes even items that may be identical in all respects but are not produced by the OEM. If the contract requires the delivery of end products produced in the United States, then the contractor is obligated to supply items manufactured in the United States. This is required even though comparable or identical items are available from foreign sources at lower costs to the contractor. Further, if the contract requires that certain tests be conducted to ensure that an item is suitable for its intended use and can be relied upon to perform as expected, those tests must be conducted. The contractor's ability to produce an item that will perform within acceptable limits regardless of whether actually tested is not relevant.

c. Contractors frequently argue that substituted goods or service delivered to the Government were "just as good" as what was contracted for, even if specifications are not met, and that, therefore, no harm is done to the government. There are several important fallacies to be noted when considering this argument. First and foremost, the substitute is usually not as good as what was contracted for. In cases of product substitution investigated to date, the substitute is usually one of inferior quality or the workmanship is extremely poor because it was done by lesser qualified and cheaper labor. Secondly, while the immediate harm that the substitute might cause or may have, in fact, caused is sometimes difficult to determine, its introduction into Defense supply channels undermines the reliability of the entire supply system. If, for example, a microchip were in use in larger components which failed, the cause of the failure might not be directly traceable to the inferior quality of the microchip. Third, even if the item is useable, there is harm to the integrity of the competitive procurement system which is based on all competitors offering to furnish the item precisely described in specifications.

6-2. Fraud potential.

a. There are a wide variety of fraudulent schemes that may involve product substitution. Many of the recent product substitution fraud allegations involve consumable or off-the-shelf items. Defense employees should be aware of similar problems that have arisen in component parts and materials used in weapon systems, ships, aircraft, and vehicles. Cases have included:

(1) The provision of inferior quality raw materials;

(2) Materials that have not been tested as required by the contract specifications;

(3) Providing foreign made products where domestic products were required; and

(4) Providing untrained workers when skilled technicians were required.

b. Product substitution cases sometimes involve Government employees. For example, gratuities and bribes have been paid to Government inspection personnel to accept items which do not conform to contract requirements.

c. The potential for a product substitution case is greatest where DoD relies on contractor integrity to ensure that the Government gets what it has paid for. For example, fast pay procedures apply to small purchases. The Government pays contractors for goods based on certification of shipment. Quality assurance is frequently limited in scope and is performed after payment has been made. Thus, small purchases are particularly susceptible to unscrupulous contractors.

d. In large dollar value procurements, Government quality personnel often rely on testing performed by the contractor. Falsification of the test documents may conceal the fact that a piece of equipment has not passed all the tests required by contract or has not been tested at all. False entries may also conceal the substitution of inferior or substandard materials in a product. When Government personnel actually witness or perform tests themselves, there is always the possibility that what they are seeing is a specifically prepared sample not representative of the contractor's actual production.

e. In August 1986, the OIG, DoD, issued a research report on Unauthorized Quality Assurance Practices by contractors. The project was conducted to identify possible systemic weaknesses in DoD quality assurance practices. The report determined Government reliance on contractor falsified documentation, inadequate Government inspection and testing, and the lack of adequate control over end items were three conditions conducive to unauthorized quality assurance practices by contractors. The report also concluded that in 22 of 24 DoD investigation cases studied, the contractors intentionally and knowingly delivered or planned to deliver products that were not in conformance with contract requirements. Related analysis in the report disclosed predominant issues that pertained to quality assurance practices. Some of the indicators of and conditions conducive to unauthorized quality assurance practices included a history of poor performance by the contractor; negative preaward survey; awards to unusually low bidders; misuse of fast pay contracts; Government quality assurance representatives' reliance on contractor falsified documentation; and insufficient Government quality assurance practices.

f. Finally, the Buy American Act (41 U.S.C. 10) generally prohibits the use of foreign manufactured articles, materials, or supplies in Government contracts.

6-3. Product substitution examples.

a. A DoD contractor provided false certifications of quality testing for coating on aluminum troop backpack frames. The backpacks are intended for use by military ground troops, and the anodized coating on frames are dyed light fast olive drab to avoid enemy detection. Inferior anodizing could endanger the lives of U.S. military personnel through the exposure of reflective metal. Investigation disclosed that no testing was performed and a sample of completed units failed at a rate of 70 percent. The owner of the company, who entered a plea of guilty to false statements, was sentenced to 3 years supervised probation, fined $6,000, and required to perform 500 hours of community service.

b. A complainant alleged that a product manufacturer of parts for Army howitzers was submitting defective items which, if installed, could produce significant safety hazards. An investigation revealed that the testing certificates being submitted by the contractor were false. The investigation kept the defective parts from being installed in Army howitzers and kept howitzers from being sold under the Foreign Military Sales program. The corporate president pled guilty to making false statements to the U.S. Government and was sentenced to one year supervised probation; the company and its president have also been debarred from contracting with the Government.

c. An investigation was conducted concerning a company that had a Navy contract to install fire-retardant decorative plastic laminate throughout the enlisted dining area of a Navy ship. The contract required the company to provide certification that the laminate was a fire-retardant material. When the company installed laminate that was not fire retardant, it seriously jeopardized the lives of the ship's crew. The investigation determined and a Federal grand jury charged that the company substituted and installed laminate that was not fire retardant and that an officer and an employee of the company conspired to falsify a certification to the Navy that the material was fire retardant. As a result of the false claims, the company fraudulently received over $23,000. Both individuals pled guilty to making false statements and claims against the Government. The president was ordered to pay restitution, and the vice president was fined $1,000.

d. A DoD investigation established that a contractor had substituted inferior check valves with the potential to damage aircraft and jeopardize personnel safety. The contractor was asked to furnish specified valves manufactured by a particular company. The scheme was discovered when the contractor billed the Government for a progress payment and billed for more valves than had been delivered. A later inspection of the delivered valves found the substitute items. The president of the company was convicted of mail fraud and submitting false statements.

e. A DoD contractor devised a scheme to deliver nonconforming and defective rifle barrels for M-14 and M-21 weapons to the DoD. Under the contract, 1,800 rifle barrels were to be provided to the Department at a price of about $245,000. The DoD inspectors were shown acceptable rifle barrels during quality assurance checks. Then the contractor substituted nonconforming rifle barrels and shipped then to DoD depots. The contractor also allegedly violated contract provisions by selling rifle barrels made for the DoD to the general public. Some of the defective barrels exploded during user tests and could have caused serious injury. A joint investigation by the Army, DoD, and Department of Justice was conducted. The president and vice president were indicted on charges of racketeering, mail fraud, obstruction of justice, and perjury. The company has been fined $400,000 and suspended from receiving future contracts.

f. Three company officials pled guilty to charges of conspiracy and filing false statements on a contract after installing pipe flanges aboard nuclear submarines without making proper tests and certifications. The defective flanges, which have a critical application aboard submarines, have been removed. The corporate president and vice president were sentenced to two years imprisonment and fined $10,000 each, and a third corporate official was sentenced to six months imprisonment and ordered to perform 500 hours community service. The corporation was debarred.

g. An investigation resulted in guilty pleas by a DoD contractor to charges of submitting false claims on Government contracts to supply aircraft parts. The company was found to have either provided nonconforming parts or to have short shipped ordered parts. The company, its owner, and two other companies that participated in the fraud, in addition to other criminal sanctions and fines, including a prison term, were debarred from receiving future Government contracts.

h. A contractor provided defective foreign-made ammunition under a Foreign Military Sales contract. The contract required 15 million rounds of 5.56mm ammunition. The first shipment of approximately 2 million rounds was according to contract specifications. However, when subsequent ammunition received from the contractor caused rifles to misfire and jam, an investigation was initiated. It was determined that the defective ammunition was produced in a foreign country, and bribery payoffs were made to facilitate acceptance of the defective product. The corporate president, vice president, and a foreign national businessman who facilitated obtaining the contracts, all pled guilty to conspiracy to defraud the U.S. Government. The president and vice president were sentenced to two and three year sentences, respectively, and the foreign national businessman was sentenced to one year confinement and fined $10,000. The corporation has been recommended for debarment.

Chapter 7. Progress Payment Fraud

7-1. Introduction.

a. Progress payments are payments made as work progresses under a contract, based on the costs incurred, the percentage of work accomplished, or the attainment of a particular stage of completion. They do not include payments for partial deliveries accepted by the Government.

b. Fraud in progress payments occurs when a contractor submits a progress payment request based on falsified direct labor charges, on material costs for items not actually purchased, or on falsified certification of a stage of completion attained/work accomplished.

c. When a DoD contract contains one of the contract clauses in FAR 52.232.16, a contractor may submit monthly progress payment requests and is entitled to receive a contractually specified percentage of its total costs.

d. Requests for progress payments are made on Standard Form 1443 (FAR 53.301-1443). On the form, the contractor identifies its contract costs and certifies that the statement of costs has been prepared from the contractor's books and records and is correct. In addition, the contractor also makes a certification concerning encumbrances against the materials acquired for the contract.

e. The purpose of progress payments is to provide contractors with a continuing source of revenue throughout contract performance, and to ensure that a contractor will have the necessary financial resoures to meet its contractual obligations. Although some progress payment requests are audited before payment, for the most part DoD relies solely on a contractor's integrity in making the payments. When a contractor requests payments for costs not actually incurred, the Government is harmed in the following ways:

(1) The contractor has the interest free use of money to which it is not entitled and which the Government itself may have had to borrow from the public.

(2) The Government may lose its advances if the contractor goes out of business and there are no materials or completed products against which the Government may assert an interest.

(3) Honest contractors lose their faith in the system and others, who are less scrupulous, are encouraged to take advantage of the system.

7-2. Progress payment fraud indicators.

a. Firms with cash flow problems are the most likely to request funds in advance of being entitled to them. Progress payments which do not appear to coincide with the contractor's plan and capability to perform the contract are suspicious. This could indicate the contractor is claiming payment for work not yet done.

b. Another type of contractor fraud in this area is to submit a progress payment claim for materials that have not been purchased. The contractor may be issuing a check to the supplier, then holding it until the Government progress payment arrives. One way to confirm the irregularity is to check the cancellation dates on the contractor's checks. If the bank received the check about the same time or later than the contractor received the progress payment, the check was probably held.

7-3. Progress payment fraud examples.

a. A contractor entered into an agreement with the Government to refurbish/overhaul heavy equipment vehicles. The contractor instructed its employees to work on the company's private commercial projects but to use a United States government time card and punch that card as though working on a Government project. The contractor received large prepayment amounts from the Government in order to support its lagging private business. The Government's monies were then used for purposes other than to repair Government vehicles. Consequently, the government vehicles either were not repaired or did receive a few repairs but not of the extent indicated on the Government repair documents and were returned to the Government as totally overhauled or refurbished equipment. The company president pled guilty to one count of making false statements, was placed on probation for two years, and fined $5,000. The company was fined $1,000. The company and its president were debarred from future business with the Government.

b. A contractor was awarded a contract to manufacture locking devices for trigger mechanisms valued at $87,000. The former president of the company allegedly submitted false invoices as proof of costs incurred, thus receiving progress payments. The president subsequently pled guilty and was sentenced to 5 years probation, fined $10,000, ordered to make restitution of $11,000, and ordered to serve 200 hours community service. The president and the company were debarred from bidding on Government contracts during his period of probation.

Chapter 8. Fast Pay Fraud

8-1. Introduction.

a. Fast pay is a special DoD procedure that allows certain contractors to be paid for contract work prior to receipt and inspection of the product by the Government. In general, the fast pay procedure is limited to contract orders that do not exceed $25,000. The fast payment procedure set forth in FAR 13.3 is designed to reduce delivery times and to improve DoD relations with certain suppliers by expediting contract payments. The procedure provides for payment based on the contractor's submission of an invoice. That invoice is a representation by the contractor that the supplies have been delivered to a post office, common carrier, or point of first receipt.

b. Fraud in fast pay occurs when a contractor submits an invoice requesting payment for supplies that have not been shipped or delivered to the Government. If the supplies are not in transit or actually delivered at the time the contractor submits his invoice, a criminal violation has occurred because the contractor submitted a false statement. It does not matter if the supplies are subsequently delivered to the Government.

c. There are specific DoD regulations regarding fast pay. Fast pay orders are usually issued on DD Form 1155. Regardless of the contract form used for the fast pay purchase, the contract will contain the following certification clause: "The Contractor agrees that the submission of an invoice to the Government for payment is a certification that the supplies for which the Government is being billed have been shipped or delivered in accordance with shipping instructions issued by the ordering officer, in the quantities shown on the invoice, and that such supplies are in the quantity and of the quality designated by the cited purchase order."

d. The fast pay procedure benefits both the contracting community and DoD. However, contractor integrity and honesty is essential. Payments are made before DoD is in a position to verify that it has received what it bargained for. In many cases, especially where overseas deliveries are involved, it may be weeks or even months before the DoD activity that actually issued the fast pay order is advised of either a nonconforming delivery or a nonreceipt. By that time, an unscrupulous contractor may have had an opportunity to defraud the Government of thousands of dollars and to drop out of sight. Because of the potential for large losses, and the effect that such losses could have on continued use of the fast pay procedure, immediate detection of those who have abused the system is necessary.

8-2. Fast pay fraud indicators.

a. How can DoD personnel dealing with fast pay identify possible fraud? The most obvious, and sometimes most difficult, thing to do is check for the correlation between the claim for payment and the delivery of goods. Since the claim for payment and receipt of goods occurs at different locations, this will require communication between paying and receiving points. An employee who becomes suspicious should check with the receiving point to verify that the goods have arrived. Some important things to check for include: not receiving the goods at all, receiving the goods later than would be expected if they were mailed when claimed, and receiving nonconforming goods. The latter sometimes occurs because the contractor has lost the incentive to perform fully to contract specifications after it has been paid.

b. DoD personnel should also be alert for indications that the invoice submitted by the contractor is forged or altered in some way to make it appear that the goods were sent. Information on the invoice may raise questions such as shipment on a weekend or holiday.

8-3. Fast pay fraud examples.

a. A DoD supply center received a shipment of bricks instead of several electronic connection plugs allegedly shipped by the contractor. A review of 13 other contracts held by the contractor identified 8 for which payment had been made, but shipments were not received at various supply centers across the country. The value of the eight undelivered shipments was over $45,000. The contractor provided alleged proof of shipment and tracer documents which, on further investigation, were determined to be forgeries. The president of the company pled guilty to three counts each of mail fraud and false claims.

He was sentenced to concurrent three year prison terms, ordered to pay $35,915 plus interest as restitution, and fined $3,000.

b. A contractor submitted fraudulent bills of lading to obtain payment for various quantities of hardware allegedly shipped to several DoD installations throughout the United States. The contractor was shipping the product at a date far after payment was received and, in some instances, never shipped the product as indicated on the bills of lading. The company, through its president, pled guilty to 93 instances of violating the provisions of the fast pay clause. The company was fined $7,500 and ordered to pay restitution of $13,753.

Chapter 9. Bribery, Gratuities, and Conflicts of Interest

9-1. Introduction.

This chapter is dedicated to the discussion of integrity awareness. It will inform managers and employees about their responsibilities to be alert for bribe offers, to avoid the acceptance of gratuities and to recognize conflicts of interest. It also calls attention to the relationship and impact of these issues in the procurement process.

9-2. Bribery and Integrity Awareness.

Federal law prohibits both the giving or offering of anything of value to influence official actions and the acceptance of such items by Government officials. The crime is complete on making the offer to a Government employee. Acceptance of the bribe does not have to be proven. In addition to being a crime, contractors who resort to bribery and gratuities in their dealings with the Government also change the nature of their business relationships with the Government. Such unethical business practices certainly bear on the issue of contractor responsibility and possibly the retention of security clearances. Much of the government procurement system relies on contractor integrity. The corruption of the procurement system by bribery is particularly damaging. Both Federal regulations and common sense dictate that the Government avoid business dealings with contractors who do not have a satisfactory record of integrity and business ethics.

a. Manager responsibilities.

(1) Managers have many responsibilities in the area of integrity awareness. They must set examples, not only of personal integrity and high ethical standards, but also of a willingness to participate in the referral and investigation process. Too often employees are discouraged from paying attention to or reporting possible bribe situations because it is thought that subsequent actions are time-consuming and disliked by managers because of the work involved. Instead of giving any impressions that they are unsympathetic to this process, managers should actively encourage their employees to be acutely aware of potential bribe overtures, encourage their employees to report bribe attempts immediately, and indicate to their employees that they will have full support from management in any efforts to assist investigators in obtaining evidence of the offense.

(2) The tendency to treat less blatant attempts at bribery as ordinary occupational hazards or as routine innuendos which can easily be ignored or

dismissed is another reason that many bribes are not reported. Another reason might include the sentiment that refusal of a bribe offer is deterrent enough. It is part of a manager's job to ensure that these conditions are not impediments to rapid, timely, and efficient reporting of attempted bribes.

b. *Employee responsibilities.* There are some primary areas that should be focused on in discussing bribery awareness with employees. The areas of concern can be grouped into several questions.

(1) *What constitutes a bribe?* A bribe is an offer to employees of something of value to (a) do something they should not do, or (b) fail to do something they should do, in their official duties. The something of value need not be money, it can be anything of value.

(2) *When is a bribe being offered?*

(a) People who offer bribes are generally astute and aware individuals. A blatant offer is a rarity. Generally, the party offering a bribe will make subtle overtures in a conventional fashion. They may begin by discussing the employee's life style, family, or salary. They are looking for a vulnerable area where they can exploit the employee. They may seek to establish that the employee has college age children and begin discussing the high cost of education. They may learn that the employee is a new homeowner and discuss high mortgage payments and the expenses of fixing up a new home. If unable to detect an area in which the employee is particularly vulnerable, they may move to more glamorous and alluring areas; cash, cars, and travel. In summary, if the employee feels the individual is getting beyond mere civility and the professional purpose for the meeting, the employee should be alert to the possibility of a bribe attempt.

(b) The preliminary conversation may be an attempt to feel the employee out. The person attempting the bribe knows that bribe offers are illegal. They also know that an employee has an obligation to report the attempted bribe. Most importantly, the offeror of the bribe does not want to get caught. If the employee is not receptive to subtle overtures and alternative attempts fail, the person may not make any overt bribe offer. An employee has an obligation to determine the nature of the person's remarks. The very subtlety of preliminary overtures makes the employee's job of detecting a bribe a delicate one.

(3) *Why not accept a bribe?*

(a) The clear answer to this question is that the acceptance of a bribe is a criminal act that can result in prosecution, dismissal, fines, and embarrassment to the family and friends of the employee.

(b) In addition, accepting a bribe leaves one at the mercy of the person who paid it. There is no such thing as a one-time favor for one who accepts a bribe. Since the employee has committed a crime, the briber can ask anything later on under the threat of reporting the bribe, claiming it was solicited, and threatening exposure.

(4) *Why not just refuse a bribe without reporting it?*

(a) When an employee rejects a bribe, the offeror of the bribe may become concerned that the employee will report the attempt. He may

decide that the best way to deal w
employee tried to solicit a bribe a
employee prosecuted or dismissed. I
attempt, it would give credence to t
the employee has done nothing wron
investigated and could cause undue pr

(b) Furthermore, since the attempt to
itself a crime, failure to report an attempte
leaves the employee open to possible prosecutio

(c) The failure to report a bribe attempt al
again with another employee of the Government
be able to resist the offer. Further, there is no de
attempt. The offeror is free to try again without
quences. Investigation and prosecution of those w
employees and our system of Government is the onl
believing that this is the way to do business with the

c. Bribes are a reality. As a demonstration that
relates to a very real problem, a few examples of re
follow:

(1) A Navy contracting officer at a Navy supply
of conspiracy to defraud the Government in connectio
approximately $21,000 in cash and other gifts in exchang
contracts. He was sentenced to two years confinement and fi

(2) An Army contracting officer's technical representative wa ... e
to five years in prison and fined $20,000 in connection with his receip of
$3,000 in bribes from a contractor performing in excess of $3 million in Ar
contracts.

(3) An Air Force inventory management specialist was fined $1,000 and required to pay $13,500 in restitution as a result of his pleading guilty to federal charges relating to his receipt of bribes to assist a contractor in transporting material unrelated to Government contracts from the United States to a foreign country at Government expense. The contractor was also convicted of Federal charges, sentenced to six years in jail, and required to pay $40,000 in restitution.

(4) A corporate sales manager was sentenced to ten years in prison, fined $1,000, and ordered to make nearly $10,000 in restitution after conviction on multiple charges of bribing a DoD civilian employee relating to a scheme of false and inflated billings.

(5) A GS-4 file clerk was convicted of receiving approximately $50,000 in bribes from various contractors to provide them inside information used to enhance their bid packages.

9-3. Gratuities.

a. Gratuities are generally distinguished from bribery in that there is usually no request for specific improper action in exchange for what is being given. Gratuities are generally given to assist in enhancing the "relationship" between the offeror and the Government employee. This "more favorable

usiness may later move the employee to "lean" in
ded. Some contractors have actually gone so far in
budget substantial sums (in excess of $150,000 for a
eate a favorable atmosphere for their dealings with

1268

those who seek to and who do business with the
be conducted in an objective manner, above reproach, and
appearance of favoritism or other impropriety. Acceptance
y kind should be avoided in order to maintain both the form
nce of objectivity in official dealings. It should also be
at the offer or acceptance of a gratuity is a felony. Further-
vision of a gratuity is in violation of a standard clause in DoD
AR 52.203), and any claim by a contractor for reimbursement of
a gratuity is a civil and criminal violation of the False Claims Act
2324(i)).

An example of illegal gratuities can be seen in the case of a Navy
ander who was responsible for keeping track of Navy flight hours used in
ort of the filming of a commercial movie. During the filming, the com-
nder received over $5,500 from the movie company through the payment of
bogus invoice for set materials. Ultimately, the commander understated the
number of hours flown in support of the movie, which resulted in over
$600,000 in lost reimbursement from the movie company. The commander
was later convicted of receiving an illegal gratuity, fined $5,000, and placed
on three years probation. The commander and the movie company were sued
in Federal court and later settled with the repayment of $400,000 in civil
damages. It was also determined that the captain of the carrier had repeatedly
accepted gratuities from the producer during filming of the movie. The
gratuities included a $1,300 hang glider and over $400 in meals, accommodations, and transportation expenses for his family to watch the filming of the
movie. The captain received a letter of caution and was required to repay all
gratuities.

9-4. Conflicts of Interest.

Employees of DoD are generally prohibited by both criminal laws and
Standards of Conduct requirements from taking official actions that deal with
businesses in which they or their immediate families have a direct financial
interest. In addition to the general prohibition, 10 U.S.C. 2397 (as amended by
the DoD Authorization Act, P.L. 99-661), imposes other post employment
restrictions on certain procurement officials, grades GS-13 or O-4 and above.
Any DoD employee who is unsure of the conflict of interest statutes and their
personal application should consult with their organization's ethics official for
guidance.

In dealing with contractors, the Government may terminate for default
any contract that was obtained as a result of a conflict of interest. Even the
appearance of a conflict of interest, although not proven in court, has been
held to be sufficient to disqualify an otherwise eligible bidder on a contract
and, by extension, may be sufficient to terminate such a contract after award
(See Chapter 11).

All DoD employees should be alert to situations in which they suspect a possible conflict of interest and report them to appropriate authorities. The following recent cases are reflective of situations to which all DoD employees should be sensitive.

a. A buyer with the Defense Electronics Supply Center (DESC), along with his wife and sister-in-law, formed a company to represent various electronics companies in their efforts to obtain contracts with DESC. On numerous occasions, the buyer, who was responsible for bid solicitation and price determination for a selected series of electronic items, recommended awards of Government contracts to those same companies. The buyer also used an affiliate of the company he had formed to sell solenoids to DESC under approximately 50 contracts with the Government. As a DESC employee, he personally participated in the award of the contracts to his own company. No disclosure of his interest in the company was made to DESC. The buyer charged DESC over $70,000 as a result of the contracts. Based on a complaint from a co-worker at DESC, the buyer was convicted under the Federal conflict of interest statute.

b. A senior medical officer, who served as a consultant to the Surgeon General of a Military Department, recommended that DoD procure an item of medical equipment on a sole source basis from one company. At no time did the officer disclose that he was a director and major stockholder in the company. When the Surgeon General agreed to the recommendation, the officer sought to recapitalize the company in anticipation of receiving a large amount of new orders. When the officer learned that he was suspected of conflict of interest, he denied his ownership in the company and had the company prepare false and backdated documents to show that he had no involvement with the company. In addition, the officer improperly received payments from various drug companies for drug tests performed at a military hospital, but failed to disclose to the hospital the receipt of that money. The allegations in this case were made by two doctors at the hospital who became aware of the medical officer's conflicts of interest. The medical officer was convicted of Federal violations of unlawfully supplementing his income.

Chapter 10. Commercial Bribery and Kickbacks

10-1. Introduction.

The payment of bribes and kickbacks by subcontractors to DoD prime contractors or higher tier subcontractors, in connection with work on Defense contracts, constitutes a serious problem. While it is similar in many ways to the bribery of a Government official, until recently commercial bribery had not had the focus of public attention and little had been done to address the problem. However, Congress recently addressed the problem, and through the passage of the Anti-Kickback Enforcement Act of 1986 has now strengthened the law in this area. The DoD is also focusing on the problem by conducting more aggressive investigations and by working with the business community for the establishment of effective company ethics programs. However, commercial bribery and kickbacks remain a problem which is not easily detected and controlled. The courts have established the presumption that the cost of any kickback activity is always passed on to the Government.

10-2. Anti-Kickback Enforcement Act of 1986.

a. With the passage of the Anti-Kickback Enforcement Act of 1986 (PL 99-634), it is illegal for any person to provide, attempt to provide, or offer any kickback to a Government contractor or contractor employee for the purpose of improperly obtaining any favorable treatment under a Government contract. The prohibition covers any money, commission, gratuity, or any other things of value, whether provided directly or indirectly, and applies equally to persons who solicit, accept, or attempt to accept kickbacks. The legislation further prohibits the inclusion of any kickback amounts in the contract price charged by a contractor.

b. In addition to providing criminal penalties, which include imprisonment for up to 10 years, the legislation also provides for civil action and administrative offsets when illegal kickbacks are involved. In a civil action, the United States may recover a penalty of twice the amount of the kickback plus $10,000 for each kickback payment. The Government contracting officer may also administratively offset the amount of any kickback against any moneys owed by the United States under the contract.

c. The Act also requires contractors to establish internal programs to detect and prevent kickback activity. Contractors are required to report any kickback activity to the Inspector General, DoD, and to cooperate fully in any investigation regarding kickbacks. Contractors are also required to allow the Inspector General, DoD, access to facilities and to audit books and records in order to determine compliance with the Act.

10-3. Other Considerations.

a. In addition to the Anti-Kickback Enforcement Act, instances of commercial bribery may also involve various other criminal statutes. The individuals paying and/or receiving the bribes may be in violation of the statute dealing with conspiracy to defraud the Government (18 U.S.C. 371), may have made false statements or certifications under the contract (18 U.S.C. 1001), or violated various other Federal or state statutes.

b. The illegal kickbacks not only affect the integrity of the procurement process and inflate Government costs, but, in some instances, the kickbacks paid may be so significant they affect the subcontractor's performance. In such cases, contract specifications may not be met or there are other performance failures due to underfunding, which results in deliveries being delayed or prevented and the ultimate user being deprived of the contracted items.

10-4. Kickback Case Examples.

A quick look at some case examples provides a clear picture of the extent to which the payments affect DoD contracts.

a. Six officials of a DoD subcontractor pled guilty to Federal charges in connection with kickback schemes involving an executive vice president of a major Defense prime contractor who, along with his assistant, received approximately $5 million in kickbacks. The corporate officer fled the country following his indictment and remains a fugitive from justice.

b. In another case, 26 people were convicted in connection with a kickback scheme operated within a major shipbuilding contractor. The scheme involved approximately $1 million in kickbacks.

c. A vice president of an advertising firm in New York City pled guilty to receiving illegal kickbacks of $60,000 in connection with the company's contract to provide national advertising for the United States Army.

d. In the aerospace industry, investigations have resulted in multiple convictions of prime contractor employees who have received kickbacks. The investigations, which developed evidence of over 70 companies where buyers for the prime contractor had received kickbacks, led the United States Attorney controlling the investigation to testify before Congress that, "It is my opinion that kickbacks on defense subcontracts are a pervasive longstanding practice which has corrupted the subcontracting process at most, if not all, defense contractors . . . ."

Chapter 11. Civil, Contractual, and Administrative Remedies for Fraud

11-1. Introduction.

a. Traditionally, Government contracting officials have relied on the criminal justice system to police fraud by DoD contractors. The reliance included forbearance from certain administrative and contractual actions until the criminal case was completed. However, the reliance was often misplaced for a number of reasons.

b. First, criminal cases must be proven beyond a reasonable doubt. While there may be insufficient information to warrant a criminal conviction, contracting officials do not need the level of proof in order to take administrative and contractual actions.

c. Second, even if criminal action is taken, many cases are plea bargained to lesser offenses. This tends to mislead people into believing that a less serious offense was proven, or that less fraudulent activity took place than really did. An example of the confusion comes from one documented case in which four nonappropriated fund officials pled guilty to accepting bribes from a contractor. The contractor, however, pled guilty to only a misdemeanor for trespassing on a Federal reservation. Contracting officials, when confronted with the fact that the contractor had been convicted of only a misdemeanor, believed that the contractor's actions had not been very serious in nature. The facts showed the seriousness of the actions despite the plea to only a minor infraction of the law.

d. Third, many contracting officials are not aware of the fact that prosecutors must set priorities for the use of their resources, and, in doing so, they are not able to prosecute every case that is brought to their attention by investigators. The decision not to prosecute a case is not always based on the failure to establish that wrongdoing has taken place. There are instances when the investigators prove a crime took place, but the circumstances do not warrant taking judicial action at that time. When a case has been declined for prosecution, contracting officials should consider the facts established by the proof the investigator has gathered to determine whether alternative action is warranted by them.

e. Fourth, the criminal justice system does not have as one of its functions the recoupment of assets lost during a fraud, or the protection of the procurement system from future dealings with the contractors who practice deception. Although a company might be convicted of or plead guilty to a crime, this does not, without action by contracting officials, prevent the company from obtaining future contracts, recoup monies paid to the contractor due to fraud, or obtain the desired or intended performance under the contract.

f. Finally, DoD officials and not the DOJ are responsible for the integrity of the DoD contracting and procurement process. The FAR and DoD implementing regulations require contracting officials to take positive action on any evidence of contractor impropriety and nonresponsibility. Therefore, it is necessary for managers and contracting officials to be aware of and effectively use the civil, administrative, and contractual powers and remedies which are available to protect the Government, to prevent further loss to the Government, and to recover Government assets and funds lost through fraud.

11-2. Coordinated approach to remedies.

a. Officials of DoD are responsible for the integrity of DoD contracts and must be prepared to take immediate action to protect the Government. This often includes positive action while a criminal investigation is under way and before an indictment or conviction has been obtained. Criminal cases often take years to complete and DoD can take many contractual and administrative actions on evidence less than that necessary for a conviction. Timely action by a contracting official, such as pre-indictment suspension or a contract default termination, will aid the Government by precluding the contractor from continuing to benefit while an investigation is under way.

b. By taking a coordinated approach to criminal, civil, contractual, and administrative actions, the Government is often able to induce guilty contractors into pleading guilty more quickly. Simultaneous consideration of all remedies available to DoD and DOJ also enables the Government and the court to fashion a single comprehensive remedy package that will punish the contractor, protect the Government from further harm, and make the Government whole from any losses suffered.

c. Early action by contracting officials is important. The action must be coordinated with a variety of officials in both DoD and DOJ. The coordination is essential to ensure that none of the actions taken will adversely affect the ability of the Government to pursue any of the other actions available. An example of how the coordination of remedies process can work is demonstrated by a recent case involving a major DoD contractor who was investigated for engaging in product substitution, cost mischarging, and defective pricing. As a result of coordinated efforts by contracting officials, investigators, the DOJ, and other DoD officials, the following results were achieved:

(1) Suspension of the contractor during the investigation to prevent the award of additional or follow-on contracts (which would have required a finding of responsibility and putting additional funds at risk).

(2) Guilty plea by the contractor to numerous felonies, resulting in criminal fines of $380,000 being paid by the contractor.

(3) Agreement by the contractor to pay restitution of over $160,000 and civil damages of over $1.6 million.

(4) Agreement by the contractor to make significant changes in its cost accounting and quality assurance procedures.

(5) Dismissal of numerous employees by the contractor for their participation in the fraud, helping to assure the Government that a repeat of the fraud was unlikely.

d. The Secretary of Defense issued DoD Directive 7050.5, "Coordination of Remedies for Fraud and Corruption Related to Procurement Activities," dated June 28, 1985, to ensure that the type of coordination discussed above takes place. The Directive requires that each Military Department and Defense Agency establish a centralized point of coordination for criminal, civil, contractual, and administrative actions in contract fraud and corruption cases. The following are some of the centralized points of coordination established under that Directive:

(1) Army—Office of the Judge Advocate General, Procurement Fraud Division. (Army Regulation 27-21)

(2) Navy—Office of the Naval Inspector General, Investigative Oversight Division (NOP-81).

(3) Air Force—Office of the Inspector General of the Air Force, Office of Review and Oversight. (Air Force Regulation 123-2)

(4) Defense Logistics Agency—Office of the General Counsel, Associate Counsel Logistics Services.

e. The Directive mentioned above requires that the centralized points of coordination be informed by the Defense criminal investigative organizations each time they open a significant investigation involving fraud or corruption in procurement or procurement related activities. The centralized point of coordination is then responsible for ensuring that a remedies plan is prepared, and updated as needed, taking into account the available remedies and the timing of their use. The coordination will involve communication between the centralized point of coordination and various officials in the investigative, prosecutive, program, and procurement areas of concern to balance the needs of each and foster communication between them. Through this process, the Government will be able to use fully the variety of remedies available for fraud and do so in a more efficient and effective manner.

f. The following segments contain a brief discussion of the many remedies for fraud that can be used by the Government. A number of these remedies have been created or changed by recent legislative action.

11-3. Available remedies.

The Government has the right to take action against contractors who engage in fraudulent activities. The Government right is based on several statutory grounds. Many of the civil actions taken based on those statutes are filed by the DOJ and may be filed in conjunction with, after, or instead of a criminal prosecution.

Under contract law and principles, the Government has the right to insist on certain standards of responsibility and business integrity from its contractors. The violation of any of those principles gives the Government the right to take a variety of actions. These actions may also be taken in conjunction with, after, or instead of a criminal prosecution.

a. Civil False Claims Act.

(1) The submission of a false claim to the Government can make a contractor liable to the Government, both criminally and civilly. The Civil False Claims Act, 31 U.S.C. 3729-3731, establishes liability for false claims. The law provides for the Government to be able to recover penalties and damages for false claims in addition to or instead of any criminal sanctions. Through such actions, the Government can recover assets lost through fraud.

(2) The statute, as recently amended, provides for penalties of $5,000 to $10,000 per false claim (previously the penalty was $2,000 per claim). Each invoice submitted by a contractor could, under appropriate circumstances, be considered as a false claim for purposes of the statute. The Government can also recover treble damages (previously it was double damages) or three times the amount of a false claim. The Government must actually suffer monetary damages to collect under that portion of the statute but not to have the civil penalties assessed. The Government is precluded from intentionally paying a claim it knows is false merely to activate the damages portion of the statute.

(3) The Government must prove, by a preponderance of the evidence, that the contractor knowingly submitted a false claim. Knowing submission means actual knowledge or deliberate ignorance of the truth (failure to take reasonable steps to find out if the claim is truthful) or reckless disregard of the truth (failure to pursue indications of falsity to find out the truth). It is not necessary to show that the contractor acted with the specific intention to defraud the Government.

b. Program Fraud Civil Remedies Act.

(1) This recently enacted law allows Federal agencies to impose administratively penalties and damages for all false claims where the damages are under $150,000, and all false statements. Government agencies are, at this writing, in the process of establishing administrative procedures to implement the provisions of the law. The procedures will be designed to protect the interests and rights of both the contractors and the Government in the determination of liability and the amount of any penalties and damages assessed against a contractor.

(2) The law provides for a penalty of $5,000 per false claim or false statement. Damages for false claims are double the amount of the provable loss (rather than the treble damages of the Civil False Claims Act which requires judicial action to obtain). The standard of proof which must be met by the Government in establishing the liability of a contractor under this law is the same as that under the Civil False Claims Act, a knowing submission of the false claim or statement.

c. Contract Disputes Act. Under the Civil False Claims Act and the Program Fraud Civil Remedies Act, the Government may only recover damages when they have actually been suffered, e.g., when a false claim is paid.

The Government is limited to the assertion of the appropriate penalty if an audit or investigation determines that a claim or statement is false and no payment is made. Under the Contract Disputes Act, 41 U.S.C. 604, a contractor is liable to the Government for the amount of any unsupported part of a claim plus the costs of reviewing the claim, if the claim is based even in part on fraud or misrepresentation of fact. The Government does not have to pay the claim in order to recover.

d. *Forfeiture of Fraudulent Claims.* The U.S. Court of Claims can, under 27 U.S.C. 2514, order the forfeiture of the entire amount of a claim in which it judges the proof, statement, establishment, or allowance thereof is based on a fraud or attempted fraud by a contractor. The Government does not have to pay a claim first for the statute to be operative. A contractor making a claim, which the contracting officer denies, risks losing the entire claim by going to the Court of Claims if the claim is based even in part on fraud.

e. *Termination for Default.*

(1) The submission of a false claim or statement on a contract is clear evidence of a contractor's nonresponsibility and failure to perform on a contract. The contracting officer has the right and obligation to terminate a contract for default under those circumstances. There is no requirement that a conviction take place for such a termination. Terminations for convenience are never appropriate when fraud is present on a contract.

(2) Furthermore, certain improper actions also give rise to a statutory right to terminate for default. The Government has the right to terminate a contract for default whenever a contractor offers a gratuity to a Government employee. The right is set forth in 10 U.S.C. 2207, and implemented in FAR 52.203-3 and DFAR Appendix D. The Government also has the right under those same provisions, in addition to all other default remedies, to penalize the contractor in the amount of three to ten times the value of the gratuity. The Navy recently convened an ad hoc gratuities board and, using the procedures in DFAR Appendix D, assessed a penalty of over $650,000 against a major DoD contractor after it was established the contractor had paid over $65,000 in gratuities to Navy personnel.

f. *Rescission of Contracts.*

(1) Rescission is a common law remedy in contracts. The remedy allows for the return of both parties to their position before the contract; that is, the contract is void and treated as if it were so from the start. The remedy has been used by the Government and upheld by the courts most frequently when there is fraud or corruption involved in the obtaining or award stage of the contract.

(2) The Government also has a right under 18 U.S.C. 218 to rescind a contract administratively under certain circumstances. The statute allows the Government to administratively rescind a contract when there has been a final conviction for bribery, gratuities, or conflicts of interest in connection with the award of a contract. The provisions of FAR Subpart 3.7 set forth in the procedures developed to accomplish the administrative voiding and rescission of contracts.

(3) A recent case serves to illustrate the use of the above provisions. The case involved a Government employee who had been awarding contracts to firms in which the employee held a financial interest. The financial interest was held in the names of aliases used by the employee to conceal any interest from audit officials reviewing the contractors. All of the contracts awarded to the contractors in which the employee held a financial interest were rescinded.

g. *Denial of Claims.* Contracting officials do not have the authority to pay claims where there is a reasonable suspicion that the claim is tainted by fraud. The Contract Disputes Act, at 41 U.S.C. 605, contains provisions under which DoD is not authorized to ". . . administer, settle, compromise or otherwise adjust any claim involving fraud." Therefore, whenever fraud is detected in a claim, contracting officials should not take any further action on any portion of the claim without coordination with DOJ. (FAR 33.009, 33.010)

h. *Findings of Nonresponsibility.* The provisions of the FAR at Subpart 9.1 state that contracts may only be awarded to responsible contractors. Contractors are required to demonstrate affirmatively their responsibility, including a satisfactory record of integrity and business ethics. Any evidence of fraud by a contractor is clearly a matter which should be considered by contracting officers in making responsibility determinations.

i. *Suspension and Debarment.*

(1) Contractors may be precluded from doing business with the Government for the commission of fraud or for various other actions indicating a lack of business integrity. The procedures for accomplishing this are found in the FAR Subpart 9.4. The Government has never had a suspension or debarment action challenged successfully so long as those procedures are followed.

(2) Suspension is an interim measure, based on adequate evidence of fraud, designated to protect the Government while a criminal investigation or trial is under way and evidence of fraud is present. A contractor may be suspended for up to 18 months while an investigation is under way. Once an indictment or civil suit is filed, the contractor can remain suspended until the completion of all legal proceedings.

(3) Debarment is a final determination of a contractor's nonresponsibility. A contractor can be debarred, based on a conviction of a crime, or on sufficient evidence that a contractor has repeatedly failed to perform properly or has committed acts which indicate a lack of business integrity and honesty. Debarment can be in effect for up to three years. A contracting officer can recommend the debarment of companies and individuals, and can impute the conduct of certain key individuals in a company to that company in recommending its debarment.

(4) Contracting offficers must forward reports of improper contractor activity to the suspension and debarment authority at the earliest opportunity in order for suspension and debarment to be effective. Reporting procedures are set forth in the DoD FAR Supplement Subsection 9.472.

(5) Each of the Military Departments and DLA require contractors to certify, as part of their bid or proposal package, that the contractor and its owners, officers, and directors are not on the suspended and debarred bidders list.

j. Disallowance of Legal Costs. Contractors who are found to have engaged in fraud on cost type contracts are not entitled, under FAR 31.205-5, to recover legal and administrative costs incurred in unsuccessfully defending against Government action. While an investigation is under way, it is important for contracting officers to take prompt action to require contractors to identify such costs as they are incurred. The contracting officer should then deny claims for such costs in all appropriate cases, which will be made easier by their earlier identification by the contractor.

k. Prohibition on Employment of Certain Felons. The employment of felons convicted of DoD contract related felonies is prohibited by 10 U.S.C. 2408. The statute states that any person convicted of a felony arising out of a Defense contract cannot work in a management or supervisory capacity on any Defense contract for a period of not less than one year from the date of conviction. Any contractor who knowingly employs such a person can be fined up to $500,000. Contracting officials should be alert to whether or not persons prohibited by the statute are involved in management or supervision of Defense contracts and report such instances through appropriate channels to the Defense criminal investigative organizations for action.

l. Contract Penalties for False Claims and Defective Pricing. Recently enacted Federal statutes allow for contract penalties for claims for unallowable costs and defective pricing. Under 10 U.S.C. 2324, a contractual penalty can be assessed whenever a contractor submits a claim for direct or indirect cost, when such a cost is specifically ruled unallowable by either statute or regulation. (See also DFAR Supplement Subpart 31.70) Similarly, 10 U.S.C. 2306a(e) authorizes a penalty for the knowing submission of defective cost or pricing data. Because violations of those statutes may also be a violation of various criminal and civil fraud laws, contracting officer actions should be coordinated with the centralized points for coordination of procurement fraud remedies and the DOJ.

m. Administrative Penalties for Conflicts of Interest. Under the provisions of 10 U.S.C. Sections 2397b and c, major DoD contractors are prohibited from employing or paying any gift, gratuity, or other form of compensation over $250 to certain covered DoD officials for a period of two years after the DoD official leaves the Government. Those DoD officials are primarily persons in grades GS-13/0-4 and above who were employed as DoD procurement officials at sites or plants owned by the contractor. Contractors who knowingly pay such compensation are subject to a $500,000 civil fine and may also be required to pay up to $100,000 in liquidated damages. Major DoD contractors are also required to file an annual report with DoD which lists all compensation paid to all former employees for a period of two years after the employee leaves DoD. Failure to file an accurate report can result in an administrative penalty of $10,000.

11-4. Personnel actions.

The Government has a variety of remedial actions it can take against employees who have colluded with contractors in fraudulent conduct or when an employee has engaged in improper actions (such as accepting or soliciting bribes or gratuities, or engaging in conflicts of interest). Some of these remedies include:

a. *Termination.* The receipt of a bribe or gratuity, or actions indicating a personal conflict of interest, can justify the immediate termination of a Federal employee. Managers should consider the gravity of the offense and its impact on the continued ability of the employee to carry out responsibilities of the position in deciding whether or not to retain employees found to have engaged in activities such as those discussed above.

b. *Revocation of a Contracting Officer's Warrant.* Contracting officers who engage in improper conduct can lose their right to contract on behalf of the Government. One contracting officer who knowingly accelerated the award of a contract to a company about to be suspended lost the authority to contract on behalf of the Government. Another contracting officer who engaged in a conspiracy to defraud the Government by preventing proper contract administration and approving false billings also lost the warrant given by the Government.

c. *Recoupment of Funds Lost.* Whenever a contractor gives a bribe or gratuity to a Government employee, both the contractor and the employee are jointly liable to the Government for an amount equal to the value of the bribe or gratuity. Action should be taken to deduct the value of any such bribe or gratuity from the pension contributions of the employee, prior to the termination of the employee (if termination action is taken). Similar actions can be taken against military personnel and retirees.

d. *Administrative Penalties for Conflicts of Interest.* Under the provisions of 10 U.S.C. 2397a and b, certain DoD procurement officials can face civil and administrative fines and penalties regarding improper negotiation regarding employment with DoD contractors, and the acceptance of compensation from such contractors. Generally, employees in grades GS-13/0-4 and above who are employed in a procurement function must immediately report any negotiations with a DoD contractor regarding future employment. Failure to report immediately the existence of negotiations, or failure to disqualify oneself from any official dealings with the contractor while such negotiations are under consideration can result in up to $20,000 in administrative penalties and a 10 year bar on employment with the contractor. Further restrictions apply to DoD employees, in grades GS-13/0-4 and above, who are engaged in a procurement function and are employed in plants owned or operated by a DoD contractor. Such employees are prohibited from accepting any employment, or any form of consideration over $250, from the contractor for a period of two years after leaving DoD. Acceptance of any form of compensation can result in a civil fine of up to $250,000.

Chapter 12. Voluntary Disclosure of Fraud

12-1. Introduction.

a. In July 1986, the Deputy Secretary of Defense announced a DoD program encouraging Defense contractors to disclose internally identified incidents involving problems affecting the acquisition process. The program encourages that disclosures of problems not involving fraud be made to the appropriate contracting officer or to DCAA. However, disclosures which involve potential criminal or civil fraud issues are to be directed to the

Assistant Inspector General for Criminal Investigations Policy and Oversight, OIG, DoD.

b. The program does not provide the disclosing contractor with any guarantees that it will not be suspended or debarred by DoD, or that it will not be prosecuted by the Department of Justice. On the other hand, the program clearly intends that both Departments will recognize voluntary disclosure, accompanied by contractor cooperation, corrective action, and restitution, as significant factors in making decisions regarding appropriate remedies.

c. In making voluntary disclosures, contractors are advised that certain "key elements" should be included in their report to DoD. The elements are designed to require the revelation of all facts that will assist the DoD in conducting its own investigation, which will seek to verify the contractor's findings. The verification process will typically require DCAA auditors to test the cost conclusions of the report, and criminal investigators to analyze the issue of whether intent to defraud is present.

d. Appendix A contains a more detailed description of the DoD voluntary disclosure program and Appendix B states the Department of Justice policy on the program.

Appendix A

THE DEPUTY SECRETARY OF DEFENSE

WASHINGTON, D.C. 20301

24 JUL 1986

Dear

During the past few years, public and congressional interest in the Department of Defense management of its programs and operations has remained intense. This is nowhere more true than in the acquisition area. These issues continue to command our personal attention and involvement. Many of the problems in the acquisition area came to light because of audits and investigations conducted by the Department of Defense. We are committed to detecting and eliminating inefficiency and improper practices in our acquisition process; we believe that most Defense contractors have institutional commitments to these same goals.

To demonstrate this commitment, a number of major Defense contractors have adopted a policy of voluntarily disclosing problems affecting their corporate contractual relationship with the Department of Defense. These disclosures are made by the contractor, without an advance agreement regarding possible Department of Defense resolution of the matter. The contractors understand the Department's view that early voluntary disclosure, coupled with full cooperation and complete access to necessary records, are strong indications of an attitude of contractor integrity even in the wake of disclosures of potential criminal liability. We will consider such cooperation as an important factor in any decisions that the Department takes in the matter.

I encourage you to consider adopting a policy of voluntary disclosure as a central part of your corporate integrity program. Matters not involving potential criminal issues should be presented to the appropriate contracting officer or Defense Contract Audit Agency auditor. Matters involving potential criminal or civil fraud issues should be directed to the Deputy Inspector General, Department of Defense.

A description of the Department of Defense program for voluntary disclosures is enclosed herewith for your consideration.

I believe that your corporate commitment to complete and timely disclosures of irregularities, regardless of their magnitude, is essential to increasing confidence in our ability to provide for the national defense effectively and efficiently.

Sincerely,

/s/

William H. Taft, IV

Enclosure

Department of Defense Program for Voluntary Disclosures of Possible Fraud by Defense Contractors

Background

Officials within the Department of Defense (DoD) have been approached by a number of contractors to determine the conditions and agreements that might be structured with the Government if a contractor sought to disclose voluntarily information that might expose the contractor to liability under Federal statutes relating to criminal and civil fraud. From the Department's perspective, the voluntary disclosure of information otherwise unknown to the Government, and contractor cooperation in an ensuing investigation, offers a number of significant advantages:

• the Government is likely to recoup losses of which it might otherwise be unaware;

• limited detection assets within the Government are augmented by contractor resources;

• consideration of appropriate remedies can be expedited by both DoD and Department of Justice when adversarial tensions are relaxed;

• voluntary disclosure and cooperation are indicators of contractor integrity; and

• contractors engaging in voluntary disclosure are more likely to institute corrective actions to prevent recurrence of disclosed problems.

Requirements on Contractors

Department of Defense recognition of a contractor as a "volunteer" will depend on four key factors:

1. The disclosure must not be triggered by the contractor's recognition that the underlying facts are about to be discovered by the Government through audit, investigation, or contract administration efforts or reported to the Government by third parties.

2. The disclosure must be on behalf of the business entity, in contrast to admissions by individual officials or employees.

3. Prompt and complete corrective action, including disciplinary action and restitution to the Government where appropriate, must be taken by the contractor in response to the matters disclosed.

4. After disclosure, the contractor must cooperate fully with the government in any ensuing investigation or audit.

Defining DoD expectations of "cooperation" in any situation will depend on the individual facts or circumstances underlying the disclosure. However, DoD may enter into a written agreement with any contractor seeking to make a voluntary disclosure where such an agreement will facilitate follow-on action without improperly limiting the responsibilities of the Government. This agreement, which may be coordinated with the Department of Justice, will describe the types of documents and evidence to be provided to DoD and will resolve any issues related to interviews, privileges, or other legal concerns which may affect the DoD ability to obtain all relevant facts in a timely manner.

Department of Defense Actions

If a contractor is recognized as a "volunteer" based on the preceding criteria, the DoD is prepared to undertake the following:

1. Identify one of the Military Departments or the Defense Logistics Agency as the cognizant DoD component to represent DoD for suspension/debarment purposes, i.e., to assess contractor integrity in light of the disclosures. Early identification of the appropriate DoD component will permit the contractor, from the outset of its cooperation, to provide relevant information relating to contractor integrity and management controls, e.g., internal controls, corrective measures, or disciplinary action taken as a result of the information disclosed.

2. The DoD, through the Office of the Inspector General and in cooperation with the Department of Justice, will seek to expedite the completion of any investigation and audit conducted in response to a voluntary disclosure, thereby minimizing the period of time necessary for identification of remedies deemed appropriate by the Government.

3. Advise the Department of Justice of the complete nature of the voluntary disclosure, the extent of contractor cooperation and the types of corrective action instituted by the contractor. As always, any determinations of appropriate criminal and civil fraud sanctions will be the ultimate prerogative of the Department of Justice.

Commencing a Voluntary Disclosure

Since initial judgments as to appropriate investigative and audit resources will be necessary in any voluntary disclosure involving possible fraud, the initial contact with the DoD on fraud-related disclosures should be with the Office of the Inspector General.

While the Office of the Inspector General will be the initial point of contact for fraud-related disclosures, other DoD components are expected to be advised or involved as circumstances warrant. Besides the Office of General

Counsel, DoD, and the appropriate suspension/ debarment authority, other DoD components that expectedly would be advised, or involved, in voluntary disclosures are the Office of the Assistant Secretary of Defense (Acquisition and Logistics) and the Defense Contract Audit Agency.

The Office of the Inspector General element that will serve as the initial point of contact is:

Assistant Inspector General for Criminal Investigations Policy and
Oversight
400 Army Navy Drive
Room 1037
Arlington, Virginia 22202
Telephone: 202-694-8958

Appendix B

Office of the Attorney General
Washington, D.C. 20530
February 5, 1987

Hon. William Howard Taft IV
Deputy Secretary of Defense
U.S. Department of Defense
The Pentagon
Washington, D.C. 20301

Dear Will:

Thank you for your letter of 18 September 1986 describing the voluntary disclosure initiative of the Defense Department. You have my assurance that the Department of Justice fully supports this program and will work with the Department of Defense for its successful implementation.

I am encouraged that many defense contractors are adopting compliance programs and disclosing problems affecting defense contracts. The willingness of contractors to adopt self-policing programs may be regarded as a constructive product of our joint efforts in uncovering and successfully prosecuting, both criminally and civilly, major contract frauds over the past several years. Your voluntary disclosure program will further encourage corporate good citizenship.

You express the view that it would be helpful for the Department of Justice to provide guidance on voluntary disclosures. I agree that such guidance would be both useful and appropriate.

As you are undoubtedly aware, it is our practice to take into consideration factors relating to the integrity of a company in assessing whether to bring charges. A voluntary corporate disclosure of wrongdoing is rarely the sole basis for a decision not to prosecute; however, it is one of a number of factors we view as relevant to the charging decision. Others include the strength of the evidence, indicia of *scienter,* level of employee or management involved, pervasiveness of the conduct, dollar impact on the taxpayers, the quality of cooperation during the investigation, the nature of the remedial actions taken in the wake of the discovery of misconduct, and the quality of the company's efforts to prevent misconduct in the first instance by a meaningful compliance program—implemented in fact, as well as recorded on paper.

Clearly, our objective is to bring prosecutions that will have a deterrent impact. At the same time we recognize the desirability of prosecutive judgments, whether at the charging stage, the plea stage, or the sentencing stage of the criminal justice process, which will encourage contractors to initiate compliance programs.

In prosecuting corporations, particularly defense contractors, deterrence is a most significant factor. Through criminal prosecution and punishment, other contractors are put on notice as to the requirements of law and encouraged to modify their behavior to conduct business in an honest and non-criminal manner. Prosecutions of contractor corporations create an incentive for management to establish preventive measures and establish clear standards of right and wrong for their employees.

On the other hand, contractors that make serious and responsible efforts to comply with the law and promptly disclose misconduct should not be discouraged from those practices by inflexible prosecutive policies. In some self-disclosure situations, criminal prosecution of the self-disclosing contractor could undermine our law enforcement objectives and would therefore be inappropriate.

With these general objectives in mind, we will be preparing guidance for our United States Attorneys in the form of a supplement to the *United States Attorneys Manual.* I will make sure you have a copy of the supplement as soon as it is issued.

On the civil side, the decision whether to pursue a False Claims Act case is governed by many of the same considerations I have just outlined. Of course, we are also interested in attempting to recover the actual funds defrauded from the Government, as well as using the "penalty" provisions of the Act to recover funds reflecting other losses to the Government, such as interest and the cost of investigations. As you know, the Congress recently passed and the President signed the False Claims Act Amendments of 1986, P.L. 99-562 (October 27, 1986). Those Amendments increase the damages the United States is entitled to recover from double damages to triple damages and the forfeiture amount from $2000 per false claim to not less than $5000 and not more than $10,000 per false claim. The Amendments specifically provide, however, that if prior to becoming aware of an ongoing investigation into a matter, a person provides appropriate investigating officials with all the information in their possession about the fraud within 30 days of discovery and fully cooperates with the Government's investigation, the court may reduce damages from triple to no less than double. Thus, on the civil side, we have a well defined statutory basis providing not only an incentive to your announced self-disclosure policy, but also appropriate treatment for persons or corporations that promptly disclose wrongdoing and cooperate with the Government.

Apart from the questions of prosecutorial judgment, I believe it is important that the Defense Department coordinate closely with the Justice

Department in administering its voluntary disclosure program. Accordingly, we have provided each United States Attorney with a copy of your July 1986 release. In addition, to assure that coordination between our Departments is properly maintained, our Defense Procurement Fraud Unit in the Criminal Division will continue as the contact point to review all voluntary disclosure issues on behalf of the Department of Justice. To assure consistency of decision making, the Defense Procurement Fraud Unit will also have responsibility for making or reviewing prosecutive decisions in cases involving voluntary disclosure by defense contractors.

I hope these remarks provide some guidance for the voluntary disclosure initiative and will aid in a successful self-policing and self-disclosure program for the industry. We look forward to our continued cooperation and success in combatting fraud in defense procurement.

Sincerely,

/s/

Arnold I. Burns

Deputy Attorney General

Handbook on Labor Fraud Indicators (Excerpted from a Handbook by the DOD Inspector General, August 1985)

The detection and elimination of fraud are critical elements in every government auditor's job. The auditor must test for and identify fraud indicators. A fraud indicator means that fraud may be present. It is not proof that fraud is present.

Labor cost that is charged either directly or indirectly to government contracts is a prime area of concern. Labor is usually the most significant cost charged to a government contract and, often, the most difficult to review.

The basic concern in every labor review is the same—Did the employee charge the project that was worked on? The work being performed determines how the cost is charged. The labor charge should not be based on a predetermined contractor policy or on an employee labor classification. Thus, it is important for the auditor to know the contractor. The auditor must understand the contractor's labor accounting system in order to evaluate the adequacy of the contractor's internal controls.

The key element in any labor review is the determination of the government's vulnerability to labor fraud and the risk assumed at the contractor's location. The Defense Contract Audit Agency (DCAA) published DCAAP 7641.81, Guidelines for a Comprehensive Audit of Labor Costs, in September 1984. This pamphlet offers excellent guidance for conducting labor audits and provides detailed information on critical area-risk and vulnerability analysis. The auditors must follow this analysis to determine whether comprehensive or traditional labor audit techniques are required.

Comprehensive audit techniques focus on a preinterview analysis of labor-charging patterns and employee interviews. Traditional audit techniques include labor reconciliations and employee floorchecks. In a comprehensive audit technique the employee interview covers a specific time period and focuses on a labor-charging pattern. The traditional floorcheck is used primarily to check employee labor-charging at a certain point in order to verify that the labor is charged to the work being performed. The floorcheck and the interview test the internal controls on labor recording.

Two key elements are necessary to conduct successful interviews. First, an interview should never be conducted without adequate preinterview analysis. Second, supporting documentation must be obtained, such as work orders, employee time logs, notes, or letters for any potential audit findings disclosed during the interview. This is why it is important for the interview to be conducted at the employee's work station. In addition to risk and vulnerability analysis, DCAAP 7641.81 provides excellent guidance on preliminary audit effort, audit techniques, and audit results reporting.

This handbook discusses the use of comprehensive labor audit techniques, such as preinterview analysis and employee interviews. The auditor needs to have a working understanding of the various labor audit techniques that are essential to a successful review for fraud indicators.

The review of labor provides the auditor an opportunity to exercise his or her creativity and ingenuity. This effort must be approached with an air of professional skepticism. There are no canned audit programs to find fraud indicators. The key to finding them is to think fraud, look for fraud indicators, and find them.

This handbook is designed to raise the auditors' level of fraud recognition and to get them to think fraud. The scenarios on labor mischarging highlight some of the fraud indicators auditors may find.

LABOR FRAUD INDICATORS

1. Mischarging of Labor Costs—Independent Research and Development

The Scenario. At a major contractor location, the auditor monitors charges to Independent Research and Development (IR&D) projects. In mid-October, only two months before year-end, a change in the contractor's time-charging pattern alerts the auditor to a possible problem. In four engineering design cost centers, a high number of employees are charging either 20 or 24 hours per week to their IR&D projects. In addition, the auditor notes a decrease in total hours charged to IR&D projects for the pay period.

The auditor presents this information to the audit supervisor who concurs with the auditor's recommendation to expand the scope of the review. The supervisor also suggests that the auditor check the idle time charges in the four cost centers. A review of idle time charges discloses some increase but not enough to account for the total decrease in IR&D charging.

A *preinterview analysis* discloses two distinct charging patterns. In two of the cost centers, engineers are charging four hours a day to IR&D and 4 hours to idle time. In the other two cost centers, engineers are charging three days (24 hours) a week to the IR&D projects and two days (16 hours) per week to a cost plus fixed fee contract.

Audit interviews with a number of the employees confirmed that the engineers had been directed to continue working on their current IR&D projects but to split their time since the IR&D projects were near or over budget.

Fraud Indicators:

• Distinctive labor-charging patterns on IR&D projects.

• Sudden, significant decreases in IR&D charging.

- Significant increases in charging to overhead accounts (idle time, downtime, nonapplied time).

- Significant increases in charging to cost type contracts.

- A high percentage of indirect charging employees.

- Employee reclassifications from direct charge to indirect.

- Misclassified IR&D projects.

General Comments. Because the IR&D is such a sensitive area, it requires periodic attention by the auditor. Many classic mischarging schemes have involved IR&D projects. Large contractors will often tell you that there is no incentive to mischarge IR&D since it goes over ceiling anyway. But often, midmanagement employees are evaluated on whether they complete their projects within budget. This emphasis provides sufficient motive and pressure to mischarge labor costs.

Changes in labor-charging patterns on IR&D programs should alert the auditor to mischarging problems. Consistent splitting of labor charges, whether it is by days or hours, usually indicates that some type of problem exists. Hence, the auditor must be alert for IR&D projects that run concurrently with design and development contracts and that have employees working on IR&D which has been improperly classified as an indirect charge. In reviewing this area, the auditor must be sure to review and understand the contractor's policy for classifying labor cost as direct versus indirect. All personnel, excluding some clerical effort, who work on IR&D projects should charge labor costs directly to the IR&D project and not to overhead or to some other general and administrative (G&A) account.

Misclassified IR&D projects may be the most common form of mischarging. Often these projects are called engineering development projects, manufacturing development programs, or planning projects and are charged indirectly to the U.S. Government through overhead allocations or G&A accounts. This type of review will require technical expertise to determine the true nature of the efforts being performed. The nature of the work performed determines how it should be charged, not a predetermined account description.

One area which cannot be overlooked or underestimated in reviewing IR&D is the necessity for understanding definitions. The contract auditor must be familiar with the Federal Acquisition Regulation (FAR) definitions. Information on the definitions and their interpretations is included in DCAAP 7641.81.

The monitoring of labor charges to IR&D projects is one of the most effective audit procedures. This may be accomplished by charting labor hours charged by IR&D projects on a weekly or biweekly basis. Charting makes the charging patterns visible and highlights any aberrations or areas for additional review. The auditor can also review charges by checking mismatched (uncleared) labor hours reports or exception reports that are generated by the contractor's system.

Most labor accounting systems have a procedure which checks the input (employee's name, identification number, project or charge numbers) against a master file of "good" inputs. Generally, if the information does not match, it will not be cleared or accepted into the system.

The input that does not clear is usually printed out and distributed for correction and reentry into the system. The auditor reviews the mismatched charges and asks: Why didn't the charges clear? Did someone close a particular charge number? If so, why was it closed? Who can close charge numbers? Who corrects the mismatched charges? What procedures are followed? What controls are in effect?

The field auditor must be aware of the policies, procedures, and practices relating to mismatched labor hours. Weak internal controls greatly increase the government's vulnerability to labor mischarging.

Timecards must be reviewed in selected cost centers based on descriptions or cost center designations (or both). The auditor must also understand the contractor's disclosed practices for IR&D, the classification of employees as direct or indirect, and any policies regarding corporate funds which may be available for research effort.

2. Mischarging of Labor Costs—Bid and Proposal Effort

The Scenario. While monitoring charges to bid and proposal (B&P) projects, the auditor notes that only one or two people are charging any time for a number of projects. Knowing that the chances of so few people putting together an entire proposal are remote, the auditor expands the scope of the review.

First, the auditor determines which cost centers the employees are assigned to and, second, which programs the B&P projects relate to. The auditor also begins a *preinterview analysis* of the questionable employees. The analysis discloses that the employees are charging a portion of their time to contract work orders for the B&P project. *Interviews* with the individuals disclose that:

● Most of the individuals working on B&P projects do not charge their time directly to B&P project charge numbers since they are indirect employees and are not required or allowed to charge any direct costs.

● Some individuals still working on the B&P project were charging to B&P until the project ran out of money. Now the employees are charging their time to a CPFF contract.

Fraud Indicators:

● Distinctive labor-charging patterns on B&P projects.

● Sudden, significant decreases in overall B&P charging.

● A high percentage of indirect charging employees.

● Large, complex pricing proposals with a minimum number of labor hours charged to them.

General Comments. A sensitive area like B&P requires the auditor's careful attention. Monitoring charges to B&P and tracking total expenditures will help to highlight fraud indicators. It is critical for the auditor to understand the contractor's disclosed practices for B&P, the classification of employees as direct or indirect, and any corporate policies for using corporate funds for bid preparation. The most critical element in this area may be the auditor's understanding of FAR definitions of B&P. This information can be found in appendix 1 of DCAAP 7641.81.

3. Mischarging of Labor Costs—Indirect to Direct

The Scenario. A contractor has recently experienced some cash flow problems and is searching for ways to improve the situation.

During a weekly program managers conference, the controller for the major in-house government contract offers a possible solution to the company's problem. He notes that a group of people who work on the contract are classified as indirect employees, either in overhead or G&A cost centers. The group includes engineering and manufacturing managers, marketing representatives, purchasing department employees, and controllers and business managers. Since it is a cost-type government contract, the controller recommends that the people be charged directly to the contract and the cost quickly recovered on public vouchers. Because the cash flow problem is expected to be temporary, the employees can charge their time directly to the contract for a few months and then be reclassified as indirect employees. Another controller comments that there are a number of other cost-type contracts which can bear the additional direct labor charges for a few months.

Fraud Indicators:

● Reclassification or reorganization of employees from indirect to direct.

● New cost centers appearing on public voucher supporting data.

● Changes in the labor-charging relationships between certain tasks or types of labor.

● Decrease in indirect expense pools.

● Increased labor hours with no corresponding increases in material used or units shipped.

General Comments. The mischarging of labor costs by reclassifying indirect employees to direct may not be the most common scheme, but it can never be ignored. In addition to increasing the contractor's cash flow, reclassification may be done to increase the base labor hours in anticipation of using actual labor costs as a basis for estimating a follow-on production contract.

This scheme can also be discovered by using the indicators in section 4 of this handbook, Mischarging of Labor Costs—Direct to Indirect.

4. Mischarging of Labor Costs—Direct to Indirect

The Scenario. During negotiations for contract XYZ-2, the contractor is being pressured for a reduction in engineering labor hours. The audit report questioned about 45,000 engineering labor hours based on a learning curve application and actuals for contract XYZ-1, a developmental contract which represented the beginning of a new long-term production series of contracts. Since the procurement is competitive and potentially lucrative, the contractor is eager to complete negotiations.

During the negotiations, the contractor's representatives caucus and counter with a 30,720-hour reduction in engineering labor. The negotiator accepts the offer and an agreement is reached.

Some time later, the resident contract auditor is monitoring engineering headcounts and direct and indirect charging status. He notes that the engineering cost center's direct charge headcount is down by eight employees, while the indirect headcount is up by eight. A check of the personnel roster discloses no change in the employees assigned to the cost center, but eight employees' charging status has been changed from direct to indirect. A review of labor-charging records reveals that the eight engineers are devoted to the XYZ-1 program which had recently received a follow-on contract. A review of the price negotiation memorandum shows that a reduction of 30,720 direct engineering labor hours was made during negotiations. After completing the necessary preinterview analysis, the auditor conducts *interviews* of the engineers and learns that all eight:

● Have been and still are devoted to the XYZ program.

● Were recently informed by their supervisor that they no longer had to complete timecards.

● Are doing the same work under the current follow-on contract that they did under the prior contract.

The auditor's interview with the program manager and his review of the negotiation folder discloses that the 30,720 direct labor hour reduction was developed in the following manner:

8	—	Design Engineering
× 160	—	Proposed Hours Per Month
1,280	—	Direct Charge Design Engineering Hours
× 24	—	Months (Duration of Contract)
30,720	—	Total Reduction of Direct Engineering Labor Hours

At this point, the auditor concludes that the engineers were reclassified from direct to indirect charge, only to accommodate the negotiated agreement, which gave the appearance of reducing the engineering costs to the government. However, because of the government's participation with this contractor, virtually all of the reclassified engineering labor costs were merely spread over other in-house government contracts.

Fraud Indicators:

● Reclassification of employees from direct charge to indirect.

● Substantial reduction of direct labor hours with no clear explanation during negotiations.

General Comments. The auditor could have discovered this scheme in one of several ways. A monthly review of headcount by cost center, including a direct and indirect charge breakdown, might disclose transfers, reorganizations, or reclassifications—all potential fraud indicators. Or the auditor could have picked up a lead from the price negotiation memorandum depending on the detail provided. Also, a review of the direct labor and overhead rates might disclose the reclassification of the employee.

5. Labor Accounting by Funding

The Scenario. While monitoring labor charges on a critical firm fixed-price contract, the auditor notes that labor charges, by internally established task, are consistently close to the budgeted amounts. Recognizing this as an indicator of potential irregular activity, the auditor expands the scope of the review to include a study of delivery schedules, exception reports (mismatched and uncleared labor hours), and *preinterview analysis* in selected cost centers.

The delivery schedule helps determine if labor charging patterns logically fit the scheduled and actual deliveries. The exception reports disclose any charged labor hours which were not accepted by the labor accounting system. The preinterview analysis provides labor-charging patterns for employees in specific cost centers.

The auditor uses the resource information during employee interviews, which disclose that employees were instructed to stop *charging* costs against their old work order, but to continue their work under a new work order.

The auditor's followup interviews with supervisors and program managers disclose that:

● The effort performed under the old work order has not stopped. The employees have only been assigned a new work order to charge against.

● The new work order is from a cost-type contract.

● The program cost analyst has informed the program manager of tasks which were nearing or at budgeted amounts.

● The program manager has directed all supervisors to divert labor charges to other work orders.

The auditor, with documentation obtained during the interview, properly notifies his supervisor and initiates action for reporting the potential fraud.

Fraud Indicators:

● Posted notices that certain work order numbers may no longer be charged.

● Actual hours and dollars consistently at or near budgeted amounts.

● Employees with timecards completed in advance.

● Employees submitting blank timecards.

General Comments. Often the pressure on midmanagement by upper management to meet or beat production and budget is only exceeded by the pressure midmanagers exert on themselves. In situations where a career is on the line, some radical attempts to "beat the line" may overshadow a prudent man's judgment and encourage irregular activity. Auditors must be alert to the contractor's policies on budgets, programs, and contracts suspected to have some budgetary problems, and aware of the character of managers and supervisors subjected to corporate budgetary pressure. Monitoring charges to critical contracts and understanding the contractor's labor accounting system will help to uncover characteristics of accounting by funding fraud schemes.

6. Adjusting Journal Entries—Labor Transfers

The Scenario. During the monthly review of the contractor's adjusting journal entries, the auditor notes transfers from a number of work orders to other work orders or overhead accounts. Recognizing this as a fraud indicator, the auditor expands the scope of his review. He requests the supporting documentation for the entries and learns which employee labor charges have been transferred, the rationale behind the transfer, and the responsible individuals. The journal entry explanation is, "Charged wrong work order." The work orders with the credit entries are from B&P projects and from a large cost-type government contract. The work orders with the debit entries are from a number of cost-type government contracts and from an overhead account. Additional research discloses that the large cost-type contract was subject to cost schedule control system criteria (CSCSC). Interviews with the responsible individuals—controllers and program managers—disclosed two important facts:

1. The B&P pool had recently reached the ceiling negotiated in the advance agreement, and

2. Work completed under the CSCSC-covered contract was behind schedule, but labor cost incurred was overbudget.

The controllers and program managers met and decided to transfer as many hours as possible to other cost-type contracts. When the other contracts could not absorb additional labor, the hours were transferred to an overhead account.

Fraud Indicators:

● Transfers from IR&D and B&P costs.

● Transfers from fixed-price government or commercial contracts.

● Transfers to cost-type government contracts.

● Transfers to overhead accounts.

● Transfers to any type of holding or suspense account.

General Comments: Labor transfers are always suspect. Auditors should review adjusting journal entries on a monthly basis and pay special attention to transfers of labor costs. Some types of transfers are more sensitive and require additional audit effort. The auditor must understand both the accounting and the labor accounting systems by knowing all the available ways to circumvent the traditional labor-charging procedures.

7. Nonconforming Goods or Workmanship

The Scenario. During the review of the contractor's overhead submission, the auditor notes a large increase in warranty costs. Realizing that the significant increase in a sensitive account represents a potentially bad situation, the scope of the audit is expanded.

The auditor reviews the contractor's Cost Accounting Standards Disclosure Statement, the accounting system's policies and procedures, and the supporting documentation for the warranty charges. The contractor's policy is that warranty costs on cost-type contracts are charged directly to the contract, while warranty costs on fixed-price contracts are charged to a G&A account, and later spread over all fixed-price contracts. The supporting documents disclose that three cost centers are charging labor to the warranty account.

The auditor's next step is to determine which individuals are charging warranty within each cost center. After identifying the individuals, the auditor begins his preinterview analysis, which discloses that:

● Labor charges are coming from two manufacturing centers and one engineering cost center.

● Before charging the warranty account, the three cost centers charged against a government fixed-price contract.

● A Cost Accounting Standard 402 noncompliance exists due to charging of warranty cost direct to cost-type contracts and indirect on fixed-price effort.

The auditor's discussions with the Administrative Contract Office disclosed that the "black box" system produced under the contract was not working in the field. The procurement plant representative was not aware that these costs were being charged to a G&A account.

Interviews with employees in the three cost centers disclosed the following information:

● The employees were directed to charge the warranty account for costs associated with the correction of defects, not repairs.

● The contractor was aware that, although the components for the "black box" would meet individual test requirements, the "black box" system would not work because of inherent design and materiel defects.

● Not only was the contractor aware of these problems, he was also aware of them before the award of the contract.

● The fraud was in the charging of costs to the government for the correction of known defects.

Fraud Indicators:

● Significant increases or decreases in charging to sensitive accounts.

General Comments. Monitoring charges to sensitive accounts must be an ongoing review. Charges to warranty accounts should be reviewed since they present an easy opportunity for mischarging. The auditor must understand the contractor's disclosed practices regarding warranty costs. It is also critical that the auditor understands applicable government procurement regulations, cost accounting standards, and the individual contract clauses for warranty costs. The auditor must remain aware of current developments and to ensure that contractors are in compliance.

8. Adjustment of Labor Standards

Introduction. Some recently disclosed schemes to defraud the Government have centered on the adjustment of labor standards. Variations have included padded standard labor routings, mischarged standard labor costs, altered standards, maintaining dual standards, and inadequate cost accounting systems, Different contractor systems may include labor routings, labor standards, standard hours, or other terms, but the meanings are basically the same. Primarily, these schemes are limited to manufacturing labor, but the auditor must assess the weaknesses in the contractor's accounting system.

The increased popularity of labor standard fraud schemes may be traced to three key factors: (1) many defense contractors have complex accounting systems which are difficult to understand, especially with time and other contraints placed on the contract auditor; (2) most contractors control the auditor's access to the accounting system and to other essential information; and (3) there are far more fraudulent schemes involving labor standards than was ever thought possible. In the past, popular schemes have involved timecards, mischarged research and development costs, and mischarged B&P effort. Now, schemes involving labor standards are more common.

Background. The auditor's key to finding fraud indicators in labor standards is to understand the contractor's system—how the standards are developed; how, when, and by whom the standards are updated; how the variance is allocated; and any weaknesses in the internal control system. The auditor must also understand which types of standards are used in proposals. Some writers have classified these standards as:

1. Fixed standard or basic cost standards. These standards are used as a base to compare costs from year to year.

2. Theoretical or ideal standards are based on performance under perfect conditions. These standards are useful in motivating program and functional managers to control costs.

3. Attainable standards are based on what can reasonably be expected under current conditions.

This type of labor fraud may be one of the most difficult to detect. It requires a thorough understanding of the contractor's accounting system, access to sensitive records and data, and sufficient time to complete the review.

Brief Descriptions. The directed padding of standard labor routings (a series of operations in a certain sequence) is fraud.

Padding may consist of adding labor cost which is not required to manufacture a given part. The additional cost may be found in two forms: including steps or tasks which are not required; or inflating labor requirements for the steps which are required.

There have been situations where standards were padded to support higher price proposal estimates. In some cases, fixed standards were altered to reflect additional requirements. And in other cases, historical standard cost records, which would have supported lower, realistic labor standards, were altered or destroyed. When inflated standards are used to support inflated cost proposals, you may have fraud.

This reemphasizes the importance of the auditor's understanding of the contractor's system and how costs are proposed. In addition, the auditor must be alert to the pressure placed on midlevel managers to stay within budget constraints. Padded standards help to ensure favorable labor efficiency variances and employee evaluations.

The mischarging of standard labor costs can also be accomplished by giving incorrect charge numbers to manufacturing employees. Many automated standard cost systems use a two-card system to charge cost objectives. The employee will punch-in with an identification card for time and attendance and punch another card to start charging a particular cost objective. If charge cards for one are substituted, the employee could be mischarging without realizing it. Periodic, random, or directed floor checks discourage individuals from trying this type of scheme. Under ideal circumstances, each employee understands the significance of his charge number and which contract it pertains to. But this is not always the situation the auditor encounters.

Another item auditors should be aware of may or may not be fraud, but it can certainly distort the flow of costs to the proper cost objective. This distortion can cause mischarging and may, in some instances, represent fraud. The allocation of variances over dissimilar product lines or contracts can be used to mischarge standard labor costs. Cost Accounting Standard 407, Use of Standard Costs for Direct Material and Direct Labor, sets forth the requirements for using standard costs. The standard requires production units, defined as follows, for the use of standard costs:

"A group of activities which either has homogeneous inputs of direct material and direct labor or yields homogeneous outputs such that the costs or statistics related to these homogeneous inputs or outputs are appropriate as bases for allocating variances."

The auditor must verify that standard costs are charged and that variances are accumulated and allocated over production units. In addition, the auditors must note whether labor variances are allocated on the basis of labor cost at standard or labor hours at standard or, if the output is homogeneous, on the basis of units of output. Manipulation of cost centers which are used as production units, can lead to mischarged labor costs and to the manipulation of the basis for variance allocation. Again, the auditor needs to understand thoroughly the workings of the contractor's accounting system.

Fraud Indicators:

● High labor efficiency (usage) variances.

● Seemingly unrelated task and steps on a statement of work (work breakdown structure, standard routing, description of effort, etc.).

● For similar tasks, low standard routings on fixed-price contracts and high standard routings on cost-type contracts.

● Labor standards not updated over periods of time when the contractor recognizes and realizes improvements in his manufacturing technology.

● Old labor standards used to support proposals.

● Unavailability of supporting documentation for proposed standards.

● The existence of duplicate employee identification cards to charge labor hours on automated systems.

● The lack of a clear audit trail to verify propriety of labor charges.

● Weak internal controls which allow numerous opportunities to adjust labor charges.

9. Other Schemes

Introduction. Whenever the auditor tries to compile any type of listing, something everyone else remembers is always left out. For that reason, this section includes a number of other fraudulent schemes the auditor *will* find if he (or she) looks for them.

Program Management Costs. The inconsistent treatment of program management costs is usually thought of as an accounting system inadequacy. But in these instances auditors cannot overlook the possibility of fraud. When the auditor finds all indirect charge managers of fixed-price and commercial contracts and finds direct charge managers on cost-type contracts, he or she must check it out. The scheme could be found in the way employees are classified as indirect or direct charge, it could be in the way a direct charge employee charges his (her) time, or it could be a combination based on the way program management costs are proposed and negotiated.

Contract Development Type Contracts. Mischarging of labor costs on contract development-type contracts is another common occurrence. During the design phase of a new program, the government may award a number of small contracts to competing contractors. At the completion of this development, the contractor with the best product at the best price may be awarded the long-term production contract. Since the emphasis is on building the best product, the incentive to devoting all possible resources during the development stage is apparent. At the same time, cost is also a critical factor. How can this paradox be resolved? The auditor may see mischarging of engineering design and development effort, mischarging of direct labor by reclassifying it to indirect charge, or mischarging of labor to contractor-sponsored projects which could end up in overhead or G&A accounts. The incentive to hold down costs is great, increasing the government's vulnerability to mischarging.

Altered Data. Another scheme which may be easily overlooked by auditors is the use of altered data or documentation to support costs on a DD-1411, "Contract Pricing Proposal Cover Sheet." This is a simple and effective way to overstate required labor costs, especially for fixed-price contracts. An example would be to use historical costs from a prior contract to estimate future requirements and to include work orders from other contracts to inflate requirements. When the contractor is accumulating historical cost and hour information, extra work or job orders may be included in the estimate. In reviewing these costs, the auditor must determine the nature of the work performed under the historical work orders and make certain that extra work orders are not included to inflate historical costs, resulting in overstated requirements.

Special Contract Clauses. Yet another scheme for the auditor to be aware of involves contracts with special clauses or provisions. At times, contractors may offer certain services or items "at no cost to the government." If this situation is encountered, the auditor must be sure that **all** of the costs included are segregated and that the government is not actually paying at least part of those costs through IR&D/B&P agreements, other contracts, or an overhead account.

Time and Material Contracts. Time and material contracts are often the key to labor mischarging schemes. The contractor may violate a personnel requirements clause, may not stay within the contract scope, or may be accounting by funding. Auditors should look for situations where, task-by-task, billings are consistently at ceiling and for any labor transfers affecting time and material contracts.

Scrap and Rework Costs. Other indicators which should alert contract auditors are high scrap and rework figures. The spreading of these charges over department-wide overhead rates can effectively mischarge potentially nonrecoverable costs.

Subcontracted Out Labor. The mischarging of subcontracted out labor is often hard to determine. These costs probably do not flow through the contractor's labor accounting system. Therefore, they may not be subject to the same internal controls or visibility.

The mischarging matrix in the Appendix serves as a useful guide for auditors.

APPENDIX
MISCHARGING MATRIX

FROM TO	GOVERNMENT FIXED-PRICE (FP) CONTRACT	GOVERNMENT COST-TYPE CONTRACT	INDEPENDENT RESEARCH AND DEVELOPMENT (IR&D) OR BID AND PROPOSAL (B&P)
GOVERNMENT FP CONTRACT	If one FP is overrun, shift to an FP with no budgetary or funding problems. If a follow-on to a current FP is anticipated, shift costs from another FP to increase "actuals" used for negotiations.	If FP is overrun, shift costs to a cost-type contract to recover.	Unusual, but if both FP and IR&D/B&P costs have exceeded the budget, shift costs to IR&D/B&P to negotiate a higher ceiling for the following year.
GOVERNMENT COST-TYPE CONTRACT	If a follow-on to a current FP is anticipated, shift costs from a cost-type contract to increase "actuals" used for negotiations.	If one cost-type contract is at a funding limitation or to minimize reported development costs on an upcoming program, shift costs to another cost.	Unusual. See comment above.
IR&D AND B&P	If IR&D/B&P costs are over negotiated ceiling, shift costs to an FP contract with sufficient funding.	If IR&D/B&P costs are at ceiling, shift "unallowable" costs to a cost-type contract.	
COMMERCIAL CONTRACT	If a commercial contract has reached full price, shift costs to an FP.	If a commercial contract is in trouble, shift costs to a cost-type contract.	Unusual. See comment above.

Handbook on Fraud Indicators: Material (Excerpted from a Handbook by the DOD Inspector General, July 1986)

The Government auditor must be alert for possible instances of fraud. The best method of accomplishing this is to test for and identify fraud indicators.

A fraud indicator only means that a given situation is susceptible to fraudulent practices. It does not mean that fraud exists. The auditor's role is not to prove fraud (the intent to deceive the Government) but to refer potential instances of fraudulent practices to the appropriate investigative organization, if he or she believes that significant evidence indicating fraud has been found.

Material includes raw material, purchased parts, subcontracts, and intercompany transfers. The cost of material is usually charged direct to a contract. In some instances, material cost can be accumulated in a pool and allocated as a direct charge.

Material is susceptible to loss and can be difficult for an auditor to review. Especially difficult for an auditor to evaluate are proposed versus actual material requirements, physical verification of material use, and proposed and actual material standards. Also, subcontractor kickbacks can be almost impossible to detect using standard audit approaches.

Material cost reviews concentrate on two areas: (1) proper charging of material cost, and (2) reasonableness of material cost. Proper charging is based on the material requirements for the item being procured. The reasonableness of the cost depends, to a large extent, on the contractor's procurement policies and procedures and their implementation. In both cases, the auditor must know the contractor's material accounting and related systems. The auditor must evaluate the adequacy of the contractor's internal controls.

The basis for any review of material costs involves a review of the internal controls and system reviews of the contractor's purchasing, receiving, and inventory systems. The auditor also must review the contractor's material requirements system to verify its accuracy.

The review of material must be approached with an attitude of professional skepticism. There are no canned audit programs to find fraud indicators. When the auditor determines that the area to be reviewed is susceptible to fraud, he or she should include audit steps to cover the applicable fraud indicators. The auditor must think fraud indicators, look for them, and find them.

This Handbook is designed to heighten the auditor's level of fraud awareness. The scenarios on material cost mischarging cases highlight some of the fraud indicators auditors may expect to find.

A. MATERIAL TRANSFERS—FINANCING INVENTORY

The Scenario. During a review of adjusting journal entries, the auditor notes transfers from a number of job orders to other job orders. Recognizing this as a fraud indicator, the auditor expands the scope of the audit review and requests supporting documentation for the entries. These records show which material costs have been transferred, the reason for the transfer, and the responsible individuals. The journal entry explanation is, "Materials transferred to work order number XXX." The charges are transferred from an ongoing contract to one just awarded. Additional questioning reveals that the new contract/work order is for a commercial contract. Interviews with responsible individuals—controller, program manager, and material requisitioning manager—disclose some important information:

1. Contractor personnel knew about the impending award of a commercial contract when they ordered the material for the Government contract.

2. Commercial and Government product lines are similar.

The company policy is to combine orders whenever possible to maximize savings. The company does not maintain an inventory except for small general-use materials. Work orders are charged for material when it is received, not used. Since material is ordered on one purchase order, all the costs are charged to the existing open work order. These costs, in turn, are billed to the Government through progress payments or public vouchers. The Government ends up paying the carrying and finance costs for the commercial job.

Fraud Indicators:

—Transfers from Government contracts to commercial contracts.

—Materials ordered and charged in excess of contract requirements.

—Initial billings for actual material costs far in excess of the negotiated material costs.

—Later billings showing a downward adjustment in material costs as labor/overhead costs increase.

—Transfers via any type of holding or suspense account.

General Comments. Material cost transfers are always suspect. Auditors should review adjusting journal entries on a continuous basis and be alert for transfers significant in volume or cost. Most transfers will require additional information and supporting documentation before acceptance. While combining material requirements to achieve cost savings is encouraged, the auditor must be assured that the material costs are charged to the appropriate work order and cost objective.

B. MATERIAL TRANSFERS—MATERIAL REQUIREMENTS SYSTEM

The Scenario. While performing an internal controls review of the material requirements system, the auditor notices an extremely large number of transfers between work orders. Recognizing that this may be a significant weakness in the contractor's system and a fraud indicator, the auditor expands the scope of the audit review in this area. Initial questioning of contractor personnel—controller and inventory/stores manager—indicates that the company's material requirements system is designed to transfer parts based on prioritized needs. For this reason, the company personnel dismiss the auditor's concern about the large number of transfers. "The system is merely operating as it was set up to do," the auditor is told. When a higher priority work order is set up, the system transfers existing parts to it from other lower priority work orders. Parts reordered for the lower priority work orders are charged the new (usually higher) prices, while the higher priority work order is charged the existing (usually lower) price.

Fraud Indicators:

—Transfers from ongoing jobs to open work orders for items previously delivered.

—Transfers from ongoing jobs to open work orders for items scheduled for delivery in the distant future.

—Transfers from Government contracts (job orders) to commercial job orders.

—Transfers from cost-type job orders to fixed-price job orders.

—Transfers at costs substantially different (higher or lower) than actual.

—Mass transfers from one job order to various other job orders. No physical inventory is left on the original job order, but it still has costs charged to it.

General Comments. Continuous internal controls and system reviews are an integral part of auditing any company. Without reliance on the integrity of the company's accounting and related operating systems, the auditor cannot rely on the information generated. Each system's integrity must be continually reviewed and verified.

C. EXCESS/RESIDUAL INVENTORY

The Scenario. The auditor is reviewing a proposal for the follow-on production of Lots 5 and 6. Lots 1 and 2 have been complete for 2 years, Lot 3 was just delivered, and Lot 4 is in production. Proposed material costs are based on actual costs for Lots 1 and 2. In reviewing the cost data for Lots 1, 2, and 3, the auditor finds the following:

1. Lots 1 and 2 show material transferred to Lot 4 with no associated costs transferred.

2. The actual costs per unit of Lot 3 are less than the costs for Lots 1 and 2.

The auditor discusses the situation with the contractor's representative and gets the following information:

1. The contractor has not yet reported excess material on Lots 1 and 2, even though the items were delivered 2 years ago.

2. The proposed costs for Lots 3 and 4 are also based on the incurred costs for Lots 1 and 2.

3. Extra material was transferred from Lots 1 and 2 to Lot 4 production at no cost.

Fraud Indicators:

—No reporting of residual/excess materials.

—Transfers from prior lot work orders to current or forecasted work orders.

—Transfers from cost-type to fixed-price work orders.

—Transfers from cost-type to commercial work orders.

—Mass transfers to scrap accounts.

—Mass transfers to inventory write-off account.

—Transfers to or via a suspense or any type of holding account.

—Poor internal controls over physical inventories.

—Disproportionate increase in the proposed scrap factor.

—Disproportionate increase in inventory write-off account.

—Large quantity of or significant costs for "found" parts.

General Comments. Excess material is material which is acquired or furnished for a contract and not used or consumed during the performance of that contract. Title to excess contractor-purchased material belongs to the Government under completed cost-reimbursable contracts. Untimely transfer of excess inventory on either cost-type or fixed-price contracts affects the proposed costs for the next follow-on contract. When the contractor bases the proposed costs on historical costs, which include excess inventory, he or she may be double-counting the cost of the excess parts. Additional problems occur if the excess is then transferred onto the follow-on job at no cost. Actual costs for the first job are overstated, while the actual costs for the follow-on job are understated.

D. INVENTORY WRITE-OFF

The Scenario. During a review of the inventory write-off account, the auditor notes a sharp increase in these costs compared to total direct material costs. The auditor takes a judgmental sample of charges to this account. He notes the items written off as obsolete and checks the purchase order history to see if like items had been recently purchased. In many cases, the same items were bought 6 months to a year later, some even sooner. Further checking reveals that the company has reacquired the parts from the same company they had sold the "obsolete" parts to. The auditor checks with the company controller and discovers the following facts:

1. Parts being written off as obsolete/scrap are not necessarily excess to the company's needs.

2. These parts are not really being "scrapped." They are being sold to a warehousing service firm for nominal prices.

3. When the company reacquires the part, it pays a substantially higher price based on a preestablished formula.

4. Within a short time, many parts are written off as excess and sold to a warehousing firm. These same parts are subsequently repurchased from the warehousing firm for contract use.

5. The company is the only party eligible to "buy" (reacquire) the parts it "sells" to the servicing firm. The company is provided a monthly listing of all its inventory being stored by the servicing firm.

Fraud Indicator:

—Significant increases or decreases to a sensitive account, such as scrap, inventory write-off, or rework.

General Comments. Monitoring charges to sensitive accounts must be done on an ongoing basis. Charges to inventory write-off or a scrap account should be reviewed since they represent an easy way to mischarge costs. In addition, improperly "scrapped" parts can be of personal gain to company employees. The auditor must thoroughly understand the company's policies, procedures, and internal controls governing obsolete or scrap material. The auditor also must know the applicable Government procurement regulations, cost accounting standards, and contract clauses.

E. FALSIFICATION OF DOCUMENTS

The Scenario. During a proposal review, the auditor is reviewing support for a proposed unit cost. The contractor has used actual cost as a basis for the proposal. The actual unit cost is supported by purchase order history. The auditor performs a statistical sample of the proposed bill of material and requests the supporting documentation for the selected items. The contractor provides copies of vendor invoices. The auditor closely reviews the copies and notices some suspicious print type which does not match that of the rest of the invoice. The auditor expands the review and requests the original invoice/document. Upon receiving the originals from the contractor, the auditor notes the following:

1. The unit prices on the original invoices do not match the unit prices on the copies. Apparently, some have been altered by putting additional numbers in front of the price or by moving decimals.

2. Discount terms at the bottom of the invoice have been "whitened out" so the auditor would not notice an offered 20 percent discount.

Fraud Indicators:

— Original documentation consistently unavailable for the auditor's review.

— Consistently poor, illegible copies of supporting documentation.

— Different supporting documents provided for the same item with unit prices varying widely for the same part, for no obvious reason.

General Comments. The auditor had performed a review of the purchasing system 2 years earlier. During that review, no significant deficiencies were noted. The auditor relied heavily on the results of that review and used only the purchase order history to verify unit prices. The contractor took advantage of the situation by altering selected invoices.

The auditor should periodically reverify the integrity of the accounting and operating systems he or she relies on. This can be done by doing transactional and compliance testing on a selected basis. In this case, it would involve requesting original documentation from the contractor to support the purchase order history. In other cases, the auditor may want to get third party confirmations from the actual vendors. This audit step might only be done on one or two transactions per proposal. The auditor also could randomly select a proposal and request the original documentation for a majority of the transactions. The auditor must be alert to changes in how a system works after he or she has reviewed and accepted it. Reliance must be based on continual review.

F. REPETITIVE BIDDING OF DUPLICATIVE MATERIAL COSTS

The Scenario. During a review, the auditor notes that the company has bid discretely for a type of material which it normally bids as a factor. Further review discloses that it was still the company's disclosed practice to bid these "abnormal supplies" by use of a factor. The auditor questions the company's controller and estimating manager on possible noncompliance with Cost Accounting Standard 402 and learns the following:

1. The contractor's disclosed practice is to estimate "abnormal supplies," i.e., the cost of supplies which do not become a part of the end product by use of a factor. This factor is calculated and applied to a base of shop labor costs.

2. Only supplies that become part of the end product are bid discretely.

3. The contractor has established a part number code (XXX) labeled "abnormal supplies" and has begun to bid this item discretely.

4. The costs accumulated in part number code XXX are for "abnormal supplies," as described by the company's original policies.

5. The auditor reviewed proposals that the contractor had submitted within the last year and confirmed that the contractor has repetitively bid "abnormal supplies" twice in each proposal.

Fraud Indicators:

— Vague terms used to bid materials discretely which are based solely on management's judgment.

— Repetitive noncompliance with the contractor's disclosed bidding/estimating practices.

General Comments. The auditor must know the contractor's disclosed estimating and accounting practices. Using this knowledge, the auditor can review proposed estimating or accounting changes and be alert for possible duplication of costs.

G. ADJUSTMENT OF MATERIAL STANDARDS

Introduction

Recently, a contractor manipulated material standards to defraud the Government. Possible schemes involved maintaining dual standards, padding material routing slips, mischarging standard material costs, altering standards, and maintaining inadequate cost accounting systems. These schemes were limited mainly to purchased parts and raw materials used in the manufacturing process. The auditor must determine the weaknesses in the contractor's accounting system and their possible effect.

Three factors have influenced material standard fraud schemes: (1) many Defense contractors have complex accounting systems which are difficult to understand, especially with time and other constraints placed on the contract auditor; (2) most contractors control the auditor's access to the accounting system and to other essential information; and (3) there are more fraudulent schemes involving material standards than was ever thought possible. Previously, popular schemes have involved courtesy bidding, mischarged material transfers, and subcontractor kickbacks. Now, schemes involving material standards are being uncovered.

Background

The auditor's key to finding fraud indicators in material standards is to understand the contractor's system—how the standards are developed; how, when, and by whom the standards are updated; how the variance is allocated; and any weaknesses in the internal control system. The auditor must also understand which types of standards are used in proposals. Some writers have classified these standards as:

1. Fixed standard or basic cost standards. These standards are used as a base to compare costs from year to year.

2. Theoretical or ideal standards are based on performance under perfect conditions. These standards are useful in motivating program and functional managers to control costs.

3. Attainable standards are based on what reasonably can be expected under current conditions.

This type of material fraud may be one of the most difficult to detect. It requires a thorough understanding of the contractor's accounting system, access to sensitive records and data, and sufficient time to complete the review.

Brief Description

The directed padding of standard material routing is fraud. Padding may consist of adding raw material costs which are not required to manufacture a given part. The additional cost may be found in two forms: including raw materials or items which are not required; or inflating existing material requirements for needed items.

There have been situations where standards were padded to support higher price proposal estimates. In some cases, fixed standards were altered to reflect additional requirements. In other cases, historical standard cost records, which would have supported lower, realistic material standards, were altered or destroyed. When inflated standards are used to support inflated cost proposals, there may be fraud.

This reemphasizes the importance of the auditor's understanding of the contractor's system and how costs are proposed. In addition, the auditor must be alert to the pressure placed on mid-level managers to stay within budget constraints. Padded standards help to ensure favorable material efficiency variances and employee evaluations.

Another item auditors should be aware of may or may not be fraud, but it can certainly distort the flow of costs to the proper cost objective. This distortion can cause mischarging and may, in some instances, represent fraud. The allocation of variances over dissimilar product lines or contracts can be used to mischarge standard material costs. Cost Accounting Standard 407, Use of Standard Costs for Direct Material and Direct Labor, sets forth the requirements for using standard costs. The standard requires production units, defined as follows, for the use of standard costs:

"A group of activities which either has homogeneous inputs of direct material and direct labor or yields homogeneous outputs such that the costs or statistics related to these homogeneous inputs or outputs are appropriate as bases for allocating variances."

The auditor must verify that standard costs are charged and that variances are accumulated and allocated over production units. In addition, the auditor must note whether material variances are allocated on the basis of standard material cost or units of output. Manipulation of cost centers, which are used as production units, can lead to mischarged material costs and to the manipulation of the basis for variance allocation. Again, the auditor needs to understand thoroughly the workings of the contractor's accounting system.

Fraud Indicators:

—High material efficiency (usage) variances.

—Seemingly unrelated materials charged on routing slips.

—Material standards not updated over periods of time when the contractor recognizes and realizes improvements in manufacturing technology or product design.

—Old material standards used to support proposals.

—Unavailability of supporting documentation for proposed standards.

—The lack of a clear audit trail to verify the propriety of material charges.

—Weak internal controls which allow numerous opportunities to adjust material charges.

H. SUBCONTRACTS

Introduction

Subcontracts continue to make up a large majority of contractor-proposed material costs. In spite of increased Government emphasis on subcontract breakout and competition, subcontract costs are on the rise. Due to the increasing complexity of major weapon systems, most large contractors are unable to supply all the needed subsystems.

Subcontracts are particularly vulnerable to fraud. Subcontract costs can be bid improperly through various means. Contractors may employ a multitude of schemes or just one. An audit of the contractor's subcontract management is usually needed for a thorough review of the basis for these costs. Proposal and postaward audit reviews can provide leads and indicators in the subcontract area, but most audits do not review the root causes of the fraud indicators. The auditor cannot rely simply on reviews performed by other groups, such as internal audit, administrative contracting officer, and/or the various procuring offices. The auditor must first evaluate the reviews and determine if they satisfy his or her concerns. Other reviews may be the starting point for a more in-depth audit.

Brief Descriptions. Below we will discuss some of the various schemes involving subcontract fraud and applicable fraud indicators. Not all of the described conditions are by themselves fraud indicators. Some situations, such as make versus buy or switching vendors, may have to be of a repetitive or pervasive nature in order to indicate fraud.

1. *Budget and Planning Quotes.* In many cases, only written quotes support the contractor's proposed material costs. No purchase order history may exist to compare the quotes. The question then arises as to the quotes' overall accuracy. An individual quote's accuracy can depend on many factors. The most influential is how definite the specifications are. Some companies ask for budget/planning quotes to gauge the highest cost limits for an item. Later a firm quote is requested. The company may have the firm quote prior to negotiations and not disclose it to the Government. If the auditor can compare proposed versus negotiated vendor prices, then he or she can determine if a wide variance exists between the two. A large variance could indicate the existence of two types of quotes.

2. *Switching Vendors.* A significant variance between proposed and negotiated vendor prices may also indicate that a contractor found a cheaper source for an item. The auditor can verify this by comparing the vendor cited in the proposal to the actual source for the item. The auditor can then expand the review to determine if the cheaper source was known prior to negotiations. This situation can also indicate a lack of competition in awarding buys.

3. *Make Versus Buy.* A contractor may change an approach to obtaining an item. Originally, the contractor may have bid the item as a purchased part or service. Later, the contractor may decide to perform the work in-house. Switching from buying to making an item is a fraud indicator, especially if the contractor knows that it would be cheaper to do the work in-house. The situation can reverse itself, with the contractor finding it cheaper to purchase

an item than make it. A pattern of switching make versus buy is a definite fraud indicator.

4. *Courtesy Bidding/Noncompetitive Bidding.* A contractor may arrange with various vendors to supply "courtesy" bids. The vendor then sends the contractor a high bid. The contractor can award the buy to the vendor that has been preselected as low bidder and still maintain an air of competition. Courtesy bidding may indicate subcontractor kickbacks or just be done as a "favor" to the company.

5. *Decrement Factors.* The contractor may propose a decrement or negotiation factor to account for any reduction in price due to bargaining with its suppliers. Normally, this factor is based on historical data or program experience. The auditor must evaluate the basis of the contractor's proposed factor carefully to assure that all relevant data have been included. The contractor can easily manipulate the data to provide a lower decrement factor than the actual experienced reduction.

Fraud Indicators:

— A significant variance between proposed versus negotiated vendor prices.

— High percentage of noncompetitive subcontract awards with poor explanations.

— Contractor policy of classifying an award as competitive with only two quotes.

General Comments. An effective audit technique which has been used to validate the completeness, accuracy and currency of the prime contractor's proposed subcontract prices is to "mail out" inquiries to subcontractors shown on the prime's bidder mailing lists. This procedure has proven successful in that it has identified lower bids received but not documented in the contractor's purchasing files.

I. SUBCONTRACTOR KICKBACKS

Introduction

Recent Senate hearings focused on abuses in subcontract management, specifically subcontractor kickbacks. It was estimated in testimony at those hearings that from 10 to 50 percent of all subcontractors are involved in some type of payment scheme. The abuses could range from paying for a buyer's lunch to payoffs in the thousands. With subcontracts for DoD procurements running $47 billion in FY 1984, subcontract kickbacks add substantial sums to the price of everything the Government buys.

Subcontractor kickbacks are apparently a widespread, longstanding, and entrenched practice. Buyers can easily disguise kickback situations by producing documentation to demonstrate and justify the award of a purchase order. Kickbacks occur most frequently in subcontracts under $100,000. Purchase orders under $10,000 are extremely vulnerable because of lack of scrutiny.

Unfortunately, standard audit approaches and contractor purchasing system reviews are not likely to uncover subcontract kickbacks. The documentation involved appears legitimate and the paid invoices usually do not reflect the kickbacks. Instead, internal control reviews should be used to assess the contractor's vulnerability in these areas. The failure of the contractor to monitor and control its employees' activities properly contributes to the problem through lack of attention and inaction.

Background

Kickback schemes are arrangements between subcontractors and the prime contractor's buyers, high level officials or even owners. The subcontractor agrees to pay a percentage of all subcontracts awarded to the subcontractor by the prime. One kickback scheme is called a "bump" agreement. In these cases, the prime's agent tells the vendor how much he or she can raise the bid and still be low bidder. Another system is courtesy bidding. Courtesy bidding revolves around various vendors taking turns being the low bidder. When a company is not designated the low bidder, it submits an artificially high bid to protect the designated vendor's bid. In other instances, the contractor's agent may disclose the legitimate bids to the designated vendor so he or she can underbid the competition. The contractor's representative may also disqualify legitimate low bids on the basis of technical or financial capability and award the subcontract to the preferred vendor.

Kickbacks can be in various forms. Cash, illegal drugs, cars, appliances, tools, airline tickets, package vacations have all been used as payoffs. In some extreme cases, the recipient of the kickback has sent bills to the subcontractor for purchased items or used the subcontractor's credit cards for purchases.

The subcontractor could also pay kickbacks to a nonexistent company or one that is created solely to facilitate payments from the subcontractor to the recipient of the kickback. These payments may be for consulting services or services and materials which appear related to the contract, however, when compared to overall costs and other actual charges, they show up as unusual.

Fraud Indicators:

—Poor contractor internal controls over key functional areas, such as purchasing, receiving, and storing.

—Lack of subdivision of duties between purchasing and receiving.

—Lack of rotation or subdivision of duties in the purchasing department. Buyers should be rotated to prevent familiarity with specific vendors.

—None or few contractor policies on ethical business practices.

—Poor enforcement of existing contractor policies on conflicts of interest or acceptance of gratuities.

—Purchasing employees maintaining a standard of living obviously exceeding their income.

—Instances of buyers or other employees circumventing established contractor procedures for competition of subcontracts.

—Poor or no established procedures for the competition of subcontracts.

—Poor documentation of sole source award of subcontract.

—Poor documentation of award of competitive subcontracts.

—Lack of competitive awards.

—Nonaward of subcontract to lowest bidder.

—A one-time payment to a company for services or materials usually bought from another vendor(s). The kickback recipient could be using the company to obtain his payoff.

General Comments. Detection of subcontract kickbacks is difficult. Standard audit procedures normally will not uncover such schemes. The auditor must be alert to obvious weaknesses in the contractor's internal controls which make taking payoffs easy instead of difficult. Audits of the contractor's material purchasing, receiving and storing systems will point out other weaknesses or noncompliance with existing contractor policies and procedures. Physical verification of the existence of inventories or materials charged direct to a job will also show how vulnerable the contractor's system is to fraud. A subcontract management review may be the best way to evaluate the contractor's policies and procedures for awarding subcontracts. This could assure that the contractor is following the proper procedures.

Handbook on Scenarios of Potential Defense Pricing Fraud (Excerpted from a Handbook by the DOD Inspector General, December 1986)

Public Law 87-653, the Truth In Negotiations Act, gives the Government the right to adjust the contract price when it is based on inaccurate, incomplete, or noncurrent cost or pricing data. All negotiated procurements exceeding $100,000 require the contractor to certify that the data supplied to the government were current, complete and accurate at the time of agreement on price, unless the price is set by law or regulation or is based on adequate price competition, on an established vendor's catalog or on the market price of commercial items sold in vast quantities to the general public. Defective pricing occurs when more current, complete and accurate data exist but are not provided to the negotiator.

The Defense Contract Audit Agency (DCAA) is responsible for establishing a program to perform reviews of selected contracts and subcontracts. The agency issues a positive defective pricing report when the auditor finds that the contract price was increased because the contractor did not follow the requirements of the Truth In Negotiations Act.

Auditors, in the past, concentrated on finding defective pricing and not on assessing the reason for it and whether it might be an indicator of wrongdoing. However, when DCAA issued written guidance to its auditors on September 19, 1983 (see Appendix A), the auditor was provided a list of indicators to use in assessing whether the condition found was an indicator of possible fraud and should be referred for investigation.

This handbook builds on the DCAA list of indicators by providing scenarios of defective pricing situations that indicate the need for investigation for fraud. All of the scenarios relate to negotiated procurements requiring certificates.

Scenario 1—Using a Vendor Other Than the One Proposed

A contractor submits a $1 million proposal to buy engine parts from vendor XYZ for $120,000, using XYZ's catalog prices to support the proposal.

Because the contractor recently has sent a similar proposal for engine parts which has been reviewed by the DCAA, the contracting officer waives an audit of the $1 million proposal and makes no exceptions to it. During contract negotiation, the contractor certifies that the contract cost complies with the Truth in Negotiations Act.

Later, the contract is selected for a defective pricing review. One of the auditor's review steps is to compare the proposed costs to the actual incurred cost by examining each cost element, such as, labor, material, other direct costs. The auditor notices a significant difference between the proposed and the actual incurred costs of material. A further check shows that every part proposed to be purchased from vendor XYZ was actually purchased from vendor ABC at lower prices, resulting in the contractor realizing higher profits than those shown in the proposal.

The auditor sends vendor XYZ a confirmation letter to determine the latest information furnished the vendor up to the certification date. Vendor XYZ replies that he has never done business with the contractor. The auditor now reviews other contracts to buy engine parts and finds that they too were purchased at lower prices from vendor ABC, and not from XYZ.

The auditor concludes that the contract was defectively priced, with indicators of potential fraud, and refers the contractor for investigation.

Scenario 2—Intentional Failure to Update Cost or Pricing Data

A prime contractor submits a proposal to the DoD which includes a subcontract for a major part, using the subcontractor's budgetary quote to support the price of the part. Within a few days of sending the budgetary quote, the subcontractor provides firm quotes in response to a request from the prime contractor.

The auditor begins a defective pricing review on the contract and finds that the price of the major part is different than the one proposed. The review also shows that, at the time of price agreement, the contractor had both budgetary quotes and firm quotes. The firm quotes were lower than the proposed prices, but this information was not disclosed to the Government. The date on the firm quotes was within a few days of the budgetary quotes and, in some instances, the quotes were received on the same day. None of the firm quotes were ever disclosed.

Scenario 3—Selective Disclosure

A contractor has a basic ordering agreement with the Government. The first three orders agreed to and certified by the contractor were fixed priced orders in which the contractor judgmentally selected completed work orders to support the proposed labor hours and cost.

The auditor making the defective pricing review on the three orders finds that the judgmentally selected completed work orders used to support the proposed labor hours do not include all work orders for the same item. Rather, the auditor discovers that the nonselected work orders show a lower number of labor hours required to complete the work.

The auditor decides the situation should be referred for investigation because it appears to be a misrepresentation of data. The selective exclusion of previous work orders with lower labor costs is an indicator of potential fraud.

After the auditor discloses the defective pricing situations, the contractor agrees to an additional four work orders under the same basic ordering agreement. Each of the orders is certified by the contractor.

The auditor reviews the four orders and finds that the contractor has used the same technique of selecting the higher work orders and excluding the lower ones to estimate his labor hours and costs.

Since the contractor has been told that the technique used on the first three orders resulted in defective pricing, the auditor concludes that the contractor has schemed to overstate the prices in a deceptive manner.

Scenario 4—Changed Dates

During a defective pricing review, an auditor notices that the actual subcontract cost is significantly less than the proposed cost.

The auditor requests all subcontract purchase orders and compares the dates of the orders with the date of the price agreement between the prime contractor and the Government. The auditor finds that out of 12 subcontracts, 10 had two dates on the purchase orders. The original purchase order date had been typed over to show a date 1 week after the price agreement. The typed-over date was 2 weeks before the price agreement. This resulted in the prices for the subcontracts being lower than those proposed by the prime contractor. Further, the negotiation memoranda between the prime and subcontractors were all undated.

The two dates on the purchase orders raised the auditor's suspicion. The undated negotiations between prime and subcontractors was another indicator of the potential for fraud. Both these situations show how a contractor can manipulate documents to increase his profits.

Scenario 5—Lost Records

A contractor submits a proposal for a follow-on contract to paint a building and says that he will use the prior contract as a basis of supporting the proposed labor costs for the follow-on contract.

The contractor uses learning curve techniques to arrive at the cost estimation for the labor hours. Everything seems to be in order and properly disclosed. The contractor prepares the proposal by using the painters' labor hours times the labor rate. The contract is negotiated based on the cost and pricing data. What the contractor fails to disclose is that on the previous contract, painters, painter helpers, and laborers were used to do the job.

During contract performance, the company sends status reports listing the hours incurred on the previous contract and the painter labor rate. As part of a defective pricing review, the auditors ask for the labor records. The contractor tells them that the timecards and other labor records have been destroyed.

An additional review of the payroll records shows that the workforce was evenly split between painters, painter helpers, and laborers. The auditors also find that other painting contracts had the same labor mix. They conclude that the contractor had to have known in advance that the labor hours would not be just for painters, as proposed. Thus, the review reveals defective pricing and indications of fraud.

Scenario 6—Lack of Support for Proposal

A contractor submits a proposal that includes a 10 percent scrap factor, an upward adjustment in material part quantities to account for scrap or spoilage during the manufacturing process. The contractor provides the records prepared at different stages of the manufacturing process for the last 6 months to support the proposed 10 percent cost increase. The auditor asks whether the scrap numbers are for this proposal only and the contractor indicates they are. The scrap rate is accepted as proposed.

During a defective pricing review, the auditor compares the costs incurred against the costs proposed to see whether there are significant variances. The auditor finds that the incurred cost of material is about 5 percent less than the proposed cost. A review of the supporting purchase orders and quotes discloses no material part pricing differences.

What the review does disclose, however, is that these same material parts were used on three other contracts during the past year. The auditor compares the supporting documentation for the scrap factor to learn if the contracts for this period were used to develop the scrap factor. The auditor asks for the scrap records for the three contracts and is told they do not exist. The auditor checks with the foreman and the supervisor at the different stages of production and asks to see the scrap records. Neither kept records on scrap nor had knowledge about a scrap factor. Later, the contract representative says that someone in production, he cannot remember the person, provided the scrap factor information for the proposal. The signature on the scrap report used to support the contractor's proposal is impossible to read.

The company admits they had no statistics to support a scrap factor. The auditor issues a defective pricing report and makes a referral to the investigator.

Scenario 7—Change in Make-Versus-Buy

A contractor submits a contract proposal that includes a decision to make certain items in-house because it will be cheaper than buying them from an outside vendor. On the prior two contracts, the contractor bought this item. The contractor proposes material and labor costs and applies the company burden rates of 200 percent for overhead and 25 percent for general and administrative. The awarded contract accepts the contractor's decision to make items in-house.

During the defective pricing review, the auditor finds that the incurred costs for the item are significantly higher than proposed costs and that the labor costs are significantly less. The auditor also finds that purchase orders for the materials are dated after the price agreement.

The auditor determines that the incurred labor rates are as proposed but that there are significant differences in the labor hours. The auditor asks about the underrun and is told that the contractor has decided to buy a greater portion of the items rather than make them in-house. The auditor asks for the file supporting the make-versus-buy decision, but it cannot be found.

The auditor sends a confirmation letter to the vendor and asks for copies of correspondence quotes or telephone quotes for the item. The vendor replies that 1 week prior to the contract award date the contractor verbally accepted the vendor's agreement to provide the items at a 10 percent discount over the contractor's previous purchases. The contractor asked if the vendor's delivery schedule could be expedited. The vendor was advised that a written order would be sent in 2 weeks. Three weeks after the award of the contract, the contractor bought the materials from the vendor.

Scenario 8—No Production Break

A contractor submits a proposal to the Government for a follow-on contract, stating that the contract price has increased because of a 6-month break in production—based on the proposed delivery schedule—before the start of the follow-on work. The price negotiation memorandum indicates that these statements are being relied upon and that the negotiated price is being increased because of the proposed break in production. Contractor management monitors production through weekly production schedule meetings and production scheduling reports.

The auditor begins a defective pricing review shortly after the follow-on contract is awarded. The auditor notices that the production scheduling report dated 2 weeks prior to contract price agreement shows no break in production, as proposed. The auditor reviews the negotiation memorandum and finds the statement about the break in production that will cause the additional manufacturing hours and, thus, the increase in contract price. From the distribution of the production scheduling reports and meetings, all levels of management are aware of the production scheduling. The auditor concludes that defective pricing is present and makes a suspected fraud referral.

Scenario 9—Catalog Pricing

Law and regulation exempt contracts for products with established catalog or market prices from the need for cost analysis if the price is based on an established catalog or market price of a commercial item sold in substantial quantities to the general public. In this case, the contractor submitted a proposal for widgets that required cost or pricing data; however, the contractor claimed an exemption and submitted a Standard Form (SF) 1412, *Claim For Exemption From Submission of Certified Cost or Pricing Data*. The SF 1412 was completed and signed by an officer of the corporation. An item is considered sold to the general public if it is sold to other than affiliates of the seller for end use by other than the Government. Items sold to affiliates of the seller and sales for end use by the Government are not sales to the general public.

The contracting officer waived the requirement for cost or pricing data and negotiated a price with the contractor based on the submitted SF 1412.

After the award the contracting officer requested the audit office to review the SF 1412 submission. As part of the review, the auditor requested the contractor to provide support for the widget sales to show they were sold in substantial quantities to the general public. The support provided showed that the widgets were not sold in substantial quantities to the general public. In fact, over 80 percent of the widgets were sold to the Government. Most of the sales to the Government were on one subcontract. The contractor told the auditor that they did not know that the end user was the Government on the one subcontract.

The auditor's review of the contractor's correspondence with the prime contractor showed the Air Force as the end user. This was confirmed by the auditor with the prime contractor. All indications were that the contractor knew that the widget was not sold in substantial quantities to the general public. The auditor referred the case to an investigative agency.

This scenario is not a true defective pricing situation. By claiming an exemption from the requirement to provide cost or pricing data, the contractor made a false statement. The Office of the Inspector General believes the false statement negates the exemption from providing cost or pricing data.

Scenario 10—Combining Items

In this case, the company proposed spare parts for a large weapon system on which they were a major subcontractor. The company negotiated six purchase orders, on the same date, for the spare parts. At the time of negotiation the company was manufacturing the same items. These items were about 90 percent complete. This information was not disclosed to the Government during negotiations. The company did tell the Government about an earlier completed order which showed significantly higher costs because of design changes on the first lot produced. Three months after awarding the six purchase orders, the company negotiated another purchase order for the same items. At that time the contractor had completed the items that were in process. The company did not disclose the cost history on the recently completed items. Because of the nondisclosure, the company negotiated higher prices for the seven purchase orders.

During the defective pricing review, the auditor determined that the company was able to consolidate the material requirements into one purchase and reduce its cost considerably. The company did not disclose the fact that most of the material requirement was ordered prior to agreement on price with the Government. In addition, they did not disclose the labor cost savings from combining the purchases. The resulting profit on the new orders when the contracts were completed exceeded 50 percent.

The auditor recognized a pattern that required the referral for investigation.

Scenario 11—Other Schemes

These alert statements highlight indicators of schemes that auditors should consider for referral to investigators:

● Intentionally eliminating support to increase the proposal prices.

● Including inflated rates in the proposal such as insurance or workman's compensation.

- Intentionally duplicating costs by proposing them as both direct and indirect.

- Proposing obsolete items that are not needed.

- Continually failing to provide requested data.

- Not disclosing an excess material inventory that is used in later contracts.

- Refusing to provide data which are requested for elements of proposed costs.

- Nondisclosing actuals for follow-on contracts.

- Knowingly using intercompany division to perform part of the contract but proposing purchase or vice versa.

- Ignoring established estimating practices.

- Suppressing studies that do not support the proposed costs.

- Commingling work orders with other work orders to hide productivity improvements.

- Requesting an economic price adjustment clause when the material is already purchased.

- Submitting fictitious documents.

- Withholding information on batch purchases.

- Failing to disclose internal documents on vendor discounts.

Appendix A

DEFENSE CONTRACT AUDIT AGENCY
CAMERON STATION
ALEXANDRIA, VIRGINIA 22314
19 SEP 1983

OPD-101

703.4.23

MEMORANDUM FOR REGIONAL DIRECTORS, DCAA

SUBJECT: Findings and Conditions in Postaward Audits that Require Further Pursuit as Potential Cases of Fraud

In his 9 June 1983 memorandum on DCAA audit and management initiatives, the Assistant Secretary of Defense (Comptroller), Mr. Vincent A. Puritano, included an action item on postaward audits. The initiative stated:

> DCAA should reevaluate its approach to potential defective pricing instances to identify conditions which might be indicators of fraud and thus pursue recoveries.

The audit guidance outlined in the subsequent paragraphs is to be used to accomplish this initiative.

During postaward audits, the auditor must be constantly alert in order to identify certain conditions which might be indicative of wrongdoing against the Government. When these conditions are observed during the course of such audits, it will be Agency policy to evaluate the situation, as delineated in 12-701, using the legal standards for fraud stated below. When an indication of fraud is found, the case will be referred to the proper investigative agencies in accordance with the CAM guidance.

Defective Pricing may be shown to be fraudulent under at least three statutory sections: the False Statements Act (18 U.S.C. 1001) and two provisions known as the False Claims Act. The False Statement Act is a criminal statute. A violation would occur when a contractor presents a statement knowing it to contain false information. The Certification of Current Cost or Pricing Data is an example of a statement subject to this Act. No filing of a claim is required.

The False Claims Act provisions include a criminal section (18 U.S.C. 287) and a civil section (31 U.S.C. 3729). The review for indications of fraud under these sections is the next step after determining that defective pricing exists. The courts have ruled that the Truth in Negotiation Act (Public Law 87-653) and the False Claims Act, are distinct and separate statutes and that there is a difference between just inflated or inaccurate cost estimates and fraudulent cost estimates. Neither is exclusive and the Government may proceed against the contractor under both for the same instance of defective pricing.

In order for a contractor to be guilty of fraud in the submission of defective data, it must have had "knowledge" of the defects. Under the False Claims Act, courts have formulated three standards to aid in determining the existence of knowledge. Any one of these may support a determination of culpable knowledge in an appropriate case. They are:

1. Intent to deceive

2. Misrepresentation

3. Actual knowledge

The first standard, "intent to deceive", is difficult to prove because it requires inquiry into the contractor's state of mind to determine liability. Though we should look for evidence of intent, because of the difficulty involved in proving this standard, concentration on the other two standards is considered the most viable approach to indicating potential fraud.

Under the "misrepresentation" standard the courts have set forth two criteria: *intentional misrepresentation* and *negligent misrepresentation*. Intentional misrepresentation, the more stringent criteria, may occur as a result of a contractor's reckless disregard for the truth or falsity of a belief. Negligent misrepresentation, which is a less stringent criteria, has been defined as a lack of reasonable care in ascertaining facts. However, carelessness which resembles a mistake will not meet the negligent misrepresentation definition. Therefore, a critical element to a finding of liability under the False Claims Act appears to be the perception of the deliberateness of the contractor's action. The negligence must be extreme enough as to be considered functionally equivalent to actual knowledge.

The standard for "actual knowlege" may be ascertained by (i) a verbal admission, (ii) correspondence or records that specifically indicate knowledge, or (iii) a clear indication of knowledge based on the related actions taken by the contractor.

The following are examples of conditions found during defective pricing audits which warranted additional review to determine if there was potential effort to defraud the Government:

High incidence of persistent defective pricing.

Repeated defective pricing involving similar patterns or conditions.

Continued failure to correct known system deficiencies.

Consistent failure to update cost or pricing data with knowledge that past activity showed that prices have decreased.

Specific knowledge, that is not disclosed, regarding significant cost issues that will reduce proposal cost; such as revision in the price of a major subcontract, settlement of union negotiations that result in lower increases on labor rates, etc.

Repeated denial by responsible contractor employees of the existence of historical records that are subsequently found.

Repeated utilization of unqualified personnel to develop cost or pricing data used in estimating process.

Indications of falsification or alteration of supporting data.

Distortion of the overhead accounts or base information by the transfer of charges or accounts that have a material impact on Government contracts.

Continued failure to make complete disclosure of data known to responsible contractor personnel.

Continued protracted delay in release of data to the Government to preclude possible price reductions.

The employment of people known to have previously perpetuated fraud against the Government.

When a condition or conditions such as those described above are found in a defective pricing audit, the auditor will examine each to determine if there is evidence of potential fraud using the aforementioned three standards for fraud.

It is requested that reviews be made of all completed positive defective pricing audit assignments for the period 1 July 1983 to present to identify suspected cases of fraud using the conditions and standards described above. The cases that have a strong basis for potential fraud through application of the standards should be submitted, in accordance with CAM 12-701, to Headquarters by 15 November 1983.

On all current and future defective pricing reviews, the auditor will use a revised audit program encompassing the aforementioned standards to identify cases of potential fraud. The identified cases will be processed in accordance with CAM 12-701 "Fraud or Other Unlawful Activity."

Each region should select several examples of the best audit programs developed and utilized in this review and submit them to Headquarters by 15 November 1983. These audit programs will form the basis for development of a standard audit program which will become an addendum to our present audit program for defective pricing compliance reviews and will be used when conditions indicate a high probability of a fraudulent contractor practice.

If you have any questions please contact Mr. Ray Czaplicki, Program Manager, Audit Programs Division, (202) 274-7344.

C.O. STARRETT, Jr.
Director

Memorandum Expiration Date: 31 August 1984

Topical Index